KEN GARNER
THE PEEL SESSIONS

BBC
BOOKS

Stefan Rousseau/PA Photos

CHAPTER 01

IT WAS A strange sound, coming from somewhere else. It took everyone by surprise. For a moment no one knew what it was. Some later said they thought for a split second it was a sound effect on the PA, or a sudden downpour of rain. Others, however, who had lived in the shadow of Anfield, Portman Road or Hampden, remembered something else. It felt like nothing so much as what happens to the air around a football ground when the veteran local hero, brought off the bench one last time at twenty to five on a Saturday afternoon, scores the home team's winning goal. It was the sound of thousands nearby cheering – a spontaneous, uncontrollable cheer of gratitude, of appreciation of talent, of respect, and love. The people who gave it were not celebrities, but fans. Most of the two thousand people who stood outside radio DJ John Peel's funeral at Bury St Edmunds Cathedral on Friday 12 November 2004 and cheered his coffin as it was borne outside at the end of the service were, simply, his listeners.

'I felt a real compulsion to be here, his death was a real shock,' Lindsay Neil told the BBC News website reporter Caroline Briggs in the Cathedral close. 'I used to listen to John Peel with my headphones on under the bedclothes. The music I got to hear, like The Smiths, became my favourite bands. John has had a big influence on my life and shaped the person I have become.' Claire Shilton said: 'I started listening to John Peel when I was 13 and got into punk music, I was still listening to him at 40. John has been a big part of my life. He was a lovely person. He had a bigger influence on my life than my parents.' Rick Howes told Briggs: 'John's death has left a big hole in my life. I have been listening to him for more than 30 years and

John at Peel Acres with Sheila and dog Bridget. Eleanor Bentall/Corbis

I've heard so many bands thanks to him. I can't believe I'm never going to hear his voice on the radio again. After my father, he was the most important man in my life. He is irreplaceable.' Briggs remembers that everyone she spoke to who had stood outside said these same things when asked: 'They had clearly come because they felt they had to be there. They felt he was their friend, they knew him. That's what I took home with me.'

Musicians came too, like John Yates and Nik Kavanagh from Liverpool band Ella Guru. They had released their debut album that August, Peel had been playing it and they had been invited to do their first session, then the terrible news came through of Peel's death while on holiday in Peru on 25 October. 'We queued but ended up standing outside,' says Yates; 'There was a real feeling of belonging in the crowd, possibly because we felt like he belonged to us all in one way or another. What was notable was the age range of the crowd. He'd served us all well. The feeling when the coffin was carried outside to the tune of "Teenage Kicks" was overwhelming. I don't mind saying that I cried. I looked around, lots of people were cheering and crying at the same time. It felt OK to.'

Dawn Of The Replicants drove down overnight from Scotland with no money, and no accommodation planned, and got there with just half an hour to spare. As one of Peel's favourite bands of recent years, the family had invited them. 'We were gobsmacked,' remembers Dave Coyle, 'and felt we couldn't possibly accept, considering who should have attended, but the word came back that John would have wanted us there.' Like everyone, they found it a very emotional day and were too tired afterwards to drive straight back, 'so we trawled Bury St Edmunds but there was no room at the inn. Then by chance we found this couple who owned a guest house across from the cathedral gates who had been to the funeral that day, and when they answered the door to a bunch of decidedly rough-looking Scotsmen they were very gracious in tidying out the room above the stables for us, and even made us breakfast the next morning.'

Listeners travelled from Holland, Germany and the USA to be there. Between them, Peel's wife Sheila and his last Radio 1 producer, Louise Kattenhorn, arranged for many listeners to get on the official list for seats inside the Cathedral – although there was not room for all. Those who did get inside heard Paul Gambaccini start his tribute by saying, 'Sorry, John, I'm not Walters.' Until the unexpected death of his long-serving producer John Walters in 2001, Peel had expected him to deliver the eulogy at his funeral. Instead, Gambaccini, who had begun his broadcasting career with the two Johns in Walters' infamously untidy Radio 1 office in the early 1970s – and who remained first-choice deputy presenter for the show into the 1980s – carried off as only he could the big, statistical, chart-rundown fact about Peel: 'You broke more artists than any broadcaster in the history of radio.' And he spoke for himself as well as bands and listeners when he said, 'You caught people at their most impressionable and their most emotional and gave them what mattered most to them, and they remembered it. Then you did it for the next generation.' The best laugh was in the children's tribute, read by their friend Charlie Bell. Peel's lovingly hoarded collection of £2 coins had been kept, they reassured him, and would now be spent on his headstone.

Later, at the family wake in a neighbour's barn, Annie Nightingale took over the turntables and put on some dub reggae. Andy Kershaw was buttonholing everyone saying (rightly) somebody had to organise a published collection of Peel's journalism. Manager Clive Selwood made cheery conversation and tried to pull people out of themselves. There were no pop stars, but session favourites and old friends like The Shend, Terry Edwards and David Gedge were there. The children, all now grown up, looked cool, despite everything.

William made me laugh by reminding me of the extraordinary care with which I had wrapped and posted back to him the toiletries he had left behind in my Partick tenement flat when he – then 14 – and his Dad had stopped over with me one night in 1990 after a gig. What I wanted to say to him then but could not, was, that's just like your Dad: making someone feel better at a difficult moment, while at the same time conveying the clear message that they are, of course, a complete nutter. John would have been proud. As night fell, it was time to head out into the cold. It was over. Now each of us would have to try to start coming to terms with our loss as best we could.

■

THERE WERE SOME there that day who had enjoyed no such period of grace. Radio is a demanding medium, and unforgiving of, pardon the phrase, dead air. Louise Kattenhorn was at home in London on the morning of Tuesday 26 October 2004 – her productions were on-air till 1am so she normally came in at lunchtime – when she had a call from Radio 1's head of specialist music Ian Parkinson, saying John had had a heart attack and died. She phoned show assistant Hermeet Chadha. They met, stunned, in a café, and got to Yalding House, Radio 1's square, four-storey converted thirties building on a corner of Great Portland Street, a few minutes' walk

John with Hermeet Chadha and Louise Kattenhorn. Louise Kattenhorn

from Broadcasting House, about midday. Hardly anyone else in Radio 1 knew yet. Parkinson asked Louise what she thought most appropriate to do? Who should come on-air in Peel's place that night? Peel's two-hour show start time was 11pm Tuesday, Wednesday and Thursday. The previous week there had been guest presenters while he'd been away – Underworld, Siouxsie, Robert Smith – and that week was set to feature Rob Da Bank, host of the *Blue Room* show, with Peel planned to return the following Tuesday, 2 November. They decided it should be someone who knew John well, and who listeners would know knew him, Steve Lamacq. Louise and Hermeet went to the Horse and Groom in Great Portland Street. Annie Nightingale had heard and came round, Lamacq joined them. When the news was announced, Louise nipped back and emailed everyone at the station: 'Now is not a day for working, we're in the pub drinking red wine.' Many joined them. Going round the corner for red wine with John had long been a daily tradition.

'I got texts from everyone I knew, saying "are you all right",' Louise remembers, 'but although it was an awful day I found myself coping.' Others struggled. Of all Peel's colleagues in the big, noisy 'specialist music' open-plan office on the ground floor of Yalding, where John would take his daily nap under the desk, and loved and was loved by the young staff, none were hit harder than Mary Anne Hobbs. She revered John, professionally and personally. On his 65th birthday a few weeks before, she had given him a neon sign reading 'Dream Dad'. By all accounts she was terribly upset, and remains deeply affected. When, two years later, I asked to talk to her about Peel for this book, she sent me a sweet note saying, 'I work every hour God sends and I can't even scratch the surface of what Peel was doing. I miss the music and the man so much. What I carry with me is his example of how to live this life. I can't say any more.'

Various people from Radio 1 stayed with the Peel team in the pub all day. Daytime presenters and staff, meanwhile, when not on-air, broke out the red wine in the old Live Lounge, then next to the presentation studios in the Yalding basement. Hermeet went back to the office late in the afternoon and started manically calling up classic Peel Session tracks from the recently digitised, online BBC archive, anything he could think of, both famous and obscure, and working through the torrent of emotional emails flooding in from listeners. Louise and Steve stayed in the pub, discussing what to do. 'Steve wrote a script. I talked to Hermeet. By 11pm we had a running order.' No one involved really wants to remember that night, or the night after, which Mary Anne did, or the Thursday, which she and Steve did together. Even while they were doing what they felt was right – 'it was an honest, personal response, not a BBC boardroom decision,' says Louise – Steve was not alone in commenting that John 'would have hated' all the gushing tributes and old tracks. But there was nothing else they could have done, that terrible day, as John's colleagues and friends. To try and pretend it hadn't happened and just play all new records would have been inhuman.

But what about next week, and the week after that? That was actually an easy decision. Right to the end, two new Peel Sessions were recorded every week, as they had been for years. The planning schedule ran about two months ahead of broadcast. Two bands might be booked to record sessions in a month's time on a Wednesday and a Thursday of one week, and those two recordings would typically 'go out' about a month later, on a Tuesday and Wednesday of the same week (Thursday's show, which Peel did from Peel Acres, his home in Suffolk, would most often feature either a repeat session, or a live act playing at the house). But because of Peel's impending two-week holiday in Peru, and after they had agreed on some 20 bands to ask, by mid-October Louise had booked sessions beyond the end of November, right up to the end of the year. Eight had already been recorded between late September and 26 October. She decided the rest of these invitations should be honoured. All the bands were asked to come in for their Peel Session as planned. There was, after all, six hours' showtime every week to be filled anyway.

More than this, before he went away, Peel had been working ahead on his programme running orders for his first two weeks back. Louise would normally ring him up once the newly recorded sessions came in on CD from the engineers, giving him the track titles and timings to put in alongside his chosen records, and at least four new sessions were in before he left for Peru. His system was methodical and somewhat obsessive. On a large sheet of lined paper in a ledger, he would first write 'Kat's Karavan' at the top – the name of the first radio show on which he appeared, as a guest expert on the blues, on station WRR, Dallas, in 1961. Next, he would write in the session tracks at set points in the otherwise blank running order down the page. Then he would start to fill the gaps with records. The first track, and the last. The one after the first session track, the one after the last. And so on, until all lines were filled, and there were, more often than not, exactly 26 tracks in all, making up a complete two-hour show. Then he'd type it up on an old manual typewriter – for which he found ribbons in a traditional stationers in Thetford – and fax it over to Louise.

When Sheila returned from Peru a few days later, Louise visited the house and with Sheila's help retrieved the draft running orders and borrowed from around his room the records Peel had planned to play. The shows for the first week back were pretty much complete, one or two thereafter had some details inked in. Rob

Da Bank would host the show until Christmas using these running orders, records, and the completed and planned new sessions. 'There was plenty to work with to try and programme records John had wanted to play,' remembers Rob Da Bank, 'because even after the running order drafts ran out, his BBC programme record boxes were full of other CDs marked-up with his 1–5 star system.' One star meant might play some time, rising to five stars meaning must play in the next show. 'Those two or three months were very hard and stressful, but we all felt we had to do it,' Louise says. 'People kept asking me if I wanted to take some time off, but this is where I wanted to be, dealing with things. The emails, calls and letters from bands, record companies and listeners were overwhelming. I couldn't answer them all individually. A lot of people just wanted to tell me what John had meant to them. That was, if you like, the role of our show in those weeks, to let listeners tell each other what they felt about John.'

There was one other thing that they knew had to be done. The show had to say its own goodbye, irrespective of whatever the BBC might arrange more formally later on. It would have to be something big, but something natural for the *John Peel Show* and its bands, DJs, listeners, engineers, producers, family and friends. There would need to be a documentary, interviews, favourite records for John and, above all, lots of live music, from bands, solo acts, and DJs. *Keepin' It Peel* would fill the Radio 1 schedule for six hours on the evening of Thursday 16 December. After that and the New Year holiday, a new schedule would come in, and the grieving would be over. There was only one conceivable location for such an event, both practically and emotionally: the home of the Peel Sessions, BBC Maida Vale Studios.

■

A FORMER ROLLER-SKATING rink in a genteel residential area of West London is as unlikely a location for a recording studio as any. By the time the BBC bought this long tin-roofed building with rococo porticos in Delaware Road, the Maida Vale Roller Skating Palace and Club had long since closed down. Seating 2,620, the rink opened in 1909, but lost its licence for 'music and dancing – no intoxicants' in 1912. In the 1920s, the Ministry of Health used the premises for National Insurance offices. When the BBC opened Studio 1 in 1934, it was, at 110 by 72 feet, the largest broadcasting or recording studio in Britain. Studios 2 to 5 were added the following year, and 1 to 3 are still the same shape as they were then. The attractions of the site in the 1930s were obvious. It was the only available building that could relieve the growing pressure on the studios in Broadcasting House, itself only opened in 1932.

The way into Maida Vale 4, where most Peel Sessions were recorded. Christian Burwood

From reception at street level, the main staircase takes you down ten feet to the ground floor. Peering through the porthole windows in the doors at the bottom of the stairs reveals Studio 1, still today the recording and rehearsal base of the BBC Symphony Orchestra. Beyond it, 30 yards along the street-side underground corridor, is the large Studio 2, also for orchestral recordings and the BBC Singers' choral work. Studio 3 is next along, famed as a jazz studio, with its original 1930s parquet flooring, and plaque commemorating it as the site of Bing Crosby's final recording in 1977. The far end of the building is the pop end, with Studio 4, last rebuilt in the late 1980s with its balcony (for guests) and windowed vocal booth; and 5, now for smaller live sessions and the Radio 1 Live Lounge acoustic sessions. Although many other places have hosted Peel Sessions, Maida Vale 4 recorded more than all the rest put together.

On Tuesday 26 October 2004, Studio 4 was booked for a Peel Session. Two engineers, Jerry Smith and Nick Fountain, were on duty from late morning. It would be a Radio 1 session day like any other. The band would have been told to arrive around noon, and would have about 90 minutes to set up their equipment, with the engineers miking up their amplifiers and drums at the same time. Recording was due to start at about 2.30pm and be completed by about 6pm. After an hour or so's break for dinner in the canteen, the engineers and band would have until almost 1am to mix the session, normally expected to produce about 15–20 minutes of material.

The band booked in were Avrocar, the tiny, part-time indie electropop Birmingham band led by Perry McDonagh. They had released three singles themselves over the previous three years, and Peel had played and praised each of them. After playing their third, he had commented on air, 'We really must get them in for a session.' The date was fixed. 'It was a big moment for us,' says Perry, 'even bigger than when he played our first single, and that was something I'd always wanted – he'd played the A-side, then the B-side, then the A-side again the next week! I was just overjoyed.' They hired a small van and drove down to London that morning in a state of great excitement. When they arrived Jerry and Nick got them set up and soundchecked fairly quickly – 'I was chuffed with the guitar sound they got me,' Perry recalls – and then, like every other band at Maida Vale for the first time, they went for a walk along the low-ceilinged corridors, amazed by the bits of equipment and instruments in corners everywhere; the jazz bands, orchestras and groups glimpsed through the other studio doors; and had lunch in the canteen.

They were back, sitting up in the MV4 gallery, just about to go down to start recording, when keyboard player Tony got a text message. 'John Peel's passed away.' Perry thought it was a mate playing a sick joke. He looked down across the studio to the control room. Through the glass he could see Jerry and Nick, and another man who had just appeared behind them and was saying something. He saw them freeze, staring at each other, in complete shock. Then he knew it was true. Thinking of the feelings of the family and the show's production team, the band went down and offered to pack up and go home. 'But Jerry and Nick were really strong and calm,' remembers Perry. 'No, they said, if John were here, he'd be the first to insist the show must go on, we'll do the session.'

So they did. Somehow, they played and recorded four numbers that afternoon. Jerry and Nick pulled out all the stops, the band felt, making them sound like they'd never sounded before. 'Those guys were just terrific that day, I don't know how they did it,' says Perry. Singer Penny was taking loads of photos, then stopped and apologised to the engineers, saying she suddenly felt ghoulish. It's OK, they said, everyone does it. Jerry and Nick worked patiently on the mix late into the evening. At one point, Tony said how strange it felt to be in this big studio, working calmly away on these little songs, completely isolated from the media frenzy going on already out there over John's death. As midnight approached, the band went for another walk round the now dark, deserted corridors and studios. They hardly spoke. There was nothing to say. Before leaving, they scrawled a message on the inside of the Studio 4 control room door, as every Peel Session band did: 'Avrocar, 26/10/04 – for John'.

There were 12 other bands like Avrocar who did their debut and therefore only Peel Session at Maida Vale, in those last three months of 2004: Lali Puna, Skimmer, Hot Snakes, the Bloody Hollies, Wolf Eyes, 65 Days of Static, Max Tundra, Ella Guru, Sunn O))), Vitalic, Stuffy & The Fuses, The Mutts. Wesley Doyle, of the Bloody Hollies, who Peel had been playing for a year, and were on their first European tour away from the USA, says, 'I see things written about us and our so-called "hard luck" story, that we somehow missed our big chance, and that things might have been different for the band if John Peel was alive and well when we recorded the session. The fact is that no one in the band ever felt this way at all. We were flattered to be asked, and treated it as an honour to play.' Max Tundra decided to 'unpack' his solo electronica music and experiment. 'I gathered my sister and six of our musically adept friends together and promptly began rehearsing full-band multi-instrumental versions of two songs from each of my first two albums. It was exciting going into Maida Vale and getting to use the BBC's lovely old Hammond organ and rotating Leslie speaker, as well as a gorgeous grand piano, a celeste, a Fender Rhodes, and all sorts of other glorious goodies that Led Zep probably played at some point. I

Ella Guru recording their Peel Session in MV4 on 2 December 2004. Christian Burwood

16

think the finished performances breathed new life into the rather dressing-gown-clad bedroom music of the originals. But I was sad that John never lived to hear it.' Ella Guru recorded the Thursday after Max. 'We did four songs, three of our own and a Lennon cover, "Oh My Love", as a tribute to John,' says John Yates. Their session went out on Wednesday 15 December. And the next night was the *Keepin' It Peel* night, live from Maida Vale, using Studios 3, 4 and 5. As dozens of favourite bands, DJs, listeners, family and friends took over almost the entire building that night, it became an understandably emotional and surreal experience for those who were there. When people arrived to see pictures of John displayed everywhere, and hear his voice coming out of the PA as part of the documentary, it was almost too much to bear. The evening most touched the heart late on, when Sheila chose to play as her record choice for John, Amsterdam's 'Does This Train Stop On Merseyside?', which was followed by William from Misty In Roots reading out live his famous spoken intro to their number 'Mankind'. Those were two songs in which John always found consolation, but that night it was those left behind who needed it most.

Half a dozen new sessions were still awaiting an airing, the last of them going out in the early weeks of 2005, on the regular new shows hosted by Rob Da Bank and Huw Stephens. The second Peel Session by The Workhouse, which went out on Rob Da Bank's show of 17 March, was the very last to be broadcast of all, the last of some 4,400 Peel Sessions since 1967, the last in what can now truly be described as a unique broadcast live music archive. There never was anything like it before and never will be again.

■

JOHN PEEL DID not invent radio sessions. He did not produce or engineer the ones that bear his name. He made no money from their commercial exploitation. Barring honourable exceptions in latter years, he was not even present when they were made. They are called Peel Sessions simply because out of the many thousands of live BBC sessions broadcast on dozens of different shows by Radio 1 they happen to be the ones that Peel and his successive producers chose to commission and broadcast. It was Peel's longevity and range of enthusiasms that made them pre-eminent.

There is a simple explanation for why there were so many sessions across the daytime and evening schedule in the first 20 years of Radio 1: needletime. Until it was eventually abolished as a notorious restrictive practice in 1988, needletime was the number of hours of music on record that the BBC and other broadcasters were allowed to play per day. It was allocated by a rights-negotiating company called Phonographic Performance Ltd (PPL), representing the record companies; who had an agreement with the Musicians' Union over how many hours broadcasters could have. Most music heard on BBC radio until the late 1970s, more than 60 per cent of musical output, was therefore not from records, but from pre-recorded live sessions.

It's one thing to be obligated to hire musicians. It's quite another to use such a system to invite new bands to contribute to the output of a national public broadcasting corporation almost the moment they emerge. But that's exactly what the Peel Sessions did. Most specialist shows on Radio 1 booked in new groups for sessions, but none of them could match Peel's curiosity, industry and obsession with the new. Often the sessions recorded by new bands on other Radio 1 programmes have had about them the whiff of the performance of promotional duties. Bands who have done sessions for both Peel and other shows admit to this difference. Certainly from the punk era onwards, and to an extent even earlier, bands valued a Peel Session in itself as an objective. Although Peel was almost never there in fact, they felt him to be there in spirit. It was him they wanted to play for and impress, it was his personal judgement and support they valued. That's why they tried especially hard to do something different – and why so many of the sessions were so good.

That means there are two ways of looking at the Peel Sessions. The obvious approach is to celebrate Peel's ability to be consistently ahead of the game. When Bowie, Fleetwood Mac, Siouxsie and the Banshees, The Smiths, Pulp, PJ Harvey, the White Stripes and Laura Cantrell recorded their first BBC sessions, very few people had heard of them. They had just released, or were about to release, their first records. They had played a few gigs. But they were booked in, with the result that millions of radio listeners, for whom these groups were then only acts they had read about in the music papers, had their first opportunity to hear what they actually sounded like. An alternative view, however, is to see the sessions as a night by night, random onslaught of musical novelties of the moment, a series of unique entertainments for radio listeners, in which the classic sessions were not necessarily by bands who went on to achieve superstar status. The best ones were often those with unexpected guests, startling one-off arrangements, very short or very long numbers, or which consisted entirely of surprising cover versions, or were just plain daft.

The Peel Sessions story is, however, both those things at the same time, a tale of glory and chance. It is beyond question a superlative sequence of musical discoveries. But it is more than that. Listeners do not tune in to a radio show because they think they might hear the new Beatles and can brag about it in ten years' time. Nor would they tune in, or stand for three hours on a cold November morning outside an English Cathedral, just for an old DJ who told funny stories about his family and his health. They loved Peel for what he brought them every night, the perky and the peculiar, the psychotic and the perverse. You tuned in precisely because you did not know what you were going to get. For every teenage generation since the 1950s, popular music discovered in those years has been taken to heart as speaking to our emerging self. It's just like Gambo said: Peel gave bands and listeners what they needed most, and they remembered it – and tuned in again, and again. *The John Peel Show* was the radio show for teenagers of all ages. Today, however, it's all just a memory of youthful desires. Rather than us abandoning him and his show as we got older, in the end he left us, suddenly. But when they bore his body from the cathedral, in that moment, that roar of devotion, his death ceased to be a private matter, as he was returned to his listeners, with whom his reputation now rests. Live music and studio sessions at BBC Radio 1 will no doubt go on, but for the Peel Sessions, the story is over. There was a beginning, a middle we dreamed would last for ever, and now there has been an end.

■

THIS BOOK IS about something that is past. It is not possible to write, as I did 14 years ago for *In Session Tonight* (IST), that 'at Maida Vale, a Peel Session is recorded every Sunday and Tuesday' or 'tonight, John Peel is talking to me and all his other listeners from Berlin'. The coldest part of editing the old text from that book which forms just over half this one, has been going through changing every verb attached to a quote from Peel or Walters from the present to the past tense. There is thus a presence and absence shaping the form of this book. His name is in the title, his face on the cover, his actions celebrated on almost every page. But he is no longer available to us in person. If he were, this book would not exist. It is foolish to wish such things other than they are, so I will only say that I hope I have done as decent a job as I can on a subject I honestly thought I would never attempt again.

Between IST going to press in spring 1993 and being published that September, I had got a lecturing job at Glasgow Caledonian University and my previous freelance life took a different course. Radio stayed with me, though. That autumn I was asked to become the radio critic of *Scotland on Sunday*, *The Scotsman*'s Sunday paper, and, after four years there, week in week out, I did the same for the *Sunday Express* until 2002. Late in the 1990s, a fringe meeting at a conference which I drifted into led to my becoming one of the first members of an academic association devoted to the study of radio, the Radio Studies Network, and I was chuffed when my mates in it later asked me to edit *The Radio Journal: International Studies in Broadcast and Audio Media*, which I did for its first four years to 2006. What with all this and the university day job, my involvement with the Peel Sessions had long felt like something I had done in a previous life. The fact that despite respectable sales and gratifying reviews the old BBC Books remaindered IST just 18 months after publishing it, had merely confirmed this.

My wife Magda and I stayed in touch with John and Sheila. Up to 1996, we would often share a Chinese meal in Loon Fung on Sauchiehall Street when they and producer Mike Hawkes and assistant – and later producer herself – Alison Howe would come to Glasgow for Peel outside broadcasts. These occasions dwindled in the late 1990s, though we did go to the epic 60th birthday party at Peel Acres in 1999, involving a hilarious 4am drive back to our hotel with Lard on top form in the back seat. After our daughter Hanna was born in 2001 and delightfully turned our world upside down, we were never all together again. Sheila sent Hanna some baby pink dungarees into which she entirely disappeared but now look like doll's clothes when she holds them up, giggling. I last met John on Thursday 29 April 2004, when he was in Glasgow for a show and an aborted DJ-set at the Tramway for the Triptych Festival. We went back to his and Sheila's hotel and chatted about what young people need to know about working in the media: John was incensed about how his son Tom's film business employers were treating him. After they'd gone to bed, I sat up drinking into the small hours in Lang's with show assistants Mark and Hermeet, and Hermeet's mate (and my former student) playwright Daniel Jackson. My one regret is that John never got to meet Hanna.

Sitting in the Cathedral waiting for the funeral to begin, I thought about all the tiny actions John had taken, insignificant to him, that had cumulatively done so much so long ago to help me. Although he did not take my finals for me, introduce me to my wife, assist with my daughter's birth or get me my job, in other, less tangible ways I know my life would not have taken the direction it has without his intervention. If he had not read out my cheeky letter in 1985 would he have agreed to my interviewing him for the student paper in 1986? If we had not met, would he have helped me get the phone contact I needed for an interview for my first magazine commission? But it was not this sense of professional indebtedness that made me momentarily lose it as the funeral ended. As the brief montage of his show and music played out, I choked for the loss of my radio friend, the broadcast voice I knew far better than the man in the flesh, who had brought companionship and surprise into my room for almost the entirety of my adult life.

John in the specialist music office at Radio 1. Louise Kattenhorn

When Roy Orbison died, Peel said he felt as if a window had been bricked up in his home. That's exactly how it was for me when Peel went. For months I could not bear to switch on the radio at night. All those last sessions passed me by. I did not hear Rob Da Bank broadcast Avrocar. I could not face listening to the *Keepin' It Peel* night. I bought all the newspapers but put them away unread. I eventually went through them while recovering from flu early in 2005 – and my grief turned to anger.

As a journalist myself who teaches the trade, and having made my own fair share of mistakes (not least in IST's sessionography), I should hardly have been shocked by the mountain of error I found, but I was. Anyone who had listened to Peel for a year or two would have spotted most of these howlers. According to the obituaries, he was demobbed in 1962 (1959). He found regular employment with station WRR in Dallas (they never paid him). Peel gave Jimi Hendrix his first broadcast (his last, yes; his first, no). He made his name with a show called 'In Session Tonight' (that made me laugh). His contract specified that his show would feature two or three BBC sessions (it said no such thing). His first session guest was Lulu (she wasn't). Peel was on four nights a week during the punk era (five). The Sex Pistols and The Clash used to visit Peel Acres to play live (they never did). Feargal Sharkey wrote 'Teenage Kicks' (John O'Neill, actually), which begins 'Are teenage dreams so hard to beat?' (it's not a question). He had recently written his biography (started). At his death, he still had two Radio 1 shows a week (three). He had one brother (two), was born on 31 August 1939 (the day before), had three children (four). His programme was 'conservative' (pardon?). There was some good stuff on other pages, moving pieces by Nicholas Lezard, Simon Garfield, Ed Vulliamy and Simon Edge. But it's the obits that become the first draft of history.

Two years later, I had cause to remember those errors and how much they had grated. One day in November 2006 I had a call out of the blue from Mathew Clayton, editorial director of BBC Books, now part of Random House. They were interested in doing a book on the Peel Sessions, an update of *In Session Tonight* but this time solely on Peel, he said. Did I think it could be done, and might I be interested in doing it? And if not, could I suggest someone else? In a flash I saw the mess that could be made of it by someone unfamiliar with the BBC archives. Having done it before, I would at least have an idea where to start on the vast documentary reconstruction required. Now could be the time to tell the whole story of the *Peel Show*. The press and public myth-making that had so annoyed me was understandable – Peel's anecdotes always bore a hazy relationship to the truth – but unnecessary. The facts of the Peel Sessions are astonishing enough. This was something I could, and perhaps should, do. It would be my way of showing my gratitude for the pleasure the show gave me. So, thanks, John, for all the listening.

■

OUR STORY, HOWEVER, is indebted to others as well. To tell it right, Peel and what he would later come to mean to us as his listeners has to slip into the background for a while. The story of the Peel Sessions is also a story of producers, engineers, studios, changing schedules, policies and BBC management – as well as bands and musicians. Some of the most important people are no longer with us, like John Walters, and Robin Scott, the first controller of Radio 1. Without them there would be much less to tell. Fifteen years ago I was amused but not surprised that my interview with Walters for IST ended up being conducted over four separate episodes and filling more than seven hours of tape. Now I only wish there were more. I have lost count of the times I have wanted to pick up the phone and check something with him.

But there is someone we can still go to, someone perhaps not quite so familiar to most Peel listeners, yet a name revered by those who know something of the inside story of live pop and rock at BBC radio over the past half-century. It's the name of a man who still lives, as he has done for more than 20 years, in quiet retirement in Dorset: Bernie Andrews. To understand the Peel Sessions story, we first have to go back to before Peel, before Radio 1, before even the pirate stations, to the heyday of the BBC's Light Programme, a time when music on the radio meant mostly dance bands and orchestras, cabaret quintets and light classical pieces. But the way Bernie organised and ran BBC pop recording dates in the early 1960s established precedents without which the sessions celebrated in this book would almost certainly never have taken place. Ask any BBC producer or engineer about sessions in the early days, and back will come the reply, 'Ah,

now, the person you really must talk to is...' He was so insistent on how things should be done that for the slot he won in the Radio 1 launch schedule in 1967 he retained the title *Top Gear* from a previous programme of his. He even re-recorded its old signature tune, first heard in 1964, performed by Sounds Incorporated, and composed by 'J Woodhouse, A Boyce' – otherwise known as Bernie himself ('I hummed it') and his chief producer, Jimmy Grant ('he played it'). And that name takes us back to the beginnings of rock 'n' roll sessions at the BBC.

■

The entrance to the Maida Vale studios. BBC

C H A P T E R   0 2

WHEN BERNIE ANDREWS joined the BBC in October 1957 at the age of 24, rock 'n' roll may have been in full swing in the USA, but it was barely beginning to encroach on the BBC. The Gramophone department operated a policy of giving airplay priority to British recordings of popular tunes – in many ways admirable, but this meant that genuine records from Elvis Presley and Little Richard were passed over in favour of covers by British dance bands. The originals would turn up only when specifically requested on programmes like Family Favourites.

There was one small sign of the way ahead. A 30-minute pre-recorded programme, *Saturday Skiffle Club*, had been launched on the Light Programme at the beginning of June that year, taking over the daily 10am theatre organ spot. The producer was Jimmy Grant of the Light Entertainment department, a skilled jazz musician, and the presenter was Brian Matthew, a new BBC staff announcer, who had left his job as an actor at the Old Vic the year before. 'The folk and jazz elements of skiffle at first made up the entire repertoire of the acts,' Grant remembers, 'but then some of the groups began introducing pop tunes such as Everly Brothers numbers, but I cannot recall whether amplifiers were ever brought into the studio.' That was yet to come.

On his way to his BBC engineering induction course on his first day that October, Bernie bumped into another new recruit outside the Langham Hotel, Johnny Beerling, a former studio technician at RAF Aden, and later controller of Radio 1, 1985–1993. They started out working the same shift in the old control room in the Broadcasting House sub-basement. After a few months, they went separate ways, Johnny becoming a studio manager and Bernie going into tape recording; a parting

(l to r) Bernie Andrews (with TR90 tape machine), Johnnie Beerling, Jack Singleton and Ken Sykora, Broadcasting House,1959. BBC

that would, ten years on, see Johnny producing the new Radio 1's top-rated *Tony Blackburn Show* and Bernie in charge of the most rebellious item in the schedule, *Top Gear*; but they have always remained friends.

The department that Bernie moved into in summer 1958 was a relatively new one, 'XP-Ops', or transportable tape machines, for playing in pre-recorded items ('inserts') from the control cubicle during programme transmissions, and for location recording at BBC theatres. At first, American Ampex recorders were used; but after a few months the department standardised on EMI TR90s, single-track mono quarter-inch, 15ips tape recorders, then new, and still the staple music-recording machine in BBC outside studios in the first years of Radio 1. The only other tape machines the BBC used in the late 1950s were also mono, BTR-2s. These huge green units, designed in the 1940s, known affectionately as 'battleships' or 'ovens', certainly weren't portable and were mainly used to tape complete programmes for later broadcast. But, in 1958, recording by tape at the BBC was only just becoming the norm. Jimmy Grant remembers producing many programmes in the mid-1950s 'with inserts played in on 78rpm acetate discs'.

Meanwhile, in summer 1958, the high listening figures for *Saturday Skiffle Club* had prompted Jimmy Grant's boss, Jim Davidson, Head of Light Entertainment, to ask Grant to put together a two-hour live programme with quite a small budget aimed at a younger audience, with half an hour's needletime. This was one of the many firsts for the show that would eventually run until January 1969, *Saturday Club*. The Gramophone department controlled all needletime, keeping nearly all of it for its own record programmes like *Desert Island Discs* and *Down Your Way*, and to give some of it to a rival programme-making department was unprecedented. Before this,

music shows from Davidson's department had all been all live or pre-recorded sessions. 'There must have been some reluctance to lose control of needletime to another department,' thinks Grant. 'I was instructed to take my list of records every week to Jack Dabbs, a producer in the Gramophone department, for approval. It was clear from the start that he wasn't concerned which records I had chosen, and we left it that I would consult him if I had any problems. Things might have been different if a less amenable gramophone producer had been chosen for me to see.'

This meant that a producer was free for the first time to play the latest genuine rock 'n' roll records from America, if only nine or ten each week. The rest of the show would be made up of one live band and four pre-recorded sessions, put down at the Playhouse, 201 Piccadilly, the Paris or Maida Vale. On the first edition, on 4 October 1958, the guests were Terry Dene and the Dene Aces; Humphrey Lyttelton and his Band in the 'Jazz cellar' (who also recorded the signature tune, 'Saturday Jump', written by Grant under another alias, Eddie James, and later re-recorded by Ted Heath); Gary Miller; Johnny Duncan and his Blue Grass Boys; and Russell Quaye's City Ramblers. Record requests were featured in 'Cats Call'. If none of this seems the sound of rock 'n' roll rebellion, it was nevertheless new for the BBC Light Programme of the late 1950s. Trad, bluegrass, folk and the beginnings of R 'n' B were all regarded as fringe cults, and to put them all together into one Saturday morning show was positively radical. As a BBC technical production, it was a total innovation. It was the first radio programme to combine live music, records and pre-recorded sessions, all of which would be presented live, from Studio 3A in Broadcasting House. Grant, Matthew, their studio manager (live sound) Ron Belchier, and first XP-operator Pete Dauncey, could look down from the control cubicle into the main studio on the floor below, where the live band, normally the trad jazz group, would be playing. In 1959, when Pete Dauncey left for an engineering course, Bernie took over as regular XP-op; Johnny Beerling came in as grams studio manager, cuing up the records; and this team ran the show for the next two years.

But the show would never have been possible without another liberating development: the Musicians' Union agreeing in 1956 to allow live music sessions to be pre-recorded. Since the opening of Broadcasting House in 1932, every music show had been live. The only music recording that went on was of complete programmes onto transcription disc, for a single re-broadcast on the Empire Service or, later, General Overseas Service, forerunners of today's World Service. During the war, the union had allowed 'substitutional' recording, the recording of a complete show at or after a final rehearsal, in case the blitz prevented the show going out live from a London studio. The union didn't want to risk the lives of its members, even for the sake of a principle. Many old BBC theatres were destroyed in the bombing. Indeed, it was to cover the loss of St George's Hall to enemy action in September 1940 that the Corporation acquired the tiny Paris Cinema in Lower Regent Street, 'for largely service audiences'. (This was still in use for Radio 1's *In Concert* recordings in the 1970s, and for BBC radio comedy shows right up to the mid-1990s; today it's a gym club, and where the auditorium was is now an indoor swimming pool.) Once hostilities were over, however, the union clamped down. 'MUSICIANS ACT AGAINST RECORDED BROADCASTS,' said the front page of the *News Chronicle* on 1 March 1946. The union, under general secretary F Dambman, argued that, instead of recordings, all shows should be live, creating jobs for de-mobbed musicians returning to civvy street from the forces.

Under the new Labour government, the union had strong political sympathy and won. The BBC agreed to abolish all pre-recording of complete programmes of music. This merely created confusion over bands playing a number or two in a variety show, which was then recorded for repeat broadcast. In 1954, the union, under a new general secretary, Hardie Ratcliffe, tried to get tough on this, and sought to ban all 'pre-recording' at the BBC. They were unsuccessful, and in this came the seeds of their undoing. For during the crisis negotiations the BBC's head of programme contracts, WL Streeton, having been asked to investigate the implications of tape recording, pointed out to his superiors in a confidential memo that it was now possible 'to make up a pre-recorded programme by a series of sessions at each of which we both rehearse and pre-record. This would involve the MU recognising a new type of session, somewhat akin to a transcription, film or gramophone recording session.' The BBC negotiators raised it with the MU immediately. Nothing happened, but two years later the point was eventually conceded. The 'pre-recording' session was created, just in time for *Saturday Club*.

Not that this new type of session was anything like as informal as the Peel Sessions would one day become. Every session was to be three hours' rehearsal followed by half an hour's continuous recording, producing some ten or twelve numbers. For *Saturday Club*, this meant two options. Either Jimmy Grant could hire an established band leader or musical director, with up to a dozen session musicians, who would back two star singers, performing five songs each, with the orchestra adding a couple of instrumentals at the end of the session; or, more problematically, two self-contained groups, who would both have to set up, rehearse and then record five numbers each, all within three-and-a-half hours. All this was to be achieved in mono, in one take, with no overdubs, no 'EQ' (tone controls) on the eight-channel BBC Type-A mixing desk, no playback for the acts to hear how they sounded, and no re-mixing before broadcast. Vocal overdubs were introduced later on, by 'bouncing' the recorded backing track onto a second tape machine, and adding the vocals at the same time; but being strictly outside the MU agreement, this frequently had to be conducted secretly, only once any regular MU session men on the date had left for the pub, thinking the session over.

'To be frank, during the early stages of the programme, the SM [studio manager] and I would be pleased if we got five numbers of broadcastable quality from a group in the limited time,' says Jimmy Grant. 'It's worth noting that prior to *Skiffle Club* practically all broadcasters in popular music were trained musicians, with 20 years' or more experience, able to cooperate in the studio with the SM to produce good results in the time available. With *Skiffle Club*, SMs had to learn to cope with inexperienced broadcasters, although in time, I suppose, talent won through.'

The question of new talent raises the spectre of the BBC Audition Unit. Every artist to be broadcast at that time first had to pass an audition. Bands who applied would be booked, along with three other hopefuls, for a three-hour session. Each band would have just 45 minutes to set up, rehearse and record up to three numbers.

The unmarked tapes would then be vetted by the Talent Selection Group, a weekly meeting of Light Entertainment producers, who would aim to pass or fail up to 20 acts in a morning's listening. 'It was generally a very fair system,' says Bernie. For records, there was an equivalent monitoring body, the Dance Music Policy Committee, later just the Popular Music Policy Committee, which sat in judgement each week on sheet music, albums and singles. It was eventually wound up at the end of 1964, when the absurdity of songs like 'Love for Sale' still being marked 'NTBB' (Not To Be Broadcast) on grounds of 'taste' became too embarrassing for the BBC to bear.

By the early 1960s, *Saturday Club* was easily the top radio show in Britain. Admittedly, it had little competition. In 1960, *Easy Beat* had been launched, with a live session included on each Saturday evening's live show from the Playhouse (later it moved to Sunday morning); and the daily lunchtime shows on the Light Programme began to feature guest pop groups; but *Saturday Club* was the biggest weekly showcase. It also had two very positive things going for it, as regular listener (and later *NME* staffer) Bob Woffinden recalled on the show's 30th anniversary in *The Listener*: Jimmy Grant's 'painstaking production work – he always tried to achieve a fast-paced show'; and 'the authority and unruffled professionalism of Brian Matthew, surely one of the outstanding voices in post-war radio'. But if the show was big already, unpredictable events, both inside and outside the BBC, were about to transform it into a legend.

On 7 March 1962, a northern group with a strong local following were booked into the Playhouse Theatre, Manchester, by BBC Light Programme producer Peter Pilbeam for their debut session, to be broadcast on *Teenager's Turn* the following day. He wrote on their audition report: 'a tendency to play music'. 'Now that was, in those days, high praise, because a hell of a lot of noise came out of most of the three guitars and drums groups,' says Pilbeam. In a tradition later continued by Peel, that group were then just another unsigned band. The Beatles didn't sign to EMI until July.

Coincidentally, the week after The Beatles' debut, Bernie Andrews, having acquired a name as the fastest tape editor around, began a three-month 'attachment' as a producer in Light Entertainment, at the suggestion of Jim Davidson himself. It was a breakthrough, for never before had a tape-op, or anyone from Engineering, moved straight into production. Tape operations then came under 'Engineering', and the established BBC promotion route was first to move out of the 'recording channel', the separate room which held the tape machines, into the control cubicle, and become a 'studio manager' or 'SM', who mixed and balanced the sound, and thence a producer. Xp-Ops, however, had brought portable machines into the control cubicle,

Bernie Andrews with The Beatles recording for Saturday Club, 17 December 1963. BBC

and talented engineers, like Pete Dauncey and Bernie, with them. Getting into the cubicle was effectively halfway to promotion. Most producers and SMs then, like the acts they were used to recording, were ex-RAF, educated, experienced musicians, with a strong bias towards jazz. Bernie's background, by contrast, was simply that of the ordinary pop fan. In a BBC environment characterised by professionalism, Bernie's common touch was to prove invaluable.

By the time The Beatles did their first session for *Saturday Club*, on 28 January 1963, several things had changed. They had two hits under their belt; Bernie had just become a full-time producer at the Aeolian Hall; and the MU, late in 1962, had agreed to allow 'discontinuous' pre-recording, whereby each number could be rehearsed, then recorded immediately, rather than taping all tracks in a single take at the end of the session. During the negotiations the union told the BBC this was 'the sacrifice of a cherished principle'. 'They undoubtedly spoke from the heart,' noted GM Turnell, Head of Programme Contracts. Yet it was clearly what union session-men wanted. For a start, verbal directions from the musical director or band leader didn't have to be remembered for up to two hours, until the red light was finally on.

One more crucial change was under way. Late in April 1963, the BBC floated

Popular Music off from Light Entertainment as a separate department, headed by Ken Baynes, with Donald MacLean as his assistant. In May, three chief producers were appointed to oversee the new department's various kinds of programmes. Not surprisingly, considering *Saturday Club*'s pre-eminence, Jimmy Grant was put in charge of pop music. He remained as co-producer of his show, but only had time to produce every other Saturday's transmission. So he delegated the alternate week's transmission – choosing the records; the session bookings; and all session production, save one a week – to his new co-producer, Bernie Andrews. 'Bernie definitely became the supremo for a period,' recalls Brian Matthew, 'and the show changed noticeably.' His co-producer saw it. 'Bernie excelled in consistently booking top-line British and American groups for the programme and matching studio facilities to their limited availability,' says Grant. 'This was against a background of a new economy regime of block bookings at fixed times, with which he struggled.'

But Bernie did a lot more than this. He had often watched in dismay, on various programmes, as a nervous young group doing their first BBC session (a far more make-or-break career moment than today) would be bustled along – 'that's fine, next number please' – not allowed to hear their takes back, and generally shown little sympathy. 'They had to do as they were told,' says Bernie, in a mock authoritative tone, 'and if they didn't, that was the last session they did. You didn't come along and tell BBC producers what to do!' The professional, cool atmosphere that worked so well for accomplished jazzers was stultifying for self-taught beat groups. Bernie began making some changes. For a start, he invited bands into the cubicle to hear their takes. This was simply not done. At first, horrified SMs of the old school would protest: 'What do you want to ask their opinion for? They're only pop musicians, what do they know about how it should sound?' But helped by his new regular SM, Vernon Lawrence, and later on, Bev Phillips, Bernie established this courtesy. Bev Phillips was already acquiring a name as the SM for getting a good drum sound. 'Originally for *Saturday Club* there'd just be one mic above the kit, and one on the bass drum as well. Then I'd be at a gig and see a mic on a specific part of the kit and think, "Hmmm...".' Bev also developed the tradition of SMs bringing in a personal suitcase of tricks to modify the spartan controls of the BBC desks; a tradition begun by the legendary SM Freddy Harris, who first stuck a fag packet down the back of a standard BBC ribbon mic, to help get a good piano sound. 'In the early sixties, there was usually only one "Response Selection Amplifier" or RSA [a basic pre-amp] per studio mixing desk, so once you had enhanced the vocal mic, you were technically stuffed,' recalls Bev. 'I used to solder resistors and capacitors between telephone jack plugs housed in my father's tobacco tins in order to create high-pass filters. There was once hell to pay when my boss came round with some engineering top-brass and saw these tobacco tins dangling from the jackfield on the wall.'

Taking more trouble to get a good electric guitar and drum sound, they found they couldn't squeeze two bands into a single session. In a move which was initially criticised by BBC management for encouraging inefficiency, self-contained bands on Bernie's show now got a session each. When The Beatles had done their first *Saturday Club* dates earlier in 1963, they'd had to share the studio, first with Alan Elsdon's Jazz Band (22/1/63), and the third with Kenny Ball and his Band (25/5/63). (The second was live from 3A on Saturday 16 March.) But on 5 October, when they came in to record for the show's special fifth birthday edition, they had a session to themselves. That show, produced by Bernie, also featured the Everly Brothers, Joe Brown, Kenny Ball, and Frank Ifield, Kathy Kirby and Tommy Roe singing with the Art Greenslade Orchestra, complete with strings – 'the most expensive pop session ever booked', recalls Bernie – and won 20.2 per cent of the adult listening population, 'and that's not counting any under-14s'. This classic broadcast is now, thanks to Bernie's foresight in making a complete tape, one of the jewels in the BBC Sound Archive.

'Before The Beatles there weren't many real electric self-contained groups, except perhaps Cliff and the Shadows, and Shane Fenton and the Fentones,' points out Bernie. So the need to allocate more time for electric group recording was an inevitable development, as Jimmy Grant recognises: 'Pop taste changed over the run of *Saturday Club* from middle-of-the-road, finally polarising towards beat groups, and, for instance, the small backing group of session musicians later proved unsuitable.'

The session-men system could still come in handy, though. After the Rolling Stones, minus Charlie Watts and Bill Wyman, fearful of losing their day-jobs, had just failed an audition early in 1963, Bernie got them back in that autumn by booking individuals from the group to back Bo Diddley. Once they were there, he gave them the first of what was to evolve into yet another mould-breaking innovation. Instead of the standard audition, he did a full session with them, and submitted that to the Audition panel, but only after it had been broadcast. 'It had to be someone already becoming "big" for the innovation to be accepted,' recalls Mary Cotgrove of Auditions; with support from her and Jimmy Grant, this 'trial broadcast' idea was rapidly adopted as more appropriate for rock acts who were already recording stars. Bill Wyman recalled on the Radio 1 documentary *The Stones at the Beeb* that one member of the panel thought Mick Jagger's vocals 'too black'; but they squeezed a pass. The session went out on *Saturday Club* on 26 October 1963.

Through winter and spring 1964, new bands like The Animals, Manfred Mann and The Kinks joined The Beatles and the Rolling Stones as regulars. In his quest for informality, Bernie was now doing such revolutionary things as, for a recording with Trini Lopez of 'If I Had A Hammer', inviting along an entire participating audience of BBC clerical staff, 'for many of whom it was clearly their first contact with real life show-biz,' remembers Bev Phillips; then he borrowed a builder's board for him and Brian Matthew to stamp along authentically behind the Dave Clark Five's 'Bits And Pieces' (the Audition panel rejected the tape); and, in February 1964, in response to press criticism of the thinness of BBC versions of current hits, Bernie announced he was adding an extra trumpet, sax, two guitars and a second drummer to the show's regular backing band, Arthur Greenslade and the G Men. He'd already added vocal backing groups on star sessions for the first time the previous year. The music press started referring to Bernie as 'ace BBC producer'. In January 1964, the BBC announced regular adult audience figures for the show had recently trebled to nine million. The total including teenagers and children, who bizarrely were not then counted, was of course much higher. The next month, Decca released its *Saturday Club* tribute LP, made up of sessions recorded specially by Jimmy Grant, featuring regular guests. And the 14 March show won *Saturday Club*'s highest ever audience, 25.1 per cent of the adult listening population.

By now the tide of beat groups was unstoppable. The BBC bowed to the inevitable, and Bernie was asked, at short notice, to produce a new show 'to reflect the group scene, a more progressive version of *Saturday Club*'. 'In other words, it didn't mix skiffle, trad-jazz – it was pretty hard rock from the word go,' recalls Brian Matthew, who was to present it. Bernie was given a two-hour slot through to midnight on Thursdays, a budget of £225 and – 'quite generous' – 45 minutes' needletime. The first show was to be on 16 July 1964, but what to call it, and who to book? 'I organised a competition through *Disc* [magazine],' says Bernie. Two winners, Margaret Swanson of Edinburgh and Susan Warne of Welwyn Garden City, suggested 'Top Gear'. Their prize, although only Susan could come, was to attend the recording session of the show's first guests, The Beatles, who also recorded some irreverent trailers. The session, on 14 July, came days after the release of the film and LP *A Hard Day's Night*. Bernie got them because by now he'd formed a close friendship with the group.

'I had got to know them very well socially, because I used to share a flat in Shepherd's Street, in Shepherd's Market, in Mayfair – sounds posh, but it was eleven quid a week for four bedrooms, kitchen and bathroom and I wish I still had it! – with a very close friend of George's, Terry Doran, who was a business associate of Brian Epstein. So both Brian and the boys used to come round to see Terry. I wouldn't kid myself they only used to come round to see me. George used to come round for egg and chips. He loved egg and chips. He couldn't go to a café because he'd get mobbed. He didn't want to know about cooking it himself, so he used to come round to Bern's for egg and chips. Paul only came round once, actually. Terry had this mynah bird in a cage just inside the door. When Paul came in, the bird said, "Hello Ringo!" I was very embarrassed, because it was the first time Paul had come round.' Cheeky birds notwithstanding, the first session for *Top Gear* was a classic. The group did five numbers from the new LP, and Paul tore through 'Long Tall Sally'. They also clowned about with Brian Matthew, launching 'Bernie's new vessel'. 'When was the accident, then?' says John.

Early in March 1965, it was also Bernie who brought the Stones back from the wilderness with a *Top Gear* session, after they were 'banned' by the BBC in December 1964 for failing to turn up to three recording sessions. The *Melody Maker* of 12 December had proclaimed 'BBC Storm: 6 month *Saturday Club* ban?' 'We are not going to book them,' a *Saturday Club* office spokesman told the paper. Light Entertainment booking manager Pat Newman wrote in a memo he would 'dearly love to impose sanctions of some sort'. Teddy Warrick, then a producer in the Gramophone department, recalls getting memos from the Popular Music department telling them not play Stones records, which is backed up by Bill Wyman recalling the band's hit, 'Little Red Rooster', being omitted from *Pick of the Pops'* Christmas and New Year shows. For all these reasons, *Top Gear* was an enormous success. But it only ran for a year. After six months, it was cut to an hour, and switched to 4pm on Saturdays. It was axed at the end of June 1965. There was a small demonstration outside Broadcasting House and, learning of the impending axe, Bob Dawbarn wrote a feature in the *Melody Maker* on 29 May, 'Is the BBC anti-pop?': 'The BBC, with remarkable generosity, has just parcelled-up its Saturday afternoon pop listeners and handed them over to the pirate stations,' he wrote. The pirates, including Caroline and London, had been broadcasting for almost a year. Bernie, today, can only put the axing down to his superiors not liking the show. Perhaps *Top Gear* took the undeserved blame for the Corporation's struggle to come to terms with the swinging sixties. Bernie got a new show, *Folk Room*. The only live shows left playing any rock were *Saturday Club* and *Easy Beat*.

■

IN 1966, IT was easily the offshore pirate stations that were leading pop radio, with all-record programming. On 20 December 1966, in the wake of the first reading of its Marine Offences Bill, the Labour government published its white paper on the future of broadcasting, recommending that the BBC should run a popular music service. And yet what both government and BBC had in mind was hardly a copy of the pirates. For the *BBC Handbook* for 1967, published late in 1966, Frank Gillard, director of Sound Broadcasting, wrote: 'Startling changes in BBC Radio in 1967 are highly improbable.' Some insiders, like Donald MacLean, assistant head of Popular Music, believed listeners wanted to hear popular tunes, and that the BBC should commission its own research into a song, rather than using charts based on record sales. Working from that research, the department's regular orchestras would record cover versions. Others, like Mark White, MacLean's opposite number at Gramophone department, and Robin Scott, who arrived as controller of what would become the new Radios 1 and 2 (the renamed Light Programme) in March 1967, argued for as much needletime as possible, believing the new stations should, ideally, be all-record.

But even with another seven hours' needletime granted by the MU and PPL, an all-disc format was impossible. Inevitably, the launch format was a compromise between Scott, White, and MacLean, enforced by needletime restrictions, which also meant the proposed new Radios 1 and 2 would have to share programmes for much of the day. There was one significant breakthrough, however, in the summer of 1967, without which, Scott was convinced, the station would never have got on air on schedule on 30 September 1967: a new deal on sessions negotiated by MacLean and Michael Standing, with an MU team led by John Morton. Essentially, it expanded an experimental deal which had been running for two Light Programme shows since late 1964, making it available for all daytime 'strip' shows. This 'item recording' agreement, as it was known, allowed producers to use tracks from one session on different days of the week – one at 4pm Monday, the next at 5.30pm Tuesday, and so on – instead of having to put it out as a lump. And this remained the basis for how most Radio 1 daytime and evening shows used their sessions, one track a night, right up to the 1990s. 'It meant we could use those items like we might use gramophone records,' Robin Scott recalled, 'but it also allowed groups not only to play both sides of their current hit, but six other numbers as well.' Nevertheless, 'departmental policy was that sessions were simply a necessity,' says Mark White.

Bernie, however, had a more positive attitude, with a secret new idea to help make Radio 1 sessions worthwhile. 'To me, it seemed silly to spend three and a half hours in a studio, recording material just for one programme, because you used a third of that setting up and getting a balance. So I had this idea for the "double-session". I'd book the studio for seven hours. That gave us twice as much time for recording; the band got twice the fee; and I'd record enough material for two programmes – I'd hold two of the tracks back for a later broadcast. I made an undertaking to the groups that if they did a session for me, I would take a lot of trouble over it, as much as I could, and get it how they wanted. I'd make sure I'd get the right sort of studio, which was the Playhouse, and the right engineer, who was sympathetic to that kind of music the heavy groups were playing, and that was Pete Ritzema.'

'Bernie was a great innovator,' says Pete Ritzema. 'The double-session was a really radical departure. The people who did those sessions were prepared to hang around for hours and hours, really producing the thing with the musicians.' Bernie knew groups were frustrated with the BBC's mono studios and time restrictions. The double-session, however, implicitly took them and their music seriously. The deal was exclusive to Bernie and the show he recreated for the Radio 1 launch schedule: *Top Gear*, now inked in for three hours every Sunday afternoon. But who was to present it? Bernie had been listening to the pirate stations, and also sounding out his music business and underground band contacts throughout the summer of 1967, about who they thought would be a good presenter for his new show. 'I knew who I wanted to do the programme,' he recalls. 'John Peel.'

■

JOHN PEEL WAS the broadcast name of John Robert Parker Ravenscroft, 27, a former public schoolboy and cotton-broker's son from the Wirral, who after national service had drifted into American commercial radio in Texas, Oklahoma and San Bernadino, California, on the back of the British pop boom led by The Beatles (thanks partly to his knowledge of Liverpool), and then got a job on the pirate ship Radio London after his return from America early in 1967. There he had developed his small-hours *Perfumed Garden* show, playing the psychedelic records he had brought back from America, reading out people's letters and poetry, and not playing the news or ads. In the Summer of Love, the show became a sensation. Peel said years later that he'd heard that the first the station boss Alan Keane knew about it was supposedly when Brian Epstein, The Beatles' manager, congratulated him on having the foresight to put such a programme out. 'At which point he listened to it, and was horrified, but by this time Radio London had only got a few weeks to run anyway, and so they decided they might as well leave things as they were.'

Peel wrote requesting work to Mark White, deputy head of BBC radio's Gramophone department, from the pirate Radio London office on 27 July, two weeks before the pirate was to close down, on the eve of the Marine Offences Act becoming law, on 15 August. He enclosed a tape of *The Perfumed Garden*. 'Basically, the programme is a forum for the "better" sounds in popular music, with the emphasis on the music rather than myself,' Peel wrote. 'By "better music", I mean the West Coast groups and British groups that are trying to do something new and imaginative. Obviously I hope that there is some possibility of my continuing with what I believe to be an important programme,' he concluded. White replied on 1 August, saying he had forwarded the tape to Mary Cotgrove, who ran BBC radio's audition panel. It then went to John Simmonds in the Light Entertainment department, and subsequently disappeared.

Nothing came of this formal approach; except, perhaps, 'more than a little reluctance to give me work', Peel suspected. 'They were probably passing the tape around for their own amusement.' Bernie remembers his first suggestion of Peel was greeted by his superiors with forceful remarks like 'no, not him'. As late as 8 August, a provisional station line-up still had a blank space next to *Top Gear*, in which an administrator had scribbled 'Mike Ahern? Mike Raven?' Meanwhile, Peel was getting worried. He turned to Clive Selwood of Elektra Records, who he had got to know through having championed Elektra's acts on *The Perfumed Garden*. Clive offered to help, the beginning of a lifelong friendship that never needed formalising with a contract. He arranged for Peel to visit Bernie in his office in the Aeolian Hall, and Bernie said he'd get Peel on *Top Gear* somehow.

Bernie couldn't just hire Peel outright, however. All 46 DJs hired to launch Radio 1 were to be on eight-week contracts, knowing that many would be weeded out thereafter. So Bernie had been instructed to try out a different compere for *Top Gear* in each of the first six weeks. Having set his mind on getting Peel, however,

Spot the man not smiling, with fellow Radio 1 DJs, 1967. BBC

Bernie suggested to Robin Scott doing a double-headed show instead, using one professional anchorman with a different guest expert 'DJ' each week. Scott agreed. Bernie then booked Peel as one of those 'guests', just in time for him to attend the famous launch line-up photo shoot on the steps of All Souls Church, opposite Broadcasting House, on 4 September. Bernie confirmed his presentation line-up to his department just five days before the on-air date: Pete Drummond as anchorman (another, authoritative-sounding ex-pirate DJ, also now managed by Selwood), with Peel as guest DJ for the first show, followed by Mike Ahern, Tommy Vance and Rick Dane. 'I liked Tommy,' Bernie remembers, 'but I was told to book Ahern and Dane by my superiors, and I knew I didn't want them.' About weeks five and six, Bernie said nothing. He was confident his joint-compere format could establish Peel, surreptitiously, as the programme's regular voice after the first four weeks because, once the station was on-air, things would quickly move beyond the control of the bureaucrats. What would listeners, deprived of the pirates, make of the new Radio 1? Which DJs would they rate the best? When it came, their voice, their taste, their preference, would come as a complete shock to most BBC management.

■

CHAPTER 03

THE ANSWER IS Tomorrow. Or Big Maybelle and the Senate. Possibly Tyrannosaurus Rex, maybe even Captain Beefheart. A case could be made for each of them being the first Peel Session. It depends on how you look at the changing presenter line-up of *Top Gear* in Radio 1's first 18 weeks on air. Tomorrow 'featuring Keith West', and Big Maybelle and the Senate – along with Pink Floyd, Traffic, Tim Rose, and The Move – featured on that first *Top Gear*, from 2 to 5pm on Sunday 1 October 1967, the network's second day of broadcasting, and those two were the first to be recorded, on 21 September. But you could just as easily call them 'Drummond Sessions'. Pete Drummond anchored the show, after all. Tommy Vance became a legendary BBC rock DJ too, and he and Peel remained on good terms, but the classic and oft-repeated Jimi Hendrix Experience session from the third edition, 15 October, which Tommy hosted with Pete, never got to be called a 'Vance Session'. The mere notion of a 'Rick Dane Session' or 'Mike Ahern Session', the two unwanted guest DJs on shows two and four, is ludicrous. It's only a consequence of Peel's eventual longevity that we now look back and call these earliest *Top Gear* sessions by his name. The truth is, in those first few weeks, Peel and the other 'comperes' had little influence over the bookings. Tyrannosaurus Rex and Beefheart would have to wait. 'It was always Bernie's show,' says his co-producer Bev Phillips. And, despite his plans, there was no certainty Peel would survive.

But Bernie had a secret ally, and a powerful one: Robin Scott, the controller himself, who sat above the Popular Music and Gramophone Departments which made the station's shows. Bernie's former assistant, Shirley Jones, was now Scott's

PA, brought in partly because she'd also worked at the pirate Radio Caroline and knew lots of the DJs the station was considering. She kept Scott informed about what Bernie was planning, and in August had independently suggested to Scott that putting Peel with Bernie might be a good idea. Shirley arranged for Peel to come in for an informal interview with Scott before the launch. 'I do remember his poverty-stricken image, what with his bumper boots being laced-up with electrical wire. I gave him a shilling for the bus fare home,' she recalls. Yet all of this influence was actually pushing at an open door. Scott already had a view of what Peel could bring to the BBC, and stuck to it. He and his wife Pat would go on in retirement to become Suffolk neighbours and family friends of Peel and his wife Sheila, his tall, genial figure and shock of white hair becoming a familiar sight at Peel Acres parties, right up to Peel's 60th birthday in 1999, not long before his death the following year aged 80. Peel read the final tribute at Scott's memorial service. 'Whilst I had from very early on wanted John Peel to do quite a lot of things,' Scott told me in the 1990s, 'I think there was a feeling in-house that maybe John was almost too much his own man to let loose.' So he popped into the studio to watch over *Top Gear* that first Sunday afternoon with, he admitted, not a little anxiety. 'I was very glad when it shook down, that afternoon programme, and became his show,' he said, 'but it was a shaky start.'

Listening to that first show, you can see Scott's point. It's not the sessions that are shaky. All 36 tracks are terrific. Every other day from 21 September, the show's two recording teams, Bernie Andrews with engineer Dave Tate, and co-producer Bev Phillips with engineer Pete Ritzema (Bernie would also do extra ones with Pete), had been working hard in BBC studios like the Playhouse Theatre in Northumberland Avenue, 201 Piccadilly (formerly the Stage Door, a Lyons Tea-House), and Maida Vale 4. Traffic, who Bernie remembers being ear-splittingly loud – 'I think Stevie Winwood brought in three Leslie cabinets' ('well, at least two,' says Pete Ritzema) – got down a swirling version of 'Hole In My Shoe'. Tomorrow, with Steve Howe on guitar and Twink on drums, recorded their summer hit 'My White Bicycle', with Bernie ringing the bicycle bell in live on the transmission, opening up a mic in the control room – 'We completely forgot to put it on at the session.' On Monday 25 September, the Pink Floyd had completed a first session at the second attempt, including versions of 'Scarecrow' and 'Set The Controls', and possibly the band's only live attempt at their next single, 'Apples And Oranges'. A previous Floyd session on the afternoon of 28 July, also at the Playhouse, which Bernie had attempted to produce for *Saturday Club*, was abandoned when Syd Barrett walked out. 'I have memories of Syd getting upset that we couldn't play loud or long enough or something, then the whole thing becoming rather disastrous,' says Nick Mason. Patrick Newman, light entertainment bookings manager, noted for his dry sense of humour, learning of the cancellation, wrote to the band's management asking 'whether you'd be good enough to find out which gentleman "freaked out" (this strange expression was heard about the studio), together with any explanatory comments which come to mind'. Bernie also used his 60 minutes' needletime to the full. The first record was 'Love Bug Leave My Heart Alone' by Martha and the Vandellas. Amidst new releases from Donovan, the Idle Race, Procol Harum and Blossom Toes, there were several records Peel had brought back from California, including Country Joe and the Fish, the Mothers of Invention, *The Velvet Underground and Nico* and Captain Beefheart and his Magic Band.

No, what makes the programme shaky is the sheer nervousness of Drummond and Peel. Although they had worked together at Radio London, they were nevertheless in competition, and it shows. Each tries to outwit the other with amusing remarks, and silly 'BBC' voices are adopted frequently. Peel remembered it being 'a rather fraught way of making programmes'. Sat at a table in a talks studio in Broadcasting House, with records and tapes played in from the control room, the formality compared to 'self-op' on the pirate ships was unnerving. 'I think we had to give a written cue for the end of our links as well,' he recalled. This formality, however, was the price Bernie had to pay to get Peel on air.

Peel may not have been involved for the next three weeks, but session production obviously carried on as normal the very next day, 2 October, with one which Bernie still feels was one of his very best: the first for a new Birmingham band, the Idle Race, led by Jeff Lynne. For the recording at the Playhouse, extra instruments hired by the BBC included '2 pedal timps, glockenspiel, Wow Pedal' (sic). The band had just released their first single, and had applied for an audition, but before one could be booked, Bernie called them in for this 'trial broadcast'. 'We'd been going for about 18 months,' says Jeff Lynne. 'We lived and played mostly in Birmingham, so going down to London to record for the BBC was a major event. We hadn't had much experience of recording, so it was a relief to find it quite easy-going. I thought it was great, you got to record and got paid for doing it. I think the fee just about covered the petrol from Birmingham. Bernie got us a good sound. At the time, I was wanting to be a producer myself, so I was learning a lot. I even got some blue corduroy trousers like Bernie's, and wore them for my first attempt as a record producer, the second Idle Race album. From then on, corduroy trousers were always called Producer's Trousers.'

That was just the Monday of the first Radio 1 week on air. Tuesday saw the Crazy World of Arthur Brown, with Ron Wood on guitar, pre-recording at the Playhouse;

and Lou Rawls and Maxine Brown at 201 Piccadilly. Wednesday was Denny Laine's Electric String Band, with Bernie and Dave Tate; and Friday the Jimi Hendrix Experience, again at the Playhouse. But it wasn't the group's first BBC session. They had done two for *Saturday Club*, in February and March that year. Chas Chandler, Jimi's manager, knew *Saturday Club* producer Bill Bebb from his days in The Animals, and had assured him, as Bill recalls, that 'this guy'll blow you away.' He did more than that. The first session, on 13 February, was in S2, a studio in the Broadcasting House sub-basement, three floors below street level, which had originally been the small 'Vaudeville' studio theatre. 'The SM (Peter Harwood) said "getting a lot of feed-back", so I opened up the talkback, and started saying, "Er, Jimi, we're getting rather a lot..." when Chas, sitting with me in the control room, leans over and says, "Shuttup man, that's his sound!"' remembers Bill. 'So quickly I said, "No, everything's fine Jimi, you just carry on." But by now the SM's having kittens. "Just shut it right down," I said; but when he switched off the monitors we could still hear Jimi through the sound-proof glass, and we could see the glass moving.' Halfway through the session, a woman appeared behind Bill to complain that the live string quartet broadcast she was doing for Radio 3

CLASSIC SESSION

THE JIMI HENDRIX EXPERIENCE

Recorded: **6.10.67**
Studio: **Playhouse Theatre**
Producer: **Bev Phillips**
Engineer: **Pete Ritzema**
First Broadcast: **15.10.67 Top Gear**
Tracks: **Little Miss Lover, Driving South, Burning of the Midnight Lamp, Hound Dog, Experiencing the Blues**
Line-up: **Jimi Hendrix (guitar & vocals); Noel Redding (bass & vocals); Mitch Mitchell (drums)**

'While at the BBC studios, we were introduced to Stevie Wonder [there to be interviewed by Brian Matthew]. When Mitch nipped off to the loo, some enterprising person suggested an "informal jam" between Jimi and myself, with Stevie on drums. We jammed two segments, then Stevie sang an old R 'n' B song. Of course, they forgot to turn the tape machines off. The jam was aired a couple of times [not on Top Gear – KG] and then bootlegged.'

from Are You Experienced? by Noel Redding & Carol Appleby (Picador).

'Stevie wanted to play the drums, to calm down before his interview. Jimi Hendrix and Noel Redding played along with a bit of 'I was made to love her', for about a minute and a half, and then about another seven minutes of mucking about. I don't remember Stevie singing, though. It's not that wonderful, but it is one of those legendary things: Stevie Wonder did jam with Jimi Hendrix on that session and it's there on tape. I don't think it was ever broadcast.

'Hendrix I remember as being rather shy, giggly and camp. He was very self-concious about doing his vocals. He insisted on having screens put up round his mic when he was overdubbing his vocals, because, otherwise, he said, Noel and Mitch would make him laugh. But he also did these blues jams on his sessions [e.g. 'Experiencing the blues' on 2nd Top Gear session, 15.12.67], where he'd get everyone along from the Hendrix office to join in, which was rather fun.'

Pete Ritzema

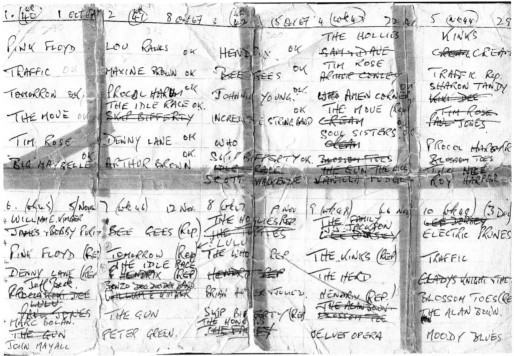

Bernie Andrews' original wallchart of planned Top Gear Session broadcasts for the first 10 weeks of Radio 1.

from the Concert Hall, two floors above, kept being interrupted by wafts of electric guitar. But, as Bill points out, for this Radio 1 & 3 simulcast, 'Jimi didn't ask for a repeat fee.'

The Hendrix session of 6 October went out on the third *Top Gear*, along with another 'first' from The Who: the first BBC session recorded outside the Corporation, in a commercial studio. Bernie remembers he had to fight for permission. The Who were keen to do it, proved by their agreeing to record five one-off jingles for the show on the date, including 'My Favourite Station' to the tune of 'My Generation', but had insisted on using stereo facilities at De Lane Lea, rather than BBC mono studios. Bernie went there to produce it on the 10th. Soon afterwards, The Who offered to redo some of their *Top Gear* jingles for regular use on Radio 1, but were prevented by the fact that there was, apparently, 'no MU/BBC agreed basis for a contract'.

After the fourth show (featuring The Nice's first session, members of whom also backed Tim Rose's recording on the same day), Bernie put Peel back on air with Drummond for two more Sundays. The 29 October *Top Gear* featured new sessions from The Cream, The Kinks, and Jeff Beck, and the debut of Roy Harper, backed by Clem Cattini on drums and Brian Brocklehurst on bass. 'The recording experience was fraught with worrying whether what I was doing would be understood by either the session musicians or the producer and engineer,' says Harper, the session ending up 'a compromise, but quite a happy one. What I managed to get together with the bass player on Zengem was excellent. The most important thing I gained, I think, was how quickly something adequate could be knocked together when necessary.'

Then came a tiny event which would inadvertently effect Peel and Bernie's entire future careers: the debut session by Tyrannosaurus Rex, booked primarily at Peel's instigation, on the sixth show, of 5 November. Two of the six numbers Marc Bolan and Steve Peregrine-Took played at the 30 October recording at 201 Piccadilly, 'Highways' and 'Pictures of Purple People' (the latter not broadcast until the repeat on 4 February 1968), did not appear later on the group's first album. Although Peel was already a fan and friend of Bolan, the Audition panel of Popular Music department senior producers were not so sure about the tape, when presented to them the day after this trial broadcast. 'Crap, and pretentious crap at that,' said one. They scored two 'No' votes; but six eventually said 'Yes', and the group passed, as 'a contemporary folk/blues duo'; with the proviso that 'the panel thought them suitable only for specialist programmes such as *Top Gear*.' It's no coincidence that two days after the panel met, Bernie was told by one of his superiors never to use Peel again. Bernie acted immediately. He phoned Clive Selwood and booked Peel for a further seven weeks. From 12 November, for the next three months, *Top Gear* would be co-hosted by Peel with Tommy Vance. There was hell to pay for Bernie when the Popular Music department found out. 'They went stark raving mad,' Bernie recalls. They tried to force him to cancel the booking but, as Clive Selwood says, 'Bernie went out on a limb with the Radio 1 bosses, by insisting that he and I had a verbal contract for a series.' And the following week the management, to their fury and astonishment, found out listeners took a diametrically opposed view of Peel's talents. The initial audience research on the network's first month, which appeared internally from the second week of November, showed that the 'sizeable minority' who liked *Top Gear* felt Peel had 'a good voice' and was 'more sincere' than all the other DJs. The duty office summarised its calls up to 21 November, saying: 'Many of the suggestions for Radio 1 were from supporters of DJs such as John Peel and Tony Prince.' Peel was safe, if only for a few weeks.

Peel and Vance's first show featured no fewer than three first broadcasts: The Gun, Peter Green's Fleetwood Mac and the Bonzo Dog Doo-Dah Band, recorded successively on the 6, 7 and 8 November. And the next week it was Brian Auger's Trinity, Honeybus and, in a session which has become an innocent subject of controversy, by Lulu. For years Peel believed that this was on his first show, and

Peel and Vance co-presenting Top Gear, November 1967.

CLASSIC SESSION

THE BONZO DOG DOO-DAH BAND

Recorded: **8.11.67**

Studio: **Maida Vale 4**

Producer: **Bernie Andrews**

Engineer: **Pete Ritzema**

First Broadcast: **12.11.67 Top Gear**

Tracks: **The Equestrian Statue, The Craig Torso Show, Mickey's Son And Daughter, Death Cab For Cutie**

Line-up: **Viv Stanshall; Neil Innes; Roger Ruskin Spear; Rodney Slater; Legs Larry Smith; Vernon Dudley Bohay-Nowell; Sam Spoons**

'We'd always do short playlets, made up specially for the sessions. They would be worked out in the BBC studio for the first time. I remember I lived round the corner from Bernie in Muswell Hill, and I used to phone him up the day before a session asking can we have such-and-such effect? Those sessions quickly took the format of three songs and one piece of recitative. I used to invent things just to break all these ridiculous BBC rules: like on the one we did later with Walters, he told us that more than five or six seconds' silence was not allowed, so I put about ten seconds into "Sofa Head", after saying, "Silence is appropriate, and it shall remain appropriate." On that first one with Bernie, "The Craig Torso Show" was a play parodying the new Radio 1 DJs, which we never recorded elsewhere.'

Viv Stanshall

'They were some of the most creative sessions I ever did, because the numbers were created in the studio, with tape editing, effects and so on. As the first ones also ran until 1am, then unheard of, and the commissionaires at Maida Vale and Piccadilly complained, they also started my undeserved reputation of running all these weird sessions through the night.'

Bernie Andrews

held it up as an example of what he claimed was the programme's brief, 'to look over the horizons of pop', which never, in truth, existed in writing. Like all BBC radio producers then, Bernie was never given a formal brief: 'They knew what I was about,' he says. In fact, Bernie booked Lulu partly at the suggestion of Donald MacLean, to reassure him *Top Gear* was open-minded in the wake of the Tyrannosaurus Rex incident, and partly because she was going through an R 'n' B phase. 'It was actually a bloody good, ballsy session,' Bernie recalls.

Two more debut sessions followed on the 26th: The Family, and Elmer Gantry's Velvet Opera. So the scoops went on. On 3 December it was the Alan Bown; Ten Years After, Fairport Convention and Nirvana on the 10th, along with a storming soul session from Gladys Knight and the Pips, backed by the Johnny Watson Concept, including then session guitarists Jim Sullivan and Jimmy Page ('they were knocked out by the guitar playing, recalls Pete Ritzema); and Cat Stevens and the Soft Machine on the 17th. That Softs debut was of the three-piece that had just released their debut LP. As Robert Wyatt was to sing on their second session, 18 months later, 'though each little song was less than three minutes long, Mike [Ratledge] squeezed a solo in somehow.' Then, on Christmas Eve, it was David Bowie's turn. Two years before, on 2 November 1965, his group David Bowie and the Lower Third had auditioned but been rejected by the Talent Selection Group, with comments on his report such as 'a singer devoid of personality' and 'amateur-sounding vocalist who sings wrong notes'. Now he was back with his debut album on Deram, in his Anthony Newley phase. Bernie liked it a lot. 'I phoned up Ken Pitt (then Bowie's manager), and the three of us met for a lunch to discuss it. David wasn't too keen to do things from the LP, because to him it was already old stuff; but he did some of them, plus new songs. He did almost everything first take.' Bernie booked a 15-piece version of the Art Greenslade Orchestra, complete with four-piece violin section to back Bowie, on that 18 December recording at 201 Piccadilly. This time, the tape passed the Audition panel.

The new year brought one of Bernie's most cunning ruses. Captain Beefheart and his Magic Band were in the UK on tour, and Peel was keen to get them in. Unfortunately, as Americans, they fell foul of the then Ministry of Labour rules on work permits. In support of the MU, the Ministry stipulated that only musicians from countries whose radio stations offered reciprocal bookings for British acts could play at the BBC. As American radio didn't do live sessions, no American bands could be recorded. Solo artists could be booked, if backed by British musicians. But Beefheart had an all-American band. Bernie persuaded the Ministry that, as the name suggested, this was a touring band of magicians. They got permission, as a

'Variety' act. The session itself, on the 24th at Maida Vale, featured 'Sure 'Nuff 'n Yes I Do', and Dave Tate remembers having to suspend a mic over Beefheart, who insisted on singing lying on his back. Later, on the band's second and final BBC radio date, in May, at the Piccadilly, Bernie recalls Beefheart being entranced by the sound made by the control cubicle light switch. 'Oh, isn't that great,' he said, switching the fluorescents on and off for three or four minutes.

But that first Beefheart broadcast, on 4 February, was notable for another reason. It was the first *Top Gear* Peel presented on his own. The show was cut to two hours, ending at 4pm. Needletime was cut to 45 minutes. Each week's show now needed only two, not three or four new sessions. Bev Phillips left at the beginning of March to become a producer on the teatime David Symonds show. Soon after, Bernie moved Peel to self-op studios in Broadcasting House, meaning he could at last play the records in himself. But this, and some other good news, had been coming to Peel for a while. As early as 5 December, a meeting of the Popular Music department had confirmed that Peel would be the sole *Top Gear* presenter 'from Week 6'. Even earlier, an idea from another producer, in a different department, meant that by March 1968, Peel, who had barely got past the first cull of DJs in November, now had not one, but two programmes. That producer was John Muir.

■

MUIR HAD JOINED the BBC from the RAF as a technical operator in 1961, and followed the usual route into engineering, then, just before Radio 1 launched, won a production attachment in the Recorded Programmes Department, or Service (RPS), later known as Archive Features. The idea was to make programmes from non-needletime archive material, such as recordings by the BBC and other broadcasters; in other words, programmes costing next to nothing in copyright payments. Muir

---

A LISTENER WRITES...

'In March 1967 I'd arrive home from school, have tea and tune in to Radio London, "The Big L", listening for an hour or so before doing my homework. One afternoon I found that the amiable Australian Norman St John, who'd just left the station, had been replaced by an interesting new voice, with a well-spoken, slightly Liverpudlian public-school accent and a droll wit, a mixture of Kenny Everett's zaniness and the 60s TV satirists. So I got to know Peel as one of the daytime Radio London team before discovering his more adventurous late-night programmes, first "London After Midnight" and then "The Perfumed Garden", which is another story. I thought once he joined the BBC that only "Night Ride", for a short time at least, developed the open-minded spirit of "The Perfumed Garden".'

Colin Ellis

discovered there was a wealth of underused, non-needletime world-music recordings. He was toying with the idea of putting them together with poetry and acoustic sessions when, about a month into Radio 1 – just after Bernie's bosses had told him never to hire Peel again – he met Clive Selwood. 'Peel thinks they're going to sack him,' he told Muir. 'Any programmes going?' Muir immediately suggested making a pilot. Peel did it, the tape was submitted, nothing happened. Muir became worried. His attachment, on which he was producing middle-of-the-road editions of RPS's after-midnight show *Night Ride*, ran out at the end of March. Late in 1967, he asked his boss, Harold Rogers, about the delay. The tape must then have got through to Robin Scott. On 1 January he told Popular Music department, 'RPS has produced a *Perfumed Garden* type show, which I am considering for a late night slot.' Peel and Muir got the first hour, midnight to 1am, of the Wednesday *Night Ride* strip, from 6 March.

This radical show would become a cult to rival *Top Gear*, and on tape and as audio files swapped by networks of listeners remains a treasured relic of the counter-culture era. Each edition had a guest poet live and one session act, normally a solo, acoustic artist or duo. John Muir, with SM Roger Derry, pre-recorded these on Monday afternoons or evenings in S1, the tiny sub-basement studio in Broadcasting House celebrated as the site of the world's first experimental television broadcast, on 22 August 1932. It also sits right on top of the Bakerloo tube line, and sessions occasionally had to be stopped as trains rumbled below. 'This is the first of a new series of programmes on which you may hear just about anything,' Peel said, introducing the Incredible String Band and Adrian Mitchell. In those first few weeks, people like all the new Mersey poets, Roger McGough, Brian Patten and the 'Liverpool Scene', Andy Roberts and Adrian Henri, were featured.

When his attachment ended after the first four shows, Muir handed Peel over to Denis O'Keeffe, a fellow SM on attachment to RPS. *Night Ride* threw up startling double bills almost every week: Champion Jack Dupree and Christopher Logue; the Occasional Word Ensemble and Roy Harper; Ron Geesin and Mike Cooper – both debuts. Through spring and summer 1968, the show also featured first sessions from Shirley and Dolly Collins, Al Stewart, Stefan Grossman, Michael Chapman, John Martyn, Bridget St John, Dave and Jo-Ann Kelly and Ian A Anderson, today editor of *Folk Roots* magazine: 'I took along harmonica player Steve Rye. He wasn't credited as there apparently wasn't the budget to pay him, but he was heard on the tapes,' he says. Many of these acoustic country-blues acts, like Anderson, had started on the South-West club scene the year before. 'Mike Cooper and I had suggested Gef Lucana of Saydisc in Bristol start a blues label called Matchbox, and when its

ONE-SESSION WONDER

Mississippi Fred McDowell

First broadcast: **Night Ride, 5.3.69**
Recorded: **26.2.69**
Studio: **Aeolian Hall Studio 1**
Producer: **John F Muir**
Engineer: **unknown**
Tracks: **Louise, Burying Ground Blues, Glory Hallelujah, Jesus On The Main Line, Way Out On The Frisco Line, Keep Your Lamps Trimmed And Burning, Good Morning Little Schoolgirl**
Line-up: **McDowell solo (electric guitar and vocal)**

McDowell (b. 1904, d. 1972) was one of the last original exponents of the bottleneck blues style, who toured Britain twice in the late 1960s, this second tour managed by Ian A Anderson. This was his only BBC session.

'I'll tell you another thing, I enjoyin' being' over here, in England. It's the second time I've been here, and I've met some nice people. Before when I was here I really had a good time, and I'm lookin' forward to having another one this time. And I hope the people like my type of playing. I don't play no rock 'n' roll. I just play old blues, that's all I play.'

– from interview pre-recorded at session

Peel confessed on air he was disappointed not to have been able to attend the session, because he'd first heard McDowell on albums recorded at his home by Alan Lomax many years before.

first compilation LP *Blues Like Showers of Rain* came out in July 1968, everything went silly,' notes Anderson; 'John Peel, then, as he ever was, the first to spot something good happening at the roots, played it every week on *Night Ride* and had most of the artists guesting.'

But what made the show a cause célèbre at the time was something quite different. Pete Carr took over production in October 1968, and decided to make the show more satirical. His first edition featured Richard Neville of *Oz*. On 6 November, John Wells, then author of 'Mrs Wilson's Diary' in *Private Eye*, came in and said to Peel, among other things, that people who had spoken to Harold Wilson had said that he wasn't interested in the Nigerian war because it would lose him votes. Across London in No 10 Downing Street the Prime Minister, apparently, was listening. He was evidently not pleased. Shortly after the broadcast, the Labour chief whip, John Silkin, complained to Sir Hugh Greene, Director-General of the BBC. On the following Monday morning, the 11th, the headline on the front page of *The Times* read 'BBC at fault over slur on Wilson'. 'The complaint is understandable. We were at fault,' the BBC apologised, via the newspaper. On the following Wednesday, Peel read out a written BBC apology, but was allowed to disassociate himself from it. A few weeks later, Pete Carr got the attachment to television he'd been seeking. John Muir was put back in charge.

Not that things calmed down. On his first show back on, Muir found John Lennon and Yoko Ono holding up to the mic a cassette

A LISTENER WRITES...

'Summer of 69. Warm Sunday evenings. The 14-year-old me cradling a transistor, wandering the empty streets of my small town. Nobody about. Shops all closed. My mind wide open and opening wider with every Top Gear. This ritual enacted every Sunday, all summer long. Two sessions stick in the mind. John Fahey deconstructing the guitar till it sounds like no guitar music I've ever heard. The post-Barrett Floyd becoming so abstract that it's barely music. For years these are my benchmarks for weirdness. Treasured memories of my questing self. And then one day not so long ago someone sent me a Top Gear tape. 17/8/69. And there they are. Both sessions. ON THE SAME SHOW. Fahey's deconstruction was simply a little note bending and detuning and slide work. Floyd's abstractions amounted to a few birdsong and seascape sound effects over their pleasant pastoral noodlings. The 50-something in me bemoaned the loss of aural innocence. The 14-year-old in me who still hears like that marvelled once more at the magic of it all.'

Rob Chapman, Manchester

---

recording of Yoko's baby's heart, which had later miscarried. A Baptist Minister, the Rev John McNicol, complained to the BBC that the interview was in bad taste. *The Times* of 17 December, under the headline 'Late Night Show "Suggestive"', said the BBC was to investigate the complaint. Nothing, however, came of it. Muir and Peel carried on. In January 1969, Muir recorded Tim Hart and Maddy Prior, the duo that would end up in Steeleye Span, and the next week captured Pete Brown and the Battered Ornaments in session. Although some listeners would phone in to complain about the show's 'deplorable' music, its range of live blues, folk, and world music showed impeccable taste. Some within the BBC were won over. Jon Curle, who would take over from Peel for the second, middle-of-the-road hour of the slot, would sometimes play the extra session tracks recorded which Peel had not been able to squeeze into his half.

But, in the wake of the Wilson affair, the show, never liked by some senior executives, was now definitely out of favour. Once its original backer Robin Scott was gone, taking over from David Attenborough as controller of BBC2 TV in December 1968, it had no friends in high places. Shortly after Muir left to take up a contract producer's job in Popular Music in March and Pete Ritzema, by now on attachment as a producer, took over, the Wednesday Peel *Night Ride* was moved, in April, to a mid-evening MW-only slot, 8.15–9.15pm. 'They moved it to kill it,' says Pete Ritzema, and he should know. Nevertheless, 'Son of *Night Ride*' as Peel called it, was allowed to continue, under sentence of death, before finally being axed in September. Ritzema and Peel made use of the stay of execution. Interviewing Tony van Den Burgh about a forthcoming Radio 4 programme on VD and the problem of people acknowledging the disease, on 28 May, Peel, to help the argument, admitted he had it. There were complaints, but Peel survived. Other interviewees that summer included a young Richard Branson and Ralph Steadman. Ivor Cutler did what was to be the first of more than a score of Radio 1 sessions; and the Paris was booked on 12 May 1969 for what would prove to be Pink Floyd's fifth and final BBC session, on which they did 'Daybreak', 'Cymbeline', 'Green Is The Colour' and 'The Narrow Way', broadcast on 14 May, and promptly repeated on the following Sunday's *Top Gear*, 18 May.

Pete Roche, a poet and regular guest, livened up the penultimate show no end. 'At first, I thought he was perhaps changing into something, as you do,' Peel remembered. 'All of a sudden there was this naked figure in the studio saying, "Hi John, look at me",' recalls Pete Ritzema. After a moment's shocked pause, fellow guest Viv Stanshall exclaimed, 'I say, what a good idea!' The last night, 24 September 1969, featured the debut of Kevin Coyne's first band, Coyne Clague. He, like many others given their first break on *Night Ride*, would return to record for Peel again. The then management of Radio 1 may have killed the show; but the idea of giving Peel a late-night slot, originating from John Muir, and backed by Robin Scott, was far from dead. It too would return.

■

BACK IN MARCH 1968 there was no sign of a threat hanging over either of Peel's new, solo-DJ programmes. Audience figures published later would show *Top Gear* regularly winning 1.6 million listeners in the first quarter of 1968. That summer would prove to be their finest hour. Once on his own, Peel's manner relaxed and the programmes sounded much more confident and, after Bev's departure, Bernie produced all the sessions, normally with Pete Ritzema at the Playhouse on Mondays; and with Dave Tate, and, from July, Allen Harris, at 201 Piccadilly on Tuesdays.

FIRST HEARD HERE...

'With A Little Help From My Friends' by Joe Cocker & the Grease Band

First heard on Top Gear 14 July 1968
Session recorded May 1968
Reached No 1 in UK singles chart November 1968
Peel Ahead of Everyone by... (PAE) Index: 16 weeks

The first-ever recording of the group's new stage favourite cover of The Beatles' song. Bernie Andrews saved it, and first put it out on the repeat on 14 July. It was only recorded commercially later that summer, released in September, and became a UK and US number one, and was famously captured on film at Woodstock – but that was more than a year later.

ONE-SESSION WONDER

Leonard Cohen

First broadcast: **Top Gear, 14.7.68**
Recorded: **9.7.68**
Studio: **Piccadilly 1**
Producer: **Bernie Andrews**
Engineer: **Dave Tate**
Tracks: **That's No Way To Say Goodbye, You Know Who I Am, Like A Bird On A Wire, So Long Marianne (Dress Rehearsal Rag, first broadcast on session repeat 11.8.68)**
Line-up: **Cohen (guitar, vocals), plus 5 musicians including Dave Cousins (banjo), 3 backing singers, director Tony Gilbert**

'We expected him to come in and sit in the corner in denims and be rather sombre,' recalled Peel, 'instead of which he appeared in a rather nice suit and really took charge of everything: "I want the singers over there where I can maintain eye contact; and if we could have those screens here please..." Just a very organised guy.'

'It was a strange re-working of the old BBC session system, because Bernie had booked this pick-up band of contemporary notables, including Dave Cousins on banjo. I just sat there enthralled at the back of the stalls. Cohen walked out for a break and I had a word with him. He was a really nice guy.' Ashley Hutchings of Fairport Convention, who had asked Bernie if he could come along.

One month later, the Fairports would do their only ever recording of their stage favourite, Cohen's 'Suzanne', in the same studio. This remains Leonard Cohen's only BBC radio session.

Harris had been one of the two regular XP-ops on the *Top Gear* sessions since the beginning, sharing running the tape machines at the Playhouse and Piccadilly with Bob Conduct; who later rose to head up 'Sound Ops Group 2', which organised all Radios 1 and 2's sound engineers. 'The Playhouse was good for loud groups,' Bob Conduct explains. 'The irregular shape of the unconverted theatre, with all its velvet-upholstered seating, even when empty, absorbed a lot of the volume.' As you entered the back of the stalls from the foyer, the control room, for producer and SM, was on your right, and the recording channel, with the tape recorders, on the left. The layout was similar at the Piccadilly, except that the two cubicles were at the front of a small balcony, reached by a spiral staircase up from the stalls. Things had developed since Bev Phillips had brought in his customised tobacco tins, but recording was still mono. The Playhouse mixing desk now had four RSAs, or BBC EQ circuits. It was also the Type B desk, which allowed you to mix at high level, every mic having its own valve amplifier. Piccadilly had a rebuilt Type A, with 'quadrant pots' instead of rotary faders. These were rather bizarre, Flash Gordon-style levers which moved through 90 degrees. Not that bands necessarily disliked the antiquated atmosphere of the theatres. Pete Ritzema remembers Tim Buckley, after his memorable first session for *Top Gear* on 4 April, at the Piccadilly, wanting to make an album there. Then he asked, "this place is stereo, right?" At this point the plan collapsed.

Nevertheless there could be technical problems which no one could blame on the

CLASSIC SESSION

FAIRPORT CONVENTION

Recorded: **26.8.68**
Studio: **Studio 1, 201 Piccadilly**
Producer: **Bernie Andrews**
Engineer: **Pete Ritzema**
First Broadcast: **1.9.68 Top Gear**
Tracks: **If You Feel Good You Know It Can't Be Wrong, Fotheringay, Gone Gone Gone, Eastern Rain, (Suzanne, first broadcast 29.9.68)**
Line-up: **Sandy Denny (vocals); Ashley Hutchings (bass & vocals); Martin Lamble (drums); Ian Matthews (vocals); Simon Nicol (guitar & vocals); Richard Thompson (guitar & vocals)**

'The care and attention that was paid to tracks was wonderful, particularly on "If you feel good"; I remember recording a kazoo and speeding it up on tape, just to get the right ragtime effect. And we took ages to record one tiny insert that was a musical joke. This involved breaking a cup, which wasn't as easy as it sounds, because it had to be just the right kind of smash, and then inserting it into the song after the line "put down your coffee cup". The whole operation took up about an hour and several BBC cups. We never recorded a lot of those tracks we did for radio sessions. We'd put down things we liked to do on stage, and we were doing a lot of cover versions then. "Suzanne" was a stage favourite, and audiences would cheer the moment we announced it; but that BBC session was the only recording we made of it. The arrangement was all based on rhythm. Martin was going round the kit with beaters, and the two guitars, drums and bass were all doing different patterns. It was a masterpiece of rhythmic interplay, and Bernie did a great job on the production.'

Ashley Hutchings

BBC's ageing recording equipment. Gilbert O'Sullivan, then just known as Gilbert, had made his first record on CBS, 'Disappear', and on the strength of it Bernie booked him for a debut recording at the Piccadilly on 14 May, backed by the 16-piece Keith Mansfield Orchestra. 'He was worried about coming in, because he'd only ever performed with his own piano, which was half a tone out,' says Bernie. 'So I OK-ed an extra £8 porterage to bring his piano in from his flat in Bayswater. Then when the musicians went to tune up with the piano, they went mad. They all had to de-tune down to it. He did about three or four songs, and it turned out OK. Afterwards, he played another three numbers on his own at the piano, and really got into it. I think that session was much better than anything he did subsequently.'

In the space of four weeks that summer, Deep Purple, Free and Jethro Tull all made their first radio appearances here. 'I think it was at Maida Vale, and I recall finding Bernie a jolly soul, who, if nothing else, put everyone at ease,' says Ian Anderson of Tull. 'We did a third of the act we were doing then at the Marquee and the blues clubs, and Mick Abrahams' interpretation of 'Cat's Squirrel'. I do remember the position the programme held within the otherwise chaperoned world of radio. It was all there was. The importance of *Top Gear* was that it created a volatile atmosphere, which reflected what was going on. At the time there was growing competition, albeit friendly rivalry, between the Marquee bands. And that was a cruel indication that out there was a manipulative world. That rather chummy friendliness that Peel and Bernie's show captured was inevitably beginning to get frayed, as bands became successful, harsh realities were coming home to roost, and record sales began to be significant.' Ian Anderson suggests that in the scene's success lay the beginning of its end. Peel sensed this too. In the *Melody Maker* late in July, he lamented the inverted snobbery into which the underground was slipping. 'The extraordinary thing is, if anybody gets anything done, he becomes unpopular.' His and Bernie's programme would soon suffer a similar fate within the BBC. *Top Gear* was about to achieve its greatest success. Yet six months later it would be dealt a body blow.

When the *Melody Maker* published the results of its 1968 Readers' Poll, in late September, John Peel won Top Disc Jockey, and *Top Gear* won Top Radio Programme. Radio 1 was stunned. They had assumed that Tony Blackburn, who came second, would win. With the exception of controller Robin Scott and one or two far-sighted

CLASSIC SESSION

FLEETWOOD MAC

Recorded: **27.8.68**
Studio: **Studio 1, 201 Piccadilly**
Producer: **Bernie Andrews**
Engineer: **Allen Harris**
First Broadcast: **1.9, 13.10 and 24.11.68 Top Gear**
Tracks: **A Mind Of My Own, I Have To Laugh, You're The One, Preachin' The Blues (all first broadcast 1.9.68); You Need Love, A Talk With You, Bo Diddley, Wine Whisky Women (all first broadcast 13.10.68); Crutch And Kane, If You Be My Baby, Crazy For My Baby (all first broadcast 24.11.68)**
Line-up: **Peter Green (guitar, vocals); Jeremy Spencer (guitar, vocals); Danny Kirwan (guitar, vocals); John McVie (bass guitar); Mick Fleetwood (drums); and guest Christine Perfect (keyboards, vocals)**

A classic session for three reasons: the band's first recording with new member Danny Kirwan; a special guest appearance by Christine Perfect, then with Chicken Shack, but also John McVie's wife-to-be; and a staggeringly productive work-out, 11 numbers, totalling 33' 50" of music, in what Bernie put down as the first 'Triple Session' for Radio 1: 'Once we set the tapes rolling, they just played and played.' 'Most of the numbers were recorded straight down in one go, live, with no overdubs,' says Allen Harris.

Recorded the day after the Fairport Convention 'Classic Session' on the previous page, in the same studio: just a typical week on Top Gear.

Peel winning Top DJ from the Melody Maker, September 1968.
Getty Images

FIRST HEARD HERE...

'Sabre Dance' by Love Sculpture

First heard here on Top Gear 6 October
Session recorded 16 September
Reached No 5 in UK singles chart end
November 1968
Peel Ahead of Everyone by... (PAE)
Index: Eight weeks

'We recorded "Sabre Dance", all six minutes of it, and I couldn't believe it: it was one of those "first-take" numbers, we did do another take, but we couldn't improve on the first. I programmed it intentionally early in the programme: I wouldn't normally, I'd rather close with it, especially if it was a long number. Now by this time, Peel was doing the transmissions by himself, and I would be at home. For the last item in the show, I put in a six-minute record, which could be cut, because I knew what was going to happen: as soon as "Sabre Dance" went out, the phone rang, and I knew it was Peel, and what he was going to ask. "Take out the last song, and you can play Sabre Dance again," I said. And that was the first and only time a pre-recorded session item was played twice in the same programme. The reason it hadn't been done before was because it incurred an immediate full repeat fee. But "Sabre Dance" justified it. Parlophone picked up on it, re-recorded it, rush-released it, and had a hit. But Dave Edmunds always said that first BBC version was the best recording.'

Bernie Andrews

others, the station's producers regarded Peel as little more than a joke, who clearly wouldn't last. Bernie himself was 'gobsmacked' at the award. The *MM* itself was sure. 'The idea that *Top Gear* is a minority appeal programme has been exploded,' it said. 'John Peel – A Victory for the Music' read the headline. 'Probably more letters to *MM* mention Peel than any other artist or deejay.' Peel claimed his contribution was simply 'to let people hear what other people are doing'. Bernie paid tribute to the programme's session sound engineers. 'A lot of our success is due to their efforts and the way they take a personal interest in getting things right.'

They carried on doing so. That autumn, Ritzema and Harris were joined as Bernie's SMs by Bob Conduct, moving up from XP-Op; and two of the earliest he did were Van der Graaf Generator's first and Caravan's first, recorded on the last day of the year. For Bernie, it was a career highlight to rank with the Idle Race. 'It was one of those where I didn't care what anyone else thought: I know they're bloody good, and I'm going to book them!' Caravan founder member Richard Sinclair's memories are mainly to do with the Maida Vale canteen. 'David Sinclair and I were both on macrobiotic diets, but the canteen didn't have gamasio salt or brown rice. Man, what a downer. Not a lentil in sight.' The very next show, 12 January 1969, featured the radio debuts of both The Strawbs and Yes; and the week after that it was the turn of Jon Hiseman's Colosseum. 'Having already played with the New Jazz Orchestra, Georgie Fame and John Mayall's Bluesbreakers, to say nothing of Graham Bond, I knew those BBC recordings were a normal and essential part of getting a band born,' says Jon Hiseman. 'The radio shows were important in that we could record a number, and then find people would clap in recognition on the first concerts following transmission,' he remembers. 'John and Bernie were particularly generous to us, and we took the shows very seriously; though the recording of material at the BBC at that time was definitely a technique that had to be developed, because, technically, the BBC lagged far behind commercial recording studios. But, because of the speed of work, the very quick balance-and-play system, a good live band could get very good results.'

Just how good was to be proved again early in March. Almost exactly a year before, *Top Gear* had featured The Yardbirds' last BBC session. Now, on 3 March 1969, Bernie did Led Zeppelin's first, at the Playhouse. It was only renewing a relationship with Jimmy Page, who had turned up on many of Bernie's BBC dates as one of the top session guitarists in London. The group had already conquered America, but their first album was only released in Britain later that month, and, save, for *Top Gear*, UK audiences were then indifferent. 'They were very loud, but it was very good,' says Bernie. In the same month, Bernie finally updated his signature tune. Sounds Incorporated had re-recorded 'Top Gear' in 1967, with an organ replacing the original reed section. Then, late in 1968, it was redone by jazz guitarist Joe Moretti. But at last Bernie got what he was looking for from The Nice. On their session of 5 March, Keith Emerson slowed it down and radically rearranged it. Allen Harris used buckets of swirling echo on the recording. The new sig was first used on 16 March, and remained Peel's *Sounds of the Seventies* hallmark until October 1975. It was to be almost Bernie's final contribution, and yet, ironically, one of the longest lasting.

About this time, Popular Music department, in its staffing plans for the third quarter of the year, allocated to Bernie a weekly *Music While You Work* session for Radio 2. The department thought that Bernie was not pulling his weight by working solely on his own programme. Other producers would do their own projects, and yet also have general duties and day-to-day session work for other programmes. Bernie refused to do it. He argued that this extra work would mean he would only be able to spend 40 hours a week on *Top Gear*, which would mean an unacceptable drop in the programme's award-winning quality. The department relented slightly, and put Bernie on 'standby', the producer to be called on in emergencies. Bernie said this too was impractical. At the end of March he was told, at short notice, to go and stand-in for a colleague on a Radio 2 session. Bernie insisted his work producing *Top Gear* meant he was unavailable. The department took him off *Top Gear*.

■

'TOP GEAR PRODUCER in BBC shake-up' read the headline on page 3 of the next week's *Melody Maker*. The paper said Bernie was believed to be unhappy about the decision, but was unable to comment. It understood the reason for his removal was 'the BBC not wanting him to devote so much of his time to the one programme'. Peel told the paper Bernie worked six days a week, often into the small hours, on the show (this was true: Sheila remembers long, intense nights of endless record-playing, John and Bernie debating which tracks to play). 'It seems a rotten thing to take Bernie off *Top Gear*,' he said. 'After all, it was his programme. He deserves credit for making it such a success.' Robin Scott privately wrote a supportive letter to Bernie, encouraging him not to lose heart.

He was given other work. In June, he produced the Joe Loss Orchestra for Sam Costa, the Ian Wright Quartet, the cinema organ at Leicester Square, the Johnny Douglas Orchestra and Ken Moule and his Music, and other sessions for *Sounds Like Tony Brandon*. The following spring, he launched the Monday evening *Sounds of the Seventies* with David Symonds. Late in 1972, executive producer Teddy Warrick reunited him with Peel for a Thursday edition of *Sounds of the Seventies*, where he fleetingly rediscovered his old flair, scooping everyone else to win for Peel the first BBC sessions by Queen, Camel, Hatfield and the North, and Richard & Linda Thompson. During 1974 he produced Alan Black's Saturday night show *Rock On*. In his last years at Radio 1, he became best known as producer of Annie Nightingale's much-loved request show.

Led Zepplin. Charles Bonnay/Getty Images

But it's fair to say that Bernie was never the same man again after he was taken off the programme he had created. His relationship with BBC management became increasingly acrimonious through the 1970s. He took early retirement in the 1980s. 'I suppose I would have played things slightly differently, looking back,' he says; 'made an effort to put on a suit, go to some meetings, been a bit more flexible.'

Mention his name today and you get varied reactions. Former BBC managers will grimace and say 'a creative genius, of course, but a right pain in the arse to manage'. BBC engineers insist that none of what came to be the Peel Sessions tradition could have happened without him. Musicians will exclaim, with delight, things like: 'Bernie Andrews! Is he still alive? How is the old bastard?' When Andy Peebles interviewed John Lennon for Radio 1 on 6 December 1980, the first thing Lennon said was 'How's Bernie?'

His track record speaks for itself. In the first 18 months of Radio 1, *Top Gear* featured more than 75 first broadcasts of new acts, including everyone from that generation of the British rock scene. He invented the double session and the trial broadcast. It was he who first invited bands to 'come and have a listen'.

Many other BBC SMs and producers, not mentioned here, worked with The Beatles, the Rolling Stones and other pop giants of the 1950s and 1960s. But most of them fall into two distinct camps. There are those for whom it was a day's work like any other; and there are those younger staff whose great days lay ahead, in the 1970s and 1980s. It is no disrespect to them to say that, as far as the Peel Sessions are concerned, Bernie Andrews is the key figure in BBC history. Jimmy Grant started the ball rolling, and Bernie ran with it. No one else was there at the beginning, and yet still delighting in booking the wildest groups in the late 1960s. By sticking his neck out for Peel at a critical moment he secured the DJ's future at the expense of his own career. Perhaps the only thing he lacked was the ability to sing the BBC's song as well as his own rebel yell. That skill, to be able to play the tune the BBC wanted to hear, and by doing so preserve a corner of the Corporation for the musically uncompromising, was to be found in ample measure in his successor as John Peel's producer, John Walters.

■

At Reading Festival. Getty Images

CHAPTER 04

HE COULD BE heard blowing his own trumpet at the BBC as early as 1966. That was even before he joined the Corporation. As trumpeter in the Alan Price Set, John Walters recorded a session himself for *Saturday Club* that year. Before that he'd been an art teacher in Newcastle. But in early 1967 he was looking for more steady income, and remembered the BBC date. 'The producer seemed to be someone who sat there with a stopwatch timing tracks. I thought: I could do that.' He wrote to Popular Music department, and was called in to see Donald MacLean, with whom he recalled having a relaxed chat. Later that summer, the department invited him to apply for one of the new producers' jobs necessitated by Radio 1. He spent the first six months as a junior 'session' producer on *Scene and Heard*; and later on David Symonds' teatime show. Then, in June 1968, he was given *Savile's Travels*, a Sunday show which preceded *Top Gear*. When Symonds was taken off daytime, in January 1969, Walters was given his new show, *Symonds on Sunday*. 'I'd felt as a listener, before I'd joined Radio 1, that the live bands were often there just because the BBC couldn't play the records,' he remembered, 'but, particularly when I started *Symonds on Sunday*, I thought, let's do something positive with the live music.' He knew there were acts, like Geno Washington, that were huge in the clubs, not getting broadcast recognition. As part of this plan, he also booked the first sessions by ex-Jethro Tull guitarist Mick Abrahams' new band Blodwyn Pig, and Mason Wood Capaldi and Frog – scoops which first brought him to the attention of a miffed Peel, and, more significantly, his own Popular Music departmental chiefs.

'I inherited Bernie's office, a secretary, and a certain amount of ill feeling,' Walters said, of when he began on *Top Gear*. He is first credited as producer for the show of 27 April 1969. He had not much cared for Peel's hippy extremes. Bernie Andrews remembers him mocking these even during a training attachment with Bernie when he joined the BBC – which ironically meant he was the only producer available who knew about the show. Management thought they were going to get a controlled Peel, and also shifted the show to Sunday evenings, but things rebounded on them. 'I went in thinking, "I've got to do the best for my client",' Walters said. He started by booking bands Peel had already had in. But one of the first sessions he produced for Peel was King Crimson's debut on 6 May. His SM remembers someone from Island Records rushing into Maida Vale with the proposed artwork for their first album. That engineer was Tony Wilson, later producer of *The Friday Rock Show* and Alan Freeman. He had first teamed up with Walters on *Symonds on Sunday*. 'The die was cast,' says Tony. The team were to produce most *Top Gear* sessions for the next year.

Coming from doing standard sessions, Walters found Bernie's double-sessions a luxury. 'It was seen as absolutely outrageous by his colleagues.' He stuck with it, as well as inviting bands in to approve their takes: 'I'd certainly never been allowed to hear my stuff when I did BBC sessions.' The benefits first emerged on Led Zeppelin's fourth and

CLASSIC SESSION

SOFT MACHINE
Recorded: **10.6.69**
Studio: **Maida Vale 4**
Producer: **John Walters**
Engineer: **Tony Wilson**
First Broadcast: **15.6.69 Top Gear**
Tracks: **Face lift/Mousetrap/Backwards/Mousetrap reprise, The Moon In June**
Line-up: **Hugh Hopper (bass guitar); Mike Ratledge (keyboards); Robert Wyatt (drums & vocals)**

'I had this song called "Moon in June" which was a reactionary song, against not having songs called things like "Moon in June", but the lyrics really were about nothing, and the joke had worn off by the time I got into the studio. So I was in a panic, I thought, "I can't sing this nonsense again, I've got to write about something that's true." I just wrote about where I was, and what was happening, and the actual circumstances. I just wrote that on top of the music I'd already written.'

Robert Wyatt

'I remember Robert scribbling away in the control room, and the result was a new verse, in praise of our Maida Vale Studios, slightly ironically thanking us for allowing the Soft Machine to play as long as they wanted to.'

John Walters

Playing now is lovely, here in the BBC,
We're free to play almost as long and as loud as a
    jazz group, or an orchestra on Radio 3.
There are dance halls, and theatres, with acoustics
    worse than here,
Not forgetting the extra facilities, such as the tea
    machine, just along the corridor.
So to all our mates like Kevin, Caravan and the old
    Pink Floyd,
Allow me to recommend Top Gear, despite its
    extraordinary name.

from 'The Moon In June', as recorded on this session (copyright control).

final BBC studio session on 24 June, at Maida Vale 4. 'I can remember Jimmy Page coming in and saying the bass was a bit too high. So, knowing we had plenty of time, they could do the whole thing again. We turned the dial down, and said, "Right, when you're ready, we'll go for a cup of tea." ... That's what they had to do, because we had no multi-tracking,' says Walters. That session, on the Tuesday, was promptly followed by the band recording the pilot for what would become producer Jeff Griffin's 'Sunday Show' concert series on the Friday (27th), presented by Alan Black at the Playhouse.

John Walters. BBC

As Jeff Griffin told readers of *The Independent* in the paper's obituary for Alan Black in March 2007, the format of that show had partly been Black's idea. Zep had already agreed to do the concert pilot but, when Jeff asked Black to host it, 'Alan said he'd heard a programme in France in which bands would both play live and be interviewed about their music, and choose an interval act. He thought that this would work in the UK. The pilot was well received but the station's management didn't want the interval act, or interview section, or Alan – they wanted Peel. I felt sorry for Alan: a few months earlier, they'd all been criticising John. The programme later had a number of presenters, each chosen according to the performer, and Alan did some of those.' The Liverpool Scene, Andy Roberts and Adrian Henri, were the 'interval' act. Roberts remembers everyone adjourning to the Sherlock Holmes pub afterwards, and Henri shouting jovially down the bar, at the top of his voice, to Jimmy Page, 'Is it true you're known as the Led Wallet?' The show went out as part of *Top Gear* on 10 August.

Walters never pretended he necessarily liked what he was recording, or enjoyed producing sessions. He saw the creative aspect of his job in booking the acts: deciding, with Peel, which bands were right or wrong to record. Nevertheless, he took pleasure in Robert Wyatt's 'ironic tribute' to Maida Vale in 'The Moon In June', on Soft Machine's second BBC session in June. And the next month saw the Bonzos' last BBC date, at which Walters recalls the band being initially suspicious of him, feeling ideologically tied to Bernie. What made this worse was Walters suggesting

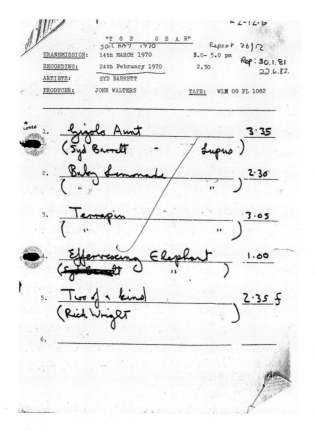

"T O P   G E A R"
30th MAY 1970   Repeat 26/5?

TRANSMISSION: 14th MARCH 1970   3.0- 5.0 pm   Ref: 30.1.81
RECORDING: 24th February 1970   2.30   22.6.82.
ARTISTE: SYD BARRETT
PRODUCER: JOHN WALTERS   TAPE: WLN 08 PL 1082

1. Gigolo Aunt   3.35
   (Syd Barrett   -   Lupus)

2. Baby Lemonade   2.30
   ("   "   )

3. Terrapin   3.05
   ("   "   )

4. Effervescing Elephant   1.00
   (Syd Barrett   "   )

5. Two of a kind   2.35 s
   (Rick Wright   )

6. _____

lines for Viv Stanshall to play on the trumpet. 'We didn't know he played,' said Stanshall, years later. Happily, this working partnership overcame these teething troubles, later to produce classic radio broadcasts.

At about the same time, BBC Records asked if Walters and Peel could put together a special *Top Gear* album. The only problem was any bands featured would have to be without a record contract, and not MU members. Walters found four unsigned acts: Bridget St John; Sweet Marriage; Welfare State; and Ron Geesin. He recorded them (except Welfare State, who provided their own tape of 'Silence Is Requested In The Ultimate Abyss') through July and early August in the huge Maida Vale 1, then the only BBC stereo studio, normally reserved for orchestral sessions, and still without any overdubbing facilities. Geesin would soon find fame as co-composer of Pink Floyd's 'Atom Heart Mother', first broadcast on the *Sunday Show* concert on 19 July 1970, Roger Waters adopting that title at the last moment at Geesin's pointed suggestion – 'You'll find a title in there' – from a headline in a copy of the *Evening Standard* lying in the control room at the Paris Cinema recording three days earlier (the story was headlined 'Atom Heart Mother Named'). But he had first attracted attention with his 1967 LP on Transatlantic, *A Raise of Eyebrows*. He was one of the first musicians of the 1960s to experiment with tapes, and create music out of the techniques of modern recording. 'Ron had a thing on that session where, to get something delayed, or echoed, we had to run the tape across all the heads of four tape recorders, and the tape ran like a washing line all round the control room,' said Walters. The *Top Gear* LP, engineered by Tony Wilson and edited by Mike Franks, also came complete with Peel's rendition on jew's harp of the old signature tune, and a sleeve featuring the bare feet of 'the Pig' ('she snorts when she laughs'), Peel's regular girlfriend of the past year, and later wife, Sheila Gilhooly. The following year the in-house label followed this up by releasing *Archive Things*, a compilation of Peel's favourite 'unusual recordings from the BBC Archives', as championed by *Night Ride*.

In September 1969, Peel and *Top Gear* again won the Best DJ and Best Radio Programme categories in the *MM* poll. Walters was maintaining the strength of the show. Yet, just one week later, Peel's Wednesday ex-*Night Ride* show was axed, and *Top Gear* was shifted again, this time to Saturday afternoons. The following month, a poll of 500 *Disc And Music Echo* readers also put Peel top, and 75 per cent of them thought Radio 1 'should promote unknown talent more actively'. Not for the first, or last time, Peel and Walters felt almost alone in championing the unknown, and they featured many first sessions early in 1970, including Medicine Head, destined to become one of the most BBC-recorded groups, and mainstay of Peel and Clive Selwood's Dandelion Record label, launched the previous September. 'I remember that John Walters did stop talking once during the whole session, something that many other *Top Gear*-ists do not believe to this day,' says Medicine Head's John Fiddler. In March, there was Syd Barrett's first solo session (14th) – 'I remember Dave Gilmore asking Syd what he wanted to do throughout,' said Walters – and The Faces' first (28th). But a week later they were no longer alone. BBC Radio 1 launched its daily *Sounds of the Seventies* programmes the following Monday, 4 April 1970.

Bringing in management consultants to improve financial control and contribute to a Policy Study Group on 'the future of national radio', sounds more like the BBC in the 1990s under John Birt, but that's what the Corporation did in the late 1960s. Consultants McKinsey arrived in November 1968. By spring 1969 they had made their suggestions, and the thinking of the Policy Study Group largely informed the decisions the Board of Management made on future programming, detailed in *Broadcasting in the Seventies*. This manifesto was published late in 1969, to protests from the arts establishment: it proposed abolishing the 'Third Programme' as a separate department. The thinking was to make each network more distinct, Radio 4 for talk, 3 for classical music, and 'to achieve a cleaner separation' between Radios 1 and 2, still sharing much programming. An early draft of *Broadcasting in the Seventies* in BBC Written Archives specifically mentions 'a daily specialist "strip" featuring mainly progressive music' on Radio 1. It didn't make the published version, but was trailed in the *BBC Handbook* for 1970. The progressive 'strip' was announced early in March. *Sounds of the Seventies* would be a daily, one-hour show, at 6pm, from Monday to Friday.

Apart from Wednesday's edition, to be a repeat of John Peel's *Sunday Show* concert which had begun in January, each show would be a DJ presenting a mix of records with two studio sessions taking up half the hour. 'We are more than doubling the amount of airtime given to progressive pop,' controller Douglas Muggeridge (who had taken over from Robin Scott) retorted, in response to criticism by George Melly and Pete Townshend in *Radio Times*. *Top Gear*, however, did not become part of the 'strip' for another 18 months, staying on Saturday afternoons. Peel and Walters now faced real competition for getting the latest bands in session first.

This was a time of considerable political change at Radio 1. In September 1970, the Popular Music and Gramophone departments were abolished, replaced by Radio 1 and Radio 2 departments. Producers from each production department had to choose their preferred network. Jimmy Grant and Bill Bebb opted for Radio 2. Most of the other names above chose Radio 1, and everyone from Popular Music moved out of Aeolian Hall and into Egton House, home of the old Gramophone Department and right next to Broadcasting House in Langham Place ('They said it was purely temporary, and I'm still in the same office today,' said Jeff Griffin in 1992, and he was still there when he retired in 1994). Mark White became the first Head of Radio 1 department. But within a little over a year, he, Donald MacLean and Grant had gone (White went to Radio 2 as Head), and Radio 1 found itself with a new hierarchy. From September 1970, the station had three executive producers, responsible to the Head: Doreen Davies, in charge of the middle-of-the-road programmes; Derek Chinnery, looking after mainstream pop; and Teddy Warrick, who, in his own words, 'was expected to deal with the sharper end'. (Chinnery became Head on White's departure, in April 1972, and Johnny Beerling took the mainstream job.) Having been chief programme organiser in Gramophone department, Teddy Warrick found himself dealing with sessions, concerts, and independent-minded producers like Bernie Andrews, Jeff Griffin and John Walters for the first time. *Sounds of the Seventies* and *Top Gear* became his main responsibilities, and he proved a consistent champion of the new.

When Peel went on holiday in August 1970, Jeff Griffin didn't fancy 'repeating a repeat' of the *Sunday Show* concerts on the Wednesday nights for a month. Instead, he offered four DJ-ed shows to a journalist, Bob Harris, who had met Jeff earlier in 1970. 'Who do you fancy having in session?' Jeff asked him. Bob chose Elton John and three new acts: Aubrey Small, Argent, and Wishbone Ash. 'At the end of the four weeks, I was feeling so excited about the idea of working for Radio 1, but that was it, there was nothing else in the pipeline at all,' recalls Bob today; 'and then David Symonds resigned, and suddenly the Monday programme became available, and the BBC offered it to me.' He kicked off on 12 October, with a session from Uriah

Heep, recorded by his producer for the next 15 months, John Muir. Muir carried off a neat trick for this new show, which was later to benefit the Peel Sessions too. Despite the fact that Radio 1 didn't yet have any stereo recording studios, Muir managed to record the groups in stereo. He did this with the help of a subsidiary department of the World Service, based in a side-street off Shepherd's Bush Green: the Transcription Service.

■

THE NAME SUGGESTS libraries of monks, transcribing by hand the utterances of distinguished contributors to BBC radio discussion programmes. The truth is slightly more complicated. The Transcription Service was set up as part of the World Service, funded by the Foreign Office and not the licence fee, to export BBC programmes to foreign broadcasters, in the cause of cultural diplomacy. Many national state broadcasters do this, but, uniquely, Transcription charged for BBC programmes. Renamed BBC Radio International (BBC RI) in 1995, it's now part of the BBC's commercial arm, BBC Worldwide. It's a measure of BBC quality that stations are still happy to pay for the programmes, making it one of the world's oldest broadcast syndication operations. As well as distributing ready-made BBC TV and

John Walters. BBC

radio shows, Transcription always made its own programmes solely for export, and this is where pop music came in.

When The Beatles and the British sound exploded onto the American pop scene in 1964, Transcription realised there was money to be made. Using BBC session tapes made for *Saturday Club* and, from July, Bernie's original *Top Gear*, a special weekly 45-minute show, strictly for export only, was released to America and the world's eager radio stations. *Top of the Pops*, not to be confused with its television namesake, was put together at Kensington House, Shepherd's Bush, Transcription's HQ. The host was Brian Matthew, who would attend the sessions and record interviews with the stars exclusively for Transcription. The show was pressed-up on 12-inch LPs, and sent off to subscribing stations by airmail. The show was still going in the 1990s. By then it was released on CD, and had not been using BBC radio sessions as its primary raw material for years, although its legacy lives on today in BBC RI's weekly show *Top of the Pops – Backstage*, which still often features live session tracks from Radio 1. But the original Transcription *Top of the Pops* was hosted for over 20 years by Brian Matthew and, until he left in spring 1992, was still made by its original producer, Pete Dauncey.

Pete Dauncey is the fifth man of the *Saturday Club* team. Jimmy Grant, Brian Matthew, Bernie Andrews and Johnny Beerling each played a part in changing the sound of BBC pop radio. The show's original tape-op, Pete Dauncey's role was to export his colleagues' achievements to the world. But his influence helped change a few things at home too, like stereo, or multi-track recording. Until the early 1970s, *Top of the Pops* got most of its raw material by sending its own engineers, like Pete Dixon, Dave 'Spot' Mulkeen and Bob Harrison, armed with a portable EMI TR90 tape recorder, to sessions for John Peel's *Top Gear*, *Saturday Club* and others; producing a weekly show on disc meant there simply wasn't time to borrow and copy master tapes. They would plug in their machine, alongside Radio 1's in the recording channel at the Playhouse, Piccadilly, or wherever, and take a direct copy of the session, live. They left the tapes running between numbers, picking up banter between the control room and studio, odd jams and out-takes, meaning Transcription's copies of sessions are often the most detailed record of what happened. Back at Kensington House, they would use the tracks to make up the next week's show.

As the Radio 1 studios were mono, this meant *Top of the Pops* had to be released in mono too, much to the frustration of American subscribing FM stations. Transcription had built its own small stereo studio in the mid-1960s, recording direct to two-track, but it was mainly used for classical music. Then, in early 1970, a new, bigger portable desk was acquired, which, with a bit of cunning 'lash-up' with cable, gave 8-track recording. Pete Dauncey hit on the idea of adding to *Top of the Pops* a full, stereo session on the flip-side of each edition, without Brian Matthew's links: 'For Your DJ' read the label. While the main part of the programme would still be in mono on the A-side, stations could dip into the complete session by the featured guest, in stereo, on the B-side. If he had enough tapes, he could even do a selection of stereo tracks. The only problem was getting enough stereo sessions to choose from each week.

John Muir had heard about the new facilities at Kensington House. 'I desperately wanted to do stereo sessions,' he says. In August 1970, he and Pete Dauncey came to an arrangement. Muir would book one or both of the new sessions he needed each week (initially for Alan Black and Bob Harris, later for Peel too), to be recorded at Transcription's stereo studio, T1. Pete Dauncey would produce the Monday evening session, with his own engineers, like Bob Harrison or Adrian Revill; and John Muir the Tuesday, or, occasionally, Wednesday evening, mainly with Nick Gomm or John White as SM. Each producer would get instant access to both sessions, Muir to broadcast on Radio 1, and Dauncey to put out on that week's *Top of the Pops*. By January 1971, the scheme was in full operation.

Dauncey had previously tried other ways of getting sessions in stereo, unsuccessfully. The most infamous experiment was on Curved Air's first session, recorded at Maida Vale 4 for *Top Gear* on 28 April 1970. In the control room, producer John Walters and SM Bob Conduct were recording the group in mono. But Bob was splitting the signals from the mics, and running them down cable, along 50 yards of Maida Vale corridor, to another room, where Pete Dauncey and Bob Harrison were simultaneously

---

FIRST HEARD HERE...

'Stairway To Heaven' by Led Zeppelin
First heard here on John Peel's Sunday Show: 4 April 1971
Concert recorded 1 April, Paris Cinema
Produced by Jeff Griffin, engineered by Chris Lycett, assistant John Etchells
Reached No 1 as track on Led Zep's untitled fourth album in UK album chart: November 1971
Peel Ahead of Everyone by... (PAE) Index: Seven months

Led Zeppelin had written and recorded 'Stairway To Heaven' for their forthcoming fourth album during the winter of early 1971, and first performed the song at Belfast Ulster Hall on 5 March as part of their UK tour that month. Their concert recording at the Paris for producer Jeff Griffin on 1 April would be their last BBC studio date. Most of the concert is now available on the double CD 'BBC Sessions' released in 1997, and even with Peel's introductions removed, listening today it's obvious this was the first time the audience had heard the song – there is no whooping or cheering at the opening notes.

recording the same session, but in stereo on a mobile desk. 'Everything went fine until we realised that one of the tracks we'd recorded was just a backing track, and the band wanted to overdub,' recalls Bob Harrison. The mono version could be 'bounced', as normal, to another tape machine, but Dauncey and Harrison would have to do the same, at exactly the same time: 'How the hell would we get the stereo tape in sync?' wondered Pete Dauncey. Eventually, communicating on headphones, the two engineering teams, with fingers poised on the recorders' capstans (drive wheels) ran both tapes, in sync, against a verbal count, while the band overdubbed. 'In the middle of all this, the new managing director of radio, Ian Trethowan, walks in,' says Bob Conduct. '"My first time at Maida Vale," he says, "but isn't this a silly way to do it?"'

Some, like Walters, thought stereo recording at that time irrelevant. 'For the average listener, it made no difference,' he said, and he had a point. Radio 1 was still, after all, only broadcasting in mono, on medium wave. This had always been the argument of the administrators. As recently as February 1969, a memo from Popular Music department had argued that multi-track equipment would unnecessarily increase producer-effort, and 'provision of even one multi-track machine would create a demand for more: 2-track would lead to the "need" for 4 tracks, and then 8.' The number of sessions for which double-tracking was 'legitimate' was 'small'. Muir may now have been able to record his sessions in stereo, but stereo broadcast of them was impossible. Even when *Sounds of the Seventies* won the 10pm-to-midnight FM slot, in October 1971, the strip only got FM mono. Yet Dauncey and Muir's arrangement still had a part to play. Muir recalls staging a demonstration for Ian Trethowan himself, showing how stereo transmission could benefit his Transcription sessions, early in 1972. FM stereo broadcasts had just started, but on Radio 3 only, with the odd test transmission on Radio 2. Soon afterwards it was decided Radios 1 and 2 would at last have to have their own multi-track studios. Two studios would be equipped with Neve 16-4 desks and 8-track Studer A80 1-inch tape recorders. Aeolian 2 was to be one of them. But it was the other chosen location that was effectively to become the home of *Sounds of the Seventies* and *Top Gear* sessions. It was a former drama studio, complete with false doors and gravel-traps, famed as the home of the long-running radio soap *Mrs Dale's Diary*, on the ground floor of the Langham Hotel, right opposite Broadcasting House: Langham 1. Only after Langham 1 opened, making multi-track recording available for all Radio 1 producers, did *Sounds of the Seventies* start going out in stereo, on Monday 6 November 1972. That, however, was more than two years after the T1 stereo tapes first rolled. And it was T1 which hosted the most famous debut BBC recording in 1970–1972, and it was for Peel: Roxy Music, on 4 January 1972.

CLASSIC SESSION

ROXY MUSIC

Recorded: **4.1.72**
Studio: **T1, Transcription Service, Kensington House**
Producer: **John Muir**
Engineers: **John White & Bill Aitken**
First Broadcast: **21.1.72 John Peel**
Tracks: **Remake Remodel, B.O.B. medley, Would You Believe,**
If There Is Something (Sea Breezes, first broadcast 18.2.72)

Line-up: **Bryan Ferry (vocals, keyboards); Andy MacKay (saxophones); Brian Eno (synthesiser, treatments); David O'List (guitar); Graham Simpson (bass guitar); Paul Thompson (drums)**

Roxy Music's first session, with David O'List on guitar. In May, then with Phil Manzanera, they recorded a second session at Kensington House with Muir, just before their first album was released.
'When the band came into the control room to listen back to the mix, I asked , "Where's Dave?" "In the studio," they said,' recalls Muir; 'and there he was, lying flat on his back.'

'Despite the strange "lashed-up" control room, the band seemed happy with this session. I remember Eno asking us about phasing effects machines. He was really into gadgets, and the only way then to get a really good flanging or phasing effect was to play back two recordings of the sound you wanted to phase off separate tape recorders, and knock one slightly out of phase with the other, by rubbing your fingers against the flange of the tape reel. At the BBC, we never had the time to attempt such convoluted techniques. Consequently, we had acquired a little box which attempted to simulate such phasing effects automatically. It didn't work very well, but it was all that was around, and I remember giving Eno the details.' Bill Aitken

■

IF THERE WERE not so many new bands appearing in the early 1970s, those that did were taken up very enthusiastically indeed. A handful of groups were recording new BBC sessions every few weeks. These universal favourites included Stone the Crows, Steeleye Span, Medicine Head, Thin Lizzy, and Lindisfarne. 'We became regulars in the canteen and almost had our own coathooks,' says Ray Laidlaw, drummer with Lindisfarne, and later with Jack the Lad. Such was the clamour for Lindisfarne that, having debuted on *Night Ride* on 6 January 1971, they recorded another two sessions before the end of the month; the second, for *Top Gear*, going out only two days before their third, on Bob Harris.

'We had a very enjoyable relationship with John Walters, who we knew slightly, as a fellow Tynesider, from his days with the Alan Price Set,' says Laidlaw. 'His constant piss-taking was a great source of amusement and one of the main attractions at Maida Vale. When asked what he would like us to record, the usual answer would be: "Oh just whack down any old shit, it all sounds the same to me anyway." On

73

many occasions we would spend most of our allotted time falling about laughing and then have to record the songs in a bit of a rush.'

Walters and Peel, in the absence of new bands, had taken *Top Gear* sessions down an experimental path. Groups like Chris MacGregor's Brotherhood of Breath, and earlier, in 1970, Ian Carr's Nucleus, had come in. 'Getting on *Top Gear* was a big break, because it got us out of the jazz-broadcasting ghetto, and into a wider field of exposure,' says Ian Carr. 'The other thing that surprised and delighted us was that we had more artistic freedom on these non-jazz programmes. Nobody seemed to worry about how long each piece was or whether it was the "right sort" of piece for the programme.' Peel and Walters also developed the idea of getting unusual combinations of musicians together on sessions, begun by Bernie: there was the Carols concert at Christmas 1970; and, in summer 1971, the 'free improvisation' session was planned. Walters wanted to get various musicians to improvise over a backing tape, originally to be a Doris Day record. But what he really needed was someone with no experience of playing an instrument: 'Chimpanzee!' he thought. He was going to get just one, but he could only find two, Bugsy and Rosie, who worked as a double act. He recorded them bashing the piano. The plan then was for Robert Wyatt to play drums, Mike Ratledge keyboards, Peel and Pig jew's harp, and

Hawkwind. Peter Sanders/Rex Features

Lennon and Yoko also agreed to take part. But then Lennon went to America and didn't come back. The session never happened. Peel kept a postcard: 'Hang onto the chimps! – John,' it said. 'A couple of years later, I read in the paper that the chimps had escaped into a school playground, police marksmen had been called, and they were shot,' said Walters.

Also that year, in another attempt to find new, different sounds for the sessions, Peel and Walters had organised a competition: best demo tape wins a session. The winners were the Cambridge band Henry Cow, and a duo, Paul Savage and John Hewitt. At around the same time, spring 1971, confirming his frustration in an interview with Michael Watts in the *Melody Maker*, Peel laid into Deep Purple, Black Sabbath, Ten Years After and ELP: 'Those bands have lost the spark somewhere down the line and are basically going through a routine ... we're going through a very sterile period ... the one distinguishing feature of Progressive music with a capital "P" is that under no circumstances should it progress an inch, because if it does people don't want to know.' Five months later, *Radio Times* announced: 'Double the radio time for "Progressive Pop".' Instead of four teatime shows, each recording one new session every week, the move of *Sounds of the Seventies* to 10pm on FM (now including *Top Gear*) from Monday 4 October 1971 meant three shows needing two each a week. From January 1972, that rose to four session-based, two-hour shows, when Peel got a second show, on Fridays, with producer John Muir, after it was agreed Peel would stop presenting the concert show – Jeff Griffin wanted to record a wider variety of bands, including some of those Peel had slagged off in the *MM*. All this demanded eight new rock sessions a week. 'Double the radio time' had doubled the sessions.

The studios, however, still 'looked like the inside of a Lancaster bomber' to a new young Scottish tape-op and former Glaswegian rock musician, Bill Aitken. Maida Vale 4 and Aeolian 2, the main rock session studios, 'looked very shabby', he recalls. The bands agreed. Dave Brock of Hawkwind, a group ahead of its time in the use of electronics, remembers finding the Maida Vale control room, on his first *Top Gear* session in August 1970, 'with its grey-painted equipment, like being in a submarine: "Full Ahead Captain!"' The band's third and final session, in May 1971 – after which they were 'blacklisted, because one of the roadies stole a microphone (the roadie was sacked)' – was in Aeolian 2, which Brock recalls as 'rather overbearing'. The year before, 201 Piccadilly had been abandoned, but the Playhouse was still in use: Rab Noakes remembers doing his first session for Peel there in May 1972. 'The Peel one was produced by Walters himself and, as a solo performance, it probably only took an hour. But those sessions were often done on the Hank Williams principle, of just calling in to the studio to put down a few tracks between shows,' says Rab.

Since Tony Wilson had become an attachment producer at Radio 1, along with Dave Tate and Pete Ritzema, in summer 1970, Walters had worked mainly with Bob Conduct as SM and Ian Sharpe as tape-op and, as Rab Noakes testifies, was still recording most Peel Sessions himself, although Pete Ritzema also did some. But in 1972, Wilson became a full-time producer, and virtually took over session production for Walters. Walters and Ritzema still did a few, but on surviving Peel Session Sheets from these years 'JOHN WALTERS' has increasingly been scored out, and 'One of Wilson's' scribbled in. Later, in the mid-1970s, Wilson producing, with, by then, SM Bill Aitken, became the standard Peel Session production unit. Wilson, from summer 1973, was also producing Alan Freeman's much-loved Saturday afternoon show, on which he would repeat many of his recent Peel productions, always trailed by Fluff as 'Tony Wilson Re-Creations'.

Back in early 1972, Bill Aitken was still a tape-op, the third man of the team recording two stereo sessions a week at Transcription Service, with producer John Muir and SMs Nick Gomm or John White. This team produced the first two of the five R1 sessions Bowie recorded between late September 1971 and late May 1972. They helped him bounce back from the 1971 low of his career, and every one of them is a classic. At the same time, the T1 team produced the first two Roxy Music

A LISTENER WRITES...

'If I hadn't listened to John Peel one night early in 1972, I'd have missed Roxy Music's first radio session. My whole world changed. Just the shock of hearing saxophones with those synthy squiggles at the same time, not forgetting Bryan Ferry's quivering crooner vocals. As a budding young saxophonist, Andy Mackay was an instant hero and I soon joined my first rock band. I pestered my local record shop after that, determined to be the first among my friends to get the album. I remember being fascinated by the sleeve. I listened to it all right there, in a scruffy sound booth they used to have in the shop, before taking it home to my crappy record player. Of all the bands I have discovered over the years, Roxy's early stuff still sounds special. I don't really know if I ever would have got to make records or work in music for my life if it wasn't for that Peel Show.'

Paul Ablett
recorded a Peel Session in Bee-Vamp, 1982

A LISTENER WRITES...

'Sometime in 1972 I was listening to Peel late at night in my lonely bedsit and he played "Listen To The Lion" from Van Morrison's new LP "St Dominic's Preview". I was totally knocked out by it and the following day was raving about it to my occasional boyfriend. A few days later when we met he said, "I bought you a present – that Van Morrison LP" – ooh goody!! – but then followed up with "but I like it so much I've decided to keep it" – what a b***er! Anyway we had a good laugh and it didn't ruin a good friendship; then a couple of years later I moved in with him telling him that it was just so that I could get "my" LP back. We're still together, married eventually, and "Listen To The Lion" is still my favourite Van Morrison track. So John Peel was kind of responsible for our long and happy life together.'

Elaine Simpson, Hebden Bridge

sessions. Aitken had an unusual role to play in the *Sounds of the Seventies* legend. For Peel's new Friday night show, 'Muir was daft enough to ask me to write some jingles,' says Bill Aitken. 'Radio 1 took over the FM slot at this time from Radio 2, and if you didn't know where you were on the dial at home, you could be tuning to the wrong station,' he says. 'To capitalise on this, the jingle began with Peter Howell (of the Radiophonic Workshop) saying in a very BBC voice, "Ladies and Gentlemen – Friday Night is Boogie Night!" (polite applause) then I would crash in, sounding like a Glasgow drunk doing a pale imitation of Little Richard to the tune of "Keep A Knockin'", except the words were "Get your boogie on a Friday night, Auntie Beeb's gonna treat you right, Johnny Peel's really out of sight, Boogie on a Friday and you'll be alright!"' Aitken had found a vocation. He followed up with the 'John Peel's Got Nice Legs' jingle, but the 'Boogie Night' jingle remains the most memorable. It was also appropriate: the show featured the first session by the 12-bar-boogie incarnation of Status Quo, on 3 March 1972. For Peel and Walters, it was a quiet time. Apart from soloists like Rab Noakes and Martin Carthy, and revivalist folk acts like the High Level Ranters and The Fureys, the only three new-name bands to debut on *Top Gear* in the first nine months of 1972 were all made up of members of former bands: Matching Mole; Plainsong; and the Albion Country Band. The long-awaited multi-track studio, Langham 1, opened in October that year. Aeolian 2 and the Playhouse had all but done their last rock sessions. And Maida Vale 4 and 5 closed for major refurbishment soon afterwards. Now they were all set up, but where was the new music going to come from? One of the first done in Langham 1 was the debut of a very shy, nervous singer-songwriter, Joan Armatrading. The week after that recording on Tuesday 31 October, the stereo transmitters were finally switched on. When a newly promoted Bill Aitken SM-ed his first sessions in Langham 1 on 17 January 1973 – 'Medicine Head in the afternoon, and Frankie Miller backed by Brinsley Schwartz in the evening, both for Bob Harris' – he became 'the first SM to

CLASSIC SESSION

JOAN ARMATRADING

Recorded: **31.10.72**
Studio: **Langham 1**
Producer: **John Walters**
Engineer: **Bob Conduct**
First Broadcast: **28.11.72 John Peel**
Tracks: **Head Of The Table, Spend A Little Time, Child Star, Whatever's For Us**
Line-up: **Joan Armatrading, acoustic guitar, piano & vocals**

The first of eight sessions Joan Armatrading was to record for John Peel up to summer 1976. Bob Conduct afterwards went round telling all his SM colleagues he'd just done this first session with an amazing singer-songwriter. Peel had gone along to listen and sat on the floor. John Walters remembers Joan communicating only by whispering to friend Pam Nestor, who would then talk to him. Gus Dudgeon, who had just produced Joan's debut album, came along and twiddled knobs.

'I remember being terribly quiet and shy then. John Peel was a big influence on a lot of people's careers. When he got stuck on someone's stuff I think it made a big difference. There was certainly a good feeling from having been on his programme. One of my happiest moments was when, years later, I did "The Secret Policeman's Ball", in 1986, I think, afterwards Peel gave me a great review. That pleased me immensely, because you know sometimes if he likes you, then you have success, and you stop doing the show, you can think he doesn't like your stuff any more. So I was really happy to read that, because I've always considered him to be a big part of my career; I know some people wouldn't think so, but I do.'

Joan Armatrading

---

cut his teeth on multi-track'. Most of the production teams had spent September getting stereo experience by doing their sessions at Kensington House. However, BBC management had made it known that extra re-mix time was not available. The thinking was still that too much mixing was unproductive, unnecessary work: hence the decision for 8-track, which 16-track in commercial studios had already rendered obsolete. 'Nevertheless, it was a giant step forward for the Beeb,' says Aitken. Fairly soon after 'the Langham' opened, all *Sounds of the Seventies* sessions were allowed to expand to Peel's 'double sessions'.

Langham 1 was only ever meant to be a stop-gap, until Maida Vale could be refurbished. But it was to remain in constant use, 15 hours a day, until summer 1981. It wasn't initially promising. Sited in a wing of the building that follows the line of Portland Place opposite Broadcasting House, it first of all had an unusual, curved shape; and the traffic meant bands faced terrible parking problems. Then, turning left from reception, roadies humping in the gear would push open the door, opening into the tiny control room, which then smashed back on the Studer tape machines, thoughtfully sited behind the door. 'However, Langham 1 is the studio I remember with most affection,' says Aitken, and he is not alone. Sharing the ground floor of the Langham with the BBC club, the atmosphere was informal. It was easy to pop out for a pint. 'Strangely, the lack of useful space seemed to work towards an effect of "closeness" rather than being cramped,' says Aitken. The BBC sold the building in the 1980s, and where the studio was is now the Chukka Bar in the Langham Hilton Hotel.

CLASSIC SESSION

BOB MARLEY AND THE WAILERS

Recorded: **1.5.73**
Studio: **Langham 1**
Producer: **John Walters**
Engineer: **Bob Conduct**
First Broadcast: **15.5.73 John Peel**
Tracks: **Slave Driver,**
Concrete Jungle, Rasta Man
Line-up: **Bob Marley, acoustic guitar & vocals; Peter Macintosh, guitar & vocals; Aston Barrett, bass guitar; Charlie Barrett, drums; Earl Lindo, keyboards; Bunny Livingstone, congos, bongos & vocals**

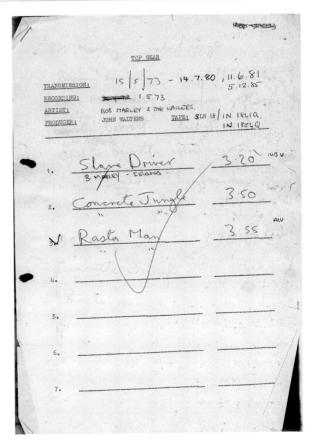

'When we got them in, people at the time said, "You're not booking that lot, are you?" When Marley arrived at the studio, you realised he was a star: very quiet, and somehow dignified. Of course, all of them were there then, Bunny Wailer, Peter Tosh. I seem to remember it took a lot of time to get started, there was a lot of sitting around, as you'd expect, and, at that time, of course, possessing marijuana was an imprisonable offence; they did everything very discreetly, but you could smell it, even through the double doors, in the control room. They were also grinding hash up and putting it in honey. What was I supposed to do? BBC training would probably have told me to call the police. Anyway, that was on their first visit to Britain, years before they were noticed. Only Island and us were onto them then.'

John Walters

At the start of October 1972, Radio 1 had at last completely separated its daytime programmes from Radio 2. *Sounds of the Seventies* was tweaked a bit too: Peel's second show was moved to Thursdays, reuniting him with Bernie Andrews as producer. There may have been new session-based programmes. There may have been a new multi-track studio. But there were fewer and fewer new bands emerging to be recorded. Even Bernie Andrews only turned up a dozen debuts in his 14 months producing Peel again. Peel and Walters, by late 1973, were picking up on the Pub Rock beginnings, with the first date by Ducks DeLuxe. But the most noticeable trend on Tuesday nights was the incoming continental experimental groups: Can, who did four sessions, plus Faust and Tangerine Dream, who both supplied special 'Private Tape' recordings from Germany. (Faust had turned up to do a session at Langham 1 on 22 May 1973 but, as Walters recalled, 'we found we didn't have enough plugs and sockets for their equipment, synthesisers and stuff, so we bought in a tape they did for us in Germany instead.') Robert Wyatt remained the most significant home-grown experimenter. Of the two sessions he did then for Peel, in late 1972 and 1974, he says, 'Those mark my metamorphosis from adolescent bipedal caterpillar to adult paraplegic flutterby. On the '72 one, I sang a Danny Kaye version of the sentimental 'Little Child', the kind of thing I wouldn't have risked in a more constricted atmosphere, certainly not on record, and a Gilbert and Sullivan-ish joke about Arts Council Grant culture. In

FIRST HEARD HERE...

'Tubular Bells' LP by Mike Oldfield

First heard here on Top Gear, 29 May 1973
Released as Virgin's first album 25 May 1973, entered UK album chart July 1974, Reached No 1 October 1974
Peel Ahead of Everyone by... (PAE) Index: 18 months

The story of how Mike Oldfield's 'Tubular Bells' was recorded at Virgin's Manor studio and then rejected by every record company until Virgin decided to release it themselves as their first album is well known. As is the legend that Peel played it in its entirety on his show, after Richard Branson had played it to him a few days earlier on his houseboat, the Alberta. Branson and Mike Oldfield then say there was a party on the boat to listen to Peel's show on the Tuesday, and everyone was amazed as Peel apparently said he was not going to play a lot of records, just this one. Peel certainly played Side 1 that night, four days after its release. But despite Branson and Oldfield's memories, there is no concrete evidence he played the entire album, though the script might be wrong. Branson says it was only after this show that record shops started ordering it in. Peel only played it this once. Seven weeks later it entered the chart, it was performed live on BBC TV at the end of November, and 18 months later eventually reached number one. In this period Peel was already regularly featuring very long session and album tracks by Can, Tangerine Dream, Faust and Shawn Phillips – although, by way of contrast, the show of 24 April had featured Merseybeat legends Gerry and the Pacemakers and Billy J Kramer in session, plus all-rockabilly classic hits, and no song in the show was longer than 2' 45"!

ONE-SESSION WONDER

Fripp & Eno

First broadcast: **Top Gear, Sounds of the Seventies, 18.12.73**
Recorded: **unknown**
Studio: **Private Tape**
Tracks: **Heavenly Music Corporation, Swastika Girls**
Line-up: **Robert Fripp (guitar, electronics), Brian Eno (synthesiser, electronics, mix)**

Fripp and Eno released their guitar-and-effects LP 'No Pussyfooting' in November 1973, and, because of the technology of the recording, Walters agreed to buy-in a 'private tape' of the album. But when he put it on in the office, it sounded strangely different. He checked with the record company, but no, it was the right tape. It must be a different take, he thought: 'Even better, that's what private tapes were supposed to be.' On the night of the show, 'Eno was, apparently, driving down the motorway and heard it. He pulled in, phoned up the BBC, and said, "I must speak to John Peel, he's playing my album backwards." "That's what they all say, sir," said the switchboard, and refused to put him through,' recalled Walters. 'We found out later and checked, and he was right! I had no experience of record companies, where tapes are kept on the take-up spool, and stored "tail-out", and the record company didn't know the BBC keeps tapes "front-out". Fortunately, only Eno noticed.'

Brian Eno. Ian Dickson/Redferns

September 1974, I went into the studio not only legless but, recklessly, without any other musicians or instruments, and just used the equipment to hand (Hammond organ, piano, marimba), to do truly solo versions of a few of my recent songs.' These included 'Sea Song', and his new hit single 'I'm A Believer'.

Elton John's infamous pub piano session, recorded for John Peel's Christmas Day show in 1973, was a sign Walters and Peel still liked to have fun. 'I think the original idea was to do what was very popular then – everyone did their singalong-a-Christmas medley, which, of course, was so inappropriate for Elton,' said Walters. 'And, at that time, don't forget, he was just peaking in worldwide popularity, and being seen very much as a serious artist.' Elton agreed to the joke. Walters got some light ales in to Langham 1, dragged along Peel and various other Radio 1 producers and managers, to get the atmosphere going around the specially hired upright pub piano, and Elton kicked off with a plinky-plonky medley of Christmas tunes. Then Walters suggested Elton do some other stuff in a pub style. 'Tell you what, I'll do a Bob Dylan medley,' he replied. The resulting truly jingle-jangle version of 'Mr. Tambourine Man' was the 'finest interpretation of Dylan's work I've ever heard,' said Walters, 'and that includes Dylan.' But that wasn't all. He went on to do a selection of pub favourites ('Down at the old Bull and Bush', etc), and then proceeded to 'do a kamikaze act' on his own standards 'Daniel' and 'Your Song'. 'He was so successful he could afford to have a tongue-in-cheek attitude to his own work,' said Walters. 'If anybody was going to have a good time destroying his own work, he might as well get the pleasure himself.' Amidst the sound of clinking beer bottles and rollicking singalong chorus on 'Your Song', Walters can clearly be heard announcing 'Last Orders!'

While Pub Rock was the only live music beginning, other things were drawing to a close. Family did their last of 14 sessions in May 1973, and yet its leaders re-emerged the next year as Chapman-Whitney Streetwalkers. This says it all. Only 24 new bands debuted on Peel in this period, Be-Bop DeLuxe being the only real stars, and all the rest consisted of ex-members of defunct groups. There were one-off scoops, solo sessions by Randy Newman and Duane Eddy. And, late in 1974, Peel experienced a minor soul explosion, with big band dates by Kokomo, Viola Wills and Gonzalez, and Ann Peebles. Notwithstanding these exceptions, though, the running orders from this period all look a bit inoffensive, unremarkable, flat.

Then, quite unexpectedly, three months after the refurbished Maida Vale reopened, with the latest generation of 24-4 Neve desks, and 8-track Studer A80s, the axe fell on *Sounds of the Seventies*. 'BBC to cut services by tenth in new year,' said the front page of *The Times* on 11 December 1974. Facing a £20 million deficit in March, and

ONE-SESSION WONDER

Bill Aitken

First broadcast: **John Peel, 8.12.75**
Recorded: **June 1975**
Studio: **Private Tape**
Tracks: **Chimney Pots, Sequel, Ghosts Of Yesterday, Open Up Your Eyes**
Line-up: **Bill Aitken (everything: acoustic guitar, guitar, bass, synthesiser, organ, drums, percussion, vocals)**

BBC studio manager Aitken recorded the numbers in his spare time earlier that year in a 16-track commercial studio. Peel, Walters and Tony Wilson liked the tape so much Aitken was given 'a papal dispensation', and his tape was broadcast on 8 December, including the famous Chimney Pots – the first documented instance of a full-time BBC employee being permitted to broadcast their own musical work. But with the advent of DJ and mix sets in the 1990s, this practice would return. Aitken left the BBC in 1981 and went on to work for SSL and later Mercury Telecommunications, where he helped found its sponsorship of the Mercury Music Prize.

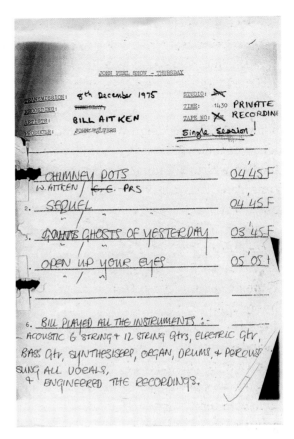

with uncertainty over the licence fee, in order to save £1 million, BBC television programmes would stop at 11.30pm, and Radios 1 and 2 would merge again in the afternoons and after 10pm. 'There will be no staff redundancies,' said the BBC, 'but Stuart Henry, Bob Harris, Alan Black and David Simmons, the Radio 1 disc jockeys, will not have their contracts renewed in the new year.' 'Radio 1 Scandal – Rock Off!' screamed the front page of the next week's *MM*. 'All this in pursuit of savings of less than £500,000 a year, out of a total budget of £140 million,' commented the paper. 'It means the end of Radio 1 stereo programmes,' said Bob Harris. 'Last week I had the best contract from the BBC I'd ever had, and then suddenly, four days later, the whole of the *Sounds of the Seventies* programmes go overboard. It's a really retrogressive step. The only real survivor will be *Top Gear*.'

So once again Peel and Walters were alone. A new early-evening strip was hurriedly created, from 5.15 to 7pm, and Peel was given Mondays and Thursdays. The other nights were presented by Alan Freeman, Annie Nightingale and Rosko. Where there had been eight new 'double sessions' a week, there were now just Peel's two. In the nine months of this regime, there were only a dozen new bands in session on Radio 1. But from Monday 29 September 1975, it was 'bedtime with Peel', announced the *Radio Times*. 'There'd been quite an outcry about the loss of the rock output late at night,' remembers Johnny Beerling, 'and Derek Chinnery [then controller] won some of it back by combining the network with Radio 2 an hour earlier, at 6pm, but reopening at 11pm for one hour only with the *Peel Show*, Monday to Friday.' The *Top Gear* subtitle was finally dropped, as was the 'sig' by The Nice, replaced by 'Pickin' The Blues' by Grinderswitch. In between spins of new albums by Rory Gallagher, Supertramp, Tangerine Dream and Joni Mitchell, there were seven debut sessions before the end of the year, including one made by SM Bill Aitken himself. And every night of the week before Christmas that year, an episode was broadcast from Viv Stanshall's *Christmas at Rawlinson End*. Aitken remembers the session overran, and everyone wondered if there was enough there on tape. Then Stanshall returned a week later. 'He started to perform monologues over the backing tracks, and the effect was hilarious: Tony Wilson, Mike Engles and I were literally falling about in the control room laughing our heads off. I even created some special sound effects for one song: "We are three vivisectionists" (F/X – Splash/Rip/Spurt).' It was a great broadcasting event. That Christmas, many tuned in every night at 11pm. But then, doing just that, turning on the radio late at night just to listen to Peel, was soon to become a vital daily ritual.

■

Keystone/Getty Images

CHAPTER 5

THE DATE IS Wednesday 19 May 1976. Most of Peel's show that night was interesting enough. There were tracks from LPs by Supercharge, the Steve Miller Band, Nils Lofgren, Streetwalkers and the Mighty Diamonds. But the last track, all 1' 30" of it, was 'Judy Is A Punk', which, as the PasB confirms, is 'Side 1. Band 3. LP: Ramones'. 'Every week I used to go down to Virgin Records at Marble Arch, and the manager, I'm sure without the approval of Head Office, used to allow me to take records out "on approval": the ones I didn't want I'd return, and those I did I would have to pay for,' Peel remembered, years later. 'One week I took out about ten LPs, one of which was the one by The Ramones, and I immediately liked several things about it: first, the simplicity of the name, it having an implication of that romantic Spanish-New York thing; and also because it was a monochrome sleeve. When I put the record on, initially, because of the aggression and brevity of the numbers, I was slightly taken aback, but sufficiently excited, that I started playing it that very night.'

And the following night he played the last three tracks from Side 2 of the LP in a row, 'Let's Dance', 'I Don't Wanna Walk Around With You' and 'Today Your Love Tomorrow The World'. On the Friday he restricted himself to playing just 'Havana Affair'. Through late May and early June, he'd kick off one or two shows a week with tracks from the album, like 'I Wanna Be Your Boyfriend' and 'Blitzkreig Bop'. Television's 'Little Johnny Jewel' was played on 9 June, The Runaways' 'Cherry Bomb' on the 18th. By the week after The Ramones' British debut at the Roundhouse on 4 July, 'Blitzkreig Bop' was being spun three nights in a row. It seemed his mind was made up. Things were changing. On the Wednesday of the next week, several tracks were played from the Jonathan Richman and the Modern Lovers LP. The next day, it was The 101ers' 'Keys

To Your Heart', on a new small British label, Chiswick Records. On the same show, there was Dave Edmunds' 'Here Comes The Weekend'. And throughout late July, Peel spun tracks from Eddie and the Hot Rods' *Live At The Marquee* EP.

But each of these only took up three minutes of an hour-long nightly show. More representative, perhaps, was the broadcast of Eric Clapton's new LP, *No Reason To Cry*, in its entirety, on 6 August. Then, for the next two weeks, each night was devoted to a band's history: The Who, Roxy Music, Fairport Convention, Soft Machine and The Faces. Everyone now knows the Sex Pistols played their first gig in 1975. Retrospectively, their gig reviews, which started appearing in the music papers from February, assume a huge significance. But at the time, they simply seemed to offer a glimpse of a bizarre new cult. Early 1976 is more accurately summed up by the new bands Peel had in session: Shanghai, Lone Star, National Health, Racing Cars, Widowmaker, AC/DC, and a couple by a jazz-rock ensemble, including a drummer from a well-known progressive group, then just gigging occasionally, Brand X.

'There were no other places that would play Brand X then; it was only people like Peel, who, whilst as "Phil Collins", he probably wouldn't be very interested in what I did, seemed to take a bit of an interest in Brand X,' Phil Collins says, 'because it was such an odd mixture of music; and it was a growing music, living and breathing – you couldn't record it and say "that's the definitive version of that song", because it just kept changing or getting better, it would never be the same thing twice, so live sessions made more sense for us.'

There were old favourites still coming in as well. The first session of the year was by Bridget St John, and others featured included Moon, Blue, the Jess Roden Band, Elkie Brooks, String Driven Thing and Caravan. 'I think I was probably relatively happy with the first part of 1976, until we got into the second part,' Peel reflected. Perhaps the only two bands to continue recording through the early punk era unscathed were Be-Bop Deluxe and Thin Lizzy. 'The punk thing never really bothered us,' says Scott Gorham of Lizzy. 'In fact, we embraced it, we were closer to the punk attitude than the pomp rock: other bands would go off-stage, have the towel draped over their shoulders, into the limo, and away. We'd stay and have parties backstage – we were a street-type band. We used to go to those sessions, get a sound, and then basically put it down live, and any overdubs were icing on the cake.'

There were also new bands who, if still drawn from a generation older than the punks about to emerge, had a more back-to-basics approach. In May, the Count Bishops, who had the first release on Chiswick at the end of 1975, did a debut session, closely followed by The Roogalator. The next month, Graham Parker and the Rumour did their first, a blistering set including 'Soul Shoes', 'White Honey' and 'Don't Ask Me Questions'. 'I do seem to remember saying in the mid-70s, prior to punk,' Peel said later, 'that I would like to see a return to the discipline that was imposed by the two-and-a-quarter minute-long single – Jerry Lee Lewis was the example I used at the time – that when you went into a studio you'd got two minutes and fifteen seconds in which you'd got to say everything you'd got to say, possibly in your life; and that seemed to me to concentrate the mind wonderfully, and produce quite extraordinarily passionate records.'

Ironically, the first British record which sought to meet this prescription was by one of the older generation, Nick Lowe's So It Goes, the first release on Stiff, 'BUY 1'. Peel played it every night of the week beginning Monday 23 August. Meanwhile, the new generation were just appearing above ground. On the Sunday of the Bank Holiday at the end of that week, the Clash played their first proper gig, supporting the Sex Pistols at the Screen on the Green. Then on Tuesday 31, the two bands played the 100 Club. In the audience was John Walters. 'When I walked in, I thought, "Well, it's over for these people now, because I've found it." If they were on at the 100 Club and I knew about it, it was no longer underground,' said Walters, echoing a comment in Caroline Coon's *MM* review the next week: 'The private party is over, they're public property now.' 'There were one or two people from record companies there, there was clearly a buzz, and obviously any purity they'd ever had was about to go,' Walters said. 'Looking back now, the whole punk movement must have been in that room. Nothing was fixed stylistically, people just looked a little odd; but there was a very conscious kicking-over of traces. I just remember it being banging and shouting, I'd never seen pogo-ing before, and all this spitting. I thought this was wonderful. Then, just as Rotten finished 'Anarchy In The UK', Dave Dee, A&R for Warners, shouted to me at the bar, "They've got no charisma!" But, to my eternal shame, I made one of the only two mistakes I've ever made,' Walters admitted. 'I thought, if I book them, I'm going to have to send them to Maida Vale. The engineers will put their fingers in their ears and say this is rubbish; but at least we'll have it on record, what they

The Damned. Platt Collection/Getty Images

sounded like. But I watched them, and all the spitting and banging, and I looked into Rotten's eyes, and remembering my past as an art teacher, I thought, there is a boy I would not trust to hand out the scissors. I wouldn't like to be in the studio with this lot. It's going to be trouble, and I'd like to have it done, but I wouldn't want to inflict this event on anybody. I'll postpone it, I thought; and by then, of course, it was too late. The old camaraderie of the producers, all mates together, got the better of me for once.'

On Tuesday 26, Peel played The Damned's 'New Rose'. It was the first real British punk record. If hearing 'Heartbreak Hotel' or 'Tutti Frutti' was the crucial moment for a previous generation, 'New Rose' was, for many of us, the record after which nothing was ever the same again. On the Thursday, The Vibrators session went out, and Peel closed the week's shows with 'Pressure' from the repeat of Aswad's date, followed by 'Teenage Depression'. And in that week's *MM*, as well as reviews of The Damned and The Rods' singles, details were announced of the first national tour by the Sex Pistols, with The Clash and The Damned. Then, on Friday 19 November, a full week before it was released, along with Richard Hell's Blank Generation (and a session by Martin Carthy), Peel played 'Anarchy In The UK'. By then, The Damned

CLASSIC SESSION

The Damned

Recorded: **30.11.76**
Studio: **Maida Vale 4**
Producer: **Jeff Griffin**
Engineer: **Mike Robinson**
First Broadcast: **10.12.76**
Tracks: **Stab Your Back, Neat Neat Neat, New Rose, So Messed Up, I Fall**
Line-up: **Dave Vanian** (vocals); **Bryan James** guitar); **Captain Sensible** (bass guitar); **Rat Scabies** (drums)

'I think I was apprehensive about it, because I hadn't seen them before or met them; but, in fact, when we got to the studio, I'm not sure who was more apprehensive, them, about being in a BBC studio, or me about working with them. The amusing thing was quite a few other people had heard that The Damned were in, and every now and again we got people creeping in through the door, looking in through the window to see if they were being sick all over the place or spitting at us. Which they weren't at all, of course; they were four of the nicest blokes I ever got to work with.'

Jeff Griffin

'I just remember it being a very fast session. Five numbers down, and Jeff away back to Radio 1 with the tapes. We finished very early.'

Mike Robinson

---

had been booked to come in for a session, to be recorded on Tuesday 30 November, just before the tour was due to start, on Friday 3 December. But the Pistols went on Thames TV's *Today With Bill Grundy* on the 1st and everything went mad. In the midst of the press hysteria over that weekend, Peel drove to Derby on the Saturday, in an attempt to catch the second night of the tour, only to be met by a sign saying 'Sorry – Not Playing'; and, on the Monday, John Walters received a phone call, in the general office 306, from Radio 1 controller Derek Chinnery.

'He had come out of a meeting and he was calling me from the Council Chamber in Broadcasting House, or the Governors' dining room, I think. Somebody had brought up this punk stuff after the Bill Grundy business on the front pages, wanting to check with Chinnery that Radio 1 wasn't getting behind this filth. "I'm just checking that you're not going to be using any, are you?" he said. "Well, we already have, Derek," I said. "What!" he exclaimed. I said we'd played several records, and the audience like them. "Yes, but you won't be getting them into BBC studios, will you?" "Well, actually," I said, "Jeff Griffin did The Damned for us last week.'"

In that week's *MM*, towards the end of a large feature on the aftermath of the Grundy incident, the paper, after reporting that 'Radio 1 is refusing to play "Anarchy In The UK" during the day,' pointed out that 'the record has been played by John Peel, who will be devoting his Radio 1 show this Friday to punk rock, with The Damned making their BBC debut.' Speaking perhaps as much to his concerned superiors as to *MM* readers, Walters told the paper: 'It's not meant to be a history of punk, but a presentation of the music, after all the remarks about the sociology of the players. It's not like the BBC is jumping on the punk bandwagon, but just some examples of what the actual artists sound like.' At a time when commercial stations up and down the land were proudly proclaiming bans on punk, that show on Friday 10 December was a triumph for Peel and Walters, and Radio 1. The Damned's five numbers were interspersed with tracks by Iggy and the Stooges, Richard Hell, Television's 'Little Johnny Jewel', 'I'm Stranded' and 'Anarchy In The UK'.

But it was too late to change listener's votes in the first-ever Peel's Festive Fifty, broadcast two weeks later, over the Christmas and New Year holidays. 'Stairway To Heaven' was voted listeners' all-time Number One. The rest of the poll was dominated by Bob Dylan (four tracks), Hendrix (three), The Beatles (three), Led Zeppelin (another two), and Pink Floyd. The only new insurgent was Jonathan Richman's 'Roadrunner' at Number 33. Nothing would change overnight, and that included the bands being booked for sessions.

■

MOST OF THE acts recorded in the first few months of 1977 were tried and tested favourites: Boys of the Lough, Be-Bop DeLuxe, John Martyn, Roy Harper, June Tabor and Supercharge. Big new releases featured included Bowie's *Low*, Pink Floyd's *Animals*, and Steve Gibbons' *Rollin' On*. Looking at the PasBs, there's a sense of a lull after the dramatic events before Christmas. 'Don't forget that in the nature of the session-booking process we would be working several weeks ahead,' Peel pointed out. Maida Vale 4 was used for all Peel Sessions at this time. It was eight-track, with Neve 24-4 desks; adapted, by BBC rules, so the faders went 'up' towards the engineer. This idiosyncrasy was introduced because the studios were also used for live broadcasts, and psychological research by Engineering suggested that the instinctive gesture to shut something off in the event of an accident, or rude word, was to jerk the hand forwards, not back. Tony Wilson was effectively in charge of Peel Sessions production. He would invariably do the Monday Peel, initially with Bill Aitken, but, increasingly through the punk period, with Dave Dade, as Aitken went on attachments. The two remained a recording team for many years on Tony's rock show sessions. Mike Robinson was the SM allocated to the Tuesday Peel, most often with Jeff Griffin producing. They, too, remained a team, later handling Live Aid and the Mandela concerts. Then, at the beginning of April 1977, Peel's show expanded to two hours a night, starting at 10pm. Nick Gomm was the SM allocated to the third Peel Session recording now required most weeks; and the producer was Malcolm Brown. The former *Sounds of the Seventies* producer had returned to Radio 1 the year before after two years' directing at BBC television: 'They weren't expecting me back, and had nothing for me to do.' Walters found him something. Through summer 1977, he and Nick Gomm, along with Jeff Griffin and Mike Robinson, were to record some of the key debut punk sessions.

Before that, Peel and Pig went to their first punk gig, Generation X at the Roxy, late in January. 'We got spat at as we walked in, and I thought, my goodness, they love me, they accept me,' Peel remembered. The Pig pogo-ed frantically and both were

FIRST AND ONLY HEARD HERE…
'God Save The Queen' by the Sex Pistols
First heard here on John Peel, 13.5.77
Reached No 2 June 1977
Peel Ahead of Everyone by… (PAE) Index: Years

The Sex Pistols' 'God Save The Queen' was released as a single on their new label Virgin on 27 May, the week before the official celebration of the Queen's silver jubilee, 7 June. The record officially got to number two by that date (although it outsold the official number one), and by then the BBC had announced they were refusing to play it because of its 'gross bad taste', and it was banned by the Independent Broadcasting Authority which regulated commercial radio and TV. So officially, and as the myth goes, the record was not broadcast anywhere. This is not true, however. Before the BBC statement, Peel had played the single pre-release, first on his show of Friday 13 May, then again on the following Monday, the 16th. He also played it as an album track on Monday 3 October, in advance of the release of 'Never Mind The Bollocks'. And again at the end of the year, on Thursday 22 December, as a surreptitious number 61 in his personal Festive Fifty of favourite records of the year (see Festive Fifty section). Over 20 years later, in June 1998, Peel was made an OBE in HM the Queen's Birthday Honours List. She clearly wasn't bothered.

ONE-SESSION WONDER

The Cortinas

First broadcast: **26.7.77**
Recorded: **18.7.77**
Studio: **Maida Vale 4**
Producer: **Tony Wilson**
Engineer: **Dave Dade**
Tracks: **Defiant Pose, Television Families, Having It, Further Education**
Line-up: **Jeremy Valentine (vocals); Nick Sheppard (guitar); Mike Fewings (guitar); Dexter Dalwood (bass); Daniel Swan (drums)**

'I would pinpoint the John Peel Session as a definite high point for the Cortinas,' says Daniel Swan. 'It came almost dead centre in the very brief life of the band. 1977 had started well for us with a string of Roxy Club performances and the recording and release of our first independent single 'Fascist Dictator'/'Television Families'. We also had some notable shows with The Damned, The Jam, The Stranglers and a successful debut as a headliner at the Marquee Club in June. We were all only 16 or 17 but had made the decision to put school and further education on hold and to pursue the band seriously. Exams were done and school ended in June 1977. Within a few days of the John Peel Session we kicked off our summer tour with Chelsea that started with a debut show in London at the Acklam Hall with Sham 69 and the Lurkers opening. From this point on the band was burdened with heavy expectations and later a major label recording contract.

'When we entered the Maida Vale studios, we were still very much having a lark and enjoying our good fortune. John Peel had recently [24 May] played and praised our single. I remember some of us were listening to his show in Dexter's bedroom, which was a converted garden shed, and when our single came on we jumped up and down with joy nearly knocking the shed off its none too sturdy foundations.

'The session takes are spirited and the energy level is high, offering a glimpse of how we sounded live at that time, and how a Cortinas album might have sounded had we had the chance to record one in the middle of 1977. Unfortunately, we were too busy touring for that to happen. Our album was recorded much later, and released in early 1978 after we broke up.'

greatly impressed. Billy Idol and Tony James' band would later record their first session, early in April. The third British punk record, after 'New Rose' and 'Anarchy', was The Buzzcocks' *Spiral Scratch* EP, which Peel played from 3 February. He was also spinning Talking Heads' 'Love Goes To Building A Fire', tracks from Television's *Marquee Moon* LP, The Damned's debut LP, Elvis Costello's 'Less Than Zero' and The Stranglers' 'Get A Grip On Yourself'/'London Lady': 'I saw them supporting Patti Smith at the Hammersmith Odeon, and people were getting up and walking out, always a good sign,' Peel said. The band recorded their first Peel Session on 1 March, first broadcast on the 7th. And Eddie and the Hot Rods finally came in for their first session in February. 'We started after 2.30pm, and I was back handing the tapes to Walters in his office at 4.30pm!' says producer Jeff Griffin. 'They did four fast numbers live, no overdubs, and that was the way to do those bands, because that was the way they played their set, and that way you captured the feel of it. Walters couldn't believe it when I handed him the tapes.'

Once the show had doubled in length, the punk bookings increased. Spring and summer 1977 would bring the final sessions from many old retainers, Medicine Head and Caravan's last of ten each, and Thin Lizzy's eleventh. 'We carried on booking a punk band and a straight band each week for quite some time,' said Walters. In the last week of April in Maida Vale 4, for example, The Adverts recorded their first on the Monday, The Jam their first the day after, and Medicine Head their last on the Wednesday. On Monday 9 May, John McLaughlin and Shakti were in, but the next day The Damned were back to do their second.

By early September, the debuts were coming thick and fast: Albertos Y Lost Trios Paranoias, The Buzzcocks and the Only Ones in three consecutive shows, and Steel Pulse and The Slits the week after. Years later, John Perry of the Only Ones told Dave Cavanagh in *Sounds*, that 'when somebody who'd never heard the Only Ones wanted to know what we sounded like I'd always play them the Peel Sessions in preference to the studio albums. They're rougher but there's more feel, because the songs were more or less recorded live. You could do more or less whatever you wanted; nobody was at all put out when I wanted to record the sound of my Strat being thrown around the room for the end of "Oh No", they just went out and set up the appropriate mics. The great thing about recording under those conditions and at that speed is that it shows whether the songs stand up for themselves.'

Walters, meanwhile, had developed a regular diary of weekly punk gigs, to go out and 'lack-of-talent spot': the Croydon Greyhound on Sundays, the Roxy (before it closed), and the Vortex on Mondays, among others. 'I did most of the going out because it rapidly became obvious that Peel was recognised and would be surrounded, as uncle John Peel, and they'd all give him tapes – we were their main platform, and they all knew it; and also he was working late anyway, and hadn't got the time.' But the Vortex went on until 2am, and when a gig featuring The Slits had been billed for 15 August, Walters said he'd take Peel down after the show. As early as March, Peel had written in *Sounds* that his 'heart was heavy' because he had yet to see the all-female Slits, already attacked in the *News of the World* simply for their name. 'They were the very essence of punk: banging and shouting, unhindered by any discernible musical ability. We thought the BBC should record them for posterity,' said Walters.

How did the Audition panel respond to this absence of 'musical ability' in punk

CLASSIC SESSION

The Slits

Recorded: **19.9.77**
Studio: **Maida Vale 4**
Producer: **Tony Wilson**
Engineers: **Nick Gomm & Bill Aitken**
First Broadcast: **27.9.77**
Tracks: **Love And Romance, Vindictive, New Town, Shoplifting**
Line-up: **Ari Up** (vocals); **Tessa Pollitt** (bass guitar); **Viv Albertine** (rhythm guitar); **Palmolive** (drums).

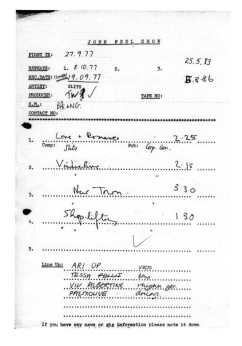

'That was the first time we'd ever been in a studio. Lots of people thought the result better than the album. It was absolutely raw, more raw than any boys' band. I almost can't believe we had that much energy. You don't expect girls of that age to have that much energy: Ari was 14, I think, and the rest of us were all under 20. "Vindictive" is not on any LP, and "New Town" was very different when re-recorded. It was also the only recording we made with Palmolive, as an all-girl band. It was years before we made an album.'

Viv Albertine

'It was everyone hitting anything as loudly as possible; vaguely in time, there was a sort of rhythm there, and then this maniac shrieking on top. On stage, at that time, it probably sounded quite good, when it was loud, but, when it came out over little speakers, fairly quietly, it just sounded painful. The tuning of the guitars was all over the place. We couldn't stand listening to these guitars, they were so badly out of tune. So myself and the other engineer, both guitarists to a certain degree, had to go out and tune them ourselves. Every now and then we'd have to go back in, and retune them, because they didn't have a clue how to. I wonder if we did the right thing.'

Nick Gomm

'The two sessions that they did are both in the Top Ten best sessions of all time. The first one they did is the best one to come out on Strange Fruit. It somehow sums up the spirit of the era.'

John Peel, 1992

acts? The panel was still meeting once a week but, since 1967, new acts had been passed with the proviso 'suitable for *Top Gear* only'. Maggie Brown, who had taken over the Unit from Mary Cotgrove, recalls the number of tapes submitted direct from rock acts dwindling by the late 1970s, with the advent of cassette demo tapes, which bands increasingly sent direct to Peel. Audition sessions were still held, and the Talent Selection Group still met, but by the time she left for Programme Contracts department at the end of 1978, Maggie Brown recalls the Unit had all but ceased to do any work for Radio 1. Responsibility devolved onto individual producers. The Unit staggered on auditioning ventriloquists and variety acts for Radio 2 shows, until it was eventually abandoned in 1981.

A few weeks before The Slits, Walters had seen Siouxsie 'strutting her stuff, with this blatant Brechtian bellowing' on a multiple bill at the Vortex. Then on 9 October he went to a Siouxsie/Slits double bill at the Croydon Greyhound. Turning up early, and listening to the Banshees' soundcheck, he remembered thinking 'these are memorable tunes, underneath it all. They were actually working as a band; you could see there were certain musical patterns, and they had plans. I booked them.' When they got to Maida Vale on 29 November, it was terrifying, Siouxsie remembers: 'It was a bit like seeing your picture for the first time, because it was the first time we'd actually "separated" anyone and listened to and laughed at each other. You ended up finding how difficult it was to come across good in a recording situation: we came from going "bleaugh!" on stage. You look back and know that the knock-on effect was a help to your career, but at the time it was just a thrill.' Steve Severin felt the same: 'It was the first real chance we had of getting across to a lot of people and to show that we were actually serious about what we did. At the time, all we were concerned with was being in a decent studio for the first time and hearing the songs.'

At the Greyhound that same night in October, Walters had met Jordan, former assistant in Malcolm Maclaren's shop Sex, and on 1 December went to a gig at the Royal College of Art by the band Jordan was managing, Adam and the Ants. 'Adam was all right, although a bit Art-School for my taste; and then suddenly Jordan came on: painted face, hair standing up about a foot in the air, and began to shriek; I thought, get that girl into the studio, and let her shriek to the nation!' He went backstage after the first half of the set, to fix up a session date with Jordan, and the two spent the entire second half locked in the band room, after Adam inadvertently slammed the door to, as he went on stage. 'This prompted much "oh, so that's how you get on the *Peel Show*" ribaldry when they came off.' The session was conditional on the band doing Jordan's song 'Lou', involving the shrieking, and the recording was set for Monday 23 January 1978. 'I felt absolutely out of my depth the moment I walked in there, because I'd never done the song in a controlled atmosphere,' Jordan told Walters years later. 'It was a song from the heart, to put it kindly, and you had to work yourself up before each performance of it, to give it its all. To sing a song like that, which is meant to be sung out of control, in a controlled atmosphere, was very difficult for me: I'd never sung it more than once on the trot, obviously. To have to do it two or three times, as I remember, was very hard on the voice, and the emotions.' The band also did 'Deutscher Girls'. The official story of Adam and the Ants describes the session broadcast, on 30 January 1978, as a 'landmark' in the group's career.

With Adam, Jordan, Siouxsie, Rich Kids, Subway Sect, The Slits, Chelsea, The Adverts, Generation X and The Damned having been in, all the bands that had emerged out of the original London punk movement had now been featured in session on John Peel, except the Sex Pistols and The Clash. By January 1978, the Pistols were on the verge of collapse, while The Clash were firmly established. What really mattered was that, in the wake of the Grundy incident, when according to Jordan 'everyone was scared witless of punk', Peel, Walters and Radio 1 alone had given it airtime. Most of the bands above were unsigned when they did their first Peel Session. No one knew then that they would go on to become stars; and that wasn't the point anyway. They were simply what was happening at the time, and Peel recorded it. By the end of 1977, each night's programme was at least 60–70 per cent punk and reggae. What happened later to the Banshees in 1978 shows the importance of Peel Sessions. For nine months, their growing public identity beyond gigs and the music press was solely constructed by the *Peel Show*. 'Within that year, all these new bands were doing sessions, and they'd never been heard by many people before, they'd just been up and down the country playing to 30 people,' says Steve Severin. 'And then suddenly it was all over the airwaves, and you couldn't really ignore it.'

■

IT WOULD HAVE been difficult indeed to ignore those Peel Sessions. By the time the Banshees' 'Hong Kong Garden' charted in autumn 1978, there had been 90 debut sessions on the programme in the 20 months since The Vibrators' first recording. It would match Bernie and Peel's achievement on *Top Gear* ten years before. The very day after Adam and the Ants' debut in January 1978, for example, Wire's first went out; and Patrik Fitzgerald, Magazine, X-Ray Spex, The Mekons and The Flys had followed them before the end of March. And the first record played in the show on which The Flys appeared, 23 March, was 'Suspect Device' by Belfast's Stiff Little Fingers. They promptly went into the most easily available small studio, which happened to be the eight-track Studio 1 at the Northern Ireland commercial radio station, Downtown Radio, and recorded a four-track 'private tape' session for Peel, which was broadcast on 13 April. Downtown's engineer Stephen Nelson recorded the tracks; and both he, and Downtown Studio 1, would famously figure again on Peel, before the year was out.

But April also brought the infamous, aborted session by The Clash. They were booked

FIRST HEARD HERE

'Hong Kong Garden'
by Siouxsie and the Banshees

First heard here on John Peel, 23.2.78

Reached No 7 August 1978

Peel Ahead of Everyone by... (PAE) Index:
6 months

Despite graffiti all over London from Christmas 1977 saying 'SIGN THE BANSHEES', the record industry wouldn't touch them: 'They hoped it would all go away,' John Walters said. On their second session, broadcast on 23 February 1978, the group did 'Hong Kong Garden'. Still the record companies weren't interested. Walters and Banshees' manager Nils Stevenson negotiated a deal for BBC records to bring out a single of the session recording. 'We thought, that'd be enough to get them on the fringes of the chart, and that would pull the finger out of the dyke, as it were, and the offers would come flooding,' Walters remembered. As soon as the labels heard about this, they jumped. Polydor signed Siouxsie up, and the BBC Records plan was dropped. 'Hong Kong Garden' was re-recorded, and promptly shot into the chart late in August that year, peaking at number seven.

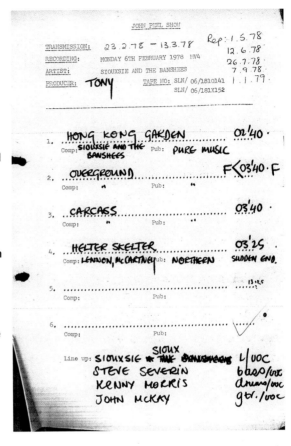

in on the 24th, with Tony Wilson producing, and Bill Aitken engineering. 'Tony was introducing me to two of the band leaders, when my eye caught Nicky Headon, who I knew as a good drummer from other bands,' says Aitken, 'and who had a very friendly little mongrel dog, who he used to love so much he would bring it along to sessions, where it would lie patiently at his feet, waiting for him to stop thumping the hell out of his kit. "Hi Nicky, how's your dog?" I said. The two leaders immediately started derisively mimicking, "how's your dog, ha! ha! ha!" then corrected me: "That's Topper." I felt sorry for Nicky, who looked extremely embarrassed by the whole thing, but couldn't afford not to conform to the collective Clash image.' The band put down some tracks, but became increasingly 'negative', says Aitken, until, towards the end, they told Tony Wilson they wanted to cancel. The explanation given was that 'it wasn't happening'. Aitken, however, is convinced the real reason was his innocent enquiry after Topper's dog.

Altogether more productive and happier were the recordings Viv Stanshall made,

ONE-SESSION WONDER

Prince Far I & Creation Rebel

First broadcast: **16.6.78**
Recorded: **7.6.78**
Studio: **Maida Vale 4**
Producer: **Jeff Griffin**
Engineer: **Nick Gomm**
Tracks: **Spoken Introduction, Black Man's Land, No More War, The Dream, Foggy Road, Front Line**
Line-up: **Prince Far I (lead vocals); Vernon (guitar); Clifton Morrisson (keyboards); Clinton Jack (bass); Dr Pablo (melodica); Charley (drums)**

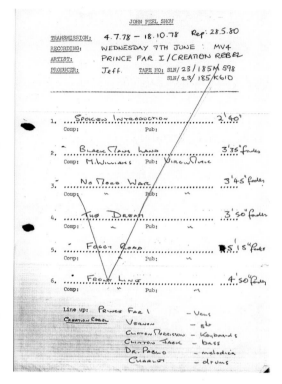

From the two Bob Marley and the Wailers sessions, through the many by Misty, Culture, Aswad, Matumbi, Reggae Regular, Gregory Isaacs, Eek-a-Mouse, New Age Steppers and others, reggae always featured in the Peel Sessions. But no session has been more talked about than this: Prince Far I's only BBC date, just after his Virgin album 'Message From The King', and recorded with backing band Creation Rebel, both of whom went on to work closely with Adrian Sherwood at On-U Sounds in the late 1970s and early 1980s. New producers would not believe Peel that there was a Prince Far-I session at all, until it was called up from the archive as proof, and promptly repeated.

From Prince Far I's Spoken Introduction: 'The publics demands, my special request, to the man John Peel. Love the torment of one, happiness of two for a fellow live in the city of three. Well these tracks is dedicated, from the Virgin album "Message From The King". Well quite likely, having your meals, which is eating your dinner or drinking your tea. It's really a grace from the Prince personally. That mean, if you don't want fi read your bible, just listen to Prince Far I.'

mainly with Malcolm Brown producing, for five *Rawlinson End* broadcasts on Peel, between 1977 and 1979. One of the most complex, involving two full recording sessions, went out that April. 'I remember on one of those Malcolm was trying to get for me the noise of a haddock being slapped across the back of Henry's head,' Stanshall remembered. 'He first of all hunted round the broom cupboards at the studios for the right kind of mop, then insisted on exactly the right amount of wetness, before it was slapped on a special piece of lino. He was really quite a whizz with the sound effects, was Malcolm.'

By now, Malcolm Brown was doing the Tuesday and the Wednesday Peel Sessions. But when he went onto producing a daytime show that summer, he had less time for Maida Vale work. One of his last regular Tuesdays produced The Skids' first session, on 16 May. At the same time, Radio 1 learned that Engineering was not going to release an SM for promotion to producing that year. Controller Derek Chinnery asked if staff knew any good freelance producers. Walters did. Coincidentally, a few days before, he'd bumped into a fellow-Tynesider and musician, who'd first turned up on Peel Sessions as keyboard player in Mick Abrahams' Band, and later in his own right, as a solo multi-instrumentalist, who had recorded for Peel as recently as June 1977: Bob Sargeant. He was hawking round his production of a demo tape of Rat Scabies' new band, The Whitecats.

Bob Sargeant thus became the first of the freelance Peel Session

The Fall's Mark E Smith. Gabor Scott/Redferns

producers, a major change in how they were done for the next decade. His first two, done as trials, were The Boys of the Lough on Wednesday 24 May, 'live-finished by 6.30pm', and The Rezillos on the 31st – 'slightly more problematic'. He started doing the Wednesday Peel regularly from 5 July. But the day before The Rezillos, a rather longer-lasting new band had been in the studio for Peel for the first time. 'You don't know me but I know you,' Walters had written to its leader on 15 May, having seen them at the Greyhound, Croydon, 'the other Sunday. The band seem to have the kind of defiant non-musical approach which ought to be encouraged. We might be able to work out something to your advantage,' he wrote. 'PS I went to see Siouxsie really but Danny Baker had recommended that I try to catch your performance.' That support band was The Fall. They were to go on to become the most recorded Peel Session band and remained Peel's favourite group. Bob Sargeant, another new boy at Maida Vale that week, did their second session that November, and ended up producing their first album *Live At The Witch Trials*.

Sargeant's beginning regular session production coincided with the last gasps of the

The Undertones. Denis O'Regan/Corbis

old guard. The only pre-punk acts to come in again were Rab Noakes, Roy Harper, Racing Cars and, last of all, Dr Feelgood, broadcast on 18 September. Their place was taken that autumn by first sessions by bands like the Pop Group, Human League, Pragvec, the Swell Maps and Scritti Politti. And Malcolm Brown's last Peel production was Stiff Little Fingers' first Maida Vale date on 12 September. But, even as they were finishing the session that night, across London at Egton House, another Northern Irish band was about to make history.

Just who got a copy of 'Teenage Kicks' to Peel is unclear. Feargal Sharkey says he had previously contacted Peel about a demo tape The Undertones had sent, so when Terri Hooley's Good Vibrations label of Belfast pressed up 2,000 copies of the *True Confessions* EP, he posted one to Peel. Terri Hooley says he spent a Friday unsuccessfully trying to sell the record to major labels in London and, late at night, left a copy for Peel at Radio 1. What happened next has become a pop legend. On Tuesday 12 September, Peel played all four tracks from the EP: 'Isn't that the most wonderful record you've ever heard?' he commented. He was so excited, he played 'Teenage Kicks' again on the Thursday and Friday. And again two days the following week. Listening to the show in his car as he drove through London was Sire Records' boss Seymour Stein, who, having signed The Ramones and The Rezillos, was looking for more acts. The next day he contacted Good Vibrations and the band in Derry. Within three weeks the band had signed to Sire, and 'Teenage Kicks' was rush re-released on Sire on 13 October. Peel used the excuse to play it again that night. 'I still maintain it's the best record ever made,' Peel always said. 'It cost us £100 to record,' says Terri Hooley. And, for just another £70, Peel had, in the meantime, already scooped Sire on a further recording by the group. Before the band had signed, and still could not afford to come to London to do a session, Peel paid for the band to go into Downtown Studio 1, and with Stephen Nelson engineering, do a three-hour 'private tape' session for the show. 'We just drove down to Belfast in an hour or so and did it,' says Feargal Sharkey. 'The first number they played, I thought, ah, that's a hit record,' recalls Stephen Nelson. 'Then they did another, and I thought, ah, now that's a hit record; and every song was like that.' The tracks recorded were 'Get Over You', 'Top 20', 'She Can Only Say No', and 'Male Model', and the tape was first broadcast on Monday 16 October. Long thought lost, in summer 1992 Peel stumbled on the tape in his attic.

Walters was still picking bands at gigs. On Sunday 26 November, he went to see 'Generation X + support' at the Greyhound, Croydon. 'Generation X had made it by then, and they'd been on tour supported by this band from Crawley,' he said. 'I was horrified to learn they were being paid a fiver for the whole band, but the manager was then having to pay Generation X's lighting and sound men a tenner, so it was costing them money to play.' Walters booked them. The band was The Cure. Shortly afterwards, Peel ran his second full listener's poll of all-time favourites, the Festive Fifty, over Christmas 1978 (he had chosen 50 of his own favourites at the end of 1977), and everything had changed. 'Anarchy In The UK' was listeners' all-time number one, and punk records filled the top ten and dominated the rest of the chart. 'Stairway To Heaven' was the highest pre-punk record, at 14. There were five Sex Pistols songs, four from The Clash, and no fewer than seven by Siouxsie and the Banshees, reflecting how they had been championed by the show since that first session in December 1977. Five times as many listeners voted as in the first poll two years before. 'The audience of two years ago was an audience growing old with me,' Peel told *MM*. 'My listeners were in their mid-to-late 20s, either students or ex-students. My existing

CLASSIC SESSION

The Cure

Recorded: **4.12.78**
Studio: **Maida Vale 4**
Producer: **Tony Wilson**
Engineer: **Dave Dade**
First Broadcast: **11.12.78**
Tracks: **Killing An Arab, 10'15 Saturday Night, Fire In Cairo, Boys Don't Cry**
Line-up: **Robert Smith (guitar & lead vocal); Michael Dempsey (bass & backing vocals); Laurence Tolhurst (drums & backing vocals)**

'After overcoming the initial disappointment in discovering the great man would not actually be there himself, the experience lived up to expectations. The four songs we recorded captured the spirit far more than the album versions. I found that the producers had exactly the right approach: if it looked like you knew what you were doing, they let you get on with it. It was this lack of meddling that made the results more like the original demos that had secured our recording contract in the first place, just better quality. All songs in the first and second session should be seen as the definitive sound of the early Cure.'

Michael Dempsey

audience did not come with me as I thought they would, and I developed a whole new audience. The audience is now a disenfranchised minority.'

■

HE SPOKE WITH SOME bitterness. Recent events at Radio 1 had led him to feel disenfranchised himself. He had just lost a show, and had nearly lost the late-night FM slot, thanks to how Radio 1 management felt it best to 'fill the in-fill'. 'Radio 1 on 247 is now joining Radio 2': for years the station had shut down at 7.30pm, joining Radio 2 for the evening, only to come back at 11pm (then 10pm from April 1977) with Peel. How to fill what was called 'the in-fill' period had occupied planners for some time, when, in autumn 1978, to coincide with the frequency shift to 275 and 285 metres, the budget eventually became available to begin evening programmes. Walters remembered the original plan had been to move Peel forward to the mid-evening, thereby losing the FM simulcast, and give Kid Jensen 10pm–midnight; this was one of the reasons Peel's later Rhythm Pal had stood in for Peel in March 1977 for those two weeks – to try him out. Walters argued against the move with controller Derek Chinnery. First he got Chinnery to accept that Peel's was the most demanding and innovative show in the schedule and should not be interfered with in programming detail. Then, he remembered, he asked whether the controller would be happy with Peel potentially playing records to children – before the 9pm watershed – by bands such as, say, The Molesters, The Vibrators and The Slits? That swung it. The show stayed at 10pm. But Peel lost his Friday-night slot from the beginning of the 'in-fill' evening schedule in November 1978, to the new *Friday Night Rock Show* hosted by Tommy Vance, produced by Tony Wilson, partly designed to replace Alan 'Fluff' Freeman's Saturday afternoon show after he had left Radio 1 that summer. Despite his previous working relationships with both Wilson and Vance, Peel was furious. He saw this as taking airtime from the hundreds of new young bands he was desperate to give airtime to and returning it to rock dinosaurs.

With hindsight a contest for creativity between the post-punk diaspora and the likes of Saxon, Samson and Iron Maiden seems no contest, but there were plenty of BBC insiders who were less than impressed by what Peel was championing. Trevor Dann, one of two new junior producers at Radio 1, along with John Sparrow, who were packed off to Maida Vale once a week to produce Peel Sessions from early 1979 for the next 18 months, remembers it as a thin time. 'Some of the groups were hideously unlistenable. I remember a series of utterly wretched groups, all of which I thought then were forgettable, and indeed who are now forgotten. The exceptions

The Cravats recording their debut session in MV4, July 1979. The Cravats

were Echo and the Bunnymen, who I thought were great; Psychedelic Furs, who overcame initial nervousness to do a good session; and Simple Minds.' Perhaps he was just unlucky in his shifts. Tubeway Army, the Gang of Four, Joy Division, Joe Jackson, Crass, Big in Japan, The Cravats, Misty, The Raincoats and Linton Kwesi Johnson all recorded first Peel Sessions early in 1979.

Robin Raymond Dalloway and The Shend of The Cravats remember the strange experience of trying to push the boundaries of their 'abrasive jazz-punk mash up sound' inside the 'time-warped Ealing Studios world' of Maida Vale in the 1970s, with its 'aircraft hangar-sized soundproofed rooms full of cables and microphones and an odd musty smell of the fifties'. 'We were young and arrogant and cheekily rewrote and rearranged stuff in the studio,' says Dalloway, 'spinning in sound samples, playing children's toy instruments and playing with all the ancient keyboards there. It felt like being in school after hours. But nothing fazed the Beeb crew. They respectfully helped us while we tested their patience way into the early hours of the morning. We particularly owed a lot to engineer Mike Robinson. He was brilliant and really got the best out of us. We loved it – Hurrah for John Peel and the *Peel Show*!' The Shend says, 'You'd spend 80 per cent of your allotted time miking up the bloody drums, blast through four tracks, whack on a couple of overdubs, mix it in the remaining

49 minutes and then load the van at midnight and head off up the M40 towards Birmingham. They always somehow ended up sounding great though, and when they were broadcast, you'd sit there with your finger poised over the record button on your crappy cassette player trying to catch John's witty intro to your masterpiece. I've still got most them somewhere.'

This was also the year when Walters felt he made his other 'mistake'. The first was not having the Sex Pistols, the second was going ahead with a session by The Police. 'I'd seen The Police in a pub and turned them down as far too retro – they were clearly going back to playing proper tunes, and singing proper songs – and although they had a following, I thought "No". Then Peel was knocked out with them at a Dutch festival ("They played particularly well," said Peel), and we got them in. They did a good session, but if you follow the philosophy of the programme, they shouldn't have been on: they summed up conformity, whereas punk was all about non-comformity.' But there were non-conformist musical movements appearing in the aftermath of punk: the ska revival, first embodied by The Specials, and later Madness, The Selecter and The Beat; the mod revival, through The Monitors, The Chords and Secret Affair; and, as *Sounds* called it in March, 'The new Merseybeat': Echo and the Bunnymen, the Teardrop Explodes, Pink Military and Orchestral Manoeuvres in the Dark; all of whom debuted on Peel in 1979. Of these, perhaps the 2-Tone bands, led by The Specials, produced the most exciting sessions, purely because their music thrived on live performance. On the night their debut session went out in May, The Specials, in Leeds for a gig, rushed into a second-hand shop to buy a radio to listen in; Peel repeated it three times before September. Madness, early in August, recorded a version of 'The Prince' that, with Bob Sargeant's production and Mike Robinson's mixing, surpassed the later record. Pauline Black of The Selecter remembers 'half the band arrived late, and the other half very late' for their debut in October: 'It was a terrible rush, but we argued our way through it, like everything else, ending up doing the fourth number, "Danger", totally live.' And at the end of the month came a band Peel and Sheila loved, The Beat.

By the first week of the new decade, such were the multiplicity of new styles emerging, that the show had established a new kind of equilibrium: new bands and independent records weren't just playing '1-2-3-4!' frantic punk, but enough of a variety for Peel's show to become a mix again. In the first week of January, UB40, Bauhaus and Simple Minds had first sessions broadcast. An average of five new bands were still being recorded each month in 1980, and far fewer of them went onto become famous household or even cult names, yet there were still stories. A day or two after the The Passions recorded their second session for the show on 7 May

CLASSIC SESSION

The Beat

Recorded: **24.10.79**

Studio: **Maida Vale 4**

Producer: **Bob Sargeant**

Engineer: **Nick Gomm**

First Broadcast: **5.11.79**

Tracks: **Tears Of A Clown, Mirror In The Bathroom, Ranking Full Stop, Click Click, Big Shot**

Line-up: **Everet Morton, drums; Dave Wakeling (guitar & lead vocals); Ranking Roger (percussion, vocal & styles); David 'Shuffle' Steele (bass); Andy Cox (guitar & optional vocals)**

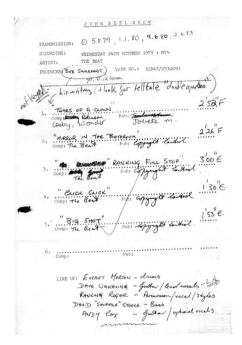

'They were very nervous, it being their first session. I tried to put them at ease. When they started to play it was immediately very fresh and exciting. I particularly thought Dave Wakeling had a great voice. We were trying to get it live and immediate, and as a result the session went very quick, and we had five numbers done by 7.30pm. Then the manager rolled in. He said the band had had a chat in the canteen, they were recording a single for 2-Tone in a few days, and would I like to produce it? I think they were simply pleased at having a very well-engineered session.'

Bob Sargeant

Bob Sargeant went on to produce the Beat's first and second albums.

The Beat. Fin Costello/Redferns

1980, Walters received a copy of a severe memo to his superiors from the House Foreman at Maida Vale: 'On my walk round the building at 20.30 last night, I heard female voices coming from the Gents toilet. I went to investigate and found two young ladies by the Gents' stand-up having their photographs taken in a most unfemale fashion. I told them to leave immediately. Outside the toilet, I told them in no uncertain manner that they were behaving in a most disgusting manner. I told the photographer what trouble he could be in for taking these pictures without permission on BBC premises, and also the group could be banned from all future recordings. The group then became most concerned over the whole incident.' *Sounds* printed the pic anyway. The world did not fall.

Edwyn Collins. Pete Cronin/Redferns

Perhaps the one truly transcendental band to appear in this period were the Birthday Party. 'I saw them at the Moonlight Club in West Hampstead,' said Peel, 'and they were stupendous, a revelation. It was also one of those gigs where you know, instantly, that this band are going to be worshipped by a certain sector of the listening public.' Their first broadcast was on 25 September. 'We'd been working at home in Australia for a couple of years, made a couple of records, then came to start from scratch in London in 1980,' remembers Mick Harvey of the Birthday Party. 'We picked up a deal with 4AD, and released two singles, but only did about eight gigs in all that year, around London. So the session was very good exposure for the band. It certainly contributed to us gaining popularity! I always remember being amused at how all the engineers would break off for their lunch and tea-breaks.'

From late that year and into early 1981, there was also a wave of Scottish bands, starting with Altered Images and closely followed by Orange Juice, Fire Engines, Josef

K and The Associates. Edwyn Collins remembers Orange Juice recording 'Falling And Laughing' 'at breakneck speed compared with the Postcard single and Polydor album versions. I don't know why that was. I think it was because we were very enthused to be doing our first Peel Session. The producer John Sparrow suggested I sing "Poor Old Soul" through a megaphone. He thought it sounded like a Twenties song, a Bonzo Dog Doo-Dah Band kind of song. I don't know where that guy's head was at! Afterwards, when our single "Blue Boy" appeared, we were investigated for fraud by the Social Security in Glasgow. They'd gathered together a lot of press cuttings – and taped this Peel Session as evidence!' Multi-instrumentalist Dennis Bovell later joined Orange Juice; he'd already appeared on sessions by Matumbi, and then improvised an extraordinary performance for Linton Kwesi Johnson in October 1981. 'The musicians that Dennis Bovell had promised did not turn up,' remembers Johnson. 'The atmosphere was nonetheless surprisingly relaxed. Dennis was very reassuring. There was no need to panic. We would do "All Wi Doin Is Defendin" as planned. The electric piano provided bass and rhythm, played by Dennis. The drums and percussion were provided by Dennis' mouth: grunts for bass drum, tongue clapping for wood block, tongue and teeth for hi-hat, etc. The sound engineer and the producer were as astonished as I was. I did my vocals and that was that.'

That first date for Orange Juice back in October 1980 was one of the very last recorded in the old eight-track Maida Vale 4. It closed down at the beginning of November 1980 for conversion to 24-track. For over a year, a team of Bob Conduct, Bob Harrison and Bill Aitken had been investigating what equipment should be chosen. They eventually plumped for a new desk design from a new Oxford company, SSL. In the end the BBC ordered quite a number of desks from SSL, which made the company's name. In fact, so pleased were they with the sale, they offered Bill Aitken a job, which he took in 1981. But in the meantime, while Maida Vale 4 and 5 were being converted, sessions were temporarily relocated back at Langham 1 for eight months. Bands would turn up and be astounded by what the engineers got out of the ageing eight-track equipment. Ageing, it was, however, the monitors being in a particularly bad way, having been hammered for 15 hours a day for ten years. Session sheets of this time are covered in engineer's doodles of exploding speakers, and credits like 'Another Blast from The Pit'. Helen McCookerybook of The Chefs remembers how at the end of their first session there in May, Mike Robinson could take it no more. 'Somebody had drawn a face in biro on one of the speakers, and cut a flap out of the fabric on the front of it where the nose would be. Mike turned on the music and started to move the fader up. As the music got louder, the nose-flap started to tremble and, eventually, it fluttered in the breeze coming from within the

A LISTENER WRITES

'When I was about 12, I used to have to go to bed too early. It was still light those summer evenings, so I used to flick through the large old radio on the bedside table while lying in bed. I was very much into music so was always intrigued by what I found at a certain part of the dial, while also being hesitant to tune in as what I heard often used to scare and haunt me. It was a darker side to music that wasn't readily available in Sevenoaks at the time and I found it sort of addictive. I felt as if I was the only person listening to this show full of obscure, never heard before music. Even now I still remember the feeling of hearing Laurie Anderson's "O Superman" and being filled with a melancholy beyond my years. I will also never forget, about 18 months later, hearing the opening drum machine rhythm to New Order's "Blue Monday" and not understanding it at all. It completely shattered my conception of how music was made. I firmly believe those nights spent listening to John in bed are the foundation of my adult musical education.'

Paul Hartnoll

John Peel started playing the import seven-inch of 'O Superman' on Bob George's 210 records in June 1981, and played it intensively through that summer. Laurie Anderson was signed by Warners and the UK-released single reached number 2 in November that year. Bob George became an occasional reporter for the Peel Show on experimental music in the USA from 1982 to 1985.

---

speaker cabinet. The music got louder and louder. Mike had a mad grin and staring eyes. We sat there speechless, looking at each other nervously. Finally at deafening volume, the speakers gave in and burst. "Right then," he said, sane again. He picked up the phone and spoke politely. "Hello, the speakers have gone in Studio 1. Could we have some new ones please?"'

This, however, was where New Order, with Tony Wilson producing and Dave Dade balancing, had recorded their famous first Peel Session in January 1981. By then, for various reasons, the number of Peel Sessions being recorded had slipped back to two a week, and would stay that way until the end. When Walters launched his own series, *Walters' Weekly*, early that year, Chris Lycett, who had begun his career at Radio 1 playing-in 'grams' (records) for *Top Gear* in 1967, took over producing John Peel's programme for two years. 'I did the Wednesday evening show, pre-recorded, to keep my hand in,' said Walters, 'but looking back it does seem to be a very slack period. It seemed to be a million-and-one bands called "Dance" something. Punk had become an historic thing. It was a trough after a peak.'

■

HAND-IN-HAND with the establishment of independent record labels, which the show also championed, the Peel Sessions of 1978–1981 permanently changed bands' perspective on worthwhile musical ambitions. From now on, a Peel Session became as much a career ambition in itself as a means to advancement. Those sessions had such impact that for a new band to record one was to gain a permanent place in an alternative tradition. Their name would be added to a unique musical roll of honour. That and making one single was often all they wanted. From punk on, the sessions were not only rare and exclusive early recordings of later superstars. Peel, Walters and Lycett were not 'picking winners'. They were giving space and time, fairly cheaply, to whoever seemed to have something to say at any particular moment. You could pick the story of any band's first session and it would be worth telling. Here, just two more will have to do.

How Que Bono got their booking in summer 1981 is now one of the few things people remember about them at all. 'Our singer, Jane, had the idea to send our demo tape to Kenny Dalglish, Peel's hero at Liverpool FC, asking him to forward it to Peel, endorsing our request for a session,' says guitarist Alan Maskell. 'We got a phone call from Peel, saying, for sheer cheek, could we do a session?' The recording itself, at Langham 1 on Tuesday 9 June, was beset by difficulties. 'We couldn't put certain things through certain channels, because they didn't work,' says Maskell. 'Even though this studio is only due to be used for a few more weeks, the monitors have deteriorated beyond all hope,' despairing producer Dale Griffin wrote (Robbo's ploy had evidently not worked). Nevertheless, the session, broadcast on the 16th, was 'a highlight of the band's career', says Maskell: 'Our later self-financed single was incorrectly pressed, six months later we had a blazing row, I left, and the band split soon after.' And then there's the story of the band, like Que Bono, from Lancashire, who had their first session broadcast the very next night, and who had been in Langham 1 the day before them: The Chameleons. The story told by Mark Burgess of their first session says everything about the value of Peel Sessions. So I leave the telling to him.

CLASSIC SESSION

The Chameleons

Recorded: **8.6.81**
Studio: **Langham 1**
Producer: **Tony Wilson**
Engineer: **Dave Dade**
First Broadcast: **17.6.81**
Tracks: **The Fan The Bellows, Here Today, Looking Inwardly, Things I Wish I'd Said**
Line-up: **Mark Burgess (bass, vocal); Dave Fielding (guitar); Reg Smithies (guitar); Brian Schofield (drums)**

'We began by simply wanting to record a session for John Peel. It wasn't that we saw this as a stepping stone to success or anything; no, all of the bands that we had grown up admiring had all recorded sessions for John Peel, and that was our main incentive. I personally never dreamt that we would get a response to the first tape we sent in. I don't think any of us did. We didn't have a regular drummer, and recorded the songs on Reg's old blaster without drums and sent it off. A few weeks later back came a letter: "Enjoyed the tape, sounds like something worthwhile is going on, if you do a studio tape be sure to send me a copy. Regards, John Peel."

'We sold everything we didn't need to make the recording: mics, stands, pa amps, everything except our guitars and back-line. Having recorded the demos, Dave and I boarded a train to London and spent the afternoon sitting on the steps of the BBC waiting for John Peel to walk past. Finally John did go by and we accosted him. Once he had established that he wasn't being attacked he became very sympathetic. He told us to give him an hour with the tape. When he came back we had a hard time convincing him that it was actually us on the tape. He seemed convinced we were playing some sort of practical joke on him, that we would suddenly declare the tape to be the work of some already established band and belittle his considerable reputation as an "underground" music guru.

'A few days later on the following Monday, at 9am, the phone rang at my parents' house and I dashed downstairs to answer it. It was John Peel! He told me he liked the tape and wanted to book us for a session, then handed me over to Chris Lycett. He told me we could wait until Maida Vale was finished and do the session in 24-track, or do it immediately in the old Langham 8-track. I consulted with the others and we decided not to wait. A date was set the next day.

'We still didn't have a permanent drummer, but a local heavy metal drummer we knew who'd played with us before, Brian Schofield, said he'd help us out. We didn't know anyone in London so it meant a ride down, record the session, then back to Manchester. That meant leaving Middleton at 6am. We made it to Langham 1 by 10am. I remember Tony Wilson as a very nice guy, but very quiet. Whenever he spoke to his engineer, Dave Dade, it was always in hushed tones. We were all very nervous and overawed by it all but Tony and Dave were very good with us. It was the first time we had worked with a producer or engineer, so for us the results sounded rather stunning. "Looking Inwardly" then had no title or lyrics, we just had the raw idea, but we didn't want the technicians to know: Dave or Reg kept them busy with guitar parts, while I lay under the grand piano with a pad and paper scribbling away. I was enjoying myself so much though, that at one point, during the take, I just threw them away: "I don't need these lyrics, what am I doing here?"

'I remember the night the session was broadcast vividly. We all met up at [roadie] Alastair's flat shortly before 10pm. We were doubly excited because the evening before John had wound up his show by telling the story of how Dave and I turned up on the BBC steps with the demo, and then urged everyone to tune-in to hear a "remarkable" session. We had been stunned. On the evening of the broadcast he heaped even more praise on the group. None of us could believe it. Because we hadn't heard the session since we'd completed it, the songs sounded more fresh and exciting than we remembered them. They leapt out of the radio. And the nerves just listening! It was like a really important gig or something. We hadn't expected a session when we first sent our tape. We certainly didn't expect the session, once done, to change our lives. Yet that is precisely what it did.'

Mark Burgess

Within days, The Chameleons were signed to Virgin Publishing and CBS Records. They released one single, and were then dropped over an argument about who should produce their LP. The band eventually recorded three albums for small independent labels, and several more Radio 1 sessions. They broke up in 1987. Most people regard their Peel Sessions as their finest recordings.

■

PEEL SESSIONS

RECORDINGS:		TRANSMISSIONS:	
MARCH	SUN. 31/3 ~~Julian Cope~~ (then weekend)	SAT. 30/3	BOSS HOG
APRIL	TUE. 2/4 Hold Hold SILVERFISH (4) ED Crouttie		PLANT BACH OF NUS APRIL ®(R)
		SUN. 31/3	CURVE
			FORCE FED ®(R)
	SUN. 7/4 PROPHECY OF DOOM ~~(Stressel 029b-279058)~~	SAT. 6/4	VIV ST.
			DATBLYGU ®(R)
	TUE. 9/4 Catherine ~~Wheel~~ (4) (Sil - 081-96_2227) G/B/DIV	SUN. 7/4	BOO RADLEYS
			A HOMEBOY A HIPPIE... ®(R)
	SUN. 14/4 BARRENCE WHITFIELD G/B/DIV	SAT. 13/4	BONGWATER
			TOP ®(R)
	TUE. 16/4 MOOSE (4) Julian Hoe 371-5633 G/B/D/V	SUN. 14/4	HEAVENLY
			MOONFLOWERS ®(R)
	SUN. 21/4 GUNSHOT (4 mx) (ROB - 792_1791) Rap/4/q/z/o-o	SAT. 20/4	HYPNOTONE
			CHARLATANS ®(R)
	TUE. 23/4 INSIDE OUT (3 mrs. USA) D/G/B/VV 0325-465309	SUN. 21/4	SLOWDIVE
			HOOVERS ®(R)
	SUN. 28/4 PITCH SHIFTER (4) 029b-277849 GG/DM/B/VV	SAT. 27/4	FAITH HEALERS
			DEPTH CHARGE ®(R)
	TUE. 30/4 70 GWEN PARTY (2) Victor 081-577-3665 D Mac/RH/G/B	SUN. 28/4	SILVERFISH
			THE THING ®(R)
MAY	SUN. 5/5 EXIT CONDITION (3) G/B/D (Richard 0782-659395)	SAT. 4/5	JULIAN COPE
			GREENHOUSE ®(R)
	TUE. 7/5 CHERRYBLADES (4) 5? Alan James 071 1083 G/G/D/D/V	SUN. 5/5	CATHERINE WHEEL
			SHAMEN ®(R)
	SUN. 12/5 BILLY BRAGG (+3/4) (Tiny - 081-860-4468)	SAT. 11/5	DR PHIBES
			MELVINS ®(R)
	TUE. 14/5 RAGGA TWINS (4/5) (Smith - Shut up + Dance) 524	SUN. 12/5	PROPHECY OF DOOM?
		NO PROG.	FIRST OFFENCE ®(R)

The Last Days of Walters: the sessions planning system on the wall of Egton 318, Spring 1991.

CHAPTER 06

1983-1991: PUTTING THE FUN BACK INTO BEING PRETENTIOUS

IT WAS ONE hell of a comeback. Discovering The Smiths in your first month back at the day job is a fairly impressive way to return to work. It was one of the first things Walters did when he resumed producing Peel full-time in 1983. After Chris Lycett moved to look after *The Breakfast Show* at the New Year, Trevor Dann had been Peel's producer for the first three months of 1983, including a week of shows from BBC Radio Merseyside. But Dann unexpectedly got the attachment to television he'd wanted, and so Walters was back in charge of all four Peel Shows, Monday–Thursday, by late April. And on 6 May he went to see The Smiths at ULU, the University of London student's union venue. 'They were a late replacement as a support act. I'd heard there was a buzz about them in Manchester, and Scott Piering, then handling The Smiths' promotion, told me about the gig at the last minute. He said, "I think you should see this band." There was a scattering of people there. I was standing next to Scott, and felt there was a kind of charisma there on stage, so I thought we'd better have a session.' He offered the band one there and then. That's the downbeat way Walters told it, but Peel remembered him returning to the office in a highly enthused state about the group.

By the time they went into Maida Vale 5 on 18 May, The Smiths had released their first one-off single on Rough Trade, 'Hand in Glove'. Their Radio 1 producer that day, Roger Pusey, was then doing quite a few Peel Sessions, and remembers 'they do stand out as being one of the better ones, certainly one of the ones we got the most out of at the session.' Engineer Nick Gomm admits he was initially slightly put off by Morrissey's singing. That didn't prevent him doing an atmospheric live mix. The first number recorded, 'What Difference Does It Make', would later be the band's third single; but that version was to feature several overdubbed layers of guitars, and some members of the band were reportedly more fond of this original, more straightforward, Peel Session recording. Years later, drummer Mike Joyce told writer Johnny Rogan: 'The Peel version is the way I wanted it to be.' It was the first time the band had even attempted to record both this number and 'Reel Around The Fountain'. (They had made a demo of 'Miserable Lie' and 'Handsome Devil', the fourth song recorded on the 18th, was the B-side of the single.)

The session went out on the first day of June. In the middle of a tour late in June, they finally signed to Rough Trade permanently, and a few days later recorded a second Radio 1 session, this time for David Jensen's *Evening Show*, commissioned by the slot's regular producer throughout the 1980s, Mike Hawkes, on Sunday 26 June. Three numbers were completed, with Dale Griffin producing. But it was the second session for David Jensen that was to prove a turning point. Hawkes booked this second one soon after repeating the first on 20 July, and the recording was set for 25 August. By then, Peel had already repeated his first session twice, the second time the very night before this third Maida Vale date for the band. The first notable thing about the recording on the 25th was that it was the first time the band met and worked with independent producer John Porter; although he had, coincidentally, already been asked, earlier that month, by Rough Trade boss Geoff Travis to remix tracks for the band's first album, following the unsuccessful Troy Tate-produced sessions in June and July. 'The way I remember it, I had listened to the tapes a few days before the BBC session,' reflects John Porter, 'then, having met the band and got on well with them at Maida Vale, particularly Johnny, I think that, knowing we liked each other, and that it would be all right, I suggested to Geoff we simply re-record the album tracks; and I think we did that very soon, perhaps only a couple of weeks after that Jensen session.' Geoff Travis thinks he only agreed the re-recording of the album after Johnny Marr had spoken highly of Porter to him, following the BBC date.

Porter would later produce The Smiths' last two BBC sessions, both for Peel, one in 1984, and the last in December 1986. 'We were working together quite a lot, and tried to make the BBC sessions as easy, and as painless, as possible. We'd try and get it good, but not get too hung up about it. I think all the numbers were done very quickly, in just a first or second take. We'd get the band sound set up, and Morrissey would come in, perhaps only for a couple of hours, and we'd just do the numbers in a very straightforward way. We never really laboured that much over them.' The working relationship that the band first developed with Porter in BBC Maida Vale studios in August 1983 was later to prove highly creative, producing their first album and several singles, including 'How Soon Is Now'. On the 25th, with Mike Robinson engineering, they recorded 'I Don't Owe You Anything', 'Accept Yourself', 'Reel Around The Fountain' and 'Pretty Girls Make Graves'.

But with baffling coincidence, on the morning of the 25th, *The Sun* published a story headlined 'Child Sex Song puts Beeb in a Spin'. The article claimed that some of Morrissey's lyrics were about paedophilia, although it mistakenly referred to the words of 'Reel Around The Fountain' as belonging to 'Handsome Devil'. Just where the paper got the idea that the BBC had already expressed reservations about either of these songs is unclear, both of them having been broadcast, either from the single or the sessions, some time before. What the article did was actually to precipitate the offence it claimed to report. 'The way I remember it, Derek Chinnery got the wind up, and finding out they were doing a session, asked Mike Hawkes if either of these songs were included,' Walters said. Hawkes is not certain of the order of events in the week following the recording. 'Chinnery might have asked me, "What's all this about?" or I might have approached him. One way or another, he got to hear the lyrics of "Reel Around The Fountain". I was arguing we should broadcast it, but as even I felt it was ambiguous, it was decided that as we weren't certain, we would not broadcast it on the first time out.' This was an upset for the band, who were seriously contemplating making it their next single.

But things ultimately turned out to the band's advantage. Walters was outraged when he heard about the dropping of 'Reel' from the broadcast. 'I got the tape out, and, on my reading of it, it was clearly about heterosexual love. And that's not the point anyway: why should Radio 1 be concerned about what *The Sun* says about anything?' He phoned Scott Piering and immediately offered the band a second Peel Session. 'The message came back from the band: "Morrissey won't forget this",' Walters recalled. And less than two weeks later, on 14 September, they delivered a classic session. Roger Pusey did check with the band about the lyrics to 'This Night', but correctly points out that this is what every Radio 1 sessions producer had to do: 'The only way round it is to make a joke of it, "Look, I'm sorry, this is the BBC, we have to tell you you can't use the F-word," and so on.' It's only sensible to know exactly what it is that is being sung and broadcast, precisely to enable Radio 1 to disregard scare stories in the tabloids about allegedly corrupting pop songs.

After their first session, Morrissey and Marr had made some disparaging remarks to the music press in July about BBC recordings (admittedly before they got to work with John Porter and Mike Robinson), reprinted years later in *Q* magazine. 'It was very, very cold,' said Morrissey. 'You can feel the weight of the BBC bearing down on

CLASSIC SESSION

The Smiths

Recorded: **14.9.83**
Studio: **Maida Vale 4**
Producer: **Roger Pusey**
Engineer: **Ted de Bono**
First Broadcast: **21.9.83**
Tracks: **This Night Has Opened My Eyes, Still Ill, This Charming Man, Back To The Old House**
Line-up: **Morrissey (vocal), Johnny Marr (guitar & harmonica), Andy Rourke (bass), Mike Joyce (drums)**

The first-ever recording of 'This Charming Man', and the other three songs were new too. Geoff Travis of Rough Trade popped into Maida Vale, heard 'This Charming Man' and immediately recommended it be the next single: 'It was certainly the first time I'd heard the song, and I remember saying that's a fantastic track, it'd make a great single, and the band said, "That sounds OK by us", a sort of happy, casual but serious decision, as things were then with the group. It was a really golden time for the group, around that session, they were just getting into the first flowering of their most creative period.'

By the time the re-recorded commercial version was released in early November, Peel had broadcast this session three times. 'You couldn't buy pre-release publicity like that,' said Scott Piering, then handling The Smiths' promotion. The single went straight into the charts.

How the band felt about the session can be deduced from the fact that all four tracks, including the unique acoustic version of 'Back To The Old House', appeared on the compilation album 'Hatful Of Hollow' the following year. The album reached no. 7 on its release in November 1984, spending almost a year in the Top 100. This session version of 'This Night Has Opened My Eyes' is the only recording of the song that has been commercially released.

The Smiths. Rex Features

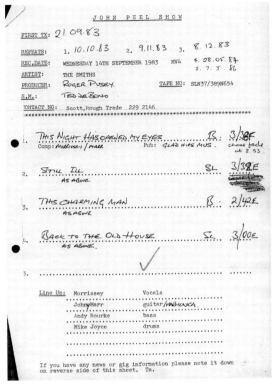

JOHN PEEL SHOW

FIRST TX: 21.09.83

REPEATS: 1. 10.10.83 2. 9.11.83 3. 8.12.83

REC.DATE: WEDNESDAY 14TH SEPTEMBER 1983 MV4 4. 28.05.84
5. 7.5.86

ARTIST: THE SMITHS

PRODUCER: ROGER PUSEY. TAPE NO: SLN37/389N654

S.M.: TED DE BONO

CONTACT NO: Scott, Rough Trade 229 2146

1. THIS NIGHT HAS OPENED MY EYES..... B.: 3/38F
Comp: MORRISSEY/MARR Pub: GLAD HIPS MUS. choose fade at 3.33

2. STILL ILL SL 3/38E
AS ABOVE

3. THIS CHARMING MAN B.: 2/42E
AS ABOVE

4. BACK TO THE OLD HOUSE SL 3/00E
AS ABOVE.

5. ....

Line Up: Morrissey Vocals
JohnyMarr guitar/HARMONICA.
Andy Rourke bass
Mike Joyce drums

If you have any news or gig information please note it down
on reverse side of this sheet. Ta.

you the whole time you're there,' said Marr. But what cannot be denied is the quality of the work they eventually produced under these constraints. Inevitably, because the BBC is an institution, and Maida Vale Studios are imposing, and sessions have to be done against the clock, they can be a traumatic experience. Yet, perhaps more than any other band, what The Smiths put into those sessions in 1983 and, crucially, what they got out of them, demonstrates how what might have felt like an oppressive way of working could actually produce results that, in some ways, say more than months and months of work in the studio. On reflection, Johnny Marr later said the sessions did give the band 'the opportunity to record our new songs very quickly'. Thanks to Walters, Peel and Mike Hawkes' enthusiasm, and, in a curious back-handed way, *The Sun*'s hysteria, The Smiths had a new session broadcast or repeated every couple of weeks for seven months, 12 transmissions in all. Tuning in, you felt, as so often when hearing Peel Sessions, a witness to pop history in the making: you knew everybody would be talking about that session the next day. You can still hear the group's original, unique character echoing in those session tapes today.

PERHAPS THE SMITHS sessions were the most famous of those in the 1980s. But another famous band, who did not have hit singles until 1990 and a no. 1 album early in 1991, actually appeared in session before The Smiths. 'The first session we recorded for Radio 1's John Peel Show was first broadcast back in May 1983, believe it or not,' Peter Hooton of The Farm told Walters, years later. It went out on the 17th, two days before The Smiths recorded their first at Maida Vale. 'It was a great opportunity for us, and also managed to help the profile of the band, because

The Farm

FIRST HEARD HERE...

'All Together Now'
by **The Farm**
First heard here on John Peel,
27 April 1983
Reached no. 4 in
December 1990
Peel Ahead of Everyone by...
(PAE) Index: 7 years

On The Farm's first Peel
Session in spring 1983 could
be heard the embryonic idea
of what would prove a Top
Ten hit for the band more
than seven years later. '"All
Together Now" was first really
demo-ed on that session,' said Peter Hooton. 'The lyrics and the melody were taken from the song
"No Man's Land"; it's obviously changed quite radically from the original, but the ideas were there.'
Similarly, the band's second Peel Session, recorded in February 1984, opened with 'Hearts And Minds',
not a hit single until 1991.

FIRST HEARD HERE...

'Two Tribes' by Frankie Goes To Hollywood
First heard here on John Peel, December 1982
Reached no. 1 in June 1984
Peel Ahead of Everyone by... (PAE) Index: 18 months

When Mike Read infamously announced live on Radio 1 in January 1984 he was no longer going to play
'Relax' by Frankie Goes To Hollywood (already in the top 10), because of its sexual content, leading
to Radio 1's ban on the record – which promptly went to no. 1 – Peel scoffed. And played the record
again. Walters immediately invited the band in for a second session – their first had been a year before
– which previewed their forthcoming no. 1 of Christmas a year later, 'The Power Of Love'. But when the
band announced their follow up to 'Relax', in spring 1984, would be a song called 'Two Tribes' and the
media began to speculate they did not play on their records and it was all the work of producer Trevor
Horn and session musicians, Peel was able to point out that the band had actually played this song on
their debut Peel Session some 18 months earlier, six months before they had ever met Horn or been
signed to his label ZTT. He and Walters promptly repeated both that and the band's second session
the very week after 'Two Tribes' reached no. 1 that summer. The Peel Session original of 'Two Tribes'
sounds very much like the single, just without the sound effects and hype.
So there, Mike Read.

in Liverpool at that time, if you did get a Peel Session, it was regarded as an achievement; and once you'd got onto that level, you got a bit more attention from the press. You certainly walked round Liverpool as if you were next in line to the throne.'

All in all, 1983 was quite a year for Peel Sessions, after a rather uneventful 1982 – save for the Cocteau Twins, Trixie's Big Red Motorbike, the Farmer's Boys, Sophisticated Boom Boom and New Order's second. Before Walters' return in April, there had been a few quirky debuts under Trevor Dann, including the Three Mustaphas Three and Sophie and Peter Johnson. But by the summer, on top of The Farm and The Smiths, there were memorable debuts by Billy Bragg and Microdisney, both in August. Bragg performed his now celebrated anglicised version of 'Route 66', a hymn to Essex: 'A13 – Trunk Road To The Sea'. And October brought the first date by James, including 'Hymn From A Village'. Generalisations are dangerous, but all these acts were characterised by a witty, melancholic disaffection with the emerging cultural orthodoxy of 1980s Britain. Songs like The Smiths' 'Still Ill', Bragg's 'A New England', Microdisney's 'Sleepless' and the aforementioned 'Hymn From A Village', all first heard in Peel Sessions that summer, while not political in any real sense, conveyed a sense of what it then was to be alive, and yet neither stupid or a yuppie. The humour around at the time was added to by Peel Session classic oddities like Twa Toots' 'Don't Play "A Rainy Night in Georgia"' and Sudden Sway's 'Let's Evolve!'

Microdisney went on to be the Peel Session band of 1984, recording three in all; including the song with the best chorus of the year, attacking English nostalgia and complacency, 'Loftholdingswood' ('Aren't you glad you were born in England?') There were notable other dates by Working Week, Bronski Beat and Yeah Yeah Noh. The last of these provided the title Peel would adopt in October for a series of gigs he

A LISTENER WRITES

'Some time in about 83 or 84 I became a regular listener to John Peel on the World Service. At the time I was living and working as a volunteer in a very remote spot in the West of Nepal. Music kept me sane for the two years I was there and hearing John Peel was like listening to an old friend. Surrounded by the Himalayan foothills I was two days' walk from the nearest road. There was no electricity, of course: I had a complicated system for joining loads of Indian batteries together to squeeze the last bit of juice out of them to be able to listen to my cassettes and Peel on the radio. Anyway, one night after playing something (I think it was perhaps by The Fall, but I can't be too sure about that), he followed up by saying "that was The Fall – and by the way, the bass player lives just up the road from my mum. I expect that's really interesting for all those of you listening to this in the middle of the Himalayas". I felt as though it was a personal message to me. I was surely the only person listening to him for a couple of hundred miles in every direction. It kept me going for a couple of months.'

Peter Branney
Edinburgh

was invited to curate and record at the ICA: 'John Peel is Putting the Fun Back into Being Pretentious' – an experiment that unfortunately would not be repeated for 14 years. But the most astonishing debut that year was by the Jesus and Mary Chain in October. 'They were down to play their first London gig the next night, the Wednesday [24 October] at the White Lion in Islington, I think,' remembers Mark Radcliffe, then a junior staff session producer at Radio 1, 'and Alan McGhee and Slaughter Joe Foster came along to Maida Vale. They all wanted to put all this feedback on the tapes, and I kept saying, "No, you don't want to do that," and they kept saying, "Oh yes we do." So in the end we did put it on, and of course they were right.'

But, apart from the Jesus and Mary Chain, Australia's Go-Betweens (October) and Triffids (November), the dominant sound of sessions that year was non-electric: 1984 was the year of cowpunk. The first of these coarse, rough-sounding acoustic bands to complete a session and have it broadcast was the Boothill Foot Tappers, closely followed by Pogue Mahone, both in April. 'Half of Pogue Mahone turned up completely pissed,' remembers producer Mark Radcliffe, 'and the bass player, Cait O' Riordan, was completely out of it: I think the accordion player redid her parts after she'd gone. I can remember her sitting with her boots over the back of Ted De Bono's chair, which Ted wasn't too keen on when he was trying to do the mix. I found them quite amiable, despite all that.' One of their four numbers recorded, 'The Boys From The County Hell', had so much swearing on it even Peel couldn't broadcast it. Next came the Skiff Skats (May), and then the Men They Couldn't Hang, in July. That same month also introduced Terry And Gerry, whom the Audition Panel, had it still been operating, might well have described as 'a humorous contemporary skiffle duo'; whose demo tape was picked up by Peel simply for the chance reason that another

---

FIRST HEARD (ANEW) HERE...

'The Green Fields Of France' by The Men They Couldn't Hang

This version first heard here on John Peel, 12 July 1984
Reached no. 3 in Festive Fifty for 1984
Peel Ahead of Everyone by... (PAE) Index: 6 months

This first session by the Men They Couldn't Hang featured their rendition of Eric Bogle's anti-war folk standard 'The Green Fields Of France'. It quickly became a highly requested repeat and was later released as a single. Regular listener Hugh Brune remembers: 'Later that summer I was travelling through Belgium on a train listening to a tape I'd made of the band's first session. In one of those time-stopping moments, "Green Fields Of France" came on just as the train went past a field, a war grave, full of endless lines of white crosses. I felt so moved as to write John a postcard. I was astonished to receive a personal note back, which I treasure to this day. The song went on to be no. 3 in that year's Festive Fifty, just about the only time one of my votes made it on to the list.'

'Terry and Gerry' were the Pig's flatmates when Peel first met her. By the end of the year, the formally renamed Pogues had come back for a second attempt.

All the bands above continued to record for Peel through 1985, but other sounds were also emerging, most notably Big Flame (February), the Cookie Crew (May), That Petrol Emotion (June), The Housemartins (July), Freiwillige Selbstkontrolle, or FSK (August), and The Primevals (September). 'We'd recently won the Rap Championship for the Best Rap group of 1985 at the Wag Club, and were doing a series of shows at the big rap festival Rap Attack at the Shaw Theatre, where we think John Peel and John Walters first saw us,' say the Cookie Crew. 'We'd probably only done about four shows, and the session was our first time in any studio that had so much equipment. We didn't have a clue. What was an engineer? We took in instrumentals and other people's rap records, had a well-written and rehearsed rap, and sung over the instrumentals,' they remember. Debbie, 'Reme-Dee', listened to and recorded every session they did, even though she only had 'a crap cassette recorder: I will always remember John Peel saying he hoped that one day we'd be making records of our own.' The Cookie Crew first recorded on the hit 'Rok the House' in 1987, and signed to London Records in 1988.

All Michael Rooney of The Primevals can remember of his classic first Peel Session is being excited at meeting Dale Griffin, being a Mott the Hoople fan, and having seen and met them years before at the Maryland in Scott Street, Glasgow: 'I was even sick in their dressing room!' But he didn't get a chance to ask Dale if he remembered him, because 'Dale was either on the phone to his garage to get his car repaired, or our French manager was on the line, throughout the day, threatening to kill me over a sum of money.' Apart from the debut of Half Man Half Biscuit that November, late in 1985 and early in 1986 the most numerous first sessions came from the bands, including The Primevals, later unfortunately labelled as 'the shambling bands' by the music press, after a passing comment by Peel, or 'C86' after the *NME*'s cassette compilation. These could be said to include the Passmore Sisters (August 1985), Age of Chance (October), Bogshed (November), A Witness (January 1986), and Stump, The Mackenzies, the Wedding Present and Twang (February). Perhaps the most memorable of these debuts was that by Stump, with its hilarious portrayal of obese female American tourists, 'Buffalo'. 'Most enjoyable newcomers for some time, wethinks,' Dale wrote across the top of the sheet. Hard on their heels came We've Got A Fuzzbox And We're Gonna Use It (March), the Happy Mondays and Head of David (April), Pop Will Eat Itself (June) and The Primitives (October). None of these, however, acquired FSK's distinction of getting an unreleased session track into Peel's listeners' Festive Fifty that Christmas. The German band's ironic cover of Dave Dudley's 'I Wish I Could Sprechen Sie Deutsch' was voted to no. 33. Commenting on the poll in his *Observer* column at the beginning of January 1987, Peel described the rendition as: 'A highlight amongst tracks which, despite their individual merits, make up a rather characterless chart.' Festive Fifty historian Mark Whitby would later write of the annual poll displaying 'an increasing conservatism as the decade wore on', discernible as early as 1984, with bands like The Smiths, New Order and Cocteau Twins dominating that chart with many entries, and almost all the rest coming from indie bands. This contributed to a growing mid-eighties perception – if only partly true – that the show itself, like the tastes of its listeners, was in a bit of a rut. It might explain Radio 1's decision to take away Peel's Thursday show at the end of September 1984, reducing his airtime to six hours a week Monday–Wednesday, which would remain the most he would ever have for the remaining 20 years of the show.

■

THAT'S NOT QUITE how Peel remembered it, though. 'They said, this guy's so good, we're going to take away his Thursday programme.' In fact, it was another stage in the desire to get Peel out of the 10pm–midnight FM slot, dating back to 1977–1978, driven by management fears that daytime listeners who would tune out at night confronted by Peel's records would therefore be lost to the Radio 1 breakfast show when they switched back on in the morning, and possibly also informed by an equivalent prejudice in those days of high Thatcherism against those perceived to be Peel's listeners, described at one meeting by then controller Derek Chinnery as 'unemployed yobbos'. However, in a stroke of fortune for discerning listeners and Walters (if not Peel personally), the show created to replace his Thursday shift, *Into the Music* with Tommy Vance, an attempt to programme melodic progressive rock, did not succeed. It was axed after only 12 months. The slot was given back to Walters, and a different new, young presenter tried out, who management may have naively hoped (he did like Springsteen, after all) would one day prove a more malleable replacement for Peel: Andy Kershaw. Kershaw has written since both Walters' and Peel's deaths of how lucky he feels to have begun his radio career in the tip that was Egton 318, a tiny office occupied by two giants of radio who were outrageous fun to work with – even if there was nowhere to sit down amid the piles of records, unopened champagne bottles, joke-shop ears and noses, out-of-date daytime DJ posters and Health & Safety and Fire Risk memos, and 16 years of promotional gifts from the music business.

And within three months of Kershaw starting, Chinnery had retired and was replaced as controller by Johnny Beerling. Beerling was the champion of daytime entertainment, the inventor of the Radio 1 Roadshow, and one of those who had long wanted to move Peel out of the 10pm–midnight slot. Several retired BBC staff recall Beerling saying to them, in despair at his scheduling problems, that he wished he could get Peel off the station. In this climate, Peel's paranoia that he was about to get fired whenever he was offered a bank holiday off or was told his show was being cancelled on a particular night to make way for *The Brits* is more easily understood. Beerling today is under no illusion about how he was viewed: 'I know Peel and Walters never really trusted me, and once prayed to their imaginary deity, the Great God Snibri [the God who distributed record company freebies], to visit a curse upon my body when I made a decision they didn't like, and I fell getting off the train and broke my arm that very night ... but I think we had a fairly productive working relationship despite all that.'

He did not axe Peel, of course. Peel had six hours a week on air when he became controller, and still had six when he left in 1993. But on top of that he gave him new things to do. He took Peel and Janice Long to Japan for a week of shows and a Peel documentary on the World Popular Song Contest in October 1986, and the next month Radio 1 repeated producer Peter Everett's acclaimed series on British teenage life since the fifties, *You'll Never Be 16 Again*, which Peel had presented on Radio 4. Following this came several documentary specials, series and overseas trips for John and Sheila in the late 1980s, including Peel's jaunt for a couple of years to the *Eurovision Song Contest*. 'I always felt there was more to Peel than just playing the music,' Beerling says. He also supported producer Dave Price in founding the Radio 1 archive in the old Egton basement, created the post of Radio 1 archivist/selector for Phil Lawton, and was instrumental in the commissioning of my book *In Session Tonight*. His old friend Bernie Andrews thinks people sometimes misunderstand his former *Saturday Club* colleague. 'Johnny knows more about the importance of the sessions, live music and encouraging specialist presenters than he's ever been given credit for,' he says. Beerling also extended Peel's annual retainer to a two-yearly contract. In latter years, Sheila recalls that he and John developed a friendly relationship. 'He's a man you can at least talk to,' Peel told me more than once. Beerling, Lycett and Peel went for a drink in the George to remember Walters just a few weeks before John died.

Back in the mid-1980s, the Peel Show settled into a familiar routine. Most shows would feature two sessions. Walters' wallchart planners, managed by assistant Sue Foster – always referred to by Peel and Walters as 'our Brian' – made the Maida Vale recordings and transmissions tick along nicely. Trevor Dann had allowed Peel to write out his own running orders for the first time and, while Walters still took the scripts in hand and tweaked things, increasingly through the 1980s Peel was left to do most of the selection himself. Walters began to go home in the evenings and listen there, not staying with Peel in the studio. The Wednesday show was often pre-recorded so Peel could get home to the family a night earlier. Perhaps the show was becoming a bit too settled, a bit like the Festive Fifty. But if character and surprise, shock even, was what was lacking at the end of 1986, then a movement spearheaded by a band that had just recorded their first session would certainly make up for this want in 1987. On 9 December 1986, The Stupids arrived at Maida Vale. The hardcore holocaust had begun.

■

'**WE TURNED UP** at Maida Vale on our skateboards, and Tommy, the drummer, had a bad crash outside the doors,' remembers Ed Wenn, alias Ed Shred, then The Stupids' fourth non-recording member, but singer and bassist-to-be, along to the session for the ride. 'We thought of ourselves as young punk rebels, and were all ready to get annoyed with the engineers. We wanted loud guitars and felt sure proper

BBC engineers wouldn't understand. We even took the band engineer along to back us up in case.' Such was The Stupids' radicalism, they didn't have any equipment. The guitar and bass were simply slung over the skateboarders' shoulders. A drum kit was arranged to be delivered to Maida Vale by the guitarist. Unfortunately, the only one he could hire that day was a synth drum kit, not exactly appropriate for the thunderous sound of hardcore. A small hand-held guitar amp was taken along, although a Marshall 100-watt stack was also hired and delivered. 'And the bass was direct-injected straight into the desk,' says Ed. 'But Dale and Mike Robinson knew what they were doing and got some good sounds out of the kit; but the session, looking back, was OK, not brilliant,' says Ed. Listeners disagreed. Their response, as Peel wrote in his *Observer* column after its first broadcast on 12 January 1987, 'was generally expressed in terms more appropriate to the casualty ward than to music criticism. "It rips," suggested one writer. "The Stupids shred," enthused another. "They truly maim," volunteered a third.'

Peel had started playing The Stupids' first LP the previous autumn, after Ed sent him a copy. More importantly, shortly after the session broadcast, Ed, now singing for the band, invited Peel and Walters along to The Stupids' first gig at the Igloo Club, at the King's Head pub on Fulham High Street, on 16 February 1987. Peel's review in the following Sunday's *Observer* alerted everyone to British hardcore, which had been born of British bands watching how American punk had split into myriad forms of 'thrash, speedcore, speedmetal', and which involved 'playing hard, fast, and with commendable brevity and lack of attention to detail'. On that memorable night, Ed's own band Bad Dress Sense, and he and Tommy's collaboration with vocalist Bobby Justice, in the band Frankfurter, supported The Stupids. Walters recalled it being like the heady days of punk: 'The band would get off stage and half the audience seemed to get on.' Most of the '40 or so revellers … seemed to be known to members of the band,' Peel wrote. Walters offered Bad Dress Sense a session on the spot. They recorded it a week later, on Tuesday 24 February, two days after Peel's seminal review, and the same night as Peel repeated The Stupids' debut for the second time. On 16 April, Frankfurter did their first, so all Tommy and Ed's bands of that night at the Igloo had been in. 'On that Frankfurter one, I remember Fred Kay was the second engineer, and she suddenly exclaimed, "I've got it! I know what this music is all about!" and Dale and Mike Engles just watched as she took over the mix. It was a wonderful moment.' Ed finally played on a Peel Session as a full Stupid on the band's second, in May. Then there was a brief lull in the storm, before the Electro Hippies' staggering debut in July. Nine tracks were recorded, none of them over 1' 40", and the last, "Mega Armageddon Death", clocking-in at exactly one second long only. 'Starts and stops rather abruptly,' Dale added helpfully on the sheet. By now, Walters was regularly going to the handful of London pub gigs that supported hardcore, once again spotting bands. Heresy recorded their first at the end of that month. Then in September came Napalm Death.

CLASSIC SESSION

Napalm Death

Recorded: **13.9.87**
Studio: **Maida Vale 4**
Producer: **Dale Griffin**
Engineer: **Mike Engles and Elizabeth Lewis**
First Broadcast: **22.9.87**
Tracks: **The Kill / Prison Without Walls / Dead (0' 55"), Deceiver / Lucid Fairytale / In Extremis (1' 45"), Blind To The Truth / Negative Approach / Common Enemy (1' 05"), Obstinate Divide / Life / You Suffer (1' 55"). Total time: 5' 40"**
Line-up: **Michael Harris (drums, vocal), Shane Embury (bass), Bill Steer (guitar), Lee Dorrian (vocal)**

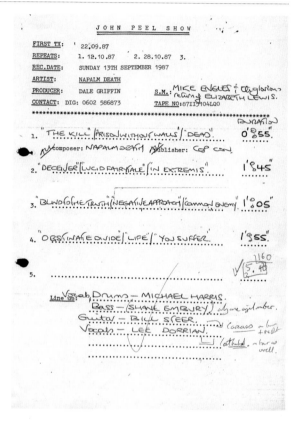

'Napam Death had been around since 1981, although in a totally different style. I joined in 1986, and the sound became faster, more aggressive, with metallic riffs: that's why I joined, to play relatively fast hardcore with metallic riffs. The band got a new singer, bassist and guitarist early in 1987 and the sound became even harder, faster, and the guitar sound even more dense. Our first LP was done then, came out that July, and Peel took a liking to the shorter tracks. He played "You Suffer", which was 0.75 of a second long, three times before we were invited to do the session.

'What happened at the session? We had to hire equipment – we had no amps, drums or cymbals – because we hadn't started touring then and had recorded on equipment available in studios. Anyway, we turned up. "How long are your songs?" Dale asked. "Pretty short, we'll do twelve numbers," we said. "Well, that's OK by us," they said, but I could see they weren't sure.

'We literally blasted our way through it. I really enjoyed it. I was so happy with the sound that day. It was just a blinding vicious sound coming straight back at you. What Dale and the engineers didn't know was that the twelve songs came to only 5' 40" in all, the shortest ever Peel Session.

'That first Napalm Death session had a huge impact. It was nearly perfect. It was like doing a great live recording, but more relaxed, a good experience. I think Peel enjoyed it too. He repeated it three times.'
Mick Harris

Extreme Noise Terror

Napalm Death's drummer and leader Mick Harris rapidly became a vital figure in the burgeoning hardcore scene after that Napalm Death debut. There was a third session by The Stupids (October), 'the first with the proper recording line-up,' says Ed Shred; Gore's astounding debut came early in November, featuring a 17-minute instrumental medley of four numbers; Mick was back at Maida Vale that same month, but now guesting on drums for Ipswich band Extreme Noise Terror, on their first Peel Session. 'It was a different style, a lot slower, with more of a punk than metallic influence, very enjoyable,' he remembers. 'There were eight numbers on that first ENT one too.' Mick would later play on Unseen Terror's Peel Session (March 1988), and several successive ENT and Napalm Death dates. After he left Napalm Death, his new band Scorn recorded a session in September 1992. But as Ed Shred points out, even as early as summer 1987, the relatively close-knit hardcore scene was fragmenting.

'Hardcore was proud of itself. At first it was very different, and nobody in Britain understood us,' says Ed. 'When we got on Peel, everyone was chuffed. Then everyone thought they could get one. What was a small cliquey thing changed after Peel started playing our records, and everyone started sending him their records. Before that the bands had been making records without a public in the UK. The original scene had changed and, by 1988, I felt we were just going through the motions really. So many bands had said, "Oh wow, we can do this" that I became a bit sceptical: lots of people had moved to the US.' Nevertheless, there were still people listening for whom there were still new hardcore bands to discover in 1988. Bolt Thrower (January), Intense Degree (February), Dr and the Crippens (May), Doom (June) and Ripcord (July) all debuted on Peel that year. Later years would bring the likes of Prong, Carcass and Deviated Instinct.

'We never really classed ourselves as a hardcore band,' says Karl Willetts, singer with Bolt Thrower, underlining Ed's point about the fragmenting scene. He joined the band just after their first Peel Session, when, on the strength of it, they were offered a record deal by Vinyl Solution. 'It was an exciting period, very different from how it is now. The scene was more integrated: Doom, Napalm Death, Extreme Noise Terror, us, we were all in the same boat.' Bolt Thrower's first session got them a deal, and their second, in November 1988, got them a better deal, with Earache, and, intriguingly, a deal with Games Workshop, the chain of role-playing games stores. 'We had a track called "Realm of Chaos", about this fantasy world of gaming,' says Karl. The company and band ended up sharing artwork over the band's second album, in an unusual bi-media marketing exercise.

The effect of all these radio sessions was to leave most listeners simply stunned. The speed, violence and brevity of the numbers made the shocking punk records of ten years before sound tame by comparison. And while hardcore, in whatever manifestation, did not cross over into mainstream success quite as punk and new wave did, the bands discovered a self-financing, separate market had grown up around them, particularly in the USA. Certainly no one else on British radio was touching this dangerous stuff, except, of course, Peel's colleague Steve Wright, who, when the Electro Hippies' session came out on record, started playing them, perhaps seeing them as a joke, in his Radio 1 afternoon show. It was a strange kind of testament to Peel Sessions' having had an exclusive, vice-like grip on this most vicious animal, born of the decaying remains of punk. Most of those hardcore sessions were done by Dale Griffin. But then you can't talk about Peel Sessions in the 1980s without mentioning him. He was, of course, doing plenty of other programmes' sessions as well. At one time in the mid-1980s, Dale would often do two Peels, a *Friday Rock Show*, an evening show recording or two, and an Andy Kershaw session, six or seven in all, every week. His name is on many, and many of them are classics. The stories about him are legion, some complimentary, some not. The Maida Vale SMs talk warmly of his professionalism and dedication. 'He would nearly always turn up early, and start setting up the mikes and rigging the studio, which is not really the producer's job at all,' says Mike Robinson. Several pop bands interviewed for this book looked back with astonishment at how Dale's opinions of the merits of some of their numbers, which they petulantly disregarded at the time, proved exactly right. His ear for a hit is not in question.

But there would be arguments, and what arguments they would be. To sum it all up, it could be argued that Dale saw his responsibility to the BBC as an important one, to deliver at least four well-recorded, exciting numbers to make a session, in just one day; and if that meant appearing a hard taskmaster or worse in order to get some of the more relaxed bands through it, then so be it. 'I changed my mind about Dale,' says Ed Shred. 'When I turned up for my third or fourth session, we hadn't even got to the studio when we bumped into Dale in the corridor. "Oh shit, not you lot again," he said. Not a happy day, really. But then he changed and became really friendly, after we'd done a few more. I think once you've gone through some sessions and got his respect he's fine. I'd be really happy now for him to produce any album for me.' Other musicians would probably disagree, finding a more relaxed, unpressured atmosphere more conducive to recording. But given the unusual time constraints on BBC sessions, who is to say definitively that the demanding approach might not, with some kinds of acts, be just as valid? It certainly helped Dale produce some of the most memorable Peel Sessions ever, like the Wedding Present's Ukrainian recordings.

CLASSIC SESSION

The Wedding Present's 'Ukrainian Sessions'

Recorded: (#1) 6.10.1987, (#2) 15.3.1988, (#3) 2.5.89
Studio: **Maida Vale 4 (#3 Wessex Studios)**
Producer: **Dale Griffin**
Engineers: **Mike Robinson and Fred Kay**
First Broadcast: (#1) 14.10.1987, (#2) 5.4.1988, (#3) 15.5.89
Tracks: (#1) Tiutiunnyk, Yichav Kozak za Dunai, Hude Dnipro Hude, Katrusya/Svitit Misyats; (#2) Minooli Dnee, Vasya Vasyl'ok, Zadumav Didochok, Verkhovyno; (#3) Cherez Richku Cherez Hai, Zavtra Ya Budu Pid Nebom Chuzhim, Sertsem I Dusheyev
Line-up: **Peter Solowka** (mandolin, accordion, tambourine and backing vocal), **Len Liggins** (vocal and violins, balalaika, sopilka (Ukrainian flute)), **Keith Gregory** (bass), **David Gedge** (guitar and backing vocal), **Simon Smith** (drums (#2 & #3)), **Roman Remeynes** (mandolin and backing vocals (#2 & #3)), **Shaun Charman** (drums (#1 only)), **Ron Rom** (backing vocals and handclaps (#1 only))

'On a previous Peel Session we'd recorded "Hopak", a tune I used to play on the guitar that I knew from my childhood, which we'd often play in the band in spare moments to warm up. After we'd done another session we were offered yet another, and felt we wanted to do something different. I suggested doing something radical, an entire session of Ukrainian folk songs, and managed to persuade the others. We practised four or five songs but the ethnic flavour wasn't coming through, so I drafted in a fiddle player friend of mine, Len Liggins, who had studied Slavonic Languages at university, and had always been crazy about everything East European; so he could do all the singing as well. After we'd done the first one we realised we'd done something rather good, although we weren't sure Peel would broadcast it. But when we heard it going out, we thought immediately, "We could do it better." Peel was startled and pleased and so we asked if we could do another. But I also got a phone call from this Ukrainian guy, that I knew of vaguely, a musician, saying, "What are you doing destroying this music?" He was quite severe, and said we could improve it. So we invited him to join us on the second one. He was a mandolin player and singer who called himself Roman Remeynes, because his real

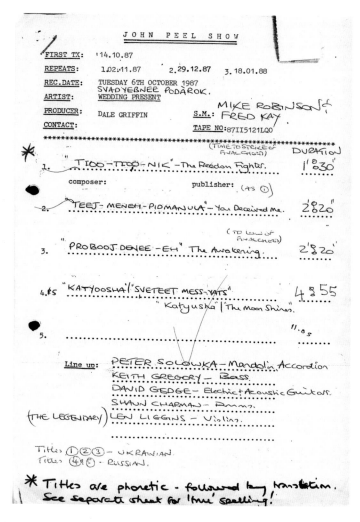

Ukrainian name is unpronounceable! So the second one, in March 1988, was much better: the intense bits more intense, the laid back bits more quiet. In front were me, Len and Roman doing the fiddly bits, backed by the solid backing of the band. After it had been broadcast, many Ukrainian people said to us they had never heard the final song, "Verkhovyno", played with such intensity. Dale and Mike worked really hard on the second session, and particularly on the mix of "Verkhovyno". Dale normally gets done by midnight, but they were still there mixing it at 2.45am. They put a lot of effort into it and it showed, it was really good.'

Peter Solowka

The first two 'Ukrainski Vistupi V Johna Peela' were released by RCA in April 1989 and reached no. 22 in the album chart, selling over 40,000 copies in the first few months of release. Peter, Len and Roman became 'The Ukrainians' permanently, releasing a debut album of their own songs in 1991, and doing two more Peel Sessions.

■

BUT IT HAS to be admitted that events like those Ukrainian recordings were unusual in featuring so many acoustic instruments. Increasing numbers of sessions in the late 1980s were based on drum machines, sequencers and sampling, with acts effectively remixing from their pre-programmed digital tracks. With the growth of house music, debuts like those by the Funky Ginger (August 1988), A Guy Called Gerald (November) and Where's The Beach (August 1989) became, along with the continuing hardcore bands, some of the most exciting sessions. A Guy Called Gerald's session was made doubly difficult by the fact that, as Dale pointed out in a note to Walters, it was booked in at the Hippodrome, which had no 'direct injection capability – it may be a good idea to keep the heavily machine-oriented stuff to MV4.'

Walters later asked Dale if the house, computer-based sessions were by definition more difficult. 'It's only more difficult if they actually haven't got their act together,' Dale replied; 'Unlike a live band, you can't suggest the drummer maybe changes this or changes that. It's really that they need to have done all their programming ahead of time, because it's not something that we can really advise on, because it's all locked up in a machine. It's really down to how together the particular artist is.' Dale was speaking from bitter experience. The session sheet files reveal that a number of machine-based bands (excluding those above), did indeed, as Dale's scribbled apologies for a session of only one or two short numbers explain, turn up at Maida Vale and only then start programming the drum machine.

But there is, above this, a professional preference among some BBC producers and engineers for live bands. Contrary to what you might expect, to be confronted with a deafening hardcore band is just the kind of challenge the SMs relish. It's something they can really get their teeth into, and work hard and fast to capture properly on tape. By contrast, for a trained broadcast sound engineer, a session which involves simply remixing digital tracks is less demanding of their particular skills. 'The only thing with machines is they play the same thing each time,' Dale told Walters. 'You never get a feel from a machine. I don't think even with the best will in the world you can build too much feeling into what's coming out of a machine output.' Many would disagree, pointing to the crucial, live human element of the mixing and treatment during performance, something which would later set apart from their rivals Peel favourites of the 1990s like Orbital, Dreadzone, Coldcut and Underworld. As the use of computers in music and on BBC Radio 1 sessions increased, Dale's view sounds retrospectively like a recipe for potential conflict. But then a certain amount of creative conflict need not necessarily be unproductive. A perfect case in point is what turned out to be one of the most extraordinary Peel Sessions ever,

CLASSIC SESSION

The Orb

Recorded: **3.12.89**
Studio: **Maida Vale 3**
Producer: **Dale Griffin**
Engineered and mixed by: **Jimmy Cauty**
First Broadcast: **19.12.89**
Tracks: **A Huge Ever Growing Pulsating Brain That Rules From The Centre Of The Ultraworld (Loving You)**
Line-up: **Jimmy Cauty (producer and mixing), Alex Paterson (DJ, samples)**

'We turned up early and, finding nobody about, started setting up the turntables and desk in the control room. Suddenly the producer appeared and bawled us out: "Get this equipment out of here!" He told us to set it up in the studio and come back at 2pm. We said we were going to generate a load of samples then mix it off the multi-track, which he didn't seem to get. We were so put off, we went round to a friend's house for an hour. But we were determined to defeat this producer, so we went back, and pulled all the sofas and lamp stands into the middle of Studio 3 and set up a little living-room set in this huge studio, like something out of Alice in Wonderland, and got the main lights switched off, to get a good atmosphere. I just started throwing all these samples at Jimmy: Waves, birdsong, jets, old Sci-Fi play excerpts, those "Aaaahs" off Grace Jones's "Slave To The Rhythm", and Minnie Ripperton's "Loving You", of course (we'd already started this thing of crediting all our samples, and virtually mixing the drums out of house music). And Jimmy did this great live mix really quick. I think we were out of the building by 7pm! I think it was the best mix we ever did of that. The head of Geffen Records was over here, and listening to it on Peel while driving and had to pull over, he was so knocked out. He tried to sign us for America, but we already had a deal. The whole thing couldn't have been planned: it was just a very vivid day, because we were finding it so entertaining to defeat this producer bloke.'

Alex Paterson

'It was almost as if they'd never had an electronic group in. Quite a lot of energy was spent at the beginning just explaining what we were going to do. Everybody was very tense. We knew, in these circumstances, we had to be really good. The other argument was when I said I was going to have to mix it myself, but I persuaded them in the end. There were just two sequences in it, the arpegiatting figure, and a 16s pulse, which I programmed on the spot, and looped everything onto 24 tracks, but there was no structure to it – you do it all in the mix, that's really important, cutting things on and off, trying to build it into an entity. It did get more relaxed later, more people came down, Alex had this living room set-up, a friend of his was videoing everything, and we started laying the sequence of samples and FX down. I just did a non-stop mix through all 20 minutes I'd laid down. It was good having the SSLs, because I could do a pass and it would memorise it on the computer. Even so I think I only did two or three passes. But because it was so long the desk crashed just before the end: the computer's memory ran out just as we'd done the final pass, so it couldn't memorise the last minute and we had to fade it. It was all so difficult that day, but I was always trying to make the thing flow, and I do remember being into it at the time.'

Jimmy Cauty

and which became the most requested for repeat for months, the first session by The Orb. 'For days after that session the phone would keep ringing in the office,' recalls Walters. 'I'd pick it up, and someone would say something like, "Ah, er, hello, er, John Peel played a very long record the other night and I was wondering if you could tell me where to get it, it's by a group called The Auburn Session."' They couldn't get it then; but fortunately The Orb-in-Session mix of 'Loving You' was released later on Strange Fruit Records, and subsequently on the triple-CD version of *Beyond The Ultraworld*.

It was not just the electronic acts which reinvigorated the show with greater musical variety in the late 1980s. There were sessions from rappers like MC Duke, Overlord X, MC Buzz B, Asher D and Daddy Freddy, the Ruthless Rap Assassins and MC 900 Foot Jesus & DJ Zero; world music acts like the Bhundu Boys, the Four Brothers, Dembo Konte & Kausu Kouyate, Zinica, Stella Chiweshe, Amayenge, Big Fayia and Shalawambe; bands from Eastern Europe such as Laibach, Zvuki Mu, and Marta Sebastyen; and Welsh-language groups like Anhrefn, Datblygu, Plant Bach Ofnus, Fflaps and Llwybr Llaethog. American bands started to appear as guests too in these years. The Pixies, Mudhoney, Sonic Youth and Nirvana all recorded Peel Sessions at Maida Vale before they crossed over to become stadium tour acts in the USA. But all this international activity was not easy. The Department of Employment would then only grant permits for live or media work for US bands if a balance of reciprocal bookings for British musicians could be demonstrated. Musicians from any other, non-EU countries would also have to wait for their work permit applications to be cleared by the ministry.

ONE-SESSION WONDER

The Would Be's

First broadcast: **19.3.90**
Recorded: **25.2.90**
Studio: **Maida Vale 3**
Producer: **Dale Griffin**
Engineer: **Mike Engles**
Tracks: **All This Rubbish Is True, Must It Be, Funny Ha Ha, My Radio Sounds Different In The Dark**
Line-up: **Mattie Finnegan (guitar), Eamonn Finnegan (bass), Paul Finnegan (guitar), Pascal Smith (drums), Aidan O'Reilly (trombone, sax), Julie McDonnell (vocal)**

This short-lived Dublin band formed by the Finnegan brothers in 1989, and managed by another brother, James, recorded and financed their debut single 'I'm Hardly Ever Wrong' on Danceline Records late that year, and Peel loved it and played it to death. Their debut (and only) session astonished Dale Griffin and Mike Engles with its charm, accomplishment and humour (the trombone is not often a lead instrument in rock): 'Paul Finnegan on guitar, only 14 years old!' Dale wrote admiringly to Peel on the sheet. Its stand-out track, 'My Radio Sounds Different In The Dark', for obvious reasons, became an immediate favourite with Peel and listeners, and very much remains so on the web as a swapped MP3 file. But after another EP or two, the band split in 1991. They re-formed for live gigs in Dublin in 2000 with new singer Karen Cunningham.

A LISTENER WRITES...

'I was a lapsed Peel listener and then in January 1987 I had to go into hospital so took with me a cassette radio and some blank tapes. I ended up recording Peel's shows at night and playing them back during the day. This, more than anything, made me really appreciate Peel and restore my passion in groundbreaking music, as after many listens, tracks and genres I originally hated grew on me and sounded fantastic. I repeated this when I had to go into hospital again a few months later and ended up with an amazing collection. After many repeated plays I just couldn't bear to tape over the tapes. Several years later, I happened to mention this to my young nephew Matt Savage and he, unbeknown to me, had taped practically every Peel Show from 1990 to 1993. For various reasons, he was about to start reusing the cassettes. Oh no! But I couldn't afford to buy all of these tapes off him, so we came to a compromise and he agreed to give me a bundle of tapes (usually about ten) as birthday and Christmas presents. He's still doing it. There are about 500 of them now. My love for new music remains and that's why I'm involved with Dandelion Radio.' Phil Edwards, Ruislip

Effectively the whole procedure made trying to bring a non-EU band in for a session more trouble than it was worth. 'But Andy Kershaw rode coach and horses through all that with his show,' Peel remembered with a wicked twinkle in his eye. 'We just kept booking the international acts until people stopped arguing,' remembers Andy. And from October 1988 the shows emanating from Walters' domain brought their new-found internationalism to a wider, younger audience. With the launch of Radio 1 FM, 6am–2am every day on its own new FM transmitters and frequencies, there was no need to argue for keeping their 10pm–midnight slot any more, and Peel and Kershaw were simply shifted forward 90 minutes in the schedule to 8.30–10.30pm, Monday–Thursday.

■

IT FELT LIKE the end of an era. With Nicky Campbell playing 'adult contemporary rock music' from 10pm, in a show which its instigator Johnny Beerling still feels is the best work Nicky's ever done, older listeners had to rearrange their listening habits to move with Peel, something they would have to get used to again and again in the 1990s. But it also undeniably brought Peel a higher profile, not just with a larger number of younger listeners – 'It got rather good figures I seem to recall,' Walters said – but in wider media perceptions. Peel was visible and (fleetingly) fashionable once more. The attention and coverage his 50th birthday received the following August was completely unexpected, and being invited around that time to be the castaway on Radio 4's *Desert Island Discs*, broadcast in January 1990, thrilled Peel and seemed to indicate esteem. By then he was back on four nights a week, 8.30–10pm only, with Kershaw having been moved to Sunday evenings. His

90-minute shows inevitably became even more high velocity, with minimal links – they averaged (yes, averaged) 11 seconds only – and the rave, jungle, rap and African tracks became more prominent, with just one session band per show. So it seemed less an Indian summer, more a new beginning. But this was a false impression. The show was about to undergo a more final ending, although it did not seem so at the time. In 1990, John Walters told the BBC he wished to take early retirement in the summer of 1991.

■

'**FOR AGES, PEOPLE** from the BBC personnel department had been writing me memos asking, "Is there anything you'd like to be in the BBC that you haven't yet been?"' Walters told me later that year, 'and I would answer, yes: 55.' It's a good story, but he was actually only 52 when he retired at the end of June 1991. Helen Walters is certain her John 'did not want to leave the Peel Show, that wasn't it at all. He just felt it was the right thing to do at his time of life. The prospect of another career was opening up for him in freelance broadcast work, and he knew he couldn't do that if he was still in the BBC.' Walters was already an award-winning broadcaster in his own right, with *Walters' Weekly* having won Best New Programme in the Broadcast Press Guild Awards of 1981, and he had contributed regular columns to *ZigZag* and *Honey*. He was a regular on *Loose Ends* on Radio 4 throughout the 1980s, and went on in the 1990s to present his own *Largely Walters* and *Idle Thoughts* on the network, as well as *Here and Now* on BBC One, and a series on cinemas for Sky TV. He died in his sleep unexpectedly at the age of 62 on 30 July 2001.

He famously described his role over 22 years as producer of the show as being Peel's 'earthly representative' or of their relationship as being that between a man and a dog, each believing the other to be the dog. What those self-mocking metaphors have in common is the sense that Walters was the one who stood up for his master when it mattered. Peel may have been idealistic and other-worldly, but Walters knew what he stood for was worth fighting for in dreary management meetings. In retirement, on Peel's *This Is Your Life* appearance, on BBC Two's *Peel Night*, he would often repeat his argument that Peel 'was the most important person in British popular music of the past half century' and his 'programme was the most important thing Radio 1 had ever done'. It's a testament to his achievement in helping keep it on air and digging up new and wildly varied acts – Ivor Cutler, Joan Armatrading, Bob Marley, the punks, The Smiths, the cowpunks, the hardcore, the electronica

ONE-SESSION WONDER

Bongwater

First broadcast: **13.4.91**
Recorded: **19.3.91**
Studio: **Maida Vale 5**
Producer & Engineer: **Mike Robinson**
Tracks: **The Power Of Pussy, You Don't Love Me Yet, White Rental Car Blues, Kisses Sweeter Than Wine.**
Line-up: **Mark Kramer (bass, vocal), Ann Magnusson (vocal), Randy Hudson (guitar), Steven Tunney aka Dogbowl (guitar), David Licht (drums)**

People still rave about this session by the wild American band – founded by Mark Kramer of Shimmy Disc Records and singer Ann Magnusson – which mixed cover versions and vocal harmonies with overladen guitars, noise and effects.

'Ann and Mark were in the vocal booth, with Mark playing his Hofner bass and singing with Ann. We started recording and tracked the first four tunes. We only did a second take on two of them, but all the first takes were used. On "You Don't Love Me Yet" and "Kisses Sweeter Than Wine", I was given another take to record other guitar parts. Then we started doing a cover of Jimi Hendrix's "Castles Made Of Sand". This was the best take we had done. There was section we added on the fly, and reharmonized another section, and we all knew we had played something special. We finished the take, and talked about it while waiting for playback. But the tape machine did not record it. The record light was on, but somehow the record head did not engage. Both the engineer and producer apologised, but it changed the vibe of the session. Mark and Ann decided to leave, saying they did not want to be present for the mixing. They told David, Steven and myself that they were going to see a play and they would meet us at the hotel later. The three of us opted to stay and at the offer of the engineer and producer we worked with them on the mixes. They were both great to work with and the mixing went really well. Both Ann and Mark were pleased when they heard them in the end. In retrospect, recording a Hendrix cover could be considered by some to be sacrilege, so maybe we were graciously spared by the recording malfunction. Over the years I've got many compliments on this date. It was a privilege to do a Peel Session, and I'm grateful to all involved, especially Ann and Mark. This band really played well together, primarily due to the fact that Ann and Mark are both great musicians, but more importantly great performers. Combined with excellent recording skills, this really came across on the mixes that day.'

Randy Hudson

– that, whereas in his Radio 1 days management colleagues would look at him as if he were mad when he spoke this way, now no one contradicted him. The truth of those statements was universally accepted, and that Walters played a major part in making them so. There would be times in the 1990s when the show would suffer from the absence of his negotiating powers.

Sheila has written in *Margrave of the Marshes* of how the Peels and Walters, who once holidayed and ate Saturday night movie dinners together, drifted apart in latter years, partly due to the rigours of Peel's working week and the inevitable

Walters, Beerling and Peel.

demands of the Ravenscroft family. Sheila wrote how, less than half an hour before he died, Peel was saying how much he missed Walters, missed him ringing him up about what was happening on telly, and how he regretted they had not spent more time together when he was alive. Helen Walters remembers the night of the last Peel Show for which her John was responsible. They were at home that last Sunday in June, setting the table for supper outside ready to listen. Walters, in many ways a hard man, the very opposite of Peel, to the complete shock of Helen, suddenly, for just a moment, choked, and wept. 'I had never seen him so emotional. It meant so much to him.' He had made Peel his life's work, and now it was over.

■

CHAPTER 07

HE WAS TIRED. He was driving to London and back four days a week. That was 16 hours a week commuting. It wasn't the pace of those new beat-packed, four 90-minute mid-evening shows that was wearing him out at the age of 50, but simply getting there to do them. And he felt he was missing out on the children during the week. In 1990, Peel asked Radio 1 if his show times could be changed. They offered him 11pm–2am Saturday and Sunday, which he accepted and, a few months before Walters retired, Peel moved to the weekends for the first time since *Top Gear* came off Saturday afternoons in autumn 1971. Walters told me later he thought Peel was daft when he said he wanted to move but somehow keep his weekends free ('where else could they have put him?'), and Sheila more or less felt the same: 'I'd got used to having the house to myself and the children during the week for 15 years, now I'd have him around too; and I might have wanted to, you know, go out with my husband at the weekends,' she said, not unaffectionately. But the change did dramatically reduce his journeying time to one trip in and back, and his health improved. He was happy enough, especially that he had lost no airtime in the switch. For his audience it was a huge change. While long-standing, grown-up regular listeners with families now knew they probably would not miss the shows and taping at home was easy to remember, at one fell stroke Peel had also removed himself from the potentially large, very young audience midweek mid-evening he had been enjoying for two years. He had voluntarily taken the graveyard shift, when radio audiences are at their very lowest, after midnight at weekends.

In terms of the show as a production, on the surface nothing much seemed to change after Walters' retirement. Mike Hawkes took over responsibility for Peel and Kershaw, but as a senior producer also in charge of Pete Tong and the Man Ezeke, Mike already had a job, and felt he didn't really have that much to do anyway, 'except make sure with [assistant] Pinky the session bookings were moving along'. Peel did his own running orders virtually unchecked from now on. This semi-detachment of producer and presenter was not helped by the layout on the third floor of Egton House. Hawkes' office 310 was beyond the notoriously gossipy open-plan assistants' office 306, where Pinky worked, while Peel (and Kershaw, and me, while I worked on *In Session Tonight* through 1992) were way along at the other end of the corridor in Walters' old office, now cleared out and usable. We could all work a whole day without ever seeing each other.

There was nothing wrong with the shows themselves. The marathon three-hour shifts each had two sessions again, and the startling variety of music continued. Acts that would become firm Peel favourites like PJ Harvey, Th' Faith Healers, Stereolab and Gorky's Zygotic Mynci all did first sessions in the early 1990s. American bands like Pavement, Smashing Pumpkins, Mercury Rev and Hole were recorded. With Peel (briefly) coming on after Kershaw, the idea of joint sessions began, with African acts like Diblo Dibala and Papa Wemba (complete with dancers!) recording thrilling long performances at Maida Vale giving each DJ a show's worth each.

And the electronica continued, most notably with Orbital's landmark first session in September 1993. Paul Hartnoll fell in love with Maida Vale immediately: 'All those labyrinthine corridors, and an orchestra and a big band playing in huge studios, I'd never seen anything like it. Then I saw the door to the BBC Radiophonic Workshop, oh my God! It was all just so steeped in history, it was, well, almost romantic. The atmosphere of the place was crowned by getting to the control room where a well-spoken Victorian explorer type [Nick Gomm] greeted us from behind his rather smart racing bike leaning on the mixing desk. He seemed a bit mystified about what we proposed to do, but we just set up our keyboards, computers and stuff right there in the control room and gave him four leads. That's it, we said, that's all you need. We'd decided to do two, long live jamming remixes off our programming. We just did one before lunch, and one after, straight off. Going for a walk later I almost expected John to materialise round a corner. I'd always dreamt of doing a Peel Session, like doing *Top of the Pops*, or Glastonbury, but this was by far the most important to me. I felt, well, I've made it now, I've arrived.'

Euros Childs of Gorky's remembers the band planning for their first session at the end of 1993 'like a tactical military manoeuvre. We rehearsed more than ever and

A LISTENER WRITES...

'One night John Peel held a raffle. A band called Buttsteak had sent him 50 copies of their great new seven-inch to give away, so I sent my name and address on a postcard to be drawn from a bucket. You could hear the shuffling of entries as the names were drawn on air. "Aidan Moffat, Falkirk," he said, live on Radio 1, in his usual casual manner as though it meant nothing at all. But John Peel had just said my name! The single didn't arrive for months and I had given up hope. It's lost in the post, I thought, or maybe the BBC just forgot – surely Peel himself wouldn't have forgotten? Of course, he hadn't – it turned up eventually with a handwritten Post-It note that read "Apologies for ludicrous delay, John (Peel)." I was so impressed that he would take the time to write this note – and presumably 49 more – by hand, and I thought the way he'd surrounded his surname in brackets was indescribably cool. The note now sits in a frame on my record shelf, which is exactly where it should be.'

Aidan Moffat
(Later recorded three Peel Sessions with Arab Strap)

taped everything leading up to the momentous occasion, the rehearsals as well us talking about the session. We also prepared ourselves for the worst, having heard stories from other bands involving producers locking the whole band out of the control room during mixing reducing the singer to tears, and of a band turning up so late they had to record the whole thing in two hours. So when the big day came we arrived four hours early (just in case) and were on our best schoolboy behaviour in front of producer Mike Engles and engineer Nick Fountain. As it happens we need not have worried, they were friendly and encouraging (as was every Maida Vale producer and engineer we were given through the years), and after a bad bout of nerves we eventually calmed down and started to enjoy ourselves.'

Under Mike Hawkes the show did tentatively begin a few small innovations. In 1991, Peel did one show from Glastonbury but with no live music. The following year the team did the first of their European trips as part of public service campaigns on work and travel in the EU for young people, with shows – and sessions – live from Berlin and Budapest (FSK and Attwenger), and Sweden (Bear Quartet, Blithe) the year after. In 1993, they took the show to the Reading Festival, again with no live music, though they did record two live sets – by The Orb and Sharon Shannon – at Glastonbury. But the most surprising event arose as a result of a bet with management, when Peel stood in for Jakki Brambles on the lunchtime show for one week in April that year. His old producer Chris Lycett, now head of Radio 1 music department, produced the shows in which Peel, as part of the bet, showed he could follow the format (playlist, news, weather, travel, etc) but filled all other available slots with his own choice of records. It was a wonderful week, which offended some listeners but surprised others. It's most celebrated, however, for when, having spun

With Clint Boon from the Inspiral Carpets and others at the Reading Festival. Alison Howe

the playlisted Chris Isaak single 'Can't Do A Thing (To Stop Me)' on the first show, Peel said, 'That's just where you're wrong pal, I can take the CD off and throw it as far as I possibly can.' The point is he had played the record first: he had done his job.

The experiment was never repeated. The station didn't want him that much. And his weekend shifts started getting shunted about, first, forward to Friday and Saturday nights, and then, in autumn 1993, the Saturday show was moved forward to the afternoon, 4.30–7pm, losing half an hour in the process. Peel always made

FIRST HEARD HERE...

'Linger' by The Cranberries
First heard here on John Peel, February 1992
Reached no. 14 in February 1994 (re-release, first released 1993)
Peel Ahead of Everyone by... (PAE) Index: at least a year

In early 1992, The Cranberries were struggling to get attention despite being signed to Island Records. On their debut and only Peel Session they recorded an early version of 'Linger', which would not be released until a year later, but unsuccessfully. It was only during a successful US tour later in 1993 that the video was picked up by MTV and the single re-released, becoming ubiquitous on FM radio in early 1994. Hardly a Peel band or act, but the song was heard here over two years before it finally reached the Top 20.

the best of schedule changes and, to the despair of his manager and agent Clive and Shurley Selwood, would not let them push Radio 1 too hard in contract negotiations. 'His fear was they'd call his bluff, he'd lose his show and wouldn't be able to get as much airtime anywhere else to play new bands and sessions, which was all he really cared about,' say the Selwoods today. But that move to Saturday afternoon can be seen as the beginning of an unsettled time for the show, which would reach a crisis in the tumultuous, traumatic year for Peel that was 1996. Two of those who would be key players in that year's events arrived on the scene in 1993. Matthew Bannister was appointed the new controller of Radio 1 that summer. And, more importantly, the show got a new production assistant that spring. She remembers vividly being astonished when, having told Peel soon after she started about a band she had just seen who she thought were really quite good and thought he'd like, Peel said immediately, 'We'd better get them in for a session, then.' 'I didn't really think that could happen, but that showed me the show wasn't just John, I thought this is great, it really opened up my confidence.' The band she'd seen was Tindersticks. The assistant would become Peel's producer herself within two years, help John successfully begin remaking the show into the lively critical success it became in its latter years, and who is now the producer of *Later with Jools Holland* and *Glastonbury* on BBC television: Alison Howe.

■

SHE HAD JOINED the BBC straight from school and college in the secretarial intake of 1988, complete with shorthand and touch-typing, two skills she would recommend to anyone contemplating a career in the media. After a spell in the copyright department she got her wish to work at Radio 1, first with Chris Lycett and then Paul Robinson, executive producer – which meant she typed up strips of paper for the musical items in the Sunday Top 40 show, possibly the last person in the BBC to learn how to document shows in that pre-computer age. But that job brought her in to the infamous Egton 306, where Pinky, Peel's departing assistant, said, 'You should work with John, you know'. And when Pinky went, she did. 'But John didn't like me at first, that was obvious. He and Kershaw used to have a go at me and I learned to give as good as I got.'

Peel and Kershaw welcomed the other new recruit, Matthew Bannister, much more warmly. They were very enthusiastic about his promise to change Radio 1 and refocus it as a very distinctive youth station, and thus justify it remaining a key part of the BBC as the Corporation headed towards Charter Renewal – the brief coming from

CLASSIC SESSION

Dreadzone

Recorded: **21.8.94**

Studio: **Maida Vale 3**

Producer: **Mike Engles**

Engineer: **Steve Bridges**

First Broadcast: **24.9.94**

Tracks: **Me Bong, Maximum, Cause & FX**

Line-up: **Greg Roberts (computer, drums),**
Tim Bran (cmp, keyboard), Leo Williams (bass),
Dan Donovan (keyboard)

The second session by the dub reggae and samples band formed by Roberts and Bran, who became firm favourites with Peel and producer Alison Howe, especially after they saw them live at Glastonbury in 1994. This session was recorded in the middle of recording their second album, 'Second Light' (1995), which remained one of Peel's top records of the decade. It was the first to feature Roberts' former colleague from the Big Audio Dynamite rhythm section, Leo Williams, and keyboard player Dan Donovan, as well as Roberts himself playing live drums. While all the tracks are strong, it was the seven-minute epic 'Maximum', never recorded elsewhere by the band, that thrilled Peel and his listeners alike, reaching no. 9 in the next year's Festive Fifty when it was released as an extra track on a CD single.

Greg Roberts: '"Maximum" was a one-take tune that captured the live energy and spirit that is hard to match from other records and is balanced finely between programmed technology and live spontaneity. Everything seemed to gel on that take as the tune builds from its trippy synth and intro speech of a US soldier on LSD, through into the simplest of basslines locked down with the jungle drums as the song gains layers of energy with dubbed fx merging with full on 303 acid lines that overlap and swell. This live favourite always produced a sweat on stage.'

Tim Bran: 'The clear picture that comes to mind of this session was setting up all our gear in the round in the huge live room at Maida Vale, then being separated by clear screens to keep the sounds from recording into each other's microphones. We still had the visual contact which was vital for a good jammed / live feel. We played through the song "Maximum" once and recorded it, and I remember at the end of the dynamic, emotional, hectic, dubbed-out tune, looking at each other and me saying, "Well, that's that one done then!" Everyone agreed. It's moments like that which will stick with me forever. The whole session seemed to flow in a magical way and was probably the happiest I have been with a Dreadzone "live" recorded performance. Thanks John. You were inspired and inspirational.'

The entire session was later released on 'The Radio One Sessions' (SFRSCD100) in 2001.

the Director-General, John Birt, who Bannister had worked for previously. To Peel and Kershaw that sounded like more new music, more live music, and less daytime nonsense. But like almost everyone else they did not quite anticipate the effect this bottom-to-top restructuring would have on their own shows, despite the new controller's glowing words about them. That would come later. Bannister's trials and tribulations in sorting out the daytime DJs and splitting commissioning from production have been well documented elsewhere. What has not been so well appreciated is one of the first things he did late in 1993 was encourage then Head of Radio 1 Department Chris Lycett to write a brief for a new department that would focus on developing and investing in even more live gigs, sessions and festivals, bringing together disparate individuals and production teams. When he'd written it, Lycett told Bannister he liked the idea so much he'd like to run it himself, please, which suited everyone. And it's this key department, Live Music & Events, with its key producers and engineers like Sam Cunningham and Andy Rogers, that went on to organise and produce the amazing variety of live sessions, outside broadcasts and festivals which make Radio 1 different to this day – including whatever of those the Peel Show wanted.

After Bannister had broken up 306 in 1994, and after he was joined by his old sidekick from BBC GLR, Trevor Dann, as the new Head of Production in January 1995, next they had a clear out of older specialist producers, and several of the old guard – like Mike Hawkes – opted to retire that spring. Which meant new blood was required, and Alison Howe was one of those 'boarded' for a new producer's job early that year, and got it. 'But there was no guarantee I'd get the Peel Show.' She did, though. And by the time she left it three years later, despite the assaults it was to suffer in the Bannister & Dann revolution, it had changed irrevocably for the better.

■ **SOON AFTER SHE** took over, she remembers a conversation with Wendy Pilmer, then the new executive producer in charge of specialist music. 'How could we develop and bring new things into John's show that he'd like and be happy with, we wondered? I thought immediately it should be more live music, it would get him out and about again, he'd like that, and it would give him more things, more stories to talk about.' So that's what they did. In fact, she had already started, in the final months of Mike Hawkes' oversight. In 1993, Radio 1 had launched its annual *Sound City* festival, and under the embryonic new Live Music & Events department had dramatically expanded its coverage of other festivals. While Peel had gone to some of those events, the show had not yet immersed itself in them. But in 1994 his show on the Glastonbury Saturday took in three live sets already recorded – Madder Rose, Dreadzone, Cheapsuitaroonies – and another five sets were broadcast over the next three weekends. More sets were recorded at Reading in August (Flaming Lips, Hole). The show came live (if with no live music) from Glasgow's Ten Day Weekend that October. 'We loved those trips to Glasgow, it became an annual thing for three or four years,' remembers Alison, 'everyone being so funny and lovely to John, especially that manager of the Chinese restaurant, saying, "Good evening, Mr Peel, let me tell you about the last album I bought."' In another innovation, which seems incredibly simple but which Peel had not featured since the days of *Night Ride*, Irish accordion star Sharon Shannon came in and did a live acoustic set with her band in the on-air studio during Peel's show on 22 October.

Once she was in charge, Alison accelerated this trend. At first, she simply helped John make more of these new events in the emerging Radio 1 calendar. Live sets were taken for the first time that year from *Sound City* in Bristol (Bluetones, Dreadzone, Pulp) the Phoenix Festival (The Fall, the Wedding Present), the Glasgow Ten Day Weekend, and Camden Live in London. By the end of 1995 no fewer than 35 live performances from British festivals had been featured. And the Glasgow connection started producing sessions too, with BBC Radio Scotland's *Beat Patrol* show, produced by Stewart Cruickshank, passing on their own recordings – like the Delgados' first, in spring 1995 – and even recording ones especially for Peel (like Uresei Yatsura, Pink Kross and Adventures in Stereo), either at BBC Glasgow or the commercial Cava Studios. This was the first time Peel Sessions by British acts had been done outside Maida Vale since the early 1980s.

But the MV4 and MV3 sessions still made up the bulk of the show's featured material and guests, week in, week out. This was, of course, the Britpop era, and while Peel did not like Oasis, and was not that keen on Blur either at first, there were other bands they enthusiastically championed, like Alison's favourites Elastica, Sleeper, Gene, Supergrass and most of all Pulp, who did their first session in 12 years in 1993, and late in 1994 recorded their then new song 'Common People' in session for Peel several months before it became a hit. 'Remember this was the time Steve Lamacq and Jo Whiley had taken over the *Evening*

FIRST HEARD HERE...

'Common People' by Pulp
First heard here on John Peel, October 1994
Reached no. 2 in June 1995
Peel Ahead of Everyone by... (PAE) Index: 7 months

The first recording of the band's biggest hit, for their third Peel Session, featuring slightly different lyrics at certain points and middle section, but absolutely recognisable. In the time of Britpop, when a Peel listener was asked who's best, Oasis or Blur, the answer was of course Pulp.

CLASSIC SESSION

Dick Dale

Recorded: **30.3.95**
Studio: **Maida Vale 4**
Producer: **Ted de Bono**
Engineers: **Ted de Bono & Lisa Softley**
First Broadcast: **8.4.95**
Tracks: **Bo, Crankin', The Wedge, Nightrider, 3rd Stone, Miserlou**
Line-up: **Dick Dale (guitar), Ron Eglit (bass), Bryan Brown (drums)**

Peel had been playing for years the instrumental surf guitar classics of Dick Dale from the early 1960s, when Dale achieved new-found fame as a result of Quentin Tarantino using his hit Miserlou for the opening titles to his 1994 film 'Pulp Fiction'. Dale came to Britain in early 1995, and Peel was determined to get him to do a session.

Dick Dale: 'After one show, when I was signing autographs, there was this gentleman leaning on the wall, just looking. He came over and said, "Excuse me, my name is John Peel." Right after he said that he explained, "I normally only spend 15 minutes to see a group or artist to see what they are all about and then I leave. You grabbed my soul from deep inside and took a lock on it and would not let it go and that is why I am still here." I said, "Thank you very much." He said, "What you do, what I witnessed on the stage was brilliant. Very difficult to explain to someone else. I would love for you to be my guest at the BBC and play on my show." I said, "Thank you for the invitation." The people who organized my tour made arrangements with John's people at the BBC and shortly after our first meeting I was recording for him at Maida Vale. They treated me like I was Elvis. John was there at the first session and introduced me to everyone and stayed and watched me perform.'

Later, after they met again at a festival in Holland, Peel and Dale began to phone each other up and have long conversations. Dale did four more sessions and a live show at the Royal Festival Hall for Meltdown.

Dale: 'We never spoke about music, what he was doing on the radio, or my music. We spoke about spiritual things, like two people talking about spiritual matters amongst themselves. I used to tease people and say I was only going to England because John Peel wanted me there. He made it clear to me, "Don't you ever come over here and not stop in for a session." It would be like bypassing my father's house after a long absence. I can hear him now saying, "What you do up there is like Picasso," and I used to say, "Don't you mean Salvador Dali?" He would shoot out a wry smile.'

SESSION DETAILS

BBC RADIO 1   ROMEO

DETAILS
Artist: DICK DALE
Programme: JOHN PEEL
Rec. Date: 30/03/1995
Rep. Date: 23/12/1995
Producer: TED DE BONO
Engineer: LISA SOFTLEY

Insert No: 94ID3594LQ0
TX Date: 08/04/1995
Program:
Location: MV4
Archive No:

LINE UP

DICK DALE : GTR
RON EGLIT : BASS
BRYAN BROWN : DRUMS

1. BO   Dur: 3.34 End
Comp(s): Dale
Pub(s): Surfbeat Music
Comment:

2. CRANKIN'   Dur: 2.24 End
Comp(s): Dale
Pub(s): Surfbeat Music
Comment:

3. THE WEDGE   Dur: 2.39 End
Comp(s): Dale
Pub(s): Surfbeat
Comment:

4. NIGHTRIDER   Dur: 1.57 End
Comp(s): Dale
Pub(s): Surfbeat Music
Comment: ** ENDS, WAIT FOR FINAL CHORD **

5. 3RD STONE   Dur: 5.55 End
Comp(s): Hendrix
Pub(s):
Comment: *** PLAY LATER ON, SLOW ONE ***

6. MISERLOU   Dur: 4.15 End
Comp(s): Dale
Pub(s): Surfbeat Music
Comment:

Name: joha   - 1 -   Date: 08/07/2007

Session and were covering this stuff too, so it was good that John could show he was still on top of these things,' says Alison. But he had the field to himself in competition with his new rival Lammo in electronica, drum 'n' bass and DJ sets, all things which Alison was also into, so 1995 brought first sessions by DJ Hell, Cristian Vogel, Laurent Garnier, Black Dog and Autechre. Alison also encouraged Peel to revive the idea of Christmas specials for the show, the two of them amazingly persuading both The Fall and Elastica to record Christmas sessions in 1994. And at the end of 1995, Jarvis from Pulp came round to Peel Acres over the holidays to be interviewed to mark their wonderful year.

Yet there were ominous signs too. The Saturday show had been cut by another 30 minutes in November 1994 and was now just two hours. Through 1995, Bannister's regime was aggressively hiring new dance music DJs and creating new R 'n' B slots around him at the weekend. Peel began to feel threatened. He'd been championing this stuff at the station as part of his shows for years. What was going on? In the meantime, he was surprised to find himself invited after almost ten years to present *Top of the Pops* once more, but found out the real reason on Wednesday 13 December 1995 when, during his closing link, he felt someone behind him irritatingly grabbing his arm. It was Michael Aspel with the big red book announcing, 'Tonight, John Peel, This Is Your Life.' The recording at TV centre was a night of bizarre and wonderful surprises for John, including afterwards in the green room a moving reunion with Bernie Andrews (they had become estranged in the 1970s) – 'It is *this* man,' John said to his children and anyone who could hear, 'you have to thank for the childhood you had secure in our house'. But by the time the show was broadcast late in January 1996 he was not feeling so secure himself. It would be the worst and yet possibly the greatest year for his show, and his life.

■

LATE IN JANUARY Radio 1 announced internally its new schedule for the second quarter which would come into effect in mid-April. To fit in new drum 'n' bass and reggae dancehall shows, Peel's shift on Friday night would be moved instead to 8–10pm Sunday evening. With his Saturday show by then already reduced to two hours, 5–7pm, Peel would now be on air for just four hours a week, the least regular airtime he had had since the three-day week at the BBC in 1975. He wrote a long, aggrieved letter to Matthew Bannister, now reproduced in full in *Margrave*. Even here though, amid his sense of injustice given his own championing of dance records and his public support for Bannister ('I think John was so hurt because he always liked and rated Matthew,' says Sheila), Peel stepped back from complaining about the location of his new show, agreeing Sunday evening was perhaps a better slot for him, once again trying to make the best of things. But he would have had every right to be even angrier. One of the most important things about radio is familiarity, knowing your favourite voices and shows will come on at the same time, so you can make an 'appointment to listen'. Yet Peel had been shunted around the weekend schedules four times in four years, and would now be on at two different, equally family unfriendly times: Saturday teatime and Sunday mid-evening. It's amazing he held on to any listeners at all in the 1990s, although he did. Whatever the strategic aims of Radio 1 at the time, you have to wonder how they could have made such a provocative decision. Did no one at the top realise how important his airtime was to him? Or was there perhaps a Machiavellian side to the plan, and Peel's paranoia justified?

Alison Howe believes not. 'I think the important thing for Radio 1 was that John was simply there, and simply by being there he did so much for them. They knew that all right. But they thought it wasn't so important how long he was on or when. So they just forgot how important that was to John, moved him around a bit too much, and he snapped.' Radio 1's reaction would seem to bear her out. Almost immediately after receiving Peel's letter, Bannister sought to make amends and promised to try and put things right later in the year, although, as Peel's letter suggests, he'd said he might try and get more airtime back for him the year before. He now said publicly that as long as he was controller there would always be a place for Peel on Radio 1 – a statement Peel took pleasure in mocking, saying he'd said that about Johnnie Walker too, who had then been axed.

But in the meantime Alison was getting Peel to try some new things for the show, kicking off with interviews, after the success of the informal Pulp visit to Peel Acres. Early in 1996 they visited DJ Dave Clarke's studio and had a long chat, broadcast on 2 February. Alison remembers Peel being reluctant, claiming – with some justification – that he couldn't do interviews, but she felt it was worth persisting. After all, late in 1995 he had completed the first short run on Radio 4 of *Offspring*, the mid-evening show about family life that led eventually to *Home Truths* more than two years later. Even more was happening for Peel beyond his show. In March he was on Radio 3's *Private Passions*, in which composer Michael Berkeley invites his guest to play and discuss the classical music that most moves them. And the very next week he did the first of three fun-filled weeks that year sitting in on Mark Radcliffe's Radio 1 show, in his old 10pm slot, live from Manchester. It wasn't just the sheer pleasure for older listeners of hearing him again at that time, nor even Lard's blustering that Peel was a candid-camera imposter sent by Mark to wind him up, that make these

Jarvis Cocker and Russell Senior at Peel Acres. Alison Howe

shows so important in retrospect. Three nights a week there was a band in session live 'in the basement', otherwise known as BBC Manchester Studio 3. Number One Cup, Tripping Daisy, Calvin Party, Super Furry Animals, Bennet – and much later in the year Half Man Half Biscuit, PJ Harvey and Flaming Stars – didn't think they were turning up to do a live Peel Session, but that's effectively what they did. Peel's delight at having the bands right there close at hand to react to was obvious. And when John Hegley did his poems and songs live in the on-air studio, Peel conducted a perfectly competent, relaxed interview, notwithstanding a few clumsy moments. He could do such things, if he was comfortable with the people, and in the place he was.

It was a lesson Alison Howe was already learning. On the very first Sunday evening show on 21 April, she introduced the second of that year's four innovations, by having Gorky's Zygotic Mynci, who were that day pre-recording a normal Peel Session in Maida Vale, play one song – Pen Gwag Glas – into the show totally live down the line. This had always been theoretically possible. Maida Vale has always been connected to the networks for broadcast play-out live to air. It's just that setting up and mixing a band for a live balanced sound is a very different process from doing a carefully recorded, multi-tracked, then sensitively remixed session – which

With Gene at the Reading Festival. Alison Howe

in that respect is far more like making a record than doing a show. Doing both at the same time on one day is both doubling the work for band and engineers, and risking technical mishap twice over. But another thing Alison was discovering was the tremendous loyalty Peel and his show brought out in the engineers. If it was for John, they'd make it work somehow. And it did. Just like when he sat in for Radcliffe, Peel loved the band being present, albeit three miles away across London. Things were looking up for the show, despite everything. At the start of June, John left for his annual trip to the TT Races on the Isle of Man with Andy Kershaw, knowing he was coming back to an exciting summer of even more festival trips, with maybe at last some good news about his airtime to come.

Everyone knows that's not quite what he came back to. The terrifying yet in the end restorative story of Sheila's near-fatal brain haemorrhage that spring has been fully told by Sheila herself elsewhere. But its deep effect on John, needing to check on her constantly thereafter, and his even greater desire to be at home whenever he could, was noticed by all those he worked with. 'If he didn't want to be away from Sheila,' Alison remembers thinking, 'how could the show maybe start to do something about that?' Meanwhile, building on the success of the one live number from Gorky's in April,

153

CLASSIC SESSION

PJ Harvey

Recorded: **5.9.96**
Studio: **Peel Acres,**
Nr Stowmarket, Suffolk
Producer: **Alison Howe**
Engineer: **Nick Fountain**
First Broadcast: **21.9.96**
Tracks: **Taut, Snake, Losing Ground, That Was My Veil**
Line-up: **PJ Harvey (guitar, vocal), John Parish (guitar, keyboard)**

The first-ever session recorded at Peel Acres. Peel and Harvey were plainly shy and nervous of each other, each admiring the other's work enormously, and the interview sections of the show with her and Parish were halting at times. But Anja Grabert's photographs of the day are intimate, touching and telling of the close relationship between artist and her champion. The interior intensity of the performances was arresting too. With just two guitars and two amps set up in the hall and John's studio, the sound is astonishingly dense and ferocious. Harvey chose three of the tracks for her 'Peel Sessions 1991–2004' compilation, a testament to their success. Her handwritten note for the CD sleeve says all that needs to be said of what Peel meant, not just to her, but to thousands of other musicians.

P J Harvey. Des Willie/Redferns

the show went a step further, a third new thing, and featured an entire session from The Bluetones live down the line from Maida Vale on Sunday 4 August. 'You wouldn't ask a new band to do that, it had to be someone who'd been in before and was also a bit better known,' says Alison; 'we were also beginning to feel doing a session live from time to time might be a way of catching up on the bookings. With only weekend shows, two a week, sometimes John and I felt the bookings were losing their impact by not being broadcast until several weeks later.' And at the same time, she came up with the solution as to how to bring the show closer to John's life, the fourth experiment of the year. Why not invite a favourite band round to Peel Acres, not just for a recorded interview, but also to play some music? They asked PJ Harvey, and she said yes. That day she and guitarist John Parrish spent at John and Sheila's home on Thursday 5 September produced a classic session. And just a week after the edited and pre-recorded programme went out on the 21st, Peel's Saturday show got an hour back in the new autumn schedule, now starting at 4pm.

So when Billy Bragg came into the on-air studios at Radio 1's new home of Yalding House for Peel's Christmas show on Sunday 22 December that year – the station had moved out of Egton House in October – to play some songs live, there were more reasons than usual for Peel to be in a festive mood. But the best news of all had just broken. Some time in the New Year, the management couldn't say when, they were all moving back into the week, saying goodbye to the weekends, taking all the show's new features with them. For his encore, Billy chose 'Deck The Walls With Bows Of Holly'. 'Tis the season to be jolly,' he sang, 'tra la-la-la-la, la-la, la-la!'

■

'**WELCOME TO YOUR** new slot!' said Jonathan Moore of Coldcut. 'Yeees!' joined in Matt Black. 'Yes, I'm very pleased to be back, I must say, I feel as though I've been pulled off the bench and given a run out with the first team,' said Peel down the line. To celebrate the show's rushed-forward move back into midweek, with an 8.30pm start time, Alison had hastily arranged for Coldcut to do a complete live mix set from Maida Vale on Tuesday 18 February 1997. It was stupendous. Ten days later, it was Carl Cox's turn. And then the show was off to Glasgow once more the very next week.

If the pace was hectic, Alison was now planning something more homely, if not exactly peaceful. When Blur's eponymous fifth album had come out that February, John had found he liked it and started playing tracks, especially the later hit single 'Song 2'. Might they consider doing a session now, he wondered, even though they

Blur visit Peel Acres 1997, with Alison Howe, Peel and Steve Lamacq. Alison Howe

were big stars? He did not know, as Alison did, that Damon would jump at the chance. 'I've got a better idea,' said Alison. 'Why don't we invite them to come and play at the house, and make it a special one-off show?' Peel loved the idea. 'And Damon thought all his Christmasses had come at once,' Alison remembers, 'he couldn't believe he was not only going to be on the show, but visit the house.' It would require a major logistical operation, though. For the discreet PJ Harvey visit, Alison and engineer Nick Fountain had just taken along a portable collection of mikes, leads, and a recorder. But that wouldn't do for a full band line-up. So Sam Cunningham from Live Music & Events booked in a mobile studio truck which would park in the drive, assigned ace engineer Miti Adhikari and, at the house, it was decided the band would play in a specially erected marquee in the garden, on 22 April. Radio 1 were thrilled too, and scheduled the planned, edited show to go out as a two-hour Bank Holiday special on Monday 5 May – a far cry from the days when the station would do anything to get Peel off the air at holiday times. Everyone gained from this absurdly ambitious event. The publicity Peel and Alison won in the music mags could not have been bought. More importantly, coming on top of the PJ Harvey visit, it showed that doing the show from Peel Acres, allowing John to be with Sheila, and let listeners in on his home life, was not absolutely impossible. Peel had a basic studio set up there for recording his shows

CLASSIC SESSION

The Delgados

Recorded: **1.7.97**
Studio: **Maida Vale 4**
Producer: **Mike Engles**
Engineered by: **Colin Marshall**
First Broadcast: **16.7.97**
Tracks: **Everything Goes Round The Water, The Arcane Model, Mauron Chanson, Pull The Wires From The Wall**
Line-up: **Emma Pollock** (guitar, vocal), **Alun Woodward** (guitar, vocal), **Stewart Henderson** (bass), **Paul Savage** (drums); and guests **Camille Mason, Alan Barr, Jennifer Christie, Emily Macpherson** (strings)

The Delgados' memorable, experimental third session, their first with their string section, which achieved astonishing impact. With the flute and strings being used as a kind of wavering wall of sound in the mix, it was not always possible to know where each sound was coming from. Peel was full of admiration on the first broadcast, and it remained one of his favourites.

'While our second session, our first in Maida Vale, was our most enjoyable, as the engineers really got into what we were doing, we knew this one was one of our most creative, even though it was a very difficult day. We were on schedule, it wasn't yet 6pm, having done three numbers, but Mike [Engles] wanted to get off early. So when we told him the final number was a different set-up, with acoustic guitar, he said we could only have one run through. Now, we'd rehearsed "Pull The Wires From Wall", but never recorded it. There was nothing for it but to just go for it. The whole thing was done live in one take, Emma's vocal included.'

Paul Savage

This original session version of 'Pull The Wires From Wall' reached no. 27 in that year's Festive Fifty, and the next year reached no. 1, in the commercially released version from the band's album 'Peloton'.

SESSION DETAILS

BBC RADIO 1   ROMEO

DETAILS
 Artist: DELGADOS
 Programme: JOHN PEEL   Insert No:
 Rec. Date: 01/07/1997   TX Date: 16/07/1997
 Rep. Date: 20/11/1997   Program:
 Producer: MIKE ENGLES   Location: MV4
 Engineer: COLIN MARSHALL   Archive No:

LINE UP
 STEWART HENDERSON : BASS
 EMMA POLLOCK : GTR/VCS
 PAUL SAVAGE : DRUMS
 ALUN WOODWARD : GTR/VCS
 CAMILLE MASON : FLUTE
 ALAN BARR : CELLO
 JENNIFER CHRISTIE : VIOLIN
 EMILY MACPHERSON : VIOLIN

      1. EVERYTHING GOES ROUND THE WATER   Dur: 4.10 End
 Comp(s): Delgados
 Pub(s): Island Music
 Comment:

      2. THE ARCANE MODEL   Dur: 4.35 End
 Comp(s): Delgados
 Pub(s): Island Music
 Comment:

      3. PULL THE WIRES FROM THE WALL   Dur: 4.00 End
 Comp(s): Delgados
 Pub(s): Island Music
 Comment:

      4. MAURON CHANSON   Dur: 3.25 End
 Comp(s): Delgados
 Pub(s): Island Music
 Comment:

 Name: joha   - 1 -   Date: 08/07/2007

for overseas stations like Radio Eins in Berlin and Radio Mafia in Helsinki, and he had secretly, with Mike Hawkes' tacit approval, been on occasion pre-recording some of his Radio 1 shows there since the early 1990s, when pressed. But it wasn't up to recording bands, and he couldn't broadcast from it. Doing the whole show there, live, would need some thought and considerable technical investment. You couldn't justify the expense of sending the mobile to deepest Suffolk once a week just for a regular Peel Show. Yet the high-profile success of the Blur visit sowed the seeds of an idea that would return.

Around the same time as the Blur session, the show and Radio 1 tried something else. Peel and Lamacq co-hosted joint four-and-a-half-hour shows during London Music Week in April, full of live gigs, and this was chosen as the model for future *Sound City* weeks, to be moved to the autumn later that year. Before then, the live session down the line from Maida Vale had become a monthly if not even more frequent regular event. Pavement, Echo and the Bunnymen (reformed), Stereolab and Eat Static had all guested in this way before October. The Future Sound Of London did two sessions live via high-quality ISDN phone line from their studio ('John and I agreed they could easily have just been playing a CD – although I don't think they were, and it wouldn't have mattered anyway!' jokes Alison). There was also a surprise live show and party from the ICA to mark John's 30 years on the

ONE-SESSION WONDER

Propellerheads

First broadcast: **23.11.96**
Recorded: **20.10.96**
Studio: **Maida Vale 4**
Producer & Engineer: **Mike Engles**
Tracks: **Take California, Dive, Props Got Skills, Bring Us Together**
Line-up: **Alex Gifford (turntables, organ), Will White (turntables, drums, human beatbox)**

An excellent, early one-off electronic dance session from this 'big beat' act, with 'Take California' being the stand-out track which blew listeners' heads off, or at least had them turning up the volume ever higher as it built. Years later it was the soundtrack to a famous iPod advert. Pity they never came back for another.

station on Wednesday 1 October, with the Delgados and Dreadzone playing live, and a presentation of many gifts including a framed letter of congratulation from one Tony Blair MP, then the country's new and first Labour Prime Minister in over 18 years. Three weeks later, Peel introduced no fewer than 20 live sets from *Sound City* Oxford on his and Lamacq's shared all-evening shift that week. Despite the plan to make things easier for Peel, it had been one hell of a year. To give John and Sheila a bit of a break, Jarvis and Pulp hosted the shows for a week in November, and Lamacq did a week in December. Then, suddenly, Alison Howe won a six-month attachment to work in BBC television, which she had always wanted to try, with the *Later with Jools Holland* show. She would leave late in March 1998.

'I've thought about this a lot since John died, and one of the things I'm sure of is, it was always John's show. It's just different people were the keeper for a time. I feel quite proud I suppose: in my time I brought a few things in that were new.' Alison is being modest. It must have taken some persistence to persuade John to try these experiments. He'd been doing fundamentally the same kind of production for years, a box of records and a session or two in a studio at Radio 1 on his own. And this was at a time when he felt under threat, with the programme being squeezed in the schedule. Theirs was not a relationship that got off to a good start. Alison was young still and unsure of herself, while John could sulk for Britain. But there was a turning point after she became producer. Peel decided as far as he could he'd try and bring her on, and Alison responded with idea after idea after idea. On the script of the final show she produced for him, on 19 March 1998, he wrote, 'Thanks for everything, love, John'. 'As you can imagine, that's now one of my most treasured possessions,' she says. His reinvigorated show was in her debt, and he knew it.

■

THEY KEPT IN touch. And they always had Glastonbury. By the turn of the millennium the BBC had secured TV rights to the festival and Alison Howe produced the epic, demanding four-day-long coverage. Peel's on-camera links with Jo Whiley and others were naturally an obvious thing for his old producer to ask of him and they became a popular feature, as John would casually rubbish the supposed groovy band coming up next, instead demanding more Lonnie Donnegan. Sheila was never there, though. By long family tradition, the Glastonbury weekend was her one quiet weekend at home of the year. But she remembers John talking with deep admiration of Alison in those last years. 'He said he would find himself watching her at Glastonbury, directing her team, calmly and nicely asking all these dozens of young staff who kept running up to her, to go and check this, please, go and ask so and so to make sure of that please, and so on, he said. "And you know," he would say, "it's wonderful to think in some very small way I'm responsible for all that.'''

■

ONE-SESSION WONDER
The Lance Gambit Trio

First broadcast: **27.8.97**
Recorded: **20.8.97**
Studio: **Own Studio**
Tracks: **D'You Know What I Mean?, Don't Go Away, Stay Young**
Line-up: **Lance Gambit (piano), Tommy Monk, Vera Stalk**

The charts had already enjoyed the Mike Flowers Pops' cover of 'Wonderwall', but the Peel Show went one step classier in the 1990s lounge music revival with this one-off session of Oasis cover versions by the Lance Gambit Trio, most famous amongst loungites as the providers of the 'gallery music' theme used on BBC TV's 'Vision On' show in the 1960s – 'Leftbank 2', composed by Wayne Hill. True to Peel Sesssion tradition, they didn't do that one here, of course.

At Glastonbury. PA Photos

CHAPTER 08

'**BUT WE ONLY** ever do one,' said Peel grumpily over the talkback. 'All you've got to do is drop one track,' replied Anita Kamath, his new producer. She saw Peel look down at the studio desk, sulkily. Oh dear, she thought, I've pushed it a bit too far. And things were going so well. She'd been producing the show for two weeks now. That night, Tuesday 7 April 1998, Yummy Fur of Glasgow were already recorded in session, and Six By Seven had just done one number live down the line from Maida Vale. It was entitled 'Something Wild', which described exactly how it sounded. Peel had loved it. While he was playing the next track in the show from CD, Anita was on the line to session producer Mike Robinson across London in the MV4 control room, telling him how pleased John was. Band leader, guitarist and singer Chris Olley just happened to be in the control room and overheard the glowing conversation. 'I shouted out that if he thought we were so good, then he should let us back on air to play another one!' 'Mike said to me, I think they're really up for it, you know,' Anita remembers. She said OK, we'll do it. And only then had she tried to sell the idea to John, who was clearly not that keen. The track ended, the red light went on, Peel lifted his head and said on air: 'Well, that last number live from Six By Seven was so fantastic, we're going to go straight back over there for another one.' Phew, what a pro, what a relief, thought Anita. 'All I remember later was hearing him moan that he had to change the whole schedule of his show because of us, typical Peel,' says Olley. But at the end of that stupendous, sizzling show, Peel had sounded ecstatic on air, and rightly so. It also tells you everything you need to know about his working relationship with his new producer who had replaced Alison Howe. Over the next three and a half years, Anita would cajole, tease and mumsy Peel through another whole raft of experiments with the show, almost all of them eventual triumphs.

She had joined Radio 1 as one of six new broadcast assistants appointed at the end of 1995, having previously had experience at both GLR and Jazz FM. She started out with Chris Lycett in Live Music & Events, working with Lycett's new producers Sam Cunningham and Andy Rogers on *In Concert*, her job being to interview fans at the gigs or catch up with them at BBC studio recordings. But in summer 1996 Lycett had some gaps in the schedule and told Anita he had always wanted a documentary series on the Peel Sessions: would she like to do it herself? She visited Peel at home to pitch the idea, 'and he said "no" for an entire day'. Eventually, however, she and his old mate Lycett twisted his arm, and thus was born *John Peel's Classic Sessions*, a thematically structured and humourous trawl through his own show's session archives. The first series that summer got rave reviews from the Radio 1 management, Matthew Bannister and Andy Parfitt asked for more, and a second batch went out over that Christmas and New Year. Anita had been a Peel listener herself since her big sister had introduced her to it when she was barely ten years old, so when she later found out she was being considered to 'stand in' for Alison for the original six months she was expected to be away (things went so well, she never came back), she was thrilled. The fact that she heard Peel was pleased when she got it made it even better. Like Alison, she wanted to develop the live music in the show, but wanted to take it further. As a listener herself, and having interviewed many bands at Maida Vale, she knew that many of them would still be disappointed when they turned up to do a session to find Peel would not be there himself. Wouldn't it be great, she thought, if somehow he could be there, if the whole show could sometimes come from Maida Vale? And the very week she started, an opportunity to do just that landed in her lap.

In early 1999, for reasons that will return in our story soon, BBC Resources was wanting to promote Maida Vale more to outside bands and companies, and planned

A LISTENER WRITES...

'I had become a regular correspondent of the Peel Show during the time I was at Cambridge studying for my PhD. One night in 2000 a friend and I went to a Monkey Steals the Drum gig in a small pub in Cambridge, and bumped into the man himself, who was there with Sheila. He insisted on buying us impoverished students drinks all night, claiming he was the one being grossly overpaid by the government. At the end of the evening he gave us his phone number and said we should go and visit Peel Acres for tea one day. A few months later we plucked up the courage and went. We had an excellent lunch followed by an afternoon looking around at the jaw-dropping amount of music in his collection. He showed such a genuine interest in what we were studying and our personal histories, that it's no wonder he was such a favourite of so many people. It was such a lovely experience which perfectly demonstrates how inclusive and kind he was to everyone who had ever listened to the show.'

Dr Kerry Knight

an Open Day. They called the Peel Show and spoke to Anita. Would Peel maybe consider, if they asked very nicely, doing a live session from there that day? Thinking on her feet, Anita told them if they paid for and provided a desk and the engineers for free, she'd get him there. She booked 60 Foot Dolls, a Welsh trio he liked a lot. And then with two weeks to go, she told John. He grumbled and said it wouldn't work. During the show itself on 21 April he made constant jokes about the temporary DJ desk constructed for him in the vocal booth, and the visiting dignatories peering through the glass at him. But it was a success. The very next week he said to Anita, 'When can we do another of those?' The one problem was, the next time, she'd have to find the budget herself. That's why, having proved it possible, there were not many more of these in 1998. Dealings with BBC Resources would play a part over the next two years and eventually a solution was found. But on 23 June 1998, Anita was able to repeat the experiment with Melys plus guests the London Welsh Male Voice Choir because, with Peel's own-curated Meltdown season of gigs at London's South Bank imminent, the show would have tons of live material over the next three months and she could afford to bring forward a later booking. Most memorably that night, Andy Rogers persuaded the choir to do 'You'll Never Walk Alone' as a surprise for John – perhaps remembering that period in the early 1980s when all Peel Session sheets requested bands to 'record verse and chorus of "You'll Never Walk Alone" for archives' and a surprising number complied – and conducted them himself up on the MV4 balcony. 'During the song, John was sat at the desk in the booth, motionless, silently crying with his head in his hands,' remembers Paul of Melys, 'it was very moving indeed. As soon as it ended he said, "I hope the choir won't mind my dedicating that to the families of the Victims of Hillsborough campaign, still seeking justice" and slammed another song on. It was a moment that we'll never forget. A moment of amazing professionalism.'

Another early scoop for Anita was getting the world-famous Jeff Mills to do a live DJ set. She knew from a friend of hers involved in a planned exhibition of Mills' photography in London that Mills knew of and admired Peel enormously, but Peel was convinced she couldn't pull this one off. 'I don't think he believed it would happen until Jeff Mills walked into the basement studio at Yalding with his three boxes of records and entourage, looking amazingly groomed, but being lovely about everything,' remembers Anita. 'We had this rather embarrassing impromptu desk set up for him because he needed three turntables. Peel was very shy and wouldn't dare go and speak to him, he was so in awe of him. Meanwhile Jeff Mills was feeling the same. Eventually John went through and expressed surprise at his three boxes of records. "We've only given you 30 minutes, you know," he said. At the end of his set,

ONE SESSION WONDER

Grandmaster Gareth

First broadcast: **17.9.03**
Recorded: **1–15.8.03**
Studio: **Own Studio**
Tracks: **Monster Melody: Entering The Monster Melody / Meet The Cartoon Monkey / War Is Not Healthy For Children / The Spinach Armada / Less Indie More Hindi / Pogo Time / The Sound Of Yourself Listening / Duelling Multi Instrumentalists / Dr Dre Has A Midlife Crisis / The Noises Made By Stupid People / A Nasty Piece Of Work / It's A Small World**
Line-up: **Grandmaster Gareth (sampling, keyboards) & guest friends**

'In 2003 I released an album called "An Introduction To Minute Melodies" on Awkward Records. I've only ever done minute melodies for my own amusement. 200 copies were pressed and of course one was sent to John Peel. A few weeks later, he played one. I was so chuffed. It was the first time I'd ever been played on Radio 1. The next night he played another, and again the following night. This continued for a few weeks. He played 17 different tracks in total including one on his World Service programme. The best was when before one he said I was "The New God"! A ridiculous thing to say but still makes me smile. Then one day I got an email from Louise Kattenhorn asking if I would be up for doing a session. I obviously jumped at the chance and decided that instead of doing minute melodies, I'd do a Monster Melody. And take up as much airtime as I could in one go! I couldn't record it at Maida Vale because I needed more than a day to write and record it. So over two hot weeks in August 2003, I recorded 17 minutes of madness in my bedroom including 24 different people making stupid noises to a click track for three minutes, free jazz pop, epic Dr Dre nonsense, the perils of being a badly drawn cartoon monkey and ending with a rousing rendition of the Disney song "It's A Small World" with plenty of bomb explosions thrown in. I managed to just meet the deadline and sent it off on a cheap CDR. A load of friends came round to listen to it when it was finally aired. I got nervous even though I knew what it was going to sound like. My nerves were increased when it took a minute to actually get it to play. It skipped and Peel had to start it again. I was very proud. My minute "Dr Dre Buys A Pint Of Milk" made it into the Festive Fifty that year. My second album, "The Party Sounds of Grandmaster Gareth", was completed shortly before John died. I was actually meant to be sending it to him when he got back off holiday.'

which involved dancing, spinning records, the whole show, Jeff looks over through the glass and says, "I used all my records, Mr Peel." Just a wonderful moment.' It was indeed the start of a wonderful relationship, with Mills happily returning for three more exclusive live DJ sets on the show over the following years. Other live DJ sets in 1998 featured Dave Angel, James Ruskin & The Drop, Si Begg, and a whole night live from Maida Vale featuring techno DJs from the Tresor label, in celebration of clocking up its first 100 releases, which got written up in the dance magazines and put Peel in *DJ* magazine's list of top DJs.

Conventional pre-recording sessions continued, producing debut sessions that year by the likes of Solex, Appliance and Hefner. Darren Hayman of Hefner remembers naively phoning up Maida Vale before his first session 'to ask whether they had a piano, and they told me they had four grand pianos and three uprights. I was quite surprised and asked what else they had, and amongst a whole list of stuff they mentioned they had nine celestes. Nine celestes? In what possible kind of recording situation would anybody require nine celestes?' But that famous and entertaining debut went out on a show notable for quite another reason. The show of Tuesday 13 October was the first show to go out back at Peel's old time, after 10pm, thanks to another new boy, or rather not-so-new boy, at Radio 1 that autumn: Andy Parfitt, who had just become the new controller of Radio 1.

■

'WHEN I CAME in I thought one thing that was important was that Radio 1 needed John Peel back at 10pm,' Parfitt remembers. 'In my listening memories and those of others it loomed large, a heritage thing, that's where he should be for listeners to find him, he needed to go back there: this is where you should be, I told John.' To Peel it was a relief after the years of scheduling turmoil in the mid-1990s. And Parfitt could genuinely claim to have some personal perspective on the show. He'd started out at the BBC in the early 1980s as a junior tape operator and second engineer at Maida Vale, assisting on many Peel Sessions of those years produced and engineered by Dale Griffin and Mike Robinson or Martin Colley. He was so junior his name did not appear on the session sheets. Later he ran British Forces Broadcasting (BFBS)'s station on the Falklands after the war in 1982, then worked in BBC Education and for the old Radio 5, before becoming Johnny Beerling's assistant. 'I was about to leave when I met Matthew Bannister who explained he was about to take over and change things, which sounded interesting, so I stuck around.' He had become managing editor, then effectively deputised for Bannister once he became Director of Radio in addition to the Radio 1 job, before giving it up in 1998.

Although Parfitt had been closely involved in two previous but very different regimes, he quickly changed a few things when he became controller. 'What I had to do was piece Radio 1 back together after the producer-choice years.' Under John Birt, BBC Director-General 1992–2000, the BBC had rigidly split operations into Broadcast (controllers, schedulers, commissioning, promotion) and Production (producers, presenters, assistants). 'But Radio 1 is a very small station in the great scheme of things, no more than 100–120 people, so that arrangement produced a lot of tensions,' says Parfitt. Producers on adjacent desks in open-plan Yalding House were often bidding against each other for slots, and sometimes being asked to contribute to decisions on each other's ideas, not exactly a recipe for a happy, creative working environment. Post-Birt, Parfitt saw his key job being to restore a sense of team spirit and purpose, 'and actually Peel was crucial to that, because he was an inspiration, a role model for younger presenters and producers of what Radio 1 at its best was all about. For someone like Huw Stephens to know they're working alongside John in the same office, the same department, for the same station, really means something.'

He remembers going out to visit Peel at Peel Acres at the start to explain some of this and what he hoped John would do. Peel remembered Andy's involvement in making the sessions, and gave him the tour of the sheds and barns containing his vast record collection. Parfitt says from that day they had a good working relationship and recalls only one crossing of swords. 'He'd been slagging off the marketing department on air, saying they all had red-rimmed glasses and pony tails. They didn't like his taking the piss out of them and neither did I and I told him to stop: they're your colleagues too, I said.' More positively, there was one technical innovation for Peel's show which did require a bit of investment from Radio 1, and it was only after Parfitt took over that the BBC did its bit in connecting Peel Acres to the Radio 1 broadcast studio network.

■

PEEL HAD TO fix his own studio first. Before a show could come from the home the desk had to be refitted and proper digital recorders installed. What the BBC brought was the ISDN high-quality digital phone line, and the connecting rack system and controllers. Early in 1999 the team were ready to start some try-outs. Chris Lycett, in one of his last favours for his old friend before he left the BBC, agreed to monitor the London studio end of the first tests, so Peel had a reassuring voice at the other end of the line during the show. Anita remembers that having told Peel that they didn't want a 'clean feed' – a version of the line that would cause problems if they needed to talkback with London – the moment the connection went live, Peel kept repeating like an automaton to the London switchroom, whatever he was asked, 'I don't want clean feed, I don't want clean feed...' Eventually they got everything to work on the night of Thursday 25 March, when Billy Bragg popped round to the house for a chat and to play some favourite records. Then, on 15 April, came the first live show from Peel Acres to feature a live music session with Tim and Charlotte from Ash playing an acoustic set (notwithstanding Sheila's memory that the first one was Cinerama, but that was on 6 May). It was a wonderful, charming show that set the trend. When Peel was doing his links, you could hear off-mike sounds of the

Nina Nastasia (r) on one of her three visits to Peel Acres to do a live session. Louise Kattenhorn

CLASSIC SESSION

Cat Power

Recorded: **18.6.00**
Studio: **Maida Vale 4**
Producer: **James Birtwistle**
Engineer: **Ralph Jordan**
First Broadcast: **20.7.00 & 31.8.00**
Tracks: **Sophisticated Lady, Hard Times In New York City, Wonder Wall, He Was A Friend of Mine, Freebird (& Deep Inside, Come On In My Kitchen, Werewolf, Up And Gone, Sister, Knockin' On Heaven's Door, 31.8.00)**
Line-up: **Chan Marshall (guitar, piano, vocal)**

A double session, providing almost half an hour of music and two broadcasts, consisting of eleven, shortish numbers, in which Cat Power recorded some of her favourite songs delicately and quietly. Peel loved this session, and it rapidly became a listener favourite too. Her version of 'Wonderwall' reached 33 in that year's Festive Fifty.

children playing table football with the band in the background at the other end of his studio, and conversation and laughter from the kitchen. Tim and Charlotte played their numbers beautifully, and a chance remark at the end of one of them led Peel to dig out and play Bridget St John's 'Ask Me No Questions', recorded for his own Dandelion record label some 30 years previously. As the massed dubbed-on birdsong and church bells effects faded out at the end, Peel said it was 'produced by me, actually'. Off-mike, from down the hall in the kitchen, Sheila could clearly be heard to shout, 'and me!'

It wasn't just the family banter that suggested this was a special moment in a special show. The gentle sound of Bridget St John prefigured something else these shows from Peel Acres in particular would champion. For the first time in decades, the show rediscovered its intimate side, with a series of absolutely unforgettable, entrancing sessions both here and at Maida Vale from solo female artists like Cat Power, Caroline Martin, Nina Nastasia, Lianne Hall, Neko Case, Laura Cantrell and others. Some older male listeners and critics saw this, *Home Truths* (which had started the previous year on Saturday mornings on Radio 4) and a more relaxed, chatty presentational style as part of a worrying, hippy softening of Peel. Indeed, it's hard to imagine some of his old male producers tolerating or encouraging this trend. Alison Howe says 'once Mike Hawkes had finished his shift, John's show was never looked after by older men again. They were fine, but they did things a certain way, and me, Anita and Louise, who came next, were young and different, we had ideas and were ambitious, and simply wanted to try different things that we thought John would like and that would develop the show.' Sheila remembers John being happier with the show than he had been for years: 'Thanks to Alison, Anita and Louise, it became at last all the things he'd always wanted it to be, connected to the bands, him going out to them, them coming in to him.'

The others who made an equal effort for these experiments were the engineers. Andy Rogers and George Thomas (who did most of the lives at Peel Acres), and at Maida Vale regular others like Simon Askew, Guy Worth, Jerry Smith, Ralph Jordan, Nick Fountain and Jamie Hart. They would all do anything for John. For the lives at Peel Acres, to keep within budget, this meant Andy and George taking along their own improvised suitcases of recording equipment, basically an 8-channel mixer, a few mikes, monitor speakers, DI boxes and headphones. 'We would normally mike-up the drum kit, always in the same place, between the stairs and John's DJ desk in John's room, by the window,' says Andy. 'Guitar amps would go in the doorway to the vinyl cupboard, and everything else sort of in a circle. We would have to take the rocking horse out if it was a big band.' For the live set itself, Andy and George

Two-sevenths of Belle and Sebastian live at Peel Acres 25 July 2002. Louise Kattenhorn

would retreat behind the sliding door into the walk-in CD cupboard where they set up the mixing desk. 'We couldn't see once we'd set up and talkback wasn't really very easy, but all we had to do was put our heads round the door. Belle & Sebastian was probably the largest set-up. We had to put Chris in the bathroom with his vibraphone. For the Christmas shows we'd have carols round the piano in the dining room at the other end of the hall, bell ringers as well, and still three or four other acts in the normal place. We loved doing those live at the house shows, and all the bands were brilliant in different ways.' George and Andy would also always pack up and drive back to London that night, no matter how late the after-show party went on in the kitchen, so their time was only charged internally as one shift and kept the show within budget. Laura Cantrell remembers wondering when she arrived for her first live show from the house in July 2000, after the winding drive down the Suffolk lanes 'where all these busy folks went when their job was over, if they stayed at a hotel in town or whatever, not realising quite yet what a family the Peel Show was. After our second show from the house in '03, we were pressed into doing a second set around the kitchen table. We didn't want to leave, even in the wee hours of the morning. It was one of the most special music evenings of my life.'

ONE-SESSION WONDER

Laura Cantrell & Ballboy Christmas Show

First broadcast live: **23.9.03**
Studio: **Peel Acres**
Producer: **Andy Rogers**
Engineer: **George Thomas**
Tracks: **Laura Cantrell – Pretty Paper, New Year's Resolution, Oh So Many Years, I Still Miss Someone. Ballboy – There Are Only Inches Between Us, Past Lovers, A Starry Night, I Lost You But I Found Country Music**
Line-up: **Laura Cantrell (acoustic guitar, vocal), Jay Graboff (guitar, mandolin), Gordon McIntyre (guitar, vocal), Nick Reynolds (bass), Gary Morgan (drums), Alexa Morrison (keyboard, vocal)**

The last Peel Acres Christmas Show. Ballboy and Laura Cantrell each did three numbers, then guested on each other's final number, producing two wonderful, unrepeatable performances.

Laura Cantrell: 'Christmas in 2003 was my last Peel Session. I am so glad I accepted the invitation. I had turned one down in 2000 because I had run out of vacation time at my office. I was very happy to be included in this Peel family radio ritual, singing the carols with the family as well as the songs we were featured on. We did a Christmas song that Roy Orbison had recorded, an original tune of mine, the old Bailes Brothers song "Oh So Many Years" morphed into the Christmas Carol "We Three Kings", and "I Still Miss Someone" as Johnny Cash had just died that fall. I did join Ballboy for their song "I Lost You But I Found Country Music", which in my mind was the most special moment in the show, and Gordon joined us for "I Still Miss Someone". Being the holidays, this evening was more family oriented than most and we really enjoyed meeting Peel's new grandson Archie.'

Handwritten note on reply slip: This is the 14th copy of this (Laura Cantrell) LP we bought. 13 have gone to friends, 1 is in my car, this is a spare. When are we going to get some new stuff? John.

IF YOU WOULD LIKE TO RECEIVE MORE INFORMATION ABOUT SHOESHINE / SPIT & POLISH ARTISTS AND RELEASES, JUST FILL IN YOUR NAME & ADDRESS, STICK ON A STAMP AND POST.

NAME ...... *John Peel* ......

ADDRESS ......

......

POSTCODE ......

E-MAIL ......

Please visit - www.shoeshine.co.uk

Peel's reply slip sent to Laura Cantrell's UK record label in 2000

Nobody else got these favours but Peel. And it showed in the programmes. The beginnings of the live sessions from Peel Acres in spring 1999 (always on Thursdays, after Peel returned from pre-recording *Home Truths* for Radio 4 all day), could be seen as the regular start of this late flowering of the show Sheila identifies, built on Alison Howe's beginnings. But this energetic period was also characterised by things like the 'Peelenium' (four records a night from one year of the twentieth century, starting in May 1999), more and more live DJ sets (from

A LISTENER WRITES...

'One abiding memory I have is of the live Melt Banana session from Maida Vale which I was lucky enough to win tickets to in October 2001. Without him, I can't imagine that the band would have got much exposure in the UK and yet the performance that evening was truly astonishing, Agata's guitar playing being one of the most amazing things I have seen in my life! The great man finished the gig by saying that those there would "remember the experience for the rest of their lives and tell their grandchildren that they were there", and he was absolutely right.'

Pat Dibben
South Norwood

the likes of the Scratch Perverts, Freddy Fresh and the annual summer showcases of the DMC World DJ Championships UK finalists), those revived Christmas Carol concerts ('We don't do that any more,' moaned Peel, when Anita had first mentioned the famous 1970 Carol Concert she'd read about in *In Session Tonight*. 'But why not?' she wondered), doing an all-time Festive Fifty for the millennium, the epic celebrations for Peel's 60th birthday in August 1999 (which produced so much live music the party lasted for three whole shows and into the following week), and new festival trips at home and abroad, like to the Noorderslag in Groningen every January. The only puzzling thing about the end of the millennium for the Peel Show was that, having started live shows from Maida Vale, they virtually dried up as regular events from mid-1998 until early 2000, apart from one-offs like the astonishing Melt Banana visit on 21 September 1999. The problem was simple: money.

Or rather, from the point of view of BBC Resources, space. Maida Vale is a huge complex and under the Birt producer-choice rules, studios were charged out to the networks at a rate according to their size. This meant, from 1998, a punitive rate, even for Maida Vale 4, which, although sizeable, has a relatively compact control room, unlike the old MV5. 'It was killing us,' remembers Sam Cunningham, 'and the one thing we feared was losing the Peel Sessions; whatever we did, we knew we had to keep those.' The rates got so high, and the bookings so thin, that in 1999 MV5 and even the historic Maida Vale 3 were mothballed, and their mixing desks, speakers and equipment removed and flogged off. MV3 was saved when, following a refit of the Golders Green Hippodrome in North London, the roof fell in shortly after reopening. The only available appropriate space for light music, jazz and MOR studio recordings was MV3, and the new Hippodrome desk was pulled out of the wreckage and reinstalled in the empty control room. There was still a danger Radio 1 would simply not be able to afford to continue sessions in MV4, until Sam, with the support of Trevor Dann, then Head of Music Entertainment, came up with the idea of the networks block-booking studios on an annual basis at a discount and reorganising personnel a bit. In the end only Radio 1 did a deal, agreeing in early 2000 to effectively buy out MV4 for an entire year at a time, use it as much as it needed, and sub-contract unwanted days to other networks and shows. From spring 2000, everything was back on an even keel and the Peel Show live nights could resume as regular events. The punitive cost of paying BBC Outside Broadcast for presentation equipment was avoided by Andy Rogers and the engineers lashing up their own improvised DJ desk set-up for John to use in the vocal booth on these nights. Finally, MV5 was reprieved in 2003 when, for reasons of space, the old basement, full-band Live Lounge sessions could no longer be fitted in at Yalding House, and with a new desk old Five was the logical temporary space to use for Jo Whiley's guests. It's still there.

■ **THAT FIRST REVIVED CHRISTMAS** concert at the end of 1999 came live from a festively bedecked MV3, Cinerama did their live night for Peel there in June 2000, and the old studio would feature again for the *25 Years Of The Festive Fifty* special – featuring live tribute numbers and a hilariously hopeless Pop Quiz on the annual polls – that December, and more sadly for the *Keepin' It Peel Night* in 2004, as would MV5. But it was the home of the Peel Sessions, MV4, that for the last four years of the show would host the overwhelming majority of both the pre-recorded and live-show session nights. Some of the wildest live shows there included Man Or Astroman insisting on dressing in their jumpsuits and doing their full stage show for John, including setting fire to a

CLASSIC SESSION

The White Stripes

Live from Maida Vale 4 on: **25.7.01**
Producer: **Simon Askew**
Engineers: **Nick Fountain & Jamie Hart**
Tracks: **Let's Shake Hands, When I Hear My Name, Jolene, Death Letter, Cannon, Astro, Hotel Yorba, I'm Finding It Hard To Be A Gentleman, Screwdriver, We're Going To Be Friends, You're Pretty Good Looking, Bollweavil, Hello Operator, Baby Blue**
Line-up: **Meg White (drums), Jack White (guitar, vocal)**

Anita Kamath: 'The day before their big gig at the 100 Club. When we arrived they were soundchecking and John decided to have a nap. I remember their expectant faces whilst they were waiting for him to get up. We went to our favourite Thai restaurant and talked about Son House, who had done a Peel Session, and Gene Vincent who John had seen. They sang three sets of songs and the sound was amazing, you just couldn't believe that there were only two of them. I asked them if they could do another track as a finale and they did three more – the last one, especially for John, was "Baby Blue" by Gene Vincent. John just welled up and afterwards he couldn't stop smiling.'

Six years later, when the band were back in Maida Vale for 'White Stripes Wednesday' in June 2007, playing live into Jo Whiley's show, Jack told Jo how he'd noticed the big photo of John outside Studio 4, and he'd remembered that first session for him.

flag, which required the continuous presence of a fire safety officer plus appropriate bucket and extinguishers. Gary Numan returned for a memorable show. And in July 2001 it was the White Stripes. By the time they came out to Peel Acres that November to repeat the favour of a live session only at the house this time ('It was incredible, but unbelievably loud,' recalls Sheila), Anita had been moved to look after two other new specialist shows at Radio 1, *The Blue Room* and *The Lock-Up*, and Peel had a new producer again: Louise Kattenhorn.

■

LOUISE ADMITS SHE was in awe of John and Radio 1 when she first started at the station as a broadcast assistant, first on daytime shows, then more regularly for Steve Lamacq, when there was still 'a bit of a thing' between him and Peel, a rivalry which was later resolved. She got a production attachment on the *Sunday Surgery* for a few months, then the Peel Show became available. 'I was very nervous when I had to go for a coffee with him and Ian Parkinson. John talked to Ian for half an hour about dub reggae. I realised I had a lot of catching up to do. I asked Ian later are we going to have a show meeting? Or an appointment interview? No, that's it, he said. It seemed I had got the job.' Louise is modest, because it was obvious Peel liked her immediately. Innumerable bands contacted for this book have given unsolicited testimonials to how great she was to work with. This book could certainly not have been done without her hard work, goodwill and support, almost day by day. She had discovered her love of radio in student broadcasting at Manchester University, devising and running an arts show, and later took the highly regarded Masters in Radio at Goldsmith's College.

'John's show, like Annie Nightingale's, was never seen as the pinnacle of demanding radio production in Radio 1,' she points out, 'but as a training ground for new producers. On the other hand, John understandably liked stability, so the new producers who've been put with him tended to stick with him a bit longer than they might have with other shows.' The main brief as she saw it was to continue Anita's energetic trying of new things to do with live music, but at the same time bring John back into the fold of the rest of Radio 1, by encouraging two-way links between him and other shows. One obvious way she did this was to develop dramatically the show's coverage of the electronic dance music Sonar festival in Barcelona each June (he had been briefly for the first time in 2001), often in partnership with Gilles Peterson's *One World* after-midnight slot. This led to joint, extended four-hour shows, loads of recorded live sets from artists from featured labels like Tigerbeat 6 and Fragile Discos and, late in 2002, the first Peel Session by the Pet Shop Boys, which Peel drolly introduced by saying, 'If you're uncomfortable about this, just pretend they're German.'

'We'd played our set at Sonar that year, and were sitting in the backstage drinks area, when two Radio 1 people next to us said they worked on the Peel Show, and he'd liked our set, and would we like to do a session?' remembers Neil Tennant. 'We've always had a liking for that, doing things the wrong way round in our career, so we liked the idea of doing a Peel Session just about the time when Radio 1 seemed to stop playing us during the daytime. I always wondered if that also had something to do with it. Peel was a great defender of the unfashionable as well as the potentially fashionable. Doing the session itself was a challenge for us because we'd normally spend four or five days on a track, instead of recording four in an afternoon. But we programmed and rehearsed, and knowing Peel would like something different, as well as what was then planned to be the next single, but in the end wasn't, "London", we did a cover of Bobby O's "(Try It) I'm In Love With A Married Man", and two other songs we'd never actually recorded.'

Tennant has a long memory as a musician, journalist and listener, remembering when very young hearing Peel play T Rex and the Incredible String Band on the Saturday afternoon *Top Gear* in the early 1970s. He loved the reggae in the late 1970s shows and, when editor of *Smash Hits* in the 1980s, always felt Peel was the best presenter *Top of the Pops* ever had. 'And don't forget, Peel was ahead of the game on eighties new pop, with Adam and the Ants, Altered Images and Orange Juice.' In the early to mid-1990s, however, he felt Peel's programmes had almost for a time become an irrelevance, because by then you could hear a lot of different music in different places. 'But he did always play rave and German and Belgian trance and other dance musics, and no one else ever played that then. That might actually be what he's remembered for most in those lost years.'

Other than Sonar and the DJ sets, Louise also saw in the introduction and recording of live sets from All Tomorrow's Parties, the alternative music festival from Camber Sands (which led to Beefheart's old Magic Band later doing a live show), as well as such Maida Vale innovations as the 'Ten Minute Men' nights, in which four or five bands would share their equipment and each play for no more than ten minutes in one show. With the addition of these events to Glastonbury, Reading, the Christmas Concerts, Noorderslag, Sonar, *One Live* (the retitled and reorganised *Sound City*), the live shows from Peel Acres and Maida Vale, from 2002 the new annual Peel calendar was complete. Memorable live shows from Maida Vale included Herman Dune in May, at which David-Ivar recalls 'I wanted a choir, so we called up Scout Niblett, Robots In Disguise and Lisa Li'Lund to sing with us. What a mess, man. I remember Sue Robots hanging from the balcony during a song she wasn't on. Russel Dufus yelled, "NYC crack and cocaine, gotta get my hair bleached" into the mike. Emma stood in the middle throwing Neman's toy percussion around. Everybody was shouting, making much more noise than the audience. It didn't scare John, though, and the songs we recorded sounded just fine.' Caroline Martin, at her more calm solo pre-recorded session that year, remembers wanting to add a sticker to the band names all over the inside of the MV4 control room door, 'but I don't have any for myself. But I did have a plaster in my bag, so I wrote my name and the date on it and added that to the collage.' Johnny Walker of the Soledad Brothers had borrowed Jack White's guitar amp for their November session, 'figuring that it would be top notch, but one of the speakers was making a terrible noise. Simon Askew just came over, diagnosed the problem, and cut the wire to that speaker.'

That year produced the most accomplished Christmas special, with Belle & Sebastian's concert from Maida Vale producing some startling, groovy covers, and a suicidally reckless attempt at a rock 'n' roll version of 'The Twelve Days of Christmas', which has to be heard to be credited. In the new year Hermeet arrived as the show assistant, having worked on shows at BBC Radio Scotland, and made a rapid contribution by suggesting a Burns Supper show special at the house. 'That was a great idea,' says Sheila, 'because we'd always celebrated it at home, because of John's Scottish grandmother.' Various Scottish bands did pre-recorded covers of

Caroline Martin recording in Maida Vale.

175

Burns songs. Later in the year he and Peel discovered the young grime dance scene, spent a fortune on records, and Hermeet put together a special live at Maida Vale night of MCs and DJs. And American one-man band Jawbone, aka Bob Zabor, did a live session too. 'When I got the invitation I was stunned. I couldn't even headline a small show in my hometown. As a one-man band any technical malfunction is deadly. Halfway into my first song, my drum pedal broke. There was no boom, boom boom. I finished the song kicking the bass drum with my toe. I had all my tools out and handy, just in case, and was able to repair it in half a minute or so, making small talk the whole time. It could've been worse.'

■

IN THE EARLY summer of 2004, Andy Parfitt wanted to squeeze in an extra specialist music slot in the evening, and asked Peel if he'd mind shifting back to an 11pm start and 1am finish each night to enable him to fit it in. He agreed. One unfortunate side effect, however, was that the monthly Wednesday night live session shows from Maida Vale were no longer possible, because the BBC's agreement with residents of Delaware Road stipulated that all live music would be finished and band equipment loaded out and removed by midnight. Instead, these shows would have to be pre-recorded in their entirety 'as live' earlier in the evening, and transmitted from CD or hard disk at 11pm. 'We did do a few like this,' says Louise, 'but it was never the same.' Despite that, the show was clearly on a roll in those last 13 weeks, from the date of the switch to an 11pm start on 27 July to Peel's last show before he left for Peru, on Thursday 14 October. Those three months had more special events and memorable sessions than his old shows of the mid-1980s or early 1990s might feature in twice the time, possibly even an entire year.

Things got off to an amazing start on the late late show with Orbital's final performance, recorded 'as live' at Maida Vale 4 on 28 July. 'When we had announced earlier that year that we were stopping, it got back to us that John had said, "Right, we've got to get them in for a last session," and how could we refuse? It would be a fitting way to finish off,' says Paul Hartnoll. 'It was one hell of a leaving party. The audience made up of our family, friends, fans and some of John's regular listeners were everywhere, all around us on the studio floor. It was a wonderful gig, made something special, charmed even, by knowing John was there, and that I could see him sitting behind us in the booth with my wife and daughter. Then, about halfway through, I looked up and suddenly spotted him now milling around at the back of the audience, getting involved. That was a thrill I'll never forget. And at the end he said on air something like "Thanks for everything, all the effort you've made for me," and he did that thing, you know, where he wells up, when you can see he's really moved. His weren't the only tears that night.'

The very next week it was the debut session by Steveless, the new band Peel was most excited about in what would be the final year of his life. Although 'band' is somehow not quite the right word. Dan Newman had originally recorded 'four improvised solo dirges of guitar, singing and some terrible casio keyboard beats' (his own description) at his parents' house, then sent his only copy on a CDR off to Peel, at the last minute scribbling 'Steveless' ('my name seemed a little lame') on a piece of paper with his mobile phone number. And forgot about it. When he eventually found out Peel loved it and was playing it, he promptly started sending in a CD every week of some of the almost 200 new pieces he had already recorded in his student bedsit in Bristol, 'which says something for the rigours of student life'. Then a few weeks later he was offered a session. He recruited a bassist and drummer and made up another nine new songs sitting on the swing in his parents' garden one day.

'We eventually recorded five tracks at Maida Vale and it was a joy to come back to the mixing room each time to find that the producer, Jerry Smith, that wonderful, wonderful man, had worked some kind of magic and managed to make us sound like a real band. All the way home down the M4 we couldn't stop raving about what an unbelievable, fine day it had been. It was simply the most magical experience of my life, perhaps rivalled only by the evening a month or so later when I sat at the radio and heard it pouring out of the speakers, a fantasy falling into my face. Now I get to drop it into conversation when I meet folk for the first time, as I act like it was just one of those things. But it wasn't one of those things, it was the thing, the most wonderful thing that could possibly have happened to me, the perfect day, dreams made real, dreams made real.'

The very next day was a beautiful duo acoustic session by Caroline Martin and Lianne Hall playing together, followed the week after by the first of three new sessions by old favourites in these last days: The Fall's 24th. David Gedge brought in the revived and roaring Wedding Present the next month (although the contract and session sheet still said 'Cinerama' at the top). 'Well, I think this is as good as anything they've ever done,' said Peel afterwards, quite rightly. And two days later The Delgados were back with an acoustic preview of some new songs, plus a powerful cover of Ewan MacColl's 'Ballad Of Accounting'. Meanwhile, Hermeet had sold to John the idea of 'showcasing' in session some DJs and MCs from Radio 1's sister digital station 1Xtra. After a slight

CLASSIC SESSION

The Fall

Recorded: **19.2.03**
Studio: **Maida Vale 4**
Producer: **Mike Walter**
Engineered by: **Ralph Jordan**
First Broadcast: **13.3.03**
Tracks: **Theme From Sparta FC, Contraflow, Groovin' With Mr Bloe / Green Eyed Locoman, Mere Pseud Mag. Ed.**
Line-up: **Mark E Smith (vocal), Dave Milner (drums, backing vocal), Jim Watts (bass, backing vocal), Ben Pritchard (guitar, backing vocal), Eleanor Poulou (organ, backing vocal)**

One of the most thrilling comebacks of any band, let alone Peel's favourite. Having been away for over four years, Mark E Smith returned with a new band line-up clearly 'on fire' as Daryl Easlea writes in the sleeve notes to the Sanctuary 'Complete Peel Sessions' set. Apparently Smith complained about the band's complacency and some of the BBC microphones, but if that's what it took to get everyone going then it was worth it. The storming 'Theme From Sparta FC' – again one of Smith's prescient songs in the year before Greece won the European Championship – reached no. 2 in that year's Festive Fifty, and the commercially released single version understandably reached no. 1 in the next year's poll, completed after Peel's death.

misunderstanding about how long their sets were to be – '45 minutes!' John raved to Hermeet in fury, 'You're giving away my programme!' – these got under way in studio Y1 next door to the on-air studio in the Yalding basement on 10 August, with Dancehall DJ Robbo Ranx assisted by MC Lady Saw. 'Everything was going fine until Lady Saw started doing all this patois rapping that was clearly sexual, mentioning John by name, more or less propositioning him,' remembers Louise. 'Poor John went bright red and didn't know where to look. Hermeet and I were struggling to stop ourselves laughing.' There was more DJ heaven when Jeff Mills and Laurent Garnier returned for a joint mix live at Maida Vale, and did two such fantastic mixes that the second one was held over to the following night. Damon Albarn popped round to Peel Acres to talk about his new solo work on the night of The Fall repeat. And on 14 October it was a repeat of Trencher. Then Peel went away.

■

SOON AFTER THE show had moved to 11pm that summer, Peel had heard some upsetting news. Andy Dickinson, drummer with Birmingham band Skimmer, had committed suicide. He had left no note. No one knew anything was wrong. The band had practised just three days before. On the morning of the funeral, bassist and singer Kev Powell received an email from Peel. 'He wrote that he'd had a similar experience himself with a friend of the family, and that we mustn't blame ourselves,' says Kev. Then a couple of weeks later, Louise Kattenhorn emailed offering the band a session. The band were both delighted and taken aback. 'We had fully intended to try and carry on,' says

Kev, 'only not quite so fast.' When the surviving trio plus a mate sitting in on drums got together for a pre-session practice, it was the first time they'd felt able to pick up their instruments since Andy's death. The date of the session was fixed for 21 October. They were not to know that theirs would be the last recorded before John's death. On the day itself, Kev had come down with a heavy cold, and struggled to get his vocals out, especially the high bits, 'but I knew I had to do my best for a Peel Session'. They started recording at 2pm and by 6.30pm had blasted down five of their power pop songs. 'We went to the pub, and when we came back, Jamie Hart and Nick Fountain got us a good mix. It was a really nice atmosphere, I was pleased with the whole day. We'd felt we'd all been lifted back up a step, after such a setback. It gave us a huge lift. We felt we could now carry on where we had left off.' A little over two years later, having changed labels, they finally managed to release the album they'd made before Andy died, and were invited to play Japan in summer 2007. They flew off to start their first Far East tour in August, and would return to record a new album in the autumn.

■

CLASSIC SESSION

Low

Live from Maida Vale 4: **8.11.00**
Producers: **Andy Rogers & Simon Askew**
Engineer: **George Thomas**
Tracks: **Will The Night, Venus, Dinosaur Act, Joan Of Arc, Immune, Over the Ocean**
Line-up: **Alan Sparhawk (guitar, keyboard, vocal), Mimi Parker (vocal, percussion), Zak Sally (bass)**

Along with perhaps Mogwai's, this is the live at Maida Vale session which presenters, producers and engineers alike rated the most superb performance of all, as the Minnesotan trio demonstrated their total grasp of intimacy and dynamics.

Chris Davison

CHAPTER 09

HE'S STILL AROUND. There are dozens of shows out there you have not heard. You can get them easily. In 2007, the listener and fan-generated tribute sites to Peel on the web mean that there is today, almost three years after his death, more Peel available than ever before. In April, for example, someone identified only as 'hills1902' popped up on the lively John Peel News Group on Yahoo (520 members and counting) announcing he had eight good-quality complete reel-to-reel off-air tapes of John Peel *Top Gear* shows from dates in 1969 and 1970. Could anyone help him convert them to digital files, and would anyone be interested in hearing them? He was nearly swamped by the deluge of offers of help from listers around the world. By July, those shows could all be heard and downloaded from one of the many blogspot websites where regular listeners put up and swap off-air show tapes. Start at johnpeeleveryday and toggle round the links. Pretty quickly you'll realise there are dozens of shows being posted all the time, sometimes in fragments, sometimes nearly complete, and, separately, many more of the sessions, mostly by acts who can never hope to have their sessions released commercially in these straitened times for the international music industry.

The new lister who offered those 1969–1970 tapes was momentarily a bit concerned about copyright. Of course, technically, such practices remain illegal. But we listers reassured him fairly quickly. Who could, or would, indict a whole wide world of bloggers? Although the BBC's 'Treasure Hunt' amnesty and request for its listeners and viewers to help restore missing and lost pre-1980 material to its archives has now officially ended (the website's still there but there is no longer an active retrieval programme), the BBC archives are still grateful to have anything they're missing, and the Corporation knows it would be on a political hiding to nothing to seek to prosecute the active goodwill of its licence-fee payers. The mere process of doing this book has incidentally restored to the Radio 1 archive at least three missing Peel Sessions, and helped date some uncatalogued Peel Show tapes awaiting digitisation at Maida Vale, as a result of listeners I found through the web, who were able to answer my questions on mystery or missing shows and sessions with an MP3 file by return: amazing! And each of those original listeners now at least has their name attached to the archive's new catalogue entry, as this particular session or show having been 'donated by...'

There is nothing ridiculous about treasuring and listening to old radio shows. No one thinks it odd to watch old films, read old books, look at old paintings. It's only the common but misplaced conception of the medium as being a solely ephemeral one – because we listen to it in the car or kitchen or bath while doing other things – that makes us feel we should not 'listen again' that much, because it's an everyday thing we do, and therefore surely can't be very important. Moreover, given the unprecedented originality and exclusive content of the Peel Show, such an activity is by no means wholly nostalgic. Like discovering an unpublished or lost story by a minor author, almost any unheard Peel Show is likely to include some music and an artist or two even informed listeners may not have heard before.

A more public face of radio celebrating Peel's Radio 1 shows has been BBC 6 Music's rebroadcast of show extracts, on top of its regular scheduling of classic sessions in its main programmes. In October 2006, it rebroadcast four extracts from Peel's final *Perfumed Garden* show on the pirate Radio London, and interviewed the listener who had restored them. Many listeners have subsequently articulated on the web the same thought: if that's possible, why not once a week play a repeat of one of the many Peel Shows that exist complete in the archive? The BBC's happy to do this with drama on its digital station BBC7, after all. And it's a lot easier in copyright terms to repeat an edited radio show than to release it commercially – given the sheer number of different copyright holders involved in a typical show. But it's thankfully a very different story trying to release any individual Peel Session.

■

IT IS AT least now commonplace for some Peel Sessions to be available commercially. Sometimes it's hard to recall how shocking it was, and how much an astonishing legal achievement and the result of years of slog, for Clive Selwood to be able to launch the official first series of Peel Session releases on 12-inch vinyl on his own Strange

Fruit label more than 20 years ago. More than 70 sessions were released on vinyl this way between 1986 and 1989, then more on CD, and then in doubles, then whole-album collections through the 1990s. Although Peel had no financial involvement (Selwood offered both him and Walters a stake in the company but they declined) he drew up lists of ones he would like to see released and requested that, in the spirit of the original sessions, the releases would not be just cherry-picking, but would also include obscurities, rarities and one-session wonders – which explains how Twa Toots, the Screaming Blue Messiahs and Girls At Our Best! were released. Initially, many celebrated pre-punk artists or their then record labels declined permission for a release. The rights to commercial exploitation – as opposed to broadcast – of any BBC session in principle reside with the artist but if at the time of the recording they had a record deal, then that company has the right to block any such release, or indeed exploit the sessions themselves. Yet within little more than a decade many such artists had evidently changed their minds, and major label BBC session releases followed from the likes of Cream and Led Zeppelin, for example. There are rumours in 2007 that plans are afoot for new sessions release sets from T Rex, Elton John and the Teardrop Explodes. Meanwhile, in the early 1990s, Clive sold Strange Fruit to its original distributor, Pinnacle, and Sue Armstrong who had helped him run the label went and ran it there. Then Pinnacle in turn was bought by Clive Calder's Zomba family of independent labels, who then sold 20 per cent to major label BMG. But in 2002 Calder obligated BMG to exercise its option to buy the rest of Zomba. BMG found they had paid too much for it so they closed all its labels down, including Strange Fruit, which, for the record, had always been profitable. The Strange Fruit catalogue in theory went in-house at BMG, but only as a dormant label. As the licence period for each title in the catalogue expired, the CDs were deleted one by one. By the time of Peel's death the whole catalogue had been junked.

But the story is not without some kind of happy ending. Out of the ashes of Strange Fruit, two Peel Session release projects emerged. First, Brian O'Reilly, who had also worked with Clive at Strange Fruit in the early days, launched Hux Records, which has in the past few years, among other archive restorations, repackaged, re-released and developed many Peel and BBC session albums by acts from the show's first 12 years, including most recently superb restoration sets of the extant BBC radio recordings by Pentangle and the Incredible String Band. If that's your period of listening, the Hux online catalogue is a delight and will no doubt do as much damage to your wallet as it has to mine. Meanwhile, Sue Armstrong pitched an idea to Universal Music. 'There's all this stuff from the old Strange Fruit catalogue and the BBC archive implicitly licensed and approved – and it could easily be out there.'

In a time when no-origination cost catalogue releases are a godsend for the record industry, the company took the point. A series of high-level talks began between Universal's and the BBC's lawyers. Eventually, the summer after Peel's death, a blanket deal was struck for anything any Universal artist did at the BBC, agreeing the percentages of everything each party – the BBC, the artist, the copyright agencies, and so on – would get, and more importantly assuming mutual 'approval' for release for anything and everything. And Universal gave Sue the job of running the BBC catalogue release programme. 'All I have to do is come up with the projects, there's no legal hassle' (although the artist's approval is formally required). Her first batch of releases in 2006 included complete Peel Session sets from Pulp, Gene, Siouxsie and the Banshees, the House of Love, and a selection personally approved by PJ Harvey. Other sets of BBC recordings including Peel Sessions have come from Free, The Housemartins, and a superb, if not absolutely complete 4-CD set from Fairport Convention. Meanwhile, across town, Steve Hammonds at Sanctuary Records Group had some plans of his own. Since Peel's death, they've brought out acclaimed *Complete Peel Sessions* sets from the Wedding Present, The Undertones and, best of all, The Fall on their Castle Music label. The news of the group's financial difficulties in 2007 and agreed sale to – coincidentally – Universal Music, means the future of this occasional programme is somewhat uncertain as this book goes to press, including a planned Cinerama Peel Sessions set. But the way things are going with the web and music, it's possible everyone's sessions could be freely downloadable within a few years. After all, as of 2001, the entire Radio 1 archive, including the Peel Sessions, has already been digitised.

■

RADIO 1 ARCHIVIST Phil Lawton was working away in his basement archive at Yalding House on the morning of 16 March 1998 – the original tape archive set up in the basement at Egton House had simply been moved round to the new building with him – when he had a rather vague phone call from reception. 'There's a bloke here to see you from management. He's asking have you got a minute?' Puzzled, Phil said, sure, send him down. Two minutes later John Birt, the BBC's Director-General, was on the steps outside the glass door into the archive. Phil ushered him in, found him a seat, and asked how he could help. Birt had heard a few things about the archive and wanted to find out what it actually constituted. So Phil started to explain about the session and concert tapes, interviews, features and documentaries. They talked for a bit, officially, then Phil thought he'd ask about Birt's TV production of a famous interview with Mick Jagger in the 1960s, 'and he completely opened up, smiling, chatty, and we had a great time.' Birt was leaving, one foot outside the door, when he paused, turned, and casually asked Phil, 'all this stuff is backed up, right?' 'No, it isn't,' said Phil. 'You're joking,' said Birt, clearly shocked – this was evidently not the answer he was expecting. 'I'm not,' said Phil, 'I've been trying to tell my bosses in Information & Archives for years that if this place goes up in flames, you lose everything, The Beatles, the Rolling Stones, the Peel Sessions, the lot.' 'We'll have to do something about that,' said Birt, and left. Phil thought nothing more of it – until the very next day he had a phone call from the directorate office asking when he would be available for meetings to discuss security and preservation issues further.

Over the next six months things moved rapidly for the juggernaut of a corporation that is the BBC. Security walls and doors were designed and fitted to make the archive secure. A business case was made for financing the dubbing of the entire archive, and approved. Phil started selecting material for a digital preservation pilot scheme. The six-month pilot went ahead in January 1999, with Phil and a colleague physically taking boxes of tapes over to Broadcasting House, then checking them back in to Yalding once they'd been converted into digital files. And in November a Radio 1 meeting announced the project to digitise the entire archive had been given the go ahead, so successful was the pilot. A new unit was set up at Maida Vale, Information and Archives (Preservations), led by Roger Olive, whose first priority was to digitise both the Radio 1 archive and as much radio drama and comedy as possible, anticipating the planned launch of the BBC's digital radio stations 6 Music and BBC7, whose programmes would rely on the archives. Finally, in summer 2001, a party was held to celebrate the completion of the digital Radio 1 archive. The whole collection is contained on seven small, Roberts-radio sized computer servers, their red lights winking from three shelves in the corner of one small room at Maida Vale. The original quarter-inch magnetic tapes were going to be dumped in a skip until Phil kicked up a fuss, and they are now housed in a proper, environmentally controlled secure facility at Television Centre along with other priceless masters from BBC radio and television.

'If it hadn't been for Birt, if he hadn't popped round, or asked that question, it wouldn't have happened,' says Phil. He's right, and in the interests of history it's only fair to say so, Birt being a much-derided figure both before and after his departure. BBC 6 Music could never have been launched on time without the digitisation of the Radio 1 archive. Uniquely, it's also all available online to Radio 1 and 6 Music producers. They can search the archive, audition or preview the files, and if they decide they want this or that session or concert track or interview clip for a show, simply click a button, and a freshly burned CD arrives in the internal post the next day. Meanwhile, up at Maida Vale, Preservations are still working away, digitising the wealth of show tapes being found and handed over, an endless task. When I visited Maida Vale in May 2007, Roger Olive showed me a metal cabinet stuffed with ROT tapes ('record of transmission', in other words, recordings of complete shows) of Mark Radcliffe's night-time Radio 1 show from Manchester in the 1990s, just one cupboard of stuff among many, waiting its turn to be ripped into the system and catalogued. At the same moment, as one, we both pointed at one dated row of tapes from 1996 and asked each other 'didn't Peel do some of those?' And that's how Roger helped me check the full details of those Manchester Peel Sessions and get them into this book. But this special place which made almost all the sessions and now keeps them secure is under threat. The BBC announced in June 2007 it was planning to sell off Maida Vale Studios for redevelopment, claiming the facility was 'unsuitable for the 21st century'. As a publicly accountable national institution, the BBC would not dream of abandoning Broadcasting House or removing Eric Gill's sculpture above the main entrance, but apparently the historic place across town where it fostered the musical life of the nation for over 70 years is just some real estate. If the home of the sessions, the studios, and the archive is not certain in the BBC, it's only logical to have some concerns about how the Corporation safeguards another, less tangible part of the Peel legacy: the broadcaster himself, his belief in what radio shows could and should be.

■

ANDY PARFITT IS confident Radio 1 can continue to honour what Peel stood for. 'We'll make sure the idea of what John stood for is respected, that individuals with taste who know and like music can get the opportunity to come on air, and, as far as possible without interference, get to showcase the music they like. We seek out broadcasters who are passionate. That'll never change as long as I'm here. It's in our DNA.' He cites as examples DJs like Rob Da Bank and Huw Stephens, among others. Without doubt they are very good, but a quick check of the schedule shows they and the likes of Annie Nightingale, Ras Kwame, Mike Davies, Fabio & Grooverider, Chris Goldfinger, Gilles Peterson and Mary Anne Hobbs are all on in the small hours of the morning, even later than Peel was pushed towards the end. Rob Da Bank doesn't think this matters, though. 'Radio 1's still the place with the best roster of specialist DJ slots at night anywhere, and we cover a hell of a lot of ground collectively, a whole gamut of styles, just not in the one show like Peel did.'

He has a point. The Radio 1 DJ roster is still strong, and Peel is irreplaceable. To even ask Radio 1 to seek out 'the new Peel' is crass. Rob Da Bank has himself had to put up with some idiotic press coverage like this, not of his or the BBC's making, when he stepped in during those difficult weeks after John's death. But there is a nagging problem here. If we accept that for various reasons – his age, the coeval development of rock with him from when he was 16 in 1955, the mere fact of his career, his decades at the microphone – that Peel was indeed a 'one-off', then that immediately lets the BBC off the hook of any obligation to try and continue what he did, because how can you repeat a one-off? If his countless awards were for anything more than just being himself – and they were, as this book has shown – then there is still a lesson in his success. More than two years after his death, he was voted Broadcaster's Broadcaster by a poll of radio presenters and producers at the 2007 Sony Radio Awards on 30 April. Accepting the posthumous award to a standing ovation, Sheila told the *Ipswich Evening Star*: 'I thought it was quite touching and very special indeed, for many reasons. It was rather good that people are still thinking about John and still recognise him as being so important in his field. You could tell everyone very much wanted him to win and John totally ran away with it, that's really lovely and it is heartwarming that his legacy continues.'

But in life Peel always occupied the place of the maverick within the BBC. The Corporation has always tolerated creative broadcasters who did not fit whatever was the currently perceived way things were done. For many years at Radio 1 he was regarded by management as at best a safety valve. If listeners complained about daytime, the station could simply say, 'Well, you can always listen to John Peel.' To understand how the BBC may or may not carry forward his legacy, it might be instructive to note how he was treated by the Corporation during his lifetime. On the one hand, he was not persecuted. Many of the perceived slights to his show existed only in his over-sensitive imagination. He was put on an annual retainer contract in 1973, which was extended to two years by Johnny Beerling in the late 1980s. As he often attested, no one ever interfered with the content of the programme. For many years he had the benefit of having as his advocate one of the sharpest minds in the BBC, John Walters. But the programme itself, and therefore by extension his own person, was never secure. At certain key moments in the late 1970s, mid-1990s, and early 2000s, successive and seemingly very different Radio 1 managements either cut his airtime or moved, or sought to move, the show to less advantageous, listener-unfriendly slots. At such times he could be forgiven for feeling hard done by.

Many of his former colleagues, long since retired or departed the BBC, believe the Radio 1 management culture, which endured unbidden across the generations, never really understood the show or rejoiced in its successes. His ratings were nearly always better than anyone else's in his allocated slots; he won awards wherever they put him; his impact on music, audiences and taste was immediate, extensive and continuous – and his reward, his friends say, was to be distrusted and even privately resented by the management, because he did it by wholly ignoring whatever the systems and values of the station were at the time, whether the desire to promote 'stars' and 'entertainment' of the Chinnery and Beerling years, or pursue specialist youth audience demographics and market segments in the Bannister and Parfitt eras.

If that's true, there is only one, surprising and seemingly reactionary conclusion to such an analysis. The only controller who simply encouraged Peel for what he was, rejoiced in his success and had no concern about the approach he took, seeing it as no slight to his own ideas or plans for the rest of the station, was the first: Robin Scott. And the BBC he represented, in which a patrician, cultured elite exercised a benign dictatorship, chose good men and let them get on with it – think of Bernie Andrews, John Walters – has long gone. It's true that, despite Scott's support, Peel barely survived the unusually hostile attitude of middle management of the time, but today someone like him, a breaker of whatever rules happen to apply, would be unlikely to last long enough to build up such critical standing as to be safeguarded from management strictures. Does the current Radio 1 specialist DJ roster genuinely constitute today's awkward squad, the true troublemakers? On the other hand, it's simply too early in their careers to judge whether Huw Stephens, say, or Rob Da Bank, will persist and become truly revered for their individualism. Peel himself was pretty flaky on air at times before 1970. Whatever he achieved, he was not without flaws, either as a broadcaster, or a man.

■

FOR SHEILA AND the family, the Peel tribute industry that has sprung up since his death – to which this book must admit belonging – has been a mixed blessing. The private and public outpouring from listeners at John's death was deeply appreciated, as was the almost spontaneous creation of Peel Day, the decision by fans to stage gigs and other activities Peel enjoyed across the country annually on an agreed date close to that of his last programme, 14 October.

Other tributes Sheila has approved as ones she knew John would be touched by have included the naming of a new kind of red tulip in his honour and, best of all, the naming of Cotswold Rail diesel locomotive no. 47813 as *John Peel*. 'John would have loved that more than anything, the idea that he could be spotted trundling around the Midlands somewhere pulling freight.' The decision in 2005 by their friends the Eavis family to rename the Glastonbury Festival's New Bands Stage after Peel was also easy to say yes to, although everyone accepts John would have probably had a difficult time approving some of the bands that have appeared on it since. The compilation albums which the family and friends have been involved with have been decent productions and representative of whatever aspect or period of Peel's career their titles claimed to celebrate. And the Channel 4 TV show *John Peel's Record Box*, an exploration of his taste and personality by exploring the contents of his singles box, produced by son Tom, got closer to what made him tick than almost anything else.

But then there have been the error-strewn obituaries and hagiographic quickie biogs. 'I had to read all those books before finishing *Margrave*, just so I knew what they were saying, but it was a sickening experience,' says Sheila, shaking her head. The production of *Margrave* itself was traumatic, but the family felt it had to be done. It's best understood in that spirit, as a family laying to rest a memory, being neither a complete autobiography nor a detached 'life'. One thing it does not claim to be is a history of his show or the sessions, hence the hoped-for place for this book. What remains to be explored here briefly is if any explanation can be found for the show in the life. Was there something in his character that made him such a good broadcaster and champion of new acts? And might there have been other consequences for his colleagues of such attributes?

On the 5 March 1969 edition of *Night Ride*, one of Peel's guests, Fraser White, did an analysis of his handwriting. The conclusions he came to were spookily accurate, as both Peel at the time and Sheila recently agreed. The full text, as read out by Peel himself, went: 'The upright slope shows lack of spontaneous emotion, an analytical mind with good reasoning powers, he has keen judgement and a dominance of intellect over emotions. He is a good creative writer. Variations in slope show moodiness. The pointed letters show him to be mentally a live-wire, but at times lacks the necessary push to get things done. The light pressure shows him to be quiet, impressionable, idealistic and dreamy. The extremely compressed writing shows him to be a poor mixer and inhibited, with indications of an inferiority complex. He has not many good friends, because he is suspicious, jealous and over-cautious. The unevenness of individual letters shows him to be changeable and moody, somewhat lacking in emotional stability, and inconsistent. The absence of finals shows self-sufficiency, reticence and an inclination to be selfish. The disconnection of letters shows him creative, with plenty of imagination. He has hunches often, and some don't come off. He forms likes and dislikes at first impression. Individual letter characteristics show modesty, dignity and fluency of thought. He lives in an idealistic world, is precise, and extremely careful.'

Idealistic, moody, creative, suspicious, selfish, precise, extremely careful – these are not a wholly charitable list of attributes, but anyone who worked with Peel will recall instances of each manifesting themselves. But only in certain contexts. For example, he was never selfish or over-cautious with his money or time, quite the reverse. And the successes of his show would seem to have been built almost entirely on hunches and first impressions. He could be analytical and intellectual, however. I used to believe he had no system or criteria for judging music because he was pathologically incapable of any such aesthetic discrimination, and only able to react in a sentimental, impressionistic way. But I now believe that after a time he deliberately chose not to analyse his musical reactions and tastes, fearing it would break the spell, and after a while this habit became so ingrained he forgot it was the result of an extremely careful decision. His journalism, for example, revealed he was quite capable of intelligent discussion of music. It seemed to me his childlike curiosity in new sounds and his faith in innocence – qualities that made him a decent and considerate friend and faithful supporter of all those he valued – were equalled by an almost childish avoidance of conflict, dispute or struggle. He was most fortunate to have people like Sheila, the Selwoods and Walters to manage his earthly and financial affairs for him. He would sooner fire off a long letter of complaint to a controller or director-general than confront his producer or executive producer face to face. Given his status in later life, who could blame him? But I am glad I was not his producer on such days, having my shortcomings implicitly rehearsed and my responsibilities undermined in front of my boss.

But what matters most for our purposes is that this active-passive, stimulated-sedated cocktail of personal attributes made him perfectly suited to life as a radio broadcaster. All the conflicts he wished to avoid were not present in the nine inches between him and the mike. All the values and ideals he believed in could be encouraged at a distance over the air. He could forget his social inhibitions, his fears of inferiority. It was all such fun his mood always lifted and the things that worried his over-cautious mind receded in importance. In music he found an outlet for his emotion. Like many millions of the shy before and since, he knew it was music that had showed him what feelings were. And radio might just bring that revelation to others, up to 26 times a show.

■

PERHAPS ALL THIS is overdoing it a bit. It was just a radio show. And one, moreover, that was fuelled by teenage dreams and aimed mainly at enthusiasts of teenage music-making. Some formerly loyal listeners recanted long ago. Sean French, journalist and author, wrote in the *New Statesman* in 1999 of how he used to tape the show religiously every night from 1978 to 1980 while at university, but then thought, 'You're insane. Stop all of this and do something constructive. And if you can't do something constructive, at least get out of your room.' He never listened to Peel again, he wrote. I asked him recently if he still felt the same way and he said yes, he did. Maybe he's right. Perhaps it has all been a juvenile waste of time. But possibly because I am also a teacher, I'm afraid I can't quite see teenage dreams as something to be shut in a box and buried for ever in the past. What listening to Peel for most of my life taught me is that there is, despite everything you learn as an adult in later life – how to hold down a steady job, how to be faithful to those you love, how to be a mum or dad – one small something to be treasured in your easily forgotten, deep-buried, seemingly solipsistic teenage self. It's something Peel had in limitless supply, something he displayed every day in many small acts of encouragement or empathy with bands, musicians, or the lonely without-knowing-it who wrote him letters in their hundreds. It's what Peel and his audience had in common. You could call it curiosity, or perhaps desire, obsession even. Here, I'd prefer another word, the verb that describes how it manifested itself in this relationship: what we did for him, but more importantly what he did for us, his listeners, his bands. It was his sign-off. Thanks for listening.

■

P A R T   2

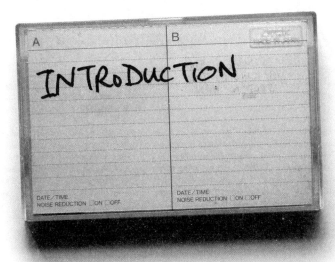

INTRODUCTION

THE PEELENIUM / THE FESTIVE FIFTIES
THE SHOWS / THE SESSIONS

The information in the remaining pages of this book was researched from the following sources, in order of importance:

- PasB (programme-as-broadcast) running order scripts, held on microfilm at BBC Written Archives, for the years 1967–1996
- Session Sheets: 1967–1996 at BBC Written Archives, more recent years held at Radio 1
- Radio Times, the complete run held by the Mitchell Library, Glasgow
- Peel's producers' production wallcharts, planners, diaries, files, notes, recollections
- BBC INfax Programme archive and catalogue
- Sue Armstrong's files of session sheets held at Strange Fruit and now Universal Music
- The Radio 1 Romeo computer system for logging shows, sessions and items
- The digitised Radio 1 archive of recordings
- Jon Small's personal website of shows and sessions 1993–2001
- The members of the John Peel News Group on Yahoo
- Many individual listeners for their diaries, tapes, tape indexes, etc

A number of websites and reference books, most notably:

- The Guinness Book of British Hit Singles (11th edition, 1997)
- Strong, Martin C. (2006) The Essential Rock Discography (Edinburgh: Canongate)
- Whitby, Mark (2005) The Festive Fifty (Widnes: Nevin Publishing)
- Myspace for bands' own websites to check titles and musicians

I am indebted to all the archivists, producers and listeners who helped me, and their names can be found in the acknowledgements. My approach to this documentary reconstruction half of the book has been driven by a key fact: no single one of the official BBC archival sources named above has all the answers. And I was never sitting listening ready with a notebook, despite what you might imagine, so I don't have them either! For example, PasBs are generally very reliable, but not perfect, because sometimes when they were microfilmed shows or pages were missing, or strips of paper for individual musical items were accidentally overlaid on others on the camera platen, obscuring some parts of the show. They also stop in 1996 for music shows, as Radio 1 moved over to doing them as basic digital music copyright reports. Session sheets are good, but very often the broadcast date is not on them because it was decided later. Radio 1's 20-year-old Romeo computer system, which has been earmarked for replacement for at least ten years, is frequently missing TX dates too. And so on. Instead I have taken the following multi-source approach:

1. Construct from the calendar, Radio Times, confirmed PasBs and existing session sheets a complete diary of all Peel show broadcast dates 1967–2004, including all session sheet data on first broadcast and repeat dates (this, now in its fifth edition since December 2006, is what follows in edited form as 'The Shows')

2. Separately enter all full session sheet data into a basic excel spreadsheet, check errors in dates against shows diary above

3. Check all blanks and obvious errors in both documents with reliable longstanding Peel listeners and tape collectors mainly via the John Peel News Group

4. Check remaining gaps and inconsistencies with PasBs at BBC Written Archives, Romeo, BBC INfax, Radio 1 digital archive, and so on

Essentially, I have worked backwards from what we can be certain listeners heard, rather than forwards from any one incomplete archival source. This means what follows has some – but not that many – unknowns. But these are unknown details about a known event. For every session except a tiny handful (less than a dozen out of 4,400) we do have a broadcast date, an artist and some titles. Everything else is gravy. And there's a helluva lot of it here. Individuals who have been particularly important for each of the sections that follow and deserving of my especial thanks are: for the 'Festive Fifties', Mark Whitby for his wonderful book, which is a must-buy for anyone who enjoyed these end-of-year polls, and the contributors to the relevant rocklist webpages; for the 'Peelenium', Lynn Macarthy, Anita Kamath and 'The Voice Of The Peelenium', aka Sheila Ravenscroft; for 'The Shows', the staff of Level 5 of the Mitchell Library, who put up with my repeated visits asking to see another 20 volumes of Radio Times with commendable forebearance, and Peel listeners Jon Small, Tim Joseph and Phil Edwards, who each contributed dozens of vital answers; for 'The Sessions', Carrie Maclennan for keying the new ones 1993–2004 for me, my brother Pete Garner who did wonders with macros saving me days of work, and my Dad Stan Garner for some sharp correcting of data inconsistencies. The mistakes that remain are all my own.

Corrections?

And, yes, there will certainly be mistakes in track titles and line-ups, despite my best efforts. All corrections and comments are welcome. I can be written to care of the publishers, found at the John Peel News Group on Yahoo, or direct on ken_garner@yahoo.com.

CHAPTER 10

ON WEDNESDAY 6 January 1999, at the top of his 'Kats' Karavan' script, John typed: 'We will celebrate the music of the century – starting on May 13th. Provided that we lose no programmes between that date and the end of the year, decade, century etc.' So the 'Peelenium' was born, on a whim. But the eventual idea of playing four tracks from one year of the 20th century per show, and the eventual title, would come later. The tracks were chosen by John & Sheila, Lynn Macarthy ('Lynntheofficejunior') and producer Anita Kamath. Sheila was 'The Voice of the Peelenium', announcing each year, and Lynn Macarthy gathered the records, and facts about the times the music was released, which often produced hilarity for their unusual news values – but that was the point. A few po-faced critics and listeners complained that until it reached the 1950s there would be no oppositional music; or debated on what basis, what scholarly system, the records were chosen? There was no such system or manifesto. It was meant to be fun, some examples of the music of each year only, and a feature to get listeners hooked – which it did – and made no pretence at definitive status. Despite this, it was frequently strikingly evocative and prescient in touching on key performers, records or styles in the pre-rock 'n' roll years – from music hall, the cinema, the blues, or dance orchestras and crooners. This became even more obvious when it reached the years 1964 and 1967, where the four compilers could not agree on a mere four records, so they did two instalments for each of these years, and had to settle on a minimum of five, or even six records in some instalments; 1962 and 1985 only got 3. Partly for these reasons, and one or two schedule changes, and indeed as Peel had feared, the feature overran. The 'Peelenium' started on 13 May, but by the turn of the millenium had only reached 1991. It eventually concluded with the bonus year 2000 on Thursday 20 January 2000. But the popularity it had won immediately prompted a further feature idea, 'Pig's Big 78', in which Sheila introduced a found 78rpm record on every show thereafter. This led to a compilation CD in 2006, 'John And Sheila: The Pig's Big 78s – A Beginner's Guide', on the German label Trikont US0350. With thanks to Lynn, Anita, and The Voice.

PEELENIUM 1900 – 2000

1900
I Want To Be A Military Man
  – **Louis Bradfield**
If It Wasn't For The 'Ouses In Between
  – **Gus Glen**
Soldiers Of The Queen – **Arthur Christian**
The Miner's Dream Of Home
  – **Peter Dawson**

1901
Knocked 'Em In The Old Kent Road
  – **Jack Morrison & The Variety Singers**
Beer, Beer, Glorious Beer / Ask A Policemen
  – **The Variety Singers**
Why Did I Leave My Little Back Room? /
  Our Lodger's Such A Nice Young Man
  – **Parlophone Quartet**
My Next Door Neighbour's Garden
  – **Herbert Darnley**

1902
Under The Deodar – **Gertie Millar**
Tell Me Pretty Maiden – **Florodra Girls**
Land Of Hope And Glory
  – **Edna Thornton with Orchestra**
Won't You Come Home Bill Bailey
  – **Arthur Collins**

1903
That's How The Little Girl Got On
  – **Marie Lloyd**
A Bird In A Gilded Cage – **Hamilton Hill**
Riding On A Motor Car – **Vesta Victoria**
I Shall Sulk – **Jack Pleasants**

1904
I Can't Do My Bally Bottom Button Up
  – **Ernie Mayne**
My Heart's At Your Feet – **Isabel Jay**

Poor Wand'ring One – **Isabel Jay**
Kashmiri Song (Four Indian Love Lyrics)
  – **Albert Sandler Trio**

1905
The Pipes Of Pan – **Winnie Melville**
Cigarette – **Robert Fear**
You And I – **Isabel Jay**
If Those Lips Could Only Speak – **George Baker with Orchestra and Male Quartet**

1906
Stop Your Tickling Jock
  – **Harry Lauder with Orchestra**
Give My Regards To Leicester Square
  – **Miss Victoria Monks with Orchestra B**
Waltz Me Round Again – **Miss Florrie Ford**
I Want What I Want When I Want It
  – **George Alexander**

1907

I Do Like To Be Beside The Seaside
  – **Miss Florrie Forde**
I Know A Lovely Garden – **Derek Oldman**
By The Side Of The Zuyder Zee
  – **Gerald Adams & The Variety Singers**
Rose In The Bud – **Eleanor Jones Hudson**

1908

Adam & Eve – **Grace Cameron**
Goodbye Molly Brown – **Maude Raymond**
The Small Town Gal – **George M Cohan**
The Dusky Salome – **Maude Raymond**

1909

Moonstruck – **Gertie Miller**
Yip-I-Addy-I-Ay – **George Grossmith Jnr**
Bring Me A Rose – **Phylis Dare**
The Jocular Joker – **G H Chirgwin**

1910

Don't Go Down The Mine Stanley
  – **Kirby & Orchestra**
Tony From America
  – **Columbia Light Opera Company**
Ginger You're Barmy
  – **Harry Champion & Orchestra**
Molly O'Morgan – **Ella Retford**

1911

I'm Shy Mary Ellen, I'm Shy – **Jack Pleasants**
The Photo Of The Girl I Left Behind
  – **Billy Merson**
Turn Your Light Off Mister Moon Man
  – **Nora Bayes & Jack Norworth**
Let Me Stay And Live In Dixieland
  – **Charles King**

1912

I'm Twenty One Today – **Unknown**
Who Were You With Last Night
  – **Mark Sheridan**
Look What Percy's Picked Up In The Park
  – **Vesta Victoria**
My Landlady – **Bert Williams**

1913

I Love The Name Of Mary
  – **Chauncey Olcott**
It's Nicer To Be In Bed – **Harry Lauder**
When Irish Eyes Are Smiling
  – **Chauncey Olcott**
Hello! Hello! Who's Your Lady Friend?
  – **Harry Fragson**

1914

Are We Downhearted? No!
  – **Harrison Latimer**
Gilbert The Filbert – **Basil Hallam**
When We've Wound Up The Watch On The
  Rhine – **Violet Loraine & Ambrose Thorne
  & Orchestra**
I Was A Good Little Girl Till I Met You
  – **Clarice Mayne and 'That' (James W Tate)**

1915

Kitty The Telephone Girl
  – **James Normouth & Orchestra**
A Little Of What You Fancy – **Marie Lloyd**
Selection Of Vesta Tilley Songs: Jolly Good
  Luck To The Girl Who Loves A Soldier
  / Following In Father's Footsteps / The
  Seaside Sultan – **Vesta Tilley with Ray
  Wallace and His Orchestra**
It's A Lovely War medley: Here We Are
  Again / Sister Susie Sewing Shirts For
  Soldiers / Never Mind / Army Of Today's
  Alright / We Haven't Seen The Kaiser
  – **Debroy Somers Band**

1916

Everybody's Crazy On The Foxtrot
  – **Walter Jeffries**
A Broken Doll – **Al Jolson**
Watching The Trains Come In
  – **Jack Pleasants**
Burlington Bertie From Bow – **Ella Shields**

1917

I Passed By Your Window – **Walter Glynne**
Love Will Find A Way – **Josie Collins**
Take Me Back To Dear Old Blighty
  – **Florrie Forde**
Smiles & Chuckles
  – **The Six Brown Brothers**

1918

First Love, Last Love, Best Love
  – **George Robey & Clara Evelyn**
Good Bye-ee – **Courtland Jeffries**
What Do You Want To Make – **Harry Weldon**
I Want A Girl – **Dorothy Ward**

1919

Omaha – **Mayfair Dance Orchestra**
That Old Fashioned Mother Of Mine
  – **Master Thomas Criddle**
Don't Have Any More Mrs Moore
  – **Lilly Morris**
Tiger Rag – **The Original Dixieland Jazz Band**

1920

I Know Where The Flies Go In Summertime
  – **Waller Williams & Vaudeville Theatre
  Orchestra**
Wyoming Lullaby – **Mayfair Dance Orchestra**
Sailing – **George Formby Snr**
Avalon – **Art Hickman's Orchestra**

1921

Arise O Sun – **Richard Crooks**
Night May Have Its Sadness
  – **Patrick Waddington**
Ours Is A Nice 'Ouse Ours Is – **Alfred Lester**
Canadian Capers – **Paul Biese Trio**

1922

My Word You Do Look Queer
  – **Ernest Hastings**
Toot Toot Tootsie – **Al Jolson**

Sheik Of Araby – **Pianola Roll**
Sally (The Sunshine Of Our Alley)
  – **Fred Barnes Baritone with Orchestra**

1923

Horsey Keep Your Tail Up – **Melville Gideon**
I Belong To Glasgow – **Will Fyffe**
Rose Of The Rio Grande
  – **I V 'Bud' Sheppard**
Dipper Mouth Blues
  – **Louis Armstrong with King Oliver**

1924

The Second Minuet
  – **Annie Zeigler & Webster Booth**
Pasadena – **Bert Firman**
Bobbed Haired Bobby
  – **Arcadian Serenaders**
Fidgety Feet – **Bix Biederbecke**

1925

When Sergeant Major's On Parade
  – **Cyril Norman & Herman Darewski**
Ogo-Pogo – **Savoy Havana Band**
Keep Right On To The End Of The Road
  – **Sir Harry Lauder**
Charleston – **Savoy Orpheans**

1926

Come On Boys Let's Do That Messin'
  Around – **Blind Blake**
Black Bottom
  – **Johnny Hamp's Kentucky Serenaders**
Bird Song At Eventide – **Henry Hall and His
  Gleneagles Hotel Band**
She Knows Her Onions
  – **The Happiness Boys**

1927

Struttin' With Some Bar-B-Q
  – **Louis Armstrong**
Black & Tan Fantasy
  – **Duke Ellington & His Orchestra**
Flapperette
  – **Nat Shilkret & His Victor Orchestra**
Dark Was The Night – Cold Was The
  Ground – **Blind Willie Johnson**

1928

Sweet Sue, Just You – **George Metaxa with
  Carroll Gibbons & His Orchestra**
Fashionette
  – **Harold Collins & His Orchestra**
Just Like A Melody Out Of The Sky
  – **Ukele Ike (aka Cliff Edwards)**
Statesboro' Blues – **Blind Willie McTell**

1929

The Admiral's Broom – **Peter Dawson**
Tip Toe Through The Tulips With Me
  – **Ambrose & His Orchestra**
I Lift Up My Fingers And I Say Tweet Tweet
  – **Stanley Lupino & The Gaiety Theatre
  Orchestra**
New Orleans Shout – **King Oliver**

1930

I'm In The Market For You – **Van Philips**
Putting On The Ritz – **Fred Astaire**
My Baby Just Cares For Me – **Jack Payne**
Bunkey-Doodle-I-Doh – **Leslie Sarony with novelty accompaniment**

1931

Oh Donna – **Clara Layton & Johnstone**
Goodnight Sweetheart – **Al Bowlly with Ray Noble & His Orchestra**
Just A Gigolo – **Bing Crosby**
Experience Blues
   – **Ruth Willis, Blind Willie McTell on guitar**

1932

Goopy Geer – **Pat O'Malley**
Try A Little Tenderness
   – **Unknown with Ray Noble**
The Clouds Will Soon Roll By – **Ambrose & His Orchestra, vocal Elsie Carlisle**
Kunz Solo Medley: Lovely To Look At / Smoke Gets In Your Eyes / Night & Day
   – **Charlie Kunz**

1933

The Wedding Of Mister Mickey Mouse
   – **BBC Dance Orchestra**
Stormy Weather – **Frances Longford**
How Come You Do Me Like You Do – **Spike Hughes and His All American Orchestra**
Jazz Me Blues – **Joe Venuti & His Blue Six**

1934

Hawkin's Rag
   – **Gid Tanner & His Skillet Lickers**
I Only Have Eyes For You
   – **Scott Wood & His Orchestra**
What A Shuffle – **Chick Webb**
Stratosphere
   – **Jimmie Lunceford & His Orchestra**

1935

Fanlight Fanny – **George Formby**
Stop That Thing – **Sleepy John Estes**
We're Frightfully BBC
   – **The Western Brothers**
Chicken & Waffles
   – **Bunny Berigan & His Blue Boys**

1936

Lotta Sax Appeal – **Andy Kirk**
These Foolish Things – **Leslie A Hutchinson**
32 20 Blues – **Robert Johnson**
I've Got You Under My Skin – **Carroll Gibbons**

1937

Steel Guitar Stomp
   – **Bob Wills & His Texas Playboys**
Once In A While – **Frances Langford**
Sing Sing Sing
   – **Benny Goodman & His Orchestra**
Hellhound On My Trail – **Robert Johnson**

1938

Goin' Down In Galilee – **Kokomo Arnold**
I Don't Do Things Like That – **Tommy Trinder**
Twinklin' – **Andy Kirk**
Panassie Stomp – **Count Basie**

1939

Your Feet's Too Big
   – **Fats Waller & His Rhythm**
I Don't Know Cripple – **Clarence Lofton**
Begin The Beguine – **Chick Henderson with Joe Loss & His Band**
King George VI's Christmas Message

1940

The Spitfire Song – **Joe Loss & His Band**
Special Stream Line – **Bukka White**
I'm Nobody's Baby – **Nat Gonella & His New Georgians**
When The Swallows Come Back To Capistrano – **The Ink Spots**

1941

When That Man Is Dead And Gone
   – **Al Bowlly & Jimmy Messene**
V Stands For Victory – **Joe Loss & His Band**
She Belongs To The Devil – **Washboard Sam**
Vine Street Blues – **Jay McShann**

1942

It Had To Be You / Paddlin' Madelin' Home
– **Ukele Ike (aka Cliff Edwards)**
Travellin' Light – **Billie Holiday with Paul Whiteman & His Orchestra**
Jersey Bounce
   – **The Royal Air Force Dance Orchestra**
Chattanooga Choo Choo – **Harry Roy & His Band, vocal Renne Lister**

1943

Pedro The Fisherman – **New Mayfair Dance Orchestra (with vocal refrain)**
You'd Be So Nice To Come Home To
– **Ambrose & His Orchestra, vocal Anne Shelton**
Evil Gal Blues – **Dinah Washington**
Pistol Packin' Mama
   – **Bing Crosby & The Andrews Sisters**

1944

Lula Mae – **Tampa Red**
Skyliner – **Charlie Barnett**
Ac-Cent-Tchu-Ate The Positive
   – **Bing Crosby & The Andrews Sisters**
Till Then – **The Mills Brothers**

1945

Nancy With The Laughing Face
   – **Frank Sinatra**
Chicago Breakdown – **Big Maceo**
Rhythm Is Our Business – **Jimmie Lunceford**
Rifftide – **Coleman Hawkins**

1946

Open The Door Richard
   – **Jack McVea & His Band**
Hamp's Walkin' Boogie
   – **Lionel Hampton & His Orchestra**

Chickery Chick
   – **Carroll Gibbons, vocal Rita Williams**
That's Alright Mama
   – **Arthur 'Big Boy' Crudup**

1947

Jumpin' With Symphony Syd – **Lester Young**
Try A Little Tenderness – **Frank Sinatra**
There I've Said It Again – **Nat King Cole Trio**
Good Rockin' Tonight – **Wynonie Harris**

1948

Twelfth Street Rag
   – **Pee Wee Hunt & His Orchestra**
My Happiness
   – **Ella Fitzgerald & The Songspinners**
So Tired – **Russ Morgan**
Some Women Do – **Eddie 'Cleanhead' Vinson & His Orchestra**

1949

Ghost Riders In The Sky – **Vaughn Monroe**
Candy Kisses
   – **Elton Britt with The Skytoppers**
'A' You're Adorable
   – **Jo Stafford & Gordon Macrae**
Drinkin' Wine Spo-Dee-O-Dee – **Stick McGhee**

1950

The Thing – **Phil Harris**
Silver Dollar – **Eve Young**
Baldhead – **John Byrd & His Blues Jumpers (Professor Longhair)**
Harry Lime Theme – **Anton Karas**

1951

Black & White Rag – **Winifred Atwell**
The Shotgun Boogie – **Tennessee Ernie Ford**
Rosemary – **Fats Domino**
Dust My Broom – **Elmore James**

1952

Delicado – **Percy Faith**
She's Allright – **Muddy Waters**
Wheel Of Fortune – **Kay Starr**
Half As Much – **Rosemary Clooney**

1953

Sleep – **Earl Bostic**
Crying In The Chapel – **The Orioles**
Answer Me (Mütterlein) – **Frankie Laine**
Broken Wings – **Art & Dottie Todd**

1954

Mr Sandman – **The Chordettes**
Boogie Disease – **Dr Ross**
Sh-Boom (Life Could Be A Dream)
   – **The Crew Cuts**
Three Coins In The Fountain – **The Four Aces**

1955

Wild Cat Blues
   – **Chris Barber & His Jazz Band**
Love Is A Many Splendoured Thing
   – **The Four Aces**
Rock-A-Beatin' Boogie – **Bill Hayley**
Baby Let's Play House – **Elvis Presley**

1956
Lost John – **Lonnie Donnegan**
Honky Tonk pt 1 & 2 – **Bill Doggett**
Race With The Devil – **Gene Vincent**
Long Tall Sally – **Little Richard**

1957
An Empty Cup (And A Broken Date)
  – **Buddy Holly & The Crickets**
Searchin' – **The Coasters**
Golden Striker – **Modern Jazz Quartet**
It All Depends – **Jerry Lee Lewis**

1958
Rumble – **Link Wray**
For Your Precious Love – **Jerry Butler**
It's Only Make Believe – **Conway Twitty**
Last Rose Of Summer – **The Symbols**

1959
Peter Gunn – **Duane Eddy**
Poor Jenny – **The Everly Brothers**
I Only Have Eyes For You – **The Flamingos**
Lavender Blue – **Sammy Turner**

1960
No Shoes – **John Lee Hooker**
The Long Walk Home – **Santo & Johnny**
There's A Moon Out Tonight – **The Capris**
At Last – **Etta James**

1961
Daddy's Home – **Shep & The Limelights**
Running Scared – **Roy Orbison**
Let's Go Trippin' – **Dick Dale**
What's Your Name? – **Don & Juan**
You'd Better Move On – **Arthur Alexander**

1962
Return To Sender – **Elvis Presley**
Stubborn Kind of Fellow – **Marvin Gaye**
Hats Off To Larry – **Del Shannon**

1963
Too Much – **Jimmy Reed**
Money – **Bern Elliot & The Fen Men**
I Saw Her Standing There – **The Beatles**
Memphis – **Lonnie Mack**

1964 – PART 1
Carol – **Rolling Stones**
So Much In Love – **The Mighty Avengers**
The One To Cry – **The Escorts**
It's Over – **Roy Orbison**
No Particular Place To Go – **Chuck Berry**

1964 – PART 2
Needle In A Haystack – **The Velvettes**
Remember (Walking In The Sand)
  – **The Shangri-Las**
Louie Louie – **The Kingsmen**
The Rise & Fall Of Flingel Blunt
  – **The Shadows**

1965
It Takes A Lot To Laugh It Takes A Train
  To Cry – **Bob Dylan**
Look Through Any Window – **The Hollies**
Ole Man Trouble – **Otis Redding**
Sail Away Ladies – **John Fahey**

1966
Sisters Of Mercy – **Leonard Cohen**
And Your Bird Can Sing – **The Beatles**
I Can Take You To The Sun
  – **The Misunderstood**
Red House – **The Jimi Hendrix Experience**
Try A Little Tenderness – **Otis Redding**

1967 – PART 1
Pat's Song – **Country Joe & The Fish**
I Am The Walrus – **The Beatles**
I Can See For Miles – **The Who**
She's A Rainbow – **Rolling Stones**

1967 – PART 2
Summertime Blues – **Blue Cheer**
Granny Takes A Trip – **Purple Gang**
Sure 'Nuff 'N Yes I Do – **Captain Beefheart**
The Castle – **Love**
Arnold Layne – **Pink Floyd**
Dark End Of The Street – **James Carr**

1968
Crossroads – **Cream**
Expecting To Fly – **Buffalo Springfield**
Canyons Of Your Mind
  – **The Bonzo Dog Doo-Dah Band**
Salamanda Palaganda – **Tyrannosaurus Rex**

1969
Pachuco Cadaver – **Captain Beefheart**
Popatop – **Andy Capp**
Hung Up Down – **Family**
Almost Liverpool 8 – **Mike Hart**

1970
An Old Raincoat Won't Ever Let You Down
  – **Rod Stewart**
Song To The Siren – **Tim Buckley**
Postcards Of Scarborough
  – **Michael Chapman**
Lowdown Popcorn – **James Brown**

1971
Maggie May – **Rod Stewart**
Hey Girl Don't Bother Me – **The Tams**
Without You – **Nilsson**
Let's Stay Together – **Al Green**

1972
Big Eyed Beans From Venus
  – **Captain Beefheart**
My Friend The Sun – **Family**
O Caroline – **Matching Mole**
Starting All Over Again – **Mel & Tim**

1973
Whisky In The Jar – **Thin Lizzy**
Stuck In The Middle With You
  – **Stealers Wheel**

Duppy Conqueror – **The Wailers**
Jessica – **The Allman Brothers Band**

1974
Down Down – **Status Quo**
It's Better To Have (And Don't Need)
  – **Don Covay**
I Can't Stand The Rain – **Ann Peebles**
I Want To See The Bright Lights Tonight
  – **Richard & Linda Thompson**

1975
Fame – **David Bowie**
Slavery Days – **Burning Spear**
Long Distance Love – **Little Feat**
Loving Arms – **Millie Jackson**

1976
They Shoot Horses Don't They – **Racing Cars**
Here Come Those Tears Again
  – **Jackson Browne**
Croaking Lizard – **The Upsetters**
I Don't Wanna Walk Around With You
  – **The Ramones**

1977
Do Anything You Wanna Do
  – **Eddie & The Hot Rods**
Shoplifting – **The Slits**
Dancing The Night Away – **The Motors**
Stretcher Case – **The Damned**

1978
Shot By Both Sides – **Magazine**
I Can't Stand My Baby – **The Rezillos**
See Them A-Come – **Culture**
Teenage Kicks – **The Undertones**

1979
At Home He's A Tourist – **Gang Of Four**
There Must Be Thousands – **Quads**
Mankind – **Misty In Roots**
You Never Heard Anything Like It
  – **The Freshmen**

1980
Twenty Four Hours – **Joy Division**
Totally Wired – **The Fall**
9–5 – **Sheena Easton**
Bloody – **Golinski Brothers**

1981
Release The Bats – **The Birthday Party**
Ghost Town – **The Specials**
(We Don't Need This) Fascist Groove Thang
  – **Heaven 17**
Dead Popstars – **Altered Images**

1982
Lion Rock – **Culture**
The Message –
  Grandmaster Flash & The Furious 5
Shipbuilding – **Robert Wyatt**
Into The Garden – **Artery**

1983
The Man Whose Head Expanded – **The Fall**
Kicker Conspiracy – **The Fall**
Leave Me Alone – **New Order**
Song To The Siren – **This Mortal Coil**

1984
Reel Around The Fountain – **The Smiths**
Lay Of The Land – **The Fall**
Between The Wars – **Billy Bragg**
Come Back – **The Mighty Wah**

1985
Never Understand – **Jesus & Mary Chain**
Gut Of The Quantifier – **The Fall**
I'm In Pittsburgh & It's Raining – **Vibes**

1986
Capture Rasta – **Culture**
Bournemouth Runner – **The Fall**
Levi Stubbs Tears – **Billy Bragg**
Trumpton Riots – **Half Man Half Biscuit**

1987
I Know You Got Soul – **Eric B & Rakim**
L Dopa – **Big Black**
Sharp As A Needle – **Barmy Army**
Hit The North Pt. 1 – **The Fall**

1988
Cadaveric Incubator Of Endo Parasites
   – **Carcass**
You Made Me Realise – **My Bloody Valentine**
Sweet Young Things Ain't Sweet No More
   – **Mudhoney**
Stakker Humanoid – **Humanoid**

1989
Wave Of Mutilation – **The Pixies**
Vanishing Point – **New Order**
The Leader Is Burning – **Pocket Fisherman**
In The Midnight Hour – **Moloko**

1990
I'm Hardly Ever Wrong – **The Would Be's**
Sliver – **Nirvana**
Summer Babe – **Pavement**
House – **Babes In Toyland**

1991
A Lot Of Wind – **The Fall**
Dress – **P J Harvey**
Lambada – **Wayne Wonder & Cutty Ranks**
Joie De Vivre
   – **Diblo Dibala & Le Groupe Loketo**

1992
Cyberdream – **Dr Devious & His Wisemen**
Tempo – **Anthony Red Rose**
Silver Shorts – **The Wedding Present**
Sugar Kane – **Sonic Youth**

1993
Statue Of Gold – **New Decade**
Stutter – **Elastica**
I Suck – **New Bad Things**
Bitumba – **Shaba Kahamba**

1994
Ping Pong – **Stereolab**
I Want You
   – **Inspiral Carpets feat. Mark E Smith**
Are We Here (industry standard mix)
   – **Orbital**
Arkines Lost – **Canopy & Matrix**

1995
Zion Youth – **Dreadzone**
Sorted For E's & Whizz – **Pulp**
Heads Of Dead Surfers
   – **Long Fin Killie & Mark E Smith**
You Can't – **Safe Deposit**

1996
Nitrus – **Dick Dale**
The State I'm In – **Belle & Sebastian**
Come Out 2 Nite – **Kenickie**
Hold Me Now – **DJ Kaos**

1997
Happy Ending – **Inter**
IPC Subeditors Dictate Our Youth – **Clinic**
Does Your Heart Go Boom – **Helen Love**
Pull The Wires From The Wall (Peel Session
   Version) – **The Delgados**

1998
Radar Intruder – **Derrero**
Du Fahrest Mich Verrückt – **Entity Squad**
Turn A Blind Eye – **Half Man Half Biscuit**
Aquarius – **Boards Of Canada**

1999
Princes & Princesses – **Cay**
It Takes A Lot To Laugh, It Takes A Train To
   Cry (special Peel 60th birthday version)
   – **Yo La Tengo**
Injured Birds – **Monkey Steals The Drum**
Alamoana Fade Away – **Princess Kaiulani**
Not Perfect – **Brian & Tony Gold**

2000
Brutal – **New Order**
Manhattan – **Cinerama**
Music For Morning People – **Kid Koala**
Sure & Simple Time – **Alfie**

■

FESTIVE FIFTY 1976 – 2004

1976

1. **Led Zeppelin** – Stairway to Heaven
2. **Derek & the Dominoes** – Layla
3. **Bob Dylan** – Desolation Row
4. **Pink Floyd** – Echoes
5. **Jimi Hendrix** – All Along the Watchtower
6. **Free** – Alright Now
7. **Racing Cars**
   – They Shoot Horses Don't They?
8. **Pink Floyd**
   – Shine on You Crazy Diamond
9. **Beatles** – A Day in the Life
10. **Bob Dylan** – Like a Rolling Stone
11. **Poco** – Rose of Cimarron
12. **Neil Young** – Cortez the Killer
13. **Rolling Stones** – Brown Sugar
14. **Beatles** – Hey Jude
15. **Legendary Stardust Cowboy** – Paralysed
16. **Jimi Hendrix** – Voodoo Chile
17. **Beatles** – Strawberry Fields Forever
18. **Captain Beefheart**
   – Big Eyed Beans from Venus
19. **Led Zeppelin** – Whole Lotta Love
20. **Lynyrd Skynyrd** – Freebird
21. **Van Morrison** – Madame George
22. **Doors** – Riders on the Storm
23. **Bob Dylan** – Visions of Johanna
24. **Jefferson Airplane** – White Rabbit
25. **Deep Purple** – Child in Time
26. **Little Feat** – Long Distance Love
27. **Grinderswitch** – Pickin' the Blues
28. **Joe Walsh** – Rocky Mountain Way
29. **Who** – Won't Get Fooled Again
30. **Misunderstood**
   – I Can Take You to the Sun
31. **Genesis** – Supper's Ready
32. **Bob Marley and the Wailers**
   – No Woman, No Cry
33. **Jonathan Richman** – Roadrunner
34. **Rod Stewart** – Maggie May
35. **Jackson Browne** – Late for the Sky
36. **Led Zeppelin** – Kashmir
37. **Jimi Hendrix** – Hey Joe
38. **Allman Brothers Band** – Jessica
39. **Rolling Stones** – Jumping Jack Flash
40. **Grateful Dead** – Dark Star
41. **Richard Thompson**
   – I Wanna See the Bright Lights
42. **Family** – The Weaver's Answer
43. **Jackson Browne** – Fountain of Sorrow
44. **Bob Dylan** – Hurricane
45. **Doors** – Light My Fire
46. **Matching Mole** – O Caroline
47. **Roy Harper** – When an Old Cricketer
   Leaves the Crease
48. **Wild Man Fischer** – Go to Rhino Records
49. **Little Feat** – Willin'
50. **Yes** – And You and I

1977

(Peel's personal choice this year)

1. **Motors** – Dancing the Night Away
2. **Althea & Donna** – Uptown Top Ranking

3. **Motors** – You Beat the Hell out of Me
4. **Rezillos** – I Can't Stand My Baby
5. **John Cooper Clarke** – Suspended Sentence
6. **Desperate Bicycles** – Smokescreen
7. **Merlyn Webber** – Right Track
8. **Neil Young** – Like a Hurricane
9. **Clash** – Complete Control
10. **Frankie Miller** – Be Good to Yourself
11. **Sex Pistols** – Holidays in the Sun
12. **Lurkers** – Shadow
13. **J. Ayes and Ranking Trevor** – Truly
14. **Pink Floyd** – Pigs
15. **Johnny Moped** – Incendiary Device
16. **Some Chicken** – New Religion
17. **Culture** – See Them Come
18. **Motors** – Emergency
19. **Yobs** – The Worm Song
20. **Boys** – Box Number
21. **Stranglers** – London Lady
22. **Sham 69** – I Don't Wanna
23. **Ramones** – Pinhead
24. **Jah Woosh** – Freedom Connection
25. **Status Quo** – Can't Give You More
26. **Jeff Beck with Jan Hammer** – Blue Wind
27. **Clash** – White Riot
28. **Iggy Pop** – Success
29. **Generation X** – Your Generation
30. **King Short Shirt** – Nobody Go Run Me
31. **Lurkers** – Love Story
32. **Bob Marley & the Wailers** – Waiting in Vain
33. **Dr Feelgood** – Paradise
34. **Five Hand Reel!** – Cruel Brother
35. **Saints** – I'm Stranded
36. **David Bowie** – "Heroes"
37. **Users** – Sick on You
38. **X Ray Spex** – Oh Bondage up Yours!
39. **The Boomtown Rats** – Lookin' After Number 1
40. **June Tabor** – No Man's Land
41. **Damned** – Neat Neat Neat
42. **Ry Cooder** – The Dark End of the Street
43. **Suburban Studs** – Questions
44. **Elizabeth Archer & the Equators** – Feel Like Making Love
45. **Dave Edmunds** – I Knew the Bride
46. **Jam** – Away from the Numbers
47. **Wreckless Eric** – Whole Wide World
48. **Roy Buchanan** – Green Onions
49. **Generation X** – Wild Dub
50. **Snatch** – I.R.T.
51. **Sex Pistols** – Pretty Vacant
52. **Oldham Tinkers** – John Willie's Ferret
53. **Peter Tosh** – Stepping Razor
54. **Clash** – Capital Radio
55. **Elvis Costello and the Attractions** – Watching the Detectives
56. **Motors** – Bringing in the Morning Light
57. **Eddie & the Hot Rods** – Beginning of the End
58. **Devo** – Jocko Homo
59. **Buzzcocks** – Whatever Happened To
60. **Little Feat** – Rocket in My Pocket

... & 61. **Sex Pistols** – God Save the Queen

1978

1. **Sex Pistols** – Anarchy in the UK
2. **Clash** – Complete Control
3. **Sex Pistols** – God Save the Queen
4. **Stiff Little Fingers** – Suspect Device
5. **Magazine** – Shot by Both Sides
6. **Sex Pistols** – Pretty Vacant
7. **Clash** – (White Man) In Hammersmith Palais
8. **Buzzcocks** – What Do I Get?
9. **Public Image Ltd.** – Public Image
10. **Undertones** – Teenage Kicks
11. **Stiff Little Fingers** – Alternative Ulster
12. **Buzzcocks** – Boredom
13. **Damned** – New Rose
14. **Led Zeppelin** – Stairway to Heaven
15. **Clash** – White Riot
16. **David Bowie** – "Heroes"
17. **Only Ones** – Another Girl, Another Planet
18. **Sex Pistols** – Holidays in the Sun
19. **Lynyrd Skynyrd** – Freebird
20. **Rezillos** – I Can't Stand My Baby
21. **Van Morrison** – Madame George
22. **Siouxsie & the Banshees** – Hong Kong Garden
23. **Clash** – Police & Thieves
24. **Jam** – Down in the Tube Station at Midnight
25. **Elvis Costello** – Watching the Detectives
26. **Bruce Springsteen** – Born to Run
27. **Ian Dury & the Blockheads** – Sex & Drugs & Rock & Roll
28. **Dire Straits** – Sultans of Swing
29. **Pink Floyd** – Shine on You Crazy Diamond
30. **Buzzcocks** – Moving Away from the Pulsebeat
31. **Derek & the Dominoes** – Layla
32. **Stranglers** – Hanging Around
33. **Stranglers** – No More Heroes
34. **Siouxsie & the Banshees** – Helter Skelter
35. **Motors** – Dancing the Night Away
36. **Bob Dylan** – Like a Rolling Stone
37. **Elvis Costello** – Alison
38. **Siouxsie & the Banshees** – Overground
39. **Who** – My Generation
40. **Stranglers** – London Lady
41. **Siouxsie & the Banshees** – Switch
42. **Siouxsie & the Banshees** – Mirage
43. **Siouxsie & the Banshees** – Jigsaw Feeling
44. **Jam** – In the City
45. **Sex Pistols** – EMI
46. **Bob Dylan** – Desolation Row
47. **Flying Lizards** – Summertime Blues
48. **Neil Young** – Like a Hurricane
49. **Thin Lizzy** – Emerald
50. **Siouxsie & the Banshees** – Metal Postcard

1979

1. **Sex Pistols** – Anarchy in the UK
2. **Undertones** – Teenage Kicks
3. **Clash** – (White Man) In Hammersmith Palais
4. **Jam** – Down in the Tube Station at Midnight
5. **Clash** – Complete Control
6. **Stiff Little Fingers** – Alternative Ulster
7. **Special AKA** – Gangsters
8. **Stiff Little Fingers** – Suspect Device

9. **Public Image Ltd.** – Public Image
10. **Damned** – New Rose
11. **Ruts** – In a Rut
12. **Undertones** – Get Over You
13. **Sex Pistols** – God Save the Queen
14. **Sex Pistols** – Holidays in the Sun
15. **Stiff Little Fingers** – Johnny Was
16. **Sex Pistols** – Pretty Vacant
17. **Magazine** – Shot by Both Sides
18. **Stiff Little Fingers** – Wasted Life
19. **Jam** – Eton Rifles
20. **Only Ones** – Another Girl, Another Planet
21. **Siouxsie & the Banshees** – Love in a Void
22. **Damned** – Love Song
23. **Gang of Four** – Damaged Goods
24. **Led Zeppelin** – Stairway to Heaven
25. **Buzzcocks** – Boredom
26. **Clash** – White Riot
27. **Jam** – Strange Town
28. **Public Image Ltd.** – Death Disco
29. **Undertones** – You've Got My Number
30. **Pink Floyd** – Shine on You Crazy Diamond
31. **Undertones** – Jimmy Jimmy
32. **Who** – My Generation
33. **Dead Kennedys** – California Uber Alles
34. **David Bowie** – "Heroes"
35. **Siouxsie & the Banshees** – Icon
36. **Specials** – Too Much Too Young
37. **Skids** – Into the Valley
38. **Siouxsie & the Banshees** – Switch
39. **Tubeway Army** – Are Friends Electric?
40. **Fall** – Rowche Rumble
41. **Mekons** – Where Were You
42. **Siouxsie & the Banshees** – Jigsaw Feeling
43. **Cure** – 10:15 Saturday Night
44. **Siouxsie & the Banshees** – Playground Twist
45. **Stranglers** – No More Heroes
46. **Siouxsie & the Banshees** – Helter Skelter
47. **Ruts** – Babylon's Burning
48. **Siouxsie & the Banshees** – Hong Kong Garden
49. **Clash** – Police & Thieves
50. **Buzzcocks** – What Do I Get?

1980

1. **Sex Pistols** – Anarchy in the UK
2. **Joy Division** – Atmosphere
3. **Joy Division** – Love Will Tear Us Apart
4. **Jam** – Down in the Tube Station at Midnight
5. **Clash** – (White Man) In Hammersmith Palais
6. **Dead Kennedys** – Holiday in Cambodia
7. **Undertones** – Teenage Kicks
8. **Damned** – New Rose
9. **Stiff Little Fingers** – Alternative Ulster
10. **Joy Division** – Transmission
11. **Public Image Ltd.** – Public Image
12. **Sex Pistols** – Holidays in the Sun
13. **Jam** – Going Underground
14. **Joy Division** – Decades
15. **Clash** – Complete Control
16. **Stiff Little Fingers** – Johnny Was
17. **Undertones** – Get Over You
18. **Cure** – A Forest
19. **Ruts** – In a Rut
20. **Joy Division** – New Dawn Fades
21. **Fall** – Totally Wired
22. **Joy Division** – She's Lost Control

23. **Sex Pistols** – Pretty Vacant
24. **Stiff Little Fingers** – Suspect Device
25. **Sex Pistols** – God Save the Queen
26. **Fall** – How I Wrote 'Elastic Man'
27. **Stiff Little Fingers** – Wasted Life
28. **Only Ones** – Another Girl, Another Planet
29. **Damned** – Love Song
30. **Adam and the Ants** – Kings of the Wild Frontier
31. **Dead Kennedys** – California Über Alles
32. **Special AKA** – Gangsters
33. **Public Image Ltd.** – Poptones
34. **Public Image Ltd.** – Careering
35. **Killing Joke** – Requiem
36. **Killing Joke** – Psyche
37. **Siouxsie & the Banshees** – Jigsaw Feeling
38. **Fall** – Fiery Jack
39. **Clash** – Armagideon Time
40. **Spizz Energi** – Where's Captain Kirk
41. **Joy Division** – Twenty-Four Hours
42. **Damned** – Smash It up
43. **Teardrop Explodes** – Treason
44. **Siouxsie & the Banshees** – Switch
45. **Siouxsie & the Banshees** – Icon
46. **Clash** – Bankrobber
47. **Siouxsie & the Banshees** – Hong Kong Garden
48. **Clash** – White Riot
49. **Fall** – Rowche Rumble
50. **Gang of Four** – Damaged Goods

1981

1. **Joy Division** – Atmosphere
2. **Sex Pistols** – Anarchy in the UK
3. **Joy Division** – Love Will Tear Us Apart
4. **New Order** – Ceremony
5. **Joy Division** – New Dawn Fades
6. **Undertones** – Teenage Kicks
7. **Joy Division** – Decades
8. **Cure** – A Forest
9. **Dead Kennedys** – Holiday in Cambodia
10. **Clash** – (White Man) In Hammersmith Palais
11. **Joy Division** – Dead Souls
12. **Damned** – New Rose
13. **Jam** – Down in the Tube Station at Midnight
14. **Joy Division** – Transmission
15. **Altered Images** – Dead Pop Stars
16. **Stiff Little Fingers** – Alternative Ulster
17. **Sex Pistols** – Holidays in the Sun
18. **Clash** – Complete Control
19. **Birthday Party** – Release the Bats
20. **Undertones** – Get Over You
21. **Specials** – Ghost Town
22. **Scritti Politti** – The 'Sweetest' Girl
23. **Jam** – Going Underground
24. **Stiff Little Fingers** – Johnny Was
25. **Theatre of Hate** – Legion
26. **Public Image Ltd.** – Public Image
27. **Killing Joke** – Requiem
28. **Killing Joke** – Follow the Leaders
29. **Heaven 17** – No Fascist Groove Thang
30. **Fall** – Fiery Jack
31. **Ruts** – In a Rut
32. **Stiff Little Fingers** – Suspect Device
33. **Fall** – How I Wrote 'Elastic Man'
34. **Laurie Anderson** – O Superman
35. **Siouxsie & the Banshees** – Jigsaw Feeling
36. **B-Movie** – Remembrance Day

37. **Siouxsie & the Banshees** – Israel
38. **Sex Pistols** – God Save the Queen
39. **Pigbag** – Papa's Got a Brand-New Pigbag
40. **Siouxsie & the Banshees** – Icon
41. **Only Ones** – Another Girl, Another Planet
42. **Dead Kennedys** – California Uber Alles
43. **Joy Division** – Twenty-Four Hours
44. **Joy Division** – Isolation
45. **Killing Joke** – Psyche
46. **Echo and the Bunnymen** – Over the Wall
47. **Fall** – Lie Dream of a Casino Soul
48. **New Order** – Procession
49. **Siouxsie & the Banshees** – Switch
50. **Altered Images** – Happy Birthday

1982

(All-time)

1. **Sex Pistols** – Anarchy in the UK
2. **Joy Division** – Atmosphere
3. **Joy Division** – Love Will Tear Us Apart
4. **Joy Division** – New Dawn Fades
5. **Cure** – A Forest
6. **New Order** – Ceremony
7. **Joy Division** – Decades
8. **Undertones** – Teenage Kicks
9. **Bauhaus** – Bela Lugosi's Dead
10. **Clash** – (White Man) In Hammersmith Palais
11. **Jam** – Down in the Tube Station at Midnight
12. **Joy Division** – Dead Souls
13. **Damned** – New Rose
14. **Dead Kennedys** – Holiday in Cambodia
15. **Siouxsie & the Banshees** – Israel
16. **Stiff Little Fingers** – Alternative Ulster
17. **Jam** – Going Underground
18. **New Order** – Temptation
19. **Clash** – Complete Control
20. **Public Image Ltd.** – Public Image
21. **Altered Images** – Dead Pop Stars
22. **Echo and the Bunnymen** – Over the Wall
23. **Joy Division** – Twenty-Four Hours
24. **Only Ones** – Another Girl, Another Planet
25. **Sex Pistols** – God Save the Queen
26. **Joy Division** – Transmission
27. **Scritti Politti** – The 'Sweetest' Girl
28. **Birthday Party** – Release the Bats
29. **Stiff Little Fingers** – Johnny Was
30. **New Order** – Procession
31. **Stiff Little Fingers** – Suspect Device
32. **Killing Joke** – Requiem
33. **Theatre of Hate** – Legion
34. **Killing Joke** – Psyche
35. **Ruts** – In a Rut
36. **Undertones** – Get Over You
37. **Sex Pistols** – Holidays in the Sun
38. **Joy Division** – Isolation
39. **Siouxsie & the Banshees** – Jigsaw Feeling
40. **Clash** – Armagideon Time
41. **Joy Division** – She's Lost Control
42. **Siouxsie & the Banshees** – Switch
43. **Specials** – Ghost Town
44. **Sex Pistols** – Pretty Vacant
45. **Siouxsie & the Banshees** – Icon
46. **Siouxsie & the Banshees** – Hong Kong Garden
47. **Magazine** – Shot by Both Sides
48. **Joy Division** – The Eternal
49. **Laurie Anderson** – O Superman
50. **Damned** – Love Song

(1982 only)

1. **New Order** – Temptation
2. **Robert Wyatt** – Shipbuilding
3. **Grandmaster Flash and the Furious 5** – The Message
4. **Echo and the Bunnymen** – The Back of Love
5. **Tears for Fears** – Mad World
6. **Clash** – Straight to Hell
7. **Wah!** – The Story of the Blues
8. **Theatre of Hate** – Do You Believe in the West World
9. **Artery** – Into the Garden
10. **Wild Swans** – Revolutionary Spirit
11. **Jam** – Town Called Malice
12. **Yazoo** – Only You
13. **Scritti Politti** – Faithless
14. **Associates** – Party Fears Two
15. **Bauhaus** – Ziggy Stardust
16. **Siouxsie & the Banshees** – Fireworks
17. **New Order** – Hurt
18. **Scritti Politti** – Asylums in Jerusalem
19. **Dexys Midnight Runners** – Come on Eileen
20. **Killing Joke** – Empire Song
21. **Farmers Boys** – Whatever Is He Like?
22. **China Crisis** – African and White
23. **Siouxsie & the Banshees** – Slow Dive
24. **Aztec Camera** – Pillar to Post
25. **Cure** – The Hanging Garden
26. **Clash** – Should I Stay Or Should I Go?
27. **Clash** – Know Your Rights
28. **Cure** – The Figurehead
29. **Psychedelic Furs** – Love My Way
30. **Simple Minds** – Promised You a Miracle
31. **Redskins** – Peasant Army
32. **Simple Minds** – Someone Somewhere (In Summertime)
33. **Cure** – A Strange Day
34. **Blancmange** – Living on the Ceiling
35. **Blancmange** – Feel Me
36. **Musical Youth** – Pass the Dutchie
37. **Cocteau Twins** – Wax and Wane
38. **Serious Drinking** – Love on the Terraces
39. **Jam** – The Bitterest Pill (I Ever Had to Swallow)
40. **Clash** – Rock the Casbah
41. **Passage** – XOYO
42. **Chameleons** – In Shreds
43. **Weekend** – A View from Her Room
44. **Shambeko! Say Wah!** – Remember
45. **Simple Minds** – Glittering Prize
46. **Bauhaus** – Third Uncle
47. **Higsons** – Conspiracy
48. **Action Pact** – Suicide Bag
49. **Siouxsie & the Banshees** – Melt
50. **Farmers Boys** – I Think I Need Help

1983

1. **New Order** – Blue Monday
2. **Smiths** – This Charming Man
3. **New Order** – Age of Consent
4. **This Mortal Coil** – Song to the Siren
5. **Cocteau Twins** – Musette and Drums
6. **Smiths** – Reel Around the Fountain
7. **Billy Bragg** – A New England
8. **Fall** – Eat Y'self Fitter
9. **Smiths** – Hand in Glove
10. **Naturalites and the Mystics** – Picture on the Wall

11. **Red Guitars** – Good Technology
12. **P.I.L** – This Is Not a LoveSong
13. **X–Mal Deutchland** – Incubus Succubus
14. **Cocteau Twins** – Sugar Hiccup
15. **Cure** – Lovecats
16. **Cocteau Twins** – From the Flagstones
17. **Echo and the Bunnymen** – Never Stop
18. **New Order** – Your Silent Face
19. **Sisters of Mercy** – Temple of Love
20. **Siouxsie & the Banshees** – Dear Prudence
21. **Fall** – The Man Whose Head Expanded
22. **Echo and the Bunnymen** – The Cutter
23. **Assembly** – Never Never
24. **Imposter** – Pills and Soap
25. **New Order** – Leave Me Alone
26. **10,000 Maniacs** – My Mother the War
27. **Sisters of Mercy** – Alice
28. **Cocteau Twins** – Peppermint Pig
29. **Aztec Camera** – Oblivious
30. **Redskins** – Lean on Me
31. **Chameleons** – Second Skin
32. **X-Mal Deutchland** – Qual
33. **Smiths** – Handsome Devil
34. **Tools You Can Trust**
    – Working and Shopping
35. **Fall** – Kicker Conspiracy
36. **Luddites** – Doppleganger
37. **Sophie and Peter Johnson** – Television
38. **Cocteau Twins** – Hithertoo
39. **S.P.K** – Metal Dance
40. **Fall** – Wings
41. **U2** – New Year's Day
42. **Danse Society** – Somewhere
43. **Birthday Party** – Deep in the Woods
44. **Cabaret Voltaire** – Fascination
45. **New Order** – The Village
46. **Birthday Party** – Sonny's Burning
47. **Strawberry Switchblade**
    – Trees and Flowers
48. **Elvis Costello** – Shipbuilding
49. **Cure** – The Walk
50. **Tom Robinson** – War Baby

1984

1. **Smiths** – How Soon Is Now
2. **Cocteau Twins** – Pearly Dewdrops Drop
3. **Men They Couldn't Hang**
   – Green Fields of France
4. **Cocteau Twins** – Spangle Maker
5. **Mighty Wah** – Come Back
6. **Membranes** – Spike Milligan's
   Tape Recorder
7. **New Order** – Thieves Like Us
8. **Sisters of Mercy** – Walk Away
9. **Fall** – Lay of the Land
10. **Redskins** – Keep on Keepin' on
11. **Nick Cave and the Bad Seeds** – St. Huck
12. **New Order** – Lonesome Tonight
13. **Billy Bragg** – Between the Wars
14. **Smiths** – Nowhere Fast
15. **Sisters of Mercy** – Emma
16. **Cocteau Twins** – Ivo
17. **Smiths** – What Difference Does It Make?
18. **Fall** – Creep
19. **Echo and the Bunnymen** – The Killing Moon
20. **New Order** – Murder
21. **This Mortal Coil** – Kangaroo
22. **Cocteau Twins** – Domino

23. **Smiths** – William It Was Really Nothing
24. **Smiths** – Heaven Knows I'm Miserable Now
25. **Frankie Goes to Hollywood** – Two Tribes
26. **Unknown Cases** – Ma Simba Bele
27. **Very Things** – The Bushes Scream
    While My Daddy Prunes
28. **Smiths** – Please, Please, Please,
    Let Me Get What I Want
29. **Billy Bragg** – The Saturday Boy
30. **Cult** – Spiritwalker
31. **Propoganda** – Dr Mabuse
32. **Yeah Yeah No** – Bias Binding
33. **This Mortal Coil** – Another Day
34. **Berntholer** – My Suiter
35. **Robert Wyatt** – Biko
36. **Smiths** – Reel Around the Fountain
37. **Jesus and Mary Chain** – Upside Down
38. **Cocteau Twins** – Pandora
39. **Flesh for Lulu** – Subteraneans
40. **Cocteau Twins** – Beatrix
41. **Special AKA** – Nelson Mandela
42. **Frank Chickens** – Blue Canary
43. **New Model Army** – Vengeance
44. **Fall** – No Bulbs
45. **Pogues** – Dark Streets of London
46. **Hard Corps** – Dirty
47. **Echo and the Bunnymen** – Thorn of Crowns
48. **Bronski Beat** – Small Town Boy
49. **Cocteau Twins** – Pepper Tree
50. **Working Week** – Venceremos

1985

1. **Jesus and Mary Chain** – Never Understand
2. **Jesus and Mary Chain** – Just Like Honey
3. **Fall** – Cruiser's Creek
4. **Cult** – She Sells Sanctuary
5. **Cocteau Twins** – Aikea-Guinea
6. **Chumbawamba** – Revolution
7. **Felt** – Primitive Painters
8. **Smiths** – The Boy with the Thorn in His Side
9. **New Order** – Perfect Kiss
10. **Housemartins** – Flag Day
11. **Men They Couldn't Hang** – Ironmasters
12. **Jesus and Mary Chain** – You Trip Me up
13. **Pogues** – Sally Maclennan
14. **Three Johns** – Death of the European
15. **Wedding Present** – Go out and
    Get 'Em Boy!
16. **New Order** – Love Vigilantes
17. **Shop Assistants** – All That Ever Mattered
18. **New Order** – Sub-Culture
19. **Woodentops** – Move Me
20. **Pogues** – A Pair of Brown Eyes
21. **Echo and the Bunnymen**
    – Bring on the Dancing Horses
22. **That Petrol Emotion** – V2
23. **Fall** – Spoilt Victorian Child
24. **New Order** – Sunrise
25. **Pogues** – I'm a Man You Don't Meet Every
    Day
26. **Rose of Avalanche** – LA Rain
27. **Cure** – InBetween Days
28. **James** – Hymn from a Village
29. **Smiths** – The Headmaster Ritual
30. **Age of Chance** – Motor City
31. **Smiths** – That Joke Isn't Funny Anymore
32. **Smiths** – Meat Is Murder
33. **Fall** – Gut of the Quantifier

34. **Beloved** – 100 Words
35. **Nick Cave and the Bad Seeds** – Tupelo
36. **Sisters of Mercy** – Marian
37. **Vibes** – I'm in Pittsburg and It's Raining
38. **Prefab Sprout** – Faron Young
39. **Fall** – Couldn't Get Ahead
40. **Billy Bragg** – Between the Wars
41. **Smiths** – Well I Wonder
42. **Fall** – LA
43. **Sisters of Mercy** – Some Kind of Stranger
44. **Primal Scream** – It Happens
45. **New Order** – Face up
46. **Hüsker Dü** – Makes No Sense at All
47. **Robert Wyatt** – The Wind of Change
48. **Woodentops** – Well Well Well
49. **One Thousand Violins** –
    Like One Thousand Violins
50. **Shop Assistants** – All Day Long

1986

1. **Smiths** – There Is a Light
   That Never Goes out
2. **Age of Chance** – Kiss
3. **Fall** – Mr Pharmacist
4. **Primal Scream** – Velocity Girl
5. **Smiths** – Panic
6. **Smiths** – I Know It's Over
7. **Smiths** – The Queen Is Dead
8. **Shop Assistants** – Safety Net
9. **Jesus and Mary Chain** –
   Some Candy Talking
10. **Fall** – US 80s 90s
11. **Smiths** – Ask
12. **Smiths** – Bigmouth Strikes Again
13. **Weather Prophets** – Almost Prayed
14. **Half Man Half Biscuit** – Trumpton Riots
15. **Fall** – Living Too Late
16. **Wedding Present** – Once More
17. **Soup Dragons** – Hang Ten!
18. **Wedding Present** – This Boy Can Wait
19. **Bodines** – Therese
20. **Fall** – Bournemouth Runner
21. **Cocteau Twins** – Love's Easy Tears
22. **Primitives** – Really Stupid
23. **Pastels** – Truck Train Tractor
24. **Billy Bragg** – Levi Stubbs' Tears
25. **Soup Dragons** – Whole Wide World
26. **Fall** – Realm of Dusk
27. **Age of Chance** – Bible of the Beats
28. **Wedding Present** – You Should Always
    Keep in Touch with Your Friends
29. **That Petrol Emotion** – It's a Good Thing
30. **Very Things** – This is Motortown
31. **We've Got a Fuzzbox** –
    Rules and Regulations
32. **The The** – Heartland
33. **Freiwillige Selbstokontrolle** –
    I Wish I Could Sprechen Sie Deutsch
34. **Mighty Lemon Drops** – Like An Angel
35. **Smiths** – Cemetery Gates
36. **Wedding Present** – Felicity
37. **Fall** – Lucifer Over Lancashire
38. **Cocteau Twins** – Those Eyes, That Mouth
39. **Half Man Half Biscuit** – Dickie Davies Eyes
40. **Elvis Costello** – I Want You
41. **Billy Bragg** – Greetings to the New Brunette
42. **Flatmates** – I Could Be in Heaven
43. **Shop Assistants** – I Don't Want to Be

Friends with You
44. **Mighty Mighty** – Is There Anyone out There?
45. **Nick Cave and the Bad Seeds**
 – By the Time I Get to Phoenix
46. **Colourbox** – The Official Colourbox
 World Cup Theme
47. **Camper van Beethoven**
 – Take the Skinheads Bowling
48. **Fall** – Dr Faustus
49. **Mission** – Serpent's Kiss
50. **Pogues** – The Body of an American

1987

1. **Sugarcubes** – Birthday
2. **Fall** – Australians in Europe
3. **Wedding Present** – Everyone Thinks
 He Looks Daft
4. **That Petrol Emotion** – Big Decision
5. **Smiths** – Last Night I Dreamt
 Somebody Loved Me
6. **Wedding Present** – My Favourite Dress
7. **New Order** – True Faith
8. **Wedding Present** – A Million Miles
9. **Fall** – Hit the North
10. **Wedding Present** – Anyone Can
 Make a Mistake
11. **I, Ludicrous** – Preposterous Tales
12. **Smiths** – Stop Me If You Think
 You've Heard This One Before
13. **Sonic Youth** – Schizophrenia
14. **Public Enemy** – Rebel Without a Pause
15. **Smiths** – Girlfriend in a Coma
16. **Jesus and Mary Chain** – April Skies
17. **Barmy Army** – Sharp as a Needle
18. **Big Black** – Colombian Necktie
19. **Primitives** – Stop Killing Me
20. **Cud** – You Sexy Thing
21. **Smiths** – Paint a Vulgar Picture
22. **Motorcycle Boy** – Big Rock Candy Mountain
23. **Smiths** – Sweet and Tender Hooligan
24. **Smiths** – Half a Person
25. **Smiths** – Death of a Disco Dancer
26. **Fall** – Athlete Cured
27. **Eric B & Rakim** – Paid in Full
28. **Railway Children** – Brighter
29. **Smiths** – I Won't Share You
30. **Bhundu Boys** – My Foolish Heart
31. **Wedding Present** – Getting Nowhere Fast
32. **Prince** – Sign o' the Times
33. **James Taylor Quartet** – Blow up
34. **Smiths** – Sheila Take a Bow
35. **McCarthy** – Frans Hals
36. **Eric B & Rakim** – I Know You Got Soul
37. **Sonic Youth** – (I Got a) Catholic Block
38. **Public Enemy** – You're Gonna Get Yours
39. **Jesus and Mary Chain** – Kill Surf City
40. **Smiths** – I Started Something
 I Couldn't Finish
41. **Jesus and Mary Chain**
 – Nine Million Rainy Days
42. **Big Black** – L Dopa
43. **New Order** – 1963
44. **Butthole Surfers** – 22 Going on 23
45. **Smiths** – Shoplifters of the World Unite
46. **M/A/R/R/S** – Pump up the Volume
47. **Colorblind James Experience**
 – Considering a Move to Memphis
48. **Gun Club** – The Breaking Hands

49. **Beatmaster/Cookie Crew** – Rok Da House
50. **Talulah Gosh** – Talulah Gosh

1988

1. **House of Love** – Destroy the Heart
2. **Wedding Present** – Nobody's Twisting
 Your Arm
3. **Jesus and Mary Chain** – Sidewalking
4. **Wedding Present** – Take Me (I'm Yours)
5. **Dinosaur Jr** – Freak Scene
6. **My Bloody Valentine** – You Made Me Realise
7. **Pixies** – Gigantic
8. **Wedding Present** – Why Are You Being So
 Reasonable Now?
9. **House of Love** – Christine
10. **Nick Cave and the Bad Seeds**
 – The Mercy Seat
11. **Inspiral Carpets** – Keep the Circle Around
12. **Morrissey** – Everyday Is Like Sunday
13. **Morrissey** – Suedehead
14. **Fall** – Cab It up
15. **Wedding Present**
 – I'm Not Always So Stupid
16. **Fall** – Bremen Nacht
17. **My Bloody Valentine**
 – Feed Me with Your Kiss
18. **House of Love** – Love in a Car
19. **Sonic Youth** – Teenage Riot
20. **Sugarcubes** – Deus
21. **Robert Floyd & the New Four Seasons**
 – Something Nice
22. **Morrissey** – Late Night Maudlin Street
23. **Morrissey** – Disappointed
24. **Fall** – Big New Prinz
25. **Billy Bragg** – Waiting For
 The Great Leap Forwards
26. **Cocteau Twins** – Carolyn's Fingers
27. **Fall** – Kurious Oranj
28. **Overlord X** – 14 Days in May
29. **Sonic Youth** – Silver Rocket
30. **Pixies** – Where Is My Mind
31. **Mudhoney** – Sweet Young Thing
 Ain't Sweet No More
32. **Spit** – Road Pizza
33. **James** – What for
34. **Pooh Sticks** – On Tape
35. **Stump** – Charlton Heston
36. **Fall** – Jerusalem
37. **Shalawambe** – Samora Machel
38. **McCarthy** – Should the Bible Be Banned
39. **Pixies** – River Euphrates
40. **Fall** – Guest Informant
41. **Loop** – Collision
42. **Flatmates** – Shimmer
43. **Mega City 4** – Miles Apart
44. **New Order** – Fine Time
45. **Pixies** – Bone Machine
46. **Primitives** – Crash
47. **Darling Buds** – Shame on You
48. **Happy Mondays** – Wrote for Luck
49. **Wedding Present** – Don't Laugh
50. **Public Enemy** – Night of The
 Living Baseheads

1989

1. **Sundays** – Can't Be Sure
2. **Wedding Present** – Kennedy

3. **Pixies** – Debaser
4. **Happy Mondays** – WFL
5. **Pixies** – Monkey Gone to Heaven
6. **Stone Roses** – I Am the Resurrection
7. **Stone Roses** – She Bangs the Drums
8. **James** – Sit Down
9. **Inspiral Carpets** – Joe
10. **House of Love**
 – I Don't Know Why I Love You
11. **Pale Saints** – Sight of you
12. **Dinosaur Jr** – Just Like Heaven
13. **Jesus and Mary Chain** – Blues from a Gun
14. **Wedding Present** – Take Me
15. **Cud** – Only a Prawn in Whitby
16. **Mudhoney** – You Got It
 (Keep It Outta My Face)
17. **Stone Roses** – Made of Stone
18. **Morrissey** – Last of the Famous
 International Playboys
19. **Wedding Present** – Brassneck
20. **Morrissey** – Ouija Board, Ouija Board
21. **Inspiral Carpets** – Find out Why
22. **808 State** – Pacific State
23. **Stone Roses** – Fools Gold
24. **Wedding Present** – Bewitched
25. **Pale Saints** – She Rides the Waves
26. **Field Mice** – Sensitive
27. **New Order** – Vanishing Point
28. **Birdland** – Hollow Heart
29. **Stone Roses** – I Wanna Be Adored
30. **Telescopes** – Perfect Needle
31. **Bob** – Convenience
32. **Jesus Jones** – Info Freako
33. **Spacemen 3** – Hypnotised
34. **De la Soul** – Eye Know
35. **Inspiral Carpets** – So This Is How It Feels
 (Peel Session)
36. **Pixies** – Wave of Mutilation
37. **Pixies** – Here Comes Your Man
38. **Fall** – Dead Beat Descendant
39. **DubSex** – Swerve
40. **Birdland** – Paradise
41. **Galaxie 500** – Don't Let Our
 Youth Go to Waste
42. **Senseless Things** – Too Much Kissing
43. **Pixies** – Dead
44. **Snuff** – Not Listening
45. **Wedding Present** – What Have I Said Now?
46. **Popguns** – Landslide
47. **Morrissey** – Interesting Drug
48. **Family Cat** – Tom Verlaine
49. **Inspiral Carpets** – Directing Traffik
50. **Inspiral Carpets** – She Comes in the Fall

1990

1. **Fall** – Bill Is Dead
2. **My Bloody Valentine** – Soon
3. **Ride** – Dreams Burn Down
4. **Ride** – Like a Daydream
5. **Sonic Youth** – Tunic (Song for Karen)
6. **Paris Angels** – (All on You) Perfume
7. **Wedding Present** – Make Me Smile
 (Come up and See Me)
8. **Happy Mondays** – Step on
9. **Wedding Present** – Corduroy
10. **Orb** – Loving You (Peel Session)
11. **Teenage Fanclub** – Everything Flows
12. **Would Be's** – I'm Hardly Ever Wrong

13. **Lemonheads** – Different Drum
14. **New Fast Automatic Daffodils** – Big
15. **Fall** – White Lightning
16. **Morrissey** – November Spawned a Monster
17. **Charlatans** – The Only One I Know
18. **Wedding Present** – Don't Talk, Just Kiss
19. **Nick Cave** – The Ship Song
20. **Wedding Present** – Heather (session)
21. **Boo Radleys** – Kaleidoscope
22. **Wedding Present** – Crawl
23. **Nirvana** – Sliver
24. **Pixies** – The Happening
25. **Ride** – Taste
26. **Ned's Atomic Dustbin** – Kill Your Television
27. **Lush** – Sweetness and Light
28. **Charlatans** – Polar Bear
29. **Dinosaur Jr** – The Wagon
30. **Fall** – Blood Outta Stone
31. **Pixies** – Velouria
32. **Happy Mondays** – Kinky Afro
33. **Fatima Mansions** – Blues for Ceaucescu
34. **Shamen** – Pro-Gen
35. **Fall** – Telephone Thing
36. **Sundays** – Here's Where the Story Ends
37. **Spiritualized** – Any Way That You Want Me
38. **Babes in Toyland** – House
39. **Wedding Present** – Dalliance
40. **Sonic Youth** – Kool Thing
41. **Fall** – Chicago, Now!
42. **Orb** – Little Fluffy Clouds
43. **Teenage Fanclub** – God Knows It's True
44. **Deee-Lite** – Groove is in the Heart
45. **Bastro** – Nothing Special
46. **Farm** – Stepping Stone
47. **Farm** – Groovy Train
48. **Pixies** – Allison
49. **Pixies** – Dig for Fire
50. **Inspiral Carpets** – Beast Inside

1991

(The Phantom 50, not broadcast until 1993)
1. **Nirvana** – Smells Like Teen Spirit
2. **PJ Harvey** – Dress
3. **Curve** – Ten Little Girls
4. **Fall** – Edinburgh Man
5. **Teenage Fanclub** – Star Sign
6. **Teenage Fanclub** – The Concept
7. **Hole** – Burn Black
8. **Wedding Present** – Dalliance
9. **Fall** – A Lot of Wind
10. **Hole** – Teenage Whore
11. **Primal Scream** – Higher Than the Sun
12. **Wedding Present** – Dare
13. **Gallon Drunk** – Some Fool's Mess
14. **Wedding Present** – Fleshworld
15. **Catherine Wheel** – Black Metallic
16. **Nirvana** – Drain You
17. **Moose** – Suzanne
18. **Babes in Toyland** – Handsome and Gretel
19. **Boo Radleys** – Finest Kiss
20. **Slowdive** – Catch the Breeze
21. **Foreheads in a Fishtank** – Happy Shopper
22. **Wedding Present** – Rotterdam
23. **Slint** – Good Morning, Captain
24. **Fall** – High Tension Line
25. **Nirvana** – Lithium
26. **Pixies** – Planet of Sound
27. **Smashing Pumpkins** – Siva

28. **70 Gwen Party** – Auto Killer UK
29. **Billy Bragg** – Sexuality
30. **Babes in Toyland** – Catatonic
31. **Babes in Toyland** – Laugh My Head Off
32. **Wedding Present** – Octopussy
33. **Chapterhouse** – Pearl
34. **Pavement** – Summer Babe
35. **Fall** – The War Against Intelligence
36. **Teenage Fanclub** – Like a Virgin
37. **My Bloody Valentine** – To Here Knows When
38. **Curve** – No Escape from Heaven
39. **Babes in Toyland** – Primus
40. **Electronic** – Get the Message
41. **Fall** – The Mixer
42. **Babes in Toyland** – Ripe
43. **Fall** – So What About It?
44. **Th' Faith Healers** – Gorgeous Blue Flower in My Garden
45. **Fieldmice** – Missing the Moon
46. **Pixies** – Motorway to Roswell
47. **Pixies** – Bird Dream of the Olympus Mons
48. **Nirvana** – Breed
49. **Mercury Rev** – Car Wash Hair
50. **Bongwater** – Nick Cave Doll

1992

1. **Bang Bang Machine** – Geek Love
2. **PJ Harvey** – Sheela-Na-Gig
3. **Ministry** – Jesus Built My Hotrod
4. **Wedding Present** – Come Play with Me
5. **Fall** – Legend of Xanadu
6. **Fall** – Free Range
7. **Sonic Youth** – Youth Against Fascism
8. **Pavement** – Trigger Cut
9. **Babes in Toyland** – Bruise Violets
10. **Pavement** – Here
11. **Future Sound of London** – Papua New Guinea
12. **Fall** – Ed's Babe
13. **Jesus and Mary Chain** – Reverence
14. **Wedding Present** – Flying Saucer
15. **Suede** – The Drowners
16. **Sugar** – Changes
17. **Sonic Youth** – Sugar Kane
18. **Wedding Present** – Silver Shorts
19. **Wedding Present** – Love Slave
20. **Orb** – Blue Room
21. **Sugar** – A Good Idea
22. **Babes in Toyland** – Handsome and Gretel
23. **Sonic Youth** – 100%
24. **Wedding Present** – Blue Eyes
25. **Dr Devious** – Cyber Dream
26. **Sonic Youth** – Theresa's Sound World
27. **Pond** – Young Splendour
28. **Drop Nineteens** – Wynnona
29. **Datblygu** – Popeth
30. **Disposable Heroes of Hiphoprisy** – Language of Violence
31. **Frank and Walters** – Happy Bus Man
32. **Arcwelder** – Favour
33. **Therapy?** – Teethgrinder
34. **Fall** – Kimble
35. **Pavement** – In the Mouth a Desert
36. **Love Cup** – Tearing Water
37. **Pavement** – Summer Babe
38. **Disposable Heroes of Hiphoprisy** – TV Drug of a Nation

39. **Boo Radleys** – Lazarus
40. **Ride** – Leave Them All Behind
41. **Wedding Present** – Sticky
42. **Pavement** – Circa 1762
43. **Drag Racing Underground** – On the Road Again
44. **KLF & Extreme Noise Terror** – 3AM Eternal
45. **Buffalo Tom** – Tail Lights Fade
46. **Wedding Present** – Falling
47. **Pavement** – Conduit for Sale
48. **Sugar** – Helpless
49. **Verve** – All in the Mind
50. **Fall** – Birmingham School of Business School

1993

1. **Chumbawamba & Credit to the Nation** – Enough Is Enough
2. **Madder Rose** – Swim
3. **Huggy Bear** – Her Jazz
4. **PJ Harvey** – Rid of Me
5. **Stereolab** – French Disko
6. **Voodoo Queens** – Supermodel Superficial
7. **Sebadoh** – Soul and Fire
8. **Breeders** – Cannonball
9. **Palace Brothers** – Ohio River Boat Song
10. **Eggs** – Government Administrator
11. **Fall** – Why Are People Grudgeful
12. **Credit to the Nation & Chumbawamba** – Hear No Bullshit
13. **New Order** – Regret
14. **Pulp** – Razzamatazz
15. **PJ Harvey** – 50ft Queenie
16. **New Bad Things** – You Suck
17. **Cornershop** – England's Dreaming
18. **PJ Harvey** – Wang Dang Doodle
19. **Fall** – Lost in Music
20. **Fall** – Glam Racket
21. **Senser** – Eject
22. **Fall** – I'm Going to Spain
23. **Archers of Loaf** – Web in Front
24. **Credit to the Nation** – Call It What You Want
25. **Hole** – Olympia
26. **Fall** – Service
27. **Tindersticks** – Raindrops
28. **Chumbawamba** – Timebomb
29. **Fall** – Ladybird (Green Grass)
30. **Tindersticks** – Marbles
31. **Radiohead** – Creep
32. **PJ Harvey** – Naked Cousin
33. **Heavenly** – Atta Girl
34. **J Church** – Good Judge of Character
35. **Boo Radleys** – Barney and Me
36. **Madder Rose** – Beautiful John
37. **Tindersticks** – City Sickness
38. **Elastica** – Stutter
39. **Stereolab** – Jenny Ondioline
40. **Nirvana** – Scentless Apprentice
41. **Fall** – A Past Gone Mad
42. **Dinosaur Jr** – Get Me
43. **Fall** – Behind the Counter
44. **Madder Rose** – Lights Go Down
45. **Nirvana** – Rape Me
46. **Pulp** – Lipgloss
47. **Hole** – Beautiful Son
48. **Fall** – It's a Curse
49. **Trans Global Underground** – Syrius B
50. **Fall** – War

1994

1. **Inspiral Carpets (featuring Mark E Smith)** – I Want You
2. **Fall** – Hey Student
3. **Veruca Salt** – Seether
4. **Elastica** – Connection
5. **Supergrass** – Caught by the Fuzz
6. **LSG** – Hearts
7. **Elastica** – Waking up
8. **Portishead** – Sour Times
9. **Stereolab** – Ping Pong
10. **Done Lying Down** – Just a Misdemeanour
11. **H Foundation** – Laika
12. **Ash** – Jack Names the Planets
13. **Pulp** – Do You Remember the First Time
14. **Pavement** – Range Life
15. **Wedding Present** – Swimming Pools Movie Stars
16. **Sebadoh** – Rebound
17. **Hole** – Miss World
18. **Shellac** – Crow
19. **Madder Rose** – The Car Song
20. **Sleeper** – Delicious
21. **Pulp** – Common People
22. **Pavement** – Gold Soundz
23. **Pulp** – Babies
24. **Shellac** – The Dog and Pony Show
25. **Mazzy Star** – Fade Into You
26. **That Dog** – One Summer Night
27. **Nirvana** – The Man Who Sold the World
28. **Ash** – Uncle Pat
29. **Sabres of Paradise** – Wilmot
30. **Wedding Present** – Click Click
31. **Orbital** – Are We Here (Industry Standard Mix)
32. **Beck** – Loser
33. **Ash** – Petrol
34. **Pavement** – Cut Your Hair
35. **Madder Rose** – Panic on
36. **Salt Tank** – Charged up
37. **Wedding Present** – So Long Baby
38. **Fall** – City Dweller
39. **Wedding Present** – Spangle
40. **Nirvana** – Where Did You Sleep Last Night
41. **Fall** – M5
42. **Elastica** – Line up
43. **Underworld** – Dirty Epic
44. **Nirvana** – About a Girl
45. **Hole** – Doll Parts
46. **ROC** – Girl with a Crooked Eye
47. **Sonic Youth** – Superstar
48. **Sleeper** – Swallow
49. **Tuscadero** – Angel in a Half Shirt
50. **Trans Global Underground** – Taal Zaman

1995

1. **Pulp** – Common People
2. **Pulp** – Sorted for E's & Wizz
3. **Wedding Present** – Sucker
4. **Ash** – Girl from Mars
5. **Dreadzone** – Zion Youth
6. **Ash** – Kung Fu
7. **Fall** – Feeling Numb
8. **Pulp** – I-Spy
9. **Dreadzone** – Maximum
10. **Long Fin Killie & Mark E Smith** – Heads of Dead Surfers

11. **PJ Harvey** – Send His Love to Me
12. **Pulp** – Mis-Shapes
13. **Supergrass** – Alright
14. **Zion Train** – Dance of Life
15. **Bluetones** – Bluetonic
16. **Dreadzone** – Fight the Power
17. **PJ Harvey** – Down by the Water
18. **Catatonia** – Bleed
19. **Gorky's Zygotic Mynci** – If Fingers Were Xylophones
20. **Elastica** – All Nighter
21. **Bluetones** – Slight Return
22. **Tricky** – Black Steel
23. **Dreadzone** – Little Britain
24. **Fall** – Don't Call Me Darling
25. **Tindersticks** – My Sister
26. **Dick Dale** – Nitro
27. **Pulp** – Disco 2000
28. **Hole** – Violet
29. **Flaming Stars** – Kiss Tomorrow Goodbye
30. **Fall** – Bonkers in Phoenix
31. **Pulp** – Underwear
32. **Spare Snare** – Bugs
33. **Stereolab** – Pop Quiz
34. **PJ Harvey** – To Bring You My Love
35. **Dreadzone** – Captain Dread
36. **Cornershop** – 6am Jullander Shere
37. **Billy Bragg** – Northern Industrial Town
38. **Van Basten** – King of the Death Posture
39. **Solar Race** – Not Here
40. **Pavement** – Father to a Sister of Thought
41. **Leftfield** – Afroleft
42. **Harveys Rabbit** – Is This What You Call Change
43. **Ash** – Angel Interceptor
44. **Dose (with Mark E Smith)** – Plug Myself in
45. **Garbage** – Vow
46. **Dave Clarke** – Red Three
47. **Bis** – School Disco
48. **Dreadzone** – Life, Love and Unity
49. **Fall** – The Joke
50. **Safe Deposit** – You Can't

1996

1. **Kenickie** – Come out 2 Nite
2. **Arab Strap** – First Big Weekend
3. **Delgados** – Under Canvas Under Wraps
4. **Kenickie** – Punka
5. **Underworld** – Born Slippy
6. **Fall** – Cheatham Hill
7. **Orbital** – The Box
8. **Gorky's Zygotic Mynci** – Patio Song
9. **Sweeney** – Why?
10. **Helen Love** – Girl About Town
11. **Stereolab** – Cybele's Reverie
12. **Billy Bragg** – Brickbat
13. **Fall** – The Chiselers
14. **Bis** – Kandy Pop
15. **Baby Bird** – Goodnight
16. **Fall** – Hostile
17. **PJ Harvey / John Parrish** – That Was My Veil (Peel Session)
18. **Flaming Stars** – 10 Feet Tall
19. **Trembling Blue Stars** – Abba on the Jukebox
20. **Stereolab** – Fluorescences
21. **Tortoise** – DJED
22. **Jon Spencer Blues Explosion** – 2 Kindsa Love

23. **PJ Harvey / John Parrish** – Taut (Peel Session)
24. **Quickspace** – Friend
25. **Dave Clarke** – No One's Driving
26. **AC Acoustics** – Stunt Girl
27. **Dick Dale** – Nitrous
28. **Belle & Sebastian** – The State I'm in
29. **Aphex Twin** – Twin Girl/Boy
30. **Force and Stars** – Fireworks
31. **White Town** – Your Woman
32. **Zion Train** – Babylon's Burning
33. **Calvin Party** – Lies, Lies and Government
34. **Broadcast** – The Book Lovers
35. **DJ Shadow** – Stem
36. **Wedding Present** – 2, 3, Go
37. **Prodigy** – Firestarter
38. **Ash** – Oh Yeah
39. **Placebo** – Teenage Angst
40. **Broadcast** – Living Room
41. **Tiger** – The Race
42. **Manic Street Preachers** – A Design for Life
43. **Half Man Half Biscuit** – Paintball's Coming Home
44. **Soul Bossa** – Sore Loser
45. **Urusei Yatsura** – Kewpies Like Watermelon
46. **Wedding Present** – Go Man Go
47. **Orbital** – Out There Somewere
48. **Flaming Stars** – The Face on the Bar Room Floor
49. **Super Furry Animals** – God Show Me Magic
50. **Stereolab** – Les Yper-Sound

1997

(Only a Festive 31 broadcast)

1. **Cornershop** – Brimful of Asha
2. **Mogwai** – New Paths to Helicon
3. **Helen Love** – Does Your Heart Go Boom
4. **Period Pains** – Spice Girls Who Do You Think You Are
5. **Belle & Sebastian** – Lazy Line Painter Jane
6. **Novak** – Rapunzel
7. **Fall** – Inch
8. **Daft Punk** – Rollin' & Scratchin'
9. **Clinic** – IPC Subeditors Dictate Our Youth
10. **David Holmes** – Don't Die Just Yet
11. **Blur** – Song 2
12. **Belle & Sebastian** – Dog on Wheels
13. **Hydroplane** – We Crossed the Atlantic
14. **Stereolab & Nurse with Wound** – Simple Headphone Mind
15. **Bette Davis & the Balconettes** – Shergar
16. **Arab Strap** – Hey Fever
17. **Fall** – I'm a Mummy
18. **Spiritualised** – Ladies & Gentlemen We Are Floating in Space
19. **AC Acoustics** – I Messiah Am Jailer
20. **Stereolab** – Fluorescences
21. **Hitchers** – Strachan
22. **Bis** – Sweet Shop Avengerz
23. **Secret Goldfish** – Dandelion Milk Summer
24. **Prolapse** – Autocade
25. **Dreamcity Film Club** – If I Die, I Die
26. **Stereolab** – Miss Modular
27. **Delgados** – Pull the Wires from the Wall (Peel Session)
28. **Propellerheads** – Velvet Pants
29. **Hybirds** – Seventeen
30. **Prolapse** – Slash/Oblique
31. **Angelica** – Teenage Girl Crush

1998

1. **Delgados** – Pull the Wires from the Wall (album version)
2. **Mogwai** – Xmas Steps
3. **Belle & Sebastian** – Boy with the Arab Strap
4. **Ten Benson** – The Claw
5. **Pop Off Tuesday** – Unwordly
6. **Cuban Boys** – Oh My God They Killed Kenny
7. **Bis** – Eurodisco
8. **Pulp** – This Is Hardcore
9. **Delgados** – Everything Goes Round the Water
10. **Helen Love** – Long Live the UK Music Scene
11. **Jesus & Mary Chain** – Crackin' Up
12. **Daniel Johnston** – Dream Scream
13. **Clinic** – Cement Mixer
14. **Badly Drawn Boy** – I Need a Sign
15. **Cinerama** – Kerry Kerry
16. **Plone** – Plock
17. **L'augmentation** – Soleil
18. **Boards of Canada** – Aquarius
19. **Solex** – All Lickety Split
20. **Evolution** – Copyright Violation for the Nation
21. **Massive Attack** – Teardrop
22. **Spiritualized (Meltdown)** – Oh Happy Day
23. **Solex** – One Louder Solex (Peel Session)
24. **Melys** – Lemming
25. **Half Man Half Biscuit** – Turn a Blind Eye
26. **Belle & Sebastian** – Sleep the Clock Around
27. **Clinic** – Monkey on Your Back
28. **Fatboy Slim** – Rockefeller Skank
29. **Super Furry Animals** – Ice Hockey Hair
30. **Billy Bragg** – Way Over Yonder in the Minor Key
31. **Freed Unit** – Widdershins
32. **Male Nurse** – My Own Private Patrick Swayze
33. **Mercury Rev** – Goddess on a Highway
34. **Elbow** – Powder Blue
35. **Gorky's Zygotic Mynci** – Sweet Johnny
36. **Gorky's Zygotic Mynci** – Hush the Warmth
37. **Melt Banana** – Stimulus for Revolting Virus
38. **Delgados** – The Actress
39. **Quickspace** – If I Were a Carpenter (Peel Session)
40. **60ft Dolls** – Alison's Room
41. **Boards of Canada** – Roygbiv
42. **Derrero** – Radar Intruder
43. **Hefner** – Pull Yourself Together
44. **Rooney** – Went to Town
45. **Soda Stream** – Turnstyle
46. **Sportique** – Kids Are Solid Gold
47. **Ten Benson** – Evil Heat
48. **Autechre** – Fold 4 Wrap 5
49. **Fall** – Shake Off (Peel Session)
50. **PJ Harvey** – Is This Desire

1999

1. **Cuban Boys** – Cognoscenti Vs Intelligentsia
2. **Hefner** – The Hymn for the Cigarettes
3. **Hefner** – Hymn for the Alcohol
4. **Fall** – Touch Sensitive
5. **Gorky's Zygotic Mynci** – Spanish Dance Troupe

6. **Elastica with Mark E Smith** – How He Wrote Elastica Man
7. **Fall** – F-Oldin' Money
8. **Flaming Lips** – Race for the Prize
9. **Murry the Hump** – Thrown Like a Stone
10. **Low** – Immune
11. **Half Man Half Biscuit** – Look Dad No Tunes
12. **Flaming Lips** – Waiting for a Superman
13. **Cinerama** – Pacific
14. **Mogwai** – Cody
15. **Orbital** – Style
16. **Sonic Subjunkies** – Do You Even Know Who You Are?
17. **Super Furry Animals** – Fire in My Heart
18. **Cinerama** – Kings Cross
19. **Salako** – Look Left
20. **Clinic** – The Second Line
21. **Godspeed You Black Emperor** – Hung Over as the Queen at Maida Vale (Peel Session)
22. **Hefner** – I Stole a Bride
23. **Bonnie Prince Billy** – I See a Darkness
24. **Super Furry Animals** – Northern Lites
25. **Mogwai** – Stanley Kubrick
26. **Kraken** – Side Effects
27. **Super Furry Animals** – Turning Tide
28. **Cuban Boys** – Flossie's Alarming Clock
29. **Dawn of the Replicants** – Science Fiction Freak
30. **Half Man Half Biscuit** – 24 Hour Garage People (Peel Session)
31. **Pavement** – Major Leagues
32. **Hefner** – I Took Her Love for Granted
33. **Gene** – As Good as It Gets
34. **Plone** – Be Rude to Your School
35. **Smog** – Cold Blooded Old Times
36. **Broadcast** – Echoes Answer
37. **Add N to X** – Metal Finger in My Body
38. **Melt Banana** – Plot in a Pot
39. **Atari Teenage Riot** – Revolution Action
40. **Blur** – Tender
41. **Badly Drawn Boy** – Once Around the Block
42. **Aphex Twin** – Windowlicker
43. **Six by Seven** – Helden
44. **Appliance** – Food Music
45. **Pavement** – Carrot Rope
46. **Stereolab** – The Free Design
47. **Marine Research** – Parallel Horizontal
48. **Miss Mend** – Living City Plan
49. **Hefner** – Hymn for the Things We Didn't Do
50. **Wheat** – Don't I Hold You

2000

1. **Neko Case & Her Boyfriends** – Twist the Knife
2. **PJ Harvey** – Good Fortune
3. **The Fall** – Dr Buck's Letter
4. **And You Will Know Us by the Trail of Dead** – Mistakes and Regrets
5. **Broadcast** – Come on Let's Go
6. **PJ Harvey** – Big Exit
7. **Hefner** – Greedy Ugly People
8. **Schneider TM** – Light 300
9. **Delgados** – No Danger
10. **Delgados** – American Trilogy
11. **Low** – Dinosaur Act
12. **Hefner** – Day That Thatcher Dies
13. **Ballboy** – I Hate Scotland

14. **Delgados** – Accused of Stealing
15. **Hefner** – Good Fruit
16. **Cinerama** – Your Charms
17. **Cinerama** – Wow
18. **PJ Harvey** – The Mess We're In
19. **Shellac** – Prayer to God
20. **Boards of Canada** – In a Beautiful Place
21. **Laura Cantrell** – Somewhere Some Night
22. **Calexico** – Ballad of Cable Hogue
23. **The Fall** – Two Librans
24. **PJ Harvey** – The Whores Hustle and the Hustlers Whore
25. **Radiohead** – Kid A
26. **New Order** – Brutal
27. **Laura Cantrell** – Two Seconds
28. **Clinic** – Second Line
29. **Cuban Boys** – Vinyl Countdown
30. **Cowcube** – Popping Song
31. **Herman Dune** – Drug Dealer in Park
32. **Half Man Half Biscuit** – 24 Hour Garage People
33. **Cat Power** – Wonderwall
34. **Cuban Boys** – Theme from Prim & Proper
35. **Lab 4** – Candyman
36. **Gorky's Zygotic Mynci** – Fresher than the Sweetness
37. **Half Man Half Biscuit** – Irk the Purists
38. **Delgados** – Witness
39. **Mighty Math** – Soul Boy
40. **Smog** – Dress Sexy at My Funeral
41. **Cinerama** – Manhattan
42. **Laura Cantrell** – Queen of the Coast
43. **The Fall** – WB
44. **Hefner** – Painting & Kissing
45. **Orbital** – Searched
46. **Bonnie Prince Billy** – Little Boy Blue
47. **Sigur Ros** – Svefn G Englar
48. **Radiohead** – Ideoteque
49. **Belle & Sebastian** – I Fought in a War
50. **Grandaddy** – Crystal Lake

(All-time)

1. **Joy Division** – Atmosphere
2. **Undertones** – Teenage Kicks
3. **Joy Division** – Love Will Tear Us Apart
4. **Sex Pistols** – Anarchy in the UK
5. **Clash** – (White Man) in Hammersmith Palais
6. **New Order** – Blue Monday
7. **Smiths** – How Soon Is Now?
8. **Nirvana** – Smells Like Teen Spirit
9. **Smiths** – There Is a Light That Never Goes out
10. **This Mortal Coil** – Song to the Siren
11. **Robert Wyatt** – Shipbuilding
12. **Pulp** – Common People
13. **Captain Beefheart & His Magic Band** – Big Eyed Beans from Venus
14. **Dead Kennedys** – Holiday in Cambodia
15. **Joy Division** – New Dawn Fades
16. **My Bloody Valentine** – Soon
17. **New Order** – Ceremony
18. **Only Ones** – Another Girl, Another Planet
19. **New Order** – Temptation
20. **Joy Division** – She's Lost Control
21. **Wedding Present** – Brassneck
22. **Smiths** – This Charming Man
23. **Sugarcubes** – Birthday
24. **Fall** – How I Wrote 'Elastic Man'
25. **Wedding Present** – My Favourite Dress

26. **Delgados** – Pull the Wires from the Wall
27. **My Bloody Valentine**
    – You Made Me Realise
28. **Joy Division** – Transmission
29. **Sex Pistols** – Pretty Vacant
30. **Pixies** – Debaser
31. **Belle & Sebastian** – Lazy Line Painter Jane
32. **New Order** – True Faith
33. **Clash** – Complete Control
34. **Fall** – Totally Wired
35. **Jam** – Going Underground
36. **Stereolab** – French Disko
37. **Jimi Hendrix Experience**
    – All Along the Watchtower
38. **Fall** – The Classical
39. **Damned** – New Rose
40. **Tim Buckley** – Song to the Siren
41. **Beach Boys** – God Only Knows
42. **Velvet Underground** – Heroin
43. **Nick Drake** – Northern Sky
44. **Bob Dylan** – Visions of Johanna
45. **Beatles** – I Am the Walrus
46. **Beach Boys** – Good Vibrations
47. **Sundays** – Can't Be Sure
48. **Culture** – Lion Rock
49. **PJ Harvey** – Sheela-Na-Gig
50. **Pavement** – Here

2001

1. **Melys** – Chinese Whispers
2. **White Stripes** – Hotel Yorba
3. **Cinerama** – Health and Efficiency
4. **Bearsuit** – Hey Charlie Hey Chuck
5. **Strokes** – Last Nite
6. **White Stripes** – Fell in Love with a Girl
7. **Strokes** – Hard to Explain
8. **Camera Obscura** – Eighties Fan
9. **New Order** – Crystal
10. **Mogwai** – My Father My King
11. **Meanwhile, Back in Communist Russia**
    – Morning After Pill
12. **Saloon** – Impact
13. **Half Man Half Biscuit** – Bob Wilson
    Anchorman
14. **Miss Black America** – Human Punk
15. **Detroit Cobras** – d'Shout bama lama
16. **Half Man Half Biscuit** – Vatican Broadside
17. **Belle & Sebastian** – Jonathan David
18. **Strokes** – The Modern Age
19. **Pulp** – Sunrise
20. **Squarepusher** – My Red Hot Car
21. **Super Furry Animals** – Rings Around
    the World
22. **Mogwai** – Two Rights Make One Wrong
23. **Cuban Boys** – Drink, Drink, Drink
24. **Greenskeepers** – Low & Sweet
25. **White Stripes** – Dead Leaves and the
    Dirty Ground
26. **Ballboy** – They'll Hang Flags from Cranes
27. **Lift to Experience** – These Are the Days
28. **Strokes** – New York City Cops
29. **Pulp** – Trees
30. **Fall** – I Wake up in the City
31. **Hefner** – Alan Bean
32. **Belle & Sebastian** – I'm Waking up to Us
33. **Ikara Colt** – One Note
34. **Cinerama** – Superman
35. **Melys** – I Don't Believe in You

36. **PJ Harvey** – This Is Love
37. **Seedling** – Sensational Vacuum
38. **Antihero** – Who's Looking out for #1?
39. **Lift to Experience** – Falling from Cloud 9
40. **Radiohead** – Pyramid Song
41. **Ballboy** – I've Got Pictures of You in Your...
42. **Miss Black America** – Don't Speak My
    Mind
43. **Shins** – New Slang
44. **Mercury Rev** – Dark is Rising
45. **Stereolab** – Captain Easychord
46. **Strokes** – Someday
47. **Hives** – Hate to Say I Told You So
48. **Rock of Travolta** – Giant Robo
49. **Saloon** – Freefall
50. **Pico** – Chard

2002

1. **Saloon** – Girls Are the New Boys
2. **Cinerama** – Quick, Before It Melts
3. **Miss Black America** – Talk Hard
4. **Nina Nastasia** – Ugly Face
5. **Antihero** – Rolling Stones T-Shirt
6. **M.A.S.S.** – Hey Gravity
7. **Laura Cantrell** – Too Late for Tonight
8. **Pinhole** – So Over You
9. = **Mark Smith v Safe & Sound** – Identify
    the Beat
9. = **Ballboy** – All the Records on the Radio
    Are Shite
11. = **Miss Black America** – Miss Black America
11. = **Yeah Yeah Yeahs** – Bang
13. **Cinerama** – Careless
14. = **Half Man Half Biscuit** – The Light at
    the End of the Tunnel (Is the Light of an
    Oncoming Train)
14. = **White Stripes** – Dead Leaves and the Dirty
    Ground
16. **Low** – In the Drugs
17. **Asa-Chang & Junray** – Hana
18. **Low** – Canada
19. = **Coin-Op** – Democracies
19. = **Belle & Sebastian** – You Send Me
    (Peel Acres Version)
21. **Datsuns** – In Love
22. **Fall** – Susan v Youthclub
23. **Jeffrey Lewis** – The Chelsea Hotel
    Oral Sex Song
24. = **Ballboy** – Where Do the Nights of Sleep
    Go (When They Do Not Come to Me)
24. = **Cornershop** – Staging the Plaguing of the
    Raised Platform
26. **Saloon** – Have You Seen the Light?
27. = **White Stripes** – Fell in Love with a Girl
27. = **Cranebuilders** – You're Song
29. **Delgados** – Mr Blue Sky (Peel Session)
30. = **Bearsuit** – Drinkink
30. = **Ladytron** – Seventeen
30. = **Boom Bip & Dose One** – Mannequin
    Trapdoor
30. = **Von Bondies** – It Came from Japan
34. **Wire** – 99.9 (Peel Session)
35. = **McLusky** – Alan Is a Cowboy Killer
35. = **Low** – (That's How You Sing)
    Amazing Grace
37. = **Antihero** – You Got Nothing (Peel Session)
37. = **Half Man Half Biscuit** – Breaking News
39. = **Cinerama** – Cat Girl Tights

39. = **McLusky** – To Hell with Good Intentions
41. = **Burning Love Jumpsuit** – Cheerleader
41. = **Interpol** – Obstacle 1
43. **Melys** – So Good
44. = **Delgados** – Coming in from the Cold
44. = **Miss Black America** – Infinite Chinese Box
46. **Eighties Matchbox B-Line Disaster**
    – Celebrate Your Mother
47. **D4** – Get Loose
48. **Mum** – Green Grass of Tunnel
49. **Aphrodisiacs** – This Is a Campaign
50. **Dawn Parade** – The Hole in My Heart

2003

1. **Cinerama** – Don't Touch That Dial
2. **Fall** – Theme from Sparta FC
    (Peel Session)
3. **Mogwai** – Hunted by a Freak
4. **Undertones** – Thrill Me
5. **Bearsuit** – Itsuko Got Married
6. **Mogwai** – Ratts of the Capital
7. **Half Man Half Biscuit**
    – Tending the Wrong Grave for 23 Years
8. **Crimea** – Baby Boom
9. **CLSM** – John Peel Is Not Enough
10. **White Stripes** – 7 Nation Army
11. **Belle & Sebastian** –
    Step Into My Office, Baby
12. **Melt Banana** – Shield Your Eyes
13. **Nina Nastasia** – You, Her & Me
14. **Ballboy** – The Sash My Father Wore
15. **Vive La Fete** – Noir Desir
16. **Sluts of Trust** – Piece O' You
17. **White Stripes** – Black Math
18. **Yeah Yeah Yeahs** – Maps
19. **Broken Family Band** – At the Back
    Of the Chapel
20. **Darkness Vs S.F.B.** – I Believe in a Thing
    Called Love
21. **Million Dead** – I Am the Party
22. **Undertones** – Oh Please
23. **Ballboy** – I Gave up My Eyes
24. **Party of One** – Shotgun Funeral
25. **Futureheads** – First Day
26. **Fall** – Green Eyed Loco Man
27. **French** – Porn Shoes
28. **Half Man Half Biscuit** – It Makes the Room
    Look Bigger
29. **Architecture in Helsinki** – The Owls Go
30. **Camera Obscura** – Suspended from Class
31. **Amsterdam** – Does This Train
    Stop on Merseyside
32. **Maher Shalal Hash Baz** – Open Field
33. **Neulander** – Sex, God, Money
34. **Black Keys** – Have Love Will Travel
35. **Mass** – Live a Little
36. **French** – Gabriel in the Airport
37. **Radiohead** – There There
38. **Ballboy** – Born in the USA
39. **Cat Power** – Werewolf
40. **Broadcast** – Pendulum
41. **Keys** – Strength of Strings
42. **Golden Virgins**
43. **Belle & Sebastian** – Stay Loose
44. **Hyper Kinako** – Tokyo Invention
    Registration Office
45. **Grandmaster Gareth** – The Minute Melodys
    (Any Of)

46. **Super Furry Animals** – Slow Life
47. **Camera Obscura** – Keep It Clean
48. **Blizzard Boys** – Ain't No Stoppin' This
49. **Freddy Fresh** – You Can See the Paint
50. **Vaults** – I'm Going

2004

1. **Fall** – Theme from Sparta FC Part 2 (Album/Single Version)
2. **Bearsuit** – Chargr
3. **Caroline Martin** – Singer
4. **Aereogramme** – Dreams & Bridges
5. **Sluts of Trust** – Leave You Wanting More
6. **Delgados** – Everybody Come Down
7. **Sons & Daughters** – Johnny Cash
8. **Half Man Half Biscuit** – Joy Division Oven Gloves (Peel Session)
9. **Graham Coxon** – Freakin' out
10. **Jawbone** – Hi-de-Hi
11. **Bloc Party** – Helicopter
12. **Texas Radio Band** – Chwareon Bwtleg Pep le Pew
13. **Martyn Hare** – Do Not Underestimate
14. **Cinerama** – It's Not You, It's Me
15. **Aereogramme** – Unravelling
16. **PJ Harvey** – The Letter
17. **Laura & Ballboy** – I Lost You But I Found County Music
18. **Jawbone** – Jack Rabbit
19. **DJ Distance** – Ritual
20. **Bloc Party** – Banquet
21. **Ballboy** – Art of Kissing
22. **Black Keys** – 10am Automatic
23. **PJ Harvey** – Shame
24. **Decoration** – I Tried It, I Liked It, I Loved It
25. **65 Days of Static** – Retreat! Retreat!
26. **McLusky** – That Man Will Not Hang
27. **Listen with Sarah** – Animal Hop
28. **XBooty** – O Superman
29. **Digital Mystikz** – B
30. **Black Keys** – Girl Is on My Mind
31. **Art Brut** – Formed a Band
32. **Delgados** – I Fought the Angels
33. **Shitmat** – There's No Business Like Propa Rungleclotted Mashup Bizznizz
34. **Magic Band** – Big Eyed Beans from Venus (Peel Session)
35. **Jon E Cash** – International
36. **Wedding Present** – Interstate 5
37. **Tunng** – Tale from Black
38. **Melys** – Eyeliner
39. **Decoration** – Joy Adamson (Peel Session)
40. **Cornershop featuring Bubbley Kaur** – Topknot
41. **Calvin Party** – Northern Song
42. **Plastikman** – Cha
43. **Kentucky AFC** – Be Nesa
44. **Bloc Party** – Little Thoughts
45. **Aphrodisiacs** – If U Want Me
46. **Mountain Goats** – Your Belgian Things
47. **Magic Band** – Electricity (Peel Session)
48. **Ella Guru** – Park Lake Speakers
49. **Ballboy** – I Don't Have Time to Stand Here with You Fighting About the Size of My Dick
50. **Vaults** – No Sleep No Need

		#	Title	Artist	Time
			"Anarchy in the U.K."	Sex Pistols	3:30
			"Atmosphere"	Joy Division	4:05
			"Love will tear us apart"	Joy Division	3:15
		4	"Down in the tube-station/midnight"	Jam	4:00
		5	"White man in Hammersmith Palais"	Clash	4:00
			"Holiday in Cambodia"	Dead Kennedys	3:45
			"Teenage kicks"	Undertones	2:25
			"New rose"	Damned	2:40
		9	"Alternative Ulster"	Stiff Little Fingers	2:40
			"Transmission"	Joy Division	3:40
			"Public image"	Public Image Ltd.	3:00
		12	"Holidays in the sun"	Sex Pistols	3:20
		13	"Going underground"	Jam	2:55
		14	"Decades"	Joy Division	6:10
		15	"Complete control"	Clash	3:10
			"Johnny was"	Stiff Little Fingers	8:05
		17	"Get over you"	Undertones	2:40
		18	"A forest"	Cure	6:00
–	11	19	"In a rut"	Ruts	3:40
		20	"New dawn fades"	Joy Division	4:50
–	–	21	"Totally wired"	Fall	3:25
–	–	22	"She's lost control"	Joy Division	3:50
6	16	23	"Pretty vacant"	Sex Pistols	3:15
4	8	24	"Suspect device"	Stiff Little Fingers	2:40
3	13	25	"God save the Queen"	Sex Pistols	3:20
		26	"How I wrote 'Elastic man'"	Fall	4:20
–	18	27	"Wasted life"	Stiff Little Fingers	3:15
17	20	28	"Another girl, another planet"	Only Ones	3:00
–	22	29	"Love song"	Damned	2:00
–	–	30	"Kings of the wild frontier"	Adam & the Ants	3:55
–	33	31	"California uber alles"	Dead Kennedys	3:25
–	7	32	"Gangsters"	Specials	2:45
		33	"Poptones"	Public Image Ltd.	7:45
		34	"Careering"	Public Image Ltd.	4:30
–	–	35	"Requiem"	Killing Joke	3:45
–	–	36	"Psyche"	Killing Joke	5:10
43	42	37	"Jigsaw feeling"	Siouxsie/the Banshees	4:40
–	–	38	"Fiery Jack"	Fall	4:45
–	–	39	"Armagideon time"	Clash	3:45
–	40	40	"Where's Capt.Kirk?"	Spizzenergi	2:20
–	–	41	"Twenty four hours"	Joy Division	4:25
–	–	42	"Smash it up"	Damned	2:50
–	–	43	"Treason"	The Teardrop Explodes	3:05
41	38	44	"Switch"	Siouxsie/the Banshees	6:50
–	35	45	"Icon"	Siouxsie/the Banshees	5:20
–	–	46	"Bankrobber"	Clash	4:35
22	48	47	"Hong Kong Garden"	Siouxsie/the Banshees	2:55
15	26	48	"White riot"	Clash	1:50
–	40	49	"Rowche rumble"	Fall	4:00
–	23	50	"Damaged goods"	Gang of Four	3:35
		51	"Love in a void"	Siouxsie/the Banshees	
		52	"Wardance"	Killing Joke	
		53	"Dog eat dog"	Adam & the Ants	
		54	"West One (Shine on me)"	Ruts	
		55	"My generation"	Who	
		56	"White mice"	Mo-dettes	
		57	"Tin soldiers"	Stiff Little Fingers	
		58	"No more heroes"	Stranglers	
		59	"Eton rifles"	Jam	
		60	"Shine on, you crazy diamond"	Pink Floyd	
		61	"Shot by both sides"	Magazine	
		62	"Death disco"	Public Image Ltd.	
		63	"Stairway to Heaven"	Led Zeppelin	
		64	"Dead soul"	Joy Division	
		65	"Better scream"	Wah! Heat	

found your entry envelope to this you wanted?

CHAPTER 11

THE SHOWS 1967–2004 is a day-by-day chronology of all John Peel's shows on Radio 1 listing briefly the main featured sessions or other main items. It is designed to be read and consulted alongside the full Session A–Z which follows. While the A–Z provides full details of the sessions themselves, 'The Shows' gives some temporal context, repeat dates, as well as much more. This section mentions all the other things the show did apart from the sessions, that therefore do not fit into the A–Z: concerts, outside broadcasts, specials, Christmas carol shows, and so on. In addition, I have added in Peel's many other documentary and feature appearances on Radio 1, appearances and series on other BBC radio networks, and occasional notable TV appearances. For the transitional years of 1975–1978, I have also added in from the PasBs details of some key records played: there were five shows a week at this time so very often there were shows with no sessions anyway. This chronology had to be produced as a research document, simply in order to write the story itself and confirm many of the dates in the A–Z, but for both Peel listeners and anyone interested in the last 40 years of British music, we felt it was a fun and fascinating thing to browse in its own right, so we decided to stick it in. I produced a rough version from PasB scripts and session sheets only for 1967–1992 in order to produce In Session Tonight, but did not complete it until after that book went to press, and so only belatedly realised with horror that the calendar and a check in Radio Times threw up almost 400 dates when Peel must have been on air but about which I knew nothing at all or had good reason to doubt what I did know was everything. It is these mystery dates, between 1978 and 1988 (mostly) which I tried to fix first for this book, with the help of the tape and diary collections of listeners found mainly via the John Peel News Group on Yahoo, then targeted searching of the PasB microfilms over three or four days in BBC Written Archives, Caversham. For 1993–2000 I am particularly indebted to Jon Small, who very kindly reactivated for me personally his old vhissue site where he carried on the index and chronology from IST via pooling ceefax listings and his and others' listening and tapes. Thanks, Jon. Louise Kattenhorn's production diaries, files and notes took over in filling the gaps from 2001 onwards. All the other stuff comes from Radio Times, the main BBC INfax programme archive catalogue, and, again, listening diaries, tapes and tip-offs from regular listeners. A final point: there are no other Peel shows or sessions outside this list. If a show in 1979 only has one session, that's because I've checked, and there was only one. Every show date where the details available looked out of the ordinary, or were queried by reliable listener-collectors, has been checked. There was no Rick Wakeman session, and no Depeche Mode session, to mention just two urban myths. This is why this chronology also indicates when there was no Peel show, when we might have expected one. This is the lot, at last.

KEY

(band) (repeat session)

All entries in brackets are session or programme repeats. The session being repeated is the immediately preceding most recent new session by that artist, except where indicated. Live concerts are excluded from this sequence. In other words, look back up the column, and the first time you find that band name not in brackets, that's the one being repeated.

(band #1)

Where sessions are repeated out of sequence, they are given a number according to their session order in the A–Z. For older repeats from more than two years previously, or to avoid ambiguity in some cases, the original first TX date is also given in brackets.

St 26/9 – St 30/10

For documentary and other series outside his main show, all information is given at the 1st TX date of episode 1.

1967

- **Top Gear, 2–5pm R1 Sundays
  produced by Bernie Andrews & Bev Phillips**

Sn 1/10/67 Tomorrow, The Move, Traffic, The Pink
Floyd, Tim Rose, Big Maybelle – Comperes Pete
Drummond with John Peel

Sn 8/10 Procol Harum, Lou Rawls & Maxine Brown,
Denny Laine and the Electric String Band, The Crazy
World of Arthur Brown, The Idle Race – Comperes
Pete Drummond with Mike A'Hern

Sn 15/10 The Who, Jimi Hendrix, Bee Gees, Skip
Bifferty, Incredible String Band, Johnnie Young and
the Word – Comperes Pete Drummond and Tommy
Vance

Sn 22/10 The Nice, Hollies, Tim Rose, The Soul Sisters
and the Clockwork Orange, The Amen Corner (The
Move) – Comperes Pete Drummond and Rick Dane

Sn 29/10 Cream, Blossom Toes, Sharon Tandy, Kinks,
Roy Harper (Traffic, Procol Harum) – Comperes Pete
Drummond and John Peel

Sn 5/11 Jeff Beck, John Mayall's Bluesbreakers, William
E Kimber, Tyrannosaurus Rex (Pink Floyd, Denny
Laine, James & Bobby Purify, 1st TX R1 8/10/67)
– Comperes Pete Drummond & John Peel

- **All shows to 28/1/68, compered by Peel and
  Vance**

Sn 12/11 Bonzo Dogs, Gun, Fleetwood Mac
(Bee Gees, Tomorrow, Idle Race)

Sn 19/11 Brian Auger's Trinity, Honeybus, Lulu
(Who, Hollies, Skip Bifferty)

Sn 26/11 Family, The Herd, Elmer Gantry's Velvet Opera,
J J Jackson (Kinks, Hendrix)

Sn 3/12 The Alan Bown, Moody Blues, Pretty Things
(Blossom Toes, Tim Rose) + i/v with Rolling Stones
Jagger, Jones, Watts, pre-rec 30/11/67

Sn 10/12 Gladys Knight, Nirvana, Ten Years After,
Fairport Convention (Cream, Gun)

Sn 17/12 Bonzo Dogs, Chris Clark, Cat Stevens, Soft
Machine (Honeybus, Fleetwood Mac)

Sn 24/12 David Bowie, Hendrix, Ice, Traffic (Family)

Sn 31/12 Eric Burdon, Pink Floyd (Moody Blues, Herd,
Alan Bown)

1968

Sn 7/1 Kaleidoscope, Manfred Mann, Amen Corner
(Pretty Things, Elmer Gantry's Velvet Opera, Spencer
Davis Group, 1st TX Saturday Club 30/12/67)

Sn 14/1 PP Arnold, Cream, Plastic Penny, Foundations
(Bonzos, Ten Years After)

Sn 21/1 Fleetwood Mac & Eddie Boyd, Donovan, Tom
Rush, Grapefruit (Traffic, Gladys Knight & The Pips)

Sn 28/1 The Move, Denny Laine, The Nice, Chicken
Shack (Bowie, Eric Burdon)

- **From 4/2 onwards Peel sole compere,
  show 2–4pm only**

Sn 4/2 Tomorrow, Moody Blues, Captain Beefheart
(Hendrix, Tyrannosaurus Rex)

Sn 11/2 Brenton Wood, Skip Bifferty, Don Partridge
(Pink Floyd, John Mayall's Bluesbreakers)

Sn 18/2 Bee Gees, Honeybus, Pentangle
(Cream, Amen Corner)

Sn 25/2 Procol Harum, Idle Race, Tim Rose
(Donovan, PP Arnold)

Sn 3/3 Traffic, Fairport Convention (Grapefruit, The
Move, Peter Anders & Vini Poncia, 1st TX R1
24/1/68)

- **From 10/3, Bernie Andrews sole Top Gear
  producer**

- **Wed 6/3/68 midnight–1am Peel's Night Ride
  begins produced by John Muir**

W 6/3 Incredible String Band

Sn 10/3 Scaffold, Yardbirds, The New Generation
(Denny Laine)

W 13/3 Tyrannosaurus Rex, Peter Roche

Sn 17/3 Spooky Tooth, Roy Harper (Captain Beefheart,
Bee Gees)

W 20/3 The End, Roger McGough

Sn 24/3 Fleetwood Mac, Tyrannosaurus Rex
(Procol Harum, The Nice)

W 27/3 Andy Roberts & Adrian Henri,
Rev Dom Robert Petitpierre

Sn 31/3 John Mayall's Bluesbreakers, The End,
Blossom Toes (Honeybus, Tim Rose)

W 3/4 Mabel Greer's Toyshop, poet Carlysle Reed,
Tim Walker & Mick Farren in studio

Sn 7/4 The Alan Bown, Ten Years After, Tim Buckley
(Traffic, Idle Race)

- **Denis O'Keeffe becomes Peel's Nightride
  producer**

W 10/4 Tony 'Duster' Bennett, Pete Brown i/v live

Sn 14/4 Small Faces & PP Arnold, Brian Auger's Trinity
(Yardbirds)

W 17/4 Fleetwood Mac, Lady Diana Dukes i/v live

Sn 21/4 Family, Love Sculpture (Skip Biffferty, Scaffold)

W 24/4 The Circus, Spike Hawkins live

Sn 28/4 Arthur Brown, Chicken Shack
(Pentangle, New Generation)

W 1/5 Davey Graham live, poet Alan Jackson

Sn 5/5 Bonzo Dogs, Barclay James Harvest
(T Rex, Spooky Tooth, Blossom Toes)

W 8/5 Shirley & Dolly Collins, Brian Patten live

Sn 12/5 Captain Beefheart, The Eclection
(Ten Years After, Roy Harper)

W 15/5 Mike Hart, poet Mike Evans

Sn 19/5 Elmer Gantry's Velvet Opera, Gilbert O'Sullivan
(Tim Buckley, Small Faces, Love Sculpture; & i/v with
Jagger & Jones, pre-rec 15/5/68)

W 22/5 Pentangle, poet Mike Horovitz

Sn 26/5 Eric Burdon, David Bowie, Mike Stuart Span
(Alan Bown, Family)

W 29/5 Al Stewart, poet Pete Morgan

- **Top Gear moves to 3–5pm**

Sn 2/6 Fairport Convention, Fleetwood Mac (Bonzos,
Barclay James Harvest)

W 5/6 Stefan Grossman, Libby Houston in studio

Sn 9/6 Idle Race, Joe Cocker and the Grease Band
(Beefheart, Eclection)

W 12/6 Mike Chapman, Roger Jones in studio

Sn 16/6 The Nice, Donovan (Gilbert O'Sullivan,
Chicken Shack)

W 19/6 Champion Jack Dupree,
poet Christopher Logue live

Sn 23/6 Spooky Tooth, The Glass Menagerie (Eric
Burdon, Elmer Gantry's Velvet Opera)

W 26/6 Incredible String Band, 1st TX 6/3/68) Tom
Pickard in studio

Sn 30/6 Traffic, Savoy Brown, Deep Purple (Fairport
Convention, Bowie)

W 3/7 Ron Geesin, poet Geoff Hill live

Sn 7/7 Kinks, Pentangle, Tim Rose
(Fleetwood Mac, Idle Race)

W 10/7 John Martyn; Gillian Barron, Ron Geesin, Dave
Symonds in studio

Sn 14/7 T Rex, Leonard Cohen, Skip Bifferty
(Joe Cocker, The Nice)

W 17/7 Spider John Koerner, Tim Rose, Peter Roche,
Richard Hill in studio

Sn 21/7 Moody Blues, Bonzo Dogs, Free
(Donovan, Glass Menagerie)

W 24/7 Occasional Word Ensemble, Roy Harper;
Harry Lund in studio

Sn 28/7 Tim Hardin, The Eclection (Traffic, Spooky Tooth)

W 31/7 Principal Edward's Magic Theatre, Mike Raven,
Harry Lund, Henry Graham

Sn 4/8 Barclay James Harvest, Family, Jethro Tull
(Kinks, Pentangle)

W 7/8 Mike Cooper, Ron Geesin, Mick Farren, Len
Grant in studio

Sn 11/8 Pink Floyd, John Dummer Blues Band
(Tim Rose, Leonard Cohen)

W 14/8 Gordon Smith, Ron Geesin, Bob Harris, John
Marshall in studio

Sn 18/8 Ten Years After, Al Stewart (Skip Bifferty,
Bonzos)

W 21/8 Ian A Anderson, Jim Eldridge in studio

Sn 25/8 Taste, The Nice (Moody Blues, T Rex)

W 28/8 Bridget St John, Tom Rayworth in studio

Sn 1/9 Fleetwood Mac, Fairport Convention, Vilayat Khan
(Tim Hardin, Eclection)

W 4/9 Jo-Ann Kelly, Chris Kennedy in studio

Sn 8/9 Procol Harum, Chicken Shack
(Pink Floyd, Barclay James Harvest)

W 11/9 Wes Magee, Marc Brierley; Nick Powells, Chris
Pierce, Hoya Hutt in studio

Sn 15/9 Honeybus (Family, Al Stewart)

W 18/9 Dave Kelly; Frances Horovitz, David Ackles,
Nirvana in studio

St 21/9 Peel presents special show on pop lyrics and
censorship, The Voice Of Pop instead of Scene And
Heard, R1 6.30–7.30pm (rpt M 23/9, 7.45–8.45pm)

Sn 22/9 Tim Rose, Idle Race (Jethro Tull, The Nice)

W 25/9 Piero Heliczer in studio, Peter Sarstedt

Sn 29/9 Joni Mitchell, Jeff Beck
(Fairport Convention, Ten Years After)

W 2/10 Libby Houston in studio, John James

Sn 6/10 Spooky Tooth, Love Sculpture
(Vilayat Khan, Procol Harum)

- **Pete Carr takes over as Peel's Nightride
  producer**

W 9/10 Jackson C Frank, David Black, Richard Neville,
Christopher Hill in studio

Sn 13/10 Joe Cocker and the Grease Band, Tim
Buckley, Fleetwood Mac (Honeybus)

W 16/10 & 23/10 Night Ride not presented by Peel

Sn 20/10 Bonzo dogs, The Bakerloo Line (Idle Race,
Tim Rose)

Sn 27/10 Brian Auger's Trinity, David Ackles, Blossom
Toes (Taste)

W 30/10 Adrian Henri & Andy Roberts, Taste

Sn 3/11 Pentangle, Duster Bennett (Jeff Beck Group,
Love Sculpture)

W 6/11 John Gourd, Anne Beresford, John Wells in
studio

Sn 10/11 T Rex, Junior's Eyes (Joni Mitchell,
Chicken Shack)

W 13/11 Amory Kane, Barry McSweeney, Lord Hunt,
HH Rogers in studio

Sn 17/11 Pretty Things, Andromeda (Joe Cocker) & live
i/v with Jagger & Richards

W 20/11 John Horder, Al Kooper in studio; Tim Hollier

Sn 24/11 Family, Fleetwood Mac, The Gun (David
Ackles)

W 27/11 Mark Talbot in studio; Elton John, David
McWilliams

Sn 1/12 The Nice, Aynsley Dunbar Retaliation
(Bonzos, Brian Auger's Trinity)

W 4/12 presented by Pete Drummond: Patrick
Dickinson, John Renbourn & Terry Cox, Sallyangie

Sn 8/12 Writing on the Wall, Eclection
(Blossom Toes, Spooky Tooth)

W 11/12 John Martyn & Harold McNair, Jackie McShee
& John Renbourne, Christopher Logue, Lennon &
Yoko i/v

Sn 15/12 Jethro Tull, Pink Floyd
(Duster Bennet, The Pentangle)

- **John Muir returns as producer of Peel's
  Nightride**

W 18/12 Roger McGough, Bert Jansch & Danny
Thompson, Harvey Matusow's Jews Harp Band

Sn 22/12 Manfred Mann, Fairport Convention
(Tyrannosaurus Rex, Andromeda)

W 25/12 Night Ride not presented by Peel

Sn 29/12 Honeybus, Van der Graaf Generator (Pretty Things, The Gun)

1969

W 1/1 Tim Hart & Maddy Prior, Third Ear Band

Sn 5/1 Ten Years After, Caravan (Junior's Eyes, Family)

W 8/1 Pete Brown and the Battered Ornaments

Sn 12/1 Strawbs, Yes (The Nice, Eclection)

W 15/1 Philip Cordell, Peggy Seeger, Harvey Matusow

Sn 19/1 Jon Hiseman's Colosseum, The Liverpool Scene (Pink Floyd, Manfred Mann)

W 22/1 Gasworks, poet Kevin Morgan (Fairport Convention, 1st TX on a non-Peel Night Ride 15/12/68)

Sn 26/1 Idle Race, Keef Hartley (Jethro Tull, Fairport Convention, 1st TX 22/12/68)

W 29/1 Anna Taylor, Dave Brock and friends

Sn 2/2 Alexis Korner & Nick South (Honeybus, Writing on the Wall)

W 5/2 Shirley Collins & the Tinderbox, Anna Lockwood, James Verner, Mike Tristram

Sn 9/2 Black Cat Bones, Deep Purple (Van der Graaf Generator)

W 12/2 Stevie Smith, David Munro, Chris Hogwood & Young Tradition, Hans Keller

Sn 16/2 Moby Grape, Bakerloo (Strawbs, Caravan)

W 19/2 R1 Club, 12 noon, introduced by David Symonds & John Peel from The Paris Cinema, with Bonzos live & guests Tyrannosaurus Rex, Dave Clark, Peter Gordeno & Clodagh Rogers

W 19/2 poet George Macbeth, Ahmad Al-Khalil & Hameed Mohammed, Kenny Everett (Stefan Grossman)

Sn 23/2 Moody Blues, Spooky Tooth (Yes, The Liverpool Scene)

W 26/2 Bob Cobbings, David Hughes, Gordon Smith, Lesley Duncan & Sweet Thursday

Sn 2/3 Mason Capaldi Wood & Frog, Terry Reid (Ten Years After, Jon Hiseman's Colosseum)

W 5/3 Mississippi Fred McDowell, Adrian Mitchell, Incredible String Band, Fraser White

Sn 9/3 Love Sculpture, Taste, The Glass Menagerie (Idle Race)

W 12/3 Dennis Lysons, Derek Brimstone, Fraser White, David Rider

Sn 16/3 Fleetwood Mac, Edgar Broughton Band (Moby Grape, Strawbs)

W 19/3 Roy Fuller, Gordon Lightfoot, Steve Scott, Wes Waring, Patrick Sky

Sn 23/3 Led Zeppelin, Free (Mood Blues, Deep Purple)

• **Pete Ritzema takes over as Peel's Night Ride producer**

W 26/3 Tammo de Jongh, Jim Haynes, Forest, Felix Scorpio

Sn 30/3 Family, Principal Edwards' Magic Theatre (Spooky Tooth, Bakerloo)

W 2/4 Colin Faber, John Harder, Patrick Sky

Sn 6/4 Fairport Convention, Mandrake Paddle Steamer (Mason Capaldi Wood & Frog, Black Cat Bones)

W 9/4 poet Bob Wood, Ron Geesin

Sn 13/4 Bonzo Dogs, Blodwyn Pig (Terry Reid, The Glass Menagerie)

W 16/4 Sadish Kumar, Duster Bennett

Sn 20/4 The Nice, Eire Apparent (Taste, Led Zeppelin)

W 23/4 Bernard Kelly, Colin Carson, Uli McCarthy from Real Camden Arts Festival Forever, Robin Scott

• **Walters appointed Top Gear producer**

• **Top Gear moved to Sn 7–9pm**

• **Peel's Night Ride moved to Wed 8.15–9.15pm MW only**

Sn 27/4 Eclection (Family, Principal Edwards Magic Theatre)

W 30/4 Mike Cooper

Sn 4/5 Juniors Eyes, Keef Hartley (Fairport Convention, Edgar Broughton Band)

W 7/5 Bob Cobbings, Ivor Cutler

Sn 11/5 T Rex, King Crimson (Fleetwood Mac, Bonzos)

W 14/5 Pink Floyd, Fairport Convention interview

Sn 18/5 Pentangle, John Dummer's Blues Band (Blodwyn Pigg, Mandrake Paddle Steamer)

W 21/5 High Tide, poet Alan Jackson

Sn 25/5 Savoy Brown Blues Band, Pretty Things (The Nice, Free)

W 28/5 John Fahey, Tony van Den Burgh interview, Teresa Lisber, poet Pete Roche

Sn 1/6 Procol Harum (Eire Apparent, The Eclection, Pink Floyd, 1st TX Night Ride 14/5/68)

W 4/6 Richie Havens, Brian Patten

Sn 8/6 Richie Havens, Nice, Roy Harper (Juniors Eyes)

W 11/6 Famous Jug Band, Marc Bolan reading poetry

Sn 15/6 Soft Machine, Ten Years After (Keef Hartley Band, T Rex)

W 18/6 Mike Chapman, Phil Ochs, Richard Branson, Don Gardner

Sn 22/6 Jethro Tull, Chicken Shack, John Fahey 3 unused tracks from session, 1st TX Night Ride 28/5/69 (King Crimson)

W 25/6 Hard Meat, Ralph Steadman, Eddie Linden, Roy Guest in studio

Sn 29/6 Idle Race, Led Zeppelin (Pentangle, Savoy Brown Blues Band)

W 2/7 Otis Spann, Michael Chapman, Paul Oliver, Mike Cooper

Sn 6/7 John Hiseman's Colosseum, Imrat Khan (Pretty Things, John Dummer's Blues Band)

W 9/7 Wizz Jones, John Esam, David Peel

Sn 13/7 Blodwyn Pigg, Steamhammer (Richie Havens, Procol Harum)

W 16/7 classical guitarist John Williams, poet Len Grant, Makunda Das, Viv Broughton

Sn 20/7 Killing Floor, Liverpool Scene (Soft Machine, The Nice)

W 23/7 The Elizabethan Jazz Trio, Charly Hart & Albert Kovitz, Edward English, James Harpham, Guy Thornton

Sn 27/7 Third Ear Band (Roy Harper, Ten Years After)

W 30/7 Patrick Sky, Eddie Linden

Sn 3/8 Family, Bonzos (Jethro Tull, Idle Race)

W 6/8 Nick Drake, Ian Sinclair in studio

Sn 10/8 Edgar Broughton Band; Led Zeppelin, whole of 2nd hour, as pilot of Jeff Griffin's concert show

W 13/8 The Egg, Miss Jane de Mendelssohn

Sn 17/8 Sweet Marriage, High Tide (John Fahey, Pink Floyd, 1st TX Nightride 14/5/68)

W 20/8 Panama Jug Band, John F Shephard

Sn 24/8 Bridget St John, Incredible String Band (Chicken Shack)

W 27/8 Young Tradition

Sn 31/8 Michael Chapman (Imrat Khan, Jon Hiseman's Colosseum)

W 3/9 Anne Briggs, Barry McSweeney, David Luddy

Sn 7/9 Blossom Toes, King Crimson, Strawbs

W 10/9 Andy Fernbach, Pete Morgan

Sn 14/9 Caravan, Battered Ornaments (Steamhammer)

W 17/9 Tim Souster, Miss Lindsay Levy & Alex Elliot, Viv Stanshall, Pete Roche

Sn 21/9 Hard Meat, Melanie (Third Ear Band)

W 24/9 Coyne Clague, Adrian Mitchell in studio

• **Wed 'Son of Nightride' mid-evening show axed**

• **Top Gear moves to Saturdays 3–5pm**

St 27/9 Humble Pie, Fairport Convention (Blodwyn Pigg)

St 4/10 (Liverpool Scene): one hour show only, from 16.00, European Pop Jury before

St 11/10 Ron Geesin, Joe Cocker and the Grease Band (Led Zeppelin)

St 18/10 Rennaissance, Doctor K (Bridget St John)

St 25/10 Fat Mattress, Keef Hartley Band (Bonzos, Edgar Broughton Band)

St 1/11 Christine Perfect, Griffin (Family, Incredible String Band)

St 8/11 Juicy Lucy, Juke Boy Bonner (Sweet Marriage, King Crimson)

St 15/11 Forest, Mike Cooper & Jo-Ann Kelly & Bob Ball (High Tide)

St 22/11 T Rex, Colosseum & Barbara Thomson (Battered Ornaments)

St 29/11 Soft Machine, Black Sabbath (Blossom Toes, Michael Chapman)

St 6/12 Skin Alley, Stone the Crows (Humble Pie)

St 13/12 Al Stewart, Free (Hard Meat, Fairport Convention)

St 20/12 Mighty Baby (Melanie)

St 27/12 (many repeats) & interview guests Robert Wyatt, Sandy Denny, Dick Heckstall-Smith, Pat Campbell 'Miss Top Gear'

1970

• **Peel 'Sunday Show' concerts begin, Sun 4–5pm produced by Jeff Griffin**

St 3/1 Roy Harper, Liverpool Scene (Fat Mattress)

Sn 4/1 Family, Tyrannosaurus Rex

St 10/1 Medicine Head, Savoy Brown (Rennaissance)

Sn 11/1 Duster Bennett, Chicken Shack

St 17/1 Edgar Broughton Band, Principal Edwards Magic Theatre (Joe Cocker & The Grease Band)

Sn 18/1 Savoy Brown, Free

St 24/1 Duster Bennett, Manfred Mann Chapter Three (Strawbs, Ron Geesin)

Sn 25/1 Keef Hartley Band

St 31/1 Graham Bond Initiation, Galliard (Keef Hartley Band)

Sn 1/2 Blodwyn Pig

St 7/2 Daddy Long Legs, Van der Graaf Generator (Soft Machine, Juke Boy Bonner)

Sn 8/2 David Bowie

St 14/2 Matthews' Southern Comfort, Arthur Crudup (Griffin)

Sn 15/2 Third Ear Band, Edgar Broughton Band

St 21/2 Mott the Hoople, Welfare State (Juicy Lucy)

Sn 22/2 Joe Cocker and the Grease Band

St 28/2 Ralph McTell, Kevin Ayers (Forest)

Sn 1/3 Brian Auger's Trinity

St 7/3 Humblebums, Nucleus (Free)

Sn 8/3 Jon Hiseman's Colosseum

St 14/3 Syd Barrett, Cochise (Stone the Crows, T Rex)

Sn 15/3 Juicy Lucy, Yes

St 21/3 Viv Stanshall's Big Grunt, Johnny Shines (Black Sabbath, Colosseum & Barbara Thompson)

Sn 22/3 Graham Bond Initiation, Jim James & Rafael Callaghan

St 28/3 Faces, Andy Roberts (Principal Edward's Magic Theatre)

Sn 29/3 introduced by Alan Black

St 4/4 John and Beverley Martyn (Edgar Broughton Band, Manfred Mann Chapter Three)

Sn 5/4 Renaissance, Elton John and Hookfoot

• **Sounds of the Seventies starts on Monday 6 April 1970**

• **Sunday Show from now on 'repeated Wednesday' at 6pm.**

• **Top Gear stays on Saturdays until Sept 1971**

St 11/4 Steeleye Span, High Tide (Liverpool Scene)

Sn 12/4 Taste, Atomic Rooster

St 18/4 East of Eden, Imrat Khan
(Matthews' Southern Comfort)
Sn 19/4 Fleetwood Mac introduced by David Symonds
St 25/4 Michael Chapman, Fotheringay
(Kevin Ayers, Mott the Hoople)
Sn 26/4 Black Sabbath, Medicine Head
St 2/5 Fairport Convention, Pete Brown and Piblokto
(Al Stewart)
Sn 3/5 Mott the Hoople, Mike Cooper
St 9/5 Curved Air (Roy Harper, Medicine Head)
Sn 10/5 Traffic
St 16/5 Soft Machine, Buddy Knox & Bad River
(Duster Bennett)
Sn 17/5 Al Stewart, Bridget St John, Kevin Ayers
St 23/5 Fleetwood Mac & Nic Pickett, Formerly Fat Harry
(Ralph McTell)
Sn 24/5 Pretty Things, Daddy Long Legs
St 30/5 Stone the Crows, Brett Marvin & the
Thunderbolts (Syd Barrett)
Sn 31/5 Soft Machine, Michael Chapman
St 6/6 Dr Strangely Strange (Faces, Arthur Crudup)
Sn 7/6 Stone the Crows, Humblebums
St 13/6 Moon (Humblebums, Andy Roberts/Mighty
Baby)
Sn 14/6 Pretty Things, Skid Row
St 20/6 Third Ear Band (Johnny Shivers, Viv Stanshall's
Big Grunt)
Sn 21/6 Procol Harum
St 27/6 Steeleye Span (Nucleus, High Tide)
Sn 28/6 Matthews' Southern Comfort, Alan Bown
St 4/7 Country Joe McDonald (Fotheringay, Cochise)
Sn 5/7 Faces, Argent
St 11/7 Kevin Ayers, Son House (East of Eden)
Sn 12/7 Free, Trader Horne
St 18/7 Supertramp (Soft Machine,
John & Beverley Martyn)
Sn 19/7 Pink Floyd: 'Atom Heart Mother' first broadcast
St 25/7 Skid Row, Incredible String Band (Curved Air)
Sn 26/7 Mungo Jerry, Simon & Steve, Jo-Ann Kelly &
Bob Hall, Brett Marvin & The Thunderbolts
St 1/8 Quartermass, Osibisa (Fairport Convention)
Sn 2/8 Van der Graaf Generator, If
St 8/8 – St 29/8 First Gear: rock 'n' roll sessions
introduced by Johnny Moran
Sn 9/8 – Sn 6/9 either not introduced by Peel,
or repeats
St 5/9 Chieftains, Family (Formerly Fat Harry)
St 12/9 Groundhogs, East of Eden (Stone the Crows)
Sn 13/9 Brinsley Schwarz, Curved Air
St 19/9 Faces, Hawkwind (Brett Marvin & the
Thunderbolts, Moon)
Sn 20/9 Humble Pie
St 26/9 Edgar Broughton Band, Keith Tippett
(Kevin Ayers)
Sn 27/9 Family
St 3/10 Blodwyn Pigg, Everyone
(Incredible String Band)

• **Concert moves to 7–8pm Sundays**

Sn 4/10 Quintessence, Cochise
St 10/10 Forest (Osibisa, Country Joe McDonald)
Sn 11/10 Caravan, Supertramp
St 17/10 Amazing Band (Dr Strangely Strange,
Son House)
Sn 18/10 Strawbs, Climax Chicago Blues Band
St 24/10 Medicine Head, Van der Graaf Generator
(Steeleye Span)
Sn 25/10 Fairport Convention, Mott the Hoople
St 31/10 Strawbs, Homesick James & Grizelda,
Wommet
Sn 1/11 James Taylor, Dr Strangely Strange
St 7/11 Cochise, T Rex (Skid Row)
Sn 8/11 Colosseum
St 14/11 Caravan (Chieftains, Quartermass)

Sn 15/11 Mick Abrahams' Band, Hawkwind
St 21/11 Bridget St John, Terry & Gay Woods
(Groundhogs, East of Eden)
Sn 22/11 Keef Hartley Band
St 28/11 Pink Fairies, Matthews' Southern Comfort
(Michael Chapman)
Sn 29/11 Faces, Wishbone Ash
St 5/12 Mr Fox, Brinsley Schwartz (Family)
Sn 6/12 Chicken Shack, Noir
St 12/12 Larry Johnson (Keith Tippett, Hawkwind)
Sn 13/12 Blodwyn Pig
St 19/12 Ralph McTell (Faces, Everyone, Edgar
Broughton Band)
Sn 20/12 Jellybread, T Rex
St 26/12 'The Carols Concert', Rudies (many repeats)
Sn 27/12 Joni Mitchell

1971

St 2/1 Soft Machine, Mike Cooper (Forest)
Sn 3/1 'Penny Concert': Comus, Demon Fuzz, Heron,
Titus Groan
St 9/1 Incredible String Band
(Cochise, Van der Graaf Generator)
Sn 10/1 Livingston Taylor
St 16/1 Holy Willie's Prayer, Wizz Jones (Mick Abrahams)
Sn 17/1 Skid Row, Third Ear Band
St 23/1 Fleetwood Mac, Delivery (Medicine Head)
Sn 24/1 Atomic Rooster, Satisfaction
St 30/1 Lindisfarne, Symbiosis
(T Rex, Terry and Gay Woods)
Sn 31/1 Kevin Ayers, Bridget St John
St 6/2 Gene Vincent & The Houseshakers, National Head
Band (Caravan, Ralph McTell)
Sn 7/2 Brian Auger's Oblivion Express, Bronco
St 13/2 Writing on the Wall, Quiver (Bridget St John)
Sn 14/2 Argent, Egg
St 20/2 Nico, Groundhogs (Larry Johnson)
Sn 21/2 Roy Young Band, Patto
St 27/2 Skid Row, Ivor Cutler (Mr Fox)
Sn 28/2 Stefan Grossman, Quiver
St 6/3 Stud (Pink Fairies, Brinsley Schwartz)
Sn 7/3 Edgar Broughton Band
St 13/3 Arc, Mickey Jupp's Legend (Wizz Jones, Soft
Machine)
Sn 14/3 Curved Air, Patto
St 20/3 Southern Comfort, Freaks (Mike Cooper)
Sn 21/3 Soft Machine '& Heavy Friends'
St 27/3 Nucleus, Steeleye Span (Fleetwood Mac,
Incredible String Band)
Sn 28/3 Incredible String Band
St 3/4 Arthur Brown's Kingdom Come (Delivery, Holy
Willie's Prayer)
Sn 4/4 Led Zeppelin: 'Stairway to Heaven' first broadcast
St 10/4 Mick Abrahams Band, Principal Edwards Magic
Theatre (Lindisfarne)
Sn 11/4 Keef Hartley Band, Brinsley Schwarz
St 17/4 Danta, Caravan (National Head Band)
Sn 18/4 Aubrey Small, Nucleus
St 24/4 Hawkwind, Gnidrolog (Quiver)
Sn 25/4 Mogul Thrash, Medicine Head
St 1/5 Cochise (Nico, Groundhogs)
Sn 2/5 Osibisa, Daddy Longlegs
St 8/5 Help Yourself (Stud, Ivor Cutler)
Sn 9/5 Groundhogs, John Martyn
St 15/5 Roy Harper, Pretty Things (Arc)
Sn 16/5 Caravan, Tir Na Nog
St 22/5 Loudon Wainwright III (Freaks, Steeleye Span)
Sn 23/5 Faces
St 29/5 Shawn Phillips, Henry Cow (Southern Comfort)
Sn 30/5 Rolling Stones, recorded by the band
themselves live at Leeds University

St 5/6 Robin & Barry Dransfield, Ian Matthews
(Nucleus, Legend)
Sn 6/6 Mick Abrahams' Band, Roy Harper
St 12/6 Medicine Head, David Parker
(Arthur Brown's Kingdom Come)
Sn 13/6 Lancaster, Help Yourself
St 19/6 Paul Savage & John Hewitt, Ron Geesin
(Caravan, Mick Abrahams Band)
Sn 20/6 David Bowie, Heron
St 26/6 Roger Ruskin Spear & the Giant Orchestral
Wardrobe, Soft Machine (Principal Edward's Magic
Theatre)
Sn 27/6 Paladin, Bell 'n' Arc
St 3/7 Dando Shaft, Edgar Broughton Band (Gnidrolog)
Sn 4/7 (Joni Mitchell, 1st TX 27/12/70)
St 10/7 Osibisa, Wishbone Ash (Help Yourself)
produced by Pete Ritzema
Sn 11/7 Heads Hands and Feet, Dando Shaft
St 17/7 Family (Loudon Wainwright III)
Sn 18/7 Southern Comfort, Lindisfarne
St 24/7 Brotherhood of Breath, Mott the Hoople
(Medicine Head)
Sn 25/7 Supertramp, National Head Band
St 31/7 Reginald (Henry Cow, Paul Savage & John
Hewitt)
Sn 1/8 Cochise, Forest
St 7/8 – St 28/8 Vivien Stanshall's Radio Flashes, co-
presented with Keith Moon; including debut sessions
by Greyhound 14/8 and Gaspar Lawal Band 28/8
(& repeats)
Sn 8/8 – Sn 29/8 Concerts introduced by Bob Harris /
Alan Black
St 4/9 Bronco, Tim Hart & Maddy Prior (Roy Harper,
Soft Machine)
Sn 5/9 If, Mr Fox
St 11/9 Lindisfarne (Hawkwind, Shawn Phillips, Robin &
Barry Dransfield)
Sn 12/9 Dion, Stackwaddy
St 18/9 Gypsy, Stone the Crows (David Parker,
Dando Shaft)
Sn 19/9 Quiver, Bridget St John
St 25/9 Mr Fox (Brotherhood of Breath, Ron Geesin)
Sn 26/9 Steeleye Span

• **Concert moves to 10pm FM on Tuesdays
from 5/10/71**

• **Top Gear moves to 10pm FM (mono) Wed
becomes part of Sounds Of The Seventies**

T 5/10 Van der Graaf Generator, Miller Anderson
W 6/10 Faces (Family, Wishbone Ash)
T 12/10 Pink Floyd: 'Echoes' first broadcast
W 13/10 Loudon Wainwright III, Incredible String Band
(Osibisa)
T 19/10 Manfred Mann, Michael Chapman
W 20/10 John Martyn, Stackridge
(Edgar Broughton Band)
T 26/10 Loudon Wainwright III, Pink Fairies
W 27/10 Stoneground, Steve Tilston
(Mott the Hoople, Bronco)
T 2/11 Stefan Grossman, Unicorn
W 3/11 Home, Thin Lizzy (Tim Hart & Maddy Prior)
T 9/11 Tom Paxton
W 10/11 Terry Reid, Natural Gas, Lol Coxhill & David
Bedford (Lindisfarne)
T 16/11 Stone the Crows, Pink Fairies
W 17/11 Nucleus, Gong (Gypsy)
T 23/11 Stoneground
W 24/11 Emitt Rhodes, Ivor Cutler, Soft Machine
T 30/11 Ralph McTell, America
W 1/12 Manfred Mann's Earth Band, Aubrey Small
(Loudon Wainwright III)
T 7/12 Lindisfarne, Stealers Wheel, Rab Noakes
W 8/12 King Biscuit Boy (Incredible String Band,
John Martyn)
T 14/12 Marmalade, Gypsy

W 15/12 Ralph McTell (Home, Stackridge)

T 21/12 Gilbert O'Sullivan, Brinsley Schwarz

W 22/12 Peace, Michael Chapman (Faces, Carol Concert)

T 28/12 Family

W 29/12 Van der Graaf Generator (Steve Tilston, Thin Lizzy)

1972

- Peel starts Fri 'boogie night' show produced by John Muir 10pm–12
- Concert moved to St 6.30–7.30pm & Peel stops presenting it
- Top Gear moves to Tuesday nights

T 4/1 Wizz Jones (Nucleus, Lol Coxhill & David Bedford)

F 7/1 Keef Hartley, Miller Anderson, Gentle Giant, Anne Briggs

T 11/1 Osibisa (Stoneground, Natural Gas)

F 14/1 Jeff Beck, Medicine Head, Arthur Brown's Kingdom Come, Barclay James Harvest

T 18/1 Danta, Dando Shaft (Gong)

F 21/1 Keith Tippett, Andy Roberts & Adrian Henri, Stray, Roxy Music

T 25/1 Southern Comfort, Matching Mole (Soft Machine)

F 28/1 David Bowie, Genesis, Manfred Mann's Earth Band, If

T 1/2 Keef Hartley, Plainsong (Aubrey Small)

F 4/2 Mick Abrahams, Lindisfarne (Miller Anderson, Gentle Giant)

T 8/2 Barclay James Harvest, Steeleye Span (Ralph McTell, Manfred Mann's Earth Band)

F 11/2 Mike Maran, Third Ear Band (Jeff Beck, Keef Hartley)

T 15/2 Jellybread (Michael Chapman, Van der Graaf Generator)

F 18/2 Mick Softley, Stackwaddy (Medicine Head, Roxy Music)

T 22/2 Gary Wright (Wizz Jones, Osibisa)

F 25/2 Roy Young Band, Budgie (Andy Roberts & Adrian Henri, Barclay James Harvest)

T 29/2 Stealers Wheel (Emitt Rhodes, King Biscuit Boy)

F 3/3 Pete Atkin, Status Quo (Arthur Brown's Kingdom Come, Keith Tippett)

T 7/3 Egg (Danta, Southern Comfort)

F 10/3 Steeleye Span, Vinegar Joe (Manfred Mann's Earth Band, Lindisfarne)

T 14/3 Pete Atkin, Groundhogs, Henry Cow

F 17/3 Edgar Broughton Band, Incredible String Band (Genesis, Mick Abrahams)

T 21/3 Mike Cooper, Stud

F 24/3 Matching Mole, Al Stewart (Stray, If)

T 28/3 Uncle Dog (Keef Hartley, Matching Mole)

F 31/3 Heads Hands and Feet, Duster Bennett (David Bowie, Roy Young Band)

T 4/4 Stackridge, Chris Hardy, Chris Spedding

F 7/4 Audience, Michael Chapman (Mike Maran, Stackwaddy)

T 11/4 Sandy Denny & Bunch (Stealers Wheel, Jellybread)

F 14/4 Kevin Ayers, Johnstons (Mick Softley, Budgie)

T 18/4 High Level Ranters (Plainsong, Barclay James Harvest)

F 21/4 Danta, Mike Cooper's Machine Gun Company (Pete Atkin, Edgar Broughton Band)

T 25/4 Argent, Bridget St John, Wishbone Ash

F 28/4 Stone the Crows, Jellybread (Al Stewart, Steeleye Span)

T 2/5 Medicine Head, Caravan (Steeleye Span)

F 5/5 John Dummer, Max Merritt & The Meteors (Incredible String Band, Duster Bennett)

T 9/5 Matching Mole (Pete Atkin, Gary Wright)

F 12/5 Ralph McTell, Clair Hammill (Status Quo, Vinegar Joe)

T 16/5 Kinks, Quiver (Groundhogs, Mike Cooper)

F 19/5 Help Yourself, Zoot Money (Kevin Ayers, Audience)

T 23/5 David Bowie, Home (Egg)

F 26/5 Slade, Paladin (Johnstons, Stone the Crows)

T 30/5 Martin Carthy (Stud, Henry Cow)

F 2/6 Country Joe McDonald, Thin Lizzy (Mike Cooper's Machine Gun Company)

T 6/6 Plainsong, Rab Noakes (Matching Mole)

F 9/6 Tir Na Nog, Brian Auger's Oblivion Express (Heads Hands and Feet, Danta)

T 13/6 Lol Coxhill, Lindisfarne (Chris Spedding)

F 16/6 Quiver (Max Merritt, John Dummer)

T 20/6 Brotherhood of Breath (High Level Ranters, Chris Hardy)

F 23/6 JSD Band, Roxy Music (Jellybread, Ralph McTell)

T 27/6 Finbar & Eddie Furey (Medicine Head, Bridget St John, Argent)

F 30/6 Natural Gas, John Baldry (Help Yourself, Claire Hammill)

T 4/7 Albion Country Band (Kinks, Caravan)

F 7/7 Bridget St John, Edgar Broughton (Zoot Money, Paladin)

T 11/7 Heads Hands & Feet, Nic Jones, Fumble

F 14/7 Ashman Reynolds, Gentle Giant (Slade, Tir Na Nog)

T 18/7 Tony Capstick, Soft Machine (Home)

F 21/7 Miller Anderson, Mark Almond (Thin Lizzy, JSD Band)

T 25/7 Cheviot Ranters, Matthew Ellis, JSD Band (David Bowie)

F 28/7 Home, Steeleye Span (Country Joe McDonald, Roxy Music) presented by Bob Harris

T 1/8 Roxy Music (Wishbone Ash, Rab Noakes)

F 4/8 Neil Innes, Pretty Things (John Baldry, Edgar Broughton Band)

T 8/8 Planxty (Martin Carthy, Lindisfarne)

F 11/8 Duster Bennett, Adrian Henri & Andy Roberts (Bridget St John, Natural Gas)

T 15/8 Pretty Things, Harvey Andrews (Plainsong)

F 18/8 Gary Wright's Wonderwheel, Mike Maran (Ashman Reynolds, Mark Almond)

T 22/8 Pete Atkin, Coulson Dean McGuinness Flint (Quiver)

T 25/8 Medicine Head (Gentle Giant, Miller Anderson)

T 29/8 Incredible String Band (Nic Jones, Lol Coxhill)

F 1/9 Bronx Cheer, Uncle Dog (Pretty Things)

T 5/9 Gentle Giant, Sutherland Brothers (Albion Country Band)

F 8/9 Matthew Ellis, Arthur Brown's Kingdom Come (Home, Steeleye Span)

T 12/9 Supertramp, Man (Soft Machine)

F 15/9 John Dummer (Adrian Henri & Andy Roberts, Neil Innes)

T 19/9 Kingdom Come, String Driven Thing (Tony Capstick)

F 22/9 Roy Young Band (Duster Bennett, Matching Mole)

T 26/9 (Entire show of session repeats, going back to 68)

F 29/9 Manfred Mann's Earth Band (Wright's Wonderwheel, Mike Maran, Uncle Dog)

T 3/10 Chieftains (Matching Mole, Lindisfarne)

- Peel Fri show moves to Thurs, prod Bernie Andrews

Th 5/10 JSD Band, Honeybus (Medicine Head, Bronx Cheer)

T 10/10 no show

Th 12/10 Stackridge (Roy Young Band, John Dummer Blues Band)

T 17/10 Tir Na Nog, Glencoe, Hockett

Th 19/10 Jimmy Stevens (Ten Years After, Gary Wright's Wonderwheel, Home)

T 24/10 Steeleye Span, Ralph McTell (Heads Hands Feet, Gentle Giant)

Th 26/10 Clifford T Ward, Stray (Honeybus)

T 30/10 Barry Dransfield (Incredible String Band, Supertramp)

Th 2/11 Glencoe, Nazareth (Gentle Giant, JSD Band)

- All 'Sounds of the Seventies' start broadcasting in stereo from Monday 6/11/72

T 7/11 Nucleus, Genesis, Boys of the Lough

Th 9/11 Roxy Music, Wild Turkey (Stackridge, Jimmy Stevens)

T 14/11 Colin Blunstone, Henry Cow, Pretty Things

Th 16/11 Uncle Dog, Holy Mackerel (Clifford T Ward, Stray)

T 21/11 Isaac Guillory, Philip Goodhand-Tait, Back Door

Th 23/11 Supertramp, Rab Noakes & Robin McKidd (Ten Years After, Glencoe)

T 28/11 Joan Armatrading, Thin Lizzy, String Driven Thing

Th 30/11 Plainsong, Mike Maran (Nazareth, Wild Turkey)

T 5/12 JSD Band, Stealers Wheel (Ralph McTell)

Th 7/12 Status Quo, Nic Jones (Uncle Dog)

T 12/12 Crowbar, Brinsley Schwartz (Steeleye Span)

Th 14/12 Babe Ruth, Gentle Giant (Holy Mackarel, Ten Years After)

T 19/12 Robert Wyatt, Dalai Lama (Glencoe, Pete Atkin)

Th 21/12 Shoot (Roxy Music, Supertramp)

T 26/12 George Melly, Tony Capstick (Colin Blunstone, Cheviot Ranters)

Th 28/12 JSD Band (Rab Noakes & Robin McKidd, Status Quo)

1973

T 2/1 Just Us (Genesis, Barry Dransfield)

Th 4/1 Good Habit (Babe Ruth, Mike Maran)

T 9/1 Finbar and Eddie Furey (Isaac Guillory)

Th 11/1 Stealers Wheel (Nic Jones, Gentle Giant)

T 16/1 Status Quo (Boys of the Lough, Henry Cow)

Th 18/1 Lindisfarne, Alan Hull (Plainsong, Shoot)

T 23/1 Bees Make Honey, John Prine (Back Door, Joan Armatrading)

T 25/1 Stackridge, Richard Thompson & Linda Peters (Good Habit)

T 30/1 Kevin Coyne (Philip Goodhand-Tait, Man)

Th 1/2 Hatfield and the North, Tir Na Nog (Stealers Wheel, JSD Band)

T 6/2 Steeleye Span, Gerry Rafferty (Thin Lizzy, Kingdom Come)

Th 8/2 Mongrel, Rory Gallagher (Alan Hull)

T 13/2 Spare Rib, Dick Gaughan (String Driven Thing)

Th 15/2 Queen, Pretty Things (Lindisfarne, Richard Thompson & Linda Peters)

T 20/2 Fairport Convention (Tir Na Nog, Brinsley Schwartz)

Th 22/2 Steeleye Span (Hatfield and the North, Stackridge)

T 27/2 Swan Arcade, Patto (Stealers Wheel)

Th 1/3 Wild Turkey, Albion Country Band (Mongrel)

T 6/3 Ron Geesin, Sutherland Brothers & Quiver, Incredible String Band

Th 8/3 Roxy Music, Martin Carthy (Tir Na Nog, Rory Gallagher)

T 13/3 Can, Boys of the Lough (Robert Wyatt)

Th 15/3 Camel, Shirley and Dolly Collins (Pretty Things)

T 20/3 Country Gazette, Chieftains (Kevin Coyne, Bees Make Honey)

Th 22/3 Supertramp, John Dummer's Ooblee Dooblee Band (Queen, Steeleye Span)

T 27/3 Shawn Phillips, Colin Blunstone (Finbar and Eddie Furey)

Th 29/3 Home, Atlantis (Roxy Music)

T 3/4 Pete Atkin, Supersister (Steeleye Span)

Th 5/4 Joan Armatrading, Nazareth (Albion Country Band)

T 10/4 Bob Sargeant (Gerry Rafferty, Fairport Convention)

Th 12/4 Robin Trower (Camel, Wild Turkey)

T 17/4 Manfred Mann, Help Yourself (John Prine)

Th 19/4 Chilli Willi and the Red Hot Peppers, Clifford T Ward (John Dummer's Ooblee Dooblee Band)

T 24/4 Billy J Kramer, Gerry and the Pacemakers, Wayne Fontana

Th 26/4 Taggett (Martin Carthy, Supertramp)

T 1/5 JSD Band (Spare Rib, Swan Arcade, Ron Geesin)

Th 3/5 Frankie Miller with Brinsley Schwarz (Home, Atlantis)

T 8/5 Henry Cow (Patto, Sutherland Brothers & Quiver)

Th 10/5 Glencoe (Joan Armatrading, Chilli Willi)

T 15/5 Bob Marley and the Wailers (Incredible String Band, Country Gazette)

Th 17/5 Stray (Nazareth, Clifford T Ward)

T 22/5 Family (Dick Gaughan, Can)

Th 24/5 Deke Leonard & Iceberg (Robin Trower, Taggett)

T 29/5 Amon Duul II, Jack the Lad (Boys of the Lough): 'Tubular Bells' first broadcast

Th 31/5 Gypsy (Glencoe, Frankie Miller)

T 5/6 Faust (The Chieftains, Colin Blunstone)

Th 7/6 Stealers Wheel, Bridget St John (Stray)

T 12/6 Loudon Wainwright III, Gong (Bob Sargeant)

Th 14/6 PFM, Harvey Andrews & Graham Cooper (Deke Leonard & Iceberg)

T 19/6 Lol Coxhill, Sonny Terry & Brownie McGhee (Shawn Phillips)

Th 21/6 Back Door, Andy Roberts (Gypsy)

T 26/6 Ducks Deluxe (Manfred Mann, Pete Atkin)

Th 28/6 Blue, Chris Hardy & The Basement Blowers (Stealers Wheel)

T 3/7 Back Door (repeats unknown – PasB missing)

Th 5/7 Fat Grapple, Supertramp (Bridget St John)

T 10/7 Bongos and the Groovies, Bob Pegg and Nick Strutt (Henry Cow)

Th 12/7 Cymande, Mick Softley (Back Door)

T 17/7 Maldwyn Pope, Na Fili, Steve Rhodes Singers

Th 19/7 JSD Band, Joan Armatrading (PFM)

T 24/7 Fela Kuti, Peter Hammill (Bob Marley and the Wailers)

Th 26/7 Sassafras (Harvey Andrews & Graham Cooper, Blue)

T 31/7 Hatfield and the North (Family, Jack the Lad)

Th 2/8 Babe Ruth (Andy Roberts, Cymande)

T 7/8 Edgar Broughton Band, Thin Lizzy (Supersister)

Th 9/8 Pete Atkin (Chris Hardy, Supertramp)

T 14/8 Martin Carthy, The Great Crash (Amon Duul II, JSD Band)

Th 16/8 Thin Lizzy, Mike Maran (Fat Grapple)

T 21/8 – T 11/9 presented by Alan Black (all repeats)

Th 23/8 – Th 13/9 presented by Alexis Korner: debuts by Nicky James Band, Duffy Power Band; new sessions by Zoot Money, Caravan, Bronco, Gasworks, John Dummer (plus repeats)

T 18/9 Kevin Coyne & Gordon Smith, Medicine Head (Help Yourself)

Th 20/9 Nic Jones, Leo Sayer (Caravan)

T 25/9 Sandy Denny, Ivor Cutler (Faust)

Th 27/9 (Thin Lizzy, Joan Armatrading, Pete Atkin)

T 2/10 Man, Boys of the Lough (Gong)

Th 4/10 (Bronco, Mick Softley, Nicky James Band)

T 9/10 Jack the Lad (Loudon Wainwright III, Family)

Th 11/10 Gypsy (Leo Sayer, Mike Maran)

T 16/10 Horslips (Ducks Deluxe, Back Door)

Th 18/10 Blue, Principal Edward's Magic Theatre (Gasworks)

T 23/10 Incredible String Band (Lol Coxhill, Na Fili)

Th 25/10 Back Door (Nic Jones, Duffy Power Band)

T 30/10 Mike Chapman (Pegg and Strut, Thin Lizzy)

Th 1/11 Duster Bennett, Home (John Dummer)

T 6/11 Colin Blunstone, Planxty (Peter Hammill)

Th 8/11 String Driven Thing, Wild Turkey (Gypsy)

T 13/11 Tir Na Nog (Edgar Broughton Band, Hatfield and the North)

Th 15/11 Glencoe (Back Door, Principal Edward's Magic Theatre)

T 20/11 Curly, Soft Machine (The Great Crash)

Th 22/11 Stackridge, PFM (Blue)

T 27/11 Be Bop Deluxe (Medicine Head, Martin Carthy)

Th 29/11 Gallagher and Lyle (Duster Bennett, String Driven Thing)

T 4/12 Bees Make Honey (Sandy Denny, Coyne & Smith)

Th 6/12 Queen, Jimmy Stevens (Home)

T 11/12 Alan Hull, Slim Chance (Man, Ivor Cutler)

Th 13/12 Alvin Lee & Mylon LeFevre (Glencoe, PFM)

T 18/12 Fripp & Eno, Bridget St John (Jack the Lad)

Th 20/12 Deke Leonard & Iceberg (Wild Turkey, Stackridge)

T 25/12 Elton John's pub piano Christmas singalong, The Shadows, Bob Marley and the Wailers

Th 27/12 Joshua Rifkin (Gallagher & Lyle, Queen)

1974

T 1/1 Pete Atkin, Bob Sargeant (Boys of the Lough)

Th 3/1 Country Gazette (Jimmy Stevens, Alvin Lee & Mylon LeFevre)

T 8/1 Gentle Giant (Horslips, Colin Blunstone)

Th 10/1 Beckett, Al Stewart & Friends (Deke Leonard & Iceberg)

T 15/1 Joan Armatrading (Be Bop Deluxe, Tir Na Nog)

Th 17/1 Sassafras (Joshua Rifkin, Queen)

T 22/1 Sutherland Brothers & Quiver (Soft Machine, Michael Chapman)

• **Walters takes over Peel's Thurs show from Bernie Andrews**

Th 24/1 Chris Hardy, Jack the Lad (Chieftains)

T 29/1 Gong (Incredible String Band, Wailers)

Th 31/1 Kevin Coyne, Nic Jones (Na Fili)

T 5/2 Rab Noakes (Slim Chance, Maldwyn Pope)

Th 7/2 Neil Innes (Back Door, Colin Blunstone)

T 12/2 Richard & Linda Thompson, Can (Bridget St John)

Th 14/2 Caravan (Peter Hammill, Boys of the Lough)

T 19/2 Horslips, Ralph McTell (Bob Sargeant)

Th 21/2 Robin Dransfield, JSD Band, Tangerine Dream

T 26/2 Steeleye Span, Christie Hennessy (Gentle Giant)

Th 28/2 Mike Maran, Chilli Willi

T 5/3 Eno & the Winkies, Peter Hammill (Pete Atkin)

Th 7/3 Martin Carthy, Isotope (Jack the Lad)

T 12/3 Philip Goodhand-Tait, The Chieftains (Sutherland Brothers & Quiver)

Th 14/3 Stomu Yamashta's East Wind (Neil Innes, Chris Hardy)

T 19/3 Roy Harper, Procol Harum (Joan Armatrading)

Th 21/3 Magma (Slim Chance)

T 26/3 Robin Trower, Maldwyn Pope (Rab Noakes)

Th 28/3 Andy Roberts (Caravan, Nic Jones)

T 2/4 Hatfield and the North (Horslips, Richard and Linda Thompson)

Th 4/4 Lindisfarne (Robin Dransfield, Chilli Willi)

T 9/4 Swan Arcade (Gong, Ralph McTell)

Th 11/4 Thin Lizzy (Kevin Coyne, Tangerine Dream)

T 16/4 Barry Dransfield (Philip Goodhand-Tait, Steeleye Span)

Th 18/4, T 23/4, Th 25/4 with Paul Gambaccini / Steve Bradshaw, produced by Teddy Warrick (repeats)

T 30/4 Blue (Can, Maldwyn Pope)

T 2/5 Global Village Trucking Company (JSD Band, Mike Maran)

T 7/5 Byzantium (Christie Hennessy, Peter Hammill)

Th 9/5 Henry Cow (Andy Roberts, Martin Carthy)

T 14/5 Eddie and Finbar Furey (Hatfield and the North, Robin Trower)

Th 16/5 Phoenix (Isotope, Arthur Crudup)

T 21/5 Isaac Guillory, Jack the Lad (The Chieftains)

Th 23/5 Be Bop Deluxe, Dave Mason (Stomu Yamashta's East Wind)

T 28/5 Pete Atkin (Procol Harum, Swan Arcade)

Th 30/5 Batti Mamzelle (Magma)

T 4/6 Ducks Deluxe (Blue, Barry Dransfield)

Th 6/6 Supertramp (Lindisfarne, Thin Lizzy)

T 11/6 Tony Capstick, Cockney Rebel (Byzantium)

Th 13/6 Bob Sargeant (Global Village Trucking Company, Henry Cow)

T 18/6 Randy Newman (Eddie and Finbar Furey, Isaac Guillory)

Th 20/6 Malicorne (Phoenix, Be Bop Deluxe)

T 25/6 Joan Armatrading, Kevin Coyne (Jack the Lad)

Th 27/6 Mike Cooper & the Trout Steel Band (Batti Mamzelle, Dave Mason)

T 2/7 John Golding, Cymande (Pete Atkin)

Th 4/7 Chapman-Whitney Streetwalkers (Supertramp)

T 9/7 Stray, Blodwyn Pig (Ducks Deluxe)

Th 11/7 The Kinks, Cheviot Ranters, Tangerine Dream

T 16/7 Andy MacKay, Slapp Happy (Tony Capstick)

Th 18/7 High Level Ranters, Carol Grimes (Bob Sargeant)

T 23/7 Michael Chapman, Heavy Metal Kids (Cockney Rebel)

Th 25/7 Brinsley Schwarz, Na Fili (Mike Cooper)

T 30/7 Duane Eddy, Kevin Ayers & the Soporifics (Randy Newman)

Th 1/8 Starry-Eyed and Laughing (Chapman-Whitney Streetwalkers, Malicorne)

T 6/8 Fairport Convention, Isotope (Kevin Coyne)

Th 8/8 Barclay James Harvest, Chilli Willi (The Kinks)

T 13/8 John Doonan, Sutherland Brothers & Quiver (John Golding)

Th 15/8 String Driven Thing (Carol Grimes, Cheviot Ranters)

T 20/8 Chris Stainton's Tundra (Cymande, Blodwyn Pig)

Th 22/8 Kokomo (Starry-Eyed and Laughing, High Level Ranters)

T 27/8 private tape of Mike Oldfield's 'Hergest Ridge'

Th 29/8 Bridget St John (Brinsley Schwarz, Tangerine Dream)

T 3/9 Peter Hammill, Viola Wills & Gonzalez (Andy MacKay)

Th 5/9 Peaches (repeats unknown, PasB missing)

T 10/9 Jess Roden (Slapp Happy)

Th 12/9 Back Door (Barclay James Harvest, String Driven Thing)

T 17/9 Robin & Barry Dransfield (Stray, Michael Chapman)

Th 19/9 Jabula (Kokomo, Ron Geesin)

T 24/9 Unicorn, Boys of the Lough (Heavy Metal Kids)

Th 26/9 Robert Wyatt, Gilgamesh (Bridget St John)

T 1/10 Jack the Lad (Kevin Ayers & the Soporifics)

Th 3/10 Martin Carthy, A Band Called 'O' (Peaches)

T 8/10 Swan Arcade, Shawn Phillips (Isotope)

Th 10/10 Ann Peebles & the Red Dog Band

T 15/10 Lol Coxhill, Can (Duane Eddy)

Th 17/10 Maldwyn Pope, Climax Blues Band (Back Door)

T 22/10 Rab Noakes (Fairport Convention, Peter Hammill)

Th 24/10 Thin Lizzy (Jabula, Robert Wyatt)

T 29/10 Cozy Powell (Chris Stainton's Tundra, John Doonan)

Th 31/10 Neutrons (Gilgamesh, Ron Geesin)

T 5/11 Etchingham Steam Band (Viola Wills & Gonzalez, Robin & Barry Dransfield)

Th 7/11 Global Village Trucking Company, Nic Jones (A Band Called 'O')

T 12/11 Ariel, Ace (Boys of the Lough)

Th 14/11 Man (Climax Blues Band, Martin Carthy)

T 19/11 Horslips, Funkees (Jess Roden)

Th 21/11 Gonzalez, Dick Gaughan (Ann Peebles)

T 26/11 Pete Atkin (Unicorn, Jack the Lad)

Th 28/11 Ivor Cutler (Neutrons)

T 3/12 Nico, Ronnie Lane & Slim Chance (Swan Arcade)

Th 5/12 Hatfield and the North, Medicine Head, Fred Frith

T 10/12 Kevin Coyne Group (Shawn Phillips, Lol Coxhill)

Th 12/12 Roy Harper (Global Village Trucking Company, Nic Jones)

T 17/12 Gentle Giant (Can, Rab Noakes)

Th 19/12 (Man, Thin Lizzy, Elton John)

T 24/12 (Gonzalez, Elton John's Christmas party from Hammersmith Odeon)

Th 26/12 (Ace, Cozy Powell, Carol Concert)

1975

- **Sounds of the Seventies axed**
- **Peel gets Mon & Thurs tea-time show 5.15–7pm**

M 6/1 Tony Capstick, Pretty Things

Th 9/1 (Bryn Howarth, Medicine Head)

M 13/1 John Martyn, Oldham Tinkers

Th 16/1 Starry-Eyed & Laughing (Hatfield and the North)

M 20/1 Michael Chapman (Ariel)

M 23/1 Baker-Gurvitz Army, Sutherland Brothers & Quiver

M 27/1 (Etchingham Steam Band, Funkees)

Th 30/1 Stackridge (Ivor Cutler)

M 3/2 Robin Trower (Horslips)

Th 6/2 Peaches (Dick Gaughan)

M 10/2 Dr Feelgood (Pete Atkin)

Th 13/2 Kursaal Flyers (Fred Frith)

M 17/2 Joan Armatrading (Ronnie Lane and Slim Chance)

Th 20/2 Brinsley Schwartz, John Golding

M 24/2 Richard & Linda Thompson (Nico)

Th 27/2 Kokomo (Roy Harper)

M 3/3 Tam Linn (Kevin Coyne)

Th 6/3 Ralph McTell (Starry-Eyed and Laughing)

M 10/3 Tim Hart & June Tabor (Gentle Giant)

Th 13/3 Groundhogs (Bryn Haworth)

M 17/3 Be Bop Deluxe (Tony Capstick)

Th 20/3 Jack the Lad (Sutherland Brothers and Quiver)

M 24/3 A Band Called 'O' (Pretty Things)

Th 27/3 Ducks Deluxe (Baker-Gurvitz Army)

M 31/3 Ace

Th 3/4 Upp (Stackridge)

M 7/4 (Oldham Tinkers, Robin Trower)

Th 10/4 Stealers Wheel (Peaches)

M 14/4 (Dr Feelgood, John Martyn)

Th 17/4 Andy Fraser Band (Kursaal Flyers)

M 21/4 (Joan Armatrading, Michael Chapman)

Th 24/4 Arthur Brown Band & The Gospelaires (Brinsley Schwarz)

M 28/4 Martin Carthy (Be Bop Deluxe)

Th 1/5 Jess Roden Group (John Golding)

M 5/5 Mike Heron's Reputation (A Band Callled O)

Th 8/5 John Cale (Kokomo)

M 12/5 Loudon Wainwright III (Tam Linn)

Th 15/5 Robin & Barry Dransfield (Groundhogs)

M 19/5 Can (Richard and Linda Thompson)

Th 22/5 (Ralph McTell, Ducks Deluxe)

M 26/5 (Ace)

Th 29/5 Alan Hull (Jack the Lad)

M 2/6 Bob Sargeant (Tim Hart and June Tabor)

Th 5/6 Thin Lizzy (Upp)

M 9/6 Global Village Trucking Company (Martin Carthy)

Th 12/6 Rab Noakes (Andy Fraser Band)

M 16/6 Terry and Gay Woods (Mike Heron's Reputation)

Th 19/6 Jet (Stealers Wheel)

Th 23/6 Roy Harper & Trigger, Gazelle

M 26/6 Mike Cooper (Arthur Brown Band & The Gospelaires)

M 30/6 Sutherland Brothers & Quiver (Loudon Wainwright III)

Th 3/7 Caravan (Jess Roden Band)

M 7/7 Isotope (Bob Sargeant)

Th 10/7 Van der Graaf Generator (Robin and Barry Dransfield)

M 14/7 Funkees (Can)

Th 17/7 Joan Armatrading & The Movies (John Cale)

M 21/7 Bryn Haworth (Global Village Trucking Company)

Th 24/7 Pretty Things (Alan Hull)

M 28/7 Moon (Terry and Gay Woods)

Th 31/7 Country Gazette (Thin Lizzy)

M 4/8 Moonrider (Roy Harper and Trigger)

Th 7/8 Malicorne (Jet)

M 11/8 Starry-Eyed and Laughing (Gazelle)

Th 14/8 (Caravan, Rab Noakes)

M 18/8 Henry Cow (Sutherland Brothers and Quiver)

Th 21/8 Blue (Mike Cooper)

M 25/8 (Thin Lizzy)

Th 28/8 Chapman-Whitney Streetwalkers (Joan Armatrading & The Movies)

M 1/9 Supercharge (Isotope)

M 4/9 Snafu (Country Gazette)

M 8/9 Kokomo

Th 11/9 Jack the Lad

M 15/9 (Bryn Haworth, Funkees)

Th 18/9 (Malicorne)

Sn 21/9 Peel presents edition of Insight, R1, 5–6pm, profiling Rod Stewart, compiled by John Pidgeon, produced by Tim Blackmore

M 22/9 Farewell to Top Gear (many session repeats)

Th 25/9 (more repeats) show ends with repeat of 1st ever record on Top Gear: Martha and the Vandellas' 'Love Bug Leave my Heart Alone'

- **Peel gets five nights a week 11pm–12 FM from Mon 29/9/75**
- **Top Gear subtitle & sig axed.**
- **New sig: 'Pickin' The Blues' by Grinderswitch**

M 29/9 'The Who By Numbers' LP

T 30/9 more 'The Who By Numbers'

W 1/10 (Pretty Things)

Th 2/10 Climax Blues Band

F 3/10 (Moon)

M 6/10 Roxy Music LP 'Siren'

T 7/10 more 'Siren'

W 8/10 (Supercharge)

Th 9/10 Pete Atkin

F 10/10 (Van der Graaf Generator)

M 13/10 Gentle Giant

T 14/10 Ivor Cutler

W 15/10 (Chapman-Whitney Streetwalkers)

Th 16/10 The Chieftains

F 17/10 (Kokomo)

M 20/10 Maddy Prior & June Tabor

T 21/10 Rory Gallagher LP 'Against the Grain'

W 22/10 (Blue)

Th 23/10 Starry-Eyed and Laughing

F 24/10 records

M 27/10 Viv Stanshall

T 28/10 (Caravan)

W 29/10 Mike Oldfield LP 'Ommadawn'

Th 30/10 (Moonrider)

F 31/10 Kursaal Flyers

M 3/11 Gilgamesh; 'Trail of the lonesome pine' ends show

T 4/11 (Mike Cooper)

W 5/11 (Henry Cow)

Th 6/11 R&L Thompson's 'Pour down like Silver', Ace's 'Time for another'

F 7/11 Supertramp LP 'Crisis? What Crisis?'

M 10/11 Boxer

T 11/11 Viola Wills and Gonzalez

W 12/11 Nic Jones; & Neil Young LP 'Zuma', incl. 'Cortez the Killer'

Th 13/11 (Snafu)

F 14/11 (Jack the Lad)

M 17/11 Andy Fairweather-Low

T 18/11 Boys of the Lough

W 19/11 20th Century Steel Band

Th 20/11 (Climax Blues Band)

F 21/11 Tangerine Dream 'Ricochet' LP side 1

M 24/11 Nasty Pop; Bob Marley LP 'Live'

T 25/11 Five Hand Reel; 'Ricochet' side 2

W 26/11 Joni Mitchell LP 'Hissing of Summer Lawns'

Th 27/11 Max Merritt & the Meteors

F 28/11 more 'Hissing of summer lawns', Pink Floyd's 'Wish you were here'

M 1/12 Miles Davis LP 'Agharta' side 1

T 2/12 Cajun Moon; Peter Frampton 'Show me the way' opens show

W 3/12 (Pete Atkin)

Th 4/12 Sutherland Brothers & Quiver; 3 from Santana LP 'Lotus'

F 5/12 Mike Oldfield 'In dulci jubilo' closes show

M 8/12 Bill Aitken; Jonathan Richman 'Roadrunner'

T 9/12 (Gentle Giant)

W 10/12 (Maddy Prior and June Tabor) more from 'Lotus'; 2 from Eno's 'Another green world'

Th 11/12 Millie Jackson 'Leftovers'

F 12/12 Stretch

M 15/12 Gavin Bryars' 'The Sinking of the Titanic'

T 16/12 Cimarrons; Neil Young 'Looking for a love' from LP 'Zuma'

W 17/12 (Viv Stanshall #2) yet more from Santana 'Lotus' LP

Th 18/12 Dransfields

F 19/12 John Peel's Top 15 singles of 1975: Peter Skellern 'Hold On To Love', Laurel & Hardy 'Trail Of The Lonesome Pine', Mike Oldfield 'In Dulci Jubilo', Joan Armatrading 'Back To The Night', 10cc 'I'm Not In Love', Bob Sargeant 'First Starring Role', Peter Frampton 'Show Me The Way', Bob Marley 'No Woman No Cry', Joan Armatrading 'Dry Land', John Lennon 'Imagine', Rod Stewart 'Sailing', Roy Harper 'When An Old Cricketer Leaves The Crease', Jack The Lad 'Gentleman Soldier', Millie Jackson 'Loving Arms', Be Bop Deluxe 'Maid In Heaven'

M 22/12 – F 26/12 (no show 25/12) Viv Stanshall's Christmas at Rawlinson End

M 29/12 (Ivor Cutler)

T 30/12 even more from 'Lotus'

W 31/12 no show

1976

Th 1/1 Be Bop Deluxe LP 'Sunburst Finish', side 1

F 2/1 (Chieftains) 'Sunburst Finish', side 2

M 5/1 (Viola Wills and Gonzalez)

T 6/1 Bob Dylan LP 'Desire'

W 7/1 Bridget St John

Th 8/1 'Roadrunner' Jonathan Richman

F 9/1 (Kursaal Flyers)

M 12/1 Andy Fairweather-Low

T 13/1 records

W 14/1 (Nic Jones)

Th 15/1 Ronnie Lane's Slim Chance

F 16/1 Nils Lofgren concert, rec'd by KSAN; Bowie 'Station To Station' LP

M 19/1 (Boys of the Lough)
T 20/1 Moon
W 21/1 (Max Merritt and the Meteors)
Th 22/1 Peaches
F 23/1 records
M 26/1 records
T 27/1 (Five Hand Reel)
W 28/1 lots of Howlin' Wolf, 'Roadrunner' again
Th 29/1 Blue
F 30/1 (Boxer)
M 2/2 (Bill Aitken)
T 3/2 (Stretch)
W 4/2 'Cortez the Killer' again
Th 5/2 (Cajun Moon)
F 6/2 Genesis LP 'Trick of the Tail', & i/v with Phil Collins
M 9/2 Maria Muldaur concert from Montreux Jazz Festival
T 10/2 Leo Kottke concert from Frankfurt Radio
W 11/2 Van Morrison concert from Montreux Festival 1974
Th 12/2 PasB missing, unknown
F 13/2 records
M 16/2 Shanghai
T 17/2 Status Quo LP 'Blue For You'
W 18/2 'Little Johnny Jewel' Television, more 'Blue For You'
Th 19/2 Robin Trower 'Live' LP
F 20/2 Ron Geesin
M 23/2 Be Bop Deluxe
T 24/2 Lone Star
W 25/2 (Sutherland Brothers and Quiver)
Th 26/2 Maddy Prior and June Tabor 'Silly Sisters' LP
F 27/2 Jess Roden Band LP 'Keep Your Hat On'
M 1/3 National Health
T 2/3 Stackridge
W 3/3 (Cimarons)
Th 4/3 'Lookin for a love' single, Neil Young
F 5/3 Talisker
M 8/3 Brand X
T 9/3 Thin Lizzy
W 10/3 records
Th 11/3 (Dransfields)
F 12/3 (Ronnie Lane's Slim Chance)
M 15/3 Poco 'live' LP, Keith Jarrett's 'Köln concert', side 2
T 16/3 (Moon)
W 17/3 Rolling Stones LP 'Black And Blue'
Th 18/3 Thin Lizzy LP 'Jailbreak'
F 19/3 records
M 22/3 Racing Cars
T 23/3 (Peaches)
W 24/3 (Bridget St John)
Th 25/3 (Elton John: 'Daniel/Your Song', from Christmas pub piano session)
F 26/3 The Bothy Band
M 29/3 String Driven Thing
T 30/3 Nils Lofgren LP 'Cry Tough'
W 31/3 (Blue)
Th 1/4 Jess Roden Band
F 2/4 LP 'No Earthly Connection' by Rick Wakeman
M 5/4 all Neil Young records
T 6/4 Alan Hull and Robert Barton
W 7/4 tracks from Chieftains LPs 1, 2, 3, 4
Th 8/4 Elkie Brooks; & 'The sinking spell' from LP 'The Hapless Child', by Michael Mantler
F 9/4 records
M 12/4 (Thin Lizzy)
T 13/4 more 'Black and Blue'
W 14/4 side 2 of 'Black and Blue'
Th 15/4 (Jimi Hendrix Experience, tracks from all BBC Radio sessions)
F 16/4 records
M 19/4 records by Chuck Berry, Ray Charles, Bo Diddley, Jimmy Reed

T 20/4 Van der Graaf Generator; side 1 of 'Rastaman Vibration' LP
W 21/4 (Be Bop Deluxe)
Th 22/4 (National Health)
F 23/4 – F 28/5 on R3, 7–7.30pm John Peel presents Where It's At, 6-part personal documentary series about the present and possible future of popular music: 1 How did it get here? beginnings, 2 Rock Art and Rock Folly (Dylan, Beatles, ELP, Mike Oldfield), 3 The Supreme Sacrifice (blues & gospel), 4 From Highlife to Dub and Skank, 5 Is there rock on the moon? Rock spreads around the world, 6 It Gives Me Great Pleasure, tax exiles and the music Peel currently likes, producer David Epps
F 23/4 side 1 of Steely Dan's 'Royal Scam', Led Zepp's 'Achilles' last stand'
M 26/4 forthcoming Toots and the Maytals LP
T 27/4 Widow Maker; & side 1 of 'Still Life' LP, Van der Graaf Generator
W 28/4 (Shanghai)
Th 29/4 Bob Sargeant; & 3 from Graham Parker LP 'Howlin' Wind'
F 30/4 (Stackridge)
M 3/5 Human Orchestra (Brand X, Lone Star, Racing Cars) 'all non-needletime' says PasB
T 4/5 records
W 5/5 (Talisker) & 'Rose of Cimmaron' by Poco
Th 6/5 A Band Called 'O'
F 7/5 Michael Chapman; & 'I can't ask for anymore than you' by Cliff Richard
M 10/5 Charlie
T 11/5 (The Bothy Band)
W 12/5 Caravan
Th 13/5 (String Driven Thing)
F 14/5 4 by The Flamin' Groovies
M 17/5 Count Bishops
T 18/5 (Elkie Brooks)
W 19/5 Steve Miller LP 'Fly Like An Eagle', 3 by Mighty Diamonds, & Ramones 'Judy is a punk' 1st play
Th 20/5 (Jess Roden Band) & 3 more from Ramones LP
F 21/5 Smiggs Band
M 24/5 Stretch; & Isley Brothers LP 'Harvest For The World'
T 25/5 'Blitzkreig Bop' opens show
W 26/5 Dodgers
Th 27/5 (Alan Hull and Robert Barton) 'I wanna be your boyfriend' opens show; 4 by Hank Mizell
F 28/5 (Van der Graaf Generator) 3 from Tubes LP 'Young And Rich', incl. 'Don't touch me there'
M 31/5 Roogalator
T 1/6 records
W 2/6 (Widowmaker)
Th 3/6 (A Band Called 'O')
F 4/6 (Bob Sargeant)
M 7/6 John Stevens' Away; & 'You drive me wild', Runaways LP; & 'Today your love' Ramones
T 8/6 Graham Central Station LP 'Mirror'
W 9/6 (Charlie) & 'Horseplay' Eddie and the Hot Rods, 'Little Johnny Jewel' Television
Th 10/6 Rod Stewart LP 'A Night on the Town'
F 11/6 Max Merritt and The Meteors
M 14/6 Supercharge
T 15/6 records: first record 'Stormtroopin' Ted Nugent, second 'Today Your Love Tomorrow The World' Ramones
W 16/6 Graham Parker and The Rumour
Th 17/6 (Michael Chapman)
F 18/6 Streetwalkers; 'Cherry Bomb' from Runaways LP
M 21/6 AC/DC; & 'Music in 12 parts' by Philip Glass
T 22/6 side 2 of 'Go' LP, Stomu Yamashta
W 23/6 Frankie Miller Band
Th 24/6 (Smiggs Band)
F 25/6 records

M 28/6 (Caravan) & 'I don't wanna go down the basement', LP Ramones
T 29/6 (Stretch)
W 30/6 'Doina de Jale' Georghe Zamfir; 'Soul Shoes' Graham Parker
Th 1/7 Budgie
F 2/7 (Count Bishops)
M 5/7 (Dodgers) 'Is it day or night?' Runaways LP
T 6/7 'Judy is a punk'; 'Dead end justice' Runaways
W 7/7 Roxy Music LP 'Viva!'
Th 8/7 Cajun Moon; 'Blitzkreig bop'
F 9/7 (Roogalator) 'Blitzkreig bop' again
M 12/7 (Supercharge) 'Blitzkreig Bop' again
T 13/7 records
W 14/7 (Max Merritt & the Meteors)
Th 15/7 Medicine Head
F 16/7 (John Stevens' Away)
M 19/7 (Graham Parker and the Rumour) Steve Miller Band LP 'Children of the Future'
T 20/7 Na Fili; 'Rose of Cimarron', again
W 21/7 'Girlfriend' & 'Here come the Martian Martians', The Modern Lovers LP
Th 22/7 Kevin Ayers; more from 'Modern Lovers' LP; 'Keys to your heart', the 101ers.
F 23/7 Nic Jones; 'Here come the weekend' Dave Edmunds; & 'Lullaby of Broadway'
M 26/7 (Streetwalkers) 'Here comes the weekend' again
T 27/7 (AC/DC)
W 28/7 records
Th 29/7 (Frankie Miller Band)
F 30/7 Steve Gibbons Band
M 2/8 Brand X
T 3/8 (Budgie) & Eddie and the Hot Rods 'Live at the Marquee' EP
W 4/8 3 tracks from Thin Lizzy LP 'Remembering'
Th 5/8 Lone Star
F 6/8 Eric Clapton LP 'No Reason To Cry'
M 9/8 – F 20/8 record retrospectives: The Who, Family, Roxy Music, Fairport Convention, Stones, Cream, Soft Machine, Faces, Yardbirds/Zeppelin, Beatles
M 23/8 Moon; 'So it goes' Nick Lowe
T 24/8 'So it goes'; 4 from Be Bop Deluxe LP 'Modern Music'
W 25/8 Joan Armatrading; 'So it goes' again
Th 26/8 Loudon Wainwright III; 'So it goes' again
F 27/8 (Cajun Moon) Eddie and the Hot Rods 'Live at the Marquee' again; 'Back to Africa' Aswad; 'So it goes' again
M 30/8 Bowles Brothers; 'So it goes' again
T 31/8 Ivor Cutler; & 3 from JJ Cale LP 'Troubadour'
W 1/9 'Long may you run' Stills-Young; 'Pickin' the Blues' single; new LPs: Crazy Cavan, June Tabor, Deaf School
Th 2/9 Aswad; 'Pickin' the blues' single again; 3 more from 'Long May You Run' LP
F 3/9 (Medicine Head) Albion Band 'Hopping down in Kent'
M 6/9 Albion Dance Band
T 7/9 Deaf School; 'Rose of Cimarron'; 'More than a feeling' Boston; 'Live at CBGBs' LP
W 8/9 'Legalize it' single
Th 9/9 (Na Fili) 'Legalize it'; lots of Jimmy Reed
F 10/9 (Brand X) 'Legalize it'; Deaf School LP; 'Rose of Cimarron'
M 13/9 June Tabor; 'Legalize it'; LP 'The Spotlights Kid', Captain Beefheart
T 14/9 Plummet Airlines; 'Cherry bomb'; 'Love & Affection'; 'She's my gal', The Gorillas
W 15/9 Bob Dylan LP 'Hard Rain'
Th 16/9 (Nic Jones) Racing Cars LP 'Downtown Tonight'
F 17/9 (Kevin Ayers) Dr Feelgood LP 'Stupidity'; 'Cherry bomb' again
M 20/9 Racing Cars; 'Cherry bomb', Stanley Clarke 'School days'
T 21/9 Martin Carthy; 'Tell it like it is' Aaron Neville; 'Rose of Cimarron'; Ry Cooder LP 'Chicken Skin Music'

W 22/9 'Play that funky music', Wild Cherry; LP 'Genuine Cowhide' Delbert McClinton; Doctors of Madness LP

Th 23/9 LPs: 'Free For All' Ted Nugent; 'L', Steve Hillage

F 24/9 Five Hand Reel

M 27/9 Robin Trower LP 'Long Misty Days' complete; 'Hey there little insect' J. Richman

T 28/9 (Steve Gibbons Band) 'Gloria/Satisfaction' Eddie and the Hot Rods

W 29/9 'I'm stranded' The Saints; 'Songs in the key of life', Stevie Wonder, 9 tracks [incl. side 2 complete]

Th 30/9 'Songs in the key of life' sides 3 & 4

F 1/10 Phil Manzanera /'801 Live' LP complete

M 4/10 (Joan Armatrading)

T 5/10 Dransfield; 'Play that funky music' again; Burning Spear LP 'Man In The Hills', 4 tracks

W 6/10 records: more Dr Feelgood, Delbert McClinton, Labelle, Cate Bros

Th 7/10 Thin Lizzy LP 'Johnny The Fox'

F 8/10 Climax Blues Band

M 11/10 Thin Lizzy

T 12/10 National Health

W 13/10 Rory Gallagher LP 'Calling Card'

Th 14/10 (Albion Dance Band) &, for umpteenth time, LP 'Napoleon's Retreat', The Chieftains

F 15/10 (Moon); 'I'm stranded' again

M 18/10 Stretch

T 19/10 (Bowles Brothers) 'Man smart woman smarter' Robert Palmer; LP 'Spirit' Earth Wind & Fire

W 20/10 'New Rose', The Damned, 1st play; 'So bad' Little Bob Story

Th 21/10 Jack the Lad; 'California sun/I don't wanna walk around with you' Ramones

F 22/10 (Loudon Wainwright III) 'Teenage depression' Eddie and the Hot Rods; 'Help' The Damned

M 25/10 (Lone Star #1)

T 26/10 'New Rose' again; LP 'Heat Treatment' Graham Parker and the Rumour

W 27/10 Fabulous Poodles

Th 28/10 Vibrators

F 29/10 (Aswad) 'Teenage depression' Eddie and the Hot Rods

M 1/11 (Ivor Cutler)

T 2/11 PasB lost

W 3/11 (Deaf School) 'Teenage depression' again

Th 4/11 (June Tabor) 3 from Wishbone Ash LP 'New England'; 'New rose' again

F 5/11 Cado Belle; 'Teenage depression' again

M 8/11 AFT; 'Teenage depression' opens show

T 9/11 (Plummet Airlines) 'New Rose' again

W 10/11 Jess Roden Band LP 'Play It Dirty, Play It Class'

Th 11/11 Roogalator; 'I'm stranded'

F 12/11 (Five Hand Reel) 'We vibrate', The Vibrators

M 15/11 Graham Parker and The Rumour; 'Little does she know' Kursaal Flyers

T 16/11 records: 3 from LP 'Max's Kansas City': The Fast 'Boys will be boys'; Pere Ubu 'Final solution'; Suicide 'Rocket USA'

W 17/11 (Racing Cars) 'Pogo dancing' Chris Spedding and the Vibrators

Th 18/11 Blue

F 19/11 (Martin Carthy) 'Blank generation', 'Anarchy in the UK' 1st play

M 22/11 Van der Graaf Generator; 'California sun/I don't wanna...' again; 'New rose' again

T 23/11 Joni Mitchell LP 'Hejira'

W 24/11 The Bothy Band; 3 from Eddie and the Hot Rods LP 'Teenage Depression'

Th 25/11 2 from ELO LP 'A New World Record'; 3 from Narada Michael Walden LP 'Garden of Love Light'

F 26/11 Bridget St John; 'Anarchy in the UK' 2nd play (day of release)

M 29/11 Bryn Haworth

T 30/11 (Climax Blues Band) 'Another world' Richard Hell

W 1/12 Eagles LP 'Hotel California'

Th 2/12 (Dransfield) 'We're the greatest' The Man Ezeke Gray; 'Come whoam to thi childer an' me' Oldham Tinkers

F 3/12 Santana LP 'Festival'; 3 from Bobby Womack LP 'Home Is Where The Heart Is'

M 6/12 Ralph McTell

T 7/12 Doctors of Madness; 'I'm stranded' opens show; 'Hotel California' track from LP of same name

W 8/12 unknown: p.2 of PasB missing

Th 9/12 Loudon Wainwright III; 'New Rose' opens show; 'I'm stranded' again

F 10/12 Damned, & the punk special, records by: Seeds, Iggy Pop, Eddie & the Hot Rods, Richard Hell, Television, Pere Ubu, Sex Pistols

M 13/12 Wes McGhee

T 14/12 'Best of' Barclay James Harvest LP

W 15/12 'Tie your mother down' Queen; 'Last resort' Eagles; 'Keep on coming' Flying saucers

Th 16/12 (Cado Belle)

F 17/12 Jess Roden Band; 3 from LP 'Milk 'n' Cookies'; 2 from Genesis LP 'Wind and Wuthering'

M 20/12 (National Health)

T 21/12 (Jack the Lad)

W 22/12 (AFT)

Th 23/12 (Thin Lizzy)

F 24/12 (Climax Blues Band, Joan Armatrading, Lone Star #1); & Rod Stewart live from Olympia

M 27/12 (Be Bop Deluxe, Jess Roden, Brand X #2, Aswad, Prior and Tabor, 1st TX 27/10/75), and first ever Festive 50 begins, numbers #44–35

T 28/12 (Stretch #3, Bill Aitken, Racing Cars #2) & Festive 50 #35–25

W 29/12 (Bowles Brothers, Graham Parker and the Rumour #2) & Festive 50 #24–19

Th 30/12 (Deaf School, Frankie Miller Band) & Festive 50 #18–11

F 31/12 no show

1977

M 3/1 (Chieftains, Thin Lizzy, Bill Aitken) & Festive 50 #10–1

T 4/1 Chris Spedding & The Vibrators

W 5/1 (Stretch) 3 from LP 'Tom Petty and the Heartbreakers'

Th 6/1 Elvin Bishop LP 'Hometown Boy Makes Good', 4 from Ace LP 'No Strings', 'All in a mouse's night' Genesis

F 7/1 (Fabulous Poodles) 3 from Emmylou Harris LP 'Luxury Liner'; 'Breaking glass' Bowie LP 'Low'

M 10/1 Streetwalkers LP 'Vicious But Fair'; Bowie's 'Low' LP – 'Subterraneans'

T 11/1 Bowie LP 'Low'

W 12/1 Original Pirates

Th 13/1 (Graham Parker and the Rumour)

F 14/1 Bowles Brothers

M 17/1 Boys of the Lough; 3 from Runaways LP 'Queens of Noise'

T 18/1 (Vibrators)

W 19/1 (Roogalator)

Th 20/1 side 1 of Pink Floyd LP 'Animals'

F 21/1 Little Bob Story; 'Animals' side 2

M 24/1 'I remember you' Ramones; 'Love goes to building on fire' Talking Heads

T 25/1 Be Bop Deluxe

W 26/1 (Van der Graaf Generator)

Th 27/1 (The Bothy Band) 'Get a grip on yourself/London Lady'; 3 from Ramones LP 'Leave Home'

F 28/1 both sides of Stranglers single again; 4 from MacGarrigles 'Dancer with bruised knees'

M 31/1 (Loudon Wainwright III) 3 from Runaways LP; 'London Lady'

T 1/2 4 from Steve Gibbons' Band LP 'Rollin' On'; 'London lady'; 3 from Coyne LP 'In Living Black and White'

W 2/2 (Damned) 'Another great divide' Split Enz; 'I think we're alone now' Rubinoos

Th 3/2 (Bryn Haworth) Bowie 'Sound and vision'; Buzzcocks 'Friends of mine'; Pink Floyd 'Dogs'

F 4/2 John Martyn

M 7/2 Andy Fairweather-Low; 'American girl' Tom Petty

T 8/2 Television LP 'Marquee Moon'; 'One of those days' Roy Harper; 'Dangerous Rhythm' Ultravox

W 9/2 Wishbone Ash

Th 10/2 Leo Kottke; 2 more from 'Marquee moon'

F 11/2 (Jess Roden Band) 3 from Bryan Ferry LP 'In Your Mind'

M 14/2 Dave Edmunds' Rockpile; 'Go your own way' single, Fleetwood Mac; 4 from Neil Young LP 'Decade'

T 15/2 Status Quo LP 'Live'

W 16/2 5 from 'Damned' LP; 3 from Uriah Heep LP 'Firefly'

Th 17/2 (Chris Spedding and the Vibrators)

F 18/2 Roy Harper and Chips

M 21/2 Eddie and The Hot Rods; 3 from Delbert McClinton LP 'Victim Of Life's Circumstance'

T 22/2 June Tabor; 4 from Nils Lofgren LP 'I Came To Dance'

W 23/2 50% rock, 50% punk records

Th 24/2 (Wes McGhee)

F 25/2 (Ralph McTell) 'Laughs on me', 'She's all mine' The Boyz; 'Cloud 149' Pere Ubu

M 28/2 Plummet Airlines; 4 from compilation LP 'The Beat Merchants'; 'Let me dream if I want to' Mink de Ville

T 1/3 (Boys of the Lough) 3 from Supercharge LP 'Horizontal Refreshment'; 4 from Jack Bruce LP 'How's Tricks?'

W 2/3 'London Lady' again; 2 from Journey LP 'Next'

Th 3/3 Steve Gibbons Band; 3 from John Martyn LP 'So Far So Good'

F 4/3 'Hurricane' from Neil Young 'Decade' LP; 3 from Deaf School LP 'Don't Stop The World'

M 7/3 Stranglers; 'Pearl's a singer' Elkie Brooks; 4 from Iggy Pop LP 'The Idiot'

T 8/3 (Original Pirates) 'White riot' The Clash

W 9/3 Roy Harper 'One of those days in England' [19' 10'], Status Quo '45 Hundred times' [16' 20"]

Th 10/3 'Birdland' Weather report

F 11/3 (Little Bob Story) 'Less than zero' Elvis Costello; 3 from MC5 LP 'Back In The USA'

M 14/3 'Best of' Barclay James Harvest LP

T 15/3 4 from LP 'Delbert and Glen'; 'Pearl's a singer'; 'Less than zero'; '1977' The Clash

W 16/3 (John Martyn)

Th 17/3 Supercharge; 3 from Saints LP '(I'm) Stranded'; 3 from Frankie Miller LP 'Full House'

F 18/3 Kevin Coyne, The 'O' Band

M 21/3 – F 1/4 'with Kid Jensen...' (repeats only)

• From Mon 4 April Peel back & now from 10pm–midnight Mon-Fri

M 4/4 Eric Clapton private tape, 8 tracks

T 5/4 (Jimi Hendrix, all surviving session tapes)

W 6/4 Viv Stanshall (Be Bop Deluxe); 3 from 'Rattus Norvegicus'; 2 from Jess Roden LP 'Blowin'

Th 7/4 (Wishbone Ash) 5 from Dave Edmunds LP 'Get It'

F 8/4 (Stranglers, Eddie and the Hot Rods)

M 11/4 Streetwalkers (Andy Fairweather-Low) 3 from 'Bunch Of Stiffs'

T 12/4 Racing Cars, Mike Chapman; 5 from Van Morrison LP 'A Period Of Transition'

W 13/4 (Dave Edmunds' Rockpile, Roy Harper and Chips) 3 from Tom Petty LP 'The Official Bootleg'

Th 14/4 (Plummet Airlines, June Tabor) 3 from 'Jeff Beck & Jan Hammer Live'

F 15/4 Deaf School; 'I don't care' The Boys; 'Smokescreen' Desperate Bicycles; 'Do the standing still' The Table

M 18/4 (Leo Kottke) Jam 'In the city' opens show; 4 from 10cc LP 'Deceptive Bends'; 4 from 'Dicky Betts Great Southern'

T 19/4 Heron (Supercharge)

W 20/4 Generation X (Boxer); Spirit LP 'Future Games' side 1; 'Erotic neurotic' The Saints

Th 21/4 Peter Hammill; 'One chord wonders' Adverts; 3 from Johnny Guitar Watson LP 'A Real Mother For Ya'

F 22/4 Motors, This Heat; Little Feat LP 'Time Loves A Hero' complete

M 25/4 (Robin Trower, Kevin Coyne) 'In the city' again

T 26/4 Nic Jones (Pretty Things #7)

W 27/4 Fabulous Poodles; 'I Bizarro', The Bizarros

Th 28/4 (John Martyn); 'Sick of you' The Users

F 29/4 Adverts (Viv Stanshall) 3 from 'Beatles at Hollywood Bowl'; Genesis 'Match of the day' EP

M 2/5 The Jam (Climax Blues Band)

T 3/5 Medicine Head (Chapman-Whitney Streetwalkers) 5 from Jam LP 'In The City'; 'Famous flower of serving men'

W 4/5 (Steve Gibbons Band) Dr Feelgood 'Sneakin' Suspicion' LP

Th 5/5 (Racing Cars, Joan Armatrading #1) Roger Daltrey LP 'One Of The Boys'

F 6/5 (Mike Chapman, Be Bop Deluxe #2)

M 9/5 (Deaf School, Bob Marley and the Wailers #1)

T 10/5 Caravan

W 11/5 (Motors, Roxy Music #3); Spirit LP 'Future Games' side 2; 'Peaches' again

Th 12/5 (This Heat, Stranglers) 'Capital Radio' The Clash

F 13/5 John McLaughlin & Shakti; 'Sheena is a punk rocker'; 'Inside and out', & 'God save the Queen'

M 16/5 Damned (Heron) 'Sheena is...' again; 'God save the Queen'

T 17/5 (Generation X, Robert Wyatt #2); 'Go buddy go'

W 18/5 Bob Marley 'Exodus' LP complete

Th 19/5 (Peter Hammill, Dr Feelgood) 'Sheena is...'

F 20/5 Radio Stars (Nic Jones) 'Time is on my side' Maze; 'Be a man' The Brats

M 23/5 Frankie Miller, Viv Stanshall; 'Welcome to the working week' Elvis Costello; 'Young savage' Ultravox

T 24/5 Neil Innes (Thin Lizzy #7) Cortinas 'Fascist dictator'; 3 from Mink de Ville LP

W 25/5 (Adverts, Ducks Deluxe #2) 'Fall out' The Police; 'Endless sleep' Nick Lowe

Th 26/5 records: 'Right to work' Chelsea, 'Remote control' The Clash, 'White line fever' Motorhead, 4 by J. Otway/W.W.Barrett

F 27/5 (Motors, Fabulous Poodles)

M 30/5 (The Jam, Caravan)

T 31/5 (John McLaughlin and Shakti, Swan Arcade #2)

W 1/6 Kingfish LP 'Live 'n Kickin' side 1

Th 2/6 (Andy Fairweather-Low, Medicine Head)

F 3/6 The Rumour, Five Hand Reel; 'Salmon song' Steve Hillage LP; 'Television families' Cortinas

M 6/6 The Tyla Gang (Genesis #2) 5 from Vibrators LP 'Pure Mania'

T 7/6 'Cranked up really high' Slaughter and the dogs

W 8/6 Albion Dance Band (Eno & the Winkies)

Th 9/6 (Radio Stars, Chapman-Whitney Streetwalkers #2)

F 10/6 (Ace, 1st TX 12/11/74)

M 13/6 (Deaf School, John Cale; 3 from Culture LP '2 Sevens Clash'

T 14/6 (Damned, Steeleye Span, 1st TX 27/6/70)

W 15/6 (Viv Stanshall, Chieftains, 1st TX 16/10/75)

Th 16/6 (Frankie Miller, Lone Star #1) 4 from Hawkwind LP 'Quark Strangeness And Charm'

F 17/6 UFO; Elvis Costello LP 'My Aim Is True'

M 20/6 Moon (Supertramp, 1st TX 6/6/74)

T 21/6 Bob Sargeant; 3 more from 'My aim is true'

W 22/6 Vibrators (Neil Innes) Mink Deville 'Spanish stroll'

Th 23/6 (The Rumour, Stealers Wheel, 1st TX 5/12/72) 'The Bitch' Slaughter and the Dogs

F 24/6 XTC (Five Hand Reel) 'Jocko homo' Devo, & Sex Pistols 'Pretty vacant' 1st plays

M 27/6 Chelsea (David Bowie, 1st TX 23/5/72)

T 28/6 (John McLaughlin and Shakti, The Tyla Gang) 4 from 'Live At The Roxy' LP

W 29/6 Chris Foster; ... & 5 more from 'The Roxy' LP

Th 30/6 (The Jam) Patrick Moraz 'Rana Batucada', Yes 'Going for the One'

F 1/7 Charlie Feathers Buddy Knox Warren Smith Jack Scott & Roger James Band; & side 1 of Rainbow LP

M 4/7 Steve Gibbons Band (Generation X) 'Rigor mortis' Cameo

T 5/7 (Frankie Miller) Yes 'Going for the One' again, & 2 more from same LP

W 6/7 (Albion Dance Band, Lone Star, 1st TX on Alan Freeman 25/6/77)

Th 7/7 Movies (Peter Hammill) 'All around the world'; J. Moped 'Incendiary device', 'Stuck on you' Electric Chairs

F 8/7 (Moon)

M 11/7 Country Joe McDonald (Faces, 1st TX 19/9/70) 'The medium was tedium' Desperate Bicycles

T 12/7 (Viv Stanshall #4 & #5, UFO) 'Looking after No.1' & 'Love comes in spurts', from LP 'New Wave'

W 13/7 Models (Man, 1st TX 14/11/74) Little Bob Story 'All or nothing'

Th 14/7 (Leo Kottke) 'Don't back the front' Desperate Bicycles; Stranglers 'Something better change'

F 15/7 Martin Simpson (Stackridge #last) 3 from 'History of Fleetwood Mac' LP

M 18/7 (Vibrators, Thin Lizzy, 1st TX 11/4/74) Mahotella Queens 'Ke ilo fata fata'

T 19/7 June Tabor; 'Cat on a wall' Squeeze

W 20/7 (XTC, Gentle Giant, 1st TX 16/10/75)

Th 21/7 Generation X (Roy Harper, 1st TX 19/3/74) 'Do anything you wanna do', 'All around the world'

F 22/7 Little Bob Story (Bob Sargeant)

M 25/7 The Jam (Racing Cars #1)

T 26/7 Cortinas (Sutherland Brothers and Quiver, 1st TX 23/1/75) 4 from 'The Boys' LP

W 27/7 Count Bishops (Caravan)

Th 28/7 (Chelsea, Chris Foster) The Killjoys 'Naive'; 3 from LP 'My Aim is True'; Only Ones 'Lovers of today'

F 29/7 (Steve Gibbons Band, John Doonan, 1st TX 13/8/74) Suburban studs 'Questions', 'Ain't bin no mo music school' Nosebleeds, 'I can't stand my baby' Rezillos

M 1/8 Elvis Costello and the Attractions; White boy 'I could puke', 5 from Lone Star LP 'Firing On All 6'

T 2/8 Dick Gaughan (Movies) 'No Russsians in Russia' Radio Stars

W 3/8 Boomtown Rats (Na Fili, 1st TX 25/7/74) 6 from Albertos LP 'Italians From Outer Space'

Th 4/8 (The Rumour); 'Johnny Mekon/All tied up' Radio Stars

F 5/8 (Led Zeppelin concert, 1st TX 4/4/71) Adverts 'Gary Gilmore's eyes'

M 8/8 Boys (Lone Star, 1st TX 25/6/77) Elvis Costello 'Red shoes'

T 9/8 (Models) 'Lovers of today' again

W 10/8 (Generation X, Oldham Tinkers, 1st TX 13/1/75)

Th 11/8 (Country Joe McDonald) Boomtown Rats 'Born to burn', Ram Jam 'Black Betty'

F 12/8 (Pink Floyd concert, 1st TX 12/10/71) Lurkers 'Shadow/Love story'; Vibrators 'London girls'

M 15/8 Blue (June Tabor)

T 16/8 (Martin Simpson, Kinks, 1st TX 11/7/74) Boomtown Rats 'Looking after No.1'

W 17/8 Ivor Cutler (Elvis Costello and the Attractions)

Th 18/8 (Little Bob Story, Kevin Coyne, 1st TX 10/12/74)

F 19/8 (Family concert, 1st TX 28/12/71)

M 22/8 Thin Lizzy; Racing Cars LP 'Weekend Rendezvous'

T 23/8 Colosseum II (Count Bishops) Generation X 'Your generation/Day by day'

W 24/8 (The Jam, Lone Star) Skatellites 'Guns of Navarone'

Th 25/8 (Frankie Miller, Motors) 3 from Iggy LP 'Lust For Life'; Wreckless Eric 'Whole wide world'

F 26/8 (Faces concert, 1st TX 23/5/71)

M 29/8 Squeeze (Cortinas, Generation X, XTC) 2nd punk special: records by Sex Pistols, Vibrators, Stranglers, Clash, Models, Desperate Bicycles,

Buzzcocks, Adverts, Users, Nosebleeds, Jam, The Table, Chelsea, Slaughter and the dogs, Boys, Rezillos

T 30/8 Adverts (Fabulous Poodles) 3 from Boomtown Rats LP, 3 from Motors LP

W 31/8 Gary Boyle (Chelsea)

Th 1/9 Roogalator (Dick Gaughan) Joan Armatrading LP 'Show Some Emotion'

F 2/9 (Feathers Knox Smith Scott & James Band; Duane Eddy)

M 5/9 – F 9/9 'with Kid Jensen' (session repeats only)

M 12/9 (Status Quo concert, 1st TX 24/3/73) The Shags 'Breathe in my ear'

T 13/9 Stranglers (Steve Gibbons Band)

W 14/9 Racing Cars (Boys) 3 from Barclay James Harvest LP 'Gone To Earth'

Th 15/9 sides 1 & 3 of Stones' 'Love You Live', 6 from Heartbreakers LP 'L.A.M.F.'

F 16/9 Alberto Y Lost Trios Paranaoias; 4 from Runaways LP 'Live In Japan'

M 19/9 Buzzcocks, Fabulous Poodles

T 20/9 Only Ones (Fairport Convention, 1st TX 6/8/74); Bowie 'Heroes' 'V2–Schneider', XTC 'Science friction', 3 from Sad Cafe LP 'Fanx Ta'ra'

W 21/9 Motors (Gary Boyle) for umpteenth time that summer, Neil Young's 'Like a hurricane'

Th 22/9 (Ivor Cutler) 'Little girl' The Banned; side 2 of Steve Hillage LP 'Motivation Radio'

F 23/9 LPs 'Introducing Sparks', Steely Dan 'Aja'

M 26/9 XTC (Thin Lizzy) 4 from Dead Boys LP 'Young Loud And Snotty', 3 from Hell LP 'Blank Generation'

T 27/9 Slits (Roogalator)

W 28/9 The Dictators recorded live at CBGB's; Skrewdriver 'You're so dumb'; Commodores 'Brick house'

Th 29/9 Steel Pulse (Boomtown Rats) Sham 69 'I don't wanna'; 3 from Wishbone Ash LP 'Front Page News'

F 30/9 (Squeeze, Adverts) Radio Active 'Alltime needletime loser'; X-Ray Spex 'O Bondage up yours!'; 3 from Randy Newman LP 'Little Criminals'; Snivelling Shits 'Terminal stupid'; Ian Dury 'Clevor Trever'; 3 from Talking Heads '77' LP

M 3/10 lots of old favourite records, & Sham 69 'Ulster', Sex Pistols 'God save the Queen'

T 4/10 lots of old records again, followed by Sex Pistols 'Anarchy in the UK'

W 5/10 Third world '96 degrees in the shade'

Th 6/10 Pistols 'Holidays in the sun' Jam 'Modern world', Damned 'Problem child' & Bowie 'Heroes' LP complete, & oldies

F 7/10 '2–4–6–8 Motorway' Tom Robinson Band, Skrewdriver 'Anti-Social', Pistols 'Satellite', oldies

M 10/10 Piano Red, Dr Feelgood

T 11/10 Wreckless Eric (XTC #1) Althea & Donna 'Up town top ranking'

W 12/10 (Albertos Y Lost Trios Paranoias) Saints '1234 demolition girl', Darts 'Daddy cool/The girl can't help it', Albertos 'Gobbing on life', Rush 'Xanadu'

Th 13/10 Downliners Sect (June Tabor) Elvis Costello 'Watching the detectives', 'Up town top ranking' again

F 14/10 Billy Boy Arnold, New Hearts; 3 from 'New Boots & Panties' LP

M 17/10 Eddie and the Hot Rods (Stranglers) 3 from Ultravox 'HaHaHa' LP

T 18/10 Killjoys (Racing Cars) 999 'Nasty nasty'

W 19/10 (Fabulous Poodles) 4 from Lofgren LP 'Night After Night', John Cooper Clarke 'Suspended sentence'

Th 20/10 Tyla Gang (Motors) Adverts 'Safety in numbers', Suburban studs 'No faith', 'Up town top ranking' again, 4 from G Parker LP 'Stick To Me', J Cooper Clarke 'Innocents'

F 21/10 (Buzzcocks) Lynyrd Skynyrd 'Free bird', 3 from Santana 'Moonflower' LP, 'Problems' from Sex Pistols LP, Zeros 'Hungry', Puncture 'Can't rock and roll', 4 from Third World LP '96 the Shade'

M 24/10 Subway Sect (John Prine, 1st TX 23/1/73) Sex Pistols LP 'Never Mind The...' complete

T 25/10 (Only Ones, Steel Pulse) 'Up town top ranking' opens show, Saints 'One way street', Chuddy Nuddies 'Do the chud', Tufty Swift 'Father's whiskers', Jam 'Sweet soul music/Back in my arms again', Deviants 'I'm coming home'

W 26/10 1st 4 records in show: Cock Sparrer 'We love you', Iggy Pop 'Success', Nick Lowe 'Halfway to paradise', Revolutionarys 'Production something'

Th 27/10 Lurkers; Scratch Band 'Uptown', 3 from Jam LP 'Modern World', 3 from Clapton LP 'Slowhand', PVC2 'Put you in the picture'

F 28/10 Skrewdriver (XTC #2)

M 31/10 (Dr Feelgood, Slits)

T 1/11 Boomtown Rats 'Mary of the IV form'

W 2/11 Van Der Graaf (The Jam) Otway/Barrett 'Really free'

Th 3/11 (Wreckless Eric) Penetration 'Don't dictate'

F 4/11 (Boys, Dick Gaughan) Lurkers 'Freakshow', Stukas 'Klean livin' kids', Larry Wallis 'Police car'

M 7/11 Rich Kids, Tom Robinson Band; 3 from Queen LP 'News Of The World'

T 8/11 Louisiana Red; Rezillos ' (My baby does) Good sculptures'

W 9/11 (Gary Boyle, Eddie and the Hot Rods) 3 from Split Enz LP

Th 10/11 Joe Gibbs LP 'African Dub Chapter 3'

F 11/11 (Squeeze, Downliners Sect)

M 14/11 Queen, Pirates

T 15/11 (The Tyla Gang) 6 from Ramones LP 'Rocket To Russia'

W 16/11 National Health (New Hearts) Menace 'Screwed up', 'Up town top ranking', 'Like a hurricane' again

Th 17/11 (Killjoys) Generation X 'Wild youth', ELP 'Show me the way to go home' from LP 'Works Vol.2'

F 18/11 Radio Stars (Subway Sect) The Stoat 'Office girl'

M 21/11 (Lurkers, Stranglers)

T 22/11 Phil Manzanera & 801 (Steel Pulse) Generation X 'Wild dub', 3 from O V Wright LP 'Memphis Unlimited', Zeros 'Don't push me round', Yobs 'The worm song', Metal Urbain 'Panik'

W 23/11 Warsaw Pakt 'Safe and warm', side 1 of Klaus Schulze 'Bodylove' soundtrack

Th 24/11 This Heat; Wasps 'Teenage treats', Some chicken 'New religion', Pigs 'National front', Alternative TV 'How much longer'

F 25/11 (Tom Robinson Band, Skrewdriver) Lockjaw 'Radio call sign', Ian Dury 'Sweet Gene Vincent', Alternative TV 'You bastard', Pigs 'Youthanasia', Wire 'Mannequin'

M 28/11 Ultravox (Eddie and the Hot Rods) Yobs 'Run Rudolph run', Telephone 'Metro'

T 29/11 (Rich Kids, Van der Graaf) Rezillos 'Flying saucer attack'

W 30/11 Zeros; 4 more from Wire LP 'Pink Flag'

Th 1/12 more from 'Pink flag', 3 from Radio Stars LP 'Sons For Swinging Lovers'

F 2/12 Suburban Studs (Motors) Pleasers ' (You keep on tellin me) Lies'

M 5/12 Siouxsie & the Banshees (Slits) Some Chicken 'New religion'

T 6/12 Sham 69 (Radio Stars)

W 7/12 (Buzzcocks, Pirates) Slaughter & the dogs 'Dame to blame'

Th 8/12 Carpettes 'Radio wunderbar/Cream of the youth', 3 from 'Live At The Vortex' LP, Soft Boys 'Wading through a ventilator', Eddie & the hot rods 'Quit this town', 4 singles by Pere Ubu

F 9/12 'Live At The Vortex' LP

M 12/12 Alternative TV, Ian Dury and the Blockheads

T 13/12 Drones (National Health) Bethnal

W 14/12 (Queen) 4 more from 'Live at the Vortex', 5 from Modern Lovers LP 'Live'

Th 15/12 lots of reggae records

F 16/12 Martin Carthy; Bethnal 'This ain't just another love song', Neon Hearts 'Regulations'

M 19/12 Viv Stanshall (Suburban Studs)

T 20/12 (This Heat) Gazoline 'Radio flic'

W 21/12 (best sessions of the year: Buzzcocks #1, Generation X #1, John McLaughlin and Shakti, Motors #1, Rich Kids, Tom Robinson Band, Sham 69, Siouxsie and the Banshees, Stranglers #1, Wreckless Eric)

Th 22/12 (Thin Lizzy Concert, 1st TX 1/9/73) Peel's personal Festive 50 for 1977

F 23/12 (Traffic Concert, 1st TX 10/5/70) Peel's personal Festive 50 for 1977

M 26/12 (Faces 5th Concert, 1st TX 21/4/73) Peel's personal Festive 50 for 1977

T 27/12 Stranglers recorded live at The Roundhouse 6/11; & Peel's personal Festive 50 for 1977 concludes

W 28/12 (best sessions of the year: Boomtown Rats #1, Colosseum II, Elvis Costello and the Attractions, Motors #2, Fabulous Poodles #2, Lurkers, Frankie Miller, Steel Pulse, Stranglers #2, June Tabor, Lone Star #3, Slits)

Th 29/12 (Phil Manzanera and 801, Roxy Music In Concert, 1st TX 16/9/72)

F 30/12 Rezillos (Blue, Five Hand Reel #3, Dick Gaughan)

1978

M 2/1 records from 76's Festive 50, alternating with best new records of 77

T 3/1 Devo 'Satisfaction', 3 from Bizarros LP 'Rubber City Rebels'

W 4/1 (Ultravox)

Th 5/1 Hiding Place (Zeros)

F 6/1 (Ian Dury and the Blockheads, Ivor Cutler)

M 9/1 (Sham 69, Siouxsie and the Banshees)

T 10/1 Greaves Blegvad, Buzzcocks 'What do I get'

W 11/1 Damned recorded live at The Roundhouse; (Viv Stanshall) Carpettes 'Radio wunderbar'

Th 12/1 Patrik Fitzgerald 'Optimism/Reject', Magazine 'Shot by both sides'

F 13/1 Bandoggs (Alternative TV) TRB 'Don't take no for an answer', Residents 'Constantinople'

M 16/1 John Martyn (Drones) Adverts 'No time to be 21', 3 from XTC LP 'White Music'

T 17/1 Mike Chapman; Jerks 'Hold my hand', 3 more from 'White music', Metal Urbain 'Paris Maquis'

W 18/1 (Rezillos, Dr Feelgood) yet another 3 from 'White music'

Th 19/1 Metal Urbain; Patrik Fitzgerald 'Safety pin stuck in my heart'

F 20/1 (Tyla Gang) ELO 'Eldorado'

M 23/1 (Stranglers) recorded live at the Roundhouse

T 24/1 Stukas

W 25/1 (Martin Carthy)

Th 26/1 (Hatfield and the North, 1st TX 2/4/74) Squeeze 'Take me I'm yours', The Unwanted 'Withdrawal', Swell Maps 'Read about Seymour'

F 27/1 (Killjoys, Only Ones) Swell Maps 'Ripped and torn black velvet'

M 30/1 Adam and the Ants (Ian Dury and the Blockheads) The Flys 'Love and a molotov cocktail'; Desperate bicycles 'Holidays/Housewife song/Cars', 6 from Sham 69 LP 'Tell Us The Truth'

T 31/1 Wire; Mekons 'Never been in a riot'; Generation X 'Ready steady go'; Nick Lowe 'The sound of breaking glass', 3 from Real Kids LP; Nasal boys 'Hot love'; Television Personalities 'Television personalities'; 4 from Virgin compilation LP 'Guillotine'

W 1/2 June Tabor (Greaves Blegvad) Mekons '32 weeks', Saints 'Know your product'

Th 2/2 (Hiding Place, Pirates) LP 'Crossing The Red Sea With The Adverts'

F 3/2 De Dannann; Bob Marley 'Is this love?' more 'Crossing the red sea with...', 3 from Squeeze LP

M 6/2 Be Bop Deluxe (Siouxsie and the Banshees) [Rezillos, Siouxsie and the Banshees, rpt on Peel's World Service show same night]

T 7/2 (John Martyn, Metal Urbain) Tubeway army 'That's too bad/Oh didn't I say', Desperate bicycles 'Advice on arrest', 4 from Little Feat LP 'Waiting For Colombus', 3 from Saints LP 'Eternally Yours'

W 8/2 Deaf School

Th 9/2 (Bandoggs, Sham 69) Clash 'Clash city rockers', Table 'Sex cells'

F 10/2 Robin and Barry Dransfield (Queen) Jam 'News of the world', Wreckless Eric 'Reconnez Cherie'

M 13/2 Killjoys (Wreckless Eric)

T 14/2 Rocks; 3 from Ranking Trevor LP '3 Piece Chicken And Chips'

W 15/2 Patrik Fitzgerald (Mike Chapman)

Th 16/2 (Stukas) Suburban studs 'I hate school'

F 17/2 (Wire, XTC) Genesis 'Follow you follow me', Attrix 'Hard times', Desperate bicycles 'Housewife song'

M 20/2 Magazine (Tom Robinson Band)

T 21/2 (Adam and the Ants, June Tabor)

W 22/2 Wasps (Viv Stanshall) Genesis 'Ballad of big'

Th 23/2 Siouxsie and the Banshees; Elvis Costello ' (I don't want to go to) Chelsea', Steel Pulse 'Ku klux klan', 3 from Blondie LP 'Plastic Letters'

F 24/2 The Jam concert tape

M 27/2 Deke Leonard and Iceberg; 8 from Buzzcocks LP 'Another Music In', 4 from 'Hope And Anchor' live LP

T 28/2 (De Dannann, Deaf School) 3 more from each of Buzzcocks & 'Hope & Anchor' live LPs

W 1/3 Kevin Coyne; Skids 'Test tube babies', Terrors 'Don't bother me'

Th 2/3 (Be Bop Deluxe, Drones)

F 3/3 John Otway 'Geneve', Joy Division 'Failures of the modern man', TRB 'Sing if you're glad to be gay'

M 6/3 X-Ray Spex, Vibrators; 2 from Albion Band LP 'Rise Up Like The Sun'

T 7/3 Peter Noel 'Rebel rock', 4 from Nick Lowe LP 'Jesus Of Cool', Pere Ubu 'Laughing'

W 8/3 Wreckless Eric and New Rockets, Sham 69 recorded live at the Roundhouse 12/2; 3 from Rutles LP

Th 9/3 (Rocks) Boomtown Rats 'She's so modern', Generation X LP, 999 LP, Albion Band 'Poor old horse'

F 10/3 (Robin and Barry Dransfield) Machines 'Everything's technical', 3 from Jubilee LP, Chelsea 'Right to work', Eno 'Slow water', Adam and the Ants 'Deutscher girls', Jam 'News of the world', Elvis Costello 'Stranger in the house'

M 13/3 (Siouxsie and the Banshees) Bee Bee Cee 'You gotta know girl' (comp. Gilhooley), 8 from Elvis Costello LP 'This Year's Model', Skids 'Charles', Johnnie Moped 'Darling, let's have another baby'

T 14/3 Mekons; 3 from Diodes LP, 4 from 'Trout Mask Replica', Blunt instrument 'No excuse'

W 15/3 (Magazine, John Martyn) 3 from LP 'The Seeds' Allen Toussaint 'Night people', 3 from Matching Mole LP

Th 16/3 4 more from 'This year's model', Joy Division 'No love lost'

F 17/3 (Patrik Fitzgerald, Wasps)

M 20/3 Elvis Costello and The Attractions

T 21/3 The Bothy Band (X-Ray Spex) 4 from Wreckless Eric LP, Stiff little fingers 'Suspect device'

W 22/3 3 from LP 'Them Belfast Gypsies'

Th 23/3 Flys; ... show opens with 'Suspect device'

F 24/3 Genesis 'Down and out' from LP 'And Then There Were Three'

M 27/3 Blue Oyster Cult recorded live in Detroit (Boomtown Rats, Sham 69, Thin Lizzy)

T 28/3 (Deke Leonard and Iceberg, Metal Urbain) show starts with 'Suspect device' again

W 29/3 The Fast 'Boys will be boys', Outcasts 'Don't want to be no adult', Bethnal 'Out in the street'

Th 30/3 with Paul Gambaccini (Kevin Coyne) Billy Joel 'Movin' out', Chris Rea 'Fool if you think'

F 31/3 Five Hand Reel; 'Suspect device' yet again; Slime 'Loony'; Subway Sect 'Nobody's scared'

M 3/4 Whitecats, Rich Kids

T 4/4 Gay and Terry Woods (Sham 69 live at the Roundhouse) 3 from Gruppo Sportivo LP '10 Mistakes'

W 5/4 Viv Stanshall (Vibrators) Magazine 'Touch and go'

Th 6/4 Sham 69 'Angels with dirty faces', Skids 'Charles/Reasons/Test tube babies', 3 from Television LP 'Adventure', X-Ray Spex 'The day the world turned dayglo'

F 7/4 (Wreckless Eric) Only Ones 'Another girl another planet', Gruppo Sportivo 'I shot my manager, Alternative TV 'Life after life', Plastic Bertrand 'Ça plane pour moi'

M 10/4 (Magazine, Elvis Costello and the Attractions)

T 11/4 XTC 'This is pop', X-Ray Spex 'I am a poseur', 'Ça plane pour moi' again

W 12/4 Ivor Cutler (Mekons) 3 from Steve Hillage LP 'Green', 'Suspect device' again

Th 13/4 Stiff Little Fingers

F 14/4 Only Ones

M 17/4 Buzzcocks

T 18/4 records, incl Thin Lizzy 'Rosalie'

W 19/4 Landscape; Jane Aire and the Belvederes 'Yankee wheels', 4 from The Band LP 'The Last Waltz'

Th 20/4 Albion Band (Subway Sect) Jilted John 'Jilted John/Going steady'

F 21/4 (Flys, The Bothy Band) TRB 'Up against the wall', Twinkle Brothers 'Free Africa', Darts 'The boy from New York City', Cramps 'Surfin' bird

M 24/4 Lurkers (Vibrators)

T 25/4 (Rich Kids) Penetration 'Firing squad', 4 from Graham Parker LP 'Parkerilla'

W 26/4 Smirks (Patrik Fitzgerald)

Th 27/4 Steel Pulse (Five Hand Reel) Manfred Mann's Earth Band 'Daddy's on the road again'

F 28/4 (Viv Stanshall) Black Slate 'Live up to late'

M 1/5 Siouxsie and the Banshees #1 & #2, Elvis Costello and the Attractions) Police 'Roxanne'

T 2/5 Detonators 'Give me a helping hand', Rudi 'Big time', Prince Far I 'No more war', Art Attacks 'I am a dalek'

W 3/5 Crabs, Matumbi

Th 4/5 (Gay and Terry Woods) Destroy all monsters 'You're gonna die', The Waitresses 'Clones'

F 5/5 (Whitecats, Ivor Cutler); 3 from Only Ones' LP, Rudi 'No.1', Bizarros 'A new order', The Germs 'Lexicon devil'

M 8/5 (Buzzcocks, Only Ones) Readymades 'Terry is a space cadet', The normal 'Warm leatherette'

T 9/5 (Albion Band, X-Ray Spex) 3 from TRB LP 'Power In The Darkness'

W 10/5 (Be Bop Deluxe) Stranglers LP 'Black And white'

Th 11/5 Elvis Costello 'Radio radio' (on CBS), Television Personalities '14th floor', Nipple Erectors 'Nervous wreck'

F 12/5 (Smirks) Augustus Pablo 'East of the River Nile', 3 from Twinkle Brothers LP 'Love'

M 15/5 Boys, Squeeze; side 2 of Kevin Burke LP 'If The Cap Fits' complete

T 16/5 (Landscape, Stiff Little Fingers) Rolling Stones 'Miss you', Dire Straits 'Sultans of swing'

W 17/5 (Lurkers) Warm Gun 'Chinese gangster', Nick Lowe 'Cruel to be kind'

Th 18/5 (Rich Kids, Steel Pulse) Squeeze 'Bang bang', 'Sultans of swing' again

F 19/5 Skids (Matumbi) Rezillos 'Can't stand my baby', Laura Logic 'Aerosol burns', Soft Boys 'Fatman's son'

M 22/5 British Lions, Slits

T 23/5 Zones (Gay and Terry Woods)

W 24/5 (Crabs, Viv Stanshall) 3 from Rab Noakes LP 'Restless', Soft Boys 'Anglepoise lamp'

Th 25/5 Clash 'Complete control', Twinkle 'Terry', 'Warm Leatherette' again

F 26/5 Boomtown Rats (Sham 69 live at the Roundhouse) Bob Seger 'Still the same'

M 29/5 Thin Lizzy LP 'Live and Dangerous'

T 30/5 Cybermen 'Where's the new wave', Magazine LP 'Real Life', The Tights 'It' [Cherry 1]

W 31/5 UK Subs (Wasps) Automatics 'When the tanks roll over Poland again'

Th 1/6 Boys of the Lough (Mekons) Boomtown Rats 'Like clockwork', Bruce Springsteen 'Prove it all night'

F 2/6 Stones LP 'Some Girls', AWB 'Your love is a miracle', 3 from Pezband LP 'Laughing In The Dark'

M 5/6 Frankie Miller (Boomtown Rats) Throbbing Gristle 'United'

T 6/6 (Albion Band, Only Ones) 3 from Springsteen LP 'Darkness On The Edge Of Town', Alternative TV 'Splitting in two', Nipple Erectors 'King of the bop'

W 7/6 (Steel Pulse) more from 'Darkness on the edge of town'

Th 8/6 Rezillos

F 9/6 records only

M 12/6 (Siouxsie and the Banshees #2, Slits #2)

T 13/6 Gruppo Sportivo

W 14/6 (Matumbi, Smirks)

Th 15/6 The Fall (Boys)

F 16/6 Prince Far I & Creation Rebel

M 19/6 Pirates (Boys of the Lough)

T 20/6 (British Lions, Squeeze) presented by Paul Gambaccini

W 21/6 (UK Subs, Frankie Miller)

Th 22/6 records only

F 23/6 Hits

M 26/6 John Otway (Boomtown Rats)

T 27/6 Roy Hill Band

W 28/6 Mickey Jupp (Skids)

Th 29/6 records only

F 30/6 (Rezillos, Albion Band)

M 3/7 Chelsea, Reggae Regular

T 4/7 (Prince Far I & Creation Rebel)

W 5/7 Rab Noakes (The Fall)

Th 6/7 records only; 'Less Of Me' Teenage Jesus and the Jerks

F 7/7 (Frankie Miller, Pirates)

M 10/7 Desperate Bicycles, Penetration

T 11/7 (Blast Furnace & the Heatwaves, 1st TX Jensen 3/7/78)

W 12/7 (Hits, UK Subs)

Th 13/7 (Mickey Jupp)

F 14/7 'Can't Stand The Rezillos' and Steel Pulse's 'Handsworth Revolution' LPs

M 17/7 Adam and the Ants (Gruppo Sportivo)

T 18/7 (Roy Hill Band, Reggae Regular)

W 19/7 records only

Th 20/7 King

F 21/7 (Chelsea, Rezillos)

M 24/7 Carpettes (Thin Lizzy, 1st TX 11/4/74)

T 25/7 Viv Stanshall

W 26/7 (Siouxsie and the Banshees #1 & #2)

Th 27/7 Alternative TV

F 28/7 (Desperate Bicycles, Rab Noakes)

M 31/7 Patrik Fitzgerald, Magazine

T 1/8 Leyton Buzzards

W 2/8 (Penetration, Reggae Regular)

Th 3/8 records only: 'Bombers' Tubeway Army

F 4/8 (Adam and the Ants, The Fall)

M 7/8 Lurkers, Spizz Oil

T 8/8 five tracks from Robin Trower LP 'Caravan To Midnight'

W 9/8 Tanz der Youth (King)

Th 10/8 The Pop Group

F 11/8 (Carpettes, Viv Stanshall)

M 14/8 (Elvis Costello and the Attractions)

T 15/8 Sean Tyla

W 16/8 Human League (Patrik Fitzgerald)

Th 17/8 Siouxsie & the Banshees 'Hong Kong Garden' on Polydor

F 18/8 (Hits, Blast Furnace & the Heatwaves)

M 21/8 Prefects, Roy Harper

T 22/8 (Alternative TV, Lurkers)

W 23/8 (Leyton Buzzards)

Th 24/8 (Spizz Oil, Only Ones)

F 25/8 Whitecats (King, Tanz Der Youth)

M 28/8 (Magazine, Thin Lizzy, 1st TX 11/4/74)

T 29/8 Pragvec (The Pop Group)

W 30/8 Punishment of Luxury (Pirates)

Th 31/8 (Desperate Bicycles)

F 1/9 Skids (Penetration)

M 4/9 – F 8/9 presented by Paul Gambaccini (repeats)

M 11/9 Racing Cars, Adverts

T 12/9 (Prefects, Sean Tyla)

W 13/9 Hot Water (Roy Harper)

Th 14/9 Radio Stars

F 15/9 UK Subs (Human League)

M 18/9 Dr Feelgood, Stiff Little Fingers

T 19/9 (Adam and the Ants, Punishment of Luxury)

W 20/9 (Pragvec, Whitecats)

Th 21/9 tracks from new LPs by The Saints, The Buzzcocks, John Cooper Clarke

F 22/9 Zones (Chelsea)

M 25/9 Motorhead (Skids)

T 26/9 (Racing Cars)

W 27/9 (Adverts)

Th 28/9 Solid Senders (Viv Stanshall)

F 29/9 Sham 69 LP 'That's Life' played in its entirety

M 2/10 Mekons

T 3/10 Wire

W 4/10 (Radio Stars, Hot Water)

Th 5/10 records only: Neil Young, XTC new LPs

F 6/10 debut LPs from Siouxsie and the Banshees, Matumbi

M 9/10 Jethro Tull recorded live in Madison Square Gardens, NY

T 10/10 Reggae Regular (Alternative TV)

W 11/10 (UK Subs)

Th 12/10 (Punishment of Luxury, Dr Feelgood)

F 13/10 new LP by Lene Lovich, 'Love Like Anthrax' Gang of Four

M 16/10 Undertones (Adverts)

T 17/10 The Stoat (Skids)

W 18/10 Split Enz (Prince Far I and Creation Rebel)

Th 19/10 Molesters (Pragvec)

F 20/10 records only, 3 tracks from Status Quo LP 'If You Can't Stand The Heat'

M 23/10 Buzzcocks (The Fall)

T 24/10 Yachts

W 25/10 Fabulous Poodles, Metal Urbain

Th 26/10 (Zones)

F 27/10 Swell Maps (Stiff Little Fingers)

M 30/10 Angelic Upstarts, Elvis Costello and the Attractions

T 31/10 (Wire, Damned #1, 1st TX 10/12/76)

W 1/11 999, Period

Th 2/11 'Don't Ring Me Up' Protex, 'Is She Really Going Out With Him?' Joe Jackson

F 3/11 (Motorhead, Reggae Regular)

M 6/11 John Cooper Clarke (Split Enz)

T 7/11 (Mekons)

W 8/11 Crisis (Roy Hill Band)

Th 9/11 (The Stoat)

F 10/11 (Molesters)

M 13/11 X-Ray Spex, Matumbi

T 14/11 (Fabulous Poodles)

W 15/11 (Yachts, Elvis Costello and the Attractions)

Th 16/11 Here and Now

• Fri 17/11 Friday Rock Show with Tommy Vance starts. Peel now Mon–Thurs only

M 20/11 XTC (Swell Maps)

T 21/11 Flys

W 22/11 (Buzzcocks)
Th 23/11 (Angelic Upstarts, 999)
M 27/11 Lene Lovich (X-Ray Spex)
T 28/11 Paul Brady (Crisis)
W 29/11 Wailing Cocks (John Cooper Clarke)
Th 30/11 (Penetration)
M 4/12 Subway Sect (Matumbi)
T 5/12 Fingerprintz
W 6/12 The Fall (Generation X #1)
Th 7/12 The Pop Group
M 11/12 The Cure (Buzzcocks)
T 12/12 (Here and Now)
W 13/12 Scritti Politti (Flys)
Th 14/12 Cimarrons (Molesters)
M 18/12 Aswad (XTC)
T 19/12 (Wailing Cocks)
W 20/12 Again Again (Paul Brady)
Th 21/12 Carpettes
M 25/12 no show
T 26/12 – M 1/1/79 (Best sessions of year)
    second Listeners' Festive 50

1979

T 2/1 (Lene Lovich)
W 3/1 Only Ones
Th 4/1 (The Fall)
M 8/1 Damned (Fingerprintz)
T 9/1 (Subway Sect)
W 10/1 (The Cure, Elvis Costello and the Attractions)
Th 11/1 (Scritti Politti, Undertones) plus tracks from
    Stiff Little Fingers LP 'Inflammable Material'
M 15/1 Prefects (999)
T 16/1 Tubeway Army (Cimarrons)
W 17/1 (XTC, Carpettes)
Th 18/1 Gang of Four
M 22/1 Leyton Buzzards
T 23/1 Members
W 24/1 Capital Letters (Again Again)
Th 25/1 (Only Ones, Aswad)
M 29/1 Ruts, Generation X
T 30/1 Lurkers
W 31/1 (Damned, X-Ray Spex)
Th 1/2 (Prefects)
M 5/2 Undertones
T 6/2 Molesters (Gang of Four)
W 7/2 Pragvec (Leyton Buzzards)
Th 8/2 records only: 'He's Frank' The Monochrome Set,
    'Into the Valley' The Skids
M 12/2 (Members)
T 13/2 (Capital Letters)
W 14/2 Joy Division (Generation X)
Th 15/2 records only: 'The Dark End Of The Street'
    James Carr, 'Sound of the Suburbs' The Members
M 19/2 Protex (Undertones)
T 20/2 Wasps (Ruts)
W 21/2 Piranhas, Essential Logic
Th 22/2 The Monochrome Set
M 26/2 Skids, Joe Jackson
T 27/2 Ivor Cutler
W 28/2 (Molesters, Lurkers)
Th 1/3 records only
M 5/3 Eddie and the Hot Rods (Lene Lovich)
T 6/3 Big in Japan
W 7/3 Penetration (The Cure)
Th 8/3 (Fingerprintz, Pragvec)
M 12/3 Tom Robinson Band (Angelic Upstarts)
T 13/3 Vipers (Piranhas)
W 14/3 (Slits #1 & #2)
Th 15/3 Hi Fi

M 19/3 Raincoats
T 20/3 (Prefects, Scritti Politti)
W 21/3 Spizz Energi
Th 22/3 Neon (Damned)
M 26/3 – Th 29/3 'Radio 1 in Yorkshire' including John
    Peel and Simon Bates reporting from down a coal
    mine: (Gang of Four, Joe Cocker, 1st TX 11/10/69)
T 27/3 (Be Bop Deluxe, Mekons #1)
W 28/3 (Human League)
Th 29/3 (Mekons, Bill Nelson's Red Noise, 1st TX Friday
    Rock Show 23/2/79)
M 2/4 Frankie Miller and his Band, Adam and the Ants
T 3/4 (Big in Japan, Essential Logic)
W 4/4 Gaffa (Eddie and the Hot Rods)
Th 5/4 Neon Hearts (Joy Division)
M 9/4 Roy Hill Band (Skids)
T 10/4 Crass (Wasps)
W 11/4 Shapes
Th 12/4 (Joe Jackson, The Monochrome Set)
M 16/4 Siouxsie and the Banshees (Generation X)
T 17/4 Patrik Fitzgerald (Vipers)
W 18/4 (Ivor Cutler, Hi Fi)
Th 19/4 records only
M 23/4 (Penetration, Tom Robinson Band)
T 24/4 Edge (Ruts)
W 25/4 (Neon, Spizz Energi)
Th 26/4 Glaxo Babies
M 30/4 Shake (Neon Hearts)
T 1/5 (Raincoats, Frankie Miller and his Band)
W 2/5 (Undertones, Roy Hill Band)
Th 3/5 (Gaffa)
M 7/5 Skids (Siouxsie and the Banshees)
T 8/5 Linton Kwesi Johnson
W 9/5 Resistance (Adam and the Ants)
Th 10/5 (Crass)
M 14/5 Magazine (Patrik Fitzgerald)
T 15/5 records only
W 16/5 The Cure (Lurkers)
Th 17/5 (Shapes)
M 21/5 Ruts
T 22/5 Swell Maps (Edge)
W 23/5 Steve Elgin and the Flatbackers (Glaxo Babies)
Th 24/5 (Shake)
M 28/5 Buzzcocks (Damned)
T 29/5 Specials (Resistance)
W 30/5 Punishment of Luxury
Th 31/5 (Capital Letters, Ruts)
M 4/6 (Linton Kwesi Johnson, Skids)
T 5/6 (Magazine)
W 6/6 (The Cure)
Th 7/6 The News
M 11/6 Undertones
T 12/6 (Buzzcocks, Steve Elgin and the Flatbackers)
W 13/6 Misty
Th 14/6 Ruts
M 18/6 Wayne County and the Electric Chairs (Specials)
T 19/6 (Punishment of Luxury)
W 20/6 Agony Column (The News)
Th 21/6 Distributors (Swell Maps)
M 25/6 Gary Numan and Tubeway Army,
    Roger Chapman
T 26/6 (Undertones)
W 27/6 Leyton Buzzards (Raincoats)
Th 28/6 UK Subs
M 2/7 Yachts (Siouxsie and the Banshees)
T 3/7 Expelaires (Specials)
W 4/7 Scritti Politti (Misty)
Th 5/7 Monitors
M 9/7 Chords, Gang of Four
T 10/7 Wayne County and the Electric Chairs
W 11/7 Vapors (The Distributors)

Th 12/7 (Agony Column)
M 16/7 Purple Hearts (Leyton Buzzards)
T 17/7 records only
W 18/7 Nicky and The Dots (Chords)
Th 19/7 Russians
M 23/7 (Gary Numan and Tubeway Army, UK Subs)
T 24/7 (Monitors, Scritti Politti)
W 25/7 Secret Affair (Expelaires)
Th 26/7 Piranhas
M 30/7 Psychedelic Furs, The Police
T 31/7 (Joy Division, Yachts)
W 1/8 Pragvec (Purple Hearts)
Th 2/8 (Resistance)
M 6/8 Jimmy Norton's Explosion (Rezillos #1)
T 7/8 (Secret Affair, Chords)
W 8/8 (The Jam #1 & #2)
Th 9/8 Cravats
M 13/8 Steel Pulse, Loudon Wainwright III
T 14/8 Dolly Mixture (The Police)
W 15/8 Cockney Rejects (Gang of Four)
Th 16/8 (UK Subs)
M 20/8 Merton Parkas (Vapors) plus tracks from
    Slits LP 'Cut'
T 21/8 (Nicky and the Dots, Piranhas)
W 22/8 Echo and the Bunnymen (Russians)
Th 23/8 (Psychedelic Furs)
M 27/8 Madness (Specials, Steel Pulse)
T 28/8 (Siouxsie and the Banshees)
W 29/8 (Undertones #2) & Peel plays first 7 of the 40
    records he'd like played at his 40th birthday party
Th 30/8 Peel's 40th birthday: completes countdown of
    his 40 party records
M 3/9 Orchestral Manoeuvres in the Dark (Leyton
    Buzzards)
T 4/9 (Pragvec, Purple Hearts)
W 5/9 2TV
Th 6/9 The Monochrome Set (Jimmy Norton's Explosion)
M 10/9 Quads (Cockney Rejects)
T 11/9 (Cravats, Loudon Wainwright III)
W 12/9 Flowers (Merton Parkas)
Th 13/9 Prats
M 17/9 Stiff Little Fingers
T 18/9 Wire (Madness)
W 19/9 Kevin Coyne
Th 20/9 records only: 6 tracks from Buzzcocks LP
    'A Different Kind Of Tension'
M 24/9 Dodgems, Peter Hammill
T 25/9 Shoes for Industry
W 26/9 Elti Fits (Gary Numan and Tubeway Army)
Th 27/9 (Echo and the Bunnymen)
M 1/10 Funboy Five, Members
T 2/10 (Flowers, The Monochrome Set)
W 3/10 records only
Th 4/10 Vitus Dance
M 8/10 Flys (Orchestral Manoeuvres in the Dark)
T 9/10 Au Pairs
W 10/10 (Stiff Little Fingers)
Th 11/10 (Quads, 2TV)
M 15/10 Teardrop Explodes, XTC
T 16/10 (Kevin Coyne)
W 17/10 A Certain Ratio
Th 18/10 Virginia Doesn't
M 22/10 The Selecter, Specials
T 23/10 records only
W 24/10 (Wire)
Th 25/10 Comsat Angels
M 29/10 Damned, Killing Joke
T 30/10 records only: 'Long shot (Kick de bucket)'
    by Pioneers
W 31/10 (Peter Hammill)
Th 1/11 (Dodgems)
M 5/11 The Beat, The Jam

T 6/11 (Elti Fits)
W 7/11 records only
Th 8/11 (Shoes for Industry)
M 12/11 Adverts
T 13/11 (Specials)
W 14/11 (Au Pairs, The Selecter)
Th 15/11 records only: Pink Floyd 'Another Brick in the
    Wall', Josef K 'Chance Meeting'
M 19/11 Mekons
T 20/11 (XTC)
W 21/11 Transmitters (The Damned)
Th 22/11 (Comsat Angels)
M 26/11 Pink Military, Secret Affair
T 27/11 Spizz Energi
W 28/11 records only: Keith Hudson 'Nuh Skin Up',
    Art Attacks 'Punk Rock Stars'
Th 29/11 Passions, Tearjerkers
M 3/12 (The Jam)
T 4/12 records only: U2 on CBS 'Out Of Control'
W 5/12 Adicts
Th 6/12 Misty, Deutsche Amerikanische Freundschaft
M 10/12 Joy Division, Lene Lovich
T 11/12 (Funboy Five)
W 12/12 (Flys)
Th 13/12 (Members)
M 17/12 PiL, NotSensibles
T 18/12 (Dodgems, Elti Fits)
W 19/12 (Comsat Angels, Echo and the Bunnymen)
Th 20/12 (Best sessions of the year) Festive 50
M 24/12 Viv Stanshall (Best sessions of year)
    Festive 50
T 25/12 & M 31/12 no shows
W 26/12 – T 1/1/80 (Best sessions of year) Festive 50

1980

W 2/1 UB40 (PiL)
Th 3/1 Bauhaus (Adverts)
Sn 6/1 John Peel's Rock Requests, R1 3–4pm, new
    series, every Sunday thereafter until Sn 29/6
M 7/1 Simple Minds (Mekons)
T 8/1 records only: Asher & Trimble 'Humble Yourself',
    Holly and the Italians 'Tell That Girl to Shut Up'
W 9/1 (Spizz Energi)
Th 10/1 XDreamysts (Misty)
M 14/1 Magazine (Adicts)
T 15/1 (Pink Military)
W 16/1 records only
Th 17/1 Lines (The Passions)
M 21/1 Leyton Buzzards (Lene Lovich)
T 22/1 (Joy Division, Secret Affair)
W 23/1 Undertones
Th 24/1 Cigarettes, Glass Torpedoes
M 28/1 Piranhas (PiL)
T 29/1 (UB40, Bauhaus)
W 30/1 records only
Th 31/1 (NotSensibles, Simple Minds)
M 4/2 Mo-Dettes (Magazine)
T 5/2 (XDreamysts)
W 6/2 (Transmitters)
Th 7/2 Original Mirrors
M 11/2 Delta 5 (Undertones)
T 12/2 (Specials, Lines)
W 13/2 Pop Rivets
Th 14/2 Stiffs, The Visitors
M 18/2 Ruts (Misty)
T 19/2 (The Damned, Glass Torpedoes)
W 20/2 records only
Th 21/2 Wire #1, Leyton Buzzards
M 25/2 Stiff Little Fingers, Cockney Rejects

T 26/2 (Cigarettes)
W 27/2 records only
Th 28/2 Psychedelic Furs
M 3/3 Elvis Costello and the Attractions (Mo-Dettes)
T 4/3 Glaxo Babies
W 5/3 (Original Mirrors, Piranhas)
Th 6/3 Scars, Any Trouble
M 10/3 The Cure (Undertones)
T 11/3 (Pop Rivets)
W 12/3 (Stiffs, Visitors)
Th 13/3 Dexy's Midnight Runners (Delta 5)
M 17/3 Revillos, Killing Joke
T 18/3 (Ruts)
W 19/3 (Stiff Little Fingers)
Th 20/3 (Cockney Rejects)
M 24/3 Chords (Elvis Costello and the Attractions)
T 25/3 Tearjerkers (Psychedelic Furs)
W 26/3 (Glaxo Babies)
Th 27/3 The Diagram Brothers (The Cure)
M 31/3 Pauline Murray (Any Trouble)
T 1/4 Swell Maps (Killing Joke)
W 2/4 (Dexy's Midnight Runners, Tubeway Army, Vapors)
Th 3/4 Bodies, Tea Set
M 7/4 (The Jam) plus 12 tracks played from The Clash's
    Rude Boy Film Soundtrack
T 8/4 (Revillos, Scars) plus private tape of Wah! recorded
    live at Eric's, Liverpool
W 9/4 (Chords, Delta 5)
Th 10/4 Moondogs, Whirlwind
M 14/4 Bodysnatchers (Diagram brothers)
T 15/4 (Pauline Murray, Mo-Dettes)
W 16/4 (UB40, Graham Parker and the Rumour #1,
    Tearjerkers)
Th 17/4 (Cockney Rejects, PiL)
M 21/4 Orchestral Manoeuvres in the Dark (Ruts)
T 22/4 (Spizz Energi, XTC)
W 23/4 The Monochrome Set (Stiff Little Fingers)
Th 24/4 The Teardrop Explodes #2 (Revillos, Visitors)
M 28/4 Basement Five (UK Subs #1)
T 29/4 UK Decay (Tea Set)
W 30/4 (Bodies, The Cure, Whirlwind)
Th 1/5 (Killing Joke, Psychedelic Furs)
M 5/5 (Dexy's Midnight Runners, Elvis Costello & the
    Attractions) plus Rude Boy Soundtrack album again
T 6/5 (Moondogs, Orchestral Manoeuvres in the Dark)
W 7/5 Steel Pulse
Th 8/5 Comsat Angels (Swell Maps)
M 12/5 Athletico Spizz 80, Laurel Aitken
T 13/5 Radio 5 (Teardrop Explodes)
W 14/5 Passions (Prefects #1)
Th 15/5 (Bodysnatchers)
M 19/5 (The Monochrome Set, Chords)
T 20/5 Idiot Dancers (Steel Pulse)
W 21/5 Mononconics (UK Decay)
Th 22/5 Echo and the Bunnymen (Basement Five)
M 26/5 Fabulous Thunderbirds (Laurel Aitken, Elvis
    Costello and the Attractions #1, Siouxsie and the
    Banshees #1)
T 27/5 All-Independent Labels special: all 7-inch single
    releases, apparently on labels called Rat Race,
    Charnel House, Rough Trade, Fetish, Ycafo,
    Woodbine Street, Dolmen, Illegal, Gogo, Voxx, Gear,
    Optimistic, Deep Water, Red Rhino, New Hormones,
    Citizens, Energy, Nadigital, Clay, Rebel, Dread At The
    Controls, Fabulous, Rampant, Damp, Fashion Music,
    Pop Aural, Deadly Boring, 021 Records, Phoney
    Gran, No Hessle, Top Ranking, Public, Quark, Swell,
    Flicknife
W 28/5 (Moondogs, Prince Far I and Creation Rebel)
Th 29/5 (Athletico Spizz 80, The Cure, Stiff Little Fingers)
M 2/6 Only Ones (Orchestral Manoeuvres in the Dark)
T 3/6 (Diagram Brothers, Mononconics)
W 4/6 records only: Jad Fair 'The Invisible Ray', The Big
    Three 'Cavern Stomp'

Th 5/6 Pink Military
M 9/6 The 2-Tone Special (The Beat, Madness, The
    Selecter, Specials, Bodysnatchers)
T 10/6 Wah! Heat (The Passions)
W 11/6 (Comsat Angels, Undertones)
Th 12/6 Au Pairs (Radio 5)
M 16/6 (Steel Pulse) & The Clash's Rude Boy
    Soundtrack again
T 17/6 (Athletico Spizz 80, Echo and the Bunnymen)
W 18/6 (Bauhaus, Idiot Dancers)
Th 19/6 Normil Hawaiians (Psychedelic Furs)
M 23/6 (Joy Division #1 & #2)
T 24/6 (UB40, Chords, Elvis Costello and the Attractions)
W 25/6 (Boomtown Rats #2, Orchestral Manoeuvres
    in the Dark)
Th 26/6 (Damned, Revillos, Sham 69)
M 30/6 (Only Ones, Diagram Brothers)
T 1/7 (Wah! Heat, Mononconics)
W 2/7 (Au Pairs, Pink Military)
Th 3/7 (Misty, Cockney Rejects)
M 7/7 (Moondogs, Normil Hawaiians)
T 8/7 (Delta 5, Radio 5)
W 9/7 (Adam and the Ants #1, Crass)
Th 10/7 (Mo-Dettes)
M 14/7 (Pauline Murray, Bob Marley & the Wailers,
    1st TX 15/5/73)
T 15/7 (Comsat Angels, The Jam #1)
W 16/7 (Glass Torpedoes, Stranglers #1)
Th 17/7 (Any Trouble, Cigarettes)
M 21/7 records only: Rulers 'Wrong Embryo', Betty
    Harris 'Ride Your Pony'
T 22/7 (Ruts #1, #2 & #3)
W 23/7 (Au Pairs, Shoes for Industry)
Th 24/7 (Elti Fits, Pink Military)
M 28/7 (Athletico Spizz 80, Echo and the Bunnymen)
T 29/7 (Bauhaus, Leyton Buzzards #3)
W 30/7 (The Cure #1, Killing Joke)
Th 31/7 (The Skids #1, Capital Letters)
M 4/8 (Passions, Elvis Costello & The Attractions #1)
T 5/8 (Basement Five)
W 6/8 (Diagram Brothers, Mekons #1)
Th 7/8 (Wah! Heat, The Damned #1)
M 11/8 (Alternative TV #1, X-Ray Spex #1)
T 12/8 (Idiot Dancers)
W 13/8 records only: Blurt 'Get', The Native Hipsters
    'There Goes Concorde Again'
Th 14/8 (Linton Kwesi Johnson, Lines)
M 18/8 Furious Pig (Piranhas #2)
T 19/8 (DAF, Metal Urbain #2)
W 20/8 I'm so Hollow
Th 21/8 Flatbackers
M 25/8 (The Jam, Siouxsie and the Banshees)
T 26/8 Young Marble Giants (Big in Japan)
W 27/8 Positive Noise (UK Decay)
Th 28/8 records only: 3 tracks from Dead Kennedys on
    'Fresh Fruit For Rotting Vegetables' LP
M 1/9 TV Personalities (Cockney Rejects)
T 2/9 (Comsat Angels)
W 3/9 records only: Orange Juice 'Lovesick', It's
    Immaterial 'Young Man Seeks Interesting Job'
Th 4/9 (Furious Pig, XTC #1)
M 8/9 Bodysnatchers (Flatbackers)
T 9/9 (I'm so Hollow)
W 10/9 records only
Th 11/9 Delta 5
M 15/9 Skids (Young Marble Giants)
T 16/9 Out on Blue Six
W 17/9 records only
Th 18/9 Martian Dance (Positive Noise)
M 22/9 The Beat
T 23/9 records only
W 24/9 The Fall

Th 25/9 The Birthday Party (TV Personalities)
M 29/9 Mo-Dettes, Misty
T 30/9 records only
W 1/10 Angelic Upstarts
Th 2/10 (Normil Hawaiians, Skids)
M 6/10 Cravats, Orchestral Manoeuvres in the Dark
T 7/10 G Lewis & B C Gilbert
W 8/10 records only
Th 9/10 Blurt (Bodysnatchers)
M 13/10 Nightingales (The Beat)
T 14/10 records only: Cathay La Creme 'I Married A Cult
    Figure From Salford'
W 15/10 (Mo-Dettes)
Th 16/10 Altered Images, Nervous Germans
M 20/10 Damned, Liggers
T 21/10 (Out on Blue Six)
W 22/10 (The Birthday Party)
Th 23/10 Petticoats (The Fall)
M 27/10 Bow Wow Wow, Peter and the
    Test Tube Babies
T 28/10 records only
W 29/10 (Martian Dance, Delta 5)
Th 30/10 TV21, Orange Juice (Viv Stanshall #6)
M 3/11 (Angelic Upstarts, Orchestral Manoeuvres
    in the Dark #2)
T 4/11 (Cravats)
W 5/11 (The Beat, G Lewis & B C Gilbert)
Th 6/11 (Young Marble Giants, Misty)
M 10/11 Professionals (Altered Images)
T 11/11 (Blurt, Nightingales)
W 12/11 Echo and the Bunnymen
Th 13/11 (Diagram Brothers, I'm so Hollow)
M 17/11 League of Gentlemen, Passions
T 18/11 (Liggers, Nervous Germans)
W 19/11 (The Fall, Peter and the Test Tube Babies)
Th 20/11 Freeze (Damned)
M 24/11 Splodgenessabounds (Bow Wow Wow)
T 25/11 Modern English (TV21)
W 26/11 (Orange Juice, The Beat)
Th 27/11 Passage (Martian Dance)
M 1/12 Specials, The Selecter
T 2/12 Minny Pops (Altered Images)
W 3/12 Department S (Petticoats)
Th 4/12 Boots for Dancing (Passions)
M 8/12 (Echo and the Bunnymen, Professionals)
T 9/12 Theatre of Hate, Undertones (Freeze)
W 10/12 Attic (Peter and the Test Tube Babies)
Th 11/12 Icarus, Postmen
M 15/12 Red Beat (The Fall)
T 16/12 In Camera (Nervous Germans)
W 17/12 Blue Orchids (Passage)
Th 18/12 Raincoats (Modern English)
M 22/12 – T 30/12 (Best Sessions of Year) Festive 50
Th 25/12 & W 31/12 no shows

1981

- Chris Lycett becomes producer, Mon, Tues
  & Thur
- Walters does Wed show, pre-recorded, 81–82

Th 1/1 (Comsat Angels, Selecter)
M 5/1 Mekons (Boots for Dancing)
T 6/1 Resistance (Mo-Dettes)
W 7/1 (Orange Juice, Theatre of Hate)
Th 8/1 Visitors (Department S)
M 12/1 TV Smith's Explorers (Adam and the Ants #1,
    Undertones)
T 13/1 The Room (Minny Pops)
W 14/1 Missing Presumed Dead (Red Beat)
Th 15/1 The Cure (Nightingales)

M 19/1 Crispy Ambulance (Attic)
T 20/1 Section 25 (Raincoats)
W 21/1 Blue Orchids, Mekons
Th 22/1 Ski Patrol (Cravats)
M 26/1 (In Camera, Passions)
T 27/1 Lines (Resistance)
W 28/1 Au Pairs (TV Smith's Explorers)
Th 29/1 (Liggers, Visitors)
St 31/1 Arena, BBC2 TV 10.45–11.25pm Today
    Carshalton Beeches... Tomorrow Croydon: study of
    phenomenon since punk of several bands in every
    town, based on Peel and Walters' experiences
    running the Peel show, who both appear, as do The
    Nightingales, The Liggers, The Skids, and Move To
    India. Director Alan Yentob, producer Anthony Wall
M 2/2 21 Guns (The Cure)
T 3/2 Diagram Brothers (Missing Presumed Dead)
W 4/2 (The Fall #1, The Room)
Th 5/2 Modern Eon (Crispy Ambulance)
M 9/2 Comsat Angels (Section 25)
T 10/2 Psychedelic Furs (Ski Patrol)
W 11/2 (Misty #1, Lines)
Th 12/2 (Red Beat, Au Pairs)
M 16/2 New Order (Rezillos #1)
T 17/2 Dead or Alive (Out on Blue Six)
W 18/2 Siouxsie and the Banshees
    (Siouxsie and the Banshees #1)
T 19/2 (Adam and the Ants #3, Diagram Brothers)
M 23/2 Girls at our Best (Modern Eon)
T 24/2 (21 Guns, David Bowie, 1st TX 23/5/72)
W 25/2 Another Pretty Face (Stiff Little Fingers #3)
Th 26/2 Blue Orchids, Psychedelic Furs)
M 2/3 Frames (Modern English)
T 3/3 Frantic Elevators (Comsat Angels)
W 4/3 (Dead or Alive, Damned #2)
Th 5/3 (A Certain Ratio, New Order)
M 9/3 Fire Engines (Siouxsie and the Banshees)
T 10/3 Ruts DC, Altered Images
W 11/3 Lucy's (Penetration #1)
Th 12/3 Gang of Four (Girls At Our Best)
M 16/3 (Dead or Alive, The Teardrop Explodes #1)
T 17/3 Restricted Code (Frames)
W 18/3 Stiff Little Fingers (Frantic Elevators)
Th 19/3 (Skids #1 & #3)
M 23/3 – Th 26/3 Radio 1 in Scotland: (Boots for
    Dancing, Altered Images)
T 24/3 Cuban Heels, Josef K
W 25/3 Positive Noise (Visitors)
Th 26/3 (Fire Engines, Orange Juice)
M 30/3 Endgames (Gang of Four)
T 31/3 The Fall (The Fall #2)
W 1/4 (Undertones, Lucy's)
Th 2/4 (Ruts DC, Restricted Code)
M 6/4 (Bodysnatchers, Stiff Little Fingers)
T 7/4 B Movie (Positive Noise)
W 8/4 records only
Th 9/4 (Glaxo Babies, Cuban Heels)
M 13/4 Members (Modern English)
T 14/4 Wah! (Scritti Politti)
W 15/4 Dead on Arrival (Endgames)
Th 16/4 Groundation (New Order)
M 20/4 Moderates (Passions #1)
T 21/4 Martian Dance (Siouxsie and the Banshees)
W 22/4 Ivor Cutler (The Fall)
Th 23/4 Blank Students (Passions)
M 27/4 Killing Joke (B Movie)
T 28/4 The Birthday Party (Members)
W 29/4 Musical Youth (Dead on Arrival)
Th 30/4 (Groundation, Syd Barrett, 1st TX 14/3/70)
M 4/5 Associates (Josef K)
T 5/5 (Blank Students)
W 6/5 (Altered Images, Wah!)

Th 7/5 (Red Beat, Martian Dance)
M 11/5 Chefs (Frames)
T 12/5 A Flock of Seagulls (Ski Patrol)
W 13/5 Revillos (Department S)
Th 14/5 (New Order, Killing Joke)
M 18/5 Moondogs (Ivor Cutler)
T 19/5 (Lucy's, Moderates)
W 20/5 (The Birthday Party)
Th 21/5 (Girls at our Best, Associates)
M 25/5 Outcasts (Musical Youth)
T 26/5 Colours out of Time (A Flock of Seagulls)
W 27/5 Black Roots (Skids #2)
Th 28/5 (Fire Engines, The Cure)
M 1/6 Higsons, Misty
T 2/6 Laura Logic (Scritti Politti #1)
W 3/6 Vice Squad (Moondogs)
Th 4/6 Scars
M 8/6 – Th 11/6 presented by John Walters (repeats)
M 15/6 Bill Nelson (Revillos)
T 16/6 Que Bono (Black Roots)
W 17/6 Chameleons (Chefs)
Th 18/6 (Outcasts, Colours out of Time)
M 22/6 Josef K (B Movie)
T 23/6 Meteors (Misty)
W 24/6 Out on Blue Six (Higsons)
Th 25/6 Cabaret Voltaire (Vice Squad)
M 29/6 Angelic Upstarts (Scars)
T 30/6 Skodas (Laura Logic)
W 1/7 (The Fall, The Birthday Party)
Th 2/7 A Certain Ratio (Bill Nelson)
M 6/7 (Graham Parker and the Rumour #1,
    Musical Youth)
T 7/7 Nightingales (Chameleons)
W 8/7 Angels 1–5
Th 9/7 Milan Station (Que Bono)
M 13/7 (Killing Joke, Josef K)
T 14/7 Bow Wow Wow, Meteors)
W 15/7 Boots for Dancing (Altered Images)
Th 16/7 (X-Ray Spex #1, Out on Blue Six)
M 20/7 Ponderosa Glee Boys (Cabaret Voltaire)
T 21/7 Mo-Dettes (Angelic Upstarts)
W 22/7 (Wah!, Higsons)
Th 23/7 Method Actors (Skodas)
M 27/7 (The Birthday Party, Boots for Dancing)
T 28/7 Artery (Angels 1–5)
W 29/7 Transmitters (The Cure)
Th 30/7 (Groundation, Vice Squad)
M 3/8 Malaria (Chefs)
T 4/8 (Frames, Frantic Elevators)
W 5/8 UK Decay (A Certain Ratio)
Th 6/8 Nuclear Socketts (Mo-Dettes)
M 10/8 Orange Juice (Milan Station)
T 11/8 Dislocation Dance (Nightingales)
W 12/8 (Girls at our Best, Ponderosa Glee Boys)
Th 13/8 (A Flock of Seagulls, Method Actors)
M 17/8 Repetition (Revillos)
T 18/8 Cravats (Artery)
W 19/8 The Freeze (Higsons)
Th 20/8 (The Birthday Party, Malaria)
M 24/8 Theatre of Hate (Transmitters)
T 25/8 Remipeds (Orange Juice)
W 26/8 The Fall (Chefs)
Th 27/8 Stimulin (Boots for Dancing)
M 31/8 (Bill Nelson, Meteors)
T 1/9 Motor Boys Motor (Dislocation Dance)
W 2/9 (UK Decay, Nuclear Socketts)
Th 3/9 Bamboo Zoo (A Certain Ratio)
M 7/9 (Mo-Dettes, Cravats)
T 8/9 Allez Allez (Repetition)
W 9/9 Talisman (Method Actors)
Th 10/9 A Formal Sigh (Nightingales)

S 12/9 Meet John Peel, various times, BBC World
Service: Robert Milne-Tyte interviews John Peel about
his life and career, 15-minute show
M 14/9 (The Freeze, Theatre of Hate)
T 15/9 Pigbag (The Fall)
W 16/9 Fire Engines, Skodas)
Th 17/9 Maximum Joy (Remipeds)
M 21/9 Rip Rig and Panic (Vice Squad)
T 22/9 Altered Images (Stimulin)
W 23/9 23 Skidoo (Motor Boys Motor)
Th 24/9 (Dislocation Dance, Slits, 1st TX 27/9/77)
M 28/9 Rudi (Bamboo Zoo)
T 29/9 Misty, Allez Allez)
W 30/9 Frantic Elevators (A Formal Sigh)
Th 1/10 Twinkle Brothers (Pigbag)
M 5/10 The Room (Altered Images)
T 6/10 (Orange Juice, Maximum Joy)
W 7/10 Comsat Angels (Meteors)
Th 8/10 (Rip Rig and Panic, 23 Skidoo)
M 12/10 Natural Scientist (The Fall)
T 13/10 Modern English (Rudi)
W 14/10 The Passage (Method Actors)
Th 15/10 Cuban Heels (Malaria)
M 19/10 (Skodas, Vice Squad)
T 20/10 (Talisman, Rip Rig and Panic)
W 21/10 (Transmitters, Maximum Joy)
Th 22/10 (Black Roots, Pigbag)
M 26/10 Slits (Frantic Elevators)
T 27/10 Linton Kwesi Johnson (Rudi)
W 28/10 (Natural Scientist, The Passage)
Th 29/10 Ellery Bop (Comsat Angels)
M 2/11 Twisted Nerve (Twinkle Brothers)
T 3/11 Jass Babies (A Certain Ratio)
W 4/11 Higsons (The Room)
Th 5/11 Gregory Isaacs and Roots Radics
(Modern English)
M 9/11 Bee Vamp (Cuban Heels)
T 10/11 Sophisticated Boom Boom (Orange Juice)
W 11/11 Schlaflose Nächte (Ellery Bop)
Th 12/11 Signorinas (Slits)
M 16/11 The Sound (Twisted Nerve)
T 17/11 Systems (The Cure)
W 18/11 Pulp (Linton Kwesi Johnson)
Th 19/11 It's Immaterial (Higsons)
M 23/11 Fire Engines (Bee Vamp)
T 24/11 The Balcony (Gregory Isaacs and
Roots Radics)
W 25/11 (The Fall, Jass Babies)
Th 26/11 (Chefs, Talisman)
M 30/11 Danse Society (Signorinas)
T 1/12 (Sophisticated Bom Boom, Comsat Angels)
W 2/12 Plain Characters (Rip Rig and Panic)
Th 3/12 Sad Lovers and Giants (Schlaflose Nächte)
M 7/12 Sinatras (Systems)
T 8/12 (Artery, Pulp)
W 9/12 (Chefs, The Sound)
Th 10/12 The Birthday Party (The Passage)
M 14/12 Ritual (Cuban Heels, Fire Engines)
T 15/12 (It's Immaterial, The Cravats)
W 16/12 Killing Joke (The Balcony)
Th 17/12 Distributors (Danse Society)
M 21/12 TV21 (Plain Characters)
T 22/12 The Teardrop Explodes (Sad Lovers And Giants)
W 23/12 – W 30/12 (Best Sessions of Year) Festive 50
Th 31/12 no show

M 4/1 Carnastoan, The Cure
T 5/1 (Fire Engines, Sinatras)
W 6/1 Steel Pulse (Slits)

Th 7/1 Little Red Duffle Coats (The Birthday Party)
M 11/1 APB (Killing Joke)
T 12/1 (Models, TV21)
W 13/1 Drowning Craze (The Teardrop Explodes)
Th 14/1 (Theatre of Hate, Distributors)
M 18/1 Pink Industry (Carnastoan)
T 19/1 (The Sound, Ritual)
W 20/1 Twinsets (The Cure)
Th 21/1 (Little Red Duffle Coats, Altered Images #1)
M 25/1 UB40 (APB)
T 26/1 The Icicle Works (Maximum Joy)
W 27/1 (Diagram Brothers, Steel Pulse)
Th 28/1 Play Dead (The Balcony)
M 1/2 Big Self (Danse Society)
T 2/2 Animal Magic (Fire Engines)
W 3/2 (Twinsets, Pink Industry)
Th 4/2 Come in Tokio (The Birthday Party #2)
M 8/2 Echo and the Bunnymen (Pulp)
T 9/2 (Drowning Craze, Siouxsie and the Banshees #1)
W 10/2 (Simple Minds, The Icicle Works)
Th 11/2 (Play Dead, UB40)
M 15/2 Artery (Animal Magic)
T 16/2 Marine Girls (Method Actors)
W 17/2 (Steel Pulse, Come in Tokio)
Th 18/2 Theatre of Hate (Sophisticated Boom Boom)
M 22/2 Action Pact (The Cure)
T 23/2 Blancmange (Cravats)
W 24/2 (Echo and the Bunnymen, 23 Skidoo)
Th 25/2 Visitors (The Teardrop Explodes)
M 1/3 Simple Minds (Marine Girls)
T 2/3 (Associates, Artery)
W 3/3 Names (Sinatras)
Th 4/3 (Higsons, Killing Joke)
M 8/3 Maximum Joy (Big Self)
T 9/3 (Action Pact, UB40)
W 10/3 Skat, Stiffs
Th 11/3 (Positive Noise, Theatre of Hate)
M 15/3 John Cooper-Clarke (TV21)
T 16/3 (It's Immaterial, Visitors)
W 17/3 (Animal Magic, Blancmange)
Th 18/3 Dead or Alive, Nightingales
M 22/3 Leisure Process (Twinsets)
T 23/3 (Misty, Simple Minds)
W 24/3 (Maximum Joy, The Birthday Party #3)
Th 25/3 Scream and Dance (Stiffs)
M 29/3 The Beat (APB)
T 30/3 (A Flock of Seagulls, Names)
W 31/3 The Au Pairs (Drowning Craze)
Th 1/4 China Crisis (John Cooper-Clarke)
M 5/4 – Th 8/4 John Peel's Week in Liverpool:
3D a Fish in Sea (Echo and the Bunnymen)
T 6/4 Cherry Boys (Come in Tokio)
W 7/4 Cross Section, Blue Poland
Th 8/4 (Jass Babies, The Teardrop Explodes)
M 12/4 Bauhaus (Skat)
T 13/4 (Leisure Process, Action Pact)
W 14/4 Boots For Dancing (Scream and Dance)
Th 15/4 (Dead or Alive, The Beat)
M 19/4 Associates (Nightingales)
T 20/4 Modernaires (Simple Minds)
W 21/4 (3D a Fish in Sea, Theatre of Hate)
Th 22/4 New Age (Au Pairs)
M 26/4 Kan Kan (China Crisis)
T 27/4 Ju Ju (UB40)
W 28/4 (Twinsets, Bauhaus)
Th 29/4 Ravishing Beauties (Cherry Boys)
M 3/5 Crabs (Boots For Dancing)
T 4/5 Michael Smith (Blue Poland)
W 5/5 Blue Orchids (Blancmange)
Th 6/5 Serious Drinking (Artery)
M 10/5 Vice Squad (Steel Pulse)
T 11/5 (Kan Kan, Cross Section)

W 12/5 1919 (Action Pact)
Th 13/5 Wild Swans (Modernaires)
M 17/5 (Buzzcocks #1, Associates)
T 18/5 Wah! (Leisure Process)
W 19/5 (The Beat, New Age)
Th 20/5 Gymslips (Animal Magic)
M 24/5 Scritti Politti (Ravishing Beauties)
T 25/5 (Associates, Blue Orchids)
W 26/5 Endgames (Ju Ju)
Th 27/5 (Serious Drinking, Michael Smith)
M 31/5 (Altered Images #1, Madness #1,
Adam & the Ants #1)
T 1/6 New Order (Vice Squad)
W 2/6 (Wild Swans, Higsons)
Th 3/6 (Crabs, The Birthday Party #1)
M 7/6 The Passage (1919)
T 8/6 Nasmak (Misty #1)
W 9/6 (Wah!, Simple Minds)
Th 10/6 Southern Death Cult (Echo and the Bunnymen)
M 14/6 – Th 24/6 with Mark Ellen (repeats)
M 28/6 Swinging Laurels (Come in Tokio)
T 29/6 (Gymslips, Maximum Joy)
W 30/6 Attila the Stockbroker, The Room
Th 1/7 Send No Flowers (Theatre of Hate)
M 5/7 Endgames, New Order)
T 6/7 Rubella Ballet (Southern Death Cult)
W 7/7 Amazulu (Scritti Politti)
Th 8/7 Kevin Coyne (Pink Industry)
St 10/7 – St 14/8 Peel's Pleasures: Peel stands-in for
Walters' Weekly, 4–5pm, featuring favourite eccentric
records, radio clips and session repeats from: (Gerry
& the Pacemakers, Ivor Cutler, Rudies, Ann Peebles,
Fleetwood Mac, Bonzo Dogs), produced by Chris
Lycett / John Walters
M 12/7 Rip Rig and Panic (Michael Smith)
T 13/7 (Echo and the Bunnymen #1, Crabs)
W 14/7 Dislocation Dance (Gymslips)
Th 15/7 Cocteau Twins (Serious Drinking)
M 19/7 Yazoo (The Room)
T 20/7 Erazerhead (The Beat)
W 21/7 (3D a Fish in Sea, The Passage) & Bob George
reports from America
Th 22/7 Diagram Brothers (Swinging Laurels)
M 26/7 (Cocteau Twins, Nasmak)
T 27/7 Popular Voice (Wah!)
W 28/7 The Happy Few, Nightingales
Th 29/7 (Amazulu, Rubella Ballet)
M 2/8 March Violets (Teardrop Explodes #1)
T 3/8 Pale Fountains (Kevin Coyne)
W 4/8 (Yazoo, Dislocation Dance)
Th 5/8 Go-Betweens (Erazerhead)
M 9/8 It's Immaterial (Diagram Brothers)
T 10/8 Three Johns (Rip Rig and Panic)
W 11/8 Shriekback (Attila the Stockbroker)
Th 12/8 Wild Weekend (Scritti Politti)
M 16/8 Action Pact (Nightingales)
T 17/8 Roman Holiday (Cocteau Twins)
W 18/8 Ludus (Popular Voice)
Th 19/8 (Gymslips, The Happy Few)
M 23/8 Mikey Dread (Go-Betweens)
T 24/8 Trixie's Big Red Motorbike (March Violets)
W 25/8 Apollinaires (Three Johns)
Th 26/8 The Fruit Machine (It's Immaterial)
M 30/8 Peel's 43rd birthday: (Altered Images #2 & #3)
T 31/8 Christians in Search of Filth (Marine Girls)
W 1/9 Tears for Fears (Amazulu)
Th 2/9 Cherry Boys (Shriekback)
M 6/9 Flesh for Lulu (Pale Fountains)
T 7/9 Sisters of Mercy (The Beat)
W 8/9 Dance Fault (Roman Holiday)
Th 9/9 (Trixie's Big Red Motorbike, Josef K #1)
M 13/9 Danse Society (The Fruit Machine)
T 14/9 Farmer's Boys (Visitors)

W 15/9 (Mickey Dread, Wild Weekend)
Th 16/9 Gymslips (Ludus)
M 20/9 (Big in Japan, Action Pact)
T 21/9 (Apollinaires, March Violets)
W 22/9 Animal Magic (Tears For Fears)
Th 23/9 (Dance Fault, Christians in Search of Filth)
M 27/9 Serious Drinking (Send No Flowers)
T 28/9 Come in Tokio, Musical Youth
W 29/9 Outcasts (Cherry Boys)
Th 30/9 no show: swinging sixties 'Heroes & Villians' concert, 'introduced by John Peel & Tony Blackburn'
M 4/10 The Mad Professor (Danse Society)
T 5/10 Strawbery Switchblade (Sisters of Mercy)
W 6/10 The High Five (The Gymslips)
Th 7/10 Sophisticated Boom Boom (Flesh for Lulu)
M 11/10 Higsons (Farmer's Boys)
T 12/10 (Nightingales, Animal Magic)
W 13/10 Icon AD (The Associates)
Th 14/10 Short Commercial Break (Musical Youth)
M 18/10 Lotus Eaters (Diagram Brothers)
T 19/10 Carnastoan (Serious Drinking)
W 20/10 Redskins (Come in Tokio)
Th 21/10 (Outcasts, The Mad Professor)
M 25/10 (New Order, Sophisticated Boom Boom)
T 26/10 Darkness and Jive (The High Five)
W 27/10 The Passage (Amazulu)
Th 28/10 Higsons, Michael Smith)
M 1/11 (Crabs, Musical Youth)
T 2/11 (Strawberry Switchblade, Icon AD)
W 3/11 The Corporation (Rubella Ballet)
Th 4/11 Laurel and Hardy, Twinsets
M 8/11 Brilliant (Lotus Eaters)
T 9/11 3D (Carnastoan)
W 10/11 The Farmer's Boys 'Live at the General Wolfe, Coventry'
Th 11/11 Sex Gang Children (Darkness and Jive)
M 15/11 Cravats (Redskins)
T 16/11 Pink Industry (Short Commercial Break)
Th 18/11 Seething Wells (The Corporation)
M 22/11 The Birthday Party (Twinsets)
T 23/11 Personal Column (The Passage)
W 24/11 Honeymoon Killers (Brilliant)
Th 25/11 Xmal Deutschland (3D)
M 29/11 Spear of Destiny (Serious Drinking)
T 30/11 (Sex Gang Children, Gymslips)
W 1/12 A Certain Ratio (Pink Industry)
Th 2/12 Frankie Goes to Hollywood (Cravats)
M 6/12 Gregory Isaacs and Roots Radics (Vital Excursions)
T 7/12 The Undertones (Farmer's Boys live at the General Wolfe)
W 8/12 Laughing Clowns (Personal Column)
Th 9/12 Palais Schaumburg (The Birthday Party)
M 13/12 Khartomb, Ellery Bop
T 14/12 (Spear of Destiny, Honeymoon Killers)
W 15/12 (Nightingales #3, UB40, Theatre of Hate)
Th 16/12 (Three Johns, Cocteau Twins, Sophisticated Boom Boom)
M 20/12 – Th 30/12 (Best Sessions of Year) All-Time Festive 50, plus Festive 50 for 1982 only

1983

- **Trevor Dann takes over Mon, Tues & Thurs production from Chris Lycett**

M 3/1 Testcard F, Misty
T 4/1 You've Got Foetus on Your Breath (Brilliant)
W 5/1 APB (A Certain Ratio)
Th 6/1 (Personal Column, Gregory Isaacs and Roots Radics)
M 10/1 Benjamin Zephaniah, The Expelled (Palais

Schaumburg)
T 11/1 Culture (Wah! Live at Eric's tape repeated, 3 songs)
W 12/1 Black (Spear of Destiny)
Th 13/1 Red Lorry Yellow Lorry, Serious Drinking
M 17/1 Amazulu (The Birthday Party)
T 18/1 (Testcard F, Ellery Bop)
W 19/1 (Laughing Clowns, You've Got Foetus on Your Breath)
Th 20/1 Three Mustaphas Three (APB)
M 24/1 (The Mad Professor, Cravats)
T 25/1 Roman Holiday (Black)
W 26/1 (Khartomb, Misty)
Th 27/1 China Crisis (The Expelled)
M 31/1 Cocteau Twins (Culture)
T 1/2 Scream and Dance (Red Lorry Yellow Lorry)
W 2/2 (Laurel and Hardy, Higsons)
Th 3/2 The Box (Amazulu)
M 7/2 Benjamin Zepheniah (Undertones)
T 8/2 Rubella Ballet (Echo and the Bunnymen #1)
W 9/2 (Three Mustaphas Three, Strawberry Switchblade)
Th 10/2 Julian Cope (Redskins)
M 14/2 Cook Da Books (Xmal Deutschland)
T 15/2 (Ellery Bop, Cocteau Twins)
W 16/2 Screen 3 (Serious Drinking)
Th 17/2 (The Birthday Party, China Crisis)
M 21/2 Orchestral Maneouvres in the Dark (Roman Holiday)
T 22/2 Sophie and Peter Johnston (The Box)
W 23/2 (Scream and Dance, Benjamin Zepheniah)
Th 24/2 Marc Almond (Testcard F)
M 28/2 (Sex Gang Children, Julian Cope)
T 1/3 (Frankie Goes to Hollywood, Misty)
W 2/3 The Icicle Works (Khartomb)
Th 3/3 Ivor Cutler (Cocteau Twins)
M 7/3 (Redskins, Undertones #2)
T 8/3 (Sophie and Peter Johnston, Serious Drinking)
W 9/3 Three Johns (Screen 3)
Th 10/3 (Marc Almond, Red Lorry Yellow Lorry)
St 12/3 You'll Never Walk Alone, 4–5pm: Peel kicks-off R1's week in Liverpool with documentary, featuring interviews/contributions from Peter Hooton, Adrian Henri, Kenny Dalglish, produced by Trevor Dann
M 14/3 (Personal Column, Orchestral Maneouvres in the Dark)
T 15/3 The Peel & Jensen Merseyside Music Show, 8–11pm, with The Icicle Works, It's Immaterial, & Wah! all live at The Royal Court Theatre Liverpool, followed by an hour of records with Peel, 11pm–midnight
W 16/3 (Cook Da Books) show shortened to one hour because concert from Liverpool by Dexy's Midnight Runners overran
Th 17/3 ('You'll Never Walk Alone' documentary rpt 7–8pm)
Th 17/3 Craig Charles, Virgin Dance
M 21/3 Newtown Neurotics (Black)
T 22/3 Big Country (Cocteau Twins)
W 23/3 The Fall (Ivor Cutler)
Th 24/3 March Violets (China Crisis)
M 28/3 Kick Partners (The Icicle Works)
T 29/3 Attila the Stockbroker (Three Johns)
W 30/3 Chevalier Brothers (Sophie and Peter Johnston)
Th 31/3 Freeze Frame (Testcard F)
M 4/4 Nightingales (Julian Cope)
T 5/4 Virgin Dance, Newtown Neurotics
W 6/4 Flying Pickets (Big Country)
Th 7/4 (Cook Da Books) & Bob George reports live from America
M 11/4 Building 44 (Screen 3)

T 12/4 Rebel Da Fe (Craig Charles)
W 13/4 Wah! (The Birthday Party #1)
Th 14/4 Loudon Wainwright III (The Fall)
M 18/4 (Attila the Stockbroker, APB)

- **Walters resumes all show production after Easter 1983**

T 19/4 Marine Girls (March Violets)
W 20/4 (Nightingales)
Th 21/4 (Chevalier Brothers, Cocteau Twins)
M 25/4 Martin Carthy (Freeze Frame)
T 26/4 Blood and Roses (Flying Pickets)
W 27/4 The Farm (Building 44)
Th 28/4 Box of Toys
M 2/5 (Bauhaus #1, Wah!)
T 3/5 Basking Sharks (Loudon Wainwright III)
W 4/5 (Big Country, Virgin Dance)
Th 5/5 Offspring (Killing Joke)
M 9/5 Marine Girls, Orchestral Maneouvres in the Dark)
T 10/5 (The Fall, Three Johns)
W 11/5 1919 (Rebel Da Fe)
Th 12/5 (Martin Carthy, Nightingales)
M 16/5 Zerra 1 (Blood and Roses)
T 17/5 (The Farm) Bob George reports live from America
W 18/5 Brigandage (Basking Sharks)
Th 19/5 Skeletal Family (Magazine #1)
M 23/5 – Th 26/5 with Mark Ellen (repeats)
M 30/5 Frank Chickens, Gymslips
T 31/5 (Offspring, 1919)
W 1/6 Smiths (Blancmange)
Th 2/6 Yip Yip Coyote (The Beat #1)
M 6/6 The High Five (Zerra 1)
T 7/6 Clock DVA (Skeletal Family)
W 8/6 Darkness and Jive
Th 9/6 (Chevalier Brothers, Diagram Brothers)
M 13/6 Naturalites (Brigandage)
T 14/6 Chameleons (Altered Images #1)
W 15/6 Sophisticated Boom Boom (Frank Chickens)
Th 16/6 (Gymslips)
M 20/6 Echo and the Bunnymen (Yip Yip Coyote)
T 21/6 (Smiths)
W 22/6 Higsons (Nightingales)
Th 23/6 Play Dead (Wah!)
M 27/6 Xmal Deutschland (The Fall)
T 28/6 Bone Orchard
W 29/6 (Building 44, Freeze Frame, Box of Toys)
Th 30/6 (Brigandage, Clock DVA)
M 4/7 Black (Naturalites)
T 5/7 (Darkness and Jive)
W 6/7 Three Mustaphas Three (Sophisticated Boom Boom)
Th 7/7 Headhunters (Chameleons)
M 11/7 (Echo and the Bunnymen, Higsons)
T 12/7 Killing Joke (Play Dead)
W 13/7 The Farmer's Boys (Loudon Wainwright III)
Th 14/7 The Wake (Misty #1)
M 18/7 Orchestra Jazira (Bone Orchard)
T 19/7 (Yip Yip Coyote, Chefs, 1st TX 11/5/81)
W 20/7 (Black)
Th 21/7 Ju Ju (Xmal Deutschland)
M 25/7 Florists (Wild Swans)
T 26/7 Three Mustaphas Three, Headhunters)
W 27/7 Popticians (Gymslips)
Th 28/7 Personal Column; & Bob George Reports live from America
M 1/8 So You Think You're a Cowboy? (Killing Joke)
T 2/8 (The Farmer's Boys)
W 3/8 Billy Bragg (Zerra 1)
Th 4/8 (Smiths, Naturalites)
M 8/8 Howard Devoto (Ju Ju)
T 9/8 (The Wake)

W 10/8 Microdisney (Florists)
Th 11/8 Red Guitars (Xmal Deutschland)
M 15/8 Redskins (Popticians)
T 16/8 (Personal Column, Three Mustaphas Three)
W 17/8 Eric Bogosian (Orchestra Jazira)
Th 18/8 New Age Steppers (So You Think
    You're a Cowboy?)
M 22/8 Test Department (Billy Bragg)
T 23/8 Pink Industry (Howard Devoto)
W 24/8 (Smiths, Microdisney)
Th 25/8 Trixie's Big Red Motorbike (Yip Yip Coyote)
M 29/8 (Lotus Eaters, Frank Chickens)
T 30/8 (Red Guitars, Michael Smith)
W 31/8 SPK (Eric Bogosian)
Th 1/9 (Joy Division #1 & #2)
M 5/9 Einstürzende Neubauten (Black)
T 6/9 (Redskins, ClockDVA)
W 7/9 Helen and the Horns (Pink Industry)
Th 8/9 (Florists, Play Dead)
M 12/9 Billy Mackenzie, The Special AKA
T 13/9 3D (Popticians)
W 14/9 (Trixie's Big Red Motorbike, Test Department)
Th 15/9 The Ex (Echo and the Bunnymen)
M 19/9 Luddites (SPK)
T 20/9 (The Farm, Farmer's Boys)
W 21/9 Smiths (Einstürzende Neubauten)
Th 22/9 Fireworks (Helen and the Horns)
M 26/9 Gene Loves Jezebel (Personal Column)
T 27/9 (Billy Bragg, Billy MacKenzie)
W 28/9 Room 101 (The Special AKA)
Th 29/9 (New Age Steppers, Pink Industry)
M 3/10 Serious Drinking (The Ex)
T 4/10 Cocteau Twins
W 5/10 Frank Chickens (Test Department)
Th 6/10 Sus (Jass Babies)
M 10/10 Lotus Eaters (Smiths)
T 11/10 (Red Guitars, Luddites)
W 12/10 Tools You Can Trust (Fireworks)
Th 13/10 (Yip Yip Coyote, Helen and the Horns)
M 17/10 Eek a Mouse and Kalabash
    (Gene Loves Jezebel)
T 18/10 A Popular History of Signs (3D)
W 19/10 James (Room 101)
Th 20/10 (Serious Drinking)
M 24/10 Echo and the Bunnymen
T 25/10 The Orson Family (Frank Chickens)
W 26/10 (Sus, Lotus Eaters)
Th 27/10 Sophie and Peter Johnston
    (Sophie and Peter Johnston #1)
M 31/10 Twa Toots (Cocteau Twins)
T 1/11 (James, Tools You Can Trust)
W 2/11 Screen 3 (Einstürzende Neubauten)
Th 3/11 (Test Department, So You Think
    You're a Cowboy?)
M 7/11 Three Johns (Eek a Mouse and Kalabash)
T 8/11 (SPK, A Popular History of Signs)
W 9/11 Twinsets (Smiths)
Th 10/11 (Microdisney, Eric Bogosian)
M 14/11 Black Roots (Echo and the Bunnymen)
T 15/11 Eton Crop (Sophie and Peter Johnston)
W 16/11 Red Lorry Yellow Lorry (Twa Toots)
Th 17/11 (The Orson Family, Personal Column)
M 21/11 It's Immaterial (Cocteau Twins)
T 22/11 (Three Johns, Screen 3)
W 23/11 Zerra 1 (Eek a Mouse and Kalabash)
Th 24/11 Sudden Sway (3D)
M 28/11 Dead Can Dance (Twinsets)
T 29/11 Marc Riley and the Creepers (Black Roots)
W 30/11 (Eton Crop, Play Dead)
Th 1/12 Quando Quango (Frank Chickens)
M 5/12 Helen and the Horns (Gene Loves Jezebel)
T 6/12 (It's Immaterial, Room 101)

W 7/12 Gymslips (Sophie and Peter Johnston)
Th 8/12 (Smiths, Red Lorry Yellow Lorry)
M 12/12 Nightingales (Zerra 1)
T 13/12 Meteors (Sudden Sway)
W 14/12 Chevalier Brothers
Th 15/12 (Marc Riley and the Creepers, Dead Can
    Dance)
M 19/12 Frankie Goes to Hollywood (Quando Quango)
T 20/12 (Gymslips, Helen and the Horns)
W 21/12 – M 2/1/84 (Best Sessions of Year) Festive
    50, except:
M 26/12 The Rhythm Pals' Boxing Day Bash: David
    Jensen & John Peel, 7.30pm–midnight

1984

T 3/1 The Fall (Chevalier Brothers)
W 4/1 New Model Army (Frankie Goes to Hollywood)
Th 5/1 Here's Johnny (Meteors)
M 9/1 The Very Things (Nightingales)
T 10/1 (Sudden Sway, Quando Quango)
W 11/1 Portion Control (Echo and the Bunnymen)
Th 12/1 Ellery Bop (Zerra 1)
M 16/1 Yip Yip Coyote (Helen and the Horns)
T 17/1 (Frankie Goes to Hollywood, It's Immaterial)
W 18/1 Play Dead (Here's Johnny)
Th 19/1 (The Fall, New Model Army)
M 23/1 Microdisney (Three Johns)
T 24/1 (The Very Things, Portion Control)
W 25/1 Bourgie Bourgie (Cocteau Twins)
Th 26/1 (Dead Can Dance)
M 30/1 Three Mustaphas Three (Yip Yip Coyote)
T 31/1 (Nightingales, Ellery Bop)
W 1/2 Guana Batz (Play Dead)
Th 2/2 (Meteors, Chevalier Brothers)
M 6/2 Inca Babies (Twinsets)
T 7/2 Pastels (Microdisney)
W 8/2 In Excelsis (Bourgie Bourgie)
Th 9/2 Shoot! Dispute (Sudden Sway)
M 13/2 Onward International (Frankie Goes to
    Hollywood)
T 14/2 Craig Charles (Three Mustaphas Three)
W 15/2 (The Fall, Here's Johnny)
Th 16/2 Four Hundred Blows (The Very Things,
    Play Dead)
M 20/2 Hagar the Womb (Guana Batz)
T 21/2 (Marc Riley and the Creepers, Inca Babies)
W 22/2 Ivor Cutler (Onward International)
Th 23/2 Papa Face (Quando Quango)
M 27/2 Billy Bragg (Shoot! Dispute)
T 28/2 Cook Da Books (In Excelsis)
W 29/2 Misty (Tools You Can Trust)
Th 1/3 (Craig Charles, Ellery Bop)
M 5/3 Autumn 1904 (Four Hundred Blows)
T 6/3 (Hagar the Womb)
W 7/3 (Gene Loves Jezebel, The Very Things)
Th 8/3 (Meteors)
M 12/3 The High Five (Papa Face)
T 13/3 The Fire
W 14/3 Shillelagh Sisters (Inca Babies)
Th 15/3 Shreikback
M 19/3 The Farm
T 20/3 White and Torch
W 21/3 (Cook Da Books, Ivor Cutler)
Th 22/3 (Guana Batz, Billy Bragg)
M 26/3 – Th 29/3 presented by Mark Ellen
M 2/4 Boothill Foot Tappers (Misty)
T 3/4 Frank Chickens (Shoot! Dispute)
W 4/4 Folk Devils
Th 5/4 (The Fire, Shillelagh Sisters)

M 9/4 Nick Cave and the Bad Seeds (Craig Charles)
T 10/4 Ex-Post Facto (Four Hundred Blows)
W 11/4 Tools You Can Trust (Autumn 1904)
Th 12/4 (The Farm)
M 16/4 Personal Column (White and Torch)
T 17/4 Pogue Mahone (Shreikback)
W 18/4 Sebastian's Men
Th 19/4 DOA (Cook Da Books)
M 23/4 no sessions, bank holiday programme
T 24/4 del Amitri (Billy Bragg)
W 25/4 Xmal Deutschland (Onward International)
Th 26/4 And Also the Trees (Frank Chickens)
M 30/4 Three Johns (Folk Devils)
T 1/5 Microdisney (Ex-Post Facto)
W 2/5 Guana Batz (Tools You Can Trust)
Th 3/5 (Hagar the Womb, Nick Cave and the Bad
    Seeds)
M 7/5 The Cowpunk Women Special (Yip Yip Coyote
    #1, Helen and the Horns #1, Boothill Foot Tappers,
    Shillelagh Sisters)
T 8/5 Pink Industry (Misty)
W 9/5 (Autumn 1904, Personal Column)
Th 10/5 Come in Tokio (Sebastian's Men)
M 14/5 Working Week (del Amitri)
T 15/5 Alien Sex Fiend (DOA)
W 16/5 Chameleons (Pogue Mahone)
Th 17/5 (Microdisney, Xmal Deutschland)
M 21/5 Moodists (Three Johns)
T 22/5 (Guana Batz, Three Mustaphas Three)
W 23/5 Skiff Skats (Pink Industry)
Th 24/5 Gene Loves Jezebel (Folk Devils)
M 28/5 (Cocteau Twins #1, Smiths #1 & #2)
T 29/5 Ut (Come in Tokio)
W 30/5 Membranes (Working Week)
Th 31/5 (White and Torch, Frank Chickens)
M 4/6 Hard Corps (Alien Sex Fiend)
T 5/6 (Killing Joke #1, The Fall #6)
W 6/6 Gymslips (Microdisney)
Th 7/6 Die Zwei at the Rodeo (Skiff Skats)
M 11/6 Julian Cope (Chameleons)
T 12/6 Dormannu (Sebastian's Men)
W 13/6 Dead Can Dance (Xmal Deutschland)
Th 14/6 Shoot! Dispute (Ut)
M 18/6 Papa Levi (Moodists)
T 19/6 March Violets (Personal Column)
W 20/6 (Working Week, Three Johns)
Th 21/6 (Hard Corps, Gymslips)
M 25/6 Higsons (Membranes)
T 26/6 Eek-A Mouse (Gene Loves Jezebel)
W 27/6 Eleven (Die Zwei at the Rodeo)
Th 28/6 (Come in Tokio, Julian Cope)
M 2/7 Frankie Goes to Hollywood #1 & #2)
T 3/7 Pink Peg Slax (Dormannu)
W 4/7 (Dead Can Dance, Nick Cave and the
    Bad Seeds)
Th 5/7 Marc Riley and the Creepers (Guana Batz)
M 9/7 Meteors (Shoot! Dispute)
T 10/7 Die Töten Hosen (Eek-a-Mouse)
W 11/7 Sisters of Mercy (March Violets)
Th 12/7 The Men They Couldn't Hang (Higsons)
M 16/7 Big Flame (Skiff Skats)
T 17/7 records only, interview with the Frank Chickens'
    Kazuko Hohki in studio
W 18/7 (Eleven, Membranes)
Th 19/7 (Pink Peg Slax, Papa Levi)
St 21/7 John Peel guests on My Top 10, R1, 1–2pm,
    presented by Andy Peebles: 'Teenage Kicks', 'Old
    Man Trouble', 'Maybe I'm Amazed' Faces version,
    'Big Eyed Beans From Venus', 'Come Back', 'You'll
    Never Walk Alone' The Kop Choir, 'Peter Gunn',
    'From The Flagstones' Cocteau Twins, 'No More
    Ghettos In America' Stanley Winston, 'Mankind'
    Misty in Roots

M 23/7 Terry and Gerry (Marc Riley and the Creepers)
T 24/7 Red Guitars (Hard Corps)
W 25/7 Yip Yip Coyote (Die Töten Hosen)
Th 26/7 Savage Progress (Die Zwei at the Rodeo, Meteors)
M 30/7 Joolz (The Men They Couldn't Hang)
T 31/7 Big Flame, Julian Cope)
W 1/8 Helen and the Horns (Sisters of Mercy)
Th 2/8 Screaming Blue Messiahs (Dormannu)
M 6/8 Damned (Pink Peg Slax)
T 7/8 Yeah Yeah Noh (Terry and Gerry)
W 8/8 (Papa Levi, Red Guitars)
Th 9/8 Smiths (Yip Yip Coyote)
M 13/8 (Wah! Heat, Wah!, Shambeko! Say Wah!, Wah!)
T 14/8 The Sid Presley Experience (Savage Progress)
W 15/8 The Icicle Works (Screaming Blue Messiahs)
Th 16/8 (Joolz, Sisters of Mercy)
M 20/8 Fire Engines #1 & #2)
T 21/8 Brilliant Corners (Helen and the Horns)
W 22/8 (Die Toten Hosen, Yeah Yeah Noh)
Th 23/8 Perfect Vision (Marc Riley and the Creepers)
M 27/8 Farmer's Boys (Smiths)
T 28/8 Inca Babies (Big Flame)
W 29/8 Screaming Blue Messiahs, The Icicle Works)
Th 30/8 Everything But The Girl (Damned)
M 3/9 Alien Sex Fiend (The Sid Presley Experience)
T 4/9 Champion Doug Veitch (Higsons)
W 5/9 Cocteau Twins (Helen and the Horns)
Th 6/9 Brilliant Corners, Meteors)
M 10/9 Chinese Gangster Element
T 11/9 (Perfect Vision, Farmer's Boys)
W 12/9 (Yeah Yeah Noh, Inca Babies)
Th 13/9 X Men (Everything But The Girl)
M 17/9 Folk Devils, The Mighty Wah!
T 18/9 (Nick Cave and the Bad Seeds, Shoot! Dispute)
W 19/9 Woodentops (Champion Doug Veitch)
Th 20/9 Billy Bragg (Alien Sex Fiend)
M 24/9 Syncbeat (The Men They Couldn't Hang)
T 25/9 (Chinese Gangster Element)
W 26/9 Float Up CP (Terry and Gerry)
Th 27/9 (Cocteau Twins, Smiths, The Mighty Wah!)

• **From Mon 1/10/84 Thurs 'Into the Music' show**

• **Peel only on Mon–Wed**

M 1/10 (Folk Devils, X Men)
T 2/10 'featuring Yip Yip Coyote, live, as part of ICA Rock Week' & see below…
W 3/10 Junior Gee and the Capital Boys (Woodentops)
M 8/10 Skeletal Family (Billy Bragg)
T 9/10 (Syncbeat, Float Up CP)
W 10/10 Guana Batz, Microdisney
M 15/10 Bronski Beat (Champion Doug Veitch)
T 16/10 (Chinese Gangster Element, Cocteau Twins)
W 17/10 Chakk (Everything But The Girl)
M 22/10 Cabaret Voltaire (Skeletal Family)
T 23/10 Folk Devils, The Mighty Wah!)
W 24/10 (Sudden Sway, Junior Gee and the Capital Boys)
M 29/10 Go-Betweens (Guana Batz)
T 30/10 (Microdisney, Bronski Beat)
W 31/10 Jesus and Mary Chain (Billy Bragg)
M 5/11 (Woodentops, Chakk)
T 6/11 (Float Up CP, Cabaret Voltaire)
W 7/11 Wailing Souls (Farmer's Boys)
M 12/11 Popticians
T 13/11 Triffids (Go-Betweens)
W 14/11 (Microdisney, Bronski Beat)
M 19/11 Live sets recorded at the ICA Rock Week 2–7/10, all bands chosen by Peel under the slogan, nicked from Yeah Yeah Noh, 'John Peel Is Putting The Fun Back Into Being Pretentious': Big Flame, SPK, Terry & Gerry

T 20/11 Eton Crop (Jesus and Mary Chain)
W 21/11 Sudden Sway
M 26/11 More live sets from Peel's ICA Rock Week: Chinese Gangster Element, Hard Corps, Shoot! Dispute, Perfect Vision
T 27/11 (Wailing Souls, Popticians)
W 28/11 Onward International (Chakk)
M 3/12 More from ICA Rock Week: Pink Peg Slax, Marc Riley and the Creepers, Woodentops
T 4/12 (Triffids, Float Up CP)
W 5/12 Tools You Can Trust (Go-Betweens)
M 10/12 ICA Rock Week: Yeah Yeah Noh, The Very Things, Helen and the Horns, Ellery Bop
T 11/12 (Wailing Souls, Sudden Sway)
W 12/12 Pogues (Eton Crop)
M 17/12 ICA Rock Week: The Men They Couldn't Hang, Ut, Nightingales
T 18/12 – T 1/1/85 (Best Sessions of Year) Festive 50
M 24/12 & M 31/12 no shows

1985

W 2/1 Juggernauts (Onward International)
M 7/1 (Skeletal Family)
T 8/1 (Pogues, Josef K, 1st TX 22/6/81)
W 9/1 (Eton Crop, The Birthday Party)
M 14/1 (Big in Japan, Frankie Goes to Hollywood #1 & #2)
T 15/1 The Beloved (Tools You Can Trust)
W 16/1 Minimal Compact
M 21/1 Lash Lariat and the Long Riders (Juggernauts)
T 22/1 (Cabaret Voltaire)
W 23/1 City Limits Crew and the Mutant Rockers (Triffids)
M 28/1 Dr Calculus (Pogues)
T 29/1 (Chameleons, Popticians)
W 30/1 Persuaders (Echo and the Bunnymen #5)
M 4/2 Test Department (The Beloved)
T 5/2 (The Beat #2, Minimal Compact)
W 6/2 The Men They Couldn't Hang (Blue Orchids)
M 11/2 no show: The British Record Industry Awards live from the Grosvenor House Hotel, London
T 12/2 (City Limits Crew and the Mutant Rockers, The Cure #5)
W 13/2 Jesus and Mary Chain (Lash Lariat and the Long Riders)
M 18/2 (The Fall #5, Persuaders)
T 19/2 (Wailing Souls, Test Department)
W 20/2 Scala Timpani (Dr Calculus)
M 25/2 Big Flame (Altered Images #3)
T 26/2 Skiff Skats (Juggernauts)
W 27/2 Everything But The Girl (The Men They Couldn't Hang)
M 4/3 Dawn Chorus and the Blue Tits (Jesus and Mary Chain)
T 5/3 (Lash Lariat and the Long Riders, The Beloved)
W 6/3 Maxi Priest (Persuaders)
M 11/3 Nightingales (Scala Timpani)
T 12/3 Frank Chickens
W 13/3 (Dead or Alive #1, Big Flame)
M 18/3 (Skiff Skats, Everything But The Girl)
T 19/3 (SPK, Junior Gee and the Capital Boys)
W 20/3 (Dawn Chorus and the Blue Tits, Dr Calculus)
M 25/3 Hula (Maxi Priest)
T 26/3 (The Men They Couldn't Hang)
W 27/3 del Amitri (Frank Chickens)
M 1/4 (UB40 #2, Tears For Fears)
T 2/4 – T 9/4 presented by Muriel Gray (repeats)
W 10/4 Terry and Gerry (Undertones #5)
M 15/4 Strawberry Switchblade (Hula)
T 16/4 Boothill Foot Tappers (Marc Almond)
W 17/4 Workforce (Maxi Priest)

M 22/4 Vibes (Nightingales)
T 23/4 Yeah Yeah Noh (The Men They Couldn't Hang)
W 24/4 Three Mustaphas Three (The Beloved)
M 29/4 The Room (Terry and Gerry)
T 30/4 (Workforce, del Amitri)
W 1/5 Pink Peg Slax (Strawberry Switchblade)
M 6/5 It's Immaterial (Big Flame)
T 7/5 Guana Batz (Vibes)
W 8/5 Cookie Crew (Echo and the Bunnymen #5, Three Mustaphas Three)
M 13/5 Xmal Deutschland (Boothill Foot Tappers)
T 14/5 The Triffids (Workforce)
W 15/5 (Yeah Yeah Noh, The Room)
M 20/5 Misty (Pink Peg Slax)
T 21/5 (It's Immaterial, Frank Chickens)
W 22/5 Fini Tribe (Yazoo)
M 27/5 – W 29/5 presented by Andy Kershaw (repeats)
M 3/6 The Fall (Cookie Crew)
T 4/6 Western Promise (Guana Batz)
W 5/6 Fuzztones (Xmal Deutschland)
M 10/6 Shriekback (Triffids)
T 11/6 Naturalites (Fini Tribe)
W 12/6 The Rose of Avalanche (Misty)
M 17/6 Xymox (It's Immaterial)
T 18/6 (Vibes, The Fall)
W 19/6 Sensible Jerseys (Big Flame)
M 24/6 That Petrol Emotion (Yeah Yeah Noh)
T 25/6 (Fuzztones, The Room)
W 26/6 Inca Babies (Western Promise)
M 1/7 10,000 Maniacs, Red Beards from Texas
T 2/7 (The Rose of Avalanche, Triffids)
W 3/7 (Cookie Crew, Shriekback)
M 8/7 Folk Devils (Sensible Jerseys)
T 9/7 (Xmal Deutschland, Naturalites)
W 10/7 Moodists (Xymox)
M 15/7 Ivor Cutler (The Fall)
T 16/7 (Western Promise, Fini Tribe)
W 17/7 Janitors (Misty)
M 22/7 (That Petrol Emotion, 10,000 Maniacs)
T 23/7 Three Johns (Red Beards from Texas)
W 24/7 The Men They Couldn't Hang (Folk Devils)
M 29/7 Housemartins (Inca Babies)
T 30/7 (Shriekback, Ivor Cutler)
W 31/7 (Fuzztones, Moodists)
M 5/8 Passmore Sisters (Janitors)
T 6/8 Freiwillige Selbstkontrolle aka FSK (10,000 Maniacs)
W 7/8 The Cure (Three Johns)
M 12/8 (Smiths #3, Folk Devils)
T 13/8 (The Fall)
W 14/8 (Housemartins, Test Department #1)
M 19/8 Jeggsy Dodd (Xymox)
T 20/8 (That Petrol Emotion, The Cure)
W 21/8 Pigbros (Passmore Sisters)
M 26/8 (The Special AKA, Echo and the Bunnymen #6)
T 27/8 Mel-o-Tones (Inca Babies)
W 28/8 Prefab Sprout (FSK)
M 2/9 Billy Bragg (Janitors)
T 3/9 (Housemartins, Echo & the Bunnymen #5)
W 4/9 Marc Riley and the Creepers (Jeggsy Dodd)
M 9/9 Woodentops (Pigbros)
T 10/9 (The Cure, Three Johns)
W 11/9 Noseflutes (Mel-o-Tones)
M 16/9 Mekons (Prefab Sprout)
T 17/9 presented by Andy Kershaw: (Passmore Sisters, Billy Bragg)
M 18/9 presented by Andy Kershaw: Primevals (FSK)
M 23/9 Cookie Crew (Marc Riley and the Creepers)
T 24/9 (Moodists, Woodentops)
W 25/9 1,000 Violins (Noseflutes)
M 30/9 Loudon Wainwright III (Mekons)
T 1/10 (Pigbros, The Cure)

W 2/10 Hula (Primevals) & Stone Roses 'So Young'
single played

• **Andy Kershaw starts London-based show
Thurs 3/10, 10pm–12 produced by Walters**

M 7/10 The Fall (Billy Bragg)

T 8/10 (FSK, Cookie Crew)

W 9/10 Terry and Gerry (1000 Violins)

M 14/10 Eton Crop (Noseflutes)

T 15/10 Prefab Sprout, Hula)

W 16/10 Sonic Youth live at Hammersmith Palais rec
28/4/95 (Loudon Wainwright III)

M 21/10 Shop Assistants (The Fall)

T 22/10 (Woodentops, Terry and Gerry)

W 23/10 The Beloved (Marc Riley and the Creepers)

M 28/10 Meat Whiplash (10,000 Maniacs)

T 29/10 Age of Chance (Primevals)

W 30/10 Meteors (Eton Crop)

M 4/11 Bogshed (Terry and Gerry)

T 5/11 June Brides (Shop Assistants)

W 6/11 Ted Chippington live at the Royal Iris ship in
Liverpool (The Fall)

M 11/11 Jesus and Mary Chain (The Beloved)

T 12/11 Prefab Sprout, Meat Whiplash)

W 13/11 Xymox (Age of Chance)

W 13/11 – W 1/1/86, R4 8.15–9pm, You'll Never Be
16 Again, Peel introduces 7-part documentary
compilation show on teenage history, produced by
Peter Everett

M 18/11 That Petrol Emotion (Meteors)

T 19/11 (Passmore Sisters, Bogshed)

W 20/11 Half Man Half Biscuit (June Brides)

M 25/11 Chills (Cocteau Twins #4)

T 26/11 (Jesus and Mary Chain, Xymox)

W 27/11 Big Flame (Age of Chance)

M 2/12 Three Mustaphas Three as 'L'Orchestre Bam!'
(Shop Assistants)

T 3/12 (That Petrol Emotion, Pogues)

W 4/12 The Ex (Bogshed)

M 9/12 The Farm (Half Man Half Biscuit)

T 10/12 Primal Scream (Chills)

W 11/12 Microdisney (Eton Crop)

M 16/12 – W 25/12 (Best sessions of year) Festive 50

T 24/12 no show

M 30/12 Lash Lariat and the Long Riders
(Three Mustaphas Three 'L'Orchestre Bam!')

T 31/12 Janice Long & John Peel's New Year's Eve Party,
7.30pm–1am

1986

W 1/1 Diatribe (Big Flame)

M 6/1 A Witness (The Ex)

T 7/1 (Jesus and Mary Chain, The Farm)

W 8/1 (Half Man Half Biscuit, Primal Scream)

M 13/1 Workforce (Microdisney)

T 14/1 Diatribe

W 15/1 Janitors (Lash Lariat and the Long Riders)

M 20/1 James (Nico, 1st TX 3/12/74)

T 21/1 (A Witness)

W 22/1 The Stars of Heaven (Big Flame)

M 27/1 Yeah Yeah Noh (Microdisney)

T 28/1 (Chills, Workforce)

W 29/1 (Age of Chance, June Brides)

M 3/2 Siouxsie and the Banshees (Janitors)

T 4/2 (Joy Division #2, James)

W 5/2 Stump (Xymox)

Sat 8/2 John Peel featured in R1 DJ profile series Radio
Radio, 2–3pm

M 10/2 MacKenzies, Cramps

T 11/2 (The Stars of Heaven, PiL, 1st TX 17/12/79)

W 12/2 Twang (Yeah Yeah Noh)

Th 13/2 (9–10pm, repeat of Radio Radio profile)

M 17/2 Jasmine Minks (A Witness)

T 18/2 (Big Flame, Siouxsie and the Banshees)

W 19/2 La Muerte (Stump)

M 24/2 Soup Dragons (James)

T 25/2 (MacKenzies, The Janitors)

W 26/2 The Wedding Present (Siouxsie and the
Banshees)

M 3/3 Half Man Half Biscuit (The Stars of Heaven)

T 4/3 (Jasmine Minks, The Fall, 1st TX 24/9/80)

W 5/3 Bogshed (Twang)

M 10/3 We've Got a Fuzzbox and We're Gonna Use It
(Workforce)

T 11/3 (The Wedding Present, La Muerte)

W 12/3 Treebound Story (Yeah Yeah Noh)

M 17/3 Laugh (Stump)

T 18/3 (Soup Dragons, Half Man Half Biscuit)

W 19/3 Champion Doug Veitch (Wah! Heat #1)

M 24/3 Servants (The Birthday Party #4)

T 25/3 (Bogshed, We've Got a Fuzzbox and
We're Gonna Use It)

W 26/3 Nightingales (The Stars of Heaven)

M 31/3 (Champion Doug Veitch, Cocteau Twins #3)

T 1/4 Wolfhounds (Treebound Story)

W 2/4 Mighty Mighty (Laugh)

M 7/4 Woodentops (Servants)

T 8/4 (We've Got a Fuzzbox and We're Gonna Use It,
Half Man Half Biscuit)

W 9/4 Happy Mondays (The Wedding Present)

M 14/4 Housemartins (Nightingales)

T 15/4 Riot of Colour (Mighty Mighty)

W 16/4 (Primal Scream, Wolfhounds)

M 21/4 Red Letter Day (Bogshed)

T 22/4 (Soup Dragons, Happy Mondays)

W 23/4 Relations (Woodentops)

M 28/4 DCL Locomotive (MacKenzies)

T 29/4 (Stump, Housemartins)

W 30/4 Head of David (Riot of Colour)

M 5/5 (Half Man Half Biscuit, Siouxsie and the Banshees)

T 6/5 Pigbros (Red Letter Day)

W 7/5 (Smiths #2, Treebound Story)

M 12/5 Big Flame (Relations)

T 13/5 (DCL Locomotive, Nightingales)

W 14/5 Primal Scream (John Cale, 1st TX 8/6/75)

M 19/5 Sonic Youth (Woodentops)

T 20/5 Misty (Head of David)

W 21/5 Ivor Cutler (Pigbros)

M 26/5 The Stars of Heaven (Big Flame)

T 27/5 Triffids (Twang)

W 28/5 (Mighty Mighty, Primal Scream)

M 2/6 Deltones (Laugh)

T 3/6 (Ivor Cutler, Riot of Colour)

W 4/6 Marc Riley and the Creepers (Misty)

M 9/6 Psylons (Billy Bragg #1)

T 10/6 (Triffids)

W 11/6 (Champion Doug Veitch, Cramps)

M 16/6 Housemartins as 'The Fish City 5'
(Housemartins #2)

T 17/6 (Deltones, The Stars of Heaven)

W 18/6 Miaow (Wolfhounds)

M 23/6 Age of Chance (Marc Riley and the Creepers)

T 24/6 Laibach (MacKenzies)

W 25/6 (Psylons, Misty)

M 30/6 Pop Will Eat Itself (Primal Scream)

T 1/7 (Buzzcocks #2, Ruts #3)

W 2/7 Shrubs (Housemartins as 'The Fish City 5')

M 7/7 Stump (Miaow)

T 8/7 (Undertones #2, Eno & The Winkies, 1st TX
5/3/74)

W 9/7 The Fall (Age of Chance)

M 14/7 Bhundu Boys (Laibach)

T 15/7 (Altered Images #1, Can, 1st TX 12/2/74)

W 16/7 Hula (Pop Will Eat Itself)

M 21/7 Inca Babies (Shrubs)

T 22/7 (Generation X #1, X-Ray Spex #1)

W 23/7 Front 242 (Stump)

M 28/7 Bogshed (Hula)

T 29/7 (Damned #1 & #5)

W 30/7 MacKenzies (Bhundu Boys)

M 4/8 Anhrefn (Inca Babies)

T 5/8 (Slits #1, Prefects #1)

W 6/8 Microdisney (Age of Chance)

M 11/8 We've Got a Fuzzbox and We're Gonna Use It
(Front 242)

T 12/8 (Magazine #1, Specials #2)

W 13/8 FSK (Bogshed)

M 18/8 Frank Chickens (The Fall)

T 19/8 (Stranglers #1, Wire #1)

W 20/8 The Farm (Anhrefn)

M 25/8 Noseflutes (MacKenzies)

T 26/8 (Only Ones #3, Sham 69)

W 27/8 Mighty Lemon Drops
(We've Got a Fuzzbox and We're Gonna Use It)

M 1/9 (Bhundu Boys, FSK)

T 2/9 (Rich Kids #1, Girls at our Best #1)

W 3/9 Mighty Mighty (Frank Chickens)

St 6/9 (Peel's 'Radio Radio' profile repeated, 2–3pm)

M 8/9 Half Man Half Biscuit (Bogshed)

T 9/9 (The Skids #2, Tanz Der Youth)

W 10/9 (Laibach, The Farm)

Th 11/9 (Peel's 'Radio Radio' profile,
repeat of repeat, 9–10pm)

M 15/9 Billy Bragg (The Noseflutes)

T 16/9 (This Heat #1, The Teardrop Explodes #2)

W 17/9 Twang (Microdisney)

M 22/9 Slab! (Mighty Lemon Drops)

T 23/9 (Elvis Costello and the Attractions #2, Crass #1)

W 24/9 Flatmates (Mighty Mighty)

M 29/9 Tender Lugers (Half Man Half Biscuit)

T 30/9 (The Jam #1, Joy Division #1)

W 1/10 Andrew Berry (Billy Bragg)

M 6/10 Head of David (Twang)

T 7/10 (Jimmy Norton's Explosion, Pink Military #1)

W 8/10 D&V (Slab!)

M 13/10 Buy Off the Bar (Flatmates)

T 14/10 (The Fall #1, Frank Chickens #3)

W 15/10 Primitives (FSK)

M 20/10 – W 5/11 presented by Andy Kershaw (repeats)

M 20/10 – Th 23/10 Janice & John In Japan 7.30–10pm
(6.30–9pm Thurs)

Sn 2/11 Peel at the World Popular Song Festival in Japan
documentary, 2.30–3.30pm

St 8/11 – 20/12 (You'll Never Be 16 Again documentary
series rpt on R1 2–3pm, rpt Th 9–10pm)

M 10/11 'Top records' says Walters' wall planner:
no sessions

T 11/11 Passmore Sisters (Tender Lugers)

W 12/11 McCarthy (Andrew Berry)

M 17/11 Foyer des Arts (Head of David)

T 18/11 Toxic Reasons (Buy Off the Bar)

W 19/11 Eton Crop (The Primitives)

Sn 23/11 – Sn 7/12 Peel sits in for Annie Nightingale on
Request Show for 3 weeks, 7–9pm

M 24/11 Railway Children (FSK)

T 25/11 The Wedding Present (Half Man Half Biscuit)

W 26/11 14 Iced Bears (Passmore Sisters)

M1/12 Weather Prophets (Billy Bragg)

T 2/12 1,000 Violins (D&V)

W 3/12 Rote Kappel (McCarthy)

M 8/12 Shop Assistants (Foyer des Arts)

T 9/12 A Witness (Toxic Reasons)

W 10/12 Three Wise Men (Eton Crop)

M 15/12 Brilliant Corners (Railway Children)

T 16/12 The Ex (The Wedding Present)

W 17/12 Smiths (Rote Kappel)

Th 18/12 Peel sits in for Kershaw (Big Flame, Bogshed)

M 22/12 – W 31/12 (Best sessions of year)
    Festive 50

1987

M 5/1 Jesus and Mary Chain (Smiths)

T 6/1 Soup Dragons (Brilliant Corners)

W 7/1 Bhundu Boys (Shop Assistants)

M 12/1 Stupids (A Witness)

T 13/1 The Shamen (The Ex)

W 14/1 That Petrol Emotion (Three Wise Men)

M 19/1 Mighty Mighty (McCarthy)

T 20/1 Janitors (Smiths)

W 21/1 (Jesus and Mary Chain, 14 Iced Bears)

M 26/1 Walking Seeds (Shop Assistants)

T 27/1 (Soup Dragons, Bhundu Boys)

W 28/1 Stump (1000 Violins)

M 2/2 Da Vincis (Stupids)

T 3/2 (Mighty Mighty, Jesus and Mary Chain)

W 4/2 Dub Sex (Janitors)

T 10/2 (That Petrol Emotion, Weather Prophets)

W 11/2 Miaow (Walking Seeds)

M 16/2 Slab! (Stump)

T 17/2 The Stars of Heaven (Smiths)

W 18/2 (Da Vincis, A Witness)

M 23/2 Mekons (Dub Sex)

T 24/2 (A House, Stupids)

W 25/2 Marc Riley and the Creepers (Bhundu Boys)

M 2/3 Three Johns

T 3/3 (Mighty Mighty, Slab!)

W 4/3 Dynamic 3 (Miaow)

St 7/3 – St 28/3 Peel presents Rebel Yell, 2–3pm,
    4-part documentary series on protest songs

M 9/3 Birdhouse (The Stars of Heaven)

T 10/3 Bad Dress Sense (Stump)

W 11/3 Bourbonese Qualk (Mekons)

Th 12/3 – Th 2/4 ('Rebel Yell' repeated, 9–10pm)

M16/3 The Bambi Slam (Three Wise Men)

T 17/3 (Marc Riley and the Creepers, Dub Sex)

W 18/3 The Wedding Present (Three Johns)

M 23/3 Robert Lloyd & the New Four Seasons (Dynamic 3)

T 24/3 Bodines (Birdhouse)

W 25/3 Holger Hiller (Smiths)

M 30/3 Last Party (Foyer des Arts)

T 31/3 (Bad Dress Sense, Bourbonese Qualk)

W 1/4 Mangrove Steel Band (That Petrol Emotion)

M 6/4 Capitols (Bambi Slam)

T 7/4 (The Wedding Present, Robert Lloyd and
    the New Four Seasons)

W 8/4 Darling Buds (Dynamic 3)

M 13/4 Primitives (Holger Hiller)

T 14/4 (Last Party, Slab!)

W 15/4 Chills (Bodines)

M 20/4 Easter Monday, no show: The Andy Peebles
    Compact Disc show, plus Level 42 In Concert

T 21/4 (Billy McKenzie, Soup Dragons #1)

W 22/4 (Stump #2, Jesus and Mary Chain)

M 27/4 Laibach (Mangrove Steel Band)

T 28/4 (Capitols, Darling Buds)

W 29/4 James Taylor Quartet (Primitives)

M 4/5 Bogshed (Robert Lloyd and the New Four
    Seasons)

T 5/5 Frank N Furter (Chills)

W 6/5 Big Black (Bad Dress Sense)

M 11/5 The Fall (Bhundu Boys)

T 12/5 Visions of Change (Laibach)

W 13/5 Datblygu (Three Johns)

M 18/5 Dog Faced Hermans (Capitols)

T 19/5 (Bogshed, Big Black)

W 20/5 Noseflutes (Frank N Furter)

M 25/5 presented by Andy Kershaw

T 26/5 Milk Monitors (Primitives)

W 27/5 Stupids (The Fall)

Sn 31/5 Peel's documentary on Eurovision Song
    Contest, 2–3.30pm

M 1/6 Brilliant Corners (Visions of Change)

T 2/6 (Datblygu, Marc Riley and the Creepers)

W 3/6 Jackdaw With Crowbar (Dog Faced Hermans)

M 8/6 The Great Leap Forward (Big Flame)

T 9/6 (Noseflutes, Frank N Furter)

W 10/6 Wolfhounds (Milk Monitors)

M 15/6 Ivor Cutler (Mekons)

T 16/6 I Ludicrous (The Wedding Present)

W 17/6 (Brilliant Corners, The Stars of Heaven)

M 22/6 Renegade Sound Wave (Stupids)

T 23/6 (Jackdaw With Crowbar, The Fall)

W 24/6 FSK (The Great Leap Forward)

M 29/6 Zinica

T 30/6 Cud (Wolfhounds)

W 1/7 Tractors (I Ludicrous)

M 6/7 Pop Will Eat Itself (Bogshed)

T 7/7 (Renegade Sound Wave, Ivor Cutler)

W 8/7 Abs (Datblygu)

M 13/7 Buy Off the Bar (The Fall)

T 14/7 (FSK, Milk Monitors)

W 15/7 Head of David (Laibach)

M 20/7 Electro Hippies (Cud)

T 21/7 (Tractors, Pop Will Eat Itself)

W 22/7 Claire (Zinica)

M 27/7 14 Iced Bears (Abs)

T 28/7 (Buy Off the Bar, Stupids)

W 29/7 AC Temple (The Great Leap Forward)

M 3/8 Heresy (The Fall)

T 4/8 (Head of David)

W 5/8 Paul Johnson (Electro Hippies)

M 10/8 Terence Trent D'Arby (Claire)

T 11/8 Premi (14 Iced Bears)

W 12/8 Butthole Surfers (FSK)

M 17/8 Death By Milkfloat (Cud)

T 18/8 (AC Temple, Heresy)

W 19/8 Loop (Tractors)

M 24/8 Dub Sex (Paul Johnson)

T 25/8 (Terence Trent D'Arby, Renegade Sound Wave)

W 26/8 Shrubs (Jackdaw With Crowbar)

M 31/8 no show

T 1/9 (Premi, Death By Milkfloat)

W 2/9 Darling Buds (Visions of Change)

M 7/9 Laugh (Loop)

T 8/9 (Butthole Surfers)

W 9/9 James (Electro Hippies)

M 14/9 Motorcycle Boy (Shrubs)

T 15/9 (Dub Sex, Terence Trent D'Arby)

W 16/9 Flatmates (Death by Milkfloat)

M 21/9 Three Mustaphas Three (Darling Buds)

T 22/9 Napalm Death (Laugh)

W 23/9 Holle Holle

St 26/9 – St 30/10 Peeling Back The Years, 6-part
    retrospective, 2–3pm, presented by Walters

M 28/9 M C Duke (James)

T 29/9 (Motorcycle Boy, Heresy)

W 30/9 Walking Seeds

Th 31/9 – Th 5/11 (Peeling Back The Years
    repeats, 9–10pm)

M 5/10 Catapult (Flatmates)

T 6/10 (Premi)

W 7/10 Milk Monitors (Three Mustaphas Three)

F 9/10 – F 13/11 (You'll Never Be 16 Again, edited
    second rpt on R1, 9–10pm)

M 12/10 Jackdaw With Crowbar (Napalm Death)

T 13/10 (MC Duke, Walking Seeds)

W 14/10 The Wedding Present Ukrainian Session

M 19/10 Robert Lloyd (Holle Holle)

T 20/10 (Catapult, Paul Johnson)

W 21/10 Stupids

M 26/10 Bogshed

T 27/10 (Milk Monitors, Jackdaw With Crowbar)

W 28/10 McCarthy (Napalm Death)

M 2/11 MDC (The Wedding Present Ukrainian Session)

T 3/11 (Robert Lloyd, MC Duke)

W 4/11 Gore

M 9/11 Rhythm Pigs (Head of David)

T 10/11 (Stupids, Bogshed)

W 11/11 Housemartins

M 16/11 Les Thugs (McCarthy)

T 17/11 Extreme Noise Terror

W 18/11 (MDC, Robert Lloyd)

M 23/11 Go Hole (Gore)

T 24/11 (Rhythm Pigs, Flatmates)

W 25/11 (Big Black, James)

M 30/11 This Poison (Housemartins)

T 1/12 Overlord X (Les Thugs)

W 2/12 (Extreme Noise Terror)

M 7/12 Tot (Bogshed)

T 8/12 The Very Things (Go Hole)

W 9/12 Sugar Cubes

M 14/12 Sink (Darling Buds)

T 15/12 (Gore)

W 16/12 Midnight Choir (This Poison)

M 21/12 (Premi, Rhythm Pigs)

T 22/12 – W 30/12 (Best sessions of year) Festive 50

1988

M 4/1 Close Lobsters (Sugar Cubes)

T 5/1 Llwybr Llaethog (Tot)

W 6/1 Ut (Sink)

M 11/1 Talullah Gosh! (The Very Things)

T 12/1 (Overlord X, Midnight Choir)

W 13/1 Bolt Thrower (McCarthy)

M 18/1 Bob (Wedding Present Ukrainian Session)

T 19/1 A Witness (Close Lobsters)

W 20/1 The Bandung File (Llwybr Llaethog)

M 25/1 TV Smith's Cheap

T 26/1 (Ut, Talullah Gosh!)

W 27/1 The Stars of Heaven

Sn 31/1 Down Your Way: Peel guides listeners round
    Combs, Suffolk, including the pub where the
    strongest man in East Anglia, the lady who taught
    Margaret Thatcher chemistry and Peel himself all
    drink, R4 LW 5–5.50pm

M 1/2 (Down Your Way rpt R4 FM 11–11.50am)

M 1/2 Wolfhounds (Bolt Thrower)

T 2/2 (Cookie Crew #1 & #2)

W 3/2 Twang (Bob)

Sn 7/2 Down Your Way: John Peel visits the Wirral
    Peninsula and talks to local people & visits Liverpool
    Botanic Gardens, an RSPB bird reserve & a shrimp
    shop, R4 LW 5–5.50pm

M 8/2 (Down Your Way rpt R4 FM 11–11.50am)

M 8/2 The Great Leap Forward (A Witness)

T 9/2 Abs (The Bandung File)

W 10/2 Asher D and Daddy Freddy

M 15/2 Bastard Kestrel

T 16/2 (The Stars of Heaven, TV Smith's Cheap)

W 17/2 Datblygu (Wolfhounds)

M 22/2 (Bhundu Boys, Triffids #3)

T 23/2 (FSK #2, Eton Crop #4)

W 24/2 (Laibach, Les Thugs)

M 29/2 records only

T 1/3 Poppi UK (The Great Leap Forward)

W 2/3 Plant Bach Ofnus
M 7/3 Slab! (Bolt Thrower)
T 8/3 (Asher Dee and Daddy Freddy, Bob)
W 9/3 Heresy
St 12/3 John Peel In Russia documentary, 2–3pm
M 14/3 Stella Chiweshe
T 15/3 Intense Degree (Datblygu)
W 16/3 (Bastard Kestrel, The Stars of Heaven)
Th 17/3 (rpt of John Peel In Russia, 9–10pm)
M 21/3 – W 30/3 records only
M 4/4 Fflaps (Poppi UK)
T 5/4 The Wedding Present Ukrainian Session #2
   (Wolfhounds)
W 6/4 (Stella Chiweshe, A Witness)
M 11/4 Unseen Terror (Plant Bach Ofnus)
T 12/4 The Shamen (Slab!)
W 13/4 Marta Sebestyen & Muzsikas (Intense Degree)
M 18/4 Viv Stanshall
T 19/4 FSK (Heresy)
W 20/4 Napalm Death (Fflaps)
M 25/4 Primitives
T 26/4 King of the Slums
   (The Wedding Present Ukrainian Session #2)
W 27/4 Senseless Things (Asher D & Daddy Freddy)
M 2/5 'Me' it says on Walters' wallplanner: presented by
   John Walters, records only
T 3/5 Pooh Sticks (Unseen Terror)
W 4/5 (Viv Stanshall, Marta Sebestyen & Muzsikas,
   Bastard Kestrel)
M 9/5 Dynamic 3
T 10/5 Wire (The Shamen)
W 11/5 Extreme Noise Terror (Viv Stanshall)
M 16/5 Pixies (FSK)
T 17/5 Dr & The Crippens, Napalm Death
W 18/5 (Senseless Things)
M 23/5 'Me' it says again: presented by Walters,
   records only
T 24/5 Cud (Pooh Sticks)
W 25/5 No Means No (King of the Slums)
M 30/5 The Wedding Present (Primitives)
T 31/5 (Dynamic 3, Heresy)
W 1/6 (Wire)
M 6/6 Benny Profane (Extreme Noise Terror)
T 7/6 (Pixies)
W 8/6 Eton Crop (Cud)
M 13/6 Jesus and Mary Chain
T 14/6 (Marta Sebastyen, Unseen Terror)
W 15/6 HDQ (The Wedding Present Ukrainian Session
   #2)
M 20/6 The House of Love (Dr & The Crippens)
T 21/6 (No Means No)
W 22/6 Firehose
M 27/6 Loop (Intense Degree)
T 28/6 Doom
W 29/6 (Napalm Death, Benny Profane)
M 4/7 Death By Milkfloat (Eton Crop)
T 5/7 Dub Sex
W 6/7 (Jesus and Mary Chain, Pooh Sticks)
M 11/7 Dan (The House of Love)
T 12/7 Amayenge
W 13/7 (The Wedding Present)
M 18/7 Buy Off The Bar (Firehose)
T 19/7 (HDQ, Loop)
W 20/7 (Doom)
M 25/7 Perfect Daze
T 26/7 (Death By Milkfloat, Pixies)
W 27/7 Ripcord (Amayenge)
M 1/8 Inspiral Carpets (Dub Sex)
T 2/8 Mega City 4
W 3/8 (Dan, The House of Love)
M 8/8 Too Much Texas (Jesus and Mary Chain)
T 9/8 (Buy Off The Bar, Dub Sex)

W 10/8 The Funky Ginger
M 15/8 Overlord X (Extreme Noise Terror)
T 16/8 (Perfect Daze)
W 17/8 The Joyce McKinney Experience
M 22/8 (Loop, Ripcord)
T 23/8 (The Wedding Present, King of the Slums)
W 24/8 Waltones
M29/8 no show
T 30/8 (The Funky Ginger)
W 31/8 (Overlord X)
M 5/9 – M 26/9 What's Love Got Do With It? Peel
   presents 4-part advice and documentary series on
   sex, in which R1 listeners talk openly about romance,
   sex and love, 9.15–10pm
M 5/9 (Mega City 4, Inspiral Carpets)
T 6/9 Amayenge
W 7/9 (Too Much Texas, Doom)
M 12/9 Shalawambe (The Joyce McKinney Experience)
T 13/9 Stump
W 14/9 The House of Love
M 19/9 Billy Bragg (Waltones)
T 20/9 Sink
W 21/9 Popinjays
M 26/9 Four Brothers
T 27/9 Butthole Surfers
W 28/9 Siddeleys (Amayenge)
F 30/9 John Peel remembers 1967 for R1's 21st
   anniversary, reviewing the hit records of the time &
   recalls the start of the station in 1967, 6.45–7pm

• **Show moves to 8.30–10.30pm Mon–Wed with
  launch of Radio 1 FM**

M 3/10 Thrilled Skinny (Stump)
T 4/10 (Shalawambe)
W 5/10 My Bloody Valentine (The Funky Ginger)
M 10/10 Da Vincis (The House of Love)
T 11/10 Band of Susans (Popinjays)
W 12/10 Young Gods
M 17/10 no show: Amnesty International Concert from
   Buenos Aires
T 18/10 Pixies
W 19/10 Sonic Youth's The Fall cover-versions session
M 24/10 The Colorblind James Experience
T 25/10 (Billy Bragg, Siddeleys)
W 26/10 (Sink, Four Brothers)
M 31/10 The Fall
T 1/11 McCarthy (Thrilled Skinny)
W 2/11 (Butthole Surfers)
M 7/11 A Guy Called Gerald
T 8/11 (My Bloody Valentine, Da Vincis)
W 9/11 Bastard Kestrel
M 14/11 Dinosaur Jr
T 15/11 (Band of Susans)
W 16/11 Bolt Thrower
M 21/11 Phil Hartley
T 22/11 (Young Gods, Shalawambe)
W 23/11 Viv Stanshall
M 28/11 Humanoid
T 29/11 (Pixies, The Colorblind James Experience)
W 30/11 A Witness
M 5/12 Sandie Shaw (Sonic Youth's Fall
   covers session)
T 6/12 Gore
W 7/12 Beatnigs (The Fall)
Th 8/12 Peel presents tribute to Roy Orbison (died 7/12),
   6–7pm, Radio 1
M12/12 George & Martha
T 13/12 Fugazi (McCarthy)
W 14/12 (A Guy Called Gerald)
St 17/12 Promised Land, R1 2–3pm, Peel presents
   a journey following the route from Norfolk, Virginia
   to Los Angeles depicted in Chuck Berry's song
   'Promised Land', with clips of American radio
   stations, produced by Kevin Howlett, researched by
   Pete Frame

M 19/12 (Viv Stanshall)
T 20/12 (Promised Land feature rpt 7.30–8.30pm)
T 20/12–W 28/12 (Best sessions of year) Festive 50

1989

M 2/1 Carcass, Culture
T 3/1 (Beatnigs)
W 4/1 Chills (Sandie Shaw)
M 9/1 Last Party
T 10/1 (Gore)
W 11/1 (Fugazi, Bastard Kestrel)
M 16/1 Nose Flutes
T 17/1 (Bolt Thrower, Phil Hartley)
W 18/1 Heresy
M 23/1–W 25/1 records only
M 30/1 Snuff
T 31/1 (A Witness, Carcass)
W 1/2 Prong
M 6/2 HDQ
T 7/2 (Culture, Chills)
W 8/2 Edsel Auctioneer
M 13/2 Robert Lloyd
T 14/2 Benny Profane (Last Party)
W 15/2 Bob
M 20/2 Darling Buds
T 21/2 (Heresy)
W 22/2 Fini Tribe
M 27/2 Happy Mondays
T 28/2 (Snuff)
W 1/3 (Prong)
M 6/3 Sundays
T 7/3 records only
W 8/3 Dub Sex
M 13/3 Cud
T 14/3 Doom
W 15/3 (Darling Buds)
M 20/3 Sonic Youth
T 21/3 (Sundays)
W 22/3 Live Skull
M 27/3 (Happy Mondays)
T 28/3 Cathal Coughlan & the Fatima Mansions
W 29/3 (Robert Lloyd)

• **Show moved to 8.30–10pm Mon–Thurs**
• **Kershaw moves to Sun 9–11pm**

M 3/4 (HDQ)
T 4/4 (Bob)
W 5/4 Inspiral Carpets
Th 6/4 (Edsel Auctioneer)
M 10/4 Thee Hypnotics
T 11/4 Benny Profane
W 12/4 The House of Love
Th 13/4 (Fini Tribe)
M 17/4 Hepburns
T 18/4 (Dub Sex)
W 19/4 Walking Seeds
Th 20/4 (Cud)
M 24/4 no show
T 25/4 (Doom)
W 26/4 (Live Skull)
Th 27/4 Heart Throbs
M 1/5 no show
T 2/5 Pixies
W 3/5 (Sonic Youth)
Th 4/5 (Four Brothers, 1st TX Kershaw 25/8/88)
M 8/5 Zvuki Mu
T 9/5 no show
W 10/5 Douze Points – John Peel at the Eurovision Song
   Contest 1989, 7.30–8.30pm, no show later

Th 11/5 (Inspiral Carpets)
M 15/5 The Wedding Present Ukrainian Session #3
T 16/5 (Hepburns)
W 17/5 (Cathal Coughlan & the Fatima Mansions)
Th 18/5 Pooh Sticks
M 22/5 Dinosaur Jr
T 23/5 Siddeleys
W 24/5 Mudhoney
Th 25/5 Pleasureheads
M 29/5 no show
T 30/5 Luna Chicks
W 31/5 (Thee Hypnotics)
Th 1/6 (The House of Love)
M 5/6 Four Brothers
T 6/6 (Heart Throbs)
W 7/6 Soundgarden
Th 8/6 no show
M 12/6 (Walking Seeds)
T 13/6 Telescopes
W 14/6 (Zvuki Mu)
Th 15/6 Head of David
M 19/6 No Means No
T 20/6 (Dinosaur Jr)
W 21/6 (Siddeleys)
Th 22/6 (Pixies)
M 26/6 Ruthless Rap Assassins
T 27/6 (The Wedding Present Ukrainian Session #3)
W 28/6 Birdland
Th 29/6 Mud Honey
M 3/7 Kiss AMC
T 4/7 (Pleasure Heads)
W 5/7 Dead Famous People
Th 6/7 (Lunachicks)
M 10/7 Frank Chickens
T 11/7 (Four Brothers)
W 12/7 (Soundgarden)
Th 13/7 Band of Susans
M 17/7 Lemonheads
T 18/7 (Cud)
W 19/7 Cranes
Th 20/7 (Head of David)
M 24/7 (Happy Mondays) next 2 weeks'
   shows 'pre-recorded' says Walters' wall log
T 25/7 (Ruthless Rap Assassins)
W 26/7 (Cathal Coughlan & the Fatima Mansions)
Th 27/7 (No Means No)
M 31/7 (Pixies)
T 1/8 Hey Paulette
W 2/8 The Shamen
Th 3/8 (Birdland)
M 7/8 Pere Ubu
T 8/8 Victim's Family
W 9/8 (Kiss AMC)
Th 10/8 (Dead Famous People)
M 14/8 Dr & the Crippens
T 15/8 Frank Chickens
W 16/8 (Band of Susans)
Th 17/8 Pale Saints
M 21/8 Mute Drivers
T 22/8 no show: The Spirits of Woodstock 1969–89
   documentary
W 23/8 (Lemonheads)
Th 24/8 (Cranes)
M 28/8 no show
T 29/8 (Telescopes)
W 30/8 Peel's 50th Birthday:
   Subterranea gig recorded previous night:
   The House of Love, The Wedding Present, The Fall
Th 31/8 Where's the Beach?
M 4/9 Buy Off The Bar
T 5/9 (Pere Ubu)
W 6/9 A Guy Called Gerald

Th 7/9 (The Shamen)
M 11/9 Anhrefn
T 12/9 (Victim's Family)
W 13/9 Bomb Disneyland
Th 14/9 (Hey Paulette)
M 18/9 Filthkick
T 19/9 (Mud Honey)
W 20/9 Company 2
Th 21/9 (Dr & The Crippens)
M 25/9 Bob
T 26/9 (Pale Saints)
W 27/9 Godflesh
Th 28/9 (Mute Drivers)
M 2/10 Dembo Konte & Kausu Kouyate
T 3/10 (Where's the Beach)
W 4/10 The Family Cat
Th 5/10 (Buy Off The Bar)
M 9/10 Inspiral Carpets
T 10/10 (A Guy Called Gerald)
W 11/10 Llwybr Llaethog
Th 12/10 (Anhrefn)
M 16/10 (Bomb Disneyland)
T 17/10 Galaxie 500
W 18/10 Charlottes
Th 19/10 Loudon Wainwright III
M 23/10 (Filthkick)
T 24/10 (Company 2)
W 25/10 Snapdragons
Th 26/10 (No Means No)
M 30/10 (Birdland)
T 31/10 Fireparty
W 1/11 (Godflesh)
Th 2/11 Silverfish
M 6/11 (Inspiral Carpets)
T 7/11 (Dinosaur Jr)
W 8/11 More Fiends
Th 9/11 (Dembo Konte & Kausu Kouyate)
M 13/11 Electribe 101
T 14/11 Tunnel Frenzies
W 15/11 (Band of Susans)
Th 16/11 (Bob)
M 20/11 Jack Tars
T 21/11 (Llwybr Llaethog)
W 22/11 Nirvana
Th 23/11 (Galaxie 500)
M 27/11 The Colorblind James Experience
T 28/11 (Loudon Wainwright III)
W 29/11 Straitjacket Fits
Th 30/11 (Fireparty)
M 4/12 Ian McCulloch
T 5/12 (Silverfish)
W 6/12 John Chibadura & the Tembo Brothers
Th 7/12 Big Fayia
M 11/12 (Electribe 101)
T 12/12 Jesus & Mary Chain
W 13/12 (More Fiends)
Th 14/12 (Snapdragons)
M 18/12 (The Family Cat)
T 19/12 The Orb
W 20/12–Th 28/12 (Best sessions of year) Festive 50

1990

M 1/1 The House of Love, The Fall
T 2/1 Tad
W 3/1 Kit
Th 4/1 (Tunnel Frenzies)
M 8/1 (John Chibadurah & the Tembo Brothers)
T 9/1 New Fast Automatic Daffodils

W 10/1 (Ian McCulloch)
Th 11/1 Sofa Head
Sn 14/1 Peel on Desert Island Discs, R4, 12.15–
   12.55pm, his 8 discs being: 'Zadok the Priest',
   Roy Orbison's 'It's Over', 'Too Much' by Jimmy
   Reed, 'Mankind' by Misty in Roots, 'Teenage Kicks',
   Rachmaninov's 2nd Piano Concerto, The Fall's 'Eat
   y'self Fitter', 'Pasi Pano Pane Zviedzo' by The Four
   Brothers
M 15/1 Benny Profane
T 16/1 (The Straitjacket Fits)
W 17/1 (Jesus & Mary Chain)
Th 18/1 (The Orb)
Fri 19/1 (Desert Island Discs rpt, R4, 9.05–9.45am)
M 22/1 (Nirvana)
T 23/1 Pop Guns
W 24/1 (Jack Tars)
Th 25/1 (Tad)
M 29/1 Bastro
T 30/1 (Kit)
W 31/1 Loop
Th 1/2 (The Fall)
M 5/2 (Birdland)
T 6/2 (Sofa Head)
W 7/2 Breeders
Th 8/2 (New Fast Automatic Daffodils)
M 12/2 Barbel
T 13/2 (Benny Profane)
W 14/2 Prophecy of Doom
Th 15/2 (The House of Love)
M 19/2 Lush
T 20/2 Adamski
W 21/2 Peel At The Brits, R1 7.30–8.30pm, John Peel
   reports from behind the scenes at the 1990 Brit
   Awards, produed by Mike Hawkes
W 21/2 (Pop Guns)
Th 22/2 Walking Seeds
M 26/2 Ride
T 27/2 (Birdland)
W 28/2 (Tunnel Frenzies)
Th 1/3 MC 900 Foot Jesus & DJ Zero
M 5/3 Kevin Coyne
T 6/3 (Bastro)
W 7/3 (Llwybr Llaethog)
Th 8/3 Extreme Noise Terror
M 12/3 Jellyfish Kiss
T 13/3 (Loop)
W 14/3 MC Buzz B
Th 15/3 (Barbel)
M 19/3 Would Be's
T 20/3 (The Fall)
W 21/3 Senseless Things
Th 22/3 (Lush)
M 26/3 Robert Lloyd
T 27/3 (Prophecy of Doom)
W 28/3 (Adamski)
Th 29/3 (Walking Seeds)
M 2/4 (Breeders)
T 3/4 STP 23
W 4/4 Half Man Half Biscuit
Th 5/4 (The Orb)
M 9/4 Charlatans
T 10/4 (Ride)
W 11/4 Cranes
Th 12/4 (MC 900 Foot Jesus & DJ Zero)
M 16/4 no show: Mandela concert
T 17/4 (Inspiral Carpets)
W 18/4 Force Fed
Th 19/4 The Fatima Mansions
M 23/4 Fieldmice
T 24/4 (Would Be's)
W 25/4 Kings of Oblivion

Th 26/4 (Birdland)
M 30/4 James
T 1/5 (Robert Lloyd)
W 2/5 Bone
Th 3/5 (Extreme Noise Terror)
M 7/5 no show
T 8/5 Orchids
W 9/5 What? Noise
Th 10/5 (Kevin Coyne)
M 14/5 (Senseless Things)
T 15/5 Deviated Instinct
W 16/5 Levellers 5
Th 17/5 (STP 23)
M 21/5 Fudge Tunnel
T 22/5 (Half Man Half Biscuit)
W 23/5 (MC Buzz B)
Th 24/5 The Farm
M 28/5 no show
T 29/5 Dawson
W 30/5 (Jellyfish Kiss)
Th 31/5 (Charlatans)
M 4/6 Terminal Cheesecake
T 5/6 Inspiral Carpets
W 6/6 (Cranes)
Th 7/6 (Force Fed)
M 11/6 Masasu
T 12/6 Nightblooms
W 13/6 (The Fatima Mansions)
Th 14/6 (Fieldmice)
M 18/6 Dandelion Adventure
T 19/6 (James)
W 20/6 Sink
Th 21/6 (Kings of Oblivion)
M 25/6 (Levellers 5)
T 26/6 My Dad Is Dead
W 27/6 Cows
Th 28/6 (Orchids)
M 2/7 (What? Noise)
T 3/7 Krispy 3
W 4/7 (Deviated Instinct)
Th 5/7 Tad
M 9/7 The Family Cat
T 10/7 (Fudge Tunnel)
W 11/7 Happy Flowers
Th 12/7 (Dawson)
M 16/7 Buffalo Tom
T 17/7 (The Farm)
W 18/7 Sex Clark 5
Th 19/7 (Sink)
M 23/7 Bastro
T 24/7 (Dandelion Adventure)
W 25/7 Pussy Galore
Th 26/7 (Nightblooms)
M 30/7 Boo Radleys
T 31/7 Colon
W 1/8 Fflaps
Th 2/8 (Inspiral Carpets)
M 6/8–Th 16/8 (The Fall, 8 session repeats)
M 20/8 Heart Throbs
T 21/8 Crane
W 22/8 (Masasu)
Th 23/8 (My Dad Is Dead)
M 27/8 no show
T 28/8 Three Mustaphas Three
W 29/8 Shut Up and Dance
Th 30/8 (Cows)
M 3/9 Swervedriver
T 4/9 Bolt Thrower
W 5/9 (Krispy 3)
Th 6/9 (Sex Clark 5)
M 10/9 Napalm Death

T 11/9 (Happy Flowers)
W 12/9 (Buffalo Tom)
Th 13/9 Simba Wanyika
M 17/9 Filthkick
T 18/9–Th 20/9 no shows – Band Explosion 90 live
M 24/9 Ifangi Bondi
T 25/9 Drive
W 26/9 Where's the Beach?
Th 27/9 Paris Angels

• Show moves to Sat & Sun 11pm–2am

St 29/9 Babes in Toyland, Ride
Sn 30/9 Teenage Fanclub, Pop Guns
St 6/10 Levellers 5 (The Farm)
Sn 7/10 Chapterhouse (Inspiral Carpets)
St 13/10 The Orb (Boo Radleys)
Sn 14/10 Bark Market (Family Cat)
St 20/10 LFO (Bastro)
Sn 21/10 Stereo MCs (Colon)
St 27/10 Les Tetes Brulés, SOB
Sn 28/10 Bridewell Taxis, The Wedding Present
St 3/11 Nirvana (3 Mustaphas 3)
Sn 4/11 Galaxie 500 (Crane)
St 10/11 Filler (Heart Throbs)
Sn 11/11 (Bolt Thrower, Simba Wanyika)
St 17/11 Mighty Force (Swervedriver)
Sn 18/11 L7 (Filthkick)
St 24/11 New Fast Automatic Daffodils
        (Where's the Beach?)
Sn 25/11 Fluke (Napalm Death)
St 1/12 Blade (Paris Angels)
Sn 2/12 Bleach (Teenage Fanclub)
St 8/12 Ned's Atomic Dustbin (Pop Guns)
Sn 9/12 (Drive, Babes in Toyland)
St 15/12 Gumball (Levellers 5)
Sn 16/12 Carcass (Ride)
St 22/12–Sn 30/12 (Best sessions of year) Festive 50

1991

St 5/1 June Tabor & The Oyster Band (Bridewell Taxis)
Sn 6/1 Scientist (Chapterhouse)
St 12/1 Robert Lloyd and the New Four Seasons (LFO)
Sn 13/1 MASS (Stereo MCs)
St 19/1 35 Summers (Nirvana)
Sn 20/1 The Ugly Music Show (The Orb)
St 26/1 Definition of Sound (Galaxie 500)
Sn 27/1 Plant Bach Ofnus (Filler)
St 2/2 Force Fed (Mighty Force)
Sn 3/2 A Homeboy a Hippie and a Funky Dredd
        (New Fast Automatic Daffodils)
St 9/2 Datblygu (The Wedding Present)
Sn 10/2 Charlatans (Bark Market)
St 16/2 Moonflowers (Ned's Atomic Dustbin)
Sn 17/2 Top (Fluke)
St 23/2 Depth Charge (Tad)
Sn 24/2 Arson Garden (Gumball)
St 2/3 Hoovers (Bleach)
Sn 3/3 Greenhouse (June Tabor and the Oyster Band)
St 9/3 The Thing (Robert Lloyd & The New Four
        Seasons)
Sn 10/3 Melvins (Carcass)
St 16/3 First Offence (MASS)
Sn 17/3 Jesus Lizard (Ugly Music Show)
St 23/3 The Shamen, The Fall
Sn 24/3 Cop Shoot Cop (Definition of Sound)
St 30/3 Boss Hog (Plant Bach Ofnus)
Sn 31/3 Curve (Force Fed)
St 6/4 Viv Stanshall (Datblygu)
Sn 7/4 Boo Radleys (A Homeboy a Hippie and
        a Funky Dredd)

St 13/4 Bongwater (Top)
Sn 14/4 Heavenly (Moonflowers)
St 20/4 Hypnotone (Charlatans)
Sn 21/4 Slowdive (Hoovers)
St 27/4 Th'Faith Healers (Depth Charge)
Sn 28/4 Silverfish (The Thing)
St 4/5 Julian Cope (Greenhouse)
Sn 5/5 The Catherine Wheel (The Shamen)
St 11/5 Dr Phibes & The House of Wax Equations
        (Melvins)
Sn 12/5 no show: Concert for Kurds
St 18/5 Gunshot (Jesus Lizard)
Sn 19/5 Inside Out (Cop Shoot Cop)
St 25/5 Pitch Shifter (Boss Hog)
Sn 26/5 70 Gwen Party (The Fall)
St 1/6 Prophecy of Doom (Shamen)
Sn 2/6 Exit Condition (Curve)
St 8/6 Cherry Blades (Heavenly)
Sn 9/6 Moose (Boo Radleys)
St 15/6 Billy Bragg (First Offence)
Sn 16/6 Ragga Twins (Bongwater)
St 22/6 Helmet (Th'Faith Healers)
Sn 23/6 Surgery (Slowdive)
St 29/6 Eon (Silverfish)
Sn 30/6 Babes in Toyland (The Catherine Wheel)

• Walters retires. Mike Hawkes takes over show
  production

St 6/7 Ivor Cutler (SOB)
Sn 7/7 Tar (L7)
St 13/7 Party Dictator (Scientist)
Sn 14/7 Unsane (Blade)
St 20/7 Stella Chiweshe (Prophecy of Doom)
Sn 21/7 Bleach (Moose)
St 27/7 Stretchheads (Gunshot)
Sn 28/7 Sun Carriage (Inside Out)
St 3/8 One By One (Pitch Shifter)
Sn 4/8 Pixies (70 Gwen Party)
St 10/8 25th of May (Exit Condition)
Sn 11/8 World of Twist (Cherry Blades)
St 17/8 Cherry Forever (Ram Shavi,
        Dr Phibes & The House of Wax Equations)
Sn 18/8 Moody Boys & Screamer (Billy Bragg)
St 24/8 Foreheads in a Fishtank (Hypnotone)
Sn 25/8 live from the Reading Festival, interviews only,
        with Peel and Mark Radcliffe
St 31/8 The Farm (Ragga Twins)
Sn 1/9 Gallon Drunk (Julian Cope)
St 7/9 Breed (Tar)
Sn 8/9 Stereolab (Ivor Cutler)
St 14/9 Raw Noise (Unsane)
Sn 15/9 Telescopes (Party Dictator)
St 21/9 Gore (Viv Stanshall)
Sn 22/9 Slowjam (Helmet)
St 28/9 Therapy? (Surgery)
Sn 29/9 Gumball (Bleach)
St 5/10 Mercury Rev (Sun Carriage)
Sn 6/10 Midway Still (Babes in Toyland)
St 12/10 (Stretchheads)
Sn 13/10 Smashing Pumpkins (One By One)
St 19/10 Zero Zero (Pixies)
Sn 20/10 35 Summers (Stella Chiweshe)
St 26/10 Boo Radleys (Cherry Forever)
Sn 27/10 Paris Angels (Moody Boys & Screamer)
St 2/11 Katch 22 (Foreheads in a Fishtank)
Sn 3/11 PJ Harvey, Nirvana
St 9/11 Subsonic 2, Dr Oloh and his Mylo Jazz Band
Sn 10/11 Bizarre Inc (The Farm)
St 16/11 Ukrainians, Spitfire
Sn 17/11 Whipped Cream (Gallon Drunk)
St 23/11 Revolver, Clouds
Sn 24/11 Altern 8, Consolidated

St 30/11 Barbel (Stereolab)

Sn 1/12 Red Ninja (Gumball)

St 7/12 Krispy 3 (Raw Noise)

Sn 8/12 The Frank & Walters (Telescopes)

St 14/12 Big Chief, Sam Dees

Sn 15/12 The House of Love, Ivor Cutler

St 21/12 – Sn 29/12 (Best sessions of year) Festive 50 abandoned, became Phantom 50 TX 1993

Sn 22/12 Babes in Toyland (Best sessions of year)

M 23/12 R4 7.05–7.15pm 'The Archers: Eddie Grundy impresses a surprise guest'. The cast list for this week's episodes of the world's longest-running radio soap opera, an everyday story of country folk, printed on F 27/12, ends with 'John Peel... himself'

Sn 29/12 (R4 10.15–11.15am The Archers Omnibus edition with Peel as himself)

1992

St 4/1 Red Hour, Leatherface

Sn 5/1 Hole, Milk

St 11/1 Th'Faith Healers (Whipped Cream)

Sn 12/1 Silverfish (Mercury Rev)

St 18/1 Dawson (Smashing Pumpkins)

Sn 19/1 Cobra, FSK

St 25/1 Shonen Knife (Clouds)

Sn 26/1 Fluke (Barbel)

St 1/2 Moose (Consolidated)

Sn 2/2 Terry Edwards (Subsonic 2)

St 8/2 Smashing Orange (Krispy 3)

Sn 9/2 Terminal Hoedown (Altern 8)

St 15/2 Bang Bang Machine, The Fall

Sn 16/2 Even As We Speak, Cranberries

St 22/2 Loudspeaker (Revolver)

Sn 23/2 Ragga Twins (Big Chief)

St 29/2 Curve (Red Ninja)

Sn 1/3 Butterfly Child (The Frank and Walters)

St 7/3 Verve (The House of Love)

Sn 8/3 Sultans of Ping FC (Red Hour)

- **Shows move forward one day to Fri & Sat 11pm–2am**

Fri 13/3 A House (Hole)

St 14/3 Spiritualized (Leatherface)

F 20/3 The Family Cat (Th'Faith Healers)

St 21/3 Papa Sprain (Silverfish)

F 27/3 Splintered (Dawson)

St 28/3 Shut Up and Dance

F 3/4 Moe Tucker (Shonen Knife)

St 4/4 Freefall (Fluke)

F 10/4 Marina Van-Rooy (Terry Edwards)

St 11/4 Jacob's Mouse (Terminal Hoedown)

F 17/4 Ween (Moose)

St 18/4 Come (Cobra)

F 24/4 Luna (Cranberries)

St 25/4 Bivouac (Ragga Twins)

F 1/5 Werefrogs (The Fall)

St 2/5 The Wedding Present (Bang Bang Machine)

F 8/5 Action Swingers (Loudspeaker)

St 9/5 Disposable Heroes of Hiphoprisy, Abana Ba Nasary live in studio

F 15/5 Buttsteak (FSK)

St 16/5 Cop Shoot Cop (Freefall)

F 22/5 Ultramarine (The Family Cat)

St 23/5 Levellers 5 (Ween)

F 29/5 God Machine (Splintered)

St 30/5 Superchunk (A House)

F 5/6 Sunchalms, The Orb

St 6/6 Bardots, Swell

F 12/6 Datblygu (Jacob's Mouse)

St 13/6 Jules Verne (Luna)

F 19/6 Fudge Tunnel (Come)

St 20/6 70 Gwen Party (Bivouac)

F 26/6 Rhythm Eternity (Curve)

St 27/6 Half Man Half Biscuit (The Wedding Present)

F 3/7 Yardstick (Disposable Heroes of Hiphoprisy)

St 4/7 Headcleaner (Cop Shoot Cop)

F 10/7 Pavement (Sultans of Ping FC)

St 11/7 Stereolab (Unsane)

F 17/7 Strangelove (Action Swingers)

St 18/7 Shonen Knife, Terry Edwards

F 24/7 Th'Faith Healers (Buttsteak)

St 25/7 Babes in Toyland (Levellers 5)

F 31/7 Seaweed (God Machine)

St 1/8 Klezmatics (Bardots)

F 7/8 Philistines Jr (Jules Verne)

St 8/8 Diblo Dibala (Swell)

F 14/8 A Small Factory (The Orb)

St 15/8 Cords (Rhythm Eternity)

F 21/8 Chumbawamba (70 Gwen Party)

St 22/8 The House of Love (Fudge Tunnel)

F 28/8 Sebadoh (Yardstick)

St 29/8 Mr Ray's Wig World (Half Man Half Biscuit)

F 4/9 Loveblobs (Stereolab)

St 5/9 Papa Wemba (Pavement)

F 11/9 Drunk Tank (Th'Faith Healers)

St 12/9 Kitchens of Distinction (Babes in Toyland)

F 18/9 Future Sound of London (Headcleaner)

St 19/9 Irresistible Force (Seaweed)

F 25/9 Pond (Philistines Jr)

St 26/9 Dr Devious (Klezmatics)

F 2/10 Shonen Knife (Chumbawamba)

St 3/10 Jacob's Mouse (Cords)

F 9/10 programme broadcast from Berlin, records/ interviews only

St 10/10 live from Berlin, as part of a Radio 1 campaign on work opportunities in Europe, with Freiwillige Selbstkontrolle in session

F 16/10 live from Budapest, as above, with Attwenger in session

St 17/10 Unrest (Diblo Dibala)

F 23/10 PJ Harvey, Scorn

St 24/10 (Sebadoh, Strangelove, Pavement) four hour show, clocks went back

F 30/10 Jesus Lizard (Loveblobs)

St 31/10 Bivouac (Mr Ray's Wig World)

F 6/11 Fun Da Mental (A Small Factory)

St 7/11 Loudon Wainwright III (Jacob's Mouse)

F 13/11 Polvo (Future Sound of London)

St 14/11 Ultraviolence (Drunk Tank)

F 20/11 Skink (Irresistible Force)

St 21/11 Flaming Lips (The House of Love)

F 27/11 Marxman (Pond)

St 28/11 Moles (Shonen Knife)

F 4/12 Breed, Where's The Beach?

St 5/12 Aphex Twin (Kitchens of Distinction)

F 11/12 Huggy Bear (Fun Da Mental)

St 12/12 Staying Single, R1 documentary on the death of the 7-inch vinyl single, presented by Peel, 2–3pm, produced by Wendy Pilmer

St 12/12 Mint 400 (Superchunk)

M 14/12 Radio 5, 9.30–10pm Chain Reaction: David Gedge of The Wedding Present interviews his hero John Peel, kicking off a new nightly series, produced by Jane Berthoud

T 15/12 Radio 5, 9.30–10pm Chain Reaction: John Peel interviews his hero, Ian Rush of Liverpool FC

F 18/12 Festive 50

St 19/12 – F 1/1/93 Festive 50 (Best Sessions of Year)

St 26/12 no show

1993

St 2/1 Bandulu (Huggy Bear)

F 8/1 Hula Hoop, Ivor Cutler; Peel starts playing one track on a show from the Phantom 50, the abandoned Festive 50 of 1991, with number 50, Bongwater's 'Nick Cave Doll'

St 9/1 Dinosaur Jr acoustic session, Drop Nineteens

F 15/1 New Fast Automatic Daffodils, Unsane

St 16/1 Leatherface, Zimbabwe Cha Cha Cha Kings

F 22/1 Voodoo Queens; Sonic Youth, recorded live at Brixton Academy 14/12/92

St 23/1 Crane (Flaming Lips)

F 29/1 Moonshake (Jesus Lizard)

St 30/1 Dr Oloh (Breed)

F 5/2 Bailterspace (Where's The Beach?)

St 6/2 Meat Beat Manifesto, Therapy?

F 12/2 In Dust, Come

St 13/2 Cell, Cornershop

F 19/2 Pavement, Strangelove

St 20/2 Even As We Speak, Ukrainians

F 26/2 Codeine, Ecstasy of Saint Theresa

St 27/2 Superchunk (FSK)

F 5/3 Pulp (Polvo)

St 6/3 Werefrogs (Marxman)

T 9/3 (rpt of Staying Single documentary R1 9–10pm)

F 12/3 PJ Harvey, Oilseed Rape

St 13/3 The Fall (Aphex Twin)

F 19/3 Pavement, recorded at Brixton Academy 14/12/92 (New Fast Automatic Daffodils)

St 20/3 Velocity Girl (Skink)

F 26/3 Skyscraper (Bandulu)

St 27/3 Foreheads in a Fishtank (Hula Hoop)

F 2/4 Transglobal Underground (Leatherface)

St 3/4 Seven Year Bitch (Dr Oloh)

M 5/4 – F 9/4 'John Peel is Jakki Brambles.' Peel sits in on R1 lunchtime show all week 12.45–3pm, produced by Chris Lycett

F 9/4 Nelories (Drop Nineteens)

St 10/4 Th'Faith Healers (Crane)

F 16/4 Hole (Zimbabwe Cha Cha Cha Kings)

St 17/4 Roovel Oobik (Dinosaur Jr acoustic session)

F 23/4 Submarine (Unsane)

St 24/4 Nectarine No 9 (Bailterspace)

F 30/4 Bikini Kill (Ivor Cutler)

St 1/5 Pitch Shifter (Voodoo Queens)

F 7/5 Fun Da Mental (Cell)

St 8/5 Sebadoh (Therapy?)

F 14/5 Edsel Auctioneer (Meat Beat Manifesto)

St 15/5 Loop Guru (Strangelove)

F 21/5 Anhrefn with Margi Clarke (Cornershop)

St 22/5 Ween (PJ Harvey)

F 28/5 Tindersticks (Come)

St 29/5 Mazey Fade (Codeine)

F 4/6 (Bivouac) 70 Gwen Party

St 5/6 Terry Edwards (In Dust)

F 11/6 Trumans Water (Ecstasy Of Saint Theresa)

St 12/6 New Bomb Turks (The Fall)

F 18/6 Dr Phibes & The House of Wax Equations, Huggy Bear

St 19/6 Tsunami (Ukrainians)

F 25/6 Half Japanese

St 26/6 Shadowy Men on a Shadowy Planet; plus The Orb, Sharon Shannon, recorded live at Glastonbury

F 2/7 Polvo (Werefrogs)

St 3/7 Rollerskate Skinny (Superchunk)

F 9/7 God Is My Co-Pilot (Pulp)

St 10/7 Remmy Ongala & Orchestre Super Matimila (Oilseed Rape)

F 16/7 Royal Trux (Foreheads in a Fishtank)

St 17/7 Bear Quartet, recorded at home in Sweden (Transglobal Underground)

F 23/7 Voodoo Queens (Skyscraper)
St 24/7 Cords (Nelories)
F 30/7 Kanda Bongo Man (Th'Faith Healers)
St 31/7 Robert Ward & The Otis Grand Blues Band
    (Seven Year Bitch)
F 6/8 (Radio 5, 9.30–10pm rpt of Chain Reaction:
    Gedge interviews Peel)
F 6/8 Madder Rose (Even As We Speak)
St 7/8 How Does It Feel? Peel presents New Order
    documentary, R1 2–3pm, prod by Saira Hussain
St 7/8 J Church (Velocity Girl)
F 13/8 (R5, 9.30–10pm, rpt of Chain Reaction,
    Peel interviews Ian Rush)
F 13/8 Datblygu (Hole)
St 14/8 Mercury Rev (Loudon Wainwright III)
F 20/8 St Johnny (Roovel Oobik)
St 21/8 Radial Spangle (Nectarine No 9)
F 27/8 Senser (Voodoo Queens) in programme
    broadcast from Reading Festival
St 28/8 Eat Static (Trumans Water) in programme
    broadcast from Reading Festival
F 3/9 CNN, Flipper
St 4/9 Bad Religion, Fiasco
F 10/9 Orbital, Bratmobile
St 11/9 (Prince Far I & Creation Rebel, 1st TX 7/6/78;
    The Fall, rpt of a Mark Goodier session TX 05/93)
F 17/9 Curve (Pitchshifter)
St 18/9 Elastica (Pavement)
F 24/9 Mega City 4 (Sebadoh)
St 25/9 Brides Make Acid (Submarine)
F 1/10 Irresistible Force, aka Mix Master Morris (Bikini Kill)
St 2/10 Magnapop (70 Gwen Party)
F 8/10 Fun Da Mental, Tindersticks)
St 9/10 Jon Spencer Blues Explosion
    (Dr Phibes & The House of Wax Equations)
Th 14/10 John Peel In Scandinavia: Peel reports from
    Stockholm as part of R1's Euro Action Special on
    jobs, study and travel in Europe, 6.30–8.30pm,
    produced by Kath Morrison
F 15/10 show broadcast live from Sweden (Bear
    Quartet)
St 16/10 pre-recorded show with Scrawl
    (Anhrefn with Margi Clarke)
F 22/10 Barry Adamson, Even As We Speak
St 23/10 Eric's Trip (Terry Edwards)
F 29/10 (Ween, Loop Guru)

• Shows move to Fri 10pm–1am, Sat 4.30–7pm

St 30/10 Stereolab (Edsel Auctioneer)
F 5/11 Trumans Water (Huggy Bear)
St 6/11 Breed (Shadowy Men On A Shadowy Planet)
F 12/11 Pushkins (Rollerskate Skinny)
St 13/11 Chumbawamba (Tsunami)
F 19/11 Gag (Polvo)
St 20/11 Senseless Things
    (Sharon Shannon's Glastonbury set)
F 26/11 Sandmen, Royal Trux
St 27/11 Palace Brothers (Madder Rose)
F 3/12 Lois (New Bomb Turks)
St 4/12 Ian Rush (Half Japanese)
F 10/12 (God Is My Co-Pilot, Cords)
St 11/12 (Elastica)
T 14/12 R4, 2.30–3pm Personal Records: John Peel
    talks about and plays some records from key
    moments in his life to Jeremy Nicholas, while showing
    him round his record collection at Peel Acres,
    produced by Andrew Mussett: Ray Martine 'Blue
    Tango', Bing Crosby 'Just A Gigolo', Earl Bostic
    'Flamingo', Rachmaninov's 2nd Piano Concerto, Roy
    Orbison 'Running Scared', The Fall 'Kimble', Bongo
    Wende 'Ze Pumpa Pumpa'
F 17/12 Fabric (Mercury Rev)
St 18/12 Here (Senser)
F 24/12 & F 31/12 no shows
St 25/12 Festive 50, 10.30pm–2am

1994

St 1/1 Butterfly Child, Done Lying Down
F 7/1 AC Acoustics, Dreadzone
St 8/1 Knights of the Occasional Table, Ivor Cutler – a
    joint Kershaw/Peel session
F 14/1 Skinned Teen (Radial Spangle)
St 15/1 Hula Hoop, That Dog
F 21/1 Ronnie Dawson (Orbital)
St 22/1 Loop Guru, Man Or Astroman
F 28/1 Pussycat Trash (St Johnny)
St 29/1 Gorky's Zygotic Mynci, Eva Luna
F 4/2 Leatherface (J Church)
St 5/2 Gunshot, The Fall
F 11/2 Banco De Gaia
    (Remmy Ongala & Orchestre Super Matimila)
St 12/2 Det-Ri-Mental (Bad Religion)
F 18/2 Sleeper (Brides Make Acid)
St 19/2 Tindersticks; Blithe, recorded at home
    in Sweden
F 25/2 Elevate (Fiasco)
St 26/2 Pavement, Swirlies
F 4/3 13th Hole (Irresistible Force)
St 5/3 Credit To The Nation, Th'Faith Healers
F 11/3 Zuvuya, Bark Market
St 12/3 Ultramarine, Submarine
F 18/3 Drum Club, Thinking Fellers Union Local 282
St 19/3 Bivouac, Senser
F 25/3 Afghan Whigs, Sons Of The Subway
St 26/3 Voodoo Queens (Barry Adamson)
F 1/4 Pet Lamb, Timeshard
St 2/4 Mummys (The Sandmen)
F 8/4 (AC Acoustics, Ivor Cutler)
St 9/4 Orchids, Nectarine No 9
F 15/4 Global Communication aka Reload
    (Jon Spencer Blues Explosion)
St 16/4 Raincoats, The Wedding Present
F 22/4 (Nirvana #1 #2 & #3)
St 23/4 Archers Of Loaf (Even As We Speak)
F 29/4 The Fall recorded 8/12/93 live at
    Manchester Roadhouse
St 30/4 Ash, Madder Rose
F 6/5 K K Kings (Scrawl)
St 7/5 Heavenly, Sebadoh
F 13/5 Pure Morning, Neuro Project
St 14/5 Po (Eric's Trip)
F 20/5 Directional Force aka Dave Clarke,
    Sex Clark Five
St 21/5 Flying Saucer Attack (Bratmobile)
F 27/5 Seefeel, God Is My Co-Pilot
St 28/5 3Ds (Breed)
F 3/6 Mazey Fade, Codeine
St 4/6 no show
F 10/6 Psychick Warriors Ov Gaia, Magic Hour
St 11/6 Uzeda, Mufflon 5
F 17/6 Trumans Water, Locust
St 18/6 Frank Black & Teenage Fanclub, Movietone
F 24/6 Madder Rose, Cheapsuitaroonies, Dreadzone,
    all recorded live at Glastonbury
St 25/6 no show
F 1/7 Orbital recorded at Glastonbury Festival; Jawbox
St 2/7 Flatback Four, Philistines Jr
F 8/7 Chumbawamba and Credit To The Nation, both
    recorded live at Glastonbury
St 9/7 Elastica; Pulp recorded live at Glastonbury
F 15/7 Tribute To Nothing; plus Transglobal Underground
    recorded live at Glastonbury
St 16/7 Fun Da Mental; plus Inspiral Carpets recorded
    live at Glastonbury
F 22/7 70 Gwen Party, Shellac
St 23/7 Rodan, Harvey's Rabbit

F 29/7 Grifters, Palace Brothers
St 30/7 Eggs, Unsane
F 5/8 Salt Tank (Magnapop)
St 6/8 Breed, Centry
F 12/8 Drome, Teenagers In Trouble (Robert Ward)
St 13/8 no show, Woodstock 94 instead
F 19/8 Scorn (Royal Trux)
St 20/8 Prolapse (Ronnie Dawson)
F 26/8 Flaming Lips recorded live at the Reading
    Festival
St 27/8 Reverend Horton Heat recorded
    live at Glastonbury
F 2/9 Boyracer, Children Of The Bong
St 3/9 Zion Train (Stereolab)
F 9/9 (Thirteenth Hole, Metal Urbain, 1st TX 11/10/78)
St 10/9 Rugrat, Blubber
F 16/9 Plastikman, 18th Dye
St 17/9 Cee Bee Beaumont, Done Lying Down
F 23/9 Luke Slater's 7th Plane (Trumans Water)
St 24/9 Smudge, Dreadzone
F 30/9 Calvin Party (Pushkins)
St 1/10 (Mega City Four, Lois)
F 7/10 show broadcast from Glasgow
    (AC Acoustics, Nectarine No 9)
St 8/10 show broadcast from Glasgow, with Shriek
    (Frank Black & Teenage Fanclub)
F 14/10 Fugees (Datblygu)
St 15/10 Hopper (Loop Guru)
F 21/10 I'm Being Good (Eat Static)
St 22/10 Pulp, plus Sharon Shannon live in on-air
    studio 5 Egton House
F 28/10 Tunic, Zeni Geva
St 29/10 Doo Rag, Jale
F 4/11 Archers Of Loaf (Voodoo Queens)
St 5/11 Spike (Heavenly)
F 11/11 Deep Turtle, Whiteout
St 12/11 Pussy Crush, Ed Hall
F 18/11 Flinch (Fabric)

• Sat show loses 30 mins, now 5–7pm

St 19/11 La Bradford (Senser)
F 25/11 Cable (Elevate)
St 26/11 Sleeper (Man Or Astroman)
F 2/12 Hole recorded live at Reading Festival 26/8/94
St 3/12 Blueboy (Hula Hoop)
F 9/12 Four Brothers (Blithe)
St 10/12 (Senseless Things, Tindersticks)
F 16/12 Uzeda (Det-Ri-Mental)
St 17/12 The Fall's Christmas session,
    Elastica's Christmas session, Festive 50 pt 1
F 23/12 Festive 50 pt 2
St 24/12 & St 31/12 no shows
F 30/12 MC Solaar

1995

F 6/1 Thrush Puppies, Smog
St 7/1 Sammy (Pet Lamb)
F 13/1 Black Dog
St 14/1 Ronnie Dawson, Diblo Dabala
F 20/1 Splintered
St 21/1 Bluetones, Urusei Yatsura
F 27/1 Xol Dog 400, AC Acoustics
St 28/1 New Decade, Golden Starlet
F 3/2 Mouse On Mars
St 4/2 Spare Snare, Supergrass
F 10/2 (Po, Prolapse)
St 11/2 American TV Cops (Pavement)
F 17/2 Mazey Fade (Calvin Party)
St 18/2 Guv'Ner (Zion Train)
F 24/2 Badgewearer, The Orb

St 25/2 Lung Leg (Mufflon 5)
F 3/3 Pure Morning (70 Gwen Party)
St 4/3 Prophets Of Da City (Elastica)
F 10/3 Innersphere (Ash, Viv Stanshall, 1st TX 5/4/78)
St 11/3 Gorky's Zygotic Mynci (Orchids)
F 17/3 DJ Hell (Th'Faith Healers)
St 18/3 Spiritualized, Hooton 3 Car
F 24/3 Today Is The Day, Sabres Of Paradise
St 25/3 Kaisers, Loop Guru
F 31/3 The Holy Ghost
St 1/4 Echobelly, Luscious Jackson
F 7/4 Black Star Liner, Mug
St 8/4 Dick Dale, Pink Kross
F 14/4 Aphex Twin, Vorhees
St 15/4 Bracket (Shriek)
F 21/4 Bluetones, Dreadzone, Pulp, live from Bristol
    Anson as part of Radio 1 Sound City
St 22/4 (Flying Saucer Attack, Movietone)
F 28/4 18th Dye, Sloy
St 29/4 Ivor Cutler, Man Or Astroman
F 5/5 Donkey, ROC
St 6/5 Det-Ri-Mental, Pond
F 12/5 Papa Wemba, Elevate
St 13/5 Crowsdell (Delgados' BBC Radio Scotland
    'Beat Patrol' session rpt)
F 19/5 Calvin Party, Huevos Rancheros
St 20/5 Transglobal Underground, Fitz Of Depression
F 26/5 God Is My Co-Pilot, Caspar Brotzmann Massaker
St 27/5 Nectarine No 9 (Fugees)
F 2/6 Solar Race (Boyracer)
St 3/6 Soul Bossa (Jale)
F 9/6 Joyrider (Plastikman)
St 10/6 (Doo Rag, Tribute To Nothing)
F 16/6 Babes In Toyland (Centry)
St 17/6 El Dorados & CJ & The House Rockers (Pulp)

• **Mike Hawkes retires. Alison Howe**
  becomes show producer

F 23/6 Ash, Sleeper, Supergrass, The Boredoms, all
    recorded live at Glastonbury
St 24/6 Diablo Dibala, Dreadzone, Zion Train,
    Sharon Shannon, all recorded live at Glastonbury
F 30/6 Broccoli, Distorted Waves Of Ohm
St 1/7 Delicatessen, Beatnik Filmstars
F 7/7 Palace Music, Sounds Of Life
St 8/7 Flaming Stars, A Guy Called Gerald
F 14/7 The Fall, recorded live at the Phoenix Festival
St 15/7 The Wedding Present, recorded live at
    the Phoenix Festival
F 21/7 Kenickie, Yummy Fur
St 22/7 Menswear (MC Solaar)
F 28/7 Bandulu (Pussycrush)
St 29/7 Mercury Rev (Four Brothers)
F 4/8 Bob Tilton (Psychick Warriors Ov Gaia)
St 5/8 Half Man Half Biscuit (Hopper)
F 11/8 Pet Lamb (Shellac)
St 12/8 Dick Dale (Dreadzone)
F 18/8 Laurent Garnier (I'm Being Good)
St 19/8 (Supergrass, Stereolab)
F 25/8 Solar Race, Hole, Cable, Beck, China Drum,
    all recorded live at the Reading Festival
St 26/8 Joyrider (rec. previous day), Spare Snare,
    Bluetones, all recorded live at the Reading Festival
Sn 27/8 Flinch, Pavement, Babes in Toyland, Mudhoney,
    all recorded live at Reading Festival, in extra show
F 1/9 AC Acoustics, Flying Saucer Attack,
    recorded at the Reading Festival
St 2/9 Delicatessen, recorded at the Reading Festival
F 8/9 Murmur; plus Prolapse recorded at Reading
    Festival
St 9/9 Goober Patrol (Sabres Of Paradise)
F 15/9 Strip Kings (New Decade)
St 16/9 (American TV Cops)

F 22/9 (Pure Morning, Eat Static)
St 23/9 (Black Star Liner, Hooton 3 Car)
F 29/9 Future Sound Of London (Elevate)
St 30/9 (Pulp #1, 1st TX 18/11/81)
F 6/10 Half Japanese, Further
St 7/10 BBC R4, 6.50–7.20pm Peel presents new
    magazine show Offspring, offering 'despatches
    from the front-line of family life' (rpt Thurs 12/10,
    11.30pm–midnight). Weekly at these times thereafter
    til St 25/11/95; series #2, 10/8/96 – 28/9/96;
    Christmas Special 24/12/96 8/30–9pm; series #3,
    26/4/97–14/6/97; series #4, 4/10/97–22/11/97,
    produced by Cathy Drysdale
St 7/10 Tunic, Manson
F 13/10 Autechre, Deluxx Unconvinced,
    Billy Bragg live acoustic session
St 14/10 Bis, Quickspace Supersport
F 20/10 Nectarine No 9, Urusei Yatsura, both recorded
    live at Glasgow Ten-Day Weekend 17/10
St 21/10 Delgados recorded live at
    Glasgow Ten-Day Weekend
F 27/10 at the Camden Live Festival: Solar Race,
    Zion Train, Dave Clarke
St 28/10 Ligament (Echobelly)
F 3/11 Alec Empire, Hood
St 4/11 Natacha Atlas (Golden Starlet)
F 10/11 Heads (Distorted Waves Of Ohm)
St 11/11 (Half Man Half Biscuit)
F 17/11 Pan@sonic (Flaming Stars)
St 18/11 Smaller
F 24/11 Supreme Dicks, Van Basten
St 25/11 Jolt (Yummy Fur)
F 1/12 Cristian Vogel
St 2/12 (Ash, Flinch)
F 8/12 Brainiac (Bandulu)
St 9/12 no show
F 15/12 Nubiles (Elastica)
St 16/12 Livingstone, The Wedding Present
F 22/12 The Fall (Prince Far I & Creation Rebel)
St 23/12 (Dick Dale, Diblo Dibala)
F 29/12 & St 30/12 Festive 50

1996

F 5/1 Chrome Cranks
St 6/1 Magoo, Gene
F 12/1 Zeni Geva (Future Sound of London)
St 13/1 Luggage (Delgados 'Beat Patrol' session)
F 19/1 (Bob Tilton, DJ Hell)
St 20/1 (Broccoli, Crowsdell)
W 24/1 BBC1 TV 7–7.30pm, Peel is surprised by
    Michael Aspel while presenting Top Of The Pops, to
    be the subject of This Is Your Life, recorded 13/12/95
Th 25/1 (rpt of This Is Your Life 2.35–3.05pm BBC1)
F 26/1 (A Guy Called Gerald)
St 27/1 (Joyrider, Thrush Puppies)
F 2/2 Beam Me Up Scotty, R4 FM 10–10.30am,
    Peel presents feature on Space Age pop culture,
    produced by Andrew Johnston
F 2/2 Dave Clarke Interview
St 3/2 Chuck (Bis)
F 9/2 (Spiritualized)
St 10/2 Movietone (Billy Bragg)
F 16/2 Grifters
St 17/2 Frank Black & The Catholics, 60ft Dolls
F 23/2 Van Basten, Quickspace Supersport
St 24/2 Cable, Stereolab
F 1/3 (Smaller, Cristian Vogel)
St 2/3 Done Lying Down, Sewing Room
F 8/3 Auteurs (Nubiles)
St 9/3 Joyrider, Kenickie
F 15/3 (The Fall #1)

St 16/3 Peel is Michael Berkeley's guest on Private
    Passions, R3 12–1pm, choosing Saint-Saens' Piano
    Concerto No 2, Allegri Misere, Gottschalk's Ojos
    Criollos Danse Cubaine, Neil Young's Rockin' In The
    Free World, Bruch's Violin Concerto & Gerhswin's
    Rhapsody in Blue; and, Peel asking to be surprised,
    Berkeley played him Conlon Nancarrow's Study for
    Player-Piano No 21
St 16/3 NUB, Zion Train & Ruts DC
M 18/3 – Th 21/3 Peel sits in for Mark Radcliffe on R1
    from Manchester 10pm–midnight with live sessions
    including Number One Cup (18/3), Tripping Daisy
    (19/3), Calvin Party (20/3)
F 22/3 Fugees (Pan@sonic)
St 23/3 Sights (The Wedding Present)
F 29/3 The North Pole, demo recorded by the Band
    in Italy
St 30/3 Loop Guru, Comet Gain
M 1/4 – Th 4/4 Peel sits in for Mark Radcliffe on R1 from
    Manchester 10pm–midnight with sessions & guests
    including Super Furry Animals (1/4), John Hegley
    (2/4), Bennet (3/4)
F 5/4 Flying Saucer Attack, Mansun
St 6/4 Wilson, Bandulu
F 12/4 Bis, Wedding Present, Orbital, all live at Leeds
    Met Uni for R1 Sound City 96
St 13/4 records-only show from Sound City Leeds

• **Fri show moves to Sun 8–10pm**

• **Peel now on-air for just 4 hrs per week**

St 20/4 Flaming Stars, Urusei Yatsura
Sn 21/4 New Bad Things, Lung Leg, plus one track live
    from Gorky's Zygotic Mynci at Maida Vale
St 27/4 Ash (Kenickie)
Sn 28/4 Hooton 3 Car (Magoo)
St 4/5 records only
St 5/5 records only
St 11/5 Sleeper, Gorky's Zygotic Mynci
Sn 12/5 Delgados, Scarfo
St 18/5 (Gene)
Sn 19/5 LA Bradford (60ft Dolls)
St 25/5 Dweeb, Simon Joyner
Sn 26/5 Solar Race, Dave Angel
St 1/6 (Stereolab)
Sn 2/6 (Zion Train & Ruts DC)
St 8/6 (Fugees)
Sn 9/6 Rumble, presented by Steve Lamacq
St 15/6 US Maple
Sn 16/6 Terry Edwards, Bis
St 22/6 Pussy Crush
Sn 23/6 no show: Sex Pistols re-union concert
    live from Finsbury Park
M 24/6 – M 5/8 John Peel's Classic Sessions 7-part
    documentary series, R1, 9–10pm, produced
    by Anita Kamath
St 29/6 Live from Tribal Gathering: Dave Clarke, Vandal
    Sound, DJ Vibes
Sn 30/6 Live from Tribal Gathering: Conemelt, Daft Punk,
    Hardfloor, Chemical Brothers
St 6/7 Die Kruz
Sn 7/7 (Flaming Stars)
St 13/7 Man Or Astroman
Sn 14/7 Philistines Jr, Van Basten
St 20/7 Live at Phoenix Festival: Fun Loving Criminals,
    Zion Train, Stereolab, Beck
Sn 21/7 Live at Phoenix Festival: Urusei Yatsura, Red
    Snapper, Linoleum, Neil Young & Crazy Horse, Baby
    Bird, The Fall
St 27/7 Bennet, Brassy
Sn 28/7 Guided By Voices
St 3/8 Autopop
Sn 4/8 Bluetones live at Maida Vale
St 10/8 Pure Morning
Sn 11/8 no show
St 17/8 Beatnik Filmstars

Sn 18/8 The Fall

St 24/8 Live from the Reading Festival with recorded
highlights from: Sebadoh, Dweeb, China Drum,
Billy Bragg

Sn 25/8 Live from the Reading Festival with recorded
highlights from: The Wedding Present, Catatonia,
Ash, Julian Cope, Flaming Lips

St 31/8 Tortoise

Sn 1/9 Quickspace

St 7/9 Conscious Sound Collective

Sn 8/9 (Delgados)

St 14/9 Tunic

Sn 15/9 records only

St 21/9 PJ Harvey & John Parish recorded at Peel Acres

Sn 22/9 (Dave Angel)

• **Sat show gets extra hour, now 4–7pm**

St 28/9 (Bennet)

Sn 29/9 (Dweeb)

St 5/10 (Van Basten)

Sn 6/10 Broadcast

• **Radio 1 leaves Egton House, Langham Place
moves to Yalding House, Gt Portland St**

St 12/10 Nil

Sn 13/10 Doo Rag

M 14/10 – Th 17/10 Peel sits in for Mark Radcliffe on R1
from Manchester 10pm–midnight with live sessions
including Half Man Half Biscuit (14/10), PJ Harvey &
John Parish (15/10), Flaming Stars (17/10)

St 19/10 – Sn 20/10 no shows: Steve Lamacq from
Ten Day Weekend, Glasgow, live sets recorded 14
& 15/10

St 26/10 Future Sound of London, live by ISDN
presented by Steve Lamacq

Sn 27/10 (Bluetones) presented by Steve Lamacq

St 2/11 (Gorky's Zygotic Mynci)

Sn 3/11 Soul Bossa

St 9/11 (Hooton 3 Car)

Sn 10/11 Live from Soho Live with Delgados, Fluke

St 16/11 Tiger

Sn 17/11 Cha Cha Cohen

St 23/11 Propellerheads

Sn 24/11 (Broadcast)

St 30/11 Scott Brown

Sn 1/12 (Quickspace)

M 2/12 – M 20/1/97 (excluding 23/12 & 30/12)
John Peel's Classic Radio 1 Sessions series #2,
produced by Anita Kamath, R1 9–10pm

St 7/12 Tindersticks

Sn 8/12 Trusty

St 14/12 Roni Size live concert set

Sn 15/12 records only

St 21/12 – Sn 29/12 Festive 50, plus:

Sn 22/12 Billy Bragg acoustic in on-air studio
session plus interview

1997

Th 2/1 (Peel on Private Passions rpt R3 6.30–7.30pm)

St 4/1 Dumb, Backwater

Sn 5/1 Radar Bros

St 11/1 Jubilee Allstars, Mogwai

Sn 12/1 Dream City Film Club

St 18/1 Bennet

Sn 19/1 (Soul Bossa)

St 25/1 The Orb live from Maida Vale

Sn 26/1 (Kenickie)

St 1/2 (Propellerheads)

Sn 2/2 Half Man Half Biscuit

St 8/2 Midget

Sn 9/2 Heads

St 15/2 Topper

Sn 16/2 Clinic

• **Show moves back into mid-week Tues, Wed,
Thurs, 8.30–10.30pm**

T 18/2 Coldcut live from Maida Vale

W 19/2 (Tindersticks)

Th 20/2 Adventures in Stereo

T 25/2 Experimental Pop Band

W 26/2 Soundman recorded at BBC Manchester

Th 27/2 Carl Cox live from Maida Vale

T 4/3 show broadcast from Glasgow,
with Magoo in session

W 5/3 Calvin Party

Th 6/3 Broken Dog

T 11/3 Beatnik Filmstars

W 12/3 no show

Th 13/3 AC Acoustics

T 18/3 (Doo Rag)

W 19/3 Flaming Stars

Th 20/3 Rome

T 25/3 Arab Strap

W 26/3 Loop Guru

Th 27/3 Black Dog

T 1/4 The Gentle People

W 2/4 Liberator DJs & The London Acid Techno Mafia

Th 3/4 Source Direct

• **Shows moved back to 8.40pm start time each
night still ending at 10.30pm**

T 8/4 Prolapse

W 9/4 Olivia Tremor Control

Th 10/4 records only

T 15/4 Number One Cup

W 16/4 Bette Davis & The Balconettes

Th 17/4 Panacea

T 22/4 Folk Implosion

W 23/4 Melys

Th 24/4 records only

M 28/4 – F 2/5 London Music Week, 6–10.30pm,
with Steve Lamacq & John Peel: Mogwai, Kenickie,
Gorky's Zygotic Mynci

T 29/4 London Music Week, with live sets from Linoleum,
AC Acoustics, Tindersticks

W 30/4 London Music Week, with live sets from Eels

Th 1/5 London Music Week: Bentley Rhythm Ace; Billy
Bragg live from Divas Bar, London N1

M 5/5 Blur recorded at Peel Acres,
Special Bank Holiday Show 6.30–8.30pm

T 6/5 Tunic & Andrew Beaujon

W 7/5 Agothocles

Th 8/5 Future Sound of London,
second live-via-ISDN session

T 13/5 Hooton 3 Car

W 14/5 God Is My Co-Pilot

Th 15/5 The Make Up

T 20/5 Kidnapper

W 21/5 Servotron

Th 22/5 John Peel & Steve Lamacq Live at Manchester
Live 97: Zion Train, Dave Angel

T 27/5 Suckle

W 28/5 Demolition Doll Rods

Th 29/5 (Panacea)

T 3/6 Cable

W 4/6 Velocette

Th 5/6 no show

Sn 8/6 Vinyl Resting Place, R2, 11pm–midnight, Peel
presents feature on Britain's vinyl junkie record
collectors, meeting Nick Hornby, Elton John and Sir
Tim Rice, among others, produced by Maud Hand

T 10/6 (Brassy)

W 11/6 DM Bob & The Deficits

Th 12/6 Inter

T 17/6 (Folk Implosion)

W 18/6 Mouse On Mars featuring Laetitia & Mary
from Stereolab

Th 19/6 Mark Eitzel & Peter Buck live acoustic session

T 24/6 (The Gentle People)

W 25/6 Fuck

Th 26/6 records-only show live from Glastonbury

St 28/6 Fab & 50! Peel presents feature on the
post-war baby boom, R2, 6.30–7.30pm

T 1/7 The Secret Goldfish

W 2/7 (Melys)

Th 3/7 Crocodile God

T 8/7 (Prolapse)

W 9/7 Male Nurse

Th 10/7 (The Black Dog)

T 15/7 Pop Off Tuesday

W 16/7 Delgados

Th 17/7 (Source Direct)

T 22/7 New Bad Things

W 23/7 Bangtwister

Th 24/7 (Scott Brown)

T 29/7 Man Or Astroman

W 30/7 record-only show

Th 31/7 Police Cat

T 5/8 Yo La Tengo

W 6/8 (Midget)

Th 7/8 Bowery Electric

T 12/8 Hitchers

W 13/8 (Flaming Stars)

T 14/8 Urusei Yatsura

T 19/8 Beatnick Filmstars

W 20/8 (Heads)

Th 21/8 Pavement, live from Maida Vale

T 26/8 Stony Sleep

W 27/8 Lance Gambit Trio's session of Oasis covers

Th 28/8 Dave Angel live

T 2/9 Salaryman

W 3/9 Dawn Of The Replicants

Th 4/9 (Velocette)

T 9/9 Period Pains

W 10/9 Done Lying Down

Th 11/9 (Mouse on Mars featuring Mary & Laetitia
from Stereolab)

T 16/9 Echo & The Bunnymen, live from Maida Vale

W 17/9 Hybirds

Th 18/9 (Inter)

T 23/9 no show

W 24/9 Stereolab, live from Maida Vale

Th 25/9 Live from the launch of Radio 1 Oxford Sound
City, with Peel and Steve Lamacq: Longpigs,
Strangelove

T 30/9 Movietone

W 1/10 Radio 1 John Peel Show 30th Anniversary
surprise gig/party, live from the ICA, London:
Delgados, Dreadzone [& Stereophonics, not TX on
Peel show]

Th 2/10 (The Secret Goldfish)

T 7/10 Black Star Liner

W 8/10 (Bowery Electric)

Th 9/10 Girlfrendo

T 14/10 Helen Love

W 15/10 (Male Nurse)

Th 16/10 Eat Static, live from Maida Vale

T 21/10 Flaming Stars

W 22/10 Rachels

Th 23/10 (Yo La Tengo)

M 27/10 – Th 30/10 Live at Oxford Sound City with
Peel & Lamacq: Ultrasound, Scarfo, Travis, Gene,
Embrace

T 28/10 Oxford Sound City: Radish, Prolapse,
Supernaturals, Sleeper

W 29/10 Oxford Sound City: Broadcast, Cable,
Spiritualized, Echobelly, Hurricane No 1

Th 30/10 Oxford Sound City: Lo-Fidelity Allstars, The

Egg, DJ Shadow, Fluke, Bentley Rhythm Ace
T 4/11 Pastels
W 5/11 (Hitchers)
Th 6/11 To Rococo Rot
T 11/11 Leopards
W 12/11 Smog
Th 13/11 (Dawn Of The Replicants)
T 18/11 (Man Or Astroman)
W 19/11 Calexico
T 20/11 (Delgados)
T 25/11 – Th 27/11 shows presented by Pulp, featuring:
    Electric Sound of Joy, one track live from Maida Vale
    session recording
W 26/11 Add N To (X)
Th 27/11 Electric Sound of Joy, rest of session
    recorded 25/11
T 2/12 (Period Pains)
W 3/12 Magic Dirt
Th 4/12 no show
T 9/12 Half Japanese presented by Steve Lamacq
W 10/12 Justin Berkovi presented by Steve Lamacq
Th 11/12 no show
T 16/12 Eska
W 17/12 (Lance Gambit Trio)
Th 18/12 Coldcut live from Maida Vale
T 23/12 Festive 31 for 1997, in 4 hour show
    (Pavement live at Maida Vale)
W 24/12 – Th 1/1/98 no shows

1998

T 6/1 Comet Gain
W 7/1 (Girlfrendo)
Th 8/1 Plaid
T 13/1 Love Junk
W 14/1 (To Rococo Rot)
Th 15/1 Cristian Vogel
T 20/1 Dustball
W 21/1 (Hybirds)
Th 22/1 no show – extended Evening Session for
    NME Live event
T 27/1 no show
W 28/1 Macrocosmica
Th 29/1 Beatnik Filmstars
T 3/2 Lillian
W 4/2 Nought
Th 5/2 (Add N To (X))
T 10/2 Polythene
W 11/2 (Calexico)
Th 12/2 (Coldcut)
T 17/2 Mogwai
W 18/2 Red Monkey
Th 19/2 (Justin Berkovi)
T 24/2 Half Man Half Biscuit
W 25/2 (Pop Off Tuesday)
Th 26/2 Male Nurse
T 3/3 The Fall
W 4/3 (Cornershop #1, 1st TX 13/2/93)
Th 5/3 Finitribe, live from Maida Vale
St 7/3 Peel presents Race With The Devil: The Gene
    Vincent Story, R2 6.30–7.30pm, produced by Ken
    Phillips
T 10/3 Arab Strap
W 11/3 Spraydog
Th 12/3 (Plaid)
T 17/3 Scarfo
W 18/3 Gene
Th 19/3 (Electric Sound of Joy)

• **Alison Howe moves to BBC2's 'Later with
  Jools Holland'. Anita Kamath becomes show
  producer**

T 24/3 Super Furry Animals, one track played in live
    from Maida Vale recording
W 25/3 (Leopards)
Th 26/3 no show
T 31/3 Clinic
W 1/4 (Bangtwister)
Th 2/4 Aerial M
T 7/4 Yummy Fur, plus 2 tracks live from Maida Vale
    recording by Six By Seven
W 8/4 (Flaming Stars)
Th 9/4 El Hombre Trajeado
St 11/4 BBC R4, 9–10am, first edition of Home Truths,
    presented by Peel, 'offering a light-hearted start to
    the weekend'. Weekly thereafter. Producer Chris
    Berthoud
T 14/4 (Dustball)
W 15/4 Velodrome 2000
Th 16/4 Thievery Corporation
T 21/4 60ft Dolls, live from Maida Vale
W 22/4 Super Furry Animals
Th 23/4 (Servotron)
T 28/4 Dawn Of The Replicants, Leopards,
    live from Maida Vale, two tracks each
W 29/4 (Polythene)
Th 30/4 Tortoise
T 5/5 The High Fidelity, plus one track live from
    Solex recording at Maida Vale
W 6/5 Travis Cut
Th 7/5 Technoanimal
T 12/5 Six By Seven, plus one track live from Magoo
    recording at Maida Vale
W 13/5 Dawn Of The Replicants, Leopards, with more
    from 28/4 recordings
Th 14/5 (Half Man Half Biscuit)
T 19/5 Jeff Mills DJ set live
W 20/5 Cable
Th 21/5 (Nought)
T 26/5 Crocodile God
W 27/5 Kerb
Th 28/5 (Pavement, 1st TX 21/8/97)
T 2/6 Plone, plus one track live from Topper
    recording at Maida Vale
W 3/6 Nectarine No 9 & Jock Scott
Th 4/6 (Lance Gambit Trio)
T 9/6 Solex
W 10/6 Sportique
Th 11/6 Ten Benson, plus Dustball track live from
    Maida Vale
St 13/6 Peel made an OBE in HM The Queen's
    Birthday Honours
T 16/6 Grandaddy, plus one track live from Boards Of
    Canada at Maida Vale
W 17/6 Delgados
Th 18/6 Silicone
T 23/6 Melys, live from Maida Vale featuring
    The London Welsh Male Voice Choir
W 24/6 Stony Sleep
Th 25/6 show broadcast from Glastonbury
    (Dreadzone at Glastonbury 97)
St 27/6 extra show from Glastonbury 6–9pm
Sn 28/6 extra show from Glastonbury 6–9pm
T 30/6 – W 8/7 recorded live at Meltdown Festival
    20/6/98, Queen Elizabeth Hall, London South Bank:
    Broadcast, Plaid, Plone, Autechre
W 1/7 Meltdown: Sonic Youth, Spiritualized, Delgados
Th 2/7 Meltdown: Culture, Blood & Fire Sound System
T 7/7 Meltdown: Blur & Silver Apples, recorded 5/7
W 8/7 Meltdown: Suicide, Jesus & Mary Chain,
    recorded 4/7
Th 9/7 Billy Bragg, live in on-air studio, Yalding House
T 14/7 Magoo, plus one track live from Hofman
    at Maida Vale
W 15/7 Topper
Th 16/7 Cinerama

T 21/7 Boards of Canada, Gorky's Zygotic Mynci
    with one track live from Maida Vale
W 22/7 Dustball
Th 23/7 more Meltdown live recordings: Add N To (X),
    Half Man Half Biscuit
T 28/7 Flaming Stars, El Hombre Trajeado with
    one track live from Maida Vale
W 29/7 Unwound
Th 30/7 (Gene)
T 4/8 Bis
W 5/8 Metrotone
Th 6/8 (Male Nurse)
T 11/8 Thomas Mapfumo & Blacks Unlimited
W 12/8 Elements of Noize
Th 13/8 (Super Furry Animals)
T 18/8 more Meltdown recordings:
    Spiritualized featuring Sonic Youth, recorded 1/7
W 19/8 Hofman
Th 20/8 (Clinic)
T 25/8 Gorky's Zygotic Mynci
W 26/8 Gilded Lil
Th 27/8 (60ft Dolls)
T 1/9 Mogwai
W 2/9 Broccoli
Th 3/9 Dave Angel live DJ set
T 8/9 Yo La Tengo
W 9/9 Twp
Th 10/9 (Scarfo)
T 15/9 Comatose
W 16/9 Conemelt
Th 17/9 no show – Lamacq from
    Sound City Newcastle launch instead
T 22/9 Broken Dog
W 23/9 PJ Harvey live from Maida Vale,
    while recording for Evening Session
Th 24/9 James Ruskin / The Drop live DJ set
T 29/9 Buckfunk 3000, aka Si Begg, live DJ set
W 30/9 Fuck
Th 1/10 (Yummy Fur)
T 6/10 Appliance
W 7/10 Astronaut
Th 8/10 Live techno DJ sets from Maida Vale celebrating
    100 releases on the Tresor label: Pacou, Neil
    Landstrumm & Tobia Schmidt, Surgeon, Regis. Show
    extended by 30 minutes, courtesy of Mary Anne
    Hobbs, to fit all the sets in

• **Shows move to 10.10pm–midnight T, W, Th**

T 13/10 Hefner
W 14/10 Tram
Th 15/10 (The High Fidelity)
T 20/10 Quickspace
W 21/10 Cornelius
Th 22/10 (Plone)
M 26/10 – Th 29/10 Live from Newcastle Sound City
    Riverside/University, with Peel & Steve Lamacq,
    featuring live sets from: Tiger, Gorky's Zygotic Mynci,
    Rocket From The Crypt, Super Furry Animals, Clinic
T 27/10 Newcastle Sound City: Six By Seven, Kelly,
    Terrorvision, Three Colours Red, Gomez, Bluetones
W 28/10 Newcastle Sound City: Magoo, Gene, Hefner,
    Symposium, Stereophonics, Solavox
Th 29/10 Newcastle Sound City: Wagonchrist,
    Plastikman, Dub Pistols, Freestylers, Fatboy Slim
T 3/11 White Hassle
W 4/11 The Fall
Th 5/11 Sea Nymphs
T 10/11 El Hombre Trajeado
W 11/11 Cay
Th 12/11 (Sportique)
T 17/11 REM recorded 'as live' in BBC Radio Theatre,
    Broadcasting House; Juan Atkins live DJ set
W 18/11 Brian Jonestown Massacre
Th 19/11 (Nectarine No 9)

T 24/11 Samurai Seven

W 25/11 Tiger

Th 26/11 (Solex)

T 1/12 Klute

W 2/12 The High Fidelity's Sean Dickson's
solo omnichord session

Th 3/12 (Cinerama)

T 8/12 Wilbur Wilberforce live DJ set

W 9/12 Wagonchrist

Th 10/12 (Boards of Canada)

T 15/12 Motor Life Co

W 16/12 Turbocat

Th 17/12 (Grandaddy)

T 22/12, W 23/12, T 29/12 Festive 50

Th 24/12 & Th 31/12 no shows

W 30/12 New Order special (pre-recorded): interview,
new studio session recorded 24/11, favourite
records, and set recorded at Reading Festival 30/8
(1st TX In Concert Mon 30/11)

1999

T 5/1 Quasi

W 6/1 Tarwater

Th 7/1 (Delgados)

T 12/1 Faust

W 13/1 Cuban Boys

Th 14/1 (Cay)

T 19/1 Godspeed You Black Emperor!

W 20/1 Caroline Martin

Th 21/1 (Mogwai)

T 26/1 Scratch Perverts live DJ set from Maida Vale

W 27/1 Fleece

Th 28/1 (Metrotone)

T 2/2 Spare Snare

W 3/2 Salako

Th 4/2 Bluetones, Gene, recorded live at Queen
Elizabeth Hall, the South Bank, London, 31/1

T 9/2 Black Star Liner

W 10/2 Woodbine

Th 11/2 (Comatose)

T 16/2 no show

W 17/2 Peel Sessions live: Clinic, Coldcut, Masonna,
recorded at Queen Elizabeth Hall, South Bank,
London

Th 18/2 (Twp)

T 23/2 Freddy Fresh live DJ set

W 24/2 Carl Cox live DJ set

Th 25/2 (PJ Harvey's Evening Session live set)

T 2/3 Derrero

W 3/3 Hefner's gospel covers session

Th 4/3 (Quickspace)

T 9/3 Ooberman

W 10/3 Fantasmagroover

Th 11/3 (Appliance) & Simon Mayo drops-in as co-
presenter, for Comic Relief

T 16/3 Bonnie Prince Billy

W 17/3 Dream City Film Club

Th 18/3 (Tram)

T 23/3 AC Acoustics

W 24/3 Digital Hardcore Night at the Queen Elizabeth
Hall, London: Atari Teenage Riot, Christoph De
Babylon and Shizuo, recorded 19/3

Th 25/3 records-only show, from Peel Acres, Billy Bragg
pops round

T 30/3 Billy Mahonie

W 31/3 (Spraydog)

Th 1/4 Peel Sessions 'almost' live from the Improv
Theatre, London: Echo & the Bunnymen, PJ Harvey
& John Parish

T 6/4 DJs Kemistry & Storm live DJ set

W 7/4 ISAN

Th 8/4 (Brian Jonestown Massacre)

T 13/4 Karamazov

W 14/4 Novak

Th 15/4 Tim & Charlotte from Ash's live acoustic
session from Peel Acres

T 20/4 18th Dye

W 21/4 Pram

Th 22/4 (Black Star Liner)

T 27/4 Orbital recorded live at Queen Elizabeth Hall,
London 24/4

W 28/4 Cornelius recorded live at Queen Elizabeth Hall,
London 24/4

Th 29/4 Ec8or

T 4/5 Hirameka Hi Fi

W 5/5 Monograph

Th 6/5 Cinerama, acoustic session live from
Peel Acres

T 11/5 To Rococo Rot

W 12/5 Reviver Gene

Th 13/5 (White Hassle) 'Peelenium', four tracks each
night from one year of the 20th century, begins with
1900

T 18/5 Marine Research

W 19/5 Terry Edwards and the Scapegoats

Th 20/5 (The Fall)

T 25/5 show broadcast from Glasgow,
with Mercury Rev session

W 26/5 The High Fidelity, Delgados, live from Glasgow
Art School, in concert as part of Music Live

Th 27/5 (Samurai Seven)

T 1/6 Lo-Fi Generator

W 2/6 Third Eye Foundation

Th 3/6 Peel Sessions 'nearly' live from the Queen
Elizabeth Hall: Cay, Solex, Stereolab

T 8/6 Flossie & The Unicorns

W 9/6 10 5 Neutron

Th 10/6 (Motor Life Co)

T 15/6 Calexico

W 16/6 Union Kid

Th 17/6 (Hefner's gospel covers session)

T 22/6 Low

W 23/6 Pilot Can

Th 24/6 four-hour live show from Glastonbury
with Peel and Lamacq

St 26/6 three-hour extra show from Glastonbury with
Peel and Mary Anne Hobbs, with recorded sets
from: Super Furry Animals, REM, Underworld, Manic
Street Preachers

T 29/6 Black Star Liner recorded live at Glastonbury

W 30/6 Billy Bragg & the Blokes recorded live at
Glastonbury

Th 1/7 (Novak)

T 6/7 Dawn of the Replicants

W 7/7 Ha-Lo live DJ set from Maida Vale

Th 8/7 (Bonnie Prince Billy)

T 13/7 Six By Seven

W 14/7 Secret Goldfish

Th 15/7 (Wagonchrist)

T 20/7 Flaming Stars

W 21/7 Frank Black & The Catholics

Th 22/7 (Klute)

T 27/7 Man Or Astroman

W 28/7 Flaming Lips

Th 29/7 Loudon Wainwright live from Peel Acres

T 3/8 Miss Mend

W 4/8 Senseless Prayer

Th 5/8 Plaid

T 10/8 John Armstrong live DJ set

W 11/8 Fokkewolf

• Thurs shows start 10 mins earlier at 10pm
from 12/8

Th 12/8 Hefner live from Peel Acres

T 17/8 Twist

W 18/8 (Flaming Lips)

Th 19/8 Jim O'Rourke presented by Steve Lamacq

T 24/8 Pastels

W 25/8 Lolita Storm

Th 26/8 Khaya

Sn 29/8 BBC2 TV 9pm–12.30am John Peel Night:
Evening of documentaries about Peel to mark his
60th birthday, produced and co-ordinated by Alison
Howe

T 31/8 Peel's 60th birthday celebrations, 8pm–2am, live
from Maida Vale with Scratch Perverts, Gene, Dave
Angel, Pavement; plus extra birthday pre-recorded
session tracks from: Quasi, Pastels, Yo La Tengo,
Cha Cha Cohen, Solex

W 1/9 Bonnie Prince Billy, live set recorded at previous
night's 60th Birthday do

T 2/9 Cinerama, Dave Clarke, recorded 31/8 as part of
Peel's 60th birthday celebrations

T 7/9 no show

W 8/9 Autechre

Th 9/9 Half Man Half Biscuit

T 14/9 Supergrass special including live set
recorded at Peel Acres 23/7

W 15/9 Atari Teenage Riot recorded live at
Reading Festival

Th 16/9 (To Rococo Rot)

T 21/9 Melt Banana live from Maida Vale, Peelenum 1951

W 22/9 Sportique

Th 23/9 (Low)

T 28/9 Broken Dog

• All shows from 29/9 start 10pm, midnight finish

W 29/9 Quickspace

Th 30/9 Hellacopters

T 5/10 Blur session recorded at Peel Acres 17/9

W 6/10 Plone

Th 7/10 Lonnie Donegan, Half Man Half Biscuit,
recorded at Queen Elizabeth Hall 1/10

T 12/10 – Th 21/10 no shows – Peel away on holiday,
replaced by Mary Anne Hobbs, Gilles Peterson, and
Andy Kershaw (21/10 only): new sessions by Light
(12/10) Rooney 13/10)

M 25/10 Extra show, 8pm–midnight, live from Liverpool
for Radio 1 Sound City, with live music from Clinic,
The Flaming Lips and Hefner; Peelenium for 1962

T 26/10 Liverpool Sound City 8pm–midnight: Marine
Research, Appliance, Surreal Madrid; & Peelenium
for 1963

W 27/10 Sound City 8pm–midnight: Tarwater, Plone, To
Rococo Rot

Th 28/10 Sound City 8pm–midnight: Salako, Stereolab,
Pavement

T 2/11 Cinerama

W 3/11 Tram

Th 4/11 Ooberman, recorded live at
Liverpool Sound City 24/10

T 9/11 Elastica

W 10/11 Butterflies Of Love

Th 11/11 Michael Hurley

T 16/11 Quasi

W 17/11 BBC1 TV / BBC News 24 / BBC World,
various times, Peel interviewed on Hard Talk by Tim
Sebastian, 23-minute show

W 17/11 Radar Brothers

Th 18/11 Pop Off Tuesday

T 23/11 Magoo

W 24/11 Woodbine, L'Augmentation, both live
from Maida Vale

Th 25/12 (Flossie & The Unicorns)

T 30/11 Echoboy

W 1/12 Murry the Hump

Th 2/12 (Calexico)

T 7/12 ('Race With The Devil: The Gene Vincent Story'
rpt R2 9–10pm)

T 7/12 Nectarine No. 9, Yo La Tengo, recorded live at
Queen Elizabeth Hall 4/12

W 8/12 Christmas Carols live from Maida Vale 3, with Gene 'Someone for Everyone', Hefner 'Lonely this Christmas', High Fidelity 'Silent Night', Broken Dog 'Joy to the World', Marine Research 'In The Bleak Midwinter'; carols by show choir plus Peel family, accompanied by Martin Rossiter and Yolisa Phahle on the piano

Th 9/12 Billy Bragg recorded at QEH 4/12, Peelenium for 1983

T 14/12 Guided By Voices

W 15/12 Beulah

Th 16/12 Pachinos

T 21/12 Black Heart Procession

W 22/12 Fonn

Th 23/12 – W 29/12 Festive 50 for 1999

Th 30/12 no show

2000

T 4/1 All-Time Festive 50, 50–46; Peelenium 1992

W 5/1 All-Time Festive 50, 45–41

Th 6/1 All-Time Festive 50, 40–36

T 11/1 The Cheap Day return to Groningen including Zdob Si Zdub, Hefner recorded 8/01

W 12/1 The Make-Up; All-Time Festive 50 35–31

Th 13/1 Bluetip; All-Time Festive 50 30–26

T 18/1 Ui; All-Time Festive 50 25–21

W 19/1 Mouse on Mars; All-Time Festive 50 20–16

Th 20/1 (Man or Astroman) All-Time Festive 50 15–11; Peelenium concludes 2000

T 25/1 Derrero; All-Time Festive 50 10–6

W 26/1 Samurai Seven; All-Time Festive 50, 5–1

Th 27/1 Clinic

T 1/2 Add N To (X)

W 2/2 Dustball

Th 3/2 Appliance

T 8/2 Monkey Steals The Drum

W 9/2 Broadcast

Th 10/2 Tystion

T 15/2 Creeping Bent 5th Birthday night live from Maida Vale with Element, Speeder

W 16/2 U-ziq

Th 17/2 Melys

T 22/2 Trans AM

W 23/2 Angelica

Th 24/2 (Quasi)

T 29/2 Samurai Seven's covers session

W 1/3 Super Furry Animals

Th 2/3 (Elastica)

T 7/3 Laika

W 8/3 Luke Slater live from Maida Vale

Th 9/3 Mira Calix

T 14/3 Live sets recorded at Chemikal Underground Records' 5th Birthday party on 12/3/00 at the Garage, Glasgow, including: Arab Strap, Bis, The Delgados, Mogwai, Suckle, Magoo, Aereogramme

W 15/3 Magnetophone

Th 16/3 (Mouse on Mars)

T 21/3 Ballboy

W 22/3 Alfie

Th 23/3 Inter

T 28/3 Hefner

T 29/3 Peel Sessions 'almost' live from the Union Chapel, London, with Solex, High Fidelity and Murry the Hump live

Th 30/3 Calexico live from Peel Acres

T 4/4 Lupine Howl

W 5/4 Gorky's Zygotic Mynci

Th 6/4 (The Make Up)

T 11/4 Bardot Pond, Sigur Ros, Wire, And You Will Know Us By The Trail Of The Dead, Papa M, Clinic, all recorded live at All Tomorrow's Parties, Camber Sands, 7–9/4

W 12/4 Persil, plus one Hefner session track not broadcast 28/3 'Everything's Falling Apart'

Th 13/4 (Appliance) (Calexico, repeat of single track interrupted by emergency tape during live session from Peel Acres 30/3)

T 18/4 Pluto Monkey

W 19/4 DJ Food

Th 20/4 One Live from the Scala, Kings Cross, London, with live music from Beulah, Luke Vibert & B J Cole, Super Furry Animals

T 25/4 Reviver Gene

W 26/4 Richie Hawtin live from Maida Vale

Th 27/4 Cats Against the Bomb

T 2/5 Fantasmagroover

W 3/5 Kid Koala

Th 4/5 Aereogramme

T 9/5 Arab Strap

W 10/5 Cuban Boys' covers session, plus one Arab Strap session track not broadcast 9/5

Th 11/5 One Live in Europe, presented from Radio Eins in Potsdam, Berlin, with Sender Berlin in session, recorded 'as live' at their flat earlier same day

T 16/5 Delgados

W 17/5 Pete Wylie

Th 18/5 People Under The Stairs

T 23/5 Presented from BBC Pebble Mill, Birmingham for One Live, with live DJ set by Surgeon

W 24/5 Live from the Irish Centre in Digbeth, Birmingham, with Plone, Magnetophone and Broadcast playing live

T 25/5 no show

T 30/5 Lianne Hall & Pico

W 31/5 Wheat

Th 1/6 Chicks On Speed

T 6/6 Khaya

W 7/6 Travis Cut

Th 8/6 Suckle

T 13/6 Lolita Storm

W 14/6 Cinerama live from Maida Vale 3

Th 15/6 (Monkey Steals the Drum)

T 20/6 Kid 606 vs The Remote Viewer

W 21/6 Brassy

Th 22/6 Radar Brothers

St 24/6 extra show from Glastonbury, with live or recorded sets from: Cay, Dave Clarke, Pete Shop Boys, Elastica, Leftfield, Travis

T 27/6 E-Z Rollers recorded at Glastonbury

W 28/6 Freestylers recorded at Glastonbury

Th 29/6 Leftfield recorded at Glastonbury

T 4/7 Delgados recorded live at the Union Chapel 13/5

W 5/7 Six By Seven

Th 6/7 Laura Cantrell & The Radio Sweethearts

T 11/7 – Th 13/7 with Gilles Peterson, Peel on holiday

T 18/7 Blonde Redhead

W 19/7 DMC World DJ Championship UK Finalists, live from Maida Vale, featuring Yo 1, Woody, Tigerstyle, Mr Thing, Plus One, Mad Cut

Th 20/7 Cat Power's covers session part one

T 25/7 Piano Magic

W 26/7 Sex Clark Five

Th 27/7 Cowcube

T 1/8 Spraydog

W 2/8 Pilote

Th 3/8 (Tystion)

T 8/8 Element

W 9/8 Whistler

Th 10/8 (Lupine Howl)

T 15/8 Pram

W 16/8 And You Will Know Us By The Trail Of Dead live from Maida Vale

Th 17/8 (Pluto Monkey)

T 22/8 Clinic

W 23/8 Hefner live from Maida Vale

Th 24/8 (Kid Koala)

T 29/8 eX-Girl

W 30/8 (Melt Banana)

Th 31/8 Cat Power's cover versions session part two

T 5/9 Broken Dog

W 6/9 Rothko

Th 7/9 no show – Gilles Peterson

T 12/9 (Delgados)

W 13/9 Neko Case and Her Boyfriends live from Maida Vale

Th 14/9 Trembling Blue Stars

T 19/9 Cinerama

W 20/9 Solex live from Maida Vale

Th 21/9 Electric Music AKA

T 26/9 Sigur Ros

W 27/9 Portal

Th 28/9 Four Brothers

T 3/10 Ten Benson

W 4/10 Kelis

Th 5/10 Dick Dale programme midnight–2am

T 10/10 Herman Dune

W 11/10 Nought

Th 12/10 Ant

T 17/10 The Kingsbury Manx

W 18/10 Heads

Th 19/10 Mukka

T 24/10 Live from Clwb Ifor Bach, Cardiff, for Radio One Live, with Melys, Reviver Gene, Gorky's Zygotic Mynci (acoustic set)

W 25/10 Live from Clwb Ifor Bach, Cardiff, Radio One Live, with Topper, Murry the Hump, Derrero

Th 26/10 Live from The Coal Exchange, Cardiff, Radio One Live, with PJ Harvey, Tystion, Clinic

T 31/10 Gene

W 1/11 Man or Astroman live from Maida Vale

Th 2/11 Radio Sweethearts

T 7/11 Richie Hawtin and John Acquaviva live from Maida Vale

W 8/11 Low live from Maida Vale

Th 9/11 Monkey Steals The Drum

T 14/11 The Wisdom of Harry

W 15/11 Do Make Say Think

Th 16/11 (Laura Cantrell & The Radio Sweethearts)

T 21/11 Sodastream

W 22/11 Tompaulin

Th 23/11 Incredible String Band

T 28/11 Clearlake

W 29/11 Echoboy

Th 30/11 (Electronic Music AKA)

T 5/12 Cay

W 6/12 Dave Clarke live DJ set at Maida Vale

Th 7/12 (Ballboy)

T 12/12 Brave Captain

W 13/12 (Cat Power's cover versions session pts 1 & 2)

Th 14/12 Lorimer

T 19/12 John Peel's 25 Years Of The Festive 50 Special, rec 13/12 MV3: including versions/covers of F50 favourites by Billy Bragg, J Mascis 'Everything flows', Hefner 'Hymn For The Alcohol', David Gedge, Gary Numan, Mansun 'Shot by both sides', plus the Festive 50 Pop Quiz

W 20/12 PJ Harvey

Th 21/12 Christmas Special live from Peel Acres, with live music from Cinerama 'Christmas Song', Murry The Hump 'Walking In A Winter Wonderland', Wisdom of Harry 'You Make Me Sick At Xmas', and Herman Dune 'Channukah In Florida', plus the handbell ringers of Bucksall and singalong carols

T 26/12 – Th 28/12 Festive 50

2001

T 2/1 – Th 4/1 records only
T 9/1 Melys recorded at the Noorderslag Festival, Groningen, Holland
W 10/1 J Mascis and The Fog
Th 11/1 (Low)
T 16/1 Hefner, including – by mistake – repeat of their David Soul cover 'Don't Give Up' from session, 1st TX 28/3/00
W 17/1 (Cowcube)
Th 18/1 Rechenzentrum
T 23/1 Alfie
W 24/1 Union Kid
Th 25/1 (Wisdom of Harry)
T 30/1 Tram
W 31/1 MC Mabon
Th 1/2 Laura Cantrell live from Peel Acres
T 6/2 Sportique
W 7/2 Gary Numan live from Maida Vale
Th 8/2 (Sodastream)
T 13/2 (PJ Harvey live at the Coal Exchange Cardiff)
W 14/2 Grover
Th 15/2 Bonnie Prince Billy
T 20/2 Add N To (X)
W 21/2 Degrassi
Th 22/2 (Neko Case and Her Boyfriends)
T 27/2 Jack Drag
W 28/2 90 Day Men
Th 1/3 (Gene)
T 6/3 (Captain Beefheart and his Magic Band #1, 1st TX 4/2/68)
W 7/3 (Captain Beefheart and his Magic Band #2, 1st TX 12/5/68)
Th 8/3 (Trembling Blue Stars)
T 13/3 El Hombre Trajeado
W 14/3 Jellicoe
Th 15/3 (Herman Dune)
T 20/3 Nectarine No 9
W 21/3 Samurai Seven
Th 22/3 Mighty Math
T 27/3 Extreme Noise Terror
W 28/3 Riviera
Th 29/3 Dead Meadow
T 3/4 El Goodo
W 4/4 DJ Bone live at Maida Vale
Th 5/4 (Bonnie Prince Billy)
T 10/4 The Aislers Set
W 11/4 (Hefner)
Th 12/4 Stephen Malkmus, Calexico with Neko Case, recorded live at ULU for One Live
T 17/4 (Alfie)
W 18/4 Derrero
Th 19/4 Zabrinski; plus Lift To Experience, recorded live at ULU for One Live 12/4
T 24/4 Cane 141
W 25/4 Interpol
Th 26/4 (Tim Buckley #1, 1st TX 7/4/68)
T 1/5 Bees
W 2/5 Spare Snare
Th 3/5 (J Mascis and the Fog)
T 8/5 Astrid
W 9/5 Live from Radio Mafia, Helsinki, with live recordings from Levitation by: Paleface, Lemonator, Kwan, plus 'the Pig's Big Bells in Vaskikolo'
Th 10/5 Ikara Colt
T 15/5 Mouse on Mars
W 16/5 Seedling and Melys live from Maida Vale
Th 17/5 Centromatic
T 22/5 Hopewell
W 23/5 Stakka & Skynet live from Maida Vale

Th 24/5 Cinerama
T 29/5 (Add N to (x))
W 30/5 Lift to Experience
Th 31/5 (Jack Drag)
T 5/6 cLOUDDEAD
W 6/6 Ash live from Maida Vale
Th 7/6 (Mighty Math)
T 12/6 Bardo Pond
W 13/6 Loves
Th 14/6 (Calexico with Neko Case live at ULU)
T 19/6 Belle and Sebastian
W 20/6 Meanwhile Back In Communist Russia
T 21/6 programme recorded at Sonar, Barcelona, with live sets from: Dave Torrida, Carl Cox
T 26/6 Chapter 13
W 27/6 Strokes
Th 28/6 Appendix Out
T 3/7 DJ Wilbur Wilburforce DJ set
W 4/7 Preston School of Industry
Th 5/7 Sean Dickson live from Peel Acres
T 10/7 (Belle and Sebastian)
W 11/7 Bearsuit
Th 12/7 Super Furry Animals live from Peel Acres
T 17/7 Aqua Vista
W 18/7 Miss Black America
Th 19/7 (The Aislers Set)
T 24/7 The Icarus Line
W 25/7 White Stripes live from Maida Vale
Th 26/7 (Centromatic)
T 31/7 (Lift to Experience)
W 1/8 Llwybr Llaethog (Son House, 1st TX 11/7/70)
Th 2/8 Kaito
T 7/8 Appliance
W 8/8 Live from Maida Vale with UK finalists in the DMC World DJ Championships: Theory, Skully, Primetime, Woody, Plus One
Th 9/8 I Am Kloot
T 14/8 Camera Obscura
W 15/8 Wagonchrist
Th 16/8 (PJ Harvey)
T 21/8 Saloon
W 22/8 (Strokes)
Th 23/8 Cat Power, live at Peel Acres
T 28/8 Pulp
W 29/8 Lift To Experience live from Maida Vale
Th 30/8 (Culture #1 & #2)
T 4/9 And You Will Know Us By The Trail Of Dead recorded live at the Reading Festival
W 5/9 Stephen Malkmus recorded live at Reading
Th 6/9 PJ Harvey recorded live at Reading
T 11/9 no show – Steve Lamacq with the latest from the Mercury Music Awards
W 12/9 presented by Mary Anne Hobbs; Peel admitted to hospital with diabetes on '9/11'
Th 13/9 presented by Steve Lamacq
T 18/9 Stereolab
W 19/9 Gene live from Maida Vale
T 20/9 Gorky's Zygotic Mynci performing live at Peel Acres
T 25/9 The Locust
W 26/9 Bearsuit and Loves live from Maida Vale
Th 27/9 Loudon Wainwright III live from Peel Acres
T 2/10 Nebula
W 3/10 Melt Banana live from Maida Vale
Th 4/10 Quasi
T 9/10 (White Stripes live at Maida Vale)
W 10/10 Lab 4 live from Maida Vale 3
Th 11/10 Peel's 40th year in broadcasting party, plus special guests, recorded on 24/9 at King's College Student's Union, London, with live guests: Billy Bragg, Nick Cave, Pulp, & New Order on video
T 16/10 Aaviko

W 17/10 Mogwai live from Maida Vale
Th 18/10 A R E Weapons
T 23/10 Magoo
W 24/10 Garlic
Th 25/10 Mull Historical Society
T 30/10 live from the Medicine Bar in Birmingham, with live guests Regis, Richie Hawtin, Surgeon
W 31/10 live music from Appliance, Pulp, Meanwhile Back in Communist Russia, at the Birmingham Academy
Th 1/11 live from the Custard Factory in Birmingham, with Hefner, Ikara Colt, Seedling
T 6/11 Fabio, live DJ set from R1 Live Lounge, Yalding House
W 7/11 Aereogramme
Th 8/11 White Stripes live from Peel Acres

• **Anita Kamath switched to produce The Blue Room and The Lock-Up**

• **Louise Kattenhorn made Peel show producer**

T 13/11 Solex
W 14/11 S I Futures aka Si Begg live from Maida Vale
Th 15/11 Mercury Rev
T 20/11 Tompaulin
W 21/11 Hives
Th 22/11 show live from Maida Vale with Von Bondies
T 27/11 Dirtbombs live 'down the line' from Maida Vale
W 28/11 Six By Seven
Th 29/11 Rock of Travolta
T 4/12 Wauvenfold
W 5/12 Unfinished Sympathy
Th 6/12 Lianne Hall & Friends
T 11/12 Hefner
W 12/12 Aspects
Th 13/12 Panoptica
T 18/12 Mr Psyche DJ mix session
W 19/12 Tystion and Llwybr Llaethog live from Maida Vale
Th 20/12 Christmas special live from Peel Acres, with Camera Obscura, Lianne Hall, and Melys, doing Christmas songs, plus carol singing, the village bellringers, and a track recorded specially by Cowcube
T 25/12 – Th 27/12 Festive 50

2002

T 1/1 (Pulp)
W 2/1 Low
Th 3/1 Smog
T 8/1 Aina
W 9/1 Cinerama live from Maida Vale
Th 10/1 (Melys acoustic session repeat from The Session In Wales)
T 15/1 Aereogramme, The Bays, from Noorderslag/Eurosonic festival in Groningen
W 16/1 Dreadzone live from Maida Vale
Th 17/1 (Mercury Rev)
T 22/1 Buick 6, & Peel starts playing a record a night from his final Perfumed Garden show from Radio London, August 1967
W 23/1 (Bearsuit)
Th 24/1 Cowcube
T 29/1 Mr T Bird
W 30/1 Shifty Disco 5th Birthday Party: AM 60, Dustball live from Maida Vale
Th 31/1 Ladytron
T 5/2 Chukki Star and the Ruff Cutt Band
W 6/2 Mos Eisley
Th 7/2 Pinhole
T 12/2 live DJ mix set from Rory Phillips
W 13/2 Clinic live from Maida Vale
Th 14/2 Loves live from Peel Acres

T 19/2 Flaming Stars

W 20/2 no show: R1 backstage at the Brit Awards instead

Th 21/2 Bong Ra recorded in own studio

T 26/2 Kanda Bongo Man

W 27/2 Ballboy, Degrassi in SL Records bash live from MV4

Th 28/2 Little George Sueref

M 4/3 BBC2 TV, 10–10.30pm, John Peel is Paul Merton's guest on 'Room 101' and tries to consign to Orwellian oblivion his pet hates including beards, shopping, men with colds and driving through Essex

T 5/3 (Mr Psyche DJ mix)

W 6/3 Bays live from Maida Vale

Th 7/3 Camera Obscura live from Peel Acres

T 12/3 – Th 4/4 Peel away for 4 weeks: instead, Mary Ann Hobbs (Tuesdays) Gilles Peterson (Wed) Fabio & Grooverider (Thurs) each week

T 9/4 Soul Centre aka Thomas Brinkmann recorded live at Fabric London 6/4

W 10/4 Ikara Colt live from Maida Vale

Th 11/4 Seedling

T 16/4 Technical Itch DJ mix

W 17/4 Cornershop live from Maida Vale

Th 18/4 Travis Cut

T 23/4 Live highlights from All Tomorrow's Parties, Camber Sands 19–21/4: Shellac, Shipping News

W 24/4 Live highlights from All Tomorrow's Parties, including Nina Nastasia

T 25/4 Live highlights from All Tomorrow's Parties: Low, Wire, Smog, Rachel's, Dianogah

T 30/4 And You Will Know Us By The Trail of Dead

W 1/5 Come-Ons, Datsuns live from Maida Vale

Th 2/5 Samurai Seven

T 7/5 live DJ set from Dave Clarke in the R1 Live Lounge, Yalding House

W 8/5 Alliance Underground

Th 9/5 Mclusky

T 14/5 Hint

W 15/5 Herman Dune live from Maida Vale

Th 16/5 cancelled, line to Peel Acres lost, repeat of show of 15/1/02 instead

T 21/5 AC Acoustics

W 22/5 Jeff Mills live DJ set from Maida Vale

Th 23/5 Ronnie Ronalde

T 28/5 Anti Hero

W 29/5 Persil

Th 30/5 no show: the Session in Scotland at Music Live, The Shetland Isles

T 4/6 Nina Nastasia engineered by Steve Albini in his own studio

W 5/6 Oxes live from Maida Vale

Th 6/6 presented by Donna Legge as link to Peel Acres lost; repeats of DJ sets by (Rory Phillips 12/2, Jeff Mills 22/5)

T 11/6 The Sex Clark Five's Marc Bolan covers session

W 12/6 Liars

Th 13/6 Goatboy

Th 13/6 Oneworld special, presented by Peel live from Sonar festival, Barcelona, 12 midnight–2am

T 18/6 Tigerbeat 6 artists recorded at the Sonar Festival: Cex, Kid 606

W 19/6 Helsinki artists recorded at Sonar Festival: Didier & Anonymous DJ, Aaviko

Th 20/6 Fragile Discos artists from Sonar Festival: DJ Lopez, Audioperu

T 25/6 Vaults

W 26/6 AM60

Th 27/6 Von Bondies in a 'Dr Peel's Driving Down to Glastonbury' Special

T 2/7 DJ Rupture recorded live at Sonar Festival

W 3/7 Miss Black America

Th 4/7 Nina Nastasia live from Peel Acres

T 9/7 Culture

W 10/7 Catheters

Th 11/7 Corvin Dalek DJ mix session

T 16/7 Loudon Wainwright III

W 17/7 Boom Bip & Dose One, cLOUDEAD live from Maida Vale 4

Th 18/7 Circle part one of session

T 23/7 Misty

W 24/7 Icarus Line

T 25/7 Belle & Sebastian live from Peel Acres

T 30/7 Coin-Op

W 31/7 Jeffrey Lewis live from Maida Vale 4

Th 1/8 Bearsuit

T 6/8 Sender Berlin recorded at Fabric 2/8

W 7/8 Track and Field label night: Dressy Bessy, Saloon live from Maida Vale 4

Th 8/8 Will Oldham

T 13/8 Bellrays

W 14/8 Eon live from Maida Vale 4

Th 15/8 Cranebuilders

T 20/8 Fixit Kid

W 21/8 The D4

Th 22/8 Yeah Yeah Yeahs

T 27/8 From the Reading/Leeds Festivals: The Icarus Line, Von Bondies, White Stripes

W 28/8 From the Reading Festival: The Breeders, Pulp

Th 29/8 Melys performing live from Peel Acres in Peel's Birthday Special Show

T 3/9 Half Man Half Biscuit

W 4/9 Caroline Martin

- **Thursday shows Sept 02 put back to midnight–2am for Showcase for 1Xtra, BBC's new digital black music station**

Th 5/9 (Cowcube) 12–2am show

T 10/9 Dick Dale

W 11/9 Herman Dune

Th 12/9 (Anti Hero) 12–2am show

T 17/9 Wire

W 18/9 Acqua Vista

Th 19/9 (Low) 12–2am show

T 24/9 Tocques

W 25/9 Aphrodisiacs

Th 26/9 (And You Will Know Us By The Trail Of Dead) 12–2am show

T 1/10 Coalition

W 2/10 Mudhoney

Th 3/10 Mum

T 8/10 The Dawn Parade

W 9/10 DJ Rupture live from Maida Vale 4

Th 10/10 Pet Shop Boys

T 15/10 Explosions in the Sky

W 16/10 Delgados cover versions session

Th 17/10 Solex

T 22/10 Circle session part two

W 23/10 (Mr Bird)

Th 24/10 Coldcut & Headspace recorded at the Pompidou Centre, Paris, France

T 29/10 Datsuns, McClusky, Wolves of Greece; live from the Boat Club, Radio One live in Nottingham

W 30/10 Bays, Echoboy, P Brothers; live from the Boat Club, Radio One live in Nottingham

Th 31/10 Bearsuit, Miss Black America, Six By Seven; live from the Boat Club, Radio One live in Nottingham

T 5/11 Laura Cantrell

W 6/11 Soledad Brothers live from Maida Vale 4

Th 7/11 Part Chimp

T 12/11 Themselves from the Live Lounge

W 13/11 Baptist Generals

Th 14/11 (Vaults)

T 19/11 Appliance

W 20/11 Dawn of the Replicants

Th 21/11 (Loudon Wainwright III)

T 26/11 MASS

W 27/11 Ikara Colt

Th 28/11 J Mascis acoustic session

T 3/12 Terrashima

W 4/12 Loves

Th 5/12 Goldchains

T 10/12 (Aphrodisiacs)

W 11/12 Ten Minute Men: Billy Mahonie, Cove, Hiramcka Hi Fi, Reynolds, Stanton; all live from Maida Vale 4 sharing the same back-line, each playing a ten-minute set

Th 12/12 (Yeah Yeah Yeahs)

T 17/12 Econoline

W 18/12 Belle & Sebastian's Christmas Carol Concert with Peel show choir live from Maida Vale 4

Th 19/12 Fluke

T 24/12, W 25/12, T 31/12 no shows

Th 26/12 Festive 50, 8pm–1am special

2003

W 1/1 (Datsuns live at Maida Vale)

Th 2/1 James Yorkston and the Athletes

T 7/1 Broken Family Band

W 8/1 Ladytron recorded 'as live' at Maida Vale 4/12/02

Th 9/1 Nina Nastasia

T 14/1 Add N To (X)

W 15/1 Xploding Plastix live from Groningen

Th 16/1 Miss Black America playing live from Eurosonic 2003

T 21/1 Bonkers mix

W 22/1 Immortal Lee County Killers live from Maida Vale

Th 23/1 Meanwhile Back in Communist Russia; plus the Burns Night Special, 2 days early, including 'Parcel of Rogues' performed by The Delgados, 'Ye Banks and Braes' by Belle & Sebastian, 'A man's a man for a 'that' by Ballboy

T 28/1 People Like Us

W 29/1 Herman Dune, plus one track from People Like Us not TX on 28/1

Th 30/1 Low live from Peel Acres

T 4/2 records only

W 5/2 The Crimea

Th 6/2 Me Against Them

T 11/2 Three Stages of Pain

W 12/2 Cat Power

Th 13/2 Mountain Goats

T 18/2 Anti Hero

W 19/2 Aereogramme

Th 20/2 (Appliance)

T 25/2 Mr Airplane Man

W 26/2 Jeff Mills' DJ set live from Maida Vale

T 27/2 (Caroline Martin)

T 4/3 Skynet in the Live Lounge

W 5/3 Exiles, Dawn Parade, both live from Maida Vale

Th 6/3 Echoboy

T 11/3 Detroit Cobras

W 12/3 Hyper Kinako

Th 13/3 The Fall

T 18/3 Michael Mayer's Kompakt Records mix

W 19/3 Yourcodenameis: Milo

Th 20/3 Ballboy

T 25/3 knifehandchop

W 26/3 Kitty Yo label night: Jeans Team, Tarwater, live from Maida Vale

Th 27/3 (Baptist Generals)

T 1/4 Boom Bip

W 2/4 Vaults

Th 3/4 (J Mascis acoustic session)

T 8/4 (Explosions in the Sky)

W 9/4 Hellacopters live from Maida Vale

Th 10/4 Venetian Snares recorded live at

All Tomorrow's Parties
T 15/4 Tigerstyle
W 16/4 Saloon
Th 17/4 Surgeon recorded live at All Tomorrow's Parties
T 22/4 Land of Nod
W 23/4 Numbers
Th 24/4 (James Yorkston & the Athletes)
T 29/4 The Magic Band recorded live at
   All Tomorrow's Parties
W 30/4 Calexico
Th 1/5 Nina Nastasia live from Peel Acres
T 6/5 25BZ
W 7/5 Black Keys
Th 8/5 Laura Cantrell live from Peel Acres
T 13/5 Aphex Twin recorded live at All Tomorrow's Parties
W 14/5 Undertones
Th 15/5 Herman Dune live from Peel Acres
T 20/5 Pram
W 21/5 Mogwai live from Maida Vale
Th 22/5 (The Fall)
T 27/5 Autechre mix
W 28/5 Prewar Yardsale
Th 29/5 (The Crimea)
T 3/6 Locus
W 4/6 Cinerama
Th 5/6 Buzzcocks
T 10/6 Rogers Sisters
W 11/6 Caroline Martin
Th 12/6 Sonar joint Peel/One World Special, 10pm–2am:
   live sets from Themselves, Sole, Pole, Komputer,
   Potrik Pulsinger
T 17/6 More from Sonar: live set from Pulseprogramming
W 18/6 Sonar: live sets from Schneider TM, Akufen
Th 19/6 Sonar: live sets from Appliance, T Raumschmiere
T 24/6 Cranebuilders
W 25/6 Soledad Brothers
Th 26/6 Magoo
T 1/7 Super Furry Animals recorded live at Glastonbury
W 2/7 Flaming Lips recorded live at Glastonbury
Th 3/7 (Cat Power)
T 8/7 Izzys
W 9/7 Clotaire K
Th 10/7 (Hyper Kinako)
T 15/7 Blizzard Boys 'in the mix'
W 16/7 Cass McCombs
Th 17/7 Of Arrowe Hill
T 22/7 Young People
T 23/7 Reprise of 'Ten-Minute Men': Bilge Pump,
   Charltiefield, I'm Being Good, Joey Fat, Twinkle; all
   live from Maida Vale, all playing ten-minute sets only
T 24/7 Seedling
T 29/7 Mos Eisley
W 30/7 Kills
Th 31/7 Black Keys live from Peel Acres
T 5/8 – Th 14/8 Peel away: replaced by Mary Ann
   Hobbs, Gilles Peterson, Fabio & Grooverider, J Da
   Flex, DJ Bailey, Ras Kwame
T 19/8 Broadcast
W 20/8 The French
Th 21/8 Kanda Bongo Man recorded live at Glastonbury
T 26/8 Exiles
W 27/8 Loudon Wainwright III
Th 28/8 Gorky's Zygotic Mynci
T 2/9 Blueskins
W 3/9 Gossip
Th 4/9 Barcelona Pavilion
T 9/9 Keys
W 10/9 DMC World DJ Championships UK-finalists live
   from Maida Vale: DJ Blakey, DJ Tiger Style, DJ 2 Tall,
   DJ Daredevil, DJ Quest
Th 11/9 Pretty Girls Make Graves
T 16/9 Si Begg
W 17/9 Grandmaster Gareth's 'Monster Melody'

Th 18/9 Marlowe
T 23/9 DJ Twitch's Optimo Mix
W 24/9 David Jack
Th 25/9 (Ballboy)
T 30/9 Golden Virgins
W 1/10 Futureheads
Th 2/10 (Soledad Brothers)
T 7/10 Camera Obscura
W 8/10 T Raumschmiere live from Maida Vale
Th 9/10 (Black Keys)
T 14/10 Four Tet
W 15/10 Forty Fives
Th 16/10 Plaid
T 21/10 Ascii Disko
W 22/10 Three Inches of Blood
Th 23/10 Pico
T 28/10 Black Keys, Stephen Malkmus & The Jicks,
   Themselves, live from the Old Market in Brighton for
   One Live; Clearlake, live from Corn Exchange
W 29/10 Electrelane, Gorky's Zygotic Mynci, Nina
   Nastasia, live from the Old Market, Brighton, for
   One Live
Th 30/10 Melt Banana, Coin-Op, Cat On Form, Michael
   Mayer, all live from Concorde 2, Brighton, for One
   Live
T 4/11 records only
W 5/11 Bilge Pump
Th 6/11 (The French)
T 11/11 Erase Errata
W 12/11 The Bug vs Soundmurderer, live 'soundclash'
   mix plus several MCs from Maida Vale
Th 13/11 (Keys)
T 18/11 Immortal Lee County Killers
W 19/11 Vaults live from Maida Vale 4
T 20/11 Freddy Fresh Mix 2003
T 25/11 Million Dead
W 26/11 Workhouse
Th 27/11 (Blizzard Boys)
T 2/12 Shesus
W 3/12 Maher Shalal Hash Baz
Th 4/12 (David Jack)
T 9/12 Young Heart Attack
W 10/12 Underworld live from Maida Vale
Th 11/12 Midnight Evils
T 16/12 Anaal Nathrakh
W 17/12 Christ, Schneider TM, live from Maida Vale
Th 18/12 (Camera Obscura)
T 23/12 Ballboy, Laura Cantrell, live from Peel Acres,
   plus carols sung live by the Peel family choir
W 24/12 & Th 25/12 Festive 50, parts one & two
T 30/12 – Th 1/1/04 no shows

2004

T 6/1 Cinerama
W 7/1 Fuck
Th 8/1 Modena City Ramblers, Carpark North, Frames,
   Franz Ferdinand all recorded live at Groningen festival
T 13/1 Cranebuilders live in Groningen
W 14/1 Unfinished Sympathy
Th 15/1 (Pico)
T 20/1 Earth the Californian Love Dream
W 21/1 (Jeff Mills)
Th 22/1 Camera Obscura live from Peel Acres in another
   Burns Supper special, 3 days early
T 27/1 Baby Woodrose, Hell on Wheels, Myslovitz,
   Minus, Modena City Ramblers, recorded live in
   Groningen
W 28/1 Thermals
Th 29/1 Electrelane
T 3/2 Jack White with live tracks from R1 Live Lounge,
   Yalding House, plus interview

W 4/2 Dave Clarke live from Maida Vale
Th 5/2 Herman Dune
T 10/2 Hells
W 11/2 Explosions in the Sky
Th 12/2 (Three Inches of Blood)
T 17/2 Sluts of Trust
W 18/2 Von Bondies
Th 19/2 (Grandmaster Gareth's Monster Melody)
T 24/2 Biffy Clyro
W 25/2 E-Z Rollers 'in the mix'
Th 26/2 (Erase Errata)
T 2/3 Secret Hairdresser
W 3/3 Ikara Colt
Th 4/3 (Million Dead)
T 9/3 Read Yellow
W 10/3 Richie Hawtin live from Maida Vale
Th 11/3 I Am Kloot
T 16/3 Broken Family Band
W 17/3 Hixxy in the Mix
Th 18/3 (Maher Shalal Hash Baz)
T 23/3 Harpies
W 24/3 Soledad Brothers
Th 25/3 (Part Chimp)
T 30/3 Live sets recorded at ATP 2004 by Part Chimp,
   Envy, Mogwai
W 31/3 Erase Errata, Lightning Bolt, live from
   Maida Vale
Th 1/4 Trans Am, Cat Power, recorded live at
   All Tomorrow's Parties
T 6/4 Cex, recorded live at All Tomorrow's Parties
W 7/4 Bays live from Maida Vale
Th 8/4 Kid 606 recorded live at All Tomorrow's Parties
T 13/4 Decoration
W 14/4 Jawbone live from Maida Vale
Th 15/4 Nebula
T 20/4 The DM Bob & Jem Finer 2 Man Band
W 21/4 Mr Airplane Man
Th 22/4 Dick Dale
T 27/4 Bardo Pond
W 28/4 Mountain Goats
Th 29/4 records-only show presented from
   BBC BH Glasgow
T 4/5 22–20s
W 5/5 Vaults
Th 6/5 (Electrelane)
T 11/5 Persil
W 12/5 Deerhoof
Th 13/5 (Izzys)
T 18/5 DJ Rupture mix
W 19/5 Morrissey, live from Maida Vale, 2 tracks only,
   shared session with Zane Lowe
Th 20/5 PJ Harvey live from Peel Acres
T 25/5 Trencher
W 26/5 Grime Night: DJ Eastwood & Friends – MC G
   Double E, MC Purple, MC I E, and MC I Q – live mix
   set from Maida Vale
Th 27/5 Datsuns live from the ICA
T 1/6 Numbers
W 2/6 Mugstar
Th 3/6 (Golden Virgins)
T 8/6 Hakan Lidbo mix
W 9/6 Jack Rose
Th 10/6 Nina Nastasia & Huun Huur Tu live
   from Peel Acres
T 15/6 Liars
W 16/6 Apparat
Th 17/6 Bullet, Fibla, Manuvers, Micro Audio Waves,
   Rec Overflow, Sesam O, Sofus Forsberg, all live
   in 4-hour special show, 10pm–2am, from Sonar,
   Barcelona
T 22/6 Doily, Drop The Lime; recorded live at Sonar,
   Barcelona, in a Broklyn Beats Label Special
W 23/6 Shitkatapult label special: Phono, Apparat, Das
   Beirben, recorded live at Sonar, Barcelona

Th 24/6 Domino label special: Four Tet, Max Tundra, recorded live at Sonar, Barcelona

T 29/6 Belle & Sebastian recorded live at Glastonbury

W 30/6 Von Bondies recorded live at Glastonbury

Th 1/7 Live from Peel Acres, with Max Tundra recorded at Sonar

T 6/7 Mclusky

W 7/7 Magic Band live at Maida Vale

Th 8/7 (Harpies)

T 13/7 Love is All

W 14/7 Noxagt

Th 15/7 (Vaults)

T 20/7 Melys

W 21/7 Fotomoto

Th 22/7 Ictus

- **Shows move back to 11pm–1am**

T 27/7 Blueskins

W 28/7 Orbital's final performance live from Maida Vale

Th 29/7 (Biffy Clyro)

T 3/8 Highlights from The Big Chill including Colleen, Isan, Easy Star All Stars

W 4/8 Steveless

Th 5/8 Caroline Martin and Lianne Hall

T 10/8 Showcasing 1Xtra's Dancehall DJ Robbo Ranx and MC Lady Saw

W 11/8 Mono

Th 12/8 The Fall

T 17/8 Showcasing 1Xtra's Garage DJ J Da Flex & MC Crazy D

W 18/8 The French's TV Themes session

Th 19/8 Mr Psyche mix

T 24/8 Showcasing 1Xtra's DJ Bailey with MC SP

W 25/8 Fort Dax

Th 26/8 Line to Peel Acres fails again: instead, Shitmat's 'Shitmix' (plus live concert set repeats: Aphex Twin from All Tomorrow's Parties 2002; WYZ from Sonar 2002; Xploding Plastik from Eurosonic 2003)

T 31/8 Darren Styles 'in the mix'

W 1/9 Graham Coxon

Th 2/9 (Deerhoof)

T 7/9 Calvin Party

W 8/9 Superqueens

Th 9/9 (Liars)

T 14/9 Detroit Cobras

W 15/9 first half of an exclusive mix by Jeff Mills and Laurent Garnier from Maida Vale

Th 16/9 second half of an exclusive mix by Jeff Mills and Laurent Garnier from Maida Vale

T 21/9 The Wedding Present

W 22/9 Little Killers and Hunches live from Maida Vale

Th 23/9 Delgados

T 28/9 EZ T

W 29/9 Forty Fives

Th 30/9 The Double

T 5/10 Aphrodisiacs

W 6/10 Super Furry Animals in show pre-recorded 'as live' from Maida Vale

Th 7/10 (The Fall) presented from Peel Acres with guest Damon Albarn

T 12/10 Polysics

W 13/10 Phillip Roebuck live mix set live from Maida Vale

Th 14/10 (Trencher)

T 19/10 Rick Smith and Karl Hyde from Underworld, guest presenters

W 20/10 Siouxsie Sioux, guest presenter

Th 21/10 Robert Smith of The Cure, guest presenter

- **John Peel dies 25/10/04, Peru**

T 26/10 Steve Lamacq hosts Peel tribute (many session repeats)

W 27/10 Mary Ann Hobbs hosts Peel tribute (many, as above)

Th 28/10 Steve Lamacq & Mary Ann Hobbs host Peel tribute (many, as above)

T 2/11 – 23/12 Rob Da Bank hosts show, using Peel's already planned running orders, and already commissioned or recorded sessions:

T 2/11 Lali Puna

W 3/11 Oxes

Th 4/11 (Mono)

T 9/11 Ballboy

W 10/11 Magoo

Th 11/11 Skimmer

F 12/11 John Peel's Funeral, Bury St Edmunds Cathedral, Suffolk

T 16/11 Half Man Half Biscuit

W 17/11 Jack Rose, Glenn Jones and Simon Joyner recorded 'as live' earlier that day at Maida Vale

Th 18/11 Hot Snakes

T 23/11 Avrocar

W 24/11 Yourcodenameis: Milo

Th 25/11 Bloody Hollies

T 30/11 Bloc Party

W 1/12 Six By Seven

Th 2/12 Shellac recorded 'as live' at Maida Vale previous day

T 7/12 FSK

W 8/12 Wolf Eyes

Th 9/12 65 Days of Static

T 14/12 Max Tundra

W 15/12 Ella Guru

Th 16/12 Keepin' It Peel Tribute Night, 7pm–1am live from Maida Vale, with documentary presented by Jarvis Cocker, records chosen by guests, and live sets from: PJ Harvey, Damon Albarn, Belle and Sebastian, Gorky's Zygotic Mynci, Hefner, Trencher, Melys, Graham Coxon, Steveless, The Wedding Present, Nina Nastasia; plus DJ sets from Coldcut, Dreadzone, DJ Fresh, Jon E Cash, Alex Patterson, Hixxy, Dave Clarke, Mike Paradinas, Shitmat, Scotch Egg, Underworld

T 21/12 Sunn O)))

W 22/12 Vitalic, live from Maida Vale

Th 23/12 Me Against Them

T 28/12 – Th 30/12 Festive 50

15/2/05 Stuffy and the Fuses

1/3/05 The Mutts

17/3/05 The Workhouse

C H A P T E R   1 2

THE SESSIONS A–Z contains full details of all sessions featured on BBC Radio 1 programmes presented by John Peel between 2 October 1967 and 14 October 2004. Also included for completeness are the 16 sessions first broadcast on three early editions of Top Gear which Peel did not present or co-present (8, 15 & 22/10/67), eight new sessions introduced by guests on Top Gear when Peel was ill or away (1970–1973), and the 25 sessions recorded or commissioned before his death and honoured by Louise Kattenhorn and broadcast by other R1 DJs between 2/11/04 and 17/3/05. I have also listed all 21 performances at the Keepin It Peel night on 16/12/04. For the years up to 1992, as featured in my previous book In Session Tonight, I have also gone back and restored some dozen or so sessions I had excluded then for reasons of puritanical zeal and purity which now seem ludicrous to me: a few private tapes, a few repeats bought in from other shows; on reflection, Peel obviously wanted to play them, so they became Peel Sessions in effect. For the purposes of this book, I have chosen to define a session as a single day's work by an artist in a BBC or other studio, broadcast later or live, where the primary intended audience are radio listeners and Peel himself. In other words, while live from Maida Vale specials from latter years are included, in which there was often an invited small audience in the studio, all live sets recorded for the show or transmitted live from Glastonbury, Reading, Sound City, Meltdown, etc where the artist was performing primarily or substantially for a present and paying public, are excluded (brief details of these can be found in the day-by-day Shows index above).

KEY

A typical entry goes like this:

ARTIST

> 1st broadcast date Track Title 1, Track Title 2, Track Title 3, Track Title 4. Musician 1 (instrument), Musician 2 (instrument), Musician 3 (instrument), Musician 4 (instrument). Recording date Studio Producer Engineer(s) Notes

Artists are in alpha-numeric order by surname, except in certain instances. All 'DJ's, 'Dr's, 'MC's & 'Mr's (there are no 'Mrs's or 'Ms's) are grouped together under those titles in D and M, except in one instance where the title and name is the person's waking identity: Dr Oloh. Some entries for artists who appear in different guises have been flipped to read in the right chronological order (Brian Auger's Trinity comes before Brian Auger's Oblivion Express), others with multiple and frequent band name changes have been grouped to an extent (Palace Brothers and Bonnie Prince Billy, Spizz Oil, Manfred Mann, etc), and in these cases the original billing is given before the line-up.

- **TX** = Transmitted, broadcast.
- Broadcast dates and recording dates are given as **dd/mm/yy**.
- Repeat dates are not given here, but can be found in the shows index, where they are given in brackets.
- Track Titles from sessions after June 1978 are normally given in the order they appear on the session sheet, ie. the order in which they were recorded or specified by the artist at the recording, which was then most often (but by no means always) the order in which they were broadcast. Track Titles before 1978 are normally entered in the order they were broadcast, because the primary source for those early years were the PasB programme scripts at BBC Written Archives in Caversham, because most sessions sheets do not survive. Many titles as documented in BBC data have been found to be slightly wrong, and where spotted these titles have been amended. If a track was formally retitled by the artist later and is more well known by this title, this has been given where known in square brackets.
- **(& Track Title 5, 1st TX dd/mm/yy)** = When a minority of tracks recorded at the session were first broadcast on a different date,

normally later but sometimes earlier, these titles and their first broadcast date are given in brackets with the appropriate date after other titles. On occasion these titles are also first broadcast on a different show and if so the title of the show is given in capitals after the date.

- **Not TX** = More rarely I can find no trace of a track being broadcast at all, and this is indicated as shown.

- Full line-ups are given for each artist's first session only, with only changes indicated for subsequent sessions, in order to save space and avoid redundancy.

- **r** = replaces.

- For acts who did several or many sessions with frequent or substantial line-up changes (eg The Fall), where appropriate I relist the entire line-up again every few sessions after any major changes, but only giving surnames of all musicians who have appeared for this artist previously.

- **&** all musicians listed after an ampersand are guest musicians and appear on that session only.

- **( )** instruments or vocal contributions by each musician are given in brackets after their name according to the key below. If the contribution is made only on one or some tracks, this is indicated by the appropriate track number after a hyphen.

- Musicians' names have been entered as on the session sheet or contract (pre-1978). The thousands of inconsistencies in this area have been resolved to the best of my ability by consulting commercial releases, reference works, online search engines and encyclopedias, and official band websites. If 3 such sources agreed on a spelling, that's the one I chose. But I am bound to have got someone's name wrong and I am sorry if it's yours.

- **U** = unknown musician(s), dates, everything.

- **Live from** = if a session was broadcast entirely live, the entry will say so instead of giving the recording date.

- **'as live'** = recorded as part of a complete live Peel show, but the whole programme timeshifted to go out at a slightly later broadcast time that date or subsequently.

- Studios, Producers and Engineers are as indicated in the keys below.

- Notes are given as appropriate. These range from the verdicts of the BBC Audition Panel up to the mid-1970s, to brief details of earlier, non-Peel sessions (ie somebody else had this lot on first), details of commercial releases, and miscellaneous curious or amusing titbits.

- ○ session has been released on CD. Where the symbol appears at the end of the artist's name at the top of the entry, it means all or almost all of their sessions have been released, and there is unlikely to ever be any more. Where it appears only after individual sessions, it means only that session has been released. In both cases, titles and catalogue numbers of releases are given at the end of the last session featured on the identified release .

- ● session has been released on vinyl.

- † indicates individual tracks that have been selected from one or more of an artist's sessions for inclusion on a vinyl or CD release, with release title given in the manner indicated above at the end of the last session from which tracks were drawn.

- § used where different tracks have been selected from the same artist's sessions for a different release.

This discographic aspect of the A–Z does not claim to be definitive, is frankly based mainly on my own collection, and I have only included either full session releases, or other collections that draw on various sessions or at least half of one session. I have sought to include all the original Strange Fruit vinyl (SFPS) and CD (SFPMACD, SFRSCD, SFRCD) releases, which were all deleted long ago, because they represent the most substantive Peel Session release programme, remain eminently collectable and traceable, and moreover were the ones that had Peel's personal approval and initial involvement in selection. More recent releases from Universal, Hux and Sanctuary are still available.

INSTRUMENTS

ab	acoustic bass guitar	**bj**	banjo	**ci**	citern
acc	accordion	**bkv**	bass, keyboards, vocals	**cl**	clarinet
afd	african drums	**blp**	balaphon	**clav**	clavinet
ag	acoustic guitar	**bnd**	bandoneon	**clo**	cello
al	alto saxophone	**bns**	bones	**cmp**	computers
b	bass guitar	**bpp**	bagpipes	**cnc**	concertina
bal	balalaika	**brs**	brass	**cnt**	cornet
barh	baritone horn	**bsn**	bassoon	**co**	cor anglais
bars	baritone sax	**bsx**	bass saxophone	**cru**	crumhorn
bck	backing vocals	**btb**	bass trombone	**d**	drums
bcl	bass clarinet	**bu**	bugle	**db**	double bass
bfl	bass flute	**bv**	bass guitar, vocals	**dig**	didgeridoo
bgo	bongos	**bz**	bouzouki	**dj**	dj
bh	bodhran	**cel**	celeste	**dm**	drum machine
		cga	conga	**dob**	dobro

dro	drones	**mnd**	mandolin	**tmbu**	tamboura
dsc	discs	**mnda**	mandola	**tp**	trumpet
dul	dulcimer	**mrm**	marimba	**tps**	tapes
dv	drums, vocals	**mx**	mixing	**tr**	triangle
e	everything	**ng**	ngoni	**ts**	tenor saxophone
el	electronics	**npp**	northumbrian pipes	**tst**	toasting
elp	electric piano	**o**	organ	**tt**	turntables
eu	euphonium	**ob**	oboe	**tu**	tuba
fd	fiddle	**om**	omnichord	**tym**	tympani
flg	flageolet	**p**	piano	**u**	unknown
flh	flugelhorn	**perc**	percussion	**uk**	ukelele
frh	french horn	**percv**	percussion, vocals	**v**	vocals
fx	effects	**picc**	piccolo	**vi**	violin
g	guitar	**pn**	pans	**vib**	vibraphone
gbv	guitar, bass, vocals	**pp**	pipes	**vla**	viola
gg	gong	**prd**	band producer	**wb**	wobble board
gha	ghatiam	**prg**	programming	**wh**	whistle
gk	guitar, keyboards	**ps**	pedal steel guitar	**wsh**	washboard
gkv	guitar, keyboards, vocals	**rd**	reeds	**ww**	woodwinds
glo	glockenspiel	**rec**	recorder	**xyl**	xylophone
glv	guitar, lead vocals	**rg**	rhythm guitar	**-v**	suffixed to any other credit (percv, syv, for example) means vocals in addition
gsy	guitar synthesiser	**rgv**	rhythm guitar, vocals		
gv	guitar, vocals	**rp**	rapping	**lv-3**	a number attached to any credit (sx-2, k-4, for example) means this musician made this contribution on that title only
hbb	human beatbox	**sc**	scratching		
hca	harmonica	**seq**	sequencer		
hmn	harmonium	**sfx**	special effects		
hn	horns	**sit**	sitar		
hp	harp	**slg**	slide guitar		
hrp	harpsichord	**smp**	sampling, samples, sampler		
jh	jew's harp	**sp**	spoons		
k	keyboards	**ss**	soprano saxophone		
kor	kora	**str**	strings		
kv	keyboards, vocals	**sty**	stylophone		
lg	lead guitar	**su**	surbahor		
lgv	lead guitar, vocals	**sx**	saxophone		
lp	laptop	**sxl**	saxello		
lsg	lap steel guitar	**sxv**	saxophone, vocals		
lt	lute	**sy**	synthesiser		
lv	lead vocals	**syv**	synthesiser, vocals		
lvg	lead vocals, guitar	**tab**	tabla		
ly	lyricon	**tamb**	tambourine		
ma	machines	**tb**	trombone		
mbi	mbira	**tbl**	tubular bells		
md	musical director	**th**	theramin		
mel	melodica	**ti**	timbales		
mll	mellotron	**timb**	timbal		

STUDIOS

1G	Studio 1G, Broadcasting House, London
AO1	Aoelian Hall, Studio 1
AO2	Aoelian Hall, Studio 2
B15	Studio B15, Broadcasting House, London
B6	Studio B6, Broadcasting House, London
BEL	BBC Belfast Studios
BHG	Broadcasting House, Glasgow
BHM	Broadcasting House, Manchester
BRM	BBC Birmingham, Pebble Mill
C19	Chem19, Hamilton, Scotland*
CDF5	BBC Cardiff Studio 5
CH	Concert Hall, Broadcasting House
CM	Camden Theatre, London
CV	Cava Studios, Glasgow*
DWN	Studio 1, Downtown Radio, Northern Ireland*
ED	Eden Sound, London*
EDN	BBC Edinburgh Studios
EG2	Studio 2, Egton House, R1
FR	Field Recording
G6	Studio G6, BH Glasgow
GLW	BBC Glasgow Studios
HP	Hippodrome, Golders Green, London
LH1	Langham 1, Portland Place, London
LL	R1 Yalding House, Live Lounge
LR	Live Room, small studio next to Maida Vale 5
MCR3	Studio 3, Broadcasting House, Manchester
MR	Moonraker Studios, Manchester*
MV1	Maida Vale Studio 1
MV3	Maida Vale Studio 3
MV4	Maida Vale Studio 4
MV5	Maida Vale Studio 5
MV6	Maida Vale Studio 6
NW	BBC Newcastle Studios
OD	Odyssey Studios, London*
OS	Artist's own studio: all OS sessions are produced and engineered by the artist themselves on a date unknown, unless indicated otherwise
PC1	201 Piccadilly, Studio 1, London
PH	Playhouse Theatre, Northumberland Ave, London
PHM	Playhouse Theatre, Hulme, Manchester
PRIV	Private Tape: session or tape produced in an unknown non-BBC studio or supplied by an unknown music business organisation (record company, band management etc) and recorded on a date unknown by unknown producers and engineers, unless indicated otherwise
PS	Paris Cinema, Lower Regent Street
RTE	RTE Dublin, Eire*
S1	S1, sub-basement, Broadcasting House
S2	S2, sub-basement, Broadcasting House
S2G	Studio S2 BBC Glasgow
SO	Southern Studios, London*
SS	Strawberry Sound, Stockport*
T1	T1 Transcription Service, Shepherd's Bush, London
T2	T2 Transcription Service, Shepherd's Bush, London
U	Unknown
VY	Vineyard Studio, London*
WX	Wessex Studios, London*
Y4	R1 Yalding House, Studio 4

(All studios BBC except*)

PRODUCERS & ENGINEERS

AA	Adam Askew
AH	Allen Harris
AHL	Andy Halstead
AHW	Alison Howe
AJ	Andre Jacquemin
AKM	Anita Kamath
AL	Andrew Lenton
AM	Andy Meeson
AP	Anthony Pugh
AR	Andy Rogers
ARV	Adrian Revill
AS	Alan Scott
BA	Bernie Andrews
BAI	Bill Aitken
BC	Bob Conduct
BJ	Barry Jordan
BP	Bev Phillips
BS	Bob Sargeant
BSU	Barry Surdan
BYA	Barry Andrews
CB	Clive Burrows
CBM	Colin Beaumont
CBO	Chrissie Boucher
CH	Charlie Hume
CL	Chris Lycett
CLE	Chris Lee
CM	Colin Marshall
CML	Chris Maclean
DD	Dave Dade
DG	Dale Griffin
DK	Denis O'Keeffe
DKI	David Kinnaird
DMC	Dave McCarthy
DP	Dave Price
DS	Dave Shannon
DT	Dave Tate
DTH	Dave Thomas
EL	Elizabeth Lewis
ER	Ed Richmond
FK	Fred Kay
GB	Graham Bunce
GP	Graham Puddifoot
GPR	Gary Parker
GR	Gregor Reid

GT	George Thomas	MWT	Mike Walter	TD	Tim Durham
GW	Graham White	NBL	Nick Bell	TdB	Ted de Bono
GYW	Guy Worth	NBU	Neil Burn	TDO	Tony Doogan
HP	Harry Parker	NF	Nick Fountain	TVD	Trevor Dann
IC	Iain Chambers	NG	Nick Gomm	TW	Tony Wilson
JB	James Birtwistle	NGR	Nick Griffiths	TWN	Tony Worthington
JBN	John Boon	NK	Nick King	U	Unknown
JE	John Etchells	NS	Nick Scripps	~	produced and engineered by
JG	Jeff Griffin	PA	Paul Allen		
JHE	John Hemingway	PC	Pete Carr		
JHT	Jamie Hart	PCG	Paul Cargill		
JL	John Leonard	PD	Pete Dauncey		
JLC	Julia Carney	PF	Paul Fahey		
JLO	Jonathan Leong	PJ	Pete Johnson		
JLY	Jane Lyons	PK	Paddy Kingsland		
JM	John Muir	PL	Paul Long		
JMK	Julian Markham	PN	Paul Noble		
JP	John Porter	PR	Pete Ritzema		
JRS	James Ross	PRB	Paul Roberts		
JS	John Sparrow	PRS	Phil Ross		
JSM	Jerry Smith	PS	Phil Stannard		
JW	John Walters	PSI	Paul Smith (London)		
JWH	John White	PSM	Paul Smith (Manchester)		
JWI	John Owen Williams	PW	Peter Watts		
KH	Kevin Howlett	PWL	Phil Ward-Large		
KR	Kevin Rumble	RBY	Rebecca Berry		
LK	Louise Kattenhorn	RD	Roger Derry		
LR	Lis Roberts	RF	Rachel Fisher		
LS	Lisa Softley	RJ	Ralph Jordan		
MA	Miti Adhikari	RK	Ro Khan		
MAP	Martin Appleby	RM	Robin Marks		
MB	Malcolm Brown	RP	Roger Pusey		
MC	Martin Colley	RPF	Rupert Flindt		
ME	Mike Engels	SA	Simon Askew		
MF	Mike Franks	SB	Steve Bittlestone		
MFA	Mark Farrar	SBR	Steve Bridges		
MH	Mike Harding	SC	Simon Clifford		
MHS	Mark Harrison	SCK	Stewart Cruickshank		
MHW	Mike Hawkes	SCO	Sue Cockburn		
MK	Martha Knight	SCT	Sara Carter		
MP	Mike Page	SCU	Sam Cunningham		
MPK	Martyn Parker	SF	Sarah Fletcher		
MR	Mike Robinson	SFX	Stephen Faux		
MRD	Mark Radcliffe	SN	Stephen Nelson		
MS	Mike Shilling	TBA	Tony Baker		
MW	Mick Wilkojc	TBK	Trevor Barker		

1-2-3-4

2TV

5/9/79 Mary Thompson, Dear Heart, Johnny Plays Up, Kids On The Street. Steve Speight (gv), Steve Barrass (g, bck), Chris Speight (b), Steve Gale (d). 22/8/79 MV4 TVD NG

3 Inches Of Blood

22/10/03 Deadly Sinners, Premonition Of Pain, Conquerors Of The Northern Sphere, Silver & Gold. Jamie Hooper, Cameron Pipes, Bobby Froese, Sunny Dhak, Geoff Trawrek, Richard Trawrek. 1/10/03 MV4 SA~

3D

5/4/82 Houdini, Some Die For Money, Alone, The Orchard. Billed as 3D A Fish In Sea: Fred Palethorpe (d), Roy Campbell (b), John Reynolds (g), Steve Spurgin (k), Phil Martin (sx), Richie Holmes (v). 27/3/82 MV4 DG MR

9/11/82 Dreaming Of You, A Child's Toy, Red Wine. Palethorpe, Reynolds, Spurgin, Dave Edge (b), John Corner (v, sx). 23/10/82 MV4 DG MR

13/9/83 Pantau, Brave Boys Paradise, Stay, Loveliest World. Edge out. 30/7/83 MV4 DG MR

3Ds

28/5/94 The Venus Trail, The Golden Grove, The Young & The Restless, Sing Song. David Mitchell (gv), Denise Roughan (bv), David Saunders (gv), Dominic Stones (d). 24/4/94 MV4 JB KR

7 Year Bitch

3/4/93 The Scratch, Rock A Bye Baby, Dead Men Don't Rape, Damn Good And Well, Knot. Valerie Agnew (d), Elizabeth Davies (b), Roisin Dunne (g), Selene Vigil (v). 9/3/93 MV4 MR~ PA

10 5 Neuton

9/6/99 Their Signature, Entrance To Exit, Identify The Driver, Opportune, Thanks John. Jon Weeks, Andrew Martin, Gez Donnelly. 9/3/99 MV4 MR GT

13th Hole

4/3/94 Face, Crocodile, Lucky, He Is III, Doyle. Stephen Lescouarnec (d), Loic Geoffroy (b), Pascal Jollivet (g), Herve L'Hostis (g, bck), Anne Jegat (v). 25/1/94 MV4 MR PA

14 Iced Bears

26/11/86 Balloon Song, Cut, Shy Like You, Train Song. Robert Sekula (v), Kevin Canham (g), Nick Roughley (g, bck), Dominic Mills (b), Nick Emery (d). 28/10/86 U DG TdB&TD

27/7/87 If I Said, Spangle, Miles Away, Hay Fever. Sekula, Canham, Steven Ormsby (b), William Cox (d). 21/7/87 MV4 DG MR&JB

18th Dye

16/9/94 Mystics II, Sole Arch, Club Madame, D, Go Song. Piet Bendtsen (d, o), Heike Radeker (bv), Sebastian Buttrich (g, o, v). 24/7/94 MV3 MR JMK

28/4/95 Merger, Galeer, Poolhouse Blue. 26/3/95 MV3 ME JMK

20/4/99 Burnt Doors, Instant Light Years, Betty. 28/2/99 MV3 ME GT

20th Century Steel Band

19/12/75 Heaven And Hell Is On Earth, Endless Vibrations, Number One, Love's Theme. Luciano Bravo (pn), Gideon Rodgers (pn), Bubbles Oliver (pn, md, lv-2), Winston Finlay (pn), Godfrun Moore (pn), Martin Farren (pn), Mikey Brumont (pn), Colin Moore (d), Trampas Williams (cga, perc, lv-1). 11/11/75 MV4 TW U

21 Guns

2/2/81 21 Guns, Dark Night, Ambition Rock. Trevor Evans (k), Johnny Rex (d), Kevin Turner (b), Stuart (g), Gary 'Judge' Chambers (v). U PRIV Produced by Neville Staples

22–20s

4/5/04 Such A Fool, Why Don't You Do It For Me, Shoot Your Gun, Devil In Me. James Irving (d), Charles Coombes (k), Glen Bartua (b), Martin Trimble (gv). 21/4/04 MV4 MA GT

23 Skidoo

23/9/81 Retain Control, Macaw Gungah, View From Here, Four Note Base. Fritz, Alex, Johnny, Sam, Tom, Tim, Tim, Richard. 16/9/81 MV4 CL NG

25BZ

6/5/03 No Turistik No Egozotick, Etnik Market Etnik Paranoia, Ampul, Serekseni. Serhat Köksal (prg, k, e). 1/1/03 OS

25th Of May

10/8/91 Made In The USA, Crackdown, Stuff The Right To Vote. Steve Swindelli (v), Ed Garbett (gv), Nigel Cope (b), James Mathias (sc), Jabba (perc, d), Steve Cowell (k). 2/6/91 U DG AM&ME Recorded debut session for Evening Session previous day, TX 10/8/91

35 Summers

19/1/91 Come Together, Good Morning And Goodbye, Discotheque. Andy Hignett (d), Robbie Fay (b), Duncan Lomax (rg, bck), Ian Greenwood (lg), Jamie Southern (k), David Pichilingi (v). 20/12/90 MV5 DG MWT&RPF

20/10/91 Loyality, Really Down, Candy, Sheep. Alan Curry (d) r Hignett. 22/8/91 MV5 DG NG&PA

60ft Dolls

17/2/96 Stay, New Loafers, P*ss Funk, Loser, Streamlined. Richard Parfitt (gv), Mike Cole (bv), Carl Bevan (d). 11/02/96 MV3 JB

21/4/98 Summer Is Gone, Biggest Kick, Baby Says Yeah, Killer Inside, Paperback Writer. & Chris (k). Live from MV4 PL NF

65 Days Of Static

9/12/04 A.O.D, I Swallowed Hard Like I Understood, Massive Star At The End Of Its Burning Cycle, Fix The Sky A Little. Paul Wolinski (g, prg), Robb Jonze (d), Simon Wright (b), Joe Shrewsbury (g). 18/11/04 MV4 GW JHT

70 Gwen Party

26/5/91 This New Model England, Hiding In The Wall, Deviling Hour, Peeping Stick. Victor N'dip (gv), Lurgin Pin (bkv). 30/4/91 MV5 MR~

20/6/92 Auto Killer UK, Howard Hughes, Stop Resurrect & Fire, Smash. 26/5/92 MV4 MR~

4/6/93 Walkabout, Like Richard Dadd, Knee Deep In Evil, Nip. 4/5/93 MV4 MR~ PA

22/7/94 A Culling For Satan, The Love Fried, The Dearl Brothers, Snatcher. 31/5/94 MV4 ME SA

90 Day Men

28/2/01 Sort Of Is A Country In Love, Hans Lucas, The Methodist, National Car Crash. Andy Lansangan, Brian Case, Cayce Key, Robert Lowe. 14/2/01 MV4 SA GT

400 Blows

16/2/84 Introduction, Conscience, For Jackie M, Still Beating That Devil. Andrew Edward Beer, Robert Taylor, Tony Thorpe. 8/2/84 MV5 DG NG

999

1/11/78 Subterfuge, Homicide, Soldier, Let's Face It. Pablo Labritain (d), Guy Days (gv), Nick Cash (gv), Jon Watson (b). 25/10/78 MV4 MR NG

1000 Violins

25/9/85 Why Is It Always December, The Candle Man, Though It Poured The Next Day I Never Noticed The Rain, The Sun Ain't Gonna Shine Anymore. Sean O'Neill (d), Colin Gregory (g, b, bck), Dave Walmsley (k, g, tp, bck), John Wood (v). 15/9/85 MV5 DG ME

2/12/86 Almost Dead And Nigh On Forty Years To Go, I Was Depending On You To Be My Jesus, If I Were A Bullet Then For Sure I'd Find A Way To Your Heart, No-one Was Saving The World. Darren Swindle (b), Peter Day (d) r O'Neill. 4/11/86 U DG ME

1919

12/5/82 After The Fall, Caged, The Ritual, Slave, Repulsion. Mark Tighe (g), Mick Reed (d), Ian Tilleard (v), Nick Hiles (b) & Steve Madden (b-1). 8/5/82 MV4 DG MR

11/5/83 Alien, Storm, Cry Wolf, Control. Madden out; & Sputnik (sy). 4/5/83 MV4 RP NG

10,000 Maniacs

1/7/85 Just As The Tide Was A' Flowin', Lily Dale, Maddox Table, Back O' The Moon. Natalie Merchant (v), Robert Buck (lg, mnd), John Lombard (ag), Steven Gustafson (b), Dennis Drew (k), Jerry Augustyniak (d). 23/6/85 MV5 DG SC

A

A R E Weapons

18/10/01 Drums Of Joy, Champion Chains, New York Muscle, Saigon Disco. Brain (v), Matt (bv), Tom (devices, v). 1/8/01 MV4 NF GYW

Aavikko

16/10/01 Uno Lira Soluzione, Sgame Over, Pizza Job/Tapettava, Leopardinnahkatakki. Tomi Kosonen (k, sx), Tomi Leppänen (d, el perc), Paul Staufenbiel (k). 10/9/01 MV3 GYW JHT

Mick Abrahams' Band

10/4/71 Not To Re-Arrange, Seasons, Winds Of Change. Mick Abrahams (gv) & probably: Bob Sargeant (kv), Walt Monahan (b), Ritchie Dharma (d). 30/3/71 U JW BC No recording information available. Files went missing in 1980. This was 3rd R1 session

4/2/72 The Good Old Days, Let Me Love You Baby, Absent Friends (& Whole Wide World, 1st TX 17/3/72). 12/1/72 U JW BC

The Abs

8/7/87 Grease Your Ralph, Hand Me Down, Fear Is The Key, Same Mistake Twice.

Bas (gv), Bryn (gv), Buzz (b), The Rev (d). 28/6/87 U DG ME&MC

9/2/88 Rock Your Tits Off!, Concrete Hits Bone, Ideetapoo!, Cunkers In My Cleft. Fatty Ashtray' (b). 31/1/88 U DG JB&ME

AC Acoustics

7/1/94 Leatherbuyer, Sister Grab Operator, King Dick, Oregon Pine Washback. Paul Campion (gv), David Gormley (d), Caz Riley (b), Roger Ward (lg), Reid Cunningham (sx). 18/11/93 MV4 CML NF

27/1/95 Fast, Atmospheric Breakfast, I Messiah Am Jailer, Side Nova. Campion, Gormley, Riley, Mark Raine (g), Sean Guthrie (g). 11/12/94 MV3 ME JHE

13/3/97 Hand Passes Empty, I Messiah Am Jailer, Bluff Drive By, Red Not Yellow. Guthrie out. 24/1/97 MCR3 TWN U

23/3/99 Crush, B2, Hammerhead, Waiter Strains. Guthrie returns. 3/1/99 MV3 ME CM

21/5/02 A Bell Of Love Rings Out For You, Hold, Clone Of Al Capone, 16 4 2010. Paul Murray (kv) r Guthrie. 3/3/02 MV4 ME GT

AC/DC

21/6/76 Live Wire, High Voltage, Can I Sit Next To You?, Little Lover. Angus Young (lg), Malcolm Young (rg), Mark Evans (b), Philip Rudd (d), Bon Scott (lv). 3/6/76 MV4 TW U

AC Temple

29/7/87 Blowtorch, Mincemeat, Fraud, America. Jane Bromley (v), Noel Kilbride (g, v-1,4), Neil Woodward (g), Andy Hartley (b), Jayne Waterfall (d). 19/7/87 U DG MS&MA

Ace

12/11/74 24 Hours, I Ain't Gonna Stand For This No More, Rock & Roll Runaway, I Know How It Feels. Paul Carrack (kv), Alan 'Bam' King (g), Phil Harris (g), Tex Comer (b), Fran Byrne (d). 22/10/74 MV4 TW BAI

31/3/75 Sail On My Brother, Get Ready, Ain't That Peculiar, Ain't Gonna Stand For This No More. 25/3/75 MV4 TW BAI

David Ackles

27/10/68 Down River, Laissez Faire, When Love Is Gone (& Road To Cairo, Be My Friend, 24/1/68). David Ackles & (o, hmn, d, 2 ag, unknown). 1/10/68 PC1 BA AH&BC

Acqua Vista

17/7/01 25 Gallons Of Paranoia, Viva Quatro, Dangerman, Tiger 100, Toxic Beach. Rapido Turismo Lusso (g), Enrico Guivars (b), Minoy Colossus (d). 24/6/01 MV4 ME~ JHT

18/9/02 Surf Creature, We're Gonna Feed Your Voodoo Ass To The Lions, Rapido A Gogo, Holidays Are The Best Days, Los Grandes Tiborones Blancos, Down Shiftin'. 6/8/02 MV4 MA NF

Action Pact

22/2/82 People, Losers, Suicide Bag, Mindless Aggression, Cowslick Blues. Joe Fungus (d), Dr Phibes (b), Wild Planet (g), George (v). 6/2/82 MV4 DG MR&MC

16/8/82 Times Must Change, Drowning Out The Big Jets, Fools Factions, These Are A Few…, Protest Is Alive, Fouled On The Footpath. 7/8/82 MV4 DG MR

Action Swingers

8/5/92 You Want My Action, Kicked In The Head, Hot Rock Action, Lexicon Devil. Bob Bert (d), Colin Todd (b), Bruce Bennett (g), Ned Hayden (gv). 22/3/92 MV3 DG SA&EL

Adam and the Ants

30/1/78 Deutscher Girls, Puerto-Rican, It Doesn't Matter, Lou. Kurt Van Der Bogarde (b), Johnny Bivouac (g), Dave Barbe (d), Adam Ant (glv), Jordan (lv-4). 23/1/78 MV4 TW DD

17/7/78 You're So Physical, Cleopatra, Friends, I'm A Xerox. Matthew (rg, p) r Bivouac; Adam (sty), Jordan out. 10/7/78 MV4 TW DD ○

2/4/79 Table Talk, Liggotage, Animals And Men, Never Trust A Man With Egg On His Face. Adam (g-4). 26/3/79 MV4 TW BAI&MPK ○ SFRCD115

Adamski

20/2/90 Something Is Happening, Genetic NRG, Rap You In The Sound. Adamski (k, prg). 2/2/90 MV3 DG MA

Barry Adamson

22/10/93 Spooky, Hunters And Collectors/Vernal Equinox, The Snowball Effect/2001. Barry Adamson (prg, g, v), Unknown (prg), Monty Messex (g), Shamus Neagen (k), Ivor Guest (prg). 7/9/93 MV4 TdB SBR

Add N to (X)

26/11/97 The Black Regent, Warm Jag, Hit Me, Sir Ape. Barry Smith (k), Ann Shenton (k), Steve Claydon (k), John Russell (d). 23/11/97 MV4 ME KR

1/2/00 Metal Fingers In My Body, Robot N Y, King Wasp, Mathematical War. Rob Allum (d) r Russell. 21/11/99 MV3 ME KR

20/2/01 Superstar, Brothel Charge, Kingdom, Poker Roll, I Wanna Be Your Dog. 31/1/01 MV4 SA GT

14/1/03 All Night Lazy, Total All Out Water, Large Number, Sir Ape. Claydon, Barry Seven (sy), Dave Williamson (sy, b, v), Jason Buckle (g, sy, v), Joe Dilworth (dv). 19/12/02 MV4 SA GT

Adicts

5/12/79 Get Addicted, Distortion, Numbers, Sensitive. Monkey (lv), Mel Ellis (gv), Pete Davison (gv), Kid Dee (dv), Tim Hocking (bv). 20/11/79 MV4 JS MR

Adventures In Stereo

20/2/97 A Brand New Day, When You're Gone, Down In The Traffic, Said You Said, Goodbye. Gayle Harrison (g, k), Brian Doherty (b), Judith Boyle (v), Jim Beattie (g), David McCluskey, John Cavanagh (cl-4). 11/2/97 G6 SCK DKI

The Adverts

29/4/77 Quickstep, Looking Through Gary Gilmore's Eyes, One Chord Wonders, New Boys, Bored Teenagers. Laurie Driver (d), Gay Advert (b, bck), Howard Pickup (g, bck), TV Smith (lv). 25/4/77 MV4 TW BAI ● SFPS034

30/8/77 We Who Wait, New Church, Safety In Numbers, The Great British Mistake. 23/8/77 MV4 MB MR

11/9/78 Fate Of Criminals, Television's Over, Love Songs, Back From The Dead, I Surrender. Rod Latter (d) r Driver. 21/8/78 MV4 TW DD

12/11/79 The Adverts, I Looked At The Sun, Cast Of Thousands, I Will Walk You Home. Tim Cross (kv), Paul Martinez (g), Nick Martinez (d) r Pickup, Latter. 16/10/79 MV4 JS MR

Aereogramme

4/5/00 Fireworks, Outside, Motion, Zionist Timing. Craig B (gv), Campbell McNeil (b), Martin Scott (d), Deepak Bahl. 2/4/00 MV4 JSM JHT

7/11/01 Shouting for Joey, A Simple Process Of Elimination, Broken Horse, Victoria Segal's Hairy Arse. Craig B, McNeil, Scott, Iain Cook (p, g, prg), Alex Grant (bck). 7/10/01 MV4 ME GYW

19/2/03 Believe Me, Snake, Inhalation Blues, Thriller. & Lynsey Scott (bck-1 via Iain's laptop), Grant out. 29/1/03 MV4 SA NS

Aerial M

2/4/98 Vivea, Safeless, Skrag Theme. David Pajo (g, o), Tim Furnish (g, p), Tony Bailey (d), Cassie Marrett (b). 3/3/98 MV4 MR NF

Afghan Whigs

25/3/94 Revenge, Easily Persuaded, My Curse, What Jail Is Like. Steve Earle (d), John Curley (b), Rick McCollum (g), Greg Dulli (gv), Douglas Falsetti (p, bck). 22/2/94 MV4 MR CBO

AFT

8/11/76 Race Horses, The Great Panjandrum Wheel Part II. Paul Macdonnell (g), Bob Cross (g), David Ball (d), Trevor Darks (b). 21/10/76 MV4 TW BAI

Again Again

20/12/78 Beached, Scarred For Life, Here We Go, Self Employed. Rob Hutchings (v), Jeff Pountain (rg), Mark Mason (lg), Roger Payne (b), Mark Broad (d). 12/12/78 MV4 TW MR

Agathocles

7/5/97 A Start At Least, Theatric Symbolisation / Mutilated Regurgitator / Consuming Endoderme Pus / The Accident, Kill Your Idols / Lay Off Me / Media Creations / Age Of The Mutants / Thy Kingdom Won't Come / Reduced To An Object, Is There A Place / He Cared / Be Your Own God / Christianity Means Tyranny. Matty (gv), Jan (bv), Burt (d). 30/3/97 MV4 ME LS

Age of Chance

29/10/85 Mob! Hut!, The Going Going Gone Man, The Morning After The Sixties, I Don't Know And I Don't Care. Jan Penny (d), Geoff Taylor (b), Neil Howbs (g), Stevie Elvidge (v). 6/10/85 MV5 DG JB

23/6/86 Be Fast Be Clean Be Cheap, How The West Was Won, From Now On This Will Be Your God, Kiss. 10/6/86 MV4 DG MR&FK

Agony Column

20/6/79 Home Movies, Dietition, Love Is A Blanket Expression, Losing My Lust. Malcolm Raeburn (v), Ian Heywood (gv), Bri Tag (b), Jon Rust (d). 12/6/79 MV4 TVD MR

Aina

8/1/02 Bipartite/Two Questions, Ice, Spring, You Shook Me All Night Long. Xavier Sola Barceo (b), Pau Santesmasses Ruiz (d), Artur Estrada Blanco (gv). 9/12/01 MV4 GYW MA

The Aislers Set

10/4/01 Mission Bells, Long Division, Walked In Line, The Walk. Amy Linton (gv), Yoshi Nakamoto (d), Wyatt Cusik (g), Jen Cohen (o), Alicia Van Den Heuvel (bv). 1/4/01 MV4 ME JHT

Bill Aitken

8/12/75 Chimney Pots, Sequel, Ghosts Of Yesterday, Open Up Your Eyes. Bill Aitken (all instruments: ag, g, b, sy, o, d, perc, v). 6/75 PRIV BAI~

Laurel Aitken

12/5/80 Big Fat Man ('New Song Written 2 Days Ago'), Rudi Got Married, Jesse James, Rock Me Baby / Caledonia. Laurel Aitken (ov), Paul Fox (g, bck), Gary Barnacle (sx, o), Segs (b), Dave Duffy (d, bck), Malcolm Owen (bck). 28/4/80 MV4 TW DD

Damon Albarn

16/12/04 Behind The Sun, Strange News From Another Star. solo (gv, harm, mbi). Live from MV3 for Keepin' It Peel Night MA GT

Albertos y Lost Trio Paranoias

16/9/77 Kill, Gobbing On Life, Snuffing In A Babylon, Sid's Song, Death Of Rock And Roll. Bruce Mitchell (d), Tony Bower (gvb), Bob Harding (gvb), Simon White (g), Chris Lea (bv, other things), Les Prior (mouth), Jimmy Hibbert (gv, sex appeal). 14/9/77 MV4 MB NG

Albion Country Band

4/7/72 New St George / St Anne's Reel, Rambling Sailor, Morris Dance Tune Medley: Morris On / Jockey To The Fair / Room For The Cuckoo / Princess Royal / Morris Off. Tiger H (bv), Simon Nicol (g), Dave Mattacks (d), Steve Ashby (wh, hca, rec), Sue Draheim (fd), Royston Wood (v). 19/6/72 PH JW BC

1/3/73 I Was A Young Man, The Gallant Poacher, Medley: Mouresque / London Pride / Maid Of The Hill / So Selfish Runs The Hare / Sheriff's Ride. Hutchings, Nicol & John Kirkpatrick (mnd, cnc, v), Sue Harris (ob, v), Martin Carthy (g, bj, v), Roger Swallow (perc). 19/2/73 LH1 BA BC

6/9/76 An Estampie, Hopping Down In Kent, The Horses' Brawl, Old Sir Simon The King. Now Albion Dance Band: Hutchings, Mattacks, Nicol, Shirley Collins (v), Eddie Upton (v), John Rodd (cnc), John Sothcott (fd) Phil Pickett (ww), Michael Gregory (d). 22/7/76 MV4 TW BAI

8/6/77 Holm's Fancy / Cuckolds All Awry (Instrumental), Poor Old Horse, Postman's Knock, Bourreé (Instrumental). John Tams (lv, ml), Ashley Hutchings (b, bck), Simon Nicol (bck, g), Graeme Taylor (g, bck, elp), Ric Sanders (vi), Phil Pickett (ww), Michael Gregory (d), Dave Mattacks (d). 31/5/77 MV4 JG MR

20/4/78 Time To Ring Some Changes, Rainbow Over The Hill, Down The Road, Albion Sunrise / Uncle Bernard's / Bacup Tune / Jenny Lind. Now just The Albion Band: & Peter Bullock (sy). 11/4/78 MV4 MB U

Alec Empire

3/11/95 Don't Lie White Girl, Firebombing, I Just Wanna Destroy, Not Your Business. Alec Empire (e). 1/9/95 OS

Alfie

22/3/00 Umlaut, Cloudy Lemonade, Two Up Two Down, Summer Lanes. Lee Gorton (v), Ian Smith (g, bck), Matt McGeever (clo, g, bck), Sam Morris (b), Sean Kelly (d, perc), Anthony Dawson (g), Caroline Latham (fl), Ben Dumville (tp). 9/2/00 MV4 MR JHT

23/1/01 You Make No Bones, Bends, Masquerade Parade, Don't Be Blue. Morris, Smith, McGeever, Dawson, Kelly. 10/1/01 MV4 SA GYW

Alien Sex Fiend

15/5/84 Attack, Dead And Buried, Hee Haw, Ignore The Machine. Nick Fiend (v), Mrs Feind (sy), Johnny Haha (d), Rodney (g). 2/5/84 MV5 RP NG

3/9/84 In God We Trust, E.S.T-trip To The Moon, Boneshaker Baby. Sheet says 'Yaxi' (g). 25/8/84 U DG MC

Ahmad Al-Khlail & Hamid Mohammed

19/2/69 Music From Hacha, Nasma, Halla Yum Abit, Dancing Of The North. 12/2/69 S1 JM U

Allez Allez

8/9/81 Turn Up The Meter, Papa Was, Stripped Portrait. Sarah Osborne (v), Robbie Bindels (d), Roland Bindi (perc), Nico Fransolet (g), Paul Delnoy (b), Christian Debusscher (g). 29/8/81 MV4 DG MC

Alliance Underground

8/5/02 Lets Party, Ready 2 Roll, Represent We, Make Me Feel. Eli T, Del P, Nomis G, Alize, Marley. 23/1/02 MV4 SA~ GT

Marc Almond

24/2/83 Empty Eyes, The Bulls, Once Was, Your Aura. Marc Almond (v) & the Mambas: Ann Hogan (k), Lee Jenkinson (b, bck), Matt Johnson (g, bck) & the Venomettes: Ann Stevenson & Virginia Hews (vi), Martin McCarrick (clo, v), Bill McGee (b). 1/2/83 MV4 TW DD

Altered Images

16/10/80 Beckoning Strings, Legionnaire (Instrumental), Insects, Dead Pop Stars. Clare Grogan (v), Caesar (g), Tony McDaid (g), Johnny McElhone (b), Michael 'Tich' Anderson (d). 7/10/80 MV4 JS MR

10/3/81 A Day's Wait, Idols, Midnight, Jeepster. 2/3/81 LH1 DG DD

22/9/81 Yellow And It Might, Pinky Blue, Little Brown Head, Song Sung Blue. Caesar out; & The Allneds (bck-4). 4/9/81 MV4 DG HP

Altern Eight

24/11/91 Frequency (Sample 8 Mix), Give It To Baby, Say It Ya'll, Activ 8 (LA Song Mix). Chris Peat, Mark Archer. 27/10/91 MV3 DG ME&BJ

Alternative TV

12/12/77 Action Time Vision, Still Life, Love Lies Limp, Life After Life. Mark Perry (gv), Dennis Burns (b), Chris Bennett (d), Kim Turner (g). 5/12/77 MV4 TW DD

27/7/78 Nasty Little Lonely, Going Round In Circles, Release The Natives, The Good Missionary. Mick Linehan (g) r Bennett, Turner. 17/7/78 MV4 TW DD

AM60

30/1/02 Intro, Fishies, Always Music 60, Just A Dream, Girl For Me, Big As The Sky, Perfect Package, Outro, Treble Bass And Mid Range. Christopher Root (gv), Charlies Treece (g), Jean Marie Brichard (b), Mackie (d). Live from MV4 AR SA

26/6/02 Policeman, Big As The Sky, Interlude, Treble Bass And Midrange, Fishes, Outro. Stephen Dahan (gv) r Treece. 3/4/02 MV4 SA NF

Amayenge

12/7/88 Chibuyubuyu, Munise Munise, Free Nelson Mandela, Filiukotuleya. Peter Banda (d), Darius Mwelwa (gv), John Mwanza (g), Adrick Silokomela (k), Davy Mwape (bv), Kris Chali (lv), Charles Kangwa, Michael Chewe, Francis Zimba, Chanda Kama (afd), Mwangala Mubiana, Alice Mumba (bck). 5/7/88 MV4 MR~ ● SFPS067

6/9/88 Madzela Madzela, Mbikulo, Children Of Africa. & Alica Mwenge, Irady Lungu, Ajessy Bwalya (v). 11/8/88 MV4 DG MA

Amazing Band

17/10/70 Find, Amazing March. Mal Dean (tp), Rob Spall (vi, acc), Top Topham (g), George Jenson (b), Ken Hyder (perc), Mick Brannan (al), Miriam Spall (v). 29/9/70 MV4 JW BC 'A band concerned with experiments in free improvisation; can hardly be failed as there is no real yardstick to measure them by' Walters to Audition unit. Failed: 'Pretentious… boring… a musical confidence trick… rubbish of the first order'

Amazulu

7/7/82 Fussin' 'N' Fightin', Cairo, Neya Neya, Amazulu, You'll Never Walk Alone. Rose Minor (lv), Sharon Bailey (perc), Lesley Beach (sx), Margo Sagov (g), Clare Kenny (b), Debbie Evans (d). 5/6/82 MV4 DG PS

17/1/83 Cairo, Tonto, Brixton, Smiley Stylee. Annie Radok (v) r Minor, Nardo (dv) r Evans. 8/1/83 MV4 DG MC

The Amen Corner

22/10/67 Let The Good Times Roll, Beauty Is Skin Deep, In The Pocket, The World Of Broken Hearts, Open The Door To Your Heart, A Man's Temptation. Andy Fairweather-Low, Neil Jones, Blue Weaver, Dennis Bryon, Alan Jones, Clive Taylor, Mike Smith & 2 trumpets. 18/10/67 U U PR

7/1/68 I Don't Want To Discuss It, Bend Me Shape Me, The Duck, Satisnok The Job's Worth, Shake A Tailfeather. & 2 trumpets. 1/1/68 U U PR

American TV Cops

11/2/95 Captain Marvel, Pervy Dymo, Cruiser, Thirst, Lipsplint. Anthony Cluer (gv), Dale Farrington (g), Sam Allsop (b), Andy Whitty (d, perc), Gavin Monaghan (guest bck). 15/1/95 MV3 ME JLC

Amon Duul II

29/5/73 Marnana, Green Bubble Raincoat Man, Dem Guten Schonen Wahren, The Trap. Renate Kanupp (v), Chris Karrer (p, g), John Weinzierl (g), Danny Fischelscher (d), Peter Leopold (d), Falk Rogner (k). 8/5/73 AO2 JW BC

Anaal Nathrakh

16/12/03 Pandemonic Hyperblast, How The Angels Fly In, Submission Is For The Weak, The Oblivion Gene. VITRIOL (v), Irrumator (instruments), The Mad Arab (bck), Battlesticks II (d). 13/11/03 MV4 SA NF

And Also the Trees

26/4/84 There Was A Man Of Double Deed, Wallpaper Dying, Impulse Of Man, The Secret Sea. Simon Jones (v), Joe Jones (g), Steve Burrows (b), Nick Havas (d). 7/4/84 MV5 DG MC

And You Will Know Us By The Trail Of The Dead

16/8/00 Prince With A Thousand Enemies, Mistakes & Regrets, Clair, Mark David Chapman, Totally Natural, Fake Fake Eyes. Kevin Allen (b), Jason Reece (dgv), Neil Busch (lv, g, d), Conrad Sobami (v, g, d). Live from MV4 AR MA

30/4/02 Innvocation, Another Morning Stoner, Baudelaire, Homage, Richter Scale Madness. Busch, Allen, Reece, Conrad Keely. 5/2/02 MV4 MWT GT

Peter Anders and Vini Poncia

3/3/68 Virgin To The Night, Sudden Creek, You Don't Know What To Do. Peter Anders & Vini Poncia & U. 1st TX on R1 at 2pm on 24/1/68

Ian A Anderson

21/8/68 It's Hard Times, Little Boy Blue, Rowdy Blues, That's All Right, Crazy Fool Woman. Ian A. Anderson (gv), Steve Rye (hca). 14/8/68 S1 DK U

Miller Anderson

7/1/72 Corina Corina, Blackbird, Ship To Nowhere. Solo 13/12/71 T1 JM&PD JWH&BAI Previous session plus band for Mike Harding TX 21/9/71

21/7/72 It Takes A Lot To Laugh It Takes A Train To Cry, Fool's Gold, Garden Of Life, Shadows Across My Wall. 20/6/72 T1 JM JWH

Harvey Andrews and Graham Cooper

14/6/73 Whisky Jack, The Mallard, Down So Long It Looks Like Up, Headlines. Harvey Andrews (gv), Graham Cooper (gv). 21/5/73 U U U Previous duo session TX 25/5/73 not by Peel

Harvey Andrews

15/8/72 Gift Of A Brand New Day, Unaccompanied, Hey Sunday, I Used To Revolve At 78rpm But Now It's Down To 33.3rpm, Don't Know The Time. Harvey Andrews (gv). 17/7/72 PH JW BC&MF

Andromeda

17/11/68 The Reason, Looking For You, Day Of The Change, Return To Sanity. John Cann (gv), Mick Hawkesworth (bv), Jack Collings (d). 29/10/68 PC1 BA AH

Dave Angel

26/5/96 Slave, Fever, Untitled, A Slice Of Enforcement. 26/5/96 OS

28/8/97 DJ set live from MV4

3/9/98 DJ set live from Y4

31/8/99 DJ set live from MV3 AR SA

Angelic Upstarts

30/10/78 We Are The People, Student Power, Upstart, Youth Leader. Mensi (lv), Mond (g), Steve (b), Sticks (d). 24/10/78 MV4 U MR

1/10/80 Guns For The Afghan Rebels, Last Night Another Soldier, Kids On The Street, Sticks' Diary. Glyn Warren (b) r Steve. 17/9/80 MV4 DG NG

29/6/81 Two Million Voices, You're Nicked, I Understand (Pt.3), New Values. Decca Wade (d) r Sticks & Simon Lloyd (sx). 23/6/81 LH1 DG MR

Angelica

23/2/00 Concubine Blues, Bring Back Her Head, Fireflies. Holly Ross (g, v, p, cel), Brigit Colton (b, v, p), Claire Windsor (g, v, cel), Rachel Parsons (d, vi). 15/12/99 MV4 ME NF

Angels 1–5

8/7/81 Cut And Dried, Accident In Studio 4, Living For The Future, Workface. Cressida Bowyer (v), Jimmy Cauty (gv), John Cook (bv), Martin Cottis (dv). 1/7/81 LH1 CL NG 'That was the last session I went along to,' said Peel in 1992; 'I think I went because the woman singer had been in another band we'd liked before. Now what were they called? … er… er… '

Anhrefn

4/8/86 Action Man, Dawns Y Duwiau, Defaid, Nefoedd Un. Sion Sebon (gv), Rhys Mwyn (b), Dewi Gwyn (g), Hefin Huws (d, bck). 22/7/86 U DG MR&MS

11/9/89 Rude Boys, Crafwr, Bach By Ben, Gwesty Cymru. 8/8/89 MV3 DG MA

21/5/93 Clutter From The Gutter, Am Unwaith Yn Dy Fywyd, Sut Fedrwch Chi Anghofio, Croeso I Gymru. Sebon, Mwyn, Margi Clarke (v-2), Dafydd Ieuan (d). 13/4/93 MV3 ME~

Animal Magic

2/2/82 No Sex In Heaven, Get It Right, Human Being, Standard Man. Gill Baker (tp), Rob Boswell (d), Mark Hollis (sx), Mark Tayler (b), James Hill (perc), Howard Purse (gv). 20/1/82 MV4 KH U

22/9/82 Bus To Bulawao, Honesty, Love Subversion, Slim Jim From The Boneyard. 8/9/82 U U U

Another Pretty Face

25/2/81 This Time It's Real, Lightning That Strikes Twice, Out Of Control, I'll Give You Fire. John Cattwell (g, vi, bck), Adrian Johnston (d), Alan Muir (b), Mike Scott (v, p, g, vi), Paul Connelly (handclaps). 18/2/81 LH1 CL NG

Ant

12/10/00 History, Any Girl Can Make Me Shine, Maybe Love Will Return, The Trick. Anthony Harding (gv, hca). 26/7/00 MV4 SA RJ

Anti Hero

28/5/02 Who's Looking Out For Number One, You Got Nothing, Try Again, Mtv. Pete Hurley (gv), Marcus Ratcliffe (lg), Davo McConville (b), Jack Hamson (d, smp). 24/2/02 MV4 ME NF

18/2/03 Don't Trust The DJ, Love Will Tear Us Apart Again, Why Do You Look So Scared, Uk Garage Girl. 5/2/03 MV4 SA NS

Any Trouble

6/3/80 Girls Are Always Right, Turn Up The Heat, Second Choice, Yesterday's Love. Mel Harey (d), Phil Barnes (b), Clive Gregson (glv), Chris Parks (lg). 27/2/80 MV4 JE NG

APB

11/1/82 My Love, Higher The Climb, Crooner's Lullabye, From You And Back To You. Iain Slater (bv), Glenn Roberts (gv), George Cheyne (dv). 23/12/81 MV4 JWI U

5/1/83 Got It In One, Play It, Wondering, Back Inside Your Heart. 13/12/82 MV4 TW DD

Aphex Twin

5/12/92 Afx6, Illumineph, T Q T, Quintute, Blue Colx. Richard D James (e). 9/9/92 OS 'Thank you very much for your help, Richard D James (age 21)' note on sheet

14/4/95 No 1, No 2, No 3, No 4. 10/4/95 OS

Aphrodisiacs

25/9/02 Against The Grain, Backbone Of Society, This Is A Campaign, Sordid Secrets. Kevin Carlin (b, d, prg), Stephen McFall (gkv), John Cairns (g). 1/9/02 MV4 ME GYW

5/10/04 Terrahawk, The Tomorrow People, The Hour Is Late But Please Consider, Do You Remember The First Time? 18/8/04 MV4 JSM GT

The Apollinaires

25/8/82 First Degree, The Feeling's Gone, Envy The Love, Dance With Your Heart. Francis (g), Tom (g), Simon (perc), Kraig (d), James (b), Paul (v) & Chris (tp), Pete (sx), Lawrence (sx), Paul (tb), Steven (fl). 12/7/82 MV4 TW MC

Apparat

16/6/04 Komponent, Not A Good Place, It's Gonna Be A Long Walk, Silizium. Sascha Ring (g, prd), Raz Ohara (v), Lisa Verena (clo), Katrin Pfaender (vi, vla). 13/5/04 Y4 SA JHT Note from Sascha: track titles changed to Phon, Van, Dis and H

Appendix Out

28/6/01 Frozen Blight, Cyclone, I Went Hunting, Ice Age. Tom Crossley (d, fl, bck), Gareth Eggie (g, o, bck), David Elcock (bv), Ali Roberts (gpv). 12/6/01 MV4 SA JHT

Appliance

6/10/98 Fast Music, Pre Rocket Science, Pacifica, Throwing A Curve Ball. James Brooks (gkv), David Ireland (perc, elp), Michael Parker (b, el, fx, tone generator). 6/9/98 MV4 ME KR

3/2/00 Slow Roller, Personal Stereo, Electra. 3/9/99 MV4 ME KR

7/8/01 Navigating The Nursery Slopes, A Little More Information, Comrades, Homing Devices. 22/7/01 MV4 ME NF

19/11/02 Tuesday's Nearly Over, Violins, Mountains 1, As Far As I Can See. 24/10/02 GT GYW

Arab Strap

25/3/97 The Smell Of Outdoor Cooking, Soaps, I Saw You, The First Big Peel Thing. Aidan Moffat (v), Malcolm Middleton (g), David Gow (d), Gary Miller (b) & Chris Geddes (k), Stuart Murdoch (b). 4/3/97 MV4 MR JB

10/3/98 Packs Of Three, Piglet, The Night Before The Funeral, Blood. 4-piece. 10/2/98 MV4 NK

9/5/00 The Drinking Eye, Pro- (Your) Life, Tiny Girls (& Leave The Day Free, 10/5/00). & Barry Burns (p). U C19 Produced and engineered by Arab Strap and Andy Miller

Arc

13/3/71 Guru, Hello Monday, Great Lager Street. Mick Gallagher (elp, o, v), John Turnbull (lgv), Rob Tait (d), Tom Duffy (bv). 1/3/71 PH JW BC 'They must surely top the bill at the News of the World Awards Concert as my brother-in-law plays the keyboards and co-writes much of the material' Walters to audition panel. Unanimous pass

Archers Of Loaf

23/4/94 Backwash, South Carolina, I'll Never Think Of You Again, Revenge. Mark Price (d), Matthew Gentling (b), Eric Johnson (g), Eric Bachmann (g). 20/3/94 MV3 ME FK

4/11/94 Thunder Fog, Bacteria, Smoking Pot In The Hot City, Mutes In The Steeple. 22/9/94 MV4 TdB JLC

Argent

25/4/72 Tragedy, Rejoice, Keep On Rolling, Liar. Rod Argent (kv), Russ Ballard (gv), Robert Henrit (d), Jim Rodford (b). 4/4/72 MV4 PR U Group's trial broadcast on John Peel's Concert 5/7/70 passed by audition panel. 5 other Sounds of the Seventies sessions followed, not for Peel

Ariel

12/11/74 Rock & Roll Seas, Yeah Tonight, What The World Needs Now Is A New Pair Of Socks, Worm-turning Blues, I'll Be Bone. John Lee (d), Harvey James (g), Phil Putt (b), Michael Rudd (gv). 29/10/74 MV4 TW BC

Joan Armatrading

28/11/72 Head Of The Table, Spend A Little Time, Child Star, Whatever's For Us. Joan Armatrading (ag, pv). 31/10/72 LH1 JW BC

5/4/73 Lonely Lady, Alice, City Girl, Lazy Day. & possibly Larry Steel (b), Henry Spinetti (d) & unknown (lg). 19/3/73 LH1 BA U

19/7/73 Spend A Little Time, Give It A Try, Steppin' Out, Catchin' Up. Solo. 25/6/73

LH1 BA U

15/1/74 Some Sort Of Love Song, Lonely Lady, Freedom. & Snowy White (g), Mike Tomich (b), Brian Glascock (d). 14/1/74 T1 JW U

25/6/74 Old But Gold, Back To The Night, Dry Land, World's Gonna Love Me Tonight. & Peter Zorn (al, fl-1). 20/5/74 LH1 JW U

17/2/75 Steppin Out, Back To The Night, No Love For Free. & Jean Roussel (k), Gerry Conway (d), Tony Reeves (b). 4/2/75 MV4 TW BAI

17/7/75 Back To The Night, Tall In The Saddle, Body To Dust, City Girl. & The Movies: Julian Diggle (perc), Greg Knowles (g), Durban Laverde (b), Dag Small (k), Jamie Laine (d). 10/7/75 MV4 TW BAI

25/8/76 Kissing And Hugging, Down To Zero, Help Yourself, People. & Pat Donaldson (b), Jerry Donahue (g), Dave Mattacks (d). 29/7/76 LH1 TW BAI

John Armstrong

10/8/99 DJ mix. OS

Billy Boy Arnold

14/10/77 I'm Ready, Baby Please Don't Go, Goin' Away Baby, Oo-wee, I Wish You Would. Gordon Smith (g), Bernie Pallo (g), Bob Davies (b), Ted Tetlow (d). 5/10/77 MV4 TW NG

PP Arnold

14/1/68 Satisfaction, Tin Soldier, If You're Think You're Grooving, You Make Me Feel Like A Natural Woman, Road To Nowhere. PP Arnold (v) & (g), (b), (d), (o, p), (fl, al), (al, ts), (ts, bars) U & Madeline Bell, Dusty Springfield (bck). 2/1/68 PC1 BA DT First solo session had been TX 18/1/68, Pop North

Arson Garden

24/2/91 Cold, Impossible Space, Kathy's In Deep, It Will Soon Be Over. Joby Barnett (d), Michael Mann (g), April Combs (v), Chip Starr (b), James Combs (g). 4/12/90 MV5 MR MR

Artery

28/7/81 The Clown, Into The Garden, Potential Silence, Afterwards. Mark Goldthorpe (v), Mick Fidler (g, sx, bck), Garry Wilson (d, bck), Neil McKenzie (b), Simon Hinkler (o). 20/7/81 MV4 TW DD

15/2/82 The Ghost Of A Small Tour Boat Captain, Lousie, The Slide, The Sailor Situation. 30/1/82 MV4 DG MR

Ascii Disko

21/10/03 Immer, Einfach, I Wanna Be Your Dog, Untitled. Daniel Holt (e). 1/10/03 OS

Ash

30/4/94 Silver Surfer, Season, Petrol, Jazz 59. Tim Wheeler (gv), Mark Hamilton (b), Rick McMurray (d). 3/4/94 MV3 ME MWT

27/4/96 I'd Give You Anything, Get Ready, Lose Control, Darkside Lightside. 14/4/96 MV3 ME KR

15/4/99 Folk Song, Something Like You, Aphrodite, What Deaner Was Talking About, Girl From Mars. Tim Wheeler (agv), Charlotte Hatherley (ag) only. Live from Peel Acres AR GT

6/6/01 Walking Barefoot, Candy, Sometimes, Pacific Pallisades, There's A Star, World Domination, Jack Names The Planets, Submission, Teenage Kicks, Melon Farmer, Girl From Mars. 4-piece & Damien O'Neill (gv-9). Live from MV4 MA NF&GT

Ashman Reynolds

14/7/72 Came Right In, Taking Off, I'm Tired I'm Cold And I'm Hungry, Work Out The Score. Rod Edwards (p), Bob Weston (lg), Keith Boyce (d), Harry Reynolds (bv), Aleki Ashman (v). 12/6/72 MV3 JM U A 2nd session was recorded for Johnnie Walker's lunchtime show on 21/6 & TX before this, on 3/7

The Aspects

12/12/01 We Get Fowl, Psycho Boogie, My Genre, Correct English, Best Music. Ian Merchant, Ben Weaver, Chris Parsons, Ryan Jarrett, Nicholas Burt. 21/9/01 SGA Studio, Bristol

The Associates ○

4/5/81 Me Myself And The Tragic Story, Nude Spoons, A Matter Of Gender, It's Better This Way, Ulcragyceptimol. Billy McKenzie (v), Alan Rankin (g, k), Mike Dempsey (b), John Murphy (d). 28/4/81 LH1 DG MR ● SFPS075

19/4/82 Waiting For The Love Boat, Australia, Love Hangover, A Severe Case Of Career Insecurity. Steve Golding (d) r Murphy; & Martha Ladly (v-3). 6/3/82 MV43 DG MR ○ both sessions on SFRSCD115

Astrid

8/5/01 Modes Of Transport, Just One Name, Fat Girl, What You're Thinking. William Campbell (gv), Charles Clark (gv), Gareth Russell (b), Neil Payne (d). 21/3/01 MV4 SA GYW

Astronaut

7/10/98 Three, You're In Love, One In A Million, Just Can't Take It. Alex Eckford (kv), Brychan Todd (g), Graeme Elston (b, bck), Dave Masterman (d). 18/8/98 MV4 MR NF

Aswad

2/9/76 Can't Stand The Pressure†, Ethiopian Rhapsody, Back To Africa†, Natural Progression†. Brinsley Forde (gv), Donald Griffiths 'Dee' (lgv), Angus Gaye 'Drummie Zeb' (dv), George Oban 'Ras' (b), Courtney Hemmings (kv), Bunny McKenzie (hca, v), Candy McKenzie (v). 10/8/76 MV4 TW BAI&NG

18/12/78 Behold†, Love Has Its Ways, It's Not Our Wish. Tony Gadd (kv), Donnal Benjamin (gv) r Hemmings, Griffiths. 10/10/78 MV4 MB TdB † ○ SFRSCD002 The BBC Sessions

Pete Atkin

3/3/72 Driving Through Mythical America, Apparition In Las Vegas, Wristwatch For A Drummer, All The Dead Were Strangers (& The Girl On The Train, A Guitar Is A Thief In The Night, 21/4/72). Lineup unknown. 15/2/72 T1 JM U Atkin's 1st session, with an 8-piece band, had been in August 1970, for David Symonds, produced by Bernie Andrews

14/3/72 Thief In The Night, 30 Year Man, Uncle Seabird, A King At Nightfall. 6/3/72 PH JW BC

22/8/72 The Wristwatch For A Drummer, Between Us There Is Nothing, All The Dead Were Strangers, Screen Freak. 31/7/w2 PH JW BC&BAI

3/4/73 Perfect Moments, The Hypertension Kid, The Beautiful Changes, The Last Hill That Shows You All The Valley. 13/3/73 LH1 JW BC

9/8/73 Ready For The Road, Be Careful When They Offer You The Moon, Between Us There Is Nothing, Senior Citizen. 30/7/73 LH1 BA U

1/1/74 The Man Who Walked Towards The Music, National Steel, Pay Day Evening, An Array Of Passionate Lovers. 20/11/73 LH1 JW BC

28/5/74 Perfect Moments, Payday Evening, Wall Of Death, The Road Of Silk. Pete Atkin (p, elpv), Les Davidson (g), Maurice Adamson (b), Andy Monroe (d). 14/5/74 LH1 TW U

26/11/74 Session Man Blues, I See The Joker, Black Funk Rex, Rain Wheels, Nothing Left To Say. 12/11/74 U U U

9/10/75 Uncle Sea Bird, Errant Knight, Lonesome Levis Lane, Stranger In Town. & Dick Levens, Neil Campbell, Roger Odell. 18/9/75 MV4 U U

Juan Atkins

17/11/98 DJ set live from Y4 U

Atlantis

29/3/73 Let's Get On The Road Again, Maybe It's Useless, My Dreams Are The Vision Of My Former Life, Rock 'n' Roll Preacher. Ingar Rumpf (v), Jean-Jacques Kravatz (op), Karl Heinz Schott (b), Udo Lindenberg (d), Klaus-Georg Meier (g). 19/3/73 LH1 BA U

Natacha Atlas

4/11/95 Diaspora, Duden, Fun Does Not Exist. Natacha Atlas (v, zils), Acker Bismillah Lazarus Dolphy (Clarins.Wind Synths), Dubulah (b), Alex Kasiek (k), Hamid Man Tu (d, Tongue Drum/Drum Pads), Essam Rashad (Oud), Neil Sparkes (Narration). 22/9/95 OS

Attic

10/12/80 The Axxe, Art 5946 Foreign, The Ability To Speak, Whenever Is It. Robert Bartlett (lv), Pete Coote (gk, bck), Mark Bushell (d), Steve Austin (b, bck), Simon Green (gk). 3/12/80 LH1 BS NG

Attila the Stockbroker

30/6/82 Cocktails / Nigel Wants To Go To C&A's, They Must Be Russians / Russians In The DHSS / Russians In McDonalds, Death In Bromley / A Bang And A Wimpy / The Night I Slept With Seething Wells, 5th Column / Russians At Henley Regatta. Attila (v). 9/6/82 MV4 RP U

29/3/83 England Are Back / Holiday In Albania, Burn It Down / Eros Products, A Very Silly East European Propaganda Station / Where You Goin' With That Flounder In Your Hand?, Sawdust And Empire. & Steve Drewett (gb), Simon O'Brien (d), Ruth O'Brien (fl), Chris Payne (k, vi, recv), Tim Vonce (recv), Lin O'Brien (acc), Johnny Smegma (v). 14/3/83 MV4 JP MC

Attwenger

16/10/92 Paf Polka, Masta Waltz, 8 Hend, Bier, De Lied. Markus Binder, Hans-Peter Falkner. 14/10/92 Budapest

The Au Pairs

9/10/79 Pretty Boy†, Come Again, Ideal Woman†, Monogamy†. Lesley Woods (gv), Paul Foad (gv), Jane Munro (b), Pete Hammond (d). 26/10/79 MV4 BS NG

12/6/80 Dear John, The Love Song, It's Obvious, Repetition. 28/5/80 MV4 DG NG

28/1/81 We're So Cool, Armagh, The Set Up, Headache For Michelle. 21/1/81 LH1 CL NG

31/3/82 America, Steppin' Out Of Line, Sex Without Stress. 15/3/82 MV4 TW DD † on ○ Stepping Out Of Line, Castle Music 2006

Aubrey Small

1/12/71 If I Were You, Seeing Believing, You'll Always Be A Dreamer, You'll Agree With Me, Questions. Rod Taylor (elp), Pete Pinckney (gv), Allan Christmas (g, bck), Dave Young (fl, bck), Graham Hunt (d). 22/11/71 U U BC 3 previous sessions for Bob Harris, 1st in September 1970

Audience

7/4/72 Trombone Gluch, Barracuda Dan, Buy Me An Island (& Thunder And Lightning, 19/5/72). Howard Werth (gv), Trevor Williams (bv), Anthony Connor (perc, v), Nick Judd, Patrick Charles. 13/3/72 T1 PD U

Brian Auger's Trinity

19/11/67 A Kind Of Love-in, Save Me, Shadows Of You, Isola Na Tale, Goodbye Jungle Telegraph. Brian Auger, Julie Driscoll & the Trinity. 10/11/67 PH BA U Passed audition, Aeolian 2, 18/10/63, line-up then: Brian Auger (p), Rick Laird (db), Phil Kinorra (d). 1st session, Jazz Club, Light Programme, rec the Paris 5/12/63, 1st TX 7/12/63, Prod Bryant Marriott. Many sessions followed

14/4/68 Why (Am I Treated So Bad?), A Day In The Life, This Wheel's On Fire, Inside Of Him, Calze Rosse. Driscoll (v-1,3,4) & unknown (g). 8/4/68 PC1 BA PR

27/10/68 Old Jim Crow, I'm Not Talkin', Road To Cairo, Lonesome Hobo. Auger & Driscoll only. 7/10/68 PC1 BA U

Brian Auger's Oblivion Express

9/6/72 Somebody Help Us, Blind Man, Just Me Just You. Brian Auger (o, p, elp), Jim Mullen (lg), Godfrey MacLean (d), Barry Dean (b). 16/5/72 T1 JM JWH 5 previous Sounds of the Seventies sessions for this band, not for Peel

Autechre

13/10/95 Milk DX, Drane, Inhake 2. Rob Brown, Sean Booth. 30/8/95 OS ○ WARP Records WAP112 CD

8/9/99 Gelk, Blifil, Gaekwad, 19 Headaches. 5/7/99 OS Titles invented by Peel during broadcast for untitled pieces on session sheet. ○ WARP Records WAP150 CD

27/5/03 Mix OS

Auteurs

8/3/96 Kids Issue, Buddha, A New Life A New Family, After Murder Park. Barny C Rockford (d), Alice Readman (b), James Banbury (cello, o), Luke Haines (gv). 20/2/96 MV4 MR JMK

Autopop

3/8/96 Tristan Dahling, Bootboy Remembers, Smile Of Fortune, Unhand Me Brother. Aidan O'Halloran (bv), Eddie Walsh (gv), Chris Catchpole (v), Rob Hague (d). 25/6/96 U U U

Autumn 1904

5/3/84 I Heard Catherine Sing, The City, Give It Time, Innocence. Keith Falconer (d), Billy Bowie (b), Allan Dumbreck (k), Ross Thom (g), Billy Leslie (v), Lisa Cameron & Indira Sharma (bck). 25/2/84 MV5 DG MC

Avrocar

23/11/04 Julius and Venona, Kinora Viewer, Romdog, Forst Zina. Perry McDonagh (gv), Penny McConnell (v), Stefan Marangoci (g), Antony Harding (k), Damian Gaffney (d). 26/10/04 MV4 JSM NF

Kevin Ayers

28/2/70 Stop This Train†, Clarence In Wonderland†, Why Are We Sleeping†, The Oyster And The Flying Fish (& Hat Song†, no record of TX). Kevin Ayers (gb, lv) & Soft Machine: Robert Wyatt (d, p-2, bck), David Bedford (p), Lol Coxhill (ss), Nick Evans (tb), Elton Dean (al), Lyn Dobson (fl). Hopper (b) & Ratledge (o) also contracted to appear. 10/2/70 MV4 JW TW

11/7/70 Derby Day†, The Interview†, We Did It Again†, Lunatic's Lament. & The Whole World: David Bedford (p), Mike Oldfield (b), Lol Coxhill (sx), Nick Fincher (d). 9/6/70 MV4 JW TW

14/4/72 Take Me To Tahiti, Whatevershebringswesing, Stranger In Blue Suede Shoes, The Interview. & 3 singers (10 in all): including Robert Wyatt, Johnny van Derek. 21/3/72 T1 JWH&BAI

30/7/74 Another Whimsical Song†, Lady Rachel†, Stop This Train†, Didn't Feel Lonely Till I Thought Of You†. & the Soporifics: Rabbit (k), Ollie Halsall (g), Archie Legget (b), Freddie Smith (d). 9/7/74 LH1 PR BAI

22/7/76 Star†, Mr Cool†, Love's Gonna Turn You Round†, Ballad Of Mr Snake†. & Andy Summers (g), Zoot Money (k, bck), Charlie McCracken (b), Rob Townsend (d). 13/7/76 MV4 JG MR † on ○ The BBC Sessions 70–76 HUX073

B Movie

7/4/81 Polar Opposites, Welcome To The Shrink, Escalator, All Fall Down. Graham Boffey (d), Paul Statham (lg), Steve Hovington (bv), Rick Holliday (k). 31/3/81 LH1 DG MR

Babe Ruth

14/12/72 Wells Fargo, Bit O'blues, King Kong. Line-up unknown, files missing. 11/12/72 LH1 BA U

2/8/73 Lady, For A Few Dollars, Cool Jerk. 9/7/73 LH1 BA U

Babes in Toyland

29/9/90 Catatonic, Ripe, Primus, Spit To See The Shine. Lori Barbero (dv), Michelle Leon (b), Kat Bjelland (gv). 9/9/90 MV3 DG ME&RPF ○

30/6/91 Pearl, Dogg, Laugh My Head Off, Mad Pilot. 11/6/91 U TdB FK&AC ○ SFMCD211 'At last! A Radio One session with a male:female ratio of 1:5!' scribbled on sheet, presumably by Fred Kay or Alison Chorley

22/12/91 Handsome And Gretel, Blood, Mother, Dirty. 18/8/91 MV3 DG MC&PRB

25/7/92 JungleTrain, Right Now, Sometimes, Magic Flute. Maureen Herman (b) r Leon. 11/7/92 MV4 JB DMC&JB

16/6/95 The Girl Can't Help it, Cauter Eyes, Deep Song, Oh Yeah. 7/5/95 MV3 ME AA

Back Door

21/11/72 Skilpered Widlash, Askin' The Way, 32–20, One Day You're Down The Next Day You're Down. Colin Hodgkinson (b), Ron Aspery (al), Tony Hicks (d). 30/10/72 T1 JW&PD U

21/6/73 Dancin' In The Van, Livin' Track, Lieutenant Loose, Back Door, Roberta. 18/6/73 LH1 BA U

3/7/73 Adolphus Beal, Walkin' Blues, It's Nice When It's Up, Cat Cote Rag, His Old Boots. 26/6/73 LH1 JW U

25/10/73 His Old Boots, Blue Country Blues, Walkin' Blues, Adolphus Beal. 1/10/73 LH1 BA U

12/9/74 Slivadiv, The Spoiler, The Dashing White Sargeant, TB, Blakey Jones. & Dave MaCrae (k). Group also recorded several sessions for R2's Jazz Club, and several R1 In Concerts, between 72–75. 5/9/74 LH1 TW U Last session on ○ The Human Bed HUX031

Backwater

4/1/97 Your Perogative, Crucify Me, Supercool, Burn Baby Burn. Barry Peak (gv), Shaun Robinson (d, k), Ryan Mcauley (b), Paul O'Shaughnessy (g). 8/12/96 MV4 ME JMK

Bad Dress Sense

10/3/87 Need To Love, Life's Demand, Always Away, Cynical Smile, Never So Funny. Jason Twitch (d), Ed Shred (gv), Nick Schozzer (v), Paul Pizza (b). 24/2/87 U DG MR&TD

Bad Religion

4/9/93 American Jesus, Recipe For Hate, Kerosene, What Can You Do. Bobby Schayer (d), Jay Bentley (b), Greg Hetson (g), Brett Gurewitz (g), Greg Graffin (v). 24/7/93 MV5 TdB AA

Badgewearer

24/2/95 One Two Look At Your View, Blue Gorillas Are The Only Jazz Gorilla, Diamonds & Dogfood, More Sore, Private Verandah, Anthem Garrison (Verse III Force 10). Leighton Cook (d), Tony Kennedy (b), Neil Bateman (g), Jim Carstairs (v), Michael Hodge (g). 24/1/95 MV4 MR RJ

Bailterspace

5/2/93 The State, Place, Graider, Tanker. Brent McLachlan (d), Alister Parker (g, b, v), John Halvorsen (g, b, v). 6/12/92 MV3 ME JLO

The Baker-Gurvitz Army

23/1/75 Help Me, Inside Of Me, Memory Lane. Ginger Baker (d), Paul Gurvitz (gv), Adrian Gurvitz (bv), Snips (v), Pete Lemer (k). 15/1/75 MV4 U U

The Bakerloo Line

20/10/68 Rock Me, Don't Know Which Way To Go, Smokestack Lightnin', Eleanor Rigby. Terry Poole (bv), Clem Clempson (lgv), John Hinch (d). 24/9/68 PC1 BA BC

16/2/69 Big Bear Ffolly, This Worried Feeling, The Last Blues, Driving Backwards. 10/2/69 U U U

The Balcony

24/11/81 The Lizard Hunt, Surprise After Surprise, She Keeps Her Secret. David Palmer (lv), Caroline Henning (bck), Paul Cavanagh (g), Pete Baker (k), Pete McAsey (b), Bert Gardener (d). 18/11/81 MV4 JWI TdB&MWT

Long John Baldry

30/6/72 Going Down Slow, A Rake And A Rambling Boy, How Long Blues, As Long As I Can Feel The Spirit, Mother Ain't Dead (& Cocaine, 4/8/72). Baldry solo. 29/5/72 T1 JM JWH Long John Baldry had been doing live Radio 1 sessions since 1968. This was his last session for which a contract exists in BBC written archives

ballboy

21/3/00 Essential Wear For Future Trips To Space, I Hate Scotland, Sex Is Boring, Stars and Stripes. Gordon McIntyre (gv), Katie Griffiths (k), Nick Reynolds (b), Gary Morgan (d). 30/1/00 MV3 ME JB

27/2/02 All The Records On The Radio Are Sh*te, Avant Garde Music, I Lost You But I Found Country Music, Olympic Cyclist, Where Do The Nights Of Sleep Go When They Do Not Come To Me, They'll Hang Flags From Cranes Upon My Wedding Day, I Wonder If You're Drunk Enough To Sleep With Me Tonight. Live from MV4 AR SA

23/1/03 A Man's A Man For A'That. OS

20/3/03 You Should Fall In Love With Me, The Time Out Guide, I Gave Up My Eyes To A Man Who Was Blind, Nobody Really Knows Anything. & Caroline Evens (vi-2, 3), Miranda Phillips (vi-2), David Edington (vi-2), Pete Harvey (clo-2, 3, 4). 16/2/03 MV4 GT NS

23/12/03 There Are Only Inches Between Us, Past Lovers, A Starry Night, I Lost You But I Found Country Music. & Laura Cantrell (v-4). Live from Peel Acres AR GT

9/11/04 We've All Had Better Days, Let's Fall In Love And Run Away From Here, Slow Days, The Art Of Kissing, Frankie And Johnny. Alexa Morrison (k, p) r Griffiths. 28/10/04 MV4 NF JSM

The Bambi Slam

16/3/87 La La La (It's Out Of Hand), Shame Of A Sad Sick Psycho, The Awful Flute Song. Roy (gv), Natalie (b, bck), Nick Maynard (d, bck), Linda Miller (clo-1&2). 1/3/87 U DG MR&MFA

Bamboo Zoo

3/9/81 Fools Listen! Consume!, Binding Wire, Ghost Party. Mick Duffy (gv), Joe Duffy (b), Gordon Holden (d), Paul Shorrock (perc), Russ Entwhistle (g). 28/8/81 MV4 DG ME

Banco De Gaia

11/2/94 Gamelah, Heliopolis, Sunspot. Toby Marks. 9/1/94 MV3 ME SCO

The Band Of Susans

11/10/88 I Found That Essence Rare, Child Of The Moon, Throne Of Blood, Hope Against Hope. Karen Haglof (gv), Page Hamilton (gv), Robert Poss (gv), Ronald Spitzer (d, bck), Susan Stenger (bv). 4/10/88 MV4 MR~

13/7/89 Because Of You, Hard Light, Which Dream Came True, Too Late. Mark Lonergan (g, bck) r Hamilton. 2/7/89 MV3 DG MR

Bandoggs

13/1/78 The Taylor In The Tea Chest / Astley's Ride Up And Away, Laird Logie, The Dragon And The Lady / Grand Duke Of York, The Swimming Song. Peter Coe (bz, ml, dul, lv-1), Christine Coe (dul, cnc, v-2), Tony Rose (cnc, mo, v-3), Nick Jones (fd, g). 14/12/77 U MB NG

Bandulu

2/1/93 Soweto 2000, Funk Waffle, Song. Jaimie Bissmire (k), John O'Connell (k), Lucien Thompson (d). 11/11/92 OS

28/7/95 Nought Response, Wha'Appen Peeel, Shenley, Invisible Wall. 22/6/95 MV4 NG GPR

6/4/96 Killer, Shroud Part 2, Sela, Deep Sea Angler. OS

The Bandung File

20/1/88 Handkerchief Toy, Tin-legged Tap Dancer, Addicted To Robert Palmer, Garbage Town. Paul Bacon (v, sx), Steve Attwell (g, bck), Pete Hendy (b, bck), Screw Sawney (prg). 12/1/88 U DG MR&PS

Bang Bang Machine

15/2/92 Justine, Monkey, A Charmed Life, Say It Again Joe. Lamp (d), Stan Wood (b), Steve Eagles (g), Elizabeth (v). 28/1/92 MV4 MR MR

Bangtwister

23/7/97 Your Dumb Life, 3 50, Grounded, Downside Up. Alf Mitchell (bv), Keef Beacon (dv), Gordon Brady (gv). 2/7/97 MV5 SA~

The Baptist Generals

13/11/02 Alcohol (Turn And Fall), Unimaginative, Feds, It's Over. Chris Flemmons (gv), Steve Hill (d, perc), Ryan Williams (g, b), Jasom Reimer (g, elp, bck). 10/10/02 MV4 MA GYW

Barbel

12/2/90 Shadow Of A Doubt, (Safe In A) Bubble, World Facts, Inferno. Roger Sinek (d), David Morgan (b), Greg Milton (gv), Alison Williams (o, elp). 2/1/90 MV3 DG MR

30/11/91 Kicker, Lay By, Income Tax, If I Was A Rich Man. & Simon Breed (g). 6/10/91 MV3 DG ME&PF

Barcelona Pavilion

4/9/03 How Are You People Going To Have Fun If None Of You People Participate, Aiden Koper, Rats, Regret / Temptation. Maggie Macdonald (v), Steven Kado (bv), Ben Stimpson (lp), Kat Collins (bv). 18/8/03 MV4 SA JSM

Barclay James Harvest

5/5/68 Mr Sunshine, Early Morning, So Tomorrow, I Can't Go On Without You (& Eden Unobtainable, 2/6/68). John Lees (gv), Mel Pritchard (d), Les Holroyd (bv), Stuart Wolstenholme (kv). 23/4/68 PC1 BA DT 'Unanimous if unenthusiastic pass' from audition panel

4/8/68 Small Time Town, Night, Need You So Bad, Pools Of Blue. 30/7/68 PC1 BA AH&BC

14/1/72 Blue John's Blues, The Poet, After The Day. 20/12/71 U JM U

8/2/72 After The Day, The Poet, Medicine Man. 1/2/72 MV4 PR BC

8/8/74 Crazy City, Mining Disaster, For No-one, Paper Wings. 1/8/74 LH1 TW U

Bardo Pond

12/6/01 Slip Away, Lancaster Gate, Amen. Michael Gibbons (g, p), John Gibbons (g), Isobel Sollenberger (v, fl), Clint Takeda (b), Ed Farnsworth (d). 20/5/01 MV4 ME KR

27/4/04 Destroying Angel, The Word, Isle. & Tom Greenwood (g-2). 25/3/04 MV4 MWT NS

The Bardots

6/6/92 Caterina, Obscenity Thing, Gloriole, Don't Let Me Down. Neil (d), Steve (b), Chris (g, bck), Andy (g), Simon (lv). 5/5/92 MV4 MR~

Barkmarket

14/10/90 Happy, Pencil, The Patsy. Rock Savage (d), John Nowlin (b), David Sardy (gv). 30/9/90 MV3 DG MA&PL

11/3/94 Curio, Hack It Off, Gatherer, Grinder, Whipping Boy. 10/2/94 MV4 NG JMK

Syd Barrett

14/3/70 Baby Lemonade, Effervescing Elephant, Gigolo Aunt, Terrapin (& Two Of A Kind, 30/5/70). Syd Barrett (gv), Dave Gilmour (o, b, g), Jerry Shirley (d). 24/2/70 MV4 JW TW ● SFPS043 & plus Bob Harris 71 session on ○ SFRSCD127

The Basement Five

28/4/80 Last White Christmas, No Ball Games, Immigration, Silicon Chip. JR (g), Leo (b), T (d), DM (v). 21/4/80 MV4 TW DD

Basking Sharks

3/5/83 View From The Hill, New Industry, Theatre War, Diamond Age. Adrian Todd, Jed McPhail & Martyn Eames (all: sy, dm, v). 25/4/83 MV4 TW MC

Bastard Kestrel

15/2/88 Pigout, BS 3704, Risk, Drinking Suicidal. Chris M (d), Keith C (bv), Dik (gv), Paul C (g). 7/2/88 U DG U

9/11/88 Slob, Dog Rabbits, Harry Hausen, Indian Train. Jimmy Perse (d) r Chris M. 1/11/88 MV4 MR~

Bastro

29/1/90 I Come From A Long Line Of Shipbuilders, Extrovert, (I've) Ben Brown, Nothing Special. John McEntire (d, bck), Clark Johnson (b, bck), David Grubbs (gv). 14/1/90 MV3 DG ME

23/7/90 Demons Begone, Krakow Illinois, Floating Home, Recidivist 2. 1/7/90 MV3 DG ME&PA

The Battered Ornaments

8/1/69 Then I Must Go, Security Blues, The Week Looked Good On Paper, Water Carrier, Station Song. Pete Brown (v), Nisar Ahmed Khan (ts, fl), Peter Bailey (cga), Robert Tate (d), Butch Potter (b), Chris Spedding (lg). 1/1/69 PC1 JM U 'Tuneless lead vocalist… a lead voice which could never be called singing… all the tricks serve only to emphasise their mediocrity'… lyrically meaningless and pretentious… material laughable… awful', audition panel: Failed

14/9/69 Sandcastle, Slag Room, Half Past Ladbroke, Going Underground. & Brian Miller (o, v), Brown out. 2/9/69 MV4 JW U Granted second trial broadcast after Brown's departure. Passed: 'avant-garde hairy group for Top Gear-type shows only'

Bauhaus

3/1/80 A God In An Alcove, The Spy In The Cab, Telegram Sam, Double Dare†. Peter Murphy (v), Daniel Ash (g), David Jay (b), Kevin Haskins (d, perc). 4/12/79 U JS MR † on 4AD LP ● In The Flat Field CAD13

12/4/82 The Party Of The First Part, Three Shadows (pt.2), Departure†. 13/3/82 MV4 DG MC † later on B side of Beggar's Banquet 12-inch BEG 91T 'She's in Parties'

The Bays

6/3/02 No titles, all tracks improvised live. Andy Gangadeen (d) & prob Nick Cohen (b), Jamie Odell (k), Simon Wadmore (vocal smp, sfx), Richard Barbieri (sy). Live from MV4 AR SA

7/4/04 No titles, all tracks improvised live. 7/4/04 MV4 AR GT

Bear Quartet

17/7/93 Spoon, High Noon, Hrrn Hrrn, Gone Gone, Sandi Morning And Lude. Mattias Alkberg (gv), Jari Haapalainen (g), Peter Nouttaniemi (b), Urban North (d), Johan Forsling (g) 5/6/93 OS Sweden

Bearsuit

11/7/01 Stop What You're Doing What You're Doing Is Wrong, Hei Jaska Hei Jokunen, Minerals Made Me, Poor Prince Neal. Cerian Hamer (cnt, k, perc), Lisa Horton (v, k, acc, perc), Matt Hutchings (d), Matt Moss (b), Jan Robertson (fl, g, perc), Iain Ross (gv). 20/6/01 MV4 MA JHT

26/9/01 A Plea, Hovercar, Trul Sheri, Hey Charlie Hey Chuck, I Thought You Said You Were Blind, Drink Ink, Poor Prince Neal. Live from MV4 SCU MA/GYW

1/8/02 I Feel The Heat Of The Light From Heaven, Tiny Barnes, Come Around, Disembowel The Demonkind, Disco For Rodents. 16/6/02 MV4 ME KR

The Beat

5/11/79 Tears Of A Clown, Mirror In The Bathroom, Ranking Full Stop, Click Click, Big Shot. Everett Morton (d), Dave Wakeling (g, lv), Ranking Roger (perc, v, styles), David 'Shuffle' Steele (b), Andy Cox (g, bck). 24/10/79 MV4 BS NG

22/9/80 Too Nice To Talk To, Walk Away, Monkey Murders (9 Mexicans), New Psychedelic Rockers. Saxa (sx), Blockhead (k-2,3,4) join. 3/9/80 MV4 BS ME

29/3/82 Spar Wid Me, Till The End Of The Party, She's Going She's Gone, Save It For Later, Sole Salvation, Patou And Roger A Go Talk. & Lionel Martin Jr (sx), Blockhead out. U PRIV

Beatnigs

7/12/88 Suffering, The Statement On Built-in Obsolescence, The Mash, Fight Fire With Water. Michael Franti (blv), Andre (k, smp, tps, bck), Henri Flood (cga, ti, perc), Rono Tse (v, tp, perc), Kelvin (d, bck, smp, perc). 4/12/88 HP DG ME

Beatnik Filmstars

1/7/95 Jam Shoes, Chips, New Boyfriend And Black Suit, A Craze Exploding, Dogstar. Ian Roughley (d), Jerry Francis (b), Andrew Jarrett (gv), John Austin (gv), Tim Rippington (g, k). 4/6/95 MV3 ME NS

17/8/96 Pilot Jack De La Zouche, Wing Off A Plane, Rumpus Throw, Milk. Tom Adams (d) r Roughley; & Paula Knight (d-3). 21/7/96 MV3 ME PN

11/3/97 Hop Boys (Into Kraut Rock), Ransack The Misfits, Now I'm A Millionaire, Mess/Is This Is Rad? 25/2/97 MV4 MR~ U

19/8/97 His Part In The Death Of A Lottery Winner, I Can Tame Lions, Squeemish, Less Than One In Ten, Goodbye Miss Barcelona. Rippington out. 3/8/97 MV4 ME PF

29/1/98 13th Annual Showdown, Pop Dramas (Camp It Up), Good Things Proud Man, Life Amongst The Cowboys, Our Celestial Pilot, Better In Space. 4-piece & Paula Knight (vi-4). 14/12/97 MV4 ME JMK

Be Bop Deluxe

27/11/73 Axe Victim, Blusey Ruby, Tomorrow The World. Bill Nelson (gv), Robert Bryan (b), Ian Parkin (g), Nick Dew (d). 6/11/73 LH1 TW BC

23/5/74 Third Floor Heaven†, Adventures In A Yorkshire Landscape†, Mill Street Junction†, Fifteenth Of July (Invisibles)†. 9/5/74 LH1 TW BAI

17/3/75 Maid In Heaven†, Stage Whispers†, Sister Seagull†, Lights. Nelson, Andrew Clark (k), Charlie Tumahai (bv), Simon Fox (d). 11/3/75 MV4 TW BAI

23/2/76 Blazing Apostles†, Crying To The Sky†, Peace Of Mind†. 10/2/76 MV4 TW MR

25/1/77 Millstreet Junction, Adventures In A Yorkshire Landscape, Still Shining. 17/1/77 MV4 TW DD

6/2/78 Super Enigmatix, Panic In The World†, Possession, Love In Flames†. 30/1/78 MV4 TW DD † ○ on Tramcar To Tomorrow HUX009

Jeff Beck Group

5/11/67 Ain't Superstitious, Beck's Bolero, Loving You Is Sweeter Than Ever, You'll Never Get To Heaven If You Break My Heart, You Shook Me (Tales Of Mickey Waller). Jeff Beck (gv), Ron Wood (b), Micky Waller (d), Rod Stewart (v). 1/11/67 MV4 BP PR 3 previous sessions earlier in 67 for Sat Club (2) and David Symmonds

29/9/68 You Shook Me, Shapes Of Things, Sweet Little Angel, Mother's Old Rice Pudding (& Rock My Plimsoul, 3/11/68). 17/9/68 PC1 BA U

14/1/72 Going Down, Got The Feeling (& Ice Cream Cokes, 11/2/72). Beck & Clive Chaman (b), Cozy Powell (d), Max Middleton (k), Bob Tench (v). 14/12/71 T1 JM NG&MF

Beckett

10/1/74 Rolling Thunder, Life's Shadow, Tiffany. U 7/1/74 U BA U Debut session for Harris Nov 73

The Bee Gees

15/10/67 In My Own Time, I Close My Eyes, New York Mining Disaster 1941, Massachussets, Mrs Gillespie's Refrigerator, To Love Somebody, Cucumber Castle (& World, 12/11/67). Barry Gibb, Robin Gibb, Maurice Gibb, Colin Peterson & Vince Maloney & 'small group'. 9/10/67 PC1 BA DT Debut session for Sat Club April 67, producing 'rave notices from the audition panel' noted Jimmy Grant

18/2/68 Birdie Told Me, With The Sun In My Eyes, The Earnest Of Being George, And The Sun Will Shine. & Tony Gilbert for the services of 19 musicians, Bill Shepherd (md) (Bill Shepherd Orchestra). 13/2/68 PH BA U

Bee Vamp

9/11/81 Lucky Grills, London Bridge (Is Falling Down), Valium Girls, Nigel Follows Barry To Bengal, Our Eyes Met Across The Disco Floor. Paul Ablett (sx), Jim Parris (db, b), Martin King (g), Rory Lynch (d). 24/10/81 MV4 DG PS

Captain Beefheart and his Magic Band

4/2/68 Sure 'Nuff 'N Yes I Do, Yellow Brick Road, Abba Zabba, Electricity. Captain Beefheart (v), John French (rg), Alex St Clair (lg), Geoffrey Hanley (d), Jeff Cotton (b). 24/1/68 MV4 BA DT&BC

12/5/68 Safe As Milk, Beatle Bones 'n' Smoke 'n' Stones, Kandy Korn, You Gotta Trust Us. 6/5/68 PC1 BA PR&AH

Bees Make Honey

23/1/73 Get On Board, The Woman From Booterstown, Bloodshot Eyes, Hanging On Hoping Strong. U 9/1/73 U U BC

4/12/73 Knee Trembler, On Virginia, The Sweet Taste Of Moonshine, Rocking Days. U 13/11/73 U U BC

The Bees

1/5/01 A Minha Menina, Punch Bag, No Trophy, This Town, Binnel Bay. Paul Butler (gv), Aaron Fletcher (b), Mick Clevett (d, perc), Warren Hampshire (o, perc), Tim Parkin (tp, bck). 22/4/01 MV4 ME~ JHT

Si Begg

29/9/98 Untitled, Untitled 2. Billed as 'Buckfunk 3000'. 29/9/98 MV4 SA~

14/11/01 Intro, This Is The Way, I Like That (Brand New), We Are Not A Rock Band, Eurostar, Freestyle Disco, I'm The Bomb. Si Begg (DJ) as S I Futures. Live from MV4 AR NF

16/9/03 U R D Best, Gerbil Trouble, Tigon And Ligers, Entertainment. 20/8/03 OS

Belle & Sebastian

19/6/01 Shoot The Sexual Athlete, The Magic Of A Kind Word (For Papa John), Nothing In Silence, (My Girl's Got) Miraculous Technique. Stuart Murdoch (gv), Stevie Jackson (v, g, hca, bj), Isobel Campbell (v, perc, glo), Sarah Martin (v, mel, vi), Chris Geddes (vib, perc, p, sy), Richard Colburn (d, perc), Mick Cooke (tp, b, frh, vib) & Charlie Cross, Ollie Langford, Vuk Kracovic, Helen Keen. 11/5/01 MV4 SA~ JHT

25/7/02 You Don't Send Me, Roy Walker, Love On The March, Sleep On A Sunbeam, Desperation Made A Fool Of Me. Murdoch, Martin, Colburn, Jackson, Geddes, Cooke, Bob Kildea (g, b). Live from Peel Acres AR GT

18/12/02 Christmas Time, Santa Claus, Step Into My Office Party, Jonathon David, Santa Claus Go Straight To The Ghetto, Photo Jenny, Silent Night, Oh Little Town Of Bethlehem, Santa Bring My Baby Back To Me, If You Find Yourself Caught In Love, The Boy With The Arab Strap, O Come O Come Emmanuel, Get Me Away From Here, Took Some Time For Christmas, 12 Days Of Christmas, Oh Come All Ye Faithful. Live from MV4 AR MA&NF

23/1/03 Ye Banks and Braes / Address To The Toothache. OS

16/12/04 Meat And Potatoes, Funny Little Frog, I Took A Long Hard Look. Live from MV4 NF RJ

Bellrays

13/8/02 Change The World, Remember, Shotgun, Rude Awakening / Thunder All The Time, The Change Is Changing, Get It Right, New Kid, Voodoo Kid. Lisa Kekaula (v), Robert Vennum (b, bck), Tony Fate (gv), Vince Meghtouni (g). 7/7/02 MV4 ME GT

The Beloved

15/1/85 The Flame, A Hundred Words, Idyll, A Beautiful Waste Of Time. Jon Marsh (kv), Steve Waddington (g), Tim Havard (b), Guy Gausden (d). 8/1/85 MV5 MRD PW

23/10/85 Josephine, Up A Tree, So Seldom Solemn, In Trouble And Shame. 13/10/85 MV5 DG ME

Bennet

3/4/96 Hello We Are Bennet, Someone Always Gets There First, Motorbike, Colossal Man. Jason Applin (gv), Andy Bennet (b), Kevin Moorey (d), Johnny Peer (g, bck). Live from MCR3 LR CLE

27/7/96 Dance The Matrimonial Polka, Jordan Bennett, Someone Always Gets There First, Karaoke. 2/6/96 MV3 ME PA

18/1/97 Air Hockey, Mums Gone To Iceland, Married With Children, Bennet Have Left The Building. & Neil McCurley (k). 5/1/97 MV4 ME JLO

Tony 'Duster' Bennett

10/4/68 Worried Mind, I've Been A Fool, Everybody Got A Friend But Me, Blues With A Feeling. U 20/3/68 U DK U

3/11/68 Worried Mind, I'm Gonna Wind Up Ending Up, Country Jam, Jumping At Shadows (& I Want You To Love Me, Sleeping In The Ground, 15/12/68). U 14/10/68 U U U

16/4/69 Further Up The Road, What A Dream, Hot Roddin', Rock Of Ages Cleft For Me, Morning Star Blues, Life Is What You Make It. U 16/4/69 S2 PR U

24/1/70 Hill Street Rag, I Chose To Sing The Blues, I Worship The Ground You Walk On, I Was Fooled. & Tony Mills, Stella Bennett. 9/12/69 PH JW U

31/3/72 I Love My Baby, Walking Pork Shops, Country Breakdown (& I Feel So Good, Watcha Gonna Do, 5/5/72). U 28/2/72 U JM U

11/8/72 Pride Of Place, Blue River Rising, Let Your Light Shine On Me (& Back In The Same Old Bag, 22/9/72). U 24/7/72 U JM U

1/11/73 Gone Gershwin, Summertime, Them That Got, Coming Home. U 24/9/73 U BA U

Benny Profane

6/6/88 Everything, Quick Draw McGraw Meets Dead Eye Dick Rob A Bank, Beam Me Up. Becky Stringer (b), Robin Surtees (g), Joseph McKechnie (g), Peter Baker (o), Dave Jackson (v), Dave Brown (d, tamb). 22/5/88 MV4 DG MA

14/2/89 Skateboard To Oblivion, Pink Snow, Fear, Man On The Sauce. Roger Sinek (d) r Brown. 29/1/89 U DG U

15/1/90 Time Bomb, Hey Waste Of Space, Jerked To Jesus, When It All Kicks In. Liam Rice (d) r Sinek. 7/1/90 MV3 DG ME

Justin Berkovi

10/12/97 Real Action, A Distant Teacher, Grey Citadel, The Institute. Justin Berkovi. OS

Andrew Berry

1/10/86 All Alone, God Bless (Your Sister), Take What You Please, Andrew Berry (gv), Vini Reilly (g, b), Simon J. Wolstencroft (d). 21/9/86 U DG ME&FK

Bette Davis

16/4/97 Feed My Ego, Surf Surf Kill Kill, White Food, Big Pussy Sound, Shergar, 898. Brian Percival (g), Tracey Rees (b), Eugene Wolstenholme (k), Joe Robinson (d). 23/3/97 MV4 ME LS

Beulah

15/12/99 Disco The Secretaries Blues, Maroon Bible, Warmer. Miles Kurosky (g, b, v), Steve La Follette (b, k), Pat Noel (k, g), Robin Bennett (fl), Steve St Cin (d), Joe Bennett (vi), Bill Evans (k, hca), Bill Swan (g, tp, v). 31/10/99 MV3 ME~

The Bhundu Boys

14/7/86 Manhenga, Writing On The Wall†, Chemedza Vana†, Let's Work Together, Kuroja Chete. Kenny Chitsvatsva (d), Davie Mankaba (b, bck), Rise Kagona (gv), Biggie Tembo (gv), Shakie Kangwena (k, bck). . 6/7/86 HP DG ME&SC † Released as single The Bhundu Boys In London JIT-5 in Zimbabwe

7/1/87 My Foolish Heart, Ndoita Sei?, Jig-a-jig, Rugare. & the Potato Five Brass section (2, 3). 21/12/86 U DG ME&FK

Biffy Clyro

24/2/04 There's No Such Thing As A Jaggy Snake, Liberate The Illiterate (A Mong Among Minger), You Can Go Your Own Way, With Aplomb. Simon Neil, James Johnston, Ben Johnston. 22/1/04 MV4 NF SCT

Big Black

6/5/87 The Newman Generator, L Dopa, Dead Billy, Ugly American. Steve Albini (gv), Santiago Durango (g), David Riley (b). U Recorded in Chicago

Big Chief

14/12/91 Destination Poon, Six Pack, Bong Wrench, Into The Void. Mike Danner (d), Matt O'Brien (b), Phil Durr (g), Mark Dancey (g), Barry Henssler (v). 20/10/91 MV3 DG ME

Big Country

22/3/83 Close Action, Inwards, 1000 Stars, Porroh Man. Stuart Adamson (gv), Bruce Watson (g), Tony Butler (b), Mark Brzezicki (d). 9/3/83 MV4 JP NG&MS Debut session for Jensen Aug 82

Big Fayia

7/12/89 Gba Nya Ma / Nga Mone Biwe, Kamo Ahmadu / Nginamudele, How Are You / Lawoseh / Look Waiu Wowo / Co Co Rose, Tiawama A Kpandei / U Deh Make Make Panme, Muana Limia / Yawolo Yiama / Sandi Manya / Heilei Nay Hun. The Big Fayia West African mask dance troup of Sierra Leone, featuring: Mustafa Joe (lv-1,2,5), Sidikie JC Kortogbou (lv-3), Tamba Musa (shengbi drum-3), Sahr Karimu (kongoma, lv-4), Daniel Lavalie (mendi shengbai, or big drum-5). Recorded 2/11/89, The British Council, Freetown, Sierra Leone

Big Flame

16/7/84 Debra, Man Of Few Syllables, Sargasso, Breath Of A Nation. Alan Brown (bv), Dil Green (d), Gregory Keeffe (g). 10/7/84 MV5 MRD MWT

25/2/85 All The Irish Must Go To Heaven, New Way, Chanel Samba, These Boots Are Made For Walking. 17/2/85 MV5 DG ME

27/11/85 Earsore, Let's Re-write The American Constitution, Cat With Cholic, Every Conversation. 17/11/85 MV5 DG HP

12/5/86 Sink (Get Out Of The Ghetto Blues Part I), Xpqwrtz, Three On Baffled Island, Testament To The Slow Death Of Youth Culture. 4/5/86 MV5 DG DD&EL

Big in Japan

6/3/79 Suicide High Life, Goodbye, Don't Bomb China Now. Jayne Casey (lv), Ian Broudie (g, bck, o), Holly (b, bck), Budgie (d, bck). 12/2/79 MV4 TW DD

Big Self

1/2/82 When The Wind Blows, Don't Turn Around, You're Not Afraid, Supervisor. Michael Morris (d), Patrick Sheeran (bv), Bernard Tohill (gv), Jim Nicholl (g). 16/1/82 LH1 DG MR

Bikini Kill

30/4/93 New Radio, Demi Rep, Star Bellied Boy, Not Right Now. Kathleen Hanna (v, d-4), Kathi Wilcox (b, bck), Bill Karren (g), Tobi Vali (d, v-4). 28/3/93 MV3 ME~ RJ

Bilge Pump

23/7/03 Up The Nest, You Make Me Feel (Like A Natural Blonde), Budda. Joe O'Sullivan (gv), Emlyn Jones (b, lv), Neil Turpin (d). Live from MV4 AR SA/GT

5/11/03 The Fall And Rise Of The Alpha Male, Archeological Diggin', Brown Ale For Sister Sarah, The F**kover. 16/10/03 MV4 SA JHT

Billy Mahonie

30/3/99 Watching People Speak When You Can't Hear What They're Saying, World Inaction, We Accept American Dollars, We Both Agreed That The Lemon Was The (rest of title lost). Howard Monk (d), Gavin Baker (g), Hywell Dinsdale (b, g), Kev Penny (b). 24/1/99 MV3 ME RJ

11/12/02 As Sure As Eggs Is Eggs, Dusseldorf. Baker, Monk, Duncan Brown (b), Tony Barrett (g, b, k). Live from MV4 MA~ GT

Birdhouse

9/3/87 Hurricane In My Head, Rev It Up, Sick Boy, Bad Love. Johnny Rev (v), Kathy Freeman (g), Mark Nicol (g), Billy Scarr (b), Max Cantara (d). 22/2/87 U DG ME&PS

Birdland

28/6/89 Paradise, White, See No Evil, Sugar Blood. Robert (v), Simon (b, bck), Lee (g, bck), Kale (d). 6/6/89 ED DG MR

5/2/90 All Over Me, Wanted, Shoot You Down, Rock 'n' Roll Nigger. Lee (lv-3). 2/1/90 MV5 DG TD

The Birthday Party

25/9/80 Cry, Yard, Figure Of Fun, King Ink. Nick Cave (v, p, sx), Rowland Howard (g), Mick Harvey (g, o, d), Phil Calvert (d), Tracy Pew (b). 10/9/80 MV4 DG NG&MC

28/4/81 Release The Bats, Roland Around In That Stuff, (Sometimes) Pleasure-heads Must Burn, Loose. 21/4/81 LH1 DG MR ○ SFPCD020

10/12/81 Big Jesus Trash Can, She's Hit, Bully Bones, Six Inch Gold Blade. 2/12/81 MV4 JWI PW ● SFPS058

22/11/82 Pleasure Avalanche, Deep In The Woods, Sonny's Burning, Marry Me (Lie! Lie!). Calvert out. 15/11/82 U DG DD

Bis

14/10/95 Super James, Icky Poo Air Raid, Kandy Pop, Teen C Power. Sci-Fi Steven (gv, dm), Manda Rin (k, v, rec, b), John Disco (g, v, k) & 'Super James' (d). 17/9/95 MV3 ME SBR

16/6/96 Sweet Shop Avengers, Antiseptic Poetry, We Love John Peel, Keroleen, Rebel Soul. 4/6/96 MV4 MR~ U

4/8/98 Making People Normal, Action & Drama, The Hit Girl, It's All New. 28/6/98 MV4 MPK NK

Bivouac

25/4/92 Drank, Two Sticks, Lead, Spine. Anthony Hodkinson (d), Granville Marsden (b), Paul Yeadon (gv). 8/3/92 MV3 DG ME&AR

31/10/92 Money Song, Popsong, Good Day Song, Bad Day Song. 4/10/92 MV3 ME~ DMC

19/3/94 Art Science & Making Things, Treppaning, Forty Five Seated Standing Nil, Heat Emittter. 5/3/94 MV4 JB JLO

Bizarre Inc

10/11/91 Controversy, Song For John, 4024, Plutonic. Meercham (k, mix), Meredith (k, mix), Turner (dm, mix). 1/9/91 OS

Black

12/1/83 Under Wraps, As Long As It Takes, Blue, Stephen For The Moment. Colin Vearncombe (gbv), David Dickie (bk, dm, bck), David Wibberly (g), Justine Shakespeare & Pauline Dickie (v). 6/12/83 MV4 TW MC

4/7/83 It's Easy, Fast Car Soundtrack, Widemouth Frog, Why Do I Do The Things I Do When They Only Get Me Done? Vearncombe, Dickie, Rachel Furness (vi). 25/6/83 MV4 DG TdB

Black Cat Bones

9/2/69 Baby Be Good To Me, I Want To Know, Train Blues, Don't Know Which Way To Go. Paul Tiller (hca, v), Bob Weston (lg), Derek Brooks (g), Stuart Brooks (b), Terry Sims (d). 13/1/69 MV4 BA U Debut session on World Service R&B show Jan 69

Black Dog

13/1/95 Shadehead, Rise Up, Simperton, Rue, Psycosyin. Edward Handley, Ken Downie, Andrew Turner. 12/12/94 OS ○ Warp WAP115 CD

27/3/97 Dissidents & Red & Black, Decline And Fall, Babylon, Julia. OS

Black Keys

7/5/03 Set You Free, Hard Row, No Trust, The Moan, John Peel Jingle. Dan Auerbach (v, g), Patrick Carney (d). 20/4/03 MV4 SA GT

31/7/03 Thickfreakness, I Cry Alone, Have Love Will Travel, No Fun, Them Eyes, Busted. Live from Peel Acres AR~ GT

Black Roots

27/5/81 Confusion, What Them A Do?, Chanting For Freedom, The Father. Charles Bryan (lv), Errol Brown (v), Barry Thompson (percv), Cordell Francis (lg), Michael Taylor (k), Arol Thompson (rg), Derek King (b), Trevor Seivwright (d). 19/5/81 LH1 DG MR

14/11/83 Far Over, Strugglin', Africa, Black Heart Man. J Ngozi (rg), Carlton Smith (k) r A Thompson, Taylor; & K Ngozi (cga, v). 7/11/83 MV4 U U

Black Sabbath

29/11/69 Behind The Wall Of Sleep, NIB, Black Sabbath (& Devil's Island, 21/3/70). Tony Iommi (g), Ozzie Osborne (v), Geezer Butler (b), Bill Ward (d). 11/11/69 U JW U

Black Star Liner

7/4/95 Harmon Session Special, Tabla Attack, Hooba Hooba, Non Stop To The Border. Choque Hosein (v), Tom Salmon (wh), Chriss Harrop (g), Tino Diplacido ('Scratch And Sniff Gee') 7/3/95 MV3 JB GPR

7/10/97 Glitter Frenzy, Gimmick Prince, Superfly & Bindi, Rock Freak. Hosein, Salmon, Harrop, Errol Rollins (d). 2/9/97 U U U

9/2/99 Yellow Funk, Swimmer, Hindu Homeboy Detective, Wheels Of Steel, Sita D. 12/1/99 MV4 MR RJ

Frank Black

18/6/94 Handyman, The Man Who Was Too Loud, The Jacques Tati, Sister Isabel. Frank Black (g, lv) & Teenage Fanclub: Paul Quinn (b, bck), Gerrard Love (b, bck), Norman Blake (g, bck), Raymond McGinley (g, bck). 14/5/94 MV4 TdB NS

17/2/96 Close Your Eyes, Skeleton Man, Man Of Steel, Everyone Is Wrong. & Scott Bontier (d), Lyle Warkman (gv), Dave McCaffrey (bv). 6/2/96 MV4 U U

21/7/99 Living On Soul, Billy Radcliffe, Changing Of The Guards, Valley Of Our Hope, Sister Isobel. & The Catholics: Boutier, McCaffrey, Rich Gilbert (lgbv). 25/5/99 MV3 MR PN

Blackheart Procession

21/12/99 It's A Crime I Never Told You About The Diamonds In Your Eyes, Destroying The City Of Hearts, Blue Tears, When We Reach The Will. Pall Jenkins (v, g, sy, saw), Tobias Nathaniel (p, g, o), Mario Rubalcaba (d, sy, thunder sheet), Dmitri Dziensuwski (o, ep). 13/10/99 MV4 MR NF

Blade

1/12/90 The Coming Is Near, It Don't Mean A Thing, Lyrical Maniac, Forward. Blade (v), Renegade (dj). 15/11/90 MV5 DG NG&JLY

Blancmange

23/2/82 I Would, Living On The Ceiling, Waves, Running Thin. Neil Arthur (g, v, el), Stephen Luscombe (k, el). 13/2/82 MV4 DG AP

Blank Students

23/4/81 Supercreeper, Don't Understand, Passionate Rap. Miles Salisbury (gv), Dog (d), Dom (sx), Harts (b), Horace (unknown). 13/4/81 LH1 TW AP

Blast Furnace and the Heatwaves

11/7/78 Can't Stop The Boy, Keep On Dancing, South Of The River, Write Me A Letter. Blast Furnace (lv, lg), Skid Marx (hca), Blitz Krieg (rg, slg), D. Based (b, bck), Tim Pani (d). 19/6/78 MV5 PR U First TX by Jensen 3/7/78

Bleach

2/12/90 Fall, Wipe It Away, Seeing, Dipping, Jingle. Steve Scott (d), Nick Singleton (b), Neil Singleton (g), Salli Carson (gv). 20/11/90 MV5 MR~

21/7/91 Decadance, Friends, Surround, Headless. 4/6/91 HP MR~

Blithe

19/2/94 Hell Of Man, Soft, Big One, Lying Awake, Allegiance. Emil Odling (gv), Mattias Norland (g), Nils Forsberg (b), Johan Nilsson (d). 7/11/93 Produced by Kjell Nasten in OS Sweden

Blizzard Boys

15/7/03 In The Mix OS

Bloc Party

30/11/04 So Here We Are, Tulips, Luno, Compliments. Kele Okereke (gv), Russell Lissack (g), Gordon Moakes (b, bck), Matt Tong (d). 4/11/04 MV4 MA NF

Blodwyn Pig

13/4/69 Ain't You Coming Home, The Modern Alchemist†, It's Only Love, Mr Green's Blues†. Mick Abrahams (lg), Andrew Pyle (b), Jack Lancaster (ss, ts, bfl, vi), Ron Burg (d). 24/3/69 PH BA AH&BC 1st session was for Symonds on Sunday, 2/3/69, prod JW

13/7/69 Summer Day, See My Way, It's Only Love†. 7/7/69 PH JW U

3/10/70 See My Way, Lonely Nights, Lovely Lady, Lady Of Liberty. Pete Banks (gv), Barry Reynolds, r Abrahams; & Eddie Lee Becker (flh). 14/9/70 PH JW U

9/7/74 Baby Girl†, Blues Of A Dunstable Truck Driver†, See My Way†, The Leaving Song†. Abrahams, Lancaster, Pyle, Clive Bunker (d). 17/6/74 LH1 TW U † on ◯ The Basement Tapes HUX019

Blonde Redhead

18/7/00 Where Is John?, Missle Me, In An Expression Of The Inexpressionable. Simon Pace (d), Amedeo Pace (gv), Kazu Makino (gv). 7/6/00 MV4 SA RJ

Blood and Roses

26/4/83 Theme From 'Assault On Precinct 13', Possession, Spit Upon Your Grave, Curse On You. Lisa Kirby (v), Bob Short (g, cel), Jez James (b, p, o), Richard Morgan (d). 20/4/83 MV4 RP NG&NR

The Bloody Hollies

25/11/04 Eleven Time Too Many, Long Distance Blues, Cut Me Loose, Whatcha Running From? Wesley Doyle (gv), Phillip Freedenberg (b), Jason Klawon (d). 3/11/04 MV4 MWT JHT

Blossom Toes

29/10/67 Listen To The Silence, The Remarkable Saga Of The Frozen Dog, What On Earth, Watchmaker. Jim Cregan (g), Brian Godding (g), Brian Belshaw (b), Kevin Westlake (d) & U (tb). 23/10/67 PC1 BA DT

31/3/68 I'll Be Your Baby Tonight, Looking Up I'm Looking Back, Love Is, The Saga Of The Frozen Dog. 25/3/68 PC1 BA PR

27/10/68 Wait A Minute, Ever Since A Memory, Peaceloving Man. 22/10/68 PC1 BA AH&BC

7/9/69 Love Bomb, Kiss Of Confusion, Peace Loving Man, Indian Summer. 18/8/69 PH JW TW

Blubber

10/9/94 Bleach, Utopia, Is She A Boy, Crush, Glug. Dick Adland (d), Rob McRobert (b), Chris Taplin (g), Andy Suggett (g, bck), Sarah George (v). 14/8/94 MV4 JB FK

Blue

28/6/73 Look Around, Someone, Little Jody, Wish I Could Fly. Hughie Nicholson (gv), Jimmy McCullough (gv), Ian MacMillan (b), Angus 'Timmy' Donald (d). 18/6/73 LH1 BA U

18/10/73 Max Bygraves, Sad Sunday, Sittin' On A Fence, Too Many Miles. 23/8/73 LH1 JM U

30/4/74 Big Bold Love, Lonesome, You Give Me Love, Sweet Memories. Robert Smith r McCullough. 9/4/74 LH1 U U

21/8/75 Dark Eyed Darling, Round And Round, I Know How It Feels. Smith out. 14/8/75 MV4 TW U

29/1/76 I'll Be Satisfied, Careless Kinda Guy, Love Has Gone. David Nicholson (b, v, p), Dean Ford (v, hca) & Jeff Allen (d, cga, ti) r Donald. 22/1/76 MV5 TW U

18/11/76 The Shepherd, Another Nightime Flight, Charlie Black Arrow, Tired Of Loving You (Silver Dollars). 9/11/76 MV4 JG MR

15/8/77 Bring Back The Love, I'm Alone, Tired Of Loving You, Women. Hughie Nicholson (g, p, hca, v), David Nicholson (b, p, v), Ian McMillan (g, b, v, hca), Charlie Smith (dv). 8/8/77 MV4 TW DD

Blue Orchids ◯

17/12/80 The House That Faded Out, Work, Low Profile. Martin Bramah (g, lv), Richard Goldstraw (g, bck), Steve Toyne (b), Ian Rogers (d, bck), Una Baines (k). 8/12/80 LH1 TW NG ◯

5/5/82 A Year With No Head, No Looking Back, Bad Education, Sun Connection. Bramah, Baines, Mark Hellyer (b), Toby (d), Philip Rainford (bck). 17/4/82 MV5 DG MR ◯ From Severe To Serene LTMCD2354

Blue Poland

7/4/82 Find Out, Household God, Time And Motion, Puppet Nation. Neil Morgan (lv), Mel Deeprose (bck), Nigel Robinson (gv), Chris Larsen (b), Steve Thomas (d, perc). 29/3/82 MV5 JWI DD

Blueboy

3/12/94 Toulouse, Good News Week, Dirty Mag's, Loony Tunes. Keith Girdler (v), Paul Stewart (g), Gemma Townley (clo), Mark Cousens (b), Harvey Williams (g), Martin Rose (d). 30/10/94 MV3 ME TD

Blueskins

2/9/03 Girl, I Wanna Know, The Stupid Ones, No 23. Ryan Spendlove (gv), Richard Townsend (rgv), Matthew Smith (bv), Paul Brown (d). 31/7/03 MV4 MA JSM

27/7/04 Seconds To None, Bound To Wait, Inspire Me, Fat Cats. 10/6/04 MV4 MA NF

Bluetip

13/1/00 Polymer, Anti Bloom, Magnetifed, Castanet. Jason Farrell (gv), David Stern (g), James Kump (b), David Bryson (d). 10/11/99 MV4 MR JHT

The Bluetones

21/1/95 Cut Some Rug, Slight Return, A Parting Gesture, Talking To Clary. Mark Morris (v), Scott Morris (b, bck), Adam Devlin (g), Eds Chesters (d). 18/12/94 MV3 ME NK

4/8/96 The Simple Things, Castle Rock, Devil Behind My Smile, Electric Vampire. Live from MV4 MR LS

Colin Blunstone

14/11/72 Andorra, I Don't Believe In Miracles, How Wrong Can One Man Ever Be? (& Say You Don't Mind, 26/12/72). Colin Blunstone (v), Gary Griffiths (lg), Pete Wingfield (elp), Terry Poole (b), Jim Toomey (d). 23/10/72 T1 JW BC&NG Debut session for Harris Sept 71

27/3/73 Pay Me Later, I Want Some More, Looking For Someone To Love. 6/3/73 LH1 JW BC

6/11/73 Wonderful, Weak For You, Shadow Of A Doubt, Setting Yourself Up To Be Shot Down. Derek Griffiths (g) r Gary Griffiths. 22/10/73 T1 JM BAI

Blur

5/5/97 Country Sad Ballad Man, Chinese Bombs, Movin On, M O R, On Your Own, Popscene, Song 2. Damon Albarn (v), Graham Coxon (g), Alex James (b), Dave Rowntree (d), Diana Gutkind (k). 22/4/97 Peel Acres AHW&SCU MA Two previous sessions for Goodier's Evening Session 90 & 92

5/10/99 Bugman, Fried, Blur E M I, 1992, Bonebag, Trim Trabb, John Peel Birthday Skank. 17/9/99 Peel Acres SCU MA

Blurt

9/10/80 Cherry Blossom Polish, Paranoid Blues, Ubu, Some Come. Peter Creese (g, tb), Ted Milton (sxv), Jake Milton (dv). 24/9/80 MV4 BS MR

Boards Of Canada

21/7/98 Aquarius, Happy Cycling, Olson (& XYZ 1st TX live 16/6/98). Mike Sandison (k), Marcos Ian (k). 16/6/98 MV4 MR FK ○ Warp WAP114 CD (XYZ not included)

Bob

18/1/88 Esmeralda Brooklyn, Kirsty, Trousercide, Brian Wilson's Bed. Simon Armstrong (gv), Richard Blackborow (gv, k), Jem Morris (b), Gary Connors (d). 7/1/88 U DG ME&PL

15/2/89 Who You Are, Scarecrow, It Was Kevin, So Far So Good. Dean Leggett (d) r Connors. 5/2/89 MV3 DG ME

25/9/89 Extension 'Bob' Please (Instrumental), Throw Away The Key, Bloodline, Wild West 9. Blackborow (o-1) & Harry Parker (p-3). 3/9/89 MV3 DG ME

Bob Tilton

4/8/95 Palm Reading, Be My Valentine, A Song About Killing, Butterfly / Orchard Bare. Chay Lawrence (g), Neil Johnson (g), Allan Gainey (g), Simon Feirn (v), Mark Simms (bg). 9/7/95 MV4 ME SB

The Bodies

3/4/80 Zone, Something, New Positions, Subtraction. Mark Adams (vsy), The Tanz (blg), Leon Thompson (rg), Tony Cobley (d). 26/3/80 MV4 U NG

The Bodines

24/3/87 Skanking Queens, Untitled, Tall Stories, Clear. Michael Ryan (v, g), Paul Brotherton (g), Tim Burwood (b), John Roland (d). 15/3/87 U DG ME&PS 2 previous sessions for Janice Long Nov 85 & July 86

The Bodysnatchers

14/4/80 What's This?, Happy Time Tune, The Boiler, The Ghosts Of The Vox Continental. Rhoda Dakar (lv), Miranda Joyce (sx), Stella Barker (g), Sarah-Jane Owen (g), Pennie Leyton (k), Nicky Summers (b), Judy Parsons (d). 8/4/80 MV4 U U

8/9/80 Hiawatha, Mixed Feelings, Private Eye, The Loser. 27/8/80 MV4 BS NG

Eric Bogosian

17/8/83 The Coming Depression, Marios, Fat Fighter, Inside Inside, Starving Children, Cancer Dessert, No Answers. Eric Bogosian. 10/8/83 MV4 BYA U

Bogshed

4/11/85 Packed Lunch To School, Oily Stack, Hell Bent On Death, Can't Be Beat. Tristan King (d), Mike Bryson (b), Mark McQuaid (g), Phil Hartley (v) & Tom Sott (sx-2). 27/10/85 MV5 DG TdB

5/3/86 The Fastest Legs†, Adventure Of Dog†, Summer In My Lunchtime, Morning Sirt / Little Car. & Mac Andrassy (sx). 25/2/86 MV4 DG JB

28/7/86 Tried And Tested Public Speaker†, Champion Love Shoes†, Little Grafter†, Gather In The Mushrooms. 15/7/86 U DG MR&MA † on ● Tried And Tested Public Speaker' LP Shelf3

4/5/87 The Gourmet Is A Baby, Raise The Girl, I Said No To Lemon Mash, Loaf. 14/4/87 U DG MR&JB

26/10/87 Six To One And Likely, Into Me, From The Stumble, Duck Flight / US Bands / Wally Wallah (Medley). 18/10/87 U DG ME&PS

Bolt Thrower

13/1/88 Forgotten Existence, Attack In The Aftermath, Psychological Warfare, In Battle There Is No Law. Al West (v), Jo Bench (b), Andy Whale (d), Gav Ward (g), Baz Thomson (g). 3/1/88 MV4 DG MWT ○

16/11/88 Drowned In Torment, Eternal War, Realm Of Chaos, Domination. Karl Willets (v) r West. 6/11/88 HP DG ME ○

4/9/90 Destructive Infinity, Warmaster, After Life, Lost Souls' Domain. 22/7/90 MV3 DG ME&FK ○ SFRCD116

Bomb Disneyland

13/9/89 Suicide 999, Twisted, Nail Mary, Faster Bastard. Simon (d, bck), Prud (bv), Mark (gv). 13/8/89 MV3 DG ME

The Graham Bond Initiation

31/1/70 Walking In The Park, Wade In The Water, Love Is The Law. Graham Bond (o, al, v), Diane Stewart (cga), Keith Bailey (d), Nigel Taylor (b), Dare Usher (fl, ts, g). 20/1/70 MV4 JW TW Graham Bond's trio, quartet and the Organisation all did BBC sessions prior to R1. The Organisation's trial broadcast was for WS R&B, Rec 19/11/64 at PH, prod. JG, TX 12/12/64

Bone

2/5/90 Amnesia Soup, Bad Line To Lebanon, 8 Legged Enemy, Cannibal Sunset. Danny (b, bck), Dave (g), Bob (v). 15/4/90 MV3 DG MC

Bone Orchard

28/6/83 Mankre, The Mission, Shall I Carry The Budgie Woman?, Fat's Terminal. Mark Horse (g), Troy Tyro (g), Paul Henrickson (b), Mike Finch (d), Chrissy McGee (v). 18/6/83 MV4 DG MR

Bong Ra

21/2/02 Kick Out The Jams, Dark Jazz, Archie Bunker Disciples, Ghettoblaster. Bong Ra. 21/2/02 OS

Bongos and the Groovies

10/7/73 Ella, First Day Of October, Lagos, The Station, Eche Une. 8-piece African group. OS

Bongwater

13/4/91 The Power Of Pussy, You Don't Love Me Yet, White Rental Car Blues, Kisses Sweeter Than Wine. David Licht (d), Neil Kramer (bv), Dogbowl (g), Randy Hudson (g), Ann Magnusson (v). 19/3/91 MV5 MR~ ○ US release as CD EP on Dutch East India 1992

Bonkers

21/1/03 Happy hardcore compilation mix by various DJs OS

Bonny Prince Billy

16/3/99 I Send My Love To You, Another Day Full Of Dread, Stablemate, O Let It Be, What's Wrong With A Zoo. Will Oldham (gv), Matt Sweeney (g), Mike Fellows (b), James Lo (d). 2/2/99 MV4 MR PN

1/9/99 Dream Of The Sea, Sweeter Than Anything, One With The Birds, Arise Therefore. Oldham, Sweeney only. 31/8/99 MV3 AR SA

15/2/01 When Die Song, Jolly One, Rich Wife Full Of Happiness, Beezle. Oldham solo. 28/1/01 MV4 ME RJ See Palace Brothers

The Bonzo Dog Doo Dah Band

12/11/67 The Equestrian Statue, The Craig Torso Show†, Mickey's Son And Daughter†, Death Cab For Cutie. Viv Stanshall (tp, eu, tu, v), Neil Innes (p, g), Roger Ruskin Spear (cnt, ts, xyl), Rodney Slater (al, ts, bars, bsx, cl, bcl, tb, tu), Vernon Dudley Bohay-Nowell (bj, b), Legs Larry Smith (d, tu), Sam Spoons (real name Martin Ash) (d, perc). 8/11/67 MV4 BA PR

17/12/67 The Equestrian Statue, Mickey's Son And Daughter, Rockalyser Baby, The Monster Mash, Jazz Delicious Hot Disgusting Cold. 5/12/67 PH BA PR&BC

5/5/68 Do The Trouser Press Baby†, Canyons Of Your Mind†, I've Found The Answer, The Urban Spaceman†. David Clague (b) r Bohay-Nowell, Spoons. 29/4/68 PC1 BA PR

21/7/68 Young Girl, Beautiful Zelda, Captain Cool, My Pink Half Of The Drainpipe, 11 Moustachioed Daughters (& Can Blue Men Sing The Whitest†, 18/8/68). 8/7/68 PC1 BA PR&BC

20/10/68 Shirt, I'm The Urban Spaceman Baby, The Bride Stripped Bare 'by The Bachelors', Excerpt From 'Brain Opera' (& Ready Mades [E's Mad Deary], 1/12/68). Clague out. 8/10/68 PC1 BA AH&BC

13/4/69 Look At Me I'm Wonderful†, Mr Apollo†, Quiet Talks And Summer Walks†, Excerpt From 'Brain Opera' Pt 3. Dennis Cowan joins. 31/3/69 PH BA AH&BC

3/8/69 We're Going To Bring It On Home†, Monster Mash†, Sofa Head†, Tent†. 29/7/69 MV4 JW TW ● SFPS051 † on ○ The Complete BBC Recordings SFRSCD108. This CD also has 4 tracks from a claimed but spurious Top Gear session recording date of 2/10/68 – Give Booze A Chance, We Were Wrong, Keynsham, I Want To Be With You – which neither Bernie Andrews nor I can locate in any Top Gear recording session or show

The Boo Radleys

30/7/90 Aldous, How I Feel, Bluebird. Steve (d), Tim (b), Martin (g, v), Sice (v). 12/7/90 MV5 DG NG&BJ

7/4/91 Alone Again Or, Something Soon She Said, Foster's Van, Eleanor Everything. Rob Cieka (d) r Steve. 12/3/91 MV5 MR MR

26/10/91 Smile Fades Fast, Towards The Light, Lazy Day, Boo Faith. 5/9/91 MV5 DG NG&PA

Boom Bip

17/7/02 Square, Dead Man's Teal, Me And People, Accapella, Birdcatcher's Return, Birdcatcher's Oath, Danger Will Robinson (& encore Mannequin Hand Trapdoor I Reminder, not TX). Bryan Hollon (k, smp, b, g, th) & Dose One: Adam Drucker (v). Live from MV4 AR RJ/GT

1/4/03 U R Here, From Left To Right, Last Walk Around The Mirror Lake, Pulse All Over. & Adam Drucker (v), Andrew Killmeier (sy, smp), Matt Johnson (g, b, sy), Hazen Frick (d). 6/3/03 MV4 AR RJ/AR

The Boomtown Rats

3/8/77 Joey, Neon Heart, Looking After Number One, Mary Of The 4th Form. Simon Crowe (d, bck), Bob Geldof (lv), Johnny Fingers (k, bck), Garry Roberts (g, bck), Gerry Cott (g), Pete Briquette (b). 26/7/77 MV4 JG MR

26/5/78 Like Clockwork, Me And Howard Hughes, Living In An Island, (Watch Out For) The Normal People. & Neil Burn (bck-4). 15/5/78 MV4 TW NBU

The Boothill Foot Tappers

2/4/84 New River Train, Long White Robe, Bowl Of Porridge, I Ain't Broke. Danny (d), Kevin (agv), Slim (acc), Chris (bj, v), Marnie (wsh, v), Wendy and Merrill (v). 24/3/84 MV5 DG MC

16/4/85 How's Jack? (Pt 1), Learning How To Dance, Sunday Evening, Coloured Aristocracy. & Lloyd Winter (db), 'Merrileggs' Heatley. 10/3/85 MV5 DG ME

Boots For Dancing

4/12/80 Timeless Tonight, The Pleasure Chant, (Somewhere In The) South Pacific, Hesitate. David Carson (lv), Michael Barclay (g), Jo Callis (g), Douglas Barry (b), James Stewart (d), Robert Last (bck), Hilary Morrison (bck). 17/11/80 LH1 TW DD

15/7/81 Shadows Of Stone, Stand, Wild Jazz Summers. Carson, Barclay, Mike Bailey (b), Simon Bloomfield (b), Dickie Fusco (perc), Pete Harris (o). 13/7/81 MV4 TW DD

14/4/82 Nobody Raves About The Salt In The Ocean, Style In Full Swing, Bend An Elbow Lend An Ear, Get Up. U 24/3/82 U U U

Boss Hog

30/3/91 Big Fish†, Sugar Bunny / Spanish Fly†, Red Bath. Charlie (d), Jens (b), John (gv), Kurt (g), Cristina (v), Remko (perc, ashtray). 3/3/91 MV3 DG SA&DMC † released as a single NR18795

The Bothy Band

26/3/76 Music Of The Glen / The Humours Of Scariff / Poll An Madadh Visce, Old Hag You Have Killed Me / Danny Delaneys / Morrisons, When I Was A Fair Maid, Am Bothan A Buaig Fionnghuala, The Maid Of Coolmore. Uncertain, save Triona (v-3,5). 9/3/76 MV4 JG MR

24/11/76 The Hare In The Heather, Bonny Kate / Jenny's Chickens, Garrett Barry's / Coppers And Brass, Billy Banker / The Shores Of Loughrea / The Laurel Tree, Michael Gormans / The Frieze Britches / All The Way To Galway / Fairhead Mary, Sixteenth Come Next Sunday. Matt Molly (fd-2 solo), Paddy Keenan (Uileann pp-3 solo), Fion (v-6). 19/10/76 MV4 JG MR

21/3/78 Lord Franklin, O'Neill's March, The Strayaway Child, Maids Of Mitchelstown. Paddy Keenan (wh, Uileann pp), Micheal O'Domhnaill (g, v-1), Trina Ni Dhomhnaill (cl, v-1), Matt Molloy (fl), Kevin Burke (vi), Donal Lunny (bz&bh-2). 14/3/78 MV4 MB MR

Bourbonese Qualk

11/3/87 Sweat It Out, Dream Decade, Northern Soul, Cupid's Itch, Call To Arms. Simon Crab, Steven Tamza, Mike Kean, Lucia Binto. 31/3/87 OS

Bourgie Bourgie

25/1/84 Careless, I Gave You Love, Here Comes That Feeling, Breaking Point. Ken McDonald (d), Keith Band (b), Ian Burgoyne (g), Michael Slaven (lg), Paul Quinn (v). 18/1/84 MV4 DG NG&PS

Bow Wow Wow

27/10/80 Radio G-string, Baby On Mars, Uomosex-Al-Apache, Fools Rush In. Matthew Ashman (g, bck), Lee Gorman (b, bck), Dave Barbarrossa (d), Annabella Lewin (v). 20/10/80 MV4 TW DD&BC

Bowery Electric

7/8/97 Slide, Electro, Blow Up. Martha Schewendener, Lawrence Chandler, Wayne Magruder. 20/7/97 MV4 AA~

David Bowie

24/12/67 Love You Till Tuesday, Little Bombadier, In The Heat Of The Morning, Silly Boy Blue, When I Live My Dream. David Bowie (v) & The Arthur Greenslade Orchestra. 18/12/67 PC1 BA DT

26/5/68 London Bye Ta Ta†, In The Heat Of The Morning†, Karma Man†, When I'm Five (& Silly Boy Blue†, 30/6/68). & Tony Visconti (md), Orchestra management Ltd for 14 musicians. 13/5/68 PC1 BA PR&AH

28/1/72 Hang On To Yourself, Ziggie Stardust, Queen Bitch, Waiting For The Man (& Lady Stardust, 31/3/72). Bowie, Mick Ronson (gv), Trevor Bolder (b), Woody Woodmansey (d). 11/1/72 T1 JM NG

23/5/72 Hang On To Yourself†, The Rise And Fall Of Ziggy Stardust†, White Light White Heat†, Suffragette City†, Moon-Age Daydream†. & Nick Graham (p). 16/5/72 MV4 PR U † on ☉ Bowie At The Beeb EMI plus much more

The Bowles Brothers

30/8/76 Nuts For Charlie, Why The Fuss, Disparate Dan, Sweeter Than Sugar. Brian Bowles (gv), Julian Smedley (g, v, vi), Richard Lee (b), Sue Jones-Davies (v). 5/8/76 MV4 TW U Previous live broadcasts on R2

14/1/77 F1 To, Roger The Dodger, Samba, Downtown Girl. 10/1/77 MV4 TW DD

Alan Bown

3/12/67 Story Book, Technicolour Dream, Love Is A Beautiful Thing (& Pandora's Golden Heebie-Jeebies, 31/12/67). Alan Bown, Jess Roden, Jeff Bannister, John Anthony, Vic Sweeney, Stan Haldane, Tony Catchpole. 29/11/67 MV4 BA U&BC Three previous sessions for Saturday Club in 67

7/4/68 Mutiny, Story Book, All Along The Watchtower, Penny For Your Thoughts. 20/3/68 MV4 BA U&BC

Box of Toys

28/4/83 When Daylight Is Over (Sunset), Time Takes Me Back, Precious Is The Pearl, I'm Thinking Of You Now. Andy Redhead (d), Roy Campbell (b), Phil Martin (al, ss, ob, fl), Brian Atherton (kv). 13/4/83 MV4 HP NG

The Box

3/2/83 Out, Strike, The Hub, Water Grows Teeth. Paul Widger (g), Charlie Collins (sx, fl), Roger Quail (d), Peter Hope (b), Terry Todd (b). 24/1/83 U DG MC

Boxer

10/11/75 Shooting Star, California Calling, All The Time In The World, More Than Meets The Eye. Mike Patto (p, elp, v), Ollie Halsall (g, clav), Keith Ellis (b), Tony Newman (d). 7/10/75 MV4 TW U

Gary Boyle ☉

31/8/77 The Dancer, Cowshed Shuffle, Almond Burfi. Gary Boyle (g), Zoë Kronenberger (k), Jeff Downes (k), Steve Shone (b), Sergio Castillo (d). 22/8/77 MV4 TW DD ☉ Isotope / Gary Boyle Live At The BBC HUX048

Boyracer

2/9/94 Advice To Young Bands About Publishing Deals, One Step Forward, Love Song For Henry Mancini / New Wave Old Hat, Pretentious Headline Band Ego Problem. Stewart Anderson (g, v, o), Matthew Green (g, bck), Nicola Hodgkinson (bv), Ged McGurn (d). 31/7/94 MV4 JB RJ

Boys of the Lough

7/11/72 The Boys Of The Lough / Slantigard, Farewell To Whiskey, Keenya Rua / Morning Dew, The Lass From Glasgow Town. Robin Morton (bh, v), Cathal McConnell (v, wh, fl), Dick Gaughan (gv), Aly Bain (fd). 16/10/72 U JW U

13/3/73 Shetland Wedding Marches, Flowers Of The Forest, Erin I Won't Say Her Name / The Whinney Hills Of Leitrin / Joe Ryan's Jig, Wee Croppy Tailor / Boy In The Gap / McMahon's Reel. 29/1/73 T1 JW U

2/10/73 A Ewe Came To Our Door Bleating / Christmas Day In The Morning, Lovely Nancy, Shetland Reels, Mason's Reel. Dave Richardson (j, mnd, ci, cnc) r Gaughan. 24/9/73 T1 JW&ARV

24/9/74 Jigs: Kincora Jig / Behind The Haystack, The Maid With The Bonnie Brown Hair, The Golden Slipper / The Stevenstown Jig / Johnny Mcl'John's Reel / Sonny's Mazurka, Hounds And The Hare. 9/9/74 LH1 JW U

18/11/75 Medley: The Laird Of Drumblair / Millbrae, Farewell To Ireland, The Darling Baby, Dovecote / The Atholl Highlanders, Lochaber No More. Finlay McNeil joins. 30/10/75 MV4 TW U

17/1/77 Torn Petticoat / The Piper's Broken Finger / The Humours Of Bally Connell, The Lament For Limerick, The Red Haired Man's Wife, The Old Favourite Jig / Bobby Gardner's Jig, Lady Anne Mongtgomery / The Highland Man That Kissed His Granny / O'Connor Donn's Reel. 9/12/76 MV4 TW U

1/6/78 Donal Og, The New Rigged Ship / Naked And Bare / The Graemsay Jig, McConnell's Gravel Walk / The Gravel Walk, The Larks March. 24/5/78 MV4 BS NG

The Boys

8/8/77 Sick On You, First Time, Cop Cars, Box Number, Livin' In The City, Rock Relic. Kid Reid (lv, b), Mat Dangerfield (lgv), Honest John Plain (rgv), Casino Steel (pv), Jack Black (d). 3/8/77 MV4 TW NG

15/5/78 TCP, Brickfield Nights, Classified Suzie, Boys. 2/5/78 MV4 MB MR

Bracket

15/4/95 My Stepson, Why Should I, G Vibe, Two Hot Dog For 99p. Ray Castro (d), Zack Charles (b, bck), Larry Tinney (g), Marty Gregori (gv). 20/3/95 MV4 MWT RF

Paul Brady

28/11/78 The Hunter's Purse / The Sailor On The Rock, The Death Of Queen Jane, Jigs, Mulqueeny's (Hornpipe) / Fergal O'Gara (16th Chieftan) / Drag Her Round The Road, Crazy Dreams. Paul Brady (g, v, mnd), Matt Molloy (fl), Kevin Burke (fd), Micheal O'Domhnaill (gv). 20/11/78 MV4 TW DD

Billy Bragg

3/8/83 A New England, Strange Things Happen, This Guitar Says Sorry, Love Gets Dangerous, Fear Is A Man's Best Friend, A13 – Trunk Road To The Sea. Billy Bragg (gv). 27/7/83 MV4 U U †

27/2/84 Lovers' Town†, St Swithin's Day, Myth Of Trust, To Have And To Have Not. & Wiggy (g-1). 21/2/84 MV5 MRD TdB

20/9/84 It Says Here, A Lover Sins†, Between The Wars†, Which Side Are You On†. 18/9/84 MV5 MRD TdB

2/9/85 Days Like These†, Jeanne†, The Marriage†, There Is Power In A Union. 20/8/85 MV5 TdB TdB

15/9/86 Greetings To The New Brunette†, Ideology, The Warmest Room, Chile Your Waters Run Red Through Soweto†. 2/9/86 U DG MR

19/9/88 The Short Answer, Valentine's Day Is Over, Rotting On Remand, She's Got A New Spell. 30/8/88 MV4 MR~ † on ◯ SFRCD117

15/6/91 The Few, Accident Waiting To Happen, Tank Park Salute, Life With The Lions. & Cara Tivey (pv), Wiggy (g, b), Grant Cunliffe (g). 12/5/91 MV3 DG U

13/10/95 Northern Industrial Town, A Pict Song, Brickbat, The Gulf Between Us. Live in on-air studio

22/12/96 Goalhanger, Levi Stubbs, The Dark End Of The Street, A New England, Deck The Halls With Bows Of Holly. Live in on-air studio AHW U

9/7/98 My Flying Saucer, Another Man's Done Gone, Black Wind, Blowing, Psalm, A Song About Law And Order, All You Fascists Bound To Lose, Ingrid Bergman, Let's Have Christ For President. Live from Y4 AKM RJ

19/12/00 Brickbat, Way Over Yonder In The Minor Key. 13/12/00 MV3 AR MA

Brainiac

8/12/95 Sexual Frustration, Go Freaks Go, A Day In the Hot Seat, I Am A Cracked Machine. Tim Taylor (v, k, g), Johna Schmersal (g), Juan Monasterio (b), Tyler Trent (d). 19/11/95 MV3 ME LS

Brand X

8/3/76 The Ancient Mysteries, Kubil Blitz (& Born Ugly, not TX). John Goodsall (g), Robin Lumley (k), Percy Jones (b), Phil Collins (d). 26/2/76 MV4 TW BAI

2/8/76 Why Should I Lend You Mine When You've Broken Yours Off Already, Malaga Virgin. & Preston Hayman (perc). 15/7/76 MV4 TW BAI&DD

Brassy

27/7/96 Straighten Out, What You Are, Route Out, Right Back. Stefan Gordon (lg), Jonny Barrington (d), Karen Frost (b), Muffin Spencer (gv). 9/6/96 MV3 KR~ U

21/6/00 Parkside, B'Cos We Rock, I Gotta Beef / Who Stole The Show, All-New, Extra Juice. 21/5/00 MV4 JSM MAP

Bratmobile

10/9/93 There's No Other Way / No You Don't, Bitch Theme, Make Me Miss America, Panik. Allison Wolfe (v), Molly Neuman (d, bck), Erin Smith (g). 25/7/93 MV4 PL AA

Brave Captain

12/12/00 Zizou, Better Living Through Reckless Experimentation, The Sound Of Nichita. Martin Carr (gv), Dave Hirst (b), Mary Wycherley (k), Andy Fung (d), Ashley Cook (g, perc), Ian Bailey (sx). 3/12/00 MV4 ME NS

Breed

7/9/91 Splinter, Perfect Hangover, Pendulum, Hard Cash. Steven Hewitt (d), Andrew Park (b), Simon Breed (gv). 28/7/91 MV3 DG ME&FK ◯ SFMCD213

4/12/92 Wonderful Blade, Shanking The Bone, Woah Woah Woa, Phantom Limb. 29/9/92 MV4 U U

6/11/93 Blood Planets, Violent Sentimental, Hell Stays Open All Night Long, Greatest Story Ever Told. 11/10/93 MV3 ME JLC

6/8/94 The Collaborateur, Little Things That Keep Us Together, The Last Fiver, All Ears And No Skin. 26/6/94 MV5 MPK GW

The Breeders

7/2/90 Hellbound, When I Was A Painter, Iris, Fortunately Gone. Kim Deal (agv), Tanya Donelly (gv), Josephine Wiggs (b), Shannon Doughton (d). 22/1/90 Boston USA

Brian Jonestown Massacre

18/11/98 Jennifer, Who, Hide & Seek, Feel It. Anton Newcombe (v, o, g), Charles Mehling (k), Adam LeBlanc (g), Billy Pleasant (d), Dean Taylor (g), Joel Gion (tamb). 25/10/98 MV3 ME NK

Brides Make Acid

25/9/93 Flying Over Frankfurt, Bulldozer, Enchanted, Flying Over Cologne. Hanni Bear (cmp, writer, technician), Sean Moffett (smp, engineer). 24/8/93 MV4 MR SA

The Bridewell Taxis

28/10/90 Spirit, Whole Damn Nation, Face In The Crowd, Aegis. Glenn Scullion (d), Simon Scott (b), Sean McElhone (g), Gary Wilson (k), Chris Walton (tb), Mick Roberts (v). 18/9/90 MV5 DG ME&JLO

Marc Brierley

11/9/68 Matchbox Men, Sunlight Sleepers Song, Welcome To The Citadel, Thoughts And Sounds, Hold On Hold On The Garden Scene Looks Good On The Floor. U 11/9/68 U DK U

Brigandage

18/5/83 Let It Rot, Heresy, Hope, Fragile. Michelle (v), Mick Fox (g), Scott Addisson (b), Ben Addisson (d). 14/5/83 MV4 DG MR

Anne Briggs

3/9/69 The Snow It Melts The Soonest, Standing On The Shore, Sullivan's John, Go Your Own Way. Anne Briggs (agv). 18/8/69 U U U

7/1/72 Tangled Man, Fire And Wine, Hills Of Greenmore. 19/12/71 PH JM JWH

Brilliant

8/11/82 Colours / Break It Down, Bells, Holst. Marcus Myers (gv), Youth (b, db), Tin Tin (b), Andy Anderson (d) & Peter Ogi (k). 11/10/82 MV4 TW MC

The Brilliant Corners

21/8/84 Tangled Up In Blue, Sixteen Years, My Baby's In Black, Trash. Bob Morris (d), Chris Galvin (b), Davey Woodward (g, hma, lv), Winston Forbes (bck). 11/8/84 MV5 DG MC

15/12/86 Arlington Villas, Would It Be Sad?, Anticipation, Trust Me. Dan Pachini (tp) joins. 23/11/86 U DG ME&FK

1/6/87 Oh!, Please Please Please, I'll Never Be The One To Break Your Heart, Teenage. 17/5/87 U DG ME&SC

Derek Brimstone

12/3/69 Back In Tobago, Little Tin Men, Mrs Fisher And Poem, Sing To Me, Streets Of London, Long Old Summertime, Fairytale, Jon Curle's Lullabye. U 4/3/69 U JM U

Brinsley Schwarz

5/12/70 Seymour I Love You, Funk Angel, The Slow One, Rock And Roll Station. Brinsley Schwarz (gv), Nick Lowe (bv), Bill Rankin (d), Rob Andrews (ov), Ian Gomm, Dave Jackson. 16/11/70 PH JW BC Debut session was for DLT May 70

12/12/72 Hooked On Love, Thirty Pounder (Do The Cod), Night Flight, Hello Mamma. Jackson out. 27/11/72 T1 JW BC

25/7/74 What's So Funny About Peace Love And Understanding (1st TX Rock On, 20/7), The Ugly Things, You Ain't Living Till You're Loving, I'll Take Good Care Of You. 11/7/74 LH1 TW BAI

20/2/75 (You've Got To Be) Cruel To Be Kind†, We Can Mess Around With Anything But Love†, Gimme Back My Love†, Everybody§. 6/2/75 MV4 TW BC † on ◯ Cruel To Be Kind HUX052 § on ◯ What's So Funny About Peace Love and Understanding? HUX023

The British Lions

22/5/78 One More Chance To Run, Break This Fool, Wild In The Streets. Buffin (d, bck), Overend Watts (b, bck), John Fiddler (lvg), Ray Major (lg, bck), Morgan Fisher (k, bck). 10/5/78 MV4 TW NG

Broadcast

6/10/96 Forget Everytime, The Note, The World Backwards, Untitled. Stephen Perkins (d), Tim Felton (g), James Cargill (b), Richard Stevens (k), Patricia Keenan (v). 15/9/96 MV4 ME~

9/2/00 Long Was The Year, Echo's Answer, Where Youth And Laughter Go. Keith York (d) r Perkins. 23/1/00 MV3 ME PN

19/8/03 Pendulum, Colour Me In, Minim, Sixty Forty. Keenan, Felton, Cargill, Billy Bainbridge (k), Neil Bullock (d). 24/7/03 MV4 MA JSM

Broccoli

30/6/95 Relent, Neglect It, Blue, Cherry Drop Club. Benni Esposito (b), Graeme Gilmour (d), Grant Myles (gv). 28/5/95 MV3 ME BSU

2/9/98 Constance, Television, Broken, Fido. Scott Stewart (bv) r Esposito. 9/8/98 MV4 SA NK

Dave Brock and Friends

29/1/69 Diamond Ring, When I Came Home This Morning, Hesitation Shuffle, Illusions, Ripley's Blues, Roll On Pete. Dave Brock (g, v, hca), Mike King, Mike Greig, Pete Judd. 21/1/69 S1 JM U Brock telephoned and asked for an audition on 22/10/68. Recorded at MV3 28/11 passed

Broken Dog

6/3/97 Stop Your Banging, In The Dark, Where Will You Go When There's Nowhere Left To, Baby I'm Lost Without You. Martine Roberts (gbv, cl), Clive Painter (g), Nick Avery (d, tamb). 16/2/97 MV4 ME SBR

22/9/98 Door, Eventually You Could Mean Nothing To Me, Halo Of Days, Well Of Comfort, Light Passing Through. & Paul Anderson (ag). 1/9/98 MV3 MWT NF

28/9/99 Slope, Stranger, Drink Was The Height Of The Day, They Were Real. Roberts, Painter, Mark Wilsher (d), Alex Morris (ag, o, k). 18/7/99 MV4 ME NS

8/12/99 Joy To The World. Live from MV3 AKM&AR SA

5/9/00 Stay On My Side, Will There Be Drinks, Never Too Far, You've Gone Over To The Other Side. Roberts, Painter, Wilsher, Andrew Blick (tp). 2/8/00 MV4 SA JHT

Broken Family Band

7/1/03 Don't Leave That Woman Unattended, When We're Dry, Gone Dark, You Were A Nightmare. Steven Adams (gv), Jason Williams (gv), Gavin Johnson (b), Mick Roman (d) & Martin Green (acc), Timothy Vicar (bj, o, v, perc). 12/12/02 MV4 MA GT

16/3/04 Happy Days Are Here Again, I Send My Love To You, O Princess, We Already Said Goodbye, Offcom Swearing Warning Jingle. & Timothy Victor (o, bj). 11/2/04 MV4 JSM GT

Bronco

4/9/71 Old Grey Shadow, Time Slips Away, New Day Avenue. Jess Roden (v), Robert Blunt (g), Kevyn Gammond (g), John Pasternak (g), Peter Robinson (d). 26/7/71 PH JW BC 3 previous sessions for Mike Harding 70/71

6/9/73 Strange Awakening, Turkey In The Straw, Steal That Gold. Paul Lockey (lv, g), Dan Fone (kg, hca) r Roden, Blunt. 13/8/73 LH1 BA BC

Bronski Beat

15/10/84 Close To The Edge, Puits D'Amour, The Potato Field, Ultra Clone. Larry Steinbachek (k, dm), Steve Bronski (k, dm), Jimmy Sommerville (v). 25/9/84 MV5 MRD TdB Previous sessions for Jensen May 84 and Saturday Live June 84

Bronx Cheer

1/9/72 Springdale Blues, KC Moan, Surprising Find, Adult Games, Flash In The Park. Brian Cookman (g, hca, v), John Reed (mnd, g, bj, v), Tony Knight (g, bj, v). 15/8/72 T1 JM U Previous sessions for R2 1970, and Pete Drummond 72

Elkie Brooks

8/4/76 Jigsaw Baby, Lilac Wine, Try A Little Love, Where Do We Go From Here. Elkie Brooks (v), Isaac Guillory (g), Pete Gage (g), Peter Van Hook (d), Steve York (b), Kirk Duncan (k), George Chandler (bck), Jimmy Chambers (bck), Lee Van Der Bilt (bck). 16/3/76 MV4 TW MR

Brotherhood of Breath

24/7/71 Union Special, Call, Kongi Theme, Think Of Something (& There Is A Spirit, not TX). Chris MacGregor (p), Louis Moholo (d), Harry Miller (db), Alan Skidmore (ts), Gary Windo (ts), Dud Pukwana (al), Mike Osborne (al), Nick Evans (tb), Malcolm Griffiths (tb), Mongesi Feza (tp), Mark Charig (tp), Harry Beckett (tp). 13/7/71 MV4 JW BC Heirs to The Blue Notes, whose radio audition 10/65 was rejected by the audition panel: 'lacking in precision' 'a cacophony' 'full of inaccuracies'. MacGregor's band did get sessions two years later.

20/6/72 Do It, The Serpent's Kindly Eye. Keith Bailey (d), Evan Parker (ts) r Moholo, Beckett. 13/6/72 MV4 PR U

The Edgar Broughton Band

16/3/69 Evil, For What You Are About To Receive†, Love In The Rain, Why Can't Somebody Love Me?† (& Crying, 4/5/69). Edgar Broughton (gv), Stephen Broughton (d), Arthur Grant (b). 27/1/69 PH BA U 'For the extreme sharp end only', audition panel borderline pass. † on Ⓞ Demons At The Beeb HUX020

10/8/69 They Carried A Star, Aphrodite, Psychopath Blues, For The Captain (& Medals, 25/10/69). 4/8/69 PH JW U

17/1/70 Old Gopher, The Moth, There's No Vibrations But Wait, Officer Dan (& Mama's Reward, 4/4/70). 5/1/70 PH JW BC

26/9/70 Freedom, What Is A Woman For, For Dr Spock, The House Of Turnabout. 1/9/70 MV4 JW U

3/7/71 Hotel Room, Look At The Mayor, Mama's Reward. Vic Unitt joins. 15/6/71 MV4 JW BC

17/3/72 What A Pity / I Got Mad, Side By Side / Sister Angela, Chilly Morning Mama. 14/2/72 T1 JM U

7/7/72 Homes Fit For Heroes, Gone Blue, The Rake, Side By Side / Sister Angela. 6/6/72 T1 JM JWH

7/8/73 Hurricane Man / Rock 'n' Roller, Green Light, Slow Down. 17/7/73 LH1 U U

Pete Brown and Piblokto

2/5/70 The Politician, Here Comes The Old Man Dressed In Flowers, Someone Like You. Pete Brown (v, perc), David Thompson (o.p, sx, perc), Jim Mullen (lg, perc), Robert Tait (d, perc), Steve Glover (b, perc). 21/4/70 MV4 JW U

The Crazy World of Arthur Brown

8/10/67 Witch Doctor, Nightmare, Devil's Trip, I Put A Spell On You, Time. Arthur Brown (v), Vincent Crane (o), Drachen Theaker (d) & guest Ron Wood (g). 3/10/67 AO2 BA U

28/4/68 Child Of My Kingdom, Come And Buy, Fire, I Put A Spell On You. & (b) unknown. 8/4/68 PC1 BA PR

Arthur Brown's Kingdom Come

3/4/71 No Time, Night Of The Pigs, Gipsy (& Sunrise, not broadcast). Arthur Brown (v), Goodge Harris (o), Andrew McCulloch (d), Des Fisher (b), Andrew Dalby (lg), Paul Brown (VCS3 sy). 22/3/71 PH PR U

14/1/72 Night Of The Pigs, Bathroom. Brown, Harris, Dalby, Martin Steer (d), Phil Shutt (b). 28/12/71 T1 JM U

8/9/72 Director General, Time Captains. Steer out; Brown (dm). 29/8/72 T1 JM U

19/9/72 Van Gogh's Not Ear, Triangles, Slow Rock. 5/9/72 MV4 U BC

Arthur Brown Band

24/4/75 We've Got To Get Out Of This Place, Dance, The Lord Will Find A Way, Crazy. Arthur Brown (v), Chris Nichols (k), Andy Dalby (g), Barry Clark (g), Steve York (b), Charlie Charles (d), Eddy Edwards (perc), George Khan (ss, ts), Stevie & Mutt Lang (bck) & 10 Gospelayres (bck-3). 17/4/75 MV4 PR U

Scott Brown

30/11/96 Spice Of Life, Andromeda, Its Our Future, Hardcore Assasin. Scott Brown (everything). 20/11/96 OS

Tim Buckley

7/4/68 I'm Coming Here To Stay, Morning Glory, Sing A Song For You, The Troubadour (& Once I Was, Hallucinations, 19/5/68). Tim Buckley (agv), Edward 'Lee' Underwood (gv), Carter CC Collins (bgo). 1/4/68 PC1 BA PR Ⓞ SFPCD082

13/10/68 Love From Room 170, Buzzin' Fly, Untitled. U 1/10/68 PC1 BA PR&BC

Budgie

25/2/72 Hot As A Docker's Armpit, The Author, Whisky River, Nude Disintegrating Parachutist Woman. Burke Shelley (bv), Tony Bourge (g), Ray Phillips (d). 1/2/72 T1 JM U

1/7/76 Sky High Percentage, In The Grip Of A Tyre Fitter's…. Myf Isaacs (g) r Brown. 15/6/76 MV4 TW U

Buffalo Tom

16/7/90 Sunflower Suit, Birdbrain, Bus, Fortune Teller. Bill Janovitz (gv), Chris Colbourn (bv), Tom Maginnis (d). 5/7/90 MV5 DG NG&RPF

The Bug vs Soundmurderer

12/11/03 Live soundclash mix between Todd Osborn (dj, lp) and Kevin Martin (dj) plus guest MCs. Live from MV4 AR~ U

Buick 6

22/1/02 Back Roads, The Mightiest, Standing In The Way, 35 Days, Brand New Morning. Craig Hamilton (gv), Jim Summerfield (gv), Anna Russell (elp, perc, v, o), Jez Ince (b, mnd), Phil Robinson (d, banana and apple shaker). 2/12/01 MV4 ME GYW see Tocques

Building 44

11/4/83 Azrael, Give Me It Back, Mr Opium. Pete Reynolds (v), Kenneth Nelson (sy, v), Tony Jones (bv), Dave Riley (d, perc). 2/4/83 MV4 DG MC

Eric Burdon and the Animals

31/12/67 All Night Long, Monterey, Orange And Red Beans, Anything, Chim Chim Cheree. Eric Burdon, John Weider, Barrie Jenkins, Danny McCullough, Victor Briggs. 21/12/67 U U U

26/5/68 White Houses, Monterey, Landscape, When Things Go Wrong (& It Hurts Me Too, 23/6/68). 21/5/68 PC1 BA DT

Butterflies Of Love

10/11/99 It's Different Now, The Brain Service, Mt Everest, Serious. Daniel Greene (gv), Jeffrey Greene (gv), Scott Amore (k), Neil O'Brien (d), Peter Whitney (b). 17/10/099 MV4 MPK SBR

Butterfly Child

1/3/92 Violin, Led Through The Mardi Gras, Ship Wreck Song, Neptune's Fork. Joseph Cassidy (g, v, b), Gary McKendry (g), Rudy Tambala (prg). 12/1/92 MV3 DG ME&PRB see Papa Sprain

1/1/94 Passion Is The Only Fruit, My Kinda Carnival, Botany Bay, Our Lady Mississippi Revisited. Joseph Cassidy (v, g, cel), James Harris (b), Pendle (g), Richard Thomas (d, sx). 14/11/93 MV3 ME JLC

The Butthole Surfers

12/8/87 Florida, Cherub, Graveyard, Shotgun. U U U U U

27/9/88 Blind Man, EDG, Neee Neee. Gibby Haynes (v), King Coffee (d), Theresa Taylor (d), Jeff Pinkus (b), Paul Leary (g). 20/9/88 MV4 TdB~

Buttsteak

15/5/92 Keith Meat Thief, The Kidd, Garnishy Wages, I Saw Him Burn His Head, Wine Dealership, Western Opera, It's. George M Bowen (gv), Julie McDermott (kv), Jim Glass (g), Scott Hedrick (b), Sergio Ponce (d). 31/3/92 MV4 MR PL&MR

Buy Off The Bar

13/10/86 Peanut Butter Boy, Commie Come Back, Too Shy To Die / That Man, Papa's Music. Loet Schilder (d), Marcelle van Hoof (b), Paul Hekkert (gv), Ingmar van Wynsberge (g), Theo van Heynsbergen (g), Michael Lemmens (sx, v), Francois Moonen (tamb). 28/9/86 U DG ME Lyrics of cover of The Fall's 'That Man' altered to refer to Peel

13/7/87 Keyboard Control, There's No Fridge On The Bristol Bridge, In The Back, No Progression. Jaj Bouwens (tp), Dirk Schouten (v, tamb) r Heynsbergen, Moonen. 5/7/87 U DG TD&NG

18/7/88 No Money For The Lavatory, Euroburger, Illegal Shed, Go Away. Heynsbergen (tp) returns, Femke Hoyng (tamb, perc) r Schouten. 3/7/88 U DG FK&MWT

4/9/89 Hi America, Pleasure Machine, Big Sleep. Schouten (g, bck) returns, Theo Van Kempen (tp) r Heynsbergen. 30/7/89 MV5 DG PL

The Buzzcocks

19/9/77 Fast Cars, Pulse Beat, What Do I Get. John Maher (d), Garth Davies (Smith) (b), Pete Shelley (lg), Steve Diggle (rg). 7/9/77 MV4 MB NG ○

17/4/78 Noise Annoys, Walking Distance, Late For The Train. Steve Garvey (b) r Davies. 10/4/78 MV4 TW DD ○ ○

23/10/78 Promises, Lipstick, Everybody's Happy Nowadays, 16 Again. 18/10/78 MV4 BS NG ○

28/5/79 I Don't Know What To Do With My Life, Mad Mad Judy, Hollow Inside, ESP. Diggle (lv-2). 21/5/79 MV4 TW DD ○ SFRCD104

5/6/03 Driving Insane, Certain Move, Lester Sands, Jerk, Breakdown, Orgasm Addict, Harmony In My Head. Shelley, Diggle, Tony Barber (b), Phil Barker (d). 2/4/03 MV4 SA NS/GYW Joint Peel / One World session, not all tracks TX on Peel

Byzantium

7/5/74 I'll Just Take My Time, Half Way There, Small World. Jamie Rubinstein (g), Mick Barakan (g), Robin Lamble (b), Steve Corduner (d). 16/4/74 LH1 TW U

Cabaret Voltaire

25/6/81 Black Mask, Greensborough, Walls Of Jericho, Jazz The Glass. Richard Kirk (gk), Stephen Malinder (bv), Mark Tattersall (d, perc). Rec. date unknown PRIV U U

22/10/84 Sleep Walking, Big Funk, The Operative. 14/10/84 MV5 DG ME

Cable

25/11/94 Seventy, Oubliette, Sports Cars & Devil Worship, Deadwood For Green, Give Them What They Want. Darius Hinks (g), Peter Darrington (b), Matt Bagguley (gv), Neil Cooper (d). 18/10/94 MV4 JB KR

24/2/96 The Colder Climate, Action Replay Replay, Whisper Firing Line, Apparently. Richie Mills (d) r Cooper. 13/2/96 MV4 MA PN

3/6/97 God Gave Me Gravity, Freeze The Atlantic, The (We Did The Music For The Sprite Ad) Blue, Ring Of Fire. & Andy Haslam (can). 13/5/97 MV4 MR SBR

20/5/98 Hexagon Eye, Blackmail, Honoloulou, A Ball Is A Ball Whichever Way You Look At It. 14/4/98 MV4 MWT RJ

Cado Belle

6/11/76 Stone's Throw From Nowhere, Rough Diamonds, Got To Love. Maggie Reilly (v), Alan Darby (g), Stuart Mackillop (k), Colin Tully (sx, fl), Gavin Hodgson (b), Davy Roy (d). 26/10/76 MV4 JG MR

Cajun Moon

2/12/75 Back Again, Calling On, Fiddler John, Losers Can Be Winners. Allan Taylor (gv), Brian Golbey (fd, v), John Gillaspie (o, clav, v, bombarde). 6/11/75 MV4 TW U

8/7/76 Underneath The Cajun Moon, Mistress Music, Sawtooth Line, Crowded City. 17/6/76 MV4 BAI BAI

John Cale

8/5/75 Taking It All Away, Darling I Need You, Fear, You Know More Than I Know. Pat Donaldson (b, bck), Chris Thomas (hrp), Chris Spedding (g, kbv), Timi Donald (d, bck), John Cale (pgv). 1/5/75 MV4 TW U

Calexico

19/11/97 Paper Route, Wash, Sanchez, Spokes, Drape. John Convertino (d, vib), Joey Burns (gv, smp), Howe Gelb (p, k, Walkman, Warbler), Lisa Germano (vi). 19/10/97 MV4 ME CH

15/6/99 Glowing Heart Of The World, Stray, Frontera/Trigger, Jesus & Tequilla. Convertino, Burns, Volker Zander (b, v, clo), Michael Lembach (g, tp), Martin Wenk (tp, vib). 27/4/99 MV4 MR RJ

30/3/00 Ballard Of Cable Hogue, Over Your Shoulder, Fade, The Crystal Frontier, Gillbert, Press Tour 2000. Convertino, Burns only. Live from Peel Acres AR GT

30/4/03 Not Even Stevie Nicks, Quattro, Alone Again Or. Burns, Jacob Valenzuela (tp, perc, vibes). 31/3/03 MV4 GT RJ

Calvin Party

30/9/94 Celebration, Life & Other Sex Tragedies, The First Thing That I Saw, Po Mo Gothic. Gavan Whelan (d), Phil Hayes (b), John Donaldson (gv), Cameron Donaldson (g), Carole Fleck (perc, bck). 23/8/94 MV4 MR FK

19/5/95 Heart And Soul, Caspar's Ballroom, Blood Simple, Repetition Number 2. 11/4/95 MV4 MR JHE

20/3/96 Caspar's Ballroom, Lies Lies And Government, Mass, Poverty. Live from MCR3 LR TWN

5/3/97 Maybe If Only, Some Words About Sexuality, Plans, Brave New Morning. 9/2/97 MV4 ME JMK

7/9/04 Loss And Gain, All Things Considered, Come Bleed, Tall Grass, Whimsy. J Donaldson, Fleck, Dave Thom (g, bj), Pez (d). 11/8/04 MV4 JSM GYW

Camel

15/3/73 Never Let Go, Arubaluba, Curiosity, Six Ate. Peter Bardens (v), Andy Latimer (gv), Andy Ward (d), Doug Ferguson (b). 19/2/73 LH1 BA U

Camera Obscura

14/8/01 Number One Son, Sun On His Back, Antiwestern, Before You Cry. Tracyanne Campbell (gv), John Henderson (v), Gavin Dunbar (b), Kenny McKeeve (g), Lindsay Boyd (o, p), Lee Thomson (d), Nigel Baillie (tp). 5/8/01 MV4 NF~ RPF

20/12/01 Happy New Year, Little Donkey. Live from Peel Acres AR SA

7/3/02 Park N Ride, Eighties Fan, Pen & Notebook, Sugartown, Let Me Go Home. Carey Lander (k) r Boyd. Live from Peel Acres AR GT

7/10/03 Greyhound Going Somewhere, Return To Send Her, Phil And Don, San Fransisco Song. 25/9/03 MV4 NF JHT

22/1/04 Love My Jean, O'That Were Where Helen Lies, A Fond Kiss, Red Red Rose, Cock Up You're Beaver. Live from Peel Acres AR GT

Can ○

13/3/73 Untitled (as Up The Bakerloo With Anne Nightingale on repeat). Irmin Schmidt (elp, o), Jaki Liebezeit (perc), Damo Susuki (v), Holger Czukay (b), Michael Caroli (g). 20/2/73 LH1 JW BC ○ First British broadcast was R1 In Concert 3/3/73

12/2/74 Tony Wanna Go. Damo out. 29/1/74 LH1 TW (orJW) U ○

15/10/74 Return To BB City, Tape Kebab. 8/10/74 MV4 TW U ○

19/5/75 Geheim, Mighty Girl. 14/5/75 MV4 TW U ○ SFRCD135

Cane 141

24/4/01 In The Sky The Lucky Stars, Jd, Metalheart, Porno Mystique, New Day Parade. Michael Smalle (lv, gk), Ger Connolly (agv), Paul Brennan (k), Shane Burke (b), Ronan Burke (k), Colm Hogan (d). 11/4/01 MV4 SA~ JHT

Laura Cantrell

6/7/00 Not The Tremblin' Kind, When The Roses Bloom, Queen Of The Coast, Blue Eyes Crying In The Rain, Somwhere Some Night. Laura Cantrell (gv) & The Radio Sweethearts: John Miller (bck, g), Francis Macdonald (d), Malcolm McMaster (ps), Kevin Key (g), Martin Hayward (b). 4/6/00 MV4 ME RJ

1/2/01 Two Seconds, Too Late For Tonight, The Whiskey Makes You Sweeter, Churches Off The Interstate, Legend In My Time. & Jon Graboff (mnd, ps), Jeremy Chatzky (b), Jay Sherman Godfrey (g). Live from Peel Acres AR GT

5/11/02 Broken Again, Hong Kong Blues, Cellar Door, Christmas Letter Home. & Godfrey, Graboff, Ivor Ottley (fd), Paul Sandy (b), Francis Macdonald (snare drum). 1/10/02 MV4 SA GYW

8/5/03 Early Years, Rainboy, Wait, Indoor Fireworks, Lee Harvey Was A Friend Of Mine. & Graboff, Macdonald, Zachary Ware (gv), Simon Cottrell (bv). Live from Peel Acres AR GT

23/12/03 Pretty Paper, New Year's Resolution, Oh So Many Years, I Still Miss Someone. & Graboff only; Gordon McIntyre of Ballboy (v-4). Live from Peel Acres AR GT

Capital Letters

24/1/79 Smokin My Ganja, Rasta Say, Fire. Rodrick Harvey (d), Junior Brown (b), George Scarlet (g), Springey (gv), Danny McKen (gv), Earl Lynch (kv), Wenty Stewart (cga), Dell Spence (perc, v), Paulette Hayden (perc, v). 16/1/79 U BS MR

The Capitols

6/4/87 I Want To Be Alone, Who Can Tell?, Every Time, Born Yesterday, Failing Again. Phil (d), Jimbo (b), Tank (g), Sue (g, lv), Maria (vi, bck). 24/3/87 U DG MR&MS

Tony Capstick

18/7/72 Sir Thomas Of Winesbury, I Drew My Ship Into A Harbour, Captain Grant, Foggy Dew, Bonny Bunch Of Roses. Tony Capstick (agv). 26/6/72 PH JW BC 1st appeared on Radio 4 North's Local Accent 19/1/68

26/12/72 Charley, Punch And Judy Man, The Seeds Of Love, The Only Friend I Own. 19/12/72 LH1 JW U

11/6/74 Lazlo Faher, Punch And Judy Man, McCafferty, Old Mollie Metcalf. 13/5/74 T1 U U

6/1/75 I Drew My Ship, Van Dieman's Land, Weak Before Easter, Rambling Sailor, Hello Hans. 16/12/74 MV4 U U

Caravan

5/11/68 Green Bottles For Marjorie, A Place Of My Own, Feeling Reeling And Squealing, Ride. Pye Hastings (gv), Richard Sinclair (bv), David Sinclair (kv), Richard Coughlan (d). 31/12/68 MV4 BA BC

14/9/69 The Clipping Of The Eighth, Why, Excerpt From The Daily Routine Of Maurice Haylett. 26/8/69 MV4 JW U

14/11/70 Golf Girl, For Richard, Hello Hello. 2/11/70 PH JW BC Also recorded special session for Transcription's Top Of The Pops show, 9/9/70, T1†

17/4/71 Nine Feet Underground. 29/3/71 PH JW BC

2/5/72 Waterloo Lily, Love In Your Eye, The World Is Yours. 11/4/72 MV4 U U

30/8/73 Head Loss, Memory Lain Hught, L'Auberge Du Sanglier / A Hunting We Shall Go / Pengola / Backwards†. John Perry (b), Geoff Richardson (vla) r R Sinclair. 20/8/73 LH1 BA U

14/2/74 The Love In Your Eye†, Virgin On The Ridiculous†, Mirror For The Day†, For Richard†. 7/2/74 LH1 TW U † on ○ Songs For Oblivion Fishermen HUX002

3/7/75 The Show Of Our Lives, Stuck In A Hole, Dabsong Conshirto. Mike Wedgewood (b, cga) r Perry. 26/6/75 MV6 TW U §

17/5/76 All The Way, A Very Smelly Grubby Little Oik / Bobbing Wide / Come On Back / Grubby Little Oik (Reprise). Jan Schelhaas (k) r D Sinclair. 6/5/76 MV4 TW BAI §

10/5/77 Behind You, The Last Unicorn, Better By Far, Nightmare. Dek Messecar (b) r Wedgwood. 2/5/77 MV4 TW DD § last 3 sessions on ○ Ether Way HUX013

Carcass

2/1/89 Crepitating Bowel Erosion, Slash Dementia, Cadaveric Incubator Of Endo Parasites, Reek Of Putrefaction. K Grumegargler (dv), J Offalmangler (bv), W G Thorax Embalmer (gv). 13/12/88 MV4 DG MR ● SFPS073

16/12/90 Empathological Necroticism, Foeticide, Fermenting Innards, Exhume To Consume. Bill Steer (g, lv), Jeff Walker (b, lv), Michael Amoit (g, bck), Ken Owen (d, bck). 2/12/90 MV3 DG ME&DMC

Carl Cox

24/2/99 DJ set live from Y4 U

Carnastoan

4/1/82 Progressive News, Natural Man, Give A Damn, Pirate. Conrad Kelly (d), Eugrall Brown (rg, lv), Neville King (k, bck), Anthony Bennett (b, bck), Nigel Bowen (bck). 1/12/81 MV4 TW DD&MC

19/10/82 Satan, Trouble On My Mind, I Don't Want To Lose You, Sufferer. Kelly, King, Bennett, Leo Green (perc), Neville Brown (lv, rg). 29/9/82 MV4 RP NG

The Carol Concert

26/12/70 God Rest Ye Merry Gentlemen, Away In A Manger, Good King Wenceslas, Silent Night, O Come All Ye Faithful. David Bedford (p) & Marc Bolan, June Child, Ivor Cutler, Sonja Kristina (& friend), Rod Stewart, Robert Wyatt, Mike Ratledge, Ron Wood, Ronnie Lane, Peel & Pig, Kenny Jones, Ian McLagan (all v). (2 – Stewart only; 3 – Lane & Wyatt solos; 4 – Kristina). 8/12/70 MV4 JW BC&IS

The Carpettes

24/7/78 Reach The Bottom, I Don't Mean It, Away From It All, Indo-China. Neil Thompson (gv), George Maddison (bv), Kevin Heard (d). 12/7/78 MV4 BS NG

21/12/78 Cruel Honesty, What Can I Do, It Don't Matter, Double Platinum, Routine. Tim Wilder (d) r Heard. 13/12/78 MV4 BS MR

Martin Carthy

30/5/72 The False Lover Won Back, King Henry, Died For Love, Trindon Grange, John Blunt. Martin Carthy (agv). 22/5/72 PH JW BC First broadcast was accompanying Shirley Collins on Light Programme's Roundabout Feb 61, followed by dozens of folk show sessions

8/3/73 John Barleycorn, Seven Yellow Gypsies, John Blunt (& Trindon Grange Explosion, Brigg Fair, 26/4/73). 19/2/73 U BA U

14/8/73 Thorneymoor Woods, Three Jolly Sneaksmen, The Famous Flower Of Serving Men, The False Lover Won Back. 6/8/73 PH JW U

7/3/74 Lucy Wan, Prince Heathen, Skewball, Geordie. 28/2/74 LH1 JW BC

3/10/74 Bonny Boy Billy Boy, All Of A Row, The Bed Making, Green Wedding. 16/9/74 U U U

28/4/75 Sweet Joan, The Trees They Do Grow High, The Unfortunate Sailor, The Famous Flower Of Serving Men. 22/4/75 MV4 U U

21/9/76 The Unfortunate Tailor, King Knapperty, Willie's Lady, Searching For Lambs. 7/9/76 MV4 TW MR

16/12/77 Willie's Lady, Bonnets So Blue, William Taylor The Poacher, Three Jolly Sneaksmen, Blown Adam. 7/12/77 MV4 MB NG

25/4/83 The Devil And The Feathery Wife, Tatty Trousers, Lady Dysie, Long John, I Sowed Some Seeds. 18/4/83 MV4 TW U

Neko Case and Her Boyfriends

13/9/00 Set Out Running, Make Your Bed, Gold And Silver, Favourite, Twist The Knife, Bought And Sold, Furnace Room Lullabye, I'll Be Around, Runnin' Out Of Fools, Lord Don't Move The Mountain, Bowling Green. Neko Case (agv), Andy Hopkins (gv), Bill Hertzog (b), Jon Rauhouse (ps), Mark Pickerell (d), Kelly Hogan (bck). Live from MV4 SA~ JHT

Cat Power

20/7/00 Sophisticated Lady, Hard Times In New York City, Wonder Wall, He Was A Friend of Mine, Freebird (& Deep Inside, Come On In My Kitchen, Werewolf, Up And Gone, Sister, Knockin' On Heaven's Door, TX 31/8/00). Chan Marshall (gkv). 18/6/00 MV4 JB RJ

23/8/01 Untitled, Baby Doll, Come On In My Kitchen. Live from Peel Acres AR~

12/2/03 Names, Funny Things, Evolution, I Don't Blame You. 23/1/03 MV4 RJ~

Catapult

5/10/87 Sink Me, Hope, Subtle And Tip, Undemocratic. Stephen Butler (gv), Martin Stebbing (b), Graham Clarke (g), Richard Knight (d). 27/9/87 U DG ME

The Catherine Wheel

5/5/91 She's My Friend, Shallow, Black Metallic, Painful Thing. Neil Sims (d), David Hawes (b), Brian Futter (g), Rob Dickinson (gv). 9/4/91 MV5 MR~

Catheters

10/7/02 Tightrope, Nothing, Clock, On The Outside. Brian Standeford (v), Leo Gebharot (b), Derek Mason (g), David Brozowski (d). 10/7/02 MV4 SA GT

Cats Against The Bomb

27/4/00 Nerys Hughes Vs The Time Tunnel, South Suffolk Super Sexy Sex Club Seven Super Nuke The Duke Of Mid Morning Mucus, Triple Lawsuit Action, Search And Destroy. Adam Flood (b), Michael Bone (g), Martin Bent. 5/3/00 MV3 KR JSM

Nick Cave and the Bad Seeds

9/4/84 Saint Huck, I Put A Spell On You, From Her To Eternity. Nick Cave (v), Hugo Race (g), Mick Harvey (b), Barry Adamson (b), Blixa Bargeld (g). 28/3/84 MV5 RP NG

Cay

11/11/98 Princes & Princesses, Live & Learn, Skool, Neurofen & Brandy. Anette Mook (gv), Mark Bullock (d), Tom Harrison (b), Nick Olofsson. 20/9/98 MV3 PL RF

5/12/00 Sung Through The Rain, Flying Fool Through Icy Attitudes, Part Of The Snow, F U N Y (A Celebration Of New York). Mook, Olofsson, Ed Sondroe, Chris Hall. 22/11/00 MV4 MA~

Cee Bee Beaumont

17/9/94 Gum Kick, N19 Mudslide, Mad Dog Glove Compartment, Swamp Dog, Dead Shot, After The Slide, Slap Dunk, The Offered Road Divide. Andrew Bourton (Chef Butch) (d), Owen Thomas (King Zero) (g), Mark Flunder (Snider) (g). 7/8/94 MV3 TD SB

Cell

13/2/93 Stratosphere, Everything Turns, Camera, Halo. Jerry Dirienzo (gv), Ian James (gv), Keith Nealy (d), David Motamed (b). 14/12/92 MV4 JB~ AS

Centromatic

17/5/01 Why Are They Playing So Loud, Without You, Flashes And Cables, Fountains Of Fire. Scott Danborn (p, bck), Mark Hedman (b), William Johnson (gv), Matt Pence (d). 6/5/01 MV4 ME~

Centry

6/8/94 Bad Boy Dub, Zion Garden, Release The Chains, The Testament. Dougie Wardrop (prg), Nigel Lake (b, g), Chris Petter (tr, p), Jon Petter (ts, cga), Daniel Spahni (d). 7/7/94 MV4 NG SA

A Certain Ratio

17/10/79 Do The Du (Casse), All Night Party, Flight, The Choir. Simon Topping (v), Martin Moscrop (g), Peter Terrell (g), Jeremy Kerr (b), Donald Johnson (d). 1/10/79 MV4 TW BAI

2/7/81 Knife Slits Water, Day One, Skipscada. & Martha Lucy. 29/6/81 LH1 TW DD

1/12/82 Who's To Say?, Piu Lento, Touch. Andy Connell (k, perc) joins. 20/11/82 MV4 DG MPK

Cha Cha Cohen

17/11/96 Spook On The High Lawn, He's Jet, Freon Short Wave, Get Lost. Jackie Cohen (v), Paul Dorrington (g), Simon Cleave (g), Keith Gregory (b), Simon Smith (d), Justine Wolfenden (k). 27/10/96 MV4 ME~

31/8/99 Interstellar Overdrive OS

Chakk

17/10/84 Cut The Dust, Sedative Ends, #3 Sound, Mother Tongues. Dee Boyle (d), Mark Brydon (b), Simeon Lister (sx), Alan Cross (k, tps), Jake Harries (v). 7/10/84 MV5 DG SC

The Chameleons ○

17/6/81 The Fan The Bellows, Here Today, Looking Inwardly, Things I Wish I'd Said. Marc Burgess (bv), Dave Fielding (g), Reg Smithies (g), Brian Schofield (d). 8/6/81 LH1 TW DD ○

14/6/83 Don't Fall, Nostalgia, Second Skin, Perfumed Garden. John Lever (d) r Schofield & Alistair Lewthwaite (k) joins. 8/6/83 MV4 BYA U ○

16/5/84 Dust To Dust (Return Of The Roughnecks), One Flesh, Intrigues In Tangiers, PS Goodbye. Lewthwaite out. 5/5/84 MV5 DG MR ○ SFRCD114

Michael Chapman

12/6/68 No One Left To Care, If I Bring You Roses, Sunday Morning, One Time Thing, On My Way Again. Michael Chapman (gv). 23/5/68 U JM DK When told this trial tape had to be submitted to the Audition unit, Chapman wrote in saying he'd already been on WS R&B on 2/2/68. However, this possible first broadcast has proved untraceable

18/6/69 Rabbit Hills, No Song To Sing, Naked Ladies In Electric Ragtime, Not So Much A Garden More Like A Maze. 10/6/69 U PR U

31/8/69 Naked Ladies In Electric Ragtime, You Say, Postcards Of Scarborough, Rabbit Hills. & Barry Morgan, Jack Asselman, Bruce Barthol. 11/8/69 PH JW U

25/4/70 Among The Trees, Lady On The Rocks, Not So Much A Garden More Like A Maze (& Landships, Soulful Lady, 28/11/70). & Rick Kemp (b), Richard Dharma (b). 7/4/70 MV4 JW U

22/12/71 Polar Bear Fandango, Night Drive, In The Valley, Time Enough To Spare. U 13/12/71 U JW U

7/4/72 Soulful Baby, The Hero Returns, Shuffle Boat River Farewell, New York Ladies. 20/3/72 U JM U

30/10/73 The Hero Returns, Fire Water Dreams, The Dawning Of The Day, Time Enough To Spare. solo. 16/10/73 LH1 TW BC

23/7/74 Time Enough To Spare, Rock And Roll Jigley, Banjo Song, Firewater Dreams. & 3 U. 1/7/74 U U U

20/1/75 Waiting For A Train, Deal Gone Down, Party Pieces, Among The Trees. U 14/1/75 MV4 TW MR

7/5/76 Shuffleboat River Farewell, Devastation Hotel, Secret Of The Locks, How Can A Poor Man Stand Such Times And Live. & Brian Chatton (p, elp), Rick Kemp (b), Keef Hartley (d) 'recorded on his birthday'. 8/4/76 MV4 MB U

12/4/77 Among The Trees, Dogs Got More Sense, Secret Of The Locks, In The Valley. & Rod Clements (b), Keef Hartley (d, dynamic tambourine 'from Woolworths'-JG). 15/3/77 MV4 JG MR

17/1/78 Falling Apart, Dogs Got More Sense, I'm Sober Now, Kodak Ghosts. & Andy Ward (d), Brian Chatton (k), BJ Cole (ps). 10/1/78 MV4 MB MR

25/6/79 Moth To A Flame, Always Gotta Pay In The End. PRIV

Chapman-Whitney Streetwalkers

4/7/74 Tokyo Rose / Hangman, Systematic Stealth, Get Out Of My Life Woman, Roxyanna. Roger Chapman (v), Charlie Whitney (g), Tim Hinkley (k), Mel Collins (sx), Ian Wallace (d), Bob Tench (b), Philip Chen (b). 27/6/74 LH1 TW U

28/8/75 Burn It Down, Toenail Draggin', Crawfish. John Plotell (b), Mick McBain (d) r Chen, Wallace, Hinkley, Collins. 21/8/75 MV4 TW MR

18/6/76 Daddy Rolling Stone, Run For Cover, Me Me Horse And Me Rum. 8/6/76 MV4 TW U Billed from now on just as 'Streetwalkers'

11/4/77 Chilli Con Carne, Mama Was Mad, Crazy Charade. Micky Feat (b, bck), Dave Dowle (d), Bryan Johnston (k, bck) r Plotell, McBain. 14/3/77 MV4 TW DD

Chapter 13

26/6/01 Transnational, Half Hearted, Alpha Male, Axel B. Paul Rothwell, Mark Russell. 3/6/01 MV4 ME JHT

Chapterhouse

7/10/90 Falling Down, Something More, Inside Of Me, Treasure. Ashley Bates (d), Russell Barrett (b), Simon Rowe (g), Stephen Patman (gv), Andrew Sherriff (gv). 23/9/90 MV3 DG MA

The Charlatans

9/4/90 Then, Always In Mind, You Can Talk To Me, Polar Bear. Tim Burgess (v), Rob Collins (o), Jon Day (b), Jonathan Brookes (d), John Day (g). 20/3/90 MV4 DG TdB

10/2/91 Can't Be Bothered, Between 10th & 11th, Opportunity. Martin Blunt (b), Jon Baker (g) r J & J Day. 22/1/91 MV5 MWT~

Craig Charles

17/3/83 Party Night, Family Way, Thought It Was, Music Scene, Oh To Be In England, In The City. Craig Charles (v) & Dave Treble (g), Pete Gray (bk), Stuart Gray (d), Alan Peters (tp-1). 2/3/83 MV4 RP MWT

14/2/84 What Can You Do, Hands Together Eyes Closed, Consulting His Notebook He Said…, Adolf Hitler. & Brian Harcombe (d), Tony Doyle (b), Paul Morgan (g), Alan Peters (tp), Mike Nelson (sx), Jason R Cunliffe (bck) (4, 5: Charles). 7/2/84 MV5 MRD TdB

Charlie

10/5/76 Fantasy Girls, Prisoners, Summer Romances. U 13/4/76 U JG MR

Charlottefield

23/7/03 Now For The Last Time Go Home And Cut Some Firewood, Again, Weevils. Tom (gv), Ashley (d), Adam (g), Chris (b). Live from MV4 AR SA/GT

The Charlottes

18/10/89 Where You're Hiding, See Me Feel, Could There Ever Be, Venus. Petra Roddis (v), Dave Fletcher (b), Graham Garfiulo (g), Simon Scott (d). 21/9/89 MV5 DG MA

The Chefs

11/5/81 One Fine Day, I'll Go Too, Love Is Such A Splendid Thing, Northbound Train, Springtime Reggae. James McCallum (g), Russ Greenwood (d), Helen McCookerybook (bv), Carl Evans (gv). 5/5/81 LH1 DG MR

Chelsea

27/6/77 No Admission, High Rise Living, Right To Work, Pretty Vacant, Blind Date. Gene October (v), James Stevenson (g), Henry Daze (b), Carey Fortune (d). 21/6/77 MV4 JG MR

3/7/78 No Flowers, Urban Kids, Come On, I'm On Fire. Dave Martin (rgv), Geoff Myles (bv), Steve Jones (d) r Daze, Fortune. 26/6/78 MV4 JG DD

The Cherry Boys

6/4/82 Why Don't You Write?, Don't Leave Me That Way, Come The Day, Kardomah Café. Howie de Minzo (d), Keith Gunson (b), John Cherry (g), Jimmy Hughes (k). 20/3/82 MV4 DG MR

2/9/82 Only Fools Die, In The Dark, Nightmare, I'll Keep On Movin'. 16/8/82 MV4 TW AP

Cherry Forever

17/8/91 Spook, Down And Around, Back To Back, Higher Than Heaven. Gaz Parker (d), Peter Vaughan (b), Mark Revell (g), David Parker (gv). 30/6/91 MV3 DG TD&AM

Cherryblades

8/6/91 On You, Make It Mean, Stodge. Tony Renyard (d), Darrin Woodford (b), Richard Larke (g), Tim Scott (gv). 7/5/91 MV5 MR~

The Chevalier Brothers

30/3/83 Barnyard Boogie, Coco Beans, Twelfth St Rag, Fat Like That. Ray Irwin (sx, lv), Maurice Chevalier (g, bck), Roger Downham (vib, bck), Anders James (b, bck), Ricky Lee Brown (d, bck). 23/3/83 U RP MC

14/12/83 On The Tip Of My Tongue, C Jam Blues / Now's The Time / Three-Handed Woman, Bartender. Irwin, Downham, Janes, Patrice Serapiglia (g, bck), Geoff Brittain (d). 7/12/83 MV4 RP TdB

Cheviot Ranters

25/7/72 Jigs: Rakes Of Kildare / Smash The Windows / The Tenpenny Bit, March: Danish Double Quadrille, Hornpipes: Ridesdale Hornpipe / King Of The Fairies / Lads Of Wickham, Reels: My Love She's But A Lassie Yet / Caddam Woods / The Rose Tree, Waltzes: Mallorea/Whittingham Green Lane / The Banks Of The Tyne. Bryce Anderson (acc), Jack Thompson (fd), Phil Sutherland (b), Geo Mitchell (p), Jock Wilson (d). 12/7/72 NW JW U

11/7/74 Rants: Corn Jigs / Aiken Drum / Island Dance, Jigs: Traditional Air / The Frost Is All Over / Pet O' The Pipers, Hornpipes, Waltzes: The Lads Who Were Reared Among Heather / Bonny Cragside / The Gentle Maiden. 3/7/74 NW JW U

John Chibadura and the Tembo Brothers

6/12/89 Shira, Diya Wangu, Mukadzi Wangu, Amai. John Chibadura (lv, g), Douglas Tsavayo & Innocent Makoni (bck), Mike Gunde (d), Bata Sintirao (g), Charles Ruwizhi (b). 19/11/89 MV5 DG ME Previous session for Kershaw Oct 89

Chicken Shack

28/1/68 Lonesome Whistle Blues, It's Okay With Me Baby, The Letter, When The Train Comes Home, San-Ho-Zay (& My Baby She Loves Me, not TX). Stan Webb (gv), David Bidwell (d), Andy Silvester (b), Christine Perfect (kv). 9/1/68 AO2 BA U 'Unanimous pass' from audition panel; 'girl singer/pianist received special praise'

28/4/68 See My Baby, Waiting On You, Love Me Or Leave Me, You Done Lost Your Good Thing Now. & Rik Gunnell (ts). 17/4/68 MV4 BA PR

8/9/68 Everyday I Have The Blues, Night Life, Side Tracked, Mean Old World (& It Takes A Woman To Make A Man Cry, 10/11/68). 4/9/68 MV4 BA U

22/6/69 Midnight Hour, Look Ma I'm Crying, Things You Put Me Through. Paul Raymond r Perfect. 17/6/69 MV4 JW TW

Chicks On Speed

1/6/00 Peel The Orange A Eurotrash Girl, Night Of The Pedestrian Starring Florian Heck, Your Car Will Take You There, Mind Your Own Business, Night Drive. Melissa Logan (v), Kiki Moorse (v), Alex Murray Leslie (v), Thies Mynther (prg, devices), Tobi Nellmann (prg, devices). 17/5/00 MV4 MA NF

The Chieftains

5/9/70 Fox Hunt, The Munster Cloak, Lord Inchiquin, Kerry Polkas, Strike The Gay Harp, An Maigdean Mara. Paddy Maloney, Sean Keane, Sean Potts, Michael Turbridy, Martin Fay, Peader Mercier. 3/8/70 PH JW U Group's first R1 broadcast was on Country Meets Folk the day before this recording

3/10/72 Lord Mayo, Sonny's Mazurka / Tommy Hunt's Jig, John Kelly's / Merrily Kiss The Quaker / Dennis Murphy's, Trip To Sligo, Planxty Johnson (& An Goach Aenas, not TX). 9/9/72 MV4 JW BC

20/3/73 Drowsy Maggie, Planxty Johnson, The Munster Cloak, Morning Dew (& Lord Mayo, not TX). Paddy Maloney (pp), Paeder Mercier (bh), Michael Tubridy (fl), Sean Potts (wh), Sean Keane (fd), Martin Fay (fd). 10/3/73 T1 JW BC

12/3/74 Humours Of Ballyconnell / Bean An Fhir Rua / Cherish The Ladies, Fanny Power, Battle Of Aughram, Three Kerry Slides. 2/3/74 AO2 JW BC

16/10/75 Samhra Samhra, The Humours Of Bally Connell / Bean An Fhir Rua / Cherish The Ladies, The Humours Of Carolan, Slides, 3 Polkas. Peadar Mercier (bh), Sean Potts (wh), Michael Tubridy (fl, cnc), Paddy Maloney (pp), Sean Keane (fd), Martin Fay (fd), Derek Bell (Irish hp). 9/10/75 MV4 TW U

Children Of the Bong

2/9/94 Polyphase (Bad Food Mix), Interface Reality (Hubble Bubble Mix), Ionospheric State. Rob Henry (prg, k), Daniel Goganian (dm, prg, sfx), DJ Marin. 26/4/94 MV5 PL CML

Chilli Willi and The Red Hot Peppers

19/4/73 Friday Song, Goodbye Nashville Hello London Town, Desert Island Woman, Truck Driving Girl. Martin Stone (gv), Philip Lithman (gpv, vi), Paul Riley (bv), Paul Bailey (bj, gv), Pete Thomas (d). 9/4/73 LH1 BA U

28/2/74 The Natural Evolution Of The Human Life Form As We Know It From Stage One To Ultimate Union With His Creator, All In A Dream, Choo Choo Ch'boogie, Fiddle Diddle. 21/2/74 LH1 U U

8/8/74 Fiddle Diddle, Just Like The Devil, Nine To Five Songwriting Man, Streets Of Baltimore. 25/7/74 LH1 TW U

The Chills

25/11/85 Rolling Man, Brave Words, Wet Blanket, Night Of Chill Blue. Martin Philips (gv), Terry Moore (b, bck), Alan Haig (d), Peter Allision (k, bck). 12/11/85 MV5 PWL MR

15/4/87 Dan Destiny And The Silver Dawn, Living In A Jungle, Rain, Moonlight On Flesh. Phillips, Justin Harwood (bv), Andrew Todd (k), Caroline Easther (d, bck). 5/4/87 U DG MR&MA

4/1/89 Part Past Part Fiction, Christmas Chimes, Effloresce And Deliquesce, Dead Web. Jimmy Stephenson (d) r Easther. 18/12/88 HP DG ME

China Crisis

1/4/82 Seven Sports For All, This Occupation, Be Suspicious, Some People I Know To Lead Fantastic Lives. Dave Reilly (d, perc), Gary Daly (v, b, k), Eddie Lundon (g, k). 22/3/82 MV4 JWI U

27/1/83 A Golden Handshake For Every Daughter, Wishful Thinking, Watching The Rainclouds, Greenacre Day. Daly, Lundon, Gary Johnson (b), Kevin Wilkinson (d), Steve Levy (ob). 15/1/83 MV4 DG MC

Chinese Gangster Element

10/9/84 Red, In My Body, Red Light, This Is Hell. Fiona McBean (kv), Mick Haymer (b), Andrew Greaves (g, bck), Kevin Greaves (d). 1/9/84 U DG NG

Ted Chippington

6/11/85 Rockin' With Rita, Drivin' Down The Road, She Loves You, I Feel Like Buddy Holly. Ted Chippington (v, tps). 1/8/85 recorded live on the Royal Iris, Liverpool Docks U

Stella Chiweshe

14/3/88 Kachembere, Kana Ndikafa, Chapfudzapasi, Vana Vako Vopera. Stella Chiweshe (v, mrm) & the Earthquake: Leonard Gwena, David Tapfuma, Tonderai Zinyawa, Joshua Araketa. 6/3/88 MV4 DG U

20/7/91 Chimbochababa, Serewende, Guuarangu, Shungu. & Earthquake: Gordon Mapika (d), Eric Makakora (b), Epharaim Saturday (g), Chinembira Chidodo (mbi), Leonard Ngwenya & Gilson Mangoma (mrm). 6/6/91 MV5 DG NG&CML

Chords (92)

15/8/92 Gasping, My Dearest Friend, Plastic Sister, The Mirror. Simone Holsbeek (gv), Marcel Morsink (g, bck), Marc Fabels (g), Arnoudt Pieters (d). 28/7/92 MV4 MA PL&MA

The Chords

9/7/79 Now It's Gone, It's No Use, Something's Missing, Maybe Tomorrow. Chris Pope (lg), Billy Hassett (rg, lv), Martin Mason (bv), Brett Ascott (d). 3/7/79 U MR ME

24/3/80 Tumbling Down, Happy Families, Far Away. 11/3/80 MV4 JE MR

Christ

17/12/03 Paperboys, Odds Evens And Primates, Pylonesque (Stripped), Ritalin, Perlandine Friday, Absolom (For Lucy), MK Naomi. Christopher Horne (k, dm, fx). Live from MV4 AR GT

Christians in Search of Filth

31/8/82 Fast Food, Super Rich, Work, Gorilla. Alex Usborne (g), Dan Rubinstein (g), Simon Lewis (d), Akinola (perc), Dave Benady (b), Reed Pimlot (sx), Rick Walker (cl). 11/8/82 MV4 JWI TdB

Chrome Cranks

5/1/96 Wrong Number, We're Going Down, 2 35, Down So Low, Back Door Maniac. Bob Bert (d), Jerry Teel (b), William Weber (gv), Peter Aaron (gv). 5/12/95 MV4 MR PA

Chuck

3/2/96 Star Attraction, Just For A Laugh, Teresa, Gone Too Far. Graham Usher (d), Mark Lyons (b, lv), Paul Sawyer (g, bck). 23/1/96 MV4 AHW DD

Chukki Starr & The Ruff Cutt Band

5/2/02 Blessings Gonna Flow, Love & Peace, Sweet Meditation, So Much Trouble / Forever Shall Praise. Tony Phillips (g), Carlton Ogilvie (k), Paul Yebuah (k), Winston Williams (d), Kenton Brown (b), Barbara Nap (bck). 2/1/02 MV4 SA GT

Chumbawamba

21/8/92 Agadoo, The Birdie Song, Knock Three Times, Y Viva Espania. Harry Hamer (d), Julian Walker (b), Boff (g), Danbert (k), Dunston Bruce (perc), Maviy Dillan (tp), Lew Watts (v). 2/8/92 MV4 TdB TdB&SA

13/11/93 Timebomb, Love Me I'm Liberal, Give The Anarchist A Cigarette, The Rain It Raineth. 21/10/93 MV4 NG SBR

The Cigarettes

24/1/80 Can't Sleep At Night, Frivolous Disguises, It's The Only Way To Live (Die), Valium World. Rob Smith (gv, p), Steve Taylor (b, bck), Adam Palmer (d). 15/1/80 U JS MR

The Cimarrons

16/12/75 Tradition, Dim The Lights, You Can't Beat Us. U 4/12/75 MV4 U U

14/12/78 Rock Against Racialism, Civilisation, Reggae Rockin'. Locksley Gichie (gv), Franklyn Dunn (bv), Carl Levy (kv), Maurice Ellis (d), Winston Reid (lv). 6/12/78 MV4 BS NG

Cinerama

16/7/98 Maniac, Honey Rider, Comedienne, You Turn Me On. David Lewis Gedge (g, lv), Sally Murrell (k, bck), Philip Robinson (k, fl, bck), Dare Mason (g), Anthony Coote (b, bck), Richard Marcangelo (d), Rachel Davies (vi), Abigail Trundle (clo). 14/6/98 MV4 ME JLO

6/5/99 Maniac, Crusoe, King's Cross, Dance Girl Dance, Pacific, Hard Fast Beautiful. Gedge, Murrell, Robinson only. Live from Peel Acres AR GT

2/9/99 Kerry Kerry, Dance Girl Dance, Kings Cross, 146 Degrees, Honey Rider, Hard Fast And Beautiful. Simon Cleave (g), Terry de Castro (b), Bryan McLellan (d) join. 31/8/99 MV3 AR SA

2/11/99 146 Degrees, Film, Reel 2 Dialogue 2, Elenore. Davies (vi), Trundle (clo) return. 15/8/99 MV3 ME GT

14/6/00 146 Degrees, Heels, 10 Denier, King's Cross, Honey Rider, Apres Ski, Superman, Your Charms, Wow. Simon Pearson (d) r McLellan (d). Live from MV3 SCU MA

19/9/00 Because I'm Beautiful, Lollobrigida, Sly Curl, Yesterday Once More. Richard Bridgemont (clo) r Trundle, Robinson out; Ilka Paetz (German narration-3). 12/7/00 MV4 SA PN

21/12/00 Christmas Song. Gedge & Murrell only. Live from Peel Acres AR GT/SA

24/5/01 Careless, Get Smart, Quick Before It Melts, Health And Efficiency. Kari Paavola (d) r Pearson; & Bill Davies (vi), Abigail Trundle (clo). 13/5/01 MV4 ME JHT

9/1/02 Cat Girl Tights, Starry Eyed, Your Time Starts Now, Apres Ski, And When She Was Bad, Suck, Get Up And Go, Quick Before It Melts, Spangle, Estrella, Wow, Health And Efficiency, Brassneck, Your Charms. 5-piece & Trundle (clo), Davies (vi), Sarah Morris (vla), Eleanor Gilchrist (vi). Live from MV4 AR SA

4/6/03 Edinburgh (aka I'm From Further North Than You), Larry's, On/Off, All The Things She Said. Maria Jefferis (k) r Murrell. 8/5/03 MV3 MA U

6/1/04 Always The Quiet One, Mars Sparkles Down On Me, Why Are Nickles Bigger Than Dimes, Groovejet. Gedge, Cleave, Paavola, Sally Crewe (b), Joy Hawley (clo-2). 27/11/03 MV4 MA RF ◯ extensive selection planned for boxed set release on Sanctuary Autumn 07

Circle

18/7/02 Valtion Salaissus, Alholan Lohikaarme (& Keskenerainen Cowboy, Le Per Ty, 22/10/02). Jyrki Laiho (g), Janne Westerlund (gv), Mika Ratto (k, v, perc), Tomi Leppanen (d), Olli Joukio (perc), Jussi Lehtisalo (bv), Teemu Korpoaa (devices). 9/6/02 MV4 KR NF

Circus

24/4/68 Who Would Love Her?, Gone Are The Songs Of Yesterday, The Patience Of A Fool, Do You Dream. Mel Collins (ts, fl), Alan Bunn (d), Ian Jelfs (lg), Phillip Goodhand-Tait (v), Kirk Riddle (b). 23/4/68 AO2 DK DT 'Outdated, square, rubbish, badly played, out of tune... NO' Unanimous fail from audition panel

City Limits Crew and the Mutant Rockers

23/1/85 Fresher Than Ever, Sucker, Money, Keep It On. Little Stevie Bee & Pretty Boy Gee (rp), Erica Harrold (bck), Damon Butcher & Ricky Rennalls (k), Paul K Edgley (g, b-2), Budd Beadle (sx). 15/1/85 MV5 MRD MR

Claire

22/7/87 Who Haunted Mrs Robbins?, Wife Lover Killer, Passions For Pamela, Filled With Fear. Ian Wilson (gv), Pete Devine (g), Ian Williams (b), Andy Williams (d), Ian Wilky (perc). 14/7/87 U DG MR&MS

Chris Clark and The Johnny Watson Concept

17/12/67 Love's Gone Bad, From Head To Toe, Do Right Baby, I Want To Go Back There Again, Gotta Get You Into My Life. U 1/12/67 U U U

Dave Clarke

20/5/94 Adagio For M3, NGC 3628, M64: The Black Galaxy, COBE Theme. Dave Clarke billed as Directional Force. OS ◯ SFPSCD092

2/9/99 Live DJ set 31/8/99 MV3 AR SA

6/12/00 DJ set live from MV4 AR SA&GPR

7/5/02 Live DJ set from LL AR~ GYW

4/2/04 DJ mix set live from MV3 AR GT

16/12/04 10–min DJ mix for Keepin' It Peel night live from MV5 GYW JHT

Clearlake

28/11/00 Sunday (With Intro), Don't Let The Cold In, Hang On To Your Ego, Life Can Be So Cruel. Butch (d), Sam (k), Woody (b), Jason (gv). 19/11/00 MV4 KR NS

Climax Chicago Blues Band

17/10/74 Shopping Bag People, Amerita/Sense Of Direction, Reaching Out, Before You Reach The Grave. Colin Cooper (v, hca, sx, fl, g), Peter Haycock (v, g, hca), Derek Holt (b, o, p), John Cuffley (d). 26/9/74 MV4 TW BAI Nine previous R1 and World Service sessions 69–74

2/10/75 Devil Knows, I Am Constant, Running Out Of Time, Using The Power. & Richard Jones (k). 9/9/75 MV4 U MR just Climax Blues Band from now on

8/10/76 Couldn't Get It Right, Chasin' Change, Together And Free, Mighty Fire. 16/9/76 MV4 TW BAI

Clinic

16/2/97 Piggy, Porno, Holiday, Big Boys. Ade Blackburn (vg), Jonathon Hartley (g), Brian Campbell (b), Carl Turney (d). 26/1/97 MCR3 TWN U

31/3/98 Lester Young, Eddie Snowman, Cutting Grass, Daddy. 15/2/98 MV4 JLO LS

27/1/00 The Second Foot, Internal Wrangler, Hippy Death Suite, T. 29/8/99 MV3 KR NS

22/8/00 The Bridge, Jouster, The Nuns, Daishiki. 23/7/00 MV4 ME~

13/2/02 Magic Boots, Internal Wrangler, Walking With Three, Mr Moonlight, Sunlight Bathes Our Home, Pet Eunuch, Evil Bill, Welcome, 2/4, Monkey On Your Back, Cement Mixer. Live from MV4 AR~ SA&GT&RJ

Clock DVA

7/6/83 Sister, Beautiful Losers, Dark Encounters. Adi Newton (tp, v), Paul Browse (sx, k), Nick Sanderson (d), John Carruthers (g), Dean Dennis (b). 25/5/83 MV4 BYA TdB

The Close Lobsters

4/1/88 Loopholes, From This Day On, What Is There To Smile About?, Mirror Breaks. Stewart McFadyen (d), Bob Burnett (b), Graeme Wilmington (g), Tom Donnelly (g), Andy Burnett (v). 15/12/87 U DG MR&MC Debut session for Janice Long July 86

Clotaire K

9/7/03 Bif Bam Boom, Maqqam, Laisse Les, Lubnan. Clotaire K (v), LNB (v, hbb), Den's (d, hbb), Ewae (tt), Do Levy (b), Suzana Ansar (v-2). 18/6/03 MV4 MA NF

cLOUDDEAD

5/6/01 Peel Intro, Dead Dog, Cold Lunch, Grey, Physics Of A Bicycle. Doseone (Adam Drucker), Why? (Yoni Wolf), Odd Nosdam (David Madson). OS

17/7/02 Apt A (Part 1: Touching Story), And All You Can Do Is Laugh (Part 1: Grey), I Promise Never To Get Paint On My Glasses Again (Part 1: Out For The View), Jimmy Breeze (Part 1: I Taught Myself To Survive), Jimmy Breeze (Part 2: Ram's Crumpled Horn), Bike (Part 2: Edison Accapella), Bike (Part 2: Dead Dog), The Sound Of A Handshake, Unknown Encore. Adam Drucker (v), Jonathon Wolf (v), David Madson (k, smp), Jordan Dalrymple (k, smp). Live from MV4 RJ GT

Clouds

23/11/91 Dude Electric Cell, Poll Tax Blues, King Of The Rocket Men. Balloon (d), Helicopter Hot-Rock (b), Bruce Starbuck (g), Vim Void (v, g), Doctor Cosmos (sy). 29/9/91 MV3 DG ME&JMK

CNN

3/9/93 Shutdown, America, Too Many Cars, Gambit. Tim Brichend (g), Neill Lambert (d), David Tomlinson (v). 27/7/93 MV4 MA~

Coalition

1/10/02 Who's Next, Be What You Wanna Be, Rain Spit, Success. Subject (prd), Jairzinho (prd), Rudie Rich (dj, tt), E (MC), Fruit Juice Genius (MC), Brainz (MC), Sen-C (MC), Selina (MC), Valorous (MC), Bill Faruh (aka Mandela) (MC). 4/9/02 MV4 SA NF

Cobra

19/1/92 Tek Him, Be Patient, Fulfillment, Yush. Don Campbell (d), Kenton Brown (b), Tony Phillips (g), Carlton Ogilvie (sy), Tony Thomas (electric perc), Cobra (v). 29/12/91 MV3 DG ME&JRS

Cochise

14/3/70 Velvet Mountain, Woodland Lifetimes, Past Loves. BJ Cole (ps), Richard Wills (b), Mick Grabham (lg), Willie Wilson (d), Stuart Brown (v). 3/3/70 MV4 JW U

7/11/70 Love's Made A Fool Of You, Why I Sing The Blues, Words Of A Dying Man, Moment And The End. John Gilbert (v) r Brown. 26/10/70 PH JW BC

1/5/71 Hummingbird, Why I Sing The Blues, The Dream, Midnight Moonshine. 20/4/71 MV4 U U

Joe Cocker and the Grease Band

9/6/68 Something's Coming On, Marjarine, Mr Bus Driver, I Shall Be Released (& With A Little Help From My Friends, 14/7/68). Joe Cocker (v), Chris Stainton (b), Mike Gee (g), Tommy Eyre (o), Tom Riley (d). 20/5/68 PC1 BA PR Recorded special audition for Aidan Day at R1, 16/5/68, passed by panel 21/5

13/10/68 Can't Be So Bad, With A Little Help From My Friends, Let's Go Get Stoned, Run Shaker Life. & 3 singers U. 7/10/68 PC1 BA U

11/10/69 Laudy Miss Clowdy, Darlin' Be Home Soon, Hello Little Friend, Delta Lady. Cocker, Stainton, Henry McCullough (g), Alan Spenner (b), Bruce Rowland (d). 29/9/69 PS JW TW

Cockney Rebel

11/6/74 Bed In The Corner / Sling It, Mr Soft, Sweet Dreams / Psychomodo. Steve Harley (gv), Paul Jeffreys (b), Stuart Elliott (d), Milton Ream James (p), Jean-Paul Crocker (vi). 28/5/74 LH1 TW U Group's first R1 broadcast was In Concert recorded 22/1/74, TX 26/1

The Cockney Rejects

15/8/79 East End, Are You Ready To Ruck, Flares 'n' Slippers, They're Gonna Put Me Away. Stinky Turner (v), Mick Geggus (g), Vince Reardon (b), Andy Scott (d). 8/8/79 MV4 TVD MR

25/2/80 Cockney Rip Off, 15 Nights, I Wanna Be A Star, Block Buster. Nigel Woolf (dv) r Scott; & the road crew (v, shouting). 13/2/80 MV4 JE NG

The Cocteau Twins ◯

15/7/82 Wax And Wane, Garlands, Alas Dies Laughing, Feathers Oar / Blades. Robin (g), Liz (lv), Will (b). 21/6/82 MV4 JWI DD&ME

31/1/83 Hearsay Please, Dear Heart, Blind Dumb Deaf, Hazel. & Cindy Talk (Gordon Sharp) (v). 22/1/83 U DG HP

4/10/83 The Tinderbox (Of A Heart), Strange Fruit, Hitherto, From The Flagstones. Fraser, Guthrie only. OS

5/9/84 Pepper Tree, Whisht, Peep Bo, Otterley. & Simon Raymonde (b). 29/8/84 U BYA NG All on ◯ BBC Sessions BELLACD14

Codeine

26/2/93 Jr, Tom, Smoking Room, Broken Hearted Wine. Josh Madell (d), Stephen Immerwahr (b, lv), John Engle (g). 22/12/92 MV4 MR~ TD

3/6/94 Median, Sure Looks That Way, Sea, Loss Leader. Souglas Scharin (d) r Madell. 27/4/94 MV5 SA MFA

Leonard Cohen

14/7/68 That's No Way To Say Goodbye, You Know Who I Am, Like A Bird On A Wire, So Long Marianne (& Dress Rehearsal Rag, 11/8/68). Leonard Cohen (agv) & Tony Gilbert for 5 musicians (incl Dave Cousins, bj) & 3 singers U. 9/7/68 PC1 BA DT

Coin Op

30/7/02 Democracies, The Make Up, Play Pen, Milk. Matt Leuw (gv), Nick Hills (gkv), Craig Robbins (bv), Matt Cooper (d). 12/6/02 MV4 SA NF

Coldcut

18/2/97 Coldcut vs Grandmaster Flash, Creatures, Shakatakadoob, Scratch Ya Head, Beats + Pieces 97. Matt Black, Jonathon Moore. Live from MV4 MR GT

18/12/97 Mix, titles unknown, live from MV4 U U

16/12/04 10–min DJ mix for Keepin' It Peel night. Live from MV3 GYW JHT

Shirley Collins

5/3/69 Nellie The Milkmaid, Fire And Wine, Ramble Away, Dreamsong, Lowlands, The Finite Time, Oliver Woodworm, The Spirit Of Christmas. Shirley Collins with the Tinderbox (2,4,6,7,8–Tinderbox only). 28/1/69 S1 JM U

Shirley and Dolly Collins

8/5/68 Whitsun Dance, Lovely Joan, Good Dog, A Blacksmith Courted Me, Over The Hills And Far Away. Shirley and Dolly Collins. 7/5/68 S1 DK U

15/3/73 Nelly The Milkmaid, The Blacksmith, Morris Dance Medley, The Banks Of The Bawn. 12/2/1973 U BA U

Colon

31/7/90 Top Quality Sturdy Bargains, Disco Bar, Corno, Sex Cadet. Nicky Smith (bv), Phil Reynolds (gv), Selwin Callister (g), Colin Christian (dm). 3/7/90 MV3 MR MR

The Colorblind James Experience

24/10/88 Polka Girl, Hey Bernadette, Havoc Theme, Wedding At Canaa. Jim McAveney (d), Ken Frank (b), Phillip Marshal (lg), Dave McIntire (sx, cl), John Ebert (tb), Colorblind James (rg, vib, v). 18/10/88 MV4 MR MR ◯ SFPCD076

27/11/89 Some Night, Rollin' 'n' Tumblin', It Didn't Work Out, I'm Never Gonna Hurt The Girl I Love. same, except 'Joe Colombo' (tb). 7/11/89 MV5 DG MR

Jon Hiseman's Colosseum

19/1/69 The Road She Walked Before, Those About To Die, Backwater Blues, A Whiter Spade Than Mayall (& Debut, 2/3/69). Jon Hiseman (d), Dick Heckstall-Smith (sx), Dave Greenslade (o, vib), Tony Reeves (b), James Litherland (gv). 17/12/68 PC1 BA AH

6/7/69 Elegy, Grass Is Greener, Hiseman's Condensed History Of Mankind, February's Valentine (& Butty's Blues, 31/8/69). & Barbara Thompson (sx, fl). 30/6/69 PH JW TW

22/11/69 Lost Angeles, Grass Is Always Greener, Arthur's Moustache. & Thompson & Dave Clempson (gv) r Litherland. 18/11/69 MV4 JW TW Four Sounds of the Seventies sessions as just Colosseum, not for Peel, followed in 70–71, before…

Colosseum II

23/8/77 Put It This Way, Intergalactic Strut, Lament, The Inquisition. Jon Hiseman (d), Gary Moore (g), Don Airey (k), John Mole (b). 15/8/77 MV4 TW DD Previous Colosseum II line-up, with Neil Murray (b) & Mike Starrs, debuted on In Concert June 76

Colours Out of Time

26/5/81 Listen To Me Now, The Waiting, Asylum, 5 4 3 2 1. Steve Reynolds (v), Dave Roberts (g, bck), Andy Pennance (g), Philip Bourne (b), John Durrant (d), Clive Williams (o). 18/5/81 LH1 TW DD

Comatose

15/9/98 Football Fanatic, Drifting, Body Part, Hopeless Dream. Alison Clough (b, bck), Hazel Stuart (glv), Adam Sherriff (d), Barbara Cunningham (g). 16/8/98 MV4 ME~

Come

18/4/92 Bell, Off To One Side, William, Dead Molly. Arthur Johnson (d), Sean O'Brien (b), Chris Brokaw (g, bck), Thalia Zedek (gv). 2/4/92 MV4 DG NG&JI

12/2/93 Sharon Vs Karen, Wrong Side, Mercury Falls, City Of Fun. 21/1/93 MV4 NG MA

Come in Tokio

4/2/82 Tokyo, Nature Call, Walk Away, Save Me From Falling. Alan Curry (d), Frank Mahon (b), John Gillin (lg), Phil Wylie (rg, lv), John Jenkins (k). 23/1/82 U DG MR

28/9/82 What Lurks Behind Old Satan's Door?, Number One, Say You'll Never Go Away Again (& Change Of Style, not TX). 15/9/82 PHM JL U

10/5/84 Say You'll Never Go Away Again, Turn Walk Away, Been Such A Long Time Waiting For Love, It Was Nothing. Craig Frank (k) r Jenkins; Gillin out. 28/4/84 MV5 DG MR

Come Ons

1/5/02 It's Alright, Hip Check, Sunday Drive, Bello Amore, Don't Tell Me, Grounded, Twine Time, I'll Show You Why. Deanne Lovan (bv), Patrick Pantano (d, perc), Jim Johnson (g, bck), Nate Caveleri (bk, o). Live from MV4 SA JHT

Comet Gain

30/3/96 Say Yes Kaleidoscope Sound, Stripped, Pier Angell. Sarah Bleach (v), David Charlie Peck (gv), Phil (d), Jax, (b, k), Sam (g). 17/3/96 MV3 ME SA

6/1/98 Emotion Pictures, Tighten Up, Young Lions, We Are All Rotten. Rachel Evans (v), David Christian (gv), Blair Cowl (b, g), Kay Ishikawa (k), Darren Smith (d). 11/11/97 MV4 MR AA

Company 2

20/9/90 I'm Breathing Thru This, Bear No Malice, Tell It As It Is. Ben Chapman (dj), David Harrow (k), Lee (Stepz) Bennett (v). 20/8/89 MV5 DG ME

Comsat Angels

25/10/79 Total War Girl, Independence Day, Baby, Ju-ju Money. Steve Fellows (lvg), Andy Peake (k, bck), Kevin Bacon (b), Mick Glaisher (d). 10/10/79 MV4 TVD NG

8/5/80 Real Story, Money Pilot, Waiting For A Miracle, Home Is The Range. 29/4/80 MV4 BS MR

9/2/81 Dark Parade, Eye Of The Lens, Be Brave, At Sea. 3/2/81 LH1 DG MR

7/10/81 Now I Know, Ju Ju Money, Our Secret, Goat Of The West. 28/9/81 MV4 KH HP

Conemelt

16/9/98 Magic Till, Letter From Ransford, Soul Tombola, Stinky Feeling. Ashley Marlowe, Grant Newman, Nat Mellors. OS

Conscious Sound Collective

7/9/96 Every Sound, Every Sound Dub, In The Sun, The Conquerer, Rebirth. All (1, 2), The Dub Specialists (3), Bush Chemists & Culture Freeman (4), Centry (5). OS

Consolidated

24/11/91 America No 1, This Is Fascism, No Censorship, Meat Kills. Adam Sherburne (gv), Mark Pistel (k), Philip Steir (d). 8/10/91 MV4 JB PL&JB

Cook Da Books

14/2/83 Low Profile, Do One, I Wouldn't Wanna Knock It, Falling. John Leggett (d), Gwen Moran (bv), Peter 'Digs' Deary (gv), Tony Prescott (k). 7/2/83 U JP U

28/2/84 Keep On Believing, Golden Age, I Wouldn't Touch You, Hurt Me Deep Inside. 18/2/84 MV5 DG MC

The Cookie Crew

8/5/85 B The Place To Be, The Cut Master Swift Rap, It's Gotta Be Fresh. Suzie Q (v), Reme-Dee (v). 28/4/85 MV5 DG ME

23/9/85 Party People, On The Beat, All You People, Radio One Tribute, Sipho. & Sipho Hah!: Sipho Jozana (hbb), Debbie Pryce (rp), Susan Banfield (rp). 10/9/85 U JWI MS

John Cooper Clarke

6/11/78 I Married A Monster From Outer Space, Readers' Wives, Health Fanatic, Spilt Beans. John Cooper Clarke (v). 31/10/78 MV4 TW MR

15/3/82 Midnight Shift, The Day My Pay Went Mad, Night People, The New Assassin. & Steve Hopkins (k), Steve Williams (b), Richard Darbyshire (g), Martin Hannet (g), Trevor Spencer (d). 24/2/82 MV4 KH NG

Mike Cooper

7/8/68 Leadhearted Blues, Tadpole Blues, Divinity Blues, The Way I Feel, Maggie Campbell. Solo (agv). 7/8/68 S2 DK U Auditioned and passed 4/68

30/4/69 Turtle Blues, Death Letter, Poor Little Annie, Electric Chair, Oh Really. 29/4/69 PH PR BC

15/11/69 Spider And The Fly, I Think She Knows Me Now, Moon Going Down, Tell Me Papa. Mike Cooper (gv), Jo-Ann Kelly (p), Bob Ball (p) (3–Cooper out). 20/10/69 PH JW BC

2/1/71 Wish She Was With Me, Black Monday, Take A Look Around, I've Got Mine (& Too Late Now, 20/3/71). 7/12/70 PH JW BC

21/3/72 3.48, Think She Knows Me Now, Time To Time, Few Short Lines. Solo. 6/3/72 PH JW BC

21/4/72 Morning Glory, The Singing Tree, Night Journey, Three Forty. Mike Cooper's Machine Gun Company: & Bill Boazman (g), Geoff Hawkins (ts), Les Calvert (b), Tim Richardson (d). 28/3/72 T1 JM U

27/6/74 Suicide Deluxe, Black Night Crash, Beads On A String. & the Trout Steel Band: Mike Cooper (rgv), Terry Clarke (g, bck), Mike Osbourne (al), Colin Boyd (b), Harry Miller (db), Louis Maholo (d). 20/6/74 LH1 PR U

26/6/75 Wild Rover, Blind Willie, Beads On A String, Rock And Roll Highway. & Les Calvert (b), Roger Keene (perc, fl). 19/6/75 MV4 U U See Uptown Hawaiins, below

Cop Shoot Cop

24/3/91 If Tomorrow Ever Comes, Drop The Bombs, Slipped Clutch, Coldest Day Of The Year. Tod (b, v-1,2,4), Natz (b, v-3), Cripple Jim (smp), Phil Pyled (d, perc). 26/2/91 MV5 MR~

16/5/92 Surprise Surprise, Nowhere, Rm 429. & KJ (bck-3). 29/3/92 MV3 DG ME&SCO

Julian Cope

10/2/83 Head Hang Low, Lunatic And Fire-Pistol, Hey High-Class Butcher, The Greatness And Perfection Of… Julian Cope (gv, sit, k, perc), E O Cas (dm), Kate St John (ww). 5/2/83 MV4 DG TdB

11/6/84 Me Singing, Sunspots, Search Party, Hobby. Cope, Donald Skinner (g). 29/5/84 MV5 MRD ME

4/5/91 Hanging Out And Hung Up On The Line, You Think It's Love, The Mystery Trend, Soul Medley: Free Your Mind / Everything / Hung Up. & Peggy Suicide: Skinner, Tim Bran (bk), Rooster Cosby (d). 11/4/91 MV5 DG NG&PL

Philip Cordell

15/1/69 Quality Street, When Summer's Here Again, That's A Mighty Road, Winning In The End, Anna Syde. Philip Cordell (agv). 8/1/69 S1 JM U

Cords

24/7/93 Taurus (Star), Second Skin, Angellust, Big Show, Storm. Simone Holdbeek (gv), Marcel Morsink (g, bck), Marc Fabels (b), Arnoudt Pieters (d). 22/6/93 MV4 MR AA

Cornelius

21/10/98 Ball In Kickoff, Lazy, Brand New Season. Keigo Oyamuda (gv, ag, seq, th), Horie Hirohisa (k, bck), Ohashi Nobuyuki (b, bck), Araki Yuko (d, perc). 8/9/98 MV4 MR~ GT

Cornershop

13/2/93 Nai Zindigi Nai Jevan (New Way New Life), Summer Fun, England's Dreaming, Trip Easy. Tjinder Singh (bv), Ben Ayres (lgv), Avtar Singh (g), John Robb (g), Anthony Saffery (sit), David Chambers (d). 17/1/93 MV3 ME JB

17/4/02 Heavy Soup, Staging The Plaguing Of The Raised Platform, Norwegian Wood, Jullander Shere, Lessons Learned From Rocky 1 To Rocky 3, Spectral Mornings, We're In Your Corner. Singh, Ayers, Nick Simms (d), Pete Downing (g), Pete Bengry (perc), Sheema Mukhergee (b), James Milne (b), Lorraine Smith (bck). Live from MV3 AR SA

The Corporation

3/11/82 Threats And Promises, Hard Times, Hip Talk, Open Season. Paul Winters (gv), Keith Robson (bv), John Alexander (d), Rob MacLagan (sx), Brian Bull (tp, g), Grahame Cusak (perc, cga). 18/10/82 U TW DD

The Cortinas

26/7/77 Defiant Pose, Television Families, Having It, Further Education. Jeremy Valentine (v), Nick Sheppard (g), Mike Fewings (g), Dexter Dalwood (b), Daniel Swan (d). 18/7/77 MV4 TW DD

Elvis Costello and the Attractions

1/8/77 Less Than Zero, Mystery Dance, Red Shoes, Blame It On Cain. Elvis Costello (lvg), Peter Thomas (d), Bruce Thomas (b), Steve Naive (po). 25/7/77 MV4 TW DD

20/3/78 (I Don't Wanna Go To) Chelsea, The Beat, Pump It Up, You Belong To Me. 13/3/78 MV4 TW DD

30/10/78 Really Mystified, Radio Radio, (I Just) Don't Know What To Do With Myself, Stranger In The House. 23/10/78 MV4 TW DD

3/3/80 High Fidelity, Possession, Beaten To The Punch, B Movie. 25/2/80 MV4 TW DD

The Count Bishops

17/5/76 Takin' It Easy, Confessin' The Blues, Wang Dang Doodle, Dust My Blues. Zenon de Fleur (rgv), Johnny Guitar (lgv), Steve Lewins (b), Paul Balbi (d). 4/5/76 U JG MR

27/7/77 Till The End Of The Day, Don't Start Me Talking, Hands On The Wheel, I Want Candy. & Dave (v). 20/7/77 MV4 U NG

Country Gazette

20/3/73 Virginia Darlin', Keep On Pushing, I Might Take You Back Again, Rawhide. Byron Berline (fd, mnd, v), Roger Bush (db, v), Alan Mundy (bj), Kenny Wertz (g, lv). 5/3/73 T1 JW U Debut session for Bob Harris earlier that month

31/7/75 Sunday Sunrise, Working On A Building, The Last Thing On My Mind, Hide Your Love Away, Improve Your Mind, Dear Old Dixie. Roland White (g, bj, v) r Wertz; David Ferguson (fd, v) r Berline. 22/7/75 MV4 TW MR

Wayne County and the Electric Chairs

18/6/79 Waiting For The Marines, Berlin, C4, Midnight Pal. Wayne County (lv), Henry Padovani (kgb), Elliot Michaels (g), Val Haller (bk), JJ Johnson (d, tp), David Cunningham (p-2). 11/6/79 MV4 TW DD

Cove

11/12/02 Untitled 1, Autumn Leaves Turn From The Dresses Of The Vampire Girls, Spelling Bee Champion, The Minuet Song. Mark Davidson (d), Patrick Lloyd (b), David CW Briggs (gv). Live from MV4 NF~ GT

Cowcube

27/7/00 Grooved For Extra Flavour, Stretchy For Penguin, Romperstomper, Bacon Beats. Paul Stimpson (e). OS

20/12/01 unknown title. OS

24/1/02 George, Ouch, Supermusicboy, Truffle Shuffle. OS

Cows

27/6/90 Big Mickey, You Are So Beautiful†, How Dry I Am†. Tony Oliveri (d), Kevin Rutmanis (bv), Thor Eisentrager (g), Shannon Selberg (v, bu). 3/6/90 MV3 DG ME&FK † On ◯ SFMCD212

Carl Cox

27/2/97 DJ set live from MV4 U U U

Lol Coxhill

13/6/72 Felicidad, Whitefield Music II, Mood, Whispering. Lol Coxhill (sx), Peter Bedford (p), Ted Speight (gp-1) John Walters (mel-4). 22/5/72 PH JW BC

19/6/73 Bath 72, Monk, Fire And Rain, Theme For Mrs Grieg. 7/5/73 U JW BC

The Lol Coxhill-David Bedford Duo

10/11/71 Pretty Little Girl, Hungerforf, It's Easier Than It Looks, Don Alfonso (& Pretty Little Girl Pt 2, 4/1/72). Lol Coxhill (sx), David Bedford (p). 25/10/71 U JW U Debut as duo for Bob Harris Aug 71

Graham Coxon

1/9/04 Min Trampolin, Right To Pop, Been Smoking Too Long, Ship Building. Graham Coxon (gv), Steven Gilchrist (d), Owen Thomas (g), Toby Mcfarlane (b), Sean Read (k, o). 19/8/04 MV4 MWT GYW

16/12/04 Just A State Of Mind, You're So Great. solo (gv). Live from MV3 MA GT

Coyne Clague

24/9/69 The Stride, I Wonder Where, Sixteen Women, Get Right Church. Kevin Coyne (v), David Clague (b), Martin Sax (lg), Nick Cudworth (p), Tat Meager (d). 28/8/69 PH PR U Passed by panel: 'A very good blues singer,' backed by band 'who did not impress the panel so much'. Band changed name to Siren 1/70, see below

Kevin Coyne

30/1/73 Mummy!, Smile, Pretty Park, Breathe In Deep. 2/1/73 LH1 JW BC

18/9/73 Karate King, Everybody's Saying, The Fat Girl, Chicken Wing. & Gordon Smith (g). 20/8/73 T1 U BC

31/1/74 Poor Swine†, Need Somebody†, Araby, Do Not Shout At Me Father†. & Smith, Tony Cousins (b), Chilli Charles (d). 24/1/74 LH1 PR BAI

25/6/74 Mrs Hooley Go Home, It's Not So Bad, The Stride, Blame It On The Night. Terry Slade, Rick Dodds r Charles. 4/6/74 LH1 TW U

10/12/74 The Miner's Song†, Evil Island Home†, Looking For The River, Dance Of The Bourgeoisie. Pete Nu (p) r Penn. 26/11/74 MV4 TW BC&MR

18/3/77 You Know Who, Araby, Rainbow Curve. 7/3/77 MV4 U U

1/3/78 That's Rock And Roll†, Lunatic, River Of Blood†, I Only Want To See You Smile. 22/2/78 MV4 U NG 'All these songs written for and sometimes during the session' KC to Peel on session sheet

19/9/79 A Leopard Never Changes Its Spots†, Nothing's Changed, Memory Lane Pt 12, Ey Up Me Duck†. & Bob Ward (g). 5/9/79 MV4 TVD MR

8/7/82 Tell The Truth, Liberation, You Won't Like It, I Talk To Myself, You'll Never Walk Alone. & Pete Kirtley (ag), Steve Bull (sy). 7/6/82 MV4 TW DD

5/3/90 Tear Me Up, City Crazy, We're Going To Heaven, I Couldn't Love You†. & Paradie Band: Martin Muller (d), Friedrich Pohrer (b), Hans Pukke (g), Henry Beck (sy). 11/2/90 MV3 DG MA † on ◯ SFRCD112

The Crabs

3/5/78 Victim, Under Pressure, Lullabys Lie, Don't Want Your Love. Tony Diggines (lv, rg), Rick Newson (lg), Ricci Titcombe (d), Ashley Morse (b). 26/4/78 MV4 MB NG

The Crabs (82)

3/5/82 Please Ask Me Out, Love's Not That Great Really, Stalemate, Rape Rap, You'll Never Walk Alone. Sarah Smith, Jeanette Purcell, Karen King, Phil Emby, David Cuff. 21/4/82 MV4 RP U

The Cramps

10/2/86 What's Inside A Girl?, Cornfed Dames, Give Me A Woman. Lux Interior, Mick Knox, Ivy Rorschach. 23/12/85 Recorded at Ocean Way Recording Studios, Hollywood

The Cranberries

16/2/92 Waltzing Back, Linger, Want, I Will Always. Dolores O'Riordan (v, ag), Fergal Lawlor (d), Mike Hogan (b), Noel Hogan (g). 16/1/92 MV4 DG NG&KR

Crane

21/8/90 Consumption, The Than Sets In, Fear Of Noise, Asleep. Shawn Richardson (d), Nick Carter (b), Steven Malley (g), Roy Fox (v). 8/7/90 MV3 DG ME&DTH

23/1/93 Buffalo, Fire Engine, Deconstruct, Indian Red. 17/11/92 MV4 MR~ PL

Cranebuilders

15/8/02 You're Song, Morning Cup, Now I Hear You, Public Space. Tommy Roberts (gv), Simon Reynolds (g), Helen Turner (kv), Matthew McPartlan (b), Steve Keast (d). 4/8/02 MV4 KR JHT

24/6/03 Advance Directive, Fallen Arches, Layoutstretched, Something Familiar, Trains Across The Sea. 12/6/03 MV3 SA U

The Cranes

19/7/89 Focus Breathe, E G Shining, Starblood, Till Tomorrow. Jim Shaw (d, b, g), Alison Jane Shaw (v), Mark Francombe (g), Simon Tufnal (b). 9/7/89 MV5 DG ME

11/4/90 Give, Da Da 331, Inescapable. Matt Cope (g) r Tufnal. 13/3/90 MV3 DG MR

Crass

10/4/79 G's Song, Mother Earth, Bomb, Shaved Women, Tired. Steve Ignorant (lv), Eve Libertine (lv), Phil Free (gv), N A Palmer (g, literal readings), Pete Wright (bv), George Tarbuck (p), Penny Rimbaud (d), Virginia Creeper (tram noises), Alan (Wind and Wit). 28/3/79 MV4 JS NG 'Recorded & mixed by Nick Gomm at 105 decibels' note on sheet

The Cravats

9/8/79 Welcome, Who's In Here With Me, Pressure Sellers, Precinct, Live For Now. Rob Dallaway (gv), Richard Yehudi (sx, other bits), The Shend (bv), Dave Bennett (dv). 31/7/79 MV4 BS MR

6/10/80 Still, In Your Eyes, You're Driving Me, Triplex Zone. 23/9/80 MV4 JS MR

18/8/81 Rub Me Out, Terminus, Firemen, Ice Cubists. Shend (b, v-1,3), Rob (g, v-2,4), F-Reg (sx, cl), Dave (d). 10/8/81 MV4 TW DD

15/11/82 The Station, Working Down Underground, There Is No International Rescue, Daddy's Shoes. Shend (bv), Arthur (lv, g), Baird Smart (sx, cl), '31' (d). 6/11/82 U DG MR

Cream

29/10/67 Take It Back†, Outside Woman Blues†, Tales Of Brave Ulysses, Sunshine Of Your Love†, Born Under A Bad Sign†. Eric Clapton (gv), Jack Bruce (bv), Ginger Baker (d). 24/10/67 AO2 BA DT Six previous sessions from Nov 66 on Saturday Club and World Service R&B show

14/1/68 Swalbr†, The Politician†, Steppin' Out†, We're Going Wrong, Blue Condition. 9/1/68 AO2 BP PC † on BBC Sessions CD included in Triple CD set ◯ I Feel Free: Ultimate Cream Polydor 2005

Credit To The Nation

5/3/94 Mr Ego Trip, Pressure, Come Dancing, Sowing The Seeds Of Hatred. Matty (pp), Neil Ferguson (g, k), Common Knowledge (k). 17/2/94 MV4 MA LS

The Crimea

5/2/03 Fred Flinstone, Isobel, Lottery Winners On Acid, Forgotten. Davey Macmanus (gv), Joe Udwin (b, bck), Andy Stafford (k, bck), Owen Hopkin (d), John Thomas (g). 16/1/03 MV4 SA NS

Crisis

8/11/78 UK 78, Alienation, White Youth, Brickwood Hospital. Phrazer (lv), Doug Pearce (rg, v), Tony Wakeford (bv), Lester Jones (lgv), The Cleaner (d), Dexter (bck), Virg (bck). 1/11/78 U MR U

Crispy Ambulance

19/1/81 Come On, Egypt, Drug User Drug Pusher, October 31st. Robert Davenport (g), Gary Madeley (d), Keith Darbyshire (b), Alan Hempsall (v). 12/1/81 LH1 TW DD

Crocodile God

3/7/97 Ladders, Hey 11/Dovetail, Of A Wall, Bridge. Mark Murphy (g), Keith Ravenscroft (b), Liam Smith (d). 22/6/97 MV4 ME NK

26/5/98 Final Song, You Don't Holds, Bucket Love Song Number Six, No Middle Eight, Dogs Trousers. 5/4/98 MV4 ME NK

Cross Section

7/4/82 Wounds Are Too Deep, The Dole, Too Many Hills, Where Is The Love. Graham Amir (lv, rg), Jr Spence (d), Lloyd Massett (b), Roddie Gillard (lg), Julie Reid (k, sx), Neil Innes (perc, bck), Steve Welsby (perc, bck). 31/3/82 MV5 RP NG

Crowbar

12/12/72 Oh What A Feeling, Listen Sister, Kilroy, Nothing Lasts Forever. Nicholas McGowan (tp), Henry Soltys (ts), Pierre Rouchon (tb), Sonnie Ernardi (dv), Kelly Jay (kv), Roland Greenway (bv), John Peter Gibbard (lcv), Rheal Lanthier (lgv), Joey Chirowski (kv). 4/12/72 T1 JW U

Crowsdell

13/5/95 Sunny Sparkle, Sugar Coated, You Want Me Dead, Spy 56. Paul Howell (b), Laurie Wall (d), Shannon Wright (gv). 9/4/95 MV4 SA~

Arthur Big Boy Crudup

14/2/70 Sunny Road, That's Alright, Rock Me Mama, All I've Got Is Gone, Nobody Wants You When You're Old And Grey. Arthur Big Boy Crudup (gv). 9/2/70 PH JW TW

Cuban Boys

13/1/99 Oh My God They Killed Kenny, Stardust (Part 3 Ariana In Space), Hanging On The Telephone, (Let's Get) Raunchier. Ricardo Autobahn (sy, prg), Skreen B (sy, v), Jenny McLaren (v), BL Underwood (g, v, k). 6/12/98 MV3 ME GT

10/5/00 From Out Of Nowhere, The Number One Song In Heaven, Ghosts, The Laughing Gnome. 22/3/00 MV4 MR~

Cuban Heels

24/3/81 Hard Times, Walk On Water, Work Our Way To Heaven, Old School Song. John Milarky (v), Nick Clark (bv), Laurie Cuffe (gv), Ali Mackenzie (d). 18/3/81 LH1 CL NG Debut session on Richard Skinner the night before

15/10/81 Call Of The Wild, The Innocents, Matthew & Son, Primitives. 10/10/81 MV4 DG AP

Cud

30/6/87 Mind The Gap, You're The Boss, Don't Bank On It, You Sexy Thing. Carl Puttnam (v), Mike Dunphy (g), William Potter (b), Stephen Goodwin (d). 16/6/87 U DG ME&TdB ● SFPS045

24/5/88 Treat Me Bad, Punishment / Reward Relationship, Living In The Past, Everybody Works So Hard. 15/5/88 U DG MA&JBN

13/3/89 Only A Prawn In Whitby, BB Couldn't C, (I'm The) Urban Spaceman, The Epicurean's Answer. 19/2/89 MV3 DG JB&MA

Culture

11/1/83 Too Long In Slavery, Two Sevens Clash, Lion Rock, Armageddon. Joseph Hill (v), Frederick Thompson (lg), Ronald Campbell (rg), Fez Walker (b), Lewis Daley (d), Harry Powell (perc), Vincent Morgan (k), Evoald (tb), Itico (tp). 11/12/82 MV4 DG MR ● SFPS024

2/1/89 Two Sevens Clash, Fussin' And Fightin', Capture Rasta. Norman Douglas, Ian Watson, Joslyn George McKenzie, Francisco Thompson, Albert Walker, Roy Silvester Dayer, Joseph Hill, Frederick Anthony Thomas. 22/11/88 MV4 MR MR

9/7/02 Fussing And Fighting, Down In Jamaica, Iron Sharpening Iron, Old Mount Zion, Lion Rock. Joseph Hill (lv), Telford Nelson (bck), Albert Walker (bck), George Kouao (k), Earl Michelin (k), Dean Pond (d), Robin Armstrong (g), Ryan Wilson (b). 5/5/02 MV4 ME RJ

The Cure

11/12/78 Killing An Arab, 10.15 Saturday Night, Fire In Cairo, Boys Don't Cry. Robert Smith (gv), Michael Dempsey (bv), Lol Tolhurst (d, bck). 4/12/78 MV4 TW DD ○ SFPCD050

16/5/79 Desperate Journalist In Ongoing Meaningful Review Situation, Grinding Halt, Subway Song, Plastic Passion, Accuracy. 9/5/79 MV4 JS TdB

10/3/80 A Forest, 17 Seconds, Play For Today, M. Matthieu Hartley (k), Simon Gallup (b) r Dempsey. 3/3/80 MV4 TW DD

15/1/81 Holy Hour, Forever, Primary, All Cats Are Grey. Smith, Gallup, Tolhurst. 7/1/81 LH1 CL NG

4/1/82 Figurehead, A Hundred Years, Siamese Twins (& A Hanging Garden, not completed or TX). 21/12/81 MV4 KH DD

7/8/85 The Exploding Boy, Six Different Ways, Screw, Sinking. Smith, Tolhurst, Gallup (b) returns, Paul Thompson (g, k, sx), Boris Williams (d). 30/7/85 MV5 JWI TdB

Curly

20/11/73 Keeping My Motor Cool, Rock Me Roll Me, High Flying Bird. Steve Farr (ts, fl, v), Stewart Blandameer (al, gv), Dave Dowle (d), Kevin Cantlon (b), Bill Roberts (gv). 29/10/73 T1 JW U

Curve

31/3/91 Ten Little Girls, No Escape From Heaven, The Colour Hurts, The Coast Is Clear. Monti (d), Dean Garcia (b, seq), Debbie Smith (g), Alex Mitchell (g), Alan Moulder (g-4), Toni Halliday (v). 10/3/91 MV3 DG ME

29/2/92 Split Into Fractions, Die Like A Dog, Horrow Head, Arms Out. Moulder out. 11/2/92 MV4 MR MR

17/9/93 Crystal, Turkey Crossing, Superblaster, Left Of Mother. & Sally Herbert (vi-3&4). 25/8/93 MV5 MPK JMK

Curved Air

9/5/70 Screw, Vivaldi, Hide And Seek. Sonja Kristina (v), Daryl Way (vi, v), Francis Monkman (gk), Robert Martin (b), Florian Pilkington-Mikse (d). 28/4/70 MV4 JW BC

Ivor Cutler

7/5/69 Trouble Trouble, Bounce Bounce Bounce, In My Room There Sits A Box. Ivor Cutler (v, p, hmn). 5/5/69 S2 PR MH

27/2/71 Trouble Trouble / I'm Going In A Field, A Second Before Is Not Now, Ivor You Are Beautiful, My Father Once Had, Life In A Scotch Sitting Room Vol II Episode 2, Sit Down / Man With The Trembly Nose, Life In A Scotch Sitting Room Vol II ep 7 (& A Lemon On The Grass, A Seal Is A Sheep, Two Balls / Two Fried Eggs For Sixpence, 8/5/71). 15/2/71 PH JW BC

24/11/71 I Believe In Bugs / That's What It's All About, Life In A Scotch Sitting Room Vol II Ep 1 & 9, The Green Rain / Mud, If All The Cornflakes / I Like Sitting / When I Entered Heaven / Poem By My Son Jeremy. 8/11/71 PH JW BC

25/9/73 Piano Tuner Song AD2000. A Wag At The Flicks, Gooseberries And Bilberries, I Worn My Elbows, Poems From 'Many Flies Have Feathers', Pearly Gleam (& Life In A Scotch Sitting Room Vol II Episode 4, 11/12/73). 3/9/73 T1 JW BC

28/11/74 Railway Sleepers / Three Sisters, I'm Walkin' To A Farm / Baby Sits, Alone / Lean / The Turn / What?, Big Jim, Yellow Fly / I Think Very Deeply, Song Of The Sky, Life In A Scotch Sitting Room Vol II Ep 6. 14/11/74 MV4 TW BAI

14/10/75 Pearly Winged Fly, Go And Sit Upon The Grass, Sleepy Old Snake, Little Black Buzzer, Life In A Scotch Sitting Room Vol II Ep 11, Fremsley, True Humility, Nigerians In A Tunnel, I Spent Ten Years, Excitement, A Hen Runs, A Bowled Over Child, A Wooden Tree. 25/9/75 MV4 TW U

31/8/76 Bicarbonate Of Chicken, Barabadabada, In The Chestnut Tree, Rubber Toy, Life In A Scotch Sitting Room Vol 2 Ep 5, Lemon Flower, Everybody Got, The Surly Buddy (Story), I Ate A Lady's Bun, Stubborn Vassals, Fish, Living Donkey, When I Stand On An Open Cart, Irk (9–14 poems). 17/8/76 MV4 U MR

17/8/77 A Great Grey Grasshopper, A Suck Of My Thumb, The Shchi, Get Away From The Wall, The Natural Height Of Cloud / If We Dug A Hole, I Had A Little Boat / I'm Going In A Field, Life In A Scotch Sitting Room Vol II ep 12 & 13. 10/8/77 MV4 TW MR ● SFPS068

12/4/78 Three Piece Suite, Lead Bell, The Head Of A Nail / The Blonde Mouse, A Mouse Asked A Rat / A Small Mouse Beckons, I Even Know What Size / The Old Lady Danced, Life In A Scotch Sitting Room Vol II Eps 3 8 &14, My Face Is Red, 'There's Got To Be Something There, The Green Rain (3–6 poems). 3/4/78 MV4 TW DD

27/2/79 The Obliging Fairy, The Man With The Trembly Nose, I Love But I Don't Know What I Mean, Bubu Bird, Pass The Ball Jim, Examine The Contents / A Saucer / A Lady Found An Insect / Lunatic / Melon, Gruts For Tea, Egg-Eater, (6, 7, 8 poems). 20/2/79 MV4 TVD MR

22/4/81 Pellets, OK I'll Count To Eight, Tomato Brain, Step It Out Lively Boys, Counting Song, Ready / A Land Of Penguins / Her Darling, Oh Quartz / How Do You Do / Dirty Sky, Life In A Scotch Sitting Room Vol II Eps 15 &16. 15/4/81 LH1 CL U

3/3/83 Pussy On The Mat / Blue Bear / Women Of The World, Halfway Through / The Wren / Creamy Pumpkins, Life In A Scotch Sitting Room Vol 2 Ep 17 & 18 (& Brenda / Mostly Tins / People Run To The Edge, Bad Eye / A Doughnut In My Hand / Old Black Dog, 23/3/83). 23/2/83 MV4 RP NG

22/2/84 All The Time, The Revelation, Her Equipment, Three Men, Just A Nuance, Life In A Scotch Sitting Room Vol 2 Ep 19, Vegetarians, Lemonade, I Jumped Over A Wall, Jelly Mountain, My Next Album, I Built A House. 15/2/84 MV5 RP NG

15/7/85 Back Home, I'm Fixed, Knockin' At My Door, It's Snowin', I'm Walkin' To A Farm, Life In A Scotch Sitting Room Vol II Ep10, Other Poems. 30/6/85 MV5 DG ME

21/5/86 Bend Down Yetta, Crunch Crunch, A Ball In A Barrel, One Of The Best, Questionnaire, Glasgow Dreamer # 3 & #4, Eggmeat, Jewish Jokes, God's Blessing, Laughter And Disbelief, Bucket And Steam, Maturity, Vermin, A New Home, Large

CLASSIC SESSIONS

Ivor Cutler

Ivor Cutler's 22 Peel Sessions were one of the constants over the longest time period of the show of any act, almost 30 years. John Walters told me once that what they liked about him was that he was always reliable, always came up with new stuff, was happy to stand in when some precious artsy-fartsy band cancelled, 'and people really liked it'. 'He was also quite canny, possibly the only person I've ever booked who read the small print on the back of their BBC contract, and realised he could charge us "carriage" for his harmonium, as a large instrument.' Speaking to me in 1992 for 'In Session Tonight', Ivor Cutler said: 'I don't remember how my first Peel Session came about, but he was playing anarchic tapes then by the likes of Ron Geesin and Lol Coxhill. I do know that he bought a copy of my LP "Ludo" in Woolworth's, Stowmarket, for 10 shillings, not long after. He stopped playing the others, eventually, but kept playing me. Thanks to Peel, I gained a whole new audience, to the amazement of my older fans, who would find themselves among 16–35s in the theatre and wonder where they came from. I've also had fan mail and lots of other work because of the sessions: Piers Plowright of Radio 3 heard me on Peel, got in touch and I wrote 13 plays for him. Then Neil Cargill got me to do six 30-minute shows, also for Radio 3. And Andy Kershaw started playing me on his Radio 1 show. I'm a member of the Noise Abatement Society and the Voluntary Euthanasia Society, if you take my meaning.' In the 1990s, his sessions started being done at his flat in North London, because he hated the air conditioning at Maida Vale, and engineer James Birtwistle went round on his bike with a rucksack of recording equipment to do them. They jokingly called these the 'Studio But and Ben' sessions – a Scottish reference explained by Ivor himself – and occasionally had to stop as traffic roared by outside. 'I offered to put some reverb on the recordings when I got back to Maida Vale, as you sometimes do for field recordings, but Ivor would have none of it: "don't put it on," he'd say, "it doesn't sound miserable enough".' Ivor Cutler died in March 2006 aged 83.

Ten Bands Who Despite What You Might Have Heard Never Did A Peel Session

- The Beatles
- The Rolling Stones
- Emerson Lake and Palmer
- The Sex Pistols
- The Clash
- U2
- Radiohead
- Oasis
- Coldplay
- Snow Patrol

Ten Acts Who You Never Would Have Believed Did A Peel Session But Did, Honest

- Lulu
- George Melly
- The Shadows
- Ronnie Dawson
- Wayne Fontana
- Joshua Rifkin
- Gerry & the Pacemakers
- Ronnie Ronalde
- Gladys Knight & the Pips
- Tony Capstick

The Acts, Artists or Individuals Who Did Most Peel Sessions

- The Fall (24)
- David Gedge of The Wedding Present and Cinerama (24)
- Ivor Cutler (22)
- Viv Stanshall in the Bonzos and solo (20)
- The Laidlaw Family Father Ray of Lindisfarne and Jack The Lad, sons Jack and Jed of Mos Eisley (17)
- Andy Roberts of The Liverpool Scene, Plainsong, Roy Harper, Viv Stanshall & solo & duos (17)
- Robert Lloyd of The Prefects, The Nightingales, and solo (16)
- Ashley Hutchings in Fairport Convention, Steeleye Span and the Albion Band (15)
- Loudon Wainwright III (15)
- Roger Chapman & Charlie Whitney in Family, Streetwalkers & solo (14)
- Damian O'Neill in The Undertones, Eleven, Dawn Chorus & the Blue Tits, That Petrol Emotion, Ash (13)

- Half Man Half Biscuit (12)
- Michael Chapman (12)
- Darren Heyman in Hefner and The French (12)
- Incredible String Band (12)
- Billy Bragg (11)
- Thin Lizzy (11)
- Caravan (11)
- Kevin Coyne (11)
- John O'Neill brother of Damian, in The Undertones and That Petrol Emotion (10)
- Robert Wyatt in Soft Machine, Matching Mole, and solo (10)
- Medicine Head (10)
- Bridget St John (10)

And Puffy, A Country Door, Are You A Tory?, The Curse, Scratch On My Back. 11/5/86 MV5 DG ME

15/6/87 The Shapely Balloon, The Clever Night Doctor, The Aggressive Onion-Vendor, Me And My Kid Brother, The Perambulating Scottish Collander, A Wag At The Flicks. 9/6/87 U DG U

6/7/91 Glasgow Dreamer #6 & #8, Beside The Fish / Footsteps / Green Light, Biltong / A Long Hard Gland / Hee Haw, Two Coy Hinnies / Insect / Seaweed. 9/5/91 MV5 DG NG&JLC

15/12/91 Thick Coat, Neighbours, Eyes Shut Tight, What A Mistake, Glasgow Dreamer #7 & #10. 31/10/91 MV4 DG TdB&RK

8/1/93 Doing The Bathroom Ep 1, The Lid, 25,000 Miles, Part Of The Ground, Between Two Walls, Your Side, Pschawa, Ros Vulgaris, A Dale Song, Two Paracetamol, Doing The Bathroom Ep 2. 25/11/92 Home JB~

8/1/94 Gym Mistress, Billy's Wife, Sharks, Slut, A High Treat, Spreadeagled, Terrific Fun, My Top 20 Words, Glasgow Dreamer #19. 16/11/93 Studio But and Ben JB~ 'Mr Cutler would like John to know a 'But and Ben' as in 'Studio But and Ben' is a sort of shack / holiday hut, or 2–bedroomed late 18th c cottage'

29/4/95 Her Body, Squashing Hard, Five Or Seven, A Long Fine, A Stuggy Pren, Glasgow Dreamer #9, The Other Half, Ben Jacob, Flies. 8/3/95 Studio But and Ben JB~

Late 1998 / early 1999? Alone, What, The Painful League, Birdswing, And So Do I, A Romantic Man, Jam, What Have You Got (Spoken Intro) (& The Darkness, Blind, Irk, A Flat Man, Smack, A Ball In The Barrel, One Of The Best, Out With The Light, TX 30/7/99 Kershaw). 12/6/98 Home JB~ Commissioned as a joint Peel/Kershaw session, Peel tracks spread over 2 or 3 shows dates unknown, not broadcast as entire session

Cymande

12/7/73 Bra, Rickshaw, The Message, Zion I. Patrick Patterson (g), Steve Scipio (b), Sam Kelly (d), Pablo Gonzalez (cga), Joey Dee (v), Derek Gibs (al, ss), Michael Rose (al, fl, bgo), Desmond Atwell (ts). 9/7/73 LH1 BA U

2/7/74 Crawshay, For Baby-Ooh, Brothers On The Slide, Breezeman. 11/6/74 LH1 TW BC

Asher D and Daddy Freddy

10/2/88 Ragamuffin Song, Run Come Follow Me, Ragamuffin Hip-hop Medley. Asher D & Daddy Freddy (v, rp, tst) & Simon Harris (rg, prg, k). 2/2/88 U DG DD&SC

D&V

8/10/86 So You Believe In West Minstawoffel, Conscious, Epsilon City Limits. Jet Antcliffe, Andy Leach, Roy Schulman, Smuff. 2/12/86 U Produced by Ray Shulman & Smuff

The D4

21/8/02 Get Loose, Baby In A Box, John Rock, No Antidote. Jimmy Christmas (gv), Dion Palmer (gv), Vaughn Williams (b), Daniel Pooley (Beaver) (d). 3/7/02 MV4 SA NF

Daddy Long Legs

7/2/70 Where Have All Your Clothes Gone?, Bad Blood Mama, Getting High Again. Steve Hayton (g), Kurt Palomski (b), Clif Carrison (d). 26/1/70 PH JW TW

Dalai Lama

19/12/72 Trying Too Hard To Score, Nimzo Witch, Spirit Of The Living Dead. Kenny George (v, perc), Morris Lares (agv), Temba Matebese (gpo), Andre Abrahamse (b), Bobby Stegnac (cga, perc), Koss Georgiou (lg), Wally Gilek (d), Stuart Spiers (sx, fl). 28/11/72 LH1 U U

Dick Dale

8/4/95 Bo, Crankin', The Wedge, Nightrider, 3rd Stone, Miserlou. Dick Dale (g), Ron Eglit (b), Bryan Brown (d). 30/3/95 MV4 TdB LS

12/8/95 Fich Taco, Kiss Of Fire, Let's Go Tripping, Peter Gunn. Walt Woodward The Third (d) r Brown. 10/7/95 MCR3 LR NBL

5/10/00 Death Ride, Dune, Wake The Dead, Dulce Corazon. Dusty Watson (d) r Woodward. 21/9/00 MV3 ME JHT

10/9/02 Avalanche, Jesse, Gremmie 02, Surftrip. 28/8/02 MV4 SA NF

22/4/04 Shakin Stomp J P, Death Of A Gremmie, D D Shuffle, Mi Corazon (My Heart), Dd Boogie. Sam Bolle (b) r Eglit. 24/3/04 MV4 JHT NS

Corvin Dalek

11/7/02 DJ mix OS

The Damned

10/12/76 Stab Your Back, Neat Neat Neat, New Rose, So Messed Up, I Fall. Dave Vanian (v), Brian James (g, bck), Captain Sensible (b, bck), Rat Scabies (d). 30/11/76 MV4 JG MR ● SFPS040

16/5/77 Sick Of Being Sick, Stretcher Case, Fan Club, Feel The Pain. 10/5/77 MV4 JG MR ◯ 1st 2 sessions now on 30th Anniversary Edition of Damned Damned

Damned CMETD1453

8/1/79 Melody Lee, Love Song, I'm A Burglar, Looking At You. Captain Sensible (gv, o), Al Ward (bv) r James. 20/12/78 MV4 BS NG

29/10/79 Just Can't Be Happy, Smash It Up, Liar, I'm So Bored. Al Ward (lg-3). 22/10/79 MV4 TW DD

20/10/80 Curtain Cali Pt I, Hit Or Miss, Therapy. Paul Gray (b) r Ward. 6/10/80 MV4 TW DD

6/8/84 Thanks For The Night, Nasty, We Love You, Is It A Dream? Bryn Merrick (b), Roman Jug (gk) r Gray. 7/7/84 MV5 DG MR

Dan

11/7/88 Blind Ignorance / Woman Of Your Dreams, Army Of Fools, Madman And The Fool / El Amour, A Dream Come True. James Clarke (d), Ian Armstrong (b), Ian Wallis (g), Julie Dalkin (v), Sarah Goddard (v). 28/6/88 MV4 MA MFA

Dance Fault

8/9/82 Tell Me It's Fine, No Surprise, Toys, Stop. Jan Smiley (lv), Susan Jones (v), Debbie Knapp (v), Jade Campbell (bv), Penny Pooley (g), Graham Cusak (d). 23/8/82 MV4 DG GP

Dandelion Adventure

18/6/90 Exit Frenzy Revisited, Bing Crosby's Cathedral, Don't Look Now, All The World's A Lounge. Geoff (d), Jason (g), Ajay (b), Stan (g), Mark (v). 13/5/90 MV3 DG MFA

Dando Shaft

3/7/71 Coming Home To Me, Shadows Cross The Moon, Never Mind The Rain, Black Prince Of Paradise (& Whispering Red, 18/9/71). U 21/6/71 PH JW BC Debut session on Folk On 1 Aug 70

18/1/72 Road Song, I Heard Somewhere, Melancholie Fervour, Don't Forget The Animal. 11/1/72 PH JW U

Danse Society

30/11/81 Sanity Career, We're So Happy, Woman's Own, Love As Positive Narcotic. Paul Gilmartin (d), Steve Rawlings (v), Lyndon Scarfe (k), Tim Wright (b), Paul Nash (g). 21/11/81 MV4 DG MR

13/9/82 Clock, Ambition, Godsend, The Seduction. 28/8/82 U DG MC

Danta

17/4/71 Queen Of Sheba, Ebeneza Nwa Nnem, The Dead. Vernon Cummings (cga), Richard Mainwaring (d), Hugh Ashton (b), Helen Denniston (tamb, v), Kenny George (v, perc), Derek Mandel (lg), Ige Adebari (rg), Denny Morris (cga). 6/4/71 MV4 JW BC

18/1/72 Mau Mau, Stormsong, Freeway. Val McDonald (d) r Mainwaring. 10/1/72 PH JW BC

21/4/72 Feeling The Heat, Anambra, Flying Out. 4/4/72 T1 JM U

Terence Trent D'Arby

10/8/87 Soul Power, Under My Thumb, Heartbreak Hotel / Mannish Boy. Terence Trent D'Arby (v), Dave (d), Cass Lewis (b), Pete (g), Christine (g, sx), Preston (perc), Ebo Ross & Frank Collins (bck). 2/8/87 U DG NG&MS Previous session for Janice Long April 87

Darkness and Jive

26/10/82 Death In Venice, Guys And Dolls, Candle, Rage In A Cage. Paul Johnstone (gv), Steve Rainey (d), Tony Kennedy (b), Gary McKenzie (sy), Louise McGuckin & Jackie Dear (bck-2). 6/10/82 MV4 RP NG

8/6/83 Shake Down, Speak Clearly, Jigsaw, Victims. Johnstone, Rainey, Kennedy, Tony Strong (sy), Jackie Dolly (bck). 1/6/83 MV4 BYA U

The Darling Buds

8/4/87 I Couldn't Remember, It's Up To You, Mary's Got To Go, The Other Night. Andrea (v), Harley (g), Simon (b), Bloss (d). 29/3/87 U DG ME&MWT

2/9/87 Shame On You, Think Of Me, My Valentine, Spin. Chris (b) r Simon. 23/8/87 U DG MA

20/2/89 The Things We Do For Love, Different Daze, She's Not Crying, It's All Up To You (Flip Flop). 7/2/89 U DG MR

Datblygu

13/5/87 Bagiau Gareth, Carpiog, Cerddoriaeth Dant, Nesaf. David Edwards (v, toys), Patricia Morgan (instruments), Wyn Davies (additional noises). 26/4/87 U DG ME&TD ◯

17/2/88 Fanzine Ynfytyn, Cristion Yn Y Kibbutz, Gwlad Ar Fy Nghefn, Dros Y Pasg Eto. 9/2/88 MV4 DG MC ◯

9/2/91 Pop Peth, Slebog Bywydeg, Nid Chwiwgi Pwdin Gwaed, Rhag Ofn I Chi Anghofio. 20/1/91 MV3 DG ME&FK ◯ on BBC Peel Sessions Ankst 027

12/6/92 Hymne Europa 1992, Dim Deddf Dim Eiddo, Rausch Gift Suchtiae, Hablador. Edwards, Morgan, John Griffiths (perc), Al Edwards (d, perc), Euros Rowlands (d, perc), Rheinallt Ap Gwynedd (b), Peredur Ap Gwynedd (p, g). 3/5/92 MV3 ME~

13/8/93 Clwb 11 18, Wastod Absennol, Mae Arian Yn Tyfu Tu Mewn Coed, Diarrhea Berfol. David Edwards (v, toys), Pat Morgan (g), Alun Edwards (d), Rheinallt Ap Gwynedd (b), Paul O'Brien (dig), Ryan Minchin (k), Euros Rowlands (d). 11/7/93 MV3 ME GT

Datsuns

1/5/02 Fink For The Man, Lady, Harmonic Generator, Super Gyration, Freeze Sucker, Transistor, Good Night Now. Dolf D Datsun (bv), Christian Livingstone (gv), Phil Buscke (gv), Matt Osment (d). Live from MV4 SA JHT

The DaVincis

2/2/87 Something Missing, Ava Gardner, When You're In, New Ways To Wear Coats. Paul McCormick (gv), Martin Ward (g), Chris Stevens (b), Iain Bickle (d). 18/1/87 U DG ME&FK

10/10/88 This Is What We Look Like, Eating Gifted Children, On And On, Second Home. Steve Ashton (d) r Bickle. 27/9/88 MV4 MR MR

The Spencer Davis Group

7/1/68 Taking Out Time, Mr Second Class, Time Sailor, Don't Want You No More, With His New Face On. Spencer Davis (d) & U 1/1/68 U U 1st TX on Saturday Club R1 30/12/67, without final track. Spencer Davis Group had done numerous Light Programme sessions since 1964

Dawn Chorus and the Blue Tits

4/3/85 Teenage Kicks, Photographs, Lovely Lips, That Silver-Haired Daddy Of Mine. Dawn Chorus (aka Liz Kershaw) (v), Al Thompson (g), David Davies (b) & Damien O'Neill (g), Andy Kershaw (whistling-3). 24/2/85 MV5 DG ME

Dawn Of The Replicants

3/9/97 Lisa Box, Diggin' Bear, Fatal Firework, Leaving So Soon. Grant Pringle (d, bck), Donald Kyle (b), Mike Small (g, bck, k), Roger Simian (g, bck), Paul Vickers (v). 12/8/97 MV4 MR GT

28/4/98 Skullcrusher, Windy Millar (& Jack Fanny's Gym, Sergeant Growly 13/5/98). Live from MV4 MR KR

6/7/99 Get A Bright Flame, Big Hefty Hounds, Candlefire, Fearless Vampire Hunters. 25/4/99 MV4 ME PN

20/11/02 Hollywood Hills, Rhinestone Cowboy, Rockefeller Center 1932, Smoke Without Fire. Vickers, Simian, Small, Dave Coyle (b), Dave Little (d, bck), Susie O'Neil (cl, p, elp, o, bck, th). 17/10/02 MV4 NF GYW

The Dawn Parade

8/10/02 Some Desperate Beat, Strung Out On Nowhere, The Dark Stuff, Moonbathers. Greg McDonald (gv), Mick Morley (g), Barney Wade (b, bck), Benjamin Jennings (d). 11/9/02 MV4 SA NF

5/3/03 The Passion, The Hole In My Heart, The Craving, Wider Than The January Skies, Olivia. Live from MV4 AR NF/RJ

Dawson

29/5/90 Molicoke Cocktail, White Colonial, Sort Of Man, Ad Nauseam, From The Loins Of Mr & Mrs Neurosis, Fifty Years. Jeremy Reid (v, g, b), Alistair Begbie (v, b, g), Richard Dempsey (d), Rhodri Marsden (bsn, perc), Marcus Nichol (tp, perc). 1/5/90 MV5 MA MA

18/1/92 Face Of W Biriyani, Booger Hall, A Statement Of Intent, From Bearsden To Baghdad (Via The Erskine Bridge). Reid, Begbie, Dempsey, Robbie McEndrick (d), Craig Bryce (perc), Ceebe Begbie (v-2). 1/12/91 MV3 DG ME&RPF

Ronnie Dawson

21/1/94 Wham Bam Jam, Down In Mexico, Rock The Blues, Action Packed, Up Jumped The Devil. Ronnie Dawson (glv), Malcolm Chapman (g), Matt Radford (b), Brian Neville (d), Boz Boorer (ag). 14/12/93 MV4 MR JLC

14/1/95 The Cats Were Jumping, Yum Yum, Party Time / Knock Down Drag Out, Ghost Riders In The Sky. 5-piece & Eddie Angel (g, bck), Barney Koumis (bck). 17/11/94 MV4 NG JLC

DCL Locomotive

28/4/86 Night And Day, (Walk Under) The Big Sky, Red, Coast To Coast. Robin Raymond (gv, k), The Shend (b), Disneytime (d). 20/4/86 MV5 DG ME&FK

De Danann

3/2/78 Trip To Durrow / The Maid Behind The Bar, The Lamentation On The Price Of The Pig, Love Will You Marry Me, The Hackler From Grouse Hall, Tom Billy's Jig/ Sean Ryan's Jig / The Sandmount Reel / The Cloghar Reel. Frankie Gavin (fd, wh), Johnny Moynihan (mnd, bz, v), Charlie Piggot (bj, mnd, wh), Alec Finn (bz, mnd, clo), Ringo McDonagh (d), Tim Lyons (v, acc). 25/1/78 MV4 MB NG Previous sessions for R2

Dead Can Dance

28/11/83 Instrumental, Labour Of Love, Ocean, Threshold. Brendan Perry (gv, perc), Lisa Gerrard (v), James Pinker (perc), Scott Roger (b), Peter Ulrich (d). 19/11/83 MV4 DG MC

13/6/84 Flowers Of The Sea, Penumbra, Panacea, Carnival Of Light. 2/6/84 MV5 DG MC

Dead Famous People

5/7/89 Postcard From Paradise, How To Be Kind, Go Home Stay Home. Donna Savage (v), Wendy Kisstrup (g), Biddy Leyland (o), Jenny Renals (b), Gill Moon (d). 11/6/89 MV3 DG ME

Dead Meadow

29/3/01 Dusty Morning, Good Moaning, Drifting, Wondering Thunder, Untitled. Jason Simon (gv), Steve Kille (b), Mark Laughlin (d). 1/1/01 OS

Dead on Arrival

15/4/81 Murder School, Rest In Peace, Helpless, Party Games. Steve Lynn (v), Carol Bayne (v), Paul Denheyer (g), Mark Webb (b), Steve Majors (d). 8/4/81 LH1 CL NG

Dead or Alive

17/2/81 Nowhere To Nowhere, Running Wild, Flowers, Number 11. Joe Musker (d), Sue Bagton-James (b), Mandingo Healy (k), Adrian Mitchley (g), Pete Burns (v). 4/2/81 LH1 CL NG

18/3/82 Misty Circles (Parts 1 & 2), Number Twelve, Untitled. Burns, Musker, Mike Percy (b), Wayne Hussey (g), Marty (k). 1/3/82 MV4 TW DD

Deaf School

7/9/76 What A Way To End It All, Where's The Weekend?, Knock Knock Knocking, Final Act. Enrico Cadillac Junior (aka Steve Allen) (v), Eric Shark (v), Bette Bright (v), Clive 'Cliff Hanger' Langer (k), Steve 'Average' Lindsay (b, p-4), Tim Whittaker (d), Ian Ritchie (sx). 19/8/76 U TW U

15/4/77 Boy's World, Hypertension, What A Jerk, Capaldi's Cafe. & Max Ripple (k). 29/3/77 MV4 MB MR

8/2/78 Working Girls, All Queued Up, English Boys, Ronny Zamora. 11/1/78 MV4 MB NG

Death by Milkfloat

17/8/87 Breakbone, Mr Obvious Wig, Blood On The Car, The Front Of Your Face. Phil Dolby (gv), Jonny Dawe (b, bck), Steve Kelly (d). 9/8/87 U DG ME&MP

4/7/88 Post Jazz Rumble Bumble, Vagrancy, Boxed Away, Too Much Feel, Wrong. 21/6/88 U MR~

Decoration

13/4/04 Pink, Oversight, Joy Adamson, 86 Tvs. Stuart Murray (gv), Steven Dickenson (g), Stephen Taylor (d), Sam Noble (b). 1/3/04 MV4 GYW GT

Deep Purple

30/6/68 Hush, One More Rainy Day, Help. Rod Evans (v), Nick Simper (b), Jon Lord (k), Ian Paice (d), Ritchie Blackmore (g). 18/6/68 PC1 BA DT 'Enthusiastic, unanimous pass' from panel: 'polished, commercial group'

9/2/69 Hey Bob-A-Roo-Bob, Emaretta, Wring That Neck, Hey Joe (& It's All Over Now, 23/3/69). 14/1/69 MV4 BA AH

Deep Turtle

11/11/94 Tun Go, Nohand, Hedless, Gnulf, Ratua, Toothpaste Tastebred. Tapio Laxtrom (b), Mikko Saaristo (d), Pentii Dassum (gv). 9/10/94 MV3 ME SA

Deerhoof

12/5/04 Desaparecere, Giga Dance, Byun Byun Byun, Come See The Duck, Dummy Discards A Heart, Jorbe B S Friend. Satomi Matsuzaki (b, v, d), Greg Saunier (d, g), John Dieterich (g), Chris Cohen (g, b). 1/4/04 MV4 SA JHT

Sam Dees' Beauty & the Beat

14/12/91 One In A Million, Homecoming, Child Of The Streets. Sam Dees (lv), Crissy Lee (d), Ruth Bitelli (b), Ayala Ciran (g), Hilary Cameron (k), Sarah Kelly (sx, fl). 7/11/91 MV4 DG NG&PA

Definition of Sound

26/1/91 Now Is Tomorrow, Wear Your Love Like Heaven, Moira Jane's Cafe, Rise Like The Sun. Crispin Taylor (d), Paul Holland (b), Ronnie Simpson (g), Adrian York (k), Kevin Clark & Donald Weekes (rp), Elaine Vassell (v), Angela Henry-Fontaine (bck). 30/12/90 MV3 DG TD&JSM

Degrassi

21/2/01 Target, Pacifics, Malkovich, Mathmos. Stuart Turner (gv), Michael Branagh (dv), Scott Smith (g), Stephen McColl (k, b), Chris Bathgate (b). 21/1/01 MV4 ME~

27/2/02 Terminal Ocean, Brownian Motion, The Emerald City, Air Force 1, No Tracks In The Snow. McColl out. Live from MV4 AR SA

del Amitri

24/4/84 Heard Through A Wall, Crows In The Wheat Field, Breaking Bread, Decieve Yourself (In Ignorant Heaven). Justin Currie (bv), Paul Tyagi (d, perc), Bryan Tolland (g), Iain Harvie (g). 31/3/84 MV5 DG MC

27/3/85 Hammering Heart, Ceasefire, This King Is Poor, Keepers. 19/3/85 MV5 U U

The Delgados ○

13/5/95 Lazar Walker, Blackwell, I've Only Just Started To Breathe, Primary Alternative. Emma Pollock (gv), Alun Woodward (gv), Stewart Henderson (b), Paul Savage (d). 5/3/95 CV SCK TDO Recorded & 1st TX March 95 for BBC Radio Scotland's 'Beat Patrol'

12/5/96 Sucrose, 4th Channel, Under Canvas Under Wraps, Teen Elf. & Gayle Harrison (vi). 23/4/96 MV4 AA JMK&MR

16/7/97 Everything Goes Round The Water, The Arcane Model, Pull The Wires From The Wall, Mauron Chanson. & Camille Mason (fl), Alan Barr (clo), Jennifer Christie (vi), Emily Macpherson (vi). 1/7/97 MV4 ME CM

17/6/98 Repeat Failure, Don't Stop, Blackpool, The Weaker Argument Defends The Stronger. & Alan Barr (clo). 25/5/98 MV4 MR SA

16/5/00 No Danger, Make Your Move, Accused Of Stealing, Aye Today. & Camille Mason (fl), Alan Barr (clo), Colin Macpherson (k), Charlie Cross (vi, vla), Jeremy Birchall (vi), Oliver Langford (vi, vla), Vuk Crakovic (vi). 29/3/00 MV4 JB GYW

16/10/02 Mr Blue Sky, California Uber Alles, Matthew And Son, Last Rose Of Summer. & Alan Barr (clo), Kobis Frick (vi), David Lang (vi), Lewis Turner (p, k). 15/9/02 MV4 GYW NF

23/1/03 Parcel Of Rogues. & Lewis Turner (p). OS

23/9/04 I Fought The Angels, Ballad Of Accounting, Is This All I Came For?, Everybody Come Down. & Alan Barr (k, p). 2/9/04 MV4 SA NS everything on ○ The Complete BBC Peel Sessions CHEM088CD

Delicatessen

1/7/95 Classic Adventure, Embalming The Dead Entertainer, Yes / No In Any Language, Inviting Both Sisters Out To Dinner. Neil Carlill (gv), Will Foster (b), Stuart Dayman (d, perc), Craig Brown (g, fl). 21/5/95 MV3 ME GT

Delivery

23/1/71 We Were Satisfied, Fools Meeting, Home Made Rain. Steve Miller (pv), Phil Miller (g), Carol Grimes (v), Roy Babbington (b), Pip Pyle (d). 4/1/71 PH JW BC Two previous World Service sessions Oct 69 and April 70 and Sunday Show Dec 70, with different line-ups

The Delta 5

11/2/80 Delta-5, Colour, Make Up, Anticipation, You. Bethan Peters (bv), Ros Allen (bv), Alan Riggs (g), Kelvin Knight (d), Julz Sale (v). 4/2/80 MV4 TW DD

11/9/80 Triangle, Journey, Try, Leaving. 2/9/80 MV4 JS MR

Deltones

2/6/86 Stay Where You Are, Make Me Smile, Party Pooper, Lemon Squeezy. Sandra Brown (d), Julie Liggett (b), Angie Risner (b-1,2), Serena Parsons (g), Sara McGuiness (k), Amanda Fenn, Jacqui Callus & Anna Maria Bianchi (v), Nicky Ford & Gilly Johns (al), Anna Keegan (ts), Penny Leyton (tp). 25/5/86 MV5 DG ME&FK

Deluxx Unconvinced

13/10/95 Train From Kenland, Eskimo Lover, Salmon Days, Nature's Wonders, On The Hutchison Trail. Mark Perretta (gv), Anne Slinn (b), Bob Fay (d). 26/9/95 MV4 JB SA

Demolition Doll Rods

28/5/97 Number 1 Feel, Lil' Naked, Got The Love, Wig Garden, Queen Bee, Good Golly. Margaret Dollrod (glv), Danny Dollrod (lgv), Christine Dollrod (perc). 29/4/97 MV4 TdB NS

Sandy Denny

11/4/72 That'll Be The Day, Love's Made A Fool Of You, Learning The Game, Crazy Arms, Jambalaya. & bunch (5) (unknown). 28/3/72 MV4 JW U 'Originally applied and passed solo audition at AO1 14/10/66, after mother Ena phoned auditions unit 18/2/66 and 'rambled on about how good her little girl was'. 1st session rec'd 7/11/66 S2 for WS Folk Music programme, TX 4/1/67, prod. BA. Did 2 more for Light's Cellar full of Folk 3, 4/67 & live on Country Meets Folk 30/12/67 PH & My Kind Of Folk 3/7/68. 1st solo session after Fairport and Fotheringay (see below) was on Bob Harris Sept 71

25/9/73 Solo, Like An Old-Fashioned Waltz†, Who Knows Where The Time Goes?† Solo. 11/9/73 LH1 TW U † on ○ The BBC Sessions 1971–1973 SFRSCD086

Department S

3/12/80 Clap Now, Ode To Cologne (The Stench Of War), Age Concern, Is Vic There? Vaughan Toulouse (lv), Michael Herbage (g), Tony Lordan (b), Eddie Roxie (sy), Stuart Mizon (d). 19/11/80 LH1 BS NG

Depth Charge

23/2/91 Depth Charge US Silver Fox, War Is Not Good, Under The Electrical Storm, Laughing At Strangers Wearing Funny Shorts. Saul Kane (prg, smp), Alan Scott (g), Donovan Hart (v-1). 27/1/91 MV3 DG ME&FK

Derrero

2/3/99 Floater, Out To Lunch, Monoman, Casket. Ashley Cooke (gv), Andy Fung (dv), Dave Hirst (b), Mary Wycherley (k, perc). 5/1/99 MV4 MR MPK

25/1/00 Pets/Cappice, Fixation With Long Journeys, Lasoe, State Messages. 17/11/99 MV4 MR SBR

18/4/01 Sound At The Rate It Fades, Dusk Brings Depth, Lean On Me for Comfort, Old Grey Skies. 21/2/01 MV4 SA~

The Desperate Bicycles

10/7/78 Smokescreen, Skill, Sarcasm, Teacher's Prayer. Dave Papworth (d), Roger Stevens (b), Nicky Steven (lg), Danny Wigley (lv). 4/7/78 MV4 MB MR

Det Ri Mental

12/2/94 Sufer In, Babylon, Righteous Preacher (Version), Dub Asian. Lallaman (v), Goldfinger (perc, bck), DJ Obeyo (mx), Raj-A-Wadi (b), Bishop Christ (smp, Box Master), DJ Goorah Harami (Hot Mini). 6/1/94 MV4 NG JM

6/5/95 Dalai Lama, Country Man, Total Revolution, Living On The Edge. Lallaman, Goldfinger, Prince Darkness (g), Raga-Man-Raj (b), Peace-Man (d), Anita Maddigan (v-1). 12/3/95 MV4 ME JLC

Detroit Cobras

11/3/03 C'Mon Over To My House, Bad Girl, I'll Keep Holding On, Village Of Love. Rachel Nagy (v), Steve Nawara (g), Maribel Restrepo (g), Matt O'Brien (b), (d, unknown). 13/2/03 MV4 MA NS

14/9/04 Hey Sailor, Hot Dog, Fall, Tonight. Nagy, Restrepo, Nawara, Joseph Mazzola (g, b), Kenny Tudrick (d). 9/9/04 MV4 MA~

Deutsche Amerikanische Freundschaft (DAF)

6/12/79 Was Ist Eine Welle?, I And I Reality, Violence, Kebab Dreams. U U PRIV

Deviated Instinct

15/5/90 Molten Tears, Dredger, (Behind) The Scaffold, Open Wound. John Adam Stevenson (d), Steven Harvey (b), Robert Middleton (gv). 17/4/90 MV5 TdB PA

Howard Devoto

8/8/83 Cold Imagination, Topless, Some Will Pay. Howard Devoto (gv), Dave Formula (k), Alan St. Clair (g), Neil Pyzer (sx, sy), Pat Ahearn (d), Martin Heath (b), Laura Teresa (bck). 1/8/83/ MV4 TW MC

Dexy's Midnight Runners

13/3/80 (Tell Me When My) Light Turns Green, Breaking Down The Walls Of Heartache, The Horse, Geno. Kevin Rowland (lv), A Archer (gv), J.B. (ts), Steve Spooner (al), Pete Williams (bv), Stoker (d), Andy Leake (ov), Big Jim Paterson (tb). 26/2/80 MV4 BS MR

The Diagram Brothers

27/3/80 Animals, Bricks, Bikers, There Is No Shower. Fraser (lv, g), Laurence (g), Jason (b) & Simon Diagram (d). 17/3/80 MV4 TW DD

3/2/81 Postal Bargains, Those Men In White Coats, I Didn't Get Where I Am Today By Being A Right Git, My Bad Chest Feels Much Better Now. Andy Diagram (b, bck) r Jason. 27/1/81 LH1 DG MR

22/7/82 Hey Dad!, Tracey, You've Got To Pick A Pocket Or Two, The Expert, You'll Never Walk Alone. 26/6/82 MV4 DG PS

Diatribe

1/1/86 Peace In Our Time, Student Rap, No Reason, Burn. Jonathan Kirby (d), Tim Kirby (bv), Andy Fenn (g). 8/12/85 MV5 DG ME

Diblo Dibala

8/8/92 Laissez Passer, Tcheke, Medisance, Extra Ball (& Matchatcha Wetu, Bolingo, Mondo Ry, Merci Papa – on KERSHAW earlier same night). Diblo Dibala (gv), JP Kinkazi (rg), Alain Dieng (v), Ringo Avom (d), Serge Bimangou (perc), Emi Laskin (v), Mondo David (v), Gwen Lemmonier, Electra Weston, Laure Anne & Antoinette Yelessa (bck, dancing). 19/7/92 MV3&4 MA MA&SA

14/1/95 Intro, Iye (An Interjection Of Happiness), Kangaroo (A Dance), Destin. Diblo Dibala (lg, v), Yelessa Antoinette, Ngomateke Martin, Bolonge Jo Mali, Mobeti Sabuela Donau, N'simba Miguel, Okala Bilounga, Lotutala Nianga, Bonane Bungu, David Kibakila, Komba Mafwala Bellow. 19/11/94 MV4 JB~

Sean Dickson

2/12/98 Cola Coca, Substitute, Commercial Suicide, Omnichord 4am. Sean Dickson (om, v) OS

5/7/01 Scream If You Wanna Go Faster, Two Up Two Down, Electro Mail, Teenage Kicks, 4am. Live from Peel Acres GT~

Die Kruz

6/7/96 Free Format, Mind Of A Maniac, Bittersweet, Sublime State. U OS

Dinosaur Jr.

14/11/88 Raisans, Does It Float, Leper, Bulbs Of Passion. Patrick Murphy (d), Lou Barlow (b), J Mascis (g). 8/11/88 MV4 MR MR

22/5/89 Budge, No Bones, Chunks. 25/4/89 WX DG DD

9/1/93 Noon At Dawn, Get Me, Keeblin, Hide. J Mascis (dgv), Mike Johnson (gv). 24/11/92 MV5 JB~

Dirtbombs

27/11/01 Chains Of Love, Motor City Baby, Ode To A Blackman, Granny's Little Chicken, Stuck Under My Shoe, Can't Stop Thinking About It, Kung Fu, Shake Shivaree, Want You Need You. Mick Collins (gv), Tom Potter (g, bck), Jim Diamond (b, bck), Ben Blackwell (d), Pat Pantano (d). Live from MV4 AR SA

Dislocation Dance

11/8/81 Friendship, Remind Me Of Those Little Things, Shoot Out At Dead Man's Creek, It Don't Mean A Thing. Andy Diagram (tp, bck), Ian Runacres (g, lv, k), Paul Emmerson (b, bck), Dick Harrison (d, bck). 5/8/81 MV4 CL NG

14/7/82 Baby Blue, Tyrannies Of Fun, You'll Never Never Know, Working The Midnight Shift, The Next Year I Returned To St. Michel But Marie Had Gone And With Her My Childhood. & Kathy Way (v, sx). 12/6/82 MV4 DG TdB

Disposable Heroes of Hiphoprisy

9/5/92 Positive, Traffic Jam, Language Of Violence, Exercise. Michael Franti (v), Rono Tse (perc, v, taste), Simone White (d). 24/3/92 MV4 MA RK&MA

Distorted Waves Of Ohm

30/6/95 Sketch Plan And Elevation, Snark, The Solution, Spirit Level Creation, Apparitions. Tony, Chris. OS

The Distributors

21/6/79 TV Me, We Have Fun, Melt Down, Wireless. Mick Switzerland (g, k, v, tps), Keith James (gv), Enzo Raphael (bv), Dave Holmes (d). 13/6/79 MV4 BS NG

17/12/81 House Party, Look At This, Keep Looking Ahead, Motionless. Holmes, James, Robert Worby (g, k), Steve Beresford (b). 14/12/81 MV4 JWI U

DJ Bailey with MC SP

24/8/04 Showcase mix set for the 1Xtra DJ & guest MC. Live from LL AR~

DJ Bone

4/4/01 DJ set live from MV4 U U

DJ Eastwood & Friends

26/5/04 Grime Night, Live DJ Mix, DJ Eastwood with MC G Double E, MC Purple, MC I E, and MC I Q. Live from MV4 AR GT

DJ Food

19/4/00 Untitled piece [34']. OS

DJ Fresh

16/12/04 10–min DJ mix for Keepin' It Peel night live from MV5 GYW JHT

DJ Hell

17/3/95 Please Get Out, Mother Funk, Risveglio Di Una Citta. OS

DJ J Da Flex & Crazy D

17/8/04 Showcase mix set for the 1Xtra DJ & guest MC. Live from LL AR~

DJ Robbo Ranx & Lady Saw

10/8/04 Showcase mix set for the 1Xtra DJ & guest MC. Live from LL AR~

DJ Rupture

9/10/02 DJ mix live from MV4 AR~ SA&GYW

18/5/04 DJ mix OS

DJ Twitch

23/9/03 Optimo mix OS

DJs Kemistry & Storm

6/4/99 Live DJ set. Kemi Olusanya (dj) & Jane (dj). Live from Y4 U Less than 3 weeks later, DJ Kemistry was killed in a car accident near Winchester on 25/4/99 while returning from a performance

The DM Bob & Jem Finer 2 Man Band

20/4/04 How Can Evil Look So Good, Bbq Bob, I've Just Been Your Good Thing, I Want To Show You, Lou Short For Loser, Girlfriend Stole My Alien. DM Bob, Jem Finer. 2/3/04 MV4 GT GYW

DM Bob & The Deficits

11/6/97 Bush Hig'n Man, Karmann Ghia, No Soy Facie, Burn'N, I'm Not Drink'n More. Robert Tooke, Guedo Bertling, Susanna Reinhardt. 26/4/97 OS

DMC World DJ Finalists

19/7/00 DJ sets by Yo 1, Woody, Tigerstyle, Mr Thing, Plus One, Mad Cut. Live from MV4 AR U

8/8/01 DJ sets by Theory, Skully, Primetime, Woody, Plus One. Live from MV4 AR MA/NF Plus One went on to win the final and be named world champion DJ for 2001

10/9/03 DJ sets by DJ Blakey, DJ Tigerstyle, DJ 2 Tall, DJ Daredevil, DJ Quest. Live from MV4 AR~

Do Make Say Think

15/11/00 Reitschule, Goodbye Enemy Airship, Class Nood Landing. Brian Cram (tp, eu), Charles Spearin (tp, b, o), James Dyment (d), Justin Small (g), Ohad Benchetrit (g, sx, fl), David Mitchell (d). 4/10/00 MV4 KR RJ

DOA

19/4/84 Burn It Down, Race Riot, A Season In Hell, General Strike. Joe Keighley (lg, lv), Dave Gregg (g, bck), Brian Goble (b, bck, lv-3), Gregg James (d, bck). 3/4/84 MV5 MRD MR

Doctor and the Crippens

17/5/88 Pink Machine Gun† / Ballad Of Farmer Vincent / The Garden Centre Murders†, Peely Backwards / Skin Tight† / Ode To A Slug, Pneumatic Geek / Death Squad / Jimmy Goes To Egypt, Don't Look In The Freezer§ / Mindsurf§ / Experiment Conclusion§. Jesus Van Gough (d, bck), Wayne Crippenski (b, bck), Tom Crippen (g, bck), Max Von Reinhart (v), Emily Danger (v-4). . 8/5/88 U DG MA&JB † On Hardcore Holocaust ○ SFRCD101 § On Hardcore Holocaust II ○ SFRCD113

14/8/89 Henrietta's Baby, The Death Of Pinocchio / Kid With The Removable Face, I'm Sop Done / Song For Guy, Braindead / Melt. Danger out. 16/7/89 U DG JB

Doctor Calculus

28/1/85 Programme 7, Killed By Poetry, Honey I'm Home. U U U U U

Doctors of Madness

7/12/76 Out, Brothers / Suicide City. Kid Strange (gv), Urban Blitz (vi, g), Stoner (bv), Peter Dilema (dv). 25/11/76 U TW U

Jeggsy Dodd

19/8/85 Welcome To Hillview Heights, No Place To Run, A Scouse Werewolf In London, Why The Clown?, The Beer Belied Bully Boys Bash The Boys In Blue, Who Killed New Brighton?, The Day My Flat Turned Wierd. Jeggsy Dodd (v). 6/8/85 MV5 JWI MR

The Dodgems

24/9/79 Muscle Beach, Gotta Give It Up, Lord Lucan, Science Fiction (Baby You're So). Gary Turner (lvb), Doug Potter (gv), Paul Birchall (k), Charlie Zuber (d). 17/9/79 MV4 BS DD

The Dodgers

26/5/76 Don't Let Me Be Wrong, I Just Wanna Love You, Get To You, Help Me Out. John Wilson (gv), Tom Evans (bv), Bob Jackson (pv), Dave Powell (dv). 11/5/76 U JG MR

Dog Faced Hermans

18/5/87 Shat On By Angels [Or 'Shore Up The Enemy'], Malcolm Rifkind's Privy, Balloon Girl, El Doggo Speaks. Marion Coutts (v, tp), Colin McLean (b), Andy Moor (g), Wilf Plum (d). 3/5/87 U DG ME&MA

Dolly Mixture

14/8/79 Dolly Mixture Theme Song / Dream Come True, He's So Frisky, New Look Baby, Ernie Ball, The Locomotion. Rachel Bor (lv, g), Debsey Wykes (bv), Hester Smith (dv). 7/8/79 MV4 BS MR

Done Lying Down

1/1/94 Quit Smacking The Baby, Fun, Slept Around, Christmas Shoplifting. Ali Mac (b), Jack Plug (gv), Frank Art (g), Miles Grey (d). 21/11/93 MV3 JB JLC

17/9/94 Choose, Pennyhead, Pasadena, Be My Brain, Symbols (Or Something). James Sherry (d) r Grey. 6/9/94 MV4 MR GT

2/3/96 Columbus Day, Star Search, Backseat Drivers License/Not My Friend, Run To You. 30/1/96 MV4 MR NG

10/9/97 Things That Make You Spin, Thrill Me, Trisexual, A Fight You've Won. & Nicholas Curs. 24/8/97 MV4 ME GT

Donkey

5/5/95 Youth Spent Using Ventolin, Warmthness, Sweet Ass (The Irony), Safe As Flames, Subslider. Jeroen Helmer (d), Ajay Saggar (b, lv), Pim Heijne (g), Bob Wijnands (clo, v). 2/4/95 MV3 MWT NK

Donovan

21/1/68 There Is A Mountain, As I Recall It, Lalena, The Timber And The Crab, Young Girl Blues. Donovan (gv) & The John Cameron group (5). 16/1/68 MV4 BA DT&BC

16/6/68 Mad John's Escape, It's Been A Long Time, The Entertaining Of A Shy Little Girl, Lalena, Hast Thou Seen The Unicorn? (& Skip-Along Sam, 21/7/68). & John Cameron, David Katz, 14 musicians. 11/6/68 PC1 BA DT

Doo Rag

29/10/94 Kick Down/Trudge, Wash, Engine Bread, Grease And All, Oh How That Bucket Is Old/Breaking Straw, Don't Need But A Little, Barn Porn Star, Rectifier. Bob Log (gv), Thermos Mailing (box, buckets, tree etc). 1/8/94 OS

13/10/96 Tire Knocker, Confidential Body, Pit Boss, Liquor Waltz, Theme From John Guy. & Walter Malling (perc). 29/9/96 MV4 ME~

Doom ○

28/6/88 Symptom Of The Universe / Multinationals, Exploitation, Circles, No Religion, Relief, Sold Out / War Crimes. Anthony Dickens (d), Peter Nash (b), Brian Talbot (g), John Pickering (v), Paul Halmshaw (v). 19/6/88 MV5 DG MR ○

14/3/89 Means To An End / A Dream To Come True, Natural Abuse / Days Go By, Life Lock / Bury The Debt, Life In Freedom / Money Drug / Fear Of The Future. Karl Willetts (v) r Halmshaw. 7/3/89 MV4 DG MWT ○ SFPMA203

John Doonan

13/8/74 3 Irish Jigs: Comb You Hair And Curl It / I Have A Wife Of My Own / Any Old Jig Will Do, Lament To Oliver Goldsmith, The Piper Through The Meadow Strayed, Fiddler Round The Fairy Tree, Jigs: Banish Misfortune / Gillian's Apples / Morrison's Jig, 'Reels: Jacky Coleman's Reel / Brennan's Reel. John Doonan (fd). 22/7/74 T1 JW U

Dormannu

12/6/84 Slam, The Dread, Pole. Simeon Warburton (gv), Wig (b), Cristine Crev (k), Marcus Stott (d), Tinley (g), Dizzy Heights (tst). 30/5/84 MV5 BYA NG

The Double

30/9/04 Idiocy, Black Diamond, What Sound It Makes The Thunder, In The Fog. Donald Beaman (gv), Gavid Greenhill (bv), Jacob C Morris (k), Jeff McLeod (d). 16/9/04 MV4 JSM GYW

The Downliners Sect

13/10/77 Talking About You, Killing Me, Richmond Rhythm And Blues, Show Biz. Paul Holm (d), Keith Grant (lvb), Terry Gibson (lg), Don Craine (rg, bck), Paul Tiller (hca, bck). 27/9/77 MV4 MB MR

Dr Devious

26/9/92 Return To Cyber Space. Dr Devious (kv), The Diddyman (kv), Cobalt. 6/9/92 MV3 ME ME&CML

Dr Feelgood

10/2/75 I Don't Mind, I'm A Hog For You, Keep It Out Of Sight, Route 66. Lee Brilleaux (v), Wilko Johnson (g), John Sparkes (b), The Big Figure (d). 21/1/75 MV4 TW BC 3 previous sessions 73–74 for Bob Harris

10/10/77 You Upset Me Baby, She's A Wind Up, Baby Jane, 99 1/2. 20/9/77 MV4 MB MR

18/9/78 Nightime, Take A Tip, Doctor, Sugar Shaker. 5/9/78 MV4 U U

Dr Phibes & The House Of Wax Equations

11/5/91 Burning Cross, Dreaming / Insomnia, LA Woman. 18/4/91 MV5 DG MWT&JB

18/6/93 Bear Hug, Transparent Hang Up, Wait For The Gripper. Howard King (gv), Lee Blesham (b), Keith York (d). 16/5/93 MV4 MR~ JB

Dr Strangely Strange

6/6/70 Jove Was At Home, Ashling, Mary Malone. Tim Goulding, Tim Booth, Ivan Pawle. 26/5/70 U U BC

Nick Drake

6/8/69 Time Of No Reply, Cello Song, River Man, Three Hours. Nick Drake (ag, v). 5/8/69 MV5 PR MH

Robin and Barry Dransfield

5/6/71 Still He Sings, Lord Of All I Behold, Who Liveth So Merry, The Wild Rover. Robin Dransfield (gv), Barry Dransfield (fd, v). 18/5/71 MV4 JW BC Trial broadcast for R1/2's first session on Friday 14/3/70, passed, more folk show sessions followed

31/10/72 A Week Before Easter, Hyde Park Mansions, The Werewolf, Girl Of Dances. Barry Dransfield only (fd, v). 3/10/72 LH1 JW BC

21/2/74 When It's Night-time In Italy It's Wednesday Over Here, It's Dark In Here, I Once Had A Dog, The Cutty Wren, Lazy Afternoon. Robin only. 14/2/74 LH1 JW U

16/4/74 Ballad Of Dickie Lubber, Old Joe, Up To Now (& Daddy Please Take Me To The Line, 4/6/74). Barry only.1/4/74 T1 JW U

17/9/74 It's Dark In Here, Medley: Roaring Mary / The Bunch Of Keys / Silver Spire, Up To Now, The Three Muscadets. Duo. 2/9/74 T1 JW U

15/5/75 Hey Hey, The Handsome Meadow Boy, The Fool's Song, Fair Maids Of February. 8/5/75 MV4 JW U

18/12/75 Christmas Is Coming, What Will We Tell Them, You Can't Change Me Now, Violin. Billed as 'The Dransfields': Robin, Barry & Brian Harrison (b). 27/11/75 MV4 TW U

5/10/76 You Can't Change Me Now, The Ballad Of Dickie Lubber, The Alchemist And The Peddler, The Blacksmith Pt I. Billed as 'Dransfield': Robin, Barry, Harrison (b) & Bob Critchley (d). 14/9/76 MV4 JG MR

10/2/78 Catch The Morning Dew, Too Much To Do, Doctor Spine, Be Your Own Man. Robin & Barry only. 31/1/78 MV4 MB MR

Dreadzone

7/1/94 Sound Man†, Cave Of Angels, Highway To The Hidden Valley†, Out Of The East†. Tim Bran (k, mx, cmp), Greg Roberts (cmp, k). 23/11/93 MV4 MR NF

24/9/94 Me Bong†, Maximum†, Cause & FX†. Roberts, Bran, Leo Williams (b), Dan Donovan (k). 21/8/94 MV3 ME SBR † on ○ The Radio One Sessions SFRSCD100

16/1/02 Straight To A Sound Boy, Return Of The Dread, Digital Mastermind, Mean Old World, Dread Pon Sound, Different Planets, Little Britain. Roberts, Herman Williams (b), Ben Middleton (mx), Earl Daley (v), Spencer Graham (v). Live from MV4 SA~

16/12/04 10–min DJ mix for Keepin' It Peel night. Bran only. Live from MV5 GYW JHT

Dream City Film Club

12/1/97 Situation Desperate, One Sweet Moment, Perfect Piece Of Trash, Stick Girl. Michael John Sheehy (gv), Alex Vald (g), Andrew Park (b), Laurence Ash (d). 29/12/96 HP JB JLO

17/3/99 Licking The Bone, Gideon Blues, Close Watch, Nobody's Fault But Mine/ Dirty Little Cherubs. 7/2/99 MV3 ME KR

Dressy Bessy

7/8/02 Better Luck, I Saw Cinnamon, Buttercups, Lookaround, Live To Tell All, Hang Out Wonderful, Just Being Me, Just Like Henry, Carry On, That's Why, Extra Ordinary. Tammy Ealom (gv), John Hill (g, bck), Rob Greene (b), Darren Albert (d, bck). Live from MV4 NF~ GT/SA

Drive

25/9/90 Grease Gun, Road, Drive Out, Fire Flaps. Jeff Egerton (d), Dan Pye (b), Iain Roche (gv). 14/8/90 MV5 MR MR

Drome

12/8/94 Once While Busy Counting Virtues Part I, Once While Busy Counting Virtues Part II. Bernd Friedman (composer), Safak Baykal (mx), Judith Ruzicka (media artist). 2/6/94 MV4 PA JMK

The Drones

13/12/77 Be My Baby, The Change, Clique, Movement. MJ Drone (lvg), Pete Lambert (d), Whisper (b, lv-2), Guss Gangrene (lg). 6/12/77 MV4 MB MR

Drop Nineteens

9/1/93 Winona, Fight For Your Right, Nausea, My Aquarium. Greg Ackel (gv), Paula Kelly (gv), Moto Yassve (g), Steve Zimmerman (b), Chris Rouf (d). 15/11/92 MV3 ME~ JB

Drowning Craze

13/1/82 In The Heat, Keep Fit, Out Of Order, He Was. Simon Godfrey (d), Simon Raymonde (b), Paul Cummins (g), Frank Nardiello (v). 2/1/82 MV4 DG HP

Drum Club

18/3/94 Crystal Express, Follow The Sun, The Drive Out. Charles Hall (k), Laurence Hammond (k), Anabel Simmons (dig), Kim Lewis (prg, engineer). 8/2/94 MV4 PA FK

Drunk Tank

11/9/92 Stranger Danger, Crooked Mile, Pin Up Girl, Accidents. David Barker (g), Julian Mills (bv), Steve Cerio (d). 18/8/92 MV4 JB PL&JB

Dub Sex

4/2/87 Then And Now, Play Street, Kristallnacht, Man On The Inside. Mark Hoyle (gv), Dave Rumney (g), Cathy Brooks (b), Roger Cadman (d). 20/1/87 U DG MR

24/8/87 Push!, Voice Of Reason, Kicking The Corpse Around, Splintered. 16/8/87 U DG ME&MC

5/7/88 Caved-in, Snapper!, I Am Not Afraid, The Big Freeze. Chris Bridgett (g) r Rumney. 5/6/88 U DG NG&ME&PS

8/3/89 Swerve, North By North East, Kumina, Time Of Life. & Tim Costigan (g). 26/2/89 U DG MR

Ducks Deluxe ○

26/6/73 Coast To Coast, Pensecola Nightmare, Bring Back That Packard Car, Fireball. Martin Belmont (lgv), Sean Tyla (gv), Nick Garvey (bv), Tim Roper (d). 12/6/73 LH1 CB BC

4/6/74 Dancing Beat, Fireball, It's All Over Now, The Cannons Of The Boogie Night. 23/4/74 LH1 PR U

27/3/75 Paris Nine, Jumping In The Fire, Something's Going On, Amsterdam Dog. Mick Groome (bv) r Garvey, McMasters. 20/3/75 MV4 TW DD ○ All sessions on HUX086 The John Peel Sessions

Dumb

4/1/97 Mr Paul, King Tubby Meets Max Wall Uptown, Thirsty, Soz. Cathy Brooks (b), Jonny Hankins (d), Beth Taylor (perc), Mark Hoyle (vg). 1/12/96 MV4 SA JLO

John Dummer Blues Band

11/8/68 40 Days And 40 Nights, Travelling Man, Standing Round Cryin', After Hours. John Dummer (d), Dave Kelly (slg, v), T. S. McPhee (gv), John O'Leary (hca), Iain Thomson (b). 2/7/68 PC1 BA U Passed by panel despite 'some criticism' of vocalist

18/5/69 Big Feeling Blues, Skin Game, Jungle Blues (& A Few Short Lines, Hard Times, 6/7/69). Adrian Pietryea r McPhee, O'Leary. 13/5/69 MV4 JW U

John Dummer Ooblee Dooblee Band

5/5/72 I Love You Honey, Shake Your Money Maker, Riding At Midnight, Walking Blues. Kelly returns, r Pickett. 17/4/72 PH JM JWH&NG

15/9/72 The Monkey Speaks His Mind, Young Blood, Be Careful, I Ain't Sorry. Pat Grover r Pietryea. 4/9/72 T1 JM U

22/3/73 Going Home, Steel Guitar Rag, Lovin' Man, Undying Love. Pete Emery (lg), Colin Earl (p), Pete Richardson (d) r Grover. 26/2/73 LH1 BA U

13/9/73 Keep It In My Mind, Bad Dream, Good Rocking Man. 10/9/73 LH1 CB U

The Aynsley Dunbar Retaliation

1/12/68 I Tried, When The Devil Drives, Call My Woman, Mean Ol' World. Aynsley Dunbar (d), Victor Brox (o, v), John Morslead (g), Alex Dmochowski (b). 15/10/68 PC1 BA AH&BC 2 previous sessions for World Service R&B show 67 & 68

Lesley Duncan

26/2/69 Exactly Who You Are, Look What You've Done, Lullabye, Sing Children Sing, Love Song, Sunshine. Lesley Duncan (ag, v) with Sweet Thursday: John Mark (g), Harvey Burns (d), Nicky Hopkins (p). 19/2/69 S2 JM U Duncan first appeared on Light's 'The Talent Spot 24/5/63

Champion Jack Dupree

19/6/68 I Haven't Done No-one No Harm, Red Beans And Rice, Whisky Look What You've Done To Me, Tippin' In, Down-Don't Worry Me. Champion Jack Dupree (gv). 5/6/68 S1 DK U

Ian Dury and The Blockheads

12/12/77 Sex And Drugs And Rock And Roll, Clevor Trever, Sweet Gene Vincent, Blockheads. Ian Dury (v), Charlie Charles (d), Norman Watroy (b), John Turnbull (g), Chas Jankel (gk), Micky Gallagher (o). 30/11/77 MV4 MB NG See Wreckless Eric

Dustball

20/1/98 My Life Thrill, Flusher, Useless, Ice Cream Soda. Jamie Stuart (gv), Tarrant Anderson (b), James Russell (d). 30/11/97 MV4 ME RJ

22/7/98 Extra Volvo – Baby I Love You, Oh Jeff, Not BK, Mr Crisps (& Like A Fool, 1st TX live 11/6/98). & Tom Havelock (clo-1). 11/6/98 MV4 MR RJ

2/2/00 Slumber, Jazz 3, Punish The Evil Merchant, Hardcore. & Ben Lloyd (g), Paul Blois (k, o). 5/12/99 MV3 ME PN

30/1/02 Building, Sunday Under Glass, Thrown Like A Stone, Senor Nachos, Xeroxy Music. Stuart, Lloyd, Anderson, Nigel Powell (d), Tom Hubberman (tp), Rory Madden (k). Live from MV4 AR SA

Dweeb

25/5/96 Theme From Dweeb, Session Fodder For John, Scouby Doo, Retard. Lara Beltrami (kv), John Stanley (gv), Chris Beltrami (gv), Sid Abuse (Narrative, bck). 28/4/96 MV3 ME JMK

Dynamic Three

4/3/87 Beat Like This, Ten MCs, Illing. Dr Phibes, Capt. T.K., E.M.D; & Ricky Rennalls (k, perc), Damon Butcher (k). 17/2/87 U DG MR&FK

9/5/88 Def Stanza, I Feel Dynamic, Gangster. Carlos Dennis (sc) credited instead of Dr Phibes. 26/4/88 U DG TdB&PS

Earth The Californian Love Dream

20/1/04 In The Garden, Girls Fighting, Easy, Black Stuff. Huw Costin, Chris Middleton, Jonny Aitken, Sam Hempton. 19/12/03 MV4 SA GT

East of Eden

18/4/70 Nymphenburger, Sphinx (& It's The Porridge They're After, 11/7/70). Dave Arbus (vi, fl), Roy Caines (sx), Geoff Nicholson (lgv), Geoff Britton (d), Andy Sneddon (b). 6/4/70 PH JW BC Group failed trial broadcast on R1 Club, 4/69, passed re-audition at end of year

12/9/70 Scott Of The Antarctic, Halloween. David Jacks (b), Jeff Allen (d) r Caines, Nicholson, Britton. 11/8/70 MV4 JW U

Eat Static

28/8/93 Zarbi, Area 51, Bioforms. Merv Pepler (prg), Joie Hinton ('ambient mayhem'), Steve Everitt (prg). 22/8/93 MV3 ME RJ

16/10/97 Science Of The Gods, Peristalsis, Interceptor, Delta Volany. Everitt out. Live from MV5 SA GT

Ec8or

29/4/99 Ec8Hours, I Wanna Peel, Please Don't Make Me Hectical. Pete Catani, Gina V d'Orio. 21/3/99 MV3 ME NK

Echo and the Bunnymen

22/8/79 Read It In Books†, Stars Are Stars, I Bagsy Yours, Villiers Terrace†§. Ian McCulloch (gv), Will Sergeant (g), Les Pattinson (b), Dave Balfe (k, perc) & (dm). 15/8/79 MV4 TVD NG ● SFPS060

22/5/80 The Pictures On My Wall, All That Jazz†, Over The Wall†. Pete Defreitas (d) r Balfe & (dm). 13/5/80 MV4 JE MR

12/11/80 All My Colours Turn To Clouds†, That Golden Smile, Heaven Up Here, Turquoise Daze. 4/11/80 LH1 JS MR

8/2/82 Taking Advantage, An Equation, No Hands§. 27/1/82 MV4 KH U

20/6/83 Silver, Seven Seas†, The Killing Moon. 6/6/83 MV4 TW MC

24/10/83 Nocturnal Me†, Watch Out Below§, Ocean Rain†, My Kingdom. 19/9/83 MV4 U U

16/9/97 Rescue†, Don't Let It Get You Down, Altamont, Villiers Terrace. Sargeant, Pattison, McCulloch, Jeremy (d), Owen Wyse (g). Live from MV4 MR GT † on limited edition ♀ 2CD set of Evergreen, London Records 1997 § on Red Rhino 4CD set ♀ Crystal Days 1979–1999

Echobelly

1/4/95 Four Letter Word, Tarantino, Pantyhose And Roses, Way Too. Sonya Aurora Madan (v), Andy Henderson (d), Debbie Smith (g), Alex Keyboardser (g), Glenn Johansson (g, bck). 3/2/95 MV4 JB~

Echoboy

30/11/99 Zero, Atonal Apples, Daylight, Frances Says The Knife Is Alive. Richard Warren (g, b, k, v), Doggen Foster (b, g), Kevin Bales (d), Lee Horsley (k, Moog, o). 19/9/99 MV3 KR SBR

29/11/00 Sudwest Funk 5, Schram And Sheddle 261, Turning On, Siobhan. Warren, Horsley, Bales, Leon Tattersall (d), Sam Hempton (g), Dan Hayhurst (b), Pete Bassman (oscillators). 5/11/00 MV4 ME NS

6/3/03 Lately Lonely, Automatic Eyes, High Speed In Love, Wasted Spaces. Warren, Horsley, Tattershall, Pauline Kirk (clo), Chris Moore (b). 12/2/03 MV4 SA NS

The Eclection

12/5/68 Mark Time, In Her Mind, In The Early Days, Morning Of Yesterday, Confusion. Mike Rosen (g, tp, v), Geoff Hultgreen (g), Trevor Lucas (b), Gerry Conway (d), Kerry Male (v). 30/4/68 PC1 BA DT&AH

28/7/68 Another Time Another Place, Nevertheless, St George & The Dragon, Will Tomorrow Be The Same? (& Violet Dew, 1/9/68). 23/7/68 PC1 BA PR&MR

8/12/68 Please, If I Love Her, Days Left Behind, Time For Love. 19/11/68 PC1 BA AH&BC

27/4/69 Both Sides Now, Restitution, Charity, Earth, Put On Your Face. John Palmer, Gary Boyle, Dorris Henderson r Male, Rosen. 21/4/69 PH BA U

Econoline

17/12/02 Dropper, Chicks Dig Scars, The Charm Offensive, Buddy Bradley. Steve Morris (b), Ian Scanlon (gv), Valentina Magaletti (d), Piers Chandler (g). 25/11/02 MV4 SA JSM

Ecstacy Of Saint Theresa

26/2/93 Fluidum, Alpha Centauri, Trance (Between The Stars). Sam Muchon (g), Jaw Gregar (b), Irna Libowitz (v), Peter Wegner (d). 24/1/93 MV4 ME~ TD

Ed Hall

12/11/94 Fanblades Of Love, Huge Giant Omen, Parallel Universe, Hybrid. Gary Chester (gv), Larry Stubb (b), Lymon Hardy III (dv). 6/10/94 MV5 NG JMK

Eddie and the Hot Rods

21/2/77 Keep On Keeping On, Why Can't It Be, Teenage Depression, On The Run. Barry Masters (v), Dave Higgs (g, bck), Paul Gray (b), Steve Nicol (d). 15/2/77 MV4 JG MR

17/10/77 Life On The Line, I Don't Know What's Going On, Telephone Girl, Beginning Of The End. & Graham Douglas (g, bck). 10/10/77 MV4 TW DD

5/3/79 Strangers On The Payphone, Power And Glory, Breathless, Living Dangerously. & Neil Burn ('extra high' bck). 5/2/79 MV4 TW NBU

Duane Eddy

30/7/74 Cannonball Rag, Dance To The Guitar Man, The Lonely One. Duane Eddy (g) & Diane M. Abbate & (o), (lg), (b), (d) unknown. 29/7/74 LH1 JW BAI Previously appeared live on Monday Monday 6/3/67 & Tony Brandon 27/1/69

Edge

24/4/79 The Edge (Instrumental), Friday, I Give Up, Who's Your Friend. Lu (gv), Glyn (bv), Gavin (kv), John (d, perc, v). 18/4/79 MV4 JS NG

Dave Edmunds Rockpile

14/2/77 Down Down Down, TV TV Man, The Art Of The City?, I Knew The Bride. Dave Edmunds (gv), Billy Bremner (g, bck), Nick Lowe (bv), Terry Williams (d). 8/2/77 MV4 PR MR

Edsel Auctioneer

8/2/89 Brickwall Dawn, Between Two Crimes, Place In The Sun, Blind Hurricane. Chris Cooper (d), Ashley Horner (b, g), Aidan Winterburn (rgv). 24/1/89 MV4 DG MR

14/5/93 Simple, State Of Grace, Filled, Summer Hit. Horner, Winterburn, Tris Williams (d), Phil Pettler (b). 11/4/93 MV3 ME~ FK

Terry Edwards

2/2/92 Four, Eighty One, Knife, You Suffer / Your Achievement / Dead / The Kill, Lubbock Texas. Terry Edwards (dm, g, bars, sx) & Mark Bedford (b), Terry Underwood (ts), Dave Woodhead (tp). 15/12/91 MV3 DG JB ○

5/6/93 Hey Louis Let's Do Lunch, Ditch, Five Years, It's Showtime. & Jem Moore (b, v-2), Dave Bryant (d, perc). 6/5/93 MV4 TdB~ JB ○

16/6/96 I Like My Low Life Low, Boots Off, Sick Thru Drink, Cover Versions, Sex Machine. & Moore (b, v-5), Ian R Watson (g, tp), Ian White (d). 12/5/96 MV3 ME~ U First 3 sessions on ○ Birth Of The Scapegoats HUX014

19/5/99 Spill The Beans, Detroit, Creosote, Ace Of Spades. & The Scapegoats: Moore (b, v-3), White (d). 30/3/99 MV4 MR GT

Eek-A-Mouse

17/10/83 Wa-do-dem, Hitler, Assassinator, Hire And Removal. Eek-A-Mouse (v) & Kalabash: Nastas Hackett (d), Hugh Miller (b), Kenneth Mackintosh (rg), Sidney Mills (lg, k), Winston Miller (p) JP Palmer (perc). 10/10/83 MV4 TW MC Debut session broadcast previous week was recorded for Jensen, same line-up, same studio, day before

26/6/84 Elizabeth, Safari, Mouse And Man, Triple Love. 'and Jah Mullah': Noel Alphonso (d), Ronald Morris (b), Michael Ranglin (k), Ronald Butler (lg), Cleon Douglas (rg), Clifton Carnegie (perc). 16/6/84 MV5 DG MC

Egg

13/8/69 Seven Is A Jolly Good Time, While Growing My Hair, McGillicuddie The Pusillanimour Or Don't Worry James Your Socks Are Hanging In The Coal Cellar. Mont Campbell (bv), Clive Brooks (d), Dave Stewart (o). 24/7/69 PH PR U Pass from the panel, despite one comment: 'cleverness here, but no entertainment'

7/3/72 Germ Patrol, Wring Out The Ground Loosely Now, Ennagram. 22/2/72 MV4 U BC

Eggs

30/7/94 March Of The Triumphant Elephants, A Pit With Spikes, Words, Maureen's Beans. John Rickman (d), Evan Surak (b), Andrew Beaujon (g), Robert Christiansen (g, tb, k). 23/5/94 MV4 PA FK

Einstürzende Neubauten

5/9/83 Kango Licht, Sehnsucht Zittern Blixa Bargold, N U Untuh, F M Einheit, Marc Chung. 24/8/83 MV4 BYA NG

Eire Apparent

20/4/69 Yes I Need Someone, Highway 61 Revisited, Gloria. Ernest Graham (lv, rg), David Taylor (lg, bck), Chris Stewart (bv), David Lutton (d). 15/4/69 PH BA AH&BC 'Unanimous pass from the panel'. Twice on R1 Club in next few weeks

Mark Eitzel & Peter Buck

19/6/97 Fresh Screwdriver, Old Photographs, Frozen, Helium, Free Of Harm. Mark Eitzel (v), Peter Buck (g). Live from 1G RJ~

El Dorados

17/6/95 Crazy Little Mama, My Lovin' Baby, Weeping Willow Blues, Framed, My Gal Is Gone. & CJ & The House Rockers: Pirkle Lee Moses Jr (lv), Norman Palm (Tenor Vocals), Larry Johnson (Tenor Vocals), Clarence Wright (Baritone Vocals),

Rufis Hunter (Bass Vocals), CJ And The House Rockers: Mike Wheeler (hca), Andy Robbins (sx), Graham Adams (g), John Weir (b), Dexter Speedy (d), Steve Clayton (p). 15/5/95 BHM PJ CLE

El Goodo

3/4/01 Honey, Stuck In The 60s, Pay Per Sound, Highschool Low. Andrew Lewis, Andrew Jones, Jason Jones, Elliot Jones, Matthew Young. 14/3/01 MV4 SA GT

El Hombre Trajeado

9/4/98 Like Quicksand, Go Faster, Diary Extract, Sleep Deep. Robert Hubbert (gv), Stevie Jones (b), Steph Sinclair (d), Ben Jones (k). 1/3/98 MV4 ME RJ

10/11/98 Neoprene, Nearly A Week Nearly Awake, Varispeed (& Nofo 1st TX live 28/7/98). 28/7/98 MV5 ME MPK

13/3/01 Tracky B, Redial, Mu Manual, Dylar. 24/1/01 MV4 MA ME

Elastica

18/9/93 Line Up† & Vaseline†, Brighton Rock†, Rock And Roll†, Spastica†, Annie†. Justine Frischmann (glv), Donna Matthews (g, bck), Annie Holland (b), Justin Welch (d, 'funny voices') 12/8/93 MV4 NG AR

9/7/94 Never Here, Four Wheeling†, Hold Me Now†, Ba Ba Ba†. 14/6/94 MV3 MR GT

17/12/94 All For Gloria†, I Wanna Be King Of Orient Aah†, Father Christmas, Blue. 6/12/94 MV3 TD FK

9/11/99 Mad Dog, KB†, Da Da Da†, Generator†, Your Arse My Place†. Frischmann, Welch, Holland, Dave Bush (k), Mew (kbv), Paul Jones (g). 22/9/99 MV4 JB NF † on ○ The Radio One Sessions SFRSCD101

Electrelane

29/1/04 Oh Sombra!, More Than This, Untitled, This Deed. Verity Susman (kv), Emma Gaze (d), Mia Clarke (g), Rachel Dalley (b). 7/1/04 MV AR GT

Electribe 101

13/11/89 Talking With Myself, Tell Me When The Fever Ended, Lipstick On My Lover. Brian Nordhoff (k), Les Fleming (k, bck), Joe Stevens (k), Roberto Cimarosti (k), Billie Ray Martin (v). 24/10/89 U HP MA

Electric Music Aka

21/9/00 Psychics F.O, Let It Flow, Look So Haunted, The First Day Of Nothing, Lose Yourself In The Crowd. Tom Doyle (gvk), Anth Brown (g), Steve (k), Derek Hood (d, perc), Daniella (d, glo) 2/7/00 U U U

Electric Sound Of Joy

27/11/97 Our Flag, Don't Waste My Time, I Can't Wait (& Play Away, 1st TX live from MV4 25/11/97). Gregory Kurcewicz (gv), Scott Nicholas (lg), Ben Rodgers (k), Daniel Hayhurst (d), John Revill (d, perc), Paul Metcalfe (d-4). 25/11/97 MV4 MR RJ

The Electro Hippies

20/7/87 Sheep, Starve The City (To Feed The Poor), Meltdown, Escape, Deadend, Thought, Chickens, Mother, Mega-Armageddon Death Part Three (Part Four). Simon (dv), Dom (bv), Andy (gv). 12/7/87 U DG DD ● SFPS042. Most of this session is also on the two Hardcore Holocaust albums

Element

15/2/00 Too Cold To Snow, Indo Make Up Technique, The Kids Just Wanna (Have Fun), Dr Bosin, Bowie Knife (Trumpet), 20 Go To 10. James Stansfield (gv), Karl Eden (g), Mark Tattersall (d). Live from MV4 U U

8/8/00 Rural Tuning, Fatty Party, Dancing Dogs, Kitten Modulation. 5/7/00 MV4 SA NF

Elements Of Noize

12/8/98 Change, Proteus, Timebomb, Unthinkable. Alan Clark (prg), Justin Maughan (prg). 2/8/98 MV4 ME NF

Elevate

25/2/94 Stuntman Bid Drag, Trinkets Oriental Objects A Certain Delicacy, Quietly Obnoxious, Misuse Of Inner Temperament. Tim Ward (g, v, tp), Paul Collier (b, g, p), Graham Miles (g, p), James Elkington (d, vi). 16/1/94 MV3 JB FK

12/5/95 Slowspeed To Harbour, 2 Days Out Of 5, Poobs' Whiskers, Sol Lewitt. Miles, Elkington, Tim Bamforth (g, v, o), Big D (b). 6/4/95 MV4 AA KR

Eleven

27/6/84 If I Was You And You Were Me, Drop That Bomb, My Metropolis, Perpetual Emotion (Love Is A...). Frederic Ravel (d), Michael Bradley (b), Damian O'Neill (g), David Drumbold (lv). 5/6/84 MV5 U TdB

Steve Elgin and The Flatbackers

23/5/79 Agony Column, Flatbacker, Miss World 79, Lies. Steve Elgin (lv, k), Julie Usher (gv), Jeannie Hay (k, bck, lv-2), Lucy Dray (b, bck), Lynn Carol (d, perc, bck). 16/5/79 MV4 JS NG

The Elizabethan Jazz Trio

23/7/69 A Toye, Sick Tune, Carmanns Whistle, Lover And His Lass. U 19/6/69 U PR U

Ella Guru

15/12/04 On A Beach, Park Lake Speakers, Tale Of The Christmas Law, Oh My Love. John Yates (gv), Chris Burwood (g, ag), Nik Kavanagh (g, bck), Kate Walsh (v, cl), Scott Marmion (ps), Bob Picken (db), Bren Moore (d). 2/12/04 MV4 MA GW

Ellery Bop

29/10/81 Ringing, Sharp Star Rising, Fight And Desire. Jamie Farrell (gv), Mark Parry (d), Junior (perc) & Ian (b), Jonathan (k). 14/10/81 MV4 CL NG

13/12/82 Jihad, Imperial Way, 51st State, Guilt. Farrell, Steve Johnson (b), Tim Whittaker (perc), Rob Jones (d). 8/12/82 U RP NG

12/1/84 Above The World, Scream To Touch, Ourselves Alone, Twisted. Farrell, Parry, Johnson, Kevin Connelly (perc). 19/12/83 MV4 TW MC

Matthew Ellis

25/7/72 Missed You Tonight, If The Cap Fits, Lady My Lady. U 10/7/72 U JW BC

8/9/72 Sea Horse, Who Needs You, Waking To Life. & 2 U. 22/8/72 T1 JM U

Elti Fits

26/9/79 Factory Room, Letter Box, Reject, Song. Sarah Keynes (v), Graham Ellis (g, kbv), Nigel Ross (b), Karl Burns (d). 4/9/79 MV4 BS MR

The End

20/3/68 Dream World, Introspection, Shades Of Orange, Mirror. Colin Giffin (ts, g), Hugh Grant (bars), David Brown (b), John Horton (d), Nicky Graham (g, o). 12/3/68 AO2 JM U Debut session for Saturday Club July 66

31/3/68 Under The Rainbow, Shades Of Orange, Mirror, Introspection. 18/3/68 PC1 BA U

Endgames

30/3/81 Both Of Us, Fading Away, Beauty #2, Pioneer. David Rudden (bv), Paul Wishart (sx, fl), David Murdoch (k), Willie Gardner (gv), David Wilde (d). 17/3/81 LH1 DG MR

26/5/82 We Feel Good (Future's Looking Fine), Darkness, First Last For Everything, You'll Never Walk Alone. Rudden, Wishart, Murdoch, Gardner, Brian McGee (d), Douglas Muirden (sx). 10/5/82 MV4 TW DD

Eno and the Winkies

5/3/74 The Paw Paw Negro Blowtorch, Baby's On Fire / Totalled, Fever. Eno (v, sy), Mike Desmarais (d), Guy Humphreys (g), Philip Rambow (g), Brian Turrington (b). 26/2/74 LH1 TW BC&MR

Eon

29/6/91 Fear The Mindkiller, Infernal Machine, Be Cool, Basket Case. Ian B, J Saul Kane, Alan Scott (all: mx). 15/5/91 OS

14/8/02 Deadeye, Chicken Store, Holy Cow, Ramadance, Absorbed, Jackbox, Spice. Ian Loveday (el, prg, k). Live from MV4 NF GT

Erase Errata

11/11/03 Ease On Over, A Passion For Acting, Retreat The Most Familiar, Boris The Spider. Ellie Erickson (b), Sara Jeffe (g), Bianca Sparta (d), Jenny Hoysten (v, tp). 15/10/03 MV5 NF GT

31/3/04 Harvester, Ca Viewing, A Thief Detects The Criminal Elements Of The Ruling Class, Driving Test, Owls, Cat and Canary / Matter No Medley, Billy Mummy, Go To Sleep, We're All Water, Marathon. Live from MV4 AR~

Erazerhead

20/7/82 I Hate You, Teenager In Love, Martian Girl, No-One Sees Me Now. Lee Drury (v), Jim Berlin (g), Billy Trigger (d), Gary Spanner (b). 14/6/82 MV4 KH DD

Eric's Trip

23/10/93 Sickness, Red Haired Girl, Lost, Float. Mark Gaudet (d), Julie Doiron (b, g, v), Rick White (gv), Chris Thompson (g, b). 16/9/93 MV4 NG RJ

Eska

16/12/97 Sure Enough, True North, Knives Slowly, Future In Monotone. Willie Mone (d), Kenny Graham (b), Chris Mack (gv), Colin Kearney (gv). 26/10/97 MV4 KR RBY

The Etchingham Steam Band

5/11/74 The Gypsy's Wedding Day, Orange In Bloom, 2 Polkas: Sheep Shearing / Buttered Peas, The Hard Times Of Old England. Ashley Hutchings (ab), Ian Holder (acc), Terry Potter (mo), Vic Gammon (wh, ml, cnc), Shirley Collins (v). 21/10/74 MV4 JW U 'Recorded in NEW 8-track Studio 4!' – Ashley's diary

Eton Crop

15/11/83 Gay Boys On The Battlefield, Boring Isms, Explain, He Didn't Say Anything. Ed Tuyl (d, tp), Corne Bos (b, sx), Erwin Blom (gv), Peter de Kwaasteniet (gp), Peter Verschueren (k), Leoneke Daalder (mel, perc), Ben Hoogendam (bck-4). 9/11/83 MV4 RP NG

20/11/84 Snobhill, Boy Meets Tractor, Get Something For Doing Nothing, Quality In The Grooves. Lukas Daalder (mel-2, bck-4), Frans Weeke (bck-4) r Hoogendam. 13/11/84 MV5 MRD MR

14/10/85 Cocacolanization, It's My Dog Maestro, You Won't Get Me Out In The

Rain, Harry Nelson Pillsbury. Bos, Blom, Verschauren, de Kwaatseneat, Le Daalder, Weeke, Susie Honeyman (vi), Michael Harding (tp). 1/10/85 MV5 PWL TdB ● SFPS063

19/11/86 A Bundle For A Dead Dog, Jolly Adventures With Janus McManus, Banana Battle, Paraffin Brain. Lu Daalder, Hoogendam return; Weeke, Harding out. 19/10/86 U DG ME

8/6/88 A Jolly Cheerful Crowd, Pavel Morozov The Bastard!, Beating The Sicilian, Trivialities. Bos, Blom, de Kwaasteniet, Spike Daalder (sy), Ingmar van Wynsberge (g, bck), Le. Daalder ('sound creator', bck). 29/5/88 U DG ME&SC

Eva Luna

29/1/94 Lover Stay, A Debt Repaid In Kind, Trains And Boats And Planes, Beautiful End. Jun (bck, acc), Graeme Elston (everything else). 12/12/93 MV4 ME NF

Even As We Speak

16/2/92 Falling Down The Stairs, Stay With Me, Straight As An Arrow, Sailor's Graves. Anita Rayner (d), Rob Irwin (b), Paul Clarke (g, bck), Matt Love (g), Mary Wyer (v). 9/1/92 MV4 DG NG&RJ

20/2/93 Air, Blue Eyes Deceiving Me, Cos I Like It, The Revenge Of Ella May Cooley. Julian Knowles (k, prg) joins. 31/1/93 MV4 ME~ JLC

22/10/93 Suddenly, Everywhere I Go, Until Tomorrow, 30 Miles. 18/7/93 MV4 PL KR

Everyone

3/10/70 Midnight Shift, Sitting On A Rock, Too Much A Loser, Trio. Andy Roberts (gv), Bob Sargeant (p), John Porter (g), Dave Richards (b), John Pearson (d). 21/9/70 PH JW U 'Borderline pass' from the panel

Everything but the Girl

30/8/84 Ballad Of The Times, Riverbed Dry, Never Could Have Been Worse, Don't You Go. Ben Watt (g, o), Tracey Thorn (v), Phil Moxham (b), June Miles Kingston (d). 18/8/84 MV5 DG MC 1st session was for Jensen, June 84

27/2/85 Are You Trying To Be Funny, Trouble And Strife, Easy As Sin, Sean. & Neil Scott (g). 19/2/85 MV5 MRD GP

Ex Girl

29/8/00 Hei Ann Kyo, Waving Scientist At Frog King, Gin Kong Ji, Aji Fry. Fuzuki (dv), Kirilo (v, b, Casiotone), Chihiro (gv). 30/8/00 MV4 MPK TdB

Ex-Post Facto

10/4/84 Actor's Warning, Innocence, It's No Show, The Last Four. Frank Sparks (k), Chris Clarke (v), Mark Coleridge (d), Paul Reason (g), Bernie Carroll (b), Judith Laity (clo), Andy Warren (bck). 17/3/84 MV5 DG MC Debut session for Jensen March 83

The Ex

15/9/83 Crap Rap, Design For Living, US Hole, Buy Buy. Jos Kley (v), Sabien Witteman (d), Joke Laarman (b), Luc Klaassen (b, p-4), Terrie Hessels (g) & Wineke T Hart (vi-4), Kees Vanden Haak (ss-4), Dolf Planteydt (g-3), John Langford (acc-3). 7/9/83 MV4 RP NG

4/12/85 Choice, Uh-Oh Africa, Hands Up! You're Free, Butter Or Bombs. Klaassen, Hessels, Langford (blp-3), Katrin Bornfeld (d), Tom Greene (g-2), G W Sok (v), Susie Honeyman (vi-1). 24/11/85 MV5 DG ME

16/12/86 Knock, Ignorance, Business As Usual, A Job / Stupid. Bornfeld, Klaassen, Hessels, Sok, John V D Weert (gv). 30/11/86 U DG ME&FK

Exiles

5/3/03 Response, Electric, The Not Gate, Black Mark, Fer De Lance, Come Too Without You, Last Word. Bob Halliwell (d), Ben Miles (gv), Adam Moss (g), Matt Dupuy (b). Live from MV4 AR NF/RJ

26/8/03 I Can't Breathe, Serotonin Burnout, How To Lose Friends, Building. 17/7/03 MV4 SA JSM

Exit Condition

2/6/91 Learning The Hard Way, Strong & True, Slow Reflex, Toiler On The Sea. Richard Stanier (d), David Ellis (b), Darren Harris (gv). 5/5/91 MV3 DG ME&FK

The Expelaires

3/7/79 Dashboard, It's Alright Mother, Nasty Media, Frequency. Carl 'Tich' Harper (d), Mark Copson (b), David Wolfenden (g), Craig Adams (k), Grape (v). 25/6/79 U BS DD

The Expelled

10/1/83 Make It Alone, This World, Government Policy, What Justice. Rick Fox (d), Macca (Craig McEvoy) (b), Tim Ramsden (g), Jewelie (v). 20/12/82 U TW DD

Experimental Pop Band

25/2/97 Mental Health Outpatients Clinic, Chewing Gum Friends, My Girlfriends Story, Skinny. Chris Galvin (b, tamb), Joe Rooney (k), Davey Woodward (gv), Keefer Chico Bailey (d, perc). 2/2/97 MV4 ME KR

Explosions In The Sky

15/10/02 First Breath After Coma, The Moon Is Down, Memorial. Munaf Rayani (g), Mark Smith (g), Michael James (b), Christopher Hrasky (d). 18/9/02 MV4 SA GYW

11/2/04 The Only Moment We Were Alone, The Long Spring, With Tired Eyes Tired Minds Tired Souls We Slept. 28/1/04 MV4 NS GT

Extreme Noise Terror

17/11/87 False Profit, Another Nail In The Coffin, Use Your Mind, Carry On Screaming, Human Error, Conned Through Life, Only In It For The Music Part 2. Mick Harris (d), Jerry Clay (b, bck), Pete Hurley (g, bck), Dean Jones (v), Phil Vane (v). 10/11/87 U DG SC&DD ○

11/5/88 Murder, Take The Strain, No Threat, Show Us You Care, Propaganda, System Enslavement. Mark Gardiner (b) r Clay. 1/5/88 MV5 DG ME

8/3/90 Work For Never, Subliminal Music (Mind Control), People Not Profit, Punk Fact Or Faction, I Am A Bloody Fool / In It For Life, Deceived, Shock Treatment. Tony Dickens (d), Mark Bailey (b) r Harris, Gardiner. 6/2/90 MV5 DG MR ○ SFMCD208

27/3/01 When Gods Burn, Awakening, Screaming Bloody Murder, Being And Nothing, One Truth One Hate, No Lomger As Sleeves. Zac Oneil (d), Ali Firouzbakht (g), Manny Butcher (b), Dean Jones (v), Adam Catchpole. 28/2/01 MV4 SA U

E-Z Rollers

25/2/04 Mix. Jay Hurren (prg, tt), Alex Banks (prg, tt) & Kelly Richards (v). OS

EZ T

28/9/04 Downs Pain, Getting Harder, Mastodon, Plastik Surgery. Colin Gagon (gkv), Nick Frank (g), Lyz Dunnebacke (b), Matt Newman (d). 1/9/04 MV4 GYW NS

Fabio

6/11/01 DJ set live from LL

Fabric

17/12/93 Friend, Without, March Of The Machine/Seven, Carried Away. Andrew Hartwell (v), Anthony Sylvester (d), Christopher Turner (d, bck), James Tilley (g), Kevin Williams (g), Hazel Jones (bck). 11/11/93 MV4 JB CBO

The Fabulous Poodles

27/10/76 Roll Your Own, Cherchez La Femme, Grow Too Old, Pinball Pinups, Opening Finale, Acapella. Richie C Robinson (b, bck), Bobby Valentino (vi, bck), Bryn B. Burrows (d). 7/10/76 U TW U

27/4/77 Workday, On The Street Where You Live, When The Summer's Through, Mr Mike. & Tony Demeur (g, hp, lv). 18/4/77 MV4 TW DD

19/9/77 Johnny The Jockey, Rum Bara Boogie, Bike Blood, Chicago Box Car, See You Later Alligator. 6/9/77 U U U

25/10/78 Convent Girls, B Movies, Mirror Star, Toytown People, We'll Meet Again. 3/10/78 MV4 BS MR

Fabulous Thunderbirds

26/5/80 Walkin' To My Baby, Runnin' Shoes, She's Tuff, Pocket Rocket. U U PRIV

The Faces

28/3/70 Wicked Messenger, Devotion, Pineapple And The Monkey, Shake Shudder Shiver. Rod Stewart (v), Ronnie Lane (b), Ron Wood (g), Ian McLagan (o, p), Kenny Jones (d). 9/3/70 PH JW U Debut session for DLT rec. 10/3/70, TX 15/3/70

19/9/70 Had Me A Real Good Time, Around The Plynth, Country Comforts. 15/9/70 MV4 PR U

6/10/71 Stay With Me, Miss Judy's Farm, Maggie May. 28/9/71 MV4 JW BC

John Fahey

28/5/69 Buckingham Stomp, Death Of The Claytown Peacock, Sunflower River Blues, In Christ There Is No East Or West, Steel Guitar Rag (& Dance Of The Inhabitants Of The Palace Of King Philip XV, Some Summer Day, Poor Boy, all TX 22/6/69 TOP GEAR). John Fahey (ag). 22/5/69 S2 PR MH

Fairport Convention ○

10/12/67 Let's Get Together, One Sure Thing, Lay Down Your Weary Tune, Chelsea Morning. Judy Dyble (v), Ashley Hutchings (b), Martin Lamble (d), Simon Nicol (gv), Richard Thompson (gv). 24/11/67 PH BA PR

3/3/68 If (Stomp), If I Had A Ribbon Bow, Time Will Show The Wiser, Violets Of Dawn. Ian Matthews (v) joins. 6/2/68 AO2 BA DT Bernie Andrews submitted this second session as trial broadcast. 'Unanimous, enthusiastic pass' from audition panel, 'compared to Harpers Bizarre'

2/6/68 Close The Door Lightly When You Go, Where I Stand, Nottamun Town, You Never Wanted Me (& Some Sweet Day, 30/6/68). Sandy Denny (v) r Dyble. 28/5/68 PC1 BA DT

1/9/68 If You Feel Good You Know It Can't Be Wrong, Fotheringay, Gone Gone Gone, Eastern Rain (& Suzanne, 29/9/68). 26/8/68 PC1 BA PR

22/12/68 Meet On The Ledge, She Moves Through The Fair, Light My Fire, I'll Keep It With Mine, Billy The Orphan Boy's Lonely Christmas. 9/12/68 PC1 BA PR

22/1/69 Things You Gave Me, Meet On The Ledge, Autopsy, Morning Glory, Bird On A Wire, Mr Lacey. 25/11/68 MV4 PC U This session was first TX on a non-Peel edition of Night Ride on 15/12/68

6/4/69 Cajun Woman, Percy's Song, Si Tu Dois Partir Va T'En, Autopsy. & guest Ric

Grech (vi, acc, o), Matthews out. 18/3/69 PH BA AH&BC

27/9/69 Sir Patrick Spens, Jigs & Reels Medley, Tamlin, The Lady Is A Tramp, Reynardine. Dave Swarbrick (vi) r Grech; & Dave Mattacks (d) r Lamble, died 12/5/69, after M1 accident. 23/9/69 MV4 JW TW

2/5/70 The Deserter, Walk Awhile, Flatback Caper, Poor Will And The Jolly Hangman (& Doctor Of Physic, 1/8/70). Dave Pegg (b, fd, mand) r Hutchings, Denny, from 1/70. 20/4/70 PH JW TW

20/2/73 Tokyo, Matthew Mark Luke John, Rosie, Possibly Parson's Green. Trevor Lucas (gv), Jerry Donahue (gv) r Thompson, Nicol. 5/2/73 T1 PD ARV

6/8/74 John The Gun, Fiddlesticks, Rising For The Moon, Down In The Flood. Sandy Denny (pv) returns. 16/7/74 LH1 TW BC Sessions 1–4, 7–8, 10–11, and some tracks from 5 & 9, are now on ○ Live At The BBC 4 CD set Universal/Island

Andy Fairweather-Low

17/11/75 If I Ever Get Lucky, Inner City Highwayman, Jump Up And Turn Around, Wide Eyed And Legless. Dave Mattacks (d, perc), John David (bv), BJ Cole (ps), Rabbit (kv), Andy Fairweather-Low (gv). 21/10/75 MV4 TW BAI Previous Sounds of the Seventies session in Nov 74

7/2/77 Checking Out The Checker, Lighten Up, Ain't No Fun, Be-Bop'N Holla, Shimme Doo Wah Sae. Andy Fairweather-Low (gv), John David (b, bck), Mick Weaver (k, bck), BJ Cole (ps), Henry Spinetti (d). 31/1/77 TW DD This session repeated on ALAN FREEMAN 25/6/77 as Matrix H Quad Experiment

Th'Faith Healers

27/4/91 Coffee Commercial Couples, Bobby Kopper, Jesus Freak. Joe Dilworth (d), Ben Hopkin (b), Tom Cullinan (gv), Roxanne Stephen (v). 24/3/91 MV3 DG ME&PA ○ SFRCD119

11/1/92 Hippy Hole, This Time, Reptile Smile, SOS. 24/11/91 MV3 DG ME&RK

24/7/92 Love In Sesh, Moona Inna Joona, I'm Ready, Get Th' F*** Out Of My Face. 5/7/92 MV4 SA NF&SA

10/4/93 Rave Track, Bulkhead, Sparkingly Chime, Serge. 16/3/93 MV4 JB~ PA

5/3/94 Ooh Lah Lah, Curly Lips, New No 2, Without You. 27/1/94 MV4 NG RPF

The Fall ○

15/6/78 Rebellious Juke Box, Mother Sister, Industrial Estate, Futures And Pasts. Mark Smith (lv), Martin Bramah (g, b, bck), Yvonne Pawlette (k), Karl Burns (d) & Steve Davis (cga-1). 30/5/78 MV4 TW MR

6/12/78 Put Away, Mess Of My, No Xmas For John Quays, Like To Blow. & Marc Riley (b). 27/11/78 MV4 BS DD&BT ● SFPS028

24/9/80 Container Drivers, Jawbone And The Air Rifle, New Puritan, New Face In Hell. Smith, Riley (g), Craig Scanlon (g, bck), Steve Hanley (b), Paul Hanley (d). 16/9/80 MV4 JS U

31/3/81 Middlemass, Lie Dream Of A Casing Soul, Hip Priest, C 'n' C / Hassle Schmuk. & Dave Tucker (cl). 24/3/81 LH1 DG MPK

26/8/81 Deer Park, Look Know, Winter, Who Makes The Nazis? 19/8/81 MV4 DG NG

23/3/83 Smile, Garden, Hexen Definitive – Strife Knot, Eat Yourself Fitter. Burns (d) returns, Riley out. 21/3/83 MV4 JP DD

3/1/84 Pat Trip Dispenser, 2 By 4, Words Of Expectation, CREEP. Brix Smith (gv) joins. 12/12/83 MV4 TW MC

3/6/85 Cruisers' Creek, Couldn't Get Ahead, Gut Of The Quantifier, Spoilt Victorian Childe. & Simon Rogers (g, k), P Hanley out. 14/5/85 MV5 MRD MWT

7/10/85 LA, Man Whose Head Expanded, What You Need, Faust Banana. 29/9/85 MV5 DG ME

9/7/86 Hot Aftershave Bop, R O D, Gross Chapel / GB Grenadiers, US 80s 90s. Smith, Smith, Scanlon, Hanley, Rogers, Simon Wolstencroft (d). 29/6/86 MV5 DG ME

11/5/87 Australians In Europe, Twister, Guest Informant, Athlete Cured. 28/4/87 U U U

31/10/88 Kurious Oranj, Dead Beat Descendant, Cab It Up, Squid Lord. Marcia Schofield (k, lv-4) r Rogers. 25/10/88 MV4 MR MR

1/1/90 Hilary, Black Monk Theme, Chicago Now (& Whizz Bang, not TX). Martin Bramah (g) r B Smith, Kenny Brady (fd) joins. 17/12/89 MV3 DG ME

23/3/91 The War Against Intelligence, Idiot Joy Showland, A Lot Of Wind, The Mixer. Bramah, Schofield out. 5/3/91 MV5 MR MR

15/2/92 Free Range, Return, Kimble, Immortality. Smith, Scanlon, Hanley, Wolstencroft, Dave Bush (k). 19/1/92 MV3 DG ME&JB

13/3/93 Ladybird (Green Grass), Strychnine, Service, Paranoia Man In Cheap Shot Room. 28/2/93 MV4 MR JB

11/9/93 Glam Racket, A Past Gone Mad, Fifteen Ways, War. 1/5/93 MV4 PL JMK Repeat of a Mark Goodier Evening Session 1st TX w/c 17/5/93

5/2/94 M5, Behind The Counter, Reckoning, Hey! Student. 2/12/93 NG PL

17/12/94 Glam Racket / Star, Jingle Bell Rock, Hark The Herald Angels Sing, Numb At The Lodge. Karl Burns (d), Brix Smith (gv) both rejoin; & Lucy Rimmer (choir girl of the year-3). 20/11/94 MV4 JB PA

22/12/95 U Pep, Oleana, The Chiselers, This City Never Sleeps At Night. Smith, Smith, Hanley, Wolstencroft, Burns, Julie Nagle (k), Lucy Rimmer (lv-4). 17/12/95 MV4 NG AA

18/8/96 Beatle Bones 'N' Smokin' Stones, DIY Meat, Spinetrack, Spencer. Rimmer out. 30/6/96 MV4 TdB LS

3/3/98 Calendar, Touch Sensitive, Masquerade, Jungle Rock. Smith, Hanley, Nagle, Burns, John Rollason (bck). 3/2/98 MV4 MR NS

CLASSIC SESSIONS

The Fall

The 24 sessions by John Peel's favourite band The Fall represent the greatest number done by a single act, and when heard collectively make you realise how right Peel was when he said they were 'always different, always the same'. The release of all 24 sessions commissioned for the Peel show on Sanctuary Records heralded an outpouring of acclaim. While as a live band they could be the worst act in the world one night, then the greatest thing you had ever heard the next, what marks the sessions out is their consistent ability to surprise. Every session has at least one, and sometimes two, new songs that seem to be spot on of the moment and times. From 'Industrial Estate' on their first to 'Wrong Place, Right Time' / 'I Can Hear The Grass Grow' on their last – taking in classics like 'LA', 'Cab It Up', 'Chicago Now', 'M5', 'Theme From Sparta FC' along the way – the collection is a lightning rod drawing bolts from previously remembered shocks. If there is one CD collection someone who wants to remember the Peel show should buy, this is it. Listen to a session a day before meals. You won't necessarily like it all, but you'll never forget it.

The Ones I Missed

The following sessions from pre-1992 were not in In Session Tonight for a variety of reasons, most commonly there being no surviving session sheet, but also some were private tapes, or repeats from other shows. They are all in now.

- Peter Anders & Vini Poncia
- Animal Magic #2
- Boots For Dancing #3
- Ted Chippington
- Spencer Davis Group
- Deutsche Amerikanische Freundschaft
- The Fabulous Poodles #3
- The Fabulous Thunderbirds
- Fripp & Eno
- Gazelle
- Hula #2

- The Kursaal Flyers #2
- Alvin Lee & Mylon Lefevre
- Bill Nelson #1
- New Age Steppers
- The Nightingales #4
- Pentangle #2
- Protex
- Pragvec #3
- James & Bobby Purify
- Simple Minds #2
- Sophisticated Boom Boom #1
- Stiff Little Fingers #5
- The Tearjerkers #1
- The Undertones #3
- Wishbone Ash #3

Top Ten Longest Intervals Between Sessions

- Incredible String Band: 27 years
  11th session in Oct 73, 12th in Nov 2000

- Faust: 26 years
  1st in June 73, 2nd in Jan 99

- Gary Numan: 21 years
  2nd in March 79, 3rd Dec 2000

- Wire: 14 years
  4th in May 88, 5th in Sept 02

- The Pastels: 13.5 years
  1st in Feb 84, 2nd in Nov 97

- June Tabor: 13 years
  5th in Feb 78, 6th in Jan 91

- Pulp: 11.5 years
  1st in Nov 81, 2nd in March 93

- Orbital: 11 years
  1st in Sept 93, 2nd in July 04

- Eon: 11 years
  1st in June 91, 2nd in Aug 02

- The Undertones: 10.5 years
  6th in Dec 82, 7th in May 03

4/11/98 Bound Soul One, Antidotes, This Perfect Day, Shake Off. Smith, Nagle, Karen Leatham (b, k), Tom Murphy (d), Nev Wilding (g), Speth Hughes (sfx). 18/10/98 MV3 ME KR

13/3/03 Sparta FC, Contraflow, Groovin' With Mr Bloe / Green Eyed Locoman, Mere Pseud Mag Ed. Smith, Dave Milner (d, bck), Jim Watts (b, bck), Ben Pritchard (g, bck), Eleanor Poulou (o, bck). 19/2/03 MV4 MWT RJ

12/8/04 Clasp Hands, Blindness, What About Us, Wrong Place Right Time / I Can Hear The Grass Grow (& Job Search, TX 31/8/04). Smith, Watts, Pritchard, Poulou, Steve Trafford (b, bck), Spencer Birtwhistle (d), Ed Blaney (g). 4/8/04 MV4 JSM NF All except 11/9/93 on ○ Complete Peel Sessions CMXBX982

The Family

26/11/67 Piece Of My Mind, Scene Through The Eyes Of A Lens, The Voyage, The Breeze, Winter. Roger Chapman (v), Charlie Whitney (g), Rik Grech (vi, bv), Rob Townsend (d), Jim King (sx, fl, p). 20/11/67 PC1 BA DT 'Unanimous, enthusiastic pass' from panel

21/4/68 See Through Windows, Hey Mr Policeman, Three Times Time, Old Songs New Songs. 16/4/68 PC1 BA PR

4/8/68 The Procession, The Weaver's Answer, Me My Friend, Three Times Time (& The Breeze, 15/9/68). 29/7/68 PC1 BA U

24/11/68 Dim†, Second Generation Woman†, How Hi The Li, Observations† (& Hometown, 5/1/69). 11/11/68 PC1 BA U

30/3/69 Love Is A Sleeper†, I Sing 'Em The Way I Feel†, Bring It On Home, A Song For Me†. 11/3/69 PH BA AH

3/8/69 Drown In Wine†, Wheels†, No Mules Fool†, The Cat And The Rat†. John Weider (v) r Grech. 28/7/69 PH JW BC

5/9/70 Hole In The Compass, Lives And Ladies, Bad News. Poli Palmer (k, vib) r King. 10/8/70 PH JW BC

17/7/71 Save Some For Thee†, Burning Bridges†, In My Own Time†, Seasons†. Weider out. 2/7/71 T1 JM JWH

22/5/73 Buffet Tea†, Boom Bang†, Check Out†. Chapman, Whitney, Townsend, Jim Cregan (bg), Tony Ashton (k). 8/5/73 LH1 JW U ● SFPS061 † on ○ BBC Radio Vol 1 & 2 HUX057 & 060

The Family Cat

4/10/89 Remember What It Is That You Love, Octopus Jr, From The City To The Sea, Sandbag Your Heart. Kev (d), John (b), Tim (g), Jelb (g), Fred (gv). 10/9/89 MV3 DG DD

9/7/90 With A War, Gameshow, Fearless, Streamroller. 26/6/90 MV5 MC RPF 'It is 10.25pm & England have just won v Belgium. We are all jumping up and down and shouting a lot. The last note was mixed and lo and behold England scored! I think they were waiting for us to finish. Three of the songs we've done today were written specially for this session. But honestly, what a night to be trying to concentrate on songs, when England are taking so long to score. Love from The Family Cat.' Note to Peel on sheet

20/3/92 Too Many Late Nights, Furthest From The Sun, Prog One, River Of Diamonds. 30/1/92 MV4 DG NG&DMC

Famous Jug Band

11/6/69 Going To Germany, Common Or Garden Mystery, Black Is The Colour, I Don't Need No Orchestra. Pete Berryman (gv), Henry 'the Eighth' Bartlett (jug, v), Jill Johnson (v), Wizz Jones (gv). 29/5/69 PS PR U

Fantasmagroover

10/3/99 Purple, Butch Reads A Pamphlet, Fix, Give Em An Inch. Babbsy (gv), John (b), Mikey (d). 10/1/99 MV3 ME~

2/5/00 I Killed Myself Today, The Wolf, Closing Down Sale At The Gun Factory, Neptune Valley Hard On. Babbsy, John, George Double (d, bck), Will Bersey (clo-1). 2/2/00 MV4 MR JSM

The Farm

27/4/83 Memories, No Man's Land, Information Man. Peter Hooton (lv), Phil Stevenson (b), Steve Grimes (g), Andy McVann (d), George Maher (tp), Tony Evans (tp), Joe Musker (perc). 17/4/83 MV4 DG MC

19/3/84 Hearts And Minds, Too Late, Somewhere, Same Old Story. Hooton, Grimes, McVann, Maher, John Melvin (g, bck), John Owens (b, p-3), Joey Musker (perc). 28/2/84 MV5 MRD TdB

9/12/85 Some People, Sign Of The Cross, Little Ol' Wine Drinking Me, Heart Of The Nation. Hooton, Grimes, McVann, Maher, Melvin, Carl Hunter (b), Steve Levy (sx), Tony Evans (tb). 26/11/85 MV5 PWL MS&MR

20/8/86 Worn Out Sayings, Power Over Me, Wearing That Smile, The Moroccan. Keith Mullin (g, bck) r Melvin. 10/8/86 U DG ME&FK

24/5/90 Groovy Train, Very Emotional (Ballad To Ray Toohey), I Don't Know, Family Of Man. Hooton, Grimes, Hunter, Mullin, Roy Boulter (d), Ben Leach (k). 6/5/90 MV3 DG ME

31/8/91 Mind, Smile, Love See No Colour, News International. & Rebecca Lee White (bck). 21/7/91 MV3 MR~

The Farmer's Boys

14/9/82 With These Hands I Built The World, Soft Drink, The Country Line, Drinking And Dressing Up, Description Of The River Waveney At Wortwell. Billed as 'Kid

Brian and his Farmer's Boys': Frog (dm), Stan (gk), Baz (lv, k), Mark (b) & Kid Brian (introductions). 6/9/82 U TW MC Debut session was for Jensen April 82

13/7/83 The Way You Made Me Cry, Matter Of Fact, Probably One Of The Best Investments I Ever Made, I Don't Know Why I Don't Like All My Friends. 9/7/83 MV4 DG MC

27/8/84 Sport For All, Walk About, All Of A Sudden, Heartache. 14/8/84 MV5 JWI TdB&PS

Fat Grapple

5/7/73 Happy In The Lord, The Opener, The Whaling Song. Nick Liddell (b), Lionel Gibson (lg), Steve Lee Bowers (d), John Pryor (p, vi), John Saxby (perc, v), Phil Welton (gv). 2/7/73 LH1 BA U Debut session was for Pete Drummond July 72

Fat Mattress

25/10/69 Naturally, Mr Moonshine, Magic Forest, Happy My Love. Noel Redding (lg, bck), Neil Lander (lv), Eric Dillon (d), Jimmy Leverton (bv). 6/10/69 PS JW TW Recorded session for DLT 7 days later, TX 6 days before Peel's

The Fatima Mansions

28/3/89 The Day I Lost Everything, Only Losers Take The Bus, The Door To Door Inspector, What. Billed as Cathal Coughlan (v, k) and the Fatima Mansions: Nick Allum (d), Seanathan O'Crocain (b), Andreas O'Gruama (g), Zac Woolhouse (k). 19/3/89 MV4 DG MA

19/4/90 Mr Baby, It Will Be Cold, Blues For Ceausescu, Broken Radio No 1. Hugh Bunker (b) r O'Crocain & Nick Bunker (k-3). 25/3/90 MV3 DG ME

Faust

5/6/73 Just A Second / Ask The Cleaning Woman She Knows The Subtitle / Foam Rubber. Werner Diermayer (d), Hans-Joachim Irmler (k), Jean-Herve Peron (b), Rudolf Sosna (g), Gunther Wusthoss (sx). Recorded in Germany, date & studio U

12/1/99 What Really Happenend To Faust Part I And II, Part 3. Diermayer, Irmler, Michael Stoll (b, db, fl), Steven Wray Cobdell (g), Lars Paukstat (iron percussion, zither). 29/10/98 MV3 TdB PN

Charlie Feathers, Warren Smith, Jack Scott, Buddy Knox and the Roger James Group

1/7/77 Ubangi Stomp, What In The World's Came Over You, Hula Love, Too Much Alike, Leroy's Back In Jail Again, Rock 'n' Roll Ruby, Bottle To The Baby, Goodbye Baby Bye Bye, Rock Your Little Baby, Blue Suede Shoes. Warren Smith (lv-1,6,10), Jack Scott (lv-2,5,8), Buddy Knox (lv-3,9), Charlie Feathers (lv-4,7) & the Roger James Group. 3/5/77 U DP&MB U

Andy Fernbach

10/9/69 Mystic Meaning, Woman Goes From Man To Man, I Feel Like Starting Again, If You Miss Your Connection. Andy Fernbach (slg, v), Dave Fernbach, Ned Bale. 27/8/69 S2 PR U

Fflaps

4/4/88 Pethau Piws, Llosg Llech, Y Dyn Blin, Blodyn Tatws. Ann Matthews (gv), Alan Holmes (vi, b), Johnny Evans (d). 13/3/88 MV4 DG ME

1/8/90 Malltod, Rhowch Hi I'r Belgwyr, Hyll Eto, Arwyr Duwiol. 19/6/90 MV3 DG ME

Fiasco

4/9/93 11th Of November, Miserable Man, You Trying To Make Me Feel Bad, Battlefield. John Jennings (d), Robbie Fay (b), Russ Taylor (g), Ian Finney (g, bck), David Pichilingi (v). 1/8/93 MV4 TdB GT

The Fieldmice

23/4/90 Anoint, Sundial, Fresh Surroundings, By Degrees. Michael Hiscock (b), Bobby Wratten (gv, dm), Harvey Williams (g), Ian Catt (k). 1/4/90 MV3 DG ME

Filler

10/11/90 First Out, Trapped Then Killed, Touched, Hurts To Say. Dave Skeen (dv), Jonathan Barry (bv), Richard Bramley (g). 4/11/90 MV3 DG ME&AA

Filthkick

18/9/89 Lynching Party / Bar Room Brawl / A A... (sheet possibly incomplete), Between The Lines / Meat Rack, The Harder You Fall / Drowning In Affluence. Ben (d), Jim (b), Mark (g), Leggo (v). 15/8/89 MV3 DG MR

17/9/90 Rise / Gein Within / Just Another Word, Mondo Delerium / Cabin Fever, Mind Games / Kill Kill Kill, This Void Of Ignorance, Brain Fry. Daz (d), Pete (b), Steve (g), Leggo. 7/8/90 MV5 MR MR

Fingerprintz

5/12/78 Sean's New Shoes (instrumental), Finger Prince, Nervz, Who's Your Friend, Sync Unit. Step Ling (lv), Jinne O'Neill (rg), Cha Burnz (lg), Kenny Dalglish (b), Bob Shilling (d). 28/11/78 MV4 MR~

Fini Tribe

22/5/85 Goose Duplicates, An Evening With Clavichords, We're Interested, Splash Care. Simon McGlynn (d), Philip Pinsky (b), John Vick (k), Andy McGregor (g), David Millar (gv), Chris Connelly (v). 12/5/85 MV5 DG ME

22/2/89 Electrolux, Disturb, Swans. Vick, Pinsky, Millar. 12/2/89 MV5 DG ME

5/3/98 Mind My Makeup, The Electrician, Frantic, Waltzer, Theme. Millar, Pinsky, Niroshini Phambar (p, vi, mel), Chris Ross (d), Katie Morrison (v). Live from MV4 MR~

The Fire

13/3/84 Stop, Dancing And Laughing, Mothers And Sons, Jimmy's Grin (Song To This Port). David Wibberley (g, lv), Jamie Dickie (b), Ian Bickle (d), Jill McCarthy (clo-3), David Dickie (k). 29/2/84 MV5 RP NG

Fire Engines

9/3/81 Untitled, Discord, Candy Skin (We Don't Need This) Fascist Groove Thang. David Henderson (gv), Russell Burn (d), Graham Main (b), Murray Slade (g). 23/2/81 LH1 TW DD

23/11/81 The Big Wrong Time, Young Tongues Need Taste, Qualitamatic, Produced To Seduce To. & Miti Adhikari (k-4). 14/11/81 MV4 DG MC&MA

Fire Party

31/10/89 Basis, How To, Are You On, Stray Bullet. Nicky Thomas (d), Kate Samworth (b), Natalie Avery (g), Amy Pickering (v, b-1). 17/10/89 MV5 DG MA

Firehose

22/6/88 She Paints Pictures, Choose Any Memory, Makin' The Freeway, Hear Me. Ed Crawford (gv), Mike Watt (b, bck), George Hurley (d). 12/6/88 U DG DD&CBM

Fireworks

22/9/83 Man Of The Times, Second Eleven, Shall We All Dance. Moose (v), Steve Norris (g), Dave Griffiths (b), Martin Watts (d). 12/9/83 MV4 JP DD

First Offence

16/3/91 Three Steps, A Brotherhood Of Man, Money, Drugs. Steven Harris (v), Ian Bent (cuts), Billy Spiby (k), Carl Adesile (prd, prg), Eric Powell (prg). 19/2/91 MV5 MR MR

Fitz Of Depression

20/5/95 She Wants To Know, Gotten Sly, Young & Free, Mask, See Me Hear Me. Mikey Dees (gv), Craig Becker (d), Brian Sparhawk (b). 23/4/95 MV3 ME JLC

Patrik Fitzgerald

15/2/78 Don't Tell Me Because I'm Young, Bingo Crowd, Little Dippers, Safety Pin Stuck In My Heart, Back Street Boys. Patrik Fitzgerald (gv). 8/2/78 MV4 MB NG

31/7/78 No Fun Football, Little Fishes, A Mixed Kid, The Sound Of My Street, Jarvis. 19/7/78 MV4 BS NG

17/4/79 Suicidal Wreck, Improve Myself, Tonight, All The Splattered Children, Dance Music / Late Night. 10/4/79 MV6 TVD MR

Five Hand Reel

25/11/75 Campbell's Farewell To Red Castle / The Duchess Of Perth / The Lads Of Mull, Slieve Gallion Braes, Wee Wee German Lairdie. U 28/10/75 MV4 TW BAI

24/9/76 Kempey's, When A Man's In Love (& others unknown, PasB damaged). 2/9/76 MV4 U U

3/6/77 A Man's A Man For All That, Carrick Fergus, P Stands For Paddy, Pinch Of Snuff. Dave Tulloch (d), Barry Lyons (b), Tom Hickland (vi, v-3), Dick Gaughan (g, v, solo v-4), Bobby Eaglesham (dul, g, v-1,2). 25/5/77 MV4 MB NG

31/3/78 The Trooper And The Maid, Jackson And Jane, My Love Is Like A Red Red Rose. 22/3/78 MV4 DP NG

Fixit Kid

20/8/02 The Big Red Machine, For The 1st Time In 15 Yrs I Bought My Own, Fingermails. Lisa C. Justin Dean (gv), Mat Davies (bv), Alex Grant (d). 14/7/02 MV4 ME NK

The Flaming Lips

21/11/92 My Two Days As An Ambulance Driver (Jets Pt 2), Hit Me Like You Did The First Time, The Sun, Life On Mars. Wayne Coyne (gv), Ronald Jones (gv), Michael Ivins (b), Stephen Drozd (d, v, p) 13/10/92 MV4 MA PL

28/7/99 The Switch That Turns Off The Universe, We Can't Predict The Future, It Remained Unrealizable. Jones out. 8/6/99 MV4 MR JHT

The Flaming Stars

8/7/95 Kiss Tomorrow Goodbye, Like Trash, The Face On The Bar Room Floor, Broken Heart, Tubs Twist. Paul Dempsey (b), Joe Whitney (d), Max Decharne (v, k), Johnny Johnson (g, hca), Mark Hosking (g). 15/6/95 MV4 U U

20/4/96 Forget My Name, Downhill Without Brakes, Back Of My Mind, 3am On The Bar Room Floor, Who's Out There. Huck Whitney (g) r Johnson. 9/4/96 MV4 MR KR

17/10/96 Ten Feet Tall, Spaghetti Junction, Bury My Heart At Pier 13, Down To You. Live from MCR3 LR PCG

19/3/97 Bury My Heart At Pier 13, Just Too Bad, Sweet Smell Of Success, London After Midnight. 2/3/97 MV4 U U

21/10/97 Better Than That, Blood Money, Street That Never Closes, New Hope For The Dead. 14/9/97 MV4 ME

28/7/98 Only Tonight, Running Out Of Time, Sing Sing, Just How It Feels. 7/6/98 MV4 ME GT

20/7/99 Lit Up Like A Christmas Tree, Breaking Down, What Do I Get, Coffined & Grave Digger Jones, The Last Picture Show. 1/6/99 MV4 MR MPK

19/2/02 Cash 22, Over And Done, Action Crime & Vision, Killer In The Rain. 13/1/02 MV4 ME GYW

Flatback 4

2/7/94 I Would, Oven Love, S F U, Ermagit, Love Potion. Jonathon Barrett (d), Darren Jones (g), Adam Rockingham (v). 17/5/94 MV4 MR RPF

The Flatbackers

21/8/80 Gary, Never Had Nuffin', I Know, Pumping Iron. Julie Usher (lg, lv-1), Lucy Dray (b, lv-2,3,4), Lynne Monk (d, percv, handclaps, chanting). 12/8/80 MV4 DG MR

The Flatmates

24/9/86 Tell Me Why, Love Cuts, Happy All The Time, Thinking Of You. Sarah Fletcher (bck, b), Debbie Haynes (lv), Martin Whitehead (g), Rocker (d, bck, sty). 14/9/86 U DG ME

16/9/87 You're Gonna Cry Too, Barbella Blue, Sportscar Girl, Shimmer. Joel O' Beirne (d) r Rocker. 6/9/87 U DG SC&JB

Fleece

27/1/99 Leanne, Heroes, The Man From Mars, A Letter To The Pope. James Mayor (gkv), Marcus Nunn (g), Adrian Blyth (d), Miles Hubbard (b), Neil Hobbs (k). 10/11/98 MV4 MR~

Peter Green's Fleetwood Mac

12/11/67 Long Grey Mare, Baby Please Set A Date, Looking For Somebody, I Believe My Time Ain't Long, Got To Move. Peter Green (lgv), Jeremy Spencer (gv), Mick Fleetwood (b), John McVie (b). 7/11/67 MV4 BP PR

21/1/68 Can't Hold Out, Blue Coat Man, Sweet Little Angel, The Stroller, Bee-I-Bicky-Bop Blue Jean Honey Babe Meets High School Hound Dog Hot Rod Man (& Where You Belong, Don't Be Cruel, The Sun Is Shining, The World Keeps Turning, 24/3/68). & guest Eddie Boyd (v-2,4,6). 16/1/68 AO2 BA DT

17/4/68 How Blue Can You Get?, My Baby Is Sweet, Long Grey Mare, Buzz Me, I'm So Lonesome And Blue. 16/4/68 AO2 DK U

2/6/68 That Ain't It, Mean Mistrusting Mama, Psychedelic Send-Up Number, Dead Shrimp Blues (& Sheila, 7/7/68). 27/5/68 PC1 BA U Billed as just Fleetwood Mac from now on

1/9/68 A Mind Of My Own, I Have To Laugh, You're The One, Preachin' The Blues (& You Need Love, A Talk With You, Bo Diddley, Wine Whisky Women, 13/10/68; & Crutch And Lean, Crazy For My Baby, 24/11/68). Danny Kirwan (lg) joins; & guest Christine Perfect (v). 27/8/68 PC1 BA AH

16/3/69 You'll Never Know What You're Missing Until You Try, Blues With A Feeling, Heavenly, I Can't Believe You Wanna Leave (& Tallahassie Lassie, Early Morning Come, 11/5/69). 10/3/69 PH BA PR

23/5/70 Sandy Mary, World In Harmony, Tiger, Only You, Leaving Her Blues. & Nick Pickett (guest). 27/4/70 PH JW TW

22/8/70 Buddy's Song, When Will I Be Loved, Jenny Lee, When I See My Baby, Honey Hash. Green out. 7/7/70 MV4 JW BC

23/1/71 Start Again, Teenage Darling, Preaching, Get Like You Used To Be (& Dragonfly, 27/3/71). Christine McVie (kv) joins. 5/1/71 MV4 U BC

Flesh for Lulu

6/9/82 Dancer, Walk Tired, Missionary, Spy In Your Mind. James Mitchell (d), Philip Ames (b, bck), Mark Ambler (k), Nick Marsh (gv). 21/8/82 MV4 DG MR

Flinch

18/11/94 I Hope, Ashtray, Two Minds, Days, Wheel. Grog Prebble (bv), Paul Smith (g), Dominic Luckman (d). 16/10/94 MV3 ME JB

Flipper

3/9/93 We're Not Crazy, Way Of The World, Telephone, Someday. Bruce Loose (v), John (b), Steve Depace (d), Ted (g). 15/8/93 MV3 ME JLO

Float Up CP

26/9/84 Pray For This, Sexy Bushes, You Make Me Wet. Sarah Sarbandi (vla), Sean Oliver (bg), Neneh Cherry (v), Gareth Sager (pg, cl), Bruce Smith (d), Oliver Moore (sx). 19/9/84 MV5 RP MPK Previous session for Jensen Dec 83

A Flock of Seagulls

12/5/81 Messages (From The Rings Of Saturn), Talking (It's Not Me Talking), I Ran, Committed. Mike Score (sy, g, lv), Paul Reynolds (g), Frank Maudsley (b, bck), Ali Score (d). 6/5/81 LH1 CL NG

Florists

25/7/83 Top Models Know, Our Much Loved Daughter, Julia, The Longest Hour. Sue Prior (v), Lawrence Diagram (g), Gary Terrell (b), Dick Harrison (perc), Andy Diagram (tp), Michael Pollard (d). 13/7/83 MV4 RP NG&EL

Flossie & The Unicorns

8/6/99 Hurricane, You Don't Own Me, Thundercloud, Queen Bee. Miss Pussycat (bk, perc), Stinger, Sparky Mittens (4), Litiffa (4), Mr Quintron (ov). 18/4/99 MV5 DD SA

The Flowers

12/9/79 Living Doll, Tunnels, The Deep End Dance, Tear Along. Hill-ray (v), Andy Copland (g), Fraser Sutherland (b), Simon Best (d). 28/8/79 MV4 BS MR

Fluke

25/11/90 Thumper†, Taxi†, Jig†, Our Definition Of Jazz†. Jonathan Fugler (v), Michael Tournier & Mike Bryant (k, smp, prg). 18/11/90 MV3 DG ME&FK

26/1/92 The Bells†, Top Of The World, The Allotment Of Blighty†, The Timekeeper†. 10/12/91 MV4 MR JB † on ○ The Peel Sessions SFMCD215

19/12/02 Switch / Twitch, Hang Tough Vs Wild Oscar / Snapshot. 8/12/02 OS

The Flying Pickets

6/4/83 Get Off My Cloud, Psycho Killer, Disco Down, Factory. Ken Gregson, Red Stripe, Rick Lloyd, Gareth Williams, Brian Hibard, David Brett (all v). 30/3/83 MV4 RP TdB At this point, regular Peel listeners might expect to find a session by The Flying Creamshots. Mysteriously, I can find no trace of one; although Billy Bragg once reported to Peel he'd just missed them in San Francisco

Flying Saucer Attack

21/5/94 Always, Feedback Song Demo, Popol Vuh III, Light In The Evening, Feedback Song. Dave Pearce (v), Rachel Brook, perc, b). OS

5/4/96 Heartbeat, Guitar Blues, Jeff Mills Blues, I Can Take You To The Sun, Resolution Island. Brook, Pearce, Rocker (see Flatmates), Dave Mercer, Kurt Jurgens. 1/3/96 OS

The Flys

23/3/78 New Hearts, Fun City, We Don't Mind The Rave, Living In The Sticks. Dave Freeman (lg), Neil O'Connor (rgv), Joe Hughes (b), Pete King (d). 15/3/78 MV4 DP MR

21/11/78 Love And A Molotov Cocktail, Name Dropping, I Don't Know, Waikiki Beach Refugees. 14/11/78 MV4 MR MR

8/10/79 Let's Drive, Energy Boy, Frenzy Is 23, I'll Survive. Graham Deakin (d) r King. 18/9/79 MV4 JS MR

Fokkewolf

11/8/99 Time To Kill, Porno Rocker (No Time For Love), Take Me Down For A Little While, Fool If Ya Think It's Over. Daz Smith (bv), Nick Clark (h, hca), Paul Earth (d). 13/6/99 U ME~

The Folk Devils

4/4/84 Where The Buffalo Roam, Beautiful Monster, Tight Sleep, What's That Smell? Kris Jozajtis (g, bck), Al Cole (d), Ian Lowery (v), Mark Whiteley (b, bck). 20/3/84 MV5 MRD TdB

17/9/84 Big Car Big Car, Wail, Broken Head, Ink Runs Dry. 5/9/84 MV5 RP NG

8/7/85 This Traitor Hand, It Drags On, Under The Bridge, Dead Heat. 18/6/85 MV5 JWI MR

Folk Implosion

22/4/97 That's The Trick, Blossom, Checking In, Barricade. John Davis, Lou Barlow, Gary Held. 6/4/97 MV4 ME GT

Fonn

22/12/99 No Pulse, Cone, Rogue (& Spoke§, Mollify§). Dave Cawley (el), Stuart Horgan (g, ag), Martin Granger (g, ag), Andrew Major (prg, vibrations), James McKechan (b, ag, g), Gavin McMillan (d, perc). 10/10/99 MV4 U U § recorded 17/10/99 at the Shed, Edenbridge, Kent

Wayne Fontana

24/4/73 The Game Of Love, Um Um Um Um Um Um, Pamela Pamela. 2/4/73 T1 JW U Last of dozens of pop sessions

Force Fed

18/4/90 Full Up, Loaded, Claustrophobia, Can't Get Out. Nigel Clark (d), Kalvin Piper (b), Nick Clark (g), Jamie Sims (v). 18/3/90 MV3 DG MR

2/2/91 I Don't Know, Burn My Back, Fast Forward, One Million Miles. N & N Clark, Neil Pitfield, Mick Knowlton (v). 8/1/91 MV5 MR

Foreheads in a Fishtank

24/8/91 British Telecom, Happy Shopper, Sex And Drugs And, Sylvester's Mother. Adrian Leaman (d), Gavin Jones (b), Jeff Leahy (gv), Jez Watts (k), Matt Brewster (k). 7/7/91 MV3 DG MFA&PRB

27/3/93 Rum, Onions, Bond, Pussy. & Julian Beeston (prg). 16/1/93 MV4 TD JLC

Forest

26/3/69 A Glade Somewhere, Pools Of Memory, Reflecting In The Sea, Mirror Of Life, Smoke, Fading Light. Martin Welham (gv, hca), Adrian Welham (gv, mand), Derek Allenby (mand, hca, wh, v). 18/3/69 S1 PR U Failed by audition panel: 'cacophony' 'appalling sound, raggy and amateur' 'messy, uninspiring, distasteful'

15/11/69 Gipsy Girl And Ramble Away, Autumn Childhood, Love's Memory Gone, Mirror Of Life. 16/9/69 MV4 JW U This 2nd trial broadcast passed by panel

10/10/70 Hares On The Mountain, Graveyard, Hermit / Guardian Angel, Hawk The Hawker (& Do Not Walk In The Rain, 2/1/71). 28/9/70 PH JW U

A Formal Sigh

10/9/81 Looking At Walls, Bleak Intrusion, Ev Rev, Ad Nauseam. Flo Sullivan (v), Greg Milton (gb), Mark Peters (b), Roger Sinek (d), Robin Surtees (g). 5/9/81 MV4 DG MR

Formerly Fat Harry

23/5/70 Honky Tonk Angel, Untitled, Seuble. Phil Greenberg (gv), Gary Peterson (gk), Bruce Barthol (b), Laurie Allan (d). 12/5/70 MV4 JW U

FortDax

25/8/04 Wolfcub, For Chou Chou Debussy, Horizon 7 7, A Beverly Mythic. Darren Durham (e). OS

The Forty Fives

15/10/03 Trying To Get Next To You, Go Ahead And Shout Now, Come On Now Love Me, Get Out. Bryan Malone (gv), Adam Renshaw (d), Mark McMurthy (b), Trey Tidwell (k). 28/9/03 MV4 SA JHT

29/9/04 Junk Food Heaven, The American Ruse, Can't Keep Up With Myself, Fast Eddie. 8/9/04 MV4 SA JSM

Chris Foster

29/6/77 The Golden Glove, Lady Maisry, William Taylor, The Famous Flower Of Serving Men, Unicorns. Chris Foster (gv). 22/6/77 MV4 U NG

Fotheringay

25/4/70 Banks Of The Nile, Ned, The Sea, Nothing More (& The Way I Feel, 4/7/70). Sandy Denny (vgp), Trevor Lucas (g), Gerry Conway (d), Jerry Donahue (g), Pat Donaldson (b). 13/4/70 PH JW U First session was for what became first edition of Folk On One, 5/4/70

Fotomoto

21/7/04 Edmund, La Planet De Gopak, Le Sport La Musique, Kes Buits Do Georgiennes. Sergey Sergeyex (g), Anton Singurov (k), Olya Volodina (v), Alex Ivanov (cmp). 16/6/04 MV4 NF JSM

The Foundations

14/1/68 A Whole New Thing, Back On My Feet Again, Help Me, 96 Tears. Peter McGrath, Alan Warner, Pat Burke, Tim Harris, Eric Allendale, Clem Vurtis, Tony Gomes, Mike Elliott. 8/1/68 PC1 BA U

The Four Brothers

26/9/88 Rugare, Uchandifunga, Vimbayi, Pahukama. Marshall Munhumumwe (d, lv), Never Mutare (b, bck), Frank Sibanda (g, bck), Aleck Chipaika (g, bck). 11/9/88 HP DG U ● SFPS070. First session – playing Serevende, Rudo Chete, Rudo Imoto, Rumbizayi – but only with three-brother line-up (Chipiaka delayed in Ethiopia), was 2 weeks earlier on Andy Kershaw, repeated by Peel 4/5/89

5/6/89 Rudo Chete, Pasi Pano Pane Zvidzo, Wakazvarwa Seyi, Ngatipindukewo. 23/5/89 MV3 DG MR

9/12/94 Wachiveiko, Tsvaga Hunhu, Takabua Neko, Mberko Yakaramba. Robrum Chauraya (rg) r Chipaika. 27/10/94 U NG~

28/9/00 Vamwene, Ndibvubamire, Regai Nditaure, Ndateterera. Mutare, Sibanda, Chapaika, Robium Chauraya (rg), Antonio Makosa (lv), Revison Chakanyuka (d). 6/9/00 MV4 SA~

Four Tet

14/10/03 She Moves She, All The Chimers, Tangle, Eat Your Own Ears. Kieron Hebden (e). 24/9/03 MV4 SA JHT

Foyer Des Artes

17/11/86 Frauen In Frieden Und Freiheit, Konnten Bienen Fliegen, Einhaus Aus Den Knochen Von Cary Grant, Schimmliges Brot. Gerd Pasemann (g), Max Goldt (v), Terry Edwards (sx, k), Frog (b), Simon Charterton (d). 12/10/86 U DG ME&SC

Frames

2/3/81 The Shock Of The New, Play It By Fear, La Chanson Ironique, Stingray. Sue Jonas (v), Nick Radford (g), Stephen Wood (d), Mike Marshfield (b). 24/2/81 LH1 DG MR

The Frank & Walters

8/12/91 Fashion Crisis In New York, Happy Busman, The World Carries On. Paul Linehan (lv, b), Ashley Keating (d), Niall Lineman (g). 3/11/91 MV3 DG DG&JLC Previous session for Goodier Sept 91

The Frank Chickens

30/5/83 Tokyo Boogie, Sake Ballad, We Are Ninjas, Woman In Harbour, UFO. Kazuko Hohki, Kazumi Taguchi. 16/5/83 MV4 TW DD

5/10/83 Fujiyama Mama, Night Of Alaska, Monster, Life Theatre, Shellfish Bamboo. with David Toop & Steve Beresford (k, dm). 28/9/83 MV4 DG AP

3/4/84 We Are Ninja, Blue Canary, Dream Theatre, Yellow Toast. & Beresford only. 14/3/84 MV5 RP NG

12/3/85 China Night, Amy Rang, Japanese Rumba, Sake Ballad, Eightman. & Elisabeth Perry (vi), Alexander Balenescu (vla), Lol Coxhill (sx). 5/3/85 MV5 MRD MR

18/8/86 Two Little Ladies, We Say You Say, Japanese Girls, Sacred Marriage, Chicken Ondo. Four piece. 5/8/86 U DG MR&MS

10/7/89 Jackie Chan, Want To See You Again, Carmen 77, Do The Karaoke. Kazuko, Atsuko Kamara (v), Hood, Adams, Cunliffe, Jah Wobble (b), David Harrow (sy, smp), Clive Bell (acc, fl, wh). 25/6/89 MV3 DG MC&SA

Jackson C Frank

9/10/68 Blues Run The Game, Jimmy Clay, Just Like Anything, Carnival, You Never Wanted Me. U 9/10/68 U PC U

Frankfurter

5/5/87 Inbred Zombies, Gimme Donuts, Hot Babes, We're Gonna Eat / John Peel. Mean Tom (d, gv), Angus Tomahawk (bv), Nick Schozza (v), RJ Justice (v). 16/4/87 U DG ME&FK

Frankie Goes to Hollywood

2/12/82 Two Tribes, The World Is My Oyster, Krisco Kisses, Disneyland. Holly Johnson (v), Paul Rutherford (v), Brian Nash (g), Peter Gill (d), Mark O'Toole (b). 24/11/82 U AP U

19/12/83 Junk Funk (Get On Down), The Other Side Of Midnight, The Power Of Love, Get It On. & Andy Richards (k). 3/12/83 MV4 DG MC

The Frantic Elevators

3/3/81 Ding Dong, Searching For The Only One, Hunchback Of Notre Dame, I Am The Man, Production Prevention. Neil Smith (g), Mick Hucknall (v), Brian Turner (b), Kevin Williams (d). 25/2/81 LH1 DG NG

30/9/81 And I Don't Care (Nobody Stays Here), After Hanging Around, What To Do?, I'm Not To See Her, Ice Cream And Wafers. 19/9/81 MV4 DG MR

Andy Fraser Band

17/4/75 Love Train, Bring It On Home, Ain't Gonna Worry, Don't Hide Your Love. Andy Fraser (bv), Nick Judd (elp), Kim Turner (d). 10/4/75 MV4 PR BAI

Freaks

20/3/71 Come Out Into The Open, Music For Rawlinson End, Rawlinson End, Bad Blood, Watcher. Viv Stanshall (v, tp), Neil Innes (k), Andy Roberts (g), Keith Moon (d), Denis Cowan (b), Bubs White (g), Shamsi Sarumi (cga), Gaspar Lawal (bgo). 2/3/71 MV4 JW BC

Freddy Fresh

23/2/99 DJ set live from Y4 U

20/11/03 Freddy Fresh In The Mix OS

Free

21/7/68 Waiting On You†, Walk In My Shadow, Moonshine, Free Me. Paul Rodgers (v, hca), Paul Kossoff (g), Andy Fraser (bv), Simon Kirke (d). 15/7/68 PC1 BA PR

23/3/69 I'm A Mover†, Song Of Yesterday†, Over The Green Hills†, Broad Daylight†. 17/3/69 PH BA AH&BC

13/12/69 Trouble On Double Time†, Mr Big, I'll Be Creepin'†, Mouthful Of Grass† (& Woman, 7/3/70). 8/12/69 PH JW TW † on ○ Free Live At The BBC Universal/Island

Freefall

4/4/92 Shine, Our Eyes, Green And Blue, Love In Idleness. Sean Shaw (d), Charles Hankers (bv), Andrew Abram (g, bck), Stuart Johnson (g). 9/2/92 MV3 DG ME&AD

Freeze

20/11/80 Quality Burning, And Then We Danced, Sunday, Lullaby In Black. Gordon Sharp (v), David Clancey (gk), Keith Grant (b), Graeme Radin (d). 27/10/80 MV4 TW TdB&NG

19/8/81 Building On Holes, From The Bizarre, Location. Sharp, Clancy, Neil Braidwood (k), Mike Moran (b). 12/8/81 MV4 CL NG

Freeze Frame

31/3/83 Fox Hole, Personal Tough, Your Voice, Today Tomorrow. Ronnie Stone (k, d, gv), Steve Byrne (v). 26/3/83 MV4 DG MR

Freiwillige Selbstkontrolle (aka FSK)

6/8/85 A Swingin' Safari†, Lieber Ein Glas Zuviel, Drunk, Trink Wie Ein Tier. Wilfred Petzi (tb, g, percv), Thomas Meinecke (cnt, g, percv), Justin Hoffman (elp, g, xyl, v), Michaela Melian (b, mel, v). 4/8/85 MV5 DG ME ● on Last Orders ZickZack ZZ1066 (German release) † on ● Continental Breakfast Ediesta CALC LP 16

13/8/86 Am Tafelberg Von Kapstadt, I Wish I Could Sprechen Sie Deutsch, Die Musik Findet Immer Nach Haus, Dr Arnold Fanck. 3/8/86 U DG MR ○ SFMCD204

24/6/87 Komm Gib Mir Deine Hand, Girl, Birthday, Don't Pass Me By. 21/6/87 U DG MR&MC ○ SFMCD204

19/4/88 In Lauterbach, Stalinbar Jodler, Die Englischen Frauleins, Cannonball Yodel. 10/4/88 U DG ME&JBN

19/1/92 Black Market, Ohne Kapitalisten Geht Es Besser, Horsti Schmandhoff, Ostblockgirl 91. Carl Oesterhelt (d) joins. 3/12/91 MV4 JB JB&MR

10/10/92 Under The Double Eagle, Franz Josef Strauss, Shiner Song, Hobo Zwiefacher. 8/10/92 Berlin

7/12/04 Fragen Der Philosophie, Im Rhythmus Der Zeit, Move Ahead, Faire Le Chicken. 10/11/04 MV4 JHT ME

The French

20/8/03 Crispy Ambulance John Peel Jingle, The English Head, The Protons And The Neutrons, When She Leaves Me, Punk Rocks Going To Die. Darren Hayman (v, uk, g, k), John Morrison (b, Moog), John Lee (v, d, mel). 3/7/03 MV3 MA GYW

18/8/04 TV Themes covers session: Theme From Hill Street Blues, Theme From Big John Little John, Crocket's Theme, Maybe Tomorrow. 29/7/04 MV4 GYW JSM

Fripp & Eno

18/12/73 Heavenly Music Corporation, Swastika Girls. Robert Fripp (g, el), Brian Eno (sy, el, mx) U PRIV The session that was broadcast backwards (see p.81)

Fred Frith

5/12/74 Please Give It Back, My Need Is Greater Than Yours, Noise Carruthers Pure Bloody Noise, In Which Case The Anxiety, Narrow Road. Fred Frith (g, vi), Anthony Moore (k), Dagmar Krause (v). 2/12/74 MV4 TW U

Front 242

23/7/86 No Shuffle, Funkadhafi, Don't Crash, Body To Body. R23 (dv), Patrick Coornys (k), Jean Luc de Meyer (v), Daniel B (k, fx). 13/7/86 MV5 DG ME&MA

The Fruit Machine

26/8/82 Take Your Medicine, I Don't Need No Doctor, Trials Of A Physical Jerk, I Think There's Something Wrong. Ludi Andrews (v), Michelle Fagan (v), David Harkins (v), Robbie Harris (b), Chris Kant (g), Ian Fraser (d) & Chicken Supremes (bck-1). 2/8/82 MV4 TW DD

Fuck

25/6/97 Shotgun Hours, Lil Hilda, Serpent, To My Girl, Thoroughfare. Geoff Soule, Kyle Statham, Timothy Prudhomme, Ted Ellison. 1/6/97 MV4 TdB SBR Session booked mainly, so Peel said, he could hear the Radio 1 Breakfast Show announce 'and later tonight on Radio 1, John Peel with Fuck in session'

30/9/98 Dieses Jahr, Whistlers Dream Date, Don't You Fret, Flapper, Panties Off, For Lori. 11/8/98 MV4 TdB GT

7/1/04 George W Hitler, No One Like You, 91 Dodge Van, Guess What, Prone To Disease, Space Probe. 3/12/03 MV4 AR GT

Fudge Tunnel

21/5/90 Sweet Meat, Boston Baby, Bedcrumbs, Sex Mammoth. Adrian Parkin (d), Dave Ryley (b, bck), Alex Newport (gv), Fudge Bear (spiritual advisor). 22/4/90 MV3 DG ME

19/6/92 Ten Percent, Good Kicking, Tipper Gore, Stuck. Fudge Bear absent. 21/5/92 MV3 ME JB&ME

Fugazi

13/12/88 Waiting Room, Break In, Merchandise, Glueman. Guy Picciotto (v), Ian MacKaye (gv), Joe Lally (b), Brendan Canty (d). 11/12/88 HP DG ME

Fugees

14/10/94 I Shot The Sherrif (Fugees Live), Rebel Rapper, Hip Hop Music, Tranziator Jazz. Lauryn Hill (v), Neal Wyclef (v, elp, g), Prakazrel Michel (v), Jerry Duplesis (b), Leon Higgins (dj), Johnny Wise Lewis (d). 8/9/94 MV4 TdB SB

22/3/96 Haitian In England, Blame It On the Sun, Freestyle. Donald Guillaume (d) r Lewis; & Christopher Spider Boswell (v), Rudolph Dabady (v). 22/2/96 MV5 TdB SBR

Fumble

11/7/72 Take Good Care Of My Baby, Teddy Bear, Teenagers In Love, Breaking Up Is Hard To Do. Des Henly (glv), Sean Mayes (pv), Barry Pike (d), Mario Ferrari (bgv). 27/6/72 MV4 U BC

Fun Da Mental

6/11/92 Peace Love And Was, Sister India, Wrath Of The Blackman. Inderjit LS Matharu (tab, perc), Amir Ali (v), Haq Naqaz Qureshi (Dat Master General), Craig Miller (dig), Nick Page (b). 8/9/92 MV4 JB~ RJ

7/5/93 Front Line, Tribal Revolution, Country Man. Propa Gandi (operator), Goldfinger (tab, perc, v), Bad-Sha Lallaman (v), Count Dubulah (b), Mojo Love (dig). 6/4/93 MV4 MR~ AA

16/7/94 Justice Or Just Defy, The Truth Commission, Mr Bubbleman. Dave Watts (aka impi-D), Aki Nawaz (aka Propaghandi), Aniruddha Das (aka Dr Das Bass) from Asian Dub Foundation Joe Cohen (sx-3). 3/7/94 MV3 ME KR

The Funboy Five

1/10/79 Life After Death, Compulsive Eater, Haircut Bob Dylan 66, Bleached Roots Of Surf. Robert Radhall (d), Bob Brimson (b), Mick Sinclair (gv), John McCrae (k). 19/9/79 MV4 BS NG

The Funkees

19/11/74 Abraka, Tule-Tule, Life, Dancing In The Nude. Tony Mallett, Danny Heibs, Jake N. Solo, Chyke Madu, Harry Agada, Sonny Akpan. 5/11/74 MV4 U U

14/7/75 Wine Festival, Lobo, Too Lay, Experience. Madu, Akpan, Solo, Heibs, Harry Mosco (gv, wooden gg). 1/7/75 MV4 TW U

Funky Ginger

15/8/88 Money Passion Vice, Jack The Knife, Slaughter House. Funky Ginger (perc, various), Dr Ross (gk), Sedley Francis (b), Doby DJ (sc). 26/7/88 MV4 MR~

Finbar and Eddie Furey

27/6/72 The Bonnet / Crowleys, Reynardine, Spanish Cloak / Dingle Regatta, Pretty Sara, Farewell To Tarwathy. 12/6/72 U U BC Several previous sessions for folk shows from 69

9/1/73 Jennifer Gentle, Bobly And Spikes Reel, Life Is Just That Way, Tattered Jack Walsh. 7/11/72 U U BC

14/5/74 Peggy And The Soldier, John Peel's Favourite Pipe Jig, Lament For Anacuion / Ace And Deuce Of Pipery, Sailor Come Home From The Sea, Crowley's Reel. 5/11/74 U U U

Furious Pig

18/8/80 Johnny's So Long, I Don't Like Your Face, The King Mother. Martin Kent, Stephen Kent, Jonathan (Cass) Davis, Dominic Weeks (all 'vocal stylists'). 11/8/80 MV4 DG DD

Further

6/10/95 Don't Know How Long, The Kids Are All Wrong, Victim Rock, J O 2, Lhs 79. Josh Schwartz, Brent Rademaker, Darren Rademaker. 28/9/95 MV4 NG JMK

Future Sound of London

18/9/92 Lifeforms, Expander, Papua New Guinea, Space Hippy. Garry Cobains & Brain Dougans (prg). 25/8/92 MV4 MR U

29/9/95 Spatial Freakout, My Kingdom, Yage. & Simon Snuff (g). 12/9/95 MV4 TdB JMK

26/10/96 Her Killing, My Kingdom, Max, Glass, Quadmar, Yage. Live by ISDN from OS

8/5/97 Tudor Oak, The Shining Path, Trying To Make Impermanent Things Permanent, Thinking About Thinking About Thinking, How To Be A Genuine Fake. Live by ISDN from OS

Futureheads

1/10/03 Le Garage, Aims, Robot, The City Is Here For You To Use. Barry Hyde (gv), David Craig (bv), Ross Millard (gv), David Hyde (dv). 11/9/03 MV4 MA JSM

The Fuzztones

5/6/85 She's Wicked, Epitaph For A Head, Bad News, Cinderella. Ira Elliott (bck, d), Michael Jay (bck, b), Rudi Protrudi (lvg, hca), Elan Portnoy (g), Deb O'Nair (bck, o). 26/5/85 MV5 DG ME

Gaffa

4/4/79 Baby Sitting, Anna Nervosa, White But Not Quite, The Rota, Gangster Tendencies. Wayne Evans (bv), John Maslen (gv), Clive Smith (g), Mick Barratt (d). 20/3/79 MV4 TVD MR

Gag

19/11/93 What Is The Reason, Ere Drij, Dance Party, Fruin, Topper, Dismissed Bill, I Understand Fully. Leighton Crook (dv), Rhodri Marsden (v, k, bsn), Stuart Cook (b), Kevin Burrows (g), Susannah Marsden (vi). 17/10/93 MV3 ME GT

Galaxie 500 ○

17/10/89 Flowers, Blue Thunder, Decomposing Trees, Don't Let Our Youth Go To Waste. Damon Krukowski (d), Naomi Yang (b), Dean Wareham (g, lv). 24/9/89 MV5 DG DD

4/11/90 Moonshot, Submission, When Will You Come Home, Final Day. 30/10/90 MV5 MWT AR&MWT Both sessions on ○ Peel Sessions 20–20–20 Records

Gallagher and Lyle

29/11/73 Shine A Light, Randolph And Me, Country Morning, Misspent Youth. Benny Gallagher (kv), Graham Lyle (gv), Jimmy Jewell, Bruce Rowlands. 19/11/73 LH1 BA U Seven previous sessions not for Peel 71/73

Rory Gallagher

8/2/73 Race The Breeze, Hands Off, Banker's Blues, Walk On Hot Coals. Rory Gallagher (gv), Rod De'ath (d), Lou Martin (k). 5/2/73 LH1 BA U Six previous sessions not for Peel, 71/72

Galliard

31/1/70 Frog Galliard, Wrapped Her In Ribbons, Near Dawn Breaking, Ask For Nothing. Richard Pannell (lg), Geoff Brown (rg), Andrew Abbott (b), Leslie Podraza (d), Lyle Jenkins (ts), David Caswell (tp). 12/1/70 U JW U

Gallon Drunk

1/9/91 Ruby, Some Fool's Mess, Drag 91, Two Wings Mambo. Max Decharne (d), Mike Delanian (b), James Johnson (g, o, v), Joe Byfield (maraccas). 14/7/91 MV3 DG DMC&JLB ○ SFMCD213

Lance Gambit Trio

27/8/97 D'You Know What I Mean?, Don't Go Away, Stay Young. Lance Gambit (p), Tommy Monk, Vera Stalk. 20/8/97 OS

Gang of Four ○

18/1/79 I Found That Essence Rare, Return The Gift, 5.45, At Home He's A Tourist. John King (lv, mel), Andy Gill (gv), Dave Allen (bv), Hugo Burnham (dv). 9/1/79 MV4 BS BAI

9/7/79 Natural's Not In It, Not Great Men, Ether, Guns Before Butter. 2/7/79 U U U

12/3/81 Paralysed, History's Bunk, To Hell With Poverty. 9/3/81 LH1 PS DD&MPK All sessions on ○ SFRCD107

Garlic

24/10/01 Waverly, Twenty One, Kathleen & Marie, Wide Open. Richard Cramp (g), Dominic Smith (b), Mike Wyzgowski (gv), Jo Hillyer (k), Marcus McCarroll (ps), Sandra Yee (dbv). 23/9/01 MV4 ME GYW

Laurent Garnier

18/8/95 The Thing, Soho, Untitled. Laurent Garnier (e). 1/6/95 OS See also Jeff Mills

Gasworks

22/1/69 These Things I Remember, Frankie Rose. John Brown (g), Michael Draper (g). 10/1/69 S1 JM U Failed by audition panel: 'a saddening waste of time'. Re-auditioned 4/9/70, failed again

13/9/73 We Three Kings, Don't Push Me, Share It Out, I Never Knew. & Brian Scott (b). 10/9/73 LH1 CB U

Dick Gaughan

13/2/73 The Gillie Mhor, Rattling Roaring Willie, Jock Of Hazeldean, Fine Flowers In The Valley. Dick Gaughan (agv). 29/1/73 T1 JW U

21/11/74 Farewell To Whiskey, Planxty Johnson, Farewell To Sicily, The Gypsy Laddie. 11/11/74 T1 JW U

2/8/77 Farewell To Whiskey, Freedom Come All Ye, Rashie Moor, Boys Of The Lough, My Donald. 27/7/77 MV4 MB NG

Gazelle

23/6/75 Tova, You Better Run, Looks Like We've Got Something Together. 6 musicians U U PRIV

Ron Geesin ○

3/7/68 Pretty Little Faces, Off The Left Cuff, Yesterday's Sheep, Very Nostalgic Piece, Devised Now. Ron Geesin (all instruments, vocals, tapes, effects). 20/6/68 S2 DK U Geesin also appeared live on Night Ride 14/8/68 as a poet, reading Wind Of Life, Railway Sleepers, and Whirls of Brain

9/4/69 The First Piece, John's Title, Three-quarter Inch Plywood Cover For Voice, Out Of Your Tune, Virtuoso Piece For Banjo. 1/4/69 S2 PR CL

11/10/69 Agitation In Anticipation Of Offspring Pts W, X & Y. 19/7/69 MV1 JW TW&MF ● On Top Gear LP BBC Records REC 52S

19/6/71 Twist And Knit For Two Guitars, Duet For Two And Street Market, Wrap A Keyboard Round A Plant, The Middle Of Whose Night, Duet For One String Banjo And Water Cistern. & Geoffrey Mitchell (counter tenor-4). OS

6/3/73 Geesin's 6/8ths, Roll 'Em Bowl 'Em, On Through Out Up, Mr Peugeot's Trot, Upon Composition. OS

19/9/74 For Sale, Where Daffodils Do Thrive, Two Part Beneficial Flop, Two Travel Moments, Paddling Steamers Across High Teacups, Nuts Bolts Several Guitars, Animal Autos, Evaporated Ballroom, Jagged Prance, Brain Twirl. 1 & 10 poems; 2–9 film soundtrack sequences. OS

20/2/76 Ab Db & Gb Black Major Throb, White Note Of Calm, Romanian Ragtome Shut, Smoked Hips, Tomorrow's People On The Move Today (From Ballet Music For 'Spaceship Earth'). OS ○ All Ron Geesin's Peel Sessions forthcoming on his own label in 2007

Gene

6/1/96 Speak To Me Someone, Save Me I'm Yours, Fighting Fit, Drawn To The Deep End. Martin Rossiter (v, p), Steve Mason (g), Keven Miles (b), Matt James (d). 14/12/95 MV4 TdB LS ○

18/3/98 As Good As It Gets, The Looker, I Need You, Little Child. 24/2/98 MV4 TdB NF ○

31/8/99 The British Disease, For The Dead, Undressed, You'll Never Walk Again, Where Are They Now, As Good As It Gets. Live from MV3 AR SA 1st 3 sessions on ○ John Peel Sessions 95–99 Universal/Polydor

8/12/99 Someone For Everyone. Live from MV3 AKM&AR SA

31/10/00 You, Walking In The Shallows, Yours For The Taking, We'll Get What We Deserve. 11/10/00 MV4 KR JSM

19/9/01 Simple Request, Is It Over, Longsleeves For The Summer, Get What You Deserve, Walking In The Shadow, British Disease, Oh Lover, Where Are They Now, Somewhere In The World, For The Dead. & Angie Pollack (p, k). Live from MV4 SA JHT

Gene Loves Jezebel

26/9/83 Pop Tarantula, Brittle Punches, Upstairs, Screaming For Emmalene. Ian Hudson (lg), Dick Hawkins (d), Ja (gv), Mike Aston (lv), Kymille (v), Steve Radwell (b). 17/9/83 MV4 DG MC Debut session was for David Jensen, June 83

24/5/84 Waves, Shame, Five Below. Kymille out. 12/5/84 MV5 DG MR

Generation X ○

20/4/77 Day By Day, Listen!, Youth Youth Youth, Your Generation. Billy Idol (lv), Bob Andrews (gv), Tony James (bv), John Towe (d). 12/4/77 MV4 JG MR

21/7/77 From The Heart, Rock On, Gimme Some Truth, No No No. Mark Laff (d) r Towe; Idol (g-3). 12/7/77 MV4 JG MR

14/2/79 Paradise West, Love Like Fire, Night Of The Cadillacs, English Dream. 15/1/79 MV4 TW DD All on ○ Radio 1 Sessions SFRSCD105

Genesis

28/1/72 Return Of The Giant Hogweed, Harold The Barrel, The Fountain Of Salmacis (& Harlequin, 17/3/72). Peter Gabriel (v, fl), Tony Banks (k), Mike Rutherford (b, gv), Steve Hackett (g), Phil Collins (d, bck). 9/1/72 T1 JM NG Original line-up won 'enthusiastic' pass from audition panel for R2 Night Ride session April 1970. Debut R1 session for second line-up was for Bob Harris in May 71

7/11/72 Watcher Of The Skies, Twilight Alehouse, Get Them Out By Friday. 25/9/72 T1 JW BC

Gentle Giant

7/1/72 Alucard, Plain Truth, Giant (& Funny Ways, 4/2/72). Phil Shulman (ts, tp, fl, v), Derek Shulman (gbv, hca), Ray Shulman (gbv, vi, tp), Kerry Minnear (k, vi, clo, percv), Gary Green (lg), Malcolm Waterman (d). 12/12/71 T1 PD U 2 previous Sounds of the Seventies sessions in 1970

14/7/72 Mr Class And Quality, Prologue, Scooldays. Jon Weathers (d) r Waterman. 13/6/72 T1 JM U

5/9/72 Plain Truth, The Advent Of Panurge, Funny Ways. 8/8/72 MV4 PR BC

14/12/72 Prologue, The Advent Of Panurge, Cry For Everyone. 11/12/72 LH1 BA U

8/1/74 Excerpts From Octopus, Way Of Life. P Shulman out. 4/12/73 LH1 TW BC ○

17/12/74 Proclamation, Experience, Aspirations, Cogs In Cogs. 10/12/74 U TW U ○

13/10/75 Just The Same, Free Hand, On Reflection. 16/9/75 MV4 U BAI ○ on Totally Out Of The Woods: The BBC Sessions HUX018

The Gentle People

1/4/97 Soundtrack Of Life, Emotion Heater, Travel Bug, Misty Waters. Laurie Lemans, Honeymink, Valentine Carnelian, Dougee Dimensional. 9/3/97 MV4 U U

George and Martha

12/12/88 I Understand, Burn, Machine, Wretch. Stephan M (v), Chris M (g), Stefan Muller (b), Frank Seele (d). 6/12/88 MV4 DG MR

Gerry and the Pacemakers

24/4/73 Ferry Cross The Mersey, How Do You Do It, You'll Never Walk Alone. Gerry Marsden (gv), Billy Kinsley (b), Joe McLaughlin (p), Pete Clarke (d). 17/4/73 LH1 U U A one-off. 'Must have been one of Peel's funny periods' said John Walters in 92. Band did many Light Programme sessions in 60s

Steve Gibbons Band

30/7/76 Rollin', Tupelo Mississippi Flash, Johnny Cool, Spark Of Love. Steve Gibbons (lv), Bob Wilson (gv), Dave Carroll (gv), Trevor Burton (bv), Bob Lamb (d). 20/7/76 MV4 JG MR

3/3/77 Right Side Of Heaven / Rollin' On, Please Don't Say Goodbye, One Of The Boys. 21/2/77 MV4 TW DD

4/7/77 Tulane, The Music Plays On, Gave His Life To Rock 'n' Roll, Boppin' The Blues. 27/6/77 MV4 TW DD

Gilbert

19/5/68 You, What Can I Do, Disappear, My Front Door, Come On Home (& I Don't Know What To Do, Better Than Valentino, 16/6/68). Gilbert O'Sullivan (pv, 5–7 solo) & The Keith Mansfield Orchestra (16). 14/5/68 PC1 BA DT&AH

Gilded Lil

26/8/98 Departure Lounge, Klang/When I Was Young (2 Song Segue), Bea, Big King Whitey. Kerry McDonald (v), Malcy Duff (gv), Ross Robertson (g), Gerry Hillman (b), Mark Bailie (d). 4/8/98 MV4 MR SA

Gilgamesh

26/9/74 One End More, Arriving Twice, Lady And Friend, Not Withstanding. U 19/9/74 LH1 JM BAI&MG

3/11/75 Jamo, Island Of Rhodes. Alan Gowen (k), Phil Lee (g), Jeff Clyne (b), Michael Travis (d, perc). 11/9/75 MV4 TW U

Girlfrendo

9/10/97 First Kiss Feelings Vs Everyday Sensations, Photo Session In A Photo Booth, Fab Gear, Not Sleepy Song. Per Idborg (glv), Sara Carneholm (lv), Josephine Olausson (lv), Anders Kwanmark (k, bck), Nicholaus Zannikis (b, bck). 26/8/97 MV4 MR NF

Girls at Our Best!

23/2/81 China Blue, This Train, Getting Beautiful Warm Gold Fast From Nowhere. Judy Evans (v), Gerard Swift (b), Carl Harper (d), James Allan (g). 17/2/81 LH1 DG MR ● SFPS029. Session for Richard Skinner recorded 4 days before, TX on same day as Peel's

The Glass Menagerie

23/6/68 One More Heartache, You Didn't Have To Be So Nice, Love Me Two Times (& Dear Mr Fantasy, 21/7/68). William Atkinson (d), Alan Kendall (lg), Keith O'Connell (opv), John Medley (bv), Ian Stonebridge (lv, hca). 5/6/68 MV4 BA U Debut session was for David Symonds May 68

9/3/69 Putting It Off 'Til Another Day, Do You Ever Think, Life Is Getting It Together, She Came From Hell. O'Connell out. 21/1/69 PC1 BA AH

Glass Torpedoes

24/1/80 Forced A Smile, Something, Tall Stories, This Is The End. Barbara Donovan (v), Mark Coleridge (dv), Gary Daly (b), Paul Reason (lg). 9/1/80 U JE NG

The Glaxo Babies

26/4/79 It's Irrational, Who Killed Bruce Lee, Burning, She Went To Pieces. Robert Chapman (rg, v), Dan Catois (g, bck), Tom Nichols (b), Geoff Allsop (d), Tony Wraften (sx, bck). 17/4/79 MV4 JS MR Robert Chapman is now the author of Selling The Sixties: The Pirates And Pop Music Radio (Routledge, 1992), a music writer, DJ and lecturer at the University of Huddersfield

4/3/80 Jihad, Limited Entertainment, Permission To Be Wrong, There'll Be No Room For You In The Shelters. Nichols, Catois, Charlie Llewelyn (sy, dv), Tim Aylett (percv), Alan Jones (g, syv). 19/2/80 MV4 JE MR

Glencoe

17/10/72 Airport, Look Me In The Eye, Telephonia, It's. John Turnbull (g), Norman Watt-Roy (b), Graham Maitland (o, p), Stuart Francis (d). 12/9/72 MV4 PR BC

2/11/72 Look Me In The Eye, Watching The Rivers Flow, Lifeline. 16/10/72 LH1 BA U

10/5/73 Born In The City, Is It You, Roll On Bliss (& Two On An Island In Search Of A New World, 31/5/73). 30/4/73 LH1 BA U

15/11/73 Roll On Bliss, To Divine Mother, It's, Airport. 5/11/73 LH1 BA BAI

Global Communication (aka Reload)

15/4/94 1st Movement, 2nd Movement, 3rd Movement. Mark Pritchard (k), Tom Middleton (k). OS

Global Village Trucking Company

2/5/74 Apple Pie, The Sun Can Always Catch You With Your Trousers Down, Watch Out There's A Mind About. Jon Owen (lv, rg), Mike Medora (lg), Jimmy Lascelles (elp, o), Jon McKenzie (b), Simon Stewart (d). 11/4/74 LH1 TW U

7/11/74 Sky Train, On The Judgement Day, Down In The Lowlands. 24/10/74 MV4 U U

9/6/75 Love Will Find A Way, Cock Of The Rocks, I Never Knew. Pete Kirtley (lg) r Medora. 27/5/75 MV4 U U

Gnidrolog

24/4/71 My Room, Time And Space, Saga Of Smith And Smythe. Stewart Goldring (lg, mand), Colin Goldring (rgv, hca, rec), Nigel Pegrum (d, fl, ob), Peter Cowling (b). 13/4/71 MV4 JW BC

Go Hole

23/11/87 Bayonet Practice, Treacherous, I'll Be Waiting. Les Clarke (lvg), John Mason (b, bck), Matt Wrigley (d, bck). 17/11/87 U DG MC&JB

Goatboy

13/6/02 Nitro, Grease Of Love, 100, Cannonball Dreaming. Nik Jenkins (gv), Steve Cullen (tt), Neil Rowling (b), Rhodri Thomas (d). 10/2/02 MV4 ME NS

The Go-Betweens

5/8/82 Near The Chimney, Metal And Shells, Ask, A Peaceful Wreck. Robert Forster (gv), Grant McLennan (bv), Lindy Morrison (d). 14/7/82 MV4 RP NG

29/10/84 The Power That I Now Have, Secondhand Furniture, Five Words, Rare Breed. Robert Vickers (b) joins. 21/10/84 MV5 DG ME ● SFPS074

God Is My Co-Pilot

9/7/93 Pulled Up To Park, Kurdish List Laulu, 55 151, 2 Meats, Katrussja, Lead With Your Chin. Sharon Topper (v, cl, ml, o), Craig Flanagin (g), Ann Rupel (bv, o), Marion Coutts (tpv), Margaret Fielder (gv), Michael Evans (d). 3/6/93 MV4 MA RF

27/5/94 Kiss & Tell, Boris, Disco By Night, Quinie Q. Alex Klein (b), Siobhan Duffy (d) r Rupel, Evans. 19/4/94 MV4 MR RJ

26/5/95 Boxstitch, Moleskin, U Doet Me Pijn, I Love My Life With An F, Code And Submit. Topper, Flanagin, Coutts, Fly (bv), Dan Brown (d). 18/4/95 MV4 AA NK

14/5/97 Menarche, Dymastica, Far More Attractive, Monkeys, Kleines Eisstuck. & Jer Reid (g), Daria Klotz (b), Sheila Sobolewski (d). 22/4/97 MV4 MR JMK

God Machine

29/5/92 Commitment, Desert Song, Double Dare, Pictures Of A Bleeding Boy. Ron Austin (d), Jimmy Fernandez (b), Robin Proper Sheppard (gv). 21/4/92 MV4 MR~

Godflesh

27/9/89 Tiny Tears, Wound (Not Wound), Pulp, Like Rats. G Christion Green (b), Justin Broadrick (g, v, prg), Kevin (sx-3). 27/8/89 MV3 DG ME

Godspeed You Black Emperor!

19/1/99 Hungover As The Queen In Maida Vale 1, Hungover As The Queen In Maida Vale 2. Aidan Girt (perc, tym), Maro Pezzente (b), Roger Tellier (g), Sophie Trudeau (vi), Efrim Menuck (g), Dave Bryant (g), Norsala Johnson (clo), Thierry Amar (b, p), Bruce Cawdron (d, glo, tym). 22/11/98 MV3 ME KR

Goldchains

5/12/02 How We Do This, Idk, Sunshine Kisses, Death. Topher Lafata (v, e). 10/11/02 OS

Golden Starlet

28/1/95 Packet Romance, Stupid Punk Boy, D I Y, Fan Club, Boy Scout, Putty In Your Hands. Nicky Peacock (d), Cheryl Shaw (d), Janet Haigh (bv), Nathan Stephenson (g), Catherine Haigh (g, lv). 3/1/95 MV4 MR MK

Golden Virgins

30/9/03 Shadows Of Your Love, Staying Sober, We'll Never Be Friends, I Don't Want No One But You. Lucas Renney (gv), Allan (b), David Younger (sy), Neil Bassett (d, xy). 4/9/03 MV4 SA JSM

John Golding

2/7/74 Oh Boy, Here's To The Summer Day, Believe What You Feel, Do You Really Need To Keep On Asking. John Golding (gv) & U (bj, mnd). 10/6/74 T1 U &DD

20/2/75 Loving Is A One-sided Thing, Good Luck And Love To You, What They Say About You, Those 'Being Far Away From You' Blues. 13/2/75 MV4 U U

Gong

17/11/71 Magic Brother, Clarence, Tropical Fish. Contracted as 'Kevin Ayers, Daevid Allan and The Gong': Kevin Ayers (bgv), Daevid Allen (gv), Gilly Smith (v), Phillip Pyle (d), Didier Malherbe (sx), Christian Tritsch. 9/11/71 MV4 JW BC

12/6/73 Can't Kill Me, Radio Gnome Direct Broadcast / Crystal Machine, Zero The Hero And The Orgasm Witch. Allen, Smith, Malherbe, Mike Howlett (b), Steve Hillage (g), Pierre Moerlen (d), Tim Blake (sy). 29/5/73 MV4 PR BC

29/1/74 Radio Gnome, Oily Way. Rob Tate (d), Di Stewart (perc, v) r Moerlen. 15/1/74 LH1 TW U

Gonzales

3/9/74 Put It Where You Want It, Ugly Man, Run To The Nearest Exit, Clapham South, A Day In The Life. with Viola Wills (lv) & Roy Davies (elp), De Lisle Harper (b), Gordon Hunte (lg), Steve Ferrone (d), Alan Sharpe (cga, perc), Ron Carthy (tp), Steve Gregory (sx, fl), Chris Mercer (ts), Geoff Beadle (bars), Michael Eves (ts), (1,4–Wills out). 20/8/74 LH1 PR U

21/11/74 Adelanto Nightride, No Way, Skyscraper, Pack It Up. Davies, Harper, Hunte, Gregory, Mercer, Beadle, Eves, Carthy, George Chandler (v), Glenn Le Fleur (d), Robert Stignac (cga, perc), Robert Ahwai (rg). 7/11/74 MV4 TW U

11/11/75 Baby Please Rescue Me, What's Going On, Stuck On You, Remember Me. with Viola Wills (lv), Malcolm Griffiths, Larry Steele, Richard Bailey (d) r Harper, Sharpe, Ferrone, Gregory, Beadle. 2/10/75 MV4 TW BAI

Goober Patrol

9/9/95 Easy Life, I'll Do Without, The Biggest Joke, Crammin', Go Away Please. Stewart Sandall (d), Tom Blyth (b), Tim Snelson (g), Simon Sandall (lgv). 22/8/95 MV4 MR NK

Good Habit

4/1/73 I Am And So Are You, I'm Going Down, Ship Of Gold, The Only Place Left To Be. Ian Thomson (sx, fl), Paul Steward (d), Alan Collier (v), Philip Blackmore (gv), John Roberts (sx), David Land (bv). 18/12/72 LH1 BA U

Philip Goodhand-Tait

21/11/72 Child Of Jesus, Leon, When Will I Be Loved, Raining Rain. Philip Goodhand-Tait (pv) 24/10/72 U U BC 5 previous sessions 71/72 not for Peel

12/3/74 Almost Killed A Man, Ready Willing And Able, Jesus Don't Only Love The Cowboys, Everybody's Gone Away. 12/2/74 LH1 U U

Gore

4/11/87 Axe Of Revenge, Loaded, Mean Man's Dream, Chainsaw, The Arena. Peter Deswart (g), Danny Arnold (d), Marij Hel (b). 27/10/87 U HP TdB

6/12/88 The Breeding, In The Garden Of Evil. Arnold, Hel, Joes Bently (g), Frankie Stoo (v). 29/11/88 MV4 DG MR

21/9/91 Rustproof Rape, Waste Taste, Treat, No Respect. Hel, Bardo Maria (d), Van Reede (g). 9/7/91 MV5 JB JB&PA

Gorky's Zygotic Mynci

29/1/94 Y Ffordd Oren, Bocs Angelica, Merched Yn Neud Gwallt Ei Gilydd, Gewn I Gorffen. Osian Evans (d), Richard James (b), John Lawrence (g, bck), Euros Childs (v, k), Megan Childs (vi). 19/12/93 MV3 ME NF

11/3/95 Paid Cheto Ar Pam, If Fingers Were Xylophones, Pethau, Mynwes Kentucky. Euros Rowlands (d) r Evans; & B J Cole (lsg). 12/2/95 MV3 ME JLC

11/5/96 Meirion Wylit, Young Girls Happy Endings, Dim Atsain (aka Patio Song) (& Pen Gwag Glas, 1st TX live 21/4/96). 21/4/96 MV3 ME GT

25/8/98 The Tidal Wave, Freckles, Spanish Dance Troupe (& Catrin 1st TX live 21/7/98). 21/7/98 MV4 ME MA

5/4/00 Honeymoon With You, The Lady And The Travelling Man (aka Lady Fair), Out On The Side, How I Long To. E & M Childs, James, Rowlands, Gorwel Owen (o), Ashley Cook (g), Rhodri Puw (b). 27/2/00 MV4 SA JSM

20/9/01 These Winds Are In My Heart, Let Those Blue Skies, Instrumental 2, My Honey, The Summer's Been Good From The Start. E & M Childs, James, Puw, Peter Richardson (d). Live from Peel Acres AR GT

28/8/03 Monica, Old Fanny Mahoney, Eyes Of Green Green Green, The Film That Changed My Wife. 30/7/03 MV4 SA JSM

16/12/04 Ladyfair, Y Ffordd Oren. E & M Childs, James, Richardson. Live from MV4 NF RJ

Gossip

3/9/03 Eyes Open, Jason's Basement, Ain't It The Truth, Yesterday's News. Beth Ditto (v), Nathan Howdeshell (g), Kathy Mendonca (d). 20/8/03 MV4 SA JSM

John Gourd

6/11/68 A Funny Love Affair, Sitting In A Den, Small Minority, Thank You Kindly, Through The Leaves. John Gourd (agv). 6/11/68 S2 PC U

Davy Graham

1/5/68 Bruton Town, Tristano, I'm Ready, Rock Me, Good Morning Blues. Davy Graham (gv, 2–instr). Live in on-air studio

Grandaddy

16/6/98 Hawaiian Island Wranglers, I'm In Love With No One, Street Bunny, Volvo In G. Jim Fairchild (g), Tim Dryden (k), Kevin Garcia (bv), Jason Lytle (gkv), Aaron Burtch (d). 17/5/98 MV4 ME JLO

Grandmaster Gareth

17/9/03 Monster Melody: Entering The Monster Melody / Meet The Cartoon Monkey / War Is Not Healthy For Children / The Spinach Armada / Less Indie More Hindi / Pogo Time / The Sound Of Yourself Listening / Duelling Multi Instrumentalists / Dr Dre Has A Midlife Crisis / The Noises Made By Stupid People / A Nasty Piece Of Work / It's A Small World. 15/8/03 OS

Grapefruit

21/1/68 Breaking Up A Dream, Dear Delilah, The Dead Boot, Trying To Make It Monday. Peter Sweetenham (rg), Geoffrey Sweetenham (d), John Perry (lg, o), George Alexander (b) & David Katz for 11 musicians, Bill Shepherd (md). 15/1/68 PC1 BA U

The Great Crash

14/8/73 She Throws It All Away, Hero Of The Beach, Regimental Reunion. Nick Smith (g), Al Grey (kv), George Benn (bv), Piers Geddes (dv). 7/8/73 LH1 JW U

The Great Leap Forward

8/6/87 Propping Up The Nose Of The King, Hope's Not Enough Son – Ask Your Parents, Haranguing The Boisterous Buffoons, When It's Cold In Summer. Nobby Normal (d), Arty Farty (bck, hn), Padraig Byrne (b), Helvetica Halbfett (gv). 24/5/87 U DG ME&MA

8/2/88 How To Be Successful In A World Of Failure, Cursing This Audacity, A Peck On The Cheek À La Politique, The Original Sin. Nobby Normal (d), John Sargeant (b), Eileen Cox (k), Big Al (gv). 26/1/88 U DG MR&MC

Greaves Blegvad

10/1/78 Mostly Twins And Trios, From The Trees To The Wheel, Actual Frenzy. Andy Ward (d, glo-3), John Greaves (bpv), Anthony Moore (sy), Peter Blegvad (gv), Tom Newman (g). 13/12/77 MV4 MB MR 'All numbers specially written for Peel', note on session sheet

Greenhouse

3/3/91 Ban The Car, Rules, New World Order, Her Too. Tom Kincaid (d, bck), Rob England (b, bck), Simon King (g, bck), John Parkes (gv). 5/2/91 MV5 MR MR

Greyhound

14/8/71 54–46 Was My Number, Moon Walk, Black And White, Singer Man. Sonny Binns (o, p), Trevor White (b), Earl Dunn (lg), Danny Smith (d), Glenroy Oakley (v). 29/6/71 MV4 JW BC 1st TX on Viv Stanshall's Radio Flashes while Peel on holiday. After failing two previous auditions under other names, finally passed with this session

Griffin

1/11/69 What A Day It's Been, The Shine, My Head Your Lies. Peter Kirtley (g), Colin Gibson (b), Graham Bell (pv), Ken Craddock (o), Alan White (d). 21/10/69 MV4 JW BC

Grifters

29/7/94 Meanwhile, Ten Thousand, Wreck, Clot. Dave Shouse (gv), Tripp Lamkins (b), Scott Taylor (gv), Stan Gallimore (d). 22/5/94 MV4 JB GT

16/2/96 Steam, Subterranean Death Ride Blues, Life Is Swell. 4/2/96 MV4 U U

Carol Grimes

18/7/74 Somebody's Sleeping In My Bed, That's What It Takes, Give It Everything You've Got, A Change Is Gonna Come. Carol Grimes (v), Tim Hinckley (p), Neil Hubbard (g), Alan Spenner (b), Ian Wallace (d), Mel Collins (sx). 4/7/74 LH1 TW U

Stefan Grossman

5/6/68 Mississippi Blues, I'm So Glad, All My Friends Are Gone, Requiem (For Pat Kilroy), You're Gonna Be Sorry. Stefan Grossman (g). 5/6/68 S1 DK U

Groundation

16/4/81 Forward, Judgement, Rebel, Juganout. Dave Miller (d), Henry Forde (rg), George Jeffers (b), Ellis Paul (k), Franklin Jeffers (lg), Terence Browne (lv), Robert Charlse (sx). 23/3/81 LH1 PS DD

The Groundhogs

12/9/70 Eccentric Man, Mistreated, Strange Town (& Gasoline, 21/11/70). Tony McPhee (gv), Peter Cruickshank (b), Ken Pustelnick (d). 4/8/70 MV4 JW TW Debut Session was for World Service R&B show, March 70. Group's UK trial broadcast was John Peel Concert May 70. Session for Mike Harding followed in July 70

20/2/71 Split Pts 1 2 & 4, A Year In The Life. 16/2/71 MV4 U BC

14/3/72 Earth Is Not Room Enough, Wages Of Peace, Music Is The Food Of Thought, Bogroll Blues. 29/2/72 MV4 U U

13/3/75 Light My Light, I Love Miss Ogyny, Soldier. 6/3/75 MV4 PR U

Grover

14/2/01 Ham Fist, I Await Your Letters And Sendings, Half Life, A Simple Misunderstanding. Simon Fox (gv), Andrew Hall (b), Simon Rider (d). 14/1/01 MV4 ME JHT

Gruppo Sportivo

13/6/78 Beep Beep Love, Rock 'n' Roll, Girls Never Know, I Shot My Manager. Hans Vandenburg (g, lv), Eric Whermeyer (b), Peter Calicher (k), Max Mollinger (d) & the Gruppettes: Meue Touw (bck), Josee Van Lersel (bck). 5/6/78 MV4 TW DD

Guana Batz

1/2/84 Zombie Walk, Jungle Rumble, Train Kept A Rollin', The Cave. Pip Hancox (v), Mick White (b), Stuart Osborne (g), Dave Turner (d). 24/1/84 MV4 TW MPK

2/5/84 No Particular Place To Go, Nightwatch, King Rat, The Overture. 24/4/84 MV5 MRD TdB

10/10/84 Dynamite, Brand New Cadillac, Rockin' In The Graveyard, Nightmare Fantasy, Rocking In My Coffin. Sam Sardi (b) r White. 30/9/84 MV5 DG GP

7/5/85 Endless Sleep, Goofing Around, Can't Take The Pressure, Got No Money. 23/4/85 MV5 MRD MR

Guided By Voices

28/7/96 Wondering Boy Poet, Party/Striped White Jets, Atom Eyes, Cut Out Witch, Man Called Aerodynamics, Wondering Boy Poet. Mitch Mitchell (g), Toby Sprout (g), Robert Pollard (v), Kevin Fennell (d), Leland Cain (b). 18/6/96 MV4 JB

14/12/99 Frequent Weavers Who Burns, Zoo Pie, Tight Globes, Much Better Mr Buckles, Dragon's Awake, Bright Paper Werewolves / Lord Of Overstock. Robert Pollard (v), Doug Gillard (g), Nate Farley (rg), Tim Tobias (b), Jim Macpherson (d). 19/10/99 MV5 MR JHT

Isaac Guillory

21/11/72 Hold On St Peter, Movin' On, Brussels, The Carbondale Strut. Isaac Guillory (agv). 31/10/72 LH1 JW BC&BAl

Gumball

15/12/90 All The Time, This Town, I Want You, Vietnam. Jay Spiegel (d), Eric Vermillion (b), Don Fleming (gv) & guest Norman Blake (g, bck). 25/11/90 MV3 DG ME&JLY

29/9/91 39 Lashes, Light Shines Through, Back Off Boogaloo, Marilyn, High Or Low. 20/8/91 MV5 MR MR

The Gun

12/11/67 Hold On, Stop In The Name Of Love, The Lights On The Wall, Most Peculiar Man. Paul Curtis, Louis Farrell, Timothy Mycroft, Gearie Kenworthy. 6/11/67 PC1 BA U

24/11/68 Sunshine, Race With The Devil, Unlock My Door, The Man Who Paints The Pictures. Adrian Curtis r Mycroft, Kenworthy; & 3 trumpets & 3 trombones. 4/11/68 PC1 BA PR

Gunshot

18/5/91 Construct / Destruct, Bullets Entering Chest, To Those Who Deserve It, Gunshot's History. Mercury (rp), Alkaline (rp), White Child Rix ('machines'), Alan Scott (prg). 21/4/91 MV3 DG ME&CML

5/2/94 Social Psychotics, Mind Of A Razor, Lockdown, Colour Code. Danny Hart (rp), Anthony Franklin (rp), Barry Blair (rp), Ricky Croucher (rp, sc), Alan Scott (g, b). 4/1/94 MV4 MR SA

Guv'Ner

18/2/95 Thespian Girl, Clear The Room, Baby's Way Cruel, I Wanna. Charles Gansa (k, v, g), Pumpkin Wentzel (bv), Michael Ramatyn (d). 17/1/95 MV4 MR GT

A Guy Called Gerald ○

7/11/88 Time Waits For No Man, Rockin' Ricki, Emotions Electric. Gerald Simpson (prg, sy) & 'Chapter': Aniff Counsins & Colin Thorpe (sy, smp) & Paulette Blake (v). 30/10/88 HP DG ME ● SFPS071

6/9/89 Johnny Roadhouse, Satisfaction, Bruford. Gerald, Edward Barton & Cola Nile (v). 6/8/89 MV5 DG PA

8/7/95 Amabruku (Bad Boy), Time Labyrinth, 3 2 B One, 1 1 2 4 Q. Gerald & MC Kusta (mc-1). Recorded in June 95 OS ○ all 3 sessions on SFRSCD083

The Gymslips

20/5/82 Erika (With A K), Renees, Big Sister, 48 Crash, You'll Never Walk Alone. Paula Richards (gv), Suzanne Scott (bv), Karen Yarnell (dv). 12/5/82 MV4 JWI NG

16/9/82 Barbara Cartland, Pie And Mash, Drink Problem, Thinking Of You, Robot Man. 1/9/82 MV4 RP NG

30/5/83 Silly Egg, Wandering Star, Up The Wall, More Tea Vicar? & Kathy Barnes (k). 30/4/83 MV4 DG SC

7/12/83 Whirlwind Flings, Love's Not The Answer, Valley Girl, Call Again. 28/11/83 MV4 DG MC

6/6/84 Leave Me, Soldier, On The Line, We're Gonna Bring Your Empire Down. Paula Richards (gv), Karen Kay (bv), Sue Vickers (k), Michelle Chowrimootoo (d). 22/5/84 MV5 MRD TdB

Gypsy

18/9/71 Don't Cry On Me, What A Day, Let Me Take You Home (& I Don't Want To See You, 17/11/71). Robin Pizer (lg), John Napp (g), David Smith (d), David McCarthy (b), Rod Reed (rg). 6/9/71 PH JW BC Debut session was for Stuart Henry, July 71

31/5/73 Let's Roll, Still You're Not Sure, You Got To Me, The Jig. Ray Martinez (g) r Reed. 21/5/73 LH1 BA U

11/10/73 Slow Down, Sorting It Out, Still You're Not Sure, I'll Be There (& You Got To Me, 8/11/73). 8/10/73 LH1 BA U

Hagar the Womb

20/2/84 Today's Miss World, Armchair Observer, By Force, A Song Of Deep Hate. Chris Knowles (d), Mitch Flacko (b), Paul Harding (g), Janet Nassim (g), Ruth Ellis, Karen Amden & Elaine Reubens (v). 11/2/84 MV5 DG PW

Hakan Libdo

8/6/04 DJ Mix OS

Half Japanese

25/6/93 Song Of Joy And Love, True Believers, All Part Of My Plan, She, If He Says He Did, Talking In My Sleep, Bashful Bob & Chicago. Tim Foljahn (g), Gilles Rieder (d), Mick Hobbs (b, midi-sx, p), Marc Baines (g), Jad Fair (v). 25/5/93 MV4 CML/AR

6/10/95 The Feeling's Getting Stronger, Den Of Sin, Do It, This Is Our Day, What About Me. Fair, Rieder, Hobbs, Steve Petter (g), John Sluggett (g), Dallas Good (b). 24/9/95 MV3 ME BJ

9/12/97 Starlight, Superman, Natalie, Vicky, Summer Nights. Fair, Rieder, Hobbs, Sluggett. 4/11/97 MV4 MR GT

Half Man Half Biscuit

20/11/85 D'ye Ken Ted Moult?†, Arthur's Farm†, All I Want For Christmas Is A Dukla Prague Away Kit†, The Trumpton Riots, Ol'tige. Paul Wright (d), Neil Crossley (bv), Nigel Blackwell (rg, lv), Simon Blackwell (lg), David Lloyd (k). 10/11/85 MV5 DG MA ● SFPS057

3/3/86 I Left My Heart In Papworth General, The Continuous Cremation Of Hattie Jacques, Reasons To Be Miserable (Part 10)†, The Bastard Son Of Dean Friedman. 23/2/86 MV5 DG ME † ● On 'Back Again In The DHSS' LP on Probe Plus

8/9/86 Rod Hull Is Alive. . . Why?, The Best Thing In Life, Dickie Davies' Eyes, I Was A Teenage Armchair Honved Fan. 31/8/86 U DG ME&FK

4/4/90 Ordinary To Enschede, Our Tune, Yipps (My Baby Got The), Pragvec At The Melkveg. 1/3/90 MV3 DG ME

27/6/92 Marsultras (You'll Never Make The Station), 4AD 3D CD, Floreat Interria, Goodnight Irene. 2/6/92 MV4 MR MR

5/8/95 Song Of Encouragement For The Orme Ascent, CAMRA Man, Get Kramer, Mr Cave's A Window Cleaner Now. Nigel Blackwell (gv), Neil Crossley (bv), Carl Alty (d). 11/7/95 MV4 KR AA

14/10/96 Bad Review, Deep House Victims Minibus Appeal, Dead Men Don't Need Season Tickets, Shropshire Lad, Paintball's Coming Home. Ken Hancock (g) joins; Carl Henry (d) r Alty. Live from MCR3 LR U

2/2/97 Monmore Here's Running, Tonight Matthew I'm Going To Be With Jesus, Prs Yearbook The Quick Drawbridge, He Who Would Valium Take. & Martyn Jones (o). 12/1/97 MV4 ME U

24/2/98 Four Skinny Indie Kids Drinking Weak Lager, You're Hard, Secret Gig, Moody Chops. Blackwell, Crossley, Hancock, Henry. 1/2/98 MV4 ME FK

9/9/99 Uffington Wassail, Gubba Look-alikes, Bottleneck At Capel Curig, Twenty Four Hour Garage People. 25/8/99 MV4 MPK NS

3/9/02 Thems The Vagaries, The Light At The End Of The Tunnel (Is The Light Of An Oncoming Train), Song To The Siren / Vatican Broadside, Breaking News. 23/6/02 BHM IC CLE Band diaries suggest this was actually done on 24/7/02 BHM, live in one take on same day as a Kershaw session

16/11/04 Asparagus Next Left, For What Is Chatteris, Epiphany, Joy Division Oven Gloves. Henry away, (dm) instead. 10/10/04 BHM PCG U

Lianne Hall

30/5/00 Warning, Alright, Stumble, Full On, Chard. Lianne Hall (gv) & Pico: Bela Emerson (clo, bck), John Gray (sx, bck), Andrew Wills (prg), Justin Wood (b). 30/4/00 MV3 RJ NF

6/12/01 Fair Enough, Rain, Trouble, Stumble, So Good. & Friends': Lianne Hall (gv), Kirsten Elliott (fl), Bela Emerson (clo, bck), Alice Eldridge (clo), Andrew Wills (prg). 14/10/01 MV4 ME RJ

20/12/01 In The Bleak Midwinter, Soul Kid. Lianne Hall (gv), Bela Emerson (clo). Live from Peel Acres AR SA. See Caroline Martin

Ha-Lo

7/7/99 Theramin Carousel, Rapid Descent, Regenerate House, Life Force. H Cullen, C Knowles. 7/7/99 MV4 MR RF

Claire Hammill

12/5/72 When I Was A Child, The Big Time Kid, Speedbreaker. Claire Hammill (gv). 14/4/72 U JM U Debut session was for Bob Harris March 72

Peter Hammill

24/7/73 Easy To Slip Away, German Overalls, In The End, Time For A Change. Hammill (gpv). 9/7/73 T1 JW U

5/3/74 Rubicon, Red Shift, A House Is Not A Home. & 2 (unknown). 18/2/74 T1 TW U

3/9/74 No More The Sub-Mariner, The Emperor In His Workroom, Faint Heart And The Sermon. 19/8/74 T1 TW U

21/4/77 Betrayed, Afterwards, Autumn. & Graham Smith (vl). 13/4/77 MV4 U NG

24/9/79 Mister X (Gets Tense), Faculty X, Mediaevil / Time For A Change. Solo. 12/9/79 MV4 JE NG

The Happy Few

28/7/82 Seven Years, 3am, Beg Forgiveness, Bucket Of Ice. Phil Emby (d, perc), David Cuff (g, b, v), Dominic Riley (g, v-1), Nick Green (g, b). 3/7/82 MV4 DG MR

The Happy Flowers

11/7/90 My Head's On Fire, Mom And Dad Like The Baby More Than Me, Ruckwerts Essen Vetzt, I Dropped My Ice Cream Cone, These Peas Are So Green. John Beers (gv), Charlie Kramer (d, b, v). 28/6/90 MV5 DG NG&RPF

The Happy Mondays

9/4/86 Kuff Dam, Freaky Dancin', Olive Oil, Cob 20. Shaun Ryder (v), Paul Ryder (b), Marc Day (g), Paul Davis (k), Gary Whelan (d), Mark Berisford (perc). 1/4/86 MV4 DG MR&JB ● SFPS084

27/2/89 Tart Tart, Mad Cyril, Do It Better. 21/2/89 U DG MR ● SFPS077

Hard Corps

4/6/84 Sacred Heart, To Breathe, Metal And Flesh, Dirty. Hugh Ashton (cmp), Clive Pearce, Robert Doran & Paul Davies (k), Régine Fetet (v). 26/5/84 MV5 DG MR

Hard Meat

25/6/69 Walking Up Down Street, Liquid Boats, Run Shakes A Life, Strange Fruit. U 6/6/69 U U U

21/9/69 Space Between, Yesterday Today And Tomorrow, Most Likely You'll Go Your Way. 8/9/69 U U U

Tim Hardin

28/7/68 Reason To Believe, Don't Make Promises, Danville Dan, Hang On To A Dream. Tim Hardin (gpv) & the Spike Heatley Quintet (1–solo). 15/7/68 PC1 BA PR&BC Recorded a previous session for Stuart Henry 14/7, TX 21/7

Chris Hardy

4/4/72 On The Wall, Tightrope, You Have Found The Way, Living Ground. Chris Hardy (agv). 27/3/72 PH JW U First broadcast was on My Kind Of Folk 13/11/68: 'Jackson C. Frank arrived for a session with a young British student who had been accompanying him, Chris Hardy, a student at Canterbury University, he recorded one solo item' said producer Frances Line; 'impressive first broadcast', said the audition panel. Then, in 1970, Hardy was in Holy Willie's Prayer.

28/6/73 Spinning Slow, Food For The Breeze, Jug Up, Early In The Morning. & the Basement Blowers (unknown). 4/6/73 LH1 BA U

24/1/74 Cold Steel Rock, It's No Crime, Nefarious Doings, In The Shadows. 17/1/74 LH1 U U

Roy Harper

29/10/67 Forever, Zengem, Midspring Dithering, Nobody's Got Any Money. Roy Harper (gv), Clem Cattini (d), Brian Brocklehurst (b). 16/10/67 PC1 BA PR&AH

17/3/68 Life Goes By, A Beautiful Rambling Mess, Night Fighter Song Writer, All You Need Is. & Keith Mansfield Group (9 musicians). 13/3/68 MV4 BA DT

8/6/69 Hey Francesca†, Hell's Angels, She's The One†, I Hate The White Man (& It's Tomorrow And Today Is Yesterday†, 27/7/69). Solo. 3/6/69 MV4 JW U † On 'Come Out Fighting, Genghis Smith', Awareness AWCD1035

3/1/70 Forever, I Hate The White Man, North Country Girl, Don't You Grieve. 15/12/69 PH JW U

15/5/71 One Man Rock And Roll Band, Same Old Rock, Kangaroo Blues. 10/5/71 PH JW U

19/3/74 Too Many Movies, Commune, Forever, Highway Blues, I'll See You Again, North Country. 11/3/74 T1 JW U

12/12/74 Too Many Movies, Home, Highway Blues, 12 Hours Of Sunset, One Man Rock And Roll Band. 5/12/74 MV4 TW BAI

23/6/75 Referendum, Hallucinating Light, The Spirit Lives. & Trigger: Chris Spedding (lg), Dave Cochran (b), Bill Bruford (d). 10/6/75 MV4 TW BC

18/2/77 Another Day, Cherishing The Lonesome, These Last Days, Grown Ups Are Just Silly Children. & Chips: Andy Roberts (g), Henry McCullough (g), Herbie Flowers (b), John Hallsey (d), Dave Lawson (k). 14/2/77 MV4 TW DD

21/8/78 The Same Old Rock, Forget Me Not, I Hate The White Man. & Andy Roberts (g). 7/8/78 MV4 TW DD

Harpies

23/3/04 Octapied, So Low, Third Time Lucky, Fawn. Nicky Honey (v), Laura Westwood (v), John Devlin (g), Paul Hunt (b), Adam Price (d), Ade Preston (from Farse) (g-4). 26/2/04 MV4 AR GT

Tim Hart and Maddy Prior

1/1/69 The Horn Of The Hunter, Who's The Fool Now, Queen Eleanor's Confession, Adam And Eve, Oats And Beans And Barley, Turkey And Rhubarb. Tim Hart (g, bj, dul), Maddy Prior (v, bj, sp). 17/12/68 PC1 JM U The rejection by the audition panel of their earlier trial broadcast tape for My Kind Of Folk in Oct 68 was personally overruled by Jimmy Grant

4/9/71 Serving Girls' Holiday, Seamus The Showman, Saucey Sailor, Polly On The Shore (& I Live Not Where I Love, 3/11/71). 27/7/71 MV4 U U

Mike Hart

15/5/68 Elsie Straus, Spiders And Larks, Is It True, The Shelter Song. 15/3/68 S1 DK U

Keef Hartley

26/1/69 Think It Over, Sinnin' For You, Half-Breed. Keef Hartley (d), Owen Finnegan (v), Spit James (lg), Peter Dines (o), Gary Thain (b). 3/12/68 PC1 BA AH Trial broadcast for World Service R & B show 30/12/68 was passed by the panel: 'very wild R&B group'

4/5/69 Waiting Around, Too Much Thinking, Me And My Woman, Sinnin' For You. & Wynder K Frog (k), Henry Lowther (tp, vi), Lyn Dobson (al), Harry Becket (tb), Barbara Thompson (ts), Dines out. 29/4/69 MV4 JW TW

25/10/69 Waiting Around, Believe In You, Spanish Fly, Too Much Thinking. & Lowther, Thain & Miller Anderson (gv), James Jewell (ts) & 2 (tp), 2 (sx) (unknown). 14/10/69 MV4 JW U

7/1/72 Marin County, Thinking Of You, Heartbreaking Woman (& Don't You Belong, 11/2/72). & Thain, Pete Wingfield (pv), Chris Mercer (sx), Nick Newell (sx), Junior Kerr (lgv). 7/12/71 T1 JM JWH

1/2/72 Don't Sign It, Heartbreaking Woman, Don't You Belong. 25/1/72 MV4 U U

Phil Hartley

21/11/88 Lord Smutty Lips, Inspector Of Crime, Prepare To Change Sandals, Purchase Nicely. 13/11/88 HP DG JB

PJ Harvey

3/11/91 Oh My Lover†, Victory†, Sheela Na Gig†, Water†. PJ Harvey (gv), Rob Ellis (d), Stephen Vaughn (b). 29/10/91 MV4 MR MR&JB ○ SFRCD119

23/10/92 Highway 61 Revisited, Me Jane, Ecstasy. 22/9/92 MV4 NG~ JLO

12/3/93 Primed And Ticking, Claudine The Inflatable One, Wang Dang Doodle†, Naked Cousin†. & Mike Smith (sx), Dennis Rollins (tb). 2/3/93 MV4 MR~ RJ

21/9/96 Taut, Snake†, Losing Ground†, That Was My Veil†. PJ Harvey (gv), John Parish (gk). 5/9/96 Peel Acres AHW NF

15/10/96 City Of No Sun, Un Cercle Autour, Urn With Dead Flowers, Civil War Correspondent. Harvey, Parish, Ellis, Jeremy Hogg (g), Eric Feldman (bkv). Live from MCR3 LR PL

23/9/98 My Beautiful Leah, Catherine, Perfect Day Elise, Electric Light, Taut (& Sky Lit Up, Joy, The Garden, TX live on 'Evening Session' earlier). Live from MV4 AR SA

20/12/00 This Wicked Tongue†, Somebody's Down Somebody's Name, Kamikaze, Beautiful Feeeling†, Nickle Under The Foot. Harvey, Ellis, Feldman, Tim Farthing (g), Margaret Fiedler (clo, g). 10/11/00 MV4 SA~

20/5/04 The Letter, Uh Huh Her, Cat On The Wall, Evol, Shame. Harvey, Ellis, Simon Archer (b), Josh Klinghoffer (g). Live from Peel Acres AR GT

16/12/04 Horses In My Dreams, Fountain, You Come Through†. Harvey, Klinghoffer (ag). Live from MV3 MA GT † on ○ The Peel Sessions 1991–2004 Island Records

Harvey's Rabbit

23/7/94 Lie So Well, Whatever Happened To, Is This What You Call Change, Thorny Place. Tim Lions (v), Mick Pullan (g), Dave Thom (g, k), David Chorlton (b), Andy Bell (d). 21/6/94 MV4 JB GT

Hatfield and the North

1/2/73 Rifferama, Fol De Rol De Rol / Licks For The Ladies, Finesse Is For Fairies / Nan True's Hole / Lything And Gracing. Phil Miller (g), Pip Pyle (d), Richard Sinclair (bv), Dave Stewart (o, p). 22/1/73 LH1 BA U

31/7/73 Medley: For Robert / For Cyrille / Son Of 'There's No Place Like Homerton', Medley: To Mum And The Gongs / Lobster In Cleavage Probe / Invasion Of The Land Crabs. 24/7/73 LH1 TW BC

2/4/74 Shaving Is Boring / Licks For The Ladies, Your Majesty Is Like A Cream Doughnut, Aigrette / Rifferama / Top Gear Commercial. & Mick Fox (hp-6). 19/3/74 LH1 TW BC

5/12/74 Do The Lethargy Shuffle (Yeah Yeah), Let's Eat (Real Soon), Fitter Stoke Has A Bath / Calyx. 21/11/74 MV4 TW U Almost everything on ○ Hatwise Choice and ○ Hattitude HATCOCD737501/2

Richie Havens

4/6/69 From The Prison, Maggie's Farm, Just Above My Hobby Horse's Head, I Can't Make It Anymore. Richie Havens (gv), Brian Brocklehurst (b), Maurice Placquet (d). 30/5/69 S2 PR U Debut session was for Symonds On Sunday 3 days earlier

8/6/69 Handsome Johnny, Things I Used To Do, High Flying Bird, Dolphin Song. 3/6/69 MV4 JW U

Hawkwind

19/9/70 Hurry On Sundown, Seeing It As You Really Are, Some Of That Stuff. Thomas Crimble (b), Terry Ollis (d), Huw Lloyd Langton (lg), Nik Turner (v, sx, fl), Dik Mik (el), Dave Brock (gv, o). 18/8/70 MV4 JW TW Recorded a Peel Sunday Concert 5/11/70 PS, TX 15/11/70 at which a roadie stole a mic, leading to the band temporarily being banned

24/4/71 Inwards Out, Dreaming / You Shouldn't Do That. Dave Anderson (b) r Crimble; Langton out. 19/4/71 PH JW BC&NG

Bryn Haworth

8/1/75 Used, Pick Me Up, Darling Cory, Ee I Love You. Bryn Haworth (agv). 12/12/74 MV4 TW BAI Debut session was for Bob Harris Dec 74

21/7/75 Dance, Good Job, How Long, Make Love Your Aim. 8/7/75 MV4 U U

29/11/76 Send Down The Rain, We're All One, I Just Can't Get Used To Your Love. & Rash Kato (g), Gordon Marshall (b, bck), Jim Russell (d). 16/11/76 MV4 JG MR

Ritchie Hawtin

16/9/94 Pp001, Dubfunk, Helikoptor, Minak. Billed as 'Plastickman', Ritchie Hawtin (k, prg). 14/7/94 MV4 NG PA

26/4/00 DJ set live from MV4 AR U

10/3/04 DJ set live from MV4 AR~

Ritchie Hawtin & John Acquavica

7/11/00 DJ set using Final Scratch software live from MV4 AR GT

HDQ

15/6/88 Through My Eyes, Those Remembered Times, Believe, Have Faith. Golly (v), Rob Berwick (b), Dickie Hammond (g), Lainey (d). 2/6/88 U DG MA&SC

6/2/89 Leaving Home, Just When I Thought, If Only / Sinking, All We Knew. 17/1/89 MV4 DG MR

Head of David

30/4/86 Snuff Rider MC, Joyride Burning X, Shadow Hills California, Newly-Shaven Saint. Reuben Burroughs (v), Eric Jurenovski (g), Dave Cochrane (b), Sharp (d). 22/4/86 MV4 DG MR ● On 'LP' BFFP10

6/10/86 Jack Nicholson, Pierced All Over, Metal Texas Psych-Out. 23/9/86 U DG MR&JB

15/7/87 Bugged, Snake Domain, Tequila, Skindrill. Justin Broadrick (d, bck) r Sharp. 7/7/87 U DG DD

15/6/89 Moonshine, Caprice, Wildwood, Snake Hands Forever. Cochrane, Jurenovski (g, dm), Burroughs. 28/5/89 MV3 DG MR

Headcleaner

4/7/92 XL5, Fear, Attitude, Ace Of Spades. Martin Willis (gv), Guy Siddle (bv), Erick Legrande (dv). 14/6/92 MV3 ME ME ○ SFPCD086

Headhunters

7/7/83 Way Of The South, Wipe Out The Funk, Disorder In The House, Landlord. Finn (g), Nick (d), Servo (v), Bulldog (b). 29/6/83 U BYA NG

Heads

10/11/95 Chipped, Widowmaker, Theme, Woke Up, Spliff Riff. Hugo Morgan (b), Simon Price (gv), Paul Allen (g), Wayne Maskell (d). 22/10/95 MV3 ME GT

9/2/97 Could Be It Doesn't Matter, Legavan Satellite, You Can Lean Back Sometimes, Post Relaxation. 26/1/97 MV4 ME SBR

18/10/00 False Heavy, You Took Me By Surprise, Fuego, 75 (Version) John Have A

Pee. & Simon 'the Hippy' Healey. 1/10/00 MV4 ME~

Heads Hands and Feet

31/3/72 I'm In Need Of Your Help, Try To Put Me On, Safety In Numbers, Road Show (& Warming Up The Band / Hot Property, 9/6/72). Tony Colton (v), Ray Smith (gv), Pete Gavin (dv), Chas Hodges (bv), Albert Lee (gv). 14/3/72 T1 JM U 2 previous Sounds of the Seventies sessions plus Sunday Show Concert in 71

11/7/72 Hang Me Bang Me, Dancer, Harlequin, Rhyme And Time. 23/5/72 MV4 PR U

The Heart Throbs

27/4/89 In Vain, Shut Down, I Wonder Why. Stephen Ward (k), Rose Carlotti (lv, g), Rachel Carlotti (b, bck), Mark Side (d), Alan Barclay (g). 11/4/89 WX DG MR Debut session was for Simon Mayo March 88

20/8/90 Pumping, Slip And Slide, Calavera. 15/7/90 MV3 DG TD&DB

Heavenly

14/4/91 And The Birds Aren't Singing, So Little Deserve, Escort Crash On Marston Street. Mathew Fletcher (d), Rob Pursey (b), Peter Montchiloff (g), Amelia Fletcher (gv). 17/3/91 MV3 DG ME&CML

7/5/94 Sacramento, Itchy Chin, Dumpster, Sperm Meets Egg So What? & Cathy Rogers (k). 9/4/94 MV4 MR BT

Heavy Metal Kids

23/7/74 Rock And Roll Man, It's The Same, Hanging On, Runaround Eyes. Ronnie Thomas (bv), Keith Boyce (d, perc), Micky Waller (g), Danny Peyronel (kv), Gary Holton (lgv). 2/7/74 LH1 TW U

Hefner

13/10/98 The Science Fiction, I Stole A Bride, You Need A Mess Of Help To Stand Alone, Lisa And Me. Darren Hayman (v, g, p), John Morrison (b), Antony Harding (dv). 27/9/98 MV3 MA SA The band persuaded BBC staff to unlock the old BBC Radiophonic Workshop at Maida Vale, and borrowed original synthesisers to use on Science Fiction

3/3/99 Gospel Covers session: Nobody Knows, Dragnet For Jesus, Better Things For You, Turkle Dove. Jack Hayter (lsg, vi, v) joins; & Anoosha Jamaratnam (p-2). 17/1/99 MV3 ME PN

12/8/99 We Love The City, Hold Me Closer Tonight, Down Street, Seafaring, Goodfruit. 4-piece. Live from Peel Acres AR GT

8/12/99 Lonely This Christmas. Live from MV3 AKM&AR SA

28/3/00 Don't Give Up, Kate Cleaver's House, Milkmaids (& Everything Is Falling Apart 12/4/00). 16/2/00 MV4 SA GT

23/8/00 Head To Your Toes, The Greater London Radio, Don't Flake Out On Me, The Good Fruit, The Greedy Ugly People, The Cure For Evil, Don't Go, She Can't Sleep No More, The Day That Thatcher Dies, The Sad Witch. Hayter (mel, moog, g, lsg) & Amelia Fletcher (v), Neil Yates (tp), Mat Colman (tb), Andrew Ross (sx). Live from MV4 SCU MA

19/12/00 Hymn For The Alcohol. 4-piece. 13/12/00 MV3 AR MA

16/1/01 King Of Summer, Peppermint Taste, Can't Help Losing You, The Nights Are Long. 29/11/00 MV4 MA~

11/12/01 Gabriel In The Airport, New French Tits, The Pines, Anne And Bill. 9/9/01 MV4 ME GYW

16/12/04 The Librarian, Hymn For The Alcohol. Live from MV3 MA GT

John Hegley

2/4/96 Amen, A Crisis Across The Street, Sandal Man, In The Name Of The Lord, My Brother In Law, Sister, Omo, Rover, The Old Scoutmaster. John Hegley (v, ag), Nigel Piper (5&8–ag, 9–mnd) (all but 5, 8&9, poems). Live from on-air studio at BHM LR TWN

Helen and the Horns

7/9/83 Pioneer Town, Footsteps At My Door, Snakebite, Freight Train. Helen McCookerybook (gbv), Marc Jordan (tp), Dave Jago (tb), Paul Davey (sx). 31/8/83 MV4 BYA U

5/12/83 Secret Love, Twice Brewed, I'd Been Hoping For A Happy Ending, Southern Belle. & Michael Riley (perc). 26/11/83 MV4 MR MR

1/8/84 Lonesome Country Boy, Two Strings To Your Bow, Girl Versus Boy, Take Five. Helen, Jago, Davey, Chris Smith (tp, flh), Simon Walker (vi). 25/7/84 MV5 SFX U

Helen Love

14/10/97 Punk Boy, Joey Ramoney, Yeah Yeah We're Helen Love, Girl About Town. Helen Jones (v), Gary Love (g), Mark Hunter (k), Tim Wheeler (v), Dave Inson (k). 28/9/97 MV4 ME RF

Hellacopters

30/9/99 Gotta Get Some Action Now, Disappointment Blues, Slow Down (Take A Look), Empty Heart. Nick Royale (g, v, maracas), Kenny (b), Robert (d), Mr Strings (lg), Boba Fett (p). 18/8/99 MV4 MR PN

9/4/03 By The Grace Of God, Better Than You, Down On Freestreet, Carry Me Home, Venue In Force, Crimson Ballroom, No Song Unheard, Toys And Flavours, All I've Got, Soulseller, (Action) Now, Search And Destroy. Anders Niklas Andersson (lv, g), Robert Dahlqvist (g), Kenny Håkansson (b), Robert Eriksson (dv) Anders Lindström (p, rg). Live from MV3 AR~

Hells

10/2/04 Johnny Digs The Devil, My Kinda Lover, Operator Operator, The Birds. Ippy (gv), Kevin (gv), Ed (d). 14/1/04 MV AR GT

Helmet

22/6/91 Unsung§, Rude†, Sinatra†, Your Head§. John Stanier (d), Henry Bogdan (b), Peter Mengede (g), Page Hamilton (gv). 26/5/91 MV3 DG ME&AM ○ † On Strange Fruit SFMCD212 § On Amphetamine Reptile SCALE 41

Help Yourself

8/5/71 Crazy Cajun Cakewalk Man, Running Down Deep, Old Man. Malcolm Morley (gv), Richard Treece (b), David Charles (d), Ernie Graham (gv), Jonathan Glemser (g). 26/4/71 PH JW BC

19/5/72 Johnny B Goode, Re-Affirmation, Let It Roll (& While Away, 30/6/72). Paul Burton (b) r Graham, Glemser (Treece now lg). 25/4/72 T1 JM U

17/4/73 Amy, Blown Away, Who Killed Paradise, Man We're Glad We Know You. Ken Whaley (b) r Burton. 10/4/73 T1 JW U

The Jimi Hendrix Experience ○

15/10/67 Little Miss Lover, Driving South, Burning Of The Midnight Lamp, Hound Dog, Experiencing The Blues (aka Catfish Blues) (& I Was Made To Love Her / Ain't Too Proud To Beg [Instrumental Jam], Driving South [Take #2], both not TX). Jimi Hendrix (gv), Noel Redding (bv), Mitch Mitchell (d) & Stevie Wonder (d-6). 6/10/67 PH BP PR ○

24/12/67 Radio One Jingle, Wait Until Tomorrow, Day Tripper, Spanish Castle Magic, Getting My Heart Back Together Again (Aka. Hear My Train A-Coming) (& Getting My Heart Back Together Again Etc [Take #1], not TX). 15/12/67 PH BP PR ● SFPS065 ○ All tracks from both Peel sessions, plus all complete takes from Hendrix's 3 other BBC Radio Sessions, plus BBC TV Lulu show Jan 69, now on 2CD set BBC Sessions from Experience Hendrix/MCA Records

Christie Hennessy

26/2/74 Far Away In Australia, The Wealthy Squire, Casey's Wake, Messenger Boy. Christie Hennessy (agv) & (dul), (fd) unknown. 11/2/74 T1 JW NG

Henry Cow

29/5/71 Hieronymo's Mad Again, Poglith Drives A Vauxhall Viva. Fred Frith (gpv, vi), Tim Hodgkinson (o, alv), Sean Jenkins (d), John Greaves (bgv). 4/5/71 MV4 JW BC A winner in our new groups competition', John Walters to audition panel: unanimous pass for 'progressive programmes'

14/3/72 Teen Beat, Rapt In A Blanket, I Came To See You. Chris Cutler (d) r Jenkins; & Geoff Leigh (ts, fl). 28/2/72 PH JW BC

14/11/72 With The Yellow Half Moon And Blue Star, With The Yellow Half Moon And Blue Star Pt 2. & DJ Perry (speech) this date only. 17/10/72 LH1 JW BC

8/5/73 Guider Tells Of Silent Airborne Machine, 9 Funerals Of The Citizen King, Bee. 24/4/73 LH1 JW U

9/5/74 Pidgeons: Ruins / Half Awake Half Asleep / Bittern Storm Over Ulm. Lindsay Cooper (ob) joins. 25/4/74 LH1 JW U

18/8/75 Beautiful As The Moon Terrible As An Army With Banners, Nirvana For Mice, The Ottawa Song, Gloria Gloom, Beautiful As The Moon Etc (Reprise). & Dagmar Krause (v), Leigh out. 5/8/75 MV4 TW BC

The Hepburns

17/4/89 Tonight The World Of Entertainment, Where You Belong, Believe Me, You Must Have Had It All. Les Mun (d), Mike Thomas (b), Nigel Boulton (g), Matt Jones (gv), Iain Davies (k). 21/3/89 WX DG MR

The Herd

26/11/67 Mixed-Up Minds, Come On Believe Me, Paradise Lost, She Loves Me She Loves Me Not, I Want You. Peter Frampton, Andy Bown, Gary Taylor, Andrew Steele. 22/11/67 MV4 BA U Debut session on Pop North from Manchester Playhouse 11/5/67

Here

18/12/93 Hold On, Tingling, Nothing To Say. Martin Pecka (d), Pavel Koutny (b), Tom Luska (g), Zdenek Marek (g), Michaela Klimkova (v). 9/11/93 MV4 MR RPF

Here and Now

16/11/78 This Time, What You See Is What You Are, Oh My God Can Be So Hard We Tried And We Tried But Couldn't Find It, Chicken Marimba. Gavin da Blitz (sy), Keith da Missile Bass (bv), Freddy Facetious (dv), Steffy Sharpsticks (gv), Suzz da Blooz & Annie Wombat ('choir of angels'). 8/11/78 MV4 MR MR

Here's Johnny

5/1/84 Hellzapoppin', World In Action, Every Mirror I See, Your Room. Colin McKay (v), Dave Knowles (k), Andy Zsigmond (g), Steve Brown (d), Dave Whittaker (b) & Caroline McKinnon (bck-4). 21/12/83 MV4 RP NG

Heresy

3/8/87 Flowers (In Concrete), Belief / Network Of Friends, Sick Of Stupidity, Too Slow To Judge / A Sense Of Freedom. Steve Charlesworth (d), Calvin Piper (b), Mitchell Dickinson (g), John March (v). 26/7/87 U DG MA&ME

9/3/88 Consume / Face Up To It, Into The Grey, When Unity Becomes Solidarity, The Street Enters The House / Cornered Rat, Open Up. Steven Ballam (g) r Dickinson. 1/3/88 MV4 DG MC

18/1/89 Everyday Madness Everyday, Break The Connection / Ghettoised, Network Ends, Release / Genocide. 10/1/89 MV4 DG MR

Herman Dune

10/10/00 Numbers 3, Don't Look Too Deeply Into My Eyes, How Things Slide, Stealing The Bride (Part 1), Lazy Boys (Don't Stand A Chance). David-Ivar Herman Dune (gv), Andre Herman Dune (gv), Ome (d, bck). 3/9/00 MV4 ME GYW

21/12/00 Channukah In Florida, plus title unknown. Neman (d) r Ome. Live from Peel Acres AR GT/SA

15/5/02 Garden Song, Sticky Fingers, Red Blue Eyes, Little Architect, Big Bad Man, Expect The Unexpected, HD-Rider, Teddy Monkey Bear, Songs About Songwriting Suck. Trio; & The Flower Choir Ensemble, including Scout Nibblett, Robots In Disguise, Dufus, Laura Hoch, Lisa Li-Lund. Live from MV4 AR/MWT JHT

11/9/02 The Static Comes From My Broken Heart, Stick Around, Your Favourite Song, Catcher In The Rye, If Someone Loves You. & Leah Hayes (bck), Amanda Gomez (bck). 17/2/02 MV4 ME GT

29/1/03 Run Like Crazy, Dust Off Your Heart, What Are You, The Neighbours, Air Drum To Pavement. & Laura Hoch aka John Courage (v), David Tattersall aka The Wave Pictures (gv). 8/1/03 MV4 SA GT

15/5/03 Song For The Family, Wake Up To The World, At Your Luau, Nothing Here, Lover Lover, Your Priorities, HD-Rider, Show Me The Roof, Winners Lose. & Q (al), Sheila Ravenscroft (v-5). Live from Peel Acres AR GT

5/2/04 Sheer Wonder Baby, Drop of Dew, Time Of Glory / NYC, Pet Rabbit, Will You Still Love Me Tomorrow? & Lisa Li Lund (v). 8/1/04 MV4 GT MA

Mike Heron's Reputation

5/5/75 Draw Back The Veil, Sold On Your Love & unknown other titles. Mike Heron (gv), Malcolm Le Maistre (v), Graham Forbes (lg), David Barker (k), Mike Tomich (b), John Gilston (d). 15/4/75 MV4 U U

19/4/77 Do It Yourself, Draw Back The Veil, Are You Going To Hear The Music. Billed just as 'Heron': Frank Usher (lg), Dave Sams (k) r Forbes, Barker. 5/4/77 MV4 JG MR

Hey Paulette

1/8/89 Our Immeasurable Differences, I Really Do Love Penelope, A Pet Day, Erstwhile Wet Blanket. Darren Nolan (d), Colom Fitzpatrick (b), Derrick Dalton (g, bck), Eammon Davis (gv). 25/6/89 MV3 DG MC

Hi Fi

15/3/79 Movie Condition, The Silence, Feel Naked, Black Taxi. Larry Berridge (g, lv), Doctor Jenkins (lg, bck), Byron Conn (b), Steve Jones (d, perc). 7/3/79 MV4 JS NG

Hiding Place

5/1/78 Lucky Seven, Roll It, The Wanderer, Looking Out. Kenny Driscoll (v), Tich (lgv), Dave Dawson (bv), Robert Allen (dv), Paul Abrahams (k). 19/12/77 MV4 U U

The High Fidelity

5/5/98 My Frequency, Whitey, Lazy B, Pelvic Rock. Sean Dickson (gv, sfx, om), Paul Dallaway (g, chimes), Adrian Barry (b, bck), Ross Mcfarlane (d, perc). 17/3/98 MV4 MR NK

8/12/99 Silent Night. Live from MV3 AKM&AR SA

The High Five

6/10/82 If They Come In The Morning, The Curse Of Revolt, Turning, No Guarantee. Rob Jones (d), Phil Jones (b), Mark Braben (g), Aza (lv, g), Jake Waksten (perc). 11/9/82 MV4 DG MC

6/6/83 Cold Steel Gang, On The Banks, Hand On My Heart, Big Village. Hamish Cameron (k, hca) r Waksten. 23/5/83 MV4 TW U

12/3/84 100 Tons, Walk Them Back, Working For The Man, Hard Line. John Hughes (p-3) r Cameron. 3/3/84 MV5 DG MC

High Level Ranters

18/4/72 A Mile To Ride / Jockey Lay Up In The Hayloft, Plains Of Waterloo, High Level Bridge Hornpipe, Felton Lonnen, The Hens March / The Broken-legged Chicken / The Black Cow Of Whickam, Gillian The Prover / Neil Gow's Wife. Johnny Handle, Tom Gilfellow, Alistair Anderson, Colin Ross. 10/4/72 PH JW U Previous sessions on folk shows 66–68

18/7/74 Fenwick Of Bywell, Marley Hill Ducks, Dance To Your Daddy, Hesleyside Reel. Johnny Handle (acc, pp, v), Colin Ross (pp, jh), Alistair Anderson (cnc), Tom Gilfellow (gv). 3/7/74 NW JW U

High Tide

21/5/69 Walking Down Their Outlook, Pushed But Not Forgotten, Missing Out. Tony Hill (g), Simon House (vi), Peter Pavli (b), Rodge Cooper (d). 9/5/69 PS PR U 'Borderline pass' from panel: 'I don't like this at all' said one producer

17/8/69 Walking Down Their Outlook, Nowhere, Futilist's Lament, Dilemma. 12/8/69 PH JW U

11/4/70 The Joke, Saneoni Mous. 24/3/70 MV4 JW U

The Higsons

1/6/81 (I Don't Want To Live With) Monkeys†, Got To Let This Heat Out†, A Dash To The Shops†, Surrender†. Switch Higson (v), Terry Edwards (g, sx, tp, bck), Stuart McGeachin (g, bck), Colin Williams (b, bck), Simon Charterton (d, bck). 27/5/81 LH1 CL NG

4/11/81 We Will Never Grow Old†, Conspiracy, Where Have All The Club A-Go-Go's Went Went?, Touchdown†. 21/10/81 MV4 U U

11/10/82 John Peel's New Sig Tune, You Should Have Run Me Down, Gangway, Annie And Billy, Put The Punk Back Into Funk. 22/9/82 MV4 RP MC

22/6/83 Push Out The Boat†, Clanking My Bucket†, Round And Round, Attack Of The Cannibal Zombie Business Men†. & Dan Higson (sx). 9/5/83 MV4 TW MC

25/6/84 Walk On Water†, 1958†, Keep The Fire Alight, It's A Wonderful Life†. 13/6/84 MV5 RP NG † on ○ It's A Wonderful Life HUX004 CD

Roy Hill Band

27/6/78 It Can Take A Lifetime, Melody Avenue, I Like I Like I Like, More, It's Only My Life. Roy Hill (glv), Colin Wilkinson (d), Gary Twigg (bv), Ross McGeeny (lgv), Mike Taylor (kv), Peter Acock (sxv) (4–Hill). 20/6/78 MV4 MB MR

9/4/79 Baby Don't Pretend, Small Adventurer, The Loser, TV Detective. Hill, Taylor, Acock, John Knightsbridge (g), Tony Fernandoz (d), Chas Cronk (b). 2/4/79 MV6 TW DD

Holger Hiller

25/3/87 Holger Hiller, Tiny Little Cloud, 48 Kissen, Warm Glas. Holger Hiller (prg, smp, v), Izumi Kobayashi (k). 8/3/87 U DG NG&PS

Hint

14/5/02 A Shout Of Blue, Words To That Effect, Quite Spectacular. Jonathan James. 31/3/02 MV4 ME NF

Hirameka Hi Fi

4/5/99 The Formalists, Scolio Sister, Osterburg, A Warning And An Ultimatum. Chris Baldwin (g, v, p), Tom Coogan (g, v, cel), Steve Nice (b), Ben Wright (d). 28/3/99 MV3 ME MPK

11/12/02 Take On The Break, All A Tremble, The Culling Song. Pete Heddle (b) r Nice. Live from MV4 MA~ GT

Hitchers

12/8/97 Human Skull, Wannabe, Urge To Kill, My Band. Andy Gallagher (lg), Niall Quinn (d, bck), Eric Fitzgerald (g), Hoss Carnage (b). 27/7/97 MV4 ME KR

Hits

23/6/78 Bring Me The Head Of Yukio Mashinaldi, Et Moi Et Moi Et Moi, Only Thirteen, Crossroads. Giovanni Dadomo (v), Dave Fudger (g), Barry Myers (b), Nick Howell (d). 6/6/78 MV4 MB MR

Hives

21/11/01 Hate To Say I Told You So, Lost And Found, Barely Homosapian, Howlin' Pelle Talks To The British People. Howlin' Pelle Almqvist (v), Nicholaus Arson (treble guitar), Vigilante Carlstroem (middle guitar), Dr Matt Destruction (b), Chris Dangerous (d). 22/10/01 MV4 MA JHT

Hixxy

17/3/04 DJ Mix Set OS

16/12/04 10–min DJ mix for Keepin' It Peel night live from MV5 GYW JHT

Hockett

17/10/72 When I Was A Little Boy, Meri It Is, Seven Yellow Gypsies. Gary Carpenter (o, fl, p), Ian Cutler (vi), Andy Tompkins (g), Bernie Murray (d), Ray Warman (bv). 9/10/72 U JW U

Hofman

19/8/98 The Friendship Song, Guanabana, Scratch My Back, Bank Of Filth (& Paid To Wait 1st TX live 14/7/98). Steven Adams (v), Jason Williams (g), Andrew Young 'Chad' (b), Neil Rogers 'Bugs' (d). 14/7/98 MV4 MR RJ

Hole

5/1/92 Violet, Forming, Drown Soda, Doll Parts. Caroline Rue (d), Jill Emery (b), Eric Erlandson (lg), Courtney Love (g, lv). 19/11/91 MV4 MR MR&CML

16/4/93 The Void, Olympia, She Walks On Me (Sic), Pee Girl. Love, Erlandson, Kristen Pfaff (b, bck), Patty Schemel (d). 25/3/93 MV4 JB~ PL

Holle Holle

23/9/87 Patli Patang, Pind Na Challia, Ankhaa Tunai Haar, Holle Holle. Chandu & Arun (Indian drums), Inder (perc), Abass (cga), Ragen (b), Deepak (g), Shatish (k), Joe (sx), Manjeet (lv), Bina & Kum Kum (bck-4). 15/9/87 U DG MR&JB

Tim Hollier

20/11/68 Bird Of Paradise, In Silence, Song To A Room, And I, I Search For Small Distractions. Tim Hollier (gv). 20/11/68 S1 PC U

The Hollies

22/10/67 Games We Play, Step Inside, King Midas In Reverse, Postcard, Charlie And Fred, Away Away Away. Graham Nash, Allan Clarke, Tony Hicks, Bobby Elliott, Bernard Calvert; & orchestra of 14, with Johnny Scott (md). 13/10/67 U U U Group's first broadcast was on 'The Talent Spot' Light Programme 7/6/63. Dozens of pop sessions followed

Holy Ghost

31/3/95 Cobol Blu, Evil Eye, The Phaser, The Ice Man. Leon Thompson (g), Greg Griffith (sy), Gary Griffith (g). 1/1/95 OS

Holy Mackerel

16/11/72 Waterfall, Spanish Attraction, On, The Boy And The Mekon. Terry Clark (v), Derek Smallcombe (lg), Anthony Wood (b), Chris Ware (lg), Roger Siggery (d). 13/11/72 LH1 BA U Had recorded daytime sessions under previous name 'Jason Crest' after passing audition 11/68

Holy Willie's Prayer

16/1/71 Willow, Very Good Time, If You Don't, Honesty. Chris Hardy (g, vi, v), Rod Cameron (p, hmn, gv). 29/12/70 MV4 U U. 'Booked as unknown duo after submitting tape', John Walters to audition panel

Home

3/11/71 Tramp, The Idol, Mother, In My Time. Laurie Wisefield (lgv), Michael Stubbs (lgv), Clifford Williams (bv), Michael Cook (d). 4/10/71 PH U U 2 previous Sounds of the Seventies sessions, the first for Stu Henry in June 71, produced by Malcolm Brown: 'I got the impression that when they really settle down they will become quite a force in the business… the guitarist is only 17,' he reported to the audition panel: unanimous pass

23/5/72 Rise Up, Red-E-Lewis And The Red Caps, Baby Friend Of Mine. 9/5/72 MV4 U U

28/7/72 Shady Lady, Baby Friend Of Mine, Knave, How Would It Feel? 28/6/72 T1 PD U

29/3/73 Dreamer, I Like What You Do To Me, How Would It Feel? 26/3/73 LH1 BA U

1/11/73 Red-E-Lewis And The Red Caps, Dreamer, Excerpt From The Alchemist. & Dave Skillen (v), Jim Anderson (p). 22/10/73 LH1 BA U

A Homeboy a Hippie and a Funky Dredd

3/2/91 Drop Your Soul, Vicious, Dream. Mark Williams (pv) & Tony Winter. 13/1/91 MV3 DG MA Debut session was for Kershaw Nov 90

Homesick James and Grizelda

31/10/70 Got To Move, Skies Are Crying, Crossroads, Dust My Broom. Homesick James (gv). 19/10/70 PH JW U

The Honey Bus

19/11/67 Maxine's Parlour, Do I Figure In Your Life, Good Day Sunshine, Arise Sir Henry, Like An Old Time Movie. Pete Dello, Ray Cane, Colin Boyd, Peter Kircher; & strings. 15/11/67 MV4 BA PR

18/2/68 Ain't That Just Bonnie For You, I Can't Let Maggie Go, Francoise, She Comes To Me. 7/2/68 MV4 BA PR

15/9/68 Looking Down, Girl Of Independent Means, Scarlet Lady, How Long, Warwick Town. & 3 extra musicians. 20/8/68 PC1 BA AH

29/12/68 Black Mourning Band, Girl Of Independent Means, She Sold Blackpool Rock, Would You Believe?, Incredibly Bad. Jim Kelly r Dello; & 2 vi, vla, tp / frh, flh. 17/12/68 PC1 BA U

5/10/72 I Can't Say It But I Can Sing It, Big Ship, The Lady's Not For Burning, Writing's On The Wall, Lady. Dello returns, r Kelly. 2/10/72 LH1 BA U

The Honeymoon Killers

24/11/82 Fonce A Mort, Histoire A Suivre, Reveillons-Nous, Romantic Evening. Marc Hollander (k), Jean François Jones (d), Yves Flon (sx), Vincent Kenis (b), Yvon Kromman (v-1&4, g-2&3), Veronique Vincent (v-2,3), Gerald Fenerberg (g). 13/11/82 U DG MR

Hood

3/11/95 I Wish I Was A Crowbar, I've Forgotten How To Live, Fashion Mistake Of The Decade, Diesel Pioneers. Andrew Johnson (d, p), John Clyde-Evans (b, tps), Richard Adams (g, b), Craig Tattersall (g, k), Chris Adams (g, v, noise). 15/10/95 MV3 ME RJ

Hooton 3 Car

18/3/95 Strained, Sound Of The Day, Disclaimer/Lucky Day, Three Steps Back. Jonathon Jesson (d, bck), Chris Petty (g, bck), Graham Williams (g, lv), Hywel Maggs (b). 23/2/95 MV4 MPK RJ

28/4/96 Hallways, Playdoh, Swim Feeder, Carpet Burn. 26/3/96 MV5 AA GT

13/5/97 Not Recognised, What If, Oinnacle, Did You Ever Think, Danny. 20/4/97 MV4 ME SBR

The Hoovers

2/3/91 Green, Comes A Time, Mr Average, Big Time. Jo So (d), Phil (g), Granty (bv), Owey (gv). 29/1/91 MV5 MR MR

Hopewell

22/5/01 There Is Something, There is Nothing, In The Small Places, Square Peg Teeth, Contact. prob. Lyndon Roeller, Rich Meyer, Jason Russo, Tyson Lewis, Jay Green. 9/5/01 MV4 SA NF

Hopper

15/10/94 Sores, Oh My Heartless, Ridiculous Day, The Bartender, Bad Kid. Rachel Morris (v), Chris Bowers (b), Paul Sheppard (g), Mark Blackmore (d). 2/10/94 MV3 ME SB

Horslips

16/10/73 An Bratach Ban, Dearg Doom, Knockeen Free. Barry Devlin (bv), Jim Lockhart (fl, kv), Johnny Fean (g), Eamonn Carr (d), Charles O'Connor (fd, mnd, v). 1/10/73 T1 JW U Debut session was for Bob Harris 3 weeks earlier

19/2/74 The Silver Spear, Charolet / The March / You Can't Fool The Beast. 28/1/74 T1 JW U

19/11/74 Mad Pat / Blind Man, Lonely Hearts, Nightown Boys. 4/11/74 MV4 TW U

Hot Snakes

18/11/04 Brain Trust, This Mystic Decade, No Hands, Automatic Midnight. Mario Rubalcaba (d), Gar Wood (b), John Reis (g), Erik Farr (gv), Nikhil Ranade (k). 14/10/04 MV4 JHT MWT

Hot Water

13/9/78 Boxer, Back To The Beach, Motorway, Dark Fooling Man. Ben (Brenda) Prescott (v), Sheila Macartney (v), John Lovering (g), Ann Williams (k), Paul Shroud (b), Jeff Taylor (sx), Roy Smith (cga, perc), Owen Hughes (d). 30/8/78 MV4 BS NG

A House

9/2/87 Call Me Blue, YOU, Hit Me Over The Head With Your Handbag Dear, Heart Happy. David Couse (v, ag), Fergal Bunbury (g), Martin Healy (b), Dermot Wylie (d). 25/1/87 U DG ME&FK

13/3/92 Endless Art, Charity, Freakshow, Force Feed. Couse, Bunbury, Healy, Dave Dawson (d), Dave Morrisey (k), Susan Kavanagh (bck). 2/2/92 MV3 DG ME&RF

The House Of Love ◯

20/6/88 Destroy The Heart, Nothing to Me, Plastic, Blind. Guy Chadwick (gv), Terry Bickers (g), Chris Groothuizen (b), Pete Evans (d). 7/6/88 MV4 DG DD

14/9/88 The Hedonist, Don't Turn Blue, Safe, Love In Car. 26/8/88 MV4 DG MA

12/4/89 In A Room, The Beatles And The Stones, Christine, Loneliness Is A Gun. Acoustic session. 2/4/89 MV4 DG MR

1/1/90 Se Dest, 32nd Floor, 7.45 Am. Bickers out. 12/12/89 MV5 DG ME

15/12/91 Into The Tunnel, Fade Away, High In Your Face. Simon Fernsby (lg) joins. 5/11/91 MV4 MR MR

22/8/92 Cruel, Burn Down The World, Crush Me. Simon Manby (g, bck) r Fensby. 4/8/92 MV4 PL PL&AA Everything on ◯ The Complete Peel Sessions Universal/ Mercury 2006

The Housemartins ◯

29/7/85 Drop Down Dead†, Flag Day†, Stand At Ease†, Joy Joy Joy. Hugh Whittaker (dv), Ted Key (bv), Stan Cullimore (gv), Paul Heaton (v) & guest Kevin Abbott (tp-2). 21/7/85 MV5 DG ME

14/4/86 Over There†, It's Happy Hour, Get Up Off Our Knees, Caravan Of Love†. Norman Cook (b, bck) r Key. 6/4/86 MV5 DG ME&FK

16/6/86 Happy Hour†, Heaven Help Us All†, He Ain't Heavy He's My Brother, When I First Met Jesus, Peel Show Sig (A Cappella)†. Billed as 'The Fish City 5', a cappella session. 3/6/86 MV4 DG TdB&FK

11/11/87 There Is Always Something There To Remind Me§, Sunday Isn't Sunday†, Build†. Dave Hemingway (dv) r Whittaker. 3/11/87 U DG U † on ◯ Live At The BBC Universal/Mercury § On ● Now That's What I Call Quite Good LP Go! Discs

Huevos Rancheros

19/5/95 Get Outta Dodge, Jack The Ripper, El Rancho Relaxo, Telstar, Rocket To Nowhere, Rumble. Brent J Cooper (g), Rich Lazarowich (d), Graham Evans (b). 25/4/95 MV3 MR JLO

Huggy Bear

11/12/92 Hop Scotch, Teen Tightens, Nu Song, Her Jazz. Chriss Rowley (v), Jo Johnson (g), Jon Slade (g), Niki Eliot (bv), Karen Hill (d). 27/10/92 MV4 MR~

18/6/93 Limit To Surf, You Don't, Untitled, Stepping On Bugs. Bald Maude (d), Nucleus Seizure (Singing Boy), Butch David Cassidy (Silent Guitar), The Rinky Dink Panther (gv), Lizzie Strychnine HRH (bv). 16/5/93 MV3 ME~ NS

Hula

25/3/85 Freeze Out, Bad Blood, Sour Eden, Gun Culture. Ron Wright (gv, mel), Simon Crump (sx, bcl), John Avery (bk, perc), Mark Albrow (k, tps), Nort (d, perc). 12/3/85 MV5 MR JB

2/10/85 Big Heat, Ninth Degree, Torn Silk, Motor City. 22/9/95 U U U

16/7/86 Burn It Out, When That Hammer Starts To Beat, Backwall Blue, Church Trumpet. Darrell D'Silva (al, ts) r Crump. 1/7/86 MV4 DG DD

Hula Hoop

8/1/93 Leave Time To Go, Sometimes I Feel Just Alright, Blues From a Vaseline Gun, Oh Toby. Stephen Jones (d), Rachel Grimes (b, bck), Chuck Geisler (glv), Eric Stoess (glv). 10/11/92 MV4 MR~ PL

15/1/94 Jodhpur, The Coolest Thing, Butterfingered, Wisteria. 30/11/93 MV4 MR NS

Alan Hull

18/1/73 The Miller's Song, The Money Game, Numbers, Tynemouth Song (& Country Gentleman's Wife, 8/2/73). Alan Hull (gpv). 8/1/73 LH1 BA NG Debuted as solo act live from PH on Country Meets Folk, 31/1/70

11/12/73 Take Good Care Of Business, Gin And Tonics All Round, Money Game, Waiting. 12/11/73 T1 U BC

29/5/75 Squire, Dan The Plan, Money Game, One More Bottle Of Wine, City Song. 22/5/75 MV4 U U

6/4/76 Walk In The Sea, Love Is The Answer, I Wish You Well, Somewhere Out There. 11/3/76 MV4 U U

The Human League

16/8/78 Being Boiled, No Time, You've Lost That Lovin' Feeling, Blind Youth. Ian Marsh (sy, k, v), Martyn Ware (sy, k, v), Philip Oakey (v), Adrian Wright (visuals). 8/8/78 MV4 BS MR

Human Orchestra

3/5/76 Games, Stop. U 3/2/76 MV4 U U

Humanoid

28/11/88 Orbital (Feeling), Slam, Jet Stream Tokyo. Brian Dougans, John Lakker. 15/11/88 MV4 MR MR

Humble Pie

27/9/69 Shakin' All Over, Shakey Jake / Walk On Gilded Splinters. Steve Marriott (gv) Peter Frampton (gv), Greg Ridley (b), Jerry Slater (d). 9/9/69 MV4 JW TW&BC Debut session was for Symonds on Sunday Aug 69

Humblebums

7/3/70 Please Sing A Song For Us, Harry, Rick Rack, Mother (& Everybody Knows That, 13/6/70). Billy Connolly, Gerry Rafferty & Daryl Runswick, Bernie Holland, Mike Travis. 23/2/70 U U U Previous broadcasts in Scotland

Hunches

22/9/04 Static Disaster, Lisa Told Me, Pinwheel Spins, Droning Fades On, Leper Parade, When I Became Yan, Lost Time Frequency, A Flower In The Ending, Where Am I. Chris Gunn (g), Sarah Epstein (b), Hart Gledhill (v, oil drum), Ben Spencer (d). Live from MV4 AR~

Michael Hurley

11/11/99 O My Stars, Driving Wheel, Nat'l Weed Growers Association, Your Old Gearbox, I Think I'll Move. Michael Hurley (gv), Dave Reisch (b, bck). 22/8/99 Sonic Studios, Dublin

Hybirds

17/9/97 24, The Only Ones, Stranded, Born Yesterday. Rich Warren (g, lv, hp), Louis Divito (d), Darren Sheldon (b), Lee Horsley (k), Sebastian Lewsley (Moog). 17/8/97 MV4 PL LS

Hyper Kinako

12/3/03 F**ksake Sujiko, Bika Lika, Two Tadgers, Popping Step, Don't Delete My Frog. Toko (v, penyoliser), Shigeto Wada (cmp, k, v), Phil Archer (g), Lisa Hotron (b), Greg Macdermott (d). 20/2/03 MV4 SA NF

Hypnotone

20/4/91 Paris, Hypnotonic, Yu Yu, Sub. Tony Martin (k, prg), Martin Duffy (k), Valerie Fisher (v), Carlos Manning (rp). 28/3/91 MV4 DG TdB&JMK

I Am Kloot ◯

9/8/01 Storm Warning, Twist, Titanic, 86 Tv's, Stop, Your Favourite Sky. John Bramwell (gv), Andy Hargreaves (d), Peter Jobson (b, p, g). 18/7/01 MV4 SA NS ◯

11/3/04 Life In A Day, This House Is Haunted, Proof, Strange Without You, Untitled 2. 5/2/04 MV4 JSM NS ◯ Skinnydog 16CD

I, Ludicrous

16/6/87 Fabulous, Quite Extraordinary, A Pop Fan's Dream, Ridiculous. Mark Crossley (b), John Procter (g, k, dm), David Rippingdale (v). 31/5/87 U DG ME&FK

Ian Rush

4/12/93 Catrin Nadolig, Unrhyw Borthladd, Drwg Yn Y Caws, Cwcwy. Sion Williams (d), Mario Trasmundi (b), Peter Bryon (gv), Geraint Williams (g). 31/10/93 MV3 ME FK

Icarus

11/12/80 Don't Put Reggae In A Bag, Shall We Roam, Tower Block Kid. Cyril Charles (lv), Ashley Charles (v), Leroy Cyrus (k), Harold Cyrus (d), Leon Modeste (b), James Nagan (lg). 26/11/80 LH1 BS NG

The Icarus Line

24/7/01 Feed A Cat To Your Cobra, Love Is Happiness, 1970, SPMC. Lance Arnao (b), Aluin Deguzman (g), Jeff Watson (d), Aaron North (g), Joe Cardamone (v). 1/7/01 MV4 ME NF

24/7/02 The Big Sleep, Liss Like Lizard/Getting Bright At Night, Miss Bliss. Troy Petry (d) r Watson. 19/6/02 MV4 SA RJ

Ice

24/12/67 Please Don't Cry, Open The Door To Your Heart, Think, Walk On The Water. Lynton Naiff (o), Steve Turner, Grant Serpall, John Carter, Glyn James, Linda Hoile (v). 19/12/67 AO2 BA DT 2 previous daytime R1 sessions, Nov/Dec 67

The Icicle Works

26/1/82 In The Cauldron Of Love, A Factory In The Desert, All Is Right, When Winter Lasted Forever. Robert Ian McNabb (gkv), Chris Layhe (bv), Chris 'Chas' Sharrock (d). 11/1/82 MV4 TW DD

2/3/83 Love Is A Wonderful Colour, Reverie Girl, Reaping The Rich Harvest, In The Dance The Shaman Led. 26/2/83 MV4 DG MC

15/8/84 Hollow Horse, Deep In The Woods, Conscience Of Kings, When You Hear The Mission Bells. 8/8/84 MV5 BYA NG

Icon AD

13/10/82 Cancer, Clockwork Orange, Face The Facts, Ransom, No Hope. Caroline & Bev Smith (v), Craig Sharp (g), Roger Turnbull (b), Mark Holmes (d). 25/9/82 MV4 DG MPK

Ictus

22/7/04 Funkything, Drumbeat (First Offence), Do It Well, Luvbug, Yeah Yeah Yeah. Andy Halstead (e). 7/7/04 OS AHL~

Idiot Dancers

20/5/80 Imagination, True Soul, 500 Years, Jealousy. Tatty (d), Mike Horsham (bv), Dave McCarthy (gv). 14/5/80 MV4 JE NG

Idle Race

8/10/67 I Like My Toys, Hey Grandma, Knocking Nails Into My House, Imposters Of Life's Magazine, Here We Go Round The Lemon Tree. Jeff Lynne (gv), Dave Pritchard (gv), Greg Masters (bv), Roger Spencer (d). 2/10/67 PH BA PR

25/2/68 The Lady Who Would Fly, The Skeleton And The Roundabout, Tell Me The Time, Don't Put Your Boys In The Army Mrs Ward. 19/2/68 MV4 BA PR

9/6/68 The End Of The Road, Blueberry Blue, On With The Show, The Morning Sunshine (& Follow Me, Lucky Man, 7/7/68). 4/6/68 PC1 BA DT

22/9/68 Follow Me Follow, The Birthday, Told You Twice, Pie In The Sky. 3/9/68 PC1 BA AH

26/1/69 Mr Crowd And Sir Norman, Days Of The Broken Arrows, Sea Of Dreams, Worn Red Carpet (& Frantic Desolation, 9/3/69). 20/1/69 PH BA U

29/6/69 Sea Of Dreams, Please No More Sad Songs, Someone Knocking, Reminds Me Of You (& Come With Me, 3/8/69). 23/6/69 PH JW U

If

28/1/72 The City Is Falling, Box, (& Reaching Out On All Sides, 24/3/72). Jim Richardson (b), Terry Smith (lg), Dick Morrissey (sx, fl), Denis Elliott (d), Dave Quincy (ts, al), John Hodgkinson (v, perc), John Mealing (pv). 3/1/72 T1 PD ARV 4 previous Sounds of the Seventies sessions for other shows, 2 Concerts

Ifangi Bondi

24/9/90 Sanjo, Faro, Sikarsi. Momadou Nying (dv), Musa Mboob (Afd), Badou Jobe (b), Bai Janha & Aliey Dian (g), Adamu Sallah (k), Paps Touray (v), Ali Harb (v, fl). 29/7/90 MV3 DG ME&DTH

Ikara Colt

10/5/01 One Note, Pop Group, The Bishops Son, From The Beginning, Strangled Kite. Jon Ball (b), Clair Ingram (gv), Paul Resende (kv), Dominic Young (d). 25/3/01 MV4 JB SBR

10/4/02 Escalate, One Note, At The Lodge, After This, City Of Glass, Bishop's Son, Rudd, Pop Group, Video Clip Show, Sink Venice, Untitled. Live from MV4 SA JHT

27/11/02 Leave This Country, Seminal Lie, I'm With Stupid, Panic. 13/11/02 MV4 SA GYW

3/3/04 White Horses, Automatic, Rewind, Wake In The City. Tracy Bellaries (b) r Ball. 19/2/04 MV4 MA MWT

I'm Being Good

21/10/94 Flying Fatso, Non Existent Huts, I Am Bongo Legs, Double You, Black Sabbath Murder Weekend. Andru Clare (gv), David Campbell (g), Jason Williams (b), Tim Hall (d). 10/9/94 MV3 ME CML

23/7/03 Owl Service, Nostalgic For Fake Times, Last Few Days, Waste Of Bullets. Clare, Campbell, Tom Barnes (b, d). Live from MV4 AR SA/GT

I'm So Hollow

20/8/80 Fashion, Monotony, Dreams To Fill The Vacuum, Which Way? Gary Marsden (b), Jane Wilson (sy, v), Joe Sawicki (d), Rod Leigh (gv). 13/8/80 MV4 DG NG

Immortal Lee County Killers

22/1/03 Said I'd Find My Way, Nothin' Hurts Me Like My Back And Side, Cool Driver, She Likes It, Sh*tcanned Again, Robert Johnson, Goin' Down South, Let's Get Killed, Rollin' And Tumblin'. Chetley Weise (gv), J R Collins (dv). Live from MV4 SA

18/11/03 Revolution Summer, Been Down So Long, Boom Boom (Yeah Yeah), Cool Driver. 18/11/03 MV4 AR GT

In Camera

16/12/80 The Fatal Day, Co-ordinates, Apocalypse. David Steiner (v), Andrew Gray (g), Pete Moore (b), Jeff Wilmott (d). 9/12/80 LH1 JS MR

In Dust

12/2/93 Hyperdeemic Nerdle, Magnet Womb, Boredom Result, Auntie Christ. Steve Nolan (prg, g, v), Ryk Irvine (lg), Alen Finnegan (lv, odd jobs). 12/1/93 MV4 MR~ JMK

In Excelsis

8/2/84 Fire, Love Lies, Vows, Bonanza. Roxy (d), Mark (b), Spon (g), Errol (v). 25/1/84 MV5 DG NG

Inca Babies

6/2/84 Grunt Cadillac Hotel, Brother Rat, Superior Spectre, Big Jugular. Alan Brown (d), Bill Marten (b), Harry Stafford (g), Mike Keeble (v). 28/1/84 MV5 DG MC

28/8/84 The Judge, She Mercenary, Cactus Mouth Informer, Blind Man (The Chiller). Stafford, Keeble, Peter Bogg (d), Bill Bonney (b). 21/8/84 MV5 DG MC

26/6/85 Crawling Garage Gasoline, Doomed Locustland, Daniella, No Sacred Sound. Bill Marten (b) r Bonney. 16/6/85 MV5 DG ME

21/7/86 Plenty More Mutants, Opium Den, The Depths, Dresden. Stafford, Bogg, Bonney, Darren Bullows (g). 8/7/86 MV5 DG MS&JB

Incredible String Band

15/10/67 Painting Box, Mercy I Cry A City, Chinese White, Night Fall. Mike Heron (g, sit, hca), Robbie Williamson (g, vi, mnd, perc). 10/10/67 AO2 BA U

6/3/68 You Get Brighter Every Day, All Too Much For Me, Ducks On A Pond, Goodnight (& Won't You Come See Me, 26/6/68). 4/3/68 AO2 JM U

5/3/69 All Sit Down, Dust B Diamonds, Theta, Fine Fingered Hand. & Christina McKechnie, Rose Simpson. 5/2/69 S1 JM U

24/8/69 The Letter, This Moment, Gather Around, Waiting For You (& Black Jack David, 1/11/69). 5/8/69 MV4 JM U

25/7/70 Won't You Come See Me, Empty Pocket Blues, Flowers Of The Forest, Beautiful Stranger (& Dark-Eyed Lady, 3/10/70). 20/7/70 PH JW U

9/1/71 Everything's Fine Right Now, Long Long Road, The Circle Is Unbroken, Raga Phuti Raga. 6/10/70 MV4 JW U

13/10/71 You Get Brighter, Jigs, How We Danced The Lord Of Weir, The Actor. Malcolm Le Maistre (mnd, gv) r Simpson. 5/10/71 MV4 JW U

17/3/72 Oh Did I Love A Dream, Restless Night, Down Before Cathay (& Secret Temple, not TX). 29/2/72 T1 JM NG

29/8/72 Black Jack David, Rends-Moi Demain, Oh Did I Love A Dream, Hangman's Medley: Witches Hat / Ladybird / I Bid You Good Night / Long Time Sunshine. Stan Lee (ps), Stuart Gordon, r McKechnie; & Jack Ingram (g). 14/8/72 PH JW BC

6/3/73 Raga June, At The Lighthouse Dance, Saturday Maybe, Maker Of Islands. Gerard Dott r Gordon. 26/2/73 T1 PD&JW ARV

23/10/73 Dreams Of No Return, Black Jack David, Jane, Dear Old Battlefield. Mike Heron (g, sit, hca), Robin Williamson (mnd, g, vi), Graham Forbes, Jack Ingram (d), Stan Lee (b), Malcolm LeMaistre (gv). 9/10/73 LH1 JW BC Lots now on Q Across The Airwaves HUX087

23/11/00 Maker Of Islands, October Song, You Know What It Could Be, Waltz Of The New Moon, Big City Blues. Heron, Williamson, Lemaistre, Lee, Ingram, Dott. 1/8/00 Bloomsbury Theatre U U

Innersphere

10/3/95 Bounce, Cosmic Jam, Out Of Body. David Hedger (soundologist), Les Bell (g-3). 7/2/95 MV4 MR LS

Neil Innes

4/8/72 How Sweet To Be An Idiot, I Give Myself To Me, Momma B, Every Time, Children's Song. Neil Innes (o, pv), Tom McGuinness (lg), Hughie Flint (d), Dixie Dean (b), Tony White (rg). 11/7/72 T1 JM U

7/2/74 Bandwagon, Twyford Vitromant, Momma B, Dream On / L'amour Perdu, Disney Waltz, This Love Of Ours. possibly & Alan Spenner (b), Ollie Halsall (g) & 2 U. 31/1/74 LH1 JG BAI

24/8/77 Drama On A Saturday Night, Randy Raquel, Queen Elizabeth, Cheese And Onions. Neil Innes (pgv), Ollie Halsall (lg, o), Brian Hodgson (b), Pete Baron (d). 18/5/77 MV4 MB NG

Inside Out

19/5/91 Loss For Words, I Cut Myself, Cold Sterile, Get The Funk Out. Cathy Carrell (d), Karen Neal (b, lv), Lynda Metz (g, bck). 23/4/91 MV5 MPK MPK&JSM

The Inspiral Carpets

1/8/88 So Far, Monkey On My Back, Greek Wedding Song, Whiskey. Craig Gill (d), Dave Swift (b), Graham Lambert (g), Clint Boon (o, bck), Steve Holt (v). 17/7/88 MV5 DG ME

5/4/89 Out Of Time, Directing Traffic, Keep The Circle Around, Gimme Shelter. Martin Walsh (b), Tom Hingley (v) r Swift, Holt. 26/3/89 MV4 DG DD&MA ● SFPS072

9/10/89 Sun Don't Shine, She Comes In The Fall, Song For A Family, So This Is How It Feels. 17/8/89 MV5 NG&MR JLO

5/6/90 Beast Inside, Grip, Weakness, Keep It In Mind. 20/5/90 MV3 DG ME ● SFPS085

Intense Degree

15/3/88 Hangin' On / Vagrants / Skate-bored, Intense Degree / All The Guys / Daydreams, Take No Chances / Future Shock / Politician, Allegiance / Bursting. Rich Hill (v), Rich Cutts (g), Rich Collins (g), Liz Thirtle (b), Frank Pendelbury (d, bck). 28/2/88 U DG JB&SA ● SFPS053

Inter

12/6/97 Radio Finland, Cherry Red Electric Blue, Think Big, Jimmy. Steven Bray (lgv), Sid Stovold (rg), Michael Boylan (b, bck), John Gill (d). 25/5/97 MV4 ME NK

23/3/00 Speed Racer, Something Criminal, Shan't Quit Rapping, Not Curious. 29/9/99 MV4 MPK RJ

Interpol

25/4/01 Hands Away, Obstacle 2, The New, NYC. Paul Banks (gv), Daniel Kessler (g), Carlos Dengler (bk). 18/4/01 MV4 SA JHT

Irresistible Force

19/9/92 Spiritual High, Space Is The Place, Mountain High. Mixmaster Morris. 30/8/92 MV3 ME ME

1/10/93 Lotus Position, I Left My Hardcore (In San Francisco). 26/8/93 MV4 NG FK

Gregory Isaacs and Roots Radics

5/11/81 The Front Door, Permanent Lover, Confirm Reservation, Substitute. Gregory Isaacs (v), Dwight Pinkney (lg), Style Scott (d), Erroll Carter (b), Eric Lamont (rg), Anthony Johnson (k). 26/10/81 MV4 TW DD&MC

6/12/82 That's Not The Way, Sad To Know You're Leaving, Cool Down The Pace, Night Nurse. 27/11/82 MV4 DG MC

Isan

7/4/99 Saysoft, Timbremaid, Little Boy Sitting Up In Bed Looking At Moon, Paintchart. Anthony Ryan, Robin Saville. 14/2/99 MV3 ME BJ

Isotope

7/3/74 Bite On This / Upward Curve, Windmills And Waterfalls, Honkey Donkey, Do The Business. Gary Boyle (g), Jeff Clyne (b), Brian Miller (p, sy), Nigel Morris (d). 28/2/74 LH1 JW BC

6/8/74 Golden Section, Spanish Sun, Lilly Kong / E-Dorian, Illusion. Hugh Hopper (b), Lawrence Scott (k) r Clyne, Miller. 23/7/74 LH1 TW U

7/7/75 Fone Bone, Atilla, Pipe Dream. & Geoff Seopardie. 24/6/75 MV4 TW U

It's Immaterial

19/11/81 A Gigantic Raft, Immitate The Worm, White Man's Hut, Rake. Paul Barlow (d), Jarvis Whitehead (g), Henry Priestman (g, k), Julian Scott (b), John Campbell (v). 11/11/81 MV4 RP NG

9/8/82 Huzah Huzah Physic Stick, Life's My Favourite Instinct, Speak, Washing The Air. Scott out. 17/7/82 MV4 DG MR

21/11/83 Let's Murder The Moonshine, Challo, White Man's Hut, The Worm Turns. 12/11/83 MV4 DG MC

6/5/85 Rope, Hang On Sleepy Town, Space, Festival Time. Brenda Airturo (perc) r Barlow. 21/4/85 MV5 DG ME

The Izzys

8/7/03 Stand Up Laughing Falling Down To Cry, Lonely, I Wanna See (The Bright Lights Tonight), Strange. Mike Storey (gv), Jesse Korwin (b), Jared Gutstadt (d, bck). 14/5/03 MV4 MA NF

J Church

7/8/93 Bomb (NB Don't Schedule Near News), Yellow Blue Green, Good Judge, Financial Zone, Priest. Lance Hahn (gv), Gardner Pope (b), Brendan Murdock (d). 5/7/93 MV3 JB ME

Jabula

19/9/74 Baclishi, Thandie, Naledi, Our Forefathers. Lucky Rankhu (lg), Ennis Mothle (b), Graham Morgan (d), Julian Bahula (afd), Vicky Mhlongo (v), Dudu Pukwane (sx). 12/9/74 LH1 U U

Jack Drag

27/2/01 We Could've Been Big, April, At The Symphony, Now Or Never. Blake Hazard (k, smp, v), Joe Klompus (b, drum loops), John Dragonetti (gv). 4/2/01 MV4 ME JHT

Jack the Lad

29/5/73 Boilermaker Blues, One More Dance, Rosa Lee, Draught Genius. Simon Cowe (lg), Ray Laidlaw (d), Rod Clements (b, vi), Mitch Mitchell (g, mand). 14/5/73 T1 JW&PD BC

9/10/73 Where The Action Is, Fast Lane Driver, Back On The Road Again. 17/9/73 T1 JW U

24/1/74 Plain Leaking, Lying In The Water, Roadie, Turning Into Winter. 17/1/74 LH1 JW U

21/5/74 Nancy, Oakey Strike Evictions, Peggy (Overseas With A Soldier) (& Weary Whaling Grounds, 25/6/74). Philip Murray, Ian Fairburn r Clements. 2/5/74 LH1 JW BC

1/10/74 Big Ocean Liner, The Ballad Of Tonto McGuire, The Old Straight Track, The Third Millenium. 17/9/74 LH1 JW U

20/3/75 The Gentleman Soldier, Captain Grant, My Friend The Drunk, Kojoke, Walters' Drop. 13/3/75 MV4 U U

11/9/75 Winston O'Flaherty, One For The Boy, Baby Let Me Take You Home, Rocking Chair. 4/9/75 MV4 U U

21/10/76 Trinidad, 8 Ton Crazy, We'll Give You The Roll, Take Some Time. Cowe out. 28/9/76 MV4 JG MR

David Jack

24/9/03 Texture Freak, Strategic Applications, Shop Cine, Mr Wonderful. David Jack (bkg), David Robertson (k), Jane Bordwell (k, fl), Jeff Hallam (d), DJ Edit (tt), Caroline Barber (clo), Laura Metcalf (vla). 3/9/03 MV4 SA JSM

Jackdaw with Crowbar

3/6/87 Iceberg, Ignorant, Turkey Shoot, Amarillo. Dan Morrison (d), David Tibbatts (b), Tim Ellis (g, bck), Fergus Durrant (gv). 19/5/87 U DG TdB&MWT

12/10/87 Tightrope, Stomach Pump, Sailor Soul Survivor. 4/10/87 U DG ME&EL

JJ Jackson and The Urchins

26/11/67 Four Walls, Sho Nuff, Come See I'm Your Man, But It's Alright, Change Is Gonna Come. U 17/11/67 PH BA U

Joe Jackson

26/2/79 One More Time, Got The Time, Fools In Love, I'm The Man. Joe Jackson (pv), Graham Maby (b, bck), Gary Sanford (lg), Dave Houghton (d, bck). 21/2/79 MV4 JS NG Previous 'network' session recreation of 'Is She Really Going Out With Him?' for Tony Blackburn show, Oct 78

Jacktars

20/11/89 Pull The Plug, Flower Powder, Millions Of Grains, Things Not Seen. Huw Williams (d), Dave Morgan (b), Pete McPartland (g), Ian Travis (gv). 19/10/89 MV5 DG MWT

Jacob's Mouse

11/4/92 Oblong, Fridge, Microflesh, Homophobe, A Thin Shound. Sam Marsh (dv), Jebb Boothby (b), Hugo Boothby (g). 24/2/92 MV3 MR MR

3/10/92 Kettle, Deep Canvas Lake, Coalmine Dig, Ghetto Queen. 20/8/92 MV3 DG ME&EL

Jale

29/10/94 Blue Train, Again, Unseen Guest, Nine Years Now. Jennifer Pierce (o, g, v), Alyson Macloed (dv), Laura Stein (bv), Eve Hartling (gv). 13/9/94 MV4 MR JMK

The Jam

2/5/77 In The City, Art School, I've Changed My Address, Modern World. Paul Weller (g, lv), Bruce Foxton (b, bck), Rick Butler (d). 26/4/77 MV4 MB MR ● SFPS080

25/7/77 All Around The World, London Girl, Bricks And Mortar. 19/7/77 MV4 JG MR

5/11/79 Thick As Thieves, The Eton Rifles, Saturday's Kids, When You're Young. 29/10/79 MV4 TW BAI&TdB

James

19/10/83 Vulture, The Chicken Wire, Discipline, Hymn From A Village. Tim Booth (lv), James Glennie (b), Paul Gilbertson (g), Gavan Whelan (d). 3/10/83 MV4 TW U

20/1/86 Insect, Scarecrow, Are You Ready, Really Hard. James Laurence Gott (g) r Gilbertson. 12/1/86 MV5 DG MPK

9/9/87 What For?, Ya Ho, Stowaway, Whoops. 3/9/87 U DG TD&NG

30/4/90 How Was It For You, Sunday Morning, Come Home. Booth, Gott, Glennie, David Baynton-Power (d), Saul Davies (rg, vi), Mark Hunter (k), Andy Diagram (tp). 10/4/90 MV3 MR MR&FK

John James

2/10/68 If Only I, Slow Fast Dog Trot, Lampeter, Girl From Liverpool, Victory Rag. John James (gv). 2/10/68 S1 DK U

Nicky James Band

30/8/73 Rock 'N' Roll Jamboree, I Guess I've Always Loved You, A Bottle Of Cheap Red Wine, My Style. Nicky James (lv), John Weider (lg), Alan Fealdman (k), Barry Martin (sx), Brother Fataar (b), Chico Greenfield (d). 20/8/73 LH1 BA U

The Janitors

17/7/85 Nowhere, Mexican Kitchen, Good To Be The King, Thunderhead Johnny. Craig Hope (g), Pete Crow (b), Tim Stirland (d), Dentover (v). 7/7/85 MV5 U U

15/1/86 Going To Be, Really Shrinking, Track Eating Baby, Let's Go Home. 7/1/86 MV5 MR MR

20/1/87 Booga Dang Thing, Gostaggerlee, Family Fantastic, It's A Chrome Ball. Jeff (b) r Crow. 6/1/87 U DG MR&MA

Bert Jansch

18/12/68 Tree Song, I Loved A Lass, I Gotta Woman, Thames Lighterman, Haitian Fight Song, Birthday Blues. Bert Jansch (gv) & Danny Thompson (b). 11/12/68 S2 JM U Jansch first broadcast on Home Service Guitar Club, produced by Bernie Andrews, 16/12/66

Jasmine Minks

17/2/86 The Ballad Of Johnny Eye, Cry For A Man, You Can Take My Freedom, I Don't Know. Thomas Reid (d, bck), Martin Keene (b), Adam Sanderson (gv), James Shepherd (gv), Derek Christie (tp). 4/2/86 MV5 MW U

Jass Babies

3/11/81 Parable, Let Me Soak It Up, My Love Make You Melt, Talk In Tongues. Steve Brown (d), Peter Coyle (v), David Whittaker (b), Rob Boardman (g). 19/10/81 MV4 TW DD

Jawbone

14/4/04 Ready Or Not, Jump Jump, 41144, Hi De Hi, If It's Rock, And Wine, What's Goin On, I'm A Man, Walter John, Jack Rabbit, Mah Wah, Window Hatchet Blues, Jack Rabbit. Bob Zabor (g, d, e). Live from MV4 AR GT

Jawbox

1/7/94 Static, Tongues, Chinese Fork Tie, Cooling Card, Six Eight. Jay Robbins (gv), Bill Barbot (gv), Kim Coletta (b), Zach Barocas (d). 15/5/94 MV3 MR TD

Jeans Team

26/3/03 Berlin Am Meer, Baby 2, Spritz Your Life, Arthur, Boat Music. Franz Schuette (bkv), Henning Watkinson (k, g), Gunther Kreis (octapad, d), Reimo Herfort (k). Live from MV4 SCU MA

Jellicoe

14/3/01 The Magicians Breakfast, Dinosaurs & Hoverboards, Aeroplane Crash, Capital D120 (Maida Vale 4), The Music Of The Sun Rise. Jay McAllister (words, g), Jot Fuller (b, g), Dave Healy (d, p). 18/2/01 MV4 ME~

Jelly Bread

15/2/72 Down Along The Cove, Nadine, Sister Lucy, Mynah Bird. Pete Wingfield (kv), Paul Butler (gv), John Best (b), Chris Waters (d). 8/2/72 MV4 PR BC Ten previous sessions elsewhere, 69–71

28/4/72 Sister Lucy, Hound Dog, Green-Eyed Gypsy Queen (& Michigan Drag, 23/6/72). Kenny Lamb (k) r Wingfield, Rock Hayward r Waters. 10/4/72 T1 JM NG

Jellyfish Kiss

12/3/90 Crazy Bong, Little Red Car, Premortem, I'm Sticking With U. Rich (v-4), Jess (v-4), Dave (g), Mark (g), Nik (b), Greg (d). 13/2/90 MV5 DG MR

The Jesus and Mary Chain ○

31/10/84 In A Hole, You Trip Me Up, Never Understand, Taste The Floor. Jim Reid (v), William Reid (g), Douglas Hart (b), Bobby Gillespie (d). 23/10/84 MV4 MRD MR

13/2/85 The Living End, Inside Me, Just Like Honey. & Karen Parker (bck). 3/2/85 MV5 DG ME

11/11/85 Some Candy Talking, Psycho Candy, You Trip Me Up†, Cut Dead†. Billed as Jim and William Reid only. 29/10/85 MV5 U U

5/1/87 Fall, In The Rain, Happy Place. 25/11/86 U DG SC&DD ○ SFMCD210

13/6/88 Side Walking, Coast To Coast, Take It, My Girl. Hart returns. 31/5/88 MV4 MR MR

12/12/89 Far Out And Gone, Silverblade, Here Comes Alice. 26/11/89 MV3 DG ME Everything except † on ○ The Complete Peel Sessions SSFRSCD092

Jesus Lizard

17/3/91 Wheelchair Epidemic, Bloody Mary, Seasick, Monkey Trick. Mac McNeilly (d), David William Sims (b), Duane Denison (g), David Yow (v). 24/2/91 MV3 DG JLC&MR

30/10/92 Gladiator, Whirl, Puss, Boiler Maker. 27/9/92 MV3 NG~ RJ

Jet

19/6/75 Brian Damage, Diamonds Are A Girl's Best Friend, Nothing To Do With Us, Around The World In 80 Mins. Andy Ellison (v), Peter Oxendale (k), Martin Gordon (b), Dave O'List (g), Mike Nicholls (d). 12/6/75 MV4 TW U

Jethro Tull

4/8/68 A Song For Jeffrey, Serenade To A Cuckoo, My Sunday Feeling, So Much Trouble (& Cat's Squirrel, 22/9/68). Ian Anderson (fl, hca, v), Mick Abrahams (gv), Glen Cornick (b), Clive Bunker (d). 23/7/68 PC1 BA AH&BC

15/12/68 Love Story, Dharma For One, Stormy Monday, Beggar's Farm. 5/11/68 PC1 BA DT

22/6/69 A New Day Yesterday, Fat Man, Nothing Is Easy. Martin Barre (g) r Abrahams. 16/6/69 MV4 JW TW

Joey Fat

23/7/03 Intro, Waiferville, The Dribbler, Kidnapped, Cartoon Lions. Jason Dormon (g), Lawrence Price (b), James Booth (d), Jon Richards (g), Matthew Cole (v), Patrick Lloyd (g). Live from MV4 AR SA/GT

Elton John

27/11/68 Lady What's Tomorrow, Vall-hala, Digging My Grave, My First Days At Hi Eaton, The Scaffold. Solo (Contract says 'sings and plays guitar'). 27/11/68 MV4 PC U Trial broadcast for Stuart Henry 3 weeks before: 'Male vocal in the 1968 feeling – thin, piercing voice with no emotional appeal… dreary songs… one key singer… pretentious material', audition panel 12/12; pass: 'first class!' AD

25/12/73 Rudolph The Red-Nosed Reindeer/ White Christmas / Jingle Bells, Blowin' In The Wind / She Belongs To Me / Mr Tambourine Man, Don't Dilly Dally On The Way / Lilly Of Laguna / Down At The Old Bull And Bush / Knees Up Mother Brown / Hokey Cokey, Daniel / Your Song. Elton John (pub piano), BBC Radio 1 staff (bck-4). 18/12/73 LH1 JW BC

Larry Johnson

12/12/70 Sitting On The Banks Of The River, The Beat From Rampart Street, Broke And Hungry, How Long (& Things I Need To Do, 20/2/71). Larry Johnson (gv). 7/12/70 PH U U

Linton Kwesi Johnson

8/5/79 Down Di Road, Want Fi Goh Rave, It Dread Inna Inglan, Sonny's Lettah, Reality Poem. Linton Kwesi Johnson (v) & 'other musicians as on LP'. 1/5/79 MV4 TVD MR

27/10/81 Independent Intavenshan, Reality Poem, Reggae Fi'Peach, All Wi' Doin' Is Defendin'. Johnson & Dennis Bovell (p, vocal perc) (1, 2, 3 'pre-recorded backing tracks'). 3/10/81 MV4 DG MR

Paul Johnson

5/8/87 Fear Of Falling, Burning, Every Kinda People, A Song For You. Paul Johnson (lv), Dave Itall (gv), Gary Sanctuary (k), Hugh McKenna (pv), Paul Powell (b), Bobby Clarke (d), Jordan Bailey & Jenny Evans (bck). 28/7/87 U DG MR&SC Debut session recorded 6 days earlier for Janice Long

Wilko Johnson

28/9/78 Everybody's Carrying A Gun, Slipping And Sliding, Blazing Fountains, All Right, Highway 61. Wilko Johnson's (gv) 'Solid Senders': Stevie Lewins (b), John Denton (p), Alan Platt (d). 19/9/78 U MB MR

Sophie and Peter Johnston

22/2/83 One Face, Television / Satellite, Rain, Paradise. Peter Johnston (sy, d, prg), Sophie Johnston (lv), Tom McCluskey (sy). 19/2/83 MV4 DG MC 'What lovely people and refreshing light music', DG & MC on sheet

27/10/83 Travel In Time, Words And Words, Open Eyes. McCluskey out. 15/10/83 MV4 DG MC

The Johnstons

14/4/72 Ready Teddy, Won't You Come With Me, Continental Trailways Bus, If I Sang My Song. U 27/3/72 U JM U

Jolt

25/11/95 Scared Of Girls, Can't Leave Without It, Call Me If You Wanna, Love & Romance, Was It Wild. Mark Keds (gv), B B Mets (bv), Martin Shaw (dv). 12/10/95 MV4 TdB KR

Jon E Cash

16/12/04 10–min DJ mix for Keepin' It Peel night. Live from MV5 GYW JHT

Nic Jones

11/7/72 Donald The Pride Of Glencoe, The Island Of Helena, The Harper Of Loch Maben, The Rufford Park Poachers. Nic Jones (agv). 5/6/72 MV4 JW U

7/12/72 The Outlandish Knight, The Greeny Mossy Banks Of The Lea, Lakes Of Shillin, William Of Winesberry. 27/11/72 U BA U

20/9/73 Isle Of France, Lass Of London City, The Harper Of Loch Maben, O'Carolan's Concerto. 6/8/73 U BA U

31/1/74 Ploughman Lads, Isle Of France, The Drowned Lover, Fare Thee Love. 24/1/74 U JW U

7/11/74 The Working Lads Of Russia, Dives And Lazarus, Jigs: Blackthorn Stick / Dr O'Neill, Bonny Banks Of Fordie. 28/10/74 U JW U

12/11/75 Bonny George Campbell, The Wanton Seed, Sammy's Bar, Lakes Of Shilin. 14/10/75 MV4 U U

23/7/76 Billy Don't You Weep For Me, Annachie Gordon, The Thousand Miles, My Grandfather Knew The Plough. 8/7/76 MV4 U U

26/4/77 William Glen, Annachie Gordon, Rose Of Allandale. 19/4/77 MV4 JG MR

Wizz Jones

9/7/69 If Only I'd Known, Time Is Flying, Weeping Willow Blues, O My Friend. Wizz Jones (agv). 12/6/69 S2 PR U Had previously appeared as member of other acts. Solo debut Nov 68 on My Kind Of Folk R1

16/1/71 The Legendary Me, Beggerman, Willie Moore, The Time Is Flying (& If Only I'd Known, 13/3/71). & Pete Berryman (g). 21/12/70 PH JW U

4/1/72 American Jones, First Girl I Loved, Mama Let Me Lay It On You, No More Time To Try. 13/12/71 PH U U

Joolz

30/7/84 At Dawn, It's Nothing, Tattoo, Mammy's Boy, Violation. Joolz (v), Jah Wobble (b, k), Dave Maltby (g), Olly Marland (k). 21/7/84 U DG MC

Josef K

24/3/81 No Glory, Endless Soul, Chance Meeting, Pictures. Paul Haig (gv), Malcolm Ross (g, vi), David Weddell (b), Ronnie Torrance (d). U PRIV

22/6/81 The Missionary, Heart Of Song, Applebrush, Heaven Sent. 15/6/81 LH1 TW DD ○ On 'Young And stupid' LTMCD2307

Joy Division

14/2/79 Exercise One, Insight, She's Lost Control, Transmission. Peter Hook (bgv), Ian Curtis (gv), Bernard Dickin (sy, g, b), Stephen Morris (d). 31/1/79 MV4 BS NG ○

10/12/79 Love Will Tear Us Apart, 24 Hours, Colony, Sound Of Music. 26/11/79 MV4 TW DD ○ SFRCD111

The Joyce McKinney Experience

17/8/88 Tanfastic, Lions And Tigers, Walk On Your Own, In The Pink. Gigs (d), Robbie (b), Charlie (g) Sharon & Yvonne (v). 31/7/88 MV5 DG MA

Simon Joyner

25/5/96 Milk, Born Of Longing, Hood, Hotter Than Satan's Jail, Parachute. Simon Joyner (v). U MV4 JMK U See Jack Rose

Joyrider

9/6/95 Vegetable/Animal/Mineral, Fabulae, Special One, D R B. Simon Haddock (b), Clifford Mitchell (g), Philip Woolsey (gv), Buc (d). 9/5/95 MV4 MR CML

9/3/96 Rush Hour, Lost In Time, Bibleblack Belt, Another Skunk Song. Carl Alty (d) r Buc; & Dave Kent (hca-4). 27/1/96 MV4 MR NS

JSD Band

23/6/72 Open Road, Peggy And The Soldier, Barney Braligon Selection, Sylvie (& Down The Road, 21/7/72). Colin Flinn (d), Jim Divers (b), Des Coffield (g, bj, v), Lindsay Scott (fd), Sean O'Rourke (bj, g, fl, v). 15/5/72 PH JM JWH&BAI Debut on Country Meets Folk March 72

25/7/72 Sarah Jane, Betsy, Irish Girl, Johnny O'Braidislay. 25/7/72 MV4 U BC

5/10/72 Fishin' Blues, Groundhog, Paddy Stacks, The Dowie Dens Of Yarrow. 2/10/72 LH1 BA U

28/12/72 Young Waters, Darlin' Corey, The Galway Races, Dig's Paddy Bar. 4/12/72 LH1 BA U

1/5/73 Galway Races, Castle Kelly, Travelling Days. Chuck Fleming (vi) r Scott. 16/4/73 U JW U

19/7/73 Little Maggie, Tune Your Fiddles, Seamus' Jig, Glasgow. 16/7/73 LH1 BA U

21/2/74 Railroad Mama, Downfall Of Paris, Sunshine Life (& The Fox, 2/5/74). 14/2/74 LH1 U U

Ju Ju

27/4/82 Doreen, Hello Good Morning, Millionaire, Messages, Walk Alone. Alex Findlow (d), Celia Hemchen von Brockhorn (sx, v), Mark Fletcher (b), Paul Barns (g), Mark Illman (g). 19/4/82 MV5 TW MC

21/7/83 Mysterious, Tap On My Brain, Zen Master, Picture Of Dorian Gray. Ralph Derijke (sxv) r Brockhorn. 27/6/83 MV4 TW MC

Jubilee Allstars

11/1/97 They're Not Coming Anymore, Foolish Guy, Keep On Chewin', Four Corners Of Hell. Lee Casey (d), Niall McCormack (gv), Barry McCormack (gv), Fergus McCormack (b). 15/12/96 MV3 ME/NG RJ

The Juggernauts

2/1/85 Mystery Train, The Body Of The Kirk, One Thousandth Part, Made My First Million. Nigel Seaford (bv), Gordon Kerr (rgv), Paul Haig (lg), James Locke (d). 11/12/84 MV5 MRD PW

Juicy Lucy

8/11/69 She's Mine And She's Yours, Just One Time, Chicago North Western, Who Do You Love. Glen Campbell (gv), Ray Owen (lv), Chris Mercer (ts), Neil Hubbard (g), Keith Ellis (b), Pete Dobson (d). 4/11/69 MV4 JW U

Juke Boy Bonner

8/11/69 I Know What's Gonna Happen, Smiling Like I'm Happy, People Think They Know Me Well (& I Didn't Know, Jumping With Juke Boy, 7/2/70). 8/11/69 MV4 JW TW

Jules Verne

13/6/92 Hollow Tomorrow, Misadventure, Hang Up, Celebrity Twister / A Wake. Daniel Hunt (gv), Paul Winstanly (g, bck), Kari Bailey (b), David Potts (d). 17/5/92 MV3 ME ME

The June Brides

20/11/84 On The Rocks, No Place Called Home, In The Rain, I Fall. Phil Wilson (lv, g), Simon Beesley (gv), Ade Carter (b), Brian Alexis (d), Frank Sweeney (vla), Jon Hunter (tp), Reg Fish (tp). 7/11/84 MV5 JS MPK

5/11/85 This Town, Waiting For A Change, We Belong, One Day. Dave Bickley (d) r Alexis; & John Hunter (tp). 22/10/85 MV5 PWL ME ● SFPS023

Junior Gee and the Capital Boys

3/10/84 Scratch, Have You Got The Time, Love Money, Check Us Out. Junior Gee (v), Ambassador (v), Scratch (v), Double D (sc, v), backed by the Funkmasters (unknown). 26/9/84 MV5 RP TD

Juniors Eyes

10/11/68 By The Tree (On The Second Dream On Your Right), White Light, Hang Loose, Imagination. Mick Wayne (lg), Steve Chapman (d), John Redfern (o), John 'Honk' Lodge (b). 28/10/68 PC1 BA U

4/5/69 Sing A Song, So Embarassed, For Adam And Eve, Miss Lizzie (& Not Far Away, 8/6/69). 28/4/69 PH JW TW

Mickey Jupp

13/3/71 I Can't Lose, Further Up On The Road, Don't You Never, It Hurts Me Too (& Lorraine Pt 1, 5/6/71). Mickey Jupp (lv, g)'s Legend: & others U. 2/3/71 U PR U

28/6/78 Cheque Book†, Switchboard Susie, Anything You Do†, Daisy Mayes†. & Mick Grabham (g), John Gordon (b), Ron Telemacque (d). 19/6/78 MV4 TW TdB&MPK on ○ Live At The BBC HUX053

Just Us

2/1/73 La Roca, Nameless, Forsoothe, Vehim. Elton Dean (al), Nick Evans (tb), Mark Charig (cnt), Louis Maholo (d), Jeff Green (g), Neville Whitehead (b). 11/12/72 U JW U

K K Kings

6/5/94 Trance Delhi Express, The Bush Of Ghosts, Dum Maro Dum, Hardkaur She Knows The Score. Radical Sista (dj, v), Balwinder Safri (Punjambi v), Karl Junga (k), Mikha K (Kaos), Palm Deep (cl), Kave Boy X (rp), Pindi (Indian v). 29/3/94 MV3 MPK GW

Doctor K

18/10/69 Country Boy, For Caroline, I've Been Here Before, Sugar Moon. Richard Kay (p), Geoff Krivit (lg), Roger Rolt (rg), Harold Vickers (b), Eric Peachey (d), Mick Haase (lv, hca). 30/9/69 MV4 JW U

Kaisers

25/3/95 Watch Your Step, Don't Come Back, Loopy Lu, Valley Of The Kaisers, Time To Go. Kaiser Matt (gv), Kaiser George (gv), Kaiser Matt (bv), Kaiser Jonny (dv). 5/3/95 MV3 ME GPR

Kaito

2/8/01 Trailous, Shoot Shoot, Succosanko, Montigola Underground. Nikki Colk (gv), David Lake (gv), Gemma Cullingford (bv), Dieta Quintrell (dv). 11/7/01 MV4 MWT NF

Kaleidoscope

7/1/68 A Dream For Julie, Dive Into Yesterday, Faintly Blowing, (Further Reflections) In The Room Of Percussion. U 13/12/67 U U U

Kan Kan

26/4/82 Apartment 100, Shot In The Dark, Somethings Never Change, Deja Vu. Patrick Deneen (v, d, k, b), Graham McGill (b, g), Flavia Malim (v). 7/4/82 MV5 RP NG

Kanda Bongo Man

30/7/93 Yesu Christu, Sai, Wallow. Bongo Kanda (v), Shaba Kahamba (b), Mbedi Mene Mandesi (g), Sheddy Nyalto Festo (rg), Massamba Nzinga (d). 16/6/93 MV4 MPK~ AR

26/2/02 Sancho, Yesu Christu, Bili. Kanda Bongo, Emmanuel Maleso (rg), Tunta Bayenge (lg), Babwaku Biasonama (d), Ilonga Nkoso (v), Kibisngoy Douglas (b), Rabbi Makuta (v). 20/2/02 MV4 SA GT

Amory Kane

13/11/68 Four Ravens, Reflections, Physically Disqualified Blues, Night, Evolution. Amory Kane (v) & unknown British backing band. 13/11/68 MV4 PC U

Karamasov

13/4/99 Reaction Man, Fengan Nemo, The Sun Always Shines In Space, Happy Hour. Joahannes Von Weizsacker (g, clo), Adam Stewart (sy, ma), Harry Rambaut (b), Berit Immig (d, v, marimba). 16/2/99 MV4 MR PN

Katch 22

2/11/91 Mindfield, Service With A Smile, The Jam, State Of Meditation. Hunt Kill Bury Finn (rp), Mad Marka (dj), DJ Brainiac (dj), DJ Kill A Man Twice (dj), Cavey ('dancer'). 17/9/91 MV5 TdB DMC

Kelis

4/10/00 Good Stuff, Get Along With You, Mafia. Kellis Rogers, Abe Fogel, Jennifer Juson, Deborah Rolle, Arnae Burton, Kiki Hawkins, Ruby Batson, Terence Thornton, Mark Batson, Gregg Mann. U Abbey Road Studios U U

Dave Kelly

18/9/68 A Few Short Lines, Arkansas Woman, When You've Got A Good Friend, Hard Times, Travelling Blues. Dave Kelly (agv). 13/9/68 MV5 DK U

Jo-Ann Kelly

4/9/68 Rock Me, Since I First Met You Baby, Shine On Rising Sun, Louisiana Blues, Roll And Tumblin' Blues. with Bob Hall (p) & Steve Rye (hca). 3/9/68 S2 DK U Jo-Ann Kelly was unanimously rejected by the panel after an audition in 3/67. Comments ranged from 'a sincere attempt' to 'discordant' 'very depressing' 'monotonous dirge' and 'who knows or cares what she's singing about?' Many sessions after this

Kenickie

21/7/95 Drag Race, Millionaire Sweep, P V C, How I Was Made. Lauren Laverne (gv), Marie Du Santiago (gv), Emmy-Kate Montrose (bv), X (d). 18/6/95 MV3 FK
9/3/96 Scared Of Spiders, Acetone, Can I Take You To The Cinema?, Come Out Tonite. 1/3/96 OS Produced by Peter Gofton, engineered by Andy Carpenter

Kerb

27/5/98 Simple & Easy Me, From A Madman, Can't Go Home Again, Let Down. Jason Nott (v), Jarrod Prosser (rg), Syd Savage (d), David Thomas (lg), Jon Lake (b). 19/4/98 MV4 ME FK

The Keys

9/9/03 From Tense To Loose To Slack, Girlfriend, Feel A Whole Lot Better, Love Your Sons And Daughters. Matthew Evans (gv), Sion Glyn (b, bck), Gwion Rowlands (lg, bck), Elliot Jones (d), Kris Jenkins (perc). 9/7/03 MV4 SA JSM

Imrat Khan

6/7/69 Kalarati, Tori. Imrat Khan (sit), Vilayat Khan (su). 1/7/69 MV4 JW TW
18/4/70 Bihag, Aheer Bnaero. Imrat Khan (sit, su), Latif Ahmed Khan (tab). 14/4/70 MV4 JW TW

Vilayat Khan

1/9/68 Shankara, Snudh Malu. Vilayat Khan & 1 other musician, possibly his brother Imrat. 2/8/68 AO2 BA U

Khartomb

13/12/82 Swahili Lullaby, Sanatogen, Daisy High, Tribal Man. Paula Crolla (v), Caroline Clayton (v, b, fl), Ali Barnes (d), Ian Christie (g, b). 4/12/82 U DG MR

Khaya

26/8/99 Wild Friends, Summer Winter, Take Off, Avoidance. Dan Mutch (gv), Greg Dodgson (kv), Ruairidh MacGlone (g), John Mackie (b), Richie Anderson (d), Caroline Evens (vi), Pete Harvey (clo, k). 20/4/99 MV4 MR SBR
6/6/00 The Vampires, Argument, I Wanna Share A Grave With You, Music Is for Pussys. MacGlone out. 5/4/00 MV4 MR GT

Kick Partners

28/3/83 Steel Workers, Granston Villas, It's Too Late, The Beats In Your Heart. Wayne Allen (gv), Chris Pearson (b), Linda Hamblin (v), Rose Eyre (sy, o, v), Paul Hardy (d), Kev Sanderson (perc). 16/3/83 MV4 RP NG

Kid 606 Vs Remote Viewer

20/6/00 Ask Me For Gift Ideas, When You Are Through Trusting Worthless Liars, You Got It I Don't Want It, Haslingden Loves The Kid, I Don't Want Your Assistance, I Don't Want To Give You Mine. Craig Tattersall, Andrew Johnson, Kid 606. 3/5/00 MV3 MA MPK

Kid Koala

3/5/00 Roboshuffle, Drunk Trumpet, Mrs Chombee, Snakeskin. Eric San (tt), Paulo Kapunan (tt), Joanna Peters (perc), Mark Robertson (g), Massimo Sansione (d), Peter Santiago (b). 19/3/00 MV3 ME NF

Kidnapper

20/5/97 Is This A Girl, Cake, On The Q T, Heaven Only Knows. Lea Andrews (v), Lyndon Holmes (g), Yasmin Sairally (g), Lisa Cook (b), Toby Sinden. 4/5/97 MV4 ME GPR

Killing Floor

20/7/69 Mind Can Ride Easy, Louis Blues, The Sun Keeps Shining. Mick Clarke (lg), Stuart McDonald (b), Bill Thorndycraft (v, hca), Bas Smith (d), Lou Martin (p). 14/7/69 PH JW U Passed audition 3/69 sessions for Mike Raven, Johnnie Walker, May & July 69

Killing Joke

29/10/79 Psyche, Wardance, Nuclear Boy, Malicious Boogie. Jazz Coleman (kv), Geordie aka A Lizzard (gv), Big Paul (dv), Youth (bv) & roadie Alex Paterson ('disco whoop' bck-4). 17/10/79 MV4 BS NG

17/3/80 Change, Tomorrow's World, Complications. 5/3/80 MV4 JE NG

27/4/81 The Fall Of Because, Tension, Butcher. 14/4/81 LH1 DG MR&MFA

16/12/81 The Hum, The Empire Song, We Have Joy, Chop Chop. 11/12/81 MV4 JWI TdB

12/7/83 Willful Days, Frenzy, Dominator, Harlequin. Paul Raven (b) r Youth. 4/7/83 MV4 JP MC

The Killjoys

18/10/77 Recognition, At Night, Back To Front, Naive. Kevin Rowland (v), Mark Phillips (g), Ghislaine Weston (b), Lee Burton (d), Heather (bck-4). 11/10/79 MV4 JG MR

13/2/78 All The Way, Smoke Your Own, Spit On Me, Ghislaine. Bob Peach (d) r Burton; & Keith Rimell (g, b-4), Rowland (g-4), Weston (v-4). 1/2/78 MV4 MB NG

The Kills

30/7/03 The Search For Cherry Red, Wait, Gypsy Death And You, Jewel Thief. Hotel (g, v, tamb, el-vla, dm), VV (gv). 19/6/03 MV4 SA JHT

William E Kimber and The Ian Green Orchestra

5/11/67 Lazy Life, A Day Of Love, Molehill Is Not A Mountain, Crazy How Love Slips Away. U 27/10/67 U U U

King

20/7/78 Antipope, Jet Boy Jet Girl, My Baby Don't Care, Baby Sign Here With Me. Captain Sensible (g, bck; p, cel-3), Henry Badowski (v, k, sx), Kim Bradshaw (b), Dave Berk (d), Alex K. (vi). 11/7/78 MV4 MR MR

King Biscuit Boy

8/12/71 Boom Boom (Out Goes The Light), Biscuit's Boogie, Hey Hey, Cross My Heart. Canadian soul singer. No contract survives. 7/12/71 U U U BC

King Crimson

11/5/69 The Court Of The Crimson King, 21st Century Schizoid Man, Talk To The Wind. Michael Giles (dv), Greg Lake (bv), Robert Fripp (lg), Ian McDonald (al, fl, k), 6/5/69 MV4 JW TW

7/9/69 The Court Of The Crimson King, Epitaph, Bearings (Get Thy). 19/8/69 MV4 JW U

King of the Slums

26/4/88 Big Girl's Blouse, Fanciable Headcase, Venerate Me Utterly, Leery Bleeder. Charley Keigher (gv), Sarah Curtis (vi), Jon Chandler (b), Ged O'Brian (d). 12/4/88 MV4 DG MR

Kings of Oblivion

25/4/90 Pay, Fear Trade, Much Too Much Two Faced, Ghost. Neil Humphries (d, bck), Darren Smith (bv), John Harris (g, bck). 3/4/90 MV3 MR MR

The Kingsbury Manx

17/10/00 Cross Your Eyes, Simplify, Drift Off, Fanfare. Kenneth Stephenson (gv), Bill Taylor (gv), Scott Myers (bk), Ryan Richardson (dv), Ajay Saggar (g). 17/9/00 MV4 ME~

The Kinks

29/10/67 David Watts, Sunny Afternoon, Suzannah's Still Alive, Autumn Almanac, Mr Pleasant, Harry Rag. Ray Davies (gv), Dave Davies (gv), Mick Avory (d), Peter Quaife (b) & (tp) (o, p) unknown. 25/10/67 MV4 BA U Trial broadcast was on Saturday Club on 19/9/64. Dozens of dates followed

7/7/68 Days, Monica, Love Me Till The Sun Shines, Waterloo Sunset. & Nicky Hopkins (o). 1/7/68 PC1 BA U

16/5/72 Holiday, Supersonic Rocket Ship, Acute Schizophrenia Paranoia Blues, Skin And Bone. R & D Davies, Avory &: John Dalton (b), John Gosling (p), John Beecham (tb), Mike Rosen (tp), Alan Holmes (fl). 5/5/72 T1 JW BC

11/7/74 Money Talks, Demolition, Mirror Of Love. Eight musicians & 2 U. 6/6/74 LH1 TW BAI

Kiss AMC

3/7/89 Rawside, Yakety Yak, Doc Martens. Anne-Marie (v), Christine (v) & the Ruthless Rap Assassins: Kermit le Freak (prg), Dangerous Hinds (kv), Carsonoba (sc, v), Paul Roberts (g). 18/6/89 ED DG SA

Kit

3/1/90 How To Break This, Up On A Wire, Cheatin' My Heart, What If I Fell. Lin Sangster (gv), Michelle Brown (b), Tony Smith (d), Kenny Manson (g), Phil Luckin (tp). 28/11/89 MV5 DG MR

Kitchens Of Distinction

12/9/92 Four Men, Mad As Snon, When In Heaven, Blue Pedal. Patrick Fitzgerald (bv), Julian Swales (g, hca), Dan Goodwin (d). 23/8/92 MV3 ME DMC&ME

The Klezmatics

1/8/92 Doyne / Freyt Aykh Yidelekh, Klezmatics Khosidl / Fisher Lid, Keyser Rtar / Terkish Yale Veyve Tamts, Honikzaft. Matt Darriau (cl, sx), David Licht (d), Frank London (tp, k, bck), Paul Morrissett (b), Lorin Sklamberg (v, acc, k), Alicia Svigals (vi, bck). 14/7/92 MV4 MR MR&MA&RJ

Klute

1/12/98 Annihilation, The Box, Got Any Beats (Top Gear '98 Mix), Faceless (The Peel VIP Edit). Tom Withers (e). OS

knifehandchop

25/3/03 Mix by Billy Pollard (dj) OS

Gladys Knight and the Pips

10/12/67 Take Me In Your Arms And Love Me, I Heard It Through The Grapevine, Just Walk In My Shoes, Everybody Needs Love. Gladys Knight (lv), the Pips (bck) & the Johnny Watson Concept, incl Jimmy Page (g), Jim Sullivan (g). 1/12/67 PH BA PR

Knights Of The Occasional Table

8/1/94 Kundalini 256, Canadee I O, Dalek In A Coma, Journey To The Placenta Of The Earth. Nigel Packett (prg, arr, comp), Matt Mosse (comp, sy, prg), Steve Radford, Peter Rile (gv), Andrew Cowen ('decomposition, mix & match'), Martin Kavanagh ('occarina, quantum tantra'). 28/11/93 MV3 ME LS

Buddy Knox and Bad River

16/5/70 Party Doll, Hula Love, Somebody Touched Me, Rock Your Little Baby To Sleep (& Muddy Water, 8/8/70). Buddy Knox (US singer) & British backing band Bad River (unknown). 11/5/70 PH U U

Spider John Koerner

17/7/68 Things Ain't Right, Eugene C From Tennesse, I Ain't Blue, Running Jumping Standing Still, I Don't Wanna Be Terrified. U 25/6/68 U DK U

Kokomo

22/8/74 I'm Sorry Babe, Forever, It Ain't Cool To Be Cool, Angel. Neil Hubbard (g), Alan Spenner (b), Tony O'Mally (kv), Frank Collins (v), Paddie McHugh (v), Dyan Birch (v), John Sussewell (d), Jim Mullen (g), Jody Linscott (cga). 15/8/74 LH1 TW U

27/2/75 Good To Be Alive, Oo-Ee-Baby, Cos We've Ended Now As Lovers, New Morning. Terry Stannard (d) r Sussewell; & Chris Mercer (sx). 20/2/75 AO2 TW BAI

8/9/75 Do It Right, Kitty, Pinch Of Salt, Happy Birthday. Mullen out. 2/9/75 MV4 PR U

Dembo Konte and Kausu Kouyate

2/10/89 Amadou Fall, Sane Jobe, President Diawara, Alla Lakhe. Dembo Konte (kor, v) Kausu Kouyate (kor, v) with the Three Mustaphas Three rhythm section: Houzam (d), Sabah Habas (b) & Hijaz Mustapha (g, md). 5/9/89 MV3 DG MR Duo on Kershaw twice previously in 87 & 88

Alexis Korner

2/2/69 The Clapping Song, Please Don't Say No, You Don't Know My Mind. Alexis Korner (gv) & Nick Smith (bv). 14/1/69 PC1 BA AH&BC Many previous and subsequent appearances on other shows

Leo Kottke

10/2/77 Scarlatti Rip Off, Easter, San Antonio Rose / America The Beautiful / Machine Gun, Mona Ray / Morning, Pamela Brown. Leo Kottke (ag). 7/2/77 MV4 TW DD

Billy J Kramer

24/4/73 I'll Keep You Satisfied, Trains Boats And Planes, Little Children, From A Window. Billy J Kramer (v), Frank Davis (g), Sandy Byers (d), Ken Buckley (b), Mick Green (ag). 17/4/73 U JW U

The Krispy Three

3/7/90 Mentally Appetising, Natch It Up, E1. Wiz (ma, v), Sonic (v), Don (v). 10/6/90 MV3 DG MA&JB

7/12/91 Answer Me Will Ya, Where We Going, Too Damn Ignorant, Hard Times. 24/10/91 MV4 DG NG&CML

The Kursaal Flyers

13/2/75 Tennessee, Route 66, Yellow Sox, Foggy Mountain Breakdown (Version). Graeme Douglas (g), Vic Collins (ps), Richie Bull (b, bj), Paul Shuttleworth (v), Will Birch (d). 30/1/75 MV4 TW BAI

31/10/75 Cross Country, Fall Like The Rain, Willin', Pocket Money. 30/9/75 U U U

Fela Kuti

24/7/73 Fefenene, Gentleman. 16 musicians, unknown. OS

Lab 4

10/10/01 Critique, Play With The Pain, Resurrection, The Bitch, I Need Your Love, Place Go Boom, Reformation, Deny My Existence. AJ Newman, LJ Elston. Live from MV3 AR RJ

Labradford

19/11/94 Starcity, Accelerating On A Smoother Road, Balanced On Its Own Flame, Comfort. Carter Brown (k), Bobby Donne (b), Mark Nelson (g). 16/10/94 MV4 SA KR

19/5/96 Battered, Voicer, Dalmacia. 5/5/96 MV3 ME~ U

Ladytron

31/1/02 Zmeyka, Holiday 601, Another Breakfast With You, Discotraxx. Helen Marnie, Mina Aroyo, Daniel Hunt, Reuben Wu. 5/12/01 MV4 SA GYW

8/1/03 True Mathematics, Playgirl, Another Breakfast With You, Cracked LCD, Black Plastic, He Took Me To A Movie, Fire, Evil, USA Vs White Noise, Turn It On, Seventeen. 4/12/02 As live' at MV4 AR SA

Laibach

24/6/86 Krvava Gruda-Plodna Zemlda, Krst, Live Is Life. Eber, Dachauer, Keller, Saliger. 15/6/86 MV4 DG MR

27/4/87 Leben-tod, Trans-national, Krvoprelitze. 7/4/87 U DG MR

Laika

7/3/00 Looking For The Jackalope, Lower Than The Stars, Badtimes, Go Fish. Margaret Fielder (g, smp, v), Guy Fixsen (k, g), John Frenett (b), Lou Ciccotelli (d, perc). 6/2/00 MV3 ME GYW

Denny Laine and the Electric String Band

8/10/67 Say You Don't Mind, Why Did You Come, Reason To Believe, Catherine Wheel, Ask The People, Guilty Mind. Denny Laine (gv), John Stein (vi), Nigel Pinkett (clo), Andy Leigh (b), Peter Trout (d). 4/10/67 MV4 BA U Group's first session was on The Light Programme 19/6/67

28/1/68 Catherine Wheel, Machine Song, Too Much In Love, Masks, Sally Free And Easy. 24/1/68 MV4 BA U

Lali Puna

2/11/04 603, Small Things, Past Machine, Nin Com Pop. Markus Acher (b), Valerie Trebeljahr (kv), Christian Heiss (k, cmp), Christoph Branoner (d, el-perc). 30/9/04 MV4 JHT JSM

The Land Of Nod

22/4/03 Half Light, Colli Di Pedona, Inducing The Sleep Sphere, Ice Station Nod. Dave Battersby (b, sy, smp), Anthony Walker (dm, g). 20/3/04 MV4 MA NS

Landscape

19/4/78 Kaptin Whorlix, Gothan City, Lost In The Small Ads, Workers' Playtime. John Walters (el-ss, perc), Peter Thoms (el-tb, perc), Andy Pask (b), Christopher Heaton (elp), Richard Burgess (d). 12/4/78 MV4 MB NG

Neil Landstrumm & Tobia Schmidt

8/10/98 Techno DJ set by Neil Landstrumm & Tobias Schmidt live from MV4 AR U

Ronnie Lane's Slim Chance

11/12/73 Ooh La La, Careless Love, Flags And Banners, How Come. Ronnie Lane, Bruce Rowlands, Chris Stewart, Bill Livesey, Jimmy Jewell, Graham Lyle, Benny Gallagher. 27/11/73 LH1 JW BC

3/12/74 Sweet Virginia, Lovely, Anniversary. Lane & Ruan O'Lochlain, Steve Simpson, Charlie Hart, Jim Frank, Brian Belshaw. 19/11/74 MV4 TW U

15/1/76 Don't Try And Change My Mind, One For The Road, Steppin' And Reelin', All Or Nothing. Lane, Simpson, Hart, Belshaw, Colin Davey (d), Chris Thomas (p-2). 8/1/76 MV4 TW U

Lash Lariat and the Long Riders

21/1/85 Oh Baby, Bitter Tears, Feel Like Yelling, Never Been So Weary. Lash Lariat (gv), Luke Lariat (db), Johnny T (fd), Matt Black (bj), Elmer Thudd (d, bck). 13/1/85 MV5 DG ME

30/12/85 Think About Me, Change, Devil's Dancer, Eloise. 10/12/85 MV5 HP~

Last Party

30/3/87 Bigger Things, Autumn Acre, Don't Even Consider It, Tin Foil Mountain. Simon Rivers (gv), Kim Ashford (sy), Daniel Ashkenazy (b), Neil Palmer (d). 17/3/87 U DG MR&MA

9/1/89 Purple Hazel, A Full English Breakfast, Platforms And Trains, Creature Lakes. 3/1/89 MV4 DG MR

Laugh

17/3/86 Never Had It So Bad, Paul McCartney, Hey I'm Still Thinking, Take Your Time Yeah. Spencer Birtwhistle (d), Martin Mittler (b), Martin Wright (gv), Craig Gannon (g). 9/3/86 MV5 DG ME&MFA

7/9/87 Time To Lose It, Interlove, Come On Come Out, The Wright Experience. Ian Bandelow (g) r Gannon. 25/8/87 U DG MWT&SC

Laughing Clowns

8/12/82 Theme From Mad Flies Man Flies, Nothing That Harms, The Year Of The Bloated Goat, Every Dog Has Its Day. Jeff Wegener (d), Edmund Kuepper (gv), Louise Elliot (sx), Peter Doyle (tp), Leslie Millar (db). 29/11/82 TW DD

L'Augmentation

24/11/99 Lunar Eclipse, Negative War, Sun Drenched, D Is For Dum Dum, Cartoon Strip. Angela Cross (d, fl), Lisa Sellick (tpv), Jim Smith (b), Simon Vincent (kv). Live from MV3 AR/SCU MR

Laura Logic

21/2/79 Wake Up, Alkaline Loaf In The Area, Quality Crayon Wax OK, Shabby Abbott. Billed as Essential Logic: Laura Logic (sx, v), Phil Lip (g), William Charles (g), Mark Turner (b), Dave Wright (sx), Richard Thompson (d). 6/2/79 MV4 BS MR

2/6/81 Pedigree Charm, Martian Man, Rat Alley. Laura Logic (v, al, ts), Phil Legg (g, b), Duncan McDonald (d, perc). 26/5/81 LH1 DG DD

Laurel and Hardy

4/11/82 Tell Her Sey Me Sorry, You're Nicked, Toast One Quick, Speeding. Laurel (v), Hardy (v), John Kpyaie (g), Spy (b), Angus Gaye (d), Reg Graham (k), Annie Whitehead (brs), Chris Layne (v). 20/10/82 MV4 RP NG

Gaspar Lawal Band

28/8/71 Ye Ye Oro, Jankulubo. Terry Poole (b), Gaspar Lawal (d, perc, v), Graham Bond (o, v), Shamsi Surami (afd, cga), Pug Weathers (xyl, cga), Derick (surname unknown) (afd, cga), Liz Wilson, Jillian, Karen & Diane Stewart (bck), Malcolm (surname unknown) (ts, fl). 23/8/71 PH JW PK 1st TX on Viv Stanshall's Radio Flashes while Peel on holiday

The League of Gentlemen

17/11/80 Inductive Resonance, Heptaparaparshinokh, Farewell Johnny Brill, Dislocated. Robert Fripp (g), Barry Andrews (o), Sara Lee (b), Johnny Toobad (d). U PRIV

Leatherface

4/1/92 I Want The Moon, Springtime, Dreaming, Peasant In Paradise. Andrew Karzi-Laing (d), Stuart Raymond (b), Dicky Kadogo-Hammond (g), Frankie Stubbs (gv). 12/11/91 MV4 MR MR

16/1/93 Games, Books, Not A Day Goes By, Cabbage. Andy Crighton (b) r Raymond. 1/11/92 MV3 ME~ DMC

4/2/94 Heaven Sent, In My Life, Do The Right Thing, Little White God. Stubbs, Crighton, Ian Syborn (d). 23/12/93 MV4 NG NF

Led Zeppelin ○

23/3/69 Communication Breakdown, You Shook Me, I Can't Quit You Baby. Jimmy Page (g), Robert Plant (v), John Paul Jones (bp, o), John Bonham (d). 3/3/69 PH BA PR&BC This trial broadcast tape passed unanimously by audition panel 22/4/69: 'Excellent', Jimmy Grant. Sessions followed for the World Service R&B show (April 69) and a R1 Sunday show (June 69)

29/6/69 What Is And What Should Never Be, Whole Lot Of Love, Travelling Riverside Blues, Communication Breakdown. 24/6/69 MV4 JW TW

10/8/69 Communication Breakdown, Can't Quit You Baby, Dazed And Confused, White Summer, You Shook Me, How Many More Times. 27/6/69 PH JG TW ○ Billed as One Night Stand, this was the pilot for Jeff Griffin's Radio 1 Concert series. Group later recorded a second live concert for the series, 1/4/71 PS, TX 4/4/71. Both concerts, slightly edited, plus most of the 3 R1 sessions, are on The BBC Sessions Atlantic Records

Alvin Lee & Mylon LeFevre

13/12/73 The World Is Changing, So Sad, On The Road To Freedom, Rockin' Till The Sun Goes Down. Alvin Lee (gv), Mylon LeFevre (lv). U PRIV

Leisure Process

22/3/82 Sweet Vendetta, Gimme That Sax Boy, The Erection Set. Ross Middleton (v, g, b), Gary Barnacle (k, sx). 10/3/82 MV4 RP NG

The Lemonheads

17/7/89 Clang Bang Clang, Circle Of One, The Door, Mallo Cup. 4/7/89 U DG U

Deke Leonard and Iceberg ○

24/5/73 Hard Way To Live, Razor Blade And Rattle Snake, Jayhawk Special, Four Corners Of Hell. Deke Leonard (gv), Brian Breeze (g), Paul Burton (b), Keith Hodge (d). 14/5/73 LH1 BA U ○

20/12/73 7171 511, In Search Of Sarah And 26 Horses, Daughter Of The Fireplace, Eddy Waring. Leonard, Breeze, David Charles (d), Martin Ace (b). 26/11/73 LH1 BA U ○

27/2/78 Map Of India, Oh!, Big Hunk Of Love, Dirty Dirty Feelin'. Leonard, Lincoln Carr (b), Howard Hughes (p), Anthony Stone (d). 15/2/78 MV4 MB NG ○ Wireless HUX064

Leopards

11/11/97 Theme E, Shout Baby, Electric Slim And the Factory Hen, Ju Ju Girl. Mick Slaven (gv), Skip Reid (d, bck), Campbell Owens (b, bck). 12/10/97 MV4 ME JLO

28/4/98 You Are The One, Leopard Freedom (& Cutting A Short Dog, Get Ready To Run, 13/5/98). Live from MV5 NG JLO

Les Thugs

16/11/87 Intro / Les Thugs / Little Kiddy, Bulgarian Blues, Legal Drugs, About Your Life. U 1/12/87 U DG JB

Levellers Five

16/5/90 Warning Shadows, Mister Tell Me, Home, Shell. Ian Almond (afd, perc), Carole Fleck (perc), Terry Walsh (b), Steven Lindley (g), John Donaldson (gv). 19/4/90 MV3 DG U ● SFPS083

6/10/90 Somewhere, What's The Matter, Clatter, Love Thing Ha. 11/9/90 MV4 MR MR

23/5/92 Pressure Drop, Messelina, Mass, Everyone For Themselves. 12/4/92 MV4 ME U

G Lewis & B C Gilbert

7/10/80 Anchors, Norde, Quicken Your Step. G Lewis, B C Gilbert (g, b, k, perc). 22/9/80 MV4 TW DD

Jefffrey Lewis

31/7/02 Heavy Heart, Seattle, Back When I Was Four, The Last Time I Did Acid I Went Insane, This Is Madness, Texas, Another Girl, Arrow, The Man With The Golden Arm, Taxi Cab Punx, The Modern Age, We Don't Want No LSD Tonight, Springtime. Jefffrey Lewis (gkv), Jack Lewis (bkv), Anders Griffin (dv). Live from MV4 SA JHT

The Leyton Buzzards

1/8/78 Through With You, I Don't Want To Go To Art School, Can't Get Used To Losing You, 17 And Mad. Kevin Steptoe (d), Vernon Austin (gv), David Jaymes (bv), Geoff Deane (lv). 26/7/78 MV4 BS NG

22/1/79 Saturday Night Beneath The Plastic Palm Trees, Baby If You Love Me Say Yes If You Don't Say No, The Greatest Story Ever Told, Love Is Just A Dream. 18/12/78 MV4 BS DD

27/6/79 Sharp Young Men, Last Tango (In Leyton), People In The Street, Sweet Dreams Little One. 6/6/79 MV4 TW NG

21/1/80 When You Walk In The Room, Telephone, Jealousy, Swanky Pop. & Milton Reame James (k), Tony Gainsborough (d) r Steptoe. 14/1/80 MV4 TW DD

LFO

20/10/90 Take Control, To The Limit, Rob's Nightmare, Lost World. Mark Bell & Jez Varley (k, prog), Susie Thorpe (v). 7/10/90 MV3 PW TD&JL

Liars

12/6/02 Catchy Like Brains On Gangs, Loose Nuts On The Velodrome, The Pillars Were Hollow And Filled With Candy, Mr You're On Fire Mr, We're Still Young Enough To Lay Face Down. Angus Andrew (v, pedals), Aaron Hemphill (g, dm), Pat Nature (b, sy), Ron Albertson (d). 14/4/02 MV4 ME JHT

15/6/04 There's Always Room On The Broom, If You're A Wizard Then Why Do You Wear Glasses, We Fenced Other Gardens With The Bones Of Our Own, Bugman Needs A Hugman. Hemphill, Andrew, Julian Gross (d). 12/5/04 MV4 SA NF

Liberator DJs & The London Acid Techno Mafia

2/4/97 Radio On One, Creeper, Dynamo City, Carbine. Liberator DJs (1), Undulator 23 (2), Urban & Free (3), Psycho Thrill (4). OS

Lift To Experience

30/5/01 Just As Was Told, Falling From Cloud 9, The Ground So Soft, With The World Behind. Josh Pearson (gv), Josh Browning (b), Andy Young (d). 15/4/01 MV4 JB~

29/8/01 Just As Was Told, Falling From Cloud 9, With Crippled Wings, Ground So Soft, Waiting To Hit, These Are the Days. Live from MV4 MA NF

Ligament

28/10/95 Ligament By Numbers, Battleships, Give It Up For Ligament, Renius. Hamilton Industry (d), Ray Hill (b, bck), Tim Cedar (g, lv). 17/10/95 MV4 MR PA

The Liggers

20/10/80 Pretty Girls, Dreams Die First, Me And Mary Jane. Patti Owens (k, v), Gina Sobers (b, k), Neil Anderson (g, d), Andrew (g), Donna Sullivan (b, k). 30/9/80 MV4 JS MR

Light

12/10/99 Hard Isn't Belief, Shining, Fire & Water, No Need No More. Dave Mercer (e). 1/2/99 OS

Gordon Lightfoot

19/3/69 If I Could, Affair On Eighth Avenue, Pussywillow Catails, The Circle Is Small, Railroad Trilogy, The Leaves Of Grass, For Loving Me, Bitter Green. Gordon Lightfoot (ag, v). 11/3/69 S1 JM U

Lightning Bolt

31/3/04 unknown titles. Brian Chippendale (dv), Brian Gibson (b). Live from MV4 AR~

Lillian

3/2/98 Teenage Whore, Peroxide Beauties, Bulimic Bitches, Rape Anthem. Nicola Major (dmv), Nicola Anison (g). 16/12/97 MV5 JB GT

Lindisfarne

30/1/71 Positive Earth, Knacker's Yard Blues, Lady Eleanor, Dream Within A Dream (& Psalm To A Secret, 10/4/71). Alan Hull (vgk), Rod Clements (b, vi), Simon Cowe (gv, mand), Ray Jackson (v, hca, mand), Ray Laidlaw (d, perc). 12/1/71 MV4 JW BC Previous audition tape for Night Ride session 6/1/71 passed by panel, with proviso 'there doesn't seem to be a lot of call for this type of ingredient in our general output'

11/9/71 Meet Me On The Corner, Uncle Sam, All Right On The Night, Fog On The Tyne (& Together Forever, 10/11/71). 31/8/71 MV4 JW BC

4/2/72 Dancing Jack Peel, Together Forever, No Time To Lose, Alright On The Night, Meet Me On The Corner (& Poor Old Ireland, 10/3/72). 17/1/72 T1 PD ARV

13/6/72 Mandolin King, Poor Old Ireland, Road To Kingdom Come, Lady Eleanor. 8/5/72 T1 JW BC ● SFPS059

18/1/73 Oh No Not Again, Train In G Major, Uncle Sam, Court In The Act. 8/1/73 LH1 BA U

4/4/74 No Need To Tell Me, Taking Care Of Business, In Your Head, North Country Boy. Hull, Jackson, Charlie Harcourt (gv), Kenny Craddock (gkv), Tommy Duffy (bv), Paul Nichols (d). 28/3/74 LH1 JW U

The Lines

17/1/80 Don't Need Surgery, Time To Go, Two Split Seconds, False Alarm. Richard Conning (gv), Mick Lineham (g), Joe Forty (b), Nicholas Cash (d). 8/1/80 MV4 JS MR&MPK

27/1/81 Bliss-tability, Transit, Bucket Brigade, Nerve Pylon. 20/1/81 LH1 BS MR

Little Bob Story

21/1/77 Like A Rock 'n' Roll, Baby Don't Cry, So Bad, High Time. Robert Pazza (v), Dominique Lelan (bv), Dominique Quertier (d), Dominique Guillon (rg, bck), Guy George Gremy (lg). 11/1/77 MV4 TW U

22/7/77 Mr Tap, Nothing Else (Can Give It To Me), All Or Nothing, Little Big Boss. 13/7/77 MV4 U MR

Little George

28/2/02 One Stop Lovin', Don't Make Me Choose, Don't You Want To Boogie, Tell Your Mother, Baby What's Wrong With You. George Sueref (gv), David Purdey (g), Matt Radford (db), Mike Watts (d). 12/12/01 MV4 SA GYW

Little Killers

22/9/04 Jenna, Mellow Down, Butter Fingers, No Reason, You Got It Made, Sheet, Come On Up, Volume, How Do You Do It, She Don't, Happy. Andy Maltz (gv), Sara Nelson (g, bck), Kari Boden (d). Live from MV4 AR~

Little Red Duffle Coats

7/1/82 Mountains, Sky The Pitch, Natasha Rumbova Buys A Kite, Enrolment. Billy Muir (d), Nick Prescott (b), Tommy McGregor (pv), Ian Macleod (g). 19/12/81 MV4 DG PS

Live Skull

22/3/89 Safe From Me, Someone Else's Sweat, Adema, Amputease. Rich Hutchins (d), Sonda Andersson (b), Mark C (g), Tom Paine (g), Thalia Zedek (v, g-2). 14/3/89 WX DG ME

The Liverpool Scene

19/1/69 Wild West, All Around My Grandmother's Floor, Tramcar To Frankenstein, The Entry Of Christ Into Liverpool (& The Raven, Colours, 23/2/69). Adrian Henri (v), Andy Roberts (g), Percy Jones (b), Brian Dodson (d), Mike Evans (sx). 6/1/69 MV4 BA PR Passed by panel, despite following comments: 'entertaining I should imagine to devotees to self-pitying ideas on current society'; 'not accurate poetry';

'one assumes this is suitable for Top Gear – certainly it would be unsuitable for anything else'

20/7/69 I've Got The Fleetwood Mac Chicken Shack John Mayall Can't Fail Blues, Winter Poem, GBS Blues. 15/7/69 MV4 JW TW

3/1/70 Home Grown, Boathouse, Night Song, Tractor. 29/12/69 PH JW TW

Livingstone

16/12/95 Gangsta, Flirt, Call Around, Female Self, Follow Me Around. Andrew Rogers (d), John Thompson (b), Morgan Pimblett (g), Andrew Meeson (gv). 31/10/95 MV4 MR RJ

Robert Lloyd

23/3/87 Something Nice, Tocatta And Fatigue, Of Course You Can't, The Part Of The Anchor. Robert Lloyd (v) and the New Four Seasons: Cara Tivey (k, bck), Dave Lowe (g, bck), Micky Harris (b), Mark Fletcher (d). 10/3/87 U DG MS&MR

19/10/87 Top Floor To Let, Sweet Georgia Black, Half A Heart. Mark Tibenham (dm, v) r Fletcher. 11/10/87 U DG ME&PS

13/2/89 Mama Nature's Skin, Nothing Matters, The Funeral Stomp, Ta Love. Lloyd, Lowe, Tibenham, Magda (g, v, bj), Bobby Bird (g), Susanne Unruh (d). 31/1/89 MV4 DG MR

26/3/90 The Race Is On, Grown So Ugly, The Man Who Couldn't Afford To Orgy, Good Boy. Lloyd, Magda, Wendy Harper (vi, sy, tamb, bck), Nick Small (b, bck), Peter Byrchmore (g, brs), Daniel S (d). 4/3/90 MV3 DG ME

12/1/91 Here Comes Mimi, Go Forth And Multiply, Kiss Me Stupid, Slags And Angels. Lloyd, Byrchmore, Small, Daniel S, Cath Eburne (k, bck), Kerry Lloyd (bck). 11/12/90 MV5 MR MR

Llwybr Llaethog

5/1/88 Tour De France 87, Cyfundrefn Gyfalafol, Megamics. John Griffiths (dv, g-1), Kevs Ford (gv, d-1), Ben (b), Debs (perc). 20/12/87 U DG ME&PS

11/10/89 Dinas Fawr, Trachwant, Byd Mor Wahanol, Fyw Dy Fywyd. 17/9/89 MV3 DG ME

1/8/01 Porthmadog, Anomie Ville, Dimbrains Dot Com, Caws. Ford, Griffiths, Steffan Cravos (v). 15/7/01 MV4 RJ U

19/12/01 Ffestiniog Dub, Kunstroc, Jessica. Ford, Griffiths only. Live from MV4 SA NF

Anna Lockwood

5/2/69 Talk And Sounds. Anna Lockwood (v). 22/1/69 S1 JM U

Locus

3/6/03 Ethyl, Igor I, Oranjsuper, Popcorn. Martin Cooper (g), Chris Holden (b), Peter Wright (d). 30/4/03 MV3 SA GT

Locust

17/6/94 Air Secondary, Pillar, Good God, All My Sadness, Fear Of God. Mark Van Hoen. OS

The Locust

25/9/01 How To Become A Virgin, Half Eaten Sausage Would Like To See You In His Office, Kill Rodger Hedgecock, Straight From The Horse's Mouth, Moth Eaten Deer Head, Priest With Sexually Transmitted Diseases Get Out Of My Bed, Cattle Mutilation, The Perils In Believing In Round Squares, 23 Schizophrenics With Delusions Of Grandeur, Stucco Obelisks Labelled As Trees, Skin Graft At 75 Mph, Get Off The Cross The Wood Is Needed, Who Wants A Dose Of The Clap?, Wet Nurse Syndrome: Hand Me Down Display Case, Gluing Carpet To Your Genitals Does Not Make You A Canteloupe, 23 Fulltime Cowboys. Justin Pearson (bv), Gabe Serbian (s), Joseph Karam (kv), Bobby Bray (gv). 19/8/01 MV4 ME NF

Lo-Fi Generator

1/6/99 Headbangers, Cha Cha Cha, Jungle Drums, Technobeam. Marcel Immel (e) OS

Lois

3/12/93 Grass Widow, Press Play And Record, Saint What's-Her-Name, Valentine, Strip Mine. Lois Maffeo (gv), Amy Farina (d). 27/10/93 MV4 MPK KR

Lolita Storm

25/8/99 You Make Me High When You Go Down Low, So Bad I Love Him, Meat Injection, I Love Speed, Feeling Inside. Rebecca (Spex), Nhung Dang (Napalm Girl), Remy Medina, Jimmy Too-Bad. 21/7/99 MV4 MR NK

13/6/00 Candy, I Love You So Much, Suzy, Boy. 14/5/00 MV3 ME RJ

Lone Star

24/2/76 Flying, A Million Stars, She Said. Tony Smith (g), Ken O'Driscoll (lv), Rick Worsnop (k), Paul Chapman (g), Pete Hurley (b), Dixie Lee (d). 29/1/76 MV4 TW U

5/8/76 Hypnotic Mover, Spaceships. 15/4/76 MV4 TW BAI

6/7/77 Bells Of Berlin, From All Of Us, Lonely Soldier. 28/2/77 MV6 TW BAI Recorded as a Matrix H Quad experiment & 1st TX on Alan Freeman's Saturday afternoon show 25/6/77

Loop ○

19/8/87 Soundhead, Straight To Your Heart, Rocket USA. Robert Wills (gv), Glen Ray (b), James Dillon (g), John Wills (d). 11/8/87 U DG ME&MP

27/6/88 Pulse, Collision, This Is Where You End. Neil McKay (b) r Ray. 14/6/88 MV4 TdB TdB

31/1/90 Afterglow, From Centre To Wave, Sunburst. Scott (g) r Dillon. 21/1/90 MV3 HP ME ○ All sessions on 'Wolf Flow' Reactor CD3

Loop Guru

15/5/93 Aphrodite's Shoes, Paradigm Shuffle Dreaming With Kings, Zahrema's House, Pandanrama, H'Ashra. Ja Muud (k, tps), Salman Gita (g, tps) & Speechless ('hypnorthymic therapy'), Count Dubula (b), Zahrema ('zahremics'), Mad Jym ('quantum metallics'). OS

22/1/94 Words Shaking, This Bird Has Flown, Under Influence, Skidoo, Sumar. & Mad Jym (quantum metalics), Jim Chase (tablatics). 1/12/93 OS

25/3/95 Soulus v The Jungle Tree Surgery Variations, 333 Getting There, Yugoslavian Expedition To Brentford, Fumi Spread Thickly, Epic Song. & Speechless, Mad Jym, Nidhal BulBul, Elmer Thud, Sandira, Inder Goldfinger (from Det-ri-mental). OS

30/3/96 Diwanatactics, The Other Side Of The Other Side, Feeling Thinking Action, White Joy Mystery. & Speechless, Mad Jym, Nidahl Bulbul, Elmer Thud, Sandira 2/3/96 OS

26/3/97 Jackdaw, Gunung, One Note Samba, Caravan. U 1/2/97 OS

Lorimer

14/12/00 Formica, Secure Unit, George Oldfield, Still Life, Nothing Changed. Phil Pettler (bv), Chris Cooper (d), Graham Naysmith (g), Robert Wallwork (g, bck). 26/11/00 MV4 ME RJ

The Lotus Eaters

18/10/82 Can You Keep A Secret?, Stranger So Far, When You Look At Boys†, The First Picture Of You. Peter Coyle (v), Gerry Kelly (g), Phil (b), Alan Wills (d), Gerard Quinn (k). . 2/10/82 MV4 DG U † On band's debut album 'No Sense Of Sin' Arista 206263

10/10/83 Alone Of All Her Sex, German Girl, You Fill Me With Need, Love Still Flows, Signature Tune (Instrumental). Coyle, Kelly, Quinn, Michael Dempsey (b), Steve Creese (d). 5/10/83 MV4 RP NG

Loudspeaker

22/2/92 Knockout, It Wasn't Me, Stripmind, No Time. Chris Douglas (d), Charles Hanson (b), Kurt Wolf (g), Matt Burruso (gv). 26/1/92 MV3 DG JB

Louisiana Red

8/11/77 Intro, I Wonder Who, The Whole World, When My Mama Was Living, My Heart's A Loser, Look At The Children Run, I Walked All Night Long. Louisiana Red (gv). 2/11/77 MV4 JG U

Love Blobs

4/9/92 Blood Control, Soul Station, Peanuts, Two Down. Paul Thorpe (gv), Colin Todd (b, bck), Tim Holdcraft (g), Tim Cedar (d). 16/8/92 MV3 ME ME&FK

Love Child

NOT TX Slow Me Down, Asking For It, Greedy, All Is Loneliness. Alan Licht (gv), Rebecca Odes (bv, g), Brendan O'Malley (d). 21/12/92 MV4 PL~ JLO No BBC data or regular listener can find a trace of this having been broadcast. Considered opinion is that the session, which is just dandy, was simply overlooked on the shelf. It happens sometimes

Love Is All

13/7/04 Make Out Fall Out Make Up, Public Transportation, Felt Tip Hip Kids, Spinning And Scratching. Josephine Olausson (kv), Nicholas Sparding (g, bck), Johan Lindwall (b, bck), Markus Gorsch (d, bck), Fredrik Eriksson (sx, bck). 3/6/04 MV4 GT NF

Love Junk

13/1/98 Harrison Ford, Parents Can't Win, Let It Slide, Closing Time. Scruff Myers (lvg), Mickey Donuts (lgv), Wolfie Leotard (b), Reado Gurt Big (dv). 2/11/97 MV4 ME KR

Love Sculpture

21/4/68 Brand New Woman, River To Another Say, Do I Still Figure In Your Life, Stumble, Sweet Little Rock 'n' Roller. Dave Edmunds (gv), John Williams (b), Bob 'Congo' Jones (d). 2/4/68 PC1 BA DT&AH

6/10/68 The Rebel, Wang Dang Doodle, Promised Land, Sabre Dance (TX twice) (& Don't Answer The Door, 3/11/68). 16/9/68 PC1 BA AH

9/3/69 Farendale, Great Balls Of Fire, Evening, Inner Light. 28/1/69 PH JG AH

The Loves

13/6/01 Little Girl Blues, Chelsea Girl, When My Baby Comes, Just Like Bobby D. Simon (gv), Liz (k), Pnoshi (gv), George (d), James (b), Catrin (v), Becky (perc). 30/5/01 MV4 MA JHT

26/9/01 Depeche Mode, She'll Break Your Heart, Boom A Bang Bang Bang, Shake Your Bones, Little Girl Blues, I'm Gonna Get F**ked Up. Dave (d) r George. Live from MV4 MA NF

14/2/02 The Sound We Make Is Love, Boom A Bang Bang, Just Like Bobby Dee, True Love Will Find You, You're My Best Friend. Becky out. Live from Peel Acres AR GT

4/12/02 Rock 'N' Roll, Just Like Bobby D, Cold Turkey, True Love Will Find You In The End. Craig Parkinson (g) r Pnoshi. 28/11/02 MV4 MA GT

Lene Lovich

27/11/78 Monkey Talk, Home, Lucky Number, Say When. Lene Lovich (v), Les Chappell (gv), Don Snow (k), Bob Irwin (d), Ron Francois (b). 21/11/1978 MV4 MR U

10/12/79 Angels, One In A Million, Birdsong. Lovich, Chappell, Justin Hildreth (d), Mark Chaplin (b), Dead Kelvatt (k). 3/12/79 MV4 TW DD

Low

22/6/99 Those Girls (Song for Nico), Liar, I Remember, Will The Night. Alan Sparhawk (gkv), Mimi Parker (v, perc), Zak Sally (b). 16/5/99 MV5 ME GT

8/11/00 Will The Night, Venus, Dinosaur Act, Joan Of Arc, Immune, Over the Ocean. Live from MV4 AR/SA GT

2/1/02 Last Snowstorm Of The Year, Canada, Lil' Argument With Myself, In The Drugs. 26/11/01 MV4 SA GYW

31/1/03 The Last Snow Storm Of The Year, That's How We Sing (Amazing Grace), Fearless, La La, Tonight, Lordy. Live from Peel Acres AR GT Peel was snowbound in London at R1, the band playing in from Peel Acres. 'They were so disappointed he wasn't here,' remembers Sheila

L7

18/11/90 Scrap, Packin' A Rod, Shove, Let's Lynch The Landlord. Dee Plakas (d), Jennifer Finch (bv), Suzi Gardner (gv), Donita Sparks (gv). 1/11/90 MV5 DG NG&JSM

The Lucys

11/3/81 No Door, Lost Animal, The Right Man, Perfect Marriage. Ann Paley (bv), Colin McMahon (bv), Joanne Melvin (v), Pete Drew (dv), Bee Berwick (perc, v), Mike Hobbs (sx), Pete Boyse (gv). 3/3/81 LH1 DG MR

Luddites

19/9/83 Just To Return, Letters, See These, 7733 (instrumental). Steve McDermott (v), Mike Stead (g), Lawrence Gill (b), Dave Stead (d). 10/9/83 MV4 DG MR

Ludus

18/8/82 Too Hot To Handle, Wrapped In Silence, Covenant, (Pride Below The Navel) Vagina Gratitude. Linder (v), Ian (g), Paul (b), Lee (ts), Graham (ss), Roy (d), Dave (k). 4/8/82 MV4 JWI NG

Luggage

13/1/96 Magic Bag, Space Of A Day, White Wheels, Beauty Spot. Joe Fahey (g), Barry O'Mahony (v), Cahal O'Reilly (d), Rachel Tighe (b). 10/12/95 MV4 ME PL

Lulu

19/11/67 Higher And Higher, Love Loves To Love Love, To Love Somebody. Lulu (v) & The George Bean Group. 14/11/67 U BA DT

Luna

24/4/92 Crazy People, Slide, That's What You Always Say, I Can't Wait. Stanley Demeski (d), Justin Harwood (b), Dean Wareham (gv). 1/3/92 MV3 DG ME&PL

Lunachicks

30/5/89 Binge And Purge, Mabel Rock, Rip You To Shreds, Public School Hell. Becky (d), Squid (b, bck), Gina (g), Sindi (g), Theo (v). 7/5/89 HP DG MA

Lung Leg

25/2/95 Palmolive, Small Screen Queen, Lungleg, Edith Massey, Kung Fu On The Internet, Blah Blah Blah. Jane Egypt (bv), Annie Spandex (gv), Jade Green (dv), Mo-Mo (gv) & Rhodri Marsden (bsn). 29/1/95 MV4 ME SA

21/4/96 Lust For Leg, The Shaver, Theme Park, Lonely Man. 4-piece. 7/4/96 MV3 ME GPR

Lupine Howl

4/4/00 Sometimes, Love Decays, The Jam That Ate Itself. Sean Cook (b, v, hp), Mike Mooney (gv), Damon Reece (d, perc, smp), John Baggot (o, Wurlitzer, Mini Moog), Adrian Utley (g, Mini Moog, dictaphone). 20/2/00 MV3 ME JHT

The Lurkers

27/10/77 Freakshow, Total War, I'm On Heat, Then I Kissed Her, Be My Prisoner. Nigel Moore (b), Esso (d), Pete Stride (g), Howard Wall (lv). 18/10/77 MV4 MB MR

24/4/78 Ain't Got A Clue, Pills, Tell Her, Jenny. & Plug (bck). 18/4/78 MV4 MB MR

7/8/78 Here Come The Bad Times, God's Lovely Men, In Room 309, Countdown. 25/7/78 MV4 BS MR

30/1/79 Whatever Happened To Mary, Take Me Back To Babylon, Out In The Dark, See The World. 24/1/79 MV4 BS NG

Luscious Jackson

1/4/95 Energy Sucker, Soixante Neuf, Rock Freak. Jill (bv), Gab (gv), Kate (d), Viv (kv), Alex (dj). 11/3/95 MV4/5 SA GT

Lush

19/2/90 Hey Hey Helen, Leaves Me Cold, Breeze. Christopher Alland (d), Steve Rippon (b), Emma Anderson (g, bck), Miki Berenyi (gv). 23/1/90 U DG MR

Mabel Greer's Toyshop

3/4/68 Beyond And Before, Electric Funeral, Images Of Me And You, Janetta. Peter Banks (g), Chris Squire (bv), Clive Bailey (lv, g), Alexander Belmont or Bob (surname lost) (d). U U U U

Andy Mackay

16/7/74 The Hour Before Dawn, Ride Of The Valkyries, Walking The Whippet. Mackay & 4 (unknown). 24/6/74 T1 JW U

Billy Mackenzie

12/9/83 Since When Do You Cook Breakfast, This Flame, God Bless The Child. U 3/9/83 U U U

MacKenzies

10/2/86 New Breed, Man With No Reason, Give Me Averything, Gobstopper. Iain Beveridge (g), Gary Weir (v), Paul Turnbull (b) & David Allen (g), Peter Ellen (sx), Scott Brown (perc). 21/1/86 MV5 MW U

30/7/86 Milk, Big Jim (There's No Pubs In Heaven), Mealy Mouths, Jingle (Slight Return). Four-piece & Ellen, Brown, Ann Quinn (perc). 20/7/86 U DG ME

Macrocosmica

28/1/98 Masada, Rusty's Arms, Nostoc Commune, Space Geek. Gavin Laird (gv), Brendan O'Hare (gv), Russell McEwan (d), Cerwyss Ower (bv), Graham from Falkirk (dictaphone & rp-1). 7/12/97 MV4 ME KR

The Mad Professor

4/10/82 Beyond The Realms Of Dub, Ghetto Pace / Elastic Plastic, John Peel Dub, In Fine Style, Funking In The Capital Dub. Mad Professor (sy), Garnett Cross (v, p, d), Preacher (b), Jah Shaka (perc), Billy Cross (d). 23/9/82 OS

Madder Rose

6/8/93 Bring It Down, Sway, 20 Foot Red, True Religion. Billy Cote (lg, rg), Mary Lorson (gv), Matt Verta-Ray (b, bck), Johnny Kick (d, bck). 4/7/93 MV3 ME~

30/4/94 Johnny Take A Ride, In The Long Grass, Before I Sleep, Star Power. Chris Giammaivo (b) r Verta-Ray. 8/4/94 MV5 DD MR

Madness

27/8/79 The Prince, Bed And Breakfast Man, Land Of Hope And Glory, Stepping Into Line. Mike Barson (k), Suggs (lv), Mark Bedford (b), Woody (d), Chris Foreman (gv), Lee Thompson (sx, v). 14/8/79 MV4 BS MR ● SFPS007

Magazine

20/2/78 Touch And Go, The Light Pours Out Of Me, Real Life, My Mind Ain't So Open. Howard Devoto (lv, g-3), Martin Jackson (d), Barry Adamson (b), John McGeoch (g), Dave Formula (k). 14/2/78 MV4 MB MR

31/7/78 Give Me Everything, Burst, Big Dummy, Boredom. 24/7/78 MV4 TW DD

14/5/79 TV Baby, Thank You For Letting Me Be Myself Again, Permafrost. Jackson out. 8/5/79 MV4 TW MR

14/1/80 A Song From Under The Floorboards, 20 Years Ago, Look What Fear Has Done To My Body, Model Worker. & John Doyle (d). 7/1/80 MV4 TW DD

Magic Band

7/7/04 Intro, Diddy Wah Diddy, Circumstances, A Woman's Gotta Hit A Man, Bass Solo, Unknown Title, Steal Softly Through Sunshine, Talking, Abba Zabba, My Human Gets Me Blues, Alice In Blunderland, Hair Pie, Evening Bell, Electricity, Floppy Boot Stomp, Mirror Man, Talking, Moonlight on Vermont, Big Eyed Beans from Venus. John 'Drumbo' French (dv), Mark 'Rockette Morton' Boston (b), Gary 'Mantis' Lucas (g), Denny 'Feelers Reebo' Walley (g), Michael Traylor (d). Live from MV4 AR GYW

Magic Dirt

3/12/97 Ice, Shrinko, X Ray, Heavy Business. Adalita (gv), Raul Sanchez (g), Dean Turner (b), Adam Robertson (d). 28/10/97 MV5/LR MR LS

Magic Hour

10/6/94 Another Day Like Today, I Had A Thought, Passing Words. Damon Krukowski (d), Naomi Young (b), Kate (g), Wayne Rogers (gv). 3/5/94 MV4 MR SA

Magma

21/3/74 Kohntarkosz, Theusz Hamtaahk. Christian Vander (d), Jannick Top (b), Klaus Blasquiz (v), Michel Graillier (p), Gerrard Bikialo (p), Claude Almos (lg). 14/3/74 LH1 TW BAI&DD

Magnapop

2/10/93 Garen, Texas, Favourite Writer, Crush. Linda Elizabeth Hopper (v), Ruth Mary Morris (g, bck), Shannon David Mulvaney (b, box), David Granville McNair (d). 2/9/93 MV4 NG JLO

Magnetophone

15/3/00 Air Methods, Come On The Phone, How I Learnt To Live The Future, May Stand Still. John Hanson, Matthew Huish Saunders. 16/1/00 MV3 ME NF

Magoo

6/1/96 Baxter Preminger, Eye Spy, Valley As A Whole, Goldwyn. David Bamford (d), Adam Blackbourn (b, g), Andrew Raynor (gbv), Owen Turner (bck, g), Simon J Swanson (g-3). 12/12/95 MV4 CML RJ

4/3/97 Billion Dollar Brain, Your Only Friend, Playing Cards With The Stars, For No Reason. Bamford, Turner, Rayner, Andrew Hodge (b). 11/2/97 MV4 MR GT

14/7/98 Implicate The Targets, Airmen Afraid, Happy Together (& Cable Tuned And Sabre Toothed, 1st TX live from MV4 12/5/98). & Adam McLauchlan. 12/5/98 MV4 MA GT

23/11/99 East Polar Opposites Can Dream, The High Castle, Nastro Adhesivo, Valley Of Tears. Rayner, Turner, Stacey Gow (d), Jenny Heagren (b), Rhys Harder (g, k, smp). 6/10/99 MV3 GT GB

23/10/01 Motorama, 2 Dearborn, Theme From Joe 90. Rayner, Turner, Blackbourn, Heagren, Gow. 16/9/01 MV4 ME~

26/6/03 Micronaut, Lana Turner, Matthew And Son, You Make My Good Days, We R Syncronised. & Gill Sandell (fl, k, bck), Steven Gilchrist (perc, bck, vla). 15/5/03 MV4 NF U

10/11/04 Peace Love And Blood, Chicken Blows, Pink Dust, Radio Shack. & Sandell & (k) name lost. 7/10/04 MV4 JSM JHT

Maher Shalal Hash Baz

3/12/03 Loving, M1, Ferry Boat, Cold Rain, Sunset/Trees, Ethiopia, Bush Warbler. Tori Kudo (g, v, Hammond, Taisho goto), Hiroo Nakazaki (eu), Reiko Kudo (v, hca), Takashi Ueno (sx, hca), Naoto Kawate (b), Hirohiko Saito (g), Namio Kudo (sfx, perc, fl), Katrina Mitchell (d). 3/12/03 MV4 JHT NF

The Make Up

15/5/97 Wade In The Water, Caught In The Rapture, Watch It With That Thing, Live In The Rhythm Hive. James Canty (g, p, o, bck), Steve Gamboa (perc), Michelle Mae (b, bck), Ian Svenonius (v). 10/4/97 MV4 U U

12/1/00 Call Me Mommy, I Am Pentagon, Every Baby Cries The Same, The Prophet. & Alex Minoff (g, bck). 7/11/99 MV4 ME RJ

Malaria

3/8/81 I Will Be Your Only One, Geh Duschen, Nimm Mich Schnell In Deine Arme, How Do You Like My New Dog? Gudrun Gut (d, g, bck), Bettina Köster (sx, v), Christine Hahn (b, d), Manon Duursma (g), Susanne Kuhnke (sy, bck). 25/7/81 MV4 DG MR

Male Nurse

9/7/97 My Idea, Too Sexy In A Bad Way, British Stuntmen, My Own Private P Swayze. Alan Cricton (g), Ben Wallers (g), Eck King (sy), Alistair Macinvin (b), Lawrence Worthington (d), Keith Farquar (v) & Paul Kearney (g-3) 17/6/97 MV4 MR NF

26/2/98 Afraid And Jarring, Male Midwife, Back On The Pills, The Vestibule Song, German Sleeps In My Bed. & Andrew Hobson (g), Cricton out. 27/1/98 MV4 MR PI

Malicorne

20/6/74 La Fille Soldat, Pierre De Grenoble, Les Livres, Dame Lombarde, Martin. Gabrielle Yacoub, Marie Yacoub, Hughes de Courson, Laurent Ver Cambre. 13/6/74 LH1 U BAI

7/8/75 J'ai Vu Le Loup Le Renard Et La Belette, La Peronelle, Le Mariage Anglais. 31/7/75 MV4 U BAI

Batti Mamzelle

30/5/74 Lament, San Juan, Get Out Of My Way, I See The Light. Miguel Baradas (pn), Russel Valdez (pn), Ralph Richardson (pn), Winston Delandro (g), Peter Earl Duprey (b), Richard Bailey (d), Frank Ince (bgo, perc), James Chambers (v). 16/5/74 LH1 TW BAI

Man

12/9/72 Come On, Life On The Road. Mick Jones (gv), Clive John (gv), Terry Williams (d), Will Youatt (bv), Phil Ryan (k). 29/8/72 MV4 PR U 1st session was for Pete Drummond Jan 72

2/10/73 A Night In Dad's Bag (1st TX Rock On, 29/9), Ain't Their Fight. Alan Lewis (g) r John. 18/9/73 LH1 TW BC

14/11/74 Many Are Called but Few Get Up, A Hard Way To Die, Day And Night. Jones, Williams, Deke Leonard (gv), Ken Whaley (b). 31/10/74 MV4 TW BAI

Man Or Astroman

22/1/94 Nitrons Burnout, Invasion Of The Dragonman, XI 3, Mermaid Love, Rovers. Starcrunch (Brian Causey) (lgv), Doctor Deleto (Jeff Goodwin) (b, rg), Birdstuff

(Brian Teasley) (d), Coco The Electronic Monkey Wizard (Rob Delbueno) (smp, b). 21/12/93 MV3 JB~

29/4/95 Sferic Waves, Untitled, Put Your Fingers In The Socket, Max Q, Inside The Head Of Mr John Peel. Bird Stuff, Coco, Star Crunch, Captain Zeno (rg, v). 19/3/95 MV4 ME PA

13/7/96 Welcome To The Wicky Wacky World Of John Peel, The Man Made Of CO2, 9 Volt, Television Fission. Coco, Birdstuff, Star Crunch. 11/6/96 MV4 CML GT

29/7/97 The Miracle Of Genuine Pyrex, Lo Batt, Don't Think What Jack, With Automatic Shut Off, Jonathan Winters Frankenstein. Dexter X (g), Star Crunch, Coco, Bird Stuff. 13/7/97 MV4 ME LS

27/7/99 Engines Of Difference, Theme From Eeviac, Oh Cha Cha Cha And Once Again Ladies & Gentlemen I'm John Peel And While Only A Minor Political Activist I'd Like To Say That Man Or Astroman Is Indeed My Favourite Band Even Moreso Than The Fall, Krasnoyask 26 (Forward Version), Many Pieces Of Large Fuzzy Animals Staggered Together At A Rave And Snoozing With A Brick. Brian Scott Teasley, Eric Dupree Hubner, Robert James Delbueno, Richard Daniel Edelson (all: g, prg). 27/6/99 MV4 MPK JSM

1/11/00 Spectrograph Reading Of The Verying Phantom, Theme From Eeviac, Song For The Two Mile Linear Particle, Television Fission, Preparation Clone, Within One Universe There Are Millions, Engines Of Difference, Many Pieces Of Large Fuzzy Mammals Gathered, Um Espectro Sem Escala, Interstellar Overdrive, Curious Constructs Of Stem Like Devices Which… Live from MV4 AR SA

Mandrake Paddle Steamer

6/4/69 The Ivory Castle Of Solitaire Huske, Cooger And Dark, Senila Lament, Janus Suite. John Web, Peter Frohlich, Michael Hutton, David Moses, Martin Woodward. 25/3/69 PH BA AH

Manfred Mann

7/1/68 Every Day Another Hair Turns Grey, Mighty Quinn, Handbags And Gladrags, Sleepy Hollow, Cubist Town. Manfred Mann (k), Tom McGuiness (g), Mike Hugg (d), Mike D'Abo (v), Klaus Voormann (b). 3/1/68 MV4 BA DT Dozens of Light Programme sessions after original line-up passed audition in 9/63

22/12/68 Abraham Martin And John, Fox On The Run, Clair, So Long (& Orange Peel, TX 19/1/69). 25/11/68 PC1 BA PR

24/1/70 Kone Kuf, Time, Sometimes. Manfred Mann's Chapter Three: Mann, Hugg & Steve York (b), Bernie Living (sx), Craig Collinge (d), Sonny Corbett (tp), Dave Coxhill (bars), Clive Stevens (ts), Carl Griffiths (ts). 19/1/70 PH JW U

1/12/71 Happy Being Me, Captain Bobby Stout, One Way Glass. Manfred Mann's Earthband: & Mick Rogers (lg), Chris Slade (d), Colin Pattenden (b) & Lisa Strike, Barry St John. 29/11/71 PH JW BC Earthband's 1st session was for DLT July 71

28/1/72 Meat, Captain Bobby Stout, Ashes In The Wind (& Mighty Quinn, 10/3/72). 10/1/72 T1 PD ARV

29/9/72 Messin', Dealer, Glorified Magnified. 5/9/72 T1 JM U

17/4/73 Father Of Day, Bubblegum And Kipling, Get Your Socks Off. 3/4/73 LH1 TW U

The Mangrove Steel Band

1/4/87 I Shot The Sherrif, Sonata In C, Josephine, Ah Want It Back. Austin Gachette (d), Victor Alleyene (cga), Laramie Green, Christopher Hunter, Annalyn Lazardi, Robert Thompson, Emery Russell, Franky Martin, Tony Andrews, Paul Joseph, Harrison Thomas, Jason Holmes, Justin Russell, Matthew Philip, Julian Green, Wayne Andain (all pn), Tony Francis (perc), Raymond Joseph (md). 22/3/87 U DG ME&JB

Mansun

7/10/95 Skin Up Pin Up, Take It Easy Chicken, Flourella, Attack Of The Grey Lantern. The Hib (d), Stove (b), Paul Draper (gv), Dominic Chad (g) & Mark Swinnerton (smp). 19/9/95 MV4 DD NK

5/4/96 The Chad Who Loved Me, Ski Jump Nose, Lemonade Secret Drinker, Egg Shaped Fred. 4-piece. 24/3/96 MV4 AA GT Same 4 tracks as on their then new Parlophone EP: 'Hah, no Tubular Bells from them, then' said Peel grumpily

19/12/00 Shot By Both Sides. 13/12/00 MV3 AR MA

Phil Manzanera and 801

22/11/77 Law And Order, Falling Feeling, Remote Control, Out Of The Blue. Phil Manzanera (gv), Simon Ainley (gv), Bill MacCormick (bv), Dave Skinner (kv), Paul Thompson (d). 14/11/77 MV4 TW DD

Thomas Mapfumo

11/8/98 Dai Pasina Satani, Chickende, Mukadzi Wemukoma, Usatambe Nenyoka. Thomas Mapfumo (v), Lancelot Kashesha (perc), Samson Mukanga (d), Allan Mwale (b), Bezil Makombe (mbi), Joshua Dube (g), Chakaipa Mhember (mbi). 7/7/98 MV4 ME RJ Previous session for Kershaw Aug 90

Mike Maran

11/2/72 Please Come In We Know You're Out There, Tiger's Looking Back, The Life And Death Of Arthur Perkins, Fair Warning (& Red School Uniform, 7/4/72). Mike Maran (agv). 18/1/72 T1 JM U Debut on Country Meets Folk 7/2/71 more folk show sessions followed

18/8/72 Please Keep The Rain Away, Lady In Black, Fool's Castle, Magic Moon Song (& Hell Bent, 29/9/72). 18/7/72 T1 JM U

30/11/72 It All Goes To Show, Tiger's Looking Back, Daughter Of Time, Monday

Boy. 6/11/72 LH1 BA U

16/8/73 Wouldn't It Be Nice, Crazy Days, Brave New World, Unchained, Ducks And Snowmen. 23/7/73 LH1 BA U

28/2/74 Crovie, Pax Vobiscum, Crazy Days, Goodbye Horseshoes And Black Cats (& Eyes Like Steve McQueen, 2/5/74). 21/2/74 LH1 JW U

The March Violets

2/8/82 Radiant Boys, Steam, 1–2–I Love You, Grooving In Green. Laurence Elliott (b), Tom Ashton (g), Simon Denbigh (v), Rosie Garland (v), Kevin Lycett (perc). 10/7/82 MV4 DG MC

24/3/83 Strange Head†, Slow Drip Lizard, The Undertow†, Crowbaby. Denbigh, Ashton, Garland, Hugh (b), Steve Atkinson (k), Chris Shoel (sx) & the Violettes: Sara James & Michaela Sanderson (bck). 19/3/83 MV4 DG U † On LP 'Rebirth' Natural History VRB25

19/6/84 Lights Go Out, Love Hit, Electric Shades, Don't Take It Lightly. Denbigh, Ashton, Elliot (b, dm), Jean Murray (v). 12/6/84 MV5 MRD TdB

The Marine Girls

16/2/82 Don't Come Back, Love To Know, Place In The Sun, He Got The Girl, Fever. Tracey Thorne (gv), Jane Fox (b), Alice Fox (v, perc). 1/2/82 U DG DD

19/4/83 Love You More, Lazy Ways, Seascape, That Day. & Tim Hall (sx, cl). 16/4/83 MV4 DG TdB

Marine Research

18/5/99 Angel In The Snow, I Confess, Bad Dreams, Capital L. Peter Momtchiloff (g), Amelia Fletcher (v, mel), Rob Pursey (b), Cathy Rogers (kv), DJ (d) & David Gedge (v-3). 18/4/99 MV3 ME~

8/12/99 In The Bleak Midwinter. John Stanley (d) r DJ. Live from MV3 AKM&AR SA

Mark Almond

21/7/72 The 11–4, Morning Always Comes Too Soon, The Little Prince. Jon Mark (ag), Johnnie Almond (fl, sx), Tommy Eyre (o, p), Roger Sutton (b). 27/6/72 T1 JM U Previous sessions for Bob Harris in Nov 70 & July 71

Bob Marley and the Wailers

15/5/73 Slave Driver, Rasta Man, Concrete Jungle. Bob Marley (ag, v), Bunny Livingstone (cga, bgo, v), Peter Mackintosh (gv), Aston Barrett (b), Carlton Barrett (d), Earl Lindo (k). 1/5/73 LH1 JW BC&MR

25/12/73 Kinky Reggae, Can't Blame The Youth, Get Up Stand Up. Livingstone out. 26/11/73 T1 JW ARV

Marlowe

18/9/03 It's Not A Porno, All Dressed Up, Stylish, Your Luck Really Matters To Me. Simon Bradshaw (gv), Paul Robinson (b), Aron McGhee (d), Chloe Mullett (sx, fl, v), Rachel Brewster (vi), Rob Strachan (gv), Clarie Swift (vi, clo). 27/8/03 MV4 GYW MA

Martian Dance

18/9/80 Stand Alone, Two Sides One Story, The Situation, Transformed. Jerry Lamont (lv), Duncan Greig (d), Daniel Grahame (b), Kevin Addison (g). 8/9/80 MV4 TW DD

21/4/81 Roses To Reno, Party Games, Claudine's. 6/4/81 LH1 TW DD

Caroline Martin

20/1/99 The Request, Look At Me, The Singer, Alien. Caroline Martin (gv) & Nic Davies (perc), Gavin Courtie (b, eg), Liz Radford (p, k, ag), Chris Cavanagh (d). 29/11/98 MV3 ME NF

4/9/02 So I Sing, The Next Day, A Doubting Song From A Dog, All I Have Left Is A Horse, Without Permission. & Phil Normansell (slg, ag), Matthew Harvey (d), Nic Davies (hca). 28/7/02 MV4 NF~ JSM

11/6/03 Flames, I Died, Monn, My Daddy's Shotgun, Bad Like Me, Look At Me. & Benjamin Shillabeer (p), Nic Davies (d). 13/5/03 MV4 KR RF

Caroline Martin & Lianne Hall

5/8/04 Winter Blues, Chain Smoking, Beautiful Boy, Like A Man, Peace. Caroline Martin (gv), Lianne Hall (g, mel, v). 14/7/04 MV4 GYW JSM

John Martyn

10/7/68 Come Along And Sing Of Summer, Fairytale Lullaby, The Gardeners, Memphis Blues, The River. John Martyn (agv). 13/6/68 S2 DK U

11/12/68 Different From The Book, Jellyroll Baker Blues, Dusty, Hello Train, Flying On Home, Seven Black Roses. & Harold McNair (fl). 9/12/68 PC1 JM U

4/4/70 Traffic Light Lady, Give Us A Ring, Road To Ruin, Tomorrow Time (& Seven Black Roses, 18/7/70). & Beverley Martin (v). 23/3/70 U U TW

20/10/71 May You Never, Bless The Weather, Inside Of Him, Singing In The Rain. Solo. 20/9/71 PH JW U

13/1/75 One Day Without You, Discover The Lover, My Baby Girl, The Message, Spencer The Rover. 7/1/75 MV4 TW MR

4/2/77 May You Never, Certain Surprise / Over The Hill, One Day Without You. 18/1/77 MV4 JG MR

16/1/78 Small Hours, Big Muff. 9/1/78 MV4 TW DD&ME

Brett Marvin and the Thunderbolts

30/5/70 Too Many Hotdogs, So Tired, Crazy With The Blues (& Going Back, 19/9/70). John Lewis (pv), Graham Hine (g), Jim Pitts (mnd), John Randall (wsh), Peter Gibson (tb), Keith Trussell ('zob stick'). 18/5/70 PH JW TW

Marxman

27/11/92 Revolution Is Not A Revolution, Drifting, Fascist. Phrase (v), Hollis (v), Oisin (prg, ma), Kay One (dj, sc). 25/10/92 MV3 ME~ PI

Masasu

11/6/90 Mbokoshi Ya Lufu, Litande, Chimbayambaya. Evans Bwalya (d, bck), Abuild Madichi (b), John Melemena (lg, v), Oswald Mwelwa (rg), Henry Lwanga (bck), PK Chishala (rg, v). 22/5/90 MV3 MR MR

J Mascis

10/1/01 Same Day, Ammaring, Waistin, I'm Not Fine (& Everything Flows, Range Life, In A Rut, TX 19/12/00 in F50 Special). J Mascis (gv) & The Fog: Mike Watt (b), George Berz (d). 13/12/00 MV4 SA~ GT

28/11/02 I Feel Like Going Home, Alone, Everybody Lets Me Down, Freak Scene. Mascis (agv) only. 20/11/02 MV4 GT JSM

Mason, Capaldi, Wood and Frog

2/3/69 Waiting On You, Crying To Be Heard, World In Changes, Leaving Blues. Dave Mason (gv), Jim Capaldi (dv), Chris Wood (sx, fl), Wynder K Frog (real name, Michael Weaver) (k). 25/2/69 PH BA AH Debut session for Symonds on Sunday produced by John Walters & TX 16/2/69

MASS

13/1/91 Sado Seduction, Someonelse, Medusa, Unnamed. Steve Beatty (d), Daz Fralikc (b, bck), Nick Ryall (g), E (v). 16/12/90 MV3 DG ME&SA

MASS (02)

26/11/02 Right Side, Live A Little, Fake Talk, Something Tells Me. Justine Berry (v), Jonny Green (gv), Paul Hegland (b), Stuart Macmillan (d), Andy Miller (gv). 31/10/02 MV4 JSM GT

Caspar Brotzman Massaker

26/5/95 Bass Totem, Peel Party. Caspar Brotzmann (g), Ingo Krauss (b), Frank Neumeier (d), Bruno Gebhard (mx). 27/4/95 MV4 AA MAP

Matching Mole ○

25/1/72 Immediate Kitten, Brandy (re-titled Part Of The Dance). Robert Wyatt (d), Bill MacCormick (b), Phil Miller (g), Dave Sinclair (o), Dave MacCrae (elp, p). 17/1/72 PH JW BC

24/3/72 No 'Alf Measures, Lything And Gracing. Sinclair out. 6/3/72 T1 JM NG

9/5/72 Marchides / Instant Pussy (& Smoke Signal, 6/6/72) [complete 19' 35' medley of all 3 items TX only on 6/6/72]. 17/4/72 T1 JW U ○ All sessions on HUX083 On The Radio

Matthews' Southern Comfort

14/2/70 My Front Pages, Blood Red Roses, Uncle Joe, Reagan's Rag, What We Say. Ian Matthews (lv), Peter Watkins (ps), Carl Barnwell (g, bj), Roger Swallows (d), Marc Griffiths (lg). 2/2/70 PH JW BC

28/11/70 I Believe In You, Sylvie, And When She Smiles, And Me. Andy Leigh, Ray Duffy r Watkins, Swallow. 17/11/70 MV4 JW BC

Ian Matthews

5/6/71 Home, There's A Woody Guthrie Song, Through My Eyes, Hearts, Never Ending. Solo. 17/5/71 PH JW BC Previous solo session for Bob Harris April 71

Matumbi

3/5/78 Music In The Air, Rock, Chatty-Chatty. Euton Jones (perc), Glaister Fagan (tamb, bck), Bunny Donaldson (d), Jah Blake (b), Dennis Bovell (g, bck), Webster Johnson (k), Lannie Fagan (lv). 28/2/78 MV4 MB MR

13/11/78 Empire Road, Bluebeat And Ska, Money, Hook Deh. Bagga Love (v), More Ears (v), Blackbeard (gv), Taz (k, v), Jah Blake (b), Jah Bunny (d), Fergus (perc), Buttons and Zeb (horns). 17/10/78 MV4 MB MR

Harvey Matusow's Jew's Harp Band

18/12/68 Talk And Instrumental, 18 Nuns, Walking Toenail Blues, Clootchunt, War Between Fats And Thins. U 18/12/68 U JM U

Max Tundra

14/12/04 Cakes, Lysine, 6161, Merman. Ben Jacobs, Becky Jacobs, James Larcombe, Richard Larcombe, Kavus Torabi, Sarah Measures, Paul Westwood, Daniel Chudley (all playing a g, ag, p, o, elp, tp, sx, rec, fl, dul, d, tbl, b, v). 25/11/04 MV4 GW JHT

Maximum Joy

17/9/81 Caveman Fly, Slip Into The Fit, Open Your Heart. Dan Catsis (b, sx, p), Tony Wrafter (sx, tp), John Waddington (g), Janine Rainforth (v, vi), Dan Shields (d), Sandy Smith (perc, v). 12/9/81 MV4 DG MR

8/3/82 In Air, All Wrapped Up, Dancing On My Boomerang. Rainforth, Wrafter, Waddington, Shields, Charlie Llewellin (d), Kevin Evans (b). 22/2/82 U TW DD

John Mayall's Blues Breakers

5/11/67 The Last Time, Suspicious, Worried Love, Supermarket Day, Snowy Word (& Jenny, 11/2/68). John Mayall (v, hca), Mick Taylor (lg), John McVie (b), Keef Hartley (d), Rip Kent, Chris Mercer. 30/10/67 PC1 BA U Original band passed audition 7/64, 1st broadcast session Saturday Club 30/10/65, several BBC dates followed

31/3/68 Picture On The Wall, Knockers Step Forward, The Last Time, Rock Me Baby. & 1 (unknown). 26/3/68 PC1 BA U

Big Maybelle and the Senate

1/10/67 Mellow Yellow, Top Gear, Show Me, Mean To Me, Skate, Baby Please Don't Go, Sweet Thing, Every Day I Get The Blues. Big Maybelle (v) & The Senate (2, 3, 5, 7, The Senate). 21/9/67 PC1 BA DT

Michael Mayer

18/3/03 Kompakt records mix OS

Mazey Fade

29/5/93 Touchdown, Porcelain Head, Anaesthesia Analgesia, Sick & Useless. Chris Lee (gv), Tony Lee (kv), Terry Green (d). 2/5/93 ME~ JLO

3/6/94 Reactionary In Full Swing, Fifteen Going On Fourteen, Angular Masochist, Instead Plough The Tractor. & Jamie Owen (k). 19/1/95 MV4 MR AA

17/2/95 Killer Portions, Friction Means Heat, Political Mermaid, Bearhead, Nightmare Soundman. & Alistair Aspinall (g). 19/1/95 MV4 MR AA

MC 900 Foot Jesus & DJ Zero

1/3/90 Truth Is Out Of Style, Slippin', Real Black Angel. MC 900 Foot Jesus (v, ma), DJ Zero (tt, sc). 18/2/90 MV3 DG JB

MC Buzz B

14/3/90 Mr Smooth, Good Mourning. Native Rhythm (prd), Sean Brathwaite (v). 15/2/90 MV3 DG TD

MC Duke

28/9/87 The Raw, Funky For You, Free. MC Duke (rp), Simon Harris (d, prg, k, smp). 20/9/87 U DG DD&MFA

MC Mabon

31/1/01 Tamed I Aros Pryd, Your'e Twisted Niblet (Featuring Little Miss), Borders Are Cool, Riff Pynci Priodas Prysor. Sophie Barras (rp-2), Gaz Williams (b, bck-3), Frank Naughton (g, k, b), Sian Williams (d, bck), Matt Wigley (saw), Gruff Meredith (ag, g, rp, v). 17/12/00 MV4 SA

MC Solaar

30/12/94 Relations Humaines, Le Free Style D'Obsolete, Quartier Nord, A La Claire Fontaine, Nouveau Western. Claude MC Solaar (rp, v), Bambi Cruz aka Gabriel Hoareau (bck), Derin Young (v), Jimmy Jay (dj). 15/12/94 EG2 MHW RK

McCarthy

12/11/86 A Child Soon In Chains, Frans Hals, An MP Speaks, Anti-Nature. Gary Baker (d), John Williamson (b), Tim Gane (g), Malcolm Eden (gv). 7/10/86 U DG ME&SC

28/10/87 Charles Windsor, The Funeral, Should The Bible Be Banned?, This Nelson Rockefeller. 20/10/87 U DG MR&TD

1/11/88 The Myth Of The North / South Divide, I'm Not A Patriot But…, Keep An Open Mind Or Else, The Lion Will Lie Down With The Lamb. Gary Brewer credited for (d). 23/10/88 HP MA FK

Cass McCombs

16/7/03 I Cannot Lie, Ayd, Not The Way, Aids In Africa. Joe Bangina (g), John Ruscoe (k), Craig Gogay (b), Brian Deran (d), Cass McCombs (gv). 28/5/03 MV4 SA RJ

Ian McCulloch

4/12/89 Faith And Healing, The Flickering Wall, Damnation, Candleland. Ian McCulloch (gv), Steve Humphreys (d, prg), Edgar Summertime (b), John McCevoy (g), Mike Mooney (g, k). 28/9/89 U DG NG

Country Joe McDonald

4/7/70 Hold On It's Coming, Balancing On The Edge Of Time, It's So Nice To Have Love, Maria, Tell Me Where You're Bound. Country Joe McDonald (gv). 29/6/70 PH JW U

2/6/72 Hold On It's Coming, Colleen Ann, Fantasy (& Memories, 28/7/72). 8/5/72 PH JM JWH

11/7/77 Sweet Lorraine, The Man From Atharbaska, Get It Together, La-Di-Dar, Tricky Dicky, Interlude With Son And Heir, Save The Whales. Solo. 29/6/77 MV4 MB MR

Mississippi Fred McDowell

5/3/69 Louise, Burying Ground Blues, Glory Hallelujah, Jesus On The Main Line, Way Out On The Frisco Line, Keep Your Lamps Trimmed And Burning, Good Morning Little Schoolgirl. Mississippi Fred McDowell (gv). 26/2/69 AO1 JM U

Wes McGhee

13/12/76 Midnight Moon, Rosemary, Long Nights And Banjo Music. Wes McGhee (gv) & others unknown. 18/11/76 MV4 U U

McGuiness Flint

22/8/72 Let Me Die In My Footsteps, Lo And Behold, Get Your Socks Off. Tom McGuiness (g), Hughie Flint (d), Benny Gallagher (gbp, al, hca), Graham Lyle (g, mnd, b), Dennis Coulson (acc, p). 1/8/72 MV4 U BC Previous sessions for DLT Nov 70, Bob Harris Dec 70, and daytime shows thereafter

John McLaughlin and Shakti

13/5/77 Kriti, Two Sisters, La Danse Du Bonheur. John McLaughlin (g), L. Shankar (vi), Zakir Hussain (tab), T. H. Vinayakram (gha), Nancy and Poona (dro). 9/5/77 MV4 TW BAI

McLusky

9/5/02 Join The Mevolution, White Liberal On White Liberal Action, When They Come Tell Them No, Alan Is A Cowboy Killer. Andrew Falkous (gv), Jonathon Chapple (bv), Matthew Harding (d). 10/3/02 MV4 ME GYW

6/7/04 You Should Be Ashamed Seamus, Falco Vs The Young Canoeist, She Comes In Pieces, That Man Will Not Hang. Jack Egglestone (d) r Harding. 6/5/04 MV4 MA NF

Ralph McTell

28/2/70 Clown, Michael In The Garden, Daddy's Here, Eight Frames A Second. Ralp McTell (gv). 9/2/70 U U U Debut live at PH on Country Meets Folk 24/8/68. Dozens of sessions followed

19/12/70 Spiral Staircase, The Ferry Man, Too Tight Rag, Chalk Dust. 9/11/70 PH U BC

15/12/71 Genesis I 20, Ferryman, Nettle Wine, Bird Man (& In Some Way I Loved You, 8/2/72). 6/12/71 PH U U

12/5/72 I Was A Cowboy, A Small Voice Calling, A Woman With One Leg, Honey Baby Now. 24/4/72 PH JM JWH

24/10/72 When I Was A Cowboy, Zimmerman Blues, Barges, First Song. 3/10/72 LH1 U U

19/2/74 When Maddy Dances, Secret Mystery, Let Me Down Easy. & Danny Thompson (b). 5/2/74 LH1 U U

6/3/75 Interest On The Loan, El Progresso, Would I Lie To You, Country Boys. & 4 (unknown). 27/2/75 MV4 U U

6/12/76 1913 Massacre, Drybone Rag, Rizraklaru, Naomi, Vigilante Man, From Clare To Here, Summer Lightning. 2/12/76 MV4 TW U

David McWilliams

27/11/68 Redundancy Blues, Lady Helen Of The Laughing Eyes, Echo Of My Heart, Twilight, In The Early Hours Of The Morning. David McWilliams (agv). 26/11/68 S2 PC U First session was for Light Programme's Roundabout 7/67 MDC

2/11/87 Chock Full Of It, Multi-death-dead Cops, Millions Of Dam Christians / Bye Bye Ronnie, South Africa Is Free. Dave Dictor (v), Gordon Fraser (g), Franco (b, v-4), Al Schvitz (d, v-4). 25/10/87 U DG ME&TD

Me Against Them

6/2/03 White Pants, Land Of Fools, Telescope Man, Readjusting Your Halo, Multiply Now. Marty Shuubel (gv), Arthur Collier (gv), Matthew Taylor (bv), Sonny Flint (dv). 30/10/02 MV4 GT JSM

23/12/04 Shoot The Messenger, Night Of The Dead Mosquitoes, Too Beautiful To Be Trusted, Black Heart. 15/12/04 MV4 GT RJ

Meanwhile, Back In Communist Russia

20/6/01 Blind Spot / Invisible Bend, Ode, Sacred Mountain, Delay Decay Attack, Acid Drops. Emily Gray (monologues), Mark Halleren (g, drum machines), Tim Croston (k), James Matthews (g, smp), Peter Williams (g), Oliver Clueit (b). 17/6/01 MV4 ME~ NF

23/1/03 Anatomies, Cat's Cradle, Rosary, Chinese Lantern. Croston, Matthews, Clueit, Gray (v), Graham Roby (d), Thaddus Skews (b). 2/1/03 MV4 SA GT

Meat Beat Manifesto

6/2/93 Soul Driver, Fure No 9, Drop, Radio Babylon. Jack Dawgers (v, sfx), Jonny Stevens (k, prg), Simon Collins (d). 13/12/92 MV3 ME NF

Meat Whiplash

28/10/85 Loss, Walk Away, Eat Me To The Core, She Comes Tomorrow. Edward Connelly (b), Steve McClean (g), Michael Kerr (d), Paul McDermott (v), Elaine Wornock (bck-4), Leslie McKay (bck-4), Richard Green (o-4). 15/10/85 MV5 PWL MR

Medicine Head

10/1/70 His Guiding Hand, Walkin' Blues, Be Blessed To Your Heart, Ooee Baby (& Goin' Home, 9/5/70). John Fiddler (vgd, wb), Peter Hope-Evans (hca, jh, perc). 15/12/69 PH JW TW

24/10/70 But The Night Is Young, Sing With The Drum, Hungry Eye, To Train Time (& Once There Was A Day, 23/1/71). 13/10/70 U JW U

12/6/71 Pictures In The Sky, You Get The Rockin' And Rollin', Don't You Worry,

Medicine Pony (& But The Night Is Young, 24/7/71). 24/5/71 U JW BC

14/1/72 Kum On, Rain, You And Me, Only To Do What Is True. 21/12/71 T1 JM JWH&JS

2/5/72 Back To The Wall, Magic Prize, You're Not Here. 25/4/72 MV4 U JWH&BAI

25/8/72 Not Like A Soldier But Like An Old Love Song, Approximately Blue Suede Shoes, Rock & Roll Kid, Through A Hole. 14/8/72 T1 JM JWH

18/9/73 Rainy Day Blues, In The Palm Of Your Hand, Be My Flier, How's It Feel. 21/8/73 U U U

5/12/74 Walkin' Blues, It's Got To Be Alright, I Just Wanna Make Love To You, Can't Live A Lie. & Roger Saunders (lg), Rob Townsend (d), Charlie McCracken (b). 28/11/74 LH1 TW U

15/7/76 Over You, It's Natural, Sun Sinking Low. & Saunders (bv) only. 29/6/76 MV4 JG U

3/5/77 His Guiding Hand, Slip And Slide, Pictures In The Sky, It's Natural. & Morgan Fisher (o, p, wb). 27/4/77 MV4 JG NG

Mega City 4

2/8/88 Severe Attack Of The Truth, Clear Blue Sky, January, Distant Relatives, Alternative Arrangements. Chris Jones (d), Gerry Bryant (b), Danny Brown (g, bck), Wiz Brown (lgv). 19/7/88 MV4 MR MR

24/9/93 Stay Dead, Clown, Prague, Slow Down. 19/9/93 MV3 ME NF

The Mekons

14/3/78 Garden Fence Of Sound, Where Were You, Letters In The Post, Lonely And Wet, Dance And Drink The Mekons, Dan Dare-Out Of Space (It's A Really Nice Place). John Langford (v), Mark Lycett (g, lv-3), Tom Greenhalph (g, bck), Andy Corrigan (lv, bck-3), Andy Sharp (bck-1,5), Mark White (lyrics, v). 7/3/78 MV4 MB MR

2/10/78 Like Spoons No More, Trevira Trousers, What Are We Going To Do Tonight, Rosanne, I'll Have To Dance Then (On My Own). Mary Jenner (bv) r Allen; & Martin Culverwell, Jo Barnett, Simon Best, and Mick Wixey (bck). 25/9/78 MV4 BS DD

19/11/79 I Saw You Dance, Watch The Film, After 6, Beetroot. 5/11/79 MV4 TW DD

5/1/81 East Is Red, Weak Chain, The Building, English White Boy Engineer. Lycett, White, Langford, Greenhalgh, Pete Barker (g), Mark Wilson (v), Minou Myling (v), Jackie Fleming (p), Brendan Peacock (gv) & Bob Sargeant (p-1). 17/12/80 LH1 BS NG

16/9/85 Hey Susan!, Beaten And Broken, Deep End, Chop That Child In Half. Langford, Stoke Newington Jr. (vi), Tommy Greene (v), Lou Edmonds (b), Ken Lite (g), Dick Taylor (lg), Rob Worry (k), Sally Smitter (bck). 3/9/85 U MR MR

23/2/87 Danton, Skid Row, Revenge, Sophie. Langford, Greenhalgh, Goulding, Lycett, Honeyman, Bell, John Gill (b, fd), Dick Taylor (g), Sally Timms (v) & Michelle Shocked (v, mnd). 10/2/87 U DG MR&MS

Melanie

21/9/69 Visit My Dreams, Up Town And Down, Baby Guitar, Beautiful People, Tuning My Guitar. Melanie (gv). 15/9/69 PH JW TW

George Melly

26/12/72 If You're A Viper, Trouble In Mind, Gimme A Pig Foot. George Melly (v) with Fawkes-Chilton Feetwarmers. 18/12/72 T1 JW U Melly's BBC contract files dated from 1954 and by 1992 stood six inches high

The Mel-O-Tones

27/8/85 Machines, Weekend In Suburbia, Wigs On The Green, Posh. Frank Martin (v), Martyn Dempsey (g), Bob Parker (b), Jon Neesan (d), David Dickie (p, k). 13/8/85 MV5 JWI TdB

Melt Banana

21/9/99 unknown titles. Yasuko Onuki (v), Ichuro Agata (g), Rika Hamamoto (b), Masaki Oshima (d). Live from MV4 AR SA

3/10/01 WEDGE, Seesaw Semiology, RRaGG, FDC For Short, Free The Bee, Flash Cube Or Eyeball, Ethar Twisted, First Contact To Planet Q, Warp / Back Spin, Third Attack, Flip And Hit, Stimulus For Revolting Virus, Tintarella di Luna, Lost In Mirror, Spathic!, Plot In A Pot. & Dave Witte (d). Live from MV3 SA GYW

The Melvins

10/3/91 Leech, Euthanasia, Theme, Way Of The World. Dale Croven (d, bck), Lori Black (bv), Buzz Osborne (gv). 17/2/91 MV3 DG MR

Melys

23/4/97 Cysur, Diwiefr, FM Eyes, Acid Queen. Paul Adams (g, k, bck), Andrea Parker (v), Gary Husband (d), Carys Jones (k). 8/4/97 MV4 MR GT

23/6/98 Ambulance Chaser, Dirty Whore, Hedfan, You'll Never Walk Alone, Matroishka. & featuring 16-piece London Welsh Male Voice Choir (4-choir only, cond. AR). Live from MV4 AR PL&RJ

17/2/00 Lullaby, Sumi Masen, Hey That's No Way To Say Goodbye, Puppet, Elenya. Parker, Adams, Husband, Rich Eardley (b, barrel bashing). 19/12/99 MV3 ME NF

16/5/01 Chinese Whispers, I Don't Believe In You, Waiting To Fall, Un Darllwenwr Lwcus, Buwch Sanctaidd. & Carys Jones, Noel Jones, John Lawrence. Live from MV4 SA JHT/GT

20/12/01 Chinese Whispers, Silent Night. 4-piece. Live from Peel Acres AR~

10/1/02 Watercolour, Buwch Sanctaidd, Chinese Whispers. 29/11/01 CDF5 ER MHS Repeat of acoustic set 1st TX live on The Session In Wales 29/11/01

29/8/02 I Don't Believe In You (So Good), Waiting To Fall, Un Darllenwr Lwcus, Baby Burn, Happy Birthday (& Chinese Whispers, not TX). Live from Peel Acres AR~ GT

20/7/04 Treading Water, Casino El Camino, Once Around Again, Girls On Film. Dean Elfryn (d) r Husband. 9/6/04 MV4 GT NF

16/12/04 You Wannit Deep, Treading Water, Chinese Whispers. Live from MV3 MA GT

The Members

23/1/79 Love In A Lift, Phone-in Show, At The Chelsea Nightclub, Sound Of The Suburbs. Jean-Marie Carroll (gv), Nigel Bennett (gv), Chris Payne (bv), Adrian Lillywhite (d), Nick Tesco (lv). 17/1/79 MV4 BS NG

1/10/79 Muzak Machine, Killing Time, Romance, Gang War. 24/9/79 MV4 BS DD

13/4/81 Boys Like Us, Chairman Of The Board, Working Girl, Birmingham. Rudi Thompson (ts), Adam Maitland (al) join. 1/4/81 LH1 CL NG&MR

Membranes

30/5/84 Shine On Pumpkin Moon, Big Nose And Howling Wind, Great Mistake, Spike Milligan's Tape Recorder. Coofy Sid (d), John Robb (bv), Mark Tilton (gv) & Nick Brown (v), David Payne (perc). 19/5/84 MV5 DG MC

The Men They Couldn't Hang

12/7/84 Walkin' Talkin', The Men They Couldn't Hang, The Green Fields Of France, Boy Named Sue. Swill Meateater (Phil Odgers) (gv), Shanne Veg (b), Stephen Cush (gv), Jon Odgers (d), Possum Wayne (g, p) & guests Chicken Kev, Carol & Frances (bck). 4/7/84 MV5 BYA U

6/2/85 The Iron Masters, Night To Remember, Scarlet Ribbons, Donald Where's Your Trousers? Swill, J Odgers, Shanne, Laughing Dog Brand (Cush) (gv), Paul Simmonds (g) & Merrills (bck), Slim (p, cnt). 22/1/85 MV5 MRD MR

24/7/85 Shirt Of Blue, Where Have All The Flowers Gone?, Greenback Dollar, Kingdom Come. & Neil Simmonds (sx), Bobby Valentino (vi), Merrill & Wendy (of the Boothill Foot-tappers) (bck). 16/7/85 MV5 JWI MR

Menswear

22/7/95 125 West Third Street, I'll Manage Somehow, Androgenie, Piece Of Me. Matt Everett (d), Stuart Black (b, ag), Chris Gentry (g), Simon White (g, bk, clicks), Johnny Dean (lv), Paul Fletcher (cel). 4/7/95 MV4 MR RJ

Mercury Rev

5/10/91 Chasin' A Bee, Syringe Mouth, Coney Island Cyclone, Fritterin. Jim Chambers (d), Dave Fridmann (b), John Donahue (gv), Sean Mackowiak (g, bck, cl), Sue Thorpe (fl), Dave Baker (v). 27/8/91 MV3 MR MR

14/8/93 Trickledown, Boys Peel Out, Downs Are Feminine Balloons. 13/7/93 MV4 MR KR

29/7/95 Everlasting Arm, I Only Have Eyes For You, Racing The Tide, Close Encounters Of The 3rd Kind. Donahue, Chambers, Thorpe, Mackowiak, Sean O'Hagan (celv), Mark Marinoff (sx, cl), Jason Russo (b), Adam Snyder (p). 2/7/95 MV3 ME BJ

25/5/99 I Don't Wanna Be A Soldier Mama I Don't Wanna, The Funny Bird / Tonite It Shows, Observatory Crest. Mackowiak, Snyder, Russo, Jonathan Vox (ag), Jeff Mercel (d), Justin Russo (mll). 5/5/99 MV4 MA NF

15/11/01 Tides Of The Moon, Little Rhymes, Spider And Flies, Planet Caravan, Gymnopedies 3, Hercules. Vox, Mackowiak, Mercel, Paul Dillon (b), Michael Schirmer (p), Antony Molina (mll). 11/10/01 MV4 SA GYW

Max Merritt and the Meteors

5/5/72 Morning Glory, Good Friend Of Mine, Ain't You Glad, Everybody Try (& Dedicated To A Friend, 16/6/72). Max Merritt (gv), Stewart Steer (d), Bob Bertles (sx, fl), Dave Russell (b). 18/4/72 T1 JM JWH&BAI 1st broadcast was In Concert recorded 2/3/72

27/11/75 King Size Rosewood Bed, Wrong Turn, Long Time Gone, Slipping Away. Merritt, Steer, Barry Duggan (sx, fl), Fuzz Deniz (b), John Gourd (g, k). 23/10/75 MV4 TW BAI

11/6/76 Let It Slide, Rosie, Tell Me Mama, Midnight Man. Lance Dixon (k) r Duggan. 18/5/76 MV4 TW MR

The Merton Parkas

20/8/79 A Face In The Crowd, Plastic Smile, Empty Room, You Need Wheels. Mick Talbot (kv), Danny Talbot (gv), Neil Hurrell (b), Simon Smith (d). 13/8/79 MV4 TW DD

Metal Urbain

19/1/78 Atlantis, E-202, Hysterie Connective, Ghetto. Nancy Luger (g), Hermann Schwartz (g), Eric Debris (dm, sy), Clode Panik (lv). 16/1/78 MV4 TW DD

25/10/78 Futurama, Numero Zero, Anarchie Au Palace, 50/50. 11/10/78 MV4 TW NG

The Meteors

23/6/81 Voodoo Rhythm, Love You To Death, Rockabilly Psychosis, My Daddy Is A Vampire, Rockhouse. P Paul Fenech (gv), Nigel Lewis (bv), Mary Robertson (d). 16/6/81 LH1 DG ME

13/12/83 Ain't Gonna Bring Me Down, You Crack Me Up, Lonesome Train, Long Blonde Hair. Fenech, Rick Ross (b), Matthew Fraser (d). 30/11/83 MV4 RP NG

9/7/84 Stampede, Deep Dark Jungle, Surf City, I'm Just A Dog. Fenech, Ross, Ian Cubitt (d, bck) & Steve Andrews (bck-1,3). 27/6/84 MV5 RP NG

30/10/85 Torture, Meat Is Meat, Bertha Lou, Maniac. Fenech, Nev Hunt (b), Spider (d). 20/10/85 MV5 DG ME

Method Actors

22/7/81 Round World, My Time, E-Y-E, Strictly Gossip / Repetition. Vic Varney (gv), David Gamble (dv). 18/7/81 MV4 DG MR

Metrotone

5/8/98 My Own Writing, When It All Comes Down, Orange Resin Tiles, Stand By Me. Simon Poole (kv), Anthony Harding (lv), John Brenton (gkv). 21/6/98 MV4 PL NK

Miaow

18/6/86 Did She?, Following Through, Three Quarters Of The Way To Paradise, Cookery Casualty. Cath Carroll (g, lv), Andy Winters (g), Ron Caine (bv), Chris Fenner (d) & Jonathan Bedford (o-4). 8/6/86 MV5 DG ME

11/2/87 Just Keep Walking, Thames At High Water, The Dreamers' Death, Fate. Steve Maguire (g) r Winters; & Terry Edwards (ss, tp). 27/1/87 U DG MR&MA

Microdisney

10/8/83 Sleepless, Moon†, Sun†, Before Famine†. Sean O'Hagan (g, b), Cathal Coughlan (kv). 3/8/83 MV4 BYA U

23/1/84 This Liberal Love, Escalator In The Rain, Dolly, Everybody Is Dead†. John Watt (b), Tom Fenner (d) join. 14/1/84 MV4 DG MC

1/5/84 Dreaming Drains†, A Friend With A Big Mouth†, Teddy Dogs†, Loftholdingswoodt†. Jonathan Fell (b) r Watt. 14/4/84 MV5 DG MC

10/10/84 Genius†, Horse Overboard†, 464†, Goodbye – It's 1987. & Nick Montgomery (k-1). 2/10/84 MV5 MRD NG

11/12/85 Town To Town†, Bullwhip Road†, People Just Want To Dream, Begging Bowl†. James Compton (k) r Montgomery. 3/12/85 MV5 PWL MR † on ◯ SFRCD105

6/8/86 Armadillo Man, Half A Day, Soul Boy, And He Descended Into Hell. Compton out, says sheet. 27/7/86 U DG ME&SC

Midget

8/2/97 Kylie And Jason, Wendyhouse, So Damn Creepy, Magic Lamp. Richard Gombault (glv), Andy Hawkins (b, bck), Lee Major (d). 19/1/97 MV4 ME GT

Midnight Choir

16/12/87 Idle, Balsawood Bob, Pig-Man, Country-Death-Clown. Matt (d), Simon (b), Nick (g), Duncan (g, o), Ziggy (v). 8/12/87 U DG MR&MC

Midnight Evils

11/12/03 5th Avenue Blues, Thunderbird, Lost Control, Staging. Curan Folsom (bv), Brian Vernderwerf (gv), Steve Cooper (gv), Jesse Tomlinson (d). 26/11/03 MV4 SA JHT

Midway Still

6/10/91 Wish, Come Down, What You Said, Making Time. Declan Kelly (d), Jan Konopka (b), Paul Thomson (gv). 1/9/91 MV3 DG ME&SA

Mighty Baby

20/12/69 I'm From The Country, India, House Without Windows. Ian Whiteman (p), Mike Evans (b), Roger Powell (d), Martin Stone (g) Alan King (v). 2/12/69 MV4 JW U

Mighty Force

17/11/90 Dive, Antarctica, Freebass. Adam West & Simon Davies (prg). 6/11/90 MV5 MR JSM&MR

The Mighty Lemon Drops

27/8/86 Open Mind, Take Me Up, Behind Your Back, Up Tight. Paul Marsh (v), David Newton (g), Tony Linehan (b), Keith Rowley (d). 19/8/86 U DG MR&PS Previous sessions for Kershaw Dec 85 and Janice Long Feb 86

Mighty Math

22/3/01 The Futurist, Soulboy, Cherry Chocolate, Quarksparking. Robert Shaw (prg, v, sy, g, devices). 25/1/01 MV4 JB NF

Mighty Mighty

2/4/86 Throwaway, Is There Anyone Out There?, Ceiling To The Floor, Settle Down. Hugh Harkin (v, hca), Russell Burton (b, bck), Michael Geoghegan (g), Peter Geoghegan (g, o), H (David Hennessey) (d). 25/3/86 MV4 DG U

3/9/86 I Don't Need You Anymore, Little Wonder, One Way, Gemini Smile. 24/8/86 U DG ME

19/1/87 I'll Get You Back, I Never Imagined, Yours Truly, Built Like A Car. 4/1/87 U DG ME&FK

Mikey Dread

23/8/82 Parrot Jungle, Problems, Zodiac Sound, Heavy Weight Sound, Rub A Dub. U OS

Milan Station

9/7/81 Imaginary Baby, This Room Is Strange, Men In The Rain, Chapter Two. Denny Pooley (gv), Colin Bendelow (b), Neil Henderson (lv), Grahame Cusack (dv), Norman (g, bck). 4/7/81 LH1 DG MR

Milk

5/1/92 Wrong Again, Pyrosulphate, Wings, Would The Real Jesus Christ Please Stand Up. Steven Keeler (d), Duncan Brown (b), Victor Kemlicz (gv). 14/11/91 MV4 DG NG&NK

The Milk Monitors

26/5/87 Don't Lean On Me, Yo! Dance With Me, Revenge, When All Else Fails. Jason Basin (Wood) (d), Max Yobitch (b), Jake Jams (g), Keef Creole (g), Marc Monitor (v). 10/5/87 U DG ME&FK

7/10/87 The Way You Move, Max Ray Traitor, Drag You Down, Hey! Hey! Hey! We're The Milk Monitors. 29/9/87 U DG U

Frankie Miller

3/5/73 I'm Ready, It's All Over, It Takes A Lot To Laugh It Takes A Train To Cry, After All (& Ann Eliza Jane, 31/5/73). 30/4/73 LH1 BA U 1st session was for Bob Harris backed by Brinsley Schwartz TX Feb 73

25/6/76 The Doodle Song, Ain't Got No Money, Sail Away, Brickyard Blues. James Hall (p), Graham Deakin (d), Chrissie Stewart (b), Ray Minhinnett (g), Frankie Miller (glv). 10/6/76 MV4 TW U

23/5/77 Ain't Got No Money, Be Good To Yourself, Jealous Guy, Down The Honky Tonk. 16/5/77 MV4 TW DD

5/6/78 Have You Seen Me Lately Joan?, Good Time Love, Stubborn Kinda Fella, Breakaway. & Tony O'Malley (p), Ray Russell (g), Chrissy Stewart (b), BJ Wilson (d), Martin Drover (tp), Chris Mercer (ts), Dianne Birch (bck), Bonnie Wilkinson (bck). 22/5/78 MV4 TW DD

2/4/79 Good To See You, A Woman To Love, Papa Don't Know, Is This Love?, Falling In Love With You. & Steve Simpson (g, acc), Ed Dean (lg), Nick Judd (p), Tex Comer (b), Fran Byrne (d). 19/4/79 MV4 TVD DD

Million Dead

25/11/03 Pretty Good Year, Sasquatch, It's A Sh*t Business, Mute Group. Frank Turner (gv), Camerson Dean (g), Julia Ruzicka (b), Ben Dawson (d). 2/10/03 MV4 MA NF

Jeff Mills

19/5/98 DJ mix live from Y4 RJ~

22/5/02 DJ mix live from MV4 AR~ JHT

26/2/03 DJ mix live from MV4 AR GT

Jeff Mills & Laurent Garnier

15/9/04 DJ Mix pt I (& pt 2, 16/9/04). 15/9/04 MV4 AR SA

Minimal Compact

16/1/85 The Well, Nada, Not Knowing, Introspection. Max Franken (d, b), Malka Spigel (b, k, bck), Rami Fortis (g, k, bck), Vincent Kenis (g, k), Luc van Lieshout (tp, mel, hca), Samy Birnbach (v, perc). 6/1/85 MV5 DG ME

Minny Pops

2/12/80 Mono, Goddess, Jets, Ice-Cube Wall. Wim Dekker (sy), Wally Van Middendorp (v, tps), Gerard Walhof (g), Lion Van Zoeren (b). 12/11/80 LH1 DG NG

Mint 400

12/12/92 Sew My Eyes, Your Snakes Like Fish, Thrister, Natterjack Joe. Karl Hussey (d), Mark Barnes (b), Seth Taylor (g), Paul Stroud (glv). 3/11/92 MV4 MR~

Mira Calix ○

9/3/00 Ithanga (Eccelsall Mix), She Keeps Her Secrets, Listless, Only, A Pinprick Away. Chantal Passamonte (el, dj, v). 2/2/00 OS ○ Peel Sessions Warp WAP140

Miss Black America

18/7/01 Miss Black America, Personal Politics, Roadkill, Talk Hard. Seymour Glass (gv), Tripod Mae (b), Neil W Baldwin (d), Gish (g). 27/6/01 MV4 MA~

3/7/02 Liquid Silk, Smile You're On Fire, Car Crash For A Soul, The White Noise Inc. Mike Smith (b) r Tripod Mae. 29/5/02 MV4 MWT NF

Miss Mend

3/8/99 The Shape Of Things To Come, Ernst Degner, Ts125, Formica. Jon Hamilton (d), Nick Neyland (b), Callahan (k), Graeme Wilson (gv), Lisa Rosendahl (v), Dino Gollnick (g). 6/6/99 MV3 JB JSM

Missing Presumed Dead

14/1/81 You Always Say No, What She Wants, 0.5 Alive, Schlimm, Walkie Talkie Eyes. Michael Ikon (g, tp), Tim Whelan (g, v, fl), Julian Treasure (d), Ian Hawkridge (b, k), Vince Cutcliffe (g). 6/1/81 LH1 BS MR

Misty

13/6/79 Oh Wicked Man, Rich Man, Salvation, Babylon's Falling. Walford Tyson

(lv), Delvin Tyson (bck), Antoinette McCalla (bck), Chesley Samson (lg), Joe Brown (lg), Delbert McKay (rg, bck), Vernon Hunt (k), Tony Henry (b, bck), Julian Peters (d). 5/6/79 MV4 TVD MR

6/12/79 True Rasta Man, Judgement Coming On The Land, Sodom And Gomorrah. D Tyson, Henry, Samson, Kong (lv), Duxey (lv), Barry Facey (lg), Dennis Augustine (rg), Ras Bedeau (tp), Bampy (d), Sam (o), Joe Brown (p), General Sparehead (tst-2). 27/11/79 MV4 JS MR

29/9/80 Bale Out, Peace And Love, Wise And Foolish. D & W Tyson, McKay, Henry, Augustine, Samson, Brown, B Facey (lg), Bolo (p), Bampy (d), Biddu (sx), Smokes (perc). 15/9/80 MV4 TW DD

1/6/81 Live Up Jah Life, Life Boat, Big City Blues, Africa. Tysons, McKay, Henry, Samson, Brown, Augustine, Peters, Godson Bedean (sx), Brother D (lg). 12/5/81 LH1 DG MR

3/1/83 New Day, Can't Stand It, Earth, Own Them Control Them. Tysons, MacKay, Henry, Augustine, Brown, Lorrance Crossfield (lg), Delford Brisco (k), Noi Norty (sx), Gilbert Sylvester (perc). 15/12/82 U RP NG

29/2/84 West Livity, City Runnings, The Wanderer. Tysons, Henry, Augustine, Crossfield, Munya (d), Tawanda (k), Duxie (v) Ngoni (v). 22/2/84 MV5 DG NG

20/5/85 Hawks On The Street, Thought For The Children, Horizon. Tysons, McKay, Henry, Brown, Crossfield, Augustine, D Briscoe (k), A Hayward (sx-3), Steve Williamson (sx-3). 7/5/85 MV5 MRD MWT

20/5/86 Envy Us, Just A Festa, Own Them Control Them†, Together. Tysons, MacKay, Henry, Crossfield, Augustin, Tawanda (k), Steve Williamson (sx). 29/4/86 MV4 DG MS&MR † On 12-inch People Unite PU00712, with two 'versions' not TX

23/7/02 Music Suite, The Way (Almighty), Dance Hall, Cover Up. Walford Tyson (v), Barry Prince (d), L Crossfield (g), Niles Hailstones (tp), Winston Rose (sx), A Henry (b), Delford Brisco (k), J Charles (g). 23/6/02 MV4 ME KR

Joni Mitchell

29/9/68 Chelsea Morning, Galleries, Night In The City, Cactus Tree. Joni Mitchell (agv) & the John Cameron Group (5). 23/9/68 PC1 BA PR Mitchell was booked for several other R1 sessions during tours in 68 & 69, but all were cancelled, for various reasons

Moby Grape

16/2/69 If You Can't Learn, Trucking Man, Ain't That A Shame, Five To Eight (& I Am Not Willing, 16/3/69). Jerry Miller (gv), Peter Lewis (gv), Bob Mosley (bv), Don Stevenson (dv). 4/2/69 PH BA AH

The Models

13/7/77 Man Of The Year, Censorship, Brainwash, Freeze. Cliff Fox (glv), Marco (lg), Mick Allen (bv), Terry Day (d). 4/7/77 MV4 MB DD

Moderates

20/4/81 Housewife For Life, Nightlife, What's That Sound (For What It's Worth), Emile. Bob Carr (g, vi), John Brady (v, k), Heidi Kure (v), John Potter (d), Tom Gould (g), Mike Pursey (b). 25/3/81 LH1 DG PW

Modern English

25/11/80 Mesh And Lace, A Viable Commercial, Black Houses, Sixteen Days. Rob Gray (v), Gary McDowell (g, bck), Mick Conroy (b, bck), Richard Brown (d), Stephen Walker (sy). 11/11/80 LH1 JS MR

13/10/81 Someone's Calling, Face Of Wood, Being Peeled. 7/10/81 MV4 RP NG

Modern Eon

5/2/81 Real Hymn, Grass Still Grows, High Noon, Mechanic. Alix Johnson (gv), Bob Wakelin (k, sy), Cliff Hewitt (d), Danny Hampson (b), Tim Lever (g, sx). 28/1/81 LH1 CL NG

The Modernaires

20/4/82 In Order To Change, Bantustan, Land Of My Fathers. Dave Baynton-Power (d, bck), Hugh Hughes (lv, k), Phil Bradley (lv, g), Heather Jades (bck), John Adams (sx), Claire Thompson (vi), Phil Lucking (tp, b). 5/4/82 MV5 DG U

The Mo-Dettes

4/2/80 Norman (He's No Rebel), Dark Park Creeping, Kray Twins, Bitter Truth. Jane Crockford (b, lv-3), Kate Corris (gv), June Miles-Kingston (d), Ramona Carlier (lv). 28/1/80 MV4 TW DD

29/9/80 Two Can Play, Raindrops And Roses (My Favourite Things), The Sparrow, Bedtime Stories. 26/8/80 MV4 BS MR

21/7/81 Nasty Children, L'intro, White Rabbit, Yellow Smile. Jane Woodgate (bv) r Crockford. 11/7/81 MV4 DG MR This was the 1st session done in new 24-track MV4

Mogwai

11/1/97 Super Heroes Of BMX†, Summer (Priority Version), Waltz For Jo, Mogwai Salute The Brilliance Of Steve Lamacq. Martin Bulloch (d, dictaphone), John Cummings (g, b, o), Dominik Aitchison (b, o), Stuart Leslie Braithwaite (g, b, p). 22/12/96 HP ME CBM

17/2/98 Procedure 4, Ex Cowboy, Don't Cry, New Paths To Helicon (Pt II)†. 20/1/98 MV4 MR NK

1/9/98 Rollerball, Kappa†, Spoon Test, Country. 23/8/98 MV4 ME KR

17/10/01 Yes I Am A Long Way From Home, Nick Drake, You Don't Know Jesus,

Radar Maker, My Father My King. Barry Burns (multi-instrumentalist) joins. Live from MV3 AR SA

21/5/03 Hunted By A Freak†, Kids Will Be Skeletons, Killing All The Flies, Stop Coming To My House†, Golden Porche, Ratts Of The Capital, I Know You Are, New Paths to Helicon Pt 1. Live from MV4 AR SA † on ○ Government Commissions: BBC Sessions 1996–2003 PIASX051CD

Moles

28/11/92 With Body Wife Seven Days, Surf's Up, You've Lost Me There, Speed. Richard Davie (gv), Warren Armstrong (b), Glenn Fredericks (po), Eddie Rayner (d), Dominic Smith (g), Paul Thornton (tp). 20/10/92 MV4 MR~ AA

The Molesters

19/10/78 Commuter Man, Disco Love, End Of Civilization, Girl Behind The Curtain. Stella Anscombe (v), Leoni Nicol (v), John Ellis (v), Paul Heyward (g), Mark Gresty (b), Wayne Calcutt (d). 4/10/78 MV4 BS NG

6/2/79 Miss USA, What's The Time, Latex Darling, PMW / Young And Rich. Carole Brooks & Tracy Spencer (v) r Anscombe, Nicol. 30/1/79 MV4 BS MR

Zoot Money

19/5/72 It Ain't Easy, Good To Be Alive, My Father (& Three Times Corner, 7/7/72). Zoot Money (p, o). 16/4/72 CM JM PK Did many sessions in 60s with his Big Roll Band. Re-started as solo in 71

23/8/73 Good To Be Alive, Open Road, Up To Now, Three Times Corner (& Heaven And Earth, 13/9/73). 13/8/73 LH1 BA U

Mongrel

8/2/73 The Road, Melting Away, Lost, Last Night. Robert Brady (pv), Stuart Scott (g), Jimmy Phillips (g), Megan Davies (bv), Vo Fletcher (d). 22/1/73 LH1 BA U

The Monitors

5/7/79 Telegram, All The Help I Can Get, Believe In You, Token Gesture. Lee Wellbrook (gv), Chris Kitchen (glv), Nick Bidgood (b), Gary Porter (d). 26/6/79 MV4 TD MR

Monkey Steals The Drum

8/2/00 My Chinese Burns, St Germaine, Disco Kill, Galileo. Chris Ashcroft (gv), Phil Lee (g, bck), Adrian Cunliffe (bv), Angela Walker (d). 12/12/99 MV3 ME NF

9/11/00 Four By Zero, Mars Moss, That's A Cool Picture, Person Of The Year. 18/10/00 MV4 SA~ GT

Mono

11/8/04 1612, Since I've Been Waiting For You, Halcyon. Takaaakira Goto (g), Yoda (g), Tamaki (b, elp), Yasunori Takada (d). 21/7/04 MV4 GYW SCT

Mono Mono

3/7/73 Make You Realise, Awareness. U OS

The Monochrome Set

22/2/79 Espresso, Noise, Love Goes Down The Drain, Ici Les Enfants† / Fat Fun†. Bid (lv, rg), Lester Square (lg, bck, laughing box), Jeremy Harrington (b, bck), John D Haney (d, perc). 14/2/79 MV4 JS NG

6/9/79 Fallout, Martians Go Home, Viva Death Row†, Goodbye Joe / The Strange Boutique, & Tony Potts (films). 21/8/79 MV4 BS MR

23/4/80 405 Lines, B-i-d Spells Bid, Apocalypso, Love Zombies†. Andy Warren (b, bck) r Harrington; & Bob Sargeant (mrm-3). 15/4/80 MV4 BS MR † On LP ● Volume, Contrast and Briliance, Cherry Red Records

Monoconics

21/5/80 Exit Stage Left, People Will Talk, Such A Shame (About You), Vox Pop. Denny Pooley (glv), Grahame Cusack (d, bck), Dave Green (b, bck). 12/5/80 MV4 TW DD

Monograph

5/5/99 The River, Holding On In Colour, Don't Gimme Shelter, You've Got A Name, Finding New Rest For The Ghost. Rob Crutchley (gv), Steve McNairn (a, ag), Surain Lokuge (b), Gethyn Jordan (d), Martine Roberts (bv, d), Clive Painter (o, d). 2/3/99 MV4 MR PN

Moodists

21/5/84 Some Kinda Jones, You Could Be His Killer, Who's The Chicken Hawk, Phantom Flight. Dave Graney (v), Mick Turner (g), Steve Miller (g), Chris Walsh (b), Clare Moore (d). 9/5/84 MV5 RP NG

10/7/85 Other Man, Bullet Train, Take The Red Carpet Out Of Town, Justice And Money Too. Turner out. 2/7/85 MV5 JWI TdB

The Moody Blues

3/12/67 Another Morning, Twilight Time, Time To Get Away, Nights In White Satin, Forever Afternoon (Tuesday?). Justin Hayward (gv), John Lodge (bv), Ray Thomas (v, fl), Graeme Edge (kv), Mike Pinder (d). 13/11/67 PH BA PR Original line-up, with Denny Laine & Clint Warwick, 1st appeared live on the Light Programme's Joe Loss Show March 65. Dozens of sessions followed

4/2/68 Forever Afternoon, Nights In White Satin, Dawn Is A Feeling, What Am I

Doing Here? 29/1/68 PC1 BA DT

21/7/68 Voices In The Sky, The Best Way To Travel, Ride My See-Saw, Dr Livingstone I Presume. 16/7/68 PC1 BA AH

23/2/69 Send Me No Wine, To Share Our Love, Lovely To See You, Never Comes The Day. 18/2/69 PH BA AH

Moody Boys & Screamer

18/8/91 140 Bpm & Running, Centre Of The World. Tony Thorpe (prg), Nick Coler (prg), Rico (tb), Tony Poddie (rp). 2/7/91 MV5 TdB PK

Moon

28/7/75 Lone Ranger, My Old Friend, Don't Let Me Be Lonely Tonight, You've Got The Love. Noel McCalla (v), Louis Salvoni (d), Laurence Netto (lg), Graham Collyer (rg), Ronald Lawrence (b), Douglas Bainbridge (cga, fl, al), Nicky Payn (ts, fl). 15/7/75 MV4 TW U

20/1/76 My Kinda Music, Makin' Love, It's Getting Better, Don't Wear It. 13/1/76 MV4 TW U

23/8/76 Too Close For Comfort, Day Dreaming, Cold Nights. 27/7/76 MV4 TW U

20/6/77 Only Sad Boys Cry, Name Of The Game, This Is Your Life (Take 2) (& This Is Your Life-Take 1, not TX). John Shearer (d) r Salvoni. 8/6/77 MV4 MB NG

Moon ('70)

13/6/70 Mississipi Woman, Voodoo Child, Making A Name. Ian McLane (d), Sid Gardner (b), Dick Stubbs (lg), Ray Owen (gv). 1/6/70 PH JW U

The Moondogs

10/4/80 School Girl Crush, Who's Gonna Tell Mary, Talking In The Canteen, Roddie's Gang. Jackie Hamilton (bv), Gerry McCandless (gv), Austin Barrett (d). 1/04/80 MV4 MR~

18/5/81 Dream Girl, Home Is Where The Heart Is, That's What Friends Are For, I'm Not Sleeping. 27/4/81 LH1 TW DD

Moonflowers

16/2/91 My Baby, Groove Power, Back Where We Belong, Higher. Toby Paso (d), Dave Vernon (g), Adam Pope (perc), Paul Waterworth (b), Sam Burns (o, sx), Sean O'Neill (lv). 23/1/91 MV5 DG NG&RPF

Moonrider

4/8/75 Our Day's Gonna Come, Danger In The Night, Gold Digger (& Having Someone, 30/10/75). U 24/7/75 MV4 U U Show presented by Bob Harris

Moonshake

29/1/93 Sweet Heart, Mugshot Heroine, Coming, Beautiful Pigeon. David Callahan (gv), Margaret Fiedler (g, v, prg), John Frennett (b), Mig Morland (d). 22/11/92 MV3 ME JMK

Moose

9/6/91 Susanne, In Every Dream Home A Heartache, Je Reve†, Do You Remember?† Damien Warburton (d), Jeremy Tishler (b), Moose McKillop (g), Russell Yates (gv), Timbo Gane (g), Laetitia Sadier (v-3). 16/4/91 MV5 MWT MWT&DMC

1/2/92 1 2 X U, Ace Conroy, Hell Is, Orange Peel†. Warburton, Yates, McKillop, Stephen Young (b). 17/12/91 MV4 MR LS&MR † on ○ SFMCD214

More Fiends

8/11/89 Vinyl Grind, Fatty Humps, Yellow Spades, Slug Juice. Rich Poor (dv), Ron Fiend (bv), Allen Fiend (gv), Elizabeth Fiend (gv). 22/10/89 U DG MC

Morrissey

19/5/04 Don't Make Fun Of My Daddy's Voice, No One Can Hold A Candle To You. Morrissey, Martin Boorer, Alain White, Gary Day. Live from MV4 SCU MA Two tracks live from a Zane Lowe live session

Mos Eisley

6/2/02 Sodastream, Cinnamon Lift, Hate To See You Cry, The Get Up Set. Robin Howe (gv), Jack Laidlaw (bv), Jed Laidlaw (d). 6/1/02 MV4 GT~ MA

29/7/03 Make It But Make It Buzz, We Are A Solution, Go Go Gadget, I'm On Fire. 22/5/03 MV4 MA RF Jack and Jed's two Peel Sessions each bring the family total of appearances to 17, when added to those by their dad Ray of Lindisfarne and Jack The Lad

Motor Boys Motor

1/9/81 Little Boy And Fatman, Hooves, Clean Shirt And A Shave, Here Come The Flintstones. U 24/8/81 MV4 TW U

Motor Life Co

15/12/98 A Bleached Frog & A Peace Badge, Long Hours Gone, Soon I Will Be Ready For The Race, Angles. Ben Ellis (bv), Matt Gilfeather (gv), Chris Grove (d), Sean Guthrie (gv). 15/11/98 MV3 ME KR

Motorcycle Boy

14/9/87 Scarlet, Some Girls, I Could Make You Happy, Under The Bridge. Alex Taylor (v), David Scott (g), Michael Kerr (g), Eddie Connelly (b), Paul McDermott (d) & Frank Sweeney (vla-2). 30/8/87 U DG ME&TD

Motorhead

25/9/78 Louie-Louie, Tear Ya Down, I'll Be Your Sister, Keep Us On The Road. Philthy Animal (d), Fast Eddie (gv), Lemmy (bv). 18/9/78 MV4 BS DD

The Motors

22/4/77 Emergency, Bringing In The Morning Light, Dancing The Night Away. Nick Garvey (gv), Rob Henry (gv), Andy McMaster (bv), Richard Wornham (d). 22/4/77 MV4 JG MR

21/9/77 Phoney Heaven, Freeze, You Beat The Hell Out Of Me, Dancing The Night Away. Bram Tchaikovsky (g, bck) r Henry. 12/9/77 MV4 TW DD

Mott the Hoople

21/2/70 Laugh At Me, At The Crossroads, Thunder Buck Ram. Ian Hunter (elp, lv), Mick Ralphs (lg, v), Verden Allen (o), Overend Watts (b), Dale 'Buffin' Griffin (d). 3/2/70 MV4 JW U Unanimous pass' from panel for this 'Dylan-influenced group'

24/7/71 Midnight Lady, Like A Rolling Stone, Angel Of 8th Avenue. 6/7/71 MV4 U BC

Mountain Goats

13/2/03 When I Get Home, Linda Blair Was Born Innocent, Cheshire County, Shadow Song. John Darnielle (lv, g, cel, Hammond), Peter Hughes (b, bck). 30/1/03 MV4 MA RJ

28/4/04 Dance Music, Hast Thou Considered The Tetrapod, Broom People, Magpie. 8/4/04 MV4 MA NF

Mouse On Mars

3/2/95 Schlecktron, Kanu, Hardcore Fee, Peeling. Andi Toma (g, prg), Jan St Werner (el, prg), Jean-Dominique Nkishi (d, perc). 29/11/94 MV4 MR NS

18/6/97 Schnick Schnack Part 1, Schnick Schnack Part 2. & featuring Mary Hansen (v) & Laetitia Sadier (v) from Stereolab. 8/6/97 MV4 CML RK

19/1/00 Pinwheel Herman, Distroia/Super Sonig Fadeout, Gogonal, Download Sofist. & FX Randomiz (cmp, el), Vert (p, el). 13/11/99 MV4 MR JSM

15/5/01 Actionist Respoke, Introduce, Duul Orgast, Presence. & Harold 'Sack' Ziegler (horns). 2/5/01 MV4 MA JHT

The Move

1/10/67 Cherry Blossom Clinic, Hey Grandma, Stephanie Knows Who, Flowers In The Rain, Do Ya Wanna Be A Rock 'n' Roll Star, Kilroy Was Here. Roy Wood (gv), Carl Wayne (v), Bev Bevan (dv), Trevor Burton (gv), Ace Kefford (bv). 21/9/67 MV4 BA PR Passed audition 20/7/66. Innumerable sessions followed

28/1/68 Cherry Blossom Clinic, Weekend, Fire Brigade, It'll Be Me, Walk On The Water. 22/1/68 MV4 BA U

The Movies

7/7/77 Yo-Yo, Big Boys' Band, Heaven On The Street. John Cole (slg, lv), Gregg Knowles (lg), Mick Parker (k), Dave Quinn (b), Jamie Lane (d, bck), Julian Diggle (perc, bck). 28/6/77 MV4 JG MR See also Joan Armatrading

Movietone

18/6/94 Heatwave Pavement, Darkness Blue Glow, Stone, Mono Valley. Kate Wright (gv), Rachel Brook (b), Matt Elliot (g, perc, p), Matt Jones (d) & Ros Walford (cl, perc). 12/5/94 MV4 NG NF

10/2/96 The Voice Came Out Of The Box And Dropped, Blank Like Snow, Summer, Chocolate Grinder. 28/1/96 MV4 ME AA

30/9/97 The Blossom Filled Streets, Hydra, Facing West From California's Shores. & Flo Lovegrove (vla, vi, b). 31/8/97 MV4 ME KR

Mr Airplane Man

25/2/03 Red Light, Up In The Room, C'Mon DJ, Sun Goin' Down. Margaret Garrett (gv), Tara McManus (bck, d, k). 6/2/03 MV4 SA NS

21/4/04 Lonely For You, Little Red Riding Hood, Black Cat Road, No Place To Go. 11/3/04 MV4 JHT NS

Mr Bird

29/1/02 Chip Shop Fox, Only U, Welcome 2 Paris, Planet Marrow. Steve Bird (prg, k, d), Jim Montague (perc), Andy Dixon (b, ag). 16/12/01 MV4 SA GT

Mr Fox

5/12/70 Mr Trill's Song, The Gay Goshawk, Susan's Song, Ballad Of Noddy Nick (& Mr Fox, 27/2/71). Bob Pegg (acc, ml, o, gv), Carole Pegg (fd, wh, v). 24/11/70 MV4 JW U Debut session was on Country Meets Folk, Aug 70

25/9/71 Silly Billy, HP Source, Gypsy. & Barry Lyons (b), Alun Eden (d). 13/9/71 PH JW BC

Mr Psyche

18/12/01 DJ mix session. Paul Thomas OS

19/8/04 DJ mix OS

Mr Ray's Wig World

29/8/92 Faster Kittykat, Synapse / Sharon Loves Charlie, Beverley Heavenly, Mad Dog. Colin Cooper (gv), Robert Cross (g), Roger Sinek (d), Michael Corcoran (b). 11/8/92 MV4 MA PA

Mudhoney

24/5/89 By Her Own Hand, If I Think / Here Comes Sickness, You Make Me Die. Dan Peters (d), Matt Lukin (b), Steve Turner (g), Mark Arm (g). 9/5/89 WX DG MR ○ Here Comes Sickness SFRSCD090

2/10/02 The Straight Life, Dyin' For It, Urban Guerilla, I Have To Laugh. Guy Maddison (b) r Lukin. 8/9/02 MV4 ME GT

La Muerte

19/2/86 I Put The Blame On You, I'm A Man, Motor Gang, Wild Thing. Thierry (d), Sisco (b), Didier (g), Marc (v). 9/2/86 MV5 DG TdB

Mufflon 5

11/6/94 Free Wheelin, Gross Feeder, Alma Guest, Fraction. Lars Johansson (b), Fabian Edmar (g), Kalle Mogren (gv), Daniel Mannheimer (d). Recorded in Sweden

Mug

7/4/95 Sitting Frog Imitator, Compilation Dog Food, Tout Est Anatomique, Parents Express Shock Attitude. Jason Boyle (d), Tony Kennedy (b), Bolino Paquito (gv), Krieger Stephan (g), Sury Caroline (v-3). 16/3/95 MV4 NG RJ

Mugstar

2/6/04 Flavin Hot Rod, Mascon, Dux, Man With Supersight, Object. Steve Ashton (d), Jason Stoll (b), Pete Smyth (gv), Neil Murphy (g, vla). 5/5/04 MV4 JHT~

Mukka

19/10/00 Hora In Doura Parti, Hora Veche, Hicaz, Lung Li Drumi, Gankino. Frank Biddulph (vi), Kate Hands (vi), Sarah Chilvers (fl), Phillipe Wittwer (acc), Oliver Baldwin (b), Frazer Watson (perc), Beatrice Parvin (finger cymbals), Dana codorean Berciu (v). 8/10/00 MV4 JB GT

Mull Historical Society

25/10/01 Asylum, Final Arrears, Mull Historical Society, Calgary Bay. Tony Beard (d), Colin Macintyre (everything else). 13/8/01 MV4 MA GYW

Mum ○

3/10/02 Scratched Bicycle / Smell Memory, Awake On A Train, Now There's That Fear Again, The Ballad Of Broken String. Kristin Valtisdottir (v, clo, xy, mel, k), Gyda Valtisdottir (v, xy, mel), Orvar Smaarason (k, mel, glo, g), Gunnar Tynes (k, g), Samuli Koskinen (d, perc). 21/9/02 MV4 ME RJ ○ Fatcat CDFAT57 The Peel Session

Mummies

2/4/94 The Fly, The Ballad Of Iron Eyes Cody, Just One More Dance, Babba Diddy Baby, High Hell Sneakers. Trent Ruane (o, lv), Larry Winther (gv), Kevin Beesley (bv), Russell Quan (dv). 13/3/94 MV3 ME JB

Murmur

8/9/95 In Need, Never One Third, Dating Fifi, Wannabe. Martin Ilja Ryum (gv), Signe Hoirup Wille-Jorgensen (gv), Emil Landgreen (d), Kasper Deurell (b), Gry Stevens Senderovitz. 20/8/95 MV3 ME AA

Pauline Murray

31/3/80 Sympathy, When Will We Learn, Dream Sequence, Shoot. Pauline Murray (v), Peter Howells (d), Robert Blamire (b), Alan Rawlings (g). 19/3/80 MV4 JE NG

Murry The Hump

1/12/99 Cracking Up, One Fine Day, Five, Kebab Or Shag. Matthew Evans (rg, v), Gwion Rowlands (lg, bck), Curig Huws (b), Bill Coyne (d). 26/9/99 MV4 ME JHT

21/12/00 Walking In A Winter Wonderland. Nathan Stone r Huws. Live from Peel Acres AR GT/SA

Musical Youth

29/4/81 Johnny Too-Bad, Can't Fight It, Don't Blame The Youth, Culture. Fred Waite (father of Patrick, below) (v, lg), Michael Grant (k age 11), Kelvin Grant (rg 9), Patrick Waite (b 12), Frederick Waite (d 13). 22/4/81 LH1 DG NG

28/9/82 Young Generation, Children Of Zion, Heartbreaker, Rub 'n' Dub. Dennis Seaton (v-2,3) r Waite senior. 18/9/82 MV4 DG MR

The Mute Drivers

21/8/89 Frustration, Burning Burning, Happy Birthday, Twenty Thousand Millionaires. David Rogers (bv), Steve Wright (g, perc, v). 8/8/89 MV5 DG TdB

The Mutts

1/3/05 Blood From A Stone, Stuck Awake, Melted, Commotion (Creedence Clearwater cover version). Chris Murtagh (v), Bryan Shore (g), Sam Burgees (b), Adam Watson (d). 12/1/05 MV4 GT NS TX on Huw Stephens, session offered before Peel's death, honoured by Louise Kattenhorn

µ-Ziq

16/2/00 Green Lanes, Toy Gun 2, Johnson's Q Fab, Sunkist 'N' Vectif. Mike Paradinas (prg, el). 10/2/99 OS

16/12/04 10-min DJ mix for Keepin' It Peel night live from MV5 GYW JHT

My Bloody Valentine

5/10/88 I Can Feel It But I Can't See It, Lose My Breath, Colm's Song, Feed Me With Your Kiss. Debbie Googe (b), Kevin Sheilds (gv), Bilinda Butcher (gv). 25/9/88 HP DG ME

My Dad Is Dead

26/6/90 Without A Doubt, Water's Edge, Nothing Special. Mark Edwards (v, g, d), Doug Gillard (d, g), Tim Gilbride (g), Chris Burgess (b). 27/5/90 MV3 DG ME

Na Fili

17/7/73 Ar Eirrinn, Jigs: Gander In The Pratie Hole / Humours Of Donnybrock / Why So?, Caitlin Triall, Mary From Ballyhaumis. Tomas O'Canainn (pp), Tom Barry (wh), Matt Cranitch (fd). 2/7/73 T1 JW ARV Group first appeared on R2's Folk On Sunday 3/9/72 and more R2 folk sessions followed
25/7/74 Polkas, Kitty Tyreel, Slip Jigs And Reel, Unknown title (PasB illegible). 13/7/74 AO2 JW U
20/7/76 Trip To Athlone, Deus Meus, Dalaighs, Calt Nt Dhuirhir. 6/7/76 MV4 U U

Names

3/3/82 Discovery, Life By The Sea, This Is Harmony, Shanghai Gesture. Michel Smordynia (bv), Marc Deprez (g), Christophe den Tandt (k), Luc Capelle (d). 17/2/82 MV4 KH NG

Napalm Death

22/9/87 The Kill / Prison Without Walls / Dead, Deceiver / Lucid Fairytale / In Extremis, Blind To The Truth / Negative Approach / Common Enemy, Obstinate Divide / Life / You Suffer. Mick Harris (dv), Shane Embury (b), Bill Steer (g), Lee Dorrian (v). 13/9/87 MV5 DG ME&EL ◯
20/4/88 Multi National Co-operations / Instinct Of Survival, Moral Crusade / Worlds Apart / Mad, Divine Death / C9 / Control, Walls / Raging In Hell / Conform Or Die / SOB. 8/3/88 MV4 DG MR ◯
10/9/90 Unchallenged Hate / Mentally Murdered, From Enslavement To Obliteration / Suffer The… (title obliterated), Retreat To Nowhere / Scum, Deceiver / Social Sterility. Harris, Embury, Jesse Pintado (g), Mitch Harris (g), Barny (Mark Greenway) (lv). 12/8/90 MV3 DG MR&AA All sessions on ◯ SFRSCD091

Nasmak

8/6/82 Plaster, No Touch And Go, Heartache Blow Up, Walkman. Joop van Brakel (g, perc, v), Toon Bressers (v), Theo van Eenbergen (b, perc, v). 19/5/82 MV4 RP MC

Nina Nastasia

4/6/02 Beautiful Day, Albert's Song, Every Time, Untitled. Nina Nastasia (agv) & Kennan Gudjonsson (winds), Stephen Day (clo), Josh Carlebach (acc), Jim White (d), Dylan Willemsa (vla), Anne Mette Iversen (b). 3/5/02 OS Engineered by Steve Albini
4/7/02 Regrets, Treehouse Song, This Is What It Is, Deck In Vegas, All Your Life, Too Much In Between, Ugly Face. Solo. Live from Peel Acres AR GT
9/1/03 Party Favour, Heavenly Heartache, A Dogs Life, Cry Baby. & John Carlback, Jim White, Dave Richards, Dylan Williamson, Stephen Day. 5/12/02 MV4 SA GT
1/5/03 Why Don't You Stay Home, unknown title, unknown title, If We Go To The West, Jim's Room, unknown title. Solo. Live from Peel Acres AR GT
10/6/04 Underground, Lee, How I Like A Fight, Dumb I Am, We Never Talked, unknown title, Too Much In Between. & Huun Huur Tu: Alexei Saryglar, Sayan Bapa, Kaigal-ool Khovalyg, Andrey Mongush (all: throat singing & igil, khomus, doshpuluur, tungur or shaman drum). Live from Peel Acres AR GT
16/12/04 It's A World Of Dirt, Bird Of Cuzco. solo. Live from MV3 MA GT

Nasty Pop

24/11/75 Stage 'N' Plays, Crow, Lonely King. U 4/11/75 MV4 U U

National Head Band

6/2/71 Country Water, Hey Look At You Now, Listen To The Music (& Buttocks, not TX). Jan Schelhaas (o, p), Dave Paull (bv), Lee Kerslake (dv), Neil Ford (lgv). 18/1/71 PH JW BC Under previous name The Gods did many R1 pop sessions. 'Specialist programmes only', audition panel

National Health

1/3/76 Paracelsus, Agrippa, Excerpt From Lethargy Shuffle And Mind Your Backs Tango. Phil Miller (g), Dave Stewart (k), Mort Campbell (b, frh), Alan Gowen (k), Bill Bruford (d, perc), Steve Hillage (g). 17/2/76 MV4 JG MR
12/10/76 Clocks And Clouds, Brujo. & Amanda Parsons (v), Neil Murray (b) r Campbell; Hillage out. 21/9/76 MV4 JG MR
16/11/77 A Legend In His Own Lunchtime, The Collapso. & Richard Sinclair (lv-1), Pip Pyle (d) r Bruford; Parsons, Gowen out. 9/11/77 MV4 MB NG

Natural Gas

10/11/71 How Long Were You There?, The Jailer, Bad Man. Terry Samde (dv), Steve

Dale (lv), Alex Sinclair (g), Tony Phillips (b, bck). 18/10/71 PH JW BC
30/6/72 Jumping Jack Flash, Long Hot Days, Little Small Time, Mastermind. 22/5/72 MV5 JM U

Natural Scientist

12/10/81 Seven Not Seventeen Ways, No Direction Home, I'm Reading This Concise Oxford Dictionary, See Through You. Dave Willan (d), Iggy (bv), Stuart Baldwin (g), Neil Crossley (k), Boris Forrest (g, lv). 5/10/81 MV4 TW MR&MC

The Naturalites

13/6/83 Jah Love This, Jah Holy Hills, I Want Your Love, Suffer. Ossie Samms, Neil I. & Jah P. (rgv), Bimus I (lg), Marcus Naphtali (o, p), Lenroy Judah (b), Alton Ricketts (d), Simba (perc), Junior Lindo (ts), Hugh Daffus (al), Eitiko (tp). 4/6/83 MV4 DG MC
11/6/85 Pull Together, Rastafari, Your Love, Guide Me With The Tide. Samms, Daffus, Wilf Fearon (d), Percy McLeod (rgv), Lenroy Guiste (b), Paul Prince (lg), Albert Barnes (tp), Winston Williams (k). 21/5/85 MV5 MRD MR

Nazareth

2/11/72 Ruby Baby, Black-Hearted Woman, Fool About You (& Red Light Lady, 30/11/72). Dan McCafferty (v), Pete Agnew (b), Manny Charlton (g), Darrell Sweet (d). 30/10/72 LH1 BA U Original audition tape rec in Glasgow failed by panel 10/70: 'very low standard' 'out of tune singer'. First broadcast was In Concert TX 22/1/72, then Drummond session TX 8/6/72
5/4/73 Alcatraz, Broken Down Angel, Razamanaz, Bad Bad Boy. 2/4/1973 LH1 BA U

Nebula

2/10/01 Do It Now, Sonic Titan, This One, All The Way, Freedom. Eddie Glass (gv), Ian Ross (g), Mark Abshire (b), Ruben Romano (d). 21/8/01 MV4 GT GYW
15/4/04 Carpe Diem, So It Goes, Paradise Engineer, Way To Venus, Fin. Glass, Romano, Isiah Mitchell (b, bck). 19/3/04 MV4 SA NS

Nectarine No 9

24/4/93 Frownland, Unloaded For You, Pull My Daisey, Going Off Someone. Ian Holford (d, ag), Phil Smeeton (o), Todd Thompson (g), Simon Smeeton (g, bv), David Henderson (glv). 24/3/93 MV4 TdB~
9/4/94 Couldn't Phone Potatoes, This Holes Been Burned Too Many Times Before, These Days, You Can't Scratch It Out. Henderson, S Smeeton, Thompson, Holford, John Thompson (b, g). 24/3/94 MV3 JB MA
27/5/95 Tape Your Head On, Firecrackers, Adjusted Timepiece, Thunder Over Kilburn Automatic. a different John Thompson (g) & Jock Scot (lv). 2/5/95 MV4 DD BJ
3/6/98 Rock No 9, Soon Be Over Soon Be Over, Adidas Francis Bacon, Three Moans At The Base Of A Crucifixion. Henderson, Smeeton, Holford, Todd Thompson (lg) Jock Scott (poetry), Dan Connolly (bv). 3/3/98 MV4 ME NF
20/3/01 Pong Fat 6, Pocketradiodrops, Found Things, Its Raining For Some Cloudy Reasons. Henderson, T & J Thompson, Smeeton, Holford, Gareth Sager (cl, g, p, o). 4/3/01 MV4 ME GYW

Ned's Atomic Dustbin

8/12/90 Selfish, Throwing Things, You, What Gives My Son. Jonathan Penney (v), Alexander Griffin (b), Daniel Worton (d), Gareth Pring (g), Matthew Cheslin (b). 13/11/90 MV5 MR MR 1st session was for Mark Goodier recorded 3 days earlier

Nelories

9/4/93 Run Free, Trampoline, Neutral Blue, Garlic. Jun Kurihara (lv, acc), Kazmi Kvbo (g, bck). 14/3/93 MV3 ME~ CML

Bill Nelson

29/3/79 Furniture Music, Stay Young, Out Of Touch, Don't Touch Me I'm Electric. Billed as 'Bill Nelson's Red Noise': 17/2/79 U U U 1st TX 23/2/79 Friday Rock Show
15/6/81 Rooms With Brittle Views, Stay Young, Sleep Cycle, Jazz. Bill Nelson (g, perc, v), Ian Nelson (sx, k), Don Snow (k), Alan Quinn (bv), Bogdan Wiczling (d), Richard Jobson (v-4). 2/6/81 LH1 DG ME

Neon

22/3/79 Confuse The News, Eyeing Up Diddies, Plum Plum Crazy, Exterminate. U 14/3/79 MV4 JS NG

The Neon Hearts

5/4/79 The Other Great Sex Prose, Roll On Deodorant, Body Language, Rings Of Confidence. Tony Deary (lgv), Steve Heart (sx), Paul Raven (b), Mark Fuller (d). 21/3/79 MV4 JS NG

Nervous Germans

16/10/80 Waiting For The Next Wave, Watch Out, Love Letter, Bogart. Micky Meuser (bv), Manni Hollander (gv), Edgar Liebert (dv), Grant Stevens (lv). 8/10/80 MV4 BS NG

Neuro Project

13/5/94 It's A Demo, 2000 Zero Zero, Flintlock, Huichol, Shawnee. David Nicoll, Simon Sprince, Stewart Quinn. OS

Neutrons

31/10/74 Take You Further, Living In The World Today, Welsh R Blunt. U 17/10/74 U U U

New Age

22/4/82 On The Inside, Ideals, Progression, Acception. Barry Morris (v, sx), Ian Morris (g), Neil Battle (b), Nigel Loxley (k), Martin Burbage (k), Andy Hendry (d). 10/4/82 MV6 DG PS 1st session was for Jensen TX 16/11/81

New Age Steppers

18/8/83 Not A Nobody, Send For Me, John Peel Session Pt 1 1983, The Riddle. Ari Up (v-1), Bim Sherman (v-4), Style Scott (d), Lizard (Keith Logan) (b), Eskimo Fox (d, perc), 'Crucial Tony' Phillips (g), Bigga (Clifton Morrison) (p, k). 12/6/83 SO Produced & engineered by Adrian Sherwood

New Bad Things

21/4/96 Montgomery, Caravan, Smile A Little Smile (Rose Marie), Cigarettes. Christine Denkewalter (sx, v), Matthew Gaunt (bv), Andrew Leavitt (d, v, elp), Luke Adcox (gv), David French (d, v, g) & Eric Van Borstal (clo, v), Matthew Hein (g, v, d). 24/3/96 MV3 ME PL

22/7/97 Yellow Orange Day, You Are, Money From Home, Relax. 5-piece. June 97 C19 Produced by Paul Savage

New Bomb Turks

12/6/93 Death Bedside Manner, Tall Order, We Need More, Never Will, I Hate People. Eric Davidson (v), Jim Weber, Matt Rebter (b), Rill Randt (d). 9/5/93 MV3 ME~ GT

New Decade

28/1/95 The Crucial Sense, Broken Keys, Waisted Day. Paul Smailes, J Trance, Pete Camfield. 22/11/94 MV4 TdB SA

New Fast Automatic Daffodils

9/1/90 Purple Haze, Man Without Qualities II, Jagger Bog, Big (instrumental). Andy (v, mel), Dolan (g), Justin (b), Icarus (perc), Perry (d). 19/12/89 MV5 DG JB O

24/11/90 Get Better, Part 4, Man Without Qualities 1. 11/11/90 MV3 DG MA&AR O SFMCD209

15/1/93 Music, Kyphos, Bruises. Perry (d), Justin (b), Dolan (g, ag, o), Andy (v), Icarus (perc). 8/10/93 MV4 DG NG/JLO

The New Generation

10/3/68 She's A Soldier Boy, Sadie And Her Magic Mr Galahad, I Saw You (At Skippy Fair), A Brush With Sister Jo, Eleanor Rigby (& Smokey Blues Away, 28/4/68). U 28/2/68 U U U

New Hearts

14/10/77 Revolution – What Revolution, Love's Just A Word, Here Come The Ordinaries, Just Another Teenage Anthem. Matt MacKintyre (d), John Harty (b, bck), Dave Cairns (lg, bck), Ian Paine (lv). 3/10/77 MV4 MB DD

New Model Army O

4/1/84 Christian Militia, Small Town England, Running, Falklands Spirit. Justin Sullivan (Slade) (gv), Stuart Morrow (bv), Rob Heaton (d). 14/12/83 MV4 RP HP 1st session was for Jensen TX 26/7/83. O Radio Sessions 83–84 Abstract LP ABT017

New Order O

16/2/81 Truth, Senses, ICB, Dreams Never End. Peter Hook (bv), Bernard Dicken (gv), Gillian Gilbert (g, sy), Stephen Morris (d). 26/1/81 LH1 TW DD ● SFPS039 O SFRCD110

1/6/82 Turn The Heater On, We All Stand, Too Late, 586. PRIV ● SFPS001 O SFRCD110

30/12/98 Isolation, Touched, True Faith, Paradise, Atmosphere. & Bobby Gillespie (bck, g). 24/11/98 MV4 MA GT O SFRSCD128

Randy Newman

18/6/74 Leave Your Hat On, Louisiana, I Think It's Gonna Rain Today, Political Science, Birmingham, Simon Smith And The Amazing Dancing Bear / Albanian Wedding Day (& My Old Kentucky Home, 22/6/74 ROCK ON). Randy Newman (pv). 3/6/74 LH1 JW BC&MF

The News

7/6/79 Fifty Per Cent Reduction, High Society, Advertise, Brain Drain. Ivor Drawmer (k, bck), Roger Harrison (d, perc, bck), Alan Quinn (b, lv), Trevor Midgley (gv). 30/5/79 MV4 JS NG

Newtown Neurotics

21/3/83 Wake Up, Agony, Life In Their Hands, March, Jimi Jingle Peel. Steve Drewett (gv), Colin Dredd (Masters) (b), Simon Lomond (O'Brien) (d). 7/3/83 MV4 TW U

The Nice

22/10/67 Flower King Or Files, Azrail, Sombrero Sam, Tantalising Maggie, Rondo, The Thoughts Of Emerlist Davjack. Keith Emerson (k), Lee Jackson (bv), David O'List (g). 18&19/10/67 MV4 BA PR

28/1/68 Daddy Where Did I Come From, For No-one, La Aresa Dia Conte, She Belongs To Me. Brian Davison (d) r Hague. 17/1/68 MV4 BA DT

16/6/68 Get To You, The Diamond Hard Blue Apples Of The Moon, The Brandenburger, Little Arabella (& Sorcery, 14/7/68). 10/6/68 PC1 BA PR

25/8/68 America, Lumpy Gravy, Aries, Ars Longa Vita Brevis. 6/8/68 PC1 BA AH

1/12/68 Happy Friends, Brandenburger, Hang On To A Dream, Intermezzo From The Korelia Suite (& Walter's Handel Music, 12/1/69). O'List out. 26/11/68 PC1 BA AH&BC

20/4/69 I'm One Of Those People My Father Tells My Sister Not To Go Out With, Azrial Revisited, Blues For The Prairies, Diary Of An Empty Day (& Top Gear Sig., 16/3/69). 4/3/69 PH BA AH&BC Group received special extra payment of £50 for re-recording Top Gear sig on this session

8/6/69 Get To You, Country Pie, For Example, St Thomas. & Roy Harper (4). 2/6/69 PH JW TW

Nicky and the Dots

18/7/79 Can't Touch Anything, She Walks There, Sitting Next To Susan, Girl Gets Nervous. Nick Dwyer (lv), Chris Douseley (g), Paul Clark (o), Dave Williams (b), Ken Hogg (d). 11/7/79 MV4 TVD NG

Nico

20/2/71 No One Is There, Janitor Of Lunacy, Secret Side, Frozen Warnings. Nico (hmn, v). 2/2/71 MV4 JW BC Recorded session for Stuart Henry next day (3/2/71) and contracted to do Peel Sunday Show concert day after that (4/2/71) but never broadcast; Henry session broadcast first, on 11/2/71 ● SFPS064

3/12/74 We've Got The Gold, You Forgot To Answer, Janitor Of Lunacy, The End. 18/11/74 MV4 JW U

The Nightblooms

12/6/90 Afraid, One Week Moment, Let Me, Butterfly Girl. Leon Morselt (d), Petra Van Tongeren (b), Harry Otten (g), Michel Vander Woude (g), Esther Sprikkelman (v). 15/5/90 MV3 MR MR

The Nightingales

13/10/80 Start From Scratch, Butter Bricks, Torn, 12 Years. Robert Lloyd (lv), Joe Crow (gv), Paul Apperley (d), Eamonn Duffy (b). 1/10/80 MV4 BS NG ● SFPS052

7/7/81 Return Journey, (One) Mistake, Bush Beat, Inside Out. Lloyd, Apperley, Steve Hawkins (b), Andy Lloyd (g, bck), Nick Beales (g, bv). 6/7/81 LH1 TW DD

18/3/82 Give 'Em Time, Which Hi-Fi, My Brilliant Career, The Son Of God's Mate. 3/3/82 MV4 RP NG ● Cherry Red 12-inch Cherry 44

28/7/82 Joking Apart, Blood For Dirt, OK Chorale / The Crunch, It Lives Again! 30/6/82 U U U

4/4/83 Urban Ospreys, Yeah It's Okay, The Bending End, The Whys Of Acknowledgement, Only My Opinion. John Nester (b) r Hawkins.28/3/83 MV4 JP MC

12/12/83 Look Satisfied, All Talk, This, Not Man Enough. 5/12/83 MV4 DG MC

11/3/85 How To Age, Heroin, First My Job, Part-Time Moral England. Howard Jenner (b), Pete Byrchmore (g, k) r Nester, Beales. 3/3/85 MV4 DG ME

26/3/86 Down In The Dumps, Coincidence, At The End Of The Day, Rockin' With Rita. Lloyd, Byrchmore, Jenner, Ron Collins (d, bck), Maria Smith (vi, bck). 18/3/86 U DG MR&MC

Nil

12/10/96 Come On Down, Lock On, Shine, Annihilation. Michael Cunningham (vg), Greg Difin (b), John Cunningham (d). 22/9/96 MV4 ME~

Nirvana

22/11/89 Love Buzz, About A Girl, Polly, Spanx Thru'. Kurt Cobain (gv), Chris Novoselic (b), Chad (d). 26/10/89 MV4&5 DG TdB

3/11/90 Son Of A Gunt, Molly's Lipst, D7§, Turnaroundt. Dave Grohl (dv) r Chad. 21/10/90 MV3 DG ME&FK

3/11/91 Dumb§, Drain, 'No Title As Yet' (Endless Nameless§). 3/9/91 MV5 DG ME&TD † on Incesticide § on With The Lights Out box set

Nirvana with the Syd Dale Orchestra (1967)

10/12/67 Take This Hand, Pentecost Hotel, Wings Of Love, We Can Help You, Satellite Jockey. A. Spyropoulos, P Campbell-Lyons (others unknown) & The Syd Dale Orchestra. 4/12/67 U BA DT

No Means No

25/5/88 Little Creep, Body Bag, Stop It, Mamma's Little Boy. John Wright (d, bck), Rob Wright (b, bck), Andy Kerr (g, lv). 17/5/88 U MR MR

19/6/89 The Day Everything Became Nothing, The Tower, Two Lips / Two Lungs And One Tongue / Rags & Bones. 30/5/89 MV3 DG MR

Rab Noakes

6/6/72 Half A Mile From Nowhere, Drunk Again, Good Night Loving Trail, Winter Song (& Hard On You, 1/8/72). Rab Noakes (agv). 15/5/72 PH JW U

23/11/72 The Way You Know, A Long Time Ago, One Bed One Purse, Wait A Minute. & Robin McKidd (agv). 30/10/72 U BA U

5/2/74 Wrong Joke Again, As Big As His Size, Branch, Clear Day. & Mark Griffiths (lg), (b), (d) (uncertain). 21/1/74 U U BC

22/10/74 Memories, Slob, Stepping Stone, Never Too Late. 7/10/74 MV4 JW U

12/6/75 Steppin' Stone, Early Morning Friends, Somebody Counts On Me, Do-Re-

Mi. & Pick Withers (d), Charlie Harcourt (lg), Rod Clements (b). 5/6/75 MV4 TW U

5/7/78 She's All I See, I Won't Let You Down, It'll Be Me, See Me Again. & Richard Brunton (b), Steve Whalley (g), Terry Stannard (d). 5/7/78 MV4 MB MR

Normil Hawaiins

19/6/80 Uncle Green Genes, The Beat Goes On, Memories, Levels Of Water. Brian Kealy (d), Laurence Henderson (b), Jim Lusted (gv), Guy Smith (gv, p), Sue Leeves (bck), Nick Rose (b-3,4). 20/5/80 MV4 BS MR

The North Pole

29/3/96 Which Side Are You On, The Dancer, She's A Boy. U Recorded in Italy

Jimmy Norton's Explosion

6/8/79 Getting Away With Murder, Just Like Lazarus, Ambition, Lost In A Landslide. Glen Matlock (b, lv), Danny Kustow (g, bck), Budgie (d). 30/7/79 MV4 TW DD

The Noseflutes

11/9/85 Taxing Out The Creases, Worthy Pious, Let Me In To Beg, Love Endures The Autumn, Bullet Enters Brad. Ron Collins (d), Chris Horton (b), John Horton (g), Dave Pritchard (g), Chris Long (vi), Martin Longley (v). 1/9/85 MV5 DG ME

25/8/86 History Of Heart Disease, Serving In Paradise, Catcheel Maskhole, Leg Full Of Alcohol, The Ravers. & Mark Rowson (d), Roger Turner (perc) for Collins. 17/8/86 U DG ME&FK

20/5/87 Body Hair, Rotting Honeymoon, Spitball On My Kisser, Thug Thug Thug. Collins returns. 5/5/87 U DG MR&MFA

16/1/89 Born In The Last Ditch, Ossified, Rum Ship, Much Decorated. Desperate Din (k) r Long. 8/1/89 MV3 DG MA

Notsensibles

17/12/79 Because I'm Mine, King Arthur, I Thought You Were Dead, I'm In Love With Margaret Thatcher. Haggis (Michael Hargreaves) (lv), Sage (Steven Hartley) (g), RC Rawlinson (k), Gary Brown (b), Kevin Hemmingway (d), Dan the Sessionman (guest appearance-3). 28/11/79 MV4 TVD NG

Nought

4/2/98 Heart Stops Twice, Nought Anthem 1, Saved By Cock Crow. James Sedwards (g, p), Alex Pickard (d), Heini Lonergan-White (b), Alex Ward (sx, k, g). 21/12/97 MV4 ME RJ

11/10/00 Red Rag, Fever Angelique, Horseshoe Face, Narcissters. James Sedwards (g), Jonny Mitchell (d), Santiago Horro (b), Susi O'Neill (op, th), Alex Ward (g, cond) & The Nought Guitar Sextet: Tenor 1 Tony Moseley, Tenor 2 Jimmy Wood, Alto 1 Tom Abbott, Alto 2 John Macmillan, Soprano 1 Andrew Robertson, Soprano 2 Pierce Gelat. 10/9/00 MV3 ME~

Novak

14/4/99 Lord Of The World, Hotter Is Faster, Relief Rain, Peggy's Well. Kirsten Morely (b), Jeremy Hepburn (g), Adele Williams (v, xy), Tamsin Snell (acc, xy, hca), Philip Robinson (d), David Gerrard (perc, k), Jane Smith (g). 9/2/99 MV4 MR NF

Noxagt

14/7/04 Titanic, Kneel Before The Golden Land, No Exit. Nils Erga (vla, p), Kjetil D Brandsdal (b), Jan Christian L Kyvik (d). 17/6/04 MV4 SA NF

NSO Force

NOT TX Notorious, Storm 10, No Sell Out. Douglas Heywoode (v-1, 2), Kenny Clements (v-3), Victor Austin (k), Stewart De Cannonville (ma), Robert Gilmore (sc), Tyrone Sinclair (human noise effects). 5/11/89 U DG ME&FK Walters told me this could not be broadcast because of 'too much swearing'. Listening to it 18 years later, it would not sound out of place on the R1 playlist

NUB

16/3/96 Il Gatto, Brown 85, Miss Jane Lane, Tenders Guild. Jeff Gerhardt (d), Tim Ineson (gv), Nat Saunders (b), Adam Ineson (g). 3/3/96 MV3 ME RJ

Nubiles

15/12/95 Kunta Kinte, Bedbound, Layabout, Mindblender, Teenage Torso. Tara Milton (bv), Danny Goddard (d), Giorgio Curcetti (g), Penny Schueller (gkv). 12/11/95 MV3 ME NK

Nuclear Socketts

6/8/81 Riot Squad, Honour Before Glory, Pretender's Zeal, Play Loud. Phil Malone (d), Brett Gurney (b), Mark Howling (g), Kes (v). 1/8/81 MV4 DG MR

Nucleus

7/3/70 Elastic Rock, 1916, Orpheus, Persephone's Jive, Twisted Track. Ian Carr (tp, flh), Brian Smith (ts, ss, fl), Karl Jenkins (elp, ob), Chris Spedding (g), Jeff Clyne (b), John Marshall (d). 2/3/70 PH JW BC

27/3/71 Snakeskin Dream, Bearded Lady, Morning Call. 15/3/71 PH JW U

17/11/71 Feel It First, Belladonna, Tall Grass, Pieces Of Me. Dave MacRae (elp) & Clive Thacker (d) r Spedding, Marshall. 2/11/71 MV4 JW U

7/11/72 Belladonna, Suspension, Mayday (& Summer Rain, 9/1/73). Alan Skidmore (ts, ss), Gordon Beck (elp), Alan Holdsworth (g), Roy Babbington (b) & Aurio de Sousa (perc) r Smith, Jenkins, Clyne. 10/10/72 LH1 JW U

Gary Numan

25/6/79 Cars, Airplane, Films, Conversation. Gary Numan (lv), Chris Payne (k), Billy Curry (k), Paul Gardiner (b), Cedric Sharpley (d). 29/5/79 MV4 TW MR ○

19/12/00 Are Friends Electric. Numan & unknown. 13/12/00 MV3 AR MA

7/2/01 Rip, Metal, Pure, My Jesus, Cars, Listen To My Voice, I Can't Breathe, Down In The Park, A Prayer For The Unborn. Gary Numan, Steve Harris, Richard Beesely, David Brooks, Ade Orange. Live from MV4 SCU JB/NF/GT ○ plus Tubeway Army session on Gary Numan: The Complete Peel Sessions, Maida Vale Records MVRCD001

Number One Cup

18/3/96 Malcolm's X-Ray Picnic, Waiting On The Lions, Astronaut, Paris. Seth Cohen (gkv, perc), Michael Lenzi (dv, el), Pat O'Connell (gkv), John Przyborowski (bv). Live from MCR3 PRS CLE

15/4/97 Countdown, Vintage Male Singer, The New Virginia, The Monkey Song. 11/3/97 MV4 DD JLO

Numbers

23/4/03 Disease, Dance Attack, Go To Show, I'm Shy, Product List. Indra Dunis (dv), Dave Broekema (gv), Eric Landmark (Moog, Buzzerk, v). 13/3/03 MV4 SA NF

1/6/04 I Will Smile More, Cry, Drunk With Pain, Anything. 29/4/04 MV4 SA GT

A Band Called 'O'

3/10/74 No Manners, Angelica, Sidewalk Ship. Derek Ballard (d), Mark Anders (b), Craig Anders (lg), Pix (gv), Peter Filleul (elp). 24/9/74 MV4 TW BC

24/3/75 Nothing I Wouldn't Do, Fine White Wine, Sleeping, Some People. 18/3/75 MV4 U BC

6/5/76 Still Burning, Paradise Blue, Feel Alright, A Smile Is A Diamond. Jeff Bannister (kv) r Filleul. 23/3/76 MV4 TW MR

18/3/77 The Knife, Time Seems To Fly, Back Alley Lightning. 22/2/77 MV4 U MR

Occasional Word Ensemble

24/7/68 Brownville Blues, George King, I'm So Glad, Mrs Jones, Georgia Skin Game. Ric Sanders, Mitch Howard, John Brown, Richard Sylvester. 24/7/68 S2 DK U

Of Arrowe Hill

17/7/03 Godfly Adolescence, To Make Yer Feel Better, Blake On A Bad Day, I Are Becoming Instinct, Breathe. Adam Easterbrook (gv), Mark Nicholas (d), Ian Johnson (b), Karl Sabino (g). 4/6/03 MV4 SA JHT

Offspring

5/5/83 One More Night, Beautiful Eyes, Baby, Round And Round. Les Paul Morrison (bv), Alan Williams (g), Sean Jones (g), Hefyn Hughes (dv). 27/4/83 MV4 RP NG

Oil Seed Rape

12/3/93 Keel Haul, Rib Donor, Nil By Mouth, Comb. Daniel Mulligan (b), Christopher Allen (g), Wayne Travis (gv). 9/3/93 MV4 MR~ MA

Oldham Tinkers

13/1/75 A Man Like Thee, Signora, Charlie Chaplin, Oldham's Burning Sands. John Howarth (bj, v), Gerry Kearns (gv), Larry Kearns (mnd, v). 30/12/74 U JW U

Olivia Tremor Control

9/4/97 Not Feeling Human, Suite 1, Suite 2. Bill Doss (g, fl, v, tb), Will Cullen Hart (g, sfx, v), Eric Harris (d, Theramin), Peter Erchick (p, o, sfx), John Fernandes (b, cl, v). 18/3/97 MV4 MR LS

Dr Oloh

9/11/91 Cobbah Me, Yawohammi, Aleluyah Tumbay, Ajuba. Mohammed Dean (perc, bck), Abdul Bangura (d, bck), Brima Kamara (d), Dr Oloh (lv), Mohammed Kamara (d, bck), Sineh Konika (lead d), Alieu Kamara (tr, bck). 10/10/91 MV4 DG NG&JT

30/1/93 Sierra Leone Unite, Mariama, Balua, Nar You Joe Me Man. Mohamed Jalloh (lv), Abdul Bangura (bass drums), Olu Cole (bass drums), Gbassay Turay (hca), Alieu Kamara (tr), Mohammed Dean (rhythm drums). 3/9/92 MV4 NG~

One By One

3/8/91 Spineless / Kneejerk, Power Of Lump / World On Fire, Satan In The Grooves / Tell Me, Weakness (Night & Day). Big Bad Sned (bv), Alec (b), Micky McGuiness (gv), Fazzy (bv, 'road machine'). 18/6/91 MV5 MR MR

Remmy Ongala

10/7/93 Waseme, Kilio, Aiyolelio, Kamata Lupembe. Ramazani (Remmy) Ongala (gv) & Orchestra Super Matimila: Ayas Hassini (g), Batti Osenga (g), Kawelee Mutimawa (g), Mussa Maepmba (b), Yusuph Iddi Subaw. 6/7/93 MV3 JLO GW

The Only Ones ○

20/9/77 Lovers Of Today, Oh No, Telescopic Love, In Betweens. Peter Perrett (lv, rg), John Perry (lg), Mike Kellie (d), Alan Mair (b). 13/9/77 MV6 MB MR

14/4/78 Another Girl Another Planet, The Beast, No Peace For The Wicked, Language Problem. 5/4/78 MV4 MB NG

3/1/79 Miles From Nowhere, Flaming Torch, From Here To Eternity, Prisoner. 19/12/78 MV4 TW MR

2/6/80 The Happy Pilgrim, The Big Sleep, Oh Lucinda (Love Becomes A Habit), Why Don't You Kill Yourself? 21/5/80 MV4 DG NG ○ All sessions on HUX030 'Darkness & Light', previously on Strange Fruit SFRCD102

Onward International

13/2/84 Nebuchadnezar, Pe'no Gelo, Sambo Doobonnay. Simon Edwards (b, perc, v), Kim Burton (p, perc), Bosco (perc, v), Roberto Pla (perc), Dave Patiman (perc), Peter Thomas (perc, tb, v), Paul D'Oliveira (tp, perc, v), Paul Spong (tp, perc), Dave Bitelli (sx, cl, fl, perc, v). 1/2/84 MV4 DG NG

28/11/84 Lagrimas, Calix Bento, Ponteio, Onward International Calypso. Bitelli, Bosco, Pla, Burton, Edwards, Patiman, Rick Taylor (tb), Mike O'Gorman (tp, flh), Steve Sidwell (tp, flh), Dawson Miller (perc). 20/11/84 MV5 DG MR

Ooberman

9/3/99 Bees, Physics Disco, Sur La Place, Buster. Danny Popplewell (v, p), Sophia Churney (v), Andy Flett (g), Alan Kelly (d), Stephen Flett (b). 31/1/99 MV3 ME KR

Orange Juice

30/10/80 Poor Old Soul, You Old Eccentric You, Falling And Laughing, Lovesick. Edwyn Collins (gv), James Kirk (gv), David McClymont (b, bck), Steven Daly (d, perc, bck). 21/10/80 MV4 JS MR ○ 'Ostrich Churchyard' compilation

10/8/81 Dying Day, Holiday Hymn, Three Cheers For Our Side, Blokes On 45. 3/8/81 MV4 TW DD

The Orb

19/12/89 A Huge Ever-Growing Pulsating Brain That Rules From The Centre Of The Ultraworld (Loving You). Jimmy Cauty (pd, mx), Alex Paterson (sc, dj). 3/12/89 MV3 DG Engineered by Jimmy Cauty ○ 1st session only now on 2006 triple CD edition of Beyond The Ultraworld

13/10/90 Backside Of The Moon (Tranquility Lunar Orbit), Into The 4th Dimension (Essences In Starlight). Paterson, Thrash (mx), Miquette Giraudy (k), Steve Hillage (g, k, prg), Andy Falconer (k, prg). 2/10/90 MV4 MR~ first 2 sessions on ○ SFRCD118

5/6/92 Oobe, No Fun. Paterson, Thrash, Simon Phillips (b), Nick Burton (d), Greg (engineer). 12/5/92 MV4 MR~

24/2/95 Montagne D'Or (Der Gut Berg), Valley. Paterson, Phillips, Burton, Andy Hughes (processing, prg), Thomas Fehlmann (k). 14/2/95 MV4 MR SA

25/1/97 Secrets, Toxygene, Delta Mk2. Paterson, Hughes only. 25/1/97 MV4 SA~ U

16/12/04 Alex Patterson's 10–min DJ mix for Keepin' It Peel night live from MV5 GYW JHT

Orbital

10/9/93 Semi-Detached / Detached, Lush 3 (Eurotunnel Disaster 94) / Walkabout. Paul Hartnoll (k), Phil Hartnoll (k), Mickey Mann (engineer). 5/8/93 MV4 NG SBR ○ Internal/FFRR Lie CD 12

28/7/04 Remind, The Girl With The Sun In Her Hair, Belfast, You Lot, The Box, Satan, Halcyon, One Perfect Sunshine, Impact, Dr Who, Chime, Remind (Rewind). Live from MV4 AR NF/GYW Band's final performance

Orchestra Jazira

18/7/83 Money, Sakabo. Kwadwo Oteng (k), Fish (tb), Jane Shorter (ts), Nicky Scott Francis (al), Isaac Tagoe (cga, v), Emanuel Odi (perc), Martin Nimoy (perc, v), Folo Graaf (rg), Ben Mandelson (lg), Opata Azu (b), Nigel Watson (d). 20/6/83 MV4 TW MC

Orchestral Manoeuvres in the Dark ○

3/9/79 Julia's Song, Messages, Red Frame White Light, Bunker Soldiers. Andy McCluskey (bv, dm), Paul Humphries (kv). 20/8/79 MV4 TW DD

21/4/80 Pretending To See The Future, Enola Gay, Dancing, Motion And Heart. David Hughes (k), Malcolm Holmes (d) join. 14/4/80 MV4 TW DD

6/10/80 Annex, The Misunderstanding, The More I See You. Martin Cooper (sy-2) r Hughes. 29/9/80 MV4 TW DD

21/2/83 Genetic Engineering, Of All The Things We've Made, ABC Auto-Industry, Bunker Soldiers†. 29/1/83 MV4 DG HP&MC All tracks (except †) on ○ The Peel Sessions Virgin CDV2908

The Orchids

8/5/90 Dirty Clothing, Frank Desalvo, And When I Wake Up, Caveman. James Hackett (v, ag), Matthew Drummond (g), John Scally (g), Chris Quinn (d). 8/4/90 MV3 DG MWT

9/4/94 The Searching, Patience Is Mine, Waiting Seems Vain, A Living Ken And Barbie (Back To Basics Mix). & Ronnie Borland (b). 24/2/94 MV4 CML CBO

The Original Mirrors

7/2/80 Reflections, Flying, Boys Cry. Steve Allen (lv), Ian Broudie (g, bck), Jonathan Perkins (k, bck), Phil Spalding (b, bck), Pete Kircher (d, bck) & Chris Hunter (al-2,3). 22/1/80 MV4 JS MR

Jim O'Rourke

19/8/99 Halfway To A Threeway, Little Island Walking, Prelude To 110 Or 220 / Women Of The World. Jim O'Rourke (e), Sean O'Hagan (p-1), Maureen Loughnane (bck-3). 1/1/99 OS

The Orson Family

25/10/83 Wear That Pointed Bra, Snakin' Along, Big Red Gretsch, Crawdad Hole. Vernon (g), Ruby (g), Skully (v), Brewster (d). 19/10/83 MV4 RP NG

Oseni

3/7/73 Naira & Kobo, In Praise Of Sonny Ade. 6-piece African group, line-up unknown OS

Osibisa

1/8/70 Aiyko Bia, Music For Gong Gong, Black Ant. U files missing. 27/7/70 U U BC

10/7/71 Oranges, Phallus C, Woyaya. 14/6/71 U U BC

11/1/72 Woyaya, Survival, Akwaba. 4/1/72 U U U

John Otway and Wild Willy Barrett

26/6/78 Place Farm Way, Oh My Body Is Making Me, Can't Complain, The Alamo. John Otway (lv, ag), Andrew Thomas (g), Paul Sandeman (b), Dave Holmes (d). 14/6/78 MV4 JG NG 'Wild Willy Barrett, booked to appear, was 'fired by telegram for saying he had measles when he was probably watching the World Cup', JG on sheet

Out on Blue Six

16/9/80 Johnny, Mascara, Soft Sarcasm, Party Mood. Kate Sekules (v, b), Sarah Cramp (bck), Tim Oliver (bck), Nigel Holland (b, v), Carl Marsh (g), Geoff Woolley (k), Mike Daly (d). 9/9/80 MV4 JS MR

24/6/81 I'm The Man, Personal Politics, Examples, Just One Face. Cramp, Oliver out. 17/6/81 LH1 CL NG

The Outcasts

25/5/81 Gangland Warfare, The End Of The Rising Sun, Programme Love, Machine Gun. Greg Cowan (b, lv), Martin Cowan (gv), Colin Cowan (d), Raymond Falls (d), Colin Getgood (g). 13/5/81 LH1 CL NG

29/9/82 Winter, Magnum Force, Sex And Glory, Frustration. Ross Graham (perc, bck) r C Cowan. 15/9/82 MV4 RP NG

Overlord X

1/12/87 I'm Deaf, X In Effect, Lyrical Content. Overlord X (dj, prd), The Don (prd). 24/11/87 U DG MR&MC

15/8/88 The Hard Core, X Posse, The Dedication, Bax The Place. Sir Premetee (sc, dj) r The Don. 2/8/88 MV4 MR MR

Oxes

5/6/02 Boss Kitty, Half Half And Half, Panda Song, Everlong, And Giraffe Natural Enemies, Dear Spirit I'm In France, I'm From Hell Open A Windle. Nat Fowler (g), Chris Freeland (d), Marc Miller (g). Live from MV4 SA~ GT

3/11/04 Riki Cream, Top Trucker, Take Care The Song, Love For The First Time. 29/9/04 MV4 RF JSM

Pachinos

16/12/99 Sweet, This Much Times The Pain, Elvis In My Room, Bomb. Phil Nelson (dv), Daniel Borscz (b), Paul Rankin (g), Pete McDonna (gv). 24/10/99 MV3 MPK~

Pacou

8/10/98 Techno DJ set live from MV4 AR U

Palace Brothers

27/11/93 Blue Eyes, Paula, Goodnight Moon, Water. Rian Murphy (dv), Will Oldham (v, g, b), Paul Oldham (bv), Henrique Prince (fd, v), David Pajo (gv). 4/11/93 MV4 PL CML

29/7/94 The Houseboat, Trudy Dies, The Cross, The Idol On The Bar, Stable Will. Will Oldham (gv) solo. 5/6/94 MV3 ME NF

7/7/95 I Am A Cinematographer, O Lord Are You In Need, West Palm Beach, O How I Enjoy The Light. Rich Schuler (d, cga), Colin Gagon (b, p, o, bck), Bobby Rabyd (lg), Son Oldham (v, rg). 11/6/95 MV3 ME NS Here billed as Palace Music

8/8/02 Jolly Five, Arise Therefore, Death To Everyone, (I Was Drunk At The) Pulpit. Oldham & David Heumann (p, v, baritone guitar). 24/4/02 MV4 JHT~ Billed now as just Will Oldham. See Bonnie Prince Billy

Paladin

26/5/72 Well We Might, Sweet Music, Get On Deck (& Get One Together, 7/7/72). Keith Webb (d), Joe Jammer (gv), Pete Becket (v), Peter Solley (gov). 2/5/72 T1 JM JWH&ME Three previous live appearances on R1 in 1971 not for Peel

Palais Schaumburg

9/12/82 3 Nach 9, Pack Die Herzenaus, Hocke (e)y, Swingin' Safari. U 28/11/82 OS

Pale Fountains

3/8/82 Lavinia's Dream, (I'm A) Long Shot For Your Love, Thank-You, The Norfolk Broads. Michael Head (gv), Chris McCafferty (b), Thomas Whelan (d), Nathan Baxter (perc), John Millor (perc), Andy Diagram (tp). 19/7/82 U TW DD

Pale Saints

17/8/89 She Rides The Waves, You Tear The World In Two, Way The World Is, Time Thief. Chris Cooper (d), Ian Masters (bv), Graeme Naysmith (g), Ashley Horner (g). 23/7/89 MV5 JW MA

Panacea

17/4/97 Vip Hetzjagd, Chrome 14/A Hybris, Chrome 14/B Hedonism. U OS

Panama Jug Band

20/8/69 38 Plug, Canned Heat, Jailhouse, Going To Germany, Round And Round. Ron Needes (mnd, jug), Brian Strachan (lgbd), Dennis Parker (lv), Gary Compton (sp, wsh), Liz Harris (v). 31/7/69 PH PR U Previous trial broadcast on folk show 20/3/68 failed by audition panel

Pan@sonic

17/11/95 Alku / Ureakemia, Gerda, Raml / Telako C S G, Rock A Billy. Mika Vainio (k), Ilpo & Sami Salo (k), Bruce Gilbert (sound manipulation), Russell Haswell (v-1). 5/11/95 MV3 ME NK

Panoptica

13/12/01 Andl, Maquila Drug, Kinky Bitsuri, Narcoteca. Roberto Mendoza (everything). OS

Papa Face

23/2/84 Hot Hot Hot, Skidip, MC Jamboree, Dedicated To I. Donald Facey with the Reprobates: Riche Stevens (d), Alan Lane (g), Chris Lane (g), Ian Austen (b), Reg Graham (p), Angus Gaye (perc) & Bionic Rhona (bck-1). 14/2/84 MV5 MRD TdB

Papa Levi

18/6/84 Mi God Mi King, The Hit, Bonnie And Clyde. Paul Robinson (d), George Oban (b), JJ Belle (g), Carlton Ogilvie (k), Papa Levi (v). 9/6/84 MV5 DG MC

Papa Sprain

21/3/92 Time Bath, I Got Stop, You Are Ten Million Needless People, Cliff Tune. Gary McKendry (b, g, v, p), Joseph Cassidy (g), Rudy Tambala (prg). 5/1/92 MV3 DG ME&RJ see Butterfly Child

Paris Angels

27/9/90 Scope, Smile, Stay. Simon Worrall (d), Scott Carey (b), Paul Wagstaff (g), Mark Adge (g), Steven Tajti (k), Rikki Turner (v), Jane Gill (bck). 26/8/90 MV3 DG MA&FK

27/10/91 Slippery Man, Chaos, Breathless, GBF. 10/9/91 MV5 PW ME&AM

Graham Parker and the Rumour ○

16/6/76 White Honey, Back Door Love, Don't Ask Me Questions, Soul Shoes. Graham Parker (ag, lv), Brinsley Schwarz (g, bck), Martin Belmont (g, bck), Bob Andrews (o, p, bck), Andrew Bodnar (b, bck), Stephen Goulding (d, bck). 1/6/76 MV4 JG MR

15/11/76 Hotel Chambermaid, Pouring It All Out, Help Me Shake It, Heat Treatment. 2/11/76 MV4 JG MR ○ Both sessions on Not If It Pleases Me HUX003

David Parker

12/6/71 Lazy, If I Ever, Conclusions, Dark-Eyed Lady. U 24/5/71 U U U

Part Chimp

7/11/02 Monkeyslaughter, Crash The High Octave, Dark Entires, Dr Horse. Tim Cedar (gv), Hamilton Industry (d), Nick Prior (b), Iain H (g). 16/10/02 MV4 JSM GYW

Don Partridge

11/2/68 I'm A Goin' Away, Old Joe Clark, The Wayward Boy. Don Partridge (gv). 30/1/68 AO2 BA BC Debut live from PH on Country Meets Folk, 20/1/68, more folk show sessions followed

Party Dictator

13/7/91 Pressure, Bagger, Dreamland, Beam Me Up. Popel (d), Matthias (b, bck), Ole (g, bck), Nick (lv). 19/5/91 MV3 DG ME&GPR

The Passage

27/11/80 Dark Times, Shave Your Head, Devils And Angels, The Shadows. Joey McKechnie (d, bck), Dick Witts (k, bck), Andy Wilson (g, sy, bck), Lizzy Johnson (lv). 18/11/80 LH1 DG MR

14/10/81 Rod Of Iron, Form And Void, Man Of War, Love Is As. Wilson, Witts only. 30/9/81 MV4 CL NG

7/6/82 A Day, Empty Words, Horse Play. & Paul Mahoney (d). 24/5/82 MV4 TW AP

27/10/82 Watching You Dance, Dark Times, Man Of War, Love Is As, Horseplay, Empty Words. McKechnie (d) returns. 11/10/82 Recorded at The Ritz, Manchester. JL U

The Passions

29/11/79 Snow, Man On The Tube, Oh No It's You, Why Me. Barbara Gogan (lv, g), Clive Timperley (gk, bck), Clare Bidwell (b, bck), Richard Williams (d). 19/11/79 MV4 TW DD

14/5/80 Hunted, Real Mean, Absentee, Lies. 7/5/80 MV4 JE NG

17/11/80 Someone Special, The Swimmer, Bachelor Girls, German Film Star. David Agar (b, bck) r Bidwell. 5/11/80 LH1 DG NG

The Passmore Sisters

5/8/85 Shatter, Story Of A Working Man, Goodbye To The Girl, Red. Adrian Lee (d), Howi Taylor (b), Peter Richardson (g), Martin Sadofski (v). 28/7/85 MV5 DG ME

11/11/86 Strong For Europe, Sally Why?, Goodbye Billy Wildt, Hit The Ground. Brian Roberts (g, bck) r Richardson. 5/10/86 U DG ME

The Pastels

7/2/84 Something Going On, Stay With Me Till Morning, Tomorrow The Sun Will Shine, Trains Go Down The Track. Stephen Pastel (McRobbie) (gv), Brian Superstar (g), Martin (bv), Bernice (d) & Aggie (v, o), Joe (from Hendon) (gv). 17/1/84 MV4 MRD MPK

4/11/97 Ship To Shore, Advice To The Graduate, On The Way, Frozen Wave. McRobbie, Aggi (bv), Katrina Mitchell (dv), Jonathon Kilgour (g), Tom Crossley (g, wurlitzer, fl). 5/10/97 MV4 ME RF

24/8/99 Star, Rundown Rendevous, Secret Music, Mechanised. McRobbie, Aggi, Mitchell, Crossley, Kevin Shields (g), Gregor Field (perc). 4/8/99 MV4 MR MPK

31/8/99 And Your Bird Can Sing, The Night They Drove Old Dixie OS

Patto

27/2/73 Holy Toledo, San Antone, Loud Green Song. Mike Patto (g), Ollie Halsall (g), Clive Griffiths (b), John Halsey (b). 12/2/73 T1 JW U Six previous sessions, not for Peel, despite a one year ban for failing to turn up for one of them

Pavement

10/7/92 Circa 1762, Kentucky Cocktail, Secret Knowledge Of Backroads, Here. Gary Young (d), Mark Ibold (b, bck), Bob Nastanovich (d), Spiral Stairs (gv), Stephen Malkmus (gv). 23/6/92 MV4 MR MR

19/2/93 Rain Ammunition, Drunks With Guns, Ed Ames, The List Of Dorms. Malkmus, Ibold, Nastanovich, Scott Kannberg (g, o). 15/12/92 MV4 JB~ RJ

26/2/94 Brink Of Clouds, Tartar Martyr, Pueblo Domain, The Sutcliffe Catering Song. Stephen West (d) joins. 11/2/94 MV5 JB PA

21/8/97 Date With Ikea, Fin, Grave Architecture, The Classical. Live from MV4 AA KR

31/8/99 Spit On A Stranger, The Hexx, Unfair, Father To The Sister Of A Thought, Folk Jam, Carrot Rope, Shady Lane. Live from MV3 AR SA

Peace

22/12/71 Heartbreaker, Like Water, Seven Angels. Paul Rodgers (gv), Stuart Macdonald (b), Mick Underwood (d). 30/11/71 MV4 U BC

Peaches

5/9/74 B For Charlie, Methley, Street Finding Man. Nick Shillito (gv), Roger Davis (gv), Nick Howard (k), Lucian Camp (b), Jim Bamber (d). 29/8/74 LH1 TW U

6/2/75 Who Dunnit, Fings, The Sturmey Archer Kid, Never Look Back. Thomas Atley (k) r Howard. 23/1/75 MV4 TW U

22/1/76 Wild Man, Lucy And The Tiger, Heart Of Steel, Just Another Song. Martin Isaacs (gv) r Davis, Atley; & Art Gar-Belcher (sx). 15/1/76 MV4 TW U

Ann Peebles and the Red Dog Band

10/10/74 You Keep Me Hanging On, Slipped Tripped And Fell In Love, Do I Need You, I Can't Stand The Rain. Ann Peebles (lv) & 6-piece Red Dog Band (unknown). 9/10/74 MV4 TW BAI

Bob Pegg and Nick Strutt

10/7/73 Kirbstall Forge, Baroque's Off, The Wild Man Of The Hill, Headrow Song. U 3/7/73 U U U

Penetration

10/7/78 Future Daze, Vision, Stone Heroes, Movement. Pauline Murray (lv), Fred Purser (lg, rg), Neil Floyd (rg), Robert Blamire (b), Gary Smallman (d). 5/7/78 MV4 BS NG

7/3/79 Danger Signs, Last Saving Grace, Coming Up For Air. 28/2/79 MV4 JS NG

Pentangle ○

18/2/68 Travelling Song, Turn Your Money Green, Soho, Let No Man Steal Your Thyme. John Renbourn (gv), Bert Jansch (gv), Jacqui McShee (gv), Terry Cox (d), Danny Thompson (db). 29/1/68 PC1 BA PR Unanimous, enthusiastic pass from audition panel

22/5/68 The Time Has Come, Mirage, Hear My Call (& Travelling Song, Let No Man Steal Your Thyme, rpt from 29/1/68 session). 9/5/68 S1 DK U

7/7/68 Every Night When The Sun Goes In, I Am Lonely, Forty-Eight, Orlando (& No More My Lord, Bransle Gay / La Rotta / The Earl Of Salisbury, 4/8/68). 2/7/68 PC1 BA DT

3/11/68 Sovay, Sweet Child, I Loved A Lass, In Your Mind (& I've Got A Feeling, 15/12/68). 23/9/68 PC1 BA U

18/5/69 Once I Had A Sweetheart, Hunting Song, Bruton Town, Sally Go Round The Roses. 12/5/69 PH JW U Dozens more pop and folk bookings, including own series Dec 69–Jan 70 ◯ all except 22/5/68 Night Ride session on HUX 049 The Lost Broadcasts

People Like Us

28/1/03 Abridged Too Far, Cattle Call, The Doody Waltz (& Do Or Diy, 29/1/03). Vicki Bennet (everything). 10/1/03 OS

People Under The Stairs

18/5/00 Live At The Fish Bucket, Afternoon Connection, Intro To Session, Time To Rock Our Sh*t, E Business. Thes One (v), Double K (ttv), Jazz Mac (v). 19/4/00 MV4 SA SBR

Pere Ubu

7/8/89 We Have The Technology, Miss You, Bus Called Happiness. Scott Krause (d), Tony Maimone (b, bck), Jim Jones (g, bck), Eric Feldman (k, bck), David Thomas (v, acc). 27/6/89 ED DG MR

Perfect Daze

25/7/88 Break It Away, Another Kind Of View, The Back Of The Line, Ticket Don't Go. Timi Ramm Bamm (b), Wolfie Retard (b), Wild Johnny Rescoe (g), Scruff Setzer (gv), Laurence Repo (v). 10/7/88 MV5 DG ME

Perfect Vision

23/8/84 On Edge, Biff Baff, Somersault Of Love, Laugh At Breakage. Steve Xerri (kv), Giles Thomas (g), James Daniel (b), John Lewin (gv). 15/8/84 MV5 JWI NG

Christine Perfect

1/11/69 No Road Is The Right Road, When You Say, Sunshine Hours, Pen In Hand. Christine Perfect (pv) & The Derek Wadsworth Orchestra. 13/16/69 U U U

Period

1/11/78 Waste Of Breath, It's The Same Thing, The Butler Did It. Will Datsun (gv), Anne (lv), Mick Anderson (d), Staniel Swutz (b). PRIV

Period Pains

9/9/97 Ex Boyfriend, Daddy, Just 17, Spice, Homework. Felicity Aldridge (g), Lara Warwick (b), Magda Przybylski (d), Chloe Alper (v). 19/8/97 MV4 AA BJ

Persil

12/4/00 Thirty Three, Agony Aunt, Snakes And Ladders, Happy. Martine Brinksma (v), David Lingerak (d, g), Ton Morsch (b, g), Toy (o), Kasper Gerlach (g). 13/2/00 MV3 ME NF

29/5/02 June, Traces Of Knots, Mum, Dear John. Brinksma, Lingerah, Gerlach. 24/3/02 MV4 ME NS

11/5/04 Quicksand, Shifty, Music, Down Down. & Arnold De Boer (g). 15/4/04 MV4 SA NF

Personal Column

23/11/82 The Same Old Situation, Friction, Red, Dangerous Places. Terry Sterling (d), Marc Vormawar (g, lv), Mike Heyes (b). 10/11/82 U RP U

28/7/83 Strictly Confidential, Sleight Of Hand, Ignorance Is Bliss, Crusade. Colin Brown (k), Rob Boardman (g) join. 16/7/83 MV4 DG MR

16/4/84 World In Action, British Style, Cosmetic Surgery, The Price You Pay. Tom Fenner (d) r Sterling, and Phil Hargreaves (sx) joins. 4/4/84 MV5 PSI NG

The Persuaders

30/1/85 Captain Of The Ship, Great Expectations, Music For Pleasure, Somethings. Brian Farrell (d), Dave Price (b), John Gillin (g), John Jenkins (k), Tony Upham (v) & the Brett Sinclair horns: Tony Peers & Tony Griffiths (tp), Andy Herd (tb), Paul Thomas (al), Karen Pettigrew (ts) & Mark Vormawah (bck). 16/12/84 MV5 DG ME

Pet Lamb

1/4/94 Son Of John Doe, Carpet Burns, My Insides, Fly's Mother Cries. Dylan Phillips (gv), Brian Mooney (gv), Kevin Talbot (b), James Lillis (d). 20/2/94 MV3 ME LS

11/8/95 Holes, Blackmail, Microscopic Lump, Nightmare On Damest. 23/7/95 MV3 ME TBA

Pet Shop Boys

10/10/02 London, If Looks Could Kill, A Powerful Friend, Try It (I'm In Love With A Married Man). Neil Tennant (gv), Chris Lowe (k), Pete Gleadall (prg), Mark Refoy (g), Bic Hayes (g). 2/10/02 MV4 MA GYW

Peter and the Test Tube Babies

27/10/80 Moped Lads, Beat Up The Mods, Elvis Is Dead, Maniac. Peter Bywaters (lv), Derek Greening (g, bck), Chris Marchant (b, bck), Nick Loizides (d, bck). 14/10/80 MV4 JS MR

The Petticoats

23/10/80 Dream, Paranoia, Life – No. Stef Petticoat (d, b, g, lv). 15/10/80 MV4 BS NG

PFM

14/6/73 Photos Of Ghosts, Mister Nine Till Five, Celebration, River Of Life. Mauro Pagani (vi, ww), Franco Mussida (gv), Flavio Premoli (kv), Giorgio Piazza (b), Franz Di Gioccio (dv). 11/6/73 LH1 BA U

22/11/73 Il Banchetto, La Carrozza Di Hans, Dove E Quando. Yan Patrick Djivas (b) r Piazza. 12/11/73 LH1 BA U

Philistines Jr

7/8/92 Big Chief, Happy Birthday Captain Coloumbus, Army Song, Thank You John Peel. Adam Pierce (d), Tarquin Katis (bv), Peter Katis (gv). 21/7/92 MV4 TdB PA&TdB

2/7/94 Kas Tos Dumus Kupinaj?, 145 Old Mill Road, If I Did Nothing But Train For 2 Years, The Cowboy Song. 22/5/94 MV3 ME TD

14/7/96 The Russians Burned My Uncle's House Down, The Ballad Of Paul Yates, Tarzan At The BBC, Surrender, John Peel Show ID. 26/5/96 MV3 ME PL

Rory Phillips

12/2/02 DJ mix OS

Shawn Phillips

29/5/71 Hey Miss Lovely, Spring Wind, Salty Tears, Withered Roses (& L Ballad, 11/9/71). Shawn Phillips (agv). 10/5/71 PH JW U

27/3/73 Troof. 19/3/73 T1 JW U

8/10/74 See You / Planscape, 92 Years, Talking In The Garden / Furthermore, January 1st. Jon Gustafson (b) r Walmesley (backing band is original line-up of Quatermass). 1/10/74 MV4 TW U

Phoenix

16/5/74 Double Whammy, Way Behind The Moon, Warm Warm Sweet Thing. David Rohoman (d), Chris Birkin (b), Chris Smith (pv), Adrian Pietryga (g), Mick Paice (hca, sx), Roy St John (v). 7/5/74 LH1 U BC

Piano Magic

25/7/00 The Return Of, The Index, Milk Teeth, Password. Glen Johnson (kgv), Miguel Martin (d, perc, el), Al Steer (b), John Cheves (g, el), Caroline Potter (v). 28/6/00 MV4 MA~

Piano Red

10/10/77 Shake Rattle And Roll, Pinetop Boogie, Dr Feelgood, St Louis Blues, I'm Leaving, Goodbye, Please Don't Talk About Me When I'm Gone, It's A Sin To Tell A Lie, Blues Blues Blues, The Right String But The Wrong Yo-Yo. Piano Red (p). 28/9/77 MV4 DP NG

Pico

23/10/03 Abandon Ship, Speed, Tether, Want You Alive. Lianne Hall (gv), Bela Emerson (clo, bck), Justin Wood (b), Susanne Lambert (d). 12/8/03 MV4 MA GYW See Lianne Hall

Pigbag

15/9/81 Me And Your Shadow, You Can Wiggle My Toe To That, The Dug-Out. Simon Underwood (b, vi), Chris Leigh (tp), Ollie Moore (ts), Roger Freeman (perc, o, tb), James Milton-Johnstone (gb, al), Chip Carpenter (d, perc). 9/9/81 MV4 DG NG 1st session was for Richard Skinner July 81

Pigbros

21/8/85 Cheap Life, Hedonist Hat, Lick Bones, War Food. Fuzz (d), Jonathan (b), Nick (gv), Richard (sx, g). 11/8/85 MV5 DG MR

6/5/86 Bad Attitude, In Doubt, Immensity Home, What Counts? Svor Naan (g, sx, cl) r Richard. 27/4/86 MV5 DG ME&TD

PiL (Public Image Ltd.)

17/12/79 Pop Tones, Careering, Chant. John Lydon (lv), Keith Levine (g, sy), Jah Wobble (b), Martin Atkins (d). 10/12/79 MV4 TW DD

Pilotcan

23/6/99 Hannah Must Die (Monkey Wrench To Jeep), Red Brick Crayola, Slave One, Western A/R (Alternate). Steve Murgatroyd (d), Kevin Rae (b), Joe Herbert (gv), Keiron Mellote (gv), Scott Macdonald (gv), Tanya Mellote from Tunic (v, vi). 4/4/99 MV3 ME SA

Pilote

2/8/00 Decca Studios, Porcelain, Group Sex, Jelly. Stuart Cullen (k, sy, prg). OS

Pinhole

7/2/02 Is This The End?, I'm So Bored Of The USA, City Living, Addicts To You. Matt McManamon (gv), Charlie Tower (bv), Ben Gordon (gv), Brian Johnson (d). 27/1/02 MV4 ME~

Pink Fairies

28/11/70 Lucille, The Snake, 3/5 Of A Mile In 10 Seconds. John 'Twink' Alder (dv), Barry Russell-Hunter (d), Paul Fraser-Rudolph (lgv), Duncan Stewart-Sanderson (b). 10&24/11/70 MV4 JW BC&IS Passed by panel, despite comments like 'a most ugly heavy noise', and 'not for general use'

The Pink Floyd

1/10/67 The Gnome, Scarecrow, Set The Controls, Matilda Mother, Reaction In G, Flaming (& Apples And Oranges, 5/11/67). Syd Barrett (gv), Nick Mason (d), Richard Wright (k), Roger Waters (bv). 25/9/67 PH BA DT First R1 broadcast was live on 'Monday Monday' (Arnold Layne, Candy And A Currant Bun), 3/4/67 PH. Bill Bebb commissioned a session at PH on 28/7 for Sat Club, but not completed after Syd Barrett's 'freak-out'. This, therefore, is the first complete Pink Floyd session. Tracks later repeated on Symonds, 13–17/11/67

31/12/67 Vegetable Man, Scream Thy Last Scream, Jug Band Blues, Pow R Toc H. 20/12/67 MV4 BA U

11/8/68 The Murderotic Woman Or Careful With That Axe Eugene, The Massed Gadgets Of Hercules, Let There Be More Light, Julia Dream. Dave Gilmore (gv) r Barrett. 25/6/68. PC1 BA DT Massed Gadgets aka A Saucerful Of Secrets

15/12/68 Point Me To The Sky, Baby Blue Shuffle In D Major, The Embryo, Interstella Overdrive. 2/12/68 MV4 BA U

14/5/69 Daybreak, Cymbeline, Green Is The Colour, The Narrow Way. 12/5/69 PS PR CL&AH Daybreak aka Grantchester Meadows, The Narrow Way became pt 3 of that piece on Ummagumma LP, Baby Blue shuffle became Narrow Way pt 1. All tracks rpt on Top Gear 1/6/69

Pink Industry

18/1/82 Enjoy The Pain, The Final Cry, Tomorrow. Jayne (v), Ambrose (b, k, clo), Dave (g, k), Tin Tin (d), Kif Cole (perc), Phil (perc). 4/1/82 MV4 TW DD

16/11/82 Creaking Doors, Holy Shit – There's A Survivor, I've Lost My Mind, New Thing. Jayne, Ambrose only. 25/10/82 MV4 TW DD

23/8/83 Don't Be Anyone's Fashion, This Is The Place, Send Them Away, Taddy Up, Two Cultures. Tadzio Jodlowski (g) joins. 13/8/83 U DG MC

8/5/84 Pain Of Pride, No Defence, Piano Ping, Don't Let Go. 25/4/84 MV5 PSI NG

Pink Kross

8/4/95 Punk Outfit, Abomination, I Wanna Be Yr Cat, Velocababy, Hot Trash. Geraldine Kane (b), Judith Boyd (gv), Victoria Boyd (dv). 24/2/95 S2G GR U

Pink Military

26/11/79 Wild West, Did You See Her?, Stand Alone. Jayne Casey (lv), Roy White (g, bck, p), Steve Torch (b, bck), Nicky (sy, v), Budgie (d), Jackie (bck). 14/11/79 MV4 BS NG

5/6/80 Everyday, Pilgrim Forest, Dance Of The Waning Moon. Jayne, Nicky, Martin Dempsey (b), Charlie Griffiths (k), Neil (perc), Dave Baynton-Power (d). 27/5/80 MV4 BS MR

Pink Peg Slax

3/7/84 Bippo Bippo (Bop Man Bop), Self Pitying Stan, Cajun Feast, Lonely Afternoon. Abner Cavanagh (d), Chet Taylor (b), Vince Berkley (gv), Martin Lefou (fd, p) & Andrew (ag), Ade & Wink (bck). 16/4/85 MV5 AJ U

1/5/85 I Saw The Light, Ooh My Little Mama, Buzz Saw Fiddle, Excuses At A Dollar A Throw. Colin Moderne (ag, p) joins. 16/4/85 MV5 AJ U

The Piranhas

21/2/79 Coloured Music, Jilly, Saxophone, Cheap And Nasty. Alan Bines (sx), John Helmer (lgv), Bob Grover (rgv), Reg Hornsbury (b), Richard Adland (d). 7/2/79 MV4 BS NG

26/7/79 Boyfriend, Getting Beaten Up, Yap Yap Yap, Happy Families. 17/7/79 MV4 BS MR&MPK

28/1/80 Anything, Final Straw, Something, Green Don't Suit Me. 16/1/80 MV4 JE NG

The Pirates

12/1/77 Drinking Wine Spodeodee, Let's Talk, Talking About You, Cat Clothes. Mick Green (g, bck), Johnny Spence (b, lv), Frank Farley (d, bck). 4/1/77 MV4 JG MR

14/11/77 I Can Tell, Gibson Martin Fender, Four To The Bar, Shakin' All Over. 8/11/77 MV4 JG MR

19/6/78 Johnny B. Goode's Good, Shake Hands With The Devil, Voodoo, Long Journey Home. 9/5/78 MV4 U MR

Pitch Shifter

25/5/91 Gritter, Tendrill, Dry Riser Inlet. Mark Clayden (b), Stuart Toolin (g), Johnathan Carter (g, bck), Jonathan Clayden (v). 28/4/91 MV3 DG ME&DMC

1/5/93 (A Higher Form Of) Killing (Radio Phuque Edit), Diable (Wayco Survival Mix), Deconstruction (Reconstruction). J & M Clayden, Carter, 'D' J Walters (perc). 30/3/93 MV4 SA~

The Pixies

16/5/88 Levitate Me, Hey, In Heaven (Lady In The Radiator Song), Wild Honey Pie, Caribou. Black Francis (gv), David Lovering (d), 'Mrs John Murphy' (Kim Deal) (bv), Joey Santiago (lg). 3/5/88 MV4 MR~ 1st session was for Richard Skinner, TX 6/1/88

18/10/88 Dead, Tame, There Goes My Gun, Manta Ray. 9/10/88 HP DG JB

2/5/89 Down To The Well, Into The White, Wave Of Mutilation. 16/4/89 MV3 DG MWT

4/8/91 Palace Of The Brine, Letter To Memphis, Motorway To Roswell, Subbacultcha. & Bobby Santiago ('3rd guitar'). 23/6/91 MV3 DG JB&PRB

Plaid

8/1/98 Scoops In Columbia, Seph, Bo Bootch, OL. Andy Turner (prg), Ed Handley (prg). 9/12/97 MV4 AA LS

5/8/99 Elidi, Kite Rider, Housework, Lazy Beams. OS

16/10/03 Cedar Dity Beatless, Barbega, Even Spring (Live), Awotm. 1/10/03 OS

Plain Characters

2/12/81 Hideaway, O, Menial Tasks, Fingerprint City. Colin Tucker (v), Paul Johnstone (g), John Hyde (b), Tim Broughton (d). 23/11/81 MV4 TW DD

Plainsong

1/2/72 Tigers Will Survive, Seeds And Stems Again, Spanish Guitar, Any Day Woman. Ian Matthews (gv), Andy Roberts (gv), Bob Ronga (gv), Dave Richards (bv). 24/1/72 PH JW BC&NG

6/6/72 Truck Driving Man†, Amelia Earhardt's Last Flight, Yo Yo Man, I'll Fly Away (& The True Story Of Amelia Earhart, not TX). 24/4/72 T1 JW&PD BC

30/11/72 Nobody Eats At Lineburgh Anymore, Old Man At The Mill / Charlie, Save Your Sorrows, Home. Ronga out. 27/11/72 LH1 BA U

Plant Bach Ofnus

2/3/88 Aflan, Llwyd, Awst, Pydredd. Fiona Owen (v), Gorwel Owen (v, tps, vi), Robin Griffith (sy). 16/2/88 MV4 DG MC

27/1/91 Saith, Curiad + Bas = Groove, Cyfnod Pump, Ailenedigaethyllygaidmewnol. Owens only. 6/1/91 MV3 DG ME&FK

Planxty

8/8/72 Planxty Irwin, Merrily Kiss The Quaker, West Coast Of Clare, The Raggle Taggle Gypsy. Christy Moore (gv, hmn, bh), Donal Lunney (bz), Liam Og Flynn (pp), Andy Irvine (mnd, v). 24/7/72 PH JW U 1st broadcast was live from PH on Country Meets Folk 6/5/72

12/3/73 Cunla, Bean Phaidin, The Hare In The Corn, The Rambles Of Kitty (& Two Reels, 14/5/73). 28/2/73 LH1 PR U

6/11/73 Ban Fawjean, Kid On The Mountain / Fishbuck, As I Roved Out (1), As I Roved Out (2). 15/10/73 T1 JW U

Plastic Penny

14/1/68 Turning Night Into Day, Everything I Am, Take Me Back, No Pleasure Without Pain My Love, Mrs Grundy. Brian Keith (lv), Paul Raymond (o), Tony Murray (b), Nigel Olsson (d), Mike Graham (lg) & Tony Gilbert for 4 musicians (String Quartet). 10/1/68 MV4 BA DT

Play Dead

28/1/82 Effigy, Metallic Smile, Pray To Mecca, Propaganda. Rob Hickson (lv), Steve Green (lg), Pete Waddleton (b), Mark Smith (d). 13/1/82 MV4 KH NG

23/6/83 The Tennant, Total Decline, Gaze. 'Wiff' credited for (d). 15/6/83 MV4 RP NG

18/1/84 Break, Return To The East, No Motive. 11/1/84 MV4 RP NG

Pleasureheads

25/5/89 She Said, There's No Chance, Frankly, Twirling Tranquiliser Chair. Joe MacColl (d), Dave Colton (b), Andy Donovan (g), Kevin Murphy (g), Pete Elderkin & Dean Nicholls (v, perc). 30/4/89 MV3 DG ME

Plone

2/6/98 Sunday Laid Moo, Plock, Electronic Beauty Parlour. Mark Cancellara (k, prg), Michael Johnson (k, vocoder), Mike Bainbridge (k, smp). 26/4/98 MV4 ME SA

6/10/99 Another One Of Them, Marbles, Busy Working, Dry Pen. 1/9/99 MV4 JB~

Plummet Airlines

14/9/76 Don't Give A Damn, You're Keeping Us Talking, Water To Wine, Stars Will Shine. Harry Stevenson (g, lv), Daryl Hunt (b, bck), Richard Booth (g), Duncan Kerr (g, bck), Keith Gotheridge (d). 31/8/76 MV4 TW MR

28/2/77 Our Last Dance, Call Out The Engine Driver, Since I Left You, Doctor Boogie. & Gaspar Lawal (perc), Derek Quin (perc). 24/1/77 MV4 TW DD

Pluto Monkey

18/4/00 Joe Meek, A Quiet Life, Rice Cake Rabbit Soul, Ping Pong Sass. Paul Vickers, Roger Simian. 23/2/00 MV4 JB PN

Po!

14/5/94 Tomboy And Cowgirl, The Mad Girl, Pop Star Wives, A New Grandma. Gary Gilchrist (b), Paul Knight (d, perc), Terri Lowe (g), Ruth Miller (gv). 17/4/94 MV3 ME CML

The Pogues

17/4/84 Streams Of Whiskey, Greenland Whale Fisheries, The Boys From The County Hell (not TX), The Auld Triangle. Shane McGowan (lv, g), Jem Finer (bj, v, g-4), Andrew Ranken (d, bck), Spider Stacy (wh), James Fearnley (acc), Cait O'Riordan (b). 10/4/84 MV5 MRD TdB Billed under their original name of Pogue Mahone for this first session only

12/12/84 Whiskey You're The Devil, The Navigator, Sally McLannan, Danny Boy. 4/12/84 MV5 MRD MR

The Police

30/7/79 The Bed's Too Big Without You, Message In A Bottle, Next To You, Can't Stand Losing You (The Bit We Left Out). Sting (b, lv), Stewart Copeland (d), Andy Summers (g). 23/7/79 MV4 TW DD 2 previous sessions, not for Peel

Policecat

31/7/97 Blue Movie, Give Us This Day, Dark Holiday, Lone Rider. Yvonne Slaven (k), Jonathan Kilgour (gv), Scott Hall (d, perc), Gordon Kilgour (gbv), John Harrington (b, sy, slg). 8/7/97 MV4 MR KR

Polvo

13/11/92 Cars, Bubbling Volvic, Tread On Me, Snake Fist Fighter. Ashley Hideyo Bowie (gv), David Thomas Brylawski (gv), Edward Powe Watkins (d), Steven Barry Popson (b). 6/10/92 MV4 MA~ PL

2/7/93 Watch The Nail, Thermal Cupid, Six Leaf Clover, Double Scorpio. 26/5/93 MV4 TdB~ JLO

Polysics

12/10/04 Kaja Kaja Goo, New Wave Jacket, My Sharona, Buggie Technica. Hiro (gv), Fumi (b), Kayo (k, v, vocoder), Yano (d). 23/9/04 MV4 JHT SCT

Polythene

10/2/98 Low Frequency Loan Shark Radar Song, Prison Chic, Fifties Anti Communist B Movies, Kill Techno (The Peel Man Version), C/Hill Thrill Pill. Darren Heer (gv), Paul Rossington (g), Kate Themen (dv). 18/1/98 MV4 ME KR

Pond

25/9/92 Cinders, Spots, Snowing, Pretty Thing. Charlie Campbell (gv), Chris Brady (bv), David Triebwasser (d, bck). 11/9/92 MV4 JB KR&JB

6/5/95 Carpenter Ant/Van, Union, Filterless, Fear Of Dogs. 2/4/95 MV4 MR PL

Ponderosa Glee Boys

16/7/81 Scream Or Change Your Mind, Creation, Ritual. Tomo (v), Brian Swenson (gv), Carl Eaton (bv), Steve Coy (dv). 15/7/81 MV4 CL NG

The Pooh Sticks

3/5/88 On Tape, Alan McGee, Heartbreak, Indiepop Ain't Noise Pollution. Paul (g, bck), Alison (b), Stephanie (b, d, g), Hue Pooh Sticks (Williams) (v) & Amelia Fletcher (bck). 19/4/88 U DG U

18/5/89 Desperado, Young People, Hard On Love, Dare-True-Kiss-Promise. Hue, Stephanie, Paul, Geraldine (g, bck). 9/4/89 MV3 DG MWT Both sessions on ● eponymous LP on Overground Records OVER018

The Pop Group

10/8/78 We Are Time, Kiss The Book, Words Disobey Me. Mark Stewart (lv), Garreth Sager (g, k), John Waddington (g, bck), Simon Underwood (b), Bruce Smith (d). 3/7/78 MV4 TW BAl

The Pop Guns

23/1/90 Someone You Love, Bye Bye Baby, Put Me Thru It, Where Do You Go. Greg Dixon (g), Pat Walkington (b), Shaun Charman (d), Wendy Morgan (v), Simon Pickles (g). 9/1/90 MV5 DG MR

30/9/90 Going Under, I'm Spoiling Everything, Those Other Things, A World Away (It's Grim Up North). Pickles out. 4/9/90 MV5 JB JB

Pop Off Tuesday

15/7/97 Mama Awaker, Unworldly, It Was A Strangely Emotional Moment For Me, Mad Tea Party. Hiroki Miyauchi (ma), Minori Odaira (gv). OS

18/11/99 Viola Fora De Moda, Adverse, Wafflehead, Ms Boo Boo's Return, A Field Of Blue Clover. 7/9/99 MV5 MR JSM

The Pop Rivets

13/2/80 Where Have All The Good Times Gone, Going Nowhere, Beatle Boots, Empty Sounds. (Wild) Billy Childish (lv), Nobby Stiles (b, bck), Zoony the Lazoon (g, bck), Cecil Batt (d). 29/1/80 MV4 JS MR

Pop Will Eat Itself

30/6/86 Inside Out, Demolition Girl, Oh Grebo I Think I Love You, Sweet Sweet Pie. Adam Mole (g, o), Clint Mansell (gv), Richard March (b), Graham Crabb (d, bck). 17/6/86 MV4 DG TdB&MA

6/7/87 There Is No Love Between Us Anymore, Grebo Guru, Beaver Patrol, Razor Blade Kisses (Evelyn). 14/6/87 U DG ME&FK

Maldwyn Pope

17/7/73 Truly, Couldn't Be Wrong, Shall We Go To Sea, Dream Castle, That Is The Question, How Can I Forget You? U 10/7/73 LH1 JW BC

26/3/74 Maybe It's Wrong, Gunfighter, All Day, Autumn. 4/3/74 U U U

17/10/74 Lazy Country Days, Don't Say, Don't You Know. 5/8/74 T1 U U

The Popinjays

21/9/88 Perfect Dream Home, Dr Fell, Fine Lines, Backward Daydream. Polly Hancock (g, k), Wendy Robinson (v, hca). 4/9/88 HP DG TdB

Poppi UK

1/3/88 Post Modern Sex Jogger, Chinese Apple Belt, You're Not The Same, Rambo's Girlfriend. Tony Sikkes (d), Hans Pieters (bv), Ger Laning (gv), Frank van den Elzen (g). 14/2/88 U DG ME&MC

The Popticians

27/7/83 Hello Everybody, Brown Paper Bag, Mobile Home, Song About Losing Your Glasses. John Hegley (gv), Russell Greenwood (dv), Susan Norton (sxv), Keith Moore (cl, v). 20/7/83 MV4 RP ME

12/11/84 Scoutmaster, Song About The Misery Of Human Existence, Private, Song About John's Brother's Glasses, Red Ken, Somehow You Look Different Tonight. 4/11/84 MV5 DG ME

A Popular History of Signs

18/10/83 Stigma, House, Christmas Island, Comrades. Andrew Jarman (bv), Pete Scammell (sy, g), Paul Clarke (perc), Mark Dean (electronic perc, seq). 12/10/83 MV4 RP NG

Popular Voice

27/7/82 Home For The Summer, Keep Winning, Possession, That Sound Is Pain. Barry Derbyshire (v), Michael Byles (sx, g), Mark Gardner (sy), Chalky Keelian (d), Daley (p). 28/6/82 MV4 TW DD

Portal

27/9/00 Silence Slow Motion, After Tomorrow Version 2, Falling, Pulse. Scott Sinfield (gv, b, prg), Rachel Hughes (v), Jon Attwood (g). 13/8/00 MV4 ME RJ

Portion Control

11/1/84 Go Talk, Rough Justice, Scramble. Dean Piavani (v), Ian Sharp, John Whybrew (sy), Pat Bermingham. 4/1/84 MV4 RP NG

Positive Noise

27/8/80 Give Me Passion, Down There, End Of A Dream, Ghosts. Ross Middleton (g, lv), Graham Middleton (k), Fraser Middleton (b), Les Gaff (d). 19/8/80 MV4 DG MR

25/3/81 Charm, Love Like Property, Treachery, 1917 (I'm In The Mood). Russell Blackstock (lgv) joins. 16/3/81 LH1 PS DD&MPK

The Postmen

11/12/80 Fishman, Mouse Etc, Uncle, Henry's Coming. U 25/11/80 LH1 JS MR

Cozy Powell

29/10/74 Keep Your Distance, Foolish Girl, Superstrut, Hold On. Bernie Marsden (g), Don Airey (k), Clive Chaman (b), Frank Aiello (v), Cozy Powell (d). 15/10/74 MV4 TW U

Duffy Power

6/9/73 Dusty Road, Love Is Gonna Go, Glad That You're Not Me, Little Soldiers. Power, Graham Quinten Jones (g, p), Chris Bailey, Peter Kirk. 3/9/73 LH1 BA BC on ○ Sky Blues HUX026

Pragvec

29/8/78 Nervous, Bits, Ruby, Stay. Nick Cash (d), David Boyd (bv), John Studholme (gv), Susan Gogan (v, sy). 23/8/78 MV4 BS NG

7/2/79 Toast, Expert, The Follower, Hijack. 29/1/79 MV4 BS DD

1/8/79 By The Sea, Rural Erotic, Third Person, Laugh. PRIV

Pram

21/4/99 Monkey Puzzle, A Million Bubble Burst, Teaching Snails To Make Pearls. Matthew Eaton (g, k), Sam Owen (k), Rosie Cuckston (v, k), Nick Sales (th, b), Darren Garrett (d), Mark Butterworth (d), Max Simpson (smp), Alex Clare (tp). 7/3/99 MV3 ME~

15/8/00 Running Shoes, Cat's Cradle, The Way Of The Mongoose, Play Of The Waves. Cuckston, Eaton, Simpson, Clare, Sales, Owen, Steve Perkins (d). 16/7/00 MV4 ME GYW

20/5/03 Sirocco, Steamwhistler, Leeward, The Archivist. Cuckston, Owen, Simpson, Eaton, Laurence Hunt (d, perc), Hannah Baines (tp). 3/4/03 MV4 MWT NS

The Prats

13/9/79 Jesus Had A Pa, Prats 2, Strange Interlude, A Day In The Life Of Me, Poxy Pop Groups, Nothing, You're Nobody, Prats 1. Greg MacGuire (lv, g), Paul McLaughlin (lg), Tom Robinson (b), Dave MacGuire (d). PRIV

Prefab Sprout

28/8/85 Cars And Girls, Rebel Land, Lions In My Garden. 'with Kevin Armstrong' (g) is all sheet says. 18/8/85 MV5 DG U

The Prefects

21/8/78 Things In General, Escort Girls, The Bristol Road Leads To Dachau, Agony Column. Robert Lloyd (lv, hca), Roots Apperley (lg, bck), Joe Motivator (rg, bck), Ted Ward (b), Ada (d). 11/8/78 MV4 TW NG

15/1/79 Motions, Faults, Total Look, Barbarellas. Lloyd, Apperley, Eamon Duffy (b), David Twist (d) & Andy Burchell (cl), Dave Whitton (sx, 'plastic squeak'). 8/1/79 MV4 TW DD ● SFPS025

Premi

11/8/87 Paliye Panjeba Waliye, Nach Di Di Godthkhulgaye, Jago Aya, Terj Ni Kali Gooth Goriye. Chani (d), Kala (cga), Jassi Lota (dholka, v), Digsy (tamb), Mike (b), Gareth (g), Thomas (ss), Raju & Jittu (k), Johal (v). 4/8/87 U DG MR&ME

The Sid Presley Experience

14/8/84 Firewater, Take A Chance, Jealously, Can't Leave Her Alone. Peter Coyne (v), Chris Coyne (b), Del Bartle (g), Kevin Murphy (d). 4/8/84 MV5 DG MC 1st session was for Kid Jensen June 84

Preston School Of Industry

4/7/01 Somethings Happen Always, Whale Bones, 10 Grains, Happiness. Scott Kannberg (gv), Mike Drake (g), Matt Harris (b), Jim Lindsay (d). 10/6/01 MV3 ME JHT

Pretty Girls Make Graves

11/9/03 More Sweet Soul, The Grandmother Wolf, The Teeth Collector, The Is Our Emergency. Andrea Zollo (v), Nick Dewitt (d, k, bck), Derek Fudesco (b, bck), Nathan Thelan (g, bck), J Clark (g, bck). 7/8/03 MV4 SA JSM

The Pretty Things

3/12/67 Turn My Head, Defecting Grey, Talking About The Good Times, Walking Through My Dreams. Phil May (lv), Dick Taylor (lg), Skip Alan (d), John Povey (o, pv), Alan Waller (b). 27/11/67 PC1 BA DT 1st broadcast was live on Parade Of The Pops 8/7/64, more Saturday Club appearances followed

17/11/68 SF Sorrow Is Born, She Says Good Morning, Balloon Burning, Old Man Going. John Alder 'Twink' (d) r Alan. 21/10/68 PC1 BA PR

25/5/69 Send You With Loving, Alexander, The Loneliest Person, No More Spring, Marilyn. 20/5/69 MV4 JW TW

15/5/71 Stone Hearted Mama, Circus Mind, Slow Beginning (& Summertime, 14/8/71). Skip Alan returns r Alder, Peter Tolson (lg) r Taylor. 27/4/71 MV4 JW BC

4/8/72 Love Is Good, Spider Woman, Don't Bring Me Down, Onion Soup. Stuart Brooks (b) r Waller. 17/7/72 T1 JM JWH&JS

15/8/72 Rosalyn, Onion Soup, All Night Sailor (& Love Is Good, not TX). & Dick (g-1). 25/7/72 MV4 PR JWH&JS

15/2/73 Religion's Dead, Love Is Good, Defecting Grey, Old Man Going, Havana Bound. 29/1/73 LH1 BA U

6/1/75 Bridge Of God, Silk Torpedo, Come Home Momma, Dream / Joey. Jack Green (bv) r Brooks; & Gordon Edwards (gkv). 17/12/74 MV4 TW BC

24/7/75 Belfast Cowboy / Bruise In The Sky, Big City, Dream / Joey, Not Only But Also. 17/7/75 MV4 TW U

Prewar Yardsale

28/5/03 Philadelphia, Kiss Loves You, 33 Ok 5, High Five, Life Of My Party. Dina Levy (b, fl, buckets), Mike Rechner (v, ag, fuzz box). 23/4/03 MV3 SA NF

Maxi Priest

6/3/85 Should I (Put My Trust In You), Throw My Corn, In The Springtime. Maxi (lv), Paul Robinson (dv), Errol Robinson (b), Jerry Robinson (p), Ewan Robinson (o), Trevor Robinson (perc), Jerry Fulgence (lg), Frank End (rg), Al Deval (sx), Peter Lamont (tb), Kevin Robinson (tp), Carroll Tompson (v), Candy McKenzie (v), Jane Eugene (v). 26/2/85 MV5 MRD MR

Primal Scream

10/12/85 Crystal Crescent, Aftermath, Subterranean, I Love You. Thomas McGurk (d), Robert Young (b), James Beattie (lg), Paul Harte (rg), Martin St John (tamb), Bobby Gillespie (v). 1/12/85 MV5 DG ME

14/5/86 Tomorrow Ends Today, Leaves, Bewitched And Bewildered. Stewart May (rg) r Harte. 6/5/86 MV4 DG MR&JB

The Primevals

18/9/85 Saint Jack, See That Skin, Spiritual, Dish Of Fish. Lefty Burnett (d), John Honeyman (b), Brother Malcolm (McDonald) (g), Don Gordon (g), Michael Rooney (v). 8/9/85 U DG MA ● SFPS014

The Primitives

15/10/86 Stop Killing Me, Shadow, Buzz Buzz Buzz, As Tears Go By. Paul Court (g, bck), Tracy Cattell (lv), Pete Tweedie (d), Stephen Dullaghan (b). 30/9/86 U DG MR&MWT Previous sessions for Janice Long and Andy Kershaw June/July 86

13/4/87 Dream Walk Baby, Ocean Blue, Everything's Shining Bright, She Don't Need You. 31/3/87 U DG MR&TD

25/4/88 Things Get In Your Way, Keep Me In Mind, Way Behind Me. Richard Tig Williams (d) r Tweedie. 17/4/88 MV5 DG U

Prince Far I and Creation Rebel

16/6/78 Spoken Introduction, Black Man's Land, No More War, The Dream, Foggy Road, Enter. Prince Far I (lv), Vernon (g), Clifton Morrisson (k), Clinton Jack (b), Dr Pablo (mel), Charley (d). 7/6/78 MV4 JG NG

Principal Edward's Magic Theatre

31/7/68 51st Day Of Spring, Motel Song, Buckle My Knee, Hey Joe, To A Broken Guitar. Vivien MacAuliffe (v), Martin Stellman (v), Michael 'Root' Cartwright (g, mnd),

Lyn Edwards (perc), Belinda Bourquin (vi, rec, k). 16/7/68 MV5 DK U Overwhelming 'No' of panel overruled, made a 'Yes', by Jimmy Grant. Some of the other producers' comments: 'who can like this, if they don't come from New Delhi?' 'ugly tuneless voice… the pseudo-eastern influence I find offensive' 'could it not be useful to the Birmingham Pakistani programme?'

30/3/69 Lament For The Earth, The Ballad Of The Big Girl Now And The Mere Boy, Third Sonnet To Sundry Notes Of Music, Pinky: A Mystery Cycle. & Jeremy Ensor, David Jones, Monica Mettles. 24/2/69 PH BA U

17/1/70 Thus Making A Change, Autumn Lady Travelling Song, Plague Of Birds, King Of The. Ensor, Cartwright, MacAuliffe, Edwards, Stellman, Bourquin. 13/1/70 MV4 JW U

10/4/71 Kettering Song, Weasel, Freef'rall. Ensor, Cartwright, Stellman, Bourquin, John Jones, Roger Swallow, Catherine Freckingham. 23/3/71 MV4 JW BC

18/10/73 Juggernaut, Milk And Honey Land. Cartwright, Bourquin & Nick Pallett (gv), Richard Chipperfield (bv), David Jones (perc), Geoff Nicholls (d). 17/9/73 LH1 BA U

John Prine

23/1/73 Clocks And Spoons, Flag Decal, Angel From Montgomery, Everybody. John Prine (gv). 22/1/73 T1 PD (for JW) U On back of session sheet, someone has scribbled 'Nominee for Grammy Award'

Maddy Prior and June Tabor

20/10/75 Four Loom Weaver, The Seven Joys Of Mary, Singing The Travels, The Doffin' Mistress. Maddy Prior (lv, bck), June Tabor (lv, bck). 23/9/75 MV4 JW BC&NG

Procol Harum

8/10/67 She Wandered Through The Garden Fence, Good Captain Clack, Homburg, Kaleidoscope, Repent Walpurgess. Matthew Fisher (o), Gary Brooker (pv), Dave Knights (b), Robin Trower (g), Barry 'B. J.' Wilson (d). 27/9/67 MV4 BP PR Previously live on the Light Programme twice in June 67

25/2/68 Quite Rightly So, Shine On Brightly, Rambling On, Skip Softly My Moonbeams. 14/2/68 MV4 BA U

8/9/68 Wish Us Well, Skip Softly My Moonbeams, Long Gone Geek, In Held 'twas In I. 19/8/68 PC1 BA U

1/6/69 A Salty Dog, Juicy John Pink, Devil Came From Kansas, Too Much Between Us. Chris Copping (o) r Fisher, Knights out. 27/5/69 MV4 JW U

19/3/74 Butterfly Boys, The Idol, Beyond The Pale, Nothing But The Truth. Mick Grabham (g) r Trower. 12/3/74 LH1 TW BC

The Professionals

10/11/80 Join The Professionals, All The Way With You, Crescendo, Kick Down The Doors. Paul Cook (d, bck), Steve Jones (lg, lv), Paul Myers (b, bck), Kid McVeigh (g, bck). 3/11/80 LH1 TW ME

Prolapse

20/8/94 Serpico, Doorstep Rhythmic Bloc, When Space Invaders Were Big, Broken Cormorant. Michael Derrick (v), Linda Steelyard (v), Mick Harrison (b), David Jeffreys (g), Pat Marsden (g), Tim Pattison (d). 17/7/94 MV5 ME MFA

8/4/97 Slash Stroke Oblique, Deanshanger, Outside Of It, Place Called Clock. Pattison, Marsden, Jeffreys, Harrison, Steelyard, Meho Deho (v, pp), Donald Ross Skinner (k). 16/3/97 MV4 ME RJ

Prong

1/2/89 Defiant, Decay, Senseless Abuse, In My Veins. Ted Parsons (d, bck), Mike Kirkland (b, lv-2,4), Tommy Victor (g, lv-1,3). 22/1/89 MV3 DG ME ○ SFRCD078

Propellerheads

23/11/96 Take California, Dive, Props Got Skills, Bring Us Together. Alex Gifford (tt, o), Will White (tt, d, human beatbox). 20/10/96 MV4 ME~

Prophecy of Doom

14/2/90 Insanity Reigns Supreme, Earth Reality Victim, Rancid Oracle, Hybrid Thought. Dean (d), Martin (b), Shrub (g), Tom (g), Shrew (v). 28/1/90 MV3 DG MA ○ SFRCD079

1/6/91 Raze Against Time, Onward Ever Backward, Acknowledge The Confusion Master, The Voice Of Tibet / Our Shame & Hypocrisy. 7/4/91 MV3 DG ME&AA

Prophets Of Da City

4/3/95 Deen Taariq Meets Da Deck Wrekka Of Boom, Brasse And Gassielams, Sound Boy Test, Dallah Flet. Deon Thomas Daniels, Shaheen Arief dien, Ramone De Wet, Nader Mogamat Hoosain, Ishmael Molifi Morabe, Allie Gafoor, Celmet Snyden. 28/1/95 OS

Protex

19/2/79 Don't Ring Me Up, I Can't Cope, Place In Your Heart, Popularity. Aidan Murtagh (gv), David McMaster (gv), Paul Maxwell (b), Owen McFadden (d). 29/1/79 MV5 DT U 1st TX Kid Jensen show w/c 12/2/79

The Psychedelic Furs

30/7/79 Imitation Of Christ, Fall, Sister Europe, We Love You. 'Butler Rep' (Richard Butler) (lv), John Ashton (g), Roger Morris (g), Duncan Kilburn (sx), Tim Butler (b), Rod Johnson (d). 25/7/79 MV4 TVD NG

28/2/80 Soap Commercial, Susan's Strange, Mac The Knife. Uncle Ely' (Vince Ely) (d) r Johnson. 18/2/80 MV4 TW DD

10/2/81 Into You Like A Train, On And Again, All Of This And Nothing. 2/2/81 LH1 TW DD

Psychick Warriors Ov Gaia

10/6/94 Break, Dust, Pull. Reinoud Van Broek (prg, k), Reinier Brekelmans (prg, k), Joris Hilckmann (prg, k), Tim Freeman (Engineer), Peter Koedoot (Assistance Engineer). 1/5/94 MV3 ME TD

The Psylons

9/6/86 Remembrance, Clearer Skies, Mockery Of Decline, Landmark. Keith Wyatt (gv), Jack Packer (g), Warren Grech (b), Carl Edwards (d). 1/6/86 MV5 DG MS&ME

Pulp

18/11/81 Turkey Mambo Momma, Please Don't Worry, Wishful Thinking, Refuse To Be Blind. Jarvis Cocker (gv, perc), Peter Dalton (sy, o, g, bck, xyl, cnt, perc), Jamie Pinchbeck (b, perc), Wayne Furniss (d, perc). 7/11/81 MV4 DG PW

5/3/93 Pink Glove, You're A Nightmare, Acrylic Afternoons. Cocker, Candida Doyle (k), Nick Banks (d), Steve Mackey (b), Russell Senior (g, vi). 7/2/93 MV4 ME~ SA

22/10/94 Underwear, Common People, Pencil Skirt. Mark Webber (g) joins. 9/9/94 MV4 DD KR

28/8/01 Sunrise, Weeds, I Love Life, Duck Diving. Senior out. 12/8/01 MV4 ME~ KR Everything on ○ The Peel Sessions Universal/Island

Punishment of Luxury

30/8/78 Funk Me, Babalon, Let's Get Married / You're So Beautiful. Brian Bond (lv), Jeff Thwaite (d), Malla Cabbala (gv), Nevil Luxury (lgv), Jimmy Giro (bv). 22/8/78 MV4 BS MR

30/5/79 Radar Bug / Metropolis, British Baboon, Secrets. Steve Secret (d, bck) r Thwaite; Cabbala out. 22/5/79 MV4 TVD MR

Pure Morning

13/5/94 Game Over, K1704, Sick Profit, But It's All Right. Ade Blackburn (gv), Hartley (g), Brian Campbell (b), Carl Turney (d). 10/4/94 MV3 ME NS

3/3/95 Guilt Lame Kicker, Dinky, Chancile, Dirge. 5/2/95 MV3 ME NK

10/8/96 Billy, Concessions, Divorcee, Other Lovers. 13/7/96 MV3 ME PN

James & Bobby Purify

5/11/67 You Don't Know Like I Know, I Take What I Want, I'm Your Puppet, Shake A Tear (Shake A Tail Feather). James & Bobby Purify (v), Steve Gray (o) and the New York Public Library. U U U U 1st TX Saturday Club 8/10/67

Purple Hearts

16/7/79 Beat That, Millions Like Us, Nothing's Left, Frustration. Simon Stebbing, Jess Shadbolt, Gary Sparks, Bob Manton. 10/7/79 U U U

Pushkins

12/11/93 Swallow, Slinky Malone, Ugly When Naked, Rub Gently. Florence (Auntie) (d), Paul Ralph (b), Jon Griffin (gv). 24/10/93 MV3 AA PA

Pussy Crush

12/11/94 Geek, I Wanna Lose Ya, Hesitatin', Brain Dead, Grunk, Mindless. Kags (v), Pilly (d), Dom (b), Andy (g). 27/9/94 MV4 TD SA

22/6/96 No Time, Pils, Get Your Kicks, Sugar Girl, Why Dontcha, Waif Of Space. Kags (v), Pilly (d), Carl Biancucci (b), Joe Mazzari (g). 28/5/96 MV4 AA NS

Pussy Galore

25/7/90 Dead Meat, Understand Me, Nothin' Can Bring Me Down, New Breed. John Spencer, Bob Bert, Neil Hagerty, Kurt Wolf. Recorded in USA

Pussycat Trash

28/1/94 1 2 3 4, Our Option, Ultraism, Pink Metro Of Oblivion. Rosie Lewis (g, d), Rachel Holborrow (bv), Simon Coxall (d, v), Peter Dale (d, g). 7/12/93 MV4 JB RK

Quads

10/9/79 Revision Time Blues, I Know You Know, There's Never Been A Night, There Must Be Thousands. Josh Jones (lvg), Jack Jones (gv), Jim Doherty (bv), Johnny Jones (dv). 29/8/79 MV4 TVD MR

Quando Quango

1/12/83 Love Tempo, Go Exciting, Triangle. Mike Pickering (sxv), Gonnie Rietveld (syv), Barry Johnson (b, d), Simon Topping (perc). 23/11/83 MV4 RP TdB

Quasi

5/1/99 Smile, The Poisoned Well, Do You Love Me Now, Under A Cloud. Sam Coombes (kgv), Janet Weiss (dv). 8/12/98 MV4 MR~

31/8/99 I Only Have Eyes For You. OS

16/11/99 Seal The Deal, The Star You Left Behind, Not Much Else, Paint It Black. 12/9/99 MV4 ME MPK

4/10/01 Master & Dog, Goblins & Trolls, No One, Queen Majesty. 15/8/01 MV4 NF GYW

Quatermass

1/8/70 One Blind Mice, Laughing Tackle, Make Up Your Mind. Pete Robinson (k), John Gustafson (bv), Mick Underwood (d). 28/7/70 MV4 JW U

Que Bono

16/6/81 Burton Wood, Houses, Twister, Siren's Scream. Pete Mulvihill (d), Jane Mulvihill (v), Alan Maskell (g), Simon Hall (b). 9/6/81 LH1 DG MR

Queen

15/2/73 My Fairy King, Keep Yourself Alive, Doing Alright, Liar. Freddie Mercury (pv), Brian May (g, bck), John Deacon (b, bck), Roger Taylor (d, bck). 5/2/73 LH1 BA JE ○

6/12/73 Ogre Battle, Great King Rat, Modern Times Rock 'n' Roll, Son And Daughter. 3/12/73 LH1 BA MF&NGR ○ on Band of Joy 'Queen at the Beeb' BOJCD001

14/11/77 Spread Your Wings, It's Late, Melancholy Blues, We Will Rock You. 28/10/77 MV4 JG MR

Quickspace

14/10/95 Mouse, Friend, Swisher, Happy Song. Billed as Quickspace Supersport: Wendy Harper (vi, lv), Tom Cullinan (lv, g), Barry Stilwell (g), Sean Newsham (b), Max Corradi (d). 8/10/95 MV3 ME LS

1/9/96 Song For The BBC, Winona, Quasi Brau, Rise. From now on, Quickspace only: Nina Pascale (gv), Tom Cullinan (gv), Paul Shilton (k), Sean Newsham (b), Chin (d). 18/8/96 MV3 ME LS

20/10/98 Would You, If I Were A Carpenter, Worth, Bath Time. Steve Denton (d) r Chin. 11/10/98 MV3 ME JLO

29/9/99 They Shoot The Horse Don't They, The Lobbalong Song, The Flat Moon Society, Gloria Clip. 27/7/99 MV4 MR SB

Quiver

13/2/71 Back On The Road Again, Ballad Of Barnes County, Down Your Way. Calvin Batchelor (lgv), Bruce Thomas (b), Tim Renwick (g), John 'Willie' Wilson (d). 19/1/71 MV4 JW BC 'Unanimous pass with no reservations… Should be used on quite a lot of Radio 1 programmes', audition panel

16/5/72 Green Tree, Gone In The Morning, Love / No Boundaries. 2/5/72 MV4 U BC

16/6/72 I Might Stumble, Love Has No Boundary, Take A Train. 8/5/72 PH JM JWH

R

Rachels

22/10/97 Rhine And Courtesan, Oh Demeter, Nocturne No 1. Jason Noble (bg), Rachel Grimes (k, p), Christian Frederickson (vla), Dominic Johnson (vla), Bob Weston (tp, bass e-bow), Edward Grimes (d), Greg King (tps). 21/9/97 MV4 DD GT

Racing Cars

22/3/76 Pass The Bottle, Calling The Tune, They Shoot Horses Don't They?, Rhondda Reggae. Gareth Mortimer (lv, ag), David Land (b), James Dodd (d), Ray Ennis (lg, slg, bck), Hedley Grosvenor (lg, bck). 2/3/76 MV4 JG MR

20/9/76 Four Wheel Drive, Moonshine Fandango, Hard Working Woman, Down Town Tonight. Graham Williams (g), Robert Wilding (d) r Grosvenor, Dodd. 9/9/76 MV4 TW U

12/4/77 Breaking The Rules, Tickin' Over, Travelling Mood, Swampy. 4/4/77 MV4 TW DD

14/9/77 Nobody's Business, Standing In The Rain, Weekend Rendezvous, Clever Girl. & Geraint Watkins (acc-1). 5/9/77 MV4 TW DD

11/9/78 Second Best, When I'm Walking Home, Takin' On The World, Bring On The Night. 14/8/78 MV4 BS DD

Radar Brothers

5/1/97 Wise Mistake Of You, Tukon, Stay, Silence And Television. Jim Putnam (gv), Senon Williams (b), Steve Goodfriend (d). 10/12/96 MV4 PA NF

17/11/99 Shifty Lies, Shovelling Sons, Five Miles, Sisters Of Property. & Eddie Ruscha (kv). 19/9/99 MV4 JB JHT

22/6/00 Open Ocean Sailing, Friend, Secrets, Underwater Culprits. & Sean Fallon (k). 23/4/00 MV4 ME JSM

Radial Spangle

21/8/93 Birthday, Snow, Turpentine. Shannon Kerr (v), Alan Laird (gv), April Tippens (nv), Kelsey Kennedy (d, bells), Julie Wood (vi). 20/7/93 MV4 MR PA

Radio 5

13/5/80 True Colours, Animal Connections, Expressionless, Dancing With Germany. Jock Cotton (v, g), Don Hayes (b), Geoff Haran (g), Chris Groves (d), Roland 707 (occasional rhythm). 6/5/80 MV4 BS MR

Radio Stars

20/5/77 Horrible Breath, Dirty Pictures, Dear Prudence, No Russians In Russia. Andy Ellison (lv, hca), Ian MacLeod (g), Martin Gordon (b, o), Gary Thompson (d). 17/5/77 MV4 JG MR

18/11/77 Good Personality, The Beast Of Barnsley, Don't Waste My Time, Is It Really Necessary? Steve Parry (d) r Thompson. 7/11/77 MV4 TW DD

14/9/78 Boy Meets Girl, Radio Stars, Sex In Chains, Sitting In The Rain. Jamie Crompton (d) r Parry. 4/9/78 MV4 TW DD

The Radio Sweethearts

2/11/00 Let Me Be Your Man Tonight, Chains Of Love, Poppin' Pills, Take Me Back To San Francisco, Way Down Town. John Miller (agv), Francis MacDonald (d, p), Malcolm McMaster (ps), Kevin Key (g), Martin Hayward (b), John McCusker (fd, mnd). 15/10/00 MV4 ME~

Gerry Rafferty

6/2/73 Over My Head, Singing Bird, Don't Get Me Wrong. Gerry Rafferty (all instruments, v). 15/1/73 T1 JW U

The Ragga Twins

16/6/91 Spiffhead & Jugglin', Wipe The Needle / Hooligans, Flinty Badman, Smiley PJ, Deman Rocker. 14/5/91 MV5 MR AR

23/2/92 Bring Up The Mic Some More / Ragga Trip, The Truth / Tansoback. The Ragga Twins (rp), Shut Up & Dance (mx, tt). 21/1/92 MV4 MR PA&MR

The Railway Children

24/11/86 Consider, Any Other Town, Listen On, Big Hands Of Freedom. Gary Newby (gv), Brain Bateman (g), Stephen Hull (b), Guy Keegan (d). 21/10/86 U DG MA&FK

The Raincoats

1/5/79 In Love, You're A Million, Adventures Close To Home, Fairy Tale In The Supermarket. Ana Da Silva (gv), Vicki Aspinall (vi, gv), Gina Birch (bv), Palmolive (d). 6/3/79 MV4 TVD MR

18/12/80 Using My Eyes, Family Treat, Baby Song. Charles Hayward (d) r Palmolive. 10/12/80 MV4 BS NG

16/4/94 No One's Little Girl, Don't Be Mean, We Smile, Shouting Out Loud. Birch, Da Silva, Anne Wood (vi), Steve Shelley (d). 29/3/94 MV4 MR TD ○ On Extended Play SLR012

Ravishing Beauties

29/4/82 Arctic Death, Futility, We Will Meet Them Again, No Need To Cry. Virginia Astley (lv), Kate St John (bck, co, ob, fl), Nicky Holland (bck, k), Ben Hoffnung (perc). 14/4/82 U CL U

Raw Noise

14/9/91 Stench Of Death (Metal), Making A Killing, Under The Influence, Ratfink, Waste Of Life. Niall Carr (d), Martin Peck (b), Alo Firouzbakht (g, bck), Tony Doy (lg), Dean Jones (v). 4/8/91 MV3 DG MA&JRS

Lou Rawls, Maxine Brown and The Johnny Watson Concept

8/10/67 Hold On I'm Coming, Yesterday's Heroes, I Was Made To Love, Street Of Dreams, Oh No Not My Baby, It's An Uphill Climb To The Bottom, One Step At A Time, On Broadway, In The Midnight Hour, Love Is A Hurting Thing. Lou Rawls (lv-2, 4, 6, 8, 10), Maxine Brown (lv-1, 3, 5,7,9) '& guitarist' & 10 & 5 extra musicians. 3/10/67 U U U

Read Yellow

9/3/04 Model America, The Art, The Easiest Part Of Surveillance, A Love Supreme. Jesse Vuona (gv), Paul Koelle (d), Evan Kenney (gv), Michelle Freivald (bv). 12/2/04 MV4 MA NS

Rebel Da Fe

12/4/83 Ascension, Hideaway, Alter And Correct, Yangtse Kiang. Brian Ellis (v), Jarvis Whitehead (g), Karen Halewood (kv), Gary Williams (b), Mark Robson (d). 6/4/83 MV4 JS U

Rechenzentrum

18/1/01 Aufbruch, Unterwegs, Noch Dabei, Wieder Unterwegs, Strecke, Kurz Vor Dem Ziel, Ankunft Bei Nacht. Marc Weiser, Christian Conrad, Lillevan. 1/8/00 OS

The Red Beards from Texas

1/7/85 Party On The Patio, I Saw Her Standing There, Automobile, Ain't That A Shame. Morton Pinkley (gv), Wild Hoss Maverick III (bv), Bud Weiser (g), Duke Delight (d). 25/6/85 MV5 JWI MR

Red Beat

15/12/80 See, Child, Tribe, The Wheel. Roy Jones (lv), Kevin Keane (g), Chris Thompson (b), Paul Jones (d). 2/12/80 MV4 JS MR

Red Guitars

11/8/83 Fact, Marimba Jive, Paris France, Dive. Jerry Kidd (v), Louise Barlow (b), Hallam Lewis (lg), Matt Higgins (d), John Rowley (rg). 6/8/83 DG MC

24/7/84 Within Four Walls, Shaken Not Stirred, Crocodile Tears, Remote Control. 14/7/84 MV5 DG MR

Red Hour

4/1/92 Almost There, All I Need, Free Fall, William Jailor. Geoff Cooke (d), Chris Hughes (b), Roger Birby (lg), Roger Lindsay (rg), Dave Canavan (lv). 17/11/91 MV3 DG MA&PA

Red Letter Day

21/4/86 Spark Of Love, Coming Home, Killing Ground, Pictures. Ade (lv, g), Davie (lg, bck), Keith (b, bck), Daryn (d). 13/4/86 MV5 DG ME

Red Lorry Yellow Lorry

13/1/83 Sometimes, Happy, Silence, Conscious Decision. Chris Reed (g), Martin Fagen (g), Mick Brown (d), Steve Smith (b), Joanna Dobson (sx). 22/12/82 MV4 U NG&AM

16/11/83 See The Fire, Strange Dream, Monkeys On Juice. Reed, Brown, Dane Wolfenden (g), Paul Southern (b, bck). 5/11/83 MV4 DG TdB

Red Monkey

18/2/98 Not For Rent, (Ain't Nothing But) An Incendiary Device, Paper Crown, Make A Mess. Marc Walker (d), Rachel Holborow (bv), Pete Dale (gv). 25/1/98 MV4 ME RJ

Red Ninja

1/12/91 Trenton Job, Bad Voicemen Of The Apocalypse, Killing At Hellz Gate, Look Black In Anger. Motion (lv), Loop T (prg, b), Sex Ninja (v), DJ Stix (bck), Wadlow (bck, smp), Peter Peter (bck, smp), Gadjet (mel), IQ (k, smp). 22/10/91 MV4 MR MR&AR

The Redskins

20/10/82 The Peasant Army, Kick Over The Statues, Reds Strike The Blues, Unionize & Pickin' The Blues (Outro). Chris Dean (gv), Nick King (d), Millicent Martin (Hewes) (b) Steve Nichol (tp), Lloyd Dwyer (sx) & guests Dagenham Pete Pixie (bck), John Mekon (bck), Colin Car (bck). 9/10/82 MV4 DG MR ● SFPS030

15/8/83 Young And Proud, Hold On, 99–And-A-Half, Take No Heroes. Five-piece. 8/8/83 MV4 TW U

Reggae Regular

3/7/78 Weed Stalk, Fool's Game / Fool's Game (Dub Version), Where Is Jah?, Not Any More. Junior Ewbanks (lg), Patrick Donnegan (rg, bck), George 'Flee' Clarke (k), Trevor 'Seal' Salmon (b), Errol Francis (d), Tony Rookwood (lv-1 and 4), Alan King (lv-2 and 3). 12/6/78 MV4 TW DD

10/10/78 Never Needed Nobody, That Little Girl, Ital Club, Victim Of Life. 27/9/78 MV4 MR NG

Reginald

31/7/71 The Weaver, Half The Story, Seelookhearfeel. John Horne (bgv), Roger Greenwood (gv), Brian Howe (o, tp, v), Walter Day (dv), Dave Almond (lg, sx, v). 20/7/71 U JW U

Regis

8/10/98 Techno DJ set live from MV4 AR U

Terry Reid

2/3/69 Tinker Tailor, Writing On The Wall, Marking Time, Without Expression. Terry Reid (lgv), Pete Shelley (o, p), Keith Webb (d). 11/2/69 PH BA AH Previous trial broadcast on Saturday Club 1/6/68, failed by audition panel as 'nothing exceptional'

10/11/71 Anyway, Thine To Try, Dreamin'. Reid & David Lindeley (ps, v), Lee Miles (b) & (d) unknown. 19/10/71 MV4 U BC

The Relations

23/4/86 Come Back Home, Mr Wonderful, Holy Water, You Can Call Me Anything. Neil (d), Vinny (b), Kelly (g), Gerry (v). 15/4/86 MV4 DG MR&MWT

REM

17/11/98 Walk Unafraid, Day Sleeper, Lotus, At My Most Beautiful. Peter Buck (g), Michael Stipe (v), Mike Mills (b, p, bck), Scott McCaughey (k), Joey Waronker (d), Ken Stringfello (b, p), BJ Cole (ps). 25/10/98 recorded 'as live' in BBC Radio Theatre MR~

The Remipeds

25/8/81 Keep Me Hanging On, Snooky, Bodily Contact, Ain't No Day. Ozzie Orzell (lv-2, 4), Rick Kulak (g, bck, lv-3), Eddie K (k, bck, lv-1), Dave Hughes (b, bck), Sugar Ray McKnight (d, bck), Glynn Bartlett (tp), Alphonso Augusto Montuori (sx). 17/8/81 MV4 CL DD

John Renbourn and Jackie McShee

11/12/68 Watch The Stars, I Can't Keep From Crying Sometimes, Every Night When The Sun Goes In, My Johnny Was A Shoeman, The Lags Song. John Renbourn (g), Jacki McShee (v). 10/12/68 S1 JM U

John Renbourn and Terry Cox

4/12/68 Moondog, Sally Free And Easy, Ladye Nothing's Toye Puffe, Lamente Di Tristram, La Rotta, Melancholy Galliard, Earl Of Salisbury. John Renbourn (g), Terry Cox (gv). 28/11/68 PC1 JM U Renbourn debuted with a solo session on the Light Programme's Folk Room TX 28/8/65 prod BA

Renegade Sound Wave

22/6/87 Kray Twins, Traitor, How To Be Hard, Blue-Eyed Boy. Gary Asquith (v), Danny Briottet (b), Carl Bonnie (g). 2/6/87 U DG MA&ME

Rennaisance

18/10/69 Island, Ballet, Innocents. Keith Relf (gv, hca), Jim McCarthy (dv) Jane Relf (v), John Hawkins (pv), Louis Cennamo (b). 7/10/69 MV5 JW U

Repetition

17/8/81 Carnival, Autumn, On The Other Side, Enchantment. Andy Hooper (k), Steve Musham (v), Jim Solar (b, g, k), Tim Transe (d). 8/8/81 MV4 DG MR

Resistance

9/5/79 Incognito, Walking Talking Abstract Man, Svengali Number Two, Closet Kings. Mark Damron (lv, g), John O'Leary (b, bck), Alain (or Iain) Reid (k, bck), Martin Saunders (d, perc). 2/5/79 MV4 JS NG

6/1/81 Don't Fraternise With The Fraternity, Ego, Black Comedy, Nuclear Family. 15/12/80 LH1 TW DD

Restricted Code

17/3/81 Monkey Monkey Monkey, We Know We Know, Yakov Bok, Shake Your Body. Tom Cannavan (v, g), Frank Quadrelli (gv), Kenny Blythe (bv), Stephen Lironi (d, perc) & Ian Duff (p). 10/3/81 LH1 DG MR

The Revillos

17/3/80 Scuba-Scuba, You Were Meant For Me, Rock-A-Boom, Voodoo. Hi Fi Harris (g), Felix (b), Robo Rhythm (d), Fay Fife (lv), Eugene Reynolds (lv), Revettes (Babs and Cherie) (bck). 10/3/80 MV4 TW DD 2 previous sessions in Sept / Oct 79 for Kid Jensen and Mike Read

13/5/81 Caveman Raveman, She's Fallen In Love With A Monster Man, Snatzo Mobile, Man Attack. credits include 'Kid Krup' (g), 'Vince Spik' (b). 29/4/81 LH1 CL U

Reviver Gene

12/5/99 Beginning To The End, Playing For Our Lives, Postcard, Just For You. Jason Nott (v), Jarrod Prosser (g), David Thomas (lg), Jon Lake (b), David 'Syd' Savage (d). 14/3/99 MV3 ME RF

25/4/00 Lazy Starter, Always, Why Go Now, Pale Male. Prosser out. 1/3/00 MV3 ME JHT

Revolver

23/11/91 Crimson, Drowning Inside, Wave†, John's Not Mad†. Mat Flint (gv), Hamish Brown (b), Nick Dewey (d). 12/9/91 MV5 DG NG&SA † on ○ SFMCD214 1st session was for Mark Goodier July 91

Reynolds

11/12/02 The Heart Wins. Phill Rodgers (b), Kevin Smith (d), Chris Summerlin (g), Joanna Woodnutt (vi). Live from MV4 NF~ GT

The Rezillos

30/12/77 (My Baby Does) Good Sculptures, No, Fight Amongst Yourselves, Top Of The Pops. Angel Patterson (d, bck), William Mysterious (b, bck), Luke Warm (John Callis) (g, bck), Fay Fife (lv), Eugene Reynolds (lv). 12/12/77 MV4 CL BAI

8/6/78 Cold Wars (Have Cooled Me Down), Destination Venus, Somebody's Gonna Get Their Heads Kicked In Tonight, I Can't Stand My Baby (Soul Version). 31/5/78 MV4 BS NG

Steve Rhodes Singers

17/7/73 Akoi Moi, Prayer For A Traveller, Ibo Native Air, Adukpo No Mo. 25 singers (unknown). OS

Emitt Rhodes

24/11/71 Bubblegum Cruiser, Birthday Lady, Love Will Scare You, Really Wanted You. U 23/11/71 PH JW BC&IS

Rhythm Eternity

26/6/92 Hold On Tight, Freedom, Pink Champagne. Lynsey Davenport (v), Scott Rosser & Paul Spencer (k, prg). 24/5/92 MV3 ME ME

The Rhythm Pigs

9/11/87 Killer Beat, New Saviour, Simple, Satan Tuned My Snare. Greg Adams (gv), Ed Ivey (bv), Bill Atwell III (d) & Terry Edwards (ts, al-4). 1/11/87 U DG ME&FK

The Rich Kids

7/11/77 Young Girls, Rich Kids, Burnin' Sounds, Bullet Proof Lover. Midge Ure (g, lv), Steve New (g), Glen Matlock (bv), Rusty Egan (d). 31/10/77 MV4 TW DD

3/4/78 Ghosts Of Princes And Towers, Lovers And Fools, Empty Words, Here Comes The Nice. Matlock (lv-3). 20/3/78 MV4 TW DD

Ride

26/2/90 Like A Daydream, Dreams Burns Down, Perfect Time, Sight Of You. Laurence Colbert (d), Stephen Queralt (b), Andy Bell (gv), Mark Gardner (gv). 4/2/90 MV3 DG MR

29/9/90 Severance, Here And Now, All I Can See, Decay. 16/9/90 MV3 DG ME&FK

Joshua Rifkin

27/12/73 Searchlight Rag, Sugar Love, Country Club, Weepin' Willow. Joshua Rifkin (p). 17/12/73 LH1 BA MF

Marc Riley and the Creepers

29/11/83 Cure By Choice, Location Bangladesh, Baby Paints, Blow Your Own Trumpet, Pickin' The Nose. Marc Riley (o, gv), Paul Fletcher (o, g), Jim Khambatta (k, bck), Eddie Fenn (d), Pete Keogh (b). 21/11/83 MV4 TW MC

5/7/84 Snipe, Hole 4 A Soul, Shirt Scene, Shadow Figure. Clive Stewart (sx-1,4) r Khambatta. 26/6/84 MV5 MRD TdB

4/9/85 Black Dwarf, Bard Of Woking, Goin' Rate, Cold Fish. Riley, Fenn, Fletcher, Keogh; & Jim Khambatta (o), Mike Gallagher (sx), Jon Hunter (tp). 25/8/85 MV5 DG ME

4/6/86 Another Song About Motorbikes, The Adventures Of Brain Glider, Bank Of Horrors, Stroke Of Genius. Riley, Fenn, Gallagher, Phil Roberts (b, hca), Mark Tilton (g). 27/5/86 MV4 DG MR&MA

25/2/87 Lucky, Yea Heavy And A Bottle Of Bread, Sparks, Tearjerker. Billed as 'The Creepers': same line-up. 8/2/87 U DG ME&TD

Riot of Colour

15/4/86 Skink, Watching, Cold Hands. Alex Osman (d), Dominic Blaazer (bv, g), Alistair Jackson (g). 8/4/86 MV4 DG MR&MS

Rip Rig and Panic

21/9/81 Symphony In Dave's Flat, A Grand Grin And A Shaky Smile Please Mr Barman, Pullover No Sox. Lambkin Shnod (vi, v), Finklebaum (ww), Miss Pib (d, perc), The Stinking Hog (b, ag), Nico (v-3). 14/9/81 MV4 DG AP

12/7/82 What Are The Toads Doing So Far From The Swamp?, Instant Sin Sheds Skin, Blasé. Gareth Sager (g), Mark Springer (p), Sean Oliver (b), Andrea Oliver (v-3), Jez, Flash & Weasel (rd), David De Fries (tp), Steve Noble (perc), Giles Leaman (perc). 19/6/82 MV4 DG MR

Ripcord

27/7/88 Barriers / Get Away, Existance Without Cause / So Strong / Aim To Please, Collision Of Vision / No Effort No Thought, Vivisection / Passer By. John Miller (d), Jim Whiteley (b), Steve Ballam (g), Steve Hazzard (v). 12/7/88 U MR MR

Ritual

14/12/81 Playtime, Mind Disease, Human Sacrifice, Brides. Jamie Stewart (g), Mark Bond (b), Errol Blyth (v), Steve Pankhurst (sx), Ray Taylor-Smith (d). 7/12/81 MV4 TW DD

Riviera

28/3/01 Pick Up Star, International Lover, Kiss No 38, Dance Alone. Alexa (v), Taylor Sloane (b), Kairo (g), Nikki Paris (k). 11/3/01 MV4 ME GYW

Andy Roberts and Adrian Henri

27/3/68 64 Canning Street, Tonight At Noon, Burdock River Run, Love Story. Andy Roberts (gv), Adrian Henri (v). Also, with other musicians, known as The Liverpool Scene (see above). 19/3/68 S1 DK U

30/10/68 See The Conquering Heroine Comes, Galactic Love Poem, Hull Poem. 30/10/68 S1 PC U

21/1/72 Ballad Of Chairman Shankly, One Of Those Days, Morning Song, Peter Pan Man. 7/1/72 AO2 JM U

11/8/72 Winter Song, The Green Green Grass Of London, I Suppose You Think It's Funny (& King For A Day, 15/9/72; & Galactic Love Poem SEQUENCE 3/11/72). 27/7/72 CM JM U

Andy Roberts

28/3/70 Just For The Record, Creepy John, John The Revelator, Cocaine (& You're A Machine, 13/6/70). Andy Roberts (gv). 10/3/70 MV4 U BC

21/6/73 Harvest Of Tears, All Around My Grandmother's Floor, Hobo Bill's Last Ride, Living In The Halls Of Zion. 11/6/73 LH1 JG U

28/3/74 Rootie Tootie, Havin' A Party, I've Got Mine, From Brown To Blue, The Great Stampede, Speedwell. & 3 (unknown). 21/3/74 LH1 U U See Roberts' other Peel gigs with Liverpool Scene, Plainsong, Viv Stanshall, Roy Harper...

The Tom Robinson Band

7/11/77 Long Hot Summer, Don't Take No For An Answer, We Ain't Gonna Take It, Martin. Tom Robinson (b, lv), Danny Kustow (lg, bck), Brian Taylor (d, bck), Mark Ambler (k). 1/11/77 MV4 JG MR

12/3/79 Black Angel, Blue Murder, All Right All Night, Crossing Over The Road, Law And Order. Robinson, Kustow, Ian Parker (k, bck, lv-5), Preston Hayman (d, perc). 5/3/79 MV4 TW DD

ROC

5/5/95 Sizewell B (Real Time), Hey Niki, Ever Since Yesterday, Dead Pool. Pete Burgess (g, b, cmp), Pat Nicholson (p, g, v, prg), Karen Sheridan (v), Justine Makin (g), Gareth Huw Davies (b, o, Juno), Frei Browning (gv). 9/4/95 MV3 ME JLC

Rock Of Travolta

29/11/01 Lukewarm Skywater, Giant Robo, Oxygen Assisted, The Body's Still There But The Mind Has Gone. Phill Honey (b, k, g), David Warrington (g, b), Jon Carter (b), Ros Murray (clo, b, k), David Crabtree (k, smp), Joe Durow (d, k). 11/11/01 MV4 ME RJ

Rocks

14/2/78 Firefly, Spectrum, Ready For Freddie, Horn Song (Who Put The Shanty On The Shimmy Loo). Mike Patto (lv, p-1,2), Chris Stainton (p-3,4; o-1,2), Fred Gandy (b), Bernie Holland (g), John Halsey (d). 7/2/78 MV4 MB MR

Rodan

23/7/94 Sangre, Big Things Small Things, Before The Train. Kevin Coultas (d), Tara Jane O'Neil, Jeffrey Mueller (g), Jason Noble (g, v-2). 3/6/94 MV5 TdB JLC

Jess Roden

10/9/74 What The Hell, Live Love And Learn, Reason To Change, Feelin' Easy. Jess Roden (v) & Iguana: John Cartwright (b), Pete Hunt (d), Bruce Roberts (g), Steve Webb (g), Ron Taylor (al), Chris Gower (tb). 27/8/74 LH1 TW U

1/5/75 Lies, Honey Don't Worry, Under Suspicion, What Took Me So Long. 24/4/75 MV4 TW U

1/4/76 Blowin', In A Circle, You Can Leave Your Hat On, On A Winner With You. Billy Livesey (k) joins. 18/3/76 MV4 U U

17/12/76 Stay In Bed, The Ballad Of Big Sally, US Dream, Me And Crystal Eye. 7/12/76 MV4 JG MR

Phillip Roebuck

13/10/04 Live one man band. Phillip Roebuck. Live from MV4 AR~

Rogers Sisters

10/6/03 45 Prayers, Fantasies Are Nice, Shadow Play, The Light, Calculation. Jennifer Rogers (gv), Laura Rogers (dv), Miyuki Furtado (bv). 7/5/03 MV3 SA RF

Rollerskate Skinny

3/7/93 Bow Hitchhiker, Abba's Song, Violence To Violence. Ken Griffin (gv), Steven Murray (b), Jimi Shields (g, d, bck), Ger Griffin (b). 29/5/93 MV3 ME~ GT

Roman Holiday

17/8/82 Motor Maniac, One More Jilt, Jive Dive, Standby. Steve Lambert (lv), John Durno (b, bck), Brian Bonhomme (g, bck), Simon Cohen (d), Mike Deacon (p), Robert Lambert (sx), John Eacott (tp), Bob Fish (v). 31/7/82 MV4 DG MR

25/1/83 Furs And High Heels, Chartreuse, No Ball Games. Fish out; Adrian York (k) r Deacon. 17/1/83 U TW MC

Rome

20/3/97 Profiteer Dispatcher, Night Of Feathers, Facing Southwest, Above The Mansions. Roman Warfield Shaw (b, k, d), Le Deuce (smp, tps, loops), JD Walker (d). 23/2/97 MV4 ME RK

Ronnie Ronalde

23/5/02 Soldiers, Tritsch Tratsch Polka, Greensleeves, O Sole Mio, Mockingbird Kill Yodel, Amazing Grace. Ronnie Ronalde (yodels, whistling). 19/5/02 MV4 JHT~

The Roogalator

31/5/76 Ride With The Roogalator, All Aboard, Tasty Two, Cincinnati Fatback. Daniel Adler (g, lv), Nick Plytas (k), Jeff Watts (b), Bobby Irwin (d). 13/5/76 MV4 TW U

11/11/76 Sock It To My Pocket, Walkin' In The Heat, If You Don't Like Smelling It You'd Better Stop Selling It. Julian Scott (b), Justin Hildreth (d) r Watts, Irwin. 28/10/76 MV4 TW U

1/9/77 Love And The Single Girl, Easy Talk, Mind Breeding, Sweet Moma. Adler (lv-3, 4), Plytas (lv-1). 16/8/77 MV4 MB MR

Room 101

28/9/83 101, I've Got Your Number, Rivers, I'm Not Your Kind. Danny Senninger (kgb, v-3,4), Mae Fortune (k, sy, v-1,2). 21/9/83 MV4 RP TdB

The Room

13/1/81 Who Are Your Friends, Waiting Room, Fever, Crash. Becky Stringer (b), Dave Jackson (v), Clive Thomas (d), Robyn Odlum (b). PRIV

5/10/81 Heat Haze, Bated Breath, Escalator, Rewind, Conversation. 26/9/81 MV4 DG AP

30/6/82 No Dream, Chat Shows, Candle, Summer Sex Signals. 22/5/82 MV4 DG MR

29/4/85 The Storm, Here Comes The Floor, But When Do We Start To Live?, Jeremiah. Jackson, Stringer, Peter Baker (k), Alan Wills (d), Paul Cavanagh (g). 14/4/85 MV5 DG ME Jackson, Stringer & Baker re-formed as Benny Profane (see above). ● SFPS062

Rooney

13/10/99 Used To It, Time Of Day, Birdsong, Touts (Leith). Paul Rooney (gv), Colin Cromer (dkp), Ian Jackson (b). 30/5/99 MV3 TdB JHT

Roovel Oobik

17/4/93 What Ever Makes You Happy, Masters Of Day Dream Machinery, Kitsch Zew Kierkegaard, Betterlife (Recreation Version). Allan Hmelnitski (g), Tarvo Hanno (b, vib), Tonu Pedaru (v), Raul Saaremets (d, g). 20/3/93 MV3 ME~ AA

The Rose of Avalanche

12/6/85 Goddess, A Thousand Landscapes, Gimme Some Lovin', Rise To The Groove. Philip Morris (v), Alan Davis (b), Paul Berry (g), Glenn Schultz (g) & Steve Allen (k). 28/5/85 MV5 MR MR

Jack Rose, Glenn Jones and Simon Joyner

17/11/04 Sad Woman, Four Birds, The Rain Asked For A Holiday, The Only Living Boy In Omaha. As live 17/11/04 MV4 AR~

Jack Rose

9/6/04 Kensington Blues, St Louis Blues, Sundogs, Black Pearls, Now That I'm A Full Grown Man. Jack Rose (agv). 20/5/04 MV4 SA JHT

Tim Rose

1/10/67 Hey Joe, Come Away Melinda, You're Slipping Away From Me, Morning Dew, Fare Thee Well. Tim Rose (ag, v), Alan Weighall (b), Dougie Wright (d). 25/9/67 PC1 BA DT

22/10/67 When I Was A Young Man, Another Side To This Life, I Gotta Do Things My Way, Morning Dew, Hello Sunshine. & David O'List (g) & 3 musicians, drums, bass, guitar, organ & Madeline Bell, Lesley Duncan, Kay Garner (all bck). 16/10/67 AO2 BA U

25/2/68 King Lonely The Blue, Cobwebs, I Got A Loneliness, Come Away Melinda, Memory Pain, Long Time Man. & The Aynsley Dunbar Retaliation, '& Lesley Duncan for 3 singers' (2 & 5: Aynsley Dunbar Retaliation only). 20/2/68 AO2 BA PR

7/7/68 I Guess It's Over, Long-Haired Boy, Roanoke, Foggy Mountain Breakdown. & 2 musicians, including Roger Coulam (o, md). 1/7/68 PC1 BA U

22/9/68 When I Was A Young Man, Angela, Kangaroo, Dim Light, Long-Haired Boy. & (d), (b), (o) unknown. 16/9/68 PC1 BA U

Rote Kapelle

3/12/86 Marathon Man, Sundays, Acid Face Baby, Jellystone Park. Jonathan Muir (d), Malcolm Kergan (b), Chris Henman (g), Ian Binns (k), Margarita Vazquez Ponte & Andrew Tully (perc, v). 9/11/86 U DG SC † On In-Tape Records IT44

Rothko

6/9/00 Pulse Of An Artery, Time Out, Metatonic, Focus Puller, Carnivore. Mark Beazley, Crawford Blair, Jon Meade. 6/8/00 MV4 JSM GT

Roxy Music

21/1/72 Remake Remodel, BOB Medley, Would You Believe, If There Is Something (& Sea Breezes, 18/2/72). Bryan Ferry (kv), Andy MacKay (sx, cl, ob), Eno (sy, el, bck), David O'List (g), Graham Simpson (b), Paul Thompson (d). 4/1/72 T1 JM JWH&BAI

23/6/72 Bitters End, 2HB, Chance Meeting, Ladytron. Phil Manzanera (g), Peter Paul (b) r O'List, Simpson. 23/5/72 T1 JM NG&BAI

1/8/72 Virginia Plain (& If There Is Something, possibly not TX). Rik Kenton (b) r Paul. 18/7/72 MV4 PR MF

9/11/72 The BOB Medley, For Your Pleasure, The Bogus Man Pt II. 6/11/72 LH1 BA U

8/3/73 Editions Of You, Pyjamerama, In Every Dream Home A Heartache. Sal Maida (b) r Kenton. 5/3/73 LH1 BA U

Royal Trux

16/7/93 Suicide Is Painless (Theme From M.A.S.H.), Esso Dame, Sometimes, Halluncination. Neil Hagerty (g, v, k), Michael Kaiser (g), The Mighty Flashlight (d), Jennifer Herrema (v). 7/6/93 MV4 ME~ PA

26/11/93 Fe Cega Faca Amolado, (Edge Of The) Ape Oven, Gett Off, Strawberry Soda. Tom Rafferty (d), Mighty Flashlight (b), Jennifer Herrema (k), Neil Hagerty (g). 26/10/93 MV4 MR PA

Rubella Ballet

6/7/82 Slant And Slide, Belfast, Ballet Dance, T, Me. Sid Attion (d, bck), Gem Stone (b, bck), Peter Fender (g, bck), Zillah Minx (v). 29/5/82 MV4 DG MR

8/2/83 Love Life, Newz, Exit, Blues. Mark Adams (g) r Fender. 26/1/83 U RP MC

Rudi

23/6/80 Time To Be Proud, Without You, The Pressure's On, Yummy Yummy. Brian Young (gv), Ronnie Matthews (bv), Graham Marshall (d). 29/5/80 MV4 CL U

28/9/81 Crimson, Tiger Land, When I Was Dead, Excitement. 21/9/81 U DG HP&GP

The Rudies

26/12/70 Moon Bug, You Make Me So Very Happy, Patches (& Oh Me Oh My, not TX). Danny Smith (d), Trevor Donnelly (b), Sonny Binns (o), Erroll Dann (g), Glenroy

Oakley (v). 23/11/70 PH JW U Auditioned 7/68 as Glenroy Oakley and the Oracles, failed. This trial b/cast failed too: 'Badly played' 'wrong chords' 'pseudo-reggae' 'out of tune' said panel. Reformed as Greyhound May 71

Rugrat

10/9/94 Tommy's Dream/Under The Ladder, In My Day, Grin, Time To Think, Little Pig. Andrew Laing (dv), Ian Armstrong (b), Graham Kirk (g), Sean Tyler (v). 3/8/94 MV4 MA PL

Rumble

9/6/96 Burn The Disco, Jake The Muss, Do Give Up Your Day Job, Chips. Peter Johnson (gv), Genny Ramone (gv), Kieran Quigley (dv), Robert Sharkey (bv). 19/5/96 MV3 ME PL

The Rumour

3/6/77 Something's Going On, Do Nothing 'til You Hear From Me, I'm So Glad, Lookin' After Number One. Brinsley Schwarz (g), Martin Belmont (gv), Andrew Bodnar (b), Steve Goulding (d), Bob Andrews (pv) & Paul Carrack (ov), John Earle (ts), Mick Hanson (tp). 23/5/77 MV4 TW DD

Tom Rush

21/1/68 Sunshine Sunshine, No Regrets, Something In The Way She Moves, Tin Angel. Tom Rush (gv) & 'The Bob Potter 12'. 10/1/68 U U U

James Ruskin & The Drop

24/9/98 DJ set live from MV4 U U

The Russians

19/7/79 Can't Explain, Meet Me After School Tonight, Manic Depression, Stop You're Killing Me. John Brassett (b, bck), Dusty Miller (g), John Lucibello (d), Julie Rebelovitch (lv). 9/7/79 MV4 TW DD

Ruthless Rap Assassins

26/6/89 Three The Hard Way, Posse Strong, Just Mellow. Dangerous Hinds (kv), Dangerous 'C' Carsonova (tt, v), M.C. Kermit le Freak (v), Paul Roberts (g). 4/6/89 MV3 DG ME

The Ruts

29/1/79 Savage Circle, Babylon's Burning, Dope For Guns, Black Man's Pinch, Criminal Mind. Malcolm Owen (lv), Paul Fox (g, bck), Vince 'Segs' Jennings (b, bck), Dave Ruffy (d, bck). 23/1/79 MV4 U MR ○

21/5/79 Sus, Society, You're Just A..., It Was Cold, Something That I Said. & Mannah (bck-1). 14/5/79 MV4 TW DD ○

18/2/80 Staring At The Rude Boys, Demolition Dancing, In A Rut, Secret Soldiers. 11/2/80 MV4 TW DD ○ SFRCD109

10/3/81 Different View, Parasites, Fools Lead The Fools, Mirror Smashed. Billed as Ruts DC from now on: Segs, Ruffy, Fox & Gary Barnacle (sx, k). 16/2/81 LH1 TW DD See Zion Train

Sabres Of Paradise

24/3/95 Blackfriars Sunday, Duke On Berwick, Stanshalls Lament. Phil Mossman (g), Keith Tenniswood (g), Nick Abnett (b), Gary Burns (k), Jagz Kooner (k), Andrew Weatherall (perc). 13/3/95 OS

Sad Lovers and Giants

3/12/81 Alice Isn't Playing, There Was No Time, Sex Without Gravity, Clint. Garcon (v), Tristian Garel-Funk (g), Cliff Silver (b), Nigel (d), David (k, sx). 25/11/81 MV4 RP NG

Bridget St John

28/8/68 To Be Without A Hitch, Ask Me No Questions, Many Happy Returns, Rochefort, Lizard-Long-Tongue Boy. Bridget St John (agv). 21/8/68 S1 DK U 'Borderline pass' from audition panel: critical comments included 'pretentious rubbish' 'her guitar-playing is inaccurate and uninspired and her voice dull'

24/8/69 Curl Your Toes, Night In The City†, Hello Again (Of Course) (& Song To Keep You Company†, The River†, Lazarus†, Like Never Before, 18/10/69). 21/7/69 MV1 JW TW&MF † On ● Top Gear LP BBC Records

21/11/70 Back To Stay, The Leaves Of Lime, City Crazy, If You'd Been There. 9/11/70 PH JW U

25/4/72 Thank You For, Happy Day, Silver Coin, Fly High. & 1 (unknown). 27/3/72 PH JW BC

7/7/72 Fly High, To Leave Your Cover, If You've Got Money In Your Pockets, Ask Me No Questions. & 3 unknown. 5/6/72 MV5 JM U

7/6/73 Sparrow Pit, Passing Thru, Jumble Queen, The Road Was Lonely On My Own. & 3 (unknown). 7/5/73 LH1 BA U

18/12/73 Curious & Woolly, Choosing You Lose One, Jumble Queen, Sparrow Pit, In The Bleak Midwinter. 3/12/73 T1 TW U

29/8/74 Want To Be With You, Waterden Widow, Some Kind Of Beautiful, I Don't Know If I Can Take It, Present Song. 12/8/74 LH1 JW U

7/1/76 Come Up And See Me Sometime, Catch A Falling Star, Untitled Song, Bumper To Bumper. & 1 (unknown). 11/12/75 MV4 U U

26/11/76 Moody, Grow, Crazy Have You Eton, Song For You. 4/11/76 MV4 U U

St Johnny

20/8/93 Bow And Arrow, Lo City, Mr Clarinet, Fields & Fields Of People. Bill Whitten (gv), Tom Leonard (g), Jim Elliot (b, Moog), Wayne Letitia (d). 18/7/93 MV3 JB GT

Salako

3/2/99 My Booroo Clow, Don't Be Afraid, Sunburst, Seeing Colours In Front Of Your Eyes, The Truth In Me. Luke Barwell (b, k, perc, cl), James Waudby (v, g, claps, whistling), Thomas Spencer (d, perc, claps), David Langdale (g, k, cel). 20/12/98 MV3 ME PN

Salaryman

2/9/97 The Companion, My Hands Are Always In Water, Thomas Jefferson Airplane, A Dresden Seventh. Richard Valentin (sy, smp), Rosanne Marshack (sy, smp), James Valentin (sy, o), Howard Kantoff (d). 10/8/97 MV4 KR LS

Sally Angie

4/12/68 Children Of The Sun, Song Of The Healer, Flee The Melancholy Flower, Lady Mary, Midsummer Night Happening. Sally Oldfield (gpv), Mike Oldfield (g). 3/12/68 PC1 PC U

Saloon

21/8/01 Spacer, Bicycle Thieves, Make It Soft, Girls Are The New Boys. Adam Cresswell (sy), Michael Smoughton (d), Alison Cotton (vla), Matt Ashton (g, th), Amanda Gomez (gv). 4/7/01 MV4 MA NF

7/8/02 Have You Seen The Light, Absence, 2500 Walden Wave, Le Weekend, The Good Life, Impact. Live from MV4 NF~ GT&SA

16/4/03 Vesuvius, Kaspian, Happy Robots, I Could Have Loved A Tyrant. 19/3/03 MV4 RJ NS

Salt Tank

5/8/94 Charged Up, Olympic, Melt Down, Isabella's Dream. Malcolm Stanners (prg, mx), David Gates (prg, mx). 12/6/94 MV3 ME SCO

Sammy

7/1/95 Babe Come Down, Inland Empire, Slim Style, Trick Mammouth. Jesse Hartman (v, g, p), Luke Wood (gb), Brendon O'Malley (d). 27/11/94 MV3 TD CBO

Samurai Seven

24/11/98 Lois Lane, Amateur Photographer, I've Lost That Loving Feeling, See You. Simon Williams (gv), Matt Williams (rgv), Jimmy Martin (bv), Chris Hayward (d). 13/9/98 MV3 ME PN

26/1/00 Bonnet, If You Only Knew, I Am Yours, Take On Me. 28/11/99 MV3 NF ME

29/2/00 Don't Go Breaking My Heart, It's Different For Girls, I'm Telling You Now, Thank You For The Music. 9/1/00 MV3 ME MPK

21/3/01 Population You, Nunnery, What Have I Said Now, And Your Bird Can Sing. & Joe Bennett (vi, tp, elp). 11/2/01 MV4 SA NF

2/5/02 Flaming Hell Blake, Lucky Pierre, Xeroxy Music, Wherewithal. & Jim Crosskey (k). 17/3/02 MV4 ME GT

Sandmen

26/11/93 Dust Devil, Bringing It All Back, Pit Bull. Patrick L Seaman (v), Richard Smith (g), Steve Baker (b), Grant McDonald (perc, bck), Charlie Moore (d). 12/10/93 MV4 MR JMK

Bob Sargeant

10/4/73 King Of The Night, Love Of A Kind, Situation. Bob Sargeant (kgv), Walt Monohan (b), Ritchie Darma (d), Jack Lancaster (ts, ss, fl). 27/3/73 U JW U

1/1/74 Sunshine Blue, Between You And Me, Situation, The Waiting Game. & Jeff Sharkey (g). 11/12/73 LH1 JW U

13/6/74 Let Yourself Go, Never Again, First Starring Role. & John Woods (d), Robin Lumley (k). 30/5/74 LH1 TW U

2/6/75 Situation, Can You Feel It, Everyday's A Lonely Day, Sunshine Blue / First Starring Role. & 3 (unknown). 21/5/75 U TW U

29/4/76 Broadway, Prisoner Of Love, The Radio Goes On Forever, Here We Go Again. & Monahan, Clive Bunker (d). 6/4/76 U JE MR

21/6/77 Dancing At The Jook Joint, City Kids, Life Theme / Story Of My Life, Open Up Your Heart. & Sharkey, Monahan, Bunker, Barbara Sargeant (bck), Pat Sharkey (bck, rec). 14/6/77 MV4 JG MR

Peter Sarstedt

25/9/68 Steel Flamingos, I Am A Cathedral, Blagged, Time Love Hope Life, The Artist. U 25/9/68 S1 U U

Sassafras

26/7/73 Busted Country Blues, Expecting Company, Beans And Things, Goose That Lays The Golden Egg (& School Days, 30/8/73). Terry Bennett (v), David Shell

(g), Richard Holt (b), Ralph Evans (g), Peter Stroud (d). 23/7/73 U BA U Group did audition tape in Birmingham 1/72; 'borderline pass' from R1 audition panel. 1st Session for Bob Harris, June 73. Files missing, no subsequent details available
17/1/74 Box Car Hobo, To Ethel, Ohio, Schooldays. 14/1/74 U BA U

Paul Savage and John Hewitt

19/6/71 Blue, Carry On, It's Been A Long Time. Paul Savage (gv), John Hewitt (gv). 7/6/71 U JW U

Savage Progress

26/7/84 Reclaim The Night, Burning Bush, Hip Parade, Ball And Chain. Glynis Thomas (v), Rik Kenton (b), Ned Morant (perc), Carol Isaacs (k), Stewart Elliott (d). 18/7/84 MV5 RP NG

Savoy Brown Blues Band

30/6/68 Louisiana Blues, Walkin' By Myself, Gnome Sweet Gnome, Mr Down Child. Chris Youlden (v), Kim Simmonds (g), David Peverett (g), Roger Earl (d), Bob Hall (p), Rivers Jobe (b). 20/5/68 PC1 BA U Verdict of panel? 'Regretfully, yes'
25/5/69 Ring In His Nose, I've Made Up My Mind, Train To Nowhere, Don't Turn Me From Your Door (& Life's One Act Play, 29/6/69). 19/5/69 PH JW TW
10/1/70 You'd Better Pray For The Lord To Guide You, A Hard Way To Go, When I Was A Young Boy. Tony Steven r Jobe, Hall. 6/1/70 MV4 U U Now billed as just Savoy Brown

Leo Sayer

20/9/73 Tomorrow, Innocent Bystander, Why Is Everybody Going Home. Leo Sayer (v), James Litherland (g), Dave Rose (k), Bill Smith (b), John Dentith (d). 3/9/73 LH1 BA MF 'Must have a Top 3 hit in the next few months!' wrote Bernie in his report to Audition Unit. He did

Scaffold

10/3/68 Yellow Book, Do You Remember, Carry On Krow, Please Don't Run Too Fast. Mike McGear, Roger McGough, John Gorman, Dave Mason (bck) & The John Cameron Group. 5/3/68 AO2 BA U 1st broadcast was on Light Programme 1966

Scala Timpani

20/2/85 Crazy, Utopian Sunday, The Underlined Reaction. Russel Courtenay (d), Alistair Broadhead (b), Chesh Wegrzynski (g), Simon Elliott-Kemp (k), Russell Bonnell (v). 10/2/85 MV5 DG ME

Scarfo

12/5/96 Bingo Engald, Ultra Paj, Safe Cracker, Latino. Jamie Hince (gv), Nick Prior (b), Al Saunders (d). 15/4/96 MV4 CML~ U
17/3/98 Good Cop Bad Cop, Sinatra Cars, One Eighty, Americana. & Tim Cedar (k). 17/2/98 MV4 MR PA

The Scars

6/3/80 She's Alive, So Strong, Author! Author!, Je T'aime C'est Le Mort. Bobby King (v), Paul Research (gv), John Mackie (b), Calumn Mackay (d). 20/2/80 MV4 JE NG
4/6/81 Remember Me, Turn Me On, Vanishing, They Came And Took Her. Steve McLaughlin (d) r Mackay. 20/5/81 LH1 PS NG&GP

Schlaflose Nachte

11/11/81 Same Mistake Twice, Touch Me, Recall. Gila Mousson (v, b, perc), Bernie von Braun (sy, g, b, perc), Peter Prima (d). 2/11/81 MV4 TW DD

Schneider TM

17/12/03 Abyss, From Toi Se, Cuba, Onkel Nokko, DJ Guy, Reality Check. Schneider (Dirk Dresselhaus), Kptmichigan. Live from MV4 AR GT

Scientist

6/1/91 The Bee, The Exorcist, The Circle. U 13/12/90 MV5 DG NG&DTH

Scorn

23/10/92 Heavy Blood, Ultra Nova, Wall of Silence. Mick Harris (d, el), Nicholas Bullen (bv), Paul Neville (g). 20/9/92 MV3 ME~ RF
19/8/94 Almost Human, Maker Of Angels, Scorpionic. James Plotkin (g, sy) r Neville. 10/7/94 MV3 ME SBR

Scotch Egg

16/12/04 10–min DJ mix for Keepin' It Peel night live from MV3 GYW JHT

Robin Scott

23/4/69 The Sun, Morning Rain, Mara's Supper, Penelope, Port Of Leaving, I Am Your Suitcase Lover. Robin Scott (gv). 21/4/69 S1 PR U

Scratch Perverts

26/1/99 Intro, DJ Mix Set pt 1, DJ Mix Set pt 2, DJ Mix Set pt 3, DJ Mix Set pt 4, DJ Mix Set pt 5, Outro. Mr Thing (Marc Bowles), Prime Cuts (Joel Clements), Tony Kelley (Tony Vagas), Paul Bruce (First Rate). Live from MV4 MR~
31/8/99 Happy Birthday (beatbox version), various other mixes. Live from MV3 AR SA

Scrawl

16/10/93 Charles, Green Beer, Absolute Torture, Great American Pastime, Love's Insecticide. Marcy Mays (gv), Sue Harshe (b, v, p), Dana Marshall (d). 12/9/93 MV3 ME RJ

Scream and Dance

25/3/82 Giacometti, Cat Scat, Sumo Man, Slow Movement. Amanda Stewart (v), Ruth George-Jones (v), John Langley (d), Julian Dale (db), John Carley (cga), Simon Preston (perc). 27/2/82 MV4 DG MR
1/2/83 Proverbs, I Get This, Unequal Portions, Let Me Out. George-Jones & Sarah Gagg (v), Marco (d), Simon Sansa Preston & Kenny Bongo Lacey (perc), Dan Catsis (bg). 19/1/83 MV4 RP NG

The Screaming Blue Messiahs

2/8/84 Good And Gone, Someone To Talk To, Tracking The Dog, Let's Go Down To The Woods And Pray. Bill Carter (gv), Chris Thompson (b, bck), Kenny Harris (d). 24/7/84 MV5 MRD MR ● SFPS003

Screen 3

16/2/83 Red Dust, Wet Playtime, Refugee, Wonders Of Wildlife. Brett Cooper (d), Richard Kett (b), Neil Dyer (gv), Peter Jay (tp), Jason Votier (tp). 9/2/83 MV4 RP NG 1st session for Jensen Jan 82
2/11/83 Broke And In Love, I'm Not Impressed, There She Goes Again, The Visitor. & Steve Osbourne (tb). 24/10/83 MV4 TW MC

Scritti Politti

13/12/78 The Humours Of Spitalfields, Knowledge And Interest, Doubt Beat, 5/12/78. Green (g), Tom (d), Nial (b). 5/12/78 MV4 TW MR
4/7/79 Messthetics, Hegemony, Scritt Locks Door, The New One. 20/6/79 MV4 JS NG
24/5/82 Asylums In Jerusalem, A Slow Soul, Jacques Derrida. Green, Tom & Joe Cang (b), Mike McAvoy (k) & Jackie Challenor (bck), Lorenza Johnson (bck), Mae McKenna (bck). 15/5/82 MV4 DG MC

Sea Nymphs

5/11/98 Sea Snake Beware, Eating A Heart Out, Lillywhites Party, The Sea Ritual. Tim Smith (bv), William D Drake (v, p, cel), Sarah Squidsmith (v, sx, k). 4/10/98 MV3 ME KR

Seaweed

31/7/92 Squint, Sit In Class, She's Cracked, Bewitched. Clint Werner (g), John Akins (b), Wade Neal (g), Bob Bulgrien (d), Aaron Staupfer (v). 12/7/92 MV3 ME SA

Sebadoh

28/8/92 Pot Doesn't Help, Close Enuff, Circle Game, Slints, Mouldy Bread. Eric Gaffney (d), Lou Barlow (gv), Jason Loewenstein (bv). 9/8/92 MV4 TdB SA&TdB
8/5/93 Fast Times At Riot Grrl High, Hassle, Sixteen, Pro Brush. 4/4/93 MV3 ME~ AA
7/5/94 Riding, Crest, Whole Hog, Beauty Of The Ride. Bob Fay (d, bck) r Gaffney. 10/4/94 MV5 TD LS

Sebastian's Men

18/4/84 Hurt So Frighten So Hate So, Horizon, Forever And Ever In The Icehouse, A Solo Prodigy. Mike McCaroll (d), Tony Elliott (b), David Hogg (g), Ian Cowpland (lg), Margie Henderson (v). 27/3/84 MV5 MRD TdB

Marta Sebestyen

13/4/88 Csardas, The Train, Dunantuli Tancok, Szeki Tancok, Szeress Egyet. Marta Sebestyen (v) 'and Muzsikas': Damiel Hamar (b, cymbalon), Peter Eri (hca, tarogata), Mihaily Sipas (vi), Sandor Csoori (bpp, vla). 5/4/88 MV4 DG MA

Secret Affair

25/7/79 I'm Not Free (But I'm Cheap), Glory World, My World, Goin' To A Go-Go. Ian Page (v, tr), Dave Cairns (g, bck), Dennis Smith (b, bck), Seb Shelton (d). 18/7/79 MV4 TVD NG
26/11/79 I'm Not Free (But I'm Cheap), Get Ready, New Dance. & Dave Winthrop (sx). 7/11/79 MV4 DS NG

Secret Goldfish

1/7/97 Four Excited People, Top Of The World, Hey Mr Fox, Pink Drone. John Morose (g, syn), Katy McCullars (v), Steven McSeveny (b), Paul Turnbull (d). 15/6/97 MV4 ME RF
14/7/99 Funny 'Bout That Aren't You, Stop That Girl, Scene Cruiser, Sea Sick. & Francis Macdonald (k). 4/5/99 MV4 MR RJ

Secret Hairdresser

2/3/04 Verse Chorus Miaow, Speed Of Snow, Coulda Shoulda Woulda, Its Not My Problem, A Peelogy Apology. Jason Badlock (gv, smp), Julia Kidd (b), Jamie Dodd (g), Lucy Painell (k, smp, v), Robert Crawford (dv). 17/2/04 MV4 GT NS

Section 25

20/1/81 Babies In The Bardo, Hit, One True Path. Larry Cassidy (bv), Vincent Cassidy (d), Paul Wiggin (g, tps). 13/1/81 LH1 BS HP

Seedling

16/5/01 Sensational Vacuum, Cool Baby My Hips Go Woo, Every Match Must Crash And Burn, High On The Downside, William Tell Me. Marg Van Eenbergen (gv), Suzanne Linssen (v, vi, smp), Bas Jacobs (b, g), Mariken Smit (d). Live from MV4 SCU SA

11/4/02 The Upshot, Attack, About To Fall, Put Your Hand Under My Shirt. & Arnold De Boer (ag, k). 20/1/02 MV4 SA KR

24/7/03 Pink Volvo, Hey Man, Headnoiz, Ms Jackson, Jingle 1, Jingle 2. 5/6/03 MV4 SA JHT

Seefeel

27/5/94 Vex, Phasemaze, Rough For Radio, Starethrough. Mark Clifford (g, seq, prg), Daren Seymour (b), Sarah Peacock (v), Justin Fletcher (perc, d). 10/4/94 MV4 DD SBR

Peggy Seeger

15/1/69 My Love And I Are One, The Children, The Song Of Choice, Che Guevara, Fill Up Your Glasses. Peggy Seeger (agv). 13/1/69 S1 JM U

The Selecter

22/10/79 They Make Me Mad, Carry Go Bring Come, Street Feeling, Danger. Pauline Black (lv), Noel Davies (gv), Gappa Hendrickson (v), Compton Amanor (g), Desmond Brown (k), Charley 'Ironfinger' Anderson (b, bck), Charlie Bembridge (alias Charley H) (d). 9/10/79 MV4 JS MR

1/12/80 Selling Out Your Future, Deep Water, Tell What's Wrong, Washed Up And Left For Dead. James Mackie (o) r Brown. 10/11/80 LH1 TW AP

Send No Flowers

1/7/82 Days Of Rage, Caprice, Ashes, Beneath The Dreams. Lyn (gv), Timmo (g, k), Paul (b), Jake (d), Alan (perc). 26/5/82 U U U

Sender Berlin

11/5/00 Three pieces, titles unknown. Torsten Litschko, Hendrik Vaak. 11/5/00 recorded 'as live' in their flat, Berlin earlier that day by AR~ Peel after session: 'No titles as far as we know… 1st time I can remember doing a programme which went out on 2 stations simultaneously, BBC Radio 1 and Radio Eins'

Senseless Prayer

4/8/99 Step Number One, Slow Breathing Still Tongue, The Sky Is Making Shapes Again, Eleven Sticks. Charlie Hildebrandt (b, k), Fyfe Hutchings (gv), Alex Rajkowski (d, bells, squeaking sounds). 2/5/99 MV3 ME~

The Senseless Things

27/4/88 Passions Out Of Town, I've Lost My Train, When You Let Me Down, The Only One. Cass Cade (d), Morgan Plusfour (b), Ben S Thing (g), Mark Oblivion (gv). 27/3/88 U DG ME&JBN

21/3/90 Tangled Lines, Leo/It Is Too Late, Tell Me What Is On Your Mind, Someone's Talking 'Bout You. 27/2/90 MV5 DG MR

20/11/93 Tough Me On The Heath, Jerk, Role Models, Christian Killer. 28/10/93 MV4 PA SBR

Senser

27/8/93 States Of Mind, Door Game, What's Going On, Switch. Heitham Al-Sayed (v, perc), Kerstin Haigh (v, fl), James Barrett (b), Nick Michaelson (g), John Morgan (d), Andy Clinton (dj). 17/8/93 MV4 MR RJ

19/3/94 No Comply, Channel Zero, Peanut Head, Chicken In My Fantasies. 8/3/94 MV4 MR MA

The Sensible Jerseys

19/6/85 Wasting My Time, Crucial Information, People All Around The World, Two-Way Radio. Simmy Richman (d), Stephen Booker (bck, b), Andrew Cunningham (gv), David Clifton (bck, g, o). 9/6/85 MV4 DG ME

Serious Drinking

6/5/82 Spirit Of '66, Love On The Terraces, Hangover, He's An Angry Bastard But I Like Him, Walk Alone. Jem Moore (b), Andy Hearshaw (g), Eugene McCarthy (v), Martin Ling (v), Simon (d). 26/4/82 MV5 TW DD

27/9/82 R.G.B, Countdown To Bilko, 12 X U / Bobby Moore Was Innocent, Drugs, Yours Or Mine. Lance Dunlop (d) r Simon. 13/9/82 MV4 TW DD

13/1/83 Don't Shoot Me Down, Revolution Starts At Closing Time, Wonderful World Beautiful People, Baby I'm Dying A Death. 10/1/83 U TW DD

3/10/83 Closer Closer, Go For The Burn, Weird Son Of Angry Bastard, Our Time. Pete Saunders (k) joins. 26/9/83 MV4 TW MC

The Servants

24/3/86 A Fleeting Visit, Rings On Her Finger, You'd Do Me Good, She Whom Once I Dreamt Of. David Westlake (gv), John Mohan (lg), Philip King (b), John Wills (d). 16/3/86 MV5 DG ME&FK

Servotron

21/5/97 Slave To The Metal Horde, Red Robot Refund (Ballad Of R5 D4), Mechanisms In The Forever Loop, I Sing The Body Cybernetic. Hayden Thais (gv), Brian Teasley (d), Ashley Teasley (kv), Andy Baker (b). 27/4/97 MV4 ME JLO

Sewing Room

2/3/96 Slide, Rope, Ghost, Borderline Vice. Eamonn Davis (gv), Stan Erraught (gv), Colm Fitzpatrick (b, bck), Dez Foley (d, bck). 25/2/96 MV3 ME PA

The Sex Clark Five

18/7/90 Microwave Music, Modern Fix, Netta Grew Up Last, Mongol Song, America Under The Mongol Yoke Prelude, Can't Shake Loose (& She Collides With Me, 6/9/90). Jamse Butler, Rick Storey, Joy Johnson, Trick McKaha. Rec. date unknown, at Birland Studio, Alabama, USA U U

20/5/94 A Chance/Crime/Dark Eyed Brooch, Ashabanipaul, Faith/Brandy On Fire, Window To The Works/Silver Wave, Alai. OS

26/7/00 Prove You're Wrong, Talent Is An Asset, Capetown Races, Radio Pretoria, Harrier, (She Loved Me) Yesterday, Moonrock, Bastille Sun, Khartoum, Antedium, She Don't Care About Time. Laura E Lee (bv) r Johnson. OS

11/6/02 All Marc Bolan covers: By The Light, Light Of Love, Fist Heart Mighty Dawn Dart, She Was Born To Be My Unicorn, For So Long / I Was Looking At Her / Cut Up Ray. OS

Sex Gang Children

11/11/82 Kill Machine, German Nun, State Of Mind, Sebastiane. Andi (v), Rob Stroud (d), Terry MacLean (g), Dave Roberts (b). 27/10/82 MV4 RP MC

The Shadows

25/12/73 Nivram, Jungle Jam, Turn Around And Touch Me, Wonderful Land. '4 & 1, Mo Foster (b)' says sheet. 10/12/73 T1 JW MR&ARV

Shadowy Men On A Shadowy Planet

26/6/93 Telepathic, They Used To Pay Him To Watch The Trains, The Jehrny, The Last Of My Hiccups, 16 Encores. Brian Connelly (g), Reid Diamond (b), Don Pyle (d). 23/5/93 MV3 ME~ GPR

Shake

30/4/79 (But) Not Mine, Glasshouse, Night By Night, Teenbeat. Angel Patterson (d), Simon Templar (bv), Troy Tate (t), Jo Callis (gv). 23/4/79 MV4 CL DD&MPK

Shalawambe

12/9/88 Mulemena, Samora Machel, Mulamu. Julius Kabwe (d), Claudie Kabwe (b), Ricky Chota (rg), Dolenzy Kabwe (lg, lv), Gerard Bwalanda (k) & Victoria, Beatrice & Agnes (cga, perc, bck). 23/8/88 U MR MR

Sham 69

6/12/77 Borstal Breakout, Hey Little Rich Boy, They Don't Understand, Rip Off, What 'Av We Got. Jimmy Pursey (lv), Dave Parsons (b, bck), Dave Treganna (g, bck), Mark Cain (d), various others (bck). 28/11/77 MV4 TW DD

The Shamen

13/1/87 Strange Day's Dream, Passing Away, Through My Window, Where Do You Go? Keith (d), Colin (bv), Derek (gv), Peter (k). 14/12/86 U DG ME&TD

12/4/88 Knature Of A Girl, War Prayer, Nothing, Misinformation. Will (b) r Derek; Colin (g). 29/3/88 U DG DD&JB

2/8/89 Transcendental, What's Going Down, Negation State, Phorward. Colin, Will, John Delafons (d). 13/6/89 ED DG MR

23/3/91 Hyperreal, Make It Mine, Possible Worlds, In The Bag. Colin, Will, Plavka (v), Ley Icon (tt, rp), Mr Mr Man (sfx, mx). 12/2/91 MV5 MR MR

Shanghai

16/2/76 Shakin' All Over, Candy Eyes, Over The Wall, Let's Get The Hell Off The Highway. Cliff Bennett (v), Mick Green (g), Brian Alterman (g), Speedy King (b, bck), Pete Kircher (d, bck). 5/2/76 MV4 MB U

Sharon Shannon

22/10/94 Sparky, Sandy River Bell, Out The Gap, Untitled, Big Mistake. Sharon Shannon (acc, fi), Donosh Hennessy (g), Mary Custy (fi), Trevor Hutchinson (db). Live from EG2 U U

The Shapes

11/4/79 Airline Disaster, Business Calls, Beans / Bedtime Stories, Leamington. Seymour Bybuss (v), Steve Richards (g), Tim Jee (g), Bryan Helicopter (b), Dave Gee (d). 3/4/79 MV6 TVD MR

Sandie Shaw

5/12/88 Girl Called Johnny, Cool About You, Flesh And Blood, Strange Bedfellows. Sandie Shaw (v), Kevin Armstrong (g), Richard Coles (k), Andrew Paresi (d), Phil Sewell (b, bck), Clare Hirst (sx, bck). 27/11/88 HP DG ME Previous recent sessions for Janice Long (86) and Liz Kershaw (88)

Shellac

22/7/94 Spoke, Canada, Crow, Disgrace. Steve Albini (gv), Bob Weston (bv), Todd Trainer (d). 14/7/94 MV3 JB JLO

2/12/04 Ghosts, The End Of Radio, Canada, Paco, Steady As She Goes, Billiard Player Song, Dog And Pony Show, 'Il Porno Star. As live 1/12/04 MV4 AR NF/GYW

Shesus

2/12/03 Geddit, Weapons Of Love Destruction, Black Cloud, Space Truckin'. Heather Newkirk (v), Kari Murphy (bv), Michelle Boding (gv), Craig Nichols (d). 6/11/03 MV4 JHT MA

Shillelagh Sisters

14/3/84 Beetle Bug Bop, Black Cadillac, Romp And Stomp. Jacquie O'Sullivan (lv), Lynder Halpin (db), Tricia O'Flynn (sx), Mitzi Ryan (d), Boz Boorer (g). 6/3/84 MV5 RP TdB

Johnny Shines

21/3/70 Kind Hearted Woman, Ramblin', No Mail Today, Dynaflow (& I Tried And I Tried, 20/6/70). Johnny Shines (gv). 17/3/70 MV4 JW U

Shitmat

26/8/04 Shitmix by Henry Collins OS

16/12/04 10–min DJ mix for Keepin' It Peel night live from MV5 GYW JHT

Shoes for Industry

25/9/79 Devil Dogs, War Of The Potatoes, Shell Shock, Fear Of Wages. John Schofield (d), Steve Lonnen (b), Andy Leighton (g), Steve Franklin (k), Paul B Davies (v, sx). 10/9/79 MV4 JE DD&MPK

Shonen Knife

25/1/92 Flying Jelly Attack, Watchin' Girl, Tortoise Brand Pot Cleaner's Theme, Antonio Baka Guy, Boys, Chinese Song. Atsuko Yamano (dv), Michie Nakatani (bv), Naoko Shibata (gv). 8/12/91 MV3&4 DG ME

2/10/92 Get The Wow, Animal Song, Ice Cream City, Elmer Elevator, I Am A Cat. Naoko Yamano (gv) r Shibita. 01/10/92 MV3 DG SA/DMC

Shoot

21/12/72 Ships And Sails, Neon Life, Stars And Sorrows (& Living Blind, 18/1/73). Jim McCarty (pv), Craig Collins (d), Bill Russell (b), Dave Green (lgv). 4/12/72 LH1 BA BC

Shoot! Dispute

9/2/84 Lack Lustre, Can't Believe, The Great Explainer, Fun Time. Cathy Lomax (v), Mark Charles (d), Steve Smith (b, bck), Denzil Daniels (perc), Scampi (sx). 4/2/84 MV5 DG PW

14/6/84 Monkey, Power Of Persuasion, Gatgun, Love For Sale. & Dylan (g, bck). 6/6/84 MV5 RP DD

The Shop Assistants

21/10/85 Safety Net, All That Ever Mattered, Almost Made It, Somewhere In China. Alex Taylor (v), David Keegan (g), Sarah Kneale (b), Laura McPhail (d), Ann Donald (d). 8/10/85 MV5 PWL MR

20/2/86 Home Again, All Of The Time, Looking Back, What A Way To Die, Nature Lover. Joan Bride r Donald. 16/2/86 MV4 BYA SC

8/12/86 Fixed Grin, I Don't Wannna Be Friends With You, Ace Of Spades, Before I Wake. Bride out. 11/11/86 U DG MFA&JB

Short Commercial Break

14/10/82 Oxo, Yorkie, Smarties, Bran Flakes. Kirsty (bck, g), Effy (d, bck), Bernie (lv), Allan (b). 18/8/82 U CL U 'Not to be broadcast' is written over the sheet, although the TX date written in suggests that it was

Shriek

8/10/94 Crush, Girl Meets Girl, Violent Mind, Silver Head. Ros Cairney (gv), Mark Welsh (b), Gordon Roberts (d). 28/9/94 MV5 ME TD

Shriekback

11/8/82 All The Greek Boys (Do The Hand Walk), My Spine (Is The Base Line), Feelers. David Allen, Barry Andrews, Carl Marsh (all 3 – b, k, g, vi, v), Martyn Barker (d, perc-1) & Stephanie Nuttall (d, perc-2), John Murphy (d, perc-3). 26/7/82 MV4 TW DD 1st session for Jensen Feb 82

15/3/84 New Home, Under The Lights, Suck. Barker out; & Emma Burnham, Linda Neville, Helen Musto (bck-1,3). 7/3/84 MV5 MRD NG

10/6/85 Everything That Rises Must Converge, Fish Beneath The Ice, Faded Flowers. Barker returns; & Clare Torry (bck). 2/6/85 MV5 DG ME

The Shrubs

2/7/86 John Corpse, Black Mailer, Animal, Assassin. John Bentley (d), Stephen Brockway (b), Julian Hutton (g), Michael Ricketts (g), Mick Hobbs (v). 22/6/86 HP DG FK&PS

26/8/87 Sullen Days Are Over, King Urn, Papa Chaperon, Ballet Gorilla. Mark Grebby (b) r Brockway. 26/8/87 U DG U

Shut Up and Dance

29/8/90 White White World, A Change Soon Come, Lamborghini, 5678. DJ Hype (tt), PJ (v), Smiley C (v). 5/8/90 MV3 DG ME&FK

28/3/92 Autobiography Of A Crack Head, Love Is All We Need, Strut Your Stuff, Green Man. 23/1/92 MV5 DG MA&AR

The Siddeleys

28/9/88 Something Almost Brilliant Happened Last Night, You Get What You Deserve, I Wish I Was Good, Every Day Of Every Week. Allan Kingdom (g), Johnny Johnson (v), David Clynch (d). 13/9/88 MV4 MC MC

23/5/89 My Favorite Wet Wednesday Afternoon, Theft, Love With Blood, When I Grow Up I'll Be A God. & Jonathan Stein (sy). 18/4/89 WX DG MR

Sights

23/3/96 Nobody Knows, Change Your Mind, Passenger 23, Elvis Loves You. Nat Perkins (d), Lee Jakeman (b), Simon Collin (g), Steve Parker (g), John Perkins (v). 13/3/96 MV4 DD KH

Signorinas

12/11/81 Neutral, Cocktail Party, Escalator, City Golfer. Richard Wise (d), Doug Hendrey (perc), Patrick Hawkins (b), Andrew White (g), Artemis Pittas (v), Iliona Outram (v). 4/11/81 MV4 RP NG

Sigur Ros

26/9/00 Track 1, Track 2, Cold. Jon Por Birgisson (gv), Georg Holm (b), Kjarton Sveinsson (k), OrriPall Dyrason (d). 20/8/00 MV4 ME KR

Silicone

18/6/98 Stranded, To The Edge, Watad Dagray, Silence, Free. Lucie Chivers (pv), Jennie Gibbs (fl), Chris Gibbs (b, g), Patrick Chivers (d, g), Jason Bromfield (g). 12/4/98 MV4 ME NK

Silverfish

2/11/89 Driller, (Shed) Out Of Luck, Fat Painted Carcass. Fuzz Duprey (g), Les Rankin (v), Chris P Mowforth (b, bck), Stuart Watson (d). 5/10/89 MV3 DG DD

28/4/91 Harry Butcher, Pink & Lovely, Big Bad Baby Pig Squeal, 3 Puppy Pie. 2/4/91 MV5 MR MR

12/1/92 Jimmy, Crazy, Vitriola, Rock On. 26/11/91 MV4 MR MR

Simba Wanyika

13/9/90 Shillingi, Sikujva Vtabadilika, Mama Maria, Pamela. George Peter Fkinyonga (gv), Wilson Peter Kinyonga (gv), Victor Boniface (b), Mike Beche (d, bck), Hassan Mwachimwengu (cga). 24/7/90 MV5 MR~ 1st session rec for Andy Kershaw 5 days before

Simple Minds

7/1/80 Changeling, Premonition, Citizen (Dance Of Youth), Room. Jim Kerr (v), Charles Burchill (g), Michael McNeil (k), Derek Forbes (b), Brian McGee (d). 19/12/79 MV4 TVD NG 1st session for Jensen April 79

1/3/82 I Promised You A Miracle, Love Song, Sons And Fascination, King Is White And In The Crowd. 15/2/82 U U U

Martin Simpson

15/7/77 Soldier's Joy, You Win Again, Green Fields Of America, The Wild Bill Jones Medley / Georgia Railroad / Cluck Old Hen, Satan Your Kingdom Must Come Down. Martin Simpson (g, bj, v). 6/7/77 MV4 MB NG

The Sinatras

7/12/81 Finding Your Own Level, That Shape, New Clothes, The Chameleon Complex. Neil Pearson (d), Tom Hamilton (bv), Nev Hunt (g, bck), Nick Hannah (k, bck) & John Barrow (sx), Dean Sargent (tp). 28/11/81 MV4 DG MR

Sink

14/12/87 Re-begin, Chocolate Love, I Hate Yourself, Baby. Ed Shred (gv), Sunil Kittur (b-3,4), Purple Paul (b-1,2), Tommy Stupid (g), Pete Whitehouse (d). 6/12/87 U DG ME&PL

20/9/88 Birthday Song, Diamonds, For Want Of…, Perspective. Shred, Paul, Def Metro Pete-Gnome (d), Blind Lorenze Hoss Cash (v), Red Wood Jim (hca, vib), Legs (tamb). 21/8/88 HP DG ME

20/6/90 Echo, One Final Kick In The Head, Amanush, Walking With Me Blues. Shred, Kermack (d), Paul Sky (hca, b), John Ruscoe (g). 8/5/90 MV3 MR MR

Siouxsie and the Banshees ○

5/12/77 Love In A Void, Mirage, Metal, Suburban Relapse. Siouxsie (lv), Kenny Morris (d), Steve Severin (b), John McKay (g). 29/11/77 MV4 MB MR ● SFPS012

23/2/78 Hong Kong Garden, Overground, Carcass, Helter Skelter. 6/2/78 MV4 TW DD ● SFPS066

16/4/79 Placebo Effect, Playground Twist, Regal Zone, Poppy Day. 9/4/79 MV6 TW BAI&MPK

18/2/81 Halloween, Voodoo Dolly, But Not Them, Into The Light. John McGeoch (g), Budgie (d) r McKay, Morris. 10/2/81 LH1 DG MR

3/2/86 Candy Man, Cannons, Lands End. John Valentine-Carruthers (g) r McGeoch. 28/1/86 MV5 MR~ ○ All sessions on Voices In The Air: The Peel Sessions Universal/ Polydor

The Sisters of Mercy

7/9/82 1969, Alice, Good Things, Floor Show. Ben Gunn (rg), Gary Marx (lg), Craig Adams (b), Andrew Eldritch (g, v, dm). 25/8/82 U RP MWT

11/7/84 Walk Away, Emma, The Poison Door, No Time To Cry. Wayne Hussey (g) r Gunn; & Doctor Avalanche (d, bck). 19/6/84 MV5 MRD TdB

Six By Seven

12/5/98 Oh Dear, 88 92 96, Brilliantly Cute (& Something Wild, Your Town, 1st TX live from MV4 7/4/98). Chris Olley (gv), Sam Hempton (g), James Flower (o, sx), Paul Douglas (b), Chris Davis (d). 7/4/98 MV4 MR NF

13/7/99 Ten Places To Die, Don't Want To Go/Slab Square, Heroes/Helden (German Version Of Heroes), Always Waiting For. 18/5/99 MV4 MR GT

5/7/00 Sleep, Another Love Song, England And A Broken Radio, Sawn Off Metallica T Shirt, Overnight Success. 31/5/00 MV4 SA RJ

28/11/01 Cafeteria Rats, Speed Is In/Speed Is Out, The Way I Feel Today, American Beer, Flypaper For Freaks. Hempton out. 4/11/01 MV4 ME JHT

1/12/04 Ocean, Catch The Rain, Sometimes I Feel Like, Around, European Me. Olley, Flower, Davis only. 16/11/04 MV4 MA GW

Roni Size and Reprazent

14/12/96 Untitled live piece/mix 31'. U U U U U

Skat

10/3/82 Honcho, Sleeping Dogs Lie, Sad Boy Style, Just A Word. Russell Greenwood (d), Helen McCookerybook (b, lv), Jim McCallum (rg), Carl Evans (lg, bck). 8/3/82 MV4 JWI U

Skeletal Family

19/5/83 Black Ju-ju, The Wind Blows, Someone New, And I. Anne Marie Hurst (v), Stan Greenwood (g), Howard Daniels (d), Roger Nowell (Trotwood) (b). 11/5/83 MV4 RP NG

8/10/84 Far And Near, Hands On The Clock, Move, No Chance. Martin Henderson (d) r Daniels; Karl Heinz (sx) joins. 22/9/84 MV5 DG MC

Ski Patrol

22/1/81 Extinguish, Where The Buffalo Roam, Cut. Nick Clift (g), Francis Cook (b), Alan Cole (d), Ian Lowery (v). 19/1/81 LH1 TW DD

Skid Row

25/7/70 After I'm Gone, Felicity, An Awful Lot Of Women. Gary Moore (lg), Brendan Shiels (b), Noel Bridgeman (d) 21/7/70 MV4 JW U Peel Sunday Concert TX 21/6/70 was their trial broadcast

27/2/71 Ramblin', If You Dip Your Wick You've Got To Pay For The Oil. 9/2/71 MV4 JW BC

The Skids

19/5/78 Of One Skin, Open Sound, Contusion, Night And Day, TV Stars. Richard Jobson (v), Stuart Adamson (lg), William Simpson (b), Thomas Kellichan (d). 16/5/78 MV4 JG MR

1/9/78 Dossier Of Fallibility, Hope And Glory, Six Times, The Saints Are Coming. 29/8/78 MV4 TW MR

26/2/79 Summer, Hang On To The Shadows, Zit, Walk On The Wild Side. 19/2/79 MV4 TW DD

7/5/79 War Poets, Withdrawal Symptoms, Hymns From A Haunted Ballroom, Masquerade. 30/4/79 MV4 TW DD

15/9/80 Filming In Africa, An Incident In Algiers, Circus Games, Snakes And Ladders (instrumental). Richard Jobson (v, g-4), Russell Webb (bg), Mike Baillie (d), John McGeoch (g-1,2,3, v-1,3; Stuart Adamson ill), Steve Severin (v-1,3). 1/9/80 MV4 DG MPK&HP

Skiff Skats

23/5/84 Cripple Creek, Hickory-Holler, Long Tall Texan, Maybelline, Jingle-Night Time Radio One (Parody Of 'Relax'). Earnshaw Cods (bj, g), Funky Texas (g), Buck Harder (wsh), T-Box Tone (b), Ringo Feathers (sx), The Old Hired Hand (dobro, fd, mnd). 16/5/84 MV5 RP NG

26/2/85 Split Personality, Hill Billy Boogie, Glendale Train, Barefoot Nelly. Pete Smith (gv), Rob Smith (bj, v), Tony Hilton (db), Tony McFadzean (lsg, dob), James Cooke (fd, mnd), John Hasler (wsh), Hector Walker ('zob stick'). 12/2/85 MV5 MRD HP

Skimmer

11/11/04 Scale Of Five, Trouble With Girls, Shimokitazawa Nights, Small Talk About Girls And Beet, Gordon And Jordan. Kevin Powell (bv), Terry Powell (g, bck), Adam Veevers (g, bck), Tom Sidwell (d). 21/10/04 MV4 JHT NF

Skin Alley

6/12/69 Country Air, All Alone, Marsha. Thomas Crimble (bv), Krzysztof Henryk Juszkiewicz (o, v), Bob James (fl, sx, gv), Giles Alvin Pope (d). 22/9/69 PH U U

Skink

20/11/92 Brian Tractor, Under Currents, Violator, Dark Side. Shib (g, d), Rob (b), Ross (v). 18/10/92 MV3 ME DMC

Skinned Teen

14/1/94 Nancy Drew, Pillow Case Kisser, C6H1206, Straight Girl (Clean Version). Layla (b, g, perc, v), Esme (g, d, v, perc), Flossy (g, b, perc, v), Miki (d, perc, bck). 5/12/93 MV3 ME AA

Skip Bifferty

15/10/67 Yours For At Least 24, On Love, Money Man, Orange Lace, I Don't Understand It. Graham Bell (lv), Tom Jackman (d), John Turnbull (g), Michael Gallagher (g), Colin Gibson (b). 29/9/67 PH BA U

11/2/68 When She Comes To Stay, In The Morning, Follow The Path Of The Stars, The Other Side Of Jesus Smith. 5/2/68 PC1 BA U

14/7/68 Once, Man In Black, Don't Let Me Be Misunderstood, The Hobbit. 9/7/68 PC1 BA DT

Skodas

30/6/81 Dog, Do It Yourself, Mouth, I'm Not Going To Give A Thing, Everybody Thinks Everybody Else Is Dead. Annie Lacey (v), Andy Moule (g, bck), Jason Pitchers (b, bck), Richard Nelson (d, bck). 24/6/81 LH1 CL NG

Skrewdriver

28/10/77 Street Fight, Unbeliever, The Only One, Anti-Social. John Grinton (d), Kevin McKay (b), Ron Hartley (g), Ian Stuart (v). 19/10/77 MV4 MB NG

Patrick Sky

2/4/69 Silly Song, Jimmy Clay, Modern Major General, She's Up For Grabs, The Dance Of Death, Many A Mile, Hangin' Round. Patrick Sky (agv). 26/3/69 S1 U U

30/7/69 Separation Blues, Love Will Endure, To Keith, Ira Hayes, Spencer The Rover. 29/7/69 U U U

Skynet

4/3/03 Unknown titles/mix. Nathan Vinall (dj, el, prg, k). Live from LL AR~

Skyscraper

26/3/93 Petrified, Choke, Red Raw, Don't Know. Vic Kemlicz (gv), Adi Vines (b), Oliver Grasset (d). 14/2/93 MV4 ME PA

Slab!

22/9/86 Mars On Ice, Painting The Forth Bridge, Dust, The Animals Are All Eating People Pie. Stephen Dray (v, sx), Paul Jarvis (g), Bill Davies (b), Robin Risson (d), Neill Woodger (tb), Hugh Rawson (tp). 12/8/86 U DG MR&MC

16/2/87 Undriven Snow, Mining Town In Lotusland, Blood Flood, Parallax Avenue. Dave Morris (g) joins; & Margaret Ward (bck, tps). 1/2/87 U DG ME&MPK

7/3/88 Big Sleeper, Last Detail, Killer For A Country, Bride Of Sloth. Scott Kiehl (d) r Risson; Woodger out. 21/2/88 U DG ME&FK

Slade

26/5/72 Move Over Baby, Let The Good Times Roll, Bye Goodbye, Darlin' Be Home Soon (& Keep On Rockin'). Noddy Holder (lvg), Dave Hill (lg), Jim Lea (b), Don Powell (d). 9/5/72 T1 JM U Recorded trial broadcast session for Symonds on Sunday June 69 as 'Ambrose Slade'. 'Entertaining, fresh musical sounds': passed by the panel. Several sessions followed

Slapp Happy

16/7/74 Europa, Me And Parvati, Little Something, War Is Energy Enslaved. Anthony Moore (k), Peter Blegvad (gv), Dagmar Krause (lv), Geoff Leigh (sx), Robert Wyatt (perc, v), Lynsey Cooper (ob, perc), Fred Frith (g), Jeff Clyne (db). 25/6/74 LH1 TW BC

Luke Slater

23/9/94 Forest, One Of Your Turns, Mask, Soup. Luke Slater's Seventh Plane: Slater, Sandra Michelle, Alan Sage. OS

8/3/00 DJ mix live from MV3 U U

Sleeper

18/2/94 Twisted, Pyrotechnician I Think I Love You, Bedside Manners, Hunch. Andy Maclure (d), Deen Osman (b), John Stewart (lg), Louise Wiener (v, rg). 11/1/94 MV4 MR PA

26/11/94 Bed Head, Little Annie, Inbetweener, Disco Duncan. 25/10/94 MV4 MR PA

11/5/96 Dress Like Your Mother, Factor 41, Nice Guy Eddie, Good Luck Mr Gorsky. & John Green (k). 13/4/96 U U U

The Slits ○

27/9/77 Love And Romance, Vindictive, New Town, Shoplifting. Ari Up (v), Tessa (b, bck), Viv Albertine (rg, bck), Palmolive (d, bck). 19/9/77 MV4 TW BAl&NG

22/5/78 So Tough, Instant Hit, FM. 17/4/78 MV4 TW U

26/10/81 Difficult Fun, In The Beginning, Earthbeat & Wedding Song. Ari, Tessa, Viv & Neneh (bck), Bruce (d), Steve (k), Sean (b-2). 12/10/81 MV4 TW DD ○ All sessions on The Peel Sessions SFRSCD52

Slowdive

21/4/91 Catch The Breeze, Song 1, Golden Hair. Simon Scott (d), Nick Chaplin (b), Christian Savil (g), Neil Halstead (gv), Rachael Goswell (gv). 26/3/91 MV4 DG ME&SA

Slowjam

22/9/91 Tex Wade, Steel Bridges, Funny Face, Little Fick. Darren Davies (bv), Matt Gray (gv), David Alderman (gv). 11/8/91 MV3 DG MA

Sloy

28/4/95 Pop, Many Things, Game, Exactly. Armand Gonzalez (gv), Virginie Peitavi (b, smp), Cyril Billbeaud (d). 28/3/95 MV4 MA CML

Sluts Of Trust

17/2/04 Greatest Gift, Tighter Than The Night, That's Right That Cat's Right, Psycho Killer. Anthony O'Donnell (d), John McFarlane. 15/1/04 MV4 GT NS

The Small Faces

14/4/68 If I Were A Carpenter†, Lazy Sunday†, Get Ready, Every Little Bit Hurts†. Steve Marriott (gv), Ian McLaglan (k), Kenny Jones (d), Ronnie Lane (bv), PP Arnold (v-1, 4). 9/4/68 PC1 BA DT&AH † on ○ The BBC Sessions SFRSCD087

Small Factory

14/8/92 Suggestions, Hopefully, Friends, Lose Your Way. Phoebe Summersquash (dv), Alex Kemp (bv), David Auchenbach (gv). 16/7/92 MV4 DG NG&JLC

Smaller

18/11/95 Wasted, Small Times, Giz A Life, What's New. Jason Riley (b), Paul Kavanagh (g), Steven Deary (d), Digsy (gv). 7/11/95 MV4 JB SBR

Smashing Orange

8/2/92 Just Before I Die, Cherry Rider, Highway, Not Very Much To See. Tim Spence or Sippke (d), Stephen Wagner (b), Rick Hodgson (g), Rob Montejo (gv). 21/11/91 MV4 DG NG&JB

The Smashing Pumpkins

13/10/91 Siva, A Girl Named Sandoz, Smiley. Jimmy Chamberlain (d), Darcy (b), James Iha (g), William Corgan (gv). 8/9/91 MV3 DG ME&RM

Smiggs Band

21/5/76 Going Down South, Just For You, Nadine, Mean Street. Gordon Smith (g, v, hca), Ruan O'Lochlainn (k, sx), Tony Cousins (b), Tim Penn (k), Bunt (d). 20/4/76 U TW U

The Smirks

26/4/78 Fool, Banking With The Bankers, OK UK, The Island Sea. Simon Milner (lv, g), Neil Fitzpatrick (lgv), Ian Morris (bv), Mike Doherty (d). 19/4/78 MV4 MB NG

Gordon Smith

14/8/68 Pearlie Blues, Worried Life Blues, Highway 51, Walkin' Blues, Rollin' And Tumblin'. Gordon Smith (g, hca, v). 31/7/68 S1 U U

26/2/69 Rollin' And Tumblin', Pearlie Blues, Diving Duck, Walkin' Blues. 4/2/69 S1 U U

Michael Smith

4/5/82 Long Time / Black And White, Roots, It A Come / Stuck / Picture Or No Picture, Me Can't Believe It, Trainer. Michael Smith (v), Tony Uter (perc). 24/4/82 MV5 DG MC

TV Smith's Cheap

25/1/88 Third Team, Silicon Valley Holiday, Luxury In Exile, Buried By The Machine. TV Smith (v), Mik Helsin (g), Andy Bennie (b), Fuzz Deniz (d). 5/1/88 U DG MR&FK

The Smiths

1/6/83 What Difference Does It Make†, Miserable Lie, Reel Around The Fountain†, Handsome Devil†. Morrissey (v), Johnny Marr (g, hca), Andy Rourke (b), Mike Joyce (d). 18/5/83 MV5 RP NG ● SFPS055

21/9/83 This Night Has Opened My Eyes†§, Still Ill†, This Charming Man†, Back To The Old House†. 14/9/83 MV4 RP TdB † on ○ Hatful Of Hollow CD

9/8/84 William It Was Really Nothing, Nowhere Fast, Rusholme Ruffians, How Soon Is Now. 1/8/84 MV5 JP NG

17/12/86 Is It Really So Strange§, London, Half A Person, Sweet And Tender Hooligan§. 2/12/86 MV4 JP U § on ○ Louder Than Bombs CD

Smog

6/1/95 My Family, A Jar Of Sand, My Shell, Your New Friend. Bill Callahan (gkv), Cynthia Dall (gv), Ron Burns (d). 20/11/94 MV3 ME SB

12/11/97 Chosen One, I Break Horses, Moonshiner, Wine Stained Lips. Callahan, Colin Gagon (p, sy), Jason Dezember (d). 14/10/97 MV4 MR JB

3/1/02 Cold Discovery, Dirty Pants, Beautiful Child, Jesus. Callahan, Mike Saenz (g), Jim White (d), Jessica Billey (vi). 10/12/01 MV4 SA NF

Smudge

24/9/94 The Wrong Pony, Impractical Joke, Rosedale, Ingrown. Tom Morgan (gv), Adam Yee (b), Alison Gallaway (d). 11/8/94 MV4 TdB JB

Snafu

4/9/75 Lock And Key, Every Little Bit Hurts, Bloodhound, Hard To Handle. Bobby Harrison (lv, bj), Micky Moody (g, mnd, v), Colin Gibson (b), Terry Popple (d), Tim Hinkley (kv). 28/8/75 MV4 TW U 3 previous Sounds of the Seventies sessions in 1974

The Snapdragons

25/10/89 Truth Is Never More Than An Opinion, Girl's Blouses, Eternal In A Moment, Quick To The Dead. James Taylor (agv), John Sullivan (gp), Spike Mullings (b), Pel Riccardi (d). 1/10/89 MV3 DG DD Previous session for Mayo in 1988

Snuff

30/1/89 Win Some, For Both Sides / I Think We're Alone Now, Another Girl, Now You Don't Remember / No One Home. Duncan (dv), Andy (b, bck), Simon (gv). U U DG ME&MFA

So You Think You're a Cowboy?

1/8/83 Poor John, Smoke Smoke Smoke, Orange Blossom Special, Don't Come Back / I Don't Need You. Annie Foy (v), Alan McDowall (gv), Tony Pilley (hca, bck, perc), Kenny Brady (fd), Robbie Bain (d), Fraser Sutherland (b). 23/7/83 MV4 DG MR

SOB

27/10/90 Over The Line, Humanity Of Stupidity, Obsessed With Wickedness, What's The Truth, Unseen Terror, Why. Yoshitomo Suzuki (v), Toshimi Seki (g), Daisuke Kawataka (b), Satdshi Yasue (d). 11/10/90 MV3 PW JLO&DB

Sodastream

21/11/00 Welcome Throw, A Drum, Mood In My Bunker, Devil On My Shoulder. Karl Smith (gv), Peter Cohen (dbv). 14/11/00 MV4 SA JHT

Sofa Head

11/1/90 It Doesn't Work, Invitation To Dinner / Infanticide, Fill, Valium Housewife. Lainey A (dv), Ian (b), Wal (gv), Claire (v). 10/12/89 MV3 DG JB

The Soft Machine ○

17/12/67 Clarence In Wonderland, We Know What You Mean, Hope For Happiness, Certain Kind (& Strangest Scene, not TX). Kevin Ayers (gb, lv-1,2), Mike Ratledge (o, p), Robert Wyatt (d, lv-3,4, 5). 5/12/67 AO2 BA DT Wildly diverging opinions from audition panel on this trial broadcast tape: 'pretentious rubbish' 'neat, pretty and charming'. Borderline pass: 'a rather ordinary contemporary pop group'

15/6/69 Face Lift / Mousetrap / Backwards / Mousetrap Reprise, The Moon In June. Hugh Hopper r Ayers; extra instrumentation: Hopper (al-1), Ratledge (fl, vib-1) & Brian Hopper (ss-1). 10/6/69 MV4 JW TW

29/11/69 Instant Pussy, Mousetrap / Noisette / Backwards Ballad / Mousetrap Reprise / Pig / Orange Skin Food / A Door Opens And Closes / 10.30 Returns To The Bedroom† ['Pig' onwards Is actually 'Esther's Nose Job']. Hopper, Ratledge, Wyatt (1–Wyatt pv solo) Elton Dean (al) & Lyn Dobson (ss), Nick Evans (tb), Mark Charig (flh). 10/11/69 PH JW TW

16/5/70 Slightly All The Time / Out Bloody Rageous / Eamonn Andrews. Four-piece only. 4/5/70 PH JW TW

2/1/71 Virtually, Fletcher's Blemish. 15/12/70 MV4 JW U

26/6/71 Grides, Dedicated To You But You Weren't Listening, Eamonn Andrews / All White. 1/6/71 MV4 JW BC

24/11/71 As If, Drop, Welcome To Frillsville. Phil Howard (d) r Wyatt. 15/11/71 PH JW BC

18/7/72 Stumble / Lbo / As If, Fanfare / All White / Me / Drop. John Marshall (d), Karl Jenkins (p, sx) r Howard, Dean. 11/7/72 MV4 U U

20/11/73 Stanley Stamp's Gibbon Album, Hazard Profile, Down The Road. Roy Babbington (b) r Hopper. 30/10/73 LH1 TW BC All sessions now on ○ BBC Radio 67–71 (HUX037) & ○ BBC Radio 71–74 (HUX047)

Mick Softley

18/2/72 I'm So Confused, If Wishes Were Horses, Travelling Man, Just Flew In On A Jet Plane (& The Land Of The Crab, 14/4/72). Mick Softley (gv) & 5 U musicians. 31/1/72 T1 JM U 2 previous sessions for Bob Harris 70/71

12/7/73 Weeping Willow, From The Land Of The Crab, Gypsy, Me And Lady Willow (& Waterfall, If You're Not Part Of The Solution You Must Be Part Of The Problem, If Wishes Were Horses, 30/7/73 on BOB HARRIS; & Just Flew In On A Jet Plane, 4/10/73). U 2/7/73 LH1 BA U

Solar Race

2/6/95 Good Enough, Out Of Time, Skewiff, Disgrace. Eilidgh Bradley (gv), Andrew Holland (b), Carl Rogers (dv). 16/5/95 MV4 MR JLO

26/5/96 Peter's Revenge, Butterfly Kisses, One Day Out, Sweet FA. 30/4/96 MV5 PL AL

Soledad Brothers

6/11/02 Mysterious Ways, Teenage Heart Attack, Break Em On Down, Rock Me Slow, Up Jumped The Devil, Johnny's Death Letter, Goin Back To Memphis, Gospel According To John, Cage That Tiger, Soledad Brother, Only Flower In My Bed, Gimme Back My Wig. Johnny Walker (gv, hca), Benjamin Swank (d), Oliver Henry (gv, k, horns). Live from MV4 AR SA/JSM

25/6/03 Bring It On Home, Handle Song, Bens Idea, Cage That Tiger. & Jessie Ebough (b), Kiny Khan (o, fuzz bass), Reuben Glaser (ag). 12/5/03 MV4 KR U

24/3/04 St Ides Of March, Jack On Fire, Lorali, Rock Me Slow. 25/2/04 MV4 GT NS

Solex

9/6/98 Solex All Lickety Split, You're So Square, Solex Is Barely Dressed, Solex Lipped (& One Louder Solex, 1st TX live from MV5 5/5/98). Elisabeth Esselink (v, k, smp), Robert Lagendijk (d), Geert De Groot (g, bck). 5/5/98 MV5 MR NF

31/8/99 Teenage Kicks. OS

20/9/00 Pastrami, Rasp, Blazers, Bassie, Escargot, Lickety Split, Oh Blimey, Pick Up, The Cutter, 1969, Snappy And Cocky, Athens Ohio. & Nina Pascale (v), Andrew Blick (tp). Live from MV4 MA JHT

13/11/01 Train Mobile, Mr Crockpot, Rico Puente Versus Tito Suave, Santa Monica, Mogli. Trio. 30/9/01 MV4 ME GYW

17/10/02 Shady Lane, Flip It, Honkey Donkey, My B Sides Rock Your World, Push Switch Up For On, Oh No I've Created A Monster. 25/9/02 MV4 SA GYW

Son House

11/7/70 My Good Gal, Spoken Intro / Death Letter, Spoken Intro / Don't You Mind People Grinnin' In Your Face. Son House (gv). 6/7/70 PH JW PR

Sonic Youth

19/5/86 Come And Smash Me, Expressway To Your Skull, Moonbeam Magic In A Glass Head Cage, Hallowed Be Thy Name. Steve Shelley (dv), Kim Gordon (bv), Thurston Moore (gv), Lee Ranaldo (gv). Rec. date unknown PRIV U U

19/10/88 All cover versions of The Fall songs: Psycho Mafia, My New House, Rowche Rumble, Victoria. & Epic Soundtracks (perc, v). 11/10/88 MV4 MA MA

20/3/89 Corporate Ghost, Rubin's Beard, Major Label Chicken Feed, Clippers. 12/3/89 MV4 DG JB&FK

Sons Of The Subway

25/3/94 Trunk A Funkz, Escape, Trunk A Funkz (Reprise), Down The Line. Lucien Thompson (k, prg), David Pitts (k, prg). OS

Sophisticated Boom Boom

10/11/81 Is It About Sex?, White Horses, Surrender To Me, Joe. Libby McArthur (v), Tricia Reid (lg, bck), Irene Brown (g), Jacquie Bradley (d), Laura Mazzolini (b). 28/10/81 U U U

7/10/82 Don't Love Me, Hearts On Skates, Stalemates, Instant Appeal. 20/9/82 MV4 TW DD

15/6/83 Singing Today, Jimmy's In Love, The Next Time, Courage. & Nick Clark (sy, g). 11/6/83 MV4 DG MR

Soul Bossa

3/6/95 Dirt Track, The Big Hurt, Hang Your Head, Wrong. Michael Ford (d), Tracy Bellaries (b), Peter Jones (gv). 14/5/95 MV3 ME JLC

3/11/96 Red Rag, Nothing, Beginning Of The End, Now. 13/10/96 MV4 ME~

The Soul Sisters and The Clockwork Orange

22/10/67 You Got 'em Beat Baby, Three Time Loser, Hold On, Blueberry Hill, Bring Me Home Love, Soulful Dress, I Can't Stand It. Teresa Cleveland (v), Ann Gissendammer (v) & The Clockwork Orange (2&5 Clockwork Orange only). 16/10/67 PC1 BA U

The Sound

16/11/81 Fatal Flaw, Skeletons, Hot House, New Dark Age. Adrian Borland (gv), Graham Green (b), Michael Dudley (d), Max Mayers (k). 9/11/81 MV4 TW AP Previous session for Mike Read 1980

Soundgarden

7/6/89 Flower, Thank You, Everybody's Got Something To Hide. Chris Cornell (gv), Kim Thayil (lg), Hiro Yamamoto (b), Matt Cameron (d). 14/5/89 HP DG MWT

Soundman

26/2/97 Quit Acting Slack, Ripchord, Shatterproof, 9 Stone Elvis. Iain Shaw, Andy McDowell, Mo McDonald, David McDonald. 8/2/97 MCR3 TWN U

Sounds Of Life

7/7/95 Hidden Rooms, Morning Light, Oblivious, A Spice Of Jazz. Jim Baker, Phil Aslett. OS

The Soup Dragons

24/2/86 Whole Wide World, Too Shy To Say, Learning To Fall, Just Mind Your Step Girl. Ross Sinclair (d), Sushil Dade (b), Jim McCulloch (g), Sean Dickson (gv) & Jacqueline (bck). 16/2/86 MV5 DG ME&FK

6/1/87 Our Lips Are Sealed, The Kids Are Alright, Purple Haze, Listen To This. 7/12/86 U DG ME

Source Direct

3/4/97 Stonekiller (Hokusai Remix), Computer State, Call And Response. Jim, Phil. OS

Tim Souster

17/9/69 Sonata 2 & 4, Sonata 5 & 6, 2nd Interlude, Sonata II. Tim Souster (p), all compositions by John Cage. 27/8/69 S2 PR U

Southern Comfort

20/3/71 Roses (Sleepwalk), The Dreadful Ballad Of Willy Hurricane, April Lady, Get Back Home. Andy Leigh, Gordon Huntley, Carl Barnwell, Ray Duffy, Mark Griffiths. 9/3/71 MV4 U BC

25/1/72 Old Rudd, Harlem Girl, Cosmic Jig, Lilly Brown. 18/1/72 MV4 U U

Southern Death Cult

10/6/82 Fat Man, Today, False Faces, Or Glory. Ian Astbury (v), Haq Qureshi (d), David 'Buzz' Burrows (g), Barry Jetson (b). 21/5/82 MV4 JWI MC

Otis Spann

2/7/69 Lucille, I'm Not Going To Sell You My Thing, Back Alley Blues. Otis Spann (gv). 1/7/69 U PR U

Spare Rib

13/2/73 Hear Me Calling, Making Light, Little Miss Femme Fatale, Probably Do. Jo Ann Kelly (v), Roger Brown (gv), Adrian Pitryga (lg), Bruce Rowlands (d), John Atkinson (b), Nick Judd (p). 6/2/73 LH1 U BC

Spare Snare

4/2/95 Wired For Sound, Super Slinky, Bugs, Call The Birds. Jan Burnett (g, v, perc, Styrophone), Alan Cormack (b, g, perc), Barry Gibson (d, g, c, Crisps) & Chip (g, v, smp). 8/1/95 MV3 ME NK

2/2/99 Profile Check, They Airbrushed My Face, Dya Ken That Bruce Hornsby And The Range Are, We Are The Snare, Holding On To The Shore. Chip out. 13/12/98 MV3 ME NF

2/5/01 Taking On The Sides, The Rattling Boy From Dublin, See It On TV, Surrender. Trio & Ross Matheson (g), Graeme Ogston (g, elpv). 29/4/01 MV4 ME~

Roger Ruskin Spear and His Giant Orchestral Wardrobe

26/6/71 On Her Doorstep, Mattress Man, Call Of The Freaks. Roger Ruskin Spear (various) & others. 8/6/71 MV4 JW BC 'I can't remember the full line-up, but Thunderclap Newman was definitely there, playing the contra-bass saxophone', John Walters

Spear of Destiny

29/11/82 Black Madonna, O-Men Of The Times, The Wake, Judgement Hymn. Kirk Brandon (gv), Stan Stammers (b), Chris Ball (d), Lascelles James (sx). 22/11/82 U TW MC

The Specials

29/5/79 Gangsters, Too Much Too Young, Concrete Jungle, Monkey Man. Jerry Dammers (k, bck), Roddy Radiation (lg), Terry Hall (lv), Horace Panter (b), Lynval Golding (lg, bck), John Bradbury (d, perc). 23/5/79 MV4 JS NG ● SFPS018

22/10/79 Rude Boys Out Of Jail, Rat Race, Long Shot Kick The Bucket / Liquidator / Moon Stomp (The Skinhead Symphony In Three Movements). & Neville Staples (v). 15/10/79 MV4 TW DD Skinhead Symphony done in one live take, no overdubs' – TW

1/12/80 Sea Cruise, Stereotypes, Raquel. & Rico Rodriquez (tb), Dick Cuthell (cnt). 29/10/80 MV4 BS NG

12/9/83 Alcohol, Lonely Crowd, Bright Lights. Now billed as The Special AKA: Dammers, Bradbury, Gary McManus (b), John Shipley (g), Andy Aderinto (sx), Rhoda Daker, Egiodio Newton & Stan Campbell (v). 22/8/83 MV4 TW MC

Chris Spedding

4/4/72 The Only Lick I Know, Dock Of The Bay, A Piece Of Pre-Recorded Music, A Hard Woman Is Good To Find. Chris Spedding (gv) & (b), (d) & 1 other (unknown). 21/3/72 MV4 PR U 2 previous sessions for Alan Black 70/71

4/1/77 Hurt By Love, Pogo Dancing, Get Out Of My Pagoda, Misunderstood, Motor Bikin'. & the Vibrators: Ian Carnochan (gv), John Ellis (gv), Pat Collier (b), Jon Edwards (d). 16/12/76 MV4 TW BAI

Speeder

15/2/00 Drag Me Down, Accordian Hugh, Karma Kids, Feelings, Take The Fun (Out Of Everything), The Underachiever, Hey What Do I Know. Jamie Cameron (g), Martin Kirwan (b), Stuart Brown (d), Scott McCluskey (lgv). Live from MV4 U U

The Jon Spencer Blues Explosion

9/10/93 Bellbottom, Blues Explosion Man, In The Red, Orange. Jon Spencer (gv), Judah Bauer (g), Russell Simins ('traps'). 9/9/93 MV4 NG JMK

Spike

5/11/94 Obsession, Love & War, Play Away, Like You Do. Michael Wallis (lv, g), Doug Holands (lg), Jason Hobart (b), Sam Kesteven (d). 3/10/94 MV4 MR LS

Spiritualized

14/3/92 Angel Sigh / Feels So Sad, Smiles. Johnny Mattock (d), Willie B Carruthers (b), Jason Pierce (gv), Mark Refoy (g), Kate Radley (o) & 'the Kick Horns': Simon Clarke (sx, fl), Tim Sanders (sx), Roddy Lorimer (tp). 7/1/92 MV5 MR MR&JB

18/3/95 Take Your Time, The Sound Of Confusion, Don't Go Stay With Me. Pierce, Radley, Damon Reece (d), Sean Cook (b), John Coxon (g), Edmund Coxon (violin). 31/1/95 MV4 MR NS

Spitfire

16/11/91 Fluid, Dive, Firebird, Hotlegs. Justin (d), Nick (b), Matt (lg), Steve (rg), Jeff (v). 15/9/91 MV3 DG ME&RJ

Spizz Oil

7/8/78 Cold City, 6000 Crazy, Pure Noise / Alien Language / Protect From Heat, Platform 3 / Switched Off. Spizz (lv, g, kazoo), Pete Petrol (lg), Frank Guest (p, perc). 1/8/78 MV4 BS MR&MPK ● SFPS022

Spizz Energi

21/3/79 European Heroes, Energy Crisis, Soldier Soldier, Life's So Safe. Alpha Scanner (b), Mark Coalfield (k), Paul Guest (g), Spizz (gv). 12/3/79 MV4 TVD MR

27/11/79 New Species, Touched, Intimate, Effortless, Where's Captain Kirk? Spizz (v), Scott (g, bck), Mark Coalfield (k, bck), Jim Solar (b), Hero Shima (d). 13/11/79 MV4 JS MR

12/5/80 Red And Black, Rythem Inside, Hot Deserts, Central Park. Now billed as Athletico Spizz 80. CP Snare (d) r Shima. 30/4/80 MV4 JE NG

SPK

31/8/83 Metal Dance, The Sandstorm Method, Metal Field, Will To Please. Sinan (v), Derek Thompson (tp, b, k, perc), Graham (perc, el). 20/8/83 MV4 DG TdB

Splintered

27/3/92 Godsend, Kill The Body So The Head Will Die, Breakdown Pt 3, Judas Cradle. Paul Dudeney (dv), Paul Wright (b), James Machin (gv), Richard Johnson (g, sy). 16/2/92 MV3 DG ME&JRS

20/1/95 Hilt, Black Dwarf, Mantle, Silence. & Colin Bradley (gsfx), Steve Pittis (wasp, k, smp, perc), David Daddy Dudeney (perc). 4/12/94 MV3 ME GT

Split Enz

18/10/78 I See Red, Mind Over Matter, Frenzy, Semi-Detached. Malcolm Green (d), Eddy Rayner (k), Nigel Griggs (b), Neil Finn (g), Noel Crombie (perc, sp), Tim Finn (v). 26/9/78 MV6 MB TdB

Splodgenessabounds

24/11/80 Rolf, Richard Freak, Malcolm's Mum Parts 1–3, Desert Island Joe. Max Splodge (v), Fred Winston Forbe (k), Miles Flat ('worst guitar'), Pat Thetic (rg), Roger Over-and-out Rodent ('attempted bass'). Baby Greensleeves (v), Whiffy Archer (sx), Desert Island Joe Lurchslive (d). 28/10/80 MV4 DG MR&HP

Spooky Tooth

17/3/68 It Hurts You So, Too Much Of Nothing, Sunshine Help Me, Tobacco Road. Gary Wright (ov), Greg Ridley (b), Mike Harrison (pv), Mike Kellie (d), Luther Grosvenor (g). 21/2/68 MV4 BP PR Passed by panel, but comments ranged from 'I liked this group, loads of attack and screaming feeling' to 'loud and pretentious psychedelic rubbish!'

23/6/68 Love Really Changed Me, Evil Women, I Can't Quit Her. 17/6/68 PC1 BA PR

6/10/68 Feelin' Bad, The Weight, I Can't Quit Her, Blues Town. 30/9/68 PC1 BA U

23/2/69 Better By You Better Than Me, Waitin' For The Wind, When I Get Home, That Was Only Yesterday. 3/2/69 PH BA U

Sportique

10/6/98 Definition 79, Just Friends, Anatomy Of A Fool, It Couldn't Last Forever. Gregory Webster (gv), Rob Purley (b), Mark Flunder (d). 31/5/98 MV4 ME SA

22/9/99 Don't Believe A Word I Say, Big Bad World, The Dying Fly, Rollercoaster. Amelia Fletcher (v). 22/8/99 MV3 ME~

6/2/01 Suture, Modern Museums, Ice Storm, Obsessive, Percy's P*ss Up. 17/1/01 MV4 ME~ SA

Spraydog

11/3/98 X Lice, Ghost Mutt, False CV, Wake Up Little Sister, San Andreas. Steve Robson (gv), Hannah Betts (v), Phil Tyler (g), Paul King (b), Chris Lanigan. 8/2/98 MV4 ME LS

1/8/00 Seeling Crax, Wait In Vain, Excuse Me Kind City Gent, These Fields May Take Forever To Fill, Durak. Robson, Tyler, Lannigan, Anika Bosanquet (v), James Atkinson (bv). 24/5/00 MV4 KR~

Squeeze

29/8/77 Cat On The Wall, Model, All Fed Up, Sex Master. Glen Tilbrook (lg), Harry Kakoulli (b), Gilson Lavis (d), Julian Holland (p), Chris Difford (rg). 17/8/77 MV4 MB NG

15/5/78 Bang Bang, Ain't It Sad, I Must Go, The Knack. 3/5/78 MV4 JG NG

Stackridge

20/10/71 Three Legged Table Pt 3, Slark. James Warren (b), Michael Slater (fl), William Bent (d), Andy Davies (gp), Mike Evans (vi). 21/9/71 MV4 JW BC 2 previous daytime sessions summer 71

4/4/72 Lummy Days, The Story Of My Heart, Syracuse The Elephant. 20/3/72 PH JW BC

12/10/72 Anyone For Tennis?, There Is No Refuge, Friendliness, Teatime. James Walter joins. 9/10/72 LH1 BA U

25/1/73 Keep On Clucking, Fourposter Bed / Orange Blossom Special, Do The Stanley, Purple Space Ships Over Yatton. 15/1/73 LH1 BA U

22/11/73 McGregor / Zorgon's Daughter, The Laughing Policeman, February In Shropshire, The Volunteer. Rod Bowkett, Keith Gemmell r Slater, Bent. 19/11/73 LH1 BA U

30/1/75 Dancing On Air, Spin Round The Room, No One's More Important Than The Earthworm, Benjamin's Giant Onion. Paul Karas, Roy Morgan, Mutter Slater r Walter, Warren, Evans. 22/1/75 MV4 JG U

2/3/76 Hold Me Tight, Hey Good Looking, Save A Red Face, Steam Radio Song. James Walter (b), Peter Van Hooke (d), Dave Lawson (k), Mutter Slater (v). 19/2/76 MV4 TW U

Stackwaddy

18/2/72 Hoochie Choochie Man, Rock Me Baby, You Really Got Me, Willie The Pimp. Mick Stott (lg), John Knail (v, hca), Stuart Banham (b), John Groom (d). 24/1/72 T1 JM U Trial broadcast for Alan Black Oct 70: 'Appalling lead voice… a lunatic shout… sounds as if he's being sick… screaming, toneless and distorted' Fail: audition panel

Stakka & Skynet

23/5/01 Drum 'n' bass DJ set by Shaun Morris & Nathan Vinall (both: el, prg, k). Live from MV4 AR SA&JHT

Viv Stanshall

21/3/70 Cyborg Signal, Blind Date, Eleven Moustachioed Daughters, The Strain. Viv Stanshall's Big Grunt: Roger Ruskin Spear (sx), Dennis Cowan (b), Ian Wallace (d), Bubs White (g). 16/3/70 AO1 JW U

27/10/75 Trails Of The Lonesome Pine, The Unbridled Suite / In The Final Analysis, Aunt Florrie Remembers from 'Giant Whelks At Rawlinson End'). Viv Stanshall (g, eu, pp, dum dum, talking drum, perc), Pete Moss (b, p, acc, vi, cel), Mox (hca, fl), Bubs White (bj, uk, g). 16/10/75 MV4 TW BAI

22/12/75 Christmas At Rawlinson End pt 1 (& pt 2 23/12, pt 3 24/12, pt 4 26/12) – including musical backing tracks Aunt Florrie Recalls, Convivial Vivisectionist, The Party's Over Now, Uncle Otto, Roar Of The End, A Half For Chuck. Stanshall, Moss, Julian Smedley (vi, mnd), Andy Roberts (dul). 2/12/75 MV4 TW BAI&ME

6/4/77 Part 34: An Absence Of Whelks, Aunt Florrie Recalls Dan, Nice And Tidy. 21/3/77 MV4 MB DD

23/5/77 Spades Balls And Sausage Trees, Wheelbarrow, Aunt Florrie Recalls. Stanshall, Zoot Money (g, p, v), Barry Dransfield (vi, clo). 11/5/77 MV4 MB NG

19/12/77 The Road To Unreason Pt 37, Aunt Florrie Recalls, Three Vivisectionists, Mrs Radcliffe. Stanshall, Money, Mox (hca, fl). 24/8/77 & 14/12/77 MV4 MB NG

5/4/78 Florrie's Waltz, Fool And Bladder, Interlewd, Smeeton. Stanshall, Smedley, Jim Cuomo (cl, rec, cel, leg). 29/3/78 MV4 U NG

25/7/78 Ginger Geyser, Socks, Stripe Me A Pinky, Fresh Faced Boys, Aunt Florrie, Piece In Toto. Moss r Cuomo. 18/7/78 MV4 MB MR

24/12/79 Gooseflesh Steps Pt 1: Sig. / Cracks Are Showing / Swelter / End Roar / Cums. Kirpatrick (acc, cnc, jews hp, bck) r Smedley. 11/12/79 MV4 MB MR

18/4/88 The Crackpot At The End Of The Rainbow, Florrie's Waltz / Under The Sea, In The Pipes, Murder Living Next Door, Private Rhythms, In The Pipes (Reprise), Cackling Gas, Florrie's Waltz / Under The Sea. Stanshall, Moss (p, d, acc), Kenny Baldock (b), Dave Swarbrick (vi, mnd). 23/2/88 U DG ME&SA

23/11/88 The Eating At Rawlinson End. Stanshall, Swarbrick, Tony Roberts, Moss, Danny Thompson. 9/8/88 MV4 MR MR

6/4/91 Crackling Gas Capers, Octavio, Tour De Farce, Achmedillo, Peristaltic Waves. Viv Stanshall, Swarbrick, Roberts, Thompson, Rodney Slater, Roger Ruskin Spear, Henry Lowther, John Megginson, Les Cirkel. 29/5/90 MV5 MR~

Stanton

11/12/02 Paw, Dead Man's Hammock, Reader Who Fights, A Free T Shirt, Electric. Simon Hughes (gv), Joe Thompson (b), Robert Davis (gv), Chris Thompson (d). Live from MV4 MA GT

Starry Eyed and Laughing

1/8/74 Money Is No Friend Of Mine, Chimes Of Freedom, See Your Face, Fifty-Fifty. Tony Poole (gv), Ross McGeeney (lgv), Iain Whitmore (bv), Mike Whackford (d). 18/7/74 LH1 U BAI

16/1/75 Nobody Home, Thought Talk, Don't Give Me A Hard Time, Since I Lost You. 9/1/75 MV4 U U

11/8/75 Down The Street, Good Love, Swarthfell Rock, Flames In The Rain. 29/7/75 MV4 TW BAI

The Stars of Heaven

22/1/86 Sacred Heart Hotel, Talk About It Now, Moonstruck, So You Know. Stanley Erraught (g), Peter O'Sullivan (b, bck), Stephen Ryan (gv), Bernard Walsh (d). 14/1/86 MV5 PRS MR ○ mini-album Sacred Heart Hotel, Rough Trade RTM173

26/5/86 28, Every Other Day, What Else Could You Do?, Paradise Of Lies. 13/5/86 MV4 DG MR

17/2/87 Wheels, Calvary Cross, Can't Seem To Make You Mine, Still Feeling Blue. 3/2/87 U DG MR&PS

27/1/88 Two O'Clock Waltz, Ammonia Train, Northern Isles, Unfinished Dreaming. 17/1/88 U DG ME&FK

Status Quo

3/3/72 Mean Girl, Na Na Na, Railroad, Someone's Leaving. Francis M Rossi (lg), Alan Lancaster (b), John Coghlan (d), Rick Parfitt (gv). 7/2/72 T1 PD ARV Previous line-up debuted on R1 in 68 and did 42 daytime sessions before end 1970!

7/12/72 Don't Waste My Time, Unspoken Words, Oh Baby, Paper Plane, Softer Ride. 20/11/72 LH1 BA U

16/1/73 Paper Plane, Don't Waste My Time, Softer Ride. 8/1/73 T1 JW U

Stealers Wheel

29/2/72 We're On The Right Track, I Get By, Jose, Mary Skeffington. Gerry Rafferty (gv), Joe Egan (ag), Ian Campbell (b), Paul Pilnick (lg), Peter Clarke (d). 14/2/72 PH JW U 3 previous R1 sessions and In Concert 71/72

5/12/72 Late Again, Midnight Rider, Chevrolet, I Get By. Rafferty, Egan, Pilnick, Luther Grosvenor (gv), De Lyle Harper (b), Rod Coombes (d). 21/11/72 LH1 U BC

11/1/73 Gets So Lonely, You Put Something Better Inside Of Me, Here Comes The Queen, Outside Looking In. 1/1/73 LH1 BA U

7/6/73 Johnny's Tune, Everything Will Be Alright, I Get By, Late Again. 4/6/73 LH1 BA U

10/4/75 Wishbone, This Morning, Monday Morning, Right Or Wrong. Rafferty, Egan & Peter Robinson, Andrew Steele, Dave Wynter, Ken Elliott. 3/4/75 MV4 TW BAI

Steam Hammer

13/7/69 When Your Friend's Gone, Passing Through, Louisiana Blues, 6/4 For Amiran. Kieran White (gv, hca), Martin Pugh (lg), Steve Joliffe (sx, fl), Steve Davy (b), Rob Tait (d). 8/7/69 MV4 JW U

Steel Pulse

29/9/77 Prodigal Son, Ku Klux Klan, Bad Man, Prediction. Steve Nesbitt (d), Ronnie McQueen (b), David Hinds (g, lv), Basil Gabbidon (lg), Selwyn Brown (o), Michael Riley (perc, bck), Alfonso Martin (perc). 31/8/77 MV4 MB NG

27/4/78 Hansworth Revolution, Rock Against Racism, Makka Splaff. 4/4/78 MV4 MB MR

13/8/79 Unseen Guests, Uncle George, Reggae Fever. Riley out. 16/7/79 MV4 TW BAI

7/5/80 Drug Squad, Shinin', Nyahbinghi. 9/4/80 MV4 JE NG

6/1/82 Ravers, Man No Sober, Blues Dance. 5/12/81 MV4 DG MR

Steeleye Span

11/4/70 A Calling-on Song, The Blacksmith, The Hills Of Greenmore, All Things Are Quite Silent, Dark Eyed Sailor. Ashley Hutchings (b), Maddy Prior (v), Gay Woods (cnc, v), Terry Woods (mand, gv), Tim Hart (g, mnd, dul, v). 31/3/70 MV4 JW U

27/6/70 The Blacksmith, Female Drummer, Rave On, I Was A Young Man, Lark In The Morning. Peter Knight (fd), Martin Carthy (g) r T & G Woods. 23/6/70 MV4 JW U

27/3/71 Two Reels, Let's Dance, Prince Charlie Stuart, Bring 'Em Down / A Hundred Years Ago. 16/3/71 MV4 JW U

8/2/72 Reels: The Oak Tree / Pigeon On The Gate, Ups And Downs, Spotted Cow, Rosebud In June, Sheepcrook And Black Dog. Rick Kemp (b) & Bob Johnson (gv) r Hutchings, Carthy. 31/1/72 PH JW U

10/3/72 Jigs, Royal Forester, John Barleycorn (& The Gamekeeper, 28/4/72). 21/2/72 T1 PD ARV

28/7/72 Rag Doll, Come Ye O'er From France, False Knight On The Road, Saucy Sailor. 4/7/72 T1 JM JWH&NG

24/10/72 New Reels: The Bank Of Ireland / Lucy Campbell, Gaudete, Truck Driving Man, Weaver. 2/10/72 T1 JW&PD ARV

6/2/73 Hello Mary Lou, Misty Moisty Morning, Three Drunken Maidens. 16/1/73 LH1 JW BC

22/2/73 Ups & Downs, One Misty Moist Morning, Hares On The Mountain, Lots Is A Bun Dance. 12/2/73 LH1 BA U

26/2/74 Thomas The Rhymer, Edwin, Long-A-Growing. & Nigel Pegram (d). 19/2/74 LH1 TW U

Stereo MCs

21/10/90 Lost In Music, The Other Side, Going Back To The Wild, Scene Of The Crime. Rob B, Head, Owen If (d), Paul O (perc). 9/10/90 MV5 JB DB&JB Previous sessions for Liz and Andy Kershaw 88/89

Stereolab

8/9/91 Super Electric, Changer, Doubt, Difficult Fourth Title. Joe Dilworth (d), Martin Kean (b), Tim Gane (g), Laetitia Sadier (lv), Gina Morris (v). 30/7/91 MV5 MR~ † ○ SFRCD119

11/7/92 Laisser Faire, Revox, Peng, John Cage Bubble Gum. Kean, Gane, Sadier, Andy Ramsey (d), Mick Conroy (k), Mary Hansen (v). 28/6/92 MV3 ME FK&ME †

30/10/93 Wow And Flutter, Anemie, Moogie Wonderland, Heavy Denim. Gane, Sadier, Ramsay, Hansen, Duncan Brown (b), Katharine Gifford (k). 28/9/93 MV4 MR SA

24/2/96 Metronomic Underground, Brigitte, Spinal Column, Tomorrow Is Already Here. Gane, Sadier, Ramsey, Hansen, Richard Harrison (b), Morgane Lhote (k). 15/2/96 MV4 MR RJ †

24/9/97 Brakhage, Flower Called Nowhere, The Light, Refractions In the Plastic Purse, Miss Modular, Metronomic Underground, John Cage Bubblegum. Live from MV4 SA GT

18/9/01 Nothing To Do With Me, Dolly Rocker, Baby Lulu, Naught More Terrific Than Man. Dominic Jeffrey (k), Simon Johns (b) r Harrison, Lhote. 16/8/01 MV3 SA GT † these 4 sessions plus more on ○ ABC Music SFRSCD111

Steveless

4/8/04 Waiting, Follow, Answers, Fool, To Hell With Boredom. Dan Newman (gv), Matt Haggett (d), Martyn Elliot (d). 1/7/04 MV4 JSM ME

16/12/04 Five improvised untitled numbers. Solo (gv, d). Live from MV4 NF RJ

Cat Stevens

17/12/67 I Love Them All, Kitty, Suns In The Sky, I'm Gonna Be King, Blackness Of The Night. Cat Stevens (ag, v) & the Art Greenslade Orchestra. 8/12/67 U BA PR Many previous appearances on Light Programme in mid-60s

Jimmy Stevens

19/10/72 Happy Birthday Sam, Allerton Towers, Paid My Dues, Tears Behind My Eyes. U 9/10/72 U BA U

6/12/73 Won't You Be My Yoko, Please Don't Let It Be, Thank You For Being A Woman, LOLA. 21/11/73 U BA U

John Stevens

7/6/76 Anni, Can't Explain, Spirit Of Peace. U 27/5/76 MV4 U U

Al Stewart

29/5/68 The Carmichaels, Swiss Cottage Maneouvres, Room Of Roots, Song For Jim, Samuel Oh How You've Changed. Al Stewart (agv). 8/5/68 S1 DK U. Debut on Light Programme 1965

18/8/68 Swiss Cottage Maneouvres, You Should Have Listened To Al, I Don't Believe You, Old Compton St. Blues (& Good As Gone, In Brooklyn, 15/9/68). & Steve Gray (o) & 3 unknown. 12/8/68 MV4 BA U

20/8/69 The Sparrow, My Enemies Have Sweet Voices, Memphis Tennessee, Clifton In The Rain, Gethsemane Again, Swiss Cottage Maneouvres, Burbling. 8/8/69 S2 PR

27/8/69 I Don't Believe You, The Ballad Of Mary Foster Pt 1, The Ballad Of Mary Foster Pt 2, Blessed, Zero She Flies, Scandinavian Girl, Ivich. 15/8/69 S2 PR

13/12/69 Zero She Flies, Burbling, Electric Los Angeles Sunset (& Manuscript 2/5/70). 1/12/69 PH U U

24/3/72 A Small Fruit Song, You Don't Even Know Me, Old Compton St. Blues, Zero She Flies (& Absolutely Sweet Marie, I'm Falling, 28/4/72). & 4 unknown. 8/3/72 T1 JM JWH&JS

10/1/74 Post World War II Blues, Soho Needless To Say, Roads To Moscow. & Francis Monkman (k), Isaac Guillory (g), Florian Pilkington Miksa (b), Pete Zorn (sx, fl), Annie Haslam (v). 7/1/74 LH1 BA U

Stiff Little Fingers

13/4/78 Alternative Ulster, Wasted Life, Johnny Was, State Of Emergency. Jake Burns (lg, lv), Henry Cluney (rg, bck), Ali McMordie (b, bck), Brian Faloon (d, concussion). U DWN SN~

18/9/78 Johnny Was, Law And Order, Barbed Wire Love, Suspect Device. 12/9/78 MV4 MB MR ○

17/9/79 Wait And See, At The Edge, Nobody's Hero, Straw Dogs. Jim Reilly (d) r Faloon. 3/9/79 MV4 BS DD ○

25/2/80 No Change, I Don't Like You, Fly The Flag, Doesn't Make It All Right. Cluney (lv-1). 12/2/80 MV4 JE MR ○ SFRCD106

18/3/81 Piccadilly Circus, Just Fade Away, The Only One, Roots Radics. 11/3/81 U U U

The Stiffs

14/2/80 Let's Activate, Brookside Riot Squad, Best Place In Town, Innocent Bystander. Phil Hendriks (gv), Ian Barnes (g, bck), John McVittie (b, bck), Tommy O'Kane (d, bck), Rankin' Juice (perc, wh, 'disco cowbells and bluffing'). 5/2/80 MV4 JS MR

10/3/82 Standing Ovation, Over The Balcony, Hook In Your Heart, Child's Play. Hendriks, Barnes, Billy Rumour (b), Bloody Rich (d). 20/2/82 MV4 DG MR&MC

Stimulin

27/8/81 Sex Object, You Get Everything, Vacuum, The Game Is Up. Alix Sharkey (lv, lg), Tony McDermott (b), John Scofield (vib, bck), Thoby Young (tp), Roger Hilton (d), Justin Langlands (cga). 22/8/81 MV4 DG MR

The Stoat

17/10/78 Tears Run Dry, No Way To Say Goodbye, Don't Say Nothing, Escorts. Richard Wall (bv), John Waters (gv), George Decsy (d). 2/10/78 MV4 BS DD

Stone the Crows

6/12/69 Raining In Your Heart, Friend, Blind Man, Touch Of Your Loving Hand. Maggie Bell (v), Leslie Harvey (g), Jimmy Dewar (b), Colin Allen (d), John McGuinnis (k). 24/11/69 PH JW U Passed by panel: 'excellent!'

30/5/70 Fool On The Hill, Freedom Road, Hollis Brown (& Danger Zone, 12/9/70). 19/5/70 MV4 JW U

18/9/71 Keep On Rolling, Aileen Mochree, Big Jim Salter, Don't Think Twice. Ronnie Leahy (k), Steve Thompson (b) r McGuinnis, Dewer. 8/9/71 MV4 JW BC

28/4/72 Going Down, On The Highway, Mr Wizard, Penicillin Blues. 11/4/72 T1 JM NG

Stoneground

27/10/71 Rock And Roll Tonight, Super Clown, Sad Man, You Must Be One Of Us. Sal Valentino (gv), Tim Barnes (lv), John Blakeley (rg), Cory Lerios (o, p), Brian Godula (b, clo), Steve Price (d) & Lyn Hughes, Diedre La Porte, Lydia Phillips, Annie Sampson. 26/10/71 MV4 TW BC

Stony Sleep

26/8/97 This Kitten Is Clean, Mid May, Wondering Why, Lady Lazarus. Ben Smith (gv), Lee Citron (b), Christian Smith (d), Steve McGuire (o). U MV4 MR LS

24/6/98 He Grows Good Grundo, Heinous Pogfrag, Sweet Decay, Dream 4. Darryn Harkness (g, k) r McGuire. 19/5/98 MV4 MR GT

STP 23

3/4/90 I'm Gonna Love You A Little More, Faithful, Good Times. Clune (k), Tim (k), Jane (v), David (g). 6/3/90 MV5 DG MR

The Straitjacket Fits

29/11/89 Quiet Come, Bad Note For A Heart, Hand In Mine, Roller Ride. Shayne Carter (gv), Andrew Brough (gv), David Wood (b), John Coulie (d). 12/11/89 U DG MC

Strangelove

17/7/92 Visionary, Hopeful, Fire, Snakes. John Langley (d), Joe Allen (b), Julian Poole (g), Alex Lee (g, bck), Patrick Duff (lv). 30/6/92 MV4 MR CML&MR

19/2/93 Frozen, Quiet Day, Walls, All Because Of You Song. Angelo Bruschini (g) r Poole. 5/1/93 MV4 MR AA

The Stranglers

7/3/77 Hangin' Around, I Feel Like A Wog, Goodbye Toulouse, Somethin' Better Change. Hugh Cornwell (gv), Jean-Jacques Burnel (bv), Dave Greenfield (o, pv), Jet Black (d). 1/3/77 MV6 JG MR

13/9/77 Dead Ringer, No More Heroes, Burning Up Time, Bring On The Nubiles. 30/8/77 MV4 TW MR

Strawberry Switchblade

5/10/82 10 James Orr Street, The Little River, Secrets, Trees And Flowers. Rose McDowall (gv), Jill Bryson (g, bck) & James Kirk (b), Shahid Starwars (d), Alex Fergusson (p, g), Babs Shores (bck-4). 4/10/82 MV4 TW DD

15/4/85 Cut With The Cake Knife, 60 Cowboys, Nothing Changes, Life Full Of Wonders. McDowall, Bryson, Balfe. 5/2/85 MV5 MRD U

The Strawbs

12/1/69 I'll Show You Where To Sleep, Poor Jimmy Wilson, The Battle, That Which Once Was Mine. Dave Cousins (gv, dul, bj), Tony Hooper (gv), Ron Chesterman (b) & Tony Visconti (md, rec). 10/12/68 PC1 BA AH Had previously appeared on R1 folk shows earlier in 68, and more followed in 69. Files for any sessions before 68 untraceable

7/9/69 We'll Meet Again Sometime, Another Day, Till The Sun Comes Shining Through. & Claire Lowther (clo). 25/8/69 PH JW TW

31/10/70 Canon Dale, The Reaper / We Must Cross The River / Antiques And Curios / Hey It's Been A Long Time, Song Of A Sad Little Girl. Rick Wakeman (k) r Lowther; John Ford (b) r Chesterman. 5/10/70 PH JW U

Stray

21/1/72 Mr Hobo, Leave It Out, How Could I Forget You. Steve Gadd (v), Ritchie Cole (g), Gary Giles (b), Del Bromham (lg). 29/12/71 T1 PD U 1st session was for Pete Drummond, Sept 71

26/10/72 Cross Country, Alone Again, I Believe It. 23/10/72 LH1 BA U

17/5/73 It's Alright Ma, Pretty Thing, Come On Air. 7/5/73 LH1 BA U

9/7/74 Mystic Lady, Right From The Start, Times Like These, Give It Up. 18/6/74 LH1 U U

Stretch

12/12/75 Can't Judge A Book, Hold On, Living On The Highway, Miss Jones. Geoff Rich (d), Steve Emery (b), Kirby (g), Elmer Gantry (v). 25/11/75 MV4 TW BAI

24/5/76 Feelin' Sad, Fixin' To Die, That's The Way The Wind Blows, Showbiz Blues. & Phil McDonnell (o-1). 29/4/76 MV4 TW BAI

18/10/76 Can't Get Enough, Hold Up The Light, Rock 'n' Roll Hoochie-Coo, The Way Life Is. McDonnell out. 30/9/76 MV4 TW U

The Stretchheads

27/7/91 Anal Beard, Skinrip, Afghanistan Bananastan, Filthy Great Yarblockodes. Mr Jason (d), Mofungo Diggs (b), Dr Technology (g), Wilberforce (v), Mr Martin (b), Mr Marcus (tp). 16/6/91 MV3 DG ME&AC

String Driven Thing

19/9/72 Regent Street, Circus, Let Me Down, Jack Diamond. Chris Adams (gv), Pauline Adams (tamb), Graham Smith (v), Colin Wilson (b). 11/9/72 PH JW U Original line-up passed trial broadcast for Tony Brandon Aug 70

28/11/72 Hooked On The Road, My Real Hero, Regent Street Incident, Let Me Down. 6/11/72 T1 JW BC

8/11/73 Two Timing Rama, Night Club, The Machine That Cried, To See You. Bill Hatje (b) r Wilson & Colin 'Billy' Fairley (d). 24/9/73 LH1 BA U

15/8/74 Overdrive, Keep On Moving, To Know You, Man Of Means, Black Eyed Queen. Jim Exell (b), Andy Roberts (g), Kim Beacon (v) r Hatje, C & P Adams. 8/8/74 LH1 U U

29/3/76 Things We Said Today, But It Do, Starving In The Tropics. 4/3/76 MV4 U U

Strip Kings

15/9/95 Hustler Bullets, Three Chord Attack, Broadway West One, Greaseball. Rich Taylor (d), Mike Quinn (b), Eddie King (gv). 5/9/95 MV4 DD RJ

The Strokes

27/6/01 The Modern Age, Hard To Explain, Barely Legal, Someday. Nick Valensi (g), Nikolai Fraiture (b), Julian Casablancas (v), Albert Hammond Jr (g), Fabrizio Moretti (d). 8/6/01 MV4 MA GT

The Mike Stuart Span

26/5/68 My White Bicycle, Children Of Tomorrow, Through The Looking-Glass. U 7/5/68 PC1 BA DT

Stud

6/3/71 Sail On, 1112235, Turn Of The Pages. Jim Cregan (lgv), Richard McCracken (ag, b), John Wilson (d). 8/2/71 PH U BC

21/3/72 Good Things, Red Wine, Samurai. 7/3/72 MV4 U U

Stuffy & The Fuses

15/2/05 Spineless, Joe C Is An Idiot, Meat Packers, Top Tim Rubies (Deerhoof cover version), Sir Wants Sex. Stuffy G (dv), Chopper Fuse (k, bck), Jen Fuse (gv), Jon Fuse (b, bck). 29/12/04 MV4 SA NF TX on Huw Stephens, session offered before Peel's death, honoured by Louise Kattenhorn

The Stukas

24/1/78 Dead Lazy, Big Boy, Motor Bike, Sport. John Mackie (d), Mick Smithers (lg), Raggy Lewis (rg), Kevin Allen (b), Paul Brown (v), John Mac and Raggy L (bck). 17/1/78 MV4 MB MR

Stump

5/2/86 Down On The Kitchen Table, Orgasm Way, Grab Hands, Buffalo. Robert McKahey (d), Kevin Hopper (b), Chris Salmon (g), Mick Lynch (v). 26/1/86 MV5 DG ME ● SFPS019

7/7/86 Tupperware Stripper, Big End, Satisfaction, Bit-Part Actor. 24/6/86 MV4 DG TdB&MC

28/1/87 Living It Down, The Eager Bereaver, Alcohol, Bone. 13/1/87 U DG MFA&MR

13/9/88 The Song Remains, Thelma, Strayte 'N' Narrow, Seven Sisters. 14/8/88 HP DG U

The Stupids

12/1/87 Layback Session, Jesus Do What You Have To Do, Root Beer Death, Memory Burns / Slumber Party. Tommy Stupid (d, v, g), Pauly Pizza (b), Marty Tuff (g). 9/12/86 U DG MR&MA

27/5/87 Life's A Drag, Heard It All Before, Shaded Eyes, Dog Love, Stupid Monday. Ed (b, bck), Tommy (d, b, g, lv), Nick (bv). 12/5/87 U DG MR&TD ● SFPS054 & most of this session is also to be found on the two Hardcore Holocaust compilations

21/10/87 You Die, You'll Never Win, Pasta Boy, Your Little World, You Don't Belong. Tommy, Ed, Stevie Snacks (b) & The Sugarbeat Crew (perc-3). 13/10/87 U DG MR&JB

Darren Styles

31/8/04 DJ Mix. OS

Submarine

23/4/93 Fading, Junior Elvis, Tugboat. Jeff Townsin (d), Rob Harron (b), Neil Haydock (gv), Claire Lemmon (gv). 23/3/93 MV4 SA~

12/3/94 The Hate Calfornia Song, Empty, Learning To Live With Ghosts. Lemmon out. 1/3/94 MV4 MR JLC

Subsonic 2

9/11/91 Unsung Heroes Of Hip Hop, Doom Of The Sonic Boom, Dedicated To The City, Tower Of Babel. Robin Morley (v), Donald Brown (v), Colin Elliot (perc, g), Steve Heyliger (k, perc), Darren Campbell (b), Simeon Lister (sx). 15/10/91 MV4 MR MR

Suburban Studs

2/12/77 Suburban Studs, I Hate School, Necro, No Faith. Eddy Zipps (lvg), Keith Owen (g), Paul Morton (b), Steve Pool (d). 22/11/77 MV4 TW MR

Subway Sect

24/10/77 Chain Smoking, Parallel Lines, I Don't Split It, Nobody's Scared. Vic Goddard (v), John Bristol (g), Paul Myers (b), Bob Ward (d). 17/10/77 MV4 TW DD ○

4/12/78 Watching The Devil, Stool Pigeon, Double Negative, Head Held High. Colin Scot (b), John Bristol (g), Steve Atkinson (k) r Miller, Myers. 29/11/78 MV4 MR NG ○ on Rough Trade compilation album

Suckle

27/5/97 Symposium, Head, Cybilla, Long Finger. Frances McKee (gv), James Seenan (b, d), Marie McKee (v), Sophie Pragnell (vla-2). 11/5/97 MV4 ME NF

8/6/00 Earth Without Pleasure, So Happy Before, To Be King, Honey Suicide. F & M McKee, Vicky Morton (b), Elanor Taylor (fl, k, whistling), Kenny McEwan (d), Brian McEwan (g), Alan Barr (clo). 12/4/00 MV4 SA NF

Sudden Sway

24/11/83 Let's Evolve, Relationships. Simon Childs (g), Peter Jostins (b), Michael McGuire (kv), Lee Shale (perc), Colin Meech (perc), Karole Meech (bck). 16/11/83 MV4 JP NG ● SFPS005

21/11/84 In The Park, A Problem Solving Broadcast (Pt 1), A Problem Solving Broadcast (Pt 2), T Minus Tranquility. McGuire, Jostins, Childs, Shale, Shawn Foreman (rg), Susan McClean (b), Lee Bailey (rg), Eliza Egee (rg, v, p, bck). 11/9/84 MV5 MRD TdB

The Sugarcubes

9/12/87 Motor Crash, Cold Sweat, Delicious Demon, Deus, Mama. Bjork Gudmundsdottir (v), Einar Benediktson (v, tp), Siggi Baldursson (d), Erikki Erlingsson (g), Bragi Olasson (b), Thor Eldon Jonsson (g). Rec. date unknown OS U U

Sultans Of Ping FC

8/3/92 Kick Me With Your Leather Boots, He Thought I Was Your Best Friend, Give Him A Ball And A Yard Of Grass, Karaoke Queen. Morty McCarthy (d), Alan MacFeely (b), Pat O'Connell (g), Niall O'Flaherty (v). 5/3/92 MV4 DG NG&BJ

Sun Carriage

28/7/91 Sick Dog Crawling Can't See Love, BABE, Kiss To Tell, Written By. Michael (d), Sarah (b), Mathew (gv). 9/6/91 MV3 DG ME&PA

The Sunchalms

5/6/92 Magic Carpet, Into The Sun, Spaceship, On Reflection. Richard Farnel (b), Matt Neale (g), John Malone (g), Chris Ridley (d), Marcus Palmer (v, tamb, hca). 26/4/92 MV3 ME ME

The Sundays

6/3/89 I Won, My Finest Hour, Skin And Bones. Harriet Wheeler (v), David Gavurin (g), Paul Brindley (b), Patrick Hannan (d). 28/2/89 MV3 DG MR

Sunn O)))

21/12/04 Candle Wolf Of The Golden Chalice. Savage Pencil (tmbu), Anthony Sylvester (hmn, sruti box), Greg Anderson (g, Moog), Stephen O'Malley (g, hmn). 9/12/04 MV4 GW NF

Super Furry Animals

1/4/96 Frisbie, Hometown Unicorn, Focus Pocus, God Show Me Magic. Gruff Rhys (gv), Dafydd Ieuan (d), Cian Ciaran (k), Guto Price (b), Huw Bunford (gv). Live from MCR3 U U

22/4/98 The Turning Tide, Phire In My Heart, The Teacher (& Y Teimlad, TX live from MV4 24/3/98). 24/3/98 MV4 MR JB

1/3/00 Y Gwyneb Iau, Ymaelodi A'r Ymylon, Charge (Theme From Das Koolies), Dx Heaven. & Tony Robinson (tr), Kevin Brown (sx). 11/1/00 MV4 SA NF

12/7/01 Zoom, Nythod Cacwn, Run Christian Run, Fragile Happiness, A Touch Sensitive. Live from Peel Acres AR GT

6/10/04 Demons, Nythod Cacwin, Cryndod Yn Dy Lais, Y Gwyneb Iau, Hometown Unicorn, The Turning Tide, Gwreiddiau Dwfn, Gathering Moss. Live from MV4 AR MA

Supercharge

1/9/75 I Believe In You, Don't Let Go, We Are Free. Dave Irving (d), Ozzie Yue (gv), Tony Dunmore (b), Iain Bradshaw (k), Graham Robertson (al, bars), Albie Donnelly (ts). 19/8/75 MV4 TW U

14/6/76 Only You, Funkier Than Thou, Back On My Feet. & Les Karski (g, v), Bob Robertson (sx) r Robertson. 20/5/76 MV4 TW U

17/3/77 Last Train, Really Quite Easy, Mess You Made. & Andy Parker (ts), Bradshaw out. 8/3/77 MV4 JG MR

Superchunk

30/5/92 Let It Go, Tie The Rope, Fishing, United. Mac McCaughan (gv), Jim Wilbur (g, bck), Laura Ballance (b), Jon Wurster (d). 14/4/92 MV4 JB PA&JB

27/2/93 Lying In State, Flawless, I Guess I Remembered Wrong, Kicked In. 2/2/93 MV4 MR TdB

Supergrass

4/2/95 Alright, Lenny, Odd?, Time. Danny Goffey (d), Mickey Quinn (b), Bobs Coombes (k), Gaz Coombes (gv). 10/1/95 MV4 MR NF 'This session is dedicated to Peter Cook' (died 9/1/95)

14/9/99 Richard III, Mary, Strange Ones, Pumping On Your Stereo, Sun Hits The Sky, Lenny, Caught By The Fuzz. 23/7/99 Peel Acres SCU MA

Superqueens

8/9/04 Mr You're A Lap Dancer, Security And Peace, The Ghost Of Billy Whizz, Cut!, Business Is Business. Michael Conroy Harris (v), Brice Magill (k, prg). 12/8/04 MV4 JSM JHT

Supersister

3/4/73 Pudding And Yesterday . Robert Jan Stips (k), Sacha Van Geest (fl, sx), Marco Vrolyk (d), Ron van Eck (b). 20/3/73 U JW BC

Supertramp

18/7/70 It's A Long Road, Try Again, Birds Of Prey. Richard Davies (o, v), Richard Palmer (gv), Dave Windthrop (sx, v), Robert Millar (d), Roger Hodgson (bv). 30/6/70 MV4 JW PR 'Enthusiastic pass' from audition panel

12/9/72 Pony Express, School, Everyone Is Listening, I Can See. Frank Farrell, Kevin Currie r Palmer, Millar. 22/8/72 MV4 U BC

23/11/72 Summer Romance, Rudy, Pony Express, Dreamer. Farrell out. 20/11/72 LH1 BA U

22/3/73 Dreamer, Black Cat, Hey Laura, Bloody Well Right. & Dougie Thompson (b). 12/3/73 LH1 BA U

5/7/73 Chicken Man, Down In Mexico, Just A Normal Day (& Land Ho, 2/3/74 ROCK ON). 25/6/73 LH1 BA U

6/6/74 Bloody Well Right, If Everyone Was Listening, School. Bob C Benberg (d) r Currie, John Anthony Helliwell (sx, cl, v) r Windthrop. 23/5/74 LH1 TW U

Supreme Dicks

24/11/95 The Fallout Song, The Eagles Ate Your Soul, Phantom Matter Part Deux, (Son Of) All That Returns, Careful With That Axe Steve. Daniel Oxenburg (gv), John Shere (gv), Steve Shavel (slg, v), Mark Hanson (dv). 1/10/95 MV3 AA RF

Surgeon

8/10/98 Techno DJ set live from MV4 AR U

23/5/00 Live DJ set live from BBC Pebble Mill, Birmingham, for One Live

Surgery

23/6/91 D Nice†, Dear Sweet Laura†, Brazier, Locust. John Leamy (d), John Lachapelle (b), M Scott Kleber (g), Sean McDonnell (v). 28/5/91 MV5 MR MR&LS 'Dear John Peel, thanks for the opportunity to record in the excellent BBC studios. Mike, the engineer/producer/magician, treated us like kings, sincerely, Surgery' † on ○ SFMCD212

Sus

6/10/83 She Seems All Right, Mr DJ, Society Says, Yearning For Your Love. Junior Bailey & Hopeton McLean (lv), Paul Hamer (tb), Baba Williams (ts), Sorenson Bellot (d), Derwent Bent (b), Len Jones (lg), Errol Shorter (rgv), Eddie Williams (perc), Franklin Fraser (k). 24/9/83 MV4 DG AP

Sutherland Brothers Band

5/9/72 Sailing, Space Hymn, Sleeping Dog, Who's Crying Now (& Change The Wind, not TX). Iain & Gavin Sutherland (both agv, b) plus Neil Hopwood (d). 7/8/72 PH JW U

Sutherland Brothers and Quiver

6/3/73 Real Love, You Get Me Anyway, Rock And Roll Show, Love Is My Religion. Iain & Gavin Sutherland & Tim Renwick (lgv), John Wilson (d), Bruce Thomas (b), Peter Wood (p). 19/2/73 T1 PD (for JW) ARV

22/1/74 Real Love, Dream Kid, Bluesy World, I Hear Thunder. 8/1/74 LH1 U U

13/8/74 World In Action, Beat Of The Street, Saviour In The Rain, Annie. Thomas out. 30/7/74 LH1 TW BC

23/1/75 Devil Are You Satisfied, Silver Sister, Something Special, Last Boy Over The Moon. 16/1/75 MV4 TW U

30/6/75 Dirty City, Little Bit Something Else, Somebody Buy The Band A Drink, Laid Back In Anger. Wood out. 17/6/75 MV4 U U

4/12/75 Mad Trail, When The Train Comes, Love On The Moon, Ain't Too Proud. 18/11/75 MV4 TW U

Swan Arcade

27/2/73 Let Bucks A-Hunting Go, Babylon, He'll Have To Go / Lunatic Asylum, Salmon Tails & Last Valentine's Day, 1/5/73). David & Heather Brady (v), Royston Wood. 13/2/73 U JW U

9/4/74 A Long Time Ago, Deliverance Will Come, So From My Window, Peat Bog Soldiers. Miller r Wood. 25/3/74 U JW U

8/10/74 The Weary Whaling Grounds, Down In The Valley To Pray, Foster's Mill, The Battle Of Sowerby Bridge. Jack French (gv), Kevin Hingston (bv), Chris Taylor (dv) r Miller. 23/9/74 MV4 JW U

Sweet Marriage

17/8/69 Titania†, Mort†, Annie's Sister. Tony Merrick (lv), Alan Doyle (g), Keith Lawless (bv), Ronald Walker (lg), Anthony McDonald (d). 11/8/69 MV1 JW TW&MF † On ● Top Gear LP BBC Records REC 52S

Swell

6/6/92 Every Day Any Day, Tell Them Why, Life's Great, There's Always One Thing. Sean Kirkpatrick (d), Monte Vallier (b), Pete Vogl (g), David Freel (v, ag). 28/4/92 MV4 MR MR

The Swell Maps

27/10/78 Read About Seymour, Harmony In Your Bathroom, Full Moon In My Pocket / Blam / Full Moon, International Rescue, Another Song. Epic (d), Jowe (b), Nikki (g), Biggles (g). 16/10/78 MV4 TW DD

22/5/79 Bandits, Vertical Slum / Forest Fire, Armadillo, Midget Submarine. & Laura Logic (sx-2,4). 15/5/79 MV4 TVD MR&MPK ◯ On LP ● Whatever Happens Next Rough Trade ROUGH21

1/4/80 Big Empty Field, Bleep And Booster Come Round For Tea / Secret Island, (Let's) Buy A Bridge, The Helicopter Spies / A Raincoat's Room. 18/3/80 MV4 BS MR

Swervedriver

3/9/90 Out, Over, Volcano Trash, Zed Head. Graham Bonnar (d), Adi Vyne (b), Jim Hartridge (g), Adam Franklin (gv). 31/7/90 MV5 MR MR

Swinging Laurels

28/6/82 Rodeo, Murder Mile, Swing The Cat, Beating Heart. Gary Birtles (v, sx, k, perc), John Barrow (sx, bck, perc), Dean Sargent (b, tp), Mark O'Hara (k). 2/6/82 MV4 RP NG

Swirlies

26/2/94 Her Life Of Artistic Freedom, Crush, Jeremy Parker. Damon Tutunjian (v, g, tps), Seana Carmody (v, g, b), Andy Bernick (b, g, k), Anthony Deluca (d). 23/1/94 MV3 ME FK

Symbiosis

30/1/71 NTU, Volume 4: Be Bop, Bass Variations On Standfast, Aura, Standfast. Robert Wyatt (d), Roy Babbington (b), Nick Evans (tb), Gary Windo (ts, fl), Mongezi Feza (tp, fl), Steve Florence (g). 11/1/71 PH JW BC 'Yes for limited use': audition panel

Syncbeat

24/9/84 Khamsin, 52nd Beat, Dominance. Andy Connell (k), Martin Jackson (d, smp), Derek Johnson (b). 15/9/84 MV5 DG MC

Systems

17/11/81 Total Recall, Can You Imagine, Wishful Thinking, Falling Up. John Hawkins (v), Kevin Brown (k), Bazz Hughes (b), Jeremy Kelly (g), Tony Elson (d), Mike Nelson (sx). 31/10/81 MV4 DG ME

T Raumschmiere

8/10/03 I'm Not Death I'm Ignoring You, The Game Is Not Over (Feat. Miss Kitten), Rabaukendiskon 1, Rabaukendisko 2, Monstertruckerdriver (Dabrye's Big Truck Rmx), Bottle Living (T Raumschmiere Rmx), A Million Brothers (Feat MC Soom T), Radio Blackout, Rabaukendisko (Bugs Dancehall Rms Feat Ras B). Marco Haas (el, prg, k. dj). Live from MV4 AR NF

June Tabor

10/3/75 Seamus The Showman, Scarborough Fair Town, Dancing At Whitsun, And The Band Played Waltzing Matilda. June Tabor (v) Tim Hart (g-1,3; 3–solo). 4/3/75 MV4 U U

13/9/76 Young Waters, Pull Down Lads, Young Allan, Short Jacket And White Trousers. & John Gillaspie (k). 26/8/76 MV4 TW U

22/2/77 Lord Bateman, The Banks Of The Sweet Dundee, The Fiddle And The Drum, Donal Og. Solo. 25/1/77 MV4 PR MR ● SFPS015

19/7/77 Derry Jail, Riding Down To Portsmouth, The Devil And The Bailiff McGlinn, Streets Of Forbes, No Man's Land, A Taboresque Utterance. 11/7/77 MV4 MB DD. 'A Taboresque Utterance was written in indignation upon hearing of John Peel's broadcast sexual and sadistic desire to bite into her neck' note by MB on sheet. Track was broadcast as follows, Tabor: 'By the way, John, if you must bite me neck, take your false teeth out of the jar first' to which Peel replied 'See if you get any more work on this programme, fatty'

1/2/78 The Overgate, Now I'm Easy, Unicorns, Flash Company, Furze Field. & Martin Simpson (g, bj), John Gillaspie (p, sy, rec, o). 24/1/78 MV4 MB MR

5/1/91 White Rabbit, Annachie Gordon, Wheels On Fire, All Along The Watchtower. June Tabor (v) & the Oyster Band: Lee (d, tamb), Chopper (b, clo), John Jones (ml), Ian Telfer (fd, cnc), Alan Prosser (g, bck). 27/11/90 MV5 MR~

Tad

2/1/90 Nuts 'n' Bolts, Daisy, Helot, Wood Goblins. Steve Wiederhold (d), Kurt Danielson (b, bck), Gary Thorstensen (g), Tad Doyle (gv). 5/12/89 MV5 DG MR

5/7/90 3D Witch Hunt, Delinquent, Plague Years, Jack Pepsi. 19/6/90 MV3 MR~

Taggett

26/4/73 Squares To A Circle, Lonely Nights Lonely Days, Buster, Time. Tim Wheatley (b), Terry Fogg (d), Peter Hansen (k), Tont Hicks (g), Colin Horton-Jennings (g). 16/4/73 LH1 BA BC 1st session for Johnnie Walker 2/4/73

Talisker

5/3/76 Diddlin' For The Bairns / The Dark Isle, Dreaming Of Glenisla, The Black Bear, Tha Cu Ban Againn (We Have A White Dog), Hey Mandu. John Rangecroft (ts, cl), Davie Webster (as), Lindsay Cooper (db), Marc Meggido (db), Ken Hyder (d, perc). 24/2/76 MV4 U MR

Talisman

9/9/81 Wicked Dem, Run Come Girl, Nothing Change. Donald De Cordova (d), Dennison Joseph (b), Leroy Forbes (lg, bck), Desmond Taylor (lv, rg), Brendan Whitmore (ts), Bill Bartlett (o, p). 7/9/81 MV4 TW DD 1st session for Richard Skinner July 81

Tallulah Gosh!

11/1/88 World's Ending, Be Your Baby, I Don't Want To Have To Break Your Face, In Love For The Very First Time, Spearmint Head. Amelia Fletcher (gv), Chris Scott (b), Peter Punk (g), Matthew (d), Eithne Farry (bck). 29/12/88 U DG U 1st session was for Janice Long Aug 86 † On ● Sarah Records 604

Tam Linn

3/3/75 Tam Linn's Opener, Gypsy Davey, Ask Me Father, Hearts Lament. 4 (unknown). 25/2/75 MV4 U U

Sharon Tandy and the Fleur de Lys

29/10/67 Go-Go Power, Crosscut Saw (instrumental), There's Always Something There To Remind Me, Our Day Will Come, Hold On. Sharon Tandy (v) & Fleur de Lys: Bryn Haworth (g) & U. 11/10/67 U BA U

Tangerine Dream

21/2/74 Mysterious Semblance At The Strand Of Nightmares, Movements Of A Visionary, Sequent C, Phaedra. U PRIV

11/7/74 Overture, Zeus, Baroque. U PRIV

Tanz der Youth

9/8/78 I'm Sorry, Why I Die, Mistaken, Delay. Brian James (g, lv), Andy Coulquhoun (b, v), Tony Moore (k, v), Alan Powell (d). 2/8/78 MV4 BS NG

Tar

7/7/91 Viaduct Removal†, Walking The King, Ballad Of The Storyteller†, Play To Win. Mike Greenless (d), Tom Zalucki (b), Mary Zablucki (g), John Moho (gv). 16/5/91 MV5 DG TdB&DMC ◯ SFMCD212

Tarwater

6/1/99 Miracle Electric, The Watersample, A Mute E, Spectra. Ronald Lippok (kv, perc), Bernd Jestram (k, b). 1/12/98 MV4 TdB RJ

26/3/03 There's A Word, 20 Rupies To Paradise Road, Miracle Of Love, Be Late, Imperator Victus. Live from MV4 SCU MA

Taste

25/8/68 Same Old Story, Blister On The Moon, Dual Carriageway Pain, Norman Invasion (& Born On The Wrong Side Of Time, 27/10/68). Rory Gallagher (gv), Eric Kitteringham (b), Norman Damery (d). 5/8/68 PC1 BA U

30/10/68 Same Old Song, Dual Carriageway Pain, Born The Wrong Side Of Time, Wee Baby Blues. Richard McCracken (b), John Wilson (d) r Kitteringham, Damery. 3/10/68 MV5 DK U

9/3/69 I'm Moving On, Sugar Mama, Leaving Blues, Hail (& Woe Woe Baby, 20/4/69). 17/2/69 PH BA U

The James Taylor Quartet

29/4/87 Blow-up, Goldfinger, Hump-Backed Bridge, One-Way Street. Simon Howard (d), Allan Crockford (b), David Taylor (g), James Taylor (o). 12/4/87 U DG MA&ME

The Tea Set

3/4/80 Keep On Running (Big Noise From The Jungle), Nelson Was A Nance, Sawtooth, Contract Killer. Cally (d), Nick Haeffner (g), Nic Egan (lv), Ron West (b), Mark Wilkins (sy). 25/3/80 MV4 BS MR

The Teardrop Explodes

15/10/79 Brave Boys Keep Their Promises, Ha Ha I'm Drowning, Went Crazy, Chance. Michael Finkler (g), Julian Cope (b, lv), Ged Quinn (k, bck), Gary 'Rocky' Dwyer (d, bck). 2/10/79 MV4 JS MR

24/4/80 Thief Of Baghdad, When I Dream, The Poppies In The Field. David Balfe (k) r Quinn. 16/4/80 MV4 JE NG

22/12/81 Soft Enough For You, Sex, The Challenger. Cope, Balfe, Dwyer, Troy Tate (g), Ron (b). 16/11/81 MV4 TW DD&MC

The Tearjerkers

29/11/79 Dressing Up, Murder Mystery, Comic Book Heroes (& Suzy, possibly not TX). Paul Maxwell (lv), The Groover (g), Brian Ranson (g), Howard Ingram (b), Nigel Hamilton (d). U PRIV

25/3/80 Is It Art, I'm Sorry, Jenny Jenny, Comic Book Heroes. 12/3/80 MV4 JE NG

Tears for Fears

1/9/82 Ideas As Opiates, The Hurting, Suffer The Children, The Prisoner. Curt Smith (bv), Roland Orzabal (g, kv), Chris Hughes (dm). 14/8/82 MV4 DG MR

Technical Itch

16/4/02 DJ mix. Mark Caro (dj, tt, el). OS

Technoanimal

7/5/98 Demonoid, King Cobra, Monomaniacal, Skulldriver. Ade Odunlami (rp), Kevin Martin, Justin Broadrick. 15/3/98 MV4 ME KR

Teenage Fanclub

30/9/90 God Knows It's True, So Far Gone, Alcoholiday, Longhair. Norman Blake (gv), Raymond McGinley (g, bck), Gerard Love (bv), Brendan O'Hare (d, bck). 28/8/90 MV4 MWT~ ○ SFPCD081

Teenagers In Trouble

12/8/94 Suite: Judy Blue Eyes, With A Little Help From My Friends, I Wanna Take You Higher, I Dreamed I Saw Joe Hill. U OS

The Telescopes

13/6/89 Sadness Pale, There Is No Floor, Suffocation, Silent Water. Stephen Lawrie (v), Dave Fitzgerald (g), Joanna Doran (g), Dominic Dillon (d), Robert Brooks (b). 16/5/89 MV3 DG MR

15/9/91 Please Tell Mother, Splashdown, Prescence Of Your Grace, To The Shore. 6/8/91 MV5 MR MR

Television Personalities

1/9/80 Silly Girl, Picture Of Dorian Gray, La Grande Illusion, Look Back In Anger. Empire (d), Joe from Hendon (b, bck), Dan (g, lv). 20/8/80 MV4 DG NG

Ten Benson

11/6/98 Evil Heat, Uncle Benson, Count The Dog, Hell This Hour. Chris Teckkam (v, g, k, sx), Napoleon Catilo (d, bck), Duncan Lovatt (g, bck). 9/5/98 MV4 ME RJ

3/10/00 Stern, I Don't Buy It, Raggedy Man, Rock Cottage. Bruce Brand (d) r Catilo. 10/5/00 MV4 SA~

Ten Years After

10/12/67 Love Until I Die, Don't Want You Woman, Sometimes I Feel Like Going Home, Losing The Dogs (& The Sounds, 14/1/68). Alvin Lee (gv), Leo Lyons (b), Rick Lee (d), Chick Churchill (o). 21/11/67 AO2 BP PR Passed audition as 3-piece 'The Jaybirds' 2/66

7/4/68 Rock Your Mama, Portable People, I Ain't Seen No Whisky (& I May Be Wrong But I Won't Be Wrong Always, 14/1/68). 13/3/68 MV4 BA PR

18/8/68 Woman Trouble, Woodchoppers Ball, No Title Blues, I'm Going Home (& Spiders In My Web, 29/9/68). 14/8/68 PH BA AH&BC

5/1/69 Don't Want You Woman, Speed Kills, A Sad Song, No Title (& Woman Trouble, 2/3/69). 30/12/68 MV4 BA U

15/6/69 Good Morning Little Schoolgirl, Woke Up This Morning, I Can't Keep From Crying Sometimes (& Crossroads, 27/7/69). 9/6/69 PH JW TW

Tender Lugers

29/9/86 Johnny / Joanne, Enjoy Yourself, A Little Protection, Teenage Cream. Tim Lewis (g), Gary Oliver (b), Jason Collingwood (g), Bruce McGregor (gv). 16/9/86 U DG MFA&MC

Terminal Cheesecake

4/6/90 Pony Boy, Blowhound, Stinky Beads, Inbreds '80. Gary (bv), Russdancrane (g, b), Ghed (perc, tab), Rudy (d). 20/4/90 OS

Terminal Hoedown

9/2/92 Superwoman, Fear Eats The Soul, Yeah, Go Go Juice. Ernie Hendricks (d), Eamonn James Duffy (b), Peter Byrchmore (lg, bck), Joe Crow (rg, bck), Robert Lloyd (v). 22/12/91 MV3 DG ME&SBR

Terrashima

3/12/02 War Machine, Say Your Prayers. Trapped Inside, 50 Reasons To Bomb America. Mark Ibbetson (v), R DelGaudio (g), Mike Cross (b), Dan Montague (d). 7/11/02 MV4 MA GYW

Sonny Terry & Brownie McGhee

19/6/73 Walkin' My Blues Away, Rock Island Line, Walk On, Life Is A Gamble. 5/6/73 PH JW BC

Terry and Gerry

23/7/84 Hello, Wolfman's Request, Clothes Shop Close, Butter's On The Bread, Wait Until You're Older. Terry Lilley (db, v), Gerry Colvin (gv), Andy Downer (gv), Doreen de-Ville (Sue Richardson) (wsh). 11/7/84 MV5 RP GP

10/4/85 Simon, Kennedy Says, Armchair Terrorist Song, A Shanty For The Gravy Boat. 24/3/85 MV5 DG ME

9/10/85 Reservation, The Last Bullet In The Gun, The Ballad Of A Nasty Man, Fashion Rodeo, Peel Jingle. Terry, Gerry, 'Doreen', Jeremy Page (gv), Chris Davies (bars), Alistair Robertson (ts), Chris Bowden (al). 24/9/85 MV5 JWI TdB

Test Department

22/8/83 Shockwork, State Of Affairs, Hunger. Angus Farquhar, Paul Jamrozy, Graham Cunnigton, Toby Burdon. 15/8/83 MV4 TW MC

4/2/85 Operation Prayer Power, Massive Kamikaze Attack. U 19/2/85 U U U

Testcard F

3/1/83 Bandwagon Tango, Blanket Expression, Ransom, Unfamiliar Room. Sue Hope (v), Pete Roberts (sy), John Hartwell (electric d), Vince Rogers (o). 18/12/82 MV4 DG MC

Les Têtes Brûlées

27/10/90 Oyili, Ekye, Ziliyan, Mindzug. Andre Afata (dv), Martin Maam (bv), Roger Bexongo (perc, gv), George Essono (kv), Jean-Marie Ahanda (tp, v). 16/10/90 MV5 U MWT&JLO

That Dog

15/1/94 One Summer Night, He Rocks, Angel, Sit On the Floor. Tony (d), Anna Waronker (glv), Rachel (bv), Petra (v, vi). 9/12/93 MV4 NG SCO

That Petrol Emotion

24/6/85 V2, Lettuce, Blind Spot, Can't Stop. John O'Neill (g), Ciaran McLaughlan (d), Raymond Gorman (g), Damian O'Neill (b), Steve Mack (v). 11/6/85 MV5 JWI MR †

18/11/85 Tight Lipped, Circusville, Cheapskate, Mouth Crazy. 5/11/85 MV5 PWL MR † on ○ SFMCD205

14/1/87 Big Decision, Swamp, Inside, Chester Burnette. 16/12/86 U DG MR

Theatre of Hate

9/12/80 Rebel Without A Brain, The Wake, 63, It's My Own Invention. Kirk Brandon (lv), Steve Guthrie (g), Stan Stammers (b), Luke Rendall (d), John Boy (sx). 1/12/80 LH1 TW DD&JB

24/8/81 Love Is A Ghost, Conquistador, Propaganda, Do You Believe In The West World? Guthrie out. 15/8/81 MV4 DG MR

18/2/82 Dreams Of The Poppy, Incinerator, The Hop, The Klan. Brandon, Stammers, Boy, Nigel Preston (d), Billy Duffy (g). 8/2/82 MV4 DG DD

Thee Hypnotics

10/4/89 Soul Trader, Love In A Different Vein, Nine Times, Let's Get Naked. Mark Thompson (d), Will Pepper (b), Ray Hanson (g), James Jones (v, hca). 28/3/89 WX DG MR

Themselves

12/11/02 This Is About The City, Only Child Explosion, Live Trap, You Devil You & ? Doseone (Adam Drucker), Jel (Jeffrey Logan). Live from LL JSM~ U

Therapy? ○

28/9/91 Innocent X / Meat Abstract, Prisonbreaker, Perversonality. Fyfe (dv), Michael (b), Andy (g). 15/8/91 MV5 DG TdB&JLO&SCO

6/2/93 Pile Of Bricks, Bloody Blue, Totally Random Man, Autosurgery. & Harvey Birell (smp). 29/11/92 MV3 JB JLC both on ○ Music Through A Cheap Transistor: The BBC Sessions, Mercury Records download 2007

Thermals

28/1/04 It's Trivia, A Stare Like Yours, Forward, Doe. Hutch Harris (gv), Kathy Foster (b), Jordan Hudson (d). 11/12/03 MV4 MA GT

Thievery Corporation

16/4/98 The Assassination, Sun Moon & Stars, Samba Tranquille, The Killers Waltz. Eric Hilton, Rob Garza. OS

Thin Lizzy

3/11/71 Raygun, The Rise And Demise Of The Funky Nomadic Tribe, Dublin, Clifton Grange Hotel. Phil Lynott (bv), Brian Downey (d), Eric Bell (g). 12/10/71 MV4 U U 1st session for Stuart Henry, July 71

2/6/72 Call The Police, Things Ain't Working Out Down At The Farm, Chatting Today. 26/4/72 T1 JM U

28/11/72 Whiskey In The Jar, Suicide, Black Boys On The Corner, The Saga Of The Ageing Orphan. 14/11/72 LH1 TW BC

7/8/73 Gonna Creep Up On You, Litle Girl In Bloom, Vagabonds Of The Western World. 31/7/73 LH1 JW U

16/8/73 Randolph's Tango, Rocker, Slow Blues. 6/8/73 LH1 BA U

11/4/74 Little Darling, Sitamoia, It's Only Money, Black Boys On The Corner, Still In Love With You. Gary Moore (g) r Bell. 4/4/74 LH1 TW BAI

24/10/74 Philomena, It's Only Money, Sha La La, She Knows. Scott Gorham (g) & Brian Robertson (g) r Moore. 3/10/74 MV4 TW BAI

5/6/75 Rosalie, Freedom Song, Half Caste, Suicide. 29/5/75 MV4 TW BAI

9/3/76 Jailbreak, Emerald, Cowboy Song, The Warrior. 12/2/76 MV4 TW BAI

11/10/76 Don't Believe A Word, Johnny The Fox Meets The Weed, Fool's Gold, Johnny. 23/9/76 MV4 TW BAI

22/8/77 Killer Without A Cause, Bad Reputation, That Woman's Gonna Break Your Heart, Dancing In The Moonlight, Downtown Sundown. & (sx) U. 1/8/77 MV4 TW BAI

Thing

9/3/91 Blu 4 U, Kiss The Sun, All Will Be Revealed, It's So Easy. Jesse Obstbaum (v), Jake Ottman (g), Salvatore Canzorieri (g), Sean Bolivar (b), Andrew Nelson (d). 10/2/91 MV3 DG ME&JLO

Thinking Fellers Union Local 282

18/3/94 Star Trek, More Glee, One Inch Tall, Father. Anne Eikelberg (bv), Brian Hageman, Hugh Swarts (gv), Jay Paget (dv), Mark Davies (g, bj, v). 13/2/94 MV3 ME AA

Third Ear Band

1/1/69 The Grove, Stone Circle, Egyptian Book Of The Dead, Pierrot. Glen Sweeney (d), Richard Coff (vi), Paul Minns (ob), Benjamin Courtland (vi). 31/12/68 AO2 PR U

27/7/69 Hyde Park Raga, Druid, Ghetto Raga. 21/7/69 PH JW U

20/6/70 Downbone Raga, Feel Your Head, Hyde Park Raga. Ursula Smith r Courtland. 8/6/70 PH JW U

11/2/72 Air, I The Key. Denim Bridges (g), Simon House (vi), Michael Marchant (gv), Peter Pavli (b) r Smith. 25/1/72 T1 JM&PD U

Third Eye Foundation

2/6/99 Goddamit You Got Too Behind, Some Pitying Angel. Matt Elliott (g, d, elec, prg). OS

This Heat ○

22/4/77 Fall Of Saigon, Not Waving But Drowning, Horizontal Hold. Charles Bullen (g), Charles Hayward (d, k), Gareth Williams (o, b). 28/3/77 MV4 TW DD

24/11/77 Makeshift, Rimp Romp Ramp, Sitting, Slither, Basement Boy. 26/10/77 MV4 B NG Both sessions on ○ Made Available 2006

This Poison

30/11/87 Question Mark, St Johnstoun, Driving Skills, It'll All Work Out. Derek MacMoir (g), Saigz MacTaylor (gv), Alistair Macdonald (b), Steve MacGray (d). 22/11/87 U DG ME&FK

Richard & Linda Thompson

25/11/73 The Little Beggar Girl, Dragging The River, The Great Valerio, Medley: The Neasden Hornpipe / The Avebury Particle Accelerator / The Flowing Tide. Richard Thompson (agv), Linda Peters (v). 1/1/73 U BA U

12/2/74 Hokey Pokey, Georgie On A Spree, I'll Regret It All. 4/2/74 T1 JW U

24/2/75 A Heart Needs A Home, Wishing, I'm Turning Off A Memory. & Ian Whitman (p), Pat Donaldson (b), Dave Mattacks (d). 11/2/75 MV4 TW U 'All vocals Linda, Richard had flu' – TW ○ Complete third session on Hokey Pokey remastered Island CD 2004

The Three Johns

10/8/82 Pink Headed Bug, Lucy In The Rain, Heads Like Convicts, No Place, You'll Never Walk Alone. John Langford (d, g), John Hyatt (v), John Brennan (bv), John Henry (tu, p), Tom Greenhalgh (g-2), Mark White ('screaming'-3), Stuart Curley & Jeremy Gilpen (bck-4,5). 21/7/82 MV4 RP AP

9/3/83 Fruit Flies, Marx's Wife, Windolene, Men-Like Monkeys, Sad House. Langford, Hyatt, Brennen; & Greenhalgh, Curley, Sally Timms (v), David Spencer (v). 5/3/83 MV4 DG MC

7/11/83 Sun Of Mud, The Day Industry Decided To Stop, A Public Song For A Friend Under Suspicion Of Fire Bombing A Private Shop, Poo-Poo-Poodle Bourgeois / Mouths To Feed. & Greenhalgh, Dave Hunt (dm), John Ridley (hca-3,4). 26/10/83 MV4 RP NG

30/4/84 Nightingales, Train, Junk, Bloop. & Greenhalgh, Mitch Hagar (bck), Karen Hagar (bck), Paul Griffiths (hca), Jeanie O'Toole (perc). 17/4/84 MV5 BYA U

23/7/85 Demon Drink, Coals To Newcastle, King Car, Torpedo, Third World War. & Kate Morath (ob), Tom Greenford (p), John Ridley (hca), John Spence (v-5). 14/7/85 MV5 DG ME

2/3/87 Key Largo, The Book Of The Dead, Computer, Never And Always. & Greenhalgh, Steve Goulding (d), Sally Timms (bck-2). 15/2/87 U DG ME&MFA

Three Mustaphas Three

20/1/83 Intro / Dobrodolska Horo / O Haralambis, Si Vous Passait Par La, Tria Pedia Voliotika / Freylich Un Lebedike, O Memetis, Czay Calypso. Hijaz (vi), Housack (d), Niaveti (acc), Ousack (clo, v) & Patrel Mustapha (lv, bz). 12/1/83 U RP NG

6/7/83 Mustapha Introduction / Pefida, A Chilling Tale Pt 2, Valjare Grave Kosovare, Haspiko Grigoro. 2/7/83 MV4 DG MR

30/1/84 Bam / Teteli, Introduction / Schnabbelleh Freilach, To Tilefono Tis Xenitias, Belz, Jingle, Theme Tune. & Isfa'ani Mustapha (perc). 21/1/84 MV4 DG MC

24/4/85 Svadba, Singe Tema, Grigoro Noz – A Chilling Tale Part 5, Ya Habaybi Ya Ghaybine. & Fat'mah Mustapha (tb). 7/4/85 MV5 DG ME

2/12/85 Niska Banja, Besarabia, Hora Lui Marin, Ainy La La/Ah Ya Assmar El Lawn, Vranjanski Ekspres, O Memetis, Cabra. L'Orchestre 'Bam' de Grand Mustapha International and Party: Uncle Patrel (bz, v), Isfa'ani (perc, md), Houzam (d, bck), Hijaz (hawaiian g, vi), Sabah Habas H (b, bck) & Niaveti Mustapha III (fl, acc, picc) & Laura Daviz (v), Kem Mustapha (p, acc), Yheric Mustapha (tp), Andreos Blake (cl, sx), Telor Borrachon Pavel (tb), '& the string ensemble 'Fat'mah', complete with EEC names and passports': Anne Stephenson & Sally Herbert (vi), Joss Pooke (vla), Rachel

Maguire (clo). † released as LP 'Local Music' on Globestyle Records Fez 003. 19/11/85 MV5 MR MR

21/9/87 A Ova / Valle Epogradecit, Musafir, Xamenhevtexia / Fien, Gankino Horo, Selver. Hijaz, Isfa'ani, Kemo (k, kaval), Sabah H. (bv), Houzam & Niaveti Mustapha. 8/9/87 U DG ME&MPK

28/8/90 Sitna Lisa, Buke E Kripe / Kalazhojne, Taxi Driver / Benga Taxi, Kopanitsa. Sabah Habas, Houzam, Niaveti, Daovdi (sx, cl), Kqno (p, qiftgli, acc) & Hija Mustapha. 10/7/90 MV5 MR~

Three Stages Of Pain

11/2/03 I Am 6 Foot 2 Inches, Death Rides The Highway, Million Times, Hull Diver. Gareth Hustwaite (v), David Fowkes (g), Daniel Walsh (g), Matthew Cretney (b), Tony Shephard (d). 9/1/03 MV4 MA GT

Three Wise Men

10/12/86 Cruising For A Bruising, Urban Hell, Refresh, Hard Bop. Jemski, Danny 'D' & AJ (rp), Cybotron (sc, dj), Phil Chil (prg). 18/11/86 U DG ME&SC

Thrilled Skinny

3/10/88 Social Climbing, So Happy To Be Alive, Love Rut / Neigh On Sea, Eat My Hat. Elliot Smoke (d, bck), Simon Goalpost (b, lv-2,3), Andy Furniture (g, lv-1,4), Utensil Realname (elp, bck). 18/9/88 HP DG MA

Thrush Puppies

6/1/95 Offside, Mayqueen, Guilty, Tart/Bint. Lauren Hyde (d), Anthony Lynch (b), Joolz McLaranon (v). 8/11/94 MV4 MR CML

Tiger

16/11/96 She's Ok, Icicle, Ray Travez, Where's The Love. Dan Laidler (v), Julie Sims (vg), Seamus Feeney (d), Dido Hallett (b, Moog), Daren Eskriett (g), Tina Whitlow (gk). 3/11/96 MV5 ME~

25/11/98 Bottle Of Juice, Candy & Andy, God It's Good, Sea Shandy. Laidler, Sims, Hallett, Whitlow, Gavin Skinner (d, perc, prg), Donald Ross Skinner (g, perc, extra bits). 13/10/98 MV4 MR KR

Tigerstyle

15/4/03 From The Pend, Tiger, Freestyle, Catch 22. Pops (dhol, dholki, vasa, tumbi, dhad), Jazz (tt), Rak (tt), Soom T (v). 27/3/03 MV4 KR NF

Steve Tilston

27/10/71 The Highway, Reaching Out, Don't Let It Get You Down (& All In A Dream, 29/12/71). Steve Tilston (ag, v). 20/9/71 PH JW BC

Timeshard

1/4/94 God Says No To Tomorrow, Oracle, Cosmic Carrot (Parts I & II). Mark Graham (p), Steven Grant (sit, k), Simon Kember. 27/2/94 MV3 MR RJ

Tindersticks

28/5/93 Raindrops, Tye Die, Her, Drunk Tank. Stuart Staples (lv), Neil Fraser (g), Dickon Hinchcliffe (b), David Boulter (vi, bck). 27/4/93 MV4 MR JB

19/2/94 Snowy In F Sharp Minor, A Night In, Dickon Steps Out, Sleepy Song. Staples, Hinchliffe, Boulter, Al McLauly (d), Mark Colwill (b). 18/1/94 MV4 MR RJ

7/12/96 Manalow, Dick's Slow Song, I Was Your Man, Don't Look Down. & Neil Fraser (o). 24/11/96 MV4 ME~ all on BBC Sessions Island/Universal ○

Keith Tippett

26/9/70 Thoughts To Geoff / Five After Dawn / Green And Orange Night Park. Keith Tippett (p), Mark Charig (cnt), Elton Dean (al, sxl), Nick Evans (tb), Roy Babbington (b), Brian Spring (d). 25/8/70 MV4 JW U Tippett's original group had debuted live on R1 Jazz Club 8/1/69

21/1/72 Chugging Brown, Yellow Buzz, Mauve Ballade (& Topless Air-Pockets, 3/3/72). Trio. 5/1/72 T1 JM U

Tir Na Nog

9/6/72 Blue Bottle Star, Piccadilly, Come And See The Show, The Same Thing Happening. Leo O'Kelly (g, bjv), Sonny Condell (g, bjv). 1/5/72 PH JM JWH

17/10/72 Teeside, Going Away, Strong In The Sun†, In The Morning, I Wanna Roo You. 4/9/72 PH JW BC

1/2/73 Cinema, Free Ride, Most Magical, In The Morning. 15/1/73 LH1 BA U

13/11/73 Free Ride†, Today We Flew†, Backwater A While†, Better Off At Home†. 23/10/73 LH1 TW U † on ○ Spotlight HUX021

To Rococo Rot

6/11/97 I'm In Training Don't Kiss Me, Esther, Days Between Stations, International Velvet. Robert Lippok (el, k), Ronald Lippok (Yamaha Sampler, d), Stefan Schneider (b, el). 30/9/97 MV4 MWT FK

11/5/99 A Little Asphalt Here And There (Featuring I), Gluck, Crosby. 11/4/99 MV3 ME~

Tocques

24/9/02 Jealous Again, In My Time Of Dying, Louise, Out There. Craig Hamilton (v, ag), Bill Summerfield (gv), Anna Russell (v, Fender Rhodes), Phil Robinson (d),

Cam Docherty (b, ag), Julian Wilson (Hammond), Leighton Hargreaves (fd), Alan MacDonald (clo), Jez Ince (mnd), Simon Alpin (dobro). 18/8/02 MV4 ME RJ See Buick 6

Today Is The Day

24/3/95 I Bent Scared, Sidewinder, Hands And Knees, Many Happy Returns, Six Dementia Sabyr. Steven Austin (g, v, smp), Michael Herrell (b), Christopher Elrod (d). 26/2/95 U ME GT

Tomorrow, featuring Keith West

1/10/67 Three Jolly Little Dwarfs, My White Bicycle, Revolution, Real Life Permanent Dream, Colonel Brown. Keith West (v), John 'Twink' Alder (d), Steve Howe (lg), John Wood (b). 21/9/67 MV4 BP PR West & Wood's previous band, The In Crowd, passed a trial broadcast on Sat Club 5/65, then no bookings until this

4/2/68 Blow Up, Strawberry Fields Forever, Now Your Time Has Come, The Incredible Journey Of Timothy Chase. 31/1/68 MV4 BP PR

Tompaulin

22/11/00 North, My Life At The Movies, Second Rate Republic, Slender. Amos Memon (d, perc), Katie Grocott (b), Simon Trought (g), Jamie Holman (gv), Stacey McKenna (v), Lee Davies (k, mel). 11/6/00 MV4 ME RJ

20/11/01 My Life As A Car Crash, Since Yesterday, Short Affairs, The Boy Hairdresser. & Giles Cooke (ag). 2/9/01 MV4 ME GT

Too Much Texas

8/8/88 Jayne, Anchor, Rogue, Harp. Tom (gv), Gordon (g), Raymond (b), Lawrence (d). 24/7/88 MV5 DG MA

Tools You Can Trust

12/10/83 The Feud, Working And Shopping, Show Your Teeth, Houses And Tools. Ben Stedman (bg, d, tps), Rob Ward (v, perc, tps) & Eddie Fenn & Colin Larn (d). 8/10/83 MV4 DG MR

11/4/84 Ranters And Preachers, Messy Body Thrust, Cut A New Seam, Blowin' Up A Storm. & Fenn (d), Claire Wilkinson (perc). 21/3/84 MV5 PSM NG&TD

5/12/84 A Knock For The Young, Crammed Down The Throat, Shazam / Sign Of The Swinging Lightbulb. & Phil Hughes (g, tp, perc), Jill Richardson (d, perc), Martin Herring (d, perc). 27/11/84 MV5 MRD U

Top

17/2/91 No 1 Dominator, Feel Good, When The Summer's Gone. Alan Wills (d), Paul Cavanagh (gv), Joe Fearon (b). 31/1/91 MV5 DG MWT&PL ● On 10-inch of 'Buzzin'' Island 10ISP504

Topper

15/2/97 Something To Tell Her, Tuneless Man, Won't Do You No Harm. Dyfrig Evans (gkv), Iwan Evans (bv), Peter Richardson (d). 28/1/97 MV4 MR PL

15/7/98 Losing My Mind, Leave Me Alone, Mystery Man, Kiss & Tell (& Just Don't Understand, 1st TX live 2/6/98). 2/6/98 MV4 MR BJ

Tortoise

31/8/96 Wait, Vaus, Tin Cans And Twine, The Taut And Tame. Johnny Herndon (d), John McEntire (d, k), Doug McCombs (b), Dave Pajo (b, g), Jeff Parker (g), Dan Bitney (perc). 13/6/96 MV4 MR RJ

30/4/98 In Sarah Mencken Christ And Beethoven There Were Women And Men, I Set My Face To The Hillside, Aldeia De Ogum, TNT. & Rob Mazurek (cnt-4), Sara P Smith (tb-4), Pajo out. 29/3/98 MV4 ME NS

Tot

7/12/87 Barney O, The Bell, To Add Up, Cling. Tony Martin (ma), Debbie Turner (v), Rachel George (v). 29/11/87 U DG ME&PS

Die Töten Hosen

10/7/84 Hip Hop Bommi Bop, Spiel Mir Das Lied Vom Tod†, Es Is Vorbei†, Reisefieber†, Bis Zum Bitteren Ende†, Hofgarten. Trini (d), Andi (b), Breiti (rg), Kuddel (k, v, lg), Campi (v), Freddy Love (rp-1). 30/6/84 MV5 DG MC † On LP ● Liebespieler Virgin TOT88

Toxic Reasons

18/11/86 White Noise, Break The Bank, No Pity, Harvest. Bruce Stuckey (gv), Tufty (bv), JJ Pearson (dv). 14/10/86 U DG MFA&TD

The Tractors

1/7/87 Caesar / Caesar, Joe, Postcard Story, Undertaker's Waltz. Andrew Cave (v), David Evans (g), Ian O'Connor (b), Jeffery Fitzhenry (b), Peter Ludden (d), Edwina Allcock (clo), Paul Boyce (cl). 7/6/87 U DG ME&FK

Traffic

1/10/67 Smiling Phases, A House For Everyone, Hole In My Shoe, Coloured Rain, Paper Sun (& Mr Fantasy, 29/10/69). Steve Winwood (ov), Dave Mason (gv), Jim Capaldi (dv), Chris Wood (sx, fl, v). 25/9/67 MV4 BA PR

24/12/67 Here We Go Round The Mulberry Bush, Heaven Is In Your Mind, No Face No Name No Number, Dealer, Hope I Never Find Me There. 11/12/67 PC1 BA DT

3/3/68 Heaven Is In Your Mind, No Face No Name No Number, Roamin' Thru The

Gloamin' With 40,000 Headmen, Blind Man (& Dear Mr Fantasy, 7/4/68). 26/2/68 PC1 BA DT

30/6/68 You Can All Join In, Who Knows What Tomorrow May Bring, Feelin' Alright (& Pearly Queen, 28/7/68). 24/6/68 PC1 BA U

Tram

14/10/98 Expectation, Too Scared To Sleep, Home, Like Clockwork. Paul Anderson (gv), Nick Avery (d), Clive Painter (g, perc), Martine Roberts (b), Bill Lloyd (k). 22/9/98 MV4 TdB RF

3/11/99 Are You Satisfied, Yes But For How Long, You Let Me Down, I've Been Here Once Before. Anderson, Avery, Painter, Ida Akesson (k). 5/9/99 MV3 ME JB

30/1/01 Now That We Can Get On With Our Lives, He Walks Alone, Underneath The Ceiling, Folk. Anderson, Avery, Painter, Fiona Brice (vi), Steve Gillard (p), Helen Thomas (clo). 10/12/00 MV4 U

Trans AM

22/2/00 I Want It All, Play In The Summer, City In Flames, Love Commander. Nathan Means (str, b, v), Phil Manely (gv), Sebastian Thomson (d). 26/1/00 MV4 MR GYW

Transglobal Underground

2/4/93 This Is My Army Of Forgotten Souls, Yallachant, Shimmer, Sirius B. Count Dubula (b, g), Natacha Atlas (v), Man-Tu (d), Neil Sparks (v), A Kasiek (prg), Goldfinger Matheru (clo). 21/2/93 MV4 ME~ JMK

20/5/95 Boss Tabla, Light Fish, Mouth Wedding, Make Me A Drum. Natacha Atlas (d, Dubalah), Coleridge (dv), Alex Kasiek (prg), Satin Singh (tab, cga). 20/4/95 MV4 AA GPR

The Transmitters

21/11/79 Dirty Harry, I Fear No-One But My Friends, Bird In The House, Blankety Blank. John Grimes (lv), Sam Dodson (g), Amanda de Grey (k), Sid Wells (b), Jim Chase (d). 30/10/79 MV4 JS MR

29/7/81 Joan Of Arc, Love Factory, Voodoo Woman In Death Plunge / The Rent Girls Are Coming, Dance Craze. Wells, Dodson, Dave Baby (sx), Julian Treasure (d), Rob Chapman (v). 22/7/81 MV4 DG NG

Travis Cut

6/5/98 Exiled, Tourniquet, Another Dumb Punk Rock Song All About A Girl, A Girl I Used To Know. Chris Guitar (v), Mac Bass (v), Bunny Ball (d). 22/3/98 MV4 ME NS

7/6/00 Closure, Eighteen Again, Run It Off, Tonight's Too Late. Mac (bv), Chris (gv), Tony (d). 16/4/00 MV3 ME NS

18/4/02 Protest & Politics, In Transit, Never Wanted Anything, M Q. 3/2/02 MV3 ME RJ

Treebound Story

12/3/86 Your Kind, Forever Green, My Life's Example, Something. Rob Gregory (d), Paul Infanti (b), Paul Currie (gv), Richard Hawley (g). 4/3/86 MV4 DG ME

Trembling Blue Stars

14/9/00 As Long As She's Needed, Before We Know It, Sometimes I Still Feel The Bruise, The Times You've Come. Bobby Wratten (gv), Harvey Williams (gk, prg), Ian Catt (b), Anne Mari Davies (v). 9/8/00 MV4 KR PN

Trencher

25/5/04 Attack Of The Sex Attackers, Delusions / Blondes Of Meth, Row Upon Row Of Leper Skulls / Deja Poo, I Lost All My Hair In A Skiing Accident / Trapp. Mark Dicker (Casio, v), Ross Sargeant (bv), Liam Sparkes (dv), Marlon McNeill (v). 28/4/04 MV4 GT NF

16/12/04 Five numbers from LP 'Lips'. Live from MV4 NF RJ

Tribute To Nothing

15/7/94 Lost Your Mind, Weight Control, Nutters, Can't Get Up, Before. Sam Turner (gv), Jim Turner (bv), Ben Turner (d), Helene Almqvist (announcements-5). 29/5/94 MV3 ME RJ

The Triffids

13/11/84 Bright Lights Big City, Monkey On My Back, Field Of Glass. Allan Macdonald (d, bck), Martyn Casey (b), Jill Birt (k), David McComb (lv, g), Rob McComb (g, bck, perc). 6/11/84 MV5 MRD MR

14/5/85 Life Of Crime, Lonely Stretch, Chicken Killer. Graham Lee (ps) joins; & Fiona Franklyn & Sally Collins (bck). 5/5/85 MV5 DG ME ● SFPS036

27/5/86 Kelly's Blues, Wide Open Road, Kathy Knows, Keep Your Eyes On The Hole. Six-piece. 20/5/86 MV5 DG MR&JB

Tripping Daisy

19/3/96 Bang, I Got A Girl, Piranha, Wiggle. Tim de Laughter (gv), Wes Berggren (g, bck), Mark Pirro (b), Mitch Drew (d). Live from MCR3 U U

Trixie's Big Red Motorbike

24/8/82 Invisible Boyfriend, Whatever Happened To The Treetops, You Took Him Away From Me, Splash Of Red. Mark Litten (dm, b, g), Jim Bycroft (k, sx), Melanie Litten (v). 28/07/82 MV4 RP MR

25/8/83 That's The End Of That, One Nation Under A Brolly, Norman And Narcissus, In Timbuktu, White Horses. Jane Fish (clo, bck, 'claps') r Bycroft. 17/08/83 MV4 BYA AP

Robin Trower

12/4/73 Twice Removed From Yesterday, Man Of The World, Daydream, Summer Song. Robin Trower (g), James Dewar (bv), Reg Isidore (d). 26/3/73 U BA BC

26/3/74 A Little Bit Of Sympathy, Bridge Of Sighs, In This Place, Alethea. 5/3/74 LH1 TW U

3/2/75 Fine Day, Confessing Midnight, It's Only Money, Gonna Be More Suspicious. Bill Lordan (d) r Isidore. 28/1/75 MV4 TW U

Trumans Water ○

11/6/93 All Wet West Of Washington, Long End Of A Firearm, Large Organs, Seven Holes, Hair Junk Fiver. Ely Loyal (d), Keven Branstetter (b, bck), Glen Galloway (gv), Kirk Branstetter (g, bck), Will Prentice (pp-1&2). 11/5/93 MV4 MR~ TD

5/11/93 Death To Dead Things, Girler Too, Suncity Girls Song (aka Esoterica Of Abyssinia), Nation Of Ulysses Song (aka Kingdom Of Heaven), No Naked Lights, True Tilt Pin Ball. K & K Branstetter, Galloway, Mike Mooradian (dv). 26/9/93 MV3 ME GT

17/6/94 Milk Train To Paydirt (aka Lick Observatory), Gogo Dancer Solidified, Electro Muerta, Talking Hockey With Strangers, Saint Job (International Gore). K & K Branstetter, Kevin Cascell (d, p, v, g-4), Dean Pritchard (exhaust pipe – 1&4). 10/5/94 MV4 MR JMK all on ○ The Peel Sessions SFRCD133

Trusty

8/12/96 Dear Diary, Dana Marie, Diving Watch, Unsnowplow. Jim Schaffer (d), Brad Long (b), James Brady (gv), Bobby Matthews (gv). 24/11/96 MV5 ME FK

Tsunami

19/6/93 460, Kidding On The Square, Water's Edge, Newspaper. Jenny Toomey (gv), Kristin Thomson (gv), Andrew Webster (b), John Pamer (d). 20/5/93 MV4 NG~ JLC

Tubeway Army

16/1/79 Me I Disconnect From You, Down In The Park, I Nearly Married A Human. Gary Numan (k, g, lv), Paul Gardiner (b), Jess Lidyard (d). 10/1/79 MV4 BS NBU ○ SFMCD202. See Gary Numan

Mo Tucker

3/4/92 Blue All The Way To Canada, Fired Up, Trains, Too Shy. John Sluggett (d), Daniel Hutchens (b), Sonny Vincent (g), Sterling Morrison (g), Mo Tucker (gv). 18/2/92 MV4 MR MR

Chris Stainton's Tundra

20/8/74 They Don't Know, Double Crossed, The Calling Of The Wind, I Want To Tell You (& Think Like A Child, 29/10/74). Chris Stainton (kg), Glen Turner (g, lv), Charlie Harrison (b), Henry Spinetti (d). 6/8/74 LH1 TW U

Tunic

28/10/94 Chandelier, Between The Lies, Locomotive, Bass Man, Tangerine Flak. Mark Gordon (g, b, v), Brian White (g, b, v), Emily Sloan (k), Jonathon Wallace (d). 20/9/94 MV4 MR RJ

7/10/95 Oh Joy, Berk Mower, Valium, The Lions In The Neighbour's Porch, Bunic In The Area. Jonathan London (d), Brian Flint (g, v, b), Marky Starr (g, v, b), Tanya Kidscape (gv), Michelle Duclef (k). 10/9/95 MV3 ME FK

14/9/96 The Man Who Would Grab Air, Stranger Boy, Geet In Dub, Wind Blows Strong. Jonathan London (dgv), Mark Karr (bgv, d, k), Tanya Kidscape (gv, vi), Brian Flint (bv), Michelle Duclef (k, rec). 27/8/96 MV4 MR~

6/5/97 L'Accord Parfait, Marche De Sacco Et Vanzetti, Le Plus Beau Jour De Ma Vie, Les Hauts Quartiers De Peine. with Andrew Beaujon (gv): Pascal McFlintoch (bv), Gilles Paris (dv), Marque De Qualite (g, v, Hammond), Michele du Clef (kv, o), Eugenie Mellot (gv, vi). 13/4/97 MV4 TdB GT

The Tunnel Frenzies

14/11/89 Turn The Screw, Drowning School, Getta Grip, Fast Dream Speeding. Simon Haden (d), Jason Bellman (bv), Mark McClenan (gv), Gary Fox (v). 29/10/89 MV3 DG ME

Turbocat

16/12/98 Psychobitch & Friends Inc., Little Dogs, Testosterone, Stupid Song. Kerry Boettcher (bv), Shaun Charman (gv), Luc Woods (dv). 8/11/98 MV3 ME KR

TV Smith's Explorers

12/1/81 The Servant, Walk Away, The Last Words Of The Great Explorer. Eric Russell (g), Mel Wesson (k), Colin Stoner (b), David Sinclair (d), TV Smith (v). 5/1/81 LH1 TW AP

TV 21

30/10/80 This Is Zero, It's Me, Waiting For Thre Drop, On The Run. Norman Roger (g, lv), Alistair Palmer (g, bck), Neil Baldwin (b), Colin MacLean (d). 22/10/80 MV4 BS. NG

21/12/81 All Join Hands, My Chance, Omei, BB's In Town. Roger, Palmer, Baldwin, Ally Paterson (d, bck), Dave Hampton (k, tp). 12/12/81 MV4 DG MR

Twa Toots

31/10/83 A New Depression, Yo-Yo, Don't Play 'A Rainy Night In Georgia', It's A Lovely Day. Philippa Richmond (gv), Sara Brown (bv) & Will Cassell (d), Frank Brown (Sarah's Father) (tb). 22/10/83 MV4 DG MR ● SFPS010

Twang

12/2/86 Big Dry Out, Eight At A Time, Lawsuit Man, Cold Tongue Bulletin. Leonard Penrose (d), John Sargeant (b), David Hindmarsh (g), Andy Ladd (v). 2/2/86 MV5 DG ME

17/9/86 Every Home Should Have One, This Is Intrusion, What's The Rap?, Here's Lukewarm. 7/9/86 U DG ME

3/2/88 Work The Word, Snapback, Yo-Ho-Delic. Albert Walton (d) r Penrose. 24/1/88 U DG MA&ME

Twinkie

23/7/03 Chaff The Queen / Hi Lo Medium, On The Verge Of Moral Collapse, Crime, Aardvark Barracuda, Columbian. Elvis Beetham Wallace (d), Dave Robert Pant (g), Debbie Fleming (gv), Moo (Paul) Bird (b, lv). Live from MV4 AR SA/GT

The Twinkle Brothers

1/10/81 I'm Longing For You, Rasta Pon Top, Me No You, Never Get Burned. Norman Grant (dv), Eric Bernard (kv), Derrick Brown (bv), Ralston Grant (rgv), Karl Hyatt (perc, v), Ashton Grant (lg), Lloyd Willacy (lg), Donovan Black (perc, v). 23/9/81 MV4 CL NG

Twinset

20/1/82 Stranded In The Jungle, Johnny Come Home, I'll Remember You, Suspicious Minds. Rory Hall (g), Norman Bell (b), Stuart Wright (d), Gaye & Rachel Spankie (v). 6/1/82 MV4 KH NG

4/11/82 Zippo, Sophisticated Boom Boom, Talk, Out Of Nowhere, Heartbeat. Gaye & Rachel, Hall, Nick Haines (g, p), Dru Farmer (d). 16/10/82 U DG MR

9/11/83 Too Too Much, Glittering New Day, Crush, Meant To Be, Girl On Her Own. G. & r Bell, Hall, Mike Berry (g), Dave Mack (d). 29/10/83 MV4 DG MR

Twist

17/8/99 Dent, Stow Down, Glistening, Lay Low. Emma Fox (gv), Vanessa White (g), Lisa Lavery (b), Leanne Taylor (bk, d). 11/7/99 MV3 ME PN

Twisted Nerve

2/11/81 When I'm Alone, Never Say Goodbye, Indecision, Five Minutes Of Fame, We Don't Need Them. Keith Hamilton (d), Gordon Munro (v), Bill McNair (g), Norbert Bass-Bin (b). 17/10/81 MV4 DG TdB

Twp

9/9/98 Dawn, Square Eyes, Bus Stop, Cool One, Falling. Gerwen Frowen (v), Spike Twp (b), Marcus Lloyd (lg), Glyn Hamer (rg), Lee Tucker (d). 30/8/98 MV4 ME TdB

The Tyla Gang

6/6/77 Young Lords, Don't Shift Tear Gear, Wizz Kid, Speedball Morning. U 30/5/77 MV4 CL U

20/10/77 On The Street, Dust On The Needle, Styrafoam, Don't Your Turn Your Radio On. Sean Tyla (gv), Bruce Irvine (lg), Brian Turrington (b), Michael Des Marais (d). 4/10/77 MV4 JG MR

15/8/78 It's Gonna Rain, Moonlight Ambulance, Spanish Streets, No Roses. Ken Whaley (b) r Turrington. Billed as 'Sean Tyla' only. 9/8/78 MV4 BS NG

Tyrannosaurus Rex

5/11/67 Scenscoft, Child Star, Highways, Hot Rod Mama, Dwarfish Trumpet Blues (& Pictures Of Purple People, 4/2/68). Marc Bolan (gv), Steve Peregrine-Took (perc). 30/10/67 PC1 BA PR

13/3/68 Beginning Of Doves, The Wielder Of Words, The Wizard, Afghan Woman, Hippy Gumbo, Frowning Atuahallpa. 28/2/68 S2 JM RD

24/3/68 Knight, Debora, Afghan Woman, Frowning Atuahallpa (& Mustang, Strange Orchestra, 3/5/68). 11/3/68 PC1 BA U

14/7/68 Stacey Grove, One Inch Rock, Salamanda Palaganda, Eastern Spell (& Wind Quartets, 25/8/68). 11/6/68 PC1 BA DT

10/11/68 The Friends, Conesuela, The Seal Of Seasons, The Evenings Of Damask (& The Travelling Tragition, Trelawny Lawn, 22/12/68). 14/10/68 PC1 BA U

11/5/69 Once Upon The Seas Of Abyssinia†, Nijinsky Hind, Misty Coast Of Albany†, Chariots Of Silk† (& Iscariot†, 15/6/69). 5/5/69 PH JW TW

22/11/69 Fist Heart Mighty Down Dart, Pavilions Of The Sun, A Day Laye, By The Light Of The Magical Moon. Mickey Finn (perc) r Peregrine-Took. 17/11/69 PH JW TW †

7/11/70 Ride A White Swan†, Jewel†, Elemental Child, Sun Eye†. 26/10/70 MV4 JW TW ● SFPS031 and † on Cube/Dakota double LP 82 Across The Airwaves, CD reissue in Canada 88

Tystion

10/2/00 Pwy Syn Rheolu'r Donfedd?, Byd Hip Hop Versus Y Byd Cymraeg, Ishe Gwybod Mwy, Gwyddbwyll. Steffan Cravos (rp), Jason Farrell (tt), Phil Jenkins (fl, b, p, ag), Frank Naughton (g, o, p, b). 19/1/00 MV4 MR RJ

19/12/01 Y Meistri, Ishe Gwybod Mwy, Pwy Sy'n Rheolu'r Donfedd, Brad A Sarhad, Yr Anwybodus, Dama Blanca. Cravos, Farrell, Gareth Williams, Clancy Pegg, Rob Mackay. Live from MV4 SA NF

UB40

2/1/80 Food For Thought, 25 Per Cent, King. Jimmy Brown (d, bck), Alistair Campbell (rg, lv), Robin Campbell (lg, bck), Earl Falconer (b), Norman Hassan (perc), Brian Travers (sx), Micky Virtue (k). 12&18/12/79 MV4 JS NG&MR

25/1/82 Politician, I Won't Close My Eyes, Love Is All Is All Right, Prince Baldhead Meets Gymslip And The School Girls At The Chemist. Astro (tp) joins. 9/1/82 MV4 DG MR

UFO

17/6/77 Too Hot To Handle, Lights Out, Try Me. Michael Shenker (g), Paul Raymond (kg), Pete Way (b), Andy Parker (d), Phil Mogg (v). 1/6/77 MV4 MB NG 3 previous sessions, not for Peel

Ugly Music Show

20/1/91 Been Here Before, White Horses, Basted, The Pie Is The Limit. Jim Robinson (lg, dm), Angus Jenner (rgv), Mike Hammer (b). 18/12/90 MV5 MR MR

Ui

18/1/00 Please Release Me, Know Your Fire Drill, Bad Ear, John Fitch Way. Sasha Frere Jones (b, g, smp), Wilbo Wright (b, k, smp), Clam Waldmann (d). 10/11/99 MV5 MW PN

UK Decay

29/4/80 Rising From The Dead, Unwind Tonight, Sexual, For My Country. Abbo (v), Steve Spon (gk), Martyn 'Segovia' Smith (b), Steve Harle (d). 22/4/80 MV4 BS MR

5/8/81 Last In The House Of Flames, Stage Struck, Glass Ice, Duel. Dutch (b) r Smith. 27/7/81 MV4 TW U

UK Subs

31/5/78 I Couldn't Be You, Tomorrow's Girls, Disease, CID, Stranglehold. Charles Harper (v), Pete Davies (d), Paul Barker (b), Nick Garratt (g). 23/5/78 MV4 MR MR

15/9/78 World War, TV Blues, Another Kind Of Blues, All I Wanna Know, Totters. 6/9/78 MV4 MR MR

28/6/79 Killer, Crash Course, Lady Esquire, IOD, Emotional Blackmail. 19/6/79 MV4 BS MR

The Ukrainians

16/11/91 Rospryahaite, Ti Moyi Radoshchi, Dity Plachut, Teper Hovorymo. Len Liggins (vi, v), Roman Remeynes (mnd, v), Stepan Pasicznyk (acc, v), Peter Solowka (g, mnd, v), Chris Harrap (b), Dave Lee (d). 24/9/91 MV3 JB PL&JB

20/2/93 Zillya Zelenenke (The Little Green Herb), Vorony (Crows), Durak (Madman) / The Leeds Waltz, Vona Moya (Ca Plane Pour Moi). Paul Briggs (b) r Harrap. 19/1/93 MV4 MR~ TD

Ultramarine

22/5/92 Saratoga, Nova Scotia, Honey, Pansy. Ian Cooper (g), Paul Hammond (b), Charlie May (k), Paul Johnson (d), Phil James (hca). 7/4/92 MV4 MR SA&MR

12/3/94 No Time, The Badger, Hooter, After. Simon Collins (d), Paul Hammond (b), Simon Key (k), Ian Cooper (k, smp), Jim Rattigan (acc), Matt Wates (sx). 1/2/94 MV4 TD JMK

Ultraviolence

14/11/92 Demons, Broken Hearted, Time To Be, We Are The Dead (instrumental). Jonathan Casey (k, el, rp). 27/8/92 OS

Ultravox

28/11/77 My Sex, The Man Who Dies Every Day, Artificial Life, Young Savage. Stevie Shears (g), Chris Cross (b, bck), Warren Cann (d, bck), Billy Curry (k, vi), John Fox (v). 21/11/77 MV4 TW DD ● SFPS047

Uncle Dog

28/3/72 Boogie With Me, You Need Somebody, Old Hat, Sweet White Wine. Terry Stannard (d), Carol Grimes (v), John Porter (b) David Skinner (p). 14/3/72 MV4 U U 1st session was in December 71 for Pete Drummond

1/9/72 River Road, Boogie With Me, Sometimes. George Butler (d) r Stannard; Paul (surname unknown) (b) r Porter; & Dick Homer (lg), Martin Stone (g), Humphrey Curtis (sx, fl). 21/8/72 T1 JM U

16/11/72 River Road, We Got Time, Old Hat (& Lose Me, 7/12/72). 13/11/72 LH1 BA BC

The Undertones ○

16/10/78 Get Over You, Top 20, She Can Only Say No, Male Model. Feargal Sharkey (lv), John O'Neill (rg), Damian O'Neill (lg, bck), Billy Doherty (d), Mickey Bradley (b, bck). 1/10/78 DWN SN~

5/2/79 Listening In, Family Entertainment, Billy's Third, Here Comes The Summer. 22/1/79 MV4 BS DD ● SFPS016

11/6/79 Nine Times Out Of Ten, The Way Girls Talk, Whiz Kids, Top 20. 7/5/79

Phoenix Studio, London, Produced by The Undertones
23/1/80 Girls That Don't Talk, Tear Proof, What's With Terry?, Rock 'n' Roll. 21/1/80 MV4 BS DD

9/12/80 The Positive Touch, You're Welcome, When Saturday Comes. 16/11/80 PRIV

7/12/82 Untouchable, The Love Parade, Luxury, The Sin Of Pride. 8/11/82 U BS U First six sessions on ○ Listening In, Sanctuary SANCD179

14/5/03 Everything But You, Thrill Me, I Need Your Love The Way It Used To Be, Girl Like You. Paul McLoone (v) r Sharkey. 14/5/03 MV4 MA JSM

Underworld

10/12/03 Leutin, Trim, 2 Months Off, Jumbo, Moaner, Nuxx / Born Slippy. Rick Smith, Karl Hyde. Live from MV4 AR GT

16/12/04 10-min DJ mix for Keepin' It Peel night live from MV3 GYW JHT

Unfinished Sympathy

5/12/01 Nicorette, Flies Came To Our Home, And A Happy New Year, Learning Imaginary Numbers. Pablo Salas (d), Guillem Hernandez (b, bck), Oriol Casanovas (g), Eric Fuentes (gv). 28/10/01 MV4 ME JHT

14/1/04 Prayers For Time, Convinced Lamarckist, Topographic, Teenage Kicks. Xavier Navarro (b) r Hernandez. 4/12/03 MV4 RF JHT

Unicorn

24/9/74 Nightingale Crescent, Take It Easy, Autumn Wine, Electric Night. Patrick Martin, Kenneth Baker, Pete Perrier, Kevin Richard Smith (g, mnd). 3/9/74 LH1 U BC Previously recorded In Concert, 10/71; & 2 sessions for Bob Harris

Union Kid

16/6/99 Pickups, He Is Mono, Grody Squad, Killer Island. Mark Keates (d), Dot (b), Sean Toohy (gv). 6/4/99 MV4 JLO RJ

24/1/01 Get This Message Back To Base, Slow Faze, 100MI/Ground Zero. Dot out. 7/1/01 MV4 ME NS

Unrest

17/10/92 Four Women Walking, Teenage Suicide, Firecracker, Three Layer Cake. Phil Krayth (d), Bridget Cross (gv), Mark Robinson (gv). 10/9/92 MV4 DG NG/AA

Unsane

14/7/91 Organ Donor / Street Sweeper / Jungle Music / Exterminator, Bath. Charlie Ondras (d), Pete Shore (bv), Chris Spencer (gv). 21/5/91 MV5 TdB DMC&TdB

15/1/93 Broke, Body Bomb, HII, Black Book (Vol II). Vincent Signorelli (d) r Ondras. 26/11/92 MV4 NG~ JT

30/7/94 Trench, S O S, Blew, Radio 1, Speak English. & P W Long (g, v-5), Jean Louis Thauvin (bck). 7/6/94 MV4 PL JLC

Unseen Terror

11/4/88 Incompatible / Burned Beyond Recognition, Oblivion Descends / Divisions, Voice Your Opinion, Strong Enough To Change / Odie's Revenge / It's My Life. Shane Embury (d), Mitchell Dickinson (bg, v-4,5,7), Mick Harris (v-1–3, 6, 8). 22/3/88 U DG MR&SC&FB ● SFPS069

Unwound

29/7/98 Hexenszene, Side Effect Of Being Tired, Kantina/Were Are And Was Or Is. Sara Lund (d), Vern Rumsey (b), Justin Tropser (g). 24/5/98 MV5 ME NK

Upp

3/4/74 Bad Stuff, I Give It To You, It's A Mystery, Get Down In The Dirt. Jim Copley (d), Andy Clarke (kv), Stephen Amazing (b), Andy Powell (g-4). 27/3/75 MV4 TW U

Urusei Yatsura

21/1/95 Teenage Dream (Proved Cursed & Wrong), Thread, Road Song, Taster, It Is. Graham Kemp (gv), Fergus Lawrie (gv), Elaine Graham (b), Ian Graham (d). 1/11/94 BHG SCK TDO

20/4/96 Skull In Action, First Day On A New Planet, The Power Of Negative Thinking, Velvey Bood. 2/4/96 MV4 JB PA

14/8/97 Hello Tiger, Dice Nae Dice, Exidor, Flaming Skull. 29/7/97 MV4 MR SA

US Maple

15/6/96 Songs That Have (No) Making Out, Home Made Stuff Melted, Knees On Morning, Snarko Bike. Pat Samson (d), Mark Shippy (hi-guitar), Todd Rittman (lo-guitar), Al Johnson (v), Yasuko (from Melt Banana), Agata (from Melt Banana). 7/5/96 MV4 MR MPK

Ut

29/5/84 Confidential, Absent Farmer, Tell It (Atomic Energy Pattern), Phoenix. Nina Canal (gbdv), Jacqui Ham (vgd), Sally Young (vgd). 15/5/84 MV5 MRD TdB

6/1/88 Evangelist, Hotel, Safe Burning. 22/12/87 U DG DD&PL

Uzeda

11/6/94 It Happened There, Well Paid, Higher Than Me, Save My Shakes, Spread, Slow. Giovanna Cacciola (v), Gulisano Raffaele (b), Davide Oliveri (d), Gianni Nicosia (g), Agostino Tilotta (g). 8/5/94 MV4 ME AA

16/12/94 Surrounded, Sleep Deeper, Right Seeds, Needle House. 6/11/94 MV3 ME JHE

Van Basten

24/11/95 Quadra Sutra, Battle Star Technology, Return To The Death Posture, Uber Alloy. Gary Webster (k, cmp), Martin Reilly (k, cmp), Gary Everatt (xyl, mute tb). 14/11/95 MV4 MR SBR

14/7/96 Speed Of Sound, Instinct, Uber Replay. OS

Van der Graaf Generator

29/12/68 People You Were Going To, Afterwards, Necromancer, Octopus. Peter Hammill (v), Keith Ellis (b), Hugh Banton (o), Guy Evans (d). 18/11/68 MV4 BA PR

7/2/70 Darkness, After The Flood. Nic Potter (b) r Ellis. 27/1/70 MV4 JW BC

24/10/70 Lost, Killer. David Jackson (ts, al, fl, v) r Potter. 12/10/70 PH JW BC

29/12/71 An Epidemic Of Father Christmasses, Lemmings, Refugees. & Chris Judge Smith (bck-1). 14/12/71 MV4 U U

10/7/75 Scorched Earth, Sleepwalkers. 3/7/75 MV4 TW U

20/4/76 Still Life, La Rossa. 1/4/76 MV4 TW U

22/11/76 When She Comes, Masks. 11/11/76 MV4 TW U

2/11/77 (Fragments Of) A Plague Of Lighthouse Keepers / Sleepwalker's End, Cat's Eye / Yellow Fever (Running), The Sphinx In The Face. Graham Smith (vi), Charles Dickie (clo, elp, sy, v), Nic Potter (b) r Banton, Jackson. 24/10/77 MV4 JG U

Marina Van-Rooy

10/4/92 All Heaven's Open, Honey Drip, Staying With Me. Marina Van Rooy (v), Ian Martin Wright (k), Peter Gyle (bck), Steven Cummerson (dm, prg). 23/2/92 MV3 DG ME&GT

The Vapors

11/7/79 Turning Japanese, Trains, Waiting For The Weekend, Cold War. Dave Fenton (g, lv), Ed Bazalgette (gv), Steve Smith (bv), Howard Smith (d). 4/7/79 MV4 TVD NG 'a goodie', Trevor Dann says on session sheet

Vaults

25/6/02 Blurred Around The Edges, In Black, And All Between, Velvet Dress. Beez Harper (v), Jimmy Vandel (gv), Richie Clark (bv), Eddy Marks (d). 7/5/02 MV4 JHT~ MA

2/4/03 Fame, Furry, The Mess Behind, Part Of You. Harper, Vandel, Richie TT Kicks (b), Eddy Treasure (d). 12/3/03 MV4 AR KR

19/11/03 She Loves, Do It Again, I'm Going, No Sleep No Need, Leaving Here, Blurred Round The Edge, Untitled, Lady Hell, Part Of You, Show And Tell. Live from MV4 SA RF

5/5/04 Show And Tell, Skiffle, Leaving Here, Untitled. Beaz (v), Richie (b, bck), Jimmi (g, bck), Mark Edwards (d). 17/3/04 MV4 SA JHT

Champion Doug Veitch

4/9/84 One Black Night, Banks Of Marble, Not The Heart, Another Place. Doug Veitch (v), Tony McDermott (b), Roger Hilton (d), Bobby Valentino (fd), Alan Dunn (acc), Jim Craig (ps), James McMillan (tp), Dave Killen (tb). 7/8/84 MV5 BYA TdB

19/3/86 Margarita, Tears On My Pillow, Rodgers And Out, Sweet Bachanaal. & McDermott, Craig, Hall, George Hinchcliffe (p, o), Bell (fd), Lawrence Woods (sx), Elms, Killen. 18/2/86 MV5 DG TdB

Velocette

4/6/97 Stepback, November, Someone's Waiting, Perfume. Phil (d), Jax (b), Sam (g), Ali (k), Sarah (v). 20/5/97 MV4 MR SCO

Velocity Girl

20/3/93 Here Comes, 57 Waltz, Copacetic, Always, Crazy Town. Jim Spellman (d), Kelly Riles (b, g), Archie Moore (g, v, b), Brian Nelson (g), Sarah Shannon (v). 23/2/93 MV4 MR MA

Velodrome 2000

15/4/98 Ivy Is A Metalhead, Sindy Sex Aid, Look Sir Droids, Yes Sir I Can Boogie, Rik Beckham. Markie Velodrome (gv), Penny (percv), Steph (d), Toniee (b), Chris (gkv). 8/3/98 MV4 ME NF

Elmer Gantry's Velvet Opera

26/11/67 Dream Starts, Reaction Of A Young Man, Flames, Mother Writes (& Long Nights Of Summer, 7/1/68). David Terry (v), Colin Forster (lg), Richard Hudson (d), Roy Stacey (b). 3/11/67 PH BP PR With James Horrocks (o), group had passed audition early in 67 as 'Five Proud Walkers'

19/5/68 Fixin' To Die, Mary Jane, Dreamy, Air (& Codine, 23/6/68). 22/4/68 PC1 BA PR

Verve

7/3/92 Slide Away, Superstar, 'Title Unknown', Already There. Peter Salisbury (d), Simon Jones (b), Nick McCabe (g), Richard Ashcroft (v). 13/2/92 MV5 DG NG&JB ○ SFMCD214

The Very Things

9/1/84 Message From Disneytime, Down The Final Flight, Phillip's World Service, Wall Of Fir. Robin Raymond (g), The Shend (bv), Disneytime (d). 17/12/83 MV4 DG MR ● SFPS046

8/12/87 Let's Go Out, There's A Ghost In My House, She's Standing Still, Walking In The Sand. & Robert Holland (k), Vincent (b). 30/10/87 Berry Street Studios, produced by Smuff & Ray Shulman

The Vibes

22/4/85 Inside Out, Looking In The Mirror, Eqyptian Thing, Judgement Day. Johnny J Beat (d), Lloyd (b), Fuzz Fury (g), Johnny 'Mother' Johnson (lg), Gaz Voola (v). 2/4/85 MV5 AJ MR

The Vibrators

28/10/76 Dance To The Music, Sweet Sweetheart, Jenny Jenny, I'm Gonna Be Your Nazi Baby, We Vibrate. Ian 'Knox' Carnochan (gv), John Ellis (gv), Pat Collier (b), Jon Edwards (d). 12/10/76 MV4 JG MR

22/6/77 Petrol, Keep It Clean, Baby Baby, London Girls, She's Bringing You Down. 13/6/77 MV4 TW DD

6/3/78 Automatic Lover, Destroy, Troops Of Tomorrow, Fall In Love. Gary Tibbs (b, bck), Eddie (d) r Collier, Edwards. 27/2/78 MV4 TW DD

Vice Squad

3/6/81 Coward†, It's A Sell Out†, 1981, Times They Are A Changing. Beki Bondage (v), Dave Bateman (g), Mark Hambly (b), Shane Baldwin (d). 1/6/81 LH1 TW DD † on 'Riotous Assembly' LP

10/5/82 Humane, Propaganda, No Right Of Reply, Sterile. 28/4/82 MV4 RP MC

Victim's Family

8/8/89 Luv Letters / Balderdash, As It Were / God Jerry And The PMRC, Burly Jalisco, Corona Belly. Eric (d), Larry (b), Ralph (gv). 11/7/89 MV5 DG DD

Gene Vincent

6/2/71 Whole Lotta Shakin', The Day The World Turned Blue, Rocky Road Blues, Say Mama. & The Houseshakers. 25/1/71 PH JW BC

Vinegar Joe

10/3/72 Ain't It Peculiar, Leg Up, Rusty Red, Early Morning Monday. Robert Palmer (v), Elkie Brooks (v), Pete Gage (g), Tim Hinkley (p), Rob Tate (d), Terry Poole (b). 22/2/72 T1 JM JWH&PK 1st session was for Pete Drummond TX 9/12/71

The Vipers

13/2/79 You're On Your Own Kid, Too Rough, You're So Strange, Playin' The Game. Paul Boyle (lv, rg), George Sweeney (lg), Dolan (b, bck), Dave Moloney (d). 27/2/79 MV4 TVD MR

Virgin Dance

17/3/83 Facts, Barriers, No Disguise, Love's Friends. Kenny Dougan (rg), Graham McMaster (b), Cliff Hewitt (d), Lorraine Gardner (k), E Hind (gv). 12/3/83 MV4 DG MC 1st session was for Janice Long, TX 25/12/82

Virginia Doesn't

18/10/79 Sanctuary, Telephone Box, Tuesday Night (On A Housing Estate), (I'd Rather) Die, The Smurf Song, Peely. Kev Robinson (v), Tweets Bird (g), Ratch Tuffin (g, bck), Craig Lindsay (b, bck), Chris Corner (d). 3/10/79 MV4 TVD NG

Visions of Change

12/5/87 Teepees In Limbo, More Than Now, Reciprocate, Visions Of Change. Gigs (d), Spencer (b), Lee Go-Go (g), Ian (v). 21/4/87 U DG MR&TdB

The Visitors

14/2/80 Pattern, Exploiting The Masters, Our Glass, The Orcadian. John McVay (kv), Colin Craigie (gv), Derek McVay (bv), Keith Wilson (dv). 6/2/80 MV4 BS NG

8/1/81 Poet's End, Compatibility, Distance. 16/12/80 LH1 JS MR

25/2/82 Flow, Third Base, Unit Of Acceptance. Malcolm Green (g, p) r Craigie. 10/2/82 MV4 KH NG

Vital Excursions

17/11/82 Just A Little Blurred, Live Show, Cat With Vertigo, Sleep. Anthony Wraster (tp, sx, fl), Angela Stewart (v), John Fairbrother (tb), Danny Sheals (d), Steven Lewis (perc), Fiona Fleck (p), Simon Edwards (b). 30/10/82 MV4 DG MR

Vitalic

22/12/04 Poney, My Friend Dario, You Prefer Cocaine, Cich Cach, Fanfares, unknown title, Warm Leatherette, La Rock, Cardboard Lamb Cover, My Friend Dario reprise. Pascal Arbez-Nicolas (e). Live from MV4 AR~

Vitus Dance

4/10/79 Down At The Park, Disgusting, Inter City Living, I'm In Control (I Think), Problem Parade. Kevin McFadden (lgv), Mark Byrne (lgv), Malcolm Young (bv), Kearin Wright (d). 25/9/79 MV4 JS MR

Cristian Vogel

1/12/95 Consumes Trousers, No One Knows, No One Goes, The Visit, My Bird In My Attic. Cristian Vogel (k, e). OS

15/1/98 They Bought You At A Party, A Slice Of Sink, Telemusica, Super Collider. OS

Von Bondies

22/11/01 Lack Of Communication, Nite Train, Sound Of Terror, Going Down, It Came From Japan, Pawn Shop Heart, My Baby's Cryin', Rock & Roll Nurse, No Sugar Mama, Please Please Mam, Ben Swankin' Lovin' It. Jason Stollmeister (gv), Marcie Bolen (gv), Carrie Smith (bv), Don Blum (dv) & Jack White (k-9). Live from MV4 SCU MA

27/6/02 Vacant As A Ghost, Save My Life, Cryin', Take A Heart. 4-piece & Austin Rhodes (ep, bck), Phil Boyd (bck), David Viner (bck), Rudolf de Borst (bck). 12/5/02 MV4 ME JSM

18/2/04 C'Mon C'Mon, Poison Ivy, Broken Man, Can't Stand It. & Steve Schmoll (g-4). 21/1/04 MV4 MA GT

Voodoo Queens

22/1/93 Kenuwee Jead (Dude Idol), Summer Sun, Princess Of The Voodoo Beat, Super Model Superficial. Anjali Bhatia (gv), Anjula Bhaskar (b), Ella Drauglis (g), Rajni Bhatia (k), Sunny (d). 10/1/93 MV3 ME~

23/7/93 Chocolate Eyes, Shopping Girl Maniac, Indian Film Star, My Favourite Handbag. Stefania Lucchesini (d) r Sunny. 20/6/93 MV3 JB RJ

26/3/94 Dream Boy Kills, Caffeine, F Is For Fame, You'll Lose A Good Thing. A Bhatia, Draiglis, Lucchesini, Rebecca Lunn (b). 15/2/94 MV4 MPK NS

Vorhees

14/4/95 Oblivion, What I'd Do, Feminist, Chinese Burns, What You Get, TV Heaven, No Self Respect, Where Did It Go?, Tied Down. Ian Leck (v), Sean Redman (g), Graeme Nicholls (g), Paul Rugman-Jones (b), Michael Gillman (d). 21/3/95 MV4 PL FK

Wagonchrist

9/12/98 REO Speedgarage, Melotronic, It Is Always Now All Of It Is Now, Memory Towel Acid Rinse. Luke Vibert (dj, k, prog). Sept 98 OS

15/8/01 Aerhaart Ahead (Remix), Chicken For Kitty, Electrogangster, Kiddies Swing. 2/8/01 OS

Wah! Heat

10/6/80 Seven Minutes To Midnight, Don't Step On The Cracks, Somesay, Other Boys. Pete Wylie (gv), Colin Redmond (g), Oddball Washington (b, bck), Rob Jones (d), KJ Tyrer (sy). 19/5/80 MV4 TW DD&MPK

14/4/81 Cut Out, Sleep, The Checkmate Syndrome, Forget The Down. Wylie, Washington, King Bluff (k), Jungle Beat Joe Musker (d). 30/3/81 LH1 TW DD

18/5/82 Papa Crak, 8–8.30 Or 10 Til 12, Satie's Faction, You'll Never Walk Alone / You'll Never Walk Again. Billed as 'Shambeko! Say Wah!': Wylie ('everything except… '), Washington (b) & Alan Peters (tp-1). 5/5/82 MV4 RP NG

13/4/83 Hope (I Wish You'd Believe Me), Sleep (Lullaby For Josie), Year Of Decision, Silver And Gold. Now, 'Wah!': Wylie, Washington, Bluff, Jay Naughton (p), Ruby, Sylvie & Shirly (bck). 14/2/83 MV4 TW DD

17/9/84 Better Scream, Weekends, Basement Blues / The Story Of The Blues, Yuh Learn. Billed as 'The Mighty Wah!': Wylie, Phil Wylie (g), Josie Jones (bck), Eugene 'Redman' Lange (bck, lv-4), Jay Naughton (k), Henry Priestman (k), Paul Steven-John Ballow (d), Joey Musker (perc), Dickie Rude (b). 22/8/84 U RP NG ● SFPS035

17/5/00 I Still Love You, Disneyland Forever, Never Loved As A Child, Alone. Now billed simply as Pete Wylie: Pete Wylie (gv), Andy Dwyer (d), John Goulbourne (b), Ian Prowse (g), Nigel Morgan (k), Natalie James (bck), Denise Harry (bck). 9/4/00 MV4 ME SBR

The Wailing Cocks

29/11/78 Positive Loving, Raffles, Listen To The Wailing Cocks, Rockin Youth. Andy Growcott (d), Alan Boyle (g, bck), Ian Rowley (b), Andde Leek (k, lv). 22/11/78 MV4 MR MR

The Wailing Souls

7/11/84 Firehouse Rock, Bredda Gravalcious, Stop Red Eye, Bandits Taking Over. Bread, Garthy, Pipe & Buddy (v), backed by the Reggae Regulars: Patrick Donegan (g), Brian Campbell (k), Trevor 'Seal' Salmon (b), Winston Williams (d). 30/10/84 MV5 MRD TdB

Loudon Wainwright III

22/5/71 Sink The Bismark!, School Days, Be Careful There's A Baby In The House†, East Indian Princess†, Medley: I Know I'm Unhappy / Suicide Song / Glenville Reel†, (& Four Is A Magic Number, 17/7/71). Loudon Wainwright III (acg, v). 18/5/71 MV4 JW U

13/10/71 Say That You Love Me, Samson And The Warden, Motel Blues, Trilogy (Circa 1967), Plane Too. 11/10/71 PH JW U

12/6/73 Clockwork Chartreuse, AM World†, Drinking At The Bar, Jerusalem Town, Lullabye. 11/6/73 T1 JW U

12/5/75 Bi-Centennial Anniversary, Detroit's A Dying City, Unrequited To The Nth Degree, Hollywood Hopeful, Have You Ever Been To Pittsburgh, Five Gold Stars. 6/5/75 MV4 TW U

24/8/76 Ingenue, Golfing Blues, Swimming Song†, Prince Hal's Dirget. 9/8/76 MV4 TW DD

9/12/76 Natural Disaster, Air Travel, Monkey In My Closet, Dick And Jane, It's Over The Hill / My Girl. 23/11/76 MV4 JG MR

13/8/79 Saturday Morning Fever, The Acid Song, Vampire Blues, April Fools' Day Morn, Dump The Dog And Feed The Garbage. 1/8/79 MV4 TVD NG

14/4/83 Outsidey, I'm All Right, Screaming Issue, Career Moves, Not John. 9/4/83 MV3 DG GP

30/9/85 Expatriot, No†, You Kids Today, I Wanna Be On MTV, Hard Day On The Planet†, Little Did I Know, I Wish It Was Met. 17/9/85 MV5 JWI NG

19/10/89 They Spelled My Name Wrong Again, Jesse Don't Like It, Sunday Times†, Sometimes I Forget. 8/10/89 MV3 DG ME † on ○ The BBC Sessions SFRSCD073

7/11/92 The Birthday Present, Happy Birthday Elvis, A Handful of Dust, So Good So Far. 1/10/92 MV4 NG~

29/7/99 When I'm At Your House, Be Careful There's A Baby In The House, One At A Time, The Doctor. Live from Peel Acres AR GT

27/9/01 I'm Not Gonna Cry, One Man Guy, Donations, Cardboard Boxes, Colours, I'd Rather Be Lonely, Surviving Twin, No Sure Way. Live from Peel Acres AR GT 'Quickest ever soundcheck at Peel Acres, so George, Louden and myself went swimming in John's pool' says Andy Rogers

16/7/02 Half Fist, Heaven, No Sure Way, Something For Nothing, The Final Frontier. 21/4/02 MV4 JHT~

27/8/03 Here Come The Choppers, To Be On TV, Nanny, When You Leave, Work In Progress. 16/7/03 MV4 JSM~

The Wake

14/7/83 Uniform, The Drill, Here Comes Everybody. Caesar (gv), Robert Gillespie (b), Carolyn Allen (sy, bck), Steven Allen (d). 6/7/83 MV4 BYA PS

The Walking Seeds

26/1/87 Huge Living Creature, Junior Acid Bait, Mark Chapman, Blathering Out. Tony Morgan (d), Lol Geoghegan (perc), Robert Parker (b), Barry Sutton (g, bck), Frank Martin (v). 11/1/87 U DG ME&FK

30/9/87 Transmaniacon MC, Eyes Too Big, El Sexorcist, Schoolfinger. Geoghegan out. 22/9/87 U DG ME&EL

19/4/89 Matchsticks, Gates Of Freedom, Cave Woman, Shaved Beatnik. Andy Rowan (b) r Sutton; Parker (g). 4/4/89 WX JW MR

22/2/90 Mortal Blues, Hairy Who, Broken Cup. Lee Webster (b) r Rowan. 30/1/90 MV3 DG MR

The Waltones

24/8/88 When You Smile, Miles Different Ways, She's Everywhere But Here, Deepest. Alex Fyans (d), Manny Lee (b), Mark Collins (g), James Knox (v). 16/8/88 MV4 MR MR

Clifford T Ward

26/10/72 Coathanger, Sam, Anticipation, Gaye, The Open University. Clifford T Ward (pv), Ken Wright (d), Derek Thomas (lg), Bev Pegg (b), David Skinner (p), Paul Booton (rg). 16/10/72 LH1 BA 1st session was for Johnnie Walker, Aug 72

19/4/73 Crisis, Gaye, Where's It Going To End, Wherewithal (& The Magician 17/5/73). & 4 unknown. 9/4/73 LH1 BA U

Robert Ward

31/7/93 White Fox, Fear No Evil, Strictly Reserved For You. Robert Ward (gv) & The Otis Grand Blues Band: Otis Grand (g), Maurice McKilroy (d), Chico Lopez (d), Steve Diamond (o), Peter Beck (ts), Lawrence Parry (tp). 1/6/93 MV4 JB TD

The Wasps

22/2/78 Teenage Treats, J-J-J-Jenny, She Made Magic, Something To Tell You. Gary Wellman (g, bck), Steve Dominic (b), Johnny Rich (d), Jessie Lynn-Dean (lv). 13/2/78 MV4 TW DD

20/2/79 Angelica, Rubber Cars, She's Alarming, This Time. Neil Fitch (gv), Dave Owen (bv), Tiam Grant (d), Jesse Lynn-Dean (lv). 13/2/79 MV4 BS MR

Wauvenfold

4/12/01 Welcome, Selenium Plus, Rebix, Clip (Clopped For Peel). Tom Hill, Noel Murphy. OS

The Weather Prophets

1/12/86 Swimming Pool Blue, Hollow Heart, She Comes From The Rain, Faithful. Peter Astor (gv), Oisin Little (g), Greenwood Golding (b), Dave Morgan (d). 2/11/86 U DG FK&SC 3 Previous sessions for Janice Long / Andy Kershaw 85–86

The Wedding Present ○

26/2/86 Felicity, What Becomes Of The Broken Hearted, You Should Always Keep In Touch With Your Friends, This Boy Can Wait. David Gedge (gv), Keith Gregory (b), Pete Solowka (g), Shaun Charman (d) & Mike Stout (g-1). 11/2/86 MV5 MW MR Previous session for Kershaw Nov 85 ● SFPS009

25/11/86 All About Eve, Don't Be So Hard, Room With A View, Never Said, Hopak. Stout (b) stands in for Gregory. 26/10/86 U DG ME&MA

18/3/87 Give My Love To Kevin, Getting Nowhere Fast, Something And Nothing, A Million Miles. & Mike Stout (g-2). 3/3/87 U DG MR&MC

14/10/87 Ukrainian Session #1: Tiutiunyk, Yichav Kozak Za Dunai, Hude Dnipro Hude, Katrusya / Svitit Misyats. Solowka (acc, mnd) & The Legendary Len Liggins (vi, lv), Ron Rom (handclaps). 6/10/87 MV4 DG MR&FK

5/4/88 Ukrainian Session #2: Minnooli Dnee, Vasya Vasyl'ok, Zadumav Didochok, Verkhovyna. Simon Smith (d) r Charman; Solowka (acc, mnd) & Len Leggins (vi, v, bal), Roman Remeynes (mnd, v). 15/3/88 MV4 DG MR

30/5/88 Unfaithful, Why Are You Being So Reasonable Now, Take Me I'm Yours, Happy Birthday. All (bck-4). 24/5/88 MV4 DG U

15/5/89 Ukrainian Session #3: Cherez Richku Cherez Hai, Zavtra Ya Budu Pid Nebom Chuzhim, Sertsem I Dusheyev. Solowka (acc, mnd) & Len Liggins (vi, v), Roman Remeynes (mndv). 2/5/89 WX DG MR

28/10/90 Dalliance, Blonde, Niagara, Heather. 14/10/90 MV3 PW NG&MFA

2/5/92 Flying Saucer, Softly Softly, Come Play With Me, California. Paul Dorrington (g) r Solowka. 17/3/92 MV4 MA MA&RJ

16/4/94 Gazebo, So Long Baby, Spangle, Him Or Me (What's It Gonna Be?). Darren Belk (bv) r Gregory; & John Parkes (g-2, 4). 22/3/94 MV4 MR JLC

16/12/95 Sports Car, Drive, Love Machine, Go Man Go. Gedge, Smith, Belk (g), Jayne Lockey (b, bck), Hugh Kelly Jr (d). 3/12/1995 MV3 ME GT

19/12/00 Swimming Pools And Movie Stars. Gedge solo (agv). 13/12/00 MV3 AR MA

21/9/04 Blue Eyes, Ringway To Seatac, Shivers, Queen Anne, White Horses. Gedge, Simon Cleave (g), Terry de Castro (b, bck), Kari Paavola (d) & Katherine Kontz (k-3, 5), Steve Fisk (k-3). 22/7/04 MV4 JSM JHT

16/12/04 Dare, The Queen Of Outer Space, What Have I Said Now? Phil Prime (d) stand-in drummer. Live from MV3 MA GT All except 19/12/00 & 16/12/04 on ○ Complete Peel Sessions Sanctuary CMXBX1447

Ween

17/4/92 Pork Roll Egg And Cheese, Nan, Captain Fantasy, Don't Get Too Close To My Fantasy. Claude Coleman Jr (d), Kramer (p, b), Mickey Melchiondo (g), Aaron Freeman (gv). 20/2/92 MV4 DG NG&AA

22/5/93 What Deaner Was Talking About, Vallejo, Take Me Away, Buckingham Green. Mickey Melchiondo, Aaron Freeman only. 25/4/93 MV4 PL~ AA

Welfare State

21/2/70 Lot's Song, Silence Is Requested In The Ultimate Abyss†, Rat Race. U PRIV † on ● Top Gear LP BBC Records REC 52S

Seething Wells

18/11/82 Titles Unknown. Seething Wells ('ranting!'), Chris Moore (g), Jon Langford (g), Martin Leon (b), Nick King (d). 7/7/82 MV4 RP MC

Papa Wemba

5/9/92 Madilamba, Zero, Maria Valencia, Ombela (& Le Voyageur, Lingo Lingo, Matinda, Annah, on KERSHAW earlier same night, joint session). Papa Wemba (lv), Amisi Mela (bck), Patrick Marie Magdelaine (g), Magid Mahdi (b), Heire ra Kotofizinga & Jean Philippa Dary (k), Roger Raspail & Lauzent Coatalen (perc), Joseph Kuo (d). 19/8/92 MV3 NG NG&PL

12/5/95 Philosophie, Matinda, Lingo Lingo / N'Fondoya. Papa Wemba (v), Celine Cheynut (bck), Pierre-Valery Lobe (d), Christian Polloni (g), Herve Rakotofirmga (k), Xavier Jouvelet (perc), Hawa Maiga (bck), Noel Ekwabi (b), Patrick Marie Magdelaine (g). 14/3/95 MV4 AA JMK

The Werefrogs

1/5/92 Spinning Felt Clouds, Sheila, Cry, Don't Slip Away. Steve Frog (d), Matthew Frog (b), Marc Frog (gv). 10/3/92 MV4 MR MR

6/3/93 Potvan, Slovenia, Revelator, H Dumpty. Marc Wolf aka Marjat Volffe (gv), Matthew Valentine aka Striped Bass (b), Steve Savoca aka Schroeder (d). 8/2/93 MV4 MHW/JB~ RJ

Western Promise

4/6/85 All The King's Horses, Running With The Saints, Burning And Looting, My War. Sean Butler (d), Dave King (b), John McGlone (rg, lv), Phil Fowler (lg). 19/5/85 MV5 DG ME

We've Got a Fuzzbox and We're Gonna Use It

10/3/86 Aaarrrggghhh! (Don't Let Us Die), Fever, Rules And Regulations, Justine. Tina (d, sx), Jo (b, g), Magz (vi, perc, d), Vix (v). 2/3/86 MV5 DG ME&MS

11/8/86 You Got Me, Preconceptions, Jackie, She, Bohemian Rhapsody. 29/7/86 U DG MR&MS

CLASSIC SESSIONS

David Gedge

With his 22 Peel Session appearances as leader and songwriter of either The Wedding Present or Cinerama, Gedge is obviously one of the musical figures of the last 20 years Peel valued most. As Peel's famous claim that Gedge had written some of the best love songs in British pop attests, it was perhaps the lyrics and the turn of phrase he liked best, explaining why he stuck with Gedge through changes of musical style. Gedge by his own admission was not the chief instigator in the band behind The Wedding Present's classic Ukrainian sessions, and he has always paid tribute to bassist Keith Gregory's driving contribution to the band's original, electric sound. But if it was the original songs Peel particularly liked, then it is Gedge we have most to thank for the impact of his first band's first, third, sixth, eighth, ninth and revived 2004 session, featuring as they did debut broadcasts of very strong new songs – not to mention several early Cinerama dates, and the fact that their 'Don't Touch That Dial' topped the Festive Fifty in 2003, the last year Peel got to hear his listeners' chart. At his best – on 'My Favourite Dress', 'A Million Miles', 'Dalliance', 'Love Slave', 'Ringway To Seatac', for example – Gedge fully delivered on Peel's public investment in his songwriting talent.

What? Noise

9/5/90 Anybody, Crash, Shit, George. Chris Nagle, Julia Nagle, Timothy Harris. 12/4/90 MV3 DG U

Wheat

31/5/00 Don't I Hold You, Death Car, More Than You'll Ever Know. Scott Levesque (gv), Richard Brennan (gv), Brendan Harney (d), Bob Melanson (b). 7/5/00 MV4 ME NS

Where's The Beach?

31/8/89 Tripping The Love Fantastic†, Suakin, Deliciously Deranged. Peter Jones & Adam Marshall (ma), Chloe Mac (v). 1/8/89 MV5 DG MR

26/9/90 Feed The Fire, Chaos At The Axe Factory, Mega Armageddon Death / Yankamantra. Angie Simmons (v) r Mac. 19/8/90 U DG PL

4/12/92 Unstoppable, Sex Slave Zombie Part Two, Oasis, Pop Killer. Adam Marshall (prg, ma), Peter Jones (prg, ma). 11/10/92 MV3 ME AR

Whipped Cream

17/11/91 Explosion, Whatever, Wait For A Minute. Lars-Erik Grimelund (d), Jonas Sonesson (b), Elisabeth Punzi (gv), Jorgen Cremonese (gv). 25/8/91 HP DG ME&TBK

Whirlwind

10/4/80 Oakies In The Pokey, Cruising Around, Nervcus Breakdown, Staying Out All Night. Nigel Dixon (g), Mick Lewis (g), Chris Emo (b), Gary Hassett (d). 2/4/80 MV4 JE NG

Whistler

9/8/00 It's Not Too Late, Thankyou, You And Me, My Kind Of Nightmare, I Saw You. Tim Weller (d), Kerry Shaw (v), James Topham (vla), Ian Dench (gbv). 9/7/00 MV4 ME RJ

White and Torch

20/3/84 Don't Be Shot, Heartbreak, No Not I, Bury My Heart. Roy White (kv), Steve Torch (v), Charlie Morgan (d), Dave Levdy (b), Jackie Robinson (bck). 10/3/84 MV5 DG MC

White Hassle

3/11/98 Life Is Still Sweet, Half Way Done With The Tour, Resolution, Futura Trance No II, The Indiana Sun. Dave Varenica (d), Marcellus Hall (g, v, hca), Alan Boyd (bck-1). 20/10/98 MV4 MR PN

White Stripes

25/7/01 Let's Shake Hands, When I Hear My Name, Jolene, Death Letter, Cannon, Astro, Hotel Yorba, I'm Finding It Hard To Be A Gentleman, Screwdriver, We're Going To Be Friends, You're Pretty Good Looking, Bollweavil, Hello Operator, Baby Blue. Meg White (d), Jack White (gv). Live from MV4 SA NF/JHT

8/11/01 Lord Send Me An Angel, Dead Leaves And The Dirty Ground, I Think I Smell A Rat, Goin Back To Memphis, Little Room, The Union Forever, The Same Boy You've Always Known, Look Me Over Closely, Looking At You, St James Infirmary Blues, Apple Blossom, Rated X, Little Girl That Says. Meg White (d), Jack White (gv). Live from Peel Acres GT~

Jack White

3/2/04 Who's To Say, Jack The Ripper, Never Far Away, Vanlear Rose. Jack White (gv). 30/1/04 LL GT~

The Whitecats

3/4/78 Escalator Of Love, Second Time Around, Teenage Dream. Kelvin Blacklock (v), Eddie Cox (g), Steve Turner (b), Rat Scabies (d). U PRIV BS U

25/8/78 Junkyard Angels, Detectives, Here I Go Again, Shotgun Lovers. & Bob Sargeant (k, gv). 16/8/78 MV4 BS NG

Whiteout

11/11/94 Every Day, Time And Again, Get Me Through, Higher. Stuart Smith (d), Paul Carroll (b, bck), Eric Lindsay (g, bck), Andrew Jones (lv). 11/10/94 MV4 MR RJ

The Who

15/10/67 Pictures Of Lilly†, Our Love Was, I Can See For Miles, Relay†, I Can't Reach You, A Quick One While He's Away†, & Jingles: Top Gear #1 & #2, Radio 1 #1† & #2†, Happy Jack†, Jingle (& See My Way†, Someone's Coming, 19/11/67). Pete Townsend (gv), Roger Daltrey (v), Keith Moon (d), John Entwhistle (bv). 10/10/67 De Lane Lea Studios BA U Failed 1st audition (applied as The Detours but recorded as The Who)9/4/64 S2 & Doug Sandon (d). Re-auditioned & Moon 12/2/65, S2, after release of 'I can't explain', 3 'no' 4 'yes' votes: 'lead guitar seemed more sure of himself than the rest. Overall not very original and below standard'. Passed. 1st appeared 2/4/65 live at PH on Joe Loss Show. This session repeated on Saturday Club & David Symonds † on ○ The BBC Sessions Polydor Records

Widow Maker

27/4/76 Such A Shame, Leave The Kids Alone, When I Met You. Steve Ellis (v), Ariel Bender (g) & (b), (d), (g) unknown. 30/3/76 MV4 JG MR

Wilbur Wilberforce

8/12/98 DJ set live from Y4 U

3/7/01 DJ set. OS

The Wild Swans

13/5/82 No Bleeding, Enchanted, Thirst. Alan Wills (d), Baz Hughes (b), Jeremy Kelly (g), Gerard Quinn (k), Paul Simpson (v). 1/5/82 MV4 DG MR Previous session for Jensen, 3/82 ● SFPS006

Wild Turkey

9/11/72 Good Old Days, Chuck Stallian & The Mustangs, Tomorrow's Friend, Eternal Mothers / The Return. Glen Cornick (b), Gary Pickford-Hopkins (v), Jeffrey Jones (d), Alan Lewis (lg), Stephen Gurl (p), Michael Dyche (g). 23/10/72 LH1 BA MH&MF

1/3/73 The Sole Survivor, Butterfly, See You Next Tuesday. 26/2/73 LH1 BA U

8/11/73 Sweet Talking Woman, Soldier Boy, Social World. Bernie Marsden (lg) r Lewis. 29/10/73 LH1 BA U

Wild Weekend

12/8/82 Hungry, Janine And The Razor Man, Scarecrow, Swimming In Mud. Ade Sleigh (d), Al Roberts (b), Keith Holian (g), Gary Horabin (k), Dave Candler (v). 24/7/82 MV4 DG MR

John Williams

16/7/69 Courant / Ballet / La Volta, Sonata, Asturias, Miller's Dance, Sonata. John Williams (ag). 17/6/69 B15 PR U The classical guitarist's 1st BBC date was in 1957

Wilson

6/4/96 Silly Season, Sylvia, Josmo King, Only The Sun. Stephen Wilson (gv), Paul Higham (g), Andy Reid (b), John Lever (d). 18/3/96 MV4 MPK GPR

Wire

31/1/78 Practice Makes Perfect, I Am The Fly, Culture Vultures, 106 Beats That. Colin Newman (vg), Graham Lewis (b), Robert Gotobed (d), Bruce Gilbert (g). 18/1/78 MV4 MB NG ○

3/10/78 The Other Window, Mutual Friend, On Returning, Indirect Enquiries. 20/9/78 MV4 BS NG ○

18/9/79 Crazy About Love. 11/9/79 MV4 JE MR ○ SFRCD108

10/5/88 German Shepherds, Boiling Boy, Drill. 24/4/88 U DG SC&SA

17/9/02 Spent, I Don't Understand, 1st Fast, 99.9. 21/7/02 MV4 ME KR

The Wisdom Of Harry

14/11/00 Shiny Shiny Pimpmobile, I'm Going To Make My Life Right, Rebellious Jukebox, Hail Tinseltown. Pete Astor (g, tps, jh, pv). 27/9/00 MV4 MA GT

21/12/00 You Make Me Sick At Xmas. Live from Peel Acres AR GT/SA

Wishbone Ash

10/7/71 Jailbait, The Pilgrim, Lady Whiskey, Lullaby. Andy Powell (gv), Ted Turner (gv), Martin Turner (bv), Steve Upton (d). 5/7/71 PH JW U 3 previous Sounds Of The Seventies Sessions, 1st for Bob Harris, 19/8/70

25/4/72 Blowing Free, Warrior, The King Will Come. 18/4/72 MV4 U U

9/2/77 Runaway, King Will Come, Lorelei, Mother Of Pearl, Blowin' Free. Laurie Wisefield (g) r Ted Turner. 16/1/77 PRIV

A Witness

6/1/86 The Loud Hailer Song, Smelt Like A Pedestrian, O'Grady's Dream, Sharpened Sticks. Vince (b), Rick (g), Keith (v) & 'Dr Umatix' (d). 15/12/85 MV5 DG ME

9/12/86 Faglane Morris Wind, Nodding Dog Moustache, Raw Patch, Hard Day's Love. 'Nobby Normal' (d). 16/11/86 U DG NG&FK

19/1/88 Zip Up, Sunbed Sentimental, Take Me Up To The Earth, McManus Octaphone. Fred Harris (d, bck). 10/1/88 U DG ME&FK ○

30/11/88 Life The Final Frontier, I Love You Mr Disposable Razors, Helicopter Tealeaf, Prince Microwave Bollard. Alan (d) r Harris. 20/11/88 HP DG ME ○ SFMCD206

Wolf Eyes

8/12/04 one unknown title (35'). Nate Young, Aaron Dilloway, John Olson. 'As live' 8/12/04 MV4 AR~

The Wolfhounds

1/4/86 Me, Anti-Midas Touch, Hand In The Till, Whale On The Beach. Dave Callahan (v), Paul Clark (g), Andy Golding (g), Andy Bolton (b, sy), Frank Stebbing (d). 23/3/86 MV5 DG ME&TD

10/6/87 Rule Of Thumb, Sandy, Boy Racers RM1, Disgusted E7. 26/5/87 U DG ME&MFA

1/2/88 Happy Shopper, Non Specific Song, Son Of Nothing, William Randolf Hearse. Martin Stebbing (b) r Bolton. 19/1/88 U DG MR&JB

Wommet

31/10/70 The Way You Look, How Can You Love Me So, City Of Gold, Greyhound Bus. Mick Abrahams (gv) & unknown. 20/10/70 U U U

Brenton Wood

11/2/68 The Oogum Boogum Song, Gimme Little Sign, Baby You've Got It, My Girl. Brenton Wood (v) & Tony Gilbert for the services of 3 musicians, Roger Coulam (md/o). 30/1/68 U U U

Woodbine

10/2/99 Neskwik, Chisellers, Outer Circle, I Hope That You Get What You Want. Susan Dillane (kgv), Graeme Swindon (dgb), Robert Healey (g, mel), Donald Adams (gb). 15/12/98 MV4 MR PN

24/11/99 Neskwik, Blue Bucket, Tricity Tiara, Outer Circle, Ban Everything, Drink Drive. Live from MV3 AR/SCU MR

The Woodentops

19/9/84 Get It On, Well Well, Everything Breaks, The Last Time. Rolo McGinty (v), Simon Mawby (g), Paul Holliday (d), Fraser Cheney (b), Alice Goodhead (k). 8/9/84 MV5 DG MC

9/9/85 It Will Come, Plenty, So Good Today, Plutonium Rock (Godzilla). Rolo, Mawby, Alice Thompson (k), Benny Staples (d), Frank De Freitas (b). 27/8/85 MV5 DG MR

7/4/86 Give It Time, Move Me, Special Friend, Have You Seen The Lights. 30/3/86 MV5 DG ME

Terry and Gay Woods

21/11/70 A Nobleman's Fair Daughter, I Feel Concerned, January Snows, Van Dieman's Land. Terry Woods, Gay Woods. 3/11/70 MV4 JW BC&lS

16/6/75 Blackbird, Winter Poem, When The Time Is Right, Song For The Gypsies, Country Girlie, The Hymn. 3/6/75 MV4 U U

4/4/78 We Can Work This One Out, Full Moon, Dream Come True, Lonesome Blue. Gay Woods (dul, v-1,2,4), Terry Woods (rg, v-3), Jim Russell (d), Kuma Hara (b) & unknown (lg). 28/3/78 MV4 CL MR

Workforce

17/4/85 Theories, Drowning Pool, Compromise. Paul Wheatcroft (v), Rod Leigh (g, k), Tim Owen (sx, perc), Terry Todd (b), Alan Fish (d). 31/3/85 MV5 DG ME

13/1/86 Cut To Pleasure, Rope Dancer, Say It Again. Clive Rowat (b) r Todd. 5/1/86 MV5 DG ME

The Workhouse

26/11/03 Last Of The Big Songs, Boxing Day, Aberdeen, Chancers. Mark Baker (g), Andy Dakeyne (g), Peter Lazell (d), Chris Taylor (bv). 22/10/03 MV4 SA NF

17/3/05 Sellafield, Coathanger, Shake 'Ands, Flyover. 30/12/04 MV4 SA GT TX by Rob Da Bank, session offered before Peel's death, honoured by Louise Kattenhorn

Working Week

14/5/84 Venceremos / We Will Win, Stella Marina, Soul Of Light. Simon Booth (g), Larry Stabbins (sx, fl), Annie Whitehead (tb), Bosco, Dawson & Neville Murray (perc), Roy Dodds (d), Kim Burton (p), Ernest Mothle (b), Claudia Figuera (lv-1), Julie Tippett (lv-1,3). 1/05/84 MV5 MRD TdB

World of Twist

11/8/91 Untitled, St Bruno, Kick Out The Jams, Blackpool Tower. Tony Ogden (v), Gordon King (g), Nicholas Sanderson (d), Pete Smith (ma). 25/6/91 MV5 MR MR Previous session for Mark Goodier Oct 90

The Would Be's

19/3/90 All This Rubbish Is True, Must It Be, Funny Ha Ha, My Radio Sounds Different In The Dark. Julie McDonnell (v), Aidan O'Reilly (tb, ts), Mattie Finnegan (lg), Paul Finnegan (g), Eamonn Finnegan (b), Pascal Smith (d). 25/2/90 MV3 DG ME

Wreckless Eric ○

11/10/77 Whole Wide World, Semaphore Signals, Personal Hygiene, Rags And Tatters, Reconnez Cherie. Eric Goulden (gv) & Ian Dury (d), Davey Payne (sx), Denise Roudette (b). 25/9/77 MV4 U DD

8/3/78 Semaphore Signals, Waxworks, Grown Ups, Brain Thieves. & New Rockets: Davy Lutton (d), Barry Payne (b), Charlie Hart (o, vi), John Glyn (sx). 1/3/78 MV4 MB NG ○ Both sessions on Almost A Jubilee: 25 Years At The BBC (With Gaps) HUX039

Gary Wright's Wonderwheel

22/2/72 I Know, Yesterday's Tomorrow, Whether It's Right Or Wrong. Gary Wright (o, pv), Bryson Graham (d), Archie Legget (b), Micky Jones (lg). 15/2/72 MV4 U U Gary Wright's Expansion had passed trial b'cast on Rosko Show 20/3/71

18/8/72 Something For Us All, Old As I Was Born, By Tomorrow, Gimme The Good Earth. 25/7/72 T1 JM (or PD) U

Writing On The Wall

8/12/68 Tasker's Successor, Shadow Of Man, Profile Of A Door, Felicity Jane (& Sha La La La La Le, 2/2/69). William Finlayson (lg), John Scott (b), William Scott (o), Linton Patterson (v), James Hush (d). 12/11/68 PC1 BA AH. For Bernie Andrews, yes, but 5.5 minute numbers are not for us… we have no discoteques': pass from panel for Top Gear only

13/2/71 Lucifer, Father Time, Mrs Cooper's Pie. 26/1/71 U U BC

Robert Wyatt

19/12/72 We Got An Arts Council Grant / Righteous Rhumba, Little Child, Godsong / Hatfield [Fol De Rol]. Robert Wyatt (v, po, perc, d), Francis Monkman (p, sy). 5/12/72 LH1 JW U

26/9/74 Alifib, Soup Song, Sea Song, I'm A Believer. Solo (v, p, o, mrm, perc). 10/9/74 LH1 JW BC ● SFPS037

X Men

13/9/84 The Witch, Little Girl, Xtramental, Count Von Black. Mark Stollar (v), Miles Aldridge (g), Tim Hosking (b), Debbie Green (bck, tamb), Susan Feighery (bck, tamb), Tom Cullinam (d, g-3), Joe Foster (g). 4/9/84 MV5 MRD TdB

X Ray Spex

6/3/78 Genetic Engineering, Artificial, I Am A Poser, Identity. Poly Styrene (v), Jak Airport (g), Paul Dean (b), Paul Heardin 'BP' (d), Steve Rudi (sx). 20/2/78 MV4 TW DD

13/11/78 Germ-Free Adolescents, Warrior, Age. 6/11/78 MV4 TW DD

XDreamysts

10/1/80 Pardoned Cry, I Don't Wanna Go, One In Every Crowd, Reality Blues. Vel Walls (v), John 'Doc' Doherty (g), Roe Butcher (b), Brian Moffatt (d). 5/12/79 MV4 TVD NG

Xmal Deutschland

25/11/82 Incubus Succubus, Geheimnis, Qual, Zinker. Fiona Sangster (k), Anja Huwe (v), Manuela Rickers (g), Manuela Svingman (d), Wolfgang Ellerbrock (b). 17/12/82 U RP NG

27/6/83 In Motion, Vito, Reigen, Sehnsucht. 22/6/83 MV4 RP AP

25/4/84 Nachtschatten, Tag Fuer Tag, Mondlicht, Augen-Blick. Peter Bellendir (d) r Svingman. 11/4/84 MV5 DG NG

13/5/85 Polarlicht, Der Wind, Jahr Um Jahr, Autumn. 30/4/85 MV5 MRD MR ● SFPS017

Xol Dog 400

27/1/95 First Red Liquid, The Chair, Little Metal. Christian Muller. 4/11/94 OS

XTC

24/6/77 She's So Square, Crosswires†, Radios In Motion, Science Friction. Andy Partridge (gv), Colin Moulding (bv), Barry Andrews (k, sxv), Terry Chambers (d). 20/6/77 MV4 MB DD

26/9/77 Into The Atom Age†, Heatwave Mk 2, I'm Bugged†, Dance Band†. 21/9/77 MV4 MB DD

20/11/78 Meccanik Dancing†, The Rhythm, New Town Animal In A Furnished Cage, Super Thief. 13/11/78 MV4 TW DD

15/10/79 Opening Sig And Speech†, Scissor Man, Roads Girdle The Globe†, Ten Feet Tall†, Real By Reel†. 8/10/79 MV4 TW DD † on ○ Transistor Blast: The Best of The BBC Sessions, Cooking Vinyl COOKCD152

Xymox

17/6/85 Stranger, Muscoviet Mosquito, Seventh Time. Ronnie Moerings (g, kv), Anke Wolbert (k, bv), Pieter Nooten (kv), Frank Weizig (k, g), Peter Haartsen (g, sfx, tps). 4/6/85 MV5 MRD MR

13/11/85 After The Call, Agonised By Love, Mesmerised. 3/11/85 MV5 DG MS

The Yachts

24/10/78 Mantovani's Hits, Yachting Type, Look Back In Love (Not In Anger), Then And Now. Martin Watson (gv), Henry Priestman (opv), Martin Dempsey (bv), Bob Bellis (dv). 9/10/78 MV4 BS DD

2/7/79 Then And Now, In A Second, Love You Love You, March Of The Moderates. 4/6/79 MV4 JS DD

Stomu Yamashta's East Wind

14/3/74 Hey Man, One By One, Optical Dream, Wind Words. Stomu Yamashta (perc), Hugh Hopper (b), Brian Gascoigne (k), Sammi Abu (fl), Mike Travis (d), Frank Tankowski (g). 7/3/74 LH1 JW BAI

The Yardbirds

10/3/68 Think About It, Goodnight Sweet Josephine, White Summer, Dazed And Confused. Keith Relf (v, hca), Jimmy Page (g), Jim McCarty (d), Chris Dreja (b). 6/3/68 PH BA PR Last of dozens: Last Sat. Club session recorded previous day, 5/3/68. 1st session recorded 29/10/64 PH (prod JG). TX 21/11/64 on World Service Rhythm and Blues

Yardstick

3/7/92 Blind Eye, Brutal Deiuxe, Double Zero, Twenty Three. Kevin Young (v), Ian O'Hare (g), Grease (b), Jim Harley (d). 9/6/92 MV4 JB PA&JB

Yazoo

19/7/82 Don't Go, Midnight, In My Room, Winter Kills. Vince Clarke (k, dm, g), Alison Moyet (pv). 16/6/82 MV4 RP TdB

Yeah Yeah Noh

7/8/84 Prick Up Your Ears, Beware The Weakling Lines, Starling Pillow-Case, Jigsaw. Graham Summers (d), Adrian Crossan (b), John Grayland (g), Sue Dorey (perc), Derek Hammond (v). 28/7/84 MV5 DG MC

23/4/85 Temple Of Convenience, See Through Nature, Crimplene Seed Lifestyle, Another Side To Mrs Quill. Craig (slg), Andrew Nicholls (p) r Summers. 9/4/85 MV5 AJ U

27/1/86 The Superimposed Man, Blood Soup, Stealing In The Name Of The Lord, (It's) Easier To Suck Than Sing. Tom Slater (g) r Craig; & Julie Dennis (bck). 19/1/86 MV5 DG ME ● SFPS026 ○ 'Fun on the Lawn Lawn Lawn' Vuggum BAD002

Yeah Yeah Yeahs

22/8/02 Maps, Y Control, Miles Away, Tick. Brian Chase (d), Nick Zinner (g), Karen O (v). 10/7/02 MV4 MA GT

Yes

12/1/69 Dear Father, Everydays, Sweetness, Something's Coming. Jon Anderson (v), Pete Banks (g), Chris Squire (b), Tony Kaye (o), Bill Bruford (d). 7/1/69 MV4 BA AH

Yip Yip Coyote

2/6/83 Pioneer Girl, Wagon Train, Dream Of The West, Red Bandana. Fifi (v), Carl Evans (g, bck), Eg White (b), Volker Vonhoff (d). 28/5/83 MV4 DG MC

16/1/84 Sho' Thing Boss, Cry Like The Wind, Son Of A Gun, Delray. 10/1/84 MV4 MRD MPK

25/7/84 The Cowboy Lament, Road To Hell, Burn The Barn Down, In The Name Of God. Tom (k) r Vonhoff. 12/7/84 MV5 MRD MR

Yo La Tengo

5/8/97 Autumn Sweater, Shadows, I Heard You Looking. Georgia Hubley (d, o, v), Ira Kaplan (gv, o), James McNew (b, o, d, perc). 15/7/97 MV4 MR KR

8/9/98 Tired Hippo, Now 2000, Autumn Sweater, You Can Have It All, Double Dare. 25/8/98 MV4 JLO GT

31/8/99 It Takes A Lot To Laugh It Takes A Train To Cry. OS

James Yorkston And The Athletes

2/1/03 St Patrick, Tender To The Blues, Six Thirty Is Just Way Too Early, La Magnifica. James Yorkston (gv), Holly Taylor (wh), Reuben Taylor (p, acc), Faisal Rahman (lsg, acc), John Bews (vi), Doogie Paul (db, v). 27/11/02 MV4 SA GT

Jessie Young & The Word

15/10/67 Spring Fever, Geno's Gone Walkabout, Come On Up, Hold On, Every Christian. U 9/10/67 U U U

The Roy Young Band

25/2/72 Rag Mama Rag, Roll It On, Slow Down, Mr Funky (& Nowhere To Go, 31/3/72). Roy Young (pv), Onnie McIntyre (lg), Nick South (b), Rick Dodd (sx), Eddie Thornton (tp), Clifford Davies (d). 8/2/72 T1 JM JWH&NG

22/9/72 Back Up Train, Boney Moronie, Annie's Back, All Around The World (& I Can't Believe It, 12/10/72). Denis Elliott, Nick Clark, George Ford, Howie Casey, Dave Casewell r McIntyre, South, Dodd, Davies, Thornton. 28/8/72 T1 PD U

Young Gods

12/10/88 L'Amourir, Jimmy, The Irrtum Boys, Fais La Mollette. Use Heistand (d), Cesare Pizzi (k, smp), Franz Treichler (v). 2/10/88 HP DG U

Young Heart Attack

9/12/03 In Luck, Radioland Hit Squad, Slut, El Camino. Chris Hodge (gv), Chris Frenchy Smith (g), Steven T Hall (bv), Jennifer Stephens (v, tamb), Joey Shuffield (d). 23/10/03 MV4 SA NF

Young Marble Giants

26/8/80 Searching For Mr Right, Brand New Life, Final Day, Nita, Posed By Models. Philip Moxham (b, dm), Alison Statton (v), Stuart Moxham (g). 18/8/80 MV4 DG DD 'Dale insisted the mono cassette recording of our drum machine had to be alchemised into stereo. This involved sending two dustcoated BBC techies into the bowels of the Maida Vale Studios to return, ages later, clutching some sort of signal splitter gizmo, covered in dust, and looking like something from Frankenstein's laboratory. But the drum machine in stereo is to die for!' – Stuart Moxham

Young People

22/7/03 The Man That Got Away, Night Nurse, Dutch Oven, Hot Horse. Katie Eastburn (v, d, b, perc), Jeff Rosenberg (g, perc), Jarrett Silberman (g, d, perc). 11/6/03 MV4 SA NF

Young Tradition

12/2/69 John Barleycorn, Wondrous Love, Banks Of The Nile, 3 Traditional Airs, 5 Cuts Jig, En Vrai Amour, Bright Morning Star, The Rolling Of The Stones, What If A Day. Pete Bellamy (v), Royston Wood (v), Heather Wood (v), 'with Chris Hogwood & David Munro.' 29/1/69 PH JM U Previous sessions for the Light Programme

27/8/69 My Dancing Day, The Husband Man & The Serving Man, Bright Morning Stars Are Rising, The Shepherd's Hymn, Claudy Banks. Munro out. 12/8/69 MV5 PR~

Yourcodenameis: Milo

19/3/03 17, Four Three, Team Radar, Scandinavia. Paul Mullen (v), Justin Lockey (g, d), Adam Hiles (g), Ross Harley (b), Paul Beresford (d, g). 28/2/03 MV4 NF NS

24/11/04 TV Is Better Than Real Life, I Am Connecting Flight, Yesterday's Head, 2 Stone. 20/10/04 MV4 NF JSM

You've Got Foetus on Your Breath

4/1/83 Today I Started Slogging Again Mk 2, Clothes Hoist, Wash It All Off Mk 2, Ignorance Is Bliss (Or Is It?). Jim Thirlwell (e). OS

Yummy Fur

21/7/95 Republic Of Salo, Klaxxen Education Film, Carry On Nurse, Delux Merseybeat Wig, Car Park, Independent Pop Song, Country Priest, The Man With The Enormous Mother, Yucky Food. Lawrence Worthington (d, bck), Mark Leighton (b), John McKeown (g, lv), Brian McDougall (g). 18/6/95 MV4 TdB~

7/4/98 Shivers, Fantastic Legs, In The Company Of Women, Shoot The Ridiculant. McKeown, Leighton, McDougall, Paul Thomson (d), Claire Gorman (k), Lorna Lithgow (sy-4), Paul Kearney (g-4). 22/2/98 MV4 ME JB

Zabrinski

19/4/01 Angen Cyfrifianell, It Was Big When It Burst, Freedom Of The Highway. Matthew Durbridge, Robyn Thomas, Pwyll Ap Stifin, Gareth Richardson, Philip Jenkins, Emyr Harris, Iwan Morgan, Dave Franklin. 18/3/01 MV4 ME~

Zeni Geva

28/10/94 Dead Sun Rising, Desire For Agony, Stigma, Death Blows, Godflesh. Kazuyuki K Null (gv), Tabata Mitsuru (g), Eito (d). 25/9/94 MV3 ME GT

12/1/96 Alienation, Tyrannycide, Luglio Agosto Settembre Nero, Implosion. 26/11/95 MV5 ME JLC

Benjamin Zepheniah

10/1/83 Problems, I Christmas Poem, Uganda's What I Mean. Solo. 7/1/83 B6 CL U

7/2/83 Dis Policeman, Riot In Progress, The Boat, Uprising Downturn, 13 Dead, Fight Them Not Me. Benjamin Zepheniah (v), Spartacus R (perc), Moses Valley (perc), Angie Parkinson (perc). 1/2/83 U RP NG

Zero Zero

19/10/91 Maximum Violence, Here's The News, The Sanity Clause. Simon Robinson, Mark Grant. 22/9/91 MV3 DG AR&ME

The Zeros

30/11/77 Nice Girls, Hungry, Easy Way Out, Solid State. Phil Gaylor (d), Steve Cotton (b), Steve Godfrey (g). 23/11/77 MV4 MB NG

Zerra 1

16/5/83 Cry, Let's Go Home, Nothing, Diaries. Andreas Grimminger (g), Paul Bell (kv), Korda (d). 7/5/83 MV4 DG MC

23/11/83 The Other Side, I Know, Dangerous Vision, Children. & Alison Kelly (clo), Adrian Wyatt (b). 14/11/83 MV4 TW U

Zimbabwe Cha Cha Cha Kings

16/1/93 Dear Maideyi, Shanduko, Makandiramba, Naome. Leonard Tsuro (d), Boma Kasinahama (b), Jacob Marwodzi (rg), Peter Mwachande (lg) David Ziome (v). 24/11/92 MV4 MR~ FK

Zinica

29/6/87 Faya Bulinky†, Mr John†, Jacket Tail†, Found You To Lose You. John Herbert (v-3,4), Anthony Nash (g, v-1,2), Landiman Omeil (acc), John Palmer (tp), Victor Perry (lead bj), Walter Lackwood (2nd bj), Edward Cattuse (b), Winston Perry (d). 23/6/87 U DG MR&SC † on ● LP Bluefields Express Club Sandino NSC001

Zion Train

3/9/94 Rousillon Inna No 7 Style, Tricky Angle Wembley '78, Through The Legs (Scottish Warrior), Super Eagles Zion Train Annual Dub Award. Cod (b), Tench (perc), Perch (mx, perc, siren), Molara (v, perc), Dave Ruffy (d), Hake (tp), Dom (perc), Minnow (perc). 26/7/94 MV4 ME PL

16/3/96 Teenage Dub, Suspect Dub, Bass Adds Growth, Waiting For The Dub. & Ruts DC: David Ruffy (d), Segs (b), Foxy (g), Cod (p, o), Forkbeard (tb), Hake (tp), Tench (perc), Molara (v), Perch (dubbing, siren). 5/3/96 MV4 MR KR

The Zones

23/5/78 Sign Of The Times, Away From It All, No Sense Of Humour, Tough At The Bottom. Willie Gardner (lgv), Russell 'Spyder' Webb (b), Billy McIsaac (k, bck), Kenny Hyslop (d). 17/5/78 MV4 MB NG

22/9/78 Anything Goes, Deadly Dolls, The End, It's Only Fashion. 13/9/78 MV4 BS NG

Zuvuya

11/3/94 Away The Crow Road, It Comes Down (Turnaround), Driving The Monkey Insane. Phil Pickering (prg, b, dig), Paul Choosmer (prg, k), Mi Quest (v). 30/1/94 MV3 ME GT

Zvuki Mu

8/5/89 Zima, Crazy Queen, Forgotten Sex, Gadopiatikna. Alexei Pavlov (d, tp), Alexander Lipnitsky (b), Alexei Bortnichuk (lg), Pavel Hotin (sy, bck), Peter Mamanov (gv). 23/4/89 MV3 DG ME

Die Zwie at the Rodeo

7/6/84 River Of No Return, Fairhaired Squaws, Western Union, Grapsch! Gerd Strass (v), Udo Strass (v), Holger Hiller (g). 23/5/84 MV5 RP PS&TD

THIS BOOK COULD NOT have been produced as it was in the seven months available without the invaluable support of a very small group of people, namely Louise Kattenhorn, Peel's last producer at BBC Radio 1; Hannah Jacobs, BBC Radio 1 media manager; Jeff Walden at BBC Written Archives, Caversham; Carrie Maclennan, research student in the Cultural Business Group of Glasgow Caledonian University, who keyed the session data 92-04 for me; Chris Lycett; Clive and Shurley Selwood; and Sheila Ravenscroft. My especial thanks to them. Other important and substantial contributions were made by Bernie Andrews, Sue Armstrong, Johnny Beerling, Hermeet Chadha, Euros Childs, Bob Conduct, Sam Cunningham, Alison Howe, Shirley Jones, Anita Kamath, Phil Lawton, Roger Olive, Andy Parfitt, Andy Rogers, Helen Walters.

I am also grateful for contributions, assistance, contacts or suggestions from Emyr at Ankst, Adam Askew, Steven at Benbecula, James Birtwistle, Stuart Braithwaite, Caroline Briggs, Paul Cargill, Iain Chambers, Rob Chapman, Rob Da Bank, Mike Engles, Andy Ferguson, Sean French, Jeff Griffin, Steve Hammonds, Jamie Hart, Mike Hawkes, Mary Anne Hobbs, Simon Keeler, Paul Long (of UCE Birmingham), Lynn Macarthy, Claire Marvin, Pat Neary, Nita at Goldstar, Adam Piggot, Ed Pybus, Brian O'Reilly, Gerard Wood.

I should also like to repeat my thanks here to all those who contributed to In Session Tonight 15 years ago, whose contributions are still essential to this work: Richard Addison, Miti Adhikari, Bill Aitken, Bill Bebb, Joe Boyd, Fiona Brazil, Maggie Brown, Malcolm Brown, Graham Bunce, Martin Colley, Mary Cotgrove, Stewart Cruickshank, Dave Dade, Trevor Dann, Pete Dauncey, Ted de Bono, Pete Drummond, John Etchells, Sue Falconer, Mike Franks, Nick Gomm, Jimmy Grant, Stuart Grundy, Mike Harding, Allen Harris, Bob Harris, Bob Harrison, Terry Hooley, Kevin Howlett, Paul Kent, Andy Kershaw, Mike King, Vernon Lawrence, Jon Lewin, Donald Maclean, Brian Matthew, Mark Melton, John Muir, Spot Mulkeen, Stephen Nelson, Mark Paytress, Bev Phillips, Scott Piering, Peter Pilbeam, Wendy Pilmer, Pinky, John Porter, Roger Pusey, Mark Radcliffe, Mary Ramonde, Pete Ritzema, Mike Robinson, Bob Sargeant, Ian Sharpe, Phil Smee, Dave Tate, Dave Taylor, Geoff Travis, John White, Mark White, John Williams, Tony Wilson; the staff of the old BBC Radio Programme Registry, long gone, especially Kay Green, Vicky Winch, Chris Pullen, and John Dredge; for help on that book's original sessionography 1967-1992, Jem Taylor, Al Calder, Sharon Fitzgerald, AJ Hull, Kerry Musselbrook, Ciaran McGonachy, Jane McWilliams; and Nicola for the use of the spare room in her flat in Marble Arch.

But there would be no story at all without the musicians who responded to my letters, calls and e-mails. Whether in 2007 or 15 years ago, whether quoted or not, they all informed the big story: Paul Ablett, Paul Adams, Viv Albertine, Ian Anderson (Jethro Tull), Ian A Anderson (fRoots), Stewart Anderson, Steve Ashton, Joan Armatrading, Tony Banks, Maggie Bell, Pauline Black, Ben Blackwell, Nigel Blackwell, Mickey Bradley, Billy Bragg, Tim Bran, Dave Brock, Mark Burgess, Brian Burrows, John Cairns, Laura Cantrell, Ian Carr, Jimmy Cauty, Euros Childs, Edwyn Collins, Phil Collins, The Cookie Crew, Mike Cooper, Dave Coyle, Rob Crutchley, Dick Dale, Robin Raymond Dalloway, Michael Dempsey, Wesley Doyle, Dave Edmunds, John Fiddler, Grandmaster Gareth, David Gedge, Ron Geesin, Lynval Golding, Scott Gorham, Dave Gregory, John Griffiths, Roy Harper, Mick Harris, Paul Hartnoll, Mick Harvey, PJ Harvey, Darren Hayman, Alan Hempsall, David-Ivar Herman Dune, Jon Hiseman, Randy Hudson, Ashley Hutchings, Nick Kavanagh, Linton Kwesi Johnson, Jim Kerr, Ray Laidlaw, Gavin Laird, Len Liggins, Jeff Lynne, Helen McCookerybook, Francis McDonald, Perry McDonagh, Owen McFadden, Ramond McGinley, Phil Manzanera, Caroline Martin, Alan Maskell, Wayne Maskell, Nick Mason, Aidan Moffat, Pat Morgan, Stuart Moxham, Dan Newman, Simon Nicol, Rab Noakes, Chris Olley, Brendan O'Malley, Andy Partridge, Alex Paterson, John Perry, Jason Pierce, Kev Powell, Andy Roberts, Greg Roberts, Michael Rooney, Denise Roughan, Mike Rutherford, Paul Savage, Steve Severin, Feargal Sharkey, The Shend, Richard Sinclair, Siouxsie Sue, Peter Solowka, Liam Sparkes, Daniel Swan, Darrell Sweet, Max Tundra (aka Ben Jacobs), Neil Tennant, Valerie Trebeljahr, Jeremy Valentine, Luke Vibert, Paul Vickers, Cristian Vogel, Johnny Walker, Ed Wenn, Karl Willetts, Bobby Wratten, Robert Wyatt, John Yates, Bob Zabor.

The vast job of producing both the shows diary and sessions A-Z was made immeasurably easier by the contributions of many long-standing regular listeners, whether made through the John Peel News Group on Yahoo; via responses direct to my appeals via Mojo, Record Collector or the Scottish press; or who wrote to me after the publication of In Session Tonight with suggested emendations and queries over possible omissions; plus there are one or two names below whose contributions to existing websites or other media I wish to acknowledge. My thanks to every one of them: David Alderman, Edward Arthur, Adrian Barber, Steve Barker, Billy Bragg, Peter Branney, John Bravin, Colin Bray, Alex Briggs, G L Brown, Guy Brown, Hugh Brune, Neil Burling, Mark Bursa, Roger Carruthers, Graham R Crawford, Richard Davies, Andrew Dean, Pat Dibben, Eddie Duffy, Tim Eames, Phil Edwards, Colin Ellis, Rob Fleay, Denis Goodbody, Michael Harding, Colin Harper, David Hill, Jon Horne, Rick Howes, Tim Joseph (and his sources Chris Ketchell and Steve O'Connor), Kerry Knight, Koogy, Ian Laycock, Clifford Loeslin, Brian Long, Stu McHugh, Dougal Mckinnon, Aidan Moffat, Stephen D Morgan, Lindsay Neil, David Parker, Adrian Perkins, Phyll, P J of Redditch, Shane Pope, Ed Powley, Russ Reid, Tom Roche, Rocker, Matt Savage, Steve Scott, Claire Shilton, Elaine Simpson, Jon Small, Philip Smith, Jimmy Stepek, Marcelle Van Hoof, Steve Walsh, Graham Webster, Paul Webster, Martin Wheatley, Mark Whitby.

For IT & database advice and editing, my brother Pete Garner of Cemex, and my Dad Stan Garner formerly of IBM, who also put me up for a few fleeting overnight stops. Lastly, I should like to thank my wife Magda and daughter Hanna for their forebearance while I virtually disappeared from family life into this for the first half of 2007.

Not forgotten: Alan Black, Ivor Cutler, Viv Stanshall, Tommy Vance, Teddy Warrick, Robin Scott, John Walters, John Peel.